MITCHELL BEAZLEY

THE new London Property Guide '05/06

The ***ONLY*** guide you need to **buying** and **selling**, **renting** and **letting** homes in London – ***PLUS*** **strategies for a changing market**

CARRIE SEGRAVE

The New London Property Guide '05/06

Published in 2005 by Mitchell Beazley,
an imprint of Octopus Publishing Group Ltd
2–4 Heron Quays, London, E14 4JP

ISBN 1 84533 072 2

A CIP catalogue copy of this book is available from the British Library.

At Mitchell Beazley

Executive Editors	Vivien Antwi, Jon Asbury
Project Editor	Peter Taylor
Proofreader	Andy Hilliard
Production	Seyhan Essen
Indexer	Ann Parry

Set in MetaPlus
Printed and bound in the UK by Mackays, Chatham

This book is for Christopher Foulkes; for Eleanor, a Londoner; and in memory of John Brennan

Carrie Segrave

Since the early 1980s Carrie Segrave has been a leading writer and commentator on London's property market. She has written for *The Daily* and *Sunday Telegraphs, The Times, The Financial Times, The Sunday Times Magazine* and many other publications. She started the city's first property paper and in 1988 founded *The London Property Guide*, whose annual editions rapidly became the standard reference on buying, selling and living in London.

Specialist writers

David Spittles is Property and Personal Finance writer for *The London Evening Standard* and *The Observer.* **Liz Lightfoot** is Education Correspondent for *The Daily Telegraph.* **Susan Ware** is an architect with a special interest in London homes and is a partner in The Chartered Practice. She teaches Professional Practice at the Bartlett School of Architecture, University College, London.

Contributors

Jane Ball, Ros Bentley, Jacqueline Castles, Liz Cheadle, Victoria Cooper, Eljay Crompton, Amanda Davies, Eddie Edwards, Rob Hadgraft, Wendy Hampshire, Dan Hayes, Jonathan Jaye, Kaori Kashiwagi, Natasha Kumar, Edmund Littlewood, Jill Macfarlane, Sam Mosedale, Jane Norris, Lucas Orme, Emma Roberts, Clare Sayer, Caroline Simpson, Janet Skidmore, Alex Smith, Emma Swann, Helen Wilding.

Acknowledgments and thanks

This book would in no way be possible without the enormous contribution made by a small army of London fanatics, prepared to tramp the streets (literally) on its behalf, and cross-examine town halls and the like: their names are above. In the course of their, and our, research well over 300 estate agents and other property people, plus experts on particular places in and aspects of London, also gave up their time to help; for their local and professional expertise we are, as ever, deeply grateful.

There are too many, alas, to thank them all individually, but among those whose assistance was invaluable are:

Gareth Archer, Sandy Barnett, Linda Beaney, Jeremy Best, Tim le Blanc-Smith, Andrew Botterill, Jason Carlon, Arnaud Cheung, Mark Chick, Greg Clarke, Paul Clarke, Julian Clark, John Connolly, Daniel Congram, Donald Crockant, Elaine Francis, Stuart Flury, Chris Fox, Patrick Glyn-Jones, Marc Goldberg, Sara Graybow, Helen James, Laura James, Colin Lowman, William Nelhams, Mark Mackenzie-Charrington, Stuart McCraw, Edward Mason, Shah Miah, Debbie Mitchell, Jo O'Sullivan, Adrian Owen, Steve Pacetti, Vanessa Pawley, John Payne, Q Abbas Raja, Kevin Ryan, David Salvi, Craig Saxton, Daren Seager, Jonathan Seal, Jon Singh, Eve Stanton, Ainsley Stephenson, Red Talidi, Charles Thompson, Peter Wetherell, James Whiteman, John Wilcox, Charles Willis, Paul Willis.

And my very special thanks to Caroline Simpson ('Boris') who has been involved with the Guide since the very first edition in 1988 and is without doubt its indispensible linchpin.

It would not do to forget, either, the contributors to earlier editions of this Guide whose foot-slogging helped provide the foundations upon which this year's is built.

Just as crucial as all of the above are the ace team at Mitchell Beazley: very many thanks this year to Peter Taylor, who unflappably took over day-to-day control, while John Asbury took over as Executive Editor. They are on the front line, along with our fast and expert indexer, Ann Parry, and proofreader Andy Hilliard, all bearing up nobly under the whirling load of nearly 700 close-packed pages as they whizz between us. As I have said, teamwork is everything on this book and it doesn't stop when editors, designers and proofreaders have done their bit. At the very end is a brilliant production team under Julie Young who have the worst job of the lot – getting it over the out-of-house hurdles of printing, binding and distributing in a timespan that makes other UK publishers blink.

C.S.

February 2005

Contents

London in 2005

London's areas A–Z

Introduction

This book is an annual report on the progress of London as a place to live. It is also, if you like, a shareholders' report on the biggest investment most Londoners will ever make: their homes, their stake in the city.

The heart of the book, starting on page 92, is an area-by-area description of London's residential districts, from 'A' for Acton to 'W' for Wimbledon. These pages describe the streets and the types of homes of each neighbourhood. Each chapter has details of prices, rents, transport, journey times, schools, boroughs . . . the facts you need to know to weigh up where in London you'd like to live – and can afford to live.

The first part of the book offers the analysis and the background information on how the market is working, and why. Here you will find major sections on matters that affect people's choice of where to live – **transport plans**, London's **schools**. You'll also find information on **buying** (freehold, leasehold, the new Commonhold), **selling**, (including choosing and instructing an estate agent, and the implications of the **HIP**: the 'Seller's Pack' mark II), **renting, investing, mortgages, planning** and **building regulations**, a guide to **architectural styles**, and more. Cross-London **price charts** allow comparison of average buying prices and rent levels.

The London property market in 2005

If someone quotes figures at you this year, ponder whether they be London or national ones. If the latter, ignore them. London's prices, having boomed first, have in fact gone nowhere much in the last five years – and the pool of sellers who, having listened with half an ear to the giddy statistics expressed nationally, are convinced that their homes must have doubled in 18 months has at last shrunk to a puddle. We don't live in Nationwide or Halifax; we live in London.

That said, there's some excuse for the confusion. First, ever since the Millennium, London prices have wavered above and below the trend line like the humps on the Loch Ness Monster. Up in the spring (with headlines to match), quietly back down by the year's end – barring 2003 when things went down in the spring and peaked in July/August (there *was* a war on).

Second, the pattern has varied not only from area to area but by home type. Thus there have still been headline-grabbing prices for the stratospheric stuff at the very top of the market, where celebrities and Russian billionaires roam with no need to consult a mortgage broker. Just below comes the continuing failure of the homes for more ordinarily wealthy types, the £850,000–2 million or so bracket, to achieve prices their owners would like.

This demonstrates a novel state of affairs: the fairytale-level prices are by and large for new, state-of-the-art stuff – since these are not bought from existing owners there is no 'trickle-down' effect from them into the domestic market, which remains patchy. Anything overpriced or with obvious drawbacks just will not sell. Good family homes, though, show little if any depreciation if close to good schools. At the bottom end, the lessening of competition from buy-to-let investors has allowed some owner-occupiers to buy their first homes – but too few as yet: prices remain out of reach for all too many without family help or dangerous levels of debt.

Rents, on the other hand (or rather, partly as a consequence), firmed up last year after three years of decline – to the relief of landlords large and small.

Which leads us on to the future: to read the runes look not at price levels but at turnover – a far better indicator of the health or otherwise of the market. The Land Registry figures for 2004 showed that London prices overall rose six per cent over 2003's – having described a wiggle as above, ending with a four per cent fall in the final quarter. But the volume of sales fell by a very worrying 20 per cent, which must point to average home prices that are still too expensive to be safe or healthy for most Londoners. The government is attempting to aid first-timers and key workers with soft loans and subsidies, but the danger is that these will only help force prices up (as they have at the cheapest end of the market) until someone magics new homes as well as new money. The Mayor of London, and the Deputy Prime Minister, are trying every spell they can find to put homes on London's ample acres of empty land (see p18 for the facts and figures). Watch out, though: their new schemes could bring big changes to sleepy areas.

Next, some certainties, then some possibilities, to watch out for:

• **HIPs**: at a point yet to be announced in 2006/2007 the Home Information Pack will become mandatory when selling your home. For some it may be a good plan to sell before it comes in. The big gainers look to be estate agents – and surveyors . . . details on page 24. Whatever its shortcomings, it heralds a major change to the way we sell homes. The mystery and guesswork is ebbing away as we can discover more, and faster, about a prospective purchase.

• Already the **Land Registry figures** are easily available on-line, so that you can see what else has sold in the street, for how much (and if recent, what the seller paid himself). Though it won't tell you why No. 4 sold for so much less/more than No. 8, in the case of flats in a block or streets of homogenous houses, establishing worth will be much easier.

• At the same time, **e-conveyancing** will soon be a reality at long last, removing the other great drag on the time it takes to sell, and thus the danger of a fall-through.

Take these three together and we could get a more fluid, better-informed market, which would put downward pressure on prices. Or we could get a bureaucratic tangle – time will tell.

At last this year there is news, and good news, on London's **transport plans**. Check out the details – starting on page 20 – before you make that big move.

And now the things to watch. We write this on the eve of a general election. Politicians being, well, politicians nothing is likely to be announced to frighten the horses this side of it. However, if re-elected will the Chancellor of the Exchequer be able to resist taxing homes? Right now, the Treasury only gains from domestic property wealth when we move (stamp duty) or die (inheritance tax), or from investment property when we sell (capital gains tax). Council tax is a property tax of a sort – and a growing burden, especially on the elderly and others on fixed incomes. But no Chancellor since the 1950s has seen fit – dared – to tax the value of our homes. This could change.

The current stamp duty set-up could change, too, with smoothing of the high steps between bands which at present distort prices. But short of a major fall in market turnover (which of course would lower the tax take) don't expect the stamp duty burden to lessen overall. Keep an eye, too, on plans to reform council tax, which could lead to higher bills for London homes as properties are revalued.

London – as pages 18–19 outlines – has a remarkable economy, one which has less to do with the nation which surrounds it than with the fortunes of its competitors – New York, Paris, Shanghai, Tokyo, Singapore. To live in a 21st century city-state is fascinating, at times nerve-wracking. But it's a place the young and the ambitious around the globe want to visit, to experience, to live in. We're lucky.

Have a good year.

CARRIE SEGRAVE
LONDON, FEBRUARY 2005

How to use this book

The first part of the book contains the analysis and reference chapters: a guide to London's property market, how it works and the factors that will shape it in the coming year. Look here for information on the transport plans and their effects, the procedures of buying and selling property, the ins and outs of mortgages on offer today, the latest factors influencing the education system . . . everything you need to know about moving house in London.

The core of this book is an alphabetical directory of London's main residential areas, from A for Acton to W for Wimbledon. Each area is profiled with descriptions of the neighbourhoods it is made up of.

To find out about an area look for it in the A–Z section, which starts on page 95. The initial letter of the area is printed in the margin of each page to help you find your way around. A list of the areas covered appears in the contents. There is also a full index of streets and neighbourhoods at the back of the book.

Maps

An overall area map of London is on page 12. Maps of individual areas are at the beginning of each area profile. A key to the symbols used in these is on page 94. See opposite for how to make best use of the maps and the information that accompanies them. These pages are for quick reference to the key facts about an area.

Prices

As it is an annual, this book is not intended to be used as a price guide. It does, however, gather together average prices for different sizes of property in each of the areas and provides a 'freeze-frame' picture taken at the start of the 2005 selling season. This gives you a basis for comparison throughout the year. For prices in a given area see the relevant area information section at the end of each chapter. See also the main price charts on pages 40–43 and 54–57, where you can search across London by price or by flat/house size.

Postal districts

These are listed on pages 14–17, each with a description of the areas it covers. Start with this list if you know only the postcode you are looking for. The postal districts are also listed in the information box alongside the maps at the start of each area profile.

Boroughs

Details about each of the inner and outer London boroughs are on pages 71–73. A map on page 73 shows where their boundaries fall, as does the area map on page 12.

Council tax

Detailed at the start of each area profile are the council tax rates of band D properties in the area. There can be a big difference from borough to borough. See pages 71–72 for a list of each borough's rate of council tax.

Future editions

This book is as accurate as the combined efforts of a large number of people could make it. We would be grateful to receive news from readers about changes to any areas and any other comments and (constructive!) criticism.

Area information

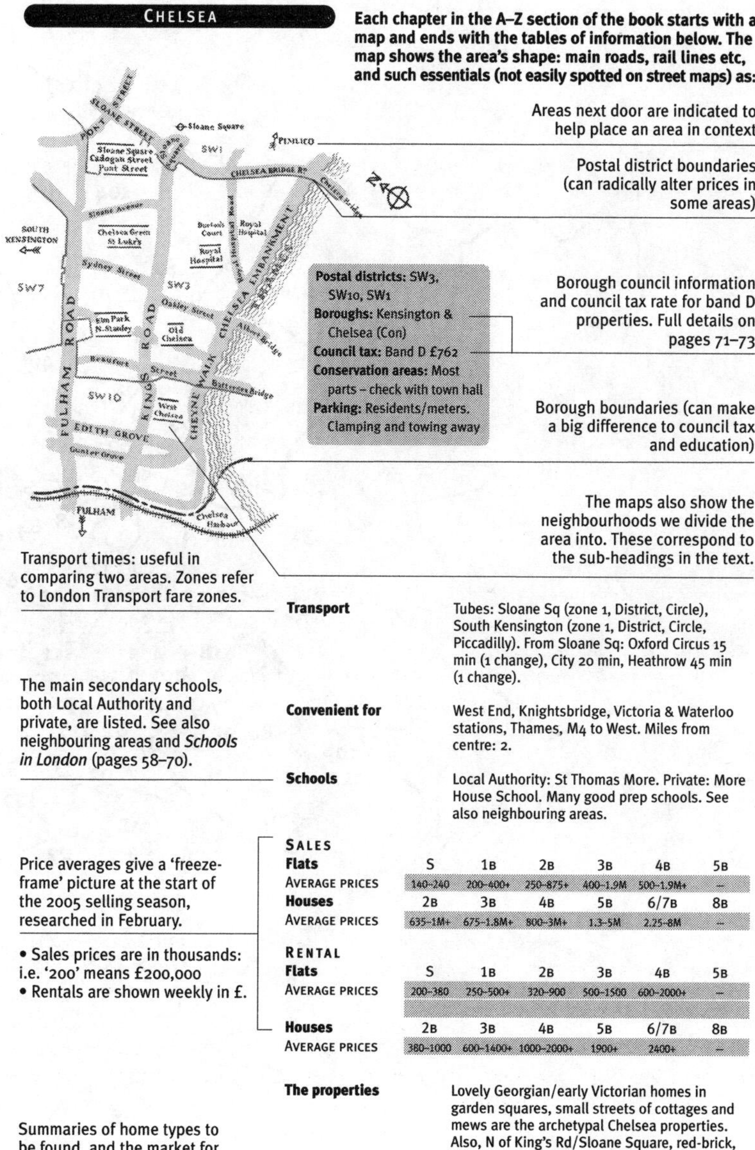

Each chapter in the A–Z section of the book starts with a map and ends with the tables of information below. The map shows the area's shape: main roads, rail lines etc, and such essentials (not easily spotted on street maps) as:

Areas next door are indicated to help place an area in context

Postal district boundaries (can radically alter prices in some areas)

Postal districts: SW3, SW10, SW1
Boroughs: Kensington & Chelsea (Con)
Council tax: Band D £762
Conservation areas: Most parts – check with town hall
Parking: Residents/meters. Clamping and towing away

Borough council information and council tax rate for band D properties. Full details on pages 71–73

Borough boundaries (can make a big difference to council tax and education)

The maps also show the neighbourhoods we divide the area into. These correspond to the sub-headings in the text.

Transport times: useful in comparing two areas. Zones refer to London Transport fare zones.

Transport Tubes: Sloane Sq (zone 1, District, Circle), South Kensington (zone 1, District, Circle, Piccadilly). From Sloane Sq: Oxford Circus 15 min (1 change), City 20 min, Heathrow 45 min (1 change).

Convenient for West End, Knightsbridge, Victoria & Waterloo stations, Thames, M4 to West. Miles from centre: 2.

The main secondary schools, both Local Authority and private, are listed. See also neighbouring areas and *Schools in London* (pages 58–70).

Schools Local Authority: St Thomas More. Private: More House School. Many good prep schools. See also neighbouring areas.

Price averages give a 'freeze-frame' picture at the start of the 2005 selling season, researched in February.

• Sales prices are in thousands: i.e. '200' means £200,000
• Rentals are shown weekly in £.

SALES

Flats	S	1B	2B	3B	4B	5B
AVERAGE PRICES	140–240	200–400+	250–875+	400–1.9M	500–1.9M+	–
Houses	2B	3B	4B	5B	6/7B	8B
AVERAGE PRICES	635–1M+	675–1.8M+	800–3M+	1.3–5M	2.25–8M	–

RENTAL

Flats	S	1B	2B	3B	4B	5B
AVERAGE PRICES	200–380	250–500+	320–900	500–1500	600–2000+	–
Houses	2B	3B	4B	5B	6/7B	8B
AVERAGE PRICES	380–1000	600–1400+	1000–2000+	1900+	2400+	–

Summaries of home types to be found, and the market for them, encapsulate the chapter for quick reference.

The properties Lovely Georgian/early Victorian homes in garden squares, small streets of cottages and mews are the archetypal Chelsea properties. Also, N of King's Rd/Sloane Square, red-brick, Dutch-gabled mansion flats. Luxury flats at King's Chelsea, part of the Duke of York's HQ, and (to come) the Barracks and Lot's Rd.

The market Buyers are now mostly City-based and prosperous: arty, upmarket locals mostly displaced by international bankers. Foreign buyers are Europeans and Americans rather than Far East, though fewer relocating families and more singles these days. Young professionals colonise West Chelsea.

Map of areas covered

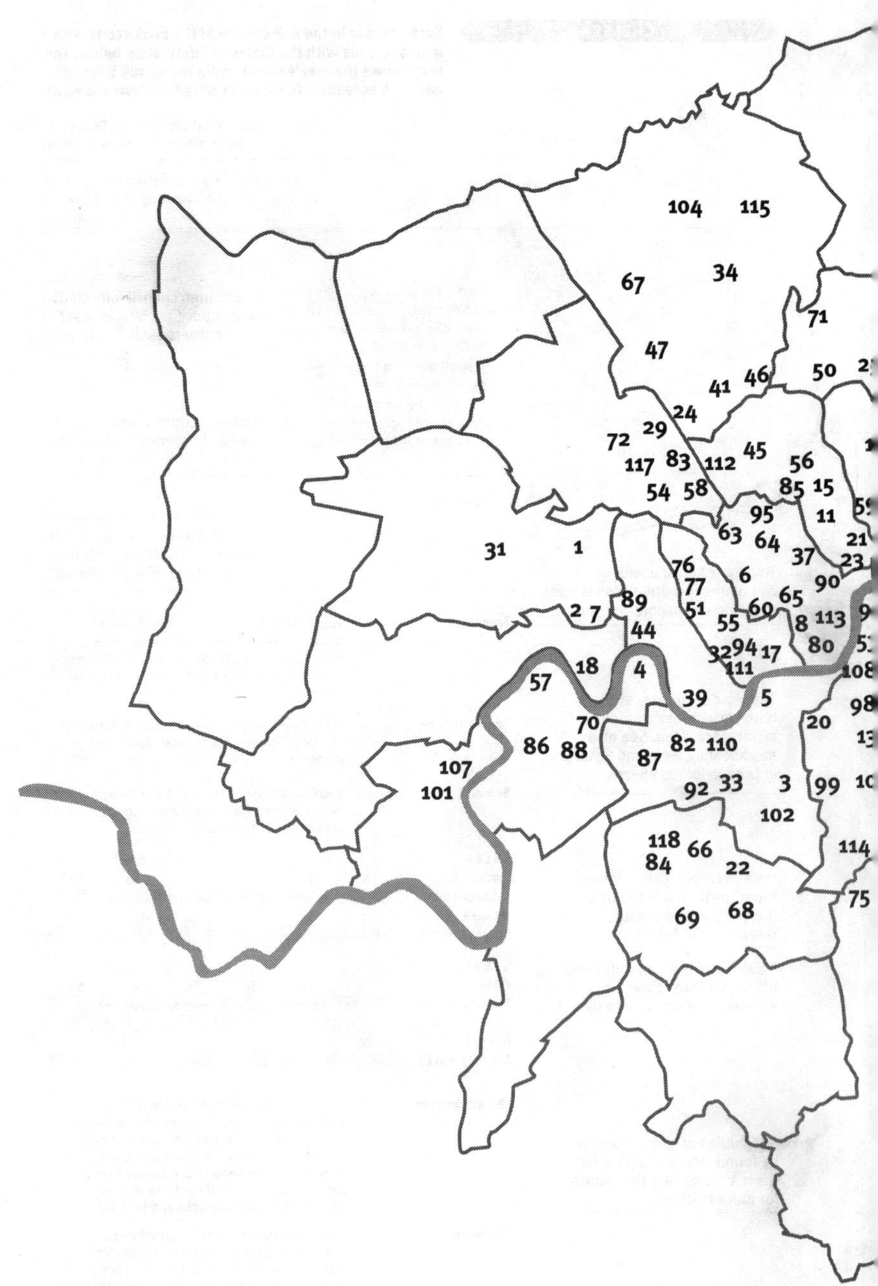

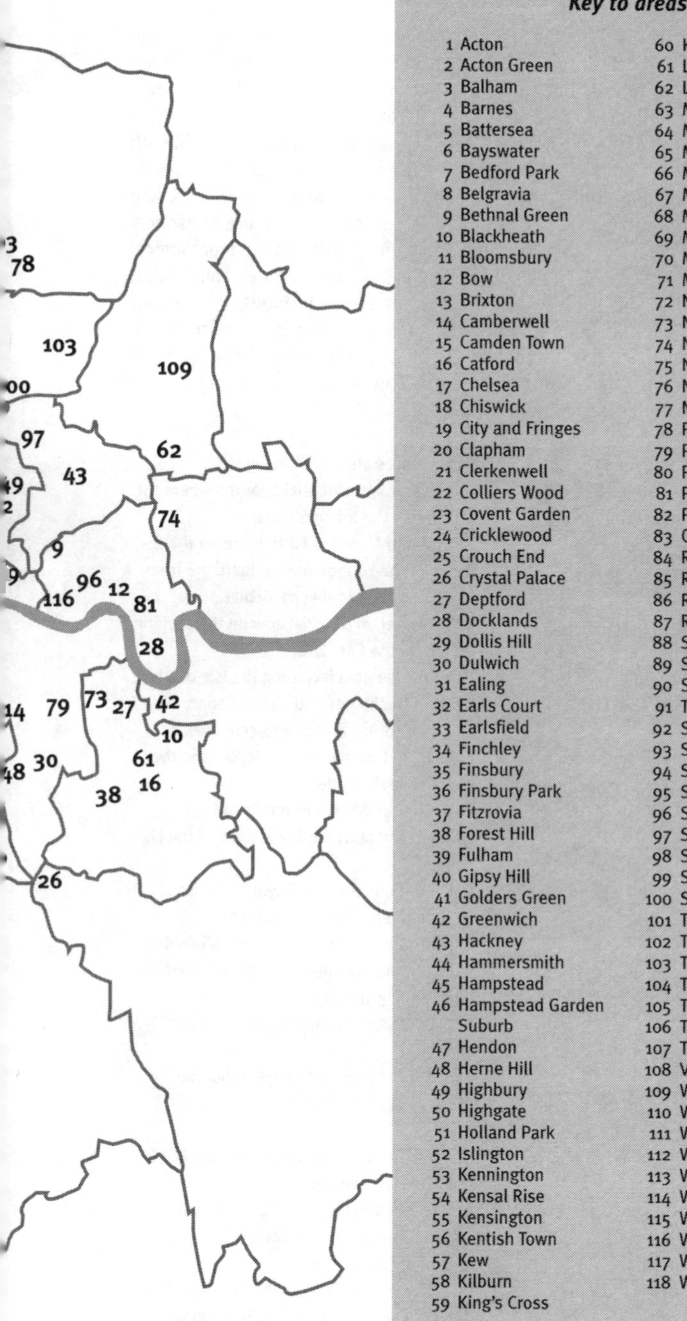

Key to areas

1 Acton
2 Acton Green
3 Balham
4 Barnes
5 Battersea
6 Bayswater
7 Bedford Park
8 Belgravia
9 Bethnal Green
10 Blackheath
11 Bloomsbury
12 Bow
13 Brixton
14 Camberwell
15 Camden Town
16 Catford
17 Chelsea
18 Chiswick
19 City and Fringes
20 Clapham
21 Clerkenwell
22 Colliers Wood
23 Covent Garden
24 Cricklewood
25 Crouch End
26 Crystal Palace
27 Deptford
28 Docklands
29 Dollis Hill
30 Dulwich
31 Ealing
32 Earls Court
33 Earlsfield
34 Finchley
35 Finsbury
36 Finsbury Park
37 Fitzrovia
38 Forest Hill
39 Fulham
40 Gipsy Hill
41 Golders Green
42 Greenwich
43 Hackney
44 Hammersmith
45 Hampstead
46 Hampstead Garden Suburb
47 Hendon
48 Herne Hill
49 Highbury
50 Highgate
51 Holland Park
52 Islington
53 Kennington
54 Kensal Rise
55 Kensington
56 Kentish Town
57 Kew
58 Kilburn
59 King's Cross
60 Knightsbridge
61 Lewisham
62 Leyton
63 Maida Vale
64 Marylebone
65 Mayfair
66 Merton Park
67 Mill Hill
68 Mitcham
69 Morden
70 Mortlake
71 Muswell Hill
72 Neasden
73 New Cross
74 Newham
75 Norbury
76 North Kensington
77 Notting Hill
78 Palmers Green
79 Peckham
80 Pimlico
81 Poplar
82 Putney
83 Queen's Park
84 Raynes Park
85 Regents Park
86 Richmond
87 Roehampton
88 Sheen
89 Shepherd's Bush
90 Soho
91 The South Bank
92 Southfields
93 Southgate
94 South Kensington
95 St John's Wood
96 Stepney
97 Stoke Newington
98 Stockwell
99 Streatham
100 Stroud Green
101 Teddington
102 Tooting
103 Tottenham
104 Totteridge
105 Tufnell Park
106 Tulse Hill
107 Twickenham
108 Vauxhall
109 Walthamstow
110 Wandsworth
111 West Brompton
112 West Hampstead
113 Westminster
114 West Norwood
115 Whetstone
116 Whitechapel
117 Willesden
118 Wimbledon

E2 or not E2? Decoding the postcodes

London's postal districts are a matter first and foremost of Post Office convenience: they act as collection and delivery zones and are based around the location of sorting offices and the ease of routes. But those few letters and numbers also convey a powerful emotional and financial message. The difference between SW1 and SW2 is more than a digit: it is all of the gap between Belgravia and Brixton. Londoners absorb these subtleties with their mother's milk. But few natives appreciate quite how remote SE2 is, or that E4 is in Epping Forest while E14 is the upwardly mobile Isle of Dogs. And the borders can be arbitrary: some of Brixton is SW2, agreed – but so are the solidly respectable mansion blocks of Streatham Hill. Some postal districts are more logical than others. The Post Office says the whole system is quite clear: it's alphabetical. It is not, and it is not. Use this list to check which areas a zone includes, and to spot anomalies. Estate agents quite frequently quote just postal districts in advertisements and by using this list you can get an idea if the area is one you want to look at. Follow the area names into the main A–Z in this book for a map, which shows postcode boundaries, and a profile of the area.

E1 The East End heartland, from the City E through Whitechapel and Stepney to Mile End. Also includes the smart warehouse conversions of riverside Wapping (see Docklands) and City fringe areas like Spitalfields and Shoreditch.

E2 North from E1, Bethnal Green and council flat-dominated Haggerston. Also a chunk of City fringe in Shoreditch.

E3 Bow, either side of the Mile End Rd in the East End.

E4 The NE fringe of London on the edge of Essex beyond the North Circular, including the suburban streets of Chingford Green and Highams Hill.

E5 The N part of Hackney borough, with Lower and Upper Clapton and a good chunk of the Hackney Marshes. Also fringes of Stoke Newington.

E6 London's eastern edge, on the way to Southend: East Ham and the Docklands suburb of Beckton.

E7 Forest Gate, the S part of Wanstead. East of Stratford East.

E8 The W side of Hackney, on the border with Islington, including the area around London Fields and the SE corner of Stoke Newington.

E9 The E part of Hackney, across the Lea Valley and the Hackney Marshes. Includes Victoria Park and Homerton.

E10 Most of Leyton, E of the Hackney Marshes from Hackney. Includes a corner of Walthamstow.

E11 Centres around Wanstead and Snaresbrook; residential suburbs where the M11 meets the North Circular.

E12 Manor Park and Little Ilford on the E fringe of the London postal district: E from here is Essex, Ilford in particular.

E13 West Ham and Plaistow on the Barking Rd E from the East End.

E14 Diverse area including the Isle of Dogs, heart of Docklands and site of Canary Wharf and other office and homes schemes, and housing in Limehouse and Poplar and the Limehouse riverside.

E15 Stratford, the metropolis of East London, and surrounding areas E of the Lea Valley.

E16 Contains the vast Royal Docks area, next on the hit-list for Docklands regeneration, as well as old-established industry and housing in riverside Silvertown and Canning Town.

E17 Walthamstow and Higham Hill in NE London.

E18 South Woodford on the suburban fringes of Epping Forest.

EC1 All four City postcodes are ECs. EC1 is the biggest, covering the relatively less prosperous tract from St Paul's N to the City Rd, and including large parts of Finsbury and all of Clerkenwell.

EC2 The money heart of the City, from the Bank of England N to Broad St. Includes the Barbican.

EC3 The E side of the City, including the Tower and the Lloyds building.
EC4 The riverside slice, including Fleet St, the Temple, Cannon St and Blackfriars.

N1 The classic Islington postcode, extending S from Highbury and Islington tube to the Angel. Includes Hoxton and De Beauvoir to the E, Barnsbury and King's Cross to the W.
N2 By contrast, the leafy streets and semis of East Finchley and Fortis Green in London's North West. Also the 'Millionaire's Row', Bishops Avenue, and the 'new' part of Hampstead Garden Suburb.
N3 Further out still, the next suburb NW covering most of Finchley.
N4 Crouch End, Stroud Green, Finsbury Park and Harringay, a widely contrasting chunk of North London.
N5 A small district covering Highbury, to the N of Islington. In Islington borough, so estate agents like to call it so.
N6 The centre of Highgate, Dartmouth Park to its S, some woods and a few streets of Fortis Green to the N.
N7 Where the Seven Sisters Rd crosses the Holloway Rd is the centre, with parts of Tufnell Park and a corner of Highbury.
N8 Hornsey, most of the 'ladder' district of Harringay, the N side of Crouch End.
N9 The N slice of Edmonton, especially Lower Edmonton.
N10 Most of Muswell Hill.
N11 Friern Barnet, New Southgate and Bounds Green: residential districts straddling the North Circular Rd.
N12 North Finchley and Woodside Park.
N13 Palmers Green, where the North Circular crosses Green Lanes due N of London.
N14 Southgate, on the northern edge of London on the Hertfordshire border.
N15 The southern part of Tottenham, at the NE end of the Seven Sisters Rd.
N16 Stoke Newington and the S part of Stamford Hill.
N17 Most of Tottenham.
N18 A slice along the North Circular N of Tottenham, including Edmonton and Upper Edmonton.
N19 Archway, from the fringes of Highgate and Crouch End in the N down to Tufnell Park.
N20 The semi-rural, prosperous and pony-infested Totteridge, Oakleigh Park and Whetstone, N of Finchley and S of Barnet.
N21 Winchmore Hill and Grange Park, suburbia plus a lot of golf courses on the fringe of North London.
N22 Wood Green, Alexandra Palace, the E side of Muswell Hill, Noel Park and the W edge of Tottenham.

NW1 One of London's most diverse districts, with the Nash villas of Regent's Park and the crowded streets of Camden Town sharing the same postcode. Starts in the S at the Marylebone Rd, takes in part of Lisson Grove in the W, the edge of Kentish Town in the NE, all of Camden Town and Primrose Hill.
NW2 One of the less helpful postcodes. Covers Cricklewood, Childs Hill, Dollis Hill, an arbritary slice of Willesden and a bit of Brondesbury.
NW3 The Hampstead postcode, and one with hardly an undesirable corner. Includes Belsize Park, part of Primrose Hill, the Finchley Rd – but not West Hampstead, which is NW6.
NW4 Hendon, from Brent Cross up along the M1 to the edge of Mill Hill.
NW5 Kentish Town, Gospel Oak and Tufnell Park, on the SE fringes of Hampstead and Highgate.
NW6 Once thought of as the Kilburn postcode – which it still is – but now associated more with West Hampstead. Also spreads W to include Queen's Park and Brondesbury Park.
NW7 Mill Hill and assorted golf courses, detached houses and green belt countryside out along the M1.
NW8 Clearly defined as St John's Wood, with only a few acres of council housing around Lisson Grove to lower the tone.
NW9 West Hendon, Colindale and Kingsbury, suburban areas NW of the Welsh Harp reservoir.

NW10 A large area extending W from Kensal Rise to the North Circular, taking in Neasden, Harlesden and parts of Willesden.
NW11 Golders Green and the older, smarter side of Hampstead Garden Suburb.

SE1 A big tract in the bend of the river opposite the City and Westminster: The South Bank from Vauxhall in the W to the Old Kent Rd in the E. Very varied: many new homes schemes, plus the National Theatre, the new Tate, the Tower Bridge quarter.
SE2 In Kent, really, E of Woolwich and even Plumstead, it comprises Abbey Wood and part of Thamesmead.
SE3 Blackheath, Blackheath Park, East Greenwich and Kidbrooke.
SE4 A small district S of New Cross and W of Lewisham, centred around Brockley.
SE5 Essentially Camberwell, though the SW end of Coldharbour Lane is better described as Brixton, the NW corner is in Kennington and the NE in Walworth.
SE6 Catford, and Bellingham to the S.
SE7 Charlton, on the river E of the Blackwall Tunnel and W of Woolwich.
SE8 Deptford, extending along the riverside opposite the Isle of Dogs and S of the Surrey Docks. Not part of the Docklands area, though similar to it. A corner of SE8 sticks down towards Lewisham, taking in St John's.
SE9 Far, suburban SE London, including Eltham and Mottingham.
SE10 Greenwich, except for East Greenwhich which is SE3. SE10 also includes the Millenium Dome peninsula to the NE beneath which the Blackwall Tunnel motorway passes.
SE11 Most of Kennington, from the Oval N to the Elephant & Castle and W to the river at Vauxhall. More SW than SE.
SE12 Lee and Grove Park, SE of Catford.
SE13 Lewisham, plus Ladywell and Hither Green to the S.
SE14 New Cross and a slice of the inland side of Deptford.
SE15 Peckham, part of Peckham Rye (the rest is in SE22), and Nunhead.
SE16 Bermondsey and Rotherhithe, including the entire Surrey Docks district of Docklands. Away from the river. SE16 includes streets on the edge of North Peckham. The NW corner, along the river, has some big new riverside developments.
SE17 Walworth, from the Elephant & Castle southwards. Includes part of Kennington in the W.
SE18 Woolwich, Plumstead and Plumstead Common.
SE19 Centres around the Crystal Palace hilltop, including Norwood New Town and the fringes of Penge.
SE20 Penge and Anerley, to the SE of Crystal Palace.
SE21 Dulwich Village, and the fringes of Tulse Hill.
SE22 East Dulwich, part of Peckham Rye and a bit of Honor Oak.
SE23 Forest Hill, to the E of Dulwich. Also Honor Oak.
SE24 Herne Hill, also extending N towards Brixton's Loughborough Junction and NW to Brockwell Park and the Poets' Estate. Some streets in the SE corner are really in Dulwich.
SE25 South Norwood.
SE26 Sydenham, from Crystal Palace E to Bell Green and S to the edge of Penge.
SE27 West Norwood and the S half of Tulse Hill.
SE28 Thamesmead, the new town on the Plumstead Marshes E down the Thames.

SW1 Perhaps the smartest code of all, the postal address of Buckingham Palace and 10 Downing St, never mind the whole of Westminster, St James's, Belgravia, Victoria and part of Knightsbridge including Harrods, squeezed in by a dramatic jink in the frontier, forming an enclave in SW3. Pimlico is SW1 and now that has 'come up' there is hardly a cheap corner left. Sloane Square is SW1 too.
SW2 Part of Brixton, the southern slice, and also Streatham Hill, the edge of Clapham Park and part of Tulse Hill.
SW3 Chelsea, though the HQ of Chelseadom, Peter Jones, is in SW1. Also a good part of Knightsbridge and some of South Ken – see the area map for the quirks of the boundaries here. SW3 stops at Beaufort St in the W and large tracts of Chelsea are in SW10.

SW4 Clapham, plus a portion of Stockwell W of Clapham Rd and a corner of W Brixton.
SW5 A small zone, essentially Earl's Court.
SW6 By contrast, the entire island cut off by the river and the railway, which is Fulham. Only in the N, where the boundary runs along Lillie Rd, is there any doubt. Some streets N of here are really in Fulham though they have W6 and W14 codes.
SW7 South Kensington, Knightsbridge (though see also SW3) and the Museums.
SW8 A mixed area, much crossed by railways, between the river and Stockwell. Includes parts of Stockwell, the Oval, Vauxhall, the E part of Battersea's Queenstown neighbourhood, and the industrial zone of Nine Elms.
SW9 The northern half of Brixton, the E side of Stockwell and a corner in the N that is really the Oval.
SW10 The western end of Chelsea, plus a patch to the N which is really West Brompton and, by sheer good luck for the developers, the big Chelsea Harbour development which physical, if not postal, geography places across the creek in Fulham.
SW11 A big slice of smart and not-so-smart South London, from Battersea Park, through Central Battersea to Wandsworth Common.
SW12 Balham, including the streets in the 'Nightingale Triangle' where people say they're in Clapham South, and the lower tier of the 'Between the Commons' neighbourhood of Battersea.
SW13 Barnes, well-defined by common, river and White Hart Lane, which forms the boundary with SW14 and Mortlake.
SW14 Mortlake by the river and the suburban streets of East Sheen on the edge of Richmond Park.
SW15 Putney, plus Roehampton in the W and some streets that are virtually Wandsworth to the E.
SW16 Streatham, plus Streatham Vale and Norbury in the S.
SW17 Tooting.
SW18 Wandsworth, part of Wandsworth Common, Southfields and Earlsfield.
SW19 A large area including Wimbledon, Wimbledon Park, Merton and Colliers Wood.
SW20 The further reaches of Wimbledon towards the Kingston bypass, including Raynes Park.

W1 Grandeur and commerce, including Mayfair, Oxford St, Regent St . . . Essentially, the West End, plus homes in Soho and Marylebone.
W2 Bayswater and Paddington, plus Little Venice S of the canal.
W3 Acton, though not Acton Green in the S or the industry of North Acton.
W4 Chiswick, including Bedford Park and Acton Green.
W5 The centre of Ealing, including South Ealing. Ealing has three postcodes: see area map.
W6 Hammersmith and the northern fringes of Fulham.
W7 The western slice of Ealing borough, including Hanwell and part of West Ealing.
W8 The heart of Kensington, around the High St and Church St.
W9 Maida Vale and Little Venice N of the canal, plus a sharply contrasting area to the W of Waterton Rd stretching up to Queen's Park.
W10 North Kensington N of the fly-over, plus Kensal as far N as Queen's Park.
W11 Notting Hill S of the fly-over and N of Notting Hill Gate. Includes the N part of Holland Park.
W12 Shepherd's Bush, plus East Acton and White City.
W13 The middle slice of Ealing, W of Ealing centre and E of Hanwell.
W14 A slice squeezed between Kensington and Hammersmith, including some of the smartest parts of Holland Park, Olympia, West Kensington and the NE quadrant of Hammersmith.

WC1 Bloomsbury, St Pancras and the W part of Finsbury.
WC2 Covent Garden, Theatreland, the Strand, part of Holborn.

London in 2005

London property market-watchers this year have the Greater London Authority (GLA) to thank for a new report which lays out London's economy for all (even non-economists) to see. It demonstrates how London's banking and finance industry operates on a world scale, how the business services sector is, in employment terms, bigger still; how both it and finance attract and support entertainment and culture, publishing, media in general, restaurants, hotels. These in their turn beget tourism, which generates more cultural and entertainment activity. What the experts call 'agglomeration effects' – mutual support – leads to yet more growth.

And all this matters to me when I am trying to buy or sell a home? Or to decide if investing in one is a sensible plan? Yes, because growth would mean more jobs, which means more people (and well-off people at that) who will need somewhere to live. It adds a positive spin to the scarcity argument: London's homes must gain in value, there are too few to go round. Does this analysis stand scrutiny? And will tomorrow's Londoners – the teachers as well as the bond traders – be able to afford the property prices?

The people who are sparking this economic growth flow into London as commuters and migrants (both from overseas and from elsewhere in the UK). The pattern is clear: young, active, often well-educated people arrive, learn, gain experience, build careers, pay their taxes and later move out (with their families), taking their skills with them. London has a younger population than, and a net outflow of people to, the rest of the UK. The numbers are kept up, indeed increased, by foreign migrants, at the net rate of 100,000 a year, of which the French are (contrary to so many perceptions) the largest single group. And of course some of the outward-movers commute back in to London daily.

The GLA statisticians link periodic surges in the numbers leaving London with rises in the capital's house prices: people cash in their stake and hightail it to the shires. Trend-watchers find in this inward flow of young, busy people an attractive source of tenants for the city's landlords, and in their frequent departure as 30-somethings a slightly less upbeat picture for owners of family homes. A study of these GLA straws in the wind (events will invariably defeat some predictions) is informative.

Counting people, counting homes

Population growth, after 40 years of decline, has become a fact in London since the mid-1990s. Population in a big city is notoriously hard to count, let alone predict, but the GLA planners reckon that it was 7.3 million in 2003, and that it will rise to 8.1 million by 2016. At the same time, the number of households is rising even faster, adding 336,000 (22,400 a year) by 2016. This is due to changes in the type of population – all those young workers. These estimates give a crude figure for the number of new homes that London needs each year. Is supply matching demand?

London at present has just over 3.1 million homes (or 'dwellings', in the jargon): 57 per cent owner-occupied, 17 per cent privately rented, the rest 'social' (council and housing association). The stock has been growing an average of 19,000 a year over the last 20 years. Not all these are new – in the last decade that number has been between 12,000 and 17,000 a year. Add conversions, or splitting up, of existing homes and you get a figure for 2004 of 24,000 – or more than the number of new households.

This would seem to knock the scarcity scenario for house price rises on the head – but not according to the Mayor of London's maths. This is based on the sums about migration and adds in those 146,000 existing households which need rehousing from unsuitable, usually overcrowded, homes. Then subtract from the housing stock homes demolished or lost to conversions (two flats may return to being one house, for instance) and you get his total of 35,000 new homes needed per annum. The mayor's target is 30,000 – half as much again as the current flow.

The Mayor's sums depend on those young, busy people continuing to knock at London's doors, and this depends on growth in London's economy. A worry is that London is becoming a one-industry town, as dependent on international finance as an old-time mill town was on cotton. Canary Wharf sneezes; we all catch a cold.

The rich are different from us

A perennial fascination is watching London's millionaire's market. What counts as expensive? Different people, different answers, but start thinking of £4 million for a home – it could well be a flat – and go on beyond £40 million (though reports of a £100 million price for Chelsea's old rectory were denied). How much does this market have to do with real London? It used to be said that the top end starts the price trends: rich buyers displace the merely well-off from their Kensington houses, and they are forced to buy in Fulham, pricing the Fulhamites out to Putney, and so on. But the difference now is so great, in level of luxury and in price, between the 'top end' and the rest of us that it is hard to find a link. Which is a pity in a way, because top prices have been rising, while the home-grown market just beneath was static. Is the supply of rich Russians inexhaustible?

And talking of the rest of us...

The Mayor, quite rightly, also reckons that not enough 'affordable' housing is coming through – a belief shared by the government, which is working on several schemes to increase provison to help first-time buyers and key workers (see page 35). He also has a map showing 'opportunity areas' where new housing could be concentrated. These cluster to the E of the city, along the Thames Gateway and the Lea Valley.

For years we have been pointing out the great white gash on London's map that is the Lea Valley, cleaving northwards from the Thames through the East End, to those who call for more building on outer-London Green Belt land. This wilderness of open space and marsh, spotted with gasworks and redundant factories, and nailed down by pylons that march miles of electricity cables above it, is flanked by traditional London areas. That's Stratford, with brand-new transport hub and soon to-be-opened Eurostar station, on its eastern shore. Here work is already under way (and the developers there are going to bury those cables). The rest is aching for equally sympathetic treatment to provide an airy, green site for the new homes we need, with transport infrastructure already to hand.

But out past the Royal Docks, the yet emptier spaces of the 'Thames Gateway' stretch all the way to Southend. Even the name is edgy as much as inspiring: gateway to London, or gateway for the river itself? We doubt many will see the charm of the Barking or Erith marshes. They are not called floodplains for nothing. As a respected colleague has it, this looks like developing along the line of least resistance. People want to be here, not there.

Transport: keeping London on the map

Three factors broke the transport log-jam in London: the Olympic Games bid, a cunning piece of financial engineering and a bout of ministerial impatience. The three came together during 2004, turning wishful thinking into firm plans, long-nurtured dreams into funded projects. Who knows, but one year soon something might actually Get Built.

Olympic bids are rare enough, and public enough, to engender a touch of panic in Whitehall. The thought of all those stern Olympians summing up London as a snarled-up mess before plumping for Paris was enough to get the East London Line bounced from the wished-for to the happening list. Then some bright sparks at City Hall set out a plausible way to pay for it: let Transport for London borrow from the banks. This bond-finance technique is common elsewere for public infrastructure, but Britain's Treasury views it with suspicion. The Olympic urgency allowed this disquiet to be quashed.

Then just up Whitehall in the Department of Transport, ministers got sick of being messed about by the Strategic Rail Authority (whose supporters would say it was messed up by the Ministry). The SRA has been duly scrapped and power to plan transport is back in the Ministry, whence it escaped a decade ago when rail was privatised.

For this last decade, thanks to the post-privatisation chaos, no single body has had the power to finance London infrastructure schemes, though half a dozen had both the power and the will to thwart them. Now, at least things are clearer: Transport for London (TfL), a province of the Mayor's empire, makes the plans and runs the services – buses, tubes; or licences them – river boats, some buses. It is angling to take on London overground rail services, at present run by various train operating companies (TOCs) like Southwest Trains. It has a Director of Rail, and now will have something to direct: the government's latest rail review (July '04, the seventh since 1997) grants TfL far more power to control train services: the first big step will be the takeover of the Silverlink Metro operation (the notoriously unreliable North London Line).

TfL has just gained the power to borrow to finance new infrastructure, thus escaping from the straightjacket tailored by the Treasury which effectively starved the Mayor (and TfL) of cash. This borrowing power will not pay for all the projects on TfL's want-list, but it goes a long way, and crucially it allows a five-year programme to be planned with the certainty that the money will be there to pay for it. Many previous transport schemes have been victims of central government spending curbs, prompted by changes of political control, financial crises or just plain Whitehall horse-trading.

TfL will borrow £3 billion over the next five years, and they expect this to be matched by the same sum from central government. An additional £4 billion is already in the budget from the PPP tube contracts and various PFI (private finance initiative) schemes.

This neatly sidelines a key obstacle to investment in London transport: why should a government, any government, spend money on the capital when the voters who elect the House of Commons are mostly elsewhere? And there are few votes in Telford or Inverness in building Crossrail.

Transport and property: dreams and realities

There is a lady in Streatham who bought two flats in 2001 and intends to sell them when the Underground opens. A good strategy. But in this case, poor tactics. The Streatham tube is the Flying Dutchman of public transport schemes: frequently reported, never proved to exist. For 20 years now, local papers and estate agents have waxed long about various tube line extensions to Streatham. The latest was the East London Line, which was being promised as recently as late 2003. It won't happen. The East London *is* being built, but only one of the three proposed branches, and Streatham is not on it.

Transport, or the lack of it, matters a lot when deciding where to live or invest. We have seen the effect that the Jubilee Line and DLR extensions had on house prices in hitherto inaccessible areas; the same, to a lesser extent, with the Croydon Tramlink. Stratford is a clear case of what investment can do, with the International station, now nearly built, sparking enormous interest in this historically deprived area. Lewisham and Greenwich gained equally from the extended DLR, and a whole swathe of the South Bank from the Jubilee Line.

Schemes and schemers

Several of the plans on these pages have been chronicled in this Guide since 1988 (and one at least goes back to 1948). They do not yet exist, except in paper form. It takes three years to gain Parliamentary powers to even begin to plan a new railway or tube, and the Public Inquiry can take another five. The new financial environment created by the mayor's borrowing power is an improvement: it lessens uncertainty. But not all the Mayor wants, can he afford. Some cherished schemes will be scrapped – especially once the Olympic excuse is blown away. So beware – schemes, proposals, firm plans all come to dust. The word 'go-ahead' is meaningless. Rarely, something gets built. Even then, it takes at least five years. Our unvarying rule: Don't Believe It till you See them Digging.

Three big plans

On from the politics: the big London rail/tube projects are Thameslink 2000, the East London Line Extension (ELLX) and Crossrail. After them come an increasingly long list of detailed, but useful, enhancements.

• **Thameslink 2000** has gone very quiet. Already the grand design, a major network within a network, with trains linking everywhere from King's Lynn to Littlehampton, Ashford to Hatfield via central London, has been shunted into a siding: it was not mentioned at all in the Government's July 2004 White Paper 'The Future of Transport', and the mayor's office has become non-committal, even though the project is on Mr Livingstone's wish-list. What is emerging is an enhanced North London commuter line with (later on) more cross-London trains. Until 2012 at the earliest, South London will make do with existing Thameslink services.

The '2000' enhancement will happen in some form: the new Eurostar terminus at St Pancras provides a new underground Thameslink station. But though 2002's planning inquiry broadly supported the scheme, it raised three big concerns about details, the most important being about the effect on the Borough Market area close to London Bridge. In mid-2004 new proposals came out, and borough planners (and doubtless after them the Mayor, and Whitehall) are considering them. Latest plans envisage work starting in January 2007, with completion in 2011. The North London part seems achievable by 2008, but it must be stressed that no funding has yet been allocated for anything beyond (admittedly detailed) planning work.

• **East London Line Extension** (ELLX) has gained from the Olympic bid and the mayor's new borrowing powers, and is now on the active list. ELLX will extend the existing East London (tube) Line at both ends, and convert it to a 'metro' service with 4-car overground-type trains. But so far only Phase One is certain.

The latest plan for Phase One, with trains per hour (tph) is:

The Northern Extension with 12 tph will run along the disused rail viaduct to the E of the Kingsland Rd. The existing Shoreditch station will close. New stations will be at: **Bishopsgate:** south of Bethnal Green Rd; on **Shoreditch High St**; at **Hoxton** on the Cremer St/Geffrye St junction, close to the Geffrye Museum; at **Haggerston** S of Lee St, close to the Kingsland Rd; in **Dalston:** south of Dalston Lane, between Kingsland Road and Roseberry Place. However, plans to run trains on via Canonbury to Highbury & Islington (where it would have had a Victoria Line interchange) have been postponed to Phase Two,

due to clashes with the busy North London Line. This means there will be no direct link for passengers between the ELLX and the North London until Phase Two is built.
The Southern Extension will run S from **New Cross Gate** to serve **Brockley, Honor Oak Park, Forest Hill** and **Sydenham.** A branch will go from Sydenham to **Crystal Palace** (4 tph). The main service would continue to **Penge West, Anerley, Norwood Junction** and **West Croydon** (4 tph). Thus the Sydenham–Surrey Quays section will have 8 tph. Phase One is planned to open by 2010. **Rotherhithe** and **Wapping** stations, both on the existing East London, were threatened with closure by the ELLX plans, but have been reprieved.

Phase Two – which has no scheduled start date, never mind a finish – involves a new line from **Surrey Quays** via a new station at Surrey Canal Rd to Queen's Road **Peckham,** then via Peckham Rye and Clapham High St through to **Clapham Junction** (but no stop at Brixton). At the N end, trains will run on from Dalston to **Highbury & Islington.**

• **Crossrail** is the most ambitious plan: a high-speed, high-capacity east–west line that would take passengers straight to the West End and the City from the edge of London, much in the manner of the Paris RER lines. It has been talked about, and planned for, since 1990. There has been much wrangling about precise routes at either end of the central tunnel, which is planned to run from **Paddington** to **Whitechapel.** A section from Kingston via Richmond to Chiswick has been dropped. So has the seemingly logical extension at the SE end from Abbey Wood, near Woolwich, on E to the new Channel Tunnel Line station at Ebbsfleet. A spur to **Heathrow** has been kept. At the W end, services would reach Maidenhead; to the E there would be two branches: via **Stratford** to Shenfield, via **Canary Wharf** to Abbey Wood.

The project was given the go-ahead by the Ministry in summer 2004, and a Hybrid Bill (granting the the necessary powers) was expected in Parliament as we went to press in February 2005. Powers there may be, plans exist in abundance, but where is the money? The Mayor has been warned off: this is a national government project. The City (and Docklands) has had their arms twisted to come up with some of the £12 billion needed, with reports suggesting government cash may be limited to £2 billion. And no-one, not even the scheme's promoters, expect it to be ready before 2013. A cheaper alternative, floated under the name Superail by a private-sector consortium, may offer a ray of hope. Crossrail has annexed (or perhaps put out of its misery) the plan for the Chelsea-Hackney Line (date of birth 1948) which will now be Crossrail 2. Or so it says here. . . .

Change at Stratford East for Paris

Yes, on this one they really are digging! At Stratford, behind King's Cross and beneath the Thames Estuary, the Channel Tunnel Rail Link (CTRL), the fast line from London to the Chunnel, is on schedule for early 2007. The tunnels are dug, the stations taking shape.

Far faster and more frequent services to Europe are the main outcome of CTRL, with **St Pancras** and the enormous new **Stratford International** stations as the starting points. The Paris journey will be 35 minutes quicker at 2 hours 20 mins, Brussels will be under 2 hours (down from 2 hrs 35 mins). Until 2007, Waterloo-bound trains are using Section One of the new line – the rural bit in Kent – shaving 20 minutes off the former Paris time and increasing Eurostar's share of all London-Paris traffic from 54 to 68 per cent in the past year. The new stations will enhance Continental connections for anyone on the N and E sides of London, of course. But Waterloo users will lose out, as Eurostar has abandoned plans to continue services from the 1993-built Waterloo International station. Eurostar passengers will have to travel by tube to the new St Pancras complex.

Faster and more frequent services from St Pancras to the **'Thames Corridor'** and Kent will also result in up to eight domestic trains an hour from 2009 (perhaps even 2007). Ebbsfleet International, close to Junction 2 on the M25, will bring Eurostar to people in **South-East** and **outer South London,** while Stratford International – to be a major interchange with domestic, London and also East of England rail services – does the same for the **North-East**. The St Pancras Eurostar station will sit above a big new deep-level Thameslink one (see above), giving excellent connections.

London's bid for the 2012 Olympics makes much, justifiably, of Stratford's excellent transport links, which would give an 'Olympic Javelin' service to St Pancras in six minutes.

Other plans

• **Docklands Light Railway** The DLR will reach the City Airport, via Silvertown (see the Royals chapter for new station sites) late this year, 2005. Next comes a new tunnel under the Thames to **Woolwich**, with an opening date in 2008. Three-car trains on the **Bank–Lewisham** section are planned for 2007. The DLR intends to extend its **Stratford** service to link up with the new International station, and it will take over the track used by the North London Line to run a service from the Royals at **Canning Town** to Stratford, with three new stations along the route. This should be in use by 2009. There are less-well-formed plans to extend the North London Line N along the Lea Valley to Tottenham Hale. A DLR extension via Barking Reach to Dagenham Dock is at the planning stage.

• **West London Line** On the other side of town, a station is being built at Chelsea Harbour/Imperial Wharf on the West London Line, offering limited peak-hour (three trains an hour) services from late this year, 2005. Another new station on the same line, at the Shepherds Bush City shopping complex, is also under construction. It's possible more frequent services could follow, a step towards the aspiration for an 'Orbirail' round-London metro. TfL's planned takeover of the Silverlink service moves in this direction. The North London Line, at present run by Silverlink, would be an important part of Orbirail. Minor changes to timetabling seem likely soon, but heavy freight use makes major passnger enhancements difficult.

• **Trams and Transits** The excellent Tramlink may grow, with a spur to **Crystal Palace** at the planning stage. Transport for London has detailed plans for four tram schemes, of which the most exciting are the **'Cross River Transit'**: from **King's Cross** to the **Elephant & Castle**, with spurs to **Peckham** and **Brixton**, and an **Uxbridge– Ealing–Shepherd's Bush** scheme. Both have been 'given the go-ahead' by the Mayor but as ever cash is short – and in the West London case locals are not keen. Expect neither before 2011. Other 'transits' (for which read buses on dedicated roads) – **Greenwich Waterfront**, **East London** – may be put on a faster track due to the Thames Gateway project. This, by the way, has sparked approval (and even cash) for the **Thames Gateway Bridge**, a new road-toll bridge between Docklands and Thamesmead, providing (by 2010?) a link between the North and South Circulars, at present joined, tenuously, by the Woolwich Ferry.

• **Heathrow** Terminal 5 at Heathrow will be ready by 2008. Public transport links will be an extended Piccadilly Line tube and an extended Heathrow Express. Beware for the next two years: Terminal 4's tube station will be closed while the work goes on, and passengers for T4 will have to get out at Hatton Cross and use a bus service.

Passengers from **Ealing** will be able to travel direct to Heathrow from this spring, 2005, using the new, half-hourly Heathrow Connect service. It will in fact start from **Paddington** – but it seems no tickets will be sold from Paddington to Heathrow to avoid competition with the premium-fare Heathrow Express. Plans, too, under the Airtrack banner for services to the S and W from Heathrow, serving Guildford and Reading, and from **Richmond** in the E. These are plans only, and cannot be expected before 2012–2015.

Just keep cool

The hot summer of 2003 prompted research on ways of cooling tube trains. It's planned that the District, Circle, Metropolitan and other 'shallow' lines will have some form of cooling from 2009, and an experiment using cool underground water and large fans may lead to relief for Victoria, Northern and other passengers – but not till around 2015.

Buying and selling in London

This year could be a good time to sell a home, especially if you are of a conservative frame of mind and distrust novelty. For next year, 2006, will see the advent of the Home Information Pack. Selling a home, or indeed buying one, will involve a whole new tranche of paperwork, a new profession, and (as is the way of new things, especially those introduced by governments) doubtless much acrimony and confusion.

All this is because of the 2004 Housing Act, which gives ministers the power to bring in the Home Information Pack regime. The timetable is not yet certain, but the government talks about early 2007, with a 'dry run', during which the HIP will not be compulsory, in mid-2006.

Yes that's right, compulsory. Market your home without a HIP, and the local Trading Standards people will be on to you, with a fine of £200 in prospect.

The tortuous, time-(dis)honoured, steam-driven method of buying, selling and how to go about both is outlined and discussed below, starting on page 30. But HIPs are the future.

Home Buying Reform

Everyone – buyers, sellers, estate agents, even solicitors – has long agreed that the present system is cumbersome and bursting with opportunities for it all to go wrong. In 1997, the present government came to power with a 'cure' for gazumping in its manifesto, and it has stuck to the promise ever since. Enter the new law, which is supposed to make it all easier and quicker (no-one is saying anything about cheaper).

The present system is usually slow and undoubtedly stressful. It allows too much time between the (non-binding) verbal agreement, the signing of the contract (still only committing the buyer to 10 per cent of the price) and (if you get there) completion. Plenty of room for sellers to accept a higher, later offer (gazumping), or buyers in a slow market to force the price down at the eleventh hour, hoping the seller will be too locked in to the move to stand firm (gazundering). Or for plain changes of heart, or circumstances.

Can I come in, I'm a Certified Home Inspector?

The key change from what we do now is the mandatory use of a 'Home Information Pack' to sell a home. This will be a legal requirement: try to sell without it, be you an estate agent or a private individual, and you will commit a civil offence. Lobbying by estate agents anxious to avoid a police record prompted a rethink of the threat to make this a *criminal* matter. Another concession is a 'reasonable endeavours' clause which will allow the pack to be supplied incomplete, and marketing to be started, if efforts to get hold of all the information are unavailing. The National Association of Estate Agents guesses that compiling a HIP will take around 14 days – *if* everyone cooperates.

If you start to sell ('market') your home before the HIP is complete, you will fall foul of the local authority's Trading Standards Office, which will have the power to levy a fixed penalty charge (predicted to be £200). There will also be a right for the buyer to sue for the cost of any item missing from the pack.

Estate agents who transgress will face unspecified 'action' by the Office of Fair Trading under the 1979 Estate Agents Act. Indeed the government seems to be using the advent of the HIP to open up a new front against 'rogue estate agents', who will be forced to join an Ombudsman or indemnity scheme to compensate the public if they commit various HIP-related misdeeds. Should the agent fail to join a scheme they will be banned, says the ministry. They go further: ministers are planning to extend the law so that all estate agency activity, not just HIPs, is covered by compulsory indemnity schemes.

The HIP is only demanded where properties are 'being sold on the open market'. 'Sales or transfers where no marketing takes place will not be affected' – so sayeth the Minister, and we foresee much broad interpretation of this: it's clear that sales between private individuals or within families, sales of tenanted properties, sales of portfolios of properties will all fall outside the net.

Estate agents, or anyone else who is in charge of compiling a HIP, have to use their judgment about who to give it out to: it must only go, says the Act, to a person who seems likely to be able to buy (that is, afford) the property in question, which in theory does not include burglars, the merely inquisitive or the local press.

The Pack will have a standard set of information and paperwork, giving potential buyers most of what they need – terms of sale, evidence of title, any planning permissions, building regulations approvals, listed building consents, local-authority searches, replies to standard preliminary enquiries – to decide if they want to buy, and get on with the deal if they do. So far, so sensible. Exceptions are made for caravans, houseboats, and new homes which carry a NHBC 10-year guarantee.

More controversial (unless you are a surveyor) is the inclusion of a Home Condition Report (HCR) based upon an inspection of the property. The Government calls this a 'professional survey', but it should not be confused with a survey as usually understood.

• **The Home Condition Report is the aspect of the seller's pack that many in the property world – and this Guide – object to. It will cost sellers money, will become useless if the home fails to sell speedily – and, instead of saving time, may lose it, possibly crucially, by delaying the putting of the home onto the market.**

This goes, too, for another Home Information Pack item, specifically for leasehold homes: copy of the lease, most recent service charge and management accounts, insurance details, and reams of legal bumpf about the management company. On top of all the rest, the seller will have to get his landlord or block management to come up with these, and quickly, when he wants to sell.

The dry run

This will take place in 2006, when estate agents will be 'encouraged', but not forced, to use HIPs. There is talk of a compulsory test in a yet-to-be chosen area of England.

An inspector calls

Only about one sale in four currently involves a survey and, to cope with the workload, a new breed of 'expert' will appear, qualified to a lower level from the fully-fledged chartered surveyor. An accreditation scheme will be run by a new Home Inspectors Certification Board – and those from non-surveying backgrounds will be able to qualify; indeed the government are encouraging 'open access' to enhance job opportunities. There will be a new NVQ Level 4 qualification for the job. It is envisaged that a two-year course will be compulsory, with shorter training for those already qualified in a relevant discipline. Qualified Chartered Surveyors may need to undertake a three-day 'bridging' course to qualify as Home Inspectors. Some 7,500 of these Home Inspectors will be needed – about 8,000 have 'expressed interest'. The Government has promised that the HCR will not be made compulsory until these people exist in the required numbers.

The reports will be stored on a national database. The HCR will not, as it turns out, have a 'sell-by date': it should be considered, says the ministry, as a 'snap-shot' of the condition of the home at a given date, and it's up to buyers and sellers to decide if a new one is needed. Other questions remain unanswered, despite five years of discussion: what happens, for instance, if the vendor (who pays for it) disagrees with the report? It is already clear that mortgage lenders will take little notice of these HCRs (though the ministry says they will be able to 'rely' on them) but continue to use their own valuers, except in cases where the loan is only a moderate proportion of the value. Then, too, the buyer may well want his own full structural survey of anything except a fairly basic property. That means three surveyors tramping through the place.

The eventual buyer will be able to 'rely' on the report in law – which means he can sue the inspector, which means they must have insurance. This is not yet in place, even the Government admits, and discussions continue: it has promised it would not introduce compulsory HCRs until it was satisfied that sufficient insurance arrangements were available.

How will the HIPs affect the London market?

Now we will have lawyers (draft contract), surveyors, lenders (for the deeds), local authorities (searches and permissions) and then perhaps landlords (lease, service charge accounts, etc etc) who could all be required to do their stuff (and collect their fees) before the HIP can be ready and the property sold.

The HIP will be prepared (says the government) by an estate agent and solicitor or licensed conveyancer. Sell your home without benefit of agent, say on the Internet, and it will be your job.

The estate agency world is hopeful that the cost will be 'absorbed' in overall selling fees, and thus 'deferred' till you settle up on completion of the sale. Indeed, the latest wheeze is to 'revise' estate agency contracts to include the costs of the pack. **Which raises the question of who pays if you are unhappy with your agent (perhaps about the poor quality of the HIP) and withdraw your property from their books. And who bears the cost if the home fails to sell? Will this end 'no sale no fee'? It all seems to give agents – especially the big agents – a stranglehold on the whole process: who would have thought a Labour government would be so inclined?**

There is also room for conflicts of interest, so often a feature of the property marketing world. Many large estate agents are owned by, or have close relationships with, mortgage lenders. If the agents compile the HIPs, offers of 'free' packs could be linked, openly or covertly, to mortgage offers.

This all seems to take little account of the cyclical nature of the selling market: by the time you've filled your Pack – even if you don't pause for a furious row with the 'inspector' over his doleful findings – it will be quietening down for the summer holidays. And all the work and expense falls to the would-be seller and his agent.

If will mean that the decision to sell your home would have to be a serious one, not something sidled into on the 'let's put it on the market to see what happens' principle. It will cost you money (around £1,000 in London), time and trouble. Claims that the 'survey' won't add to costs are fatuous: 75–80 per cent of current deals are done without one.

- **First conclusion: quite a lot of homes will simply not come to the market at all.**

What the government has forgotten is that many deals are chivvied, jollied, worried along by estate agents. The vendor is a little half-hearted (and very often one half of a couple will be more enthusiastic than the other). A generous offer is extracted from a rather carried-away buyer, who has not been forced up against too much reality in the form of surveys, deeds and service charge accounts. The offer is accepted – and then the vendor is forced to rush about to get the paperwork together, something no amount of persuasion would have got him started on otherwise.

The HCR survey aside, other aspects of the Pack will indeed help speed things up and can be easily adopted by any keen seller right now (see Selling, below). But it has one other great flaw. All the onus seems to be on the seller, not the buyer. For every gazump-accepting seller, there is also a gazundering buyer. While the pack would undoubtedly help to bring him/her more swiftly up to the mark, there is no financial compulsion to prevent him stalling, keeping the seller (or several sellers, unbeknown to each other) dangling, while he sees who he can tie down to the best deal. He, meanwhile, does not even have the cost of a survey to lose.

- **But why not a sum lodged by both sides – buyer and seller – on the acceptance**

of an offer, forfeitable should the deal fall through, to cover the frustrated party for wasted legal and surveying fees? (Insurance could pay if the reason's a good one). The Government seems to have lost sight of this idea. The prospect of giving up, say, £1,000 would at least halt frivolous or cynical time-wasters.

Freehold, leasehold – and Commonhold

A new form of tenure – Commonhold – is to added to, and in some cases will supplant, the venerable duo of freehold/leasehold. The foundations of leasehold have been seriously undermined: a succession of new laws, culminating in the 2002 Act, grant leaseholders more and more rights. This latest Act is still being implemented, with Commonhold only having started from September 2004, and further clauses being introduced during 2005. For the latest, consult the Office of the Deputy Prime Minister's Housing Division (www.odpm.gov.uk).

The 2002 Act simplifies rules whereby flat-owners can collectively buy a block's freehold; gives all leaseholders the right to join in running their blocks; strengthens leaseholders' rights to manage; relaxes the qualifications needed to get a new, longer, lease (see below); gives house leaseholders right of first refusal if the freehold is sold; confers the right to buy on those house lessees who extended leases under the 1967 Act.

Commonhold provides a new way to own and manage blocks of flats and other 'interdependent buildings' – those with shared services and common parts. Commonhold is available for new developments, and the Act allows existing leaseholders to convert to Commonhold. Conversion will only be possible where all of the leaseholders agree to participate and to buy out any other interests involved: see below.

The Government is aware that this may be a tough requirement to meet, so the Act also makes key changes to the former leasehold law that help the large number of leaseholders who are unable or unwilling to convert to Commonhold. Virtually all leases now confer the right to extend, or to enfranchise (buy the freehold). This has caused waves in the property market as both buyers and sellers attempt to value homes under the new regime. Short leases seem to be gaining value as buyers consider the gains to be made from extending the lease. But to do so is not cost-free, of course: see below. The removal of the residence test makes investing in short leases more viable.

Perhaps the most far-reaching changes are in the more technical provisions of the Act, which extend the rights of leaseholders to manage their own blocks, or to hold managing agents and freeholders to account. The 'right to manage' applies to any building with two or more homes in it, including houses split into two or more flats.

The background

Londoners have got used to the idea, which seems extraordinary to foreigners, that you can buy slices of houses for a chunk of years. Leasehold – which is what this is – is still the norm for flats. (This goes right back to the basic assumption, built deep into the nation's psyche, that property ownership equates to owning a physical piece of land. When flats arrived, the Brits couldn't conceive of owning a home suspended in mid-air.)

In many parts of London, due to quirks of history, the houses are leasehold too, which is what really surprises out-of-town buyers. In strict legal terms, you pay what can easily be a freehold price for a house – but you don't own what you buy. You're just a tenant who pays the landlord a large one-off premium to live in his property for as long as the lease lasts, plus a small (usually), annual ground rent for the land it stands on.

Behind this anomaly is another one: the surviving ownership of many areas of London by ancient estates. These are relics of the days when the fields around London were private property. When they were built on, the landlords kept the ownership of the land, granting long leases to developers who built and sold the houses – again on leases. Some of these estates belong to aristocratic families, some to charities, some to schools, some to the Church of England. The leading landlord, in size as well as status, is the Crown. This continuous ownership by such landlords has by and large been beneficial, safeguarding the character and appearance of areas such as Belgravia and Regent's Park – though on some of the other estates it did in the past lead to neglect as leases became very short and tenants saw no point in maintaining their buildings.

The development of the fields around London began in earnest in the late 17th century and continued apace until the 19th. Landlords granted leases to developers in return for an annual ground rent. The developers laid out the streets and built the houses, and then sold slightly shorter leases on the houses to the public at slightly higher ground rents. If a building lease was for 100 years, for instance, and the houses took a year to build, they'd be sold on 99-year leases. And if the ground rent the developer paid to the landlord worked out at £5 a building plot, the developer would ask a ground rent of say £15 from the house-buyers to provide himself with an income as well as capital. Finally when the 99-year leases ran out, the houses reverted to the freehold landlord, who could sell a new lease to a developer or new leases to the public.

(Some landlords fell into the trap centuries ago of permitting leaseholders to renew their leases whenever they wished at a fixed ground rent and premium, which means a very few, very lucky people still pay ground rent at 1750s levels on leases which can be as long as they like: truly a virtual freehold.)

Only now is this basic leasehold/freehold pattern being seriously challenged by the recent legislation. The estates of many of the great landlords are changing. The word 'freehold' is now to be found on sale details in Belgravia, in Marylebone, in Mayfair. Increasingly, flats come with a share of the freehold. And there have been important changes in the 'enfranchisement' rules, whereby leaseholders gain the right to buy a new 90-year lease or the freehold (see below). Note the word 'buy': no law can force a freeholder to *give* you a new lease; it's a market-place transaction, and while the law may say you have the right to buy (the estates prefer the word 'enfranchise'), the freeholder has a right to sell – at the best price he can get – within the rules laid down.

Leases can be for any length of time, and obviously the shorter they are, the lower the price. There are two exceptions to this. First, really short leases in good areas can be viewed as so many years' rent – paid, but therefore also fixed, in advance. This makes good sense to companies (who in any case don't have to worry about the difficulties the rest of us would have in getting a mortgage for a short lease). Second, buying a short lease makes even more sense if you will eventually qualify to buy the freehold from the landlord, or – a cheaper option – to extend your lease. The new law makes some leases more valuable, because it makes qualifying for a lease extension easier, and allows leaseholders of houses who have previously extended to buy their freehold.

Most landlords and developers sell new, or newly modernized, flats on 99-year or 999-year leases. A long leasehold can be as costly as an equivalent freehold property.

If you are a leaseholder, your landlord will not necessarily be the freeholder. When a freeholder originally granted a lease to a developer, the lease the developer sold to the public was a sub-lease, making him the sub-leaseholders' landlord. But today the chain of leaseholds can be even longer. In some cases freeholders sold long head-leases to companies that specialized in getting vacant possession, and as houses fell empty, these companies sold sub-leases to development companies which converted them into flats. Once the flats were finished, they were sold to owner-occupiers on sub-sub-leases. . . . But although being a sub-sub-leaseholder sounds horrendously complicated, all it really means in practice is that the ground rent will have been bumped up a bit at every stage. Where the 'chain' can cause problems is when you try to extend your lease or buy the freehold: **it's important to identify exactly who owns what.**

There are rare cases when a freehold *does* exist 'up in the air'. An example of what is known as a 'flying freehold' might be a house, long ago split into two – not vertically, but in such a way that an upper room in one half extends over a downstairs room in the other. This may work perfectly well in practice, but is legally murky. Take advice before buying.

Leasehold is the most complex subject in the London property world – even more so with the new law coming into force in bits – and very few people claim to understand all aspects fully. Take well-qualified advice before buying a leasehold property, and before attempting to extend the lease or buy the freehold. You can be sure the freeholder will have the best advice, and these expensively suited professionals will be looking after the freeholder's interests, not yours.

The new Commonhold

The 2002 Act introduces Commonhold, a new form of tenure for any property with shared services and common parts. This can be a block of flats, an estate with shared parking spaces and grounds, a shopping centre. It can apply to new buildings, and to existing leasehold ones if *all* the tenants agree (this 100 per cent rule will probably restrict the use of Commonhold to very small blocks). Commonhold should be simpler – and cheaper – to administer than an existing 'share of freehold' as it will use a standard set of terms, a 'Commonhold Statement', but is otherwise similar: the freehold is held by a company of which you are automatically a member when you buy. Apart from doing away with an outside landlord, this solves the traditional problems with leasehold value diminishing as the term shortens – and of leases varying wildly: even those within the same block can have gained an accretion of different clauses as they changed hands over the years.

Not everyone is content: developers worry that it will restrict the right of buyers to let out their flats, which may discourage investors. And the developer, by the way, will decide whether to sell on traditional leasehold terms or the new Commonhold. Be aware, too, that Commonhold means that neighbours will have to enforce the rules on each other, there being no landlord to take the blame.

The procedure was only introduced in late September 2004, so it is too soon to know how Commonhold will work. For a full account of its terms, consult the Leasehold Advisory Service (70-74 City Rd, EC1, tel 020-7490 9580, www.lease-advice.org).

Extending the lease, buying the freehold

As things currently stand, if you do qualify to buy your freehold and want to do so, there's nothing your landlord can do to stop you (although he can make things difficult, or at least expensive). The 2002 Act extends the qualifications considerably: no more residence test, no more low rent test, less demanding rules on majorities and on mixed-use properties. Under the 1993 Act, flat-owners already have the right to join with their neighbours and buy the freehold of their blocks even if the landlord doesn't want to sell.

Owners of leasehold houses that met certain conditions won the right to buy in 1967; the 2002 Act broadens these conditions and will allow those who have purchased lease extensions to buy their freehold. It also removes the residence test, stipulating only that you must have owned the lease for at least two years.

If you don't qualify to buy the freehold (and under the Act most tenants will, providing the *original* lease was for more than 21 years), you also have the right to extend your lease by up to 90 years – an important right because the shorter your lease gets, the less valuable your property and the trickier it is for any potential buyer to get a mortgage. Unlike buying the freehold, flat-owners can apply individually for a lease extension. Some great estates, including the Grosvenor and the Cadogan, will now grant new leases of up to 99 years – in some cases up to 125.

The big landlords have reluctantly accepted changes in legislation and now sell freeholds to qualifying residents – although they admit they don't go out of their way to encourage it. And some residents who have bought their freeholds on great estates have been outraged to discover that the erstwhile freeholder can still compel them to comply with estate management schemes set up to protect the appearance of some of the grandest neighbourhoods of London, including Belgravia, Mayfair and parts of Kensington. The estates argue that they have a duty to make sure people don't paint their houses purple or replace Georgian iron railings with chain-link fencing.

Leasehold enfranchisement is an area fraught with complications, not least over the valuation of the new lease or freehold. It's well worth while having an expert solicitor and/or surveyor on your side before starting negotiations; you will almost certainly be liable for the landlord's costs, so do your sums before starting the process. The Leasehold Advisory Service (see Commonhold above) offers free information and advice. Leaflets and fact-sheets on the Act are also available from the Office of the Deputy Prime Minister (www.odpm.gov.uk).

The big traditional landlords are found in central London, and in one or two suburbs:
Crown Estate: Regent's Park (where you have no right to buy the freehold), plus homes in Pimlico, Kensington (including 'Millionaire's Row') and Victoria Park, Hackney.
Duchy of Cornwall: now only directly controls around 50 homes in the Kennington lands that this royal estate has held since the Black Prince's days. The rest have been turned over to housing associations, or sold on the open market.
Church of England: Hyde Park Estate (see Bayswater), a scattering of homes in Chelsea, Kensington, Belsize Park; three properties in Maida Vale (they used to own it all).
Grosvenor Estate: Belgravia and much of the northern half of Mayfair.
Cadogan Estate: 90 acres including a large slice of Chelsea around Sloane St.
Portman Estate: 110 acres north of Oxford St and east of Edgware Rd.
Howard de Walden: the 'medical district' around Harley St, and Marylebone High St.
Duke of Bedford: 20 acres of Bloomsbury.
Wellcome Trust: now owns the former Henry Smith's Charity estate in South Kensington.
Tonbridge School, **Bedford School** and **Rugby School** all own small pockets of WC1.
Eton College: 60 acres around Swiss Cottage.
Dulwich College: most of Dulwich. **Eyre Estate**: Primrose Hill, Chalk Farm.
Gunter Estate: used to own swathes of South Kensington (e.g the Boltons); sold in 2001.

Service charges, low and high

To ensure a building divided into flats is well maintained, each leaseholder, as a condition of his lease, has to pay a bi-annual or annual service charge. This generally covers their share of any outgoings on structural repairs; having the exterior painted; heating (if the central heating is communal); paying for the cleaning and lighting of common areas such as hall, stairs, gardens; and seeing that the building is fully insured. The service charge is usually made by a managing agent who arranges for work to be done when needed, and includes his fee – usually 10–15 per cent of the money spent.

Buying a flat over-stretches many people financially, and it's tempting to choose one where the service charge is low; but unless the flat was recently converted, it's probably low because it is geared to the everyday matters above, not to covering major outlay. Maintenance may have been neglected. As a result, tenants get hit with an astronomical one-off charge once the problem becomes too serious to ignore. Sudden demands for £40,000 apiece to fund new lifts and roof are apt to come as a shock . . . . Note, too, that such neglect of capital outlay may by no means be apparent in the general appearance of the building. **It is essential to check, before buying, that your regular payments contribute to an adequate 'sinking fund': a provision against major expenses.**

Abuse by landlords, with problems of poor management, shoddy repairs and high service charges, forced changes in the law recently. The Act gives tenants a clear 'right to manage': they can take over the running of their block without having to prove the landlord is at fault, or paying him compensation. The unscrupulous landlord uses a number of methods, usually beginning by issuing unsuspecting leaseholders with huge service-charge bills. Any repairs actually done are shoddy and carried out by cowboy builders – often working for companies linked to the landlord. Protests from leaseholders are countered with threats that they would forfeit their leases and lose their homes unless they paid. The old laws were so poorly drafted that landlords flouted them with impunity, knowing that leaseholders would have to take them to court to stop them.

The 2002 Act adds further safeguards to the 1996 law. Landlords must provide annual statements showing income and expenditure of the service charge fund – and leaseholders will have the right to withhold payment if they don't. It is a criminal offence for landlords to fail to use separate Client Accounts. Leaseholders' right to be consulted before works are begun are strengthened.

Leaseholders protesting about poor management and high service charges have the right to take landlords and their agents to Leasehold Valuation Tribunals (LVTs) rather than to county courts. Taking a case to an LVT will cost leaseholders a maximum of £500 per block, and neither side will be forced to pay the costs of the other, thus removing the main obstacle for leaseholders trying to exercise their legal rights.

Leasehold Valuation Tribunals are the key to a number of important safeguards for leaseholders, and their powers are further extended by the 2002 Act. Your landlord can no longer serve you with a notice forfeiting your lease because you refuse to pay high service charges, unless the charges have been accepted as 'reasonable' by an LVT. You can apply to the LVT (020 7446 7700) for a new manager for your block if whoever is managing it (the landlord or his agent) is demonstrably incompetent, unscrupulous or both, and there's nothing to stop you and your neighbours forming yourselves into a company and applying to manage the block yourselves. But such an arrangement won't rid you of your landlord, who will still own the block unless you go the whole way and buy the freehold.

Buying a home in London

Buying your first home may seem an overwhelming step; in fact, once you have scraped up enough cash for a deposit and evidence of reliability to satisfy a mortgage lender, it will likely prove the most straightforward property deal you'll ever make. You will find a wealth of advice, in print and in person, on this subject. Everyone smiles kindly, and offers anything from free leaflets to better mortgage terms, special rates and money-off deals.

Estate agents in particular will be assiduous in their care, once you have convinced them that you have the money and the definite intention of buying. They'll escort you to view, ring afterwards to enquire politely as to your reactions, helpfully suggest alternatives. This is only partly tender solicitude on your behalf: you have, as a first-time buyer, one inestimable advantage: you are not encumbered with a home to sell before you can buy their client's. It is worth remembering this advantage that you have: it can clinch you a good deal if the seller is in a hurry to move, or otherwise desperate.

Remember too when looking for the first time that an estate agent is just that – an *agent*. Not yours, but the seller's (or 'vendors', as they are known) by whom he/she is employed. It is the agent's job to present the goods in the best light. He is bound not to lie; he is *not* bound to point out that the tube line lies below, shakes the foundations and rattles the windows. A good agent with a reputation to maintain is nevertheless keen to have satisfied customers on both sides. His clients will then often come from people to whom he has sold.

You should also bear in mind the following:

• **Agents are legally bound to pass on any offers they receive to the vendor** (but will advise you if your offer is likely to meet with a dusty answer). These days agents are also

likely to suggest you talk to their mortgage advisors (and make them some more money).
• **Be clear: you do not have to use the agent's mortgage services. To suggest otherwise is illegal.** They must *not* imply that only those who get their mortgages through the agency will be put forward to vendors as copper-bottomed buyers. 'It's our duty to ensure that potential buyers are able to proceed' they may say, piously. If you find that an agent is trying this one on, the Director General of Fair Trading and the local Trading Standards Office would be interested to hear from you.

Choosing an area

General pointers: London is luckily a very well-mapped city. Many people – and not just first-time buyers – will need to keep an open mind about their choice of areas. If you are free to live anywhere within reasonable lines of communication, it's worth bearing in mind that some areas have been altering well ahead of their reputation; the road you remember as the scruffy place where a friend had a bedsit may have changed out of all recognition. But journeying to far-flung corners can be frustrating if you find the place backs onto the rail line that carries the Channel Tunnel trains. A good look at a decent (and recent) map alongside this book can fill in the gaps in the property details. Look too at our section on transport (page 20): a new or improved transport link can, in effect, 'move' an area a lot closer to the heart of things.

That being said, one man's drawback is another soul's way into an area above his means. If you are hell-bent on a certain area, there are likely to be cheaper corners; the essential thing to remember, though, is that anything inexpensive for an unalterable reason – views from the bedroom over the local fire station, perhaps – will likely not just stay relatively cheaper but also take longer to sell. To sum up – and it's the best tip of all:
• **always look at a home with a view to having, one day, to sell it to somebody else – fast.**

The more newspaper ads and estate agents' details (which are at least free – and most can be had via their websites) you can wade through, the better idea you will get of what is going on in the market in a given area at a given time. The one golden rule when looking at a procession of properties is always to make brief notes at the time or immediately on leaving; three flats further on and you won't be able to recall which was the one that smelt damp; which overlooked a noisy playground. Sketch the layout on the back of the details, if no floorplans are included. If you consider a place is a contender, don't be afraid to ask if you can wander round again on your own. When you think you've found the one, visit the locality at different times. Many people who only have weekends for home-hunting can find on moving in that the street is a solid traffic-jam on weekdays.

Buying step by step

The anatomy of a purchase – until the government changes the rules – goes:

1. **Budgeting for the move** Talk to a mortgage lender or broker *as soon as you start looking*, – if not before. They will advise on how much you are likely to be able to borrow (for further details, see *Mortgages* chapter.) Remember that you will need money for a deposit. You may be able to borrow up to 95 per cent (worse, even more) of the property valuation over 25 years, but the more money you can put down as a deposit the better. For one thing, lenders will offer you better rates with a larger deposit. For another, you run a greater risk of being trapped in negative equity (your mortgage higher than the value of your home) if you borrow a large proportion of its value, and the market then slumps. For a third, you might, with some lenders, still be forced to take out expensive insurance (to cover your lender, not you!) if you borrow over 90 per cent (sometimes as low as 75 per cent) of the value. See, too, the Mortgages chapter.

Then, remember that all the attendant fees – searches, stamp duty, valuation, survey, solicitor – and the cost of the move will absorb another 2.5 per cent or more. Stamp duty, in particular, can be an unwelcome shock: there is nothing in London now that falls into the nil bracket (below £60,000) bar the odd parking space. You'll pay 1 per cent of the purchase price between that and £250,000 – whereupon it jumps straight to 3 per cent. £500,000-plus grabs 4 per cent, and families faced with a move into that bracket fall to thinking that the £20,000 might be better spent on an extension than on moving and giving same to the Chancellor.

However, in some 'disadvantaged areas' (defined by local council wards) there's a waiver of stamp duty up to £150,000: check with the Inland Revenue website (www.inlandrevenue.gov.uk) for the current, enlightening list.

Price does not equal value, as you may well discover when your mortgage lender gets a valuer round. Try to get the lender to use the surveyor who you instruct for your own survey – especially if the house is not typical of the area. A surveyor not familiar with the area needs 'comparables' to value the property. In a quiet market, with few if any recent sales, no such figures will exist – so the value will be cut to be on the safe side. At busy times, valuers can be under pressure to survey six homes a day. Even if Land Registry figures show that No. 43 sold for far less, unless they really know the area they cannot tell that No. 29, which you want, is nevertheless worth the difference in price.

2. Making an offer, and what happens next: Make an offer through the agency (see above). If it's accepted, get the details of the property immediately to your lender and to your waiting solicitor, who will start the searches and conveyancing process (see below). Remind yourself that although your offer has been accepted, neither side is legally committed. Even if a 'Sold' sign goes up, it will say, in small letters, '*subject to contract*'.

From that point, there are two definite stages to acquiring the property: the first, up to exchanging contracts and putting down a deposit and the second, up to completion and paying the balance of the price. **Until you've exchanged contracts neither side is bound to the deal and there's nothing to stop your seller accepting a higher offer.**

The longer this period, the more danger of such 'gazumping' – hence the government's attempt to cut it short (see above). Hence, too, the need to make sure your solicitor keeps the deal moving. In the run-up to exchange of contracts, your solicitor and the seller's solicitor will (under the current, pre-HIP, set-up) be juggling a number of papers (or electronic files) between them:

(a) **Title deeds:** The seller's solicitors will retrieve the title deeds to the house and the Land Registry certificate (nearly all London homes are registered) to confirm that the seller actually owns the property and has good title – i.e., is free to sell it.

(b) **Drawing up the contract:** They will then draw up a contract containing information from the deeds and send it to your solicitor. At the same time, yours sends a list of pre-contract enquiries to the seller to get basic information about the property. This should answer such questions as who owns and is responsible for boundary fencing, whether the property is properly insured, who the managing agent or freeholder is (if the property is leasehold: see above) and whether service-charge bills are disputed or up-to-date. You should also find out if boilers have been serviced and get confirmation that the property is connected to all utilities (gas, electricity, water, telephone).

(c) **Local authority search:** Your solicitor will also arrange for a local search, which should tell you if there's a motorway planned at the back of your garden or a compulsory purchase order on the property. Search questions are set out on a standard printed form, but the answers will only relate to the area *directly adjacent to your property*: so a road planned nearby, but not directly next to it, won't show up even though it could make your road a traffic nightmare. Check yourself with the town-hall planning dept; note that some now also have excellent websites where you can search back for the history of planning permission, etc, for 'your' house – and neighbouring sites: see page 71.

(d) **Surveys:** In the meantime, you're arranging your mortgage and getting a survey done. Lenders will insist on a valuation to make sure the property's worth the amount you want to borrow – but this is to protect them, not you. Particularly if the house is old, you should arrange your own structural survey: you need a Building Surveyor member of the RICS, or a structural engineer. This is expensive, but should highlight any major problems that need dealing with. The results may make you reconsider the deal as it stands: you might not have enough money left to renew the roof immediately (even if you have, the cost of doing so, when added to the purchase price, may be too far above the house's value). You have not exchanged contracts; you are free to try to negotiate a lower price, or back out of buying altogether. (Note: surveys are hedged about with disclaimers and err on the pessimistic side, since you can sue if some glaring fault is missed; discuss the implications with someone experienced in reading them if this is your first.)

3. **Exchanging contracts:** When all this is done, you exchange contracts and put down a 10 per cent deposit: if you back out now, you lose this. You have bought a home; you must insure it immediately – even though you have not moved in, it's now your responsibility. Note that 'exchange' is usually done by post, but if you are really keen to secure a property (or just don't quite trust the vendor not to gazump you) you can pay your solicitor to arrange an 'attended exchange', where someone from your solicitor's office goes along to the vendor's solicitor in person.

4. **Completion:** A month or so later (though it can be done in days if both sides are willing and able to move home fast) completion takes place, the balance of the purchase price is handed over and the deal is done. You are free to move in.

Buying a newly built home

The basic process of buying a home is the same whether the house is Georgian or brand new. The main difference is that with a new home you will probably be dealing with the developer, via a sales office on site, rather than with a private individual.

New homes in London are nearly always either conversions – of everything from riverside warehouses, Victorian schools, factories, old depositories to long-despised 1960s office blocks – or new buildings on re-used land. Such sites tend to be former hospitals, gas- or water-works, power stations, sewage farms, flood plains . . . . This raises the question of what level of decontamination has been done to the land. The Environment Act has a lot to say about this: quiz the builder and the local authority.

When assessing value, remember that fringe areas could be the first to suffer if there's a downturn. **Be cautious about developments aimed at 'investors'.** If you plan to own and live in such a block yourself, adjacent flats may stand empty while buy-to-let owners try to find tenants – and tenants, as neighbours, have less of a stake, and thus less interest, in the community. If you yourself are buying to let, you will be in competition with a raft of others for tenants as soon as the flats complete. It can be hard to sell, too, in any new homes scheme, until all the units have been sold by the developer – he can offer inducements and deals that a private seller can't match. Oh, and treat with a big pinch of salt all those cliams, on billboards, ads and by sales staff, that the block is '80 per cent sold'.It has been known for the developer to transfer a tranche of properties to an associate company, and 'buy' them back if demand warrants it.

Whatever you buy, check out the development and its builder. Check the terms of any special mortgage deal or discount carefully: any 'cheap' finance is almost certainly reflected in the price – there's no such thing as a free lunch.

For all developments, a chat with existing dwellers as to the standards of after-care service can be informative. And ask the selling agents for names of schemes the developer has done before. Go and have a look to see how they are faring. Whoever you are buying from, check the specifications in the brochure: do not assume you will get the standard of fittings in a show flat unless they are specifically listed. Do not assume room sizes are accurate: they have been known to be a good bit smaller than the show flat – or even the brochure plans. Keep checking – and don't order the fitted furniture yet. . . .

In any newly built home, there are certain simple checks – like, for example, jumping up and down in the centre of the floor (see if the pictures fall off the show-flat walls). Send your partner to the next room, and upstairs, and see how loudly you hear footsteps and conversation. Most new homes (not all, about 85%) carry a 10-year warranty from the National House Building Council (NHBC). But this isn't a guarantee, regardless of what the developer might tell you. It's an insurance policy, mainly to cover the builder. The cover is fairly basic and may not include what you might think are pretty glaring defects. The NHBC was forced to revise its warranty in 1997 to clarify its cover and has also extended it to conversions. Cover was further increased for homes registered from 1 July 2000. Since April 2003, in an arrangement with the Council of Mortgage lenders, lenders will not release mortgage funds for a new home unless the builder can provide a 'cover note' stating that a final inspection has been passed, and that warrantyt cover is in place. You can get up-to-date details of the NHBC cover, and check if a builder is registered, from: www.nhbc.co.uk (01494 735363).

Ask searching questions about the future of the development. The model and plans may show a lovely new pool and gym, but when will it be built, and is there anything in your contract with the developer to say it must be? What is going up next door? Check, and don't believe assurances from the (often part-time) staff in the sales office. Most town halls have helpful planning offices: they will tell you what else is planned for the neighbourhood and let you see local development plans. This will avoid buying under the impression that the site over the road is to be (as the sales lady put it) 'local shops' when it has permission for a 50,000-sq ft superstore and 'leisure complex'. It happened.

Onto the housing ladder: shared ownership, housing associations

The 'Social Housing' world is if anything more complex than the private side of housing. Gone are the simple days when boroughs built and then rented homes to the deserving. Councils build hardly any homes now, and many that they once owned have been bought by their tenants. Others – in many cases whole estates – have been transferred to housing associations. It is these, and other 'RSLs' (registered social landlords: charities like Peabody, for instance) who are building new homes – and are offering them in a far more imaginative range of tenures. The problem is not the quality (which can sometimes be cutting-edge, far better than some private developers manage, and to innovative designs) but the quantity – or rather lack – of these homes.

More and more Londoners find that buying a home in the capital is beyond their means. This particularly affects two groups: young people starting out on their careers, and families moving from elsewhere in the country. Neither group, however, is targeted by most mainstream RSLs, which concentrate on disadvantaged families. There is help to be had – buried in an increasingly complex web of 'schemes' and 'initiatives'. 'Key Workers' in the jargon, meaning those in public-sector jobs, get most help. Shorthand in this *Guide* for all such schemes is Affordable Housing.

Help for first-time buyers Look out for the government's 'First Time Buyer Initiative', new this year. It envisages using publicly-owned land, mostly from the English Partnerships land-bank, to build homes. Buyers will pay a price excluding land value; the landowner retains a stake in the property for which, after three free years, the buyer will have to pay an annual charge. It's a bit like reinventing leasehold, only the headline price for the first-time buyer is low. The London component of this scheme is included in the 'Londonwide Initiative' announced by the Office of the Deputy Prime Minister whereby 15 sites, from Wandsworth to Barking, will provide 2,000 homes: half will be for first-timers.

Key worker housing has become a buzzword in an attempt to keep teachers, nurses, etc, in London. Your starting point for current schemes is www.keyworkerliving.co.uk. Eligible are those in education, health, police, prison or probation services, and Local Authority planners, social workers, occupational therapists, educational psychologists. Each profession has different qualifying factors, such as salary level, though £60,000 a year household income is usualy the cut-off point: the website tells all. Four RSL groups are involved in London: see the website for their schemes, which are summarised here:

• **Homebuy** provides an equity loan of at least 25 per cent of the home's value up to a limit of £50,000. It helps first-time buyers (and maybe others: see scheme details) on the open market with a loan to use as/add to your deposit. No interest is charged on the loan until you sell, when you repay it plus any increase in value on the percentage it represents.
• **Key Teacher Homebuy** £100,000 loans for a small highly targeted group of teachers.
• **Intermediate Renting** is run by housing associations: rent is set at a level between that charged by social and private landlords. See cost rent schemes, below.
• **Shared Ownership** is available on new homes built by housing associations.

Shared ownership is a halfway-house between renting or buying, widely available both in the current 'key worker' schemes and from other providers (who will of course have different criteria...) You buy a share in a home, with the rest held by the housing trust/RSL or other body. You raise a mortgage for your share, repaid in the normal way; you pay rent on the rest. You can buy extra shares when you can afford it, at the price set by the District Valuer. When you come to sell, the profit on the share you own is yours. It is best to take at least a 50 per cent stake if you can; otherwise the rent, and the small proportion of the profit, can make it uneconomic. You can increase your share later on ('staircasing') if you want. Contact your local council: eligibility varies.

The RSLs usually work in conjunction with councils, and in specific localities – though some of the larger ones operate in several boroughs. Notting Hill Home Ownership, for instance, works across seven; Peabody Trust works right across London, provides both usual shared-ownership homes and its own variant of Homebuy, Peabody Home Equity.

Peabody, like many RSLs, mixes tenures in its modern schemes. This means that (indistinguishably) shared-ownership homes stand next to those for outright sale, for rent at market levels and for subsidized rent. Their big canalside scheme in W10 has 308 homes of which some are for open-market sale, others for rent, 104 for shared ownership. The open-market homes fund the others; the mixed tenure means no ghettos.

The DIY shared-ownership scheme, designed for people who want to buy on the open market yet need help to finance the home, works on a borough-by-borough basis, and there are some schemes whereby if you are a council tenant you can get grants (**Cash Incentive** schemes) to help you buy on the open market.

Cost rent schemes are built and run by RSLs and are just what the name says: rents are more than the social-housing 'Fair Rent' norm, yet less than the private-market level. An example is the Hackney Now scheme, where seven sites have been handed over by the council to an RSL which has built flats and is letting them to 'key workers' – nurses, for example. The rent is able to be lower than open-market levels as the sites come free and government regeneration money helped fund building costs. Another variant is Keep London Working, a consortium led by Peabody, which plans to build 175 homes, ranging from studios to 5-bed houses, over the next three years. These will be let at between 60 and 75 per cent of the market rents for similar properties.

• ***To find out more:*** first, contact the local council – where you live now, or where you work, your employer, and your trade union. Many RSLs also have websites (Peabody's lists homes available). And the Housing Corporation site (www.housingcorp.gov.uk) allows on-line access to the register of social landlords, sorted by borough and by type of provision, including those running the government-backed key worker schemes.

Selling a home in London

There is always limitless advice available for the guidance of first-time buyers, from free leaflets from the building society to whole books on the subject. Strangely, there is almost nothing to help the seller – especially first-time ones. This is surprising: selling a home is even more likely to be carried out under stress, since in most cases you are also trying to buy your next/coordinate it with the sale/arrange for the move. Yet even before the coming reforms, there is much that can be done in order to get off to a good, fast start – and speed is generally all-important to one party or the other in a London property deal.

For example, a problem peculiar to London is the length of time it takes to get the **local authority searches** carried out. Councils vary widely in the time they take to complete this bit of form-filling: the City of London, with only a few residents, has been known to reply in one day; others drag their feet. With such councils, it's best if possible to do the searches in person: ask at the town hall. The official target date is 10 working days, which is what the councils tend to say they achieve, but this is not always true. These searches, by the way, are a task generally undertaken by the prospective buyer, but there's no reason why the seller shouldn't get a search carried out: a small extra expense that can save weeks. The results are valid for three months.

Your solicitor can of course arrange this for you – which is a second point. **Alert your solicitor** to the fact that a move is impending: people often forget to do this, assuming that there will be time enough when a buyer is in view. That is a bad time at which to discover that your solicitor is on holiday or even – as has been known – has died, retired or sold his firm since you needed him last. Once notified, he/she can also draw up a **draft contract** in readiness, and can **retrieve the deeds** to your property from bank, building society or other mortgagor (you, by this time, have probably forgotten that whoever lent you the money holds the deeds – and that they, too, can take their time about getting them out of the system). All the above, which this *Guide* has always recommended, will soon become mandatory under the new Home Information Pack (see above). But don't wait: doing all this now may save your sanity and the sale.

Whether you use a solicitor or a licensed conveyancer, **keep ringing** to ensure they're getting on with things. If the ball seems to be stuck in the other court, ask your estate agent to chase it and let you know what's holding things up.

A top London estate agent added the interesting rider that not only can such preparation hasten the conclusion of a sale, it helps the agent to test the true worth of the would-be buyer. If the seller's side isn't ready to proceed, it can be weeks before you discover that the apparently eager buyer's own home isn't, after all, quite sold, or that they haven't, after all, got access to quite enough money.

A good agent will point all this out to you, and in London there is no shortage of agents to choose from. Like the little girl in the old rhyme, when they are good they are very, very good, and can seriously increase your wealth. When they are bad. . . .

Choosing an estate agent

A lot hinges on the seller's ability to pick the right agent and then instruct them properly. **You should see at least four.** If you don't already have strong ideas on which are the most favoured locally, it can help to go window-shopping, checking for offices in a prominent position, with properties of the calibre of your own, well displayed, and run by welcoming staff. You can go in, describe your own place and ask for details of anything of that type on their books. This serves the dual purpose of finding what the competition is, and how much – and what their reception of your potential buyers is going to be like. You can get confirmation of your own feelings, and further recommendations, by asking people who come into contact with estate agents, such as building societies, banks, builders and solicitors – and local friends and neighbours. Don't rely on Internet sites alone: while most people start their home searches on-line, physical presence in an area certainly matters: people still find their ideal home after an idle perusal of the local agents' windows on a Sunday afternoon.

Showing prospective agents your home is a good practice-run for showing potential buyers. Remember that agents are human too: they, like buyers, see many different properties; they, too, can be put off by an untidy, uncleaned shambles smelling of last night's dinner. Light, warmth, flowers and furniture polish (the old-fashioned smelly sort) really can do wonders to underline a welcoming atmosphere. And tidy up – at least – outside: buyers can, and have, been put off before they've even got through the door. Inside, clutter is a real turn-off; what's worse, it makes the place look smaller.

Everyone knows that anyone can currently set up stall as an estate agent: there are no mandatory qualifications. There are, though, two professional bodies: good agents belong to either the Royal Institution of Chartered Surveyors (RICS) or the National Association of Estate Agents (NAEA) – both useful sources of information. Members will have undergone courses and passed professional exams (the NAEA's members are not necessarily qualified; with RICS it's a condition). The bodies also guarantee deposits held by their members and can be approached if you have a dispute with a member agent.

If you have a problem with an agent, there is an **ombudsman scheme**. The trouble is that membership is voluntary: only some 40 per cent of agents belong. The ombudsman can, though, award dissatisfied customers of the scheme's members up to £50,000 compensation. Ask if the firm you instruct is a member.

• **The Estate Agents Act of 1979 was tightened up in 1991 to clamp down on a number of nefarious practices, including failure to pass on all offers and omitting to tell sellers about potential conflicts of interest. The Director General of Fair Trading has the power to ban agencies from practising, or to remove consumer credit licenses. He has warned agents that if they continued with two sins – trying to link mortgage sales to viewings (or even receiving details), and insisting on vendors signing restrictive agreements – they could and would be banned.**

The Property Misdescriptions Act, implemented in 1993, outlaws the florid exaggeration which passed for marketing in the 1980s. Fear of being caught out under this Act may make estate agents' particulars duller reading, but at least they should be more accurate. One problem, highlighted by reputable agencies is that since it is companies, not individuals, that are prosecuted for estate agency sins, the usual result is that the employee concerned is sacked – only to resurface in another firm. Perhaps one day we will see more formal licensing requirements for entry into a profession that can, to say the least, have profound effects on the health, wealth and sanity of its clients, and equally some system for its practitioners to be 'struck off'.

The Misdescriptions Act is, by the way, supposed to cover developers' details too, though few of them seem to realize this: one big builder was fined for omitting the huge trees between his flats and the river on billboards and in brochures. Note that, while the Act does not directly cover home-owners, they are bound to answer all enquiries truthfully – and not just on the concrete facts. Vendors have been sued for omitting to inform their buyers about the state of open warfare with the neighbours.

Fixing a price

Having decided to sell and picked an agent, what do you need from them? First, of course, you want to know what price they suggest. A house is worth only what someone is willing to pay at that time. The agent needs to take into account not only what appears to be the going rate, but the state of the overall market and your personal circumstances, too. If you *must* sell by the week after next, both marketing and price will be different.

When you get your property valued, **don't necessarily go for the agent predicting the highest price.** They may be desperate to get instructions and inflate the price that they say they can get just to entice you. (Their commission is also calculated on the price of the property.) It's no good putting your property on the market at an inflated price only to see it hang heavy for months. Ask the agent how he's arrived at that price and what evidence of other sales of similar properties there is to substantiate his view. The internet now allows access to actual selling prices, so insist on chapter and verse.

Conversely, there is the very low price that should in certain circumstances raise an eyebrow – perhaps suggested for the large, old, empty property you're selling on behalf of your dear departed aunty? Luckily it is, of course, illegal these days for agents to fail to disclose conflicts of interest – such as the existence of a developer who's paying him a backhander to look out for large, old, cheap properties. . . .

Ask what the agent proposes to do to sell your home. Do they have a regular contract with national or local magazines/newspapers? It can indicate the level the agency is working on. Maybe expensive brochures will be appropriate. Some firms have press offices who will send a release to the press about interesting homes. Does the firm have its own magazine? Or an attractive, professional Internet site – and if so how often is it updated? Will your home be included – and if so, how quickly and for how long? Will it have a photograph? Look at existing advertisements by the firm. Are the photographs clear? Have they been clumsily distorted? Is the wording precise (and proof-read)?

Fees come last. Some agents make a point of a lower percentage, but take this on the 'you get what you pay for' principle. A skilled agent's negotiating acumen can easily save you the half a per cent extra he charges (you can of course try haggling, if you've got something they really want to sell – or build in a reward for success).

What *will* vary the rate charged is whether you appoint one firm **sole agent** or, as you are perfectly entitled to do, instruct several at once. Agencies charge less if they get sole agency, and they work harder, because all the effort they put in will be rewarded if they get a sale. Appoint more than one, and only one will get a fee from the transaction; all of them will know this and it will be reflected in the intensity of their efforts.

Don't listen if an agent says you are legally bound to sign his standard agreement. This is a negotiable contract, not a legal document. If you don't like the terms, haggle or go somewhere else – and that goes not just for their charges but the clauses. Buried in the small print may be **'sole selling rights'** (as opposed to the more usual 'sole agency'). *Do not agree to this: it means you pay their commission even if you sell it yourself to your brother.* There will also be conditions about fees payable if you withdraw your home after a buyer has been found. These should not be unreasonable: a major firm had such a case found against them recently.

You'll find that agencies come in all shapes and sizes. Weigh local knowledge against marketing skill, the personal touch against chain-breaking clout. With big firms, ensure that the people you deal with know your area and have not just been transferred in from Sidcup. All this said, choosing an agent is a personal business. Whatever the firm, it is only as good as the people in your local branch: choose those who impress you most.

However expert the agent, you know your home best. He/she should therefore look to you to check draft particulars. These should be set out clearly and logically – and remember that items mentioned in them are generally understood to be included in the price unless otherwise specified. If you are going to be showing people around, the agent should brief you, because (s)he can provide an objective list of selling-points to mention. If you are not showing buyers round, who is? Can you meet them first, and are they both personable and intelligent (an elusive combination in junior staff in estate agents)? Who should you contact for progress reports? You should expect regular news, but remember that they have other places to sell too: don't ring them *every* day. Conversely, make sure they get off the mark fast: a lot of time can be wasted while particulars are drafted, checked, etc.

Selling tends to be fraught with excitements, and it's wise to keep cool. But what if you have appointed an agent and nothing seems to result? Give the agent a set number of weeks of sole agency, and if there is no action call him in for a progress report. There may be good reasons for the dearth of buyers. At this point decide whether to give him

•Turn the page for the buying and selling price charts: a snapshot of the state of the London market at the start of 2005, area by area.

Price charts: sales

The charts on the following pages consolidate the data in the Area Profiles in this book, showing broadly what certain kinds of homes cost in each of the areas covered. This gives you a freeze-frame picture across London at the start of the 2005 selling season: a basis for comparison throughout the year.

The prices given are for typical examples of each type of home. Where a range of figures is shown, this reflects price variations within the area. Thus the range is also an indicator of the scope of the properties in the area: if the figures for, say, a

FLATS — SALES STARTING PRICES FOR 2005

90–130: range in £1000s — too few for price average → price carries over

	STUDIO	1 BEDROOM	2 BEDROOM	3 BEDROOM	4 BEDROOM	5+ BEDROOM
Acton	110–150	120–220	140–300	180–350	–	–
Balham and Tooting	100–180	120–250	180–350+	200–350+	250–400	–
Barnes, Mortlake and Sheen	110–160	180–275	190–700+	250–700+	400+	–
Battersea	110–220	120–325	180–500	200–650+	–	–
Bayswater	135–220	215–365	250–600	290–1M	450–1.2M	900–3M
Bedford Park and Acton Green	130–180	160–250	220–400	250–450	300–800	–
Belgravia	–	350–750	450–1.7M	700–2.9M	1–3M+	–
Bethnal Green	100–140	130–200	150–250	140–280	–	–
Bloomsbury and King's Cross	150–190	200+	250+	320+	–	–
Bow	120–150	130–200	140–280	160–310	–	–
Brixton, Herne Hill and Tulse Hill	100–130+	145–200+	180–300+	200–350	270–350	–
Camberwell	85–120	120–190	140–250	175–300	180+	–
Camden Town and Primrose Hill	130–200	145–450	200–650	240–1M	–	–
Chelsea	140–240	200–400+	250–875+	400–1.9M	500–1.9+	–
Chiswick	100–180	130–300	185–500	240–500+	350–850	–
City and Fringes	150–180	160–300	250–380	300–500+	–	–
Clapham	110–165	170–260	220–400+	260–400+	–	–
Clerkenwell and Finsbury	160–180	200–310	280–400	420–900	–	–
Cricklewood	100–130	145–200+	175–320	270–400	–	–
Crouch End and Stroud Green	110–150	160–220	170–350	280–400	320—500	–
Crystal Palace	95–110	120–180	150–205	160–245	–	–
Dollis Hill and Neasden	95–135	120–170+	160–240	200–280	–	–
Dulwich	100–140	125–220	150–300	280–400	–	–
Ealing	120–160	150–250	170–350	220–450	375–500	–
Finchley	120–150	140–200	180–325	225–40	–	–
Forest Hill	80–120	100–170	130–230	140–260	–	–
Fulham	150–220	180–250	230–350	300–450	375–1.2M	→
Golders Green	130–175	150–225	190–310	225–400	335–500	–
Greenwich and Blackheath	120–180	140–220	180–290	220–400+	–	–
Hackney	100–135	130–200	170–270	200–300	220–330	–
Hammersmith	120–180	130–275	200–400	300–500	400–700	600+
Hampstead	160–200	240–320	340–1M+	450–1M+	650+	–
Hampstead Garden Suburb	130–160	170–225	200–400	250–500+	350–500+	–
Hendon and Mill Hill	120–150	150–200	180–400	200–400+	–	–
Highgate	120–175	190–250	220–600+	280–600+	500+	–
Holland Park	150–250	215–500	280–800	450–1.3M	650–2M	900–2M+
Islington and Highbury	140–220+	175–250	210–400+	250–400+	500+	–
Kennington, Vauxhall and Stockwell	100–150	140–200	225–350+	170–400	–	–

1-bed flat are 120–150, it is likely to be a fairly homogeneous area; £120–150,000 should give you a choice of such flats here. If 180–450, it is clear that there are some neighbourhoods that warrant a good premium, or perhaps there is a supply of recently developed, more luxurious flats. In all brackets you will be likely to find cheaper homes, and exceptional ones at the other end of the scale: a plus sign is used where we have not included the prices for a small number of unusual examples which would distort the averages.

HOUSES — SALES STARTING PRICES FOR 2005

90–130: range in £1000s — too few for price average → price carries over

	2 BEDROOM	3 BEDROOM	4 BEDROOM	5 BEDROOM	6–7 BEDROOM	8+ BEDROOM
Acton	230–360	250–450	350–650+	400–900	600–900	→
Balham and Tooting	200–400+	250–450+	300–1M+	→	→2M	—
Barnes, Mortlake and Sheen	250–430+	325–800+	400–1.3M	500–1.95M	850–3M+	—
Battersea	210–450	250–550	280–800	400–1M	800+	—
Bayswater	500–700	500–1.5M	800–2M	900–2.5M	1–3M	2–3.5M
Bedford Park and Acton Green	325–450	380–700	500–1M+	650–1.5M+	800–2M	—
Belgravia	800–1M+	1–2.5M+	1.1–3M+	1.8–5M	2.2–11M	—
Bethnal Green	240–280	280–350	320–450	—	—	—
Bloomsbury and King's Cross	525+	550+	750+	1M+	→2M+	—
Bow	220–280	240–400	300–800	550–850	—	—
Brixton, Herne Hill and Tulse Hill	220–400	240–450	300–550	400–850	—	—
Camberwell	250–300	250–450	300–600	450–900	600–1M	—
Camden Town and Primrose Hill	350–600+	400–900+	450–1.2M+	550–2M+	—	—
Chelsea	635–1M+	675–1.8M+	800–3M+	1.3–5M	2.25–8M	—
Chiswick	250–450	350–600+	400–1M	500–2M+	600–3M	—
City and Fringes	300–500	500–800	800–1.2M	1M+	—	—
Clapham	300–450+	350–650	425–650	475–1M+	700–1M+	—
Clerkenwell and Finsbury	350–480	450–700	650–1.2M	800–1.3M	—	—
Cricklewood	220–280	250–450	360–500+	450+	—	—
Crouch End and Stroud Green	250–390	350–460	400–600	550–850	650–1M	800–1M+
Crystal Palace	175–250	200–320	220–400+	300–700+	850–1.3M	—
Dollis Hill and Neasden	200–250	220–400	250–500	400–550	—	—
Dulwich	220–375	240–600	300–600	380–800	450–1M+	700–1.5M+
Ealing	200–350	260–450	300–700	450–1M	700–1.5M	1–1.8M
Finchley	230–350	275–475	350–650	450–800	—	—
Forest Hill	180–230	180–350	240–450	250–600	300–600	—
Fulham	350–425	400–500	500–750+	600–1.2M	—	—
Golders Green	250–350	325–500	380–750	450–1M	700–1M+	800+
Greenwich and Blackheath	250–450	320–600	500–800+	600–1M+	600–1.5M	1.5–2M
Hackney	210–325	240–450	240–500	350–700+	—	—
Hammersmith	330–600	390–750	450–1M	650–1.5M	850–2M	—
Hampstead	450–600+	650–1M	850–3M	1–3M+	1.5M+	1.7M+
Hampstead Garden Suburb	250–450	350–650	510–850	700–2M	800–4M	2M+
Hendon and Mill Hill	200–270+	280–500	340–600	400–1.5M	500–2.5M	—
Highgate	350–500	400–700+	550–1M+	500–1.2M+	→2M+	—
Holland Park	400–900	550–2M	750–3M	1.1–5M	3.5–10M+	8–15M+
Islington and Highbury	300–600	350–600+	450–1M	650–1M+	1.5M+	—
Kennington, Vauxhall and Stockwell	220–400	250–500	400–600+	400–1M	500–1M	800–1.5M

FLATS — SALES

690–130: range in £1000s — too few for price average → price carries over

	STUDIO	1 BEDROOM	2 BEDROOM	3 BEDROOM	4 BEDROOM	5+ BEDROOM
Kensington	165–285	250–350	350–1M+	420–1.5M+	1.2–3M	–
Kentish Town and Tufnell Park	120–175	160–250	200–400	230–450	350–450	–
Kilburn, Kensal Green and Queen's Park	120–160	160–220	220–400	250–450	300+	–
Knightsbridge	290–400	350–1M+	550–1.7M+	800–2.6M+	1.5–5M+	2–13M+
Lewisham and Catford	85–115	100–140	125–170	145–200	165–280	–
Leyton and Walthamstow	100–115	120–150	135–190	180–220	–	–
Maida Vale and Little Venice	150–240	190–320+	250–650+	350–1M+	450–1M+	1M+
Marylebone and Fitzrovia	140–220	175–350	300–600+	380–1M+	700+	850–3M
Mayfair and St James's	200–300+	300–750	400–900+	750–2.5M+	1.5–3.5M	1.5M+
Morden, Mitcham and Colliers Wood	100–120	125–160	130–225	165–250	–	–
Muswell Hill	120–140	130–240	160–350	245–450	360–500	–
New Cross and Deptford	80–120	110–130	120–220+	145–250+	–	–
Notting Hill and North Kensington	175–250	190–450+	250–750+	300–1.3M+	700–1.4M	–
Peckham	90–110	125–185	155–230	170–250	–	–
Pimlico and Westminster	130–200	180–350	240–500	300–1M	→1M	–
Poplar	90–130	115–190	130–250	140–200	–	–
Putney and Roehampton	100–160	150–280+	180–450+	200–500+	400–650+	–
Regent's Park	170–200+	240–700	400–1M+	535–3.5M	650–3.5M	1.3–4M+
Richmond and Kew	110–200	180–300	220–500	300–600	500–1M	1M+
Royal Docks and South Newham	130–220	145–230+	200–400	250–535+	→	–
Shepherd's Bush	130–160	130–250	190–350	210–400	220–400	–
Soho and Covent Garden	175–250	220–500	300–1M+	400–1.5M	–	–
The South Bank	160–200	180–300	220–400+	250–450+	–	–
South Kensington, Earl's Court and West Brompton	180–270+	220–650	285–1M	450–1.5M	750–1.5M	–
Southfields and Earlsfield	125–160	145–250	180–300	200–350	210–350	–
Southgate and Palmers Green	80–120	100–180	120–280	250–350	–	–
St John's Wood	160–250	190–400	275–500	325–1M+	800–2M+	–
Stepney and Whitechapel	120–150	130–200	170–270	200–320	–	–
Stoke Newington	120–160	150–230	190–290	260–335	300–350+	350–410
Stratford and North Newham	100–105	120–190	140–250	→	200–350	–
Streatham	100–130	130–165	160–240	190–250	200–275	–
Tottenham and Finsbury Park	90–120	125–170	150–210	160–325	300–350	–
Totteridge and Whetstone	120–150	125–225	150–400	200–500	250–500+	–
Twickenham and Teddington	100–170	160–260	175–500+	270–600+	→1M	–
Wandsworth	120–150	200–270	250–400	290+	380+	–
West Hampstead	100–170	165–280	220–400	300–500+	400–1M+	550–1.5M+
West Norwood, Norbury and Gipsy Hill	95–110	120–165	140–200	150–225	–	–
Willesden and Brondesbury Park	130–170	120–240	145–340	160–450	160–490	–
Wimbledon, Raynes Park and Merton Park	110–180	165–280	180–500	250–700	–	–

HOUSES — SALES

90–130: range in £1000s **— too few for price average** **→ price carries over**

	2 BEDROOM	3 BEDROOM	4 BEDROOM	5 BEDROOM	6–7 BEDROOM	8+ BEDROOM
Kensington	600+	600–1.5M+	1–3M	1.5–3.5M+	1.5–5M+	—
Kentish Town and Tufnell Park	300–450	400–600	450–850	550–1.4M	1.2M+	—
Kilburn, Kensal Green and Queen's Park	260–400	340–550	400–800	600–1M	—	—
Knightsbridge	800–1.7M	1–2.5M+	1.5–3M+	2–10M	3.5–10M+	5–10M+
Lewisham and Catford	200–230	210–260	250–300	300–450	400–500+	500–800
Leyton and Walthamstow	170–230	200–300	260–400	300–500	—	—
Maida Vale and Little Venice	340–1M	600–1.5M+	800–1.5M+	→	1–2.5M+	—
Marylebone and Fitzrovia	450–750+	700+	800–1M+	1M+	1.3M+	2–3M+
Mayfair and St James's	800–1.6M+	1–2M+	1.5–3M+	2.5–5M+	3–8M+	→15M
Morden, Mitcham and Colliers Wood	165–220	185–300	250–375	300–350+	—	—
Muswell Hill	220–350	260–475+	330–575+	430–900+	625–1.5M	—
New Cross and Deptford	175–250	190–325	240–450	350–550	400–600+	—
Notting Hill and North Kensington	450–1M+	575–1.9M+	650–2.75M	1–4.25M	3M+	→
Peckham	200–270	200–300	220–330	300–550	500–800	—
Pimlico and Westminster	420–700	500–900	600–1M	800+	1M+	—
Poplar	190–270	230–350	250–450	—	—	—
Putney and Roehampton	250–450+	300–650+	400–1M+	500–2M+	1.5–2.5M	1.5–3.5M+
Regent's Park	575–1M+	850–3M+	1.25M+	3–9M	→	6.5–18M
Richmond and Kew	225–500	350–650	400–1M	600–2M	1M+	—
Royal Docks and South Newham	150–220	185–250+	270–350	–	—	—
Shepherd's Bush	250–400	275–550	370–700	450–750	700–1M	—
Soho and Covent Garden	900–1M	900–2M	1.5–3M	2–3M	—	—
The South Bank	200–300	250–450	350–500	—	—	—
South Kensington, Earl's Court and West Brompton	445–1.1M	700–2M	1–2M+	1.5–2.2M+	3M+	4–12M
Southfields and Earlsfield	230–350	250–450	315–500	450–1M	600–1M+	750–1.5M
Southgate and Palmers Green	165–340	180–350	280–600	550–1.8M	—	—
St John's Wood	450–700	500–1M+	900–4M	1.2–5M	1.5–4M+	—
Stepney and Whitechapel	230–280	275–350	330–500	—	—	—
Stoke Newington	250–330	300–420	400–500	450–600	525–670	—
Stratford and North Newham	150–210	165–300	200–340	250–400	—	—
Streatham	190–250	220–350	300–450	350–600	500–800	—
Tottenham and Finsbury Park	185–250	220–350	250–400+	350–600+	→	—
Totteridge and Whetstone	230–400	275–500+	350–800+	475–1M+	700–1.5M	—
Twickenham and Teddington	225–375	285–750	400–775+	500–1.5M	750–2M+	—
Wandsworth	250–390	350–500	450–600	600+	750+	1.5M
West Hampstead	300–500	400–600	500–700+	600–1M+	600–1.5M	700–2M
West Norwood, Norbury and Gipsy Hill	150–250	160–300	250–400	300–500+	→	—
Willesden and Brondesbury Park	180–270	220–450	300–600	350–1M	650–1M+	—
Wimbledon, Raynes Park and Merton Park	250–500	300–700	350–800+	500–1.5M	750–2.5M	—

Mortgages

by David Spittles

Once you got a mortgage and stuck with it. But no more: this chapter should perhaps be called Remortgages. Brand loyalty has virtually disappeared in the home loans market. Why stick with your existing lender when you can get a better deal, often with all associated fees paid, by switching to another one?

While existing home-owners juggle with an increasingly complex set of choices, buyers – especially first-timers – searching out a loan also have some fast learning to do, just at at time when they have plenty else on their minds.

Banks and building societies continue to poach business from each other by offering better rates to new customers. The remarkable fact is that two in three existing borrowers do not succumb to the temptation – and therefore continue to pay much more than they need to. About 30 per cent of all borrowers are on the lender's standard variable rate (SVR) and fail to take advantage of fixed or discounted rates. Apathy and inertia are the main reasons.

Hefty savings can be made by taking action. A borrower with a £150,000 interest-only mortgage on an SVR of six per cent would pay £750 per month. By switching to a discount mortgage at four per cent, payments would fall to £500 a month.

'Remortgaging should be an integral part of every borrower's financial planning,' says Ray Boulger of Charcol, a leading broker. At least review your mortgage every year. Charcol offers a free Remortgage Check service (call 0800 718191).

You do not always have to change company to get a better rate; check out what your current lender is offering. If you threaten to go elsewhere, they may give you a rate normally reserved for new customers.

The good news for borrowers – from a start of '05 perspective – is that there should be no interest rate shocks for the time being. Rates are more likely to fall than rise, say analysts.

So the message is shop around, even at your local supermarket. Tesco has entered the mortgage fray, offering a no-frills deal – a three-year discount, with the rate guaranteed to be the same as the Bank of England base rate during the offer period.

The internet is a valuable research tool. You can get quick information on thousands of deals. But most websites do not provide advice, so always think twice before clicking the 'apply' icon. For comparisons try www.moneysupermarket.com or www.easy-quote.co.uk.

Brokers can help if your needs are unusual (buying a wreck to renovate, say) or you want to borrow more than is normally allowed. Most brokers charge a fee of between 0.5 per cent and one per cent of the loan, though there may be a minimum of £250. Always ask for written confirmation of how fees are charged and when they are due.

How much can you borrow? How much will it cost?

Traditionally, buyers have been able to borrow about 3.5 times a single salary or 2.75 times joint income – but some lenders are more flexible: Northern Rock, for instance, will lend 5.7 times income if your earn more than £100,000 a year. Bradford & Bingley even has a deal through its Mortgage Express subsidiary where first-time buyers can borrow 130 per cent of purchase price. This is aimed at people who have built up debts – credit cards, say, or student loans – and thus have no deposit. B & B says it has worked well in a two-year trial in Northern Ireland. But any such loan puts you in negative equity before you even move in. If prices fall, or even stay still, it could be hard for you to move house.

Newcastle Building Society offers a 'guarantor' mortgage to first-time buyers whose parents back them; this is only available to graduates who enter traditional professions such as law, medicine and accountancy. Norwich & Peterborough Building Society offers a 'green' mortgage to eco self-builders. And so on: there are thousands to choose from.

Loans that don't require proof of income are called 'self-certified' mortgages. These are designed for the self-employed and contract workers, and tend to be easier to obtain through brokers. Lenders take the borrower's word about their income and run a credit score test – and charge higher rates. There are fewer such loans about since the Financial Services Authority (FSA) began to regulate mortgage lending in November 2004. Well-publicised cases where brokers connived with borrowers to inflate 'incomes' led some lenders to stop granting such loans altogether.

Being aware of the best deals in the marketplace is imperative, but do not be tempted to chase cheap short-term discounts and ignore the overall cost of borrowing during the life of the loan. *Always read the small print.* Arrangement fees can reach £500, valuation fees can be high too. Is there a sting in the tail – such as redemption penalties or a lock-in period after the discount ends?

When comparing rates, remember that standard variable rates are normally about 1.5 per cent above the Bank of England base rate. But some fixed and discount rates are two per cent below.

One of the best ways to identify the cheapest rates is to study the 'best buy' tables in the personal finance pages of weekend newspapers. Don't just compare APRs: get figures from different lenders for the loan amount you want to borrow and what the monthly repayments will be. Lenders charge interest in different ways (either daily, monthly or yearly), and this can make a big difference.

The best interest-rate deals are open to those who want to borrow less than 90 per cent of the property's value. Lower percentage loans can, too, attract deals like free valuations (the lender just looks up your home on a price database, rather than doing an individual valuation, reasoning that if it is only exposed to, say, 60 per cent of the value it need not worry too much). If you need to borrow a higher percentage loan (more than 75 per cent of the property's value) choose a lender that doesn't apply a 'mortgage indemnity' premium – which could cost more than £3,000 as a one-off payment.

Multiple choice

Choosing the right loan at the outset is something you could still be benefiting from 25 years later. The first priority is to take out a mortgage that helps you achieve your aims. The Council of Mortgage Lenders points out that a suitable loan for one person may be quite wrong for another. For example, some people want to pay off the debt quickly over a set period, while others want flexible terms that allow them to overpay when times are good and underpay in leaner periods. Many first-time buyers' priority is simply to minimise their current outgoings.

So no-one should jump in without doing some detective work or taking independent advice from a regulated broker. First get to know the different types of mortgage. And remember that sensible mortgage planning is not just a matter of finding the lowest rate. Look beyond the headline rate, or inducement, or monthly payment.

Mortgages come in different shapes and sizes and it is important to get the one that fits best. A mortgage is two things: the interest you pay on the loan, and the repayment 'vehicle' (the latter is the means by which you repay the capital sum you have borrowed).

Most borrowers have simple needs. All they require is a straightforward loan at a competitive rate of interest. Usually it is a mistake to opt for something exotic like a currency mortgage. Here are the main types you will come across:

- **Standard variable rate** mortgages fall or rise in accordance with the Bank of England base rate. Most lenders charge about 1.5 per cent above this.
- **Discount** loans are where the interest rate is reduced by a set amount below the variable rate for a specified time. The downside is that you may get a payment shock when the discount ends and you are locked into the variable rate.

• **Fixed rate** loans are attractive because they provide certainty. You can fix the interest rate for as little as one year or as long as 25 years. Most experts advise against fixed rates of more than five years because the marketplace is so dynamic.
• **Capped rates** are popular when the interest rate trend is upwards. The amount you pay is guaranteed not to rise above the cap, but can drop if there is a reduction in interest rates. To an extent, this gives you the best of both worlds – provided the cap is not too high.
• **Tracker** loans are linked to the Bank of England base rate – you pay a set margin over and above this rate. The appeal is that you know you will always be paying a reasonably competitive rate. But you may miss out on a better deal.
• **Cashbacks** are useful for borrowers operating on a shoestring – say, first-time buyers who need money for a deposit or furniture. The drawback is that the interest rate you'll pay is higher than average.
• **Flexible** mortgages are offered by a growing number of lenders. These allow you to increase or reduce your monthly repayments, or take payment holidays if you are short of money. Making extra payments can save staggering amounts in interest.

Some flexible mortgages are linked to current accounts – meaning that you can use the account like a bank and benefit from the 'salary effect'. All income going into your account helps to pay off some of your mortgage, and your savings effectively earn you interest at the mortgage rate – with no savings tax to pay.

The danger is that you get complacent and don't make high enough payments, thereby eating into the equity that has built up. Experts say if you are not a disciplined borrower, it is probably best to avoid flexible mortgages.
• **Mix and match**: If you cannot make up your mind between a fixed or variable loan, you can hedge your bets by taking out both. Most lenders allow you to select more than one type. For example, you could fix half your mortgage and leave the other half on a tracker rate. If interest rates fall, your monthly repayments will drop on the tracker portion of the loan. But the fixed deal provides an element of security if rates rise.

Paying it back

The safest and often the cheapest way to repay your loan is a traditional Repayment mortgage. You pay interest, and pay back capital, each month and take out separate life insurance to cover the loan in the event of death. You don't have to stick to a 25-year term. If you can afford to pay more each month, it makes sense to opt for a shorter repayment schedule – perhaps 15 years. This will result in a much lower interest bill over the life of the loan. Ask your lender to quote you figures for different repayment periods.

The alternative to a Repayment loan is one where capital and interest are dealt with separately. You pay interest each month, then pay the capital back at the end of the term, using some kind of savings vehicle – for example an endowment, a pension or a series of ISAs. Endowments have been discredited and for most people there is little point in them. Instead consider building up savings through an ISA or some other equity investment.

Here too there is nothing to stop you repaying in a combination of ways. Say you have a £200,000 loan: you could arrange £100,000 on a repayment basis and the other £100,000 on an interest-only basis backed by ISAs or unit trusts.

Some lenders accept 'interest-only' mortgages, whereby there is no requirement to have a repayment vehicle in place. These are sometimes used by people expecting an inheritance, or some other windfall, or who plan to sell their home and 'downsize' in the future.

David Spittles is Property and Personal Finance writer for The London Evening Standard and The Observer.

Renting and investing in London

London's rental scene is rather odd. In most of the world's cities, renting your home is the norm. In London it is the exception. Only 17 per cent of London homes are privately rented, with rather more rented by social landlords (councils and housing associations). That leaves over half London's homes owned by their occupiers.

If you wonder why there has been so much fuss recently about investing in rented property, the so-called Buy-to-Let (BTL) phenomenon, reflect that it is a novelty. That 17 per cent figure, small though it is, is an increase on that prevailing ten years back, and (more visible, this) the character of landlords has changed.

Why has renting been such a shy flower? Because in the years 1915–1974 a series of laws intended to protect tenants had the back-handed effect of making renting to anyone other than a company insecure and usually unprofitable. The 1988 Housing Act (amended 1996) made the rebirth of the private rented sector possible. For the first time, landlords could sign up tenants for just six months at a market rent, with no security of tenure after the initial period. Eviction of tenants for non-payment or abuse of properties was made feasible and, providing the right contract is signed, there is now no danger of creating a 'sitting tenancy'.

This generated a much more open, and much larger, market. At last, homeseekers had a decent alternative to buying. The 1996 changes also gave comfort to the banks, which realized that a whole new source of business had emerged: loans to amateur landlords. The BTL brigade seized on this chance to invest in the Englishman's favourite: property.

Back in 1996, this made fair good sense, with returns that were well worth having even if property prices stayed at what hindsight shows were low levels. But prices went up, while rents did not. New investors were buying more and more in hope of further price rises than in certainty of a steady yield. This *Guide*, and other commentators, warned from early 2003 onwards that investment in London property was hard to justify for new entrants. This advice was given with extra urgency as rents fell steadily. The rise in interest rates during 2004 skewed the equation still further against new landlords.

Despite this, there are still plenty of people telling us that investing in property is a good idea. They would say that, wouldn't they – they have properties and loans to sell. Here, in the interests of balance, we first set out the arguments for caution. Caution in London, at this time. Then follow the facts and figures for you to make up your own mind, and the practicalities of being a landlord – and of being a tenant.

Why invest in property?

Why do people invest in property? The key reason is gearing. A bank will lend you 75 per cent, sometimes 85, of the cost of an investment property. Try doing the same to buy a portfolio of shares or gilts. So the investor has all the (surely certain!) uplift in value in return for putting down one pound in four. And the rent will pay the mortgage. That's the attraction, and for many people it has worked. But note the past tense.

Those who bought in London before 1998, say, and who have worked hard to manage their properties well and keep them tenanted, can look with some complacency at the current market. They have preserved, indeed enhanced, their capital (their deposit) while other investments have seen 50 per cent falls. They can still enjoy a net yield of 8–10 per cent on their buying price, enough to cover even this year's increased mortgage costs. And those longer-term landlords are in most cases sitting on vastly more valuable portfolios – though it's worth noting that some, at least, have cashed in their chips since 2000 and walked away from what they saw as an increasingly uncertain market.

But it is the last-in amateurs for whom the sums look less than appetising. Buying in 2001–3 at a time of historically low interest rates, and declining tenant demand, they effectively took a geared bet on property price rises. The only 'up' potential in their equation was capital value. But the equation in many cases failed to allow for another variable, the rise in interest rates. At 3.5 per cent base rate, a one per cent rise meant a 20 per cent hike in repayments. Many buy-to-let balance sheets could not, cannot, survive that. Some have been learning a new, scary term, negative cash flow: more money going out to your lender than coming in from tenants. Like negative equity... only more immediate in its effects.

Tightening yields mean more investors go for interest-only loans to cut their outgoings. Which means they are not repaying the debt. It's no use calling a flat or two 'your pension' if, still owing what you borrowed when you retire, you have to sell – thus giving up your income stream. Such investors are simply gambling on prices going up. And on finding a tenant, this month and every month, for 20 years....

The past decade's surge in buy-to-let was driven by two contradictory urges: the desire for capital gain, riding the property escalator, and the need for a better income than other investments could provide. It is a lucky property investor whose timing works out to give him/her both. It is also noticeable that the sort of people who feel happy with property investment are often uneasy about being in debt. Borrowing to buy property does not seem like debt to them, somehow – perhaps because it's called a mortgage.

Behind BTL is an unspoken assumption: that property will go on rising in price faster than inflation. So it has overall, in the UK, since 1955. In Japan, and Germany, since 1990 it has done the reverse, just like in the UK from 1900 to 1955. Imagine your position 20 years on when prices have trickled down by one or two per cent a year, you end up selling for half what you paid, and you still owe that six-figure sum to the bank....

And one last homily: don't borrow to buy property just because you can't think of another way to invest. Not when you can earn 5 per cent from an Internet bank account – which has no boiler to maintain, roof to replace... and no need of tenants.

Residential property as a business

The 30-year history of modern London property investment began with the petro-dollars of the mid-1970s. Suddenly, a whole class of exotic investors looked at London homes from a new perspective and began to buy, becoming a flood that triggered the '80s boom. The Arabs of the 1970s have been suceeded at various times in the last three decades by Japanese, Hong Kong, even Canadian and Irish investors, all eager for their own particular reasons to buy a stake in London real estate. Their reasons were their own, drawn from their own domestic economic imperatives; London merely gained from the fallout.

In the mid 1990s (after, you will recall, the prolonged recession and property-market crash) home-grown investors, the buy-to-let brigade, joined in, fuelling the last boom. This wave has now subsided; as we have observed, the economics do not add up. Yet London still seems attractive from the point of view of Beijing, Zurich, Moscow.

There have been frequent predictions that the City would get in on the act with residential property funds. These are common in the commercial property market, but have so far failed to make a dent in residential. The reason is that funds are out-gunned by private investors, both domestic and foreign, who are prepared to pay higher prices. They can do this because they borrow – gear up their investments – in a way no prudent fund mamager would contemplate. It might be sobering for some individual investors to think that they are venturing where the City fears to tread.

Strong hints have emerged from government about tax changes to make it easier for individuals to invest in property via what America and Australia know as REITs (real estate investment trusts), and via the new pension regime due in 2006. In both cases we still await the vital small print. This might add further stability – though only if regulation improves. The thought of London's estate agents, mortgage brokers, IFAs and developers let loose on a selling spree on the lines of 'invest in bricks and mortar: property is your pension' sends shivers down the spine.

What are the figures?

No-one really knows how many rented homes there are in London, who owns them and who rents them for how much. Individual estate agents' research fill some gaps, but the growing practice of multi-listing, and the (unknown) number of landlords who don't use agents, makes figures unreliable. There is no real way of knowing how much is borrowed on mortgage to finance residential investment, as the practice of equity withdrawal from individuals' main homes has led to (again unknown) sums flooding into the market. Even in London, no-one has a decent run of rental figures: eight to ten years is as far back as even the blue-chip agents can go.

Gathering what data one can, it's noteworthy that rents did not rise fast in the 1980s, despite the big increase in property prices. Rents tracked inflation, then stayed level during the property slump of 1988-92. From 1992 to '96 rents grew faster than inflation, but after 2000 steady declines were seen – a trend that only began to stabilize in '04. Rents in central and other 'prime' districts rose during 2004, for the first time since 2000. This trend continued into the early weeks of 2005. Some – not all – top agents' indices showed rises of 4 per cent for 2004 – about the same percentage as they had dropped in 2003. Despite this rise, renting a flat in the City or Mid-Town is one of the few things in London to be cheaper than in 1998, though the price of such a property has doubled over the same seven years. Rents in the prime central and western areas in early '05 were 'only' 13 per cent below the peak reached in mid-2001.

More to the point, from an investor's point of view, tenant demand seems to have grown in 2004. At the start of that year, 88 per cent of Association of Residential letting Agents (ARLA) central London members reported having more properties than tenants. During the year, demand increased steadily and when ARLA asked the same question in December 62 per cent said homes to let outnumbered tenants.

The current yield on central London property, estimated by property industry statisticians at around 5 per cent, is less than the cost of financing. This makes new investment pointless – as even lenders such as UCB Homes Loans, Nationwide's BTL subsidiary, admit. Unsurpisingly, 26 per cent of ARLA's central London landlords said they were selling properties, with only three per cent buying.

Against this nervousness must be set London's consistent status as a safe haven for wealth. Plenty of foreigners look to London as a sensible place to stash a portion of their assets, especially in troubled times – though London's properties must these days compete on a global scale, with investors in the Gulf weighing their burgeoning local market against the charms of London, where prices are perceived as high. London developers are seeking off-plan sales in China, a step beyond their traditional markets in the overseas Chinese communities in Taiwan, Singapore and Hong Kong. Irish investors are still active, and Russians are conspicuous at the very top end of the market.

Perhaps this is the wrong place to say this, but Paris has been a better bet in the past couple of years: house prices rose by 16 per cent in the 12 months to June 2004...

Investing in property: the details

First, the economics. You have two vital figures: the cost of the property and the rent it can earn. To the price you pay must be added Stamp Duty (see Buying & Selling), legal fees, preparation (cleaning, furnishing to good standard, etc). If you borrow to finance the purchase then lender's costs including valuation fee must be added. Don't forget the foregone interest on the sum you use as a deposit.

Most BTL lenders will insist on you putting up a deposit of 25 per cent. Some relax this to 15 per cent, especially when demand for loans is slack. The lender will demand that the rent coming in is at least 130 per cent of the interest going out. Some lenders insist that the property is assessed for rental yield by a professional letting agent (this will cost you money) and some go further and insist that the property be managed by an agent.

You may be able to use the gross rental yield to convince the lender, but to reassure yourself you ought to calculate a realistic *net* yield. The yield on a property is simply the percentage of its cost (or value) that can be earned in rent. This is the gross figure. From it you deduct all the costs: agents' fees, service charges (if it's a flat), ground rents (if any), insurance, repairs and maintenance.

Some properties cost more to maintain: gardens, lavish common parts and lifts in blocks will run up service charge bills. Allow for regular upgrading and refurbishing. And expect void periods (time when the property is un-let): even if new tenants are found straight away, it takes at least 10 working days to take up references and process the paperwork. Prudent landlords reckon on a month's void per year.

Another kind of yield equation – one amateur landlords are keen on – is to see if the monthy rent will pay the mortgage. If it does, this is expressed as 'letting the tenants buy me a flat'. True – if you are on a repayment loan, and if you are honest with yourself about costs. Many investors have additional motives for buying: a place for the kids to live, maybe letting rooms to other students, while at college; or perhaps to keep a stake in London while working abroad, or on moving to the country.

The eventual sale of investment property will attract Capital Gains Tax. The calculations are complex and there are various reliefs – especially if the property has been your principal private residence (PPR) at some point: get a good accountant.

Choosing the property

If you are a professional investor, the big agents have specialist units with lots of advice. But if you're an amateur, thinking along the lines above, what should you be looking for? If you are going to manage the place yourself, look close to home. A plumbing crisis at 3 a.m. is more easily coped with close by, and you will probably know the tradesmen you need to keep the place running. You will know the best streets, and those to avoid.

If you choose a property a long way from home, portered blocks of flats seem a good bet: there's someone to let the plumber in, and keep an eye on things. Ensure that common parts and block management are good quality, and be aware that your tenants will have to adhere to the block's lease conditions (rules can be strict). *But* beware of big new developments – especially in less-than-prime locations. These are often marketed aggressively (and internationally) at buy-to-let purchasers just like you, who then find that they're competing for tenants with just about every flat in the block. Your investment aims may not be shared by other, perhaps foreign, buyers. Look hard at new schemes: are they 'step-out friendly' in the jargon (is it a nice place to walk back to at midnight?). Is transport right to hand? Is there adequate parking?

Also, smart new flats attract the famous 'young professionals': well-paid workers in the finance and services sector – but they are just the people to be affected by a downturn in the economy (as 2001-3 proved). Teachers, medical staff, students will be here when the bankers have gone back to New York or Frankfurt: consider humbler homes aimed at sharers (but see below for new licencing rules) close to hospitals say, or colleges.

Rents are more stable for family homes in the suburbs, and – paradoxically – at the cheaper end of the market. Sharers can often afford more than the single professional or couple that most landlords have preferred, which explains why weekly rents of around £100–120 per bedroom are common for non-luxury properties. Such tenants look for convenient locations first: the fare band of the local tube station is a key factor.

Buy with your head, not your heart: this is business, not nest-building. You are not just an investor, you are a landlord. Look at a property through the eyes of potential tenants: is it very convenient? Is the tube really close? Do your research: stick to areas you know, or can get to know. Read the relevant chapters in this *Guide*. Speak to several agents: who's renting what, in what numbers? Get hold of all lists of homes for sale, and rent, from agents and Internet. Pay for a survey for the place; quiz the surveyor on price compared to like properties: this is as important as looking for dry rot in the basement. Be sure about areas, neighbourhoods, postcodes: the information is all in this book.

Compare prices with re-sales (ask local agents, use the Internet to find actual selling prices), check rents with independent sources, see how many flats in the block are on the lettings market (Internet property sites are the place to look). If buying in Phase III of a big scheme, find out what buyers in the first phases paid (if a lot less, they can and will undercut your rent). Only put down money where you expect the developer to stick around to complete. Quite a few went bust in 1990, taking deposits with them.

Recognize the conflicts: if you walk into a marketing suite, or deal with an agent who is selling on behalf of a developer, you are not in an impartial environment. The agent aims for the highest price for his paymaster, the developer. He will also want icing on the cake: he wants you to arrange a loan through him, possibly a solicitor too. And once the sale is done he will hope to manage the flat on your behalf for a steady percentage of your rent. In most commercial spheres this would be called a conflict of interest. The agent has a stake in you paying the highest possible price, which inevitably means that when you come to let you receive a lower yield. Consider appointing an agent, ideally a chartered surveyor who is also a specialist in rented property, to represent you in the negotiations. You will almost certainly save his fee, and he may well spot flaws in the development – from an investment standpoint – that put you off the deal entirely.

Licencing for HMOs and homes rented by sharers

A potential threat to the sharers' market comes from legislation on Houses in Multiple Occupation (HMOs) in the new Housing Act. The Scottish experience, where licensing has already been introduced, is not encouraging. The law in England and Wales is not so draconian, with 3-storey houses and/or those shared by five or more the targets: these must be licenced ('Mandatory Licence') from a start-date some time in 2005. But local councils will also gain the power to licence all HMOs in areas they decide ('Additional Licence'), and this covers groups of sharers, whatever the size of the property. It is not yet clear what this will cost landlords, nor how the landlord will be assessed (he or she must be a 'fit and proper person'). Before a council can impose a licencing regime it needs to consult with interested parties, including landlords, and it must have a reason, such as thinking that a good proprtion of HMOs are badly managed. There is also a power to impose Selective Licencing on an area, if a council decides that it would help combat anti-social behaviour there. No such licences have yet been introduced.

Being a landlord

As a landlord, you enter into a legal agreement with your tenants in the terms outlined above. Landlords should insist that sharers all sign the **Assured Shorthold Tenancy** so that they are **jointly and severally liable**. If a sharer leaves and a new one comes in, a new agreement should be drawn up. A good lettings agent, or your solicitor, will give advice on this. If using a standard agreement, ensure that it covers the particular needs of the property, such as looking after gardens, exclusion of pets if necessary (in some cases children), security such as alarms and locks and the precise number who will live there. Don't use an onerous agreement, however impressive it looks (some produced by agents are this way inclined): antagonising good tenants is not in your interest. It can also be illegal; make sure your wording is up to date – there have been recent changes in the law.

Be aware that the 2004 Housing Act changes the way landlords must handle deposits. A start-date for this change has yet to be announced: it may well be in 2006. But after that date, you must either pay the deposits into a special custody scheme, or take out insurance. Penalties for not doing so include a fine three times the deposit.

Another change: the new Home Condition Report (see Buying & Selling chapter) due in January 2007 will include a certificate of energy efficiency. Once these are in use, landlords must show them to each tenant at the start of each tenancy.

Landlords need to insure the property: both structure and your (not tenants') contents. You must also inform the insurer when it is let and check that cover continues if it is vacant between lets. Be sure that your insurance covers third-party and public liability risks. Insurance is also available to cover legal expenses and loss of rent due to damage such as a fire. If the property is mortgaged, the lender too will need to be informed of your intention to let, and may charge a fee (and/or a higher rate) for permission.

As a landlord you have to comply with the safety legislation designed to protect tenants. You must have all gas appliances (boilers, cookers, fires) inspected every year by a CORGI-registered gas fitter. This is expensive, and may lead you to consider avoiding gas and installing electrical heating and cooking. *Note, though, that since January 1 2005 electrical work is also subject to new, tighter rules: see page 74.* You must also ensure that all your soft furnishings, such as beds, chairs and sofas, comply with fire regulations, which outlaw everything made before 1988 (antique furniture is OK: check the details). If you fail to comply and tenants are injured as a result, you could be sued by them and/or prosecuted – with, if convicted, a prison term of up to six months or a fine of £5,000.

You should, in theory, find it possible under current legislation to repossess if the tenants are in arrears or are wrecking the place. In practice, it's not that simple. It takes months for courts to handle repossession cases, even under the 'accelerated possessions procedure'. You can use the accelerated procedure if the tenant is refusing to leave after the end of the agreement when you've served the correct notices. Otherwise there are two types of court proceedings for possession: discretionary and mandatory. For being at least two months in rent arrears repossession is mandatory, while for other reasons (e.g. riotous parties, or using the property as a business) it is discretionary.

The National Landlords Association (NLA), set up in 1973 as the Small Landlords Association, is a very real source of help and advice for private landlords, including guidance on the complexities of legislation, leases and so on. They can also point members towards good sources of insurance and finance. Contact them at 78 Tachbrook St, SW1V 2NA; tel 0870 241 0471; www.landlords.org.uk.

Agents

Some landlords find tenants themselves, and handle the management of, and the paperwork for, their property (the latter should be with the help of a solicitor). The NLA (see above) is a source of information. Others use an agent for a range of services up to full management and rent collection. Landlords (not tenants) pay agents a percentage of the rent, which varies according to the level of service.

There are plenty of lettings agents competing for landlords' custom, and established sales agencies have lettings departments. As a result, fees have dropped. Don't be afraid to negotiate, especially if you have, or intend to have, several properties.

Agents like their fee as soon as the agreement is signed – and in advance. This can cause cash-flow problems on a new tenancy; also, problems may arise if the tenant leaves early. So try to negotiate payment of fees monthly in arrears, as your rent is paid. Reputable firms are quoting fees circa 10 per cent for finding a tenant and collecting rent, with full management up to 15 per cent, though there does seem to be a downward trend in fees, with cut-throat competition in areas with plentiful rented property. If you are retaining an agent just to introduce tenants, offer a fixed fee (a certain number of weeks' rent, say four weeks) instead of a percentage (some agents try for 10 per cent) of the rent.

Be clear at the outset, before you sign anything, about how much you are contracted to pay to the agent. Consult your solicitor if in doubt. Do not just accept all terms offered: when the Consumers' Association scrutinized documentation from six agents (another 17 refused to cooperate) it described some 'standard' terms as 'simply outrageous'.

Membership of ARLA (Association of Residential Lettings Agents) and/or one of the two main estate agents' bodies, the RICS (Royal Institution of Chartered Surveyors) or the NAEA (National Association of Estate Agents), are good signs. Members of ARLA must hold professional indemnity insurance and run separate client accounts (as must RICS members); it has an arbitration service to settle disputes. All members are also signed up to the independent housing ombudsman scheme. Some mortgage lenders insist that property they finance be managed by an ARLA-approved agent, while others only ask that the property be vetted for rental level and suitability by an approved agent.

ARLA has a bonding scheme which works on a 'first resort' basis that protects clients' money (rent or deposits) held by agents. This means that landlords are first in the queue to get their money back if things go wrong. A member-firm must have a qualified person in each office. For members or further details: 0845 345 5752, or www.arla.co.uk.

Being a tenant

Landlords and tenants sign an Assured Shorthold Tenancy (AST) Agreement. This is for a minimum initial period of six months, after which the two sides can sign a further contract if everything is going well. An agreement is assumed (under the 1996 law) to be an AST unless the landlord specifically states otherwise. To end the contract, the landlord or the tenant has to give notice (usually two months) in writing. The landlord has the right to raise the rent at the end of any six-month period. The tenant can refer his rent to a rent assessment panel if he thinks it's excessive, but only during the first six months of the tenancy. The panel must consider market rents for similar properties in the locality. The rules differ when the landlord lives in the same building.

Sharers should all sign the tenancy agreement so that they are jointly and severally responsible: since this means that two of you can't just shrug your shoulders if the third fails to pay up, you should be careful about who you're sharing with! The agreement should be drawn up by a solicitor or a reputable letting agency. The agency will also advise on matters such as deposits and references.

Before you are granted a tenancy the landlord or their agent typically asks for three references, one of which must be from your bank and another from your employer. A deposit of four to six weeks' rent is needed, to cover any breakages or unpaid bills. This deposit is held by the landlord/agent and you should get a receipt for it. The landlord or agent should handle the transfer of utility and phone accounts into your name(s). Meters should be read on 'get-in'. You are responsible for council tax, and single occupiers can get a 25 per cent discount: apply to the town hall. Tenants should insure their possessions; the landlord should insure the building and his furniture, fittings etc.

Rents are normally paid monthly, in advance. Most agents quote rents in weekly amounts, and the tables in this book use weekly figures. There is no introductory fee payable by tenants, but there will be costs for leases and inventories. Lease costs will occur whenever a new lease is drawn up.

Although the AST Agreement gives the framework, the details of leases can differ as much as properties do. As well as the main terms such as the period of notice required on either side, it will specify such obligations as keeping windows clean and maintaining the garden. This is a legally binding document: check it well, and raise any queries, before signing. You should also get, and check well, the inventory of contents and a schedule of condition, setting out the state the place is in. Once you have signed these, they form the basis for any deductions for breakages and 'dilapidations', so if something is well worn or damaged from the outset, this should be noted: write it in yourself, if it is not. When the tenancy ends and you are about to leave, the inventory should be checked by the landlord, the agent or a specialist inventory clerk working for them. After allowance for wear and tear, any breakages or damage will come out of your deposit.

Rentals Price Charts, overleaf, give a snapshot of the London market at the start of 2005.

Price charts: rentals

The charts on the following pages consolidate the data in the Area Profiles, showing broadly what certain kinds of homes cost to rent per week in each of the areas covered. This gives you a freeze-frame picture across London at the start of 2005: a basis for comparison throughout the year.

The prices given are for typical examples of each type of home. Where a range of figures is shown, this reflects rent variations within the area. Thus the range is also

FLATS — RENTALS STARTING PRICES FOR 2005

weekly rent in £s — too few for price average → price carries over

	STUDIO	1 BEDROOM	2 BEDROOM	3 BEDROOM	4 BEDROOM	5+ BEDROOM
Acton	140–200	160–225	200–300	230–350	320–400	–
Balham and Tooting	130–200	190–250	190–300	230–430	300–600	–
Barnes, Mortlake and Sheen	140–180	170–320	210–360	260–400+	330–400+	–
Battersea	150–250	170–350	210–450+	275–500+	350+	–
Bayswater	165–275	215–400	300–675	400–1000	550–1450	1500+
Bedford Park and Acton Green	150–250	200–350+	230–400+	300–600	450–1000+	–
Belgravia	200–400	250–575	420–1000+	650–1600	1000+	–
Bethnal Green	130–150	170–210	200–270	240–350	–	–
Bloomsbury and King's Cross	170–200+	200–350+	270–550	450+	500+	–
Bow	140–160	160–220	200–280	240–340	–	–
Brixton, Herne Hill and Tulse Hill	120–150	150–250	180–300	220–370	–	–
Camberwell	115–145	140–200	165–250	200–280	230+	–
Camden Town and Primrose Hill	160–220	200–350	250–600	300–600+	400–600+	–
Chelsea	200–380	250–500+	320–900	500–1500	600–2000+	–
Chiswick	150–200	160–300	195–500	200–600	350–600+	–
City and Fringes	180–220	225–300	280–400	350–500	–	–
Clapham	150–180	170–260	200–350	320–390	380–460	500+
Clerkenwell and Finsbury	170–210	220–320	300–500	450–550	–	–
Cricklewood	125–140	150–190	200–250	275–350	350+	–
Crouch End and Stroud Green	150–190	175–230	200–280	250–360	375–450	–
Crystal Palace	100–130	120–185	150–200	175–250	–	–
Dollis Hill and Neasden	120–150	140–175	170–225	230–250	–	–
Dulwich	125–160	150–200	185–230	200–300	275–350	–
Ealing	100–185	150–250	180–300	200–400	300–400	450+
Finchley	130–160	160–210	175–300	225–325	400+	–
Forest Hill	100–150	125–175	150–200	175–300	230–350	325–370
Fulham	150–250	200–325	230–425	320–500	375–800	400+
Golders Green	125–180	175–225	200–320	280–420	350–500	–
Greenwich and Blackheath	150–180	160–250	170–285	260–450	300–400+	–
Hackney	120–140	160–200	200–250	250–320	300–450	350–550
Hammersmith	150–200	180–300	240–450	300–500	400–750	–
Hampstead	175–220	220–350	300–650	350–850	750+	–
Hampstead Garden Suburb	150–200	175–250	225–400	350–650	475–700	–
Hendon and Mill Hill	100–170	160–210	200–400	240–300+	–	–
Highgate	150–230	180–250	200–550	300–700	350–500+	–
Holland Park	150–300	250–600	300–800+	450–1500	750–4000	1500–4000
Islington and Highbury	175–200+	200–300+	250–400+	300+	450+	–
Kennington, Vauxhall and Stockwell	155–220	190–300	210–400	290–500	400–675	–

an indicator of the scope of the properties: a small range indicates a fairly homogeneous area; a wide one either that there are some neighbourhoods that warrant a premium, or perhaps there is a good supply of recently developed, more luxurious flats. In all brackets you are likely to find cheaper homes, and exceptional ones at the other end of the scale: a plus sign is used where we have not included the rents for a small number of unusual examples, which would distort the averages.

HOUSES — RENTALS STARTING PRICES FOR 2005

weekly rent in £s — too few for price average → price carries over

	2 BEDROOM	3 BEDROOM	4 BEDROOM	5 BEDROOM	6–7 BEDROOM	8+ BEDROOM
Acton	230–350	280–400	330–450	420–600	500+	—
Balham and Tooting	200–375	255–425	255–600	325–600+	400–800	—
Barnes, Mortlake and Sheen	270–400	335–475	500–800	675+	900+	—
Battersea	280–600	350–600	400–800	550–1000	650+	—
Bayswater	450–750	500–950+	700–1200	1300–4000	—	—
Bedford Park and Acton Green	300–600	350–600	450–800	600–2500	700–2500+	—
Belgravia	575–1000+	750–2000	1100–2000	2600+	4000+	—
Bethnal Green	230–300	330–400	400–500	—	—	—
Bloomsbury and King's Cross	—	—	—	—	—	—
Bow	240–300	300–350	350–450	450–600	—	—
Brixton, Herne Hill and Tulse Hill	180–330	230–390	330–550	390–600+	—	—
Camberwell	200–270	230–370	275–400	400+	—	—
Camden Town and Primrose Hill	280–600	400–800+	500–1200+	550+	600–3000	—
Chelsea	380–1000	600–1400+	1000–2000+	1900+	2400+	—
Chiswick	200–500	230–600	350–1000	400–2500	600–2500	—
City and Fringes	300–600	500+	600+	800+	—	—
Clapham	300–400	380–500	350–600	600+	—	—
Clerkenwell and Finsbury	375–500	400–800	800–1300	1000–1500	—	—
Cricklewood	250–300	275–400	300–450	400–500+	—	—
Crouch End and Stroud Green	200–300	280–400+	350–500+	450–650	600–800	—
Crystal Palace	175–250	185–300	230–450	300–600+	—	—
Dollis Hill and Neasden	190–240	230–350	275–400	300–600	—	—
Dulwich	190–275	275–325	300–450	325–500	350–500+	650+
Ealing	200–300	250–450	300–600	400–700	650+	—
Finchley	250–325	275–400	325–600	500–850	—	—
Forest Hill	175–220	210–275	260–350+	300–370	350–400	350–450
Fulham	350+	370–550	525–850	700–1200	—	—
Golders Green	280–375	350–500	350–750	450–1000	750–1000+	900+
Greenwich and Blackheath	200–450	250–500	400–600	500–600+	→1000	—
Hackney	180–250	250–350	320–475	450–550	—	—
Hammersmith	300–400	400–700	450–800+	500–1200	1000–2000	—
Hampstead	285–750	350–1000	1000–3000	1500–5000	→	—
Hampstead Garden Suburb	250–375	350–575	550–1000	750–1500	1000+	2000+
Hendon and Mill Hill	200–400	300–500	400–600	600+	—	—
Highgate	250–450	350–575	400–1000+	500–2000+	600–5000	—
Holland Park	350–850	500–1500	700–4000	1300–5000	3000–5000	—
Islington and Highbury	350+	450+	500+	700+	900+	—
Kennington, Vauxhall and Stockwell	230–400	300–500	400–625	400–600	450–700	570–1300

Flats — Rentals

weekly rent in £s — too few for price average → price carries over

	STUDIO	1 BEDROOM	2 BEDROOM	3 BEDROOM	4 BEDROOM	5+ BEDROOM
Kensington	250–350	300–550	350–800	600–1500	800–1600	—
Kentish Town and Tufnell Park	150–200	180–250	220–475	300–600	380–600	—
Kilburn, Kensal Green and Queen's Park	100–200	160–250	210–350	275–400	275–500	—
Knightsbridge	180–300	280–500+	370–950	650–1500	800–2300+	—
Lewisham and Catford	115–140	140–175	160–210	185–230	210–250	—
Leyton and Walthamstow	100–130	150–170	165–200	190–280	—	—
Maida Vale and Little Venice	150–250	200–400	280–600	300–700+	700–1000+	1000+
Marylebone and Fitzrovia	150–400	250–475	350–650	450–800	600–1200	850–3000
Mayfair and St James's	200–350	250–600	400–1200	600–2000	1000–3000	—
Morden, Mitcham and Colliers Wood	115–140	140–175	165–225	185–250	265–375	→390
Muswell Hill	140+	175–200	190–300	250–400+	400–700	—
New Cross and Deptford	115–150	140–175	175–240	210–325	275–350	—
Notting Hill and North Kensington	150–270	200–470	230–750	350–1000+	450–1400	550–1500+
Peckham	120–150	140–195	175–250	195–275	—	—
Pimlico and Westminster	170–250	250–400	200–500+	500+	→1000	—
Poplar	120–150	140–200	170–250	230–350	—	—
Putney and Roehampton	150–210	190–300	200–500	250–600	450+	600+
Regent's Park	240–290	275–450	280–700	425–1400	550–1500	2000+
Richmond and Kew	145–200	185–300	200–500	200–800	700+	1000+
Royal Docks and South Newham	130–150	150–200	170–225	210–260	300+	—
Shepherd's Bush	140–160	170–250	230–400	260–500	400–450	→500
Soho and Covent Garden	200–300	250–600	325–1000	450–2000	—	—
The South Bank	170–250	190–350	230–450+	325–800	—	—
South Kensington, Earl's Court and West Brompton	200–400	280–500+	350–1400	575–1600	750–1550	850+
Southfields and Earlsfield	140–225	165–280	210–320	250–350	275–400	—
Southgate and Palmers Green	100–140	135–185	160–210	200–350	—	—
St John's Wood	180–250	250–400	350–800	300–1500	400–2500	—
Stepney and Whitechapel	130–160	160–220	230–280	270–350	—	—
Stoke Newington	120–160	150–210	210–270	250–330	330–400	430–500
Stratford and North Newham	100–130	140–160	160–190	190–220	220–260	250–300+
Streatham	110–150	140–180	160–230	200–300	230–300	—
Tottenham and Finsbury Park	120–150	170–220	180–250	200–400	—	—
Totteridge and Whetstone	110–180	130–200	180–275+	225–350+	—	—
Twickenham and Teddington	120–210	150–250	230–400	250–420	—	—
Wandsworth	150–190	200–240	250–350	320–380	400+	—
West Hampstead	150–190	180–300	220–400	300–650	375–750	550–1000
West Norwood, Norbury and Gipsy Hill	100–140	115–160	150–210	175–270	210–370	—
Willesden and Brondesbury Park	110–175	135–230	180–300	220–370+	280–500+	350–550
Wimbledon, Raynes Park and Merton Park	140–185	175–275	230–450	275–550	—	—

HOUSES — RENTALS

weekly rent in £s — too few for price average → price carries over

	2 BEDROOM	3 BEDROOM	4 BEDROOM	5 BEDROOM	6–7 BEDROOM	8+ BEDROOM
Kensington	500–700+	750–900	900–1000	1000–4500	3500+	—
Kentish Town and Tufnell Park	320–400	375–500	450–650	500–850	—	—
Kilburn, Kensal Green and Queen's Park	275–300	350–600	375–700	500–750	—	—
Knightsbridge	475–1000+	700–2000	1150–2000	2300+	2500–4500+	—
Lewisham and Catford	175–220	200–275	230–400	250–450	275–475	—
Leyton and Walthamstow	180–220	200–260	240–300	280–340	—	—
Maida Vale and Little Venice	350–500	400–800+	800–2500	1000–4000	2000–5000	—
Marylebone and Fitzrovia	500–700	600–1000	750–2000	1200–1800+	—	—
Mayfair and St James's	500–1200	800–2000	1000–2500+	2000–4000	2500–5000	—
Morden, Mitcham and Colliers Wood	185–225	210–260	275–350	350–400	—	—
Muswell Hill	250–350	300–450	400–600+	450–800	600–1300	—
New Cross and Deptford	180–280	200–325	275–350	350–400	375–550	—
Notting Hill and North Kensington	450–950	500–1400	600–1600	800–1900+	1500–2500	→
Peckham	195–230	230–275	275–370	345–400	350–500+	—
Pimlico and Westminster	500–800	600–900	800+	800+	—	—
Poplar	200–250	250–350	250–400	—	—	—
Putney and Roehampton	300–500	350–600	450–900	600–1300	725–1800+	900+
Regent's Park	500–1000	650–1000+	950–1250+	1900–3000+	3000–6000+	—
Richmond and Kew	250–450	300–700	300–900	350–1000+	1300+	1500+
Royal Docks and South Newham	200–400	240–290	260–320	300–450	—	—
Shepherd's Bush	300–400	325–400+	380–650	500–750	—	—
Soho and Covent Garden	500–1000	800–2000	1300–3000	2500+	—	—
The South Bank	195–450	300–550	350+	—	—	—
South Kensington, Earl's Court and West Brompton	400–650	500–1200+	1000–3000	1700–5000+	2000–5000+	—
Southfields and Earlsfield	200–350	240–350	275–500	450–600	600+	—
Southgate and Palmers Green	185–230	205–320	250–415	300–580	—	—
St John's Wood	450–950	500–1500	900–2500	1000–5000	→	→
Stepney and Whitechapel	230–300	300–370	300–450	—	—	—
Stoke Newington	220–240	250–350	330–410	480–550	550–620	—
Stratford and North Newham	160–210	190–240	250–300	275–325	350+	—
Streatham	200–230	250–300	375–415	325–450	400–500	—
Tottenham and Finsbury Park	185–300	210–400	230–450	280–450	—	—
Totteridge and Whetstone	200–425	275–500	300–600+	400–1000	1000+	—
Twickenham and Teddington	220–350	260–450+	350–900	350–1000+	→2000	—
Wandsworth	250–400	350–500	400–700	600+	650+	1000→
West Hampstead	250–400	320–650	400–750+	500–1000	—	—
West Norwood, Norbury and Gipsy Hill	185–210	200–300	275–450	→	→	—
Willesden and Brondesbury Park	220–300	230–400	320–450	350–650	—	—
Wimbledon, Raynes Park and Merton Park	250–450	300–700	350–925	450–1100	→1600	—

Schools in London

by Liz Lightfoot

The first co-ordinated admissions system for the 33 boroughs which run schools in the capital comes into effect this year – and should make finding a secondary place a lot easier for parents.

Eight local authorities bordering on the London boroughs, including those with sought-after grammar schools, have agreed to join the scheme which will allow families to apply to schools in any of the 41 areas on a single form.

When applying, parents list six schools in order of preference and are allocated the highest one on their list prepared to offer a place. All applicants will be given offers of places on the same day in March.

The officials running the London Schools Admissions System promise that it will greatly reduce the number of children who end up without a place – an unfortunate feature of education in some parts of the capital in recent years – and prevent parents holding on to places they do not really want while they wait to hear from their first choice of school.

It uses advanced computer techniques to match children to schools – but what it can't do, unfortunately, is guarantee that each family gets their first preference or even their second preference place. In London, the best schools are oversubscribed by as much as ten times because of parental disappointment with standards at others.

Parents in the capital cannot assume that there will be a reasonable state school within walking distance of their homes. London has some of the best state and independent schools in the country – 37 of its primary and secondary schools appeared this year in Ofsted's first list of the best schools in England – but it also has a disproportionate share of the worst. The struggle to separate the wheat from the chaff and secure coveted places at sought-after primaries and secondaries is a major source of heart-searching for parents.

Good schools, particularly in inner London, generate a large premium on house prices in their catchment areas. An extensive survey by a London newspaper found a good local primary could add up to 57 per cent to the price of a family home. The London School of Economics, in a separate study, put the premium at 30 per cent for being in the catchment area of a top primary and 18 per cent for being near good secondary schools.

While these schools are testimony to what the state sector can achieve, parents know that too many schools in the capital offer a diet of mediocrity. The lucky parents research the best schools, fulfill the entry criteria and have little to complain about. Others have to ferry their children across town or spend a fortune on private tutors to get them through a myriad of different entrance tests.

Some desperate parents buy or rent a home in the catchment area of a good school and then move out once their first child has been accepted knowing that most (though not all) schools give priority to brothers and sisters of existing pupils. The Government is urging schools to review this policy, however, and deny places to the siblings of pupils if their parents have moved out of the area since the first child was accepted.

The academies

This year buyers of family homes must pay extra attention to what is happening in education because new academies are coming on stream. They are likely to re-arrange the demand for family homes in some of the most deprived parts of the capital. The new super-schools cost between £25 million and £30 million to build. They are the means by which the Government hopes to improve education in the inner cities and attract back the middle classes to state education. The academies are funded by the state and are free to parents, but run independently of local education authorities. Their outstanding facilities, strict discipline and longer hours have already made them sought after and over-subscribed.

Who runs London's schools?

There is no single education authority for London. Schools are run by 33 different education authorities comprising the 32 boroughs and the City of London Corporation. Each borough council is a discrete education authority, legally responsible for educating all the children within its boundaries, but parents can and do choose schools in other areas.

The boroughs don't like this cross-border drift and have to recoup the cost of educating pupils from each other, but they are bound by the 'Greenwich Judgement', a High Court decision that it is unlawful under the legislation regulating parental choice for councils to give preference to their own residents. It means a family living in a neighbouring authority will get precedence over the borough's own residents if they live nearer to the school.

The 'Greenwich Judgement' is good news for someone living, for example, on the borders of Lambeth who wants to use Wandsworth's more highly rated schools, but bad news for someone in Camden who has to compete with applicants from Haringey. Most of the movement is from inner to outer London, which does not have the same level of socio-economic deprivation, and where the authorities have been running their own schools for longer and are generally better at it.

An attempt by Camden to break ranks and defy the spirit of the Greenwich judgement by giving pupils at its primary schools priority admission to its secondaries has failed because of a challenge by three other boroughs which complained to the Office of the Schools Adjudicator. More than half the 5,000 pupils at Camden's secondary schools travel in from other boroughs making it harder for the council's residents to get places. The adjudicator, however, rejected Camden's attempt to circumvent the Greenwich judgement, saying that proximity to a school was more important than loyalty to a particular borough. She ordered Camden to scrap its change to the 2005 admission rules.

One in seven inner-London pupils attends a school outside the borough in which he or she lives, according to the Greater London Authority. The biggest exporters of children are Lambeth, Hackney, Haringey, Islington and Southwark who lose 33,609 pupils. They import 19,826 from elsewhere which means a 13,783 shortfall. The main inner London importers are Westminster, which takes in an extra 3,679 pupils, Wandsworth with 2,907 and Camden with 2,720 more than it should be educating.

In outer London the biggest net importer of pupils is Bromley, where 23 per cent are from outside the borough, many lured by its two grammar schools, Newstead Wood girls and St Saviour's & St Olave's boys.

It makes bus and train links an important consideration; even more so now the congestion charge is in place (see Transport chapter), greatly adding to the cost of the school run between inner and outer London. The congestion charge is not just a factor for parents, but also for teachers who will have to bear the financial burden or make difficult and sometimes dangerous journeys by public transport and foot through some of the roughest areas. Headteachers complain that they are losing staff and find it more difficult to recruit because of the charge.

Some boroughs have a much better reputation for providing sound education than others, but even within the worst performers there are good schools where children are well behaved and motivated. There were 37 London schools named by Ofsted this year in its first list of outstanding schools which have been commended twice in the annual reports of Her Majesty's chief inspector. Names of those within the London

Property Guide area are given in the tables at the end of this chapter. Others can be found on Ofsted's internet website: http://www.Ofsted.gov.uk.

The Ofsted site also includes reports on how well the boroughs support their schools. Hackney, Lambeth, Southwark and Islington have all received damning reports and have been forced by the government to hand over all or part of their services to outside consultants and private firms.

The reports contain useful profiles of the boroughs, including such facts as the number of children speaking English as a second language, the socio-economic make-up of the area and provision for children with special needs.

The two authorities with the best reputations are Barnet and Richmond-upon-Thames, but the success of their schools may be due mainly to the affluent, professional parents who have high expectations of their children and supplement what they learn at school with the use of private tutors.

Certainly Richmond, which tops primary league tables, does less well at secondary level where its 11–16 comprehensives achieve only just above or below the national average. A significant proportion of local parents use the borough's primaries plus tutors to help their children gain entry to the two grammar schools in neighbouring Kingston upon Thames or to the fee-paying sector.

Another complicating factor for parents trying to work out where their children are likely to get places when they consider moving to an area is the role played by the churches. Most of the high-achieving primaries and many of the most sought-after secondaries are run by the Roman Catholic church or the Church of England. These voluntary aided schools are part of the local state provision but have more say over their own affairs and are in charge of their own admissions, able to make devotion to the faith the main entrance criterion.

Being a practising Roman Catholic is a definite advantage in London because it opens up access to these voluntary aided schools across the capital. Tony Blair, the Prime Minister, for example, lived in Islington but was able to send his sons across town to The London Oratory School, the former grant-maintained comprehensive in Hammersmith and Fulham which has retained its traditional ethos and high academic standards.

A word of caution: one of the Government's latest proposals is that schools in inner London should join together in 'federations' sharing teachers and facilities. The aim is to persuade the many parents who do not get their first choice of school that their children will still have access to them through the federation. There is a potential conflict, however, with the stress also being put on firm leadership by head teachers and the importance of a strong school ethos and identity. This may be another idea which falls by the wayside.

The good, the bad and the escape route

Schools in the outer London boroughs tend to do better, partly because of their more affluent intake and less severe teacher shortages, but also because they escaped the legacy of the now defunct Inner London Education Authority, which was a maelstrom of teacher-union militancy, trendy teaching methods and lack of focus on what the children were actually learning until it was abolished by Margaret Thatcher's government in 1990.

Academically able children may be able to secure places at the few remaining grammars or Wandsworth's partially selective comprehensives. Then there are an increasing number of specialist schools which are allowed to select up to 10 per cent of their intake on the basis of aptitude for their chosen subject. Though few are using this provision at the moment, it is likely that selection will come more into play as more schools chase able pupils with keen parents.

However, the Government disapproves of selection and from September 2005 has decided that no new design and technology specialist school will be allowed to select by aptitude, though the existing ones will retain the right. The remaining grammar schools are to be omitted from the fast-tracking procedure by which the Government intends to provide more places at the most popular schools by allowing them to expand quickly even when there are spare places at others nearby.

The fact that a school has specialist status and calls itself a specialist school or college does not make it better than ordinary comprehensives, though it is likely to be better resourced through the extra cash it gets from the Government.

The biggest unknown factor for parents settling in London are the new 'Academy' secondary schools. Most of the 10 academies already open in London have been built on the site of comprehensives whose past records have driven out middle-class parents. The Government wants both to provide a much better start for children from the most deprived homes and to lure back the middle class families to bring a better social mix at the new schools.

The new schools are run independently of the local borough councils and are funded directly from Whitehall. Many of them pay teachers extra for more hours and expect children to work a longer day and participate in after-school activities. Buidings and facilities are new and lavish. Such is the competition for places that when Mossbourne Academy opened last year in Hackney the headteacher was bombarded with letters and visits from parents whose children were turned down. Families across London requested details of the catchment area so they could move to be within it. The school started with 11- and 12-year-old, Year Seven pupils only and takes its second cohort of 180 Year Sevens in September 2005. Such is the demand for places that 4,000 parents attended its open day.

Most academies test applicants in order to put children into ability bands, recruiting a proportion from each band in order to reflect the profile of the general population, a further complication for parents. A bright child in the top band will not get a place, however well he or she does in the test, if the available places for that band have been filled. This is a much harder entrance hurdle for parents to jump than proximity to the school.

Parents will also need to watch what is happening to comprehensives in areas where the super-schools spring up. Academies do not come under the same pressure to take children with behavioural and emotional difficulties and are freer to permanently exclude pupils who misbehave. Some educationalists fear that local comprehensives will lose well-motivated pupils to the academies and end up taking their rejects with consequent damage to their reputations.

Ten of the 17 academies which have opened so far are in London and Stephen Twigg, the School Standards Minister, has promised another 20 for the capital by 2008. The first to take pupils in London was Greig City Academy in Haringey, followed in September 2003 by the Capital City Academy in Brent, a sports college; West London Academy in Ealing, the City of London Academy in Southwark and the Bexley Business Academy. Last year came The Academy at Peckham, Mossbourne Academy in Hackney, Stockley Academy in Hillingdon, The London Academy, Barnet and the Lambeth Academy in Clapham.

House prices tend to rise as soon as the building work starts and some far-sighted buyers are finding out where they are planned and taking a gamble. According to the Department for Education there is a design and technology academy in the pipeline for Croydon, replacing the Stanley Technical High School, a business and enterprise college for Enfield, and an academy in Greenwich to replace St Paul's Academy in Abbey Wood. For academies in development see the ministry's Standards site (www.standards.dfes.gov.uk/academies).

There are also plans to build two other academies in Hackney, one on the site of Kingsland School which will specialise in healthcare and medicine, and another specializing in maths and music in Shoreditch on the site of Laburnum Primary school. Hillingdon is likely to get one specializing in sports science in Harefield, while Islington is to have an academy taking pupils from the ages of five to 16. Lewisham is to get a business and enterprise college and a sports science and music college, while Waltham Forest is seeking a sponsor for an academy on the site of McEntee in 2007. Two are planned for Westminster: one of them in Westbourne Green opening next year and specialising in business and enterprise, and another in Paddington for media and the arts plus business and enterprise.

Finding a school

By far the easiest way to find out about local schools is through the internet. The excellent site for parents provided by the Department for Education has an invaluable search facility which allows you to put in a postcode and access information on schools within a radius of your choice. The site, http://www.dfes.gov.uk/parents, allows you to click on the name of a school and access information about its test and exam results and how they compare with others in the local authority and with the national figures.

There's a link to Ofsted, the school inspection service, where you can read the latest reports on the school and also to individual school websites. These reports give a picture of the socio-economic intake of pupils, which is useful background when assessing their results. They grade schools on the basis of their test and exam results both in relation to schools nationally and others in similar circumstances, such as around the same proportion of pupils eligible for free school meals or speaking English as a second language.

It's important not to take the reports as gospel. Plenty of schools later discovered to be coasting on the back of an able intake with supportive parents, have had glowing reports after impressing the Ofsted inspectors. Interestingly, several of the primary schools judged to be adding the least value to pupils in a pilot of 340 schools run by the Department for Education, have recently been praised by Ofsted as good and effective.

The new Ofsted framework of inspection has also thrown up some strange decisions. Grey Court, one of the highest achieving comprehensives in Richmond-upon-Thames in terms of its GCSE results and value added between the ages of 11 and 14, was put in special measures after being failed by Ofsted inspectors in September 2003. The local authority points out that the school was one of the first to be awarded Beacon status for the quality of its education and that Her Majesty's Inspectors, the most senior Ofsted inspectors, had recommended its status be renewed three months earlier and had approved its application to specialize in computing and science, the subjects for which it was later failed. Grey Court now has a new head teacher.

Once you have a school in mind, put its name into your browser's search engine to call up any news stories or pieces of information that might help you decide. Has it been in the news for bullying, or did it close at short notice to give the teachers a day off for Christmas shopping the day after they had closed the school by industrial action? Does it compete in local or national sports fixtures? Is it involved in any national initiatives, such as the pilot on world-class tests for able and talented children, or the use of mentors? Has it got a reputation for educating children with special needs? Any item, however small, can help build up a picture and help you assess whether it would be the right place for your child.

If you don't have access to the internet and cannot use the computers at a local library, then it is possible to order the performance tables in booklet form from local authorities. Each school produces an annual report to governors which contains more detailed information on the test scores.

Take whatever opportunity you can to talk to local people, in the shops, in the pub, or even at bus stops. That said, schools do fall in and out of fashion and in the present fast-moving scene local people are not always up to date on changes taking place, so treat what they say with caution, using it as a pointer for further research.

Don't rely on out-of-date information. Several schools which have gained a bad reputation and been failed by Ofsted have been transformed by a new headteacher and change of staff. A good inspection report or improved showing in the league tables of exam and test results can bring a flood of applications and reduce the catchment area. The trick is to get your child in before the good news spreads!

There are many different local factors involved in admissions, so if you are serious about a property don't forget to ask the seller where their children, and the neighbours', go to school. You can then visit the nearest newsagent and see what the staff have to say about the pupils, and call in at the offices of the local paper to see what articles they have carried about it.

Understanding the data

Never before have parents been able to access so much information about school performance, but the official data can be confusing and misleading. The Government's tables – http://dfes.gov.uk/performancetables/ – include value-added measures alongside the raw test and exam scores for secondary schools, and a point score for the average attainment of primary pupils.

The primary tables, published in November, are based on the national curriculum tests 11-year-old children sit in May to assess their mastery of English, maths and science. They are marked externally and accepted as generally accurate, if broad-brush, in their approach. Secondary schools often complain, however, that they give an inflated and over-optimistic picture of what children can do once they transfer to them, suggesting that pupils are coached and taught to the tests.

The data tells you the proportion of children achieving Level Four, the standard expected for their age in the three core subjects. Nationally, 74 per cent reached the standard for maths, 78 per cent for English and 86 per cent for science. There is also a cumulative score out of 300 for each school, calculated on the percentage of pupils reaching the required level in each subject.

One limitation of the tables is that they do not tell you how many children reached a higher level than expected, an important factor for parents in affluent areas such as Richmond-upon-Thames, which tops the table for England, because they want to know that their children are being stretched and challenged. Ideally, parents should be able to know whether a third, or half, or two-thirds reached the higher Level Five, which is supposed to equate to the average attainment of a thirteen- to fourteen-year-old but in practice measures different things. There is some indication through the new point score per pupil which is given in the tables for each primary school, but it is difficult to interpret with much accuracy. We are told by the Department for Education that a score of 30 means on average pupils at the school attained Level Four, the standard expected for their age, but less than Level Five, the standard expected of a child two to three years later. We are also told that if 100 per cent of pupils at a school reached Level Four for all three subjects, then a proportion of them reached the higher Level Five. As I say, it's not easy to interpret, but generally a score more than 30 is a good one.

The point score provides another useful indicator, however, as it enables parents to discriminate between primary schools where similar percentages of children reach the expected Level Four. Some will have higher point scores than others, suggesting that more pupils exceeded the normal expectation and gained Level Five.

It's important, when reading the data, to look at the columns showing how many children were absent for each test, as they will count as failures. If 100 children took the test, and two were absent, they would reduce the score for that subject by two per cent. If there were 20 in the year group, however, the missing pair would bring a significant 10 per cent reduction in the proportion reaching the level.

Children with special needs are also included in the tables and are expected to reach the expected level unless the school is successful in getting them 'disallowed' because they were physically unable to sit the papers. Children newly arrived in the country speaking English as a second language are also excluded from the results. Those not disallowed, however, appear in the results even if they have been awarded statements of special educational need (SEN), suggesting a serious handicap to their learning.

Another column shows how many children are on the school's special-needs register, a difficult statistic to factor in because some schools are more ready than others to record fairly minor problems. Some children who cannot read properly because they have been badly taught also appear under this heading in some schools. On the other hand, some schools will have fewer children 'statemented' because their local education authorities are following the Government's advice on statementing and discouraging it, saying they will provide the resources without the need for the lengthy and expensive quasi-legal process.

The secondary school tables are published in January. These give GCSE and A-level results for each school, plus a value-added measure showing the progress pupils make between the national curriculum tests they take at 14 and public examinations at 16. The Government is working on a model for the future which will track each pupil and show his or her progress from 11 to 16. Information on how well the pupils do in the curriculum tests is given in a different table, published in December.

Armed with the official tables and a school's Ofsted report showing the profile of its intake, parents are at least able to spot danger signals, such as a school of indigenous English-speaking children which does much better at maths than literacy, and pick out those in poor areas reaching the same or better standards than others in middle-class suburbs.

Admissions: the tricks and the pitfall

Parental choice may be a reality in some parts of the country, but in London it would be more accurate to say that schools choose children.

• **Primary schools** Most primary schools take children living nearest to them, but the catchment areas they set are not easy to understand and change from year to year as people move in and out. A good Ofsted report or a rise up the league table of national curriculum tests can have a dramatic effect on a school's popularity, and lead to a shrinking of the catchment as the boundaries are drawn more tightly.

Despite all your careful research, it may be that even if you live nearer to a secondary school than another family, their child is given precedence because he or she went to the 'right' primary. This 'link' policy between secondary schools and feeder primaries is a feature of admissions in some boroughs. In these circumstances, parents have to consider the respective merits of secondary schools at the point at which they choose a nursery or reception place for their child.

There are a large number of Roman Catholic primary schools in London and for them commitment to the faith is more important than proximity to the building. The outstanding success of most church schools means that most are massively oversubscribed. It has not been established whether the achievements of their pupils is due to religious ethos, superior teaching or the fact that the schools can interview parents and children and demand references from local priests, but this does not affect their popularity. Church of England primary schools are generally more relaxed about the religious affiliations of their parents, seeing themselves as fulfilling a mission to provide education, particularly in the inner city where families of all faiths or none are often welcomed.

Children must start school in the term after their fifth birthday, but generally they begin in reception classes when they are four. The government promises nursery-school places for all four-year-olds whose parents want them, either in pre-school playgroups, nursery schools or primary-school reception classes. It's against the spirit of the rules, but some schools persuade parents to send four-year-olds to their nursery or reception classes by warning that places might not be available later, once the children turn five. Such threats should be reported to the local authorities and to the Department for Education, which wants parents to have the choice of voluntary, private or school nursery classes.

• **Secondary schools** Children transfer to the secondary state schools at 11 years old, and at 11 or 13 in the independent sector. Admissions are complicated by the three types of schools within the state sector: **Community** (run by local authorities), **Foundation** (funded by local authorities but with a measure of independence over admissions and fewer local-authority nominees on the governing body), and **Aided** (owned and partly funded by the churches). Parents complete a secondary transfer form in the autumn before their child is due to start in the secondary sector, and are asked to list up to six schools in order of preference. They can be in any of the 41 authorities participating in the scheme.

The schools match the applications against their admission criteria and tell the authorities the children to whom they want to offer places. The admissions system's new computer system will match offers against first-choice preferences. Later on, if there are still places, parents who put a school second and failed to get their first choice may be offered a place.

Parents are strongly advised by the authorities to include at least four and preferably six schools because those who nominate just one or two may end up without a place.

Those living on the borders of the catchment area for a school are particularly vulnerable as they may find that there are not enough places for all those putting the school first and that proximity is taken into account. If the second-choice school is also over-subscribed then it is likely to fill up with first choices leaving the family with their third choice. For this reason parents sometimes choose second-best on the basis that they are more likely to be successful. A high-stakes poker game can be less stressful.

Those applying to some church schools, especially the Roman Catholic ones, have to apply direct to the school for an application form which is used to assess devotion to the faith. Some of the schools insist that they be put first choice in order to avoid becoming the safety net for children who do not get into grammar schools.

The **City Academies** (se page 61, above) also run their own admissions and parents need to contact them directly.

Almost all schools give preference to the brothers and sisters of present pupils. Next comes proximity to the school premises, but as we have seen, catchment areas vary from year to year as families move in and out of the area.

Some authorities are able to advise parents on the likelihood of their street being included in the catchment for each school. Bexley's admissions service has drawn up a useful guide for parents to inform them how near to the school pupils have had to live to gain admittance in the past. It enables them to see, for example, that pupils admitted to the non-selective stream of Erith school lived within one and a third mile, and that the catchment for Beths Grammar School, which relies on selection tests, was four miles.

Geography is not the only consideration. Moving to the same road as a school will not guarantee a place if, as we have seen, the school is run by one of the churches which traditionally recruit more widely, valuing religious commitment more than proximity. Some authorities, such as Kensington and Chelsea, are particularly affected by the lure of their church schools. Three of the four secondary schools in Kensington and Chelsea belong to the Roman Catholic Church and bring in so many children from outside that the borough can only find places for 27 per cent of its 11-year-olds.

Nor will proximity to a school help if it is one of the 19 remaining state-run (and thus non-fee paying) grammar schools in London which recruit solely on the basis of a competitive examination. A sprinkling of partially selective schools, such as the three in Wandsworth, allocate a proportion of places to those with the best scores in entrance tests, again limiting the numbers taken from the local population. If you choose the selective schools, then your ten- or eleven-year-old could face a term of exhausting examinations for different schools, ending up without a place at any of them. Then you face a scramble to get what's left of the comprehensives. Specialist schools, meanwhile, are allowed to select 10 per cent of pupils on the basis of aptitude for the subject in which they specialize. Up to now, few have used this device, but a few language colleges are experimenting with a language aptitude test and it is likely that more will make use of it in future as they seek to meet Government targets and justify the extra money they receive.

Campaigns run by parents who want local authorities to build new, local secondary schools have had some success over the last few years. The Charter School in Dulwich and Alexandra Park School in Muswell Hill have opened in response to parental demand, but time will tell whether they can meet middle-class expectations.

Private Schools

London is fortunate to have many excellent independent preparatory ('prep') and secondary schools. Most of the secondary schools are single-sex, at least until the sixth form, and they are almost exclusively day schools, though some have embraced weekly boarding with the children returning home for the weekends. There is fierce competition for places despite the high fees, with some parents registering their offspring while they are still in the womb. Head teachers tend to take note of others in the profession, so consider asking your child's present school to contact them if you are moving to London. The south and south-west of London has more independent schools than the east, but even these are over-subscribed and usually unable to expand because of land costs. Over the last couple of years there has been an increase in the number of London pupils boarding on a weekly basis at schools in other parts of the south-east of England. The government's performance tables give the exam results for independent secondary schools, but no amount of pressure has yet persuaded prep schools to publish the scores their pupils achieve in Common Entrance, the exam they take for entry to independent secondary schools.

Competition between London prep schools to get pupils into the most sought after secondary independent schools makes most of them reluctant to take children with special needs, especially those who have emotional and behavioural difficulties which might disturb other children. In an interesting development, Wetherby, the prep school in Notting Hill attended by Princes William and Harry, has opened a new school designed as a booster for children with special needs judged capable of returning to mainstream education after a period of targeted help.

Many people moving into London use the advice and placement services of the Independent Schools Information Service (ISIS) or Gabbitas, the firm of educational consultants, both of which have extensive knowledge of the schools and the

How the boroughs perform

School-by-school 'league tables' are now widely published in newspapers and on the Internet, and here we offer an analysis of how boroughs perform. This brings together data from Ofsted, the Department for Education and the Audit Commission to give a brief sketch of each local authority's education performance. We also list the top-rated primary and secondary schools in each borough. Note that primary schools are ranked according to the Level Two cumulative points score – a rather more sophisticated measure than the sum of the test scores in the three core subjects which is usually used.

KEY

- *The first line shows the rating given to each borough by the Audit Commission based on its judgement of the efficient delivery of education and Ofsted's view of school standards, with the top score being 4.*
- *The borough average % of 11-year-olds reaching at least Level 4, the standard expected for their age, in English, where the national rate is 75%, maths where the national rate is 73% and science where it is 87%. In England as a whole the proportions reaching Level 5 are English 27%, maths 29%, and science 41%.*
- *Top primaries rated by average point score per pupil in the Key Stage Two tests.*
- *Percentage of children gaining at least five GCSEs grades A*–C. (The average in England is 53%.)*
- *Top state schools rated by percentage of 16-year-olds gaining five A*–C GCSEs.*
- *Schools on Ofsted's 2005 list of tbe best 234 schools in England.*

BARNET

Audit Commission/Ofsted rating: 3
Primary results: LEA average point score per pupil: 28.4; English 84%; maths 81%; science 90%
Top primaries: Mathilda Mark Kennedy (31.5), Independent Jewish Day (31.2), St Joseph's RC (31.2), Trent CofE (30.7), St Paul's CofE (30.9)
Secondary results: pupils attaining 5 or more A*–C GCSEs: 59.1%
Top secondaries: St Michael's Catholic (sel) 100%, Queen Elizabeth's 99%, Henrietta Barnet (sel) 95%, Top comprehensives: Hasmonean High (87%), Mill Hill County High (84%)
Ofsted commended: Compton School, Henrietta Barnet, Queen Elizabeth's

BRENT

Audit Commission/Ofsted rating: 3
Primary results: LEA average point score per pupil: 27.3; English 78%; maths 74%; science 83%
Top primaries: Mount Stewart (30.8), Oakington Manor (30.3), Leopold (30.2), North West London Jewish (29.9), Oliver Goldsmith (29.8)
Secondary results: Pupils attaining 5 or more A*–C GCSEs: 49.6%
Top secondaries: Jewish Free School 80%, Claremont High 70%, Preston Manor 70%, Convent of Jesus and Mary Language College 64%
Ofsted commended: Convent of Jesus and Mary Language College

CAMDEN

Audit Commission/Ofsted rating: 4
Primary results: LEA average point score per pupil: 27.3; English 77%, maths 73%; science 86%
Top primaries: Fleet (30.6), Christ Church (32.3), Emmanuel CofE (30.2), St Paul's CofE (30.0), Fitzjohn's (30.0).
Secondary results: Pupils attaining 5 or more A*–C GCSEs: 48.4%
Top secondaries: La Sainte Union RC 80%, Camden School for Girls 74%, Parliament Hill 66%
Ofsted commended: Camden School for Girls, La Sainte Union Catholic, Swiss Cottage School, St Aloysius RC infant

EALING

Audit Commission/Ofsted rating: 3
Primary results: LEA average point score

per pupil: 27.3; English 78%; maths 73%; science 83%
Top primaries: St Gregory's RC (30.7), Perivale (30.3), North Ealing (30.1), Berrymede (30.0), St John Fisher RC (30.0)
Secondary results: Pupils attaining 5 or more A*–C GCSEs: 49.8%
Top secondaries: Cardinal Wiseman RC 90%,Twyford CofE High 73%, Ellen Wilkinson School for Girls 68%

ENFIELD
Audit Commission/Ofsted rating 4
Primary results: LEA average point score per pupil: 27.4; English 77%; maths 73%; science 84%
Top primaries: Grange Park (31.4), Walker (31.2), St Andrew's CofE, Enfield (30.9), St George's RC (30.6), St Paul's CofE (30.6)
Secondary results: Pupils attaining 5 or more A*–C GCSEs: 46.2%
Top secondaries: Latymer (sel) 100%, Enfield County 76%, Broomfield 72%

GREENWICH
Audit Commission/Ofsted rating: 3
Primary results: LEA average point score per pupil: 26.5; English 78%; maths 74%; science 86%
Top primaries: Christ Church CofE, Shooters Hill (31.0), Halstow (30.6); Gordon (30.3), St Thomas More (29.7), Eltham CofE (28.7), Rockliffe Manor (28.7), St Mary's Catholic (28.7).
Secondary results: pupils attaining 5 or more A*–C GCSEs: 33.3%
Top secondaries: St Ursula's Convent 73%, St Thomas More RC 69%, St Paul's Catholic 53%

HACKNEY
Audit Commission/Ofsted rating: 3
Primary results: LEA average point score per pupil: 26.0; English 70%; maths 65%; science 75%
Top primaries: Simon Marks Jewish (28.9), Colvestone (28.8), Grasmere (28.7), Parkwood (28.7), Ruth Lunzer Lubavitch (28.2), Simon Marks Jewish (28.2)
Secondary results: Pupils attaining 5 or more A*–C GCSEs: 31.1%
Top secondaries: Our Lady's Convent RC 78%, Stoke Newington 57% , Cardinal Pole RC 56%
Ofsted commended: Haggerston

HAMMERSMITH AND FULHAM
Audit Commission/Ofsted rating: 3
Primary results: LEA average point score per pupil: 27.3; English 77%; maths 73%; science 86%
Top primaries: Avonmore (32.2), London Oratory (30.6), St Augustine's RC (30.6), St Mary's RC (29.8), Holy Cross RC (29.6)
Secondary results: pupils attaining 5 or more A*–C GCSEs: 50.3%
Top secondaries: Lady Margaret 97%, London Oratory 93%, Sacred Heart 89%,
Ofsted commended: The London Oratory

HARINGEY
Audit Commission/Ofsted rating: 3
Primary results: LEA average point score per pupil: 26.5; English 70%; maths 67%; science 77%
Top primaries: Tetherdown (31.4), St Martin of Porres RC (31.3), Coleridge (31.1), Rhodes Avenue (30.9), St James' CofE (30.0)
Secondary results: pupils attaining 5 or more A*–C GCSEs 35.4%
Top secondaries: Fortismere 77%, Hornsey Girls' 53%, Highgate Wood 51%
Ofsted commended: St Francis de Sales RC infant

HOUNSLOW
Audit Commission/Ofsted rating: 3
Primary results: LEA average point score per pupil: 27.4; English 77%; maths 73%; science 85%
Top primaries: St Michael & St Martin RC (30.7), St Mary's RC (30.1), Belmont Primary (29.8), Chatsworth Junior (29.8), Feltham Hill Junior (29.8)
Secondary results: pupils attaining 5 or more A*–C GCSEs: 49.5%
Top secondaries: Gurnley House RC Convent 81%, St Mark's RC 78%, The Heathland 75%
Ofsted commended: St Mark's Catholic

ISLINGTON
Audit Commission/Ofsted rating: 3
Primary results: LEA average point score per pupil: 26.6; English 71%; maths 68%; science 79%
Top primaries: St John's Highbury Vale CofE (31.1), St Peter's and St Paul RC (29.7), St Joseph's RC (29.5), Grafton (29.4), Yerbury (29.3)
Secondary results: pupils attaining 5 or more A*–C GCSEs: 32.9%
Top secondaries: Highbury Fields 65%, Central Foundation Boys' 62%, Mount Carmel RC Girls 52%
Ofsted commended: Margaret McMillan nursery, North Islington nursery

KENSINGTON AND CHELSEA
Audit Commission/Ofsted rating: 4
Primary results: LEA average point score per pupil: 28.4; English 86%; maths 82%; science 92%
Top primaries: St Barnabas and St Philip's (30.9), St Mary Abbots CofE (30.4), Oratory RC (29.7), Thomas Jones (29.6), Servite RC (29.5)
Secondary results: pupils attaining 5 or more A*–C GCSEs: 55.7%
Top secondaries: Cardinal Vaughan Memorial RC 94%, Saint Thomas More RC 65%, Sion-Manning Girls 50%

KINGSTON UPON THAMES
Audit Commission/Ofsted rating: 4
Primary results: LEA average point score per pupil: 28.4; English 86%; maths 82%; science 92%
Top primaries: Coombe Hill (31.1), Fern Hill (30.9), St Andrew's & St Mark's (30.6), St Luke's CofE (30.3), Our Lady Immaculate (30.2)
Secondary results: pupils attaining 5 or more A*–C GCSEs: 60%
Top secondaries: Tiffin Boys' (sel) 100%, Tiffin Girls' (sel) 99%, Coombe Girls' 74%
Ofsted commended: Alexandra Infant School

LAMBETH
Audit Commission/Ofsted rating: 3
Primary results: LEA average point score per pupil: 27.0; English 76%; maths 70%; science 80%
Top primaries: Sudbourne (31.1), Stockwell (30.3), Corpus Christi (30.2), Macaulay CofE (30.1), Reay (29.7), St Helen's (27.9), St John the Divine (29.7)
Secondary results: pupils attaining 5 or more A*–C GCSEs: 40.1%
Top secondaries: Dunraven 66%, La Retraite RC 61%, Archbishop Tenison's 60%
Ofsted commended: Sudbourne Primary

LEWISHAM
Audit Commission/Ofsted rating: 4
Primary results: LEA average point score per pupil: 26.9; English 73%; maths 70%; science 82%
Top primaries: All Saints' CofE (31.6), John Ball (30.5), Turnham (30.6), Our Lady and St Philip Neri Roman (29.8), Brindishe (29.7)
Secondary results: pupils attaining 5 or more A*–C GCSEs: 38.7%
Top secondaries: Haberdashers' Aske's Hatcham 86%, Bonas Pastor RC 59%, Prendergast 70%

MERTON
Audit Commission/Ofsted rating: 3
Primary results: LEA average point score per pupil: 27.2; English 75%; maths 72%; science 84%
Top primaries: Merton Park (31.0), Holy Trinity CofE (30.8), St Matthew's CofE (30.8), St John Fisher RC (29.8), St Mary's Catholic (29.8).
Secondary results: pupils attaining 5 or more A*–C GCSEs:40.9%
Top secondaries: Ursuline High 73%, Wimbledon College 64%, Ricards Lodge High 60%
Ofsted commended: Wimbledon Chase

NEWHAM
Audit Commission/Ofsted rating: 4
Primary results: LEA average point score per pupil: 26.7; English 71%; maths 70%; science 82%
Top primaries: St Joachim's RC (29.9), Godwin Junior (29.1), St Michael's RC (28.9), West Ham Church (28.9), Ellen

Wilkinson (28.8), Portway (28.8), St Winefride's RC (28.8)
Secondary results: pupils attaining 5 or more A*–C GCSEs: 42.4%
Top secondaries: St Angela's Ursuline Convent 88%, Sarah Bonnell 72%, Plashet 72%

RICHMOND UPON THAMES
Audit Commission/Ofsted rating: 3
Primary results: LEA average point score per pupil: 28.8; English 87%; maths 83%; science 92%
Top primaries: Sacred Heart RC (31.2), St James's RC (31.2), The Queen's CofE (31.2), St Mary Magdalen's (30.9), St Mary's & St Peter's (30.7)
Secondary results: pupils attaining 5 or more A*–C GCSEs: 51.4%
Top secondaries: Waldegrave 83%, Teddington 66%, Grey Court 61%, Christ's 61%

SOUTHWARK
Audit Commission/Ofsted rating: 3
Primary results: LEA average point score per pupil: 26.2; English 69%; maths 64%; science 77%
Top primaries: Dulwich Hamlet (30.5), St Anthony's Catholic (30.1), Friars Foundation (29.7), St Joseph's RC (29.5), Boutcher CofE (29.3)
Secondary results: pupils attaining 5 or more A*–C GCSEs:35.7%
Top secondaries: Bacon's College 75%, Notre Dame RC Girls 69%, Sacred Heart RC 69%
Ofsted commended: Notre Dame RC

TOWER HAMLETS
Audit Commission/Ofsted rating: 3
Primary results: LEA average point score per pupil: 27.2; English 77%; maths 75%; science 85%
Top primaries: Stewart Headlam (30.5), Cubitt Town (29.8), Halley (29.6), St Elizabeth RC (29.6), William Davis (29.5)
Secondary results: pupils attaining 5 or more A*–C GCSEs: 43.6%
Top secondaries: Sir John Cass Redcoat 87%, Oaklands School 75%, St Paul's Way 59%

WALTHAM FOREST
Audit Commission/Ofsted rating: 2
Primary results: LEA average point score per pupil: 26.6; English 73%; maths 69%; science 80%
Top primaries: St Mary's Catholic (30.3), Handsworth (30.2), Dawlish (29.3), Yardley (29.0), St Patrick's Catholic (28.7)
Secondary results: pupils attaining 5 or more A*–C GCSEs: 44.3%
Top secondaries: Highams Park 69%, Walthamstow Girls 66%, Chingford Foundation 62%
Ofsted commended: Walthamstow Girls

WANDSWORTH
Audit Commission/Ofsted rating: 4
Primary results: LEA average point score per pupil: 27.1; English 75%; maths 71%; science 83%
Top primaries: Our Lady of Victories (32.0), St Boniface RC (30.6), All Saints CofE (30.4), St Anselm's Catholic (30.4), St Michael's CofE (29.7)
Secondary results: pupils attaining 5 or more A*–C GCSEs:48.6%
Top secondaries: ADT College 77%, Graveney 85%, Burntwood 65%
Ofsted commended: Burntwood, Graveney

WESTMINSTER
Audit Commission/Ofsted rating: 3
Primary results: LEA average point score per pupil: 27.8; English 82%; maths 77%; science 85%
Top primaries: St Joseph's RC (31.4), St Mary of the Angels RC (31.1), St Vincent's RC (30.9), Hampden Gurney (30.3), St Peter's CofE (30.2)
Secondary results: pupils attaining 5 or more A*–C GCSEs: 41.5%
Top secondaries: St Marylebone CofE 90%, Grey Coat Hospital 67%, Westminster City 47%
Ofsted commended: Grey Coat Hospital, St Joseph's RC primary

The Boroughs

London has a Mayor and Assembly once more. Together they form the Greater London Authority (GLA). The Mayor's job description is to prepare strategies to deal with Londonwide issues, and coordinate action on a Londonwide basis. The Assembly scrutinizes the Mayor's activities, questioning his/her decisions. It can also investigate other issues of importance to Londoners, and make proposals to the Mayor. The GLA's role covers transport, planning in the wider sense, police and fire services, economic development and regeneration. Most were formerly the job of central government.

The 32 London boroughs still exist, and wield the same powers: now, though, they have to forge a relationship with the GLA as well as with central government. The Mayor can intervene in – indeed over-ride – borough planning decisions for important sites. As a resident, however, the local borough will be your main concern: the council determines whether you can build that extension or put dormer windows in the roof. The planning officers are experts who will advise, and ensure that what you want to do is within planning law and building regulations (see that chapter). Planning permission is then granted by the committee of elected council members – which is where the political complexion of the borough may play a part.

How much you pay for services is set by the borough: as a point of comparison between boroughs, we give the Band D council tax figure here (for the year ending 31 March 2005; this includes a cut for the GLA), and in the information box at the start of each chapter. Check where boundaries fall – living across the road could be expensive.

Barnet
Controlling party: Conservative
Town Hall tel: 020 8359 2000
Search: 2 working days, £250
Council tax, band D: £1,213
Website: www.barnet.gov.uk

Brent
Controlling party: Labour
Town Hall tel: 020 8937 1234
Search: 5–10 working days, £170
Council tax, band D: £1,141
Website: www.brent.gov.uk

Bromley
Controlling party: Conservative
Town Hall tel: 020 8464 3333
Search: 1–2 working days, £165
Council tax, band D: £1040
Website: www.bromley.gov.uk

Camden
Controlling party: Labour
Town Hall tel: 020 7278 4444
Search: 10 working days, £151
Council tax, band D: £1,200.
Website: www.camden.gov.uk

Corporation of London
Controlling party: Apolitical
Town Hall tel: 020 7606 3030
Search: 4–5 working days, £190
Council tax, band D: £773
Website: www.cityoflondon.gov.uk

Croydon
Controlling party: Labour
Town Hall tel: 020 8686 4433
Search: 5 working days, £195
Council tax, band D: £1,165
Website: www.croydon.gov.uk

Ealing
Controlling party: Labour
Town Hall tel: 020 8825 5000
Search: 5 working days, £195
Council tax, band D: £1,191
Website: www.ealing.gov.uk

Enfield
Controlling party: Conservative
Town Hall tel: 020 8366 6565
Search: same day, £177
Council tax, band D: £1,193
Website: www.enfield.gov.uk

Greenwich
Controlling party: Labour
Town Hall tel: 020 8854 8888
Search: 10 working days, £175
Council tax, band D: £1,140
Website: www.greenwich.gov.uk

Hackney
Controlling party: Labour
Town Hall tel: 020 8356 5000
Search: 5 days, £191
Council tax, band D: £1,221
Website: www.hackney.gov.uk

Hammersmith & Fulham
Controlling party: Labour
Town Hall tel: 020 8748 3020
Search: 3–4 working days, £201
Council tax, band D: £1130
Website: www.lbhf.gov.uk

Haringey
Controlling party: Labour
Town Hall tel: 020 8489 0000
Search: 4 working days, £190
Council tax, band D: £1,259
Website: www.haringey.gov.uk

Hounslow
Controlling party: Labour
Town Hall tel: 020 8583 2000
Search: 2–3 days, £195
Council tax, band D: £1,262
Website: www.hounslow.gov.uk

Islington
Controlling party: Liberal Democrat
Town Hall tel: 020 7527 2000
Search: 4–5 working days, £190
Council tax, band D: £1,107
Website: www.islington.gov.uk

Kensington & Chelsea
Controlling party: Conservative
Town Hall tel: 020 7937 5464
Search: 10 working days, £229
Council tax, band D: £944
Website: www.rbkc.gov.uk

Lambeth
Controlling party: Liberal Democrat
Town Hall tel: 020 7926 1000
Search: 2–4 working days, £220
Council tax, band D: £1050
Website: www.lambeth.gov.uk

Lewisham
Controlling party: Labour
Town Hall tel: 020 8314 6000
Search: 3–4 working days, £150
Council tax, band D: £1,141
Website: www.lewisham.gov.uk

Merton
Controlling party: Labour
Town Hall tel: 020 8543 2222
Search: 1–2 working days, £200
Council tax, band D: £1,206
Website: www.merton.gov.uk

Newham
Controlling party: Labour
Town Hall tel: 020 8472 1430
Search: 10 working days, £150
Council tax, band D: £1,059
Website: www.newham.gov.uk

Richmond
Controlling party: Conservative
Town Hall tel: 020 8891 1411
Search: 7 working days, £196
Council tax, band D: £1,339
Website: www.richmond.gov.uk

Southwark
Controlling party: Liberal Democrat
Town Hall tel: 020 7525 5000
Search: 5–10 working days, £150
Council tax, band D: £1070
Website: www.southwark.gov.uk

Tower Hamlets
Controlling party: Labour
Town Hall tel: 020 7364 5000
Search: 8–10 working days, £200
Council tax, band D: £1008
Website: www.towerhamlets.gov.uk

Waltham Forest
Controlling party: Labour/Lib Dem
Town Hall tel: 020 8527 5544
Search: 5–6 working days, £207
Council tax, band D: £1,244
Website: www.lbwf.gov.uk

Wandsworth
Controlling party: Conservative
Town Hall tel: 020 8871 6000
Search: 8 working days, £206
Council tax, band D: £596
Website: www.wandsworth.gov.uk

City of Westminster
Controlling party: Conservative
Town Hall tel: 020 7641 6000
Search: 3–5 working days, £175
Council tax, band D: £605
Website: www.westminster.gov.uk

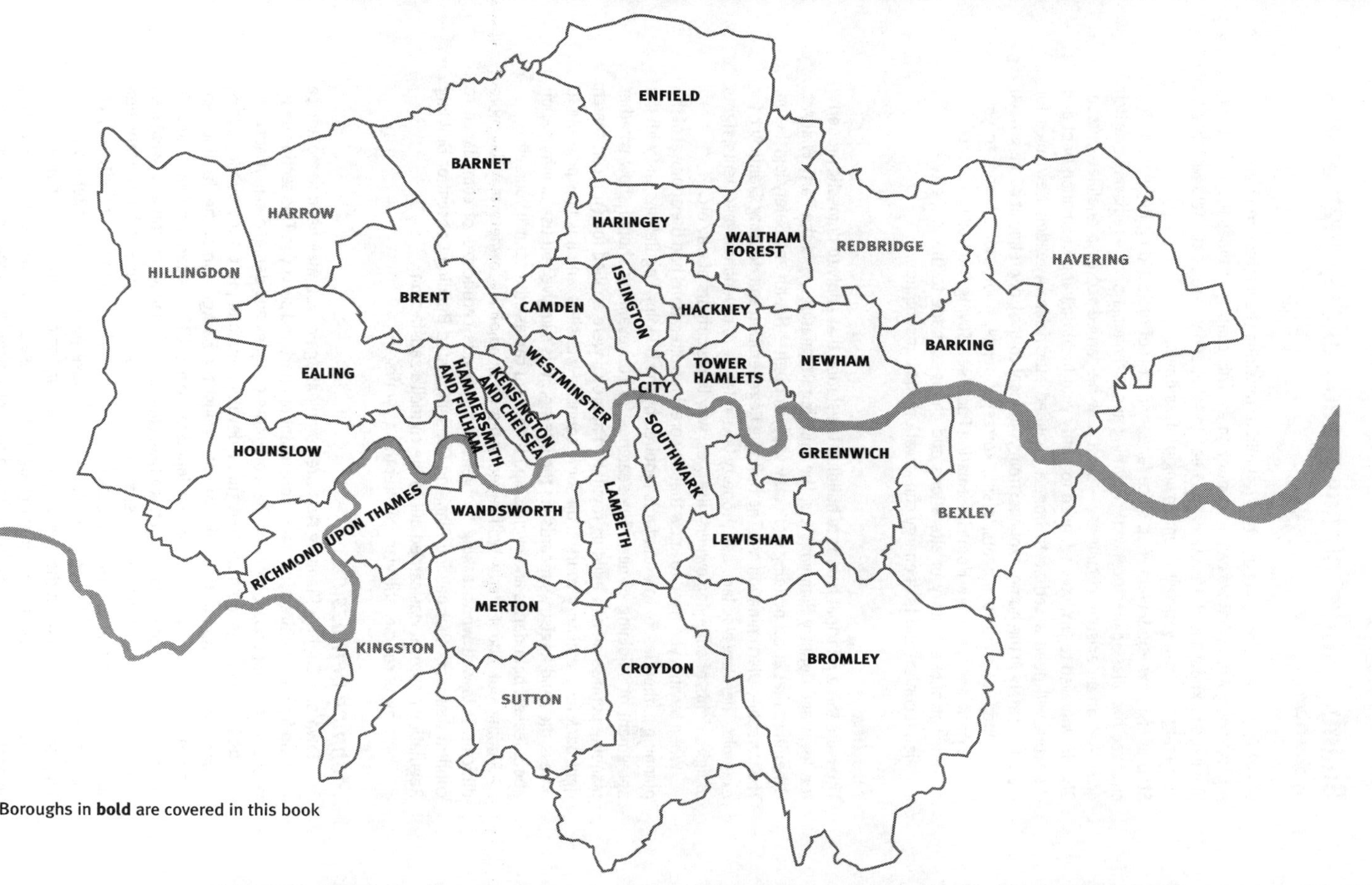

Boroughs in **bold** are covered in this book

Building works, planning and building regulations

by Soo Ware

Whether you're undertaking a virtual re-build or re-wiring the kitchen, rules and regulations govern what we can do to our homes. This chapter outlines the legislation you need to know about, the steps you need to take, and where to get help whether managing the work yourself or employing professionals.

Stop press: new regulations First, since January Part P of the Building Regulations has changed the rules on electrical work: anything above the most basic – replacing a switch or socket on an existing circuit, say – must now be carried out by a qualified person. Should you wish to DIY, you will need to notify your local Building Regulation Dept and the work will need a certificate from a qualified electrician. A leaflet, New rules for electrical safety in the home, explains: from your local council, or on-line at odpm.gov.uk.

Second, keep all documents, plans, correspondence, photos of all work to your home: come 2007, the new Home Information Pack (see Buying and Selling chapter) will require not only a history of alterations and changes made to the property but also certified technical audits of energy conservation and consumption.

The law

There are three principal groups of building legislation that apply to domestic property: the Town and Country Planning Acts, the Building Regulations, and the Party Wall Act. Other laws that affect building work may apply, though – Health and Safety legislation, The Disability Discrimination Act, The Building Regeneration and Housing Grants Act, for example. There are also land and property laws relating to covenants, easements, rights of light, rights of adjoining owners, licences, way leaves, rights of way etc.

When buying, you need to know that any previous alterations had the approval of the planning authorities, to the standards required by the Building Regulations and with the agreement of adjoining owners. The searches for conveyancing should show whether planning permission and building regulation approval were applied for. (You can search right back for the history yourself on some councils' websites, and it is now possible to access the Land Registry's records via the internet: this can give you useful information about leases, boundaries and ownership.) If not, you can ask the council yourself.

Finding out about Party Wall agreements with adjoining owners may be more difficult. It is well worth asking the vendor to provide certificates of compliance to confirm that work that needed Planning Consent, Listed Building Consent or Building Regulation Approval was carried out to the council's satisfaction.

You may, of course, still want to alter things yourself:

Planning permission

The Town and Country Planning Acts are complex: again, you may need some advice early on from an architect, planning consultant or chartered surveyor. This section deals with controls on houses; blocks of flats are more complex and demand expert advice.

The Planning Acts are there to regulate development and protect the public interest in land use. Each application is looked at against the background of the development plan, usually called the Unitary Development Plan (UDP), prepared by each London borough. Copies can be had from town halls, and can be viewed on councils' websites. Usually the council produces a separate, stricter policy document for conservation areas. Buildings that are listed (i.e. buildings of historic or architectural interest) are even more tightly controlled: you may need to have permission for alterations from English Heritage through the Conservation Officer in the council planning department.

What might seem a very minor change to a house can in fact have a far-reaching impact on adjoining homes and the appearance of a whole neighbourhood. For instance, motley roof conversions or new dormer windows on front elevations of terraces can change the look of an entire street. A planning application may be necessary for:

- Extensions, alterations, garages, conservatories, roof gardens, balconies, loft conversions.
- Garden fences, walls and felling trees (if either the subject of tree preservation orders – TPOs – or in conservation areas). But garden sheds, greenhouses, swimming pools, saunas and summer houses may not need permission if certain conditions are met.
- Alterations to road access, drives and off-street parking. Additional consent from the highway authority may also be needed.
- Alterations to a previous planning consent or a change of use – for example, dividing a house into flats, or flats back into a house.

You also need to make a planning application if:

- The building is in a conservation area, or covered by an Article 4 Direction (an order placed on a whole street to maintain the integrity of its appearance). This can include changing doors, windows or roofs; pebbledashing, sandblasting, painting brickwork, etc.
- The building is listed: a separate listed Building Consent will also be required. Make initial enquiries to the planning department of the council. A Conservation, or Historic Buildings, officer will advise whether or not you need to contact English Heritage. It is a criminal offence to make alterations (even to undertake some forms of maintenance) to a listed building without approval from English Heritage, who can and do serve enforcement notices requiring the work to be removed or re-done, or issuing a hefty fine.

Permitted development

Not all building work needs planning permission: some modest extensions or alterations fall into the category of 'permitted development'. This can include extending your home by less than a certain volume, providing that you can comply with certain conditions to do with height and location and (usually) you make no changes to the front elevation.

The volume of a house relates to the 'original' house – as it was when first built or on 1 July 1948 (if any extensions have taken place since then, the allowance may have been exceeded). The figure is based on the external dimensions of the house including roof and cellar. At present, the allowance for extensions to a terraced house is 1,765 cu ft or 10 per cent of the original volume of the house up to 4,061 cub ft; for a semi-detached or detached, it is 2,472 cu ft, or 15 per cent of the original volume of the house up to 4,061 cu ft. There are no such rights for flats: planning permission for extensions or alterations will be necessary for these, as will consent from the freeholder.

Note that even if the proposals fall within the volume for permitted development, it is advisable to consult the planning officer who deals with your area first to confirm this.

Planning permission is also often necessary for demolitions – even for such things as garden walls or fences, or for changes to railings and gates: check with the council.

Even where planning permission may not be needed, Building Regulation approval will probably be required: a separate application should be made to the Building Control Dept. A Party Wall agreement, or at least formal consent by your neighbours, may also be needed. This is obtained by negotiation: again, you can get expert help for this.

How to apply

All boroughs have a planning enquiry office, and most produce leaflets explaining their requirements for different types of work. Whenever possible, it is a good idea to have a preliminary talk with the borough before making any application. It's possible, in theory, to contact the planning office to discuss your proposals before lodging a planning application (also talk to the Conservation Officer if appropriate). In some cases you may be able to arrange to meet an officer on site. However, the huge volume of planning applications and appeals made in London means that many boroughs are no longer able to offer these services until a formal application has been lodged.

Four sets of forms and a scale of fees can be obtained from the planning office. For your submission, you will need to provide four sets of drawings and details of the materials to be used. It is also useful to include photographs of both the property concerned and the surrounding buildings, as well as a description of the proposed work.

The drawings are very important and must be done well. A location plan showing the street and surrounding area on the Ordnance Survey map at a scale of 1:1250 is required, together with the drawings of plans, elevations and sections differentiating between the proposed new work and existing buildings, plus details of the materials. For work to be carried out in conservation areas and on listed buildings additional detailed, large-scale drawings will also be needed. There is a statutory fee payable on application, which varies according to the type of alterations.

How long should it take?

In theory, planning applications should be processed within eight weeks: this is a statutory requirement. It is possible to check up on the progress of your application after four weeks from receipt of acknowledgement.

Your application will normally be considered by a planning committee (this may have a different name), though minor issues can be determined by the planning officer. The borough is obliged to consult with immediate neighbours and, in some circumstances, more distant neighbours as well. Letters may be sent to adjacent properties and notice may be posted on the boundary of the property (a town hall euphemism for the front gate-post or fence) or a nearby lamp-post so that local people are informed and can comment. Usually the council also puts notices about planning applications received in local newspapers. The procedures for public consultation vary from council to council.

Once responses to consultations have been received it is possible to get some idea of the council's view of your application. Many London boroughs are taking considerably longer than the eight weeks to process (technically called 'determine') applications – in some cases up to six months. What's more, the eight weeks is counted from the time the council acknowledges receipt of your application – and some take weeks just to do this.

The first hint of a possible delay over the eight weeks may come in the form of a letter from the council requesting a time extension. You can then either accept the delay or appeal to the Office of the Deputy Prime Minister (ODPM) on the basis that the council has effectively refused the application because it has not decided in the required time.

There are three types of appeal: a written appeal; a hearing, where an inspector listens to the case presented by the parties involved; or an inquiry – which is like a court case and may involve the appointment of a planning QC to act on your behalf.

All are a lengthy and expensive business. It is usually quicker to negotiate with the borough to determine your application rather than appeal to the Secretary of State. However, if you are reasonably certain the borough is going to refuse your application and you feel you have a good case, you can refuse a time extension and appea. Once you have set the appeal in motion, the borough will not process the application any further.

Building regulations

To some extent, making an application for building regulation approval is more straightforward than a planning application. There are two clearly defined procedures for obtaining approval: a building notice and full plans submission. It is worth knowing a little about the background to the legislation and the kinds of work which need approval. Your solicitor's searches should indicate if work has been undertaken which required Building Regulation consent; however, you should also ask the vendor for evidence that the work was carried out to the satisfaction of the Building Control Officer, who may have issued a certificate of compliance when the work was completed.

What do you need building regulation approval for?

The procedures for obtaining building regulation approval are administered through each borough Building Control Dept. The kind of work for which it is necessary includes:

- The erection of a building.
- Extension of a building (also splitting into flats, loft conversions, some conservatories).
- 'Material' alterations to a building – alterations to structural walls (for example, knocking two rooms together, taking down a chimney breast), means of escape and fire resistance, particularly in relation to conversion to flats and loft extensions.
- Provision, extension or 'material' alteration to: sanitary equipment (i.e., putting in a new bathroom, shower or WC), drainage, unvented water systems, electrical and gas systems, and putting in a stove, boiler or fire which runs on solid fuel, oil or gas.
- Provision, extension or 'material' alteration of energy conservation (including double glazing), insulation (including cavity wall systems) and ventilation (particularly when installing an internal bathroom, WC or kitchen), ventilation of heating appliances.
- Disabled access provisions.
- Provision for restriction of noise through acoustic insulation.

How to set about it

Using forms from your local authority, you need to submit an application with a fee. Except in the case of very simple work, the services of an architect or chartered surveyor will be necessary to supply detailed drawings, with calculations and technical information on structural work, materials, energy and insulation values, drainage and fire protection. You can make an appointment with the Building Control Officer, before putting in an application, to discuss the proposals and to find out what specific information should be included. Sometimes the officer (still called District Surveyors in some boroughs) will be happy to meet you on site if this is easier.

Building Notice route: For buildings where it is not necessary to obtain a fire certificate before occupation – that is most homes – it is possible to follow the Building Notice route (80 per cent of applications). You should submit a completed application form, two sets of drawings and calculations, the appropriate fee and notice that you will commence work 48 hours later without waiting for approval. You should arrange a meeting immediately afterwards to establish whether or not there are any difficulties. As work progresses, the Building Control Officer will pay regular visits to the site to ensure everything is done to his/her satisfaction.

A certain amount of confidence is needed to take this course, for if the regulations are not complied with, the local authority can enforce them up to a year after the work is completed, and this can prove to be extremely expensive for you. Less information needs to be shown on the drawings than on the Full Plan route, but the Building Control Officer, during inspections, can (and does) insist on additional works being incorporated to ensure that the regulations are complied with as the work goes along. These people have very wide powers, and they use them.

Some work may require additional applications. 'Temporary and special buildings' need a licence (a boundary wall over 6ft, a steel balcony or external fire escape). For flats or maisonettes over shops, applications have to be made to the fire brigade: your Building Control Officer will give you details of these. You will also need a licence for scaffolding, hoardings, a skip, for a crane, should you need one for a loft conversion, together with over-sailing rights negotiated with your neighbours.

Full Plan route: This is best used if you wish to have very tight control over the cost, and want all details sewn up before work starts to minimize extra expenses. You'll need a reasonably long lead-in – at least five to eight weeks for the application to be processed.

Here, building regulation approval is in two stages: first, drawings must be passed. For complex submissions where a relaxation of the regulations is required, or inadequate information is provided, approval can take much longer than eight weeks.

Second, when work begins a Notice of Commencement must go to the Building Control Officer along with a further fee to cover inspection. The officer may need to be told when certain work is taking place (e.g. building foundations, damp-proof courses, laying new drains, covering up structural work), in which case further notices (but no fee) need to be served with one full working day's notice.

For the first stage, two sets of drawings and information should be submitted together with a letter (or, in some boroughs, a form requesting that the proposals are considered for approval) along with the appropriate fee. During the period before the Full Plan approval is given, a Building Control Officer may ask for additional information and it is possible to have discussions about the best way to meet requirements.

Whichever route you select, when the works are completed you will need to write to the Building Control Dept asking for confirmation that the work was constructed in accordance with the regulations: a letter of confirmation will usually be sent to you.

What happens if you decide to go without Building Control approval? You will find the property difficult to sell, as solicitors' searches may reveal that the work was done without the proper approval, licences, or Party Wall Awards. Or you may be caught red-handed doing work, as Building Control Officers take an eagle-eyed interest in the contents of skips. This may lead to the council taking legal action.

The Party Wall Act 1997

Since the Great Fire of 1666, there has always been special legislation for the Inner London boroughs relating to the rights of adjoining owners and covering joint concerns such as party walls which provide support between dwellings and the prevention of the spread of fire. The legislation also covers party fence walls between properties. Formal procedures worked very successfully in the prevention of neighbourly disputes. In 1997 a Party Wall Act extended the procedures throughout the country.

The procedures set out in the Act formalize agreements between owners when one building owner is undertaking work to a party wall or fence or within certain distances of adjoining owners' foundations. The Act sets out the process for agreeing the condition of the buildings involved, the nature of the work proposed and the apportionment of costs. This involves serving appropriate notices on the adjoining owner on a very specific timescale, and agreeing the appointment of architects or surveyors to act on behalf of the building owner and adjoining owner to ensure that the latter's property does not suffer as a result of the work. It is specialized work and if you are considering any work which involves a Party Wall Award (meaning an agreement) you will need an architect or surveyor with the appropriate expertise.

Work which would require a Party Wall Award include loft extensions, underpinning, extensions along the boundary (or within certain distances of the boundary depending on the type of foundations proposed), works to the boundary walls, taking down chimney breasts, opening up between rooms where new beams are required bearing on the party wall, and cellar/basement conversions.

It's worth remembering that skips, and sometimes hoardings and scaffolding, require a licence from the local authority. If deliveries of materials by crane or lorry are necessary, again the relevant permissions have to be sought from the Building Control or Highways departments.

Controlling the work: contracts

Organizing building work can be as stressful as moving itself. You can 'go it alone' and manage the whole process on your own, but building legislation is increasingly complex and dealing with builders, well, unpredictable. So proper contracts are important, both for any experts you employ to advise you and for the builder working on your property.

Architects or chartered building surveyors can not only design and specify the job, but also help with the forms of building contract to protect your interests once work begins.

There are a number of published building contracts which suit work to homes. If you are 'going it alone' without an architect or surveyor, then the JCT Building Contract for Home Owner/Occupier may be suitable. This is a clearly-expressed contract between building owner and the builder, where there are no experts administering the contract. It is easy to order through a bookshop or on-line.

If you are going to use an architect or building surveyor, then there's a choice. The first is the JCT Building Contract and Consultancy Agreement pack, also clearly written. It contains two sets of contract documents: one for the agreement between you and your expert who will be running the work, the other a contract between you and the builder. The alternative is the more widely used JCT Minor Works (MW98) contract between the building owner and the builder. You should, though, also have an agreement or contract with your expert. If you are using an architect, the RIBA Small Works Appointment is usual, and sets out the services to be provided and fees to be charged. The RIBA also produces a wide range of useful booklets on hiring an architect and organizing your building work.

The RICS, too, produce similar documentation if you are going to use a chartered building surveyor. Either of these experts can also help with building cost management, since work to existing buildings can be unpredictable and result in additional costs. They will also make the applications for the necessary statutory consents that affect the development of residential property.

Where to get help and advice

Councils produce free leaflets available from their enquiry offices which explain the borough's own planning policies: these cover the UDP proposals, Conservation Area Policy documents, Borough Design Guides, and often a handbook explaining the procedures. Many councils also have excellent websites with details of their policy documents and procedures.

• **The Royal Institute of British Architects** (RIBA) provides leaflets describing services that architects offer for planning applications, and leaflets describing how drawings are prepared. These are available from the Clients Advisory Service, Royal Institute of British Architects, 66 Portland Place, London W1N 4AD. Tel: 020 7580 5533, www.architecture.com.

The Clients Advisory Service can also provide you with lists of local architects with special planning expertise. Further information is also available by e-mail or by phone (as above).

• **The Royal Institution of Chartered Surveyors** (12 Great George St, London SW1, Tel: 020 7222 7000) also produces lists of chartered surveyors and estate agents with expertise in planning matters.

• **The Royal Town Planning Institute** has leaflets about planning application procedure and appeals, lists of sources of planning advice in London, and can give lists of planning consultants who will help with applications.

They can also put people in touch with **Planning Aid for Londoners**, a free advice service manned by chartered town planners (The Royal Town Planning Institute, 41 St Botolph Lane, London EC3R 8DL. Tel 020 7929 9494, www.online@rtpi.org.uk).

Soo Ware is an architect with a special interest in London property and is a director of The Chartered Practice Ltd (CPA Ltd). She is Director of Professional Studies at the Bartlett School of Architecture, University College, London.

Architectural styles

by Soo Ware

Docklands apart, the welter of new flats and houses that have sprung up in Inner London have had to conform to a street-plan that is largely Georgian and Victorian. It is still true that the majority of the wider city's houses are pre-1919; however, there has been a real increase in new building, and there is, too, a wide choice converted from redundant industrial or commercial buildings. Such schemes can result in interesting and unusual homes – often mixing the converted and the new – particularly in and around the City (where homes have been scarce), but increasingly to be found in most areas.

Some new developments currently under way are on a very large scale, and include a mix of housing, commercial and offices: as some balance to Docklands' transformation, West London now has the extensive redevelopment of Paddington Basin round the canal. Many developments have also mushroomed (literally: towers are de rigueur) along the Thames. Right across from Greenwich to Kingston, its banks are being built up by the private sector to provide upmarket flats and houses on once-industrial 'brown' sites.

Away from the river, developers search out small infill sites (new 'mews' pop up where none was before), or convert Victorian schools, hospitals, etc, to flats and 'loft' shells. On Kings Road, Chelsea, an old College site near World's End has become a major luxury homes development, as has a former water-company HQ near Sadler's Wells in Finsbury. These are the epitome of 'gated' developments: enclaves with considerable security provisions, only accessible through sophisticated access systems; they boast porters or concierge arrangements, plus luxurious pools, health clubs, etc.

Some new estates of conventional family homes or flats get squeezed into surplus land by railways. The architectural style of these developments ranges from the high-tech avant-garde, through post-modernism to classical pastiche and bijou traditional.

An alternative housing form making a welcome appearance is the live/work unit: often very attractive, frequently with parking for business use, these are usually a large workshop with home above – not unlike a modern version of the mews. These may have restrictive covenants that only allow certain groups of people and/or work, and are sometimes sold, sometimes on short lease, or renting only.

Increasingly, to get planning permission developers are required to provide a mix of social housing for Housing Associations in with their new homes for open-market sale, in order to encourage a mixed community and to provide affordable homes.

The 'Right to Buy' legislation of the mid-'80s brought council-built homes, hitherto only available to rent by local-authority tenants, into the mainstream market. This widens the choice of homes: a generally less expensive layer of modern properties (some simply convenient, some in fact excellent in both style and soundness) in central locations.

There is, however, still a strong market for the modernized or extensively refurbished older houses, as well as demand from those who look out for a wreck to 'do up'. Most buyers, now and in the future, will be buying 'period' homes. This is a phrase widely used by estate agents who have no idea how old a house really is.

But it is often useful to know the vintage of a property – not just for interest but because different kinds of homes were built at different periods. Some are spacious, some cramped. Some were usually well built; others a hurried response to fashion. Some kinds of architecture throw up more maintenance problems than others.

It should be said that there is some cause for sympathy with the agents' 'period' tag. First, some styles (i.e. 'Georgian') were built, with little discernible evolution, for decades. Some were derived from earlier periods than when they were built – take the turn-of-last-century's 'Queen Anne'. This is still going on, with even high Victorian or Edwardian style being replicated. So the illustrations here are a starting point, a framework for reference. It can be impossible even for experts to date a London house by appearance only.

18th-century Georgian

These very elegant and much sought-after houses are found in small pockets. Some in Mayfair, many used as offices are now being converted back into homes. Others in Islington, Hackney, Greenwich, Kennington, Kew, Clapham, Battersea, Peckham, Clerkenwell, Bermondsey, Southwark, Richmond, Highgate, Hampstead. Detached or in terraces, each house is different. Flat-fronted, of classical proportions, 2- or 3-storey with a slate mansard attic storey, usually three or five sash windows on each floor, often simple in appearance, soft yellow or red bricks, weathered in appearance. Often a fine front door with a carved wood doorcase with classical details – pediments, columns and fan lights. Principal rooms on the first floor are reached by an elegant staircase. These buildings are invariably listed.

Georgian, late 18th and early 19th centuries

Built from the 1780s to the 1840s: often hard to date accurately without local knowledge. Found in Islington, Camden Town, Chelsea, Kensington, Bloomsbury, Kennington, Stockwell, Clerkenwell, Peckham and parts of the West End. Usually in terraces, sometimes in squares and crescents, always in groups arranged as a whole. Three- or 4-storeys; sometimes an attic behind a parapet and a basement behind railings. Ground floor often stucco in an ashlar pattern. Other features: fanlight above front doors and ironwork balcony. Two sash windows per floor, brickwork usually soft London stocks, sometimes rendered with stucco and painted. Rooms are often modest-sized, main ones on first floor.

Regency villas and cottages

Built in the early 19th century, these pretty villas and terraces were intended to reflect a rural idyll in urban or suburban surroundings. Normally 2-storey, terraced or semi-detached, with ironwork canopies and wooden or cast-iron conservatories, trellises, sash windows and decorative railings. The front doors and porches often have delicate canopies. Slate roof, shallow-pitched with wide eaves. Rooms pretty but small. Found in pockets (Putney, Richmond, Kew or Twickenham), though a few survive in Chelsea, Mayfair and Regent's Park. A style much sought after.

Regency terraces

In contrast to the picturesque Regency villas and cottages, there are also the more formal and magnificent terraces around Regent's Park and elsewhere in London and the river front at Richmond. These are buildings of classical proportions, with 3, 4 or 5 storeys in sweeping crescents, terraces or lodges and substantial villas. Terraces are formed by a number of identical houses joined together, with the end of the terraces being defined separately like full stops. They are generally part of large estates, and are stucco-faced with identical decorations. Some are still single homes of truly magnificent proportions, others are converted into smart flats. Many are now used as offices or as company/diplomatic accommodation. Some have been rebuilt behind the original facade. Sometimes hard to distinguish from the early Victorian equivalent (see next page).

Early Victorian

Vast areas of London were built at this period, forming a ring stretching from Kensington and Chelsea through Camden and Islington, down through Hackney and to a lesser degree in South London: Blackheath, Camberwell, Kennington. They form part of the great estates of the time: Grosvenor, Gunter, Pimlico. Three-, 4- or 5-storey flat-fronted terraces or squares, usually with semi-basements, with classical leanings: porticoes, Doric or Ionic columns, pediments and brackets. Almost always with a stucco, symbolic ashlar ground-floor storey, and sometimes painted above. Frequently whole areas are painted with the same colours. Now mostly flats, but planned as family homes for the burgeoning middle classes. Rooms often very large and well-proportioned, with attractive plasterwork, fireplaces and staircases.

Mews

Surviving mews date mostly from the 1830s to the 1890s. They were built to provide stabling and servants' housing, behind the terraces and squares in Belgravia, Knightsbridge, Mayfair, Marylebone and other parts. Today, they are converted to cottages in a hotchpotch of styles, with the coach house or stable used for garaging and the upper floor(s) forming 1 or 2 bedrooms. Some have been virtually rebuilt as larger houses. Usually brick, maybe painted or rendered or with a stucco finish. During conversion, they often gain features such as bay windows, shutters, ironwork, window boxes, hanging baskets. Some mews are still cobbled streets entered through an archway which once defined the estate.

Mid Victorian

These large villas were typically built in pairs with the front door to the side, usually approached up some steps. They have a pitched roof with elaborate overhang or eaves. Detailing is 'classical' stucco around windows and on the ground floor, with some being clad in stucco all over. Vestigial balconies, with ironwork, are found below sash windows. These are found in Chelsea, Kensington and other areas. Terraced houses in the same style, with similar classical details, are widely seen. They are the result of a building boom in the 1850s and '60s and are found all round inner London. Some, in less fashionable areas, fell into disrepair but many are now being restored. They are frequently turned into flats.

Late Victorian

Houses of this period fall into three kinds: small, medium and large. Together, they are by far the most common type of house found in inner London and many outer suburbs. It is difficult to imagine what London must have been like towards the end of the 19th century, with thousands of these houses being built all within 20 years. While the middle of the 19th century saw the construction of houses decorated with classical 18th-century architectural details, the houses of this later period follow the Gothic fashion, with columns decorated with foliage, stained-glass windows, pointed arches and generally fussy detailing. They are usually built of yellow London stock brick or with stucco or red-brick dressing, mostly with slate roofs. Their front doors are set back in decorated porches. However, despite the Gothic detailing, most have sash windows. They are found particularly in a ring round London within the North and South Circular Rds.

The smallest houses (pictured on page 84) were working-class terraces, 2-storeys high, usually with white stucco bay windows on the ground floor to the front parlour, with columns carrying foliage capitals, a narrow frontage and with rooms usually 2 up, 2 down.

The medium-sized houses are the most common (pictured below), usually 2-storeys, sometimes with an extra room in the roof with dormer windows. These houses are found either in terraces or semi-detached. They often have stucco

bay windows on both ground and first floors, with a small pointed hip roof to the gable. These houses have wider frontages, extend far back and usually have 3 or 4 bedrooms. The main rooms have high, moulded ceilings and iron fireplaces with marble surrounds. Generally the small and middle-sized houses have small front gardens and modest back gardens or yards.

The large detached, semi-detached or terraced versions (pictured below) can be very grand, like the red-brick lion houses of Peterborough Estate, Fulham, and the similar ones around Barnes Pond, Tooting Common, Highgate, Dulwich, Sydenham and Crystal Palace. They have 5 or 6 bedrooms, are usually 3 storeys high with very attractive decorative mouldings both inside and out. Double-fronted or asymmetrical they are set back from the road with medium-to-large back gardens, square bay windows with gables, large rooms with high ceilings and attractive proportions. About half of all these three sizes of houses are still family homes, but many have been converted into flats – the large houses making excellent conversions into three flats.

Late-19th-century Dutch style

These tall, usually narrow-fronted soft terracotta-coloured brick houses, with elaborate moulded brick or faience decorations, are found in Knightsbridge and tucked away in Holland Park, South Kensington and Chelsea. Now softened with weathering, they were built at the end of the 19th century in a very free and eclectic style, usually in terraces (although sometimes semi-detached), but each house having varied features. Normally 4- or 5-storeys, with enormous chimneys and wiggly 2-storey gables (decorated with everything but the kitchen sink), and an elaborate porch up a few steps. The main rooms are on the first floor, very much following the plan of the mid-19th-century stucco estates. The windows have a different design on each floor, often with fiddly glazing patterns. The first floor sometimes has decorative ironwork, and rather fine railings separate the semi-basement from the street. Although some are still private houses, most are now flats or offices.

Mansion flats

These very large blocks of flats, usually 4, 5 or 6 storeys high, were built around the end of the 19th century and the beginning of the 20th (1880–1910). Usually built of red bricks, with a horizontal stripy appearance formed by white stone banding and rows of windows picked out in white with white reveals. Facades are broken up with elaborate gable ends, bay windows, balconies and other features, giving an overall exuberant effect. They often have 'interesting' window designs, with glazing bars forming attractive patterns for both sash and casement windows. Arranged with two or four flats off a central staircase, often with well-proportioned rooms on the street frontage and secondary rooms facing rather dreary light wells. Mansion blocks range from very scruffy and poorly maintained to the extremely luxurious. Found all over London, examples include Prince of Wales Drive facing Battersea Park, around Baker St and behind the Royal Albert Hall in Kensington.

Early 20th century

These large detached and semi-detached houses were built for the wealthy middle classes who commuted from the healthy suburbs by train or tube. Many are found in such areas as Wimbledon, Putney, Hampstead, Dulwich, Greenwich and Streatham. They display the individuality of their original owners and a wide range of features were often used in one house. Usually 2- or 3-storeys with 5 or 6 bedrooms, large reception rooms and entrance halls and generous staircases. Often double-fronted, built of brick or brick with render. Features include bay windows, steep gabled pitched tiled roofs, a variety of different types of casement window. Fewer Gothic touches than the late-Victorian buildings. More modest versions have a similar approach.

Nondescript 'Georgian'

Much loved by estate agents who call them 'period', which means they are unable to date them accurately or to define precisely the architectural style. Built in the 20th century, in the 1920s and '30s, and still being built. Very large, 2-storey, double-fronted houses, detached, with attic rooms in the steep pitched roof. Set back from the road, with a sweeping drive, a full flight of steps and an imposing classical front door. Many 'Georgian' features are incorporated: pediments, the Palladian window. Several large reception rooms, bedrooms with en suite bathrooms as standard, staff quarters, large gardens. Found in Bishops Avenue in Hampstead, St John's Wood, Wimbledon Common, Bromley and Finchley.

Mock-Tudor

Built in large quantities around the perimeter of London mainly during the 1930s. More interesting examples occur nearer the centre of London and were built early in the 20th century. Even now, still a popular style with the speculative developer. 1930s examples are found in ribbon development along arterial roads and on large estates. Detached, semi-detached or terraced, many with garages, and almost all family houses with 3 or 4 bedrooms and often substantial back gardens and smaller front gardens with off-street parking. Features: leaded lights in casement windows, steep pitched tiled gabled roofs, black and white timber decoration on white rendered walls, usually red brick on the ground floor and often with fussy brick decoration. Many now heavily altered with new windows etc.

1930s blocks of flats

These very large and rather anonymous blocks of flats, 5 to 7 storeys high, were widely built during the 1930s. Some were private developments (for example, those around Baker St, Maida Vale, Dolphin Square, Streatham). Others were built by the LCC or charitable trusts and are now coming on the market as individual flats. Built from yellow or red bricks with horizontal and vertical bands of render giving a stripy effect. Often they have balconies or bay windows. Windows sometimes are Georgian-type sash, but steel casement windows with very thin glazing bars also common. Blocks are set back a little from the street, with a landscaped area for parking or an entrance drive, and are often U-shaped or courtyard buildings with a central landscaped or paved area. Flats vary from 1- to 4-bedrooms.

Loft apartments

This was the new inner-city domestic building form of the 1990s. Whether it goes on being fashionable will depend on how easy it is to resell these flats when the original buyers move on. The location of these conversions, often on the riverside or in up-and-coming city locations, should ensure continuous interest. Converted from redundant industrial buildings, offices and schools, these highly individual flats were often sold as 'shells' to be fitted out by the purchaser with idiosyncratic results. Frequently these shells are double-height, allowing open plan, modern interiors. The structure, e.g. bare brickwork, roof construction and columns, is exposed to indicate the building's original use.

Modern private estates

Security and pastiche sum up the appearance of these modern developments. Prime sites in good locations, these estates are enclosed by a discreet security envelope and make no reference to any characteristic London vernacular. The developments, which include flats, maisonettes and houses, feature electronic gates, security personnel, private roads with garages and parking, all in well-landscaped surroundings offering an anonymous secure environment. These new estates are on land purchased from the Health Authorities, public utilities and educational bodies, freed up by privatization legislation. Many (though not all) are located in prestigious areas, including sites strung along the riverbank.

Glossary of architectural terms

Beetle infestation: timber in buildings can become infested with insect life. The most common is woodworm, which is often found in floor joists and roof timbers. The infected timber has numerous small holes, a little smaller than a pinhead in size. Depending on the amount of damage, the timber can be chemically treated or replaced. Other wood-boring beetles found in houses cause damage, usually identified by the size and shape of the flight holes in the timber left by the hatching insects.

Bricks: London stock bricks are the most common, made from yellowish clay in Kent. They weather down to greyish black but are often cleaned up and have a soft appearance. Red bricks are also widely used, often with London stocks as a decorative feature.

Casement window: a window with the opening part hinged on one side. Traditionally wood, but in the '20s they were made of steel and now also of aluminium or plastic.

Columns and capitals: vertical pillars with decorative tops (called 'capitals'). Can be either in Doric, a simple geometric style, or Ionic, a more elaborate style with curled motifs. Occasionally the third order, Corinthian, is seen: an elaborate design decorated with leaves. The Victorians decorated their capitals in a Gothic style with natural forms using plants, birds, insects and even reptiles.

Doorcase: a wooden surround to a door opening, often very elaborate with carving or mouldings and classical decorative features – e.g. pediments or columns.

Dormer window: a vertical window (sash or casement) with upright sides coming through a sloping roof, having its own pitched or flat roof.

Dry rot: a fungus affecting timber in older houses. This is serious as all infected timber usually needs to be removed and destroyed and associated areas of brickwork chemically treated. Dry rot is often invisible and not detected until alterations reveal its existence, although the sensitive nose may detect a smell. The fungus spreads in hairline strands behind plasterwork and in brickwork courses. Timber becomes dry and powdery and loses its strength.

Faience: decorative moulded bricks, usually terracotta-coloured or yellowish, sometimes glazed; used in late-Victorian times for picking out features.

Frieze: a band of mouldings around a building usually at high level.

Gabled end or gable: a triangular end wall of a pitched roof, often becoming a decorative feature in its own right, for example, Dutch gables.

Glazing bars: the narrow strips of moulded timber or metal which hold the panes of glass together.

Leaded lights: small panes of diamond-shaped glass held together with narrow strips of lead.

Mansard roof: first rises steeply, almost vertically, with windows in it, and then has a flat top.

Moulding: continuous groove or ridge which forms a decorative feature with an original functional purpose, eg. to throw water away from the face of a building. Can be in any material – brick, timber, stone, stucco. Internally, the term applies to decorative plasterwork or joinery, externally to many design features.

Palladian window: a composite window, designed to look like one big window but made up of three, of which the middle section has a semi-circular fanlight over.

Parapet: a small wall guarding the edge of a roof or, alternatively, the wall of the building extended above the roof line to conceal the gutters.

Pediment: triangular decorative motif usually found over doors and windows.

Pointing: the finish given to the mortar that holds together the brickwork, masonry, etc. It needs to be checked and kept in good repair to keep outside walls weatherproof.

Render: a thick finish, usually sand and cement or pebbledash, which covers all the brickwork and can be painted as well. Popular on Edwardian or mock-Tudor houses with areas of brickwork or tile hanging.

Sash window: a window in which the opening parts slide up and down. They are usually balanced with ropes and weights concealed inside the frame. Traditionally wood, but replacement windows are now aluminium or plastic.

Slates: thin sheets of grey rock, once used extensively for roofing in London. Slates deteriorate after about a hundred years; many have been replaced with artificial slates. Most new properties will also have artificial slate.

Stucco: similar to render, but popular in the 18th and 19th centuries as a smooth finish covering large areas of a building (often the whole wall), sometimes with classical mouldings or details. Normally painted cream or white.

Tiles: made of clay, traditionally plain tiles, rusty-red, small, rectangular and flat in shape, have been used in some areas for hundreds of years, and are seen on all styles of houses. They are used on roofs or can be hung vertically on walls as a decorative feature. In modern times, a wide variety of much larger profiled clay tiles have been used for replacement of old slate or tile roofs.

Velux window: a manufacturer's name for a window inserted into the sloping part of a roof, frequently used in loft conversions.

Wet rot: another fungus affecting timber in buildings. Usually more obvious than dry rot and found in areas where timber becomes wet, e.g. windowsills, the bottom of doors, the ends of joists in external walls, skirting boards on inside walls, in bathrooms and kitchens where there is condensation. The timber becomes wet and spongy and loses its strength. When the timber is painted the surface looks crazed if wet rot is present. Infected timber can be cut out and new pieces inserted. Generally not as serious as dry rot.

Soo Ware is an architect with a special interest in London property and is a director of The Chartered Practice Ltd (CPA Ltd). She is Director of Professional Studies at the Bartlett School of Architecture, University College, London.

A B C D E F G H I K L M N P R S T W

London's Areas A–Z

How to use the A–Z section

This central section of the *Guide* is an alphabetically organized guide to London's areas. The system is a two-tier one: each chapter covers an area of London, and each chapter is subdivided into the various neighbourhoods within the area. Parson's Green can thus be found under 'F' for Fulham, of which it is a part. This division, although less clear-cut than using the hard-and-fast boundaries of postal districts or boroughs, makes for more sense since, on the ground, areas refuse to stop at bureaucratic boundaries.

Indexes

Streets, areas and neighbourhoods are listed in the **Main Index** at the end of the book. If you only know the postal district of the place you are looking for, check **Decoding the postcodes**, which starts on page 14.

The chapter contents

Within each chapter you will find:

Maps

An outline map of London appears on pages 12–13. This shows the areas covered in the guide. The first page of each area chapter has a locator map and an information box. The map is designed to be a guide to the shape of the area, its main roads, railways and stations, the neighbourhoods it divides into, and which areas lie next door. Borough and postal district boundaries are also shown. These are not always shown on street maps but can be important when house-hunting. There is a key to the maps on page 94. Our maps cannot, of course, be street maps; you will no doubt need a full London Street Atlas when searching for your property.

Boxed information

The postal district(s) of the area is given, and so is the borough(s) and controlling political party. Further details on both postcode and borough can be found on pages 14–17 and 71–73 respectively.

A B C D E F G H I K L M N P R S T W

Conservation areas are indicated where relevant. These are zones subject to special planning protection and where new building is generally not allowed unless it is in harmony with the existing architecture. Check with the local town hall (see **Boroughs**, page 71, for phone numbers) for exact boundaries.

Car parking restrictions are listed where information is available. The note on parking refers to residential, not commercial, streets. In most areas, there are restrictions on parking in shopping areas and on main through-routes.

Area profiles

The text on each area consists of an area profile and sub-sections on neighbourhoods. These are the areas that people who live in the area divide it up into. Some have 'proper' names, others are defined as, for example, west or east of a certain point. See the area map for an indication of next-door areas. And note that the neighbourhoods are marked on the maps.

At the end of each area chapter there is a list of some of the main estate agents active in the area. This is neither an endorsement of the agents mentioned nor does it (or could it) mention all those you might encounter.

Each chapter ends with a summary of further useful information:

Transport

At the end of each chapter you will find transport details giving the area's tube stations and local rail stations, and the fare zone the stations are in. The London Transport network is split into Zones 1, 2, 3, 4, 5 and 6 with 1 at the centre. Times are given from a central station in the area to three key points: the City (Bank station), Oxford Circus and Heathrow Airport. Where local rail lines are available, their main central destinations are given. Note that official journey times assume no hold-ups! Use the times given as a point of comparison with other areas. See the **Transport** section of **London in 2005** (pages 20–23) for the latest news on new routes and improvements to existing ones: these can affect an area, and its property prices, profoundly.

The 'miles from centre' note under 'Convenient for' is the distance from the centre of the area to Charing Cross. The purpose of this figure is to give an immediate picture of an area's relationship to the centre of London, and as a quick point of comparison between areas.

Schools

At the end of each area profile we also list the main secondary schools and private secondary schools in the area. For more information see **Schools in London** (page 58) with the borough performance tables and **Boroughs** (pages 71–73) to find out who to contact.

Prices

Average prices are given for both sales and rentals of flats and houses of all sizes in the area. These prices give a 'freeze-frame' picture of where prices stood at the start of the 2005 selling season and are based on data collated in January. They indicate the price range into which each size of home mainly falls, not the price of the meanest slum or the grandest palace. Thus a narrow or a wide range for, say, a 2-bed flat is in itself an indication of the range of homes to be found in the area, and of the different neighbourhoods within the area. See also **How to Use this Book** (page 10).

Below the price bands is a note on the kinds of homes to be found in the area and on the state of the property market there.

A B C D E F G H I K L M N P R S T W

Finding a street

To find a particular street, refer to the **Main Index**, which lists the streets, areas and neighbourhoods mentioned in this book.

How to use the maps

Maps are not to scale and are intended for orientation and general reference. Check north point for orientation. Only main roads are shown. The neighbourhoods are those discussed in the accompanying text.

To locate a map, see arrows for surrounding areas and see the key map at the start of the A–Z section. For full details refer to the *A–Z London Street Atlas*.

NIO

Postal district

East
ulwicl

Neighbourhood

N

North point

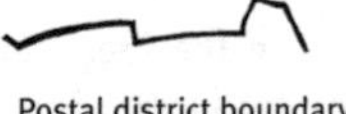

Postal district boundary

Road

Dockland light railway station

Borough

Railway

Rail station

Borough boundary

Open space

Underground station

ACTON

Postal districts: W3
Boroughs: Ealing (Lab)
Council tax: Band D £1,192
Conservation areas: Acton Park, Acton centre, Creffield, Mill Hill Park, Gunnersbury Park, Hanger Hill Garden estate
Parking: Residents' round East Acton station, Acton Town, The Vale, Acton central, S. Acton. W. Acton still free.

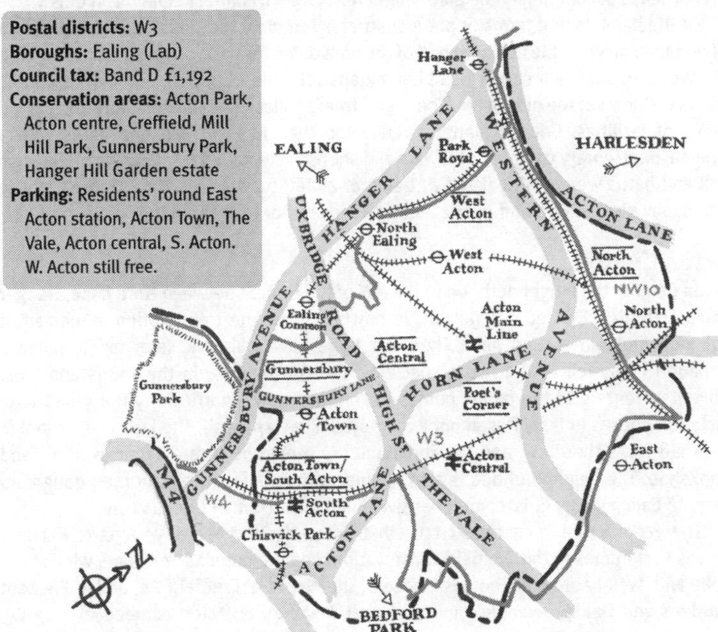

Rents are lower here in one of West London's buy-to-let hotspots. Rents matter as much as prices, since so much property has been bought by investors. The question for this year is will lower yields lead to lower buying prices, and thus to the re-entry of first time buyers into a market they've been wary of? Or will landlords accept that five per cent gross is a sensible rate of return (last year it was six)?

Tenants have been plentiful – Antipodeans in the private sector, and five-year deals with the council and housing asociations. But demand from the latter is easing, say agents – thus the fall in rents. First-time buyers, hunting in couples and small packs, are still competing with landlords for anything ex-council and/or cheap – which around here starts around £185,000 for a 2-bed.

The W3 postcode lacks the cachet of its neighbours W4, Chiswick, or W5, Ealing. Yet Acton is surprisingly close in: next door is Shepherd's Bush; beyond it the rich and starry lands of Holland Park, Kensington, Notting Hill. . . . And the big employers anchor the area: the BBC at White City, plus the burgeoning office towers along the A40, create enduring demand for homes.

And if the young renters and buyers who visit Acton's good ethnic restaurants are not high-flying City whizz-kids, at the top end of the family homes market there's a different picture. Schools are the draw (the Japanese School, the King Fahad Academy, some good comprehensives) and have pushed these houses to very un-Acton prices. However, some of the large, old houses are rented, and often brim-full of young (and sometimes noisy) Australians, South Africans and other fairly transient folk – their presence reflected in local pubs with names such as The Redback and The Captain Cook. Enclaves of neat, lovingly done-up, usually terraced, homes exist, as everywhere in London: one, the 'poets' corner' described below, has become a positive ghetto of BBC types.

There are also fast communications, thanks to Acton's many rail lines. These, though, conspire with main roads to carve the area into small, badly linked pieces, eroding any overall sense of community the place might have. Again, contrast Ealing, and Chiswick.

Of the hamlets and farms of pre-industrial Acton, only the skeleton of the old **High St** remains: much of the northern half of the area dates from the 1920s or later, and even the Victorian southern corner has been extensively rebuilt in parts. St Mary's Church marks the heart of the old village. The High Street still lacks an 'anchor' store and a good range of facilities. Council plans to redevelop the old town hall and baths with a cinema/pool/library complex, plus flats and shops, were halted last year when the town hall and baths were swiftly listed as being of architectural merit. Back to the drawing board, say planners, to find a scheme that keeps rather than razes them.

Acton Central

Acton Central, the neighbourhood to the NW of the High St between **Horn Lane, Hanger Lane, Uxbridge Rd** and the railway, is nowhere near the train station so-named: a common problem around here. There are large Edwardian and later family houses, although many fell to the Acton speciality, flat conversions, in the 1980s and '90s. Buyers or renters of the family homes in central Acton – particularly the 5-bed late-Victorian houses in leafy **Rosemont Rd** – may well be Japanese. The Japanese school in **Creffield Rd** is the draw, and the community is served by estate agencies, delis and bookshop. The neighbourhood is also popular with families who want their daughters to go to Ealing's only girls' comprehensive, Ellen Wilkinson, in **Queens Drive**.

The general rule in central Acton – that prices rise the nearer you get to Ealing – means that homes in the Creffield conservation area are popular. These are wide roads lined with well-kept family homes. Those at the W end of **Creffield Rd**, and in **Western Gardens** and **Oakley Avenue**, come with that dream of an Acton homebuyer. . . a W5 postcode. Creffield Rd gains further tone from the Ealing Lawn Tennis Club. There's also a sports ground with tennis courts E of **Twyford Avenue**, which bisects the area.

Shop-lined, busy **Uxbridge Rd** leads W to Ealing: it grows more respectable as it leaves Acton behind. Ealing Common tube station is here. A strip of green divides the main road from **Twyford Crescent** with its big, handsome Edwardian houses. Further E, **Horn Lane** is a dirty, noisy main road; but **Pierrepoint Rd, Rosemont Rd** and nearby streets could be in another world – secluded, green and quiet: a 4-bed semi might be £450,000, with £500,000-plus 5-bedders in nearby streets such as **Buxton Gardens**.

Lynton Rd to the N is a mixture – a busy road with some '30s and '40s houses, some Edwardian, with an equal mix of flat conversions and houses. Prices unchanged on last year: c. £180,000 for a 1-bed flat, £230,000 for a 2-bedroomed one; a 4-bed semi might be £460,000. Check which side of the street it's on: the railway line lies to the N. Parking is slightly easier in this long, wide road than in most of Acton – though there's no residents' zone here: plans were thrown out. **Horn Lane** is the location of Wimpey's 'Springfield Square', with town-houses and flats and 11 Housing Association homes: a 4-bed town-house re-sale was £440,000 last autumn. Opposite Acton mainline station a new block has retirement flats for sale and some shared-ownership homes.

Acton Town/South Acton

The triangle S of **Acton High St**, E of **Gunnersbury Lane** and W of the railway line is dominated both physically and in reputation by the South Acton Estate (some call it the Authors Estate). The council estate's jumble of low-rise blocks and the least attractive of towers and slabs loom above the pleasant Edwardian rows E of Acton Town tube station, reach as far S as South Acton Station and N nearly up to the High Street. One tower has been demolished, with more set to go this year, as the council tries to revive the place as part of a 15-year programme. Next year, 2006, work starts on 745 new homes.

The main attraction for buyers of the terraced Edwardian houses, or the flats carved from them, in pleasant **Avenue** or **Mill Hill Rds** is the nearby tube station. These streets date from after 1877 and are collectively called Mill Hill Park. The terraced houses of various styles are mostly smart, the roads are tree-lined, and there's a garden and playground in Mill Hill Park itself. This corner is cut off from the South Acton Estate by one-way and closed-off roads, keeping streets quiet, and there is residents' parking. Three-bed houses in this conservation area maintain a stable, c. £360–380,000, price. Acton Housing Association is busy in **Mill Hill Rd** and above shops in the High St.

Off Avenue Rd lies **Heathfield Rd**, which continues as **Avenue Gardens**, forming a secluded crescent with a mix of purpose-built flats, large and rather gaunt late-Victorian houses, a few 1930s semis, the odd interesting Edwardian house, and a few Arts and Crafts, cottagy ones. **Roman Close** has 1970s town-houses off Avenue Gardens.

Poets' Corner

Estate agents wax lyrical about Poets' Corner – it is central, pleasant, full of pretty if small houses and converted flats, and a tight-knit community dominated by BBC workers. The area stretches N of the **High St**, between **Horn Lane** and **East Acton Lane**. The streets grouped (appropriately) around **Shakespeare Rd** offer a cultural menu which includes **Chaucer**, **Spencer**, **Milton** and **Cowper**. (Who, though, was **Myrtle**?) Agents aver that the grid of streets N of **Woodhurst Rd** is in Poets' Corner, too: they must have an unusually comprehensive anthology. Homes are mostly pretty, small-scale terraces, which can be expanded to 4-beds with a loft job, in tree-lined streets. **Cowper Rd** and **Milton Rd** have little 2-bed versions: too small to be turned into flats and with tiny gardens, but a delightfully cottagy feel. Poets' prices are up a bit having been fairly static in 2002–4, with 2-bed houses £300–340,000-plus, 3-beds £350–400,000-plus. **Shakespeare Rd** is a better bet for flats: some have big rooms and elegant facades.

South, across **Churchfield Rd**, the huge 3-storey Victorian terraces in **Alfred Rd** and **Birkbeck Rd** are smartening up. Some have been bought by housing associations, while others have been done up for sale. Prices are much as last year: a 2-bed flat may cost £225,000, a 1-bed £170–180,000 – but these streets link to the High St one-way system, so traffic is heavy. Bigger houses in streets such as **Cumberland Rd** and **Maldon Rd** (part of Poets' Corner, some claim – and not a rhyming couplet between 'em) were once grand family homes, but are now almost all 2- or even 3-bed flats. One whole house in **Cumberland Park** was advertised last year by an Ealing agent for £1.2 million – but the million-pound hurdle has proved hard to leap in Acton . . .

Goldsmith Rd turns, northwards, into **Goldsmith Avenue** and an even more favoured corner: the Goldsmith estate's Victorian and Edwardian homes, where 5-bed houses are c. £550,000. The clutch of streets N of **Birkbeck Avenue** are popular: Victorian semis and terraceds, quite a few split into flats. Across the railway to the E, the streets around **Shaa Rd**, N from Acton Park, are popular with Arab families because of **East Acton Lane**'s exclusive school for Arab children – the same street also has the well-known Barbara Speake Stage School and East Acton Primary – and a 4-bed house with 'parking for six or seven cars' priced at £999,000 last winter. The little green and pub at the junction of East Acton Lane and **Friars Place Lane** create a village atmosphere.

Around **Beech Avenue**, across East Acton Lane, there are some modern homes. At the E end of **The Vale**, Somerfield's supermarket is being redeveloped with a new store – plus a cache of 129 live/work units. **Beech Avenue**, along with **Larch** and **Maple Avenues**, form the Vale Estate: grim-looking council blocks, popular with investors.

East Acton Lane has the spacious grounds of Acton Sports Association, with cricket, tennis, football. The association joined up with a health-club company to renew facilities and to create a smart fitness centre: The Park Club. Lots of new homes on **Bromyard Avenue:** Berkeley Homes is carving 500-plus flats from an old office, ready 2006: studios from £150,000, 1-beds from £215,000, 2-beds from £275,000, penthouses £500,000-plus. Just across the road, a Virgin fitness centre awaits all these keen young buyers.

West Acton

West Acton was the scene of a property buyer's dream in the early '80s – 3-bed semis were sold off for just a few thousand each, a fraction of the market price. These were the 'railway cottages': homes between **Saxon Drive** and **Noel Rd**, built in the 1920s by the Great Western Garden Village Society for workers to rent, and 60 years later sold to the tenants. Today these fetch £270–320,000, depending on condition.

West Acton, in the angle between **Horn Lane** and **Western Avenue**, is dominated by rail lines – but it is greener than the rest of Acton, with several sports and playing fields. And W of West Acton station is the Hanger Hill garden estate – impeccable 1930s mock-Tudor, unique in Ealing or Acton, its black-and-white half-timbered houses and flats amid plenty of green space. Families love it for its 3-bed, £350–400,000 houses in roads such as **Queens Drive, Monks Drive** and **Princes Gardens.** Japanese families come here: their school is just to the S, and the City is accessible by tube. Across the tracks, the grand Hanger Hill estate (as opposed to 'garden estate') rises up the hill: see Ealing chapter.

North Acton and East Acton

North Acton might be called Leamington Park by some estate agents, but don't let the upmarket name blind you to the drawbacks. It has none of the Ealingesque atmosphere to which many in Acton are drawn, not least because it is mostly industrial estates and railways. There *are* homes: up in NW10, isolated amid rail lines, **Wells House Rd** forms an enclave of neat flat-fronted Victorian cottages with gardens. East of **Victoria Rd**, the early-'90s 4–5 storey blocks in **Shaftesbury Gardens**, are £185–190,000 for a 2-bed: location is against them, but agents say people buy once they've taken a look. Westcott Park in **Cotton Avenue**, built in the late '80s, is another source of studios and 1- and 2-bed (£180–200,000) flats – but prices in traffic-choked **Leamington Park** are lower.

The action is tucked away between **Western Avenue** and the **North Circular**: the Park Royal neighbourhood, where a few streets of homes struggle on amid a vast industrial estate. Diageo and LRP are building 'Firstcentral', a major office scheme. Offices are the main component – nine gleaming, head-office-sized blocks – but it will also include some homes, a 150-bed hotel,even a new tube station (Central and Piccadilly Lines). At Gypsy Corner, where **Victoria Rd** meets the A40, another big commercial scheme is under way, – with, as well, 167 housing-trust homes (half shared ownership) close to N Acton station.

East Acton is a small neighbourhood in the midst of railway lines and bordered to the S by the busy A40 Western Avenue. It straddles the Hammersmith borough boundary, close to Wormwood Scrubs Prison and the common to the E. These two dozen roads have a pleasantly villagy feel – most homes were built in the 1920s by public bodies, and were or are owned by the council or housing associations, though some were built by developers for sale. Local agents say people either love it – for its value and convenience – or hate it, for its still rather grim appearance. Families buy here and tend to stay put. It now has a residents' parking scheme. Three-bed houses are stable at c. £300,000.

Running N from **Western Avenue, St Andrews Rd** has 1930s red-brick terraces with square bays. Council-built properties dominate **The Fairway** (street names here refer to the golf course they were built on), which runs W–E between the main line and **Old Oak Common Lane.** The majority are stone-clad semis and terraces, but some are of a warmer brown brick. Nearby, on the pleasant green, the homes – 1930s once again – are privately owned and arranged in both terraces and semis. Moving N through **The Bye** to **Long Drive,** clusters of a dozen or so semis are grouped around small greens in closes. Further down Long Drive towards **Western Avenue** are one or two larger detached houses, rare in East Acton. **Brassie Avenue** offers a mix of council-built and private semis. The main

shopping area is in nearby **Old Oak Common Lane** to the E, near the A40. The tube station is in **Erconwald St**, also to the E. All the essentials are there for a quiet, pleasant corner.

Borders: Gunnersbury

Rather a no-man's-land between Ealing and Acton, trapped in the triangle of **Gunnersbury Lane, Uxbridge Rd** and **Gunnersbury Avenue**, Gunnersbury is nevertheless a pleasant area. It boasts some quiet roads of detached homes with large gardens that fetch high prices: **Lillian Avenue, Gunnersbury Gardens, Gunnersbury Crescent**. The area is very convenient for the huge Gunnersbury Park, also Acton Town tube, the focus of a small shops/restaurants strip. The 4-bed mock-Tudor homes of **Carbery Avenue** are especially popular, as are those of the 'Gunnersbury Triangle', the local agents' name for **The Ridgeway, Park Drive** and **Princes Avenue**, three streets E of the North Circular grouped around a tennis club. Traffic seeking relief from the North Circular can be a problem.

For Acton Green, cut off by rail lines and in W4, see the Bedford Park chapter.

Transport Tubes: Acton Town (zone 3, Piccadilly, District), North Acton (zone 2/3, Central), others see map. From Acton Town: Oxford Circus 30 min (1 change), City 45 min, Heathrow 20 min. Trains: Acton main line (Paddington 15 min), Acton Central and South Acton on N London Line, Silverlink. Miles from centre: 6.5.

Convenient for Heathrow, routes to Oxford and the West, BBC in Shepherd's Bush.

Schools Ealing Education Authority: Acton High School, Ellen Wilkinson (g), Twyford C of E. Private: Japanese School, King Fahad Academy, Greek School. See also Ealing.

SALES

Flats	S	1B	2B	3B	4B	5B
Average prices	110–150	120–220	140–300	180–350	–	–
Houses	2B	3B	4B	5B	6/7B	8B
Average prices	230–360	250–450	350–650+	400–900	600–900	→

RENTAL

Flats	S	1B	2B	3B	4B	5B
Average prices	140–200	160–225	200–300	230–350	320–400	–
Houses	2B	3B	4B	5B	6/7B	8B
Average prices	230–350	280–400	330–450	420–600	500+	–

The properties Mix of late-Victorian and Edwardian terraces and inter-war suburbia, plus ex-council. Fewer large houses. Ample 1- and 2-bed flats. Some new-build, including several big schemes.

The market Family homes in defined enclaves, flats everywhere, many bought to let. Best parts of Acton can approach Ealing prices. These are bought by BBC types or rented to families who move here for the Japanese School or King Fahad Academy.

Among estate agents active in this area are:

- Bushells
- Rolfe East
- Churchill
- Haart
- Landsdowne
- Winkworth
- Northfields
- Foxtons
- Bellengers
- Grimshaw
- Ludlow Thompson
- Oaktree
- Hantons• Robertson Smith & Kempson

BALHAM AND TOOTING

B

Postal districts: SW12, SW17
Boroughs: Wandsworth (Con), Lambeth (Lib)
Council tax: Band D Wandsworth £597 Lambeth £1,050
Conservation areas: Several, including Heaver, Hyde Farm, Totterdown Fields, Trinity Rd
Parking: Residents' zones now widespread

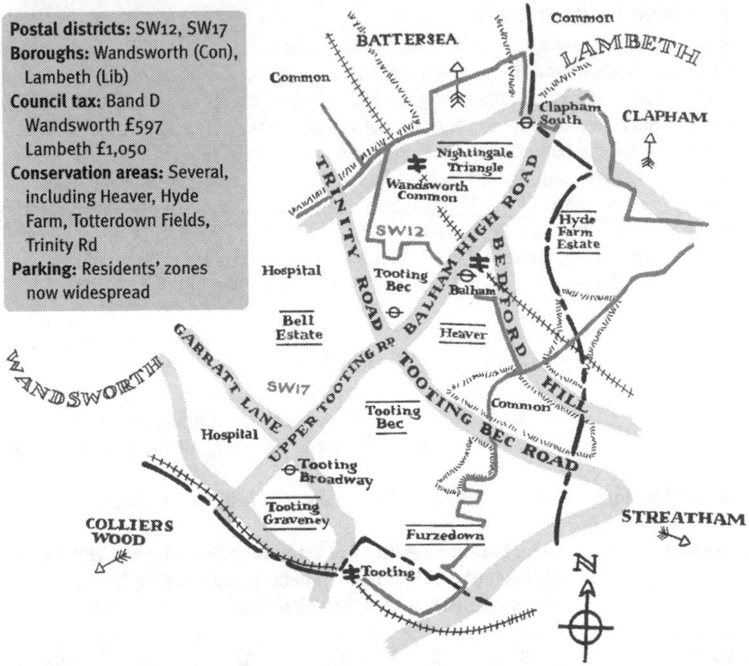

Balham and Tooting are growing apart. Indeed, some say they have nothing but their Commons in common. Like a long-married couple they are finding new friends, new directions. The Northern Line and Wandsworth borough still tie them together, but for many Balhamites, the glamour of face-lifted Clapham has a far stronger pull than the faded charms of dear old Tooting. And Tooting, in any case, is finding new lovers of its own.

Bankers, lawyers and the like have been spending serious money in Balham, and carefully defined parts of its southern neighbour Tooting, since the mid-1990s. They follow a trail marked, around 1985, by brave pioneers to what was then a seriously unfashionable, humdrum stretch of South London.

Now, in several clearly defined enclaves, in leafy streets or off commons, million-pound-plus homes cluster. The reason? Here, growing families find big houses, with just that touch of late-Victorian grandeur to fuel Trollopian fantasies. Nightingale Square may not be Eaton Square, but it's a passable run back by BMW from the West End at night, and the Northern Line takes one into the City or Docklands. Between these posh enclaves there are tracts of everyday but fast-smartening terraces; some very busy, sometimes seedy but increasingly tidy main roads and a growing supply of new homes from studios to 4-bed houses. The terraces are attracting a whole range of newcomers: first-time buyers head for ripe-for-revival Tooting Graveney, middle-rank families for the less obvious bits of Balham and the up-and-coming Tooting Bec corner. Young graduates rent here because their parents have heard of it and their friends live nearby. And the smart new flats in the Hill or the High Road go to singles displaced down the tube line from Clapham – and to buyers who previously rented locally.

The Northern Line – better than it was, with new trains and more reliable timetable – connects the two areas with both Waterloo and the City. Wandsworth borough brings a smart name and a history of low council tax to much of the area, and up-and-come Clapham and Battersea are neighbours. Within the twin areas, Tooting Bec station provides the frontier point: travel on S, and you are in Tooting.

Balham is now self-possessed enough to stop claiming to be 'Clapham South' (the name of the tube station at the tip of the common), while the smart bits of SW17 – the Heaver estate, Trinity Road – trade on the Wandsworth (borough) name and try to forget Tooting altogether. Indeed, careless estate agents now often advertise the Heaver Estate as Balham, not Tooting. More humdrum corners are happy that both names now sound acceptable – and that Balham (at least in contrast to Tooting) is considered smart.

Like a lot of South London, Balham and Tooting spent much of the 20th century asleep in seedy respectability, of interest only to strictly local buyers until the '80s boom started people prospecting pastures new (to them). In some parts the market is very local still, particularly among the thriving Asian community, which adds many shops and a round dozen restaurants, plus temples and mosques, along **Upper Tooting Rd**. Here, the biggest bank is not NatWest but the Bank of Baroda.

In the mid-19th century, Balham and Tooting were merely rural hamlets on the main road into London, favoured spots for the country residences of the professional classes: this accounts for the impressive houses near to the commons still standing today. The later Victorian and Edwardian terraces crowd around the spine of the area, the A24, which runs SW from the bottom tip of Clapham Common and is called successively **Balham Hill**/**Balham High Rd**/**Upper Tooting Rd**/**Tooting High St**.

Away from the main road, the area is fringed with greenery: Tooting Bec, Tooting Graveney, Wandsworth and Clapham Commons, plus a golf course – and a couple of large cemeteries. There is also a major teaching hospital, St George's.

Both areas had reputations for being cheaper than neighbouring Clapham and Battersea. This is no longer true at the top end of the market: the big family houses in the best-regarded enclaves push up well beyond a million pounds. You can spend a lot less, though: you can still find little 2-bed terraced houses from £200,000 in Tooting, though the better ones reach £260,000. Or you can choose one of the many new homes: some large ex-hospital sites have sprouted whole new neighbourhoods.

Broadly speaking, prices drop as you go south. Proximity to stations raises prices. A home in a 'known' enclave – see the detailed text below – will always command a premium. Several of these 'estates' are conservation areas.

Most homes in Balham are Victorian, whereas Tooting ranges from the 1800s to the

B

present day – the bulk, though, are mainly Victorian, Edwardian and 1930s. The 1980s contributed, first, widespread flat conversions and then small pockets of new homes – mainly in Balham – and the late '90s saw further development, which continues. Tooting Bec has the area's first really large-scale new housing: on the site of the old hospital are some 750 new flats and houses. Now comes 'Heritage Park', the Springfield Hospital site in Upper Tooting, on the W edge of the area: some 'surplus land' is being used for homes (including care homes, rather than the usual Affordable Housing).

Balham's bustling **High Rd**, though small, provides an increasing tally of lively bars and pubs and a Sainsbury's, and is being smartened up with new pavements and crossings. It even has a town centre manager. **Bedford Hill**, off the High Rd, is also smartening up and has some hip bars and restaurants. Charming, villagey **Bellevue Rd**, at the foot of Wandsworth Common, has the fashionably smart shops, pubs and restaurants. Neighbouring areas supply the cinemas (Clapham, Streatham), theatres and pub theatres (Wimbledon, Battersea). Indeed Wandsworth Council's policy is now to try to restrict the increasing number of new bars and cafés in several hot-spots across the borough – **Bellevue** and **Balham High Rd** among them.

Traffic is a downside. The A24 is always congested along its entire length, and the many railway lines – with few road bridges – shape the area, making car journeys tortuous and bus travel erratic at best. Parking is a big problem across both areas, especially close to tube and rail stations and hospitals. Both councils have brought in residents' zones, which have expanded as commuters discover their boundaries.

Balham

People like saying they live in Balham now. It is even alleged to be trendy. Smart developers are building modern flats. The process began around 1985 when a local estate agent confided 'it's all right to talk about Balham'. The combined efforts of Peter Sellers ('Gateway to the South') and Nikolaus Pevsner ('nothing of interest on Balham Hill except the Odeon') had damned the place into a sort of property limbo. Then the climb-back began: Clapham South tube lent its name to a swathe of Balham, and the pleasant streets between **Nightingale Lane** and **Balham High Rd** migrated upwards to become the 'Nightingale Triangle'. Finally, locals have come full circle, foresworn the name Clapham South and become born-again Balhamites.

Balham has all the attributes of a real place: a High Road, a station (mainline trains and Northern Line tube), a parish church (St Mary's, 1805) and a library. The railway line, running W–E on its embankment, divides Balham in half and contributes largely to traffic congestion: there are only three bridges over or under it.

Nightingale Triangle

This is the most exclusive area in Balham (if not *quite* as smart as **Balham Park Rd**): quiet, attractive, convenient for transport, and bordering Clapham and Battersea. It is bounded by **Nightingale Lane**, **Balham High Rd** and the railway. Prices here are among the highest in the two areas: think in terms of £500,000-plus for a 3-bed house; the best homes exceed seven figures, with £1.5 million-plus being mooted for the really big/really smart ones, and a steady trickle asking £1 million-plus.

On the SW side, the roads between **Ravenslea Rd** and **Chestnut Grove** contain neat Victorian terraced 3/4-bed houses, popular but smaller than some in the Triangle. Those in **Calbourne Rd** and **Mayford Rd** have larger gardens.

Nightingale Lane itself starts on the brow of the Wandsworth Common railway bridge; it holds very large and distinctive semi-detached 5/6/7-bed houses – some, opposite **Endlesham Rd**, by TE Collcutt (1879). Some are flats, with a few big 3-bed duplexes, and others taking up entire floors of the big old houses. Then come '30s 4-bed houses leading on to mansion flats near Clapham South tube, including Clapham

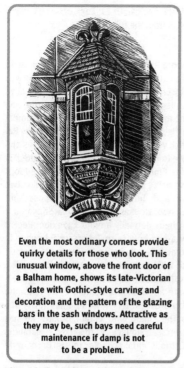

Even the most ordinary corners provide quirky details for those who look. This unusual window, above the front door of a Balham home, shows its late-Victorian date with Gothic-style carving and decoration and the pattern of the glazing bars in the sash windows. Attractive as they may be, such bays need careful maintenance if damp is not to be a problem.

Mansions (2/3/4-bed flats) and Art Deco Hightrees House, looking out over the cricket ground. Service charges are quite high – but these include insurance, porterage and use of gym and pool.

Western Lane, leading southwards from the popular Nightingale pub, is a leafy alley with mid-19th-century cottages, attractively paved and boasting handsome Victorian-style lamp posts. Through to **Linnet Mews** – built 1983 – with its smart 1/2-bed red-brick houses and flats. South is the picturesque **Nightingale Square** – coveted, spacious Victorian houses that surround a garden for residents. Despite the bustle of two schools and a church at the far end, the square is a popular corner. A 5-bed, 3-bath house here was £950,000 last autumn. **Endlesham Rd** has some double-fronted Victorian houses: these 6/7-beds go for £750,000, a hundred thou less for a 4/5-bed.

Chestnut Grove, running on to the S, has pleasant cottagey terraces and a large school on the W side. It gets less popular as it nears busy **Balham High Rd** and the tube. **Ramsden Rd**, cutting through the middle of the triangle, has a variety of red-brick and flat-fronted Victorian houses and terraces, some large (5-bedroomed) and some small. The houses are generally larger at the two ends of the road, but the **High Rd** end does get congested, with the supermarket's car-park entrance on the E side. **Old Dairy Mews**, 20 2-, 3- and 4-bed houses, some with classy features such as double-height conservatories, appeared in 2003 on the old Unigate Dairy site.

Two-bed cottages (once workmen's quarters) feature in **Bellamy St**, **Pickets St**, **Balham Grove** and **Temperley Rd**. Stretched to provide 3 beds/2 baths, they go for £350,000-plus. **Bracken Avenue** is leafy and pleasant. **Badminton Rd** has period red-brick homes on the E side (3-bed £525,000), unusual early 20th-century double-fronted maisonettes on the W. Front gardens on the E side are smaller (Nos. 1–54). **Balham Grove** has the supermarket's goods entrance at the S end, but then a couple of lovely Georgian houses – one now apartments. The old paper factory here became smart new flats in '02, and also in the Grove are the Blueprint Apartments by Bermondsey developers Angel: 2-bed flats £335,000. Off **Oldridge Rd,** eight new 'loft-style' houses were built in 2004 round a courtyard.

Large Victorian houses follow, plus a small '80s estate in **Ainslie Walk**. The Lochinvar Estate ('60s, concrete, low-rise) is an affordable, if uninspiring, first-time buy. **Liberty Mews**, built in the '80s, is off **Malwood Rd** at the apex of the triangle and just around the corner from the tube, Malwood Rd's Victorian 3-storey, 4- and 5-bed houses sell for c. £700,000. At 18–20 **Balham Hill**, a 1990 mews has cottages and flats opening out around a courtyard, behind some small office units developed in the late 1990s. **Clarence Mews** off Balham Hill was new in '03: 29 flats with underground parking. Also on the Hill is 'The Foyer', the conversion of part of the 1930s Odeon cinema into eight 2- and 3-bed flats. The Majestic Wine warehouse is staying put on the ground floor. Next door is to be 'The Cube' – new flats, details as yet unclear. Or for £255,000 you can get an ex-local authority flat on the Hill a short walk from the tube.

B

East Balham & the Hyde Farm Estate

Hyde Farm is a rectangle bounded by **Hydethorpe Rd**, **Emmanuel Rd** and **Radbourne Rd** in the eastern part of Balham and in Lambeth, not Wandsworth, borough. Building was begun in 1901 by speculative developers, led by Ernest Hayes-Dashwood, on land leased from Cambridge University's Emmanuel College. Today, parts of **Radbourne** and **Telferscot Rds** are still set aside as rent-free housing for retired servicemen. Conservation area status has been granted to the roads S of, and including, **Burnbury Rd**.

This network of streets consists of red-brick Victorian 3/4-bed terraced houses and maisonettes, with only slight variations in style from road to road (more 'bell-fronted' in **Haverhill Rd** than in **Scholars Rd**, for example). **Emmanuel Rd** is popular – it overlooks Tooting Bec Common, the railway line beyond being screened by trees, and holds two Infant/Junior schools – Henry Cavendish and Telferscot: many purpose-built maisonettes along here, selling at £275–325,000. Houses go for around £425,000 if smartened to 4-bed, 2-bath standard, with 3-beds normally around £375,000. Recent additions include a courtyard with five new 4-bed houses to **Telferscot Rd**, while in **Radbourne Rd** an Edwardian school has become loft-style homes courtesy of Sapcote.

The area N of Hyde Farm is more mixed, with an industrial estate in **Zennor Rd**. **Weir Rd** is industrial at its W end but soon calms down to Victorian terraces on the S side and **Molly Huggins Close** on the N, with an '80s development of 40 flats and houses for rent on an old hospital site. 'Fryday Grove Mews' off Weir Rd has new 3-bed flats at £325,000. **Belthorn Crescent** has the smart Weir estate. **Atkins Rd** has pleasant 20th-century semi-detached and terraced houses on the right – mainly in good repair, some mock-Tudor. Also two Catholic girls' schools: the St Bernadette Primary and the La Retraite secondary.

The roads running E from the **High Rd** to **Cavendish Rd**, between **Englewood Rd** (which is really in Clapham) to the N and **Rossiter Rd** (S), are almost entirely terraces of 3/4/5-bed houses of various vintages. Prices for flats start at c. £235,000; around £260–310,000 for 2-beds. Exceptions to the period rule include gated, cobbled **Anchor Mews** off **Hazelbourne Rd** (just around the corner from Clapham South tube and Clapham Common), with loft-style flats with garages. **Yukon** and **Dinsmore Rds** form a small Conservation Area with their neatly detailed 1899 terraces: some are maisonettes (2-bed £245,000). There are recent flats in **Hanson Close**, but it's back to period in **Ravenswood Rd**. **Old Devonshire Rd** has a mosque and some industrial buildings giving way to a mix of period and recent properties. With next-door **Old Balham Road** it forms a conservation area: some homes date from the 1820s, others from a little later. **Laitwood Rd**, **Ormeley Rd** and **Ranmere St** form a quiet, pretty enclave, close to the tube and rated the best 3-bed houses in the Wandsworth borough side of the neighbourhood. On either side of the railway line, **Fernlea Rd** and **Byrne Rd** have attractive, flat-fronted upper facades, early Victorian in style, leading to more Victorian terraces.

Bedford Hill runs off the High Rd close to the station. It now boasts a leading music/comedy pub and a couple of smart new bars. An accolade for the Hill is the purchase by media/film club Soho House of three Victorian buildings which they've converted into a big new bar/brasserie with flats above. New flats, too, at the old market. Moving S, the Hill has large period houses – some very grand, with ornamental brickwork. Many were split into flats (1-beds go for £175–210,000), or be your own developer with the double-fronted ready-to-split-up monster where Hill meets Heaver: only £1.3 million. The 1980s added some purpose-built flats such as those on the corner of **Culverden Rd** and twelve more for a housing association in the shadow of the railway bridge. More new flats (1- to 3-bed) on the Hill in 2002 from Metropolis: recent asking price £430,000 for a 2-bed. The Priory, a gothic-revival mansion on the edge of Tooting Bec Common, dates from 1822 and is now much-in-demand flats.

Leafy **Culverden Rd** has some handsome 1880s semi-detached villas, most now split into flats, though a handful survive as 6/7-bed homes. Those on the E side overlook Tooting Bec Common. Neat terraces in **Dornton Rd** (some Victorian purpose-built flats with balconies) and **Fontenoy Rd** – reckon on £600,000-plus for a 4-bed house in these roads. Smart new maisonettes on the E of **Brierley Rd** are opposite period terraces. The Ryde Vale Estate (entrance **Ryde Vale Rd**) has a mix of styles – small blocks of terraced flats, low-rise concrete blocks and bungalows.

The area E of Hyde Farm, and S of the **South Circular** with the wide **Kings Avenue** running N–S, has generally large, pleasant inter-war and post-war housing with some flats scattered around. **Thornton Rd** is semi-detached mock-Tudor (6-bed house for £625,000); **Thornton Gardens** is a small estate. There is also a late-'80s development off Thornton Rd: **St Stephens Mews** is 1- and 2-bed flats. The flats at the S of **Kings Avenue** give way to large modern houses with garages. More 20th-century houses in **Copthorne Avenue** and **Parkthorne Rd.** This area has aspirations to be Clapham Park, or perhaps Streatham Hill.

Balham High Road & St James's

Marius Rd, W of the High Rd, has attractive period houses and Cecil and Marius Mansions – impressive Victorian flats, 3-beds c £325,000 – at the far end. More mansion flats are to be found at the S ends of **Nevis Rd** and **Wontner Rd** (Stanley Mansions). **Boundaries Rd** has Boundaries Mansions. There are many period terraces and some modern ones – notably the pleasant brick houses in **Ashdown Way** and the not-so-pretty yellow **Flowersmead** council-built estate (1940s) opposite, where many homes are in private ownership.

On the E side of **Balham High Rd** is the '02-vintage 'The Hub' with both flats and mews houses. Next to Balham Spiritualist Church, on the corner of **Elmfield Rd,** Laing contributed a mix of 30 2-bed flats and 3-bed mews houses, marketed under the name 'Lumiere', and exactly opposite, between **Marius Rd** and **Upper Tooting Park,** is Falconbrook Mansions, a block of 12 flats. Fairview's 'The Connection' on the High Rd close to Tooting Bec tube had 1- and 2-bed flats from £250,000 last winter.

The N end of **St James's Drive** boasts large, covetable homes overlooking Wandsworth Common – popular because they are also close to the train station, the good local schools (private and state) and the amenities of pretty, villagey **Bellevue Rd. St James's Close** is an attractive 1980s group of houses and flats around a garden; **Old Hospital Close** is similar, but bigger. **Balham Park Rd,** leading E from St James's Drive back to the High Rd, has large and highly prized houses (some of the priciest in the area, with numbers like £1.3 million cropping up) by the common, Victorian terraces, and towards the E end more modern flats and houses. Du Cane Court on the **High Rd** – once the largest block in Europe – is a '30s warren of 650 studio and 1/3-bed flats: studios come in two sizes (small and minute) at prices around £125,000 and £100,000 respectively, while 1-beds go for c. £185,000. For the W side of **Trinity Rd** see Upper Tooting, below.

Balham Borders

Working from N to S a few corners are debatable Balham. The roads N of **Nightingale Lane** and S of **Thurleigh Rd**, while still in SW12, have been annexed into the area known these days as 'Between the Commons' in Battersea – see Battersea chapter.

At the foot of Wandsworth Common, in the triangle between **St James's Rd**, deeply fashionable **Bellevue Rd** and **Trinity Rd**, are tucked some neat, prosperous, very pricey, grey-brick terraced mid-Victorian cottages. In SW17 rather than SW12, and emotionally Wandsworth Common (see Wandsworth chapter) rather than Balham.

B

Tooting

The name Tooting excites a certain amusement, but the place has more history than Balham and can boast a past back to Domesday. Little remains of the medieval villages of upper Tooting (Tooting Bec) and lower Tooting (Tooting Graveney); the place stayed small and rural well into the 19th century, and the big development of houses happened relatively late. The result is a district of orderly grids of late-19th-century homes, some spacious, some small, all well served by the Northern Line tube.

Tooting's two commons, Bec (the biggest) and Graveney, boast lido, sports and tennis (and a fishing lake sheltering monster carp). Bec Common has been tidied up with new planting, CCTV cameras and extra lighting. Both are sadly split by rail and roads. They do, however, give Tooting a clear boundary to the E. To the N is Balham; W, beyond Springfield University Hospital and the Streatham Cemetery, is Earlsfield. To the S, the rail line forms the boundary with Colliers Wood. Tooting rail station is right on the (SE) edge of the district it is named after.

The commercial spine of the area is **Upper Tooting Rd/Tooting High St**, centring on the crossroads with **Mitcham Rd/Garrat Lane**, where you'll find Tooting Broadway tube station. **Tooting Broadway** is less domestic than its outlying districts and more closely resembles a typical South London inner-city high street. The two Northern Line stations are at either end of Upper Tooting Rd. Now, with the redevelopment of the Tooting Bec Hospital site ('Heritage Park/Heritage Gate'), on the south-western edge of Tooting Bec Common – see below – Tooting's main public landmark has become the enormous, sprawling, ever-growing, congestion-causing complex of St George's Hospital on the Wandsworth/Merton border.

Heaver

By far the grandest neighbourhood in Tooting and Balham, with house prices a good jump above anything else except the smarter bits of Nightingale and the St James's Drive corner. Alfred Heaver was a local builder, who laid out and developed the grid of houses in the 1890s (local legend has it that he was assassinated by his brother-in-law, who then committed suicide, during the development: who said Tooting was boring?).

The conservation area lies between **Balham High Rd**, **Tooting Bec Rd**, the Common and **Ritherdon Rd**; with the neat terraces between **Ritherdon** and **Elmfield Rds** claimed by agents as outliers (see below) though they are not in the official zone. The handsome double- and single-fronted 2- and 3-storey houses (and some maisonettes) are all in red-orange brick with stucco details. Some are detached, some semi-, most in terraces. Around half have been split into flats, and these too make for very generous-sized homes.

The undivided houses are enormous – a typical property would have six to eight bedrooms, two bathrooms, kitchen plus three reception rooms and a huge garden. Many original features remain, inside and out – note the ornate front doors with stained-glass insets. The Heaver Estate is largely intact, the main exceptions being infill maisonettes in **Manville Gardens** and **Carnie Hall**, and smart flats at N end of **Hillbury Rd**, which also boasts some modern 3-bed town-houses and some 4/5-bed 'mock-Heaver' houses, built in 1989. Families wishing to escape cramped modern housing find havens in these popular, individually distinctive streets – for example, the S end of **Elmbourne Rd** (ornate brickwork framing door arches and windows), which overlooks the Common, as does the E side of **Hillbury Rd**, or the wide, tree-lined **Streathbourne Rd** (each house name inlaid in decorative plaques). House prices in these three roads start around £500,000 for an unmodernised mid-sized house, with £1.5 million being asked for the really big, really smart ones. (Back in the boom year 1988, the record Heaver house hit £450,000, and prices dropped to £190–300,000 during the early 1990s.)

The roads directly N of the Heaver Estate, from **Ritherdon Rd** up to **Elmfield Rd**, are neat period terraces apart from some '60s flats at the N ends of **Carminia Rd** and **Childebert Rd**. At the W end of **Elmfield Rd** there are mansion flats of impressive red brick, recently smartened up. Ravenstone School (primary) opposite and Balham Leisure Centre (pool, gym, solarium, etc) are the other features of the road. **Cheriton Square** is opposite the leisure complex: its curving terraces always enjoy top billing in estate agents' ads. It is also around the corner from Balham station and tube.

Tooting Bec

The stretch enclosed by **Tooting Bec Rd** (N) to **Mitcham Rd** (S), **Upper Tooting Rd** (W) and **Rectory Lane** (E), this includes the area's biggest cache of modern homes, built on the ex-Tooting Bec Hospital site. Fairview re-christened this swathe between **Tooting Bec Rd**, **Franciscan Rd**, **Mantilla Rd** and **Church Lane** 'Heritage Park': it contains a mix of everything from studio flatlets to 4/5-bed houses, beginning with a handsome crescent. It has proved very popular with buyers, with those who got in early seeing big uplifts. Local agents warn that the homes vary markedly: check position and aspect with care. One-bed flats start at £180,000, 2-beds at £230,000, while a 4-bed, 3-bath town house in the crescent was £475,000 last winter. The second phase, at the N end, goes under the name Heritage Gate: 12 houses and 234 flats, including some for the over-60s ('Doulton Place'). This new district has children's' nursery, medical centre etc.

This corner also holds an earlier, innovative, development – the delightfully named Totterdown Fields (streets between **Derinton Rd** and **Cowick Rd**), which has the distinction of being the first cottage council estate in the world – started in 1903. A pity, some say, councils didn't stick to this style: now a conservation area, the 1,200 houses are an 'olde-worlde' mixture of red-brick and grey stucco. They were designed in four grades, from 'first class' to 'fourth class': the latter are 3-room flats.

To the N, close to Tooting Bec tube, the corner N of **Foulser Rd** is smartening up and becoming a tad bohemian: the red-brick Victorian terraces are colourfully painted. There's Edwardian and '30s in **Lynwood Rd**; more cottage-council in **Topsham Rd**. An ex-army building in **Brudenell Rd** has been smartly converted into ten 2-bed flats.

South of the Totterdown Fields comes more century-old streets of 3-bed houses and purpose-built maisonettes (spot these in the ads by the words 'own front door'). **Vant Rd** has modern maisonettes at the S end. **Franciscan Rd**, running S through the neighbourhood from **Tooting Bec Rd** to **Mitcham Rd**, is mainly period with a few modern 'pockets' – the latest at the Common end. At its N end is **Barringer Square**, yellow 7-storey flats surrounded by smaller, pleasant, brown-brick blocks, with a communal garden for residents. **Bruce Hall Mews** is a small, smart clutch of 20 houses and flats around a courtyard and **Groomfield Close** is '80s maisonettes opposite the church. St Benedict's, in the triangle between **Mitcham Rd**, **Rectory Lane** and **Church Lane**, is popular; built mainly by Laing in 1984, it's made pleasant by trees and landscaping, and has off-street parking. It has spacious 1-, 2- and 3-bed houses and flats.

Furzedown

Running between **Links Rd** to the S, **Rectory Lane**, **Thrale Rd** and **Mitcham Lane**, Furzedown is filled with Edwardian/Victorian homes popular with families, plus some students' halls of residence for the London Institute and St George's Medical School. No tube nearby, so prices tend to be lower than elsewhere in Tooting. As a rule of thumb pay £100,000 a bedroom for Furzedown houses, ten thousand a room more for really smart ones, but less than the benchmark if scruffy. However the popular Graveney and Penwortham schools lift prices in adjacent streets. The feel is generally a bit down-market compared to Tooting Bec. Approximately half is counted as Tooting – the area S of **Southcroft Rd** plus **Crowborough Rd, Idlecombe Rd, Salterford Rd** and **Freshwater Rd.** The remainder is thought of as Streatham – which chapter see.

B **Southcroft Rd** has at its eastern end older terraces (£240,000 for a 2-bed house), giving way as you go W to post-war rows on the right and a series of pleasant 2-storey ex-council red-brick flats on the left. On the corner of **Nimrod Rd** is a low-rise block of modern flats. Both sides of **Southcroft Rd** are flats. Ditto **Freshwater Rd** and roads off. We regain Victorian terraces at the W end of **Southcroft Rd** and adjoining roads running to the N, parallel with **Mitcham Rd**.

The borough boundary runs E–W between **Southcroft Rd** and **Seely Rd**, along the course of the River Graveney. **Seely Rd** and **Links Rd**, running parallel, have identical terraces of solid, deep-porched turn-of-the-century houses. East of the junction with **Eastbourne Rd**, however, **Seely Rd** changes to less appealing, and often badly modernized, 20th-century terraces (£270,000 for a 3-bed) and then to bay-windowed, gabled homes. Running between **Seely Rd** and **Links Rd** are orderly rows of uniform terraces. Their regimentation is reflected in the road names, which run alphabetically from 'A' (for **Ascot Rd**) to 'J' (for **Jersey Rd**). The only breaks in the regularity are the striking Links Primary School and the modern orange-brick flats of St Andrews Hall at S end of **Hailsham Rd** – horribly inappropriate amongst such general order. **Vectis Gardens** surrounds a small rectangle of fenced-off grass. The whole section has an air of well-cared-for, quiet suburbia. The S side of **Links Rd** backs onto the railway. Over the tracks in **Bruce Rd**, close to Tooting station, newly-built Stanley Court has a few flats left: 1-beds £185,000, 2-beds £225,000.

Tooting Graveney

West of Furzedown is Tooting Graveney, named after the Gravenel family who owned the manor in the 12th century. This, bounded by the Wimbledon–Streatham railway to the S, **Tooting High St** to the W and **Mitcham Rd** to the N, is the cheaper end of Tooting. First-time buyers hunt here, not worrying too much about its prevailing scruffiness.

At the E end of **Longley Rd** there is a small block of red-brick flats/houses on the right – Kilmarnock Court – with a play-area for the kids. Handsome Victorian terraces continue left and right, plus some later-period houses on the right. The railway runs behind the S side of **Longley Rd**. The area to the N is a maze of period terraces and maisonettes with modern infills. **Bickersteth Rd**, leading N from **Longley Rd**, contains a veritable cocktail of architecture in places, and thus looks a little ragged. **Otterburn St** (off **Byton Rd**) has well-cared-for large mock-Tudor houses opposite Edwardian maisonettes. The school in **Selincourt Rd** (Infants and Junior) stands among terraced maisonettes (generally 2/3-bed: pay c. £235,000). These provide a popular source of often rented homes; also found in **Trevelyan Rd. Mellison Rd** and **Trevelyan Rd** encompass a small conservation area: a handful of semi- and detached houses built of flint, in South Downs style, in the 1870s.

Central Tooting

Across the A24 (here **Tooting High St**), **Garratt Lane** leading W from Tooting Broadway tube is lined with large, flat-fronted, period, semi-detached houses (first few with front gardens) and smaller terraces. Parking is a big problem on this main road and larger properties have the usual uneasy mixture of garden and parking space. Smaller terraces without gardens on the left side have, however, garages behind in **Garratt Terrace**. Opposite these garages is a long row of Victorian 2-storey houses, curving round to **Tooting High St** (resembling a pale imitation of the Royal Crescent, Bath). These include some flat conversions. A few smart modern houses stand at the top on the left. Roads to the S of **Garratt Terrace** have similar rows of period housing, but modern maisonettes appear in **Recovery St** and smart-looking '30s flats in **Tooting Grove**. Quaint cottagy terraces line **Aldis** and **Carwell Sts. Aldis Mews** was a 1980s development.

Blackshaw Rd, SW of St George's Hospital, has smart 2/3-bed Edwardian terraces – these tend to be cheaper as they're next to Lambeth Cemetery. Anderson House (1931) on the corner of **Fountain Rd** is a handsome-looking 3-storey ex-local authority block of red- and cream-brick flats. An archway in the block leads through to a public recreation ground. More Victorian terraces in **Fountain Rd**, plus some earlier flat-fronted 2-storey stucco houses (perhaps the cheapest houses around here at £225,000). **Cranmer Terrace**, off **Fountain Rd**, leads to Tooting Gardens – a small park with swings, etc – quite a surprise among such intensive housing. Period terraces lie W of **Fountain Rd**, some quite quaint: for instance the cottage rows of **Bertal Rd. Alston Rd** has Edwardian terraces. **Hazelhurst Rd** has a school (Smallwood Junior and Infants) and the imposing grey concrete of the Hazelhurst council estate. **Greaves Place**, E of **Fountain Rd**, holds the striking 'geometrics' of Tooting Leisure Centre (swimming, gym, etc).

The Bell Estate and Upper Tooting

The Bell Estate, to the W of **Upper Tooting Rd**, belonged to an old family trust that was developed during the 1930s and '40s by the Bell in question. Comprising **Fishponds Rd, Ansell Rd, Hebdon Rd** and **Lingwell Rd**, its neat 3/4-bed terraced houses are now popular with families (especially as some house prices still start with a two) and convenient for Tooting Bec tube station. It is a stable community with a low turnover of properties: agents rate it 'desirable'. Houses in **Ansell Rd** have small roof extensions. **Lingwell Rd** and **Hebdon Rd** tend to be slightly cheaper as they back onto Springfield Hospital (built as Surrey County Lunatic Asylum, 1840s) and Streatham Cemetery respectively. **Holmbury Court**, at the N end of **Fishponds Rd**, has uninspiring maisonettes. **Fishponds Rd** itself has the occasional Edwardian property.

The roads between **Broadwater Rd** and **Garratt Lane** have Victorian terraces, most of which have been painted, giving a multi-coloured effect to the streets. Endearing cottage terraces at the E end of **Graveney Rd**, and modern maisonettes opposite the junction with **Selkirk Rd. Graveney Rd** has a new gated development: five 3-bed houses from £330,000 – the same money buys a Victorian 3-bed house in the same street. Ungainly semi-detached maisonettes line **Rogers Rd** and the top of **Broadwater Rd** as it turns E to the A24. On the corner of **Rogers Rd** and **Garratt Lane** stands Bellamy House: council flats, stylish in red-brick and white detail.

Glenburnie Rd on the other, northern, side of the Bell Estate has mainly smart Edwardian homes, but on the S side of **Beechcroft Rd** are some large, attractive, mock-Tudor detached houses. These have been joined, in the angle of the two roads, by Barratt's gated 'Trinity Square': handsome, pedimented Georgian-style 3-bed/3-bath town-houses and 4-bed/3-bath houses set around a garden complete with fountain. A further development, Bellway's **Chancery Mews**, has added 37 more houses. Then there's **Pavilion Square**: yet another gated clutch of 3- and 4-bed town-houses and flats. The houses came onto the market at £690,000, but settled down at around £600,000. **Beeches Rd** has pleasant red-brick terraces (Victorian), plus less special, small, beige-brick maisonettes (c. 1983). To the left is **Parkhill Court** – an impressive '30s block of large 2/3-bed flats.

The roads between **Trinity Rd** and **Beechcroft Rd**, to the N of the Bell Estate, are part of a conservation area filled with large, appealing Victorian properties lining leafy streets. Red-brick dominates, although **Brodrick Rd** has some lovely Georgian-style 3-storey stucco houses. **Crockerton Rd** and **Dalebury Rd** have stately red brick courtesy of the Heaver brothers. Modern flats at S end of **Crockerton Rd.** Ernest Bevan School is opposite in **Beechcroft Rd.** To the N of the school is the College Gardens Estate, built 1983: an attractive clutch of 1/2-bed houses and flats similar to Balham's

Ashdown Way, but slightly cheaper as further from the Northern Line tube.

At the N end of **Trinity Rd**, where it crosses into Wandsworth, are shops and restaurants facing a playing field. Then, going S, come impressive mid-19th-century flat-fronted stucco terraces and houses. Victorian red-brick continues. Tooting Bec fire station and police station are close to the junction with **Trinity Crescent**, one of the most expensive roads in the area with fine mid-19th-century stucco houses of 7/8-beds and large gardens: people have asked £1.5 to £2 million for these. Impressive mansion flats on the right-hand side. **Holderness Rd** has mock-Tudor houses, terraced and semi-detached, and the faithful Victorian terrace reappears in **Chetwode Rd**.

Transport Tubes: Balham, Tooting Bec, Tooting Broadway (zone 3, Northern) direct to City, Charing Cross, Waterloo. From Tooting Bec: Oxford Circus 30 min (1 change), City 30 min, Heathrow 1 hr 30 min (1 change). Trains: Balham to Victoria 15 min; Tooting to London Bridge, Blackfriars 20 mins.

Convenient for South Coast, Gatwick and tube into town. Miles from centre: 5.

Schools Local Authority: Graveney, Ernest Bevin (b), Burntwood (g). Private: Upper Tooting High, La Retraite RC (g), Streatham Hill & Clapham High (g).

SALES

Flats	S	1B	2B	3B	4B	5B
Average prices	100–180	120–250	180–350+	200–350+	250–400+	–
Houses	2B	3B	4B	5B	6/7B	8B
Average prices	200–400+	250–450+	300–1M+	→	→2M	–

RENTAL

Flats	S	1B	2B	3B	4B	5B
Average prices	130–200	190–250	190–300	230–430	300–600	–
Houses	2B	3B	4B	5B	6/7B	8B
Average prices	200–375	255–425	255–600	325–600+	400–800	–

The properties Balham is Victorian, Tooting Edwardian/'30s, with a (very) few older homes in both. Terraced houses of all sizes (including some very large, as in Heaver), plus conversions and some p/b flats. Inter-war suburban homes, areas of '80s, '90s and current 'developer' housing and a rash of smart new flats.

The market Buyers have traditionally been first-timers plus families seeking big, more affordable homes. Nightingale Triangle and Heaver Estate, and now a swathe of new homes, are popular for big, even grand, houses. New flats and mews bring cool to Balham; Tooting Broadway is cheaper, more cosmopolitan: a more local market.

Among estate agents active in this area are:

- Douglas & Gordon
- Barnard Marcus
- Jacksons
- Heaver
- Winkworth
- Ludlow Thompson
- Bells
- Haart
- Nightingale Estates
- J Hollingsworth
- Vanstons
- Courtenay
- Kinleigh Folkard & Hayward
- C James
- Lauristons
- Bushells
- John G Dean

BARNES, MORTLAKE AND SHEEN

Postal districts: SW13, SW14
Boroughs: Richmond upon Thames (Con)
Council tax: Band D £1,339
Conservation areas: Include Barnes Pond, Green and Common, Mortlake Green
Parking: Controlled zones N and S of Church St and in North Barnes; meters on High St

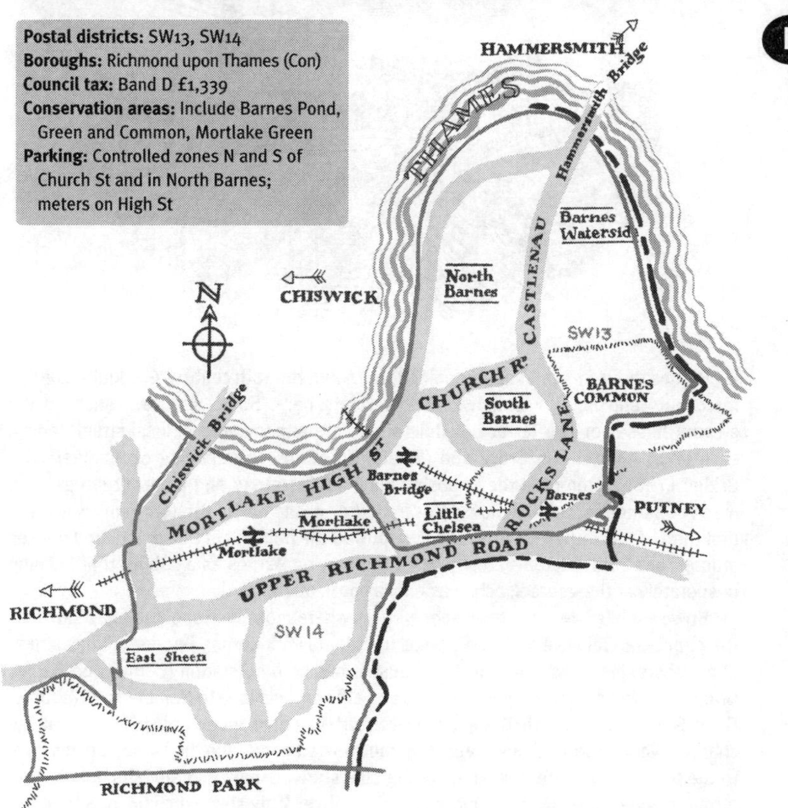

Fly in to Heathrow, look down and you will see the point of Barnes. The meandering Thames snaking up to coil protectively round it on three sides, green parks and commons almost completing the circle on the other make the attractions obvious. Look more closely, and two further points catch the airborne eye: the swirling patterns of water and marshland at the superb Wetland Centre, and the scarcity of road bridges across the encircling Thames.

Were it not for the road congestion and the lack of a tube, this would be the ideal London location. Barnes is a recognizable village still, with much open space and a continuous riverside towpath. Mortlake, another ex-village lining the river bank to the W, is more built-up. Sheen, away from the river, borders Richmond Park and adjoining commons – the great green tract that defines the whole area to the south.

Barnes

Here – a stone's throw across the bridge from busy, noisy Hammersmith – we are in bourgeois heaven: river, green spaces, pretty houses (from cottage to mansion), interesting shops and atmospheric pubs. . . . Barnes, some feel, even for this idyll, goes just a little over the top with its village duck pond – never mind the W I market (Fridays), the farmers' market (Saturdays) and a Common Warden to keep it all neat.

Barnes thrived on market gardening throughout the 18th century. Gradually, London merchants and nobility built weekend retreats here. Some survive – such as the elegant houses of **The Terrace** – while others are remembered in local street names, such as **St Anne's, Elm Grove** and **Ranelagh Avenue**. The opening of Hammersmith Bridge in 1827 prompted the imposing villas of **Castelnau** and adjacent streets, but much of Barnes as we see it now dates from the second half of the 19th century and the first third of the 20th, when the railways spurred the building of those 'little red houses in long rows' which led a 1920s novelist to describe Barnes as a suburb that, 'aiming desperately at the genteel, achieves only a sordid melancholy'.

However, later decades have seen virtues where more metropolitan ages saw only the mundane. Only five and a half miles from Hyde Park Corner, Barnes still has a rural atmosphere: locals say that this is because it has no tube station (Barnes and Barnes Bridge rail stations make up for this, plus an efficient bus lane to Hammersmith's tube). Once S of Hammersmith Bridge, however, urban grime gives way to Surrey-village charm, complete with village green, that much-loved pond (one thousand families gave to the appeal to restore it when it sprung a mysterious leak) and au pairs pushing all-terrain buggies. (The local fishmonger has a notice: 'only six pushchairs at a time'.)

Barnes is indeed a family favourite. Leafy riverside walks, more than 100 acres of its own pretty common, Leg of Mutton Reservoir (NW) where swans breed, award-winning Barn Elms Wetland Centre, with all kinds of aquatic wildlife. . . and Kew Gardens, Richmond at its foot, are close. And, key to life here, there are good local schools: St Paul's (boys) in Lonsdale Rd; Godolphin & Latymer (girls), Latymer Upper (boys) and St Paul's (girls) in nearby Hammersmith. The Swedish School (again in Lonsdale Rd) draws in expatriate and diplomatic families. The Harrodian School (independent, 4–16-year-olds) is just along the same road. The German School in Petersham is not far off. Richmond borough's own schools achieve good ratings in the league tables, especially at primary level, and there's a popular Church of England secondary, Christ's, where East Sheen meets Richmond.

There are a few black spots. One penalty of living 30 minutes' drive from Heathrow is some aircraft noise – an effective pressure group, supported by a local MP, monitors problems. Alternate use of the N and S runways at Heathrow ensures occasional relief, but inhabitants pray for an east wind, which removes the planes entirely. The building of Terminal 5 at Heathrow, and the threat of a third runway, is raising the temperature of this debate; locals predict yet more planes, yet longer hours. Back on the ground, remember that only four roads lead into Barnes across its ramparts of river, greenery and rail-lines.

The real point about Barnes is the wide range of its family homes. Unusually, it has a good number of 5- to 8-bed houses – but coveted locations near river or common mean prices can top £2.5 million. The best houses sell fast, often without involving agents or appearing on the open market.

Smaller Victorian or Edwardian terraced family houses, though, form the bulk. They greatly outnumber flats or maisonettes – though new developments are adding to these. Larger flats can be found in purpose-built blocks, especially those with prime locations close to Hammersmith Bridge and the blocks beside the river in the village, such as Elm Bank Mansions. But the usually ubiquitous 2-bed flat conversion is rare in Barnes.

The most enviable streets are **Castelnau, The Terrace, Lonsdale Rd, Woodlands, The Crescent, Vine Rd** and some of **Station Rd**. But there are desirable homes everywhere, with peaceful, leafy locations more than compensating for those that boast only humdrum architecture. Values fall somewhat where properties are near the rail line – though the cottages of rail-begirt 'Little Chelsea' seem expensive enough. In the last decade The Waterside development on the old filter beds site (see below) has added a new district of several dozen lovely, spacious detached villas to the top end of the market, plus some handsome town-houses, also apartments; and the Harrods Village scheme (again detailed below) further boosted the supply of upmarket flats.

Actors and writers of the more successful sort find Barnes congenial, and the new developments in the N of the area attract an international/City clientele. One and all, though, newcomers join long-serving locals in defending Barnes's 'village' status. The whole area benefits from an abnormally active, well-supported community association, which is behind the Green and pond warden scheme (a vacancy, at time of writing) and much else. The typical newcomer starts in a mansion flat or Little Chelsea cottage, and trades up to a family home. Schools tend to lock families into the area; many homes sell to locals, though City money increasingly makes its presence felt. Once the bonuses stack up, there are elegant early Victorian, gravel-drived villas in **Castelnau**. . . .

The High Street was one of the first in SW London to regain good local butchers, cheese shops, delis etc – but now seems a little tired and run down; the chi-chi shops are round the corner in Church Rd or have migrated to the quieter White Hart Lane on the Mortlake side. However, neither Barnes nor Mortlake goes in for chain stores or formula coffee bars: look to Sheen or Richmond for those.

North Barnes; Castelnau

Castelnau – a boulevard named after the French lands of the Boilieu family, once the landowners here – forms the spine of Barnes, leading S from Hammersmith Bridge via **Rocks Lane** down to the **Upper Richmond Rd**, with **Church Rd** forming the rough divide between the N and S neighbourhoods of Barnes. The large 1840s semi-detached villas of **Castelnau** are set well back; driveways and trees mask them from the road, which has a well-policed and well-used N-bound bus lane (fast rides to Hammersmith and the tube). Early Victorian styles (not Regency, whatever the estate agents say) near the bridge lead down to later double-fronted, tall-gabled houses towards the Red Lion pub (junction of **Rocks Lane/Church Rd**). The double-fronted monsters are not often on the market, though a 7-bed was £2.5 last autumn. The later, still big, Victoriana ranges from £1.25 million (5-bed) upwards. Right at the N end of Castelnau, by the bridge, a well-placed clutch of Edwardian mansion blocks lurks in **Riverview Gardens** and **Clavering Avenue**: a 3-bed flat on a long lease might be £400–450,000; a bit more for a river view. Next S is **Arundel Terrace**: Victorian cottages and, for lower-priced flats, some 1960s blocks: c. £280,000 will buy a 2-bed here, or in The Spinney – pleasant brick '60s flats set well back from Castelnau. Off Castelnau Place is **Fielding Mews**, with nicely detailed '80s 2-storey mews houses.

Across the main road, **Trinity Church Rd** leads to an unexpected enclave: the Barnes Waterside estate is an eight-year-old complex of 320 homes on a lovely, hidden 34-acre site E of Castelnau. The S part of the site is the 105-acre nature reserve formed from the

B

old waterworks filter beds. In this suddenly airy, open setting, along **Wyatt Drive** are terraces, a crescent (Regency in style, as far as the ironwork goes) and enviably large sub-Palladian villas that are priced to compete with **Castelnau**, plus blocks of flats overlooking the Thames. These, (disappointingly, given this site) form a dull rampart; behind them, several stand-alone blocks seem to take their architectural inspiration from century-old Peabody housing. A 2-bed flat might be £335,000 upwards – more for a river view; seven figures for a big penthouse. The water lies to the S, jutting into the site as reed-lined ponds.

Adjoining is the gated **Harrods Village**, complete with little Grecian temple and concierge in green waistcoat. Here are 250 homes: 2000-vintage flats and houses, and the conversion of the giant, looming, faïence-decorated warehouse that recalls the parent store, only marooned amid trees. Two-bed flats can be from £335,000, 3-beds £850,000; penthouses ask £1.5 million. Back in the real world, the once-humble Victorian cottages of **Merthyr Terrace** have been smartly done up to match all this magnificence, which they overlook. Even the allotments have gained posh iron gates.

Next, explore to W of Castelnau: the long sweep of **Lonsdale Rd** boasts more Victorian villas, some with stunning white exteriors and Italianate towers (next to St Paul's playing fields). Some are now flats (1-bed £275,000). Close to the Castelnau end, Thirlstone's 5-bed houses were £1 million when new in 2002; the 19th-century versions might be twice that. Octagon are building two big, classy (5-bed/4 recep) villas and four mews houses opposite St Paul's; prices in the £800,000–£2.2 million band. **St Hilda's Rd** leads off to a couple of streets of small-scale terraces (N side of **Lilian Rd** the prettiest; a 2-bed cottage £430,000) in a peaceful corner bounded by St Paul's School grounds. Two commercial sites in **Glentham Rd** here look set to become flats and offices. As **Lonsdale Rd** follows the river's curve, a variety of homes face open land on the riverside – some low council-built flats, '30s and Edwardian (5-beds, £800,000–£1 million plus) houses – down to the Bull's Head pub and **The Terrace** – of which more below.

Lonsdale Rd and **Castelnau** are linked by a lattice of streets – including **Suffolk Rd**, double-width **Nassau Rd, Lowther Rd, Westmoreland Rd** and **Baronsmead Rd** – where buyers hunt hard for a range of 3- to 5-bed, £800,000-plus family houses; a mix of Edwardian/'30s/Victorian. Some, in **Nassau Rd** especially, can easily top a million, with a 6-bed last autumn asking £1.4 million – but around **Verdun Rd**/**Barnes Avenue**/ **Stillingfleet Rd** and across to **Boileau Rd** lies a cottagy, 1920s council-built estate: here, 4-bed houses are c. £360-400,000, 3-beds c.£335,000. As Boileau Rd continues S, the council-built homes merge with private-built 1920s semis and short terraces. **Suffolk Rd** and its neighbours offer mixed 1920s–30s suburban homes. Houses get bigger and older once more – and streets leafier – as you go S into the turnings off **Westmoreland Rd. Kitson Rd**, just to the N of Church Rd, has 6-bed Edwardian houses.

South Barnes

South of **Church Rd** (with art gallery, French café, restaurants, greengrocer called 'Two Peas in a Pod'. . .) is what many feel is the heart of family-home Barnes: a grid of Victorian houses bounded to S and W by the Common. These come in various styles: some, in **Glebe Rd** and its neighbours, are in gothicky, square-bayed red brick, boasting stone lions on balconies and rooftops (just like those found in Fulham's Peterborough Estate). These are among the most requested local homes: a 6-bed was £1.4 million last autumn. A linked pair of Lion houses in **Hillersden Avenue** was £3.6 million in the autumn. Other houses are in 'tudorbethan' style, or – in **Ranelagh Avenue** facing the common – tall 3-storey, £2-million-plus terraces. **Bellevue Rd, Rectory Rd** (2-storey terraced homes) and **Elm Grove Rd** lead onto the Common, and have a touch of Little Venice as Beverley Brook passes beneath them. To the W **Laurel Rd** and **The Crescent** branch on to the Green; the W end of the latter having views across the pond (a 'rarely available, needs refurb' 4-bed was £1.2 million late last year). Back on **Church Rd**, an Edwardian detached house sold for £3.4 million last summer.

Wonderfully isolated amid a wild bit of Common is **Mill Hill**: a clutch of cottages, a pair of Victorian villas . . . and a beautiful, big, painstakingly restored 7-bed Regency house: £3.5 million when it came up for sale a while back in winter 2003.

West of Barnes Green is **Station Rd**; overlooking the pond is 17th-century Milbourne House, where Henry Fielding lived. On its way S to the station it holds a mixed bag of handsome Georgian houses, bay-windowed Victorian terraces, workers' flat-fronted cottages; pretty 18th-century cottages and, down close to the common, large and imposing Victorian mansions. On the Common side of the road is a good conversion of the former postal sorting office into art gallery, restaurant, offices and 12 flats.

The corner between **Station Rd** and Barnes Bridge railway line – once the 'wrong' side of the village – is now firmly OK. This is worth exploring: small 2-bed cottages give way to flat-fronted 3-storey houses and 4-bed mid-Victorian semis (c. £800,000) in **Cleveland Rd**, with an outcrop of eight 'Lion' houses (£800–900,000) marooned at the corner of **Cleveland Gardens** (itself with 3-bed terraces at £600–725,000). **Beverley Rd** has 2-bed flats and houses. Then at the end of **Brookwood Avenue** (1920s semis) is a small, neatly-arranged council-built corner of houses and flats and, across the brook via a bridge, **Sheridan Place**, a neat enclave of modern houses built by Lovell. Another enclave – marketed (with truth for once) as 'The Enclave'– is Laing's 2004 clutch of six flats and a 4-bed house, approached via another private bridge over Beverley Brook.

North of Station Rd is **Barnes High St**, which runs down to the river. Laing (again) have just built 21 flats, some with river views, plus 15 Housing Association homes on the old police station site running from the High St right through to **Lonsdale Rd**. Remaining flats were £330–740,000 last autumn. Turn left into wonderful, riverside **The Terrace**, and a sweep of pastel-coloured 18th-century houses – wisteria wrapped around wrought-iron balconies – gives a whiff of Regency Brighton. These rarely change hands, though a 4-bed was £1.25 million, and a 6-bed £3 million, last autumn. Those closest to the rail bridge are a bit less. A recent block near the bridge is named River House. Past Barnes Bridge (said by the unkind to be the ugliest to span the Thames) and the station are **Elm Bank Gardens** (large 4- and 5-bed houses), Elm Bank Mansions (red-brick Edwardian blocks), and more ivy-clad Georgiana. **The Terrace** ends at the White Hart pub; **White Hart Lane** cuts S, marking the boundary with Mortlake. Barnes continues S of the railway crossing down to the **Upper Richmond Rd**, with streets such as **Rosslyn Avenue** offering more early 20th-century homes. **Eleanor Grove** is earlier, with 2-bed flat-fronted terraces.

Back towards the Common, two rail lines converge and frustrate drivers on **Vine Rd** with a pair of level crossings (the S one, the Richmond line, especially busy). The road, though, boasts some handsome, almost countrified homes overlooking a cricket ground. Off it, **The Elms** is a gated enclave, while **Westwood Rd** has pretty 1920s homes. North of the rail lines (and thus close to the station) Vine Rd is bordered by the private, unsurfaced **Scarth Rd**, with its gaunt but spacious Victorian villas sheltering behind a belt of trees.

Little Chelsea

In the V between two railway lines and the river lie **Charles St**, **Thorne St**, **Archway St** and **Westfields Avenue**. The vogue for doing up these 2-bed (some run to three) cottages was apparently started by a Polish builder in the '60s. His wife saw the potential of the area, comparing the brewery workers' homes with their mewsy counterparts in Chelsea. An irregular style – they were added to as the Victorian workforce grew – makes them less stately than their namesakes, but prettier. Extensive renovation means some have an extra bedroom or conservatory, and are priced accordingly. Prices are little changed from last year: 2-beds start around £300,000, but smart/secluded/extended/3-bed ones go up to £450,000. Skirting the area are **Thorne Passage** and **Beverley Path** – reached on foot (the railways preclude driving in anyway); cottages here are smaller or have the Hounslow loop rail line running behind their garden – factors which may give a discount. The same drawback applies to the **Railwayside** cottages, though their line is the busier. **Westfields**, also reached from the W via a path, has 3- and 4-storey council-built 1950s flats (2-beds remain c. £200,000) plus the highly rated Westfields primary school on its pretty site. The Little Chelsea streets run up to White Hart Lane, the border with Mortlake.

B

Mortlake

Best known as the end of the Oxford and Cambridge Boat Race (rowed upstream from Putney), Mortlake is historically more important than Barnes. Brewing has been a local industry since the 15th century, and a large modern brewery still dominates the river bank towards Chiswick Bridge. The boundary with Barnes to the E is the postal district, with Barnes in SW13 and Mortlake in SW14. **White Hart Lane** marks the border and has a range of interesting shops – more villagy than Barnes High St, though the pub is now a 'café/bar/restaurant' full of mummies and babies, and the shops are chi-chi designer. The railway line hems Mortlake in to the S: some of its prettier homes are unfortunately closest to the busy line. White Hart Lane itself has some little 3-bed Victorian houses and some 3-storey ones, many divided into flats (2-beds range from £230–265,000) but asking £600,000-ish when intact and done-up.

Large houses are scarce, but there are plenty of modest terraces and some pretty cottages. The more expensive streets are **First** and **Second Avenues**, with **Cowley**, **Ashleigh** and **Victoria Rds** also popular. Riverside houses rate the highest prices. The **High St** along the river has many large and interesting flats, some in council-built blocks.

There are gems in Mortlake for those who care to look – particularly the cottages of varying sizes in the network of paths and lanes close to the old parish church: **Church Path**, **Fitzgerald Rd**, **Victoria Rd**, **James Terrace** (2-bed cottage, £325,000). **Wrights Walk** has larger cottages with unusually big gardens; **Worple St** has tiny flat-fronted cottages facing a Catholic primary school and a convent; **Ripley Gardens** has 1914 terraces. **Rosemary Cottages** (a row of pretty ex-almshouses: £340,000 for a 2-bed) is sandwiched between blocks of flats and overlooks Mortlake station. Off the **High St**, which belies its name, **Cowley**, **Ashleigh** and **Avondale Rds** are mostly Edwardian terraces with 2-bed flats. Cowley Mansions has a range of flats from 1- to 3-bed (£180–310,000). It's worth noting that homes along **North Worple Way** face the railway.

The green and the area to E and W are a conservation area. **Tideway Yard**, on the river near the White Hart pub, is a good redevelopment of an old refuse depot/power station. There are offices in a courtyard, and a busy riverside wine bar, plus 18 new-build riverside flats. A handsome 18th-century Thames-side house is now flats and offices.

Some rather more recent additions here, too: Dukes Reach is a new, gated Berkeley scheme on the river bank with 26 flats (£240,000 for a 1-bed), most with river views, plus some Affordable Homes; Vineyard Heights has 42 smart, modern flats (2-bed £400,000) in an award-winning converted office tower. **Parliament Mews**, off **Thames Bank**, is a quiet, handsome but unnecessarily gated enclave with smart houses and flats with river views. They share the views with more lovely period homes and pub in this quiet waterfront street, reached past the brewery – its enormous old riverside warehouse must, one day, become flats, surely? Those parking should beware tidal flooding, however. Curve on round and a Georgian riverside house is now seven small houses, accessed from **Varsity Row**. Backing onto **Willows Lane** is the large 1930s Combe House flats block. Overlooking Mortlake Green, a large Victorian building holds flats.

Sheen

East Sheen lies either side of the **Upper Richmond Rd West** (the local name for the ever-busy, red-routed South Circular). To the S are Sheen and Palewell Commons, both of which merge into Richmond Park's rolling acres. In the W, the streets around **Clifford Avenue** and **Derby Rd** blend into Richmond. Sheen may not be as fashionable an address as Barnes or Richmond, but it attracts young families and flat-buyers who enjoy much the same facilities and at rather lower prices. The 1990s saw the start of a generational shift in the area's character, as older people moved away to be replaced by professional-classes families. Once dug in, schools and other ties mean they stay.

East Sheen was a hamlet until around 1900. There is nothing rural about the **Upper Richmond Rd West** today – a sprawl of '30s shops, with supermarkets and restaurants attracting people from both Richmond and Barnes, and flats above the shops and in mansion blocks (budget for £200,000 for a 1-bed, £230,000-plus for a 2-bed). **Sheen Lane** has developed into a useful street of specialist shops. There are opulent houses in the more suburban-feeling tract to the S on the fringes of Richmond Park (with prices to match) and relative bargains on the N, Victorian/Edwardian, Mortlake side.

Between South Worple Way and Upper Richmond Rd West lie **Trehern Rd, Lewin Rd, Kings Rd**, **Princes Rd** and **Queens Rd** (known as The Royals). These are 2-bed cottages that mirror those found in Little Chelsea, but slightly cheaper (2-beds £280,000-plus, 3-beds £330–380,000) and some a little larger. A pretty 2-bed cottage along **South Worple Way** may be less, but all the houses face a main railway line which runs along the N side.

Further W, where **Vernon Rd** joins **Portman Avenue** and **Thornton Rd**, is an area of 3/4-bed Edwardian property. Across Sheen Lane is **St Leonard's Rd** (some pretty mid-Victorian houses), which swings into a curve before meeting **Clifford Avenue** (at this end another pseudonym for the South Circular – and the reason why its 4-bed semis can be suspiciously cheap). At the Sheen Lane end of **St Leonard's Rd** is some 3-storey, semi-detached, flat-fronted Edwardiana, painted in pastel shades, while **Little St Leonard's** and **The Byeway** have some surprisingly large houses, Victorian and later. Despite the railway it is surprisingly quiet. As **Clifford Avenue** goes on towards Chiswick Bridge, there are '30s mansion flats in Chertsey Court at affordable prices (but check the leases).

Behind St Leonard's Rd and Elm Rd is a pathway called **Model Cottages**. These pairs of cottages, their pretty front gardens full of fruit trees and lavender bushes, were built for poor labourers in the 1850s. Many have been extended to provide garages or extra rooms. In the angle formed by the South Circular and St Leonard's Rd is a grid of interesting late Victorian/Edwardian homes: **Graemsdyke Avenue** has quite plain terraced houses made pretty by tiny bay windows; **Holmesdale Avenue** has unusual cottages, with Dutch-style gables, and facing doorways slightly at a slant; **Ormonde Rd** and **Carlton Rd** have grey houses enclosed by white wooden fences. Converted flats are scattered throughout this area, but particularly along **Elm Rd** and **St Leonard's Rd**.

Parkside

South of the Upper Richmond Rd, between **Stanley Rd** (with pretty cottages at the bottom and the Common end) and **Hertford Avenue**, a neighbourhood of leafy roads snakes up to the Common. Roads are typically wide and curving, and houses are semi- or detached with drives. **Stanley Rd** and **Derby Rd** begin, however, with terraced cottages (£340,000 for 2-beds, £430,000 for 3) and '30s blocks. **Deanhill Rd** has Edwardian semis with good gardens; **Coval Rd** more of the same, plus some terraces.

From here on S towards Richmond Park, there's a general rule: the closer to the green spaces, the newer the homes and the higher the prices. Some big old Victorian and early 20th-century houses survive, however, and these are among the most expensive: look along **Fife Rd** and **Christ Church Rd**, which both border Richmond Park, if you want to spend £2 million-plus on a 6-bed. (The latter road has the well-regarded Sheen Mount primary school.) Most Parkside homes, though, date from the 1930s or later. You'll find them in sub-Arts-and-Crafts style, pseudo-Mediterranean with copper-green cupolas, and (most common) what you might call Done-Up Surrey Vernacular.

Note that two new Conservation Areas here will restrict what can be done from now on: too late to add that outsized portico. . . .

B

All gain from proximity to the Park and to Palewell and East Sheen Commons – both of which lead into it. Palewell has tennis courts; there are more off **The Mall** with its distinguished 1920s houses in the grounds of an old country estate. **Vicarage Rd, Stonehill Rd** and **Hood Avenue** have large post-war family houses enjoying the kind of space associated with the Surrey suburbs. **Park Avenue** and **Sunbury Avenue** have smaller, 1930s, semis: less smart, but leafy and quiet; **Hertford Avenue,** which runs from Palewell Common to **Upper Richmond Rd** a range of house sizes, plus two schools. **Enmore Gardens** has smaller homes, some in pretty Arts-and-Crafts-ish terraces. Enmore Court is a big Victorian house, now flats. **Palewell Park** and adjoining roads offer big Edwardian houses. Further N you might pay £550–650,000 for a 4-bed, while grand homes along the park shore command prices above £2 million.

Transport Trains: From Barnes, Barnes Bridge, Mortlake to Waterloo 16–20 min. Tube stations at Hammersmith and Richmond.

Convenient for Richmond Park, River Thames, Kew Gardens. Richmond theatres and shopping. Miles from centre: 6.

Schools Richmond Education Authority: Shene School, Christ's School. Private: Swedish School, St Paul's School (b), Harrodian School.

SALES

Flats	S	1B	2B	3B	4B	5B
Average prices	110–160	180–275	190–700+	250–700+	400+	–
Houses	2B	3B	4B	5B	6/7B	8B
Average prices	250–430+	325–800+	400–1.3M	500–1.95M	850–3M+	→

RENTAL

Flats	S	1B	2B	3B	4B	5B
Average prices	140–180	170–320	210–360	260–400+	330–400+	–
Houses	2B	3B	4B	5B	6/7B	8B
Average prices	270–400	335–475	500–800	675+	900+	–

The properties Charming cottages and 3/4/5-bed terraces; some huge, very early Victoriana in Barnes, also splendid 18th-century and modern riverside homes. Mortlake is more Victorian; smaller houses on the whole. Sheen has Edwardian and other 20th-century homes: cottages via '30s flats to mini-mansions. Wide range of styles and sizes reflected in price bands above: Harrods Village and Waterside homes break out above these ranges.

The market Barnes is the most expensive area, but none is cheap. Media, sporting and political people diluted by European (especially Scandinavians) and US businessmen/diplomats. Sheen is seeing a steady influx of professional families as older residents move on.

Among estate agents active in this area are:

- Featherstone Leigh
- Chesterton
- Friend & Falcke
- Gascoigne Pees
- Boileau Braxton
- Dixon Porter
- Michael Gregory
- James Anderson
- Geoffrey Jardine
- Savills
- Priory Management
- Sargent & Young

BATTERSEA

Postal district: SW11
Borough: Wandsworth (Con)
Council tax: Band D £597
Conservation areas: Numerous – check with town hall
Parking: CPZs around Junction, Battersea Park, Clapham Common; Battersea Village; Red Routes on Battersea Park & Bridge Rds

How much is that view of the river? Is it worth more than twice the view of Battersea Park from a Victorian mansion flat? Or four times the park view if you take the square footage of the flat into account?

Until 2003, the answer was obvious: riverside swank seriously outbid parkside comfort. Investors bit at the bait so glossily offered: the fitness suites, the concierges, the sparkling newness of it all. This year, a more cautious air prevails. Investors are a much-depleted band, now that interest rates have risen. Talk of £1,000 per sq ft – Mayfair prices – for new flats with a busy rail line on one side and a derelict power station at the back, is no longer heard. Last year, we reported a figure of £700 per sq ft, though £800 per sq ft, even in one case £1,000, was still being asked. This year, informed opinion – the agents trying to sell these flats and their competitors – reckons £600, at most £720, is tops. And there are plenty to choose from.

Chelsea Bridge marks the eastern end of this riverside strip of smart and super-smart modern flats, both current and gleam-in-the-eye, which runs all the way to the Wandsworth boundary and beyond. Montevetro, the Richard Rogers-designed glass slab dwarfing the riverside St Mary's Church, has been joined by Norman Foster's curvacious Albion Wharf in **Hester Rd** between Battersea and Albert Bridges, the Berkeley Homes complex mentioned above, Barratt's Oyster Wharf next to the heliport and Wimpey's Falcon Wharf next door. And a dozen or more towers of 'luxury apartments' between Wandsworth Bridge and Battersea Power Station are planned, or building. . . .

There is of course more to Battersea than riverside flats: there are the pleasant terraced houses of all sizes from cottage to ponderous late-Victorian mini-mansion, the sylvan Common-side Edwardiana, the 'lofts' carved out of old factories and schools, the remaining council estates (Wandsworth council has sold quite a few). However most Battersians live in Victorian terraces. Quite a few rent – especially the well-heeled young, drawn here by fast acess to the City and an established population of people-like-us.

The snag with all the Batterseas is transport: there is no tube, the river gets horribly in the way (however useful it is for selling flats) and the rail system, which Battersea relies on to get its working population into Waterloo, creaks under the strain. The railways also add a subtler form of glue to the congestion morass: there are very few road bridges under or over them, making car and bus travel a frustrating experience. That heliport on the river down near Battersea village could be getting a lot busier.

The slick riverside strip is just one of several neighbourhoods. The old village, heart of an interesting mix of (mostly ex-) council homes and neat terraces, is just discernible around pretty, triangular **Battersea Square**, at the top of the old **High Street**. Next, the park: refugees from Chelsea prices bagged the roomy mansion flats around leafy Battersea Park back in the '70s, and these have been an OK address since before most local estate agents were born or thought of. Then there's Clapham Junction, which provides the transport and shopping, and is the hub of a big tract of Victorian houses and flats. Then climb the hill to the S, passing the **Lavender Hill** mob: row upon tight-packed row of terraced Victoriana rise to the shores of Clapham Common. This and Wandsworth Common hem in the 'Between the Commons' tract – or 'Nappy Valley': a heaving anthill of fecund middle-class couples which (urban legend relates) has one of the highest birth rates in Europe. **Northcote Rd**, its heart was, a mere dozen years ago, a large, cheery South London street market: shrunk to a few occasional fruit-and-veg barrows, it now has bars, restaurants and more bars, wine merchants, bespoke tailors and wall-to-wall estate agents. And, inevitably, a café called Boiled Eggs & Soldiers.

If there is one thing that exemplifies the changes here, it's the number of private schools. Prep schools are cheek by jowl along Clapham Common North Side, and more are packed into the streets further south. Fifteen years back, there were none.

Central Battersea and the river

From Clapham Junction station and shopping centre, Falcon Rd leads N into the heartland of Battersea. The original village is to the N, across the York Rd/Battersea Park Rd junction. Off **Falcon Rd** to the E, in a loop formed by a railway embankment, is the conveniently-sited enclave of 'Little India': 3- and 4-bedroom Victorian £380,000-plus terraces with road names straight from the Raj – **Cabul Rd**, **Afghan Rd**, **Khyber Rd** and **Candahar Rd**. Houses on the N side of **Rowena Crescent** are nearest the tracks. **Takhar Mews**, off Cabul Rd, has smart loft-style homes converted from a Victorian school. To the W of **Falcon Rd**, with a fine view of Clapham Junction railway station, are the tower blocks of The Falcons, a '60s council estate bought from Wandsworth Council by Regalian in the '80s and tidied up for sale. Many are rented, but if buying pay £170,000 for a 1-bed (2-beds were half that in 1990). Pool and gym are shared by residents. Eight new flats in 'St Lukes Court', small 2-beds, sold fast in Falcon Rd last autumn. On **Plough Rd**, at the junction of **Grant Rd**, an 11-storey tower with 66 key-worker flats is planned.

Frere St, N of the railway, has some pleasant 2-bed, 3-storey houses and a small terrace of town-houses (with garages). **Abercrombie St** – small late-Victorian terraces, £350–380,000 for a 3-bed – is another Battersea road embraced by a railway. The 1980s town-houses of **Ambrose Mews** also nestle beside the rail line.

To the N of traffic-plagued, restaurant-ridden, Red-Routed **Battersea Park Rd** lies the oldest part of Battersea, a sometimes uneasy mixture of high-rise council estates and conservation areas. At the heart of the 'village' is **Battersea Square** – the charming if choked junction of **Battersea High St** (almost entirely residential at this point), **Vicarage Crescent** and **Westbridge Rd**. The confluence of these three streets in fact make for a Triangle, rather than a Square: either way, it's cobbled and café-tabled. The little brick flat-fronted 3- and 4-bed houses may look early Victorian, but virtually all were reconstructed by a sympathetic developer in the '80s. Most are let. The Dutch-gabled pub, though, is extremely old. Space above some **High St** shops has been turned back to homes: 1- and 2-bed flats. Restoration Square, the latest batch, has flats and six houses, some new, some restored, behind the varied Victorian frontages.

Across the High St to the E, off **Shuttleworth Rd**, is a grid of five streets running S from **Orbel St** – among the most popular in Battersea, but hidden in an impenetrable road system. Agents dub these roads 'The Sisters': if you don't fancy **Edna**, take your pick from **Octavia**, or **Ursula**.... They offer 3- and 4-bed late-Victorian semi-detached houses with creamy gold brickwork at £450–475,000. In **Shuttleworth Rd** are smaller, £260,000 2-bed terraced houses and the 2-bed flats of Burns House. Round on **Bridge Lane**, one of the area's Victorian school conversions offers huge flats: 4,000 sq ft, with 18ft ceilings.

Overlooking the Thames and Chelsea Harbour, Valiant House on **Vicarage Crescent** is a popular block of early '70s brick-built flats. On the other side of **Vicarage Crescent**, still overlooking the river, are some of Battersea's oldest buildings – including the early 18th-century Devonshire House, and Old Battersea House which dates from 1699.

'Battersea Village', at the junction of **Vicarage Crescent** and **Lombard Rd**, is a pre-war estate of brick-built flats, pleasantly set around courtyards, that was sold by the council to Regalian in the 1980s. Across the road, Groveside Court is an '80s block of flats and maisonettes. Riverside, yes. Good-sized flats, yes – but buy at the end away from the Channel Tunnel freight line (paying c. £365,000 for a 2-bed). Inland, Windsor Court is a charming conversion of an old school. The Fred Wells Garden is an asset to this corner, with playground and tennis court.

Westbridge Rd, another conservation area, has some attractive early-Victorian villas and the pretty, late-18th-century Battersea Laundry (close to the junction with **Battersea High St**): now flats with a (small) outdoor swimming pool. It fronts the high-rise Surrey Lane Estate, whose towers gave planners the excuse to allow the building of Montevetro (see below) on the riverbank behind. The Somerset Estate, across the road, has a fairly high owner-occupier rate and offers 2-and 3-bed split-level flats at £200–220,000.

And so back to the river. Either side of the **Vicarage Crescent** area, the entire Battersea riverside from Wandsworth Bridge to Albert Bridge is alive with homes developments, replacing the old industrial wasteland. These run the gamut: the imaginative, the sadly pedestrian, the gross – in design, bulk and relationship to the river. As yet, the infrastructure – shops, places to eat – lags behind the homes in many cases. Apply the famous 'pint of milk' test and many fail – unless you get the car out.

One of the first and nicest schemes was **Plantation Wharf**, built in the late '80s halfway between Wandsworth Bridge and the heliport: a large and attractive mix of business and residential to create, in effect, an entire new village with Thames-side flats (2-bed £380–395,000), £950,000 penthouses and 4-bed 'atelier' work-homes. Further S, Riverside Plaza off **Chatfield Rd** has 74 flats, while Mendip Court in **Mendip Rd**, just inland, has among its flats a remarkable apartment with its own gym and cinema. To the N of Plantation Wharf, the riverside end of the Price's Candles factory has been replaced by 118 flats, all sold. Back on **York Rd**, 'the Horizon Building' is new: 1- and 2-beds £310–325,000, with shared roof terrace and parking underground. Wimpey are marketing the 'Candlemakers' scheme: loft-style flats £380–650,000.

Between the heliport and the railway bridge, **Lombard Rd** bounds riverside Grove Wharf, where Barratt are building 149 flats (125 for sale, the balance shared-ownership) in Oyster Wharf, due to be finished by early 2005. These flats are reckoned smaller than those of competitors, and prices have been 'soft': re-sales of 2-beds can be had at less than £400,000. Wimpey's Falcon Wharf scheme next door is a cruciform-plan 17-storey block with 124 flats, each with a glazed 'winter garden', ready by 2006 – no prices yet.

Back N of Battersea Square, **Battersea Church St** swings down to the river and one of the gems of the area, the Grade I-listed parish church of St Mary's, built in 1777 but with origins back to Domesday. Its fate is now to be flanked by modern slabs: white-rendered Old Swan Wharf to the S (penthouse £1.1 million), reasonable in scale – to the N, where once the great manor house stood, Lord Rogers' Montevetro 'statement' tower, rears its wedge-shaped head, stepping down to the church from its 18-storey height. A 2-bed flat, £600,000 – or (much) more. Its mass cuts off vistas with, inland, custard-coloured cladding rather more in evidence than glass. Early talk of a jetty and river buses has evaporated, and can now be seen as the marketing hype that it was.

A return to a more family, domestic scale can be found in earlier schemes like the 1970s flats and houses of successful Morgan's Walk next to Battersea Bridge (which was just about the first). Street names in this gated estate include riverside **Thorney Crescent** and **Whistler's Avenue**. Stanton Gate on **Battersea Church Rd** added some 5-bedroomed modern houses to the area.

The riverside tract across **Battersea Bridge Rd** to the E is the stamping ground of that other architectural eminence, Lord Foster. His company plans a new office scheme fronting **Battersea Bridge Rd** and flanked by **Howie St** and **Hester Rd.** This would house the architects themselves, who at present luxuriate in a glass-walled riverside box, Riverside One, which originally had some £1.8 million-ish flats and will now gain ten more (the change-of-use application was successful). These join the next-door (again, Foster-designed) monster 11-storey, but comfortably curving, futuristic Albion Riverside block of 190 flats. There are 45 Affordable Housing flats in a lower building behind its inward-sloping back. As well as flats, there are offices, shops, restaurants and, naturally, a leisure centre. A 2-bed might be £850,000, or £950,000. At least for that you get a view of Chelsea, not Fulham.

East of Albion comes the **Ransome's Dock** area: this L-shaped dock was pleasingly restored in 1991, with new dock gates plus bridge to carry the riverside walk: it now shelters some 'interesting' boats. Most of the land around the dock has been redeveloped: Lord Foster's plate-glass palace guards one side of the entrance. Across the dock, Waterside Point runs along the river with houses inland; flats including vast penthouses (£4 million-plus; own swimming-pools) on the river, inland ones at six-figure prices and some 3/4-bed houses. Another block better to look out of than at. And finally, Albert Bridge House added another 30 flats and penthouses to the tally in 1999.

Battersea Park

Between Albert and Chelsea Bridges, the riverside oasis of Battersea Park, laid out by spacious-minded Victorians, is at least inalienable. The favoured **Prince of Wales Drive** late-Victorian mansion flats run the entire length of the park. Service charges can be high, and there have been problems in the past with maintenance bills, so leaseholders got together as the law changed and bought out their landlords. Today, virtually all flats are sold with a share in the freehold of their block. The flats often have balconies from which to enjoy the park views; best of all are those with sweeping windows in the corner turrets. Here you can find 4-double-bed flats that make the new ones on the river look poky. The best block is York Mansions (the only one with a lift), followed by Overstrand. Cyril Mansions has well-kept communal gardens. Pay around £215–285,000 for a 1-bed, £325–375,000 for 2-beds, £550–625,000 for those 4-beds. Behind are more such blocks in **Lurline Gardens** and **Warriner Gardens.** Roads leading off, like **Soudan Rd, Alexandra Avenue** and **Kassala Rd**, feature big 3-storey, 4- to 7-bed red-brick houses.

The 200 acres of Battersea Park offers an art gallery, children's zoo, lake, running track, tennis courts and the splendid Peace Pagoda, gift of Japanese Buddhists.

On the other side of traffic-plagued **Battersea Park Rd** lie the high-rise Doddington and Rollo council-built estates. One tower block was in the late '80s sold off to developers and renamed Park South and another, Park Court, was comprehensively refitted by the council, who sold the flats as starter homes. Now, Park South residents enjoy 24-hour porterage and sports facilities. The blocks still loom, however. Turpin House, on the corner of **Queenstown Rd**, has been smartened up. On **Battersea Park Rd** itself, an old school is now 'Lofthaus': 29 lofts (2-beds c. £450,000) and live/work units. A business centre in the street is to become 57 new flats, 14 affordable.

The mansion flats that run most of the length of **Albert Bridge Rd** face E, thus benefiting from more light (but also more traffic) than **Prince of Wales Drive**, and they too overlook the park. Best blocks are probably Albert and Albany, but all are popular. Council-built blocks lie just to the rear. **Parkgate Rd** runs between **Albert** and **Battersea Bridge Rds**, with large plain 3-storey houses, mainly converted to flats. On the corner of **Anhalt Rd** and **Albert Bridge Rd**, Prince Regent House is five recent flats.

Back on the riverside, the landmark Battersea Power Station is a site with a history all right. The 1980s grand plan to transform it and its 35 acres into a massive fantasy-land leisure centre turned out itself to be a fantasy. Despite 12 years of subsequent ownership by Hong Kong-based group Parkview International, the 'upside-down table' remains sadly open to the elements (though the owners insist it is 'stable').

A flurry of action last autumn led to approval of some revised plans (the planning history of this site is a book in itself) and announcements by Parkview that tenants have been found for 20% of the space. Parkview have planning consent for two hotels, flats, a 4,400-seat multiplex cinema plus one or two theatres, a post-production film studio, smart shops ('more Knightsbridge than Oxford St'). A legal agreement insists the developer will undertake complete restoration of the Grade II-listed power station and build a new rail station, before any part of the scheme is occupied. Latest plans show 655 flats, including some work/live, in two buildings at the SE corner of the site, away from the river. Completion date? '2008' (this time last year it was '2007'). Watch this space.

Other developers work to a less glacial timescale. On the river, neatly sandwiched between Chelsea Bridge and the Grosvenor rail bridge (which takes all the trains into Victoria), Berkeley Homes is finishing its major scheme at Battersea Wharf (marketed as Chelsea Bridge Wharf – memo to developers, get Chelsea into the name wherever possible). There are 700 flats (166 Affordable Homes), hotel, offices, cinemas, shops, restaurants and a health club. The five buildings range from 9–12 storeys in height. Sample prices last winter: 1-bed £365,000, 3-bed duplex penthouse £2.5 million. Back on **Queenstown Rd**, opposite the park by the roundabout, is London Town's The Bridge.

Queenstown

Leaving the river, busy **Queenstown Rd** leads on up from Chelsea Bridge, past Battersea Park and Queenstown train stations, to Lavender Hill. Much changed from its grimy past, these days it boasts a good parade of shops and smart restaurants from St Philip Square to Lavender Hill. The mainly flat-fronted Victorian houses and flats along the road have been steadily renovated and improved for sale/rent. Between busy **Silverthorne Rd** on the E, across Queenstown Rd over to **Stanley Grove** and **Broughton Rd** in the W is the Park Town estate, now a conservation area, and also known (to estate agents) as the 'Diamond'. This tract dates from the 1860s–1870s. Most homes in Stanley Grove are owned, and rented out, by the Peabody Trust. At the Silverthorne Rd end of **Tennyson St** the houses are 3-storey flat-fronted. Most of the estate has cottagy Victoriana (c. £375,000 for a 3-bed); some are purpose-built flats, with roof terraces for the first-floor ones (c. £275,000 for a 2-bed garden flat). On the corner of **Thackeray Rd**, Laing inserted seven new houses as part of a Victorian school development, with 41 flats in the school. Another school conversion on **Silverthorne Rd** adds to the local stock of 'double-height loft apartments'. The large houses with ornate carved balconies overlooking **St Philip Square** and the church have been modernized and converted.

On W from **Stanley Grove** and S from **Eversleigh Rd** lie the perfect Gothic cottages of

B

the Shaftesbury estate (built in the 1870s by the Artisans, Labourers and General Dwellings Co). Enclosed by the rail tracks, Lavender Hill and traffic-snarled **Latchmere Rd,** this popular enclave is convenient for the Junction. The 2- and 3-bedroom terraced cottages – so small as to be better described as vertical flats – fetch £275–300,000 (a 2-bed), c. £320,000 (3-beds); some are owned by Peabody and rented. **Eland Rd,** leading down into the Shaftesbury estate from **Lavender Hill,** has some of the larger houses in the area, up to 4-bed. For more space try the school conversion in **Wycliffe Rd.**

Separated from the Shaftesbury estate by the railway line behind **Eversleigh Rd** lies a triangle made up of **Poyntz Rd, Knowsley Rd** and **Shellwood Rd.** Approached from **Latchmere Rd** and cut off by railway sidings on three sides are small 2- and occasionally 3-bedroom mainly flat-fronted cottages. The area is useful for access to the excellent (council-owned) Latchmere Leisure Centre off **Sheepcote Lane.** Prices have caught up with the Shaftesbury estate, despite the train lines (2-beds, £325–350,000) – these cottages have two decent reception rooms is why.

Busy **Latchmere Rd** features flats (3-storey blocks) at the upper (Lavender Hill) end – Victorian one side, modern on the W – and the usual flat-fronted cottages, generally comparatively reasonable because of traffic noise. However, the roar of the road and the constant trains proved no bar to the success of two Victorian school conversions: The Village (in **Amies St**) and Southside Quarter. Village is considered seriously posh, with security, parking, proximity to the Junction and above all large, light-flooded spaces. Southside Quarter, near the leisure centre in **Burns Rd,** added new-build 'loft houses' to the school: conventional from the front, galleried and floor-to-rafters glass at the back (4-bed, 4-floors, priced at a million in 2003; now reckon on £850,000).

Clapham Common North Side

South of **Lavender Hill,** bordered by **Cedars Rd, Lavender Sweep** and **Clapham Common North Side** is the grid of late-Victorian terraced houses known by local estate agents as the North Side Square. **Lavender Hill** has sprouted shops, wine bars and cafés, with a good parade close to **Cedars Rd/Queenstown Rd** junction. To the W, along Lavender Hill between the library and Battersea Arts Centre, estate agencies are almost wall-to-wall. Space above some of the offices and other businesses has become 'loft-style' flats.

Virtually the entire North Side area consists of terraced 2- and 3-storey homes – although some are converted into flats. Most roads have been 'traffic-calmed', but **Elspeth Rd** is a through-route for South Circular traffic heading for Battersea Bridge. A standard 'North Side Square' 4-bed falls into the £450–550,000 bracket, while those with loft conversions/ extensions/garages (like hens' teeth) go up to £650,000. The whole tract is popular with renters.

Larger houses, mainly converted into flats, are found in wide **Sisters Avenue,**

This handsome Gothic tower stands somewhat incongruously above a shop on the Shaftesbury Estate. One of a pair, it marks the entrance to the estate of little cottages built a century ago as low-rent housing for the working classes. Today, the neat little homes are fashionable with young buyers. Pointed gables and other cottagey details set these terraces apart from the norm.

Mysore Rd, **Lavender Gardens** and **Altenburg Gardens**. Homes in **Lavender Gardens** near **Lavender Hill** could experience late-night excitement from Jongleurs, the cabaret venue. This does not prevent prices of £1 million plus for the 6-bed houses. On **Lavender Hill**, the old Battersea Town Hall is now the excellent Battersea Arts Centre. The flats in Avenue Mansions, **Sisters Avenue**, are unusually spacious, and the top ones offer good views across London. At the top of **Lavender Gardens** is The Shrubbery, a stunning late-Georgian mansion, complete with ballroom (and more useful hereabouts off-street parking), converted to 16 flats (typical 2-bed £400,000, biggest 2-beds £600,000). On the **Elspeth/Lavender** corner 'Lavender Buildings' has somewhat cheaper flats.

B

Stormont Rd has an unusual mix of traditional terraced houses and rather odd modern ones. **Sugden Rd** is untypical, and much in demand, for its semi-detached, pastel-painted houses with bigger-than-average gardens. **Parma Crescent** and **Eccles Rd** – more early Edwardian terraces – are popular for their easy access to Clapham Junction (prices drop as distance grows). The E side of this area is served by Clapham Common tube. **Nansen** and **Gowrie Rds**, parallel to the common, have 3-storey, 4-bed £500,000 houses; **Garfield Rd** is slightly cheaper. **Wix's Lane** holds spacious purpose-built Victorian flats and some new mews houses (3-bed and parking £400–445,000); also the borough and postal boundaries. Eastward lies SW4 and Clapham.

Clapham Junction

Clapham Junction's busy station and shops form a local centre, though little is now being heard of the plans to rebuild the station at enormous expense, with the inevitable smart shopping/office development to pay for it. Leading off **Lavender Sweep**, with its 3-bed houses, roads like **Barnard Rd** and **Eckstein Rd** offer spacious, purpose-built early-Edwardian 2- and 3-storey red-brick flats and maisonettes, the upper floor ones with big roof terraces. Carrington Court is an enclave of flats and some peaceful, 3-bed duplexes set round a courtyard (with parking under) in the angle of **Limburg Rd**. **Ilminster Gardens** and **Beauchamp Rd** feature plain 3-storey Victorian houses, virtually all converted to flats. Both suffer somewhat from their proximity to Arding & Hobbs, the area's very own department store, expensively re-vamped to keep up with the Junction's new image. The store may split into three units some time soon. Persimmon are replacing its carpet warehouse with 4-bed houses and 2-bed flats ('Ilminster Place'): no prices yet, but planned completion May '05. This development follows a long planning row: residents of **Ilminster Gardens** are unimpressed.

The tight little triangle between **Boutflower Rd**, **St John's Hill** and **St John's Rd**, once a cheaper corner, now sees close proximity to the Junction as a benefit. Just across Battersea Rise, in the corner between it and Northcote Rd, **Cairns Rd** might prove a quieter location: it borders the cemetery. Here in 1999 Laing tucked in a gated development of 2- and 3-bed mews cottages.

Back across St John's Hill, past Plough Rd, are **Louvaine Rd**, **Cologne Rd** and **Oberstein Rd**, which feature some imposing early Edwardian and late-Victorian terraced houses – some, notably in **Louvaine**, ornate 3-storey-plus-basement with porticoes. Virtually all are flats. Houses in the N leg of **Harbut Rd** (smaller 3- and 4-bed Edwardian – and mostly still family homes) will hear the passing trains. The prettiest – and most popular – road in the area is tree-lined **St John's Hill Grove**, with some charming Regency and early Victorian cottages, some semi-detached. **Plough Terrace** has rather cramped, garden-less (but with parking!) newish houses in a gated scheme. On **Plough Rd**, really handy for the station, there are new flats: 1-beds £210,000, 2-beds £335,000.

Strathblaine Rd, **Vardens Rd** and **Sangora Rd**, running between **St John's Hill** and the railway line, are quite smart now and still improving. On the Hill itself, an old church is now seven homes. There are more big 3-storey Victorian houses here. Some, notably in cut-off, leafy **Vardens Rd**, are large semi-detached 3-storey semi-basement affairs, most split up into very pleasant flats, while the few intact survivors command £1 million as 6-bed houses. Houses to the S side of **Strathblaine Rd** back onto the railway.

B *Between the Commons*

Northcote Rd is the spine of a more peaceful area properly called Northcote, but now known as 'Between the Commons' (less kindly as Nappy Valley – and many locals claim they live in Clapham). It runs from **Battersea Rise** to **Thurleigh Rd** and is flanked to E and W by Clapham and Wandsworth Commons. These protect the area from through traffic, and the leafy streets are filled with prosperous and fertile families, who send their children to nurseries with names like The Mouse House, then on to the rash of prep schools that have moved into Clapham Common. The Wandsworth borough schools are good, and the pull of Honeywell primary in **Honeywell Rd** is so strong that families have been known to sell up and move across the street to get into its catchment area.

The mainly late-Victorian/early-Edwardian terraced houses sweep down from the Commons to **Northcote Rd** which, from Battersea Rise to Salcott Rd, features a fruit and vegetable market twice a week. The once humdrum shops are now cafés, delis, restaurants, excellent butchers, a serious cheese shop. . . . The S end is the smarter.

The majority of houses are 2-storey, 3- or 4-bed Edwardian homes – some of considerable charm inside. Prices for these 'mainstream' houses are around £570–600,000. There are pockets of larger, 3-storey mainly flat-fronted houses (some with coveted semi-basement: Nappy Valley families are always cramped for space due to nannies, third child etc) notably in **Mallinson Rd, Bennerly Rd** and **Salcott Rd.** Really big houses, mostly at the S end of the area, have achieved serious seven-figure prices, but this end of the market softened during 2004, with reports of 10% falls over a million.

Little, if any room here for newbuild, but on **Clapham Common West Side**, and running back to form a continuation of **Roseneath Rd**, is Rialto's clutch of 30 houses on the old Walsingham School site. All have parking and garages; the grandest face out over the common and are in SW4.

Broomwood Rd is reckoned to be best at the two ends, rather than the middle: some 5-bed houses here have pushed past £1 million. Broomwood and **Thurleigh Rd** are the E–W through-roads; despite this the latter has houses up to £2 million. **Webb's Rd**, where there are local shops (lots of 2-bed flats above them), has traffic running N–S between Battersea Rise and Broomwood Rd. However the traffic-calming is effective, and traffic speeds are further slowed by the solid ranks of parked 4x4s.

South of Broomwood Rd, **Hillier, Devereux, Gayville** and **Montholme Rds** are the Broomwood House estate: terraces dating from the 1880s. **Chatham Rd** boasts a row of attractive Victoriana: Hyde's Cottages, 1863 (facing a small, low-rise council estate) and one of the oldest pubs in the area, The Eagle. These 2-bed, £500,000 cottages are joined by Michael Shanly's Amhurst Mews: six 4/5-bed town houses. **Stonell's Rd** (a cul-de-sac off Chatham Rd), offers tiny flat-fronted early- Victorian cottages facing a school playground. There are virtually no private purpose-built flats in the area with the exception of Broomwood Chambers off **Broomwood Rd**, but former council flats fill the gap. Ex-council properties also include the 4-bed terraced houses in a quiet cul-de sac off **Bolingbroke Grove.**

The largest houses in the area are on and just off **Bolingbroke Grove**, which runs along the length of Wandsworth Common. Most are late-Victorian semi-detached and terraced. Those on Bolingbroke Grove itself balance road noise with open views over the common: they nudge £2 million. Low street numbers are best. The large 3-storey red-brick terraced or semi-detached Victorian houses of **Gorst Rd** and **Dents Rd** are quieter – and can be around £1.6 million. **Blenkarne Rd** has a few large houses with the use of a communal garden: these have been known to be pricier still. The N end of **Bolingbroke Grove** has smaller mid-Victorian houses. Off **Chivalry Rd**, which forms an L-shape between **Battersea Rise** and **Bolingbroke Grove**, is Commonside, a small estate of houses and flats. **Chivalry Rd** has attractive late-Victorian houses.

South of **Thurleigh Rd** is SW12 and the parish boundary, and thus Balham; but the streets between **Thurleigh** and **Nightingale Lane** belong to 'Between the Commons'. There are some big houses down here: detacheds on the N side of **Thurleigh** and in **Sudbrooke Rd**, where prices can also nudge £2 million.

Transport No tubes; nearest are Clapham Common, Clapham South. Trains: Clapham Junction to Victoria 9 min, Waterloo 7 min; Queenstown Rd to Waterloo 7 min; Battersea Park to Victoria 5 min.

Convenient for Victoria and Waterloo, Gatwick Airport (28 min), Sloane Square, Thames, Clapham Common, Battersea Park. Miles from centre: 3.

Schools Local Authority: Battersea City Technology, Salesian College RC (b). Private: Emanuel School, St Francis Xavier RC.

SALES

Flats	S	1B	2B	3B	4B	5B
Average prices	110–220	120–325	180–500	200–650+	–	–
Houses	2B	3B	4B	5B	6/7B	8B
Average prices	210–450	250–550	280–800	400–1M	800+	–

RENTAL

Flats	S	1B	2B	3B	4B	5B
Average prices	150–250	170–350	210–450+	275–500+	350+	–
Houses	2B	3B	4B	5B	6/7B	8B
Average prices	280–600	350–600	400–800	550–1000	650+	–

The properties Terraced late-Victorian houses, flat conversions and smart new town-house/flat developments. Five-bed-plus houses and larger flats are scarce (try round the park for bigger mansion flats, 'Twixt Commons' for houses). Smartest new homes are the new riverside flats and loft-style conversions of old Victorian schools.

The market Demand for riverside flats much subdued as investors re-do sums. Tenants and owner-occupiers have a wide choice of flats, from ex-council to sub-Manhattan. Clapham Junction (despite the name) is in Battersea: this draws City types who compete for the smarter terraced and (a few) bigger houses with Fulham's children, while 'Twixt Commons' heaves with polite families.

Among estate agents active in this area are:

- John Thorogood
- Foxtons
- John Hollingsworth
- Bairstow Eves
- Winkworth
- Barnard Marcus
- John D Wood
- Edwin Evans
- Bishop Beamish
- Douglas & Gordon
- Thresher Owen
- Andrew Kent & Ptnrs
- Kinleigh Folkard & Hayward
- Bells
- Wellingtons
- Savills
- Robert Trindle
- Chesterton
- Courtenay
- Lauristons

BAYSWATER & PADDINGTON

B

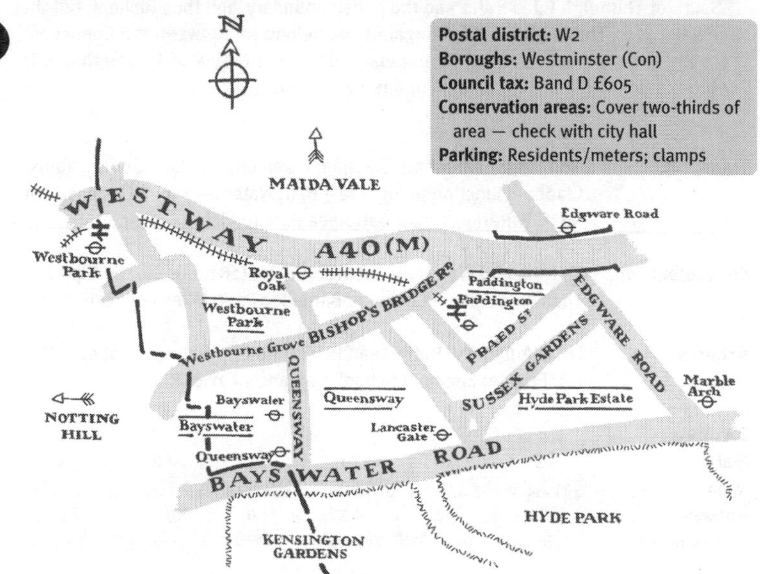

Postal district: W2
Boroughs: Westminster (Con)
Council tax: Band D £605
Conservation areas: Cover two-thirds of area – check with city hall
Parking: Residents/meters; clamps

Above Hyde Park sits a microcosm of London. Everything (and everyone) is here: one of the capital's main gateways, Paddington Station, with the usual somewhat seedy surroundings, sits at one end; at the other lies a discreet, tucked-away Regency village of multi-million-pound houses toothsome enough to tempt the Prime Minister.

It also has its brave new world: the ongoing transformation of a once-derelict canal basin and ex-railyards as dramatic, if smaller in scale, than Canary Wharf's. In Paddington Basin – or Paddington Waterway, as it would now like to be known – the towers are a little shorter, waterscapes more confined, but the buildings are as opulent. A new district is emerging from the ruins of a previous century's infrastructure: shops and squares and homes are arriving; blue-chip businesses are colonizing statement buildings. Canary Wharf showed that if you throw money at architecture and infrastructure even an initially dodgy location can come good. Paddington has a head start: it is part of established Bayswater, on the West End's doorstep and a fast train-ride from Heathrow. The once-grey Basin is now stitched across with glass walkways and witty bridges.

Then there are the dramas: the community gain from the Basin regeneration is meant to be the renaissance of the adjacent St Mary's Hospital, to be merged with the Brompton and Harefield heart hospitals and Imperial College as the 'Paddington Health Campus'. This troubled plan, dogged by controversy and costs that have more than doubled, is back under review. And while Marks & Spencer's new HQ is here, Orange changed their minds; some buildings are on hold, and Terry Farrell's striking 10-storey 'The Point', first destined for Orange and then for the Health Campus, looks set to remain empty for now.

Just as in Docklands, here too the commercial towers are complemented by blocks of smart flats. The initial speculative frenzy for these has died back from the peak of the 2001 hype; but thanks to the position and the 15-minute Express to Heathrow there are still investment buyers for blocks like Park West – Russians to the forefront, currently –

and renters. The best flats now let on a par with South Kensington's ('there's fewer people with long enough memories to be prejudiced against Paddington' as one agent opined cheerfully). But in keeping with the mood of the London market, residential prices – measured by re-sales, not the rather opaque pricing of the new properties – have stayed some 10 per cent down over the year with only the very best showing an increase. For your first tour of this new neighbourhood, see New Paddington below.

Bayswater is the larger area, the doughnut round the Paddington hole. It has its own considerable attractions, whatever happens round the back of the station. It is, after all, closer to the heart of things than Notting Hill, has a similar mix of homes, and sits atop Central London's biggest green space – the combined acres of Hyde Park and Kensington Gardens. Add that Heathrow Express, and you have a prime address.

So, to define Bayswater: its southern boundary is the broad sweep of Park and Gardens stretching to Marble Arch. East, the **Edgware Rd** is the frontier with Marylebone. To the N, beyond the elevated M40, the railway and the canal, is Little Venice and Maida Vale. To the W Bayswater blends into Notting Hill. The entire area is within Westminster City Council's jurisdiction, and the W2 postcode boundary also neatly encompasses it.

Until recently an image of transience held Bayswater back – it still has probably the fastest population turnover of any London district. It has long been a quarter of hotels of all descriptions, of short-stay flats, of rooming-houses and bedsits – the sort of thing that mainline stations always attract. . . . But concealed among these are several close-knit, long-established neighbourhoods, some fast-improving ones, an increasing store of desirable flats – and some of London's grandest properties. In short, Bayswater offers just about every kind and status of home, with two things in common: you can't get much more central, and they're all in W2.

Some of the West End's most luxurious homes are here, fronting Hyde Park and hidden behind in the area's best-kept secret: the Hyde Park Estate. But this select triangle ends at **Sussex Gardens**: N of it is fast-changing Paddington. And from its W tip at **Lancaster Gate** across to the borders of Notting Hill there spreads, away from the park, a lively and very mixed web of streets – but amid the bustle (plenty of that) are pretty corners, garden squares and a clutch of lovely, quiet, tucked-away mews. This has at its heart **Queensway**, a cosmopolitan shopping and restaurant street that never closes. The **Edgware Rd** quarter to the E is the centre of London for prosperous Arab visitors and expats.

The wider area also takes in fascinating neighbourhoods such as **Westbourne Grove** (now as fashionable as next-door Notting Hill) and the elegant parkside terraces. It still, though, has deprived (and some would claim depraved) corners – mainline rail stations attract cheap hotels and all that goes with them. It is home to more nationalities than you

B

can count – and always has been; early on it was a centre for Greeks and Russians. At the same time it's surprisingly parochial: home for many long-term residents – in council-built homes, as well as million-plus flats. There are many tiny but vociferous residents' associations, some covering single streets. Community events burgeon, with summer parties, Christmas fairs, fireworks. Good primaries and London's international schools draw families.

Bayswater's building boom took place in the mid-19th century, when the grand squares and terraces were laid out and acres of cream stucco was applied to endless pompous facades. The grandeur always had a very slightly démodé air: Bayswater was stigmatized as 'the wrong side of the park' by the upper-crust denizens of Knightsbridge and Belgravia. Now it's the right side for Notting Hill and, via the Express, Heathrow.

Like so much of central London, Bayswater spent most of the 20th century in decline. But by the end of the 1980s the huge decaying houses, split up into scores of seedy bedsits, were beginning to be tidied up, and pockets of smart flats appeared. The northern part of the area, especially, attracted grants from the council to promote housing improvements. Now, its future has never looked brighter.

Renting is the other dimension to the Bayswater scene, thanks to its splendidly central position: the choice is vast. For those buying – particularly flats – this is an area where it pays to check the age and quality of the conversion or upgrade. Standards have risen sharply over the years, as developers recognized the demand for more spacious, and higher-standard, homes. Because there is such a huge variety, and such a variation in quality and in the length of leases, prices, taken in isolation, can often be misleading.

Traffic and parking are contentious issues here, as the number of flats and hotels put pressure on the available road space and the Congestion-Charging Zone abuts to the E. However, much has been achieved by no-through-roads and one-way streets, as any outsider trying to navigate through by car discovers. The best advice is to go by public transport – or take a taxi. Or walk. Or cycle: Hyde Park offers traffic-free routes.

Bayswater – Westbourne Grove

Bounded by **Westbourne Grove** (N), **Queensway** (E), the borough boundary (W) and **Bayswater Rd**, this neighbourhood, with its once-gracious 5-storey stucco terraces, was the heart of Bayswater's traditional bedsit land. As the London market boomed in the 1980s the larger houses were split and sold off as flats, especially in the S close to Hyde Park and convenient for the West End. Those that are still single homes can command very high prices – in the right street.

To begin in the S, **Orme Square** opens onto the busy **Bayswater Rd**, but thus gains views over Kensington Gardens. It has large Regency houses, plus studio flats in Orme Court: a particularly large studio, £195,000 last autumn. As you head N into the district from **Bayswater Rd** and the Park, the noise level drops dramatically. Quiet, leafy streets and mews meander up to **Moscow Rd**, which has Bayswater tube at its Queensway end, and the Orthodox Cathedral that serves the Greek community. Alexandra Court here is a smart 1989 development (2-bed flats, c. £400,000). Plenty of big mansion flats in this road: 2-beds in Burnham Court c. £450,000, 4-beds up to £875,000. Some of the mansion blocks are distinctly Manhattan-smart and attract star names; portered Palace Court has 2-beds for £400–700,000. **Garway Rd**, running N towards Westbourne Grove, has 3-storey 19th-century semis which have fetched up to £2 million; more modestly, a 1-bed flat in one of them, £235,000. **St Petersburgh Place**, running S, has an attractive terrace of period maisonettes, plus Georgian houses and mansion blocks (a 2-bed, with shared garden, £550,000). It's also home to the imposing New West End Synagogue and St Matthew's Church. Cobbled **St Petersburgh Mews** has some little 2-bed houses.

Further W is **Hereford Rd**: smaller, less ornate, houses with wrought-iron balconies, and large, pillared-portico ones: a 5-floored example, £2.3 million. A few small shops and restaurants, too. Cobbled **Hereford Mews** adds some new homes to its cottages.

Three very much larger squares dominate the N part of the neighbourhood – **Leinster Square, Princes Square** and **Kensington Gardens Square**. For many years very down-at-heel, these: improvement has been slow and patchy, with some buildings still shabby-genteel. Now, though **Kensington Gardens Square** still holds some busy (and recently smartened) hotels, most of the tall houses are split into smart flats. **Princes Square** combines the two with an 'apart-hotel', Vancouver Studios. Each square has a large communal garden to which neighbouring residents have access – an oasis of peace in a noisy area (much of it emitting from foreign students at the area's many language schools). Nearby, in **Redan Place** behind Whiteley's, a 1998 Barratt's development has flats with basement parking: a 2-bed/2-bath here, £395,000.

Westbourne Grove itself is now positively chi-chi. This was not always so: it was known in the 1860s as 'bankruptcy avenue' and described, politely, in this Guide's 1989 edition as 'cosmopolitan'. New bars and restaurants have joined those serving Chinese, Malaysian, Indian, Greek, Lebanese food. Dotted about this gastronomic mecca are specialist shops for cooks or collectors of Oriental furnishings, an Arabic bookshop (though the current wave of international business buyers is less Arabic, more Indian/ Pakistani, and Russian) and more and more up-market fashion stores. The W end of the Grove is part of the smart Notting Hill antiques district. With Queensway, this is an ideal part of town for the nocturnal, rivalling Earl's Court and Soho in its ability to stay up late.

Where W2 runs into W11, at the N ends of **Chepstow Place** and **Hereford Rd** (full of design studios), Regalian's 'Baynards' has 80 'open-plan' flats (2-beds c. £550–600,000, with porter, gardens and gym) carved in 1999 from a Victorian department store plus modern additions. **Westbourne Grove Terrace** has a 16-flat scheme behind the facades of four stucco-fronted houses. Right on the edge of the area, where **Chepstow Rd** meets **Westbourne Grove**, 'The Corner' is 32 flats and two live/work 'villas', just completing: the three units left range from £785,000–£1.4 million – oh, and £40,000 if you want a garage.

Queensway – Lancaster Gate

The neighbourhood bounded by **Queensway** in the W, **Bayswater Rd** to the S, **Gloucester Terrace** (E) and **Bishop's Bridge Rd** (N) reflects the tremendous social mix that is characteristic of this part of town. 'The bewildering cosmopolitanism of Queensway,' observes Peter Ackroyd in his *London: the Biography* 'where the Tower of Babel might once more be constructed'. Here, it seems as if every one of London's 200-plus nationalities has its representative bar/café/restaurant/shop.

In the N is the council-built Hallfield Estate, stretching along **Bishop's Bridge Rd** from **Inverness Terrace** to **Gloucester Terrace**: 6- and 10-storey blocks of flats angled away from the roads in a classic 1950s garden layout – very daring for its time – and now a conservation area. The estate has a strong community feeling, its own health centre and school (which is listed Grade II-starred); a 1-bed flat here sold last autumn for £199,000. **Inverness Terrace** itself holds Park Gate, a big, recent development of 37 flats. Wide **Gloucester Terrace** sweeps up from Lancaster Gate, taking traffic from Central London out the M40 via the Westway; its large, well-kept creamy stucco rows, most now flats, mingle with brick terraces. Also mansion flats: a 3-bed in Maitland Court, £545,000.

In parallel **Westbourne Terrace** most of the enormous houses, for long hotels, have reverted to homes. Expect to pay from c. £220,000 for a 1-bed flat, up to a million-plus for a big maisonette – but prices vary enormously depending on quality. **Bishop's Bridge Rd** has distinctive Bishop's Court, handsomely clad in stock brick above stucco, providing 49 flats on seven floors. Where Gloucester Terrace meets **Craven Rd**, another small 'village' begins. Going W along Craven Rd, there's a cluster of local shops. And on either side are mews with steeply sloped entrances: **Gloucester Mews**, **Smallbrook Mews**, **Upbrook Mews** and **Craven Hill Mews**, whose former stables make smart little houses.Then there's **Brook Mews North**, with 18 2- and 3-bed flats by Berkeley in a smart 2003 conversion of a row of old houses. **Chilworth St** has some small stucco houses; a little 2-bed here, £425,000.

B

Around the corner off **Leinster Gardens**, **Craven Hill Gardens** and **Queens Gardens** have more large, 5-storey buildings; some opulent flats have been carved from grand old houses in **Cleveland Square** whose rear terraces lead directly into the square gardens. A lateral 2-bed here, £565,000. **Devonshire Terrace** in the main has smaller, 3-storey houses.

The most desirable homes in Bayswater – beside those of the Hyde Park Estate – are in the **Lancaster Gate** and **Porchester Terrace** areas. Porchester Terrace, which runs N from the park, contains an intriguing mix of grand period mansions with well-maintained gardens, interspersed with the occasional modern one with off-street parking. Semi-detached houses here are around £2 million plus. Dotted among the big houses are flat-fronted brick blocks of flats; the modern Hyde Park Towers block has wide views across Kensington Gardens. **Fulton Mews**, off Porchester Terrace, has kept its cobbles.

Lancaster Gate is a street (or triangle) of surprises. Here the large hotels have solid, respectable frontages. The square itself surrounds an eye-catching clutch of luxury – some seven-figure – flats created in the 1980s from a former church. On the corner, another opulent-level development produced 24 flats carved out of several 5-storey, colonnaded terraced houses. This sort of scheme allows for Tardis-like lateral conversions – one boasts 4/5-bedrooms and a 43ft living room. Likewise, behind the facade of the old Football Association office at No. 17 are five big lateral flats and a mews house. And planning permission has now been passed to convert the 390-bed Lancaster Gate Hotel, and a terrace of former houses, into 139 flats and 15 Affordable Homes.

In contrast to the atmosphere and scale of Lancaster Gate is neighbouring **Lancaster Mews**, reached from **Craven Terrace.** Its sloping entrance is topped by the Mitre pub. Its attractive, pastel-washed cottages are beautifully maintained, with Mediterranean blue paintwork and abundant window boxes completing the picture of this busy commercial/ residential 'village'.

Back on **Queensway** itself, at the W end of the neighbourhood, the traditional night life continues with restaurants pulling in tourists and visitors, and small shops catering for locals. Thirties brick apartments, served by walkways, top the shopping arcades at the lower end of Queensway. The famous Whiteley's department store – London's first, opened 1863 – was reborn in 1989 as a shopping/leisure complex, with shops, Marks & Spencer food hall and cinema. A Tesco Metro has appeared for good measure.

Westbourne Park

Porchester Rd takes you N from the Queensway neighbourhood and up towards Royal Oak tube station, the motorway and Harrow Rd. Pass by the local landmark of Porchester Hall, council-owned and always busy. Everything from A-level exams to Indian weddings takes place here – you too can hire this splendid venue. Behind this is the Porchester Baths (public and private), with a luxurious health club. A surviving detached period house was on the market for £1.45 million last winter.

To the E, this end of **Gloucester Terrace** (see above) is the motorway access route: once an elegant terrace of large 4-storey 1850s houses, now the elevated Westway A40(M) overshadows them. The buildings were restored and split into flats by the old GLC back in the 1960s and '70s. **Porchester Square** and **Porchester Place** are tucked into a corner N of Bishop's Bridge Rd: worth a look, with 2-bed flats in a 16-storey block plus the usual period conversions. The GLC was active here too. **Porchester Square** has a busy communal garden with playground. In **Orsett Terrace** 90 flats were carved from the houses in the late '80s. The Colonnades has 1975-built town-houses and maisonettes (4-beds £440,000 plus: leases vary) with underground parking opposite the Hallfield Estate.

To the W of Porchester Rd, **Westbourne Park Rd** has a curious mixture of homes ranging from flat-fronted brick apartment blocks to terraces and detached villas with ornate, oriental-inspired decorations and colonnaded entrances. **Celbridge Mews** off Porchester Rd has 1980s mews houses and offices. **Westbourne Gardens** gets smarter as it goes W and becomes **Sunderland Terrace**, leading on round to stylish **Alexander St**, with its Victorian terraces still in use as whole houses: one was £1.7 million last autumn – unmodernised. **Kildare Terrace** is reached by car from Talbot Rd, the N end, and is a tranquil enclave of 4-storey houses set back behind open terraces. It leads into **Kildare Gardens** which has 4-bed Victorian terraced houses and flats.

West of the triangle bounding the church, **St Stephens Crescent** has an attractive curve of stucco 5-storey houses with steps up to front entrances guarded by columns. **St Stephens Mews** boasts two year-old 4-storey houses: one was on at £1,375,000 last autumn. Around the corner, just off **Talbot Rd**, lies **Bridstow Place,** a tiny row of colour-washed Victorian cottages behind little gardens. Small-scale homes again in **Shrewsbury Mews**, where the tiny, modern cottages have garages. But turn the corner, and you're back with **Chepstow Rd**'s tall, 5-storey houses, scene of many a flat-conversion scheme.

Talbot Rd itself has seen homes expensively renovated in recent years. This corner, in fact, is now distinctly fashionable, numbering musicians and the odd pop star among its residents; from c. £475,000 for a 2-bed flat hereabouts. Between Talbot and tree-lined Artesian Rd, **Courtnell St** has more attractive colour-washed, brick-fronted homes, overlooked by copper beeches. Flats in a 1980s block in **Artesian Rd** include duplexes; also communal gardens, underground parking and commensurate prices. West of here is the boundary of the W2 district and of Westminster borough: across it lies Notting Hill.

New Paddington

Between them, the Paddington Goods Yards site, N of the station, and the Paddington Basin area to the E, behind St Mary's Hospital, add up to 40 hitherto-redundant acres. Add in station, hospital and peripheral sites and you have 80 acres – a neighbourhood the size of Soho. New Paddington (our name) has been ripe for redevelopment since the 1970s and there have been several false starts. Now, buildings are at last up and occupied. However, the building work could go on for another 10 years, so a tranquil environment it is not. In all, there are or will be 1,300 homes, 75% private, and a very large amount of office space – in picturesque barges as well as tower blocks.

Paddington Station, which bounds the development area to the W, is a key part of the scheme, boasting the Heathrow Express as well as tube/main line trains. The latest plans, following on from the refurb of the W side of the station, are to rebuild the E side with an extra platform, new links through to the Basin, and offices above. The canal basin is the heart of the area, and is now virtually surrounded by new homes and offices. New bridges, a footpath to Little Venice, boat moorings, cafés and restaurants, public access to the waterside – all are complete, under way or promised.

The big Hilton Metropole on the **Edgware Rd** has been extended and is now Europe's largest convention hotel (1,000 rooms). Between the hotel and the E end of the basin is the Grand Union complex: six interlinked blocks, rising to a mere 29 storeys (from a proposed 49), plus 291 homes (115 of them Affordable Housing) and a further block, The Winding, with 200 flats (30 for key workers) yet to come. Next along the quayside is the Waterside building, Marks & Spencer's new HQ – but now that Orange have pulled out, who will get The Point, on the W corner of the basin? Going N, away from the water, Paddington Walk has 197 flats, 1- to 3-beds, plus six penthouses, in four 11–15 storey towers, now completing: prices from a 1-bed, £310,000, to penthouses between £1.4–3.5 million. This **Hermitage St** site also has Peabody's 79 homes for rent/shared ownership.

The first homes scheme to complete was **West End Quay**: 468 flats in three blocks between the Basin and **Praed St.** The flats are modernistic, with sliding internal walls, all the latest electronics, air conditioning.

The 11-acre goods-yard site N of the station – Paddington Central – has St George's twin 12-storey blocks totalling 219 flats, plus offices and shops. The flats are at the E end overlooking the canal (and the Westway). The penthouses – with rooftop hot tubs – are sold; but 2-bed flats overlooking canal and plaza are £630–650,000, 3-beds £750,000. At the W end Sheldon Square, Visa's Europe HQ, has grass, open space, shops, health club.

On the southern side of the canal basin, the St Mary's Hospital site will become a 'health campus' uniting St Mary's, Harefield and Brompton Hospitals. This ambitious, £800 million plan has run into problems, but in any event will take till at least 2008. . . .

Paddington

Paddington station is the hub of the neighbourhood bounded by **Eastbourne Terrace, Harrow Rd, Edgware Rd** and **Sussex Gardens.** Like the area round most major stations, there is a mix of expensive homes, services and run-down property catering to transients. Now, though, it has good reason for an upward climb: see New Paddington above.

South of bustling **Praed St** is a network of little Victorian cottages, in **Sale Place, St Michael St** and **Star St.** Most were once owned by St Mary's Hospital or by the railway companies for their workers – but some cottages date back before the railway to the canal boom of the early 19th century. Over time these homes fell into disrepair; housing associations acquired some; in the early '90s this corner even attracted special funds as a Housing Action Area. Now the cottages' charm and undeniable convenience (Paddington three minutes) can command dizzying prices: c. £750–875,000.

New homes are being added: houses in **Praed Mews** date from 1988 and 1998. More appeared around a courtyard off **Star St. Southwick Mews** has 1970s cottages (a 3-bed, £880,000): business users with flats above. **Conduit Mews**, off **Spring St**, has a 2001 scheme by St George – 17 £1.7 million-ish houses – along the whole of the W side.

But **Praed St**, next to the station, reflects the dominant trend of the area: exchange bureaux, instant photos, heel bars and dealers in gold, silver and second-hand goods abound. However the street has smartened recently: a slick conversion has carved flats out of two of the old buildings. Leafy **Norfolk Square**, a cul-de-sac, lies S of **Praed St** and has small hotels plus some new housing-association homes round a communal garden.

South again, **Sussex Gardens** is a major road linking Lancaster Gate and the Edgware Rd, its once-grand 4-storey terraces now flats and bed-and-breakfast hotels full of bus-loads of students. What peace remains to Sussex Gardens and flanking streets is eroded somewhat by the continuation of Paddington's traditional form of commerce. However, the Frontline Club nearby is named for its war-reporter clientele, not the neighbourhood.

Hyde Park Estate

From Marble Arch walk up busy **Edgware Rd**, turn left into **Sussex Gardens**, left again at the towering Royal Lancaster Hotel onto **Bayswater Rd**, and back along the Park to Marble Arch. You have thus circumnavigated the Hyde Park Estate. Better, branch to your left and penetrate the Estate's peace and quiet.

The Estate owes its character to its long-time landlords, the Church Commissioners. Once, the Bishop of London owned nearly all of Paddington. At the start of the 19th century the Bishop's architect built an elegant Regency estate of squares and crescents – and called it, rather inauspiciously, Tyburnia. The Church Commissioners, heirs of the bishops, sold off all their Paddington land except this Hyde Park patch in the 1950s. Much of ecclesiastical Paddington had sunk into a slum, populated largely by prostitutes (one corner, W of the station, was known as 'Sin Triangle'). Concentrating on the Hyde Park Estate, the Commissioners started widespread rebuilding. The result is a neighbourhood mixing lovely Regency white stucco terraces, quiet little mews, handsome (some, anyway) modern houses and flats and – most notably forming a protective rampart to shut out the **Edgware Rd** – tower block apartments.

The key is the Regency street-plan, with its crescents and squares, which survived the rebuilding. The Estate's lack of through-routes, and its clearly-defined borders, keep it quiet and pleasant. It is a tribute to the Commissioners, or more especially to their agents and architects, that the Estate remained a desirable place to live.

Prices on the Estate are governed by whether they are for a freehold – still less common than elsewhere – or, if not, length of lease. Also by period: the modern homes amid the stucco may seem less attractive to the Brits, but are more so to the international set: nearly all post-war flats and houses have underground parking. Thanks to rebuilding and conversions, there are flats, flats, flats of every size, period, lease length, and thus price: generalizations are difficult. Despite Leasehold Reform Acts, the Commissioners still hold sway: even freeholds are liable to come under an estate management scheme.

The centre of life is the Connaught 'village', with its mix of small smart shops, offices and homes; **Connaught St** is its 'high street'. Where **Sussex Place** meets **Hyde Park Gardens Mews** is another picturesque hive of activity for eating, meeting and drinking, where on warm summer evenings people sit out at tables – in (almost) Parisian style.

The centrepiece of the Estate is **Hyde Park Crescent**, and the lovely old church of St John's, which can be seen as a long-distance vista from as far as **Sussex Square**. The Crescent adds space and dignity to the church. Mirroring it to the E is **Norfolk Crescent**. The two form an elongated circle embracing the church, two squares (**Oxford** and **Cambridge**) and two high-rise blocks. **Norfolk Crescent**, a post-war rebuild of tall thin family houses, feels slightly crammed in contrast to **Hyde Park Crescent**.

Garden squares are a feature of the Estate, each with a character and atmosphere of its own. **Oxford Square** and **Cambridge Square**, for example, are bordered by '60s town-houses and tall blocks of flats with underground garages. **Hyde Park Square** on the other hand is larger and has a range of styles, from grandiose 5-storey stucco houses, these days split into flats, to spacious modern family homes, to apartment blocks (a large 2-bed maisonette here, £950,000). **Sussex Square** has an even more spacious feel about it, with a circular green at the centre. One of the handsomest – and the earliest – is **Connaught Square**, enclosed by classic Regency terraces. Its houses are large; most are now flats, but not all (a whole one, £3–4 million). While being just a stone's throw from the Marble Arch madness, it manages to retain its dignity and much-prized leafy peace – residents were highly unamused by the publicity when one T. Blair bought here last year.

But the jewel in the crown is probably **Gloucester Square.** One can walk around the perimeter and not always be aware that it *is* a square: some of the houses have the luxury of backing directly onto the central green, concealing the communal garden from the untutored eye. A recent block of de luxe flats added onto the end of a cream stucco terrace were all eagerly snapped up. Some large 5-storey homes to be found here, too.

Many of the Estate's classic London town-houses, once occupied by the wealthy families from the pages of history books and by the merchant classes and empire builders, have now been converted into ultra-luxurious flats. Among the most exclusive are the stucco-fronted Regency buildings in **Hyde Park Gardens,** having their own huge communal garden opposite Hyde Park. Grand apartments here (some vast), with their high ceilings, huge windows and Park views come up both for buying and renting.

In contrast to this elegance and opulence, there is a variety of purpose-built modern blocks on the Estate. At the cheaper end is the workaday Park West (from £215,000 for 1-beds) in **Kendal St.** The Water Gardens and the Quadrangle, both bordering on **Sussex Gardens**, are more pricey. The Water Gardens is a complex of towers and smaller blocks, with a '60s split-level feel and a profusion of pools and fountains (2-bed flats from c. £365,000). Earlier mansion blocks such as Albion Gate in **Albion St** have house-size flats: a 4-bed (one for the maid), 3-reception, roof-gardened penthouse, £1.75 million.

Mews are ever more popular, providing compact, easily manageable homes in villagy cobbled streets, retaining their period frontage and 19th-century atmosphere – helped, in

B

most cases, by being cul-de-sacs. Some of the most charming and coveted mews are **Hyde Park Gardens Mews**, off Hyde Park Square, and two smaller mews off Albion St – **Albion Mews** and **Albion Close**. The Estate is lucky to have a mews that is still used for its original purpose: **Bathurst Mews** houses a riding school, where you can hire horses and go riding in Hyde Park. Apart from the charm, mews houses often have their own garages.

Despite the Christmas fair in **Porchester Place** the Estate, once intimate, slow-moving and villagy, has become rather more cosmopolitan and anonymous over the years. Within a few paces you'll hear languages from American to Russian, Swedish to Swahili: many diplomats live here. Wealthy Arabs, who kept London bases here for the summer months, are now increasingly replaced by Indian and Pakistani businessmen. The estate agents, banks, clothes shops, cinemas and restaurants of the **Edgware Rd** reflect the diversity.

Transport Tubes, zone 1: Bayswater (District, Circle); Lancaster Gate, Queensway (Central); Paddington (District, Circle, Bakerloo, Hammersmith & City). From Lancaster Gate: Oxford Circus 6 min, Bank 20 min. Trains: Paddington–Heathrow Express 15 min.

Convenient for Hyde Park, West End, City, M40, Heathrow. Miles from centre: 2.5.

Schools Local Authority: North Westminster Community School. Private: Pembridge Hall School (g). See also neighbouring areas.

SALES

Flats	S	1B	2B	3B	4B	5B
Average prices	135–220	215–365	250–600	290–1M	450–1.2M	900–3M
Houses	2B	3B	4B	5B	6/7B	8B
Average prices	500–700	500–1.5M	800–2M	900–2.5M	1M–3M	2–3.5M

RENTAL

Flats	S	1B	2B	3B	4B	5B
Average prices	165–275	215–400	300–675	400–1000	550–1450	1500+
Houses	2B	3B	4B	5B	6/7B	8B
Average prices	450–750	500–950+	700–1200	1300–4000	→	–

The properties 'New Paddington' brings smart modernity to an already varied area. White terraces were once all grand; currently a total mix: everything from pristine millionaires' squares (Hyde Park Estate) to hostels. Flats most common. Houses either small (lovely hidden mews homes; modern town-houses), *very* expensive – or both. The rest were converted to flats.

The market The 15-min rail link to Heathrow, plus Notting Hill's rise to fame, set the seal on this fast-changing area. Its excellence as a London base attracts the international business set. Westbourne Grove (Notting Hill borders) now almost as pricey as Hyde Park Estate.

Among estate agents active in this area are:

- Cluttons
- Chesterton
- Lurot Brand
- Savills
- Kinleigh, Folkard & Hayward
- Beaney Pearce
- Knight Frank
- Plaza Estates
- John D Wood
- Keith Cardale Groves
- Winkworth
- Jackson-Stops
- Kenwoods
- Anscombe & Ringland
- Tyser Greenwood
- Westbourne
- Springfields
- Faron Sutaria
- Foxtons
- Granvilles

BEDFORD PARK AND ACTON GREEN

Postal districts: W4
Boroughs: Ealing (Lab), Hounslow (Lab)
Council tax: Band D Ealing £1,192, Hounslow £1,262
Conservation areas: Bedford Park
Parking: Controlled parking zone

B

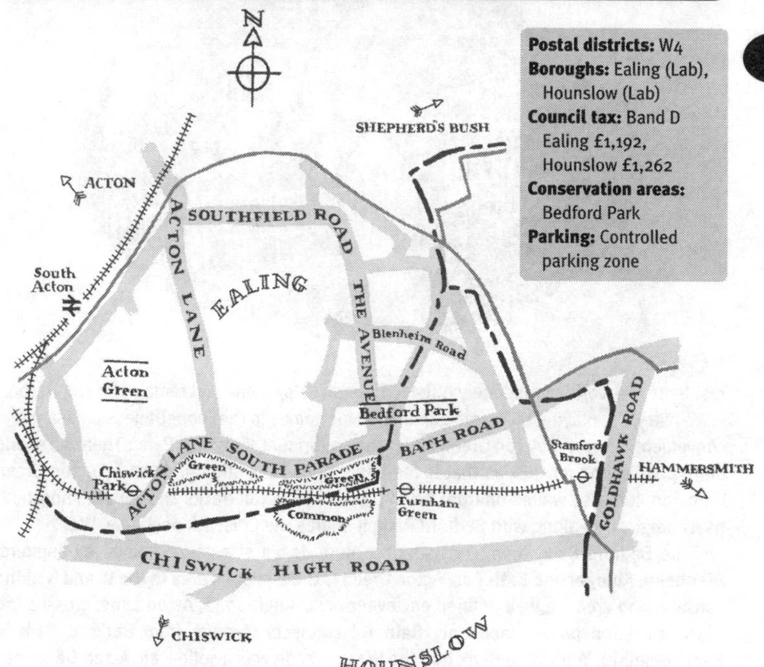

The celebration of Bedford Park's heritage is a way of life for its inhabitants. It is, of course, quite possible to live in the Park without being keen on architecture, but it would be rather a waste. For this was London's first purpose-built suburb – laid out to the highest artistic standards in the 1870s for those of aesthetic (*the* in-word of the day) tendencies. The aesthetic movement rebelled against the gloomier excesses of high-Victorian Gothic, reverting instead to a romantic, Queen Anne-cottagey, vernacular.

The Park has survived virtually intact, an island in the less creative sprawl of West London. And its residents spend a good part of their time protecting their patch against philistine encroachment from all sides – including above: relatively free of aircraft noise, they are fighting a third Heathrow runway and more night flights. They helped defeat the Crossrail spur that would have chewed up their southern shores and demolished a row of shops in Turnham Green Terrace (it will go through Acton, still close enough to be convenient), and now are working to improve Acton Green Common. The Bedford Park Society is also fighting to safeguard their local shops, destabilised by the closure of the Post Office – a hub of Park life. But the 'celebration' side is equally strong, culminating in a two-week festival in June, with art exhibitions, plays, concerts, guided tours of the Park . . . artistic activity continues throughout the year, centred on St Michael and All Angels'.

Convenient position at Turnham Green (just N of leafy Chiswick – under which you will almost certainly find it listed in estate agents' ads), a distinctive charm and family-sized – some outsized – houses are the solid attractions of this corner. Corner it is: Bedford Park is not very big, and its cachet leads to an extension of the name into Acton Green. 'Bedford Park borders' or 'West Bedford Park' are terms to beware of – if you have set your heart on the conservation area. Some roads outside the original estate belong in spirit – indeed the N part of **Esmond Rd** has just been incorporated – but to the true Park

B

residents the world immediately outside their streets is, and will remain, forever Acton.

While we're playing the name game, look for homes in the (nonetheless pleasant and convenient) streets of Acton Green under the soubriquet 'Chiswick Park'. There's a shade more justification for this, as that is the name of its tube station, down by Acton Green Common. It is also walled off from Acton *proper* by the rail tracks and – more important, psychologically – along with Bedford Park, it shares the Chiswick postcode, W4.

True Bedford Park, then, consists of a mere dozen streets, contained by **Esmond, Blenheim, Abinger** and **Bath Rds.** Acton Green is the L-shaped area to the W and N of the conservation area – a well-defined enclave: only a single road, **Acton Lane**, crosses the tracks to Acton proper (and only **Bath Rd** connects through from Bedford Park to Hammersmith). You would think that the W4 postcode was a solid wall. Acton Green has popular and peaceful (apart from the odd train rumble) family homes – ever more so, as Chiswick prices shot up – particularly the corner to the W, which has the tube.

The open space of Acton Green Common itself lies S of **South Parade**, leading up to Bedford Park's tube – which *has* retained the area's original name, Turnham Green. In its turn, the once-thriving hamlet of Turnham Green seems to have been subsumed entirely into Chiswick (which see); its name is only commemorated, sadly, by the tube station (being revamped), a Civil War battle, its green (which lies away to the S of **Chiswick High Rd**) and **Turnham Green Terrace** – a busy street of shops, restaurants and estate agencies that leads northwards across the tracks to **The Avenue**, the spine of Bedford Park.

Bedford Park

Founded in 1875 by Jonathan Carr, a cloth merchant with a taste for speculation and art, this was the prototype garden suburb. Carr employed well-known architects such as (principally) Norman Shaw, plus EJ May, EW Godwin, Maurice B Adams to design houses in the Queen Anne Revival style – all red-brick, dormer windows, Dutch gables, hanging tiles, balconies and pretty porches. Some 400 buildings, mostly Grade II listed, make up the conservation area. Despite the odd bit of war damage and modern infilling, the estate remains remarkably homogeneous; the most obtrusive new building is St Catherine's Court, a '30s block on the site of Carr's magnificent home, the Tower House. Conservation rules extend to trees, and Hounslow council brought in Article 4.2 directives, which mean you need planning permission to paint your home a different colour. Ealing, which covers the remainder, follow suits this year: if yours is in Ealing, paint it purple now. . . .

There is a great variety in homes, from little 2-storey, 3-bed cottages to 6/7-bedroom detached mansions, semis and terraces of up to 4 storeys. There are a couple of large blocks, but otherwise very few flats: those of the bigger houses that were split into flats in the '80s have wherever possible been reunited. Homes here are owner-occupied: only a few are rented. Despite its soubriquet of garden suburb, many of the gardens are disappointingly small ('Though not for Central London, which for practical purposes we are!' objected one resident), and prices can reflect garden, as much as house, size and position. Check, though, that that huge, overshadowing tree is not protected.

Houses on street corners, often set at an angle to the road, have enviable extra garden space and beautiful detailing: perhaps a conservatory, or pleasing gables, or balconies. One of the earliest EJ May-designed houses, on a coveted corner plot in **Newton Grove**, shows the scale of the largest homes: it boasts 6 bedrooms, 3 baths, 3 reception rooms, plus gardens fore and aft – and off-street parking. Lack of a parking space can be the other problem here: the aesthetic types for whom the estate was planned were plainly proto-Greens (or just plain poor): they were not expected to 'set up their carriages'. . . . The average **Priory Avenue** house, for example, is a semi-detached that boasts 4/6 beds, 2 receps, 2 baths – but no garage or off-street parking. The neighbourhood is all a controlled parking zone.

The whole estate with its irregular layout (designed by Norman Shaw to preserve existing trees) was modelled on the ideal of a village complete with shops, pub – the Tabard – church of St Michael and All Angels', church hall (restored and extended: now a super concert venue) and club. Even the Tabard's theatre is to gain a new resident company. The village ethos means lots of social/cultural activities, plus a friendly atmosphere in which everyone seems to know everyone else's business. The community spirit is fostered by the Bedford Park Society , which zealously protects the architectural heritage. Its logbook scheme to record the listed houses is a success that others emulate; it covers everything from the technical data to planning advice and how to 'corrrect past mistakes'. It is also to be kept online: you should be able to 'dial a house' and discover its history.

Originally built, then, as homes at modest rents for the 'aesthetic' middle classes, Bedford Park from the first attracted many artists (the occasional purpose-built artist's studio can be seen) and personalities of the day. Nowadays it is more likely to house media folk, professionals such as architects, and others who can afford the considerably less-than-modest prices. Because there is such a good size mix, people often move within the area: most sales are to locals, many houses selling through the grapevine ('over the dinner-table' said one agent ruefully), which is why some move to the Park's borders before working their way in. That said, some 15 were for sale last winter: lots, for the Park. However, some were just 'testing the market' and few were dropping their prices – though one 5-bed 'in need of work' in a top street made £1.35, not £1.7, million.

Carr chose the spot because of its proximity to the newly-opened Turnham Green station; these excellent links to West End and City remain, with the added advantage of a 20-minute drive (on a good day) to Heathrow down the M4 (note that Piccadilly Line trains only stop at Turnham Green in the very early/very late hours). The area is within walking distance of the shops and restaurants on **Chiswick High Rd**, too, as well as other W4 facilities. Acton Green Common, abutting the tube line, is the nearest open space, but the river, Kew Gardens, and even Richmond Park are only a short drive away.

Bath Rd, The Avenue and **South Parade** are the main routes, with buses; while the latter, along with **Flanders Rd**, lies close to the tube line. **Blenheim, Bedford** and **Abinger Rds** and streets off **South Parade** are busy; it follows that roads in the heart of the area, such as **Queen Anne's Gardens** or **The Orchard**, are quiet – but all roads have covetable houses. A curiosity is a building in **The Avenue** which pre-dates the suburb: it is the stables (now flats) of the original Bedford House – in the grounds of which Bedford Park was built.

Prices vary not only with size of home (anything from 3–7 beds), but also desirability of road and purity of architecture. Thus smaller houses can range from around half a million in the 'just-outside' fringes up to c. £700,000 in the top streets; with £800,000 to £1 million for good-sized family homes. It goes up and up from there, with classic Norman Shaw houses rarely for sale and priced accordingly: one, a 5-bed in **Woodstock Rd**, £3.5 million last autumn, while another 5-bed, this one by EJ May – but 'a restoration project rather than refubishment', was yours for £1 million. House-sized, 3- and 4-bed flats in the balconied, red-brick, Queen Anne-gabled Bedford Park Mansions can fetch house-sized prices, too: c. £500–800,000. Other flats are found in the handsome, modern St James's Court in **Bedford Rd**.

B

Bedford Park borders; Acton Green

Non-listed houses, such as those in streets off **Flanders Rd** to the SE, along with mansion blocks and houses just outside the conservation area in **Blandford Rd**, **Fielding Rd**, **Vanbrugh Rd** to the N, and **Esmond Rd**, **Ramillies Rd**, **Rusthall Avenue**, and **St Albans Avenue** were built later than Bedford Park proper, with some inter-war additions. Homes here – 'West Bedford Park' in estate-agent parlance – are cheaper in design as well as price (say, c. £600,000), though still above the more everyday homes of the 'borders' streets further N and W. Note, though, that the conservation area has been reviewed, and **Esmond Rd**'s northern section now joins some substantial houses at its southern end within it.

West of **St Albans Avenue** are the first streets of Acton Green – a peaceful corner that you'll find described as 'Chiswick Park' by agents – the name of the tube station (and the svelte new designer office complex: see below). The streets run off **Acton Lane**, but are kept distinct from Acton proper by the railway line that curls protectingly round to the NW. Lots of people (on good salaries, or with parent power) search here for their first homes.

There is a difference between the streets to the W, which are wider and have some good-sized houses amid the terraces, and those just E of Acton Lane, which tend to be narrower, with smaller homes. The homes are more run-of-the-mill than Bedford Park's, but some are of much the same date, with a good sprinkling of Edwardian and some mid-20th century. It is here, and to N of the area, that any new homes can be found; also terraces converted to flats. One-bed flats can be had in Acton Green for £200–230,000; 2-beds for up to £250,000, while 'loft'-style flats command a hefty premium.

Acton Green may well want to resume its proper name, however, to avoid confusion with the new Chiswick (business) Park, across the tracks, which has now dropped the 'Business' and titled itself plain 'Chiswick Park': this has turned the old Gunnersbury bus depot site into a 'thoughtful and surprising workplace' for 7,000 souls; a 'happy campus' of Richard Rogers hi-tech (but mercifully low-level) office blocks, with health club, cafés and shoplets, set airily around lakes and a feature waterfall. Half of the dozen planned buildings are complete: locals are still fighting a bid to make two of the forthcoming ones nine and 12 storeys, not eight as planned. A footpath goes through to **Bollo Lane** (the office folk head for the Bollo pub for lunch), a road is also planned, and the entire scheme is throwing the spotlight on these sleepy streets.

To the W of **Acton Lane**, **Church Path** winds through the area; at one point **Cleveland Rd** joins it to run parallel behind a paved and tree'd strip: a nicely villagey spot with the Swan pub as a meeting-place. At the head of this is a pretty corner house at the end of opulent-sounding, and certainly pleasant, **Rothschild Rd**, where a 3-bed house 'needing work' sold for £415,000 last winter. Done up, 3-beds sell for up to £450,000; you can, though, still find the occasional unmodernised little 2-bed house, c. £330,000. **Kingswood Rd** and **Cunnington St** cut through: wide roads with better-than-average architecture. **Antrobus Rd** is also well regarded. **Bridgeman** and **Weston Rds**, running beside the increasingly noisy railway, are popular. **Ivy Crescent**, which backs onto the railway, is a fertile field for flat conversions. Controlled parking now blankets most of the area.

Fashionable warehouse conversions appeared in 1999: 18 1-, 2- and 3-bed flats on the corner of **Acton Lane/Fletcher Rd**, close to the rail line in the N of the area. Next, an old transformer station was itself transformed into the classy flats of 'Chiswick View'. Off

Steele Rd, a refurbished/rebuilt mews is tucked in behind smart (and firmly shut) gates. Round the corner off **Church Path**, **Chapter Close** is a modern mews development; Laing added another: behind the gates of Amblemede Court there are eight 3-bed houses and a 2-bed bungalow. Tucked behind the Acton Green Common/South Parade end of **Acton Lane**, first-time buyers find the ex-council maisonettes of **Clement Close** a good way to get a foot in the area: a 1-bed here, £185,000 last winter, 2-beds c. £200,000.

The northern borderlands centre on **Southfield Rd**, a continuation of The Avenue, which leads on round to Acton Lane past a primary school and a large recreation ground with tennis courts: one more barrier that again cuts this corner off from Acton proper to the N. **Southfield Rd** boasts some 1980s homes and a 1990 cache of 3-bed, 2-bath mews houses, as well as its square-bayed 1914 terraces (some are purpose-built 3-bed maisonettes); **Fielding Rd**, close to the conservation area, is similar. **Speldhurst Rd** and the N end of **St Alban's Avenue** have slightly earlier homes.

Transport Tube stations: Turnham Green, Stamford Brook, Chiswick Park (zone 2, District). From Turnham Green: Oxford Circus 25 min (1 change), City 40 min, Heathrow 25 min (1 change). Trains: South Acton on N London Line/Silverlink.

Convenient for Heathrow and M4. Miles from centre: 4.

Schools Ealing and Hounslow Education Authorities: Chiswick School, Acton School. Private: Latymer (b), Godolphin & Latymer (g), St Paul's (g), Arts Educational School.

SALES

Flats	S	1B	2B	3B	4B	5B
Average prices	130–180	160–250	220–400	250–450	300–800	–

Houses	2B	3B	4B	5B	6/7B	8B
Average prices	325–450	380–700	500–1M+	650–1.5M+	800–2M	–

RENTAL

Flats	S	1B	2B	3B	4B	5B
Average prices	150–250	200–350+	230–400+	300–600	450–1M+	–

Houses	2B	3B	4B	5B	6/7B	8B
Average prices	300–600	350–600	450–800	600–2500	700–2500+	–

The properties Distinctive enclave of pretty, late-19th century Queen Anne-style houses, from 3-bed cottages up to mansion-sized homes; prized, though gardens can be small, and parking lacking. Pleasant bordering streets are more everyday Victorian/Edwardian, plus mansion-flat blocks and little pockets of new houses and flats.

The market The small number of genuine, conservation-area Bedford Park houses for sale attracts devotees who join a lifestyle as well as a neighbourhood. Surrounding streets, and Acton Green, also popular family homes. These are at cheaper end of above prices.

Among estate agents active in this area are:

- Barnard Marcus
- Winkworths
- Bushells
- Chesterton
- Townends
- Bellenger
- Whitman & Co
- Borthwicks
- Foxtons
- Fitz-Gibbon
- Fletcher Estates
- Tyser Greenwood

BELGRAVIA

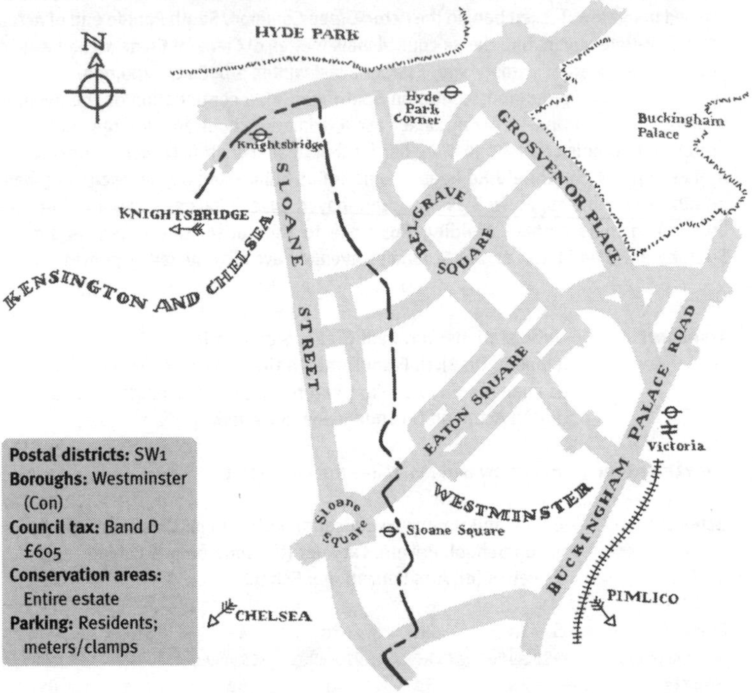

Postal districts: SW1
Boroughs: Westminster (Con)
Council tax: Band D £605
Conservation areas: Entire estate
Parking: Residents; meters/clamps

Length (of lease), Level (of service charge) and Luxury (state of) are the vital Three Ls of Belgravia property. Location is taken for granted here, between Buckingham Palace and Sloane Square, between Knightsbridge and Hyde Park Corner. Belgravia is a true enclave, a place of cream stucco and confident prosperity, minutes from Westminster and the West End yet miles, in atmosphere if not distance, from the traffic, the bustle, the crowds.

It offers homes of all sizes from little flats to monster mansions, from cottages to penthouses. Size and style may vary, status does not. But leases do: many homes are offered on short leases (see below). Before jumping at a low price, ascertain lease length: estate agents' details can be coy about this, though some worthy firms are precise and up-front. Ask too about service charges and ground rent: two seemingly identical flats on offer last winter had ground rents of £600 and £5,000 per annum. Another pair of one-beds, admittedly at opposite ends of the luxury spectrum, had service charges of £60 – and £10,000.

Which brings up the third L, luxury. A home with 'silk walls, marble and oak floors' (to quote from a Chester Sq example) can be twice the price of one that's just ordinarily smart – location, lease and size being identical. Whatever exalted standards you aspire to, somewhere in Belgravia can match them. Recently, Russian buyers have been testing the limits of opulence but Belgravia's developers and designers have proved up to the challenge. If you want a blank canvas for your creativity, unmodernised properties, such as a 12,000 sq ft, £12 million Belgrave Square house, still exist – but your efforts will still be subject to Listed Building approval.

Lease length raises the issue of leasehold reform, the process by which it has become steadily easier (if not cheaper) to extend leases and even buy freeholds (for more details of the latest law see Buying and Selling chapter). The Grosvenor Estate, which owns Belgravia, is central to life here. Belgravia is built on land held since 1677 by the Grosvenor family, the Dukes of Westminster (dukes since 1874).

The Duke's inheritance has been nibbled at of late by tenants exercising their rights under the Leasehold Reform Acts to buy the freehold of their houses, rather than pay the Estate (or a head-lessee) for a lease. The Estate now accepts the inevitability of enfranchisement; while it doesn't go out of its way to offer freeholds, it is 'happy to negotiate' with leaseholders who approach it – and will sell new leases of 99 years for houses, 125 for flats. Those in the know say the Estate is more relaxed about the situation than it was – but it still requires (and gets) large sums for extended leases.

So in the past few years, for the first time in two centuries, the word 'freehold' appears increasingly in Belgravia: about half the houses you will be offered these days will be freehold (partly because some who obtain freeholds sell on to crystalize their capital gain). The Grovesnor Estate office is still very much in charge, however: controlling tenancies, developing its own properties and stipulating just how the inhabitants – even the new freeholders – behave (try standing around drinking outside one of the few Belgravia pubs). The control of the Estate office may be discreet, but it is firm. Whatever their personal tastes, householders must paint their facades regularly, and paint them cream – not just any old cream, either, but the precise British Standard shade of magnolia that is the official Grovesnor Estate colour. Whether or not the Grovesnor Estate still owns the property, goes the thinking, safeguarding the integrity of the area protects everybody's investment. To protect its own the estate is developing flats to let as Assured Shorthold tenancies – these don't attract the right to enfranchise.

In Regency times the Grosvenors developed the 'Five Fields' just W of the new Buckingham Palace with the help of builder and architect Thomas Cubitt. Much of London was built up at this time or a little later, but no other district has kept its character in quite the same way. The credit goes partly to Cubitt, whose building standards were, if not exactly high, then better than those of Nash. But the main upholder of the Belgravian character has been the Grosvenor Estate, and the snowy sweep of stuccoed terraces and squares stands seemingly unchanged.

Central Belgravia is almost wholly residential. The Estate's policy is to use the fringes for offices and shops and hotels, but to keep the heartland free of commerce – unless you count embassies. Shops are to be found in a few streets: **Elizabeth St** and **Motcomb St** have the majority – and of course you can commission your furniture from Viscount Linley's shop among the galleries and antique shops on Belgravia's southern borders, around 'Pimlico Green' down on the **Pimlico Rd**. There are a few discreetly hidden pubs in mews. But the rest is houses and flats.

The properties vary considerably in size. The grandest homes, those in **Belgrave Square**, have virtually all become embassies or institutes. Nearly all of the only slightly more modest **Eaton Square** mansions are now flats. Smaller-scale houses often survive as single homes, as do many of the mews cottages – which were originally the stables for the grand streets and squares.

There are more freeholds available now, particularly of houses. But for the time being the standard commodity on sale here is the lease, either direct from the Estate or a sub-lease. Some can be very short, but those expecting a 15-year lease to be one-fifth the cost of a 75-year one are doomed to disappointment. For one thing, a short lease should qualify you to buy the freehold or a new lease in due course. Then there are those buyers of short leases, usually companies, who view the price as so many years' rent paid upfront, rather than as a purchase. On the third hand, private foreign buyers hate leasehold, so prices for freehold houses have rocketed. Understandably, all these considerations make price comparisons a tricky sport in Belgravia. Leasehold means paying ground rent, to add to a service charge which can shoot up in a year when the Estate decides the facade needs painting. 'Service charges,' comments a local, 'reassure one that neighbours will be like-minded people.' Except, that is, when the residents rebel – as happened in 2003 when some Eaton Square dwellers successfully challenged the Estate's programme of works which would have landed the leaseholder of one 2-bed flat with a bill for £45,000.

The area is very popular with foreign diplomats and businesspeople: Russians are the latest and most high-profile group. Owing to the positive ghetto of embassies in and around Belgrave Square there is a plethora of police, including the always-armed Diplomatic Protection Group. This reassures foreigners, say estate agents.

For a generation, until the 1970s, Belgravia's grand mansions were in decline, considered too big to inhabit without a legion of servants. They have been brought back into use by the great improvement in the art of conversion. The splendid old buildings are often just facades, concealing flats which are equally large and grand – and in some cases vast. Sometimes the conversions are lateral, running behind two or even three house facades to give whole-house-sized apartments on a single floor.

Southern Belgravia

Once, the Grosvenor family also owned the whole tract S from Victoria station down to the Thames: Pimlico was developed at the same time and was once considered part of Belgravia. The railway cut it off, however, and it never achieved the same status as its senior neighbour. The Estate sold Pimlico, known as the 'southern estate', in 1950 to cover death duties and to fund other, international investments – partly in Canada.

Belgravia thus starts at **Buckingham Palace Rd**, an anonymous, workaday through-route which runs alongside Victoria station. The strip between this road and **Ebury St**, which parallels it to the N, differs in character from central Belgravia. The occasional mews, and some flats in **Ebury Square**, compete for space with the Victoria Coach Station. Chantrey House on **Buckingham Palace Rd**, right on the edge of the Estate and facing Victoria Station, was redeveloped in 2003 by the Grovesnor Estate to yield 27 flats for letting plus nine more Affordable Homes. And just behind, in **Dorset Mews**, the Estate in partnership with Mountcity built five 3-bed houses around a courtyard with underground parking (c. £1.8 million apiece when sold in 2002). Now, the second half of the scheme yields three modern houses fronting onto Wilton St.

Ebury St ends, to the W, at **Pimlico Rd**, heading off to Chelsea. Going S, and outside the Estate, between it and the river the 12-acre Chelsea Barracks site will be developed at some point (the Army is reluctant to give it all up so roughly half may become homes), and work is under way on the Grosvenor Dock scheme – see Pimlico chapter. Between them they will add a whole new quarter, of which the only remaining original homes are likely to be the homely brick flats of the Peabody Trust Buildings.

Back to **Ebury St**, then, and the Belgravia heartland: a domestic-scale road that has been revitalized by a new road scheme, diverting the through-traffic away and slowing what remains right down. Conversion and restoration work is in evidence ('becoming much more Belgravia', nods a local) on its small – for Belgravia – early terraced houses, some of which are hotels. A few little shops and restaurants here, too. Human-scale, charming houses are mostly brick, not stucco, and some pre-date the rest of Belgravia; they can, paradoxically, boast some of the area's largest gardens. Mozart stayed in Ebury St, giving rise to the name Mozart Terrace for one short row, where a 2-bed flat was £695,000 last winter (65-year lease). Modern flats blocks are another option in Ebury St. The street ends near Victoria at **Grosvenor Gardens**, busy but convenient: its Victorian buildings house both offices and flats.

Between **Ebury St** and **Eaton Square** comes the first slice of Belgravia proper. And how proper it is, with quiet, pretty **Chester Square** as its showpiece. These houses were built as 'second rank' homes (second, that is, to the monster ones of Belgrave and Eaton Squares), but are today considered to be some of the best in the area. Nearly all are still single houses, but there are some equally large flats. Take your choice from last winter's offerings: a 3,800 sq ft lateral flat, height of *grande luxe*, £5.25 million for a 54-year lease, or a whole freehold house, 4,850 sq ft and mere everyday luxury rather than top opulence – for the same price. Another house, 6 beds, was £11 million. **Chester Row** is similar, but the houses are on a smaller scale: c. £2.2 million will buy a 5-bed freehold.

Eccleston St, which bisects Chester Square, is a one-way road taking traffic up to Hyde Park Corner. This is where the mews begin: the Belgravia 'back streets' where the little cottages, built to house the gentry's horses, now house the gentry. These – often cul-de-sacs boasting arched entrances and cobbles – can have enormous charm (not to mention garages). **Ebury Mews**, running through from Eccleston St to Elizabeth St, is typical, although not a cul-de-sac. It has a mix of mews cottages of greater and lesser degrees of smartness, plus some new-build homes in mews style. The latest are a row of six, reconstructed behind the facades into state-of-the-art luxury a couple of years back by Octagon. Belgravia's peaceful mews offers your own front door for under a million; witness a 1-bed cottage in **Minerva Mews**, off **Chester Row**, on the market for £750,000 freehold, and the **Eaton Mews South** 3-bed for £850,000 (but just 22 years).

Lower Belgrave St is another busy road, southbound this time, with plain but handsome brick houses. **Elizabeth St** has very upmarket shops (including some serving quite everyday needs such as food – a deliberate Estate policy is to encourage the 'village' nature of the street) and, increasingly, some good restaurants. Its homes include a very beautiful, low-built house – its style more reminiscent of the Nash villas of Regent's Park than of the usual lofty Belgravia terraces. There are also flats above shops.

To the W, houses in **Eaton Terrace** range from 4- to 7-beds, and for a good-standard house you can expect to pay between £2.5 and £3.5 million depending on lease. **Caroline Terrace** has more handsome brick and stucco houses – most still single homes: typically 3- to 4-bed, with gardens and (a few) with garages.

Between **Eaton Terrace** and the Chelsea borders are some smaller homes. **Bourne St**'s 2-storey plus semi-basement houses are 2/3-beds. **Graham Terrace**, too, has more modest sizes. **Belgrave Place** is off here: a new development (2002) – a rarity in this area – on an old school site. It has 28 town-houses, 3-, 4-, 5- and 6-beds (some boast pools and £4 million-plus price tags), and thirteen 1-, 2-, 3- and 4-bed flats. To the W **Bunhouse Place**, tucked behind Bourne St, has 1970s neo-Georgian town-houses: quiet and popular. Look out for **Grosvenor Cottages**, tucked away off Eaton Terrace: a delightful gated mews with a row of sweet 2-bed cottages, some double-fronted – and at the far end an elaborate, discreetly hidden, 3-bed house.

But **Eaton Square** is the centrepiece on which Belgravia turns. It has, to say the least, considerable presence. The buildings, in long, dignified terraces, entered via large and pillared porches, are enormous. It could more properly be called 'Eaton Squares': it is on so large a scale that inhabitants hardly seem to notice the slight disadvantage of the main King's Rd running down the middle en route to Chelsea. And two smaller roads cross at right angles, thus dividing the central garden into six – all of good size. Only a handful of houses (eight out of 118, to be precise, say the Estate) are still single homes. The Estate itself refurbished (rebuilt would be a better word) two of them in 2003: prices were around the £20-million mark. One is on the market now at £15 million (you get the mews house at the back thrown in). The rest of these towering terraces have yielded some 350 flats. Penthouses, often sprawling across two or three houses, top most of them. The Grosvenor Estate also recently developed Nos. 1–4 Eaton Square, which added a further thirteen 2- to 5-bed flats. Flats in the square come in all sizes, prices and leases. A 1-bed (930 sq ft) flat with just 11 years on the lease was £175,000, while 46-year leases on a couple of 2-beds were £725,000 and £850,000 – but each had service charges of nearly £10,000 a year. The sky is the limit for the penthouses.

B

Eaton Place, on the way northwards towards the centre of the Estate, runs parallel to Eaton Square; its large houses, most divided into grand flats, are second only in scale to those of the square.

Central Belgravia

Belgrave Square was planned as homes, but is today mostly embassies and institutions. This is principally due to an earlier restrictive planning policy, which decreed that the buildings could only be used for diplomatic or charitable purposes. Embassies saved this gracious square from decline: since World War II, several dozen 'new' countries have set up shop in London – and all, to the relief of the Grosvenor Estate at the time, needed rather imposing buildings – and those are certainly what they found here. Three enormous mansions, set slant-wise across the square's corners, are as big as any in London and are home to the likes of the Portuguese and Spanish ambassadors.

However, over the past decade a few of the institutional buildings have, now that that policy has been relaxed, reverted to homes or offices. One was on the market last winter at £12 million, which included the mews house behind. Both main house (12,000 sq ft) and the 4,000sq ft mews needing renovation. A 'done-up' Belgrave Square house was rumoured to have been bought by a Russian for £25 million last Christmas. A 29-year lease on a 2-bed penthouse flat was on offer at £1.38 million.

North of Belgrave Square are more mews – on a grander scale this time – with the stucco continuing behind the scenes. The arched entrances cut the mews off from the busy main streets. **Wilton Crescent** is the queen of this corner, its grand Regency sweep breaking the tempo of the streets and squares – as does its facade, distinctively refaced with stone a century ago. A 7-bed house here, mews included, was £10 million last winter. **Wilton Terrace** leads back into Belgrave Square. The N end of **Wilton Place** has some rare early, pre-Cubitt brick houses: a 31-year lease on an unrestored one was £1.7 million last winter – but please budget for the £7,500 per annum ground rent.

Little, villagey **Kinnerton St**, leading off, has concealed surprises: it is the entrance to an unusual warren of old and new cottages in mews and courtyards. Look here for pretty cottages (4-bed, £1.8 million freehold), and for surprisingly smart flats, both recent and period, in the courts: **Kinnerton Yard** has low-built 1970s flats around courtyards, £450,000 for a 36-year lease on a 2-bed. Kinnerton St boasts a couple of pubs, art gallery, village stores. To the S are some big blocks of flats with car parking (3-bed £695,000 for 58 years), then **Motcomb St** with more shops, including the novelty of a Waitrose supermarket (supermarkets were previously unknown in the estate). The succession of mews and terraces continues on past **West Halkin St** back to **Eaton Square. Chesham Place** runs E to the corner of Belgrave Square: an 18,000sq ft house, returned to a home from offices and provided with a generous 13 bedrooms and two swimming pools, attracted competing bids late in 2002 before selling for £19 million.

The E corner of Belgravia also has a cut-off collection of mews and little streets with a villagey feel, a couple of good pubs and even a general store. Streets such as **Groom Place** and **Wilton Mews** have all the Belgravia assets, plus a little extra atmosphere (a linked pair of Groom Place mews houses: £5.25 million freehold). **Montrose Place**, where there is a car park, has a newly-rebuilt mews house at £1.65 million (freehold) and will soon gain 14 flats in a venture linking Grosvenor and Clan Estates. **Chester St**, by contrast, which runs through the middle of this mewsy corner, has double-fronted Chandos House and tall, 6-storey brick and stucco terraces.

The NE corner is dominated by the Lanesborough Hotel, on **Hyde Park Corner**. A nest of little mews cottages behind it offers more charming and very desirable homes: some of these, in **Grosvenor Crescent Mews**, are deceptive – the Estate created 17 new homes behind the original facades six years ago, with more sybaritically-sized rooms. One at least is a mews house in address only: it has a swimming pool and five bedrooms. Some really small 1-bed cottages can be found in charming **Old Barrack Yard**, a flagstoned path through to **Knightsbridge** from **Wilton Row**. Those with grand ambitions should enquire about the row of eight 6-floor terraced houses for sale in **Grosvenor Crescent**.

To the W, the borough boundary running down **Lowndes St** and **Chesham St** marks, more or less, the end of the Duke's remit. **Lowndes Square**, often called Belgravia, is in Knightsbridge (see that chapter). The end of the Estate's control is marked.

Transport Tubes, all zone 1: Knightsbridge (Piccadilly), Sloane Sq (District, Circle), Victoria (District, Circle, Victoria). From Sloane Square to Oxford Circus 15 min (1 change), City 20 min, Heathrow 55 min.

Convenient for West End, Hyde Park. Miles from centre: 1.5.

Schools Local Authority: Pimlico School, Greycoat Hospital C of E (g). Private: Francis Holland (g), The American International School, Westminster School (b), More House School (g).

SALES

Flats	S	1B	2B	3B	4B	5B
Average prices	–	350–750	450–1.7M+	700–2.9M+	1–3M+	–
Houses	2B	3B	4B	5B	6/7B	8B
Average prices	800–1M+	1–2.5M+	1.1–3M+	1.8–5M	2.2–11M	–

RENTAL

Flats	S	1B	2B	3B	4B	5B
Average prices	200–400	250–575	420–1000+	650–1600	1000+	–
Houses	2B	3B	4B	5B	6/7B	8B
Average prices	575–1000+	750–2000	1100–2000	2600+	4000+	–

The properties Mainly owned by the Grosvenor Estate; longer leases and freeholds now, thanks to Leasehold Reform Acts. Grand Regency homes provide equally grand converted apartments. Also houses of all sizes from mews cottage to embassy.

The market 'Average' prices here are a very general guide: all depends on length of lease, degree of luxury and location. Discounting embassy-sized houses, Eaton Square commands highest prices and kudos. Mainstream prices for long lease or freehold equate to £1,000-plus psf. Short leases now offer scope to enfranchise.

Among estate agents active in this area are:

- George Trollope
- Beaney Pearce
- Strutt & Parker
- Ayrton Wylie
- John D Wood
- Chesterfields
- Knight Frank
- Friend & Falcke
- Savills
- W A Ellis
- Aylesford
- Hamptons
- Cluttons
- Lane Fox
- Douglas Lyons & Lyons
- Lord Francis Russell & Co
- Chesterton
- Foxtons
- Anscombe & Ringland
- De Groot Collis
- Best Gapp & Cassells
- Henry & James

BETHNAL GREEN

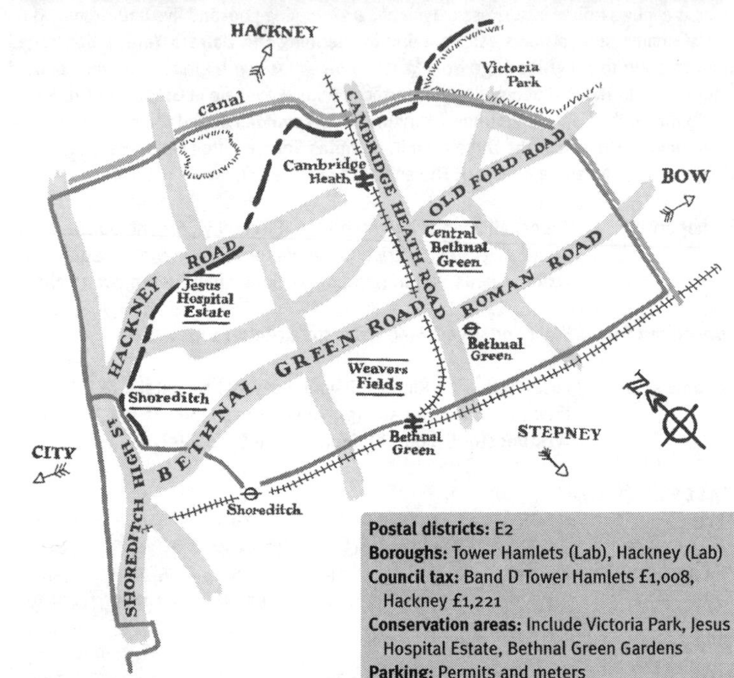

Postal districts: E2
Boroughs: Tower Hamlets (Lab), Hackney (Lab)
Council tax: Band D Tower Hamlets £1,008, Hackney £1,221
Conservation areas: Include Victoria Park, Jesus Hospital Estate, Bethnal Green Gardens
Parking: Permits and meters

The East End's traditional role is to be a staging-post for successive waves of new Londoners. Bethnal Green, right beside the City, is doing its share. Current incomers are of several sorts, of which the most vividly contrasting are the buyers of smart new £300,000 flats on the one hand and refugees from every continent's miseries on the other. Add these to the traditional Cockney population – itself an amalgam of incomers dating back to Huguenot silk weavers and beyond – and you get one of London's most diverse communities.

The resurgence in inner-city living that made Clerkenwell a residential area once again and brought loft-dwellers to Hoxton is bringing one sort of newcomer to Bethnal Green. Here you can live a tube-stop or a bike-ride from the City, and walk home from the nightlife and restaurants of Shoreditch and Brick Lane. Indeed, many of the young (they are mostly young, and single) incomers both work and live here: arts, media, communications shape their lives and form their livelihoods. New blocks of 'loft-style' flats are adding to the genuine factory and warehouse conversions; the big builders have their smart sales suites and show-flats to tempt the timid.

Those on smaller budgets find myriad ex-council flats, and rather fewer houses. These are the result of another population shift: as a local puts it, 'Bethnal Green's not the place it used to be; everyone moves further east along the District Line as they become more affluent'. Their affluence comes in part from selling-on the council flat bought under Right to Buy. And, as in other inner London areas, if on the one hand the City's boom years have seeded regeneration and an influx of cash into what was for so long a run-down and neglected area, on the other there's understandable cynicism about 'all the trendy types moving in with trust funds, trying to slum it and patronizing the locals'. This is, after all, the spiritual heart of the East End, with a vivid past of gangsters, boxing and poverty. The picture is changing. The rash of building includes joint ventures between the area's traditional landlords, the councils and the philanthropic trusts, to help local people find affordable local homes via fair-rent and shared-ownership deals. The gangsters, these days, live in Chigwell (or Marbella). Artists, by contrast, are moving in.

The opening of offices here by Clerkenwell-based agents is evidence of the move of homeseekers into the area from the likes of Clerkenwell, Shoreditch and Islington. Here they find cheaper flats and rows of sturdy 2-storey, 1840–60s terraced houses – those that survived the Blitz and 1960s 'slum' clearance now command £300,000 plus. The new inhabitants are mainly couples: Tower Hamlets' schools (while improving) are as yet no draw to families (though among local primaries William Davis and Bonner are doing well).

Bethnal Green – the green is still there, and marks the centre of the old village – and Shoreditch abut the NE corner of the City; Hackney is to the N, Bow to the E, and Stepney to the S. The main thoroughfares are (W—E) **Hackney Rd**, **Bethnal Green Rd** and (N—S) **Cambridge Heath Rd**, which runs from Stepney through to Hackney; where the latter two and **Roman Rd** meet, lies the ancient green (now Bethnal Green Gardens, one of four conservation areas) with the Bethnal Green Museum of Childhood at its top. The brave new world of Docklands, and the river, lie a mere mile or so to the SE.

Bethnal Green

The western corner of lovely Victoria Park forms part of Bethnal Green's NE boundary; it is edged, on the Bethnal side, by the Grand Union Canal: homes in the conservation area with views over canal and park command a premium. **Sewardstone** and **Approach Rds**, where 3- and 4-storey Victorian houses have been converted into flats, are popular, but **Cyprus St** is more sought after. Some of its neat 2- and 3-bed terraced homes, built before World War I, are Grade II listed, with original shutters adding to their tidy appearance; these days they reach £300,000-plus. The well kept Victorian rows have immense character; a plaque, dedicated to the memory of the men of **Cyprus St** who died in two world wars, hangs between Nos. 76–78. The terrace is continued by the Duke of Wellington pub, and further S is the Cranbrook Estate of council homes, largely 2- and 3-bed flats.

Roman Rd, a busy thoroughfare which runs E into Bow, has more council homes to the S and Meath Gardens, a welcome relief from the blocks of flats. Some low, modern council-built blocks in **Morpeth St** offer 3-bed duplexes. Before the canal bridge in the corner of the Cranbrook Estate is the Twig Folly development of canalside flats. These proved a success, and a second tranche completed in 2001. Next to this is Bow Brook, an old school turned into loft-style flats. The area W to Bethnal Green tube is known as Globe Town: the London Buddhist Centre, a Thai restaurant on **Burnham St**, photographic and art galleries on the Roman Rd itself, mix with pie-and-mash shops and discount butchers. Victoria Wharf, in **Palmers Rd** off Roman Rd, will have flats and work-homes. The biggest new tranche is 'Base E2' in **Warley St**, overlooking Meath Gardens: 258 new-last-year homes by Copthorn. It joins Caesar Court (14 flats) and Justine Place (22 live/work units) in Palmers Rd.

Victoria Park Square, which is actually off **Old Ford Rd** and behind Bethnal Green Museum, has bigger, 4-bed Victorian (naturally) houses and 1940s council-built flats. Opposite York Hall Baths in **Old Ford Rd** is an imposing Georgian house, The Terraces, part of which has been made into flats. Terraced houses, many refurbished, are on either side. On E down Old Ford Rd is **Bonner Rd**, with a row of impressive council-built houses.

At the junction of Roman Rd with Cambridge Heath Rd, the tube station stands in the splendour of Bethnal Green Gardens, another conservation area. Victoria Park Square leads to Sugar Loaf Walk and then a cluster of close-knit red-brick terraced houses in **Moravian St, Gawber St, Welwyn St, Globe Rd**. South of Roman Rd, in **Sceptre Rd** Park View, late '90s, has 1-, 2- and 3-bed flats. North of the railway on **Hadleigh St** are new

Peabody Trust flats for rent – and some very Victorian, and still-functioning, stables.

North along **Cambridge Heath Rd** is Millennium Place, a new gated flats development, and more council-built homes in **Patriot Square**, opposite the town hall. These command good prices and quick sales when they come onto the market. On the corner of **Bishop's Way** is a recent block of a dozen flats for rent. Over the road is Cambridge Heath station (trains to Liverpool St), and across Hackney Rd is a large refurbished council estate that takes in **Pritchard's Rd**, **Coate St**, **Teale St** and **Emma St**. Close by, **Wharf Place** has a canalside warehouse conversion of 2-bed flats, London Wharf. Next door, Regent's Wharf is an '80s apartment block. Both are very popular.

To the W, the Jesus Hospital Estate is on the S side of Hackney Rd and includes **Columbia Rd, Wellington Row, Durant St, Baxendale St, Quilter St, Elwin St, Ezra St, Wimbolt St**. These pretty, flat-fronted, two-up, two-down Victorian terraced cottages are very popular and sell fast – a 2-bed house goes for c. £320,000. Many boast hanging baskets of flowers in summer: **Columbia Rd** holds the famous Sunday-morning flower market. Columbia Rd itself has seen some new, much sought-after developments and is becoming positively desirable: art galleries, frock shops, etc. In contrast, council towers a street away in **Ravenscroft St** offer 1-bed flats. Another former pub in **Barnet Grove** has just been split into flats, and Providence Yard on **Ezra St** has three new live-work units. To the S, in **Claredale St**, is the tidied-up, iconic Grade II-listed ex-council tower block, Keeling House, where flats were sold off in 2000: resales include 2-beds at around £230,000.

Off **Hackney Rd** are a number of small developments – two by Peabody – and a clutch of new studio/workshops. **Cheshire St** has some tidied-up flats above shops. Here, too, Furlong Homes added the Portrait Place live/work units, and Galliard plan a big flats scheme. London Terrace, again off Hackney Rd, is a courtyard scheme of 2-bed flats.

On S, bustling **Bethnal Green Rd** has a street market (and a Tesco Metro), and 14 flats being built by Higgins Homes. A short stroll to the S is another contrast in **Derbyshire St**, where delightful 2- and 3-storey Victorian terraced houses fringe green Weavers Fields. Chicksand St has the new 'Vibeca' lock with 2-bed flats at £247–289,000. **Buckfast St**, just off Bethnal Green Rd, has a new development: a mix of flats and mews houses called Ebony House. In **Wilmot St**, opposite Hague Primary School (which has a good name), is the Waterlow estate, a 1980s Barratt conversion of a Victorian terrace into studio, 1- and 2-bed flats: around 400 homes including some sheltered homes. The **Ainsley St/Wilmot Square** corner has handsome 1900 stock-brick blocks of flats in tree-lined streets: £235,000 for a 2-bed. At the bottom of Wilmot St, in Three Colts Lane, is Bethnal Green train station. Across in **Dunbridge St**, the handsome Edwardian public baths are now 1- and 2-bed flats: pay c. £240,000 this year (as last year) for a 2-bed. East along **Bethnal Green Rd**, at the junction with Punderson's Gardens, is the City View block. This big converted bakery now holds 110 flats (2-bed £245,000), while the old police station, too, is nowadays 2- and 3-bed flats. **Paradise Row**, where Bethnal Green Rd meets Cambridge Heath Rd, lives up to its name with 3- and 4-storey Georgian terraced houses. At the end of **Birkbeck St** off Cambridge Heath Rd, a converted soap factory: Sunlight Square has 1-, 2- and 3-bed flats: 2-beds £235,000-plus, 2-bed penthouse c. £335,000.

Shoreditch

Across the busy **Kingsland Rd,** the old Roman road due N out of the City, Shoreditch has reinvented itself – replete with trendy bars, galleries and new-media companies. Most of the action takes place W of **Shoreditch High St** and the **Kingsland Rd**: see City chapter.

On the eastern, Bethnal Green side of Shoreditch, most of the homes are council-owned: the Boundary Estate conservation area is the oldest council-built housing in London, dating from the 1890s when the old London County Council (LCC) cleared a notorious slum. It includes **Palissy St, Rochelle St, Navarre St, Calvert Avenue** and

Montclare St. These streets, containing mostly flats, ring **Arnold Circus** with its bandstand; a 1-bed ex-council flat in the Circus might be c. £150,000, a 4-bed £280,000. North of the Circus is the Mildmay Mission Hospital; next door are 14 new flats.

B

Calvert Avenue leads W to Shoreditch High St and Shoreditch Church, with the picturesque St Leonard's Gardens. **Boundary St** itself has just acquired Anlaby House, a new flats block. **Hackney Rd** is fast improving; a Georgian terrace, formerly owned by the NHS, has been split into flats, new flats are under way and surviving Georgian houses can be had. Off it, **Waterson St** is the scene of much activity: 34 new flats, and more to come here and in **Long St.** North of Hackney Rd, E of Kingsland Rd, is mostly light-industrial, though Peabody and Hackney Council have a joint scheme with 69 flats for sale in **Cremer St**, behind the splendid, revamped Geffrye Museum, and Telford's large new scheme is now complete in **Goldsmiths Row.**

Bethnal Green covers part of **Brick Lane,** billed as 'the Portobello of the East': the old Truman brewery – now artists' and designers' workspaces – together with the rebranding of this Asian community area as 'Bangla Town', is transforming its character. Period homes survive; new flats have been built in **Quaker St**, with more to come, plus live/work units, in the big new Eagle Works scheme. See also City & Fringes chapter.

Transport Tubes: Bethnal Green (zone 2, Central), Shoreditch (zone 2, East London line). From Bethnal Green: Oxford Circus 15 min, City 5 min, Heathrow 1 hr 20 min (1 change). Trains: Cambridge Heath, Bethnal Green – trains to Liverpool St, Essex and Herts.

Convenient for The City, Docklands, Victoria Park. Miles from centre: 3.

Schools Local Authority: Morpeth School, Raine's C of E, Sir John Cass & Redcoat, Swanlea School. Independent: Madani School.

SALES

Flats	S	1B	2B	3B	4B	5B
Average prices	100–140	130–200	150–250	140–280	–	–
	2B	3B	4B	5B	6/7B	8B
Houses	240–280	280–350	320–450	–	–	–

RENTAL

Flats	S	1B	2B	3B	4B	5B
Average prices	130–150	170–210	200–270	240–350	–	–
Houses	2B	3B	4B	5B	6/7B	8B
Average prices	230–300	330–400	400–500	–	–	–

The properties Two- and 3-bed terraces, plus new and ex-council flats. Large houses rare. Increasing: smaller flats and smart, Docklands-style warehouse conversions and new-build.

The market Buy the best as you'll have plenty of competition when selling from all the developments here and in Docklands. Lack of good schools deters families. Tube excitement on W edge of area.

Among estate agents active in this area:

- Land & Co
- Meade
- Alex Neil
- Mitchelson McCarthy
- Winkworth
- Hamilton Fox
- Keatons
- Bridge Estates
- Mark James
- Spicer McColl

BLOOMSBURY AND KING'S CROSS

Postal districts: WC1, N1
Boroughs: Camden (Lab), Islington (Lib Dem)
Council tax: Band D Camden £1,200, Islington £1,107
Conservation areas: Most of area
Parking: Residents/meters; most of area inside Congestion Charge zone.

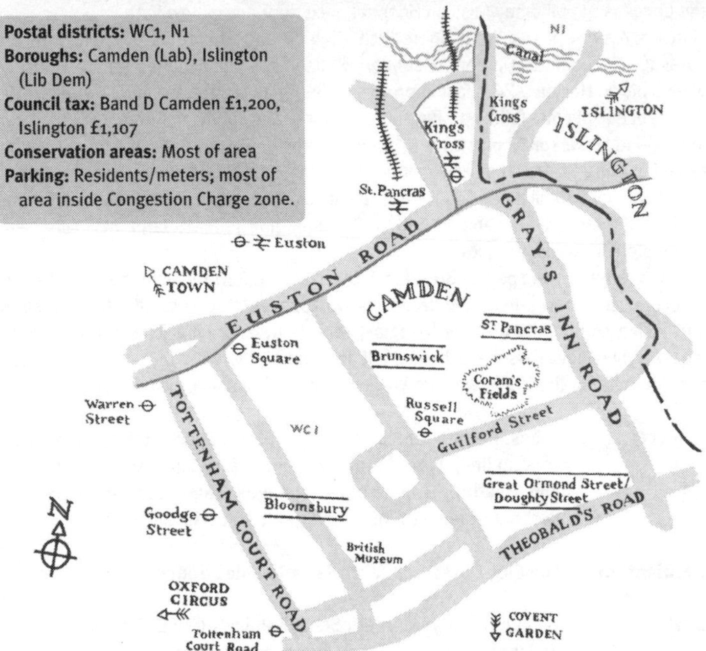

The new Central London neighbourhood now arriving at King's Cross will be a great place to live. But that's future, not present: for the next few years, living in King's Cross will be like joining one of those trains that sits in the station, going nowhere, with lights and heating intermittent. The area's eventual success will be down to superb transport – trains to everywhere from Paris to Perth, a tube hub with five lines, direct rail links to three of London's five airports. . . . All due by 2007, and suprisingly enough on schedule (at the moment).

Meanwhile, there will be digging, and dirt, and noise, and disruption, and much wandering down half-finished tube subways. And only in 2007 will the real building start, on the giant new King's Cross Central district, with a time span of 15 years. That's 2022.

So why buy there now? True, King's Cross itself is a mile from the City, a mile from the West End. But right now it is seedy, traffic-choked, and low on every kind of amenity except train stations. The off-plan buyers who have signed up for half the available new flats might be taking a long view – or perhaps a very short one, hoping that the pre-Eurostar hype (January '07, they say) will boost prices.

So should you join them? Or perhaps place a bet on Bloomsbury, which is bigger, quieter, closer in, and has been a residential district for three centuries. King's Cross is, after all, just up the road, a single tube stop away.

Emerge from Russell Square tube through a sea of bemused tourists and you could be forgiven for writing Bloomsbury off as a place to live. But turn a couple of corners and discover a district of elegant squares and hidden mews, offering a wide range of flats and the occasional superb period house.

Here you can live in the very heart of London: E lies the City, SW is the West End and theatreland. You can walk to both. The British Museum, London University, British Library

and dozens of academic institutions lie scattered around an area with Georgian bone-structure and, for so central a location, green and peaceful corners. This mix of academia and offices heavily dilutes the residential, which is why the area is not so well known. Many handsome homes are now offices; many of the less-smart ones are small hotels. Bloomsbury does not appeal to international buyers or those after a fashionable address. It attracts pied-à-terre seekers, childless couples, busy singles, romantics.

As a glance at its street names shows, Bloomsbury owes its existence to the nobility: the Southampton and Bedford families, to be exact, who developed the area as one of London's very first planned suburbs. **Bloomsbury Square**, named after the Earl of Southampton, was laid out in the 1660s, after the restoration of Charles II: alas, none of the houses from that era remain. The Southampton family estates were joined by marriage to those of the Russells, the Dukes of Bedford. Add in the Lady Gower who married the fourth Duke and you have a complete gazetteer of Bloomsbury names, though only a small part remains in Russell hands today. Other streets are (or were) owned by public school trusts – Rugby, Tonbridge and Bedford – though Camden Council has bought and restored large chunks of these rather moribund estates (one row of neglected Georgian houses on the Rugby Estate actually collapsed in the 1970s).

As well as the British Museum – here since 1755 – the University of London takes up large tracts, and there are several hospitals. The university's buildings form an almost solid block between the **Euston Rd** in the N, **Gower St** in the W, **Woburn Place** in the E, and **Russell Square/Montague Place** in the S. Last year the university sold off some outlying buildings off **Hunter St**: see below. . . .

Many of the surviving Georgian buildings spent most of the 20th century as offices, though a few return to domestic use each year, and much of the housing has – for the past 30 or so years – been controlled by the council and housing associations. But now, would-be denizens, and developers, stalk the streets. There's a brisk rental market – all those hospitals and colleges – and demand for both flats as pieds-à-terre (people often pay cash) and the rare houses. Bloomsbury received a boost from the revival of next-door Clerkenwell; then came the rediscovery of Marylebone and Fitzrovia to the W. Another catalyst has been a policy change by the Bedford Estate, which saw the offices begin to recede: one 5-storey Georgian house in **Great James St**, with planning permission to revert at last to a home, sold last winter for £1.5 million. Note that there's an optimistic attempt by some agents to rebrand the area, along with Holborn, as 'Mid-Town'.

The most common dwelling in Bloomsbury is the flat, with whole houses rare, and priced accordingly. Studios, 1- and 2-beds can be had either in purpose-built blocks (mostly from Edwardian times and the 1930s) or as conversions, new and old.

B

The area, for our purposes, is bounded by **Tottenham Court Rd** in the W, **King's Cross Rd/Farringdon Rd** in the E, **Theobalds Rd** and **New Oxford St** in the S and the **Euston Rd** to the N. This is a larger area than 'traditional' Bloomsbury, taking in streets which are allied to, but not quite part of, the old estate.

Bloomsbury can be divided into four distinct neighbourhoods that radiate out from **Brunswick Square** and **Russell Square**, which lie together at the heart of the area: St Pancras in the NE, Great Ormond St/Doughty St to the SE, and Brunswick and Bloomsbury to the W. The SW quadrant, towards Bedford Square, is the most expensive, with the NE, towards King's Cross, remaining less so.

Great Ormond St/Doughty St

Sheltering between the busy main routes of **Southampton Row**, **Guilford St**, **Theobalds Rd** and the **Gray's Inn Rd** is a lovely quiet part of London with wide pedestrian-only streets and an abundance of pâtisseries, cafés and small shops. The Rugby School Estate owns the residue of its historic eight acres around **Great Ormond** and **Lamb's Conduit Sts**; Camden Council is also a big landlord (of, among others, some superb early 18th-century houses built by the Rugby Estate).

Guilford St is only partly Georgian: 1960s hospital and college buildings replace some of the originals (a studio in a '70s block, £193,000), with an abundance of small hotels at the E end. Much of the surviving Georgiana has belonged for years to the famed Great Ormond Street hospital for children: they are completing the renovation of the run-down but beautiful, and fundamentally intact, 1790s houses in Guilford St and **Lansdowne Terrace**. Some, on the corner of **Grenville St**, have already been entirely replaced by impeccable fake-Georgian homes.

Take a footpath S from **Guilford St** to delightful, little-known **Queen Square**. Most of it is lined by offices and hospitals (and a good pub), but on the N side some handsome 1930s flats have excellent views across the square's gardens (a 1-bed, £320,000), as does Guilford Court, a 1970s block. The S side has some council-built flats: a 2-bed, £300,000 last autumn. One or two of the early Georgiana on the W side hold flats; some, too, in little **Cosmo Place**, which leads through to **Southampton Row**, busy and hotel-lined – but with 1900s and '30s mansion flats too: an unmodernised 3-bed, £500,000.

Millman St runs S from Guilford St and has a row of modern council-built maisonettes opposite some flats carved from 3-storey Victorian houses: a 2-bed lateral conversion, £415,000. It runs into **Rugby St**, which combines shops and offices with very ornate, terraced 4-storey Victoriana, again now flats. **Lamb's Conduit St**, which is partly pedestrianized, is the haunt of the area's café society, with designer shops, galleries, good pubs, restaurants. There is a recent block of flats above the shops at the N end; this links with a conversion of several houses on the corner, adding in 2002 14 new flats to a stock which includes some 1930s ones. The remaining property is shops with flats – often spacious – above; most is part of the Rugby estate.

Dombey St leads W, with houses built in 1884 and quiet courtyards at the back, and some Georgian houses split into flats. **New North St** has some big blocks of 1950s council-built flats – now often for sale, and reasonably priced. **Orde Hall St**, running N from Dombey St, again has 19th-century 3/4-storey sand-coloured houses decorated with red brick – nowadays converted to flats. Orde Hall runs into **Great Ormond St**, which splits the area in half. The W part of this has the famous children's hospital, but there are still 18th-century houses (a couple unrestored still), with flats at the E end.

Doughty St, which crosses Guilford St, is most famous for once housing Dickens at No. 48. But now there are few private residents – although the lucky ones have 3- and 4-storey Georgian buildings with grand pillared porches: a 6-bedroomed example, £2.6 million. There are a few flats. **John St** is a continuation of Doughty St to the S: similar but slightly older houses – a 5 bed here, £2.5 million last winter – though many are offices.

Behind Doughty St is cobbled **Doughty Mews**, which has some small houses with roof gardens above garages (and a good pub). A 3-bed was £725,000 last winter; a 4-bed was on at £710,000. There is also Mytre Court, a '30s block of flats at the junction with **Roger St** which overlooks a primary school. There's a number of other mews in the neighbourhood, but they are mostly commercial.

Gray's Inn Rd is a busy mix of modern office blocks, small shops and surviving period houses. Flats in plenty: slices of Georgiana, conversions above shops, late-Victorian mansion blocks, smart modern ones; latest are six flats, £270,000 plus, over a refurbished pub. **North Mews**, off to the W, has six 1980s town-houses, with some flats opposite; a 3-bed 1997 house here, £725,000. **Northington St** has more converted Georgiana.

Holborn

South of **Theobalds Rd** and E of **Kingsway**, the Holborn district has a few homes dotted among the shops, offices and lawyers' chambers. **Red Lion Square** has some surviving 17th-century houses, built when the square was laid out in 1684. A newly refurbished modern block here is a cache of 16 flats, largely to rent. A careful look S and E from here, towards **High Holborn**, will reveal some superbly central homes, mostly flats above shops. The really beautiful Georgian houses of **Bedford Row** are nearly all offices (there are some flats at the N end); a few have been returned to residential glory – and £3-millionish price tags. In **Red Lion St**, 12 flats in a white modern block add to the 1930s mansion blocks, and you can even live on **High Holborn** these days, as offices on the corner of **Chancery Lane** became flats. Another change of use in **Three Cups Yard**, where a Victorian school is now 19 homes: a 2-bed flat and a 2-bed house were both £410,000 last autumn. Next-door **Hand Court**, off High Holborn, also has converted flats.

St Pancras/Coram's Fields

Like Holborn, St Pancras was once a borough, and its town hall stands in **Judd St**. The area is best known for its station, and for the British Library building next door to it. The astonishing architecture of the old Midland Grand Hotel that fronts the station looks set to come into its own again when the Eurostar terminus is complete: a hotel, it is hoped, will reopen, while Manhattan Lofts plan 68 loft flats in the topmost floors.

Judd St and its continuation to the S, **Hunter St**, form the border of St Pancras. The socially mixed St Pancras side, to the E, contrasts with Brunswick to the W. A lot of the N part, round **Cromer St** and **Argyle Walk**, has council-built housing, but with courtyards often adorned with small trees, plants and bright wall paintings. The homes date from the very early 20th century and from the big building programme which followed bombing in World War II. **Argyle Square** and other streets round it are mid-19th century, and most of the houses are small hotels. One or two are homes: handsome, Grade II-listed terraced houses – an unmodernised 5-bed in **Crestfield St**, £925,000. **Judd St** has some flats above shops and three large blocks, including the popular Queen Alexandra Mansions at the N end. Clare Court is a 1930s block (2-bed, £300,000).

Going S, **Regent Square** is not as its name implies: much is 1950s council-built flats. The S, **Sidmouth St**, side does, though, have a lovely row of late Georgian houses overlooking St George's Gardens (1-bed conversion flats here, £160–170,000). The Gardens, which run through to **Wakefield St**, have been tidied with lottery cash, and the council has spent a deal on refurbishments hereabouts: witness the flats in Wakefield St.

In **Hunter St** are more large, 1930s or Edwardian blocks such as Jenner House (2-bed £300,000); also surviving Georgiana currently being refurbished. This includes a batch of properties owned by the university (here and on into **Handel St**). These have already yielded five 1- and 2-bed flats; ten more are due this year, from £315,000 up. Brunswick Court, again ex-UCL, is now a source of flats from c. £270–370,000. Another straw in the wind: Galliard are selling off a block of £100,000 studios in Albany House, previously let.

The best homes in this corner are in the S and W: some lovely 3-storey Georgian houses line quiet, tree-lined **Mecklenburgh Square**, though the whole N side is owned by the university. There's a purpose-built block of flats on the square, facing the open space of Coram's Fields – a haven of green space with playground and animals, including sheep, for the delight of local kids. No adults allowed without a child. In **Heathcote St**, N of the Square, is attractive neo-Georgian Grayland Court, with flats and maisonettes.

B

Crossing **Gray's Inn Rd** E into **Calthorpe St**, there are flats carved from large 4-storey Georgiana. One of the last to be smartened up, it's now traffic-calmed, cobbled and tidy. Adjacent **Wren St** has smaller 2-storey houses with white facades and basements; and in **Green Yard Mews** are some smartly designed flats in that very 1999 colour, turquoise. In curving **Cubitt St**, a new development has flats to buy (2-bed, £400,000) or rent.

Brunswick

To the W, the Brunswick neighbourhood is arranged around the busy **Tavistock Place/ Marchmont St** crossroads: small bookshops, an art gallery, grocers, barbers and so on cluster here and on down Marchmont St, with flats above the shops: a characterful corner with a community feel despite the sad loss of street trees. A first-floor, 1-bed flat, £240,000 last winter. In **Tavistock Place** a cache of modern flats lurks behind a restored Victorian facade, and there are some council-built blocks. **Leigh St** runs E out of Marchmont St, and again has flats in 3-storey buildings above shops and restaurants, with a modern block of flats and shops on the corner.

Thanet St and **Sandwich St**, which run N from Leigh St, have some small early 19th-century houses, some split into flats; also a big double-fronted house – with a garage. There is, too, a large purpose-built block on the corner of **Thanet** and **Hastings Sts**; however, people scour these streets for the popular, well-priced Edwardian mansion blocks – well-run Thanet House, for example; Rashleigh House and Sandwich House.

Leigh St leads into the elegant Regency crescent of **Cartwright Gardens**, which features tennis courts surrounded by (mostly rented) flats, hotels and student hostels. Tucked behind is **Burton Place**, with **Woolf Mews**, a little enclave of modern, somewhat suburban homes built by Camden Council. **Burton St** has Tiger House, a recent luxury scheme with flats (often to rent) and underground car park behind the original terrace facade. **Duke's Rd** and **Woburn Walk** have some delightful surviving Regency shops and houses. North is some council-built housing and the roaring **Euston Rd**.

The great news here is that at long last a £22 million refurbishment has begun of the **Brunswick Centre**, which dominates the S of the area. Built around 1970 in a striking stepped pattern (it's Grade II listed, but resembles 'a five-storey gun emplacement') around a raised, paved square, this complex encompasses flats, shops, offices, a cinema, cafés with public car park beneath. Camden Council (which leases it from the freeholder) is undertaking the much-needed revamp. Art galleries and small media businesses are encouraged (the Cartoon Gallery is a local favourite); and a starry list of new shops are lined up. There are flats to rent and buy here (a 2-bed, £325,000), though two-thirds are still council-owned. Startlingly, the biggest transformation will come if, as promised, the entire grey concrete mass will be painted cream – as, apparently, was originally intended.

The hotel district is centred here, around **Bernard St** and Russell Square tube: the station, served by lifts, is incredibly busy in the tourist season. Bernard St has been renovated: the beautiful Georgiana now houses hospital staff. The cobbled mews to the S, **Colonnade**, has been seeing much new building activity.

Bloomsbury

Bloomsbury *proper* is reckoned to cover the area from **Russell Square** and **Woburn Place** W to **Tottenham Court Rd**. The regular grid of streets betrays its 18th-century Bedford Estate origins, but London University's buildings have replaced many of the terraces and squares. Many of the homes in Bloomsbury today are purpose-built blocks consisting of studios, and 1-, 2- and 3-bed flats. Typical of these blocks are Endsleigh Court on **Woburn Place** (60 per cent studios at c. £190,000, 30 per cent 1-bed and 10 per cent 2-bed flats) and Russell Court, a big complex of 1930s blocks with ingeniously designed, if tiny, studios (c. £160,000) and a few 1-beds. The studios are snapped up as pieds-à-terre, but investors are, happily, deterred by rules that allow renting only one year in two.

Russell Square itself has big mansion flats and has seen a series of developments along the S side – for example, a refurbishment of Nos. 54–56 as a mix of offices and flats. In 1998, an office building at Nos. 13–16 transformed into Bloomsbury Mansions, 58 luxurious 1- to 3-bed flats (3-beds, c. £600,000). Russell Square's gardens are public, but **Bloomsbury Square**'s are private: homes there and close by have the right to buy a key.

Other popular blocks in this neighbourhood include Bedford Court Mansions, the vast Ridgmount Gardens between **Ridgmount St** and **Huntley St** (a 4-bed £525,000) and those in **Southampton Row.**

Apart from the mansion flats, there are converted flats in houses in many of the area's quiet backstreets. Running N off Store St is **Ridgmount St**, which has a number of recent flats above garages. These are a development by the Bedford Estate – to this day the ground landlord in this area. To the N, several of the mansion blocks are council-owned: Gordon Mansions to the E and W of **Huntley St**, for example. **Chenies St** also has Camden Council-owned mansion flats, which have been joined by a dozen smart new private flats perched above a new dance studio for RADA, the acting school. **Store St** has flats over shops. **Chenies Mews** is part residential, with a mansion block and the back gardens of Gower St; eight houses built here in 1991/2 were the first in Bloomsbury for a century; a 3-bed, with garage and garden, £735,000 last winter. The N end of the mews is industrial, hospital and college premises. At the N end of **Huntley St** a row of flat-fronted 3-storey houses is split into flats.

Chenies St runs E into **Gower St.** The buildings in this busy thoroughfare are mostly early 19th-century and are now used as hotels or for commercial or university purposes, with a few rather run-down flats. Look here for cheap end-of-lease flats, though you may have to pay as much again for a new 90-year extension; a 2-bed with long lease rated a £369,000 price tag last autumn. One of the quieter streets in the neighbourhood is **Gower Mews**, with Gower Mews Mansions: small '30s flats above garages. And to the S of here is **Bedford Square**, which is nearly all commercial – though 19 new flats were created behind an original facade in 1987. Bedford Court Mansions has large flats, while Bloomsbury Plaza, a newish block on **Bloomsbury St**, has 1-bed flats. **Adeline Place** and **Bedford Avenue**, which run directly off it, hold Bedford Court: blocks of well-appointed 1900-vintage flats. Penthouses have been added to these: a 3-bed one, £675,000.

At the S end of the neighbourhood, between the British Museum and High Holborn, a small and increasingly popular area includes some interesting old houses as well as flats above shops. In **Coptic St**, just S of the museum, the occasional freehold Georgian house appears on the market. More period buildings in **Little Russell Street**; it also has some smart 1990 homes. And so to handsome **Bloomsbury Square**, where it all began. Today the earliest remaining homes are the Regency terraces with which James Burton replaced the Southamptons' great house; one of these will set you back several million.

King's Cross

Waiting in its weed-overgrown siding to join modern London, the vast area of under-used and partly derelict land to the N of King's Cross and St Pancras stations has for decades been one of London's great lost opportunities – a giant site reaching, in the N, right up to Camden Town. At last work is well under way here for the Channel Tunnel rail link and the vast new St Pancras station to serve it, and the Argent St George consortium has sweeping plans for the hinterland. So we will see a brand-new London quarter that

B

could, if permission is granted, contain 1,800 new homes, no less. Nothing will be done until 2007, when the Eurostar terminal and Thameslink station are complete. But it is ongoing – and will unlock the whole area for development over a 15-year cycle. For starters, there's Regent Quarter: see below.

The King's Cross neighbourhood, as it stands at the moment, is a blend of commercial and small business premises, with a scattering of homes to the E of **York Way**. The Camden/Islington borough boundary runs through the area, down York Way. This has been part of the area's problems: it's no-one's baby. Even the big Regent Quarter scheme has had to satisfy both planning committees. Across the Grand Union Canal, which acts as the N boundary, lie the select realms of Camden Town, Barnsbury and Islington. The S part ends at **Argyle St** and **Swinton St**, while to the SE is Finsbury (see Clerkenwell).

Despite the potential, King's Cross is not as yet a home for the faint-hearted, or for families. There's all the colourful (if you are selling) and threatening (if buying) life that revolves around rail stations: cheap hotels and all-night traffic are but the start of it. Those who live here get into the habit of taking a taxi home at night. A new police station and video surveillance have had a positive impact, but Chelsea this is not. Just as a pointer, the developers are using see-through hoardings round their site to stop 'illicit activities' going on in the shadow of solid ones. Local reports suggest that things have got better as the traditional denizens move on.

The area's greatest advantage is of course its extraordinary convenience. Apart from King's Cross, St Pancras is next door, Euston station down the road. You can stroll to the City. King's Cross also runs a close second to Oxford Circus as the single most useful tube station on the entire network. The Thameslink station provides further options: S to the City and Gatwick, N to Luton and Bedford. All this will be enhanced by the monster works in progress – but also disrupted, for the next couple of years at least.

Many of the houses have been split into flats. Small two-bed houses and ex-council flats form the rest of the current stock. The best houses tend to be in small, secluded groups and can surprise with the quality of their architecture. The handsome houses attract people who feel the area must 'come up' (some have been waiting for 20 years). The closest thing to a residential neighbourhood in King's Cross is around the S part of the busy **Caledonian Rd**: it includes quiet backwaters such as **Keystone Crescent** and **Balfe St**. The southern part of **Northdown Rd** runs down from the Caledonian Rd and features a clutch of mostly 1-bed flats with original facade intact. The northern part, across the Caledonian Rd, has 2-bed houses dating from 1845. This is one of the nicest streets in the area. **Keystone Crescent**'s curve is echoed in the rounded windows of its pretty 2-storey houses. **Caledonian Rd** has some converted flats and flats above shops – almost exclusively studios and 1-beds. **Balfe St** runs S from **Wharfdale Rd** and is similar to Northdown Rd with modernized flats and some small houses. Here, too, 3-storey houses have been well converted into 1-bed flats behind the early-Victorian facades. This street also has some modern homes.

Regent Quarter, P&O Developments' scheme on six acres alongside the station, between **Wharfdale Rd, Balfe St, York Way** and **Pentonville Rd**, is just completing Phases I and II. The best of the existing buildings are being kept – including some warehouses and courtyards to be open to the public and used for artists' and craft workshops – plus shops, cafés, hotel, 138 homes. The first people have moved in – sales ran 57:43 investors:owner-occupiers – the Travel Inn and a Tesco Metro are open. Security is, necessarily, a very big feature in this as-yet totally unreconstructed area. Current releases, £315–620,000. The offices have proved popular, though P&O taking a big chunk itself may be seen either as a vote of confidence or as a failure to find anyone else.

Other areas of small, existing 2-bed houses include those of the **Southern St** and **Killick St** area. There are several new and slick commercial buildings in this corner. A 14-flat conversion on **King's Cross Rd** supplements a clutch of 3-storey Victorian houses at the bottom end of **Wicklow St. Swinton St** and **Acton St** have some big houses: two recently £670,000 and £895,000. There are also council flats such as the Derby Lodge Estate on **Britannia St**. The N part of the **Gray's Inn Rd** has a new Travelodge, with a few flats for sale (up to £450,000 for a 3-bed). The area bounded by **Argyle St/Gray's Inn Rd/Euston Rd** is dominated by the Birkenhead Estate, a complex of seven 1960s blocks. The remainder is a mix of 3-storey Victoriana, some Georgian houses, B & Bs, small hotels.

Explore to the N, where several new and converted blocks along the canal offer 'loft-style' living. **Thornhill Bridge Wharf** (see also Islington chapter) was among the first. **New Wharf Rd** is dominated by the recent Ice Wharf: nearly 100 1- to 4-bed flats, some with canal views. Gattis Wharf, a smaller scheme, is in the same road. Look, too, along **All Saints Rd** for other similar developments. **York Way** has a Victorian school N of the canal split, in 2002, into 21 loft-style flats, with four new houses and 19 flats built in the grounds, in an innovative scheme by the North British Housing Association.

Transport Tubes, all zone 1: King's Cross (Victoria, Piccadilly, Northern, Hammersmith & City, Circle), Russell Square (Piccadilly), others see map. From King's Cross: Oxford Circus 8 min, City 15 min, Heathrow 1 hr 10. Rail: King's Cross, St Pancras, Euston.

Convenient for Everywhere: British Museum, British Library, City, West End, St Pancras interchange. Miles from centre: 1.5.

Schools University College School, South Camden Community School.

SALES

Flats	S	1B	2B	3B	4B	5B
Average prices	150–190	200+	250+	320+	–	–
Houses	2B	3B	4B	5B	6/7B	8B
Average prices	525+	550+	750+	1M+	2M+	–

RENTAL

Flats	S	1B	2B	3B	4B	5B
Average prices	170–200+	200–350+	270–550	450+	500+	–
Houses	2B	3B	4B	5B	6/7B	8B
Average prices	–	–	–	–	–	–

The properties Many of Bloomsbury's gorgeous Georgian and early-Victorian houses have been offices for years, but the occasional gem of a home comes up for sale. Flats, however, abound, in mansion, '30s or more recent blocks. King's Cross has some surprising corners of handsome Victoriana. King's Cross/St Pancras redevelopment, at last beginning, will boost the area as a whole.

The market Young, single people, couples without children, academics and businesspeople find homes here to buy or rent from student-poor to quiet luxury. King's Cross is the cheaper end of the scale, and scene of much development – and long-term potential.

Among estate agents active in this area are:

- Callum Roberts
- Copping Joyce
- Hudsons Property
- Bloomsbury Property
- Hurford Salvi Carr
- Banbury Ball
- Frank Harris
- Property Bureau
- Stickley & Kent

B

Bow

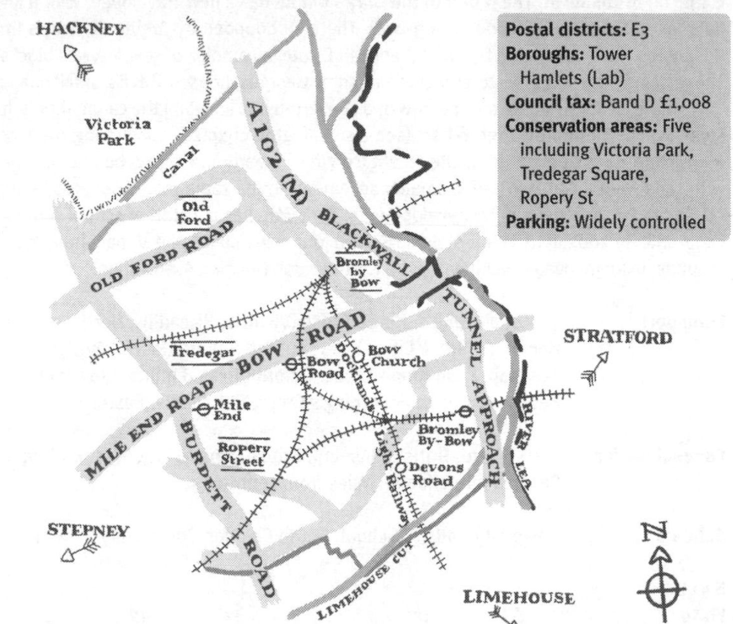

Postal districts: E3
Boroughs: Tower Hamlets (Lab)
Council tax: Band D £1,008
Conservation areas: Five including Victoria Park, Tredegar Square, Ropery St
Parking: Widely controlled

Bow has traditionally looked west, to the City, for its homebuyers. The last decade has seen it look south, to Docklands. The next will see it look east, to the burgeoning city-within-a-city at Stratford. Poised at the centre of this triangle of wealth, Bow offers the East End's best choice of homes, both period and new.

Bow has always been the tidier end of the East End, and was the least damaged by the Blitz – which is why so much period property remains. But it is still a widely varying mixture of gaunt council towers, fine Georgian terraces and more modest Victorian ones, industry, railway tracks and street markets. Homes in Bow are not grouped in neat neighbourhoods, they are scattered in pockets between all the other things jostling for space in this crowded corner. Typical inner London, in fact.

This year you can choose between 'Bow Central' and 'The Heart of Bow', two big schemes by national builders which add smart new flats and houses to the local mix.

Mile End in Bow has gained from the third-biggest lottery-funded Millennium project in London. Victoria Park, on the Hackney borders, and Tredegar Square to the south, are already well known caches of fine period houses (cheap now only by comparison with very much more 'established' areas); and now the splendid, £33.5-million Mile End Park project is consolidating the renaissance of this East End heartland. This 85-acre linear park runs southwards from Victoria Park, making a green corridor along the Grand Union Canal; a 'green bridge' spans the Mile End Road to join the two main segments, and the new attractions include a children's park, a play area, leafy cycle-ways and even an electric go-kart track. The streets bordering the southern, Burdett Rd end of the park see the greatest benefits.

To add to the remaining Georgiana and the Victorian rows, the last 15 years have seen a veritable boom in the provision of new homes, cementing this area's status as a residential area that attracts locals to owner-occupation as well as incomers from other, pricier, parts of town. The first, and the biggest, was the triumphant, prescient '80s conversion of the giant Victorian Bryant & May match factory, re-named the Bow Quarter: this added 700 homes to the local stock. Recent developments have included homes with workspace attached, and a sprinkling of fashionable loft apartments; also the building of new terraced houses on traditional streets.

At the same time, the renovation programme for hundreds of existing council homes is in full swing, many having been transferred to housing associations, with a joint Bow and Poplar housing action plan coordinating the projects. More than 2,000 student homes have been built for Queen Mary College on the canal overlooking the park.

The demolition of the last few slums (artist Rachel Whiteread's award-winning 'house' sculpture was a cast of an old terraced house, the last in its row to be pulled down) is a good symbol of the modern East End. The artistic/professional classes are infiltrating previously working-class space. The Chisenhale Gallery and the Bow Wharf development – including bars and comedy club – are symptomatic. Transport is fairly good, with Central, District and Hammersmith & City Line tubes, and the DLR for the rapidly growing N–S traffic. Bow is now an established rung on the conventional property ladder.

Bow, as described here, is essentially the E3 postal district, but the name is used rather sporadically. People who live in the Tredegar conservation area are proud to say so; others nearby talk of living in Mile End. Victoria Park is a prestigious name attached to streets in the N of the area – it adds a premium to house prices – while in the S, along Limehouse Cut, new canalside developments annexe the name Limehouse, made smart by Docklands. Of the old village of Bow, a crossing place over the River Lea, virtually nothing survives except the name. Just to confuse, there is also a corner called Bromley-by-Bow, complete with tube station and high street, but a long way from Bromley.

The Lea Valley, to the E of Bow, is a sprawling flood-plain covered by industry, derelict, but still extant; gasworks ditto; railways and sundry waterways. But just across it is Stratford, scene of many exciting changes including the vast new Channel Tunnel station, completing now. The 650 acres of virtually unused land in the Lea Valley allow plenty of scope, and the Eurostar station (opening early 2007) will, it's hoped, provide the spur. London's bid for the 2012 Olympic Games is centred around this land.

Mile End & Tredegar Square

Tredegar Square, N of the busy **Bow Rd** and within a stone's throw of Mile End tube station, is the pride of the East London property market. This delightful Georgian garden square is a conservation area and boasts the area's most impressive – and expensive – houses, some of which have five or six bedrooms. The most expensive are on the N side of the Square – and the best can, these days, reach £850,000, though £700,000-plus is a more usual price. The square also boasts seven modern houses; but these, tucked on the corner, don't disrupt the unbroken Georgiana overlooking the central gardens. The latest new homes, in neo-Georgian style, are ten flats and three mews houses.

The square is the centrepiece of a conservation area that includes **Lichfield Rd**, **Alloway Rd**, **Aberavon Rd**, **Rhondda Grove**, **Tredegar Terrace**, **College Terrace** and **Coborn Rd**. It is sometimes referred to by estate agents as Mile End village, or the Coborn Conservation Area. At Aberavon Rd, a 2-bed Georgian house was reckoned optimistically priced last winter at £425,000. In **Coborn St** Tredegar Villas, a recent development of 2-bed terraced houses and flats around a central courtyard, were carefully built in a similar style to neighbouring houses; likewise gated **Coborn Mews**. **Morgan St**, too, has new homes: particularly **Pembroke Mews**, a neo-Georgian cache built around a cobbled courtyard with 2- and 3-bed houses (2-bed £310,000 last winter).

On **Bow Rd** and still within the conservation area is Tredegar House itself, a fine 19th-century brick building that was first a shipbuilder's mansion, then a college and then came full circle, recently, back to a dwelling – but as flats this time, 20 of 'em: two 1-beds, 17 2-beds (about £240,000) and a penthouse.

At the S end of Aberavon Rd, almost opposite the tube, is (would you believe) **Eaton Terrace**, a row of 1980s 4-storey houses, with ornamental pillars at each entrance. **Ropery St**, another conservation area, lies S of Bow Rd and E of Burdett Rd, and has Victorian terraced homes, as do **Mossford St, Maritime St** and **Lockhart St. Brokesby St**, on the S side of Bow Rd, has an attractive recent loft-style development. **Bow Common Lane** leads on down to the Limehouse canal and Poplar. More terraced houses, but this time new ones, were inserted by Furlong between the Lane and **Ropery St**.

B

South of Victoria Park

Over the railway line, N of the Tredegar Square conservation area, are the popular 2-storey bay-fronted Victorian houses of **Antill Rd, Strahan Rd, Lyal Rd** and **Medway Rd**. In nearby **Arbery Rd** is the award-winning 1980s development of **School Bell Mews**, a converted school that provides a perfect setting for new flats with galleries and houses. **Haverfield Rd** (with four new 4-bed town-houses) crosses Mile End Park, which runs alongside the canal, where the Millennium project has constructed the wonderful 'green bridge': this spans the Mile End Rd, which slices the long, thin park in two; now trees, shrubs and bushes, kept verdant by automatically recycled water, nod down from the bridge at the traffic passing below. Shops have been constructed under it, including a Budgens supermarket. Ongoing work includes the landscaping of Grove Rd, which runs alongside the park northwards to cross Victoria Park. Over in the SE corner of the neighbourhood, towards the railway, Berkeley's big 'Bow Central' scheme in **Ordell Rd** has 1- and 2-bed flats and 3- and 4-bed town-houses (flats start at £180,000).

Three-storey Victorian properties, some of which have been converted into flats, in **Old Ford Rd** and **Chisenhale Rd** are made more appealing by backing onto the canal. Roads from **Hewlett Rd** across to **Vivian Rd**, including **Driffield Rd** and **Ellesmere Rd**, make up the North Bow Conservation Area, where 2-storey-plus-basement Victorian terraces offer 3/4-bed houses around £400,000. Printers' Mews, **Old Ford Rd**, has modern flats with canal-view balconies. Roach Works on **Roach Rd** has 75 new canalside live/work units. Even the Cricketers pub, on **Old Ford Rd** opposite the park, has become flats, as has another pub in **Vivian Rd**, and here too is Connaught Works, a big modern flats scheme where the homes are a mix of converted warehouses and new-build. Round the corner, **Driffield St** has 3-bedroom Victorian houses. **Kenilworth Rd** holds Nightingale Mews, a recent development of a dozen 3- and 4-bed houses. It is not just the canal that makes this corner popular, of course; across it lies lovely Victoria Park, one of the largest parks in London.

On the S side of the canal is a 4-acre site, extending from **Parnell Rd** in the E to **Gunmakers Lane** in the W. Ongoing development here involves the refurbishing of close on 400 existing council tower-block and low-built homes, and the building of nearly 500 new housing-association ones. More Affordable Homes – new flats to rent – were added, on **Old Ford Rd; Royal Victor Place** is a 1990 development in the same road.

Bow Wharf is the canalside scheme which holds not only homes but both a bar and a branch of Jongleurs comedy club – proof of the changing nature of the area. Off Parnell Rd is the optimistically named **Hampstead Walk**, with 3-bed 1994-vintage terraceds. Empire Wharf is another recent block of flats with both park and canal views.

The canal runs along Victoria Park's S border to **Cadogan Terrace**, where 3-storey Victorian homes, overlooking the park, command a premium (£375,000 for a 3-bed last winter) although parking can be a problem, and the busy A102(M) motorway is just behind. **Morville St**, off **Tredegar Rd**, is the site for 69 fair-rent flats, developed by Wimpey and the Tower Hamlets Action Trust. Yallops Yard, a former scrapyard off **Tredegar Rd**, is reborn as 'the Heart of Bow' 262 flats and houses by Lovell. Fifty of these are Affordable Homes, the open-market flats including 2-bed flats (708sq ft) at £238,000. Completion 2007. The Hermitage, a 1989 development of flats and houses in **Wrexham Rd**, is appealing despite being near the motorway.

The extraordinary old Bryant & May match factory is vast, stretching back over six acres from **Fairfield Rd**. It has created its own environment, and community, and given a considerable boost to the area. The factory itself, now known as the **Bow Quarter**, was cleverly converted and extended in the late 1980s into 730 flats around landscaped, fountain-filled squares. It boasts swimming pools plus a sports complex, The Powerhouse, and has a bar, shop and a laundry. About half the homes are rented, often through the on-site agency owned by the leaseholders. Sale prices vary widely with size and position: a 1-bed with gallery in the old factory is about £165,000, much as last year, and the year before (1994 price for the same-sized flat, £65,000) while flats in the 1980s block are a little less. Opposite Bow Quarter, Durkan has built 72 1- and 2-bed flats and 10 live/work units. Once thought of as so far out, this corner can now look just over its shoulder across to Stratford: next stop, Paris. . . .

Also in **Fairfield Rd** is a 1980s development of a dozen houses, joined by (yet another) pub conversion and The Courtyard, a clutch of 2-bed flats round the corner in **Blondin St**. West from here, a conservation area includes the flat-fronted cottages of **Cardigan Rd**. Red-brick bay-fronted houses in **Baldock St**, **Ridgdale St** and **Jebb St** lead to Grove Hall Park with its children's playground and football pitch. Alongside the park, a development of new flats appeared in **Baldock St** in 1999.

Along **Bow Rd**, which is part of the main route E to Stratford, there are some handsome early-Victorian and Georgian houses. Wellington Way has some smart Victorian-Gothic houses, some split into flats. A big conversion, 'The Theatre Building' has 200 flats close to the town hall – just joined by 14 penthouses grafted onto it.

Bow Church

Bow police station is on the opposite side of **Bow Rd** to the **Tomlin's Grove** conservation area, where steps lead up to the 3-storey Victorian houses, some with atticky rooms under the mansard roof. In Tomlin's Grove itself you can choose between a 4-bed Victorian terraced house at £470,0000 or a 2-bed flat for £270,000 in a small, new 'ecologically designed' block. The DLR station of Bow Church stands on the corner of **Campbell Rd**, part of which falls within the conservation area. Over to the E, close to the motorway junction, is oddly named (and rather forlorn) **Bromley High St**, where a scheme called 'Tudor Lodge' has just added 10 new flats. Most of this corner is the council-built homes of the Bow Bridge and Devon Estates.

South of the railway line is the Lincoln Estate, which includes council-built flats and houses in **Rounton Rd**, part of **Campbell Rd**, **Devons Rd**, **Blackthorn**, **Whitethorn** and **Tidey Sts**, **Bow Common Lane**, **Fern St** and **Swaton**, **Spanby**, **Fairfoot** and **Knapp Rds**. These are some of Bow's less desirable properties, along with the Coventry Cross council estate. This estate includes **Devas St**, **Brickfield Rd**, **Empson St** and **St Leonard's St**. However, the estate is steadily being redeveloped and refurbished, and new housing-association homes are appearing on a large tract of land beside the DLR, between the Limehouse Cut and **Devons Rd**. Some of the nicer homes are the 1950s 3-bed ex-council houses with gardens in **St Leonard's St**.

There have been good conversions of Victorian homes in **Devons Rd**, among others. A church hall in **Blackthorn St** has become All Hallows, seven loft-style flats, and more new flats are just complete in **Mornington Grove**. The canal is the focus for several live/work schemes, including Enterprise Works, in **Hawgood St**, a scheme where both houses and flats include their own workspaces. Also here are Telford Homes' new 2-bed flats. Off this street is **Alphabet Square**, a development of industrially styled flats. Telford Homes have added 1- and 2-bed flats to **Devons Rd**.

B

The valley of the River Lea is slowly struggling into life again after decades as a post-industrial wasteland. A corner in E3 (just) is called Fish Island – streets include **Roach Rd** and **Dace Rd** – which it almost is: it lies in the angle of the Grand Union and River Lea Navigation canals, and is cut off from Victoria Park and the rest of Bow by the A102 motorway. Here 'Omega 3' offers 48 work-homes (branded 'mycitypad') in a new block with water on both sides, and a footbridge to the nearby Hackney Wick station; prices were £230–425,000 last winter. To the S, **Three Mills Lane** leads into the Lea Valley to another cut-off 'island', with a film studio and 'Urban Island', a scheme with 47 1- and 2-bed flats from £320,000 to £365,000 (a penthouse, £450,000).

Transport Tubes: Mile End (zone 2, Central, Hammersmith & City, District); Bow Rd, Bromley-by-Bow (zone 3, Hammersmith & City, District). From Mile End: Oxford Circus 20 min, City 10 min, Heathrow 75 min (1 change). DLR: links to Stratford, Tower, Isle of Dogs, Bank, Greenwich & Lewisham.

Convenient for City, Docklands, City Airport & Stansted, Stratford centre & stations, Blackwall Tunnel. Miles from centre: 4.5.

Schools Local Authority: Bethnal Green Technology College, Mulberry School (g), Morpeth School, St Paul's Way Community School.

SALES

Flats	S	1B	2B	3B	4B	5B
Average prices	120–150	130–200	140–280	160–310	–	–
Houses	2B	3B	4B	5B	6/7B	8B
Average prices	220–280	240–400	300–800	550–850	–	–

RENTAL

Flats	S	1B	2B	3B	4B	5B
Average prices	140–160	160–220	200–280	240–340	–	–
Houses	2B	3B	4B	5B	6/7B	8B
Average prices	240–300	300–350	350–450	450–600	–	–

The properties Bow's Georgian glories, among the myriad 2/3-bed terraced houses, have long since been rediscovered. Old housing stock is now much improved; untouched property harder to find. Real action to renovate/rebuild council housing is restoring whole areas. Several new and recent developments – the 700-home Bow Quarter is an example of regeneration at its best, recently joined by conversions of church halls, factories, warehouses.

The market Owner-occupation is higher than other parts of Tower Hamlets, and rising in this increasingly popular, well-placed East End heartland. Best properties are mainly N of Bow Rd, especially the Roman Rd to Victoria Park stretch, and new-build.

Among estate agents active in this area are:

- Alex Neil
- Land & Co
- Keatons
- Mitchelson McCarthy
- Winkworth
- W J Meade
- LMD
- Look Property Services
- Strutt & Parker
- Spicer McColl
- Mark Murray

BRIXTON, HERNE HILL AND TULSE HILL

B

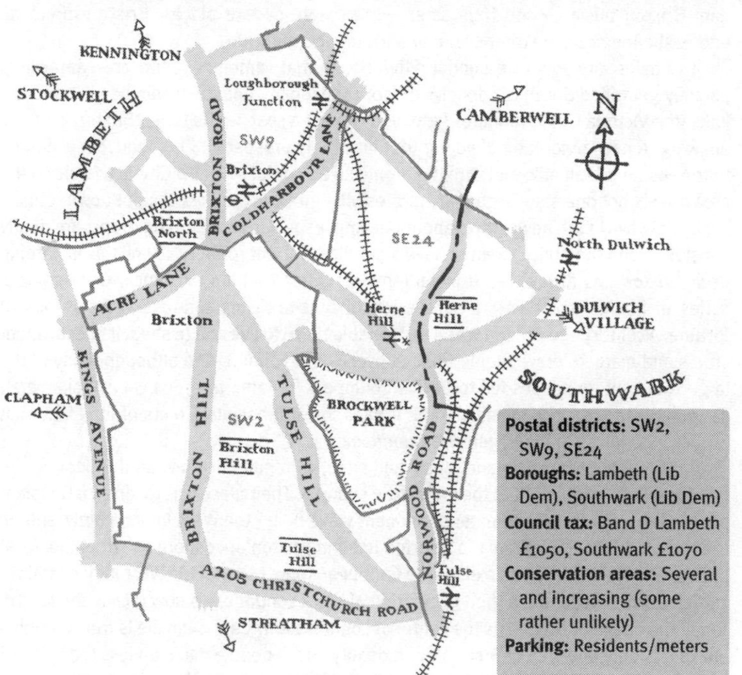

Postal districts: SW2, SW9, SE24
Boroughs: Lambeth (Lib Dem), Southwark (Lib Dem)
Council tax: Band D Lambeth £1050, Southwark £1070
Conservation areas: Several and increasing (some rather unlikely)
Parking: Residents/meters

The best mix of people in London – that's one admiring local's take on Brixton. Others are more cautious, citing downsides as varied as a growing plague of rich incomers and lack of sleep from police sirens. That said, big strides do seem to have been made in curbing the area's more outrageously illegal excesses. You do need to visit Brixton, to spend time there, get to know it, before you buy or rent – indeed agents say that the most typical buyer is someone who has rented here first. Fascinating it may be, but – some fringe neighbourhoods apart – polite it ain't. Not everyone is a Brixton person. 'Brixton reacts to you as you do to it' says another denizen. No longer, though, is Brixton a cheaper alternative to Clapham: people move here because they want to.

What's the fascination? The truth is that, unusually for London, Brixton is a truly urban place. Here, no-one pretends they are living in the country (head on south for Herne Hill, or Dulwich). It is the nearest thing London has to the downtown districts of an American city – with all that implies. Fast-changing, a crucible of new ideas and a magnet for the young and unconventional, its social mix strikes the staid as explosive. But for others it works: for a lot of people, Brixton is liberated London.

Brixton, what's more, has great bone structure. It has a proper centre – not a shapeless sprawl like the amorphous straggles of Stockwell or Kennington. And now the Mayor of London has included it in his '100 Public Spaces' scheme: a redesign should give birth to 'Brixton Central Square', linking Tate Gardens, Windrush Square and St Matthew's Peace Garden, with the possible pedestrianisation of Effra Rd. Watch, as they say, this space. . . .

Meanwhile, those with neat suburban instincts will recoil from the traffic, the patchwork of homes of every age (from glorious Georgian through to modern chic) and state of repair, the street life that undeniably deserves the term 'vibrant'. Those with a need for sleep will avoid a district that doesn't. Those who like being out at all hours find 4am Brixton busier – and thus safer – than more sedate places. Brixton offers an endlessly imaginative street scene and acclaimed nightlife.

It remains an oasis of essential difference, a real community, in a grey, sprawling, patchily gentrified South London. Next door to Clapham, boasting even better transport links (the Victoria Line terminates here: you can get a seat on the tube), Brixton is on the upswing. A new generation of young (but inevitably prosperous) homebuyers is adding to the cosmopolitan mix, and with the promised advent of two new City Academies – the area boasts not one state secondary at present – growing families can put down roots.

It is always in the news: rows about policing, especially concerning drugs, are finally subsiding, and the police seem to have a handle on street robbery. . . . All this is nothing new; Brixton has always led a melodramatic, larger-than-life existence, undergoing a series of booms and busts, a succession of rags-to-riches-and-rags-again swings of fortune. A century ago Brixton was a fashionable place to live and to shop. Its department stores and markets drew people from all over South London. And although many of the large 19th-century houses fell to German bombers (or later, to 1960s council planners), its underlying structure remains good. It had, and still has, its streets of little Victorian terraces as well as grander, genuine Georgiana.

But the City commuters and music-hall stars, who had once favoured Brixton for its transport links, moved out to the green new suburbs. Their place was taken by a transient population – the latest and most permanent wave being the West Indian immigrants of the '50s and '60s. Melodrama reasserted itself in Brixton once more as street life, local politics and rhetoric took on a distinctly Caribbean tone. Many of the West Indian families settled down here, and the third generation of black Londoners is now raising the fourth. Today the image of Brixton as the centre of London's Afro-Caribbean life is true enough – but that is only one side of Brixton's personality. Black people make up less than a third of the residents. Whites are the biggest single group, and there is a thriving gay community; but these broad figures conceal a place where everyone is a minority, where there are communities of Chileans and Chinese, City workers and anarchist squatters, flash lofts and still-grim council blocks, artists and – well, every other kind of -ist and -ian.

The latest Brixton renaissance has been driven, with a typical twist of irony, by the movement of young people into the area, not Whitehall mega-bucks. The new century saw a new wave of incomers, attracted by lifestyle and the lure of a young, lively population. School and factory conversions add lofts to the local choice; clubs and bars are always opening, young and clever people are remaking Brixton the way they want it. Many settle, and move on from flats to family houses – still more affordable here.

The growing family population – young radicals become middle-class parents – is shown by the sophisticated and energetic campaign to create a new secondary school. At the moment, most Brixton kids (indeed most Lambeth kids) leave the area at age 11, for there are no local state secondary schools. A new one has however just opened up by Clapham Common – and now, at last, the Cleanaway depot in **Shakespeare Rd** looks set to become a new, much-needed Academy comprehensive. In the meantime families head for Herne Hill, and Dulwich's schools.

At its heart, the imposing town hall looks out from the corner of **Acre Lane** and **Brixton Hill** over a wide green triangle, with St Matthew's (church plus arts centre/ nightclub/restaurant) as its focal point. A park links the centre to the green strip of Rush Common, which runs beside Brixton Hill. The triangle's apex points north, to the high-street shops of **Brixton Rd** and the famous market. By the station is the leisure centre – there are lots of good sports facilities in the area. And there's also the wide, pleasant hilly expanse of Brockwell Park with its outdoor swimming pool, tennis courts and a walled garden.

The Post Office confuses the geography of Brixton. It is often thought that Brixton equals SW2, but a glance at the map shows that Brixton station, and most of the town centre, lies in SW9, while SW2 takes in the positively suburban streets of Streatham Hill as well as Brixton Prison. Much of **Railton Rd**, the street dubbed the 'Front Line' when police/black tension was highest in the 1980s, is in SE24 – a district known more for the solid respectability of Herne Hill, rubbing shoulders with top-notch desirable Dulwich. And chunks of West Brixton stray into SW4, home of the Claphamites.

There are several conservation areas in Brixton, protecting pockets of outstanding architectural quality. Homes in these corners command a premium. Examples are found in Angell Town, Loughborough Park and – a definite hot spot – pretty, pricy **Trinity Gardens**. Lambeth has also been tidying the town centre, though locals are *still* waiting (as they were this time last year) for the tube station facelift to be finished. Residents' schemes have lessened the problem of commuter parking, long suffered by many Brixton streets. However, locals claim that these have only partly alleviated the problems, and feel that their main aim is raise council revenue. They do help homes to sell more quickly: parking is a must for many Brixton buyers, and there is less off-street parking hereabouts.

Thanks to those once-grand houses that remain, compared to neighbouring areas Brixton's 2-bed flats can be roomier, 3-bed ones are not unusual, and there are the 5- and 6-bed houses that Clapham generally lacks as well as ample 2-, 3- and 4-bed ones. The most desirable homes lie just off either side of **Brixton Hill**, offering quiet streets only 10 minutes from the centre. They are handy for the frequent buses to the town centre, the Victoria Line tube and central London. There are, however, pockets of interesting houses all over Brixton, though surroundings can sometimes still be on the grim side.

New-build has come to Brixton, with several recent schemes. However, the lure of the period home is strong: for one thing the room sizes are often better. Developers should note that flats are best built with a good-sized second bedroom: Brixtonians want to house a lodger if things get tough, not a very small baby or a bijou home office.

Acre Lane

Broad **Acre Lane** itself, which runs westwards to Clapham Park and the shores of 'Abbeville Village' (see Clapham), is a busy highway with everything from Tesco's and plumbers' merchants to the odd remnant of Georgiana and row of pretty almshouses. Also, increasingly, new homes. On its northern side, the Victorian streets enclosed by **Bedford Rd** to the W, **Ferndale Rd** to the N and **Brixton Rd** to the E hold small 3- and 4-bed terraces, plus larger 3- and 4-storey ones, many converted into flats. The W side of the neighbourhood, including the W half of **Ferndale Rd**, is in SW4 and used to harbour aspirations to be Clapham until Brixton got more trendy (a 3-bed in Ferndale, £325,000). Indeed, many of these streets are closer to Clapham North tube than they are to Brixton.

Ferndale Rd is a through-route; to the N it backs onto a rail line taking the Dover trains into Victoria and Eurostar into Waterloo, plus a lot of freight. Gaunt 3- or 4-storey Victorian terraces predominate, getting bigger at the W end, as they do on the parallel **Sandmere Rd**. These try to compensate for being too tall for their site by adorning their unfortunate brickwork with every possible high-Victorian twiddle – but they make for roomy flat conversions. New homes have squeezed into every corner: on Ferndale Rd, Persimmon's 'Trinity Court', 18 new 1- and 2-bed flats behind a gated entrance, launched at £200–275,000 in 2004. And appropriately, the old LCC School of Building is now '138 Ferndale', courtesy of developer Charles Church: 22 smart 1-, 2- and 3-bed flats (resales from c. £200,000), plus 52 newbuild ones behind in 'Reubens Place'.

From here, the terraces are smaller, plainer and more attractive in style. **Tintern St**, likewise, is small 3-bed flat-fronted Victorian terraces, as are **Ducie St**, **Medwin St** and

B

Allardyce St. Ducie St has gothicky houses with pointed-arched doorways and decorative brickwork. A 4-bed house in **Raeburn St** was £495,000 last winter; **Ballater Rd** has plenty of flat conversions. The names (if not the architecture) of **Plato Rd** and **Solon Rd** have earned them the tag of Philosophers' Corner; again, many houses have been split into flats (£187,000 for a 1-bed with garden). The higher plane is also catered for round the corner, by the Church of the First-Born and the Seventh-Day Adventists.

LondonGreen converted the old Victorian primary school in **Santley St** into loft apartments in 1999 (queues formed, and the whole lot sold instantly). Its grounds now hold Alpha and Beta Houses – new flats. Interestingly LondonGreen's smart new **Marlborough Mews** houses, tucked away off Acre Lane, sold rather slower. In 2002 came small 2- and 3-bed town-houses, as a change from flats, in the gated **Regis Place**. Just along **Acre Lane** are a pair of large, white stucco houses, now flats: one is late Georgian, the other a complete facsimile built next door by Rialto, who then used the deep plot of land at the back, behind the homes on **Concannon Rd**, for two more blocks; a 2-bed flat in **Belvedere Place** was £220,000 last winter. The once-grand Cedars House, too, in 2001 became 'The Cedars': 14 more flats.

Next, the other-worldly appearance of Trinity Almshouses heralds the potential gem of the neighbourhood – behind hides **Trinity Gardens**, a Regency square of little 3-bed cottages, with own pub. Sadly one corner also holds Daisy Dormer Court (dispiritingly 1960s), and a one-way system means struggling in via Brixton's high street, **Brixton Rd**, instead of from Acre Lane. However, that means shops and tube are a stroll away from this enclave. Homes here are much-desired, highly priced, rarely for sale – but one 3-bed last autumn was £595,000. Round the corner, on the Acre Lane exit leg from the Square, a small warehouse became three live/work homes: each 2,500 sq ft.

South West Brixton

South of **Acre Lane**, across to **Lyham Rd** in the W, **Brixton Hill** in the E and Windmill Gardens to the S, lies a mixed area of large Victorian houses, Edwardian maisonettes and inter-war semis. The land rises towards the S, where a windmill stands in a park. Beyond again is Brixton Prison. All this is SW2. It is one of the quietest parts of Brixton; to its W is Clapham Park – and the possibility of a new local secondary school on the Glenbrook Primary, Clarence Avenue, site. Estate agents have, naturally, taken to stretching Clapham Park to cover the Lyham Rd corner, which is attracting increasing attention.

Lyham Rd branches off Clapham Park's processional route, **Kings Avenue**; streets of small Victorian terraces – **Kildoran Rd, Margate Rd, Mauleverer Rd, Mandrell Rd** – run off eastwards; again, Clapham agents (and prices: a 2-bed flat, £240,000) much in evidence. 'Park Court' is six 2-bed flats on Lyham Rd by Buxton Homes. Also at this end, three new 4-bed houses in contemporary style. Further S, **Lyham Rd** has council homes on both sides, with the spreading low-rise Blenheim Gardens Estate running up to Ramilles Close and the windmill. A big new complex of care homes is close to the windmill. Things went quiet over the plans for a new secondary school here, on waterworks land, and a new site has now been earmarked for one in Shakespeare Rd: watch this space. . . .

Next come some pretty, flat-fronted brick cottages, followed by the back wall of Brixton Prison (less overwhelming than some prisons one could mention). New homes in this long road have been provided by Sapcote, who transformed the Ashby Mill Primary School into 40 loft apartments, sold in shell form , plus four new houses, in a gated complex. Some eye-watering prices have been asked on resales here.... A 1-bed loft in **Ashby Mews** was £300,000 last winter.

South of the prison, **Dumbarton Rd** has 1914-ish purpose-built flats in 2-storey terraces, fairly un-spruced, with gables and fancy porches; a 3-bed maisonette here, £212,000. Some of those in the N side of the road back onto the prison wall. **Doverfield**

Rd has similar flats (and a clutch of four new 2-bed mews houses under way) while **Felsberg Rd** has more – this time with an Arts-and-Crafts air: a 3/4-bed maisonette, £235,000. Dumbarton Court, a big block of inter-war flats, runs round onto **Brixton Hill**. In **Morrish Rd**, Barratt has contributed uninspired, and not cheap, 2- and 3-bed flats.

This district is quite high up, and some homes in these peaceful, hilly streets have good views across London to the N and W. It is convenient for the buses that run down **Brixton Hill** to the tube station, and for Streatham's shops.

The furthest SW corner of the neighbourhood lies across **Lyham Rd** to the W, in the angle between it and **Kings Avenue**. This is Clapham Park borders: leafy streets of predominantly 3- and 4-bed late-Victorian terraces. These roads, and **Kingswood Rd**, are typical of this area of clean, narrow streets full of family-sized housing (a 4-bed in Kingswood Rd, £380,000). There are relatively few flat conversions here. Nearby Windmill Gardens and the sports ground provide a welcome bit of greenery.

Back, now, down the hill to the N. In the angle between **Brixton Hill** and **Acre Lane**, behind the town hall, another grid of streets is almost cut off from those of **Lyham Rd** described above. **Blenheim Gardens** has 4-bed houses; the scale changes in **Hayter Rd** with big 3-storey, double-fronted Victorian houses, many now flats (2-bed £265,000), and eight vast detached 6-bed-plus, 4-storey, Victorian mansions. **St Saviours Rd**, **Bonham Rd**, **Lambert Rd** and the tree-lined **Haycroft Rd** follow a similar pattern: a 6-bed in St Saviours, £675,000 last autumn. **Sudbourne Rd** is very popular: it has as its focus one of London's most successful primary schools. A 4-bed house here, c. £400,000; again, large houses make for roomy flat conversions: c. £225–300,000 for a 2-bed in this corner.

Just to the N, **Baytree Rd** is a good example of suburban-type inter-war semi-detached housing, a quiet leafy street yet close to Brixton centre, with 4-bed 1930s houses. The Tesco store on **Acre Lane** backs onto some of these.

Brixton Hill

Brixton's most coveted homes lie in their biggest concentration to the E of **Brixton Hill**, around the **Brixton Water Lane** conservation area. It's close to the town centre, but the streets are quiet and leafy. Even the presence of a crack house (now closed down) failed to deter buyers in 2003. In the sweep of lovely **Josephine Avenue** and **Helix Gardens** (also a conservation area) some of the large, handsome, Victorian terraced houses have 75 feet of garden frontage. These grandly curving, leafy streets were spaciously planned by the Victorian builders – who were constrained by a covenant from building on much of the land: thus the large gardens. Fifteen years back they were the subject of a highly successful community architecture scheme. The long front gardens were reclaimed from the dumped-car-dotted wastelands they had become. New reproduction railings, improved street lighting, parking spaces appeared, and made a dramatic difference. The houses are 3-storey, and quite wide. They make big family homes of 4/6 beds; many are now roomy flats (£230,000 for a 2-bed garden flat, £280,000 for a 3-bed one). Some whole houses, too, in the long curve of **Leander Rd**: a double-fronted 6-bed, £495,000.

The nearby loop of **Appach Rd** is made up of small 3-, 4- and 5-bed Victorian terraces, with some charming 2-storey double-fronted houses (one just split into two neat 2-bed flats: £230,000; with garden, £240,000). Many houses in this area have managed to hang onto their period marble fireplaces, ornate plaster ceilings and picture rails.

Brixton Water Lane itself is busy, but has some of the area's most charming homes. They include a Georgian farmhouse (smell that country air!) and some similar-period cottages – and all with Brockwell Park close by. Views across it from a handsome 4-storey Georgian house complete with lift, 150ft garden, garage: £595,000 last winter. The enclave of **Brailsford** and **Arlingford Rds** contains big Victorian houses, some converted to flats – a 2-bed, c. £215,000. A quiet corner –

and the homes on the E of **Brailsford Rd** back onto the Park.

The area further S, between **Brixton Hill** to the W and **Tulse Hill** to the E, is disputed between those two neighbourhoods. **Holmewood Rd**, which runs E from **Brixton Hill**, is a wide road of rather ordinary Victorian terraced brick-and-stucco houses. But it leads into surprising **Holmewood Gardens**, where the same terraces suddenly open out to surround an irregular green (a 1-bed flat here, £160,000). The road is wide, the effect spacious and cut off – even before the traffic-restricting Homezone. **Maplestead Rd** has similar houses.

Upper Tulse Hill winds across these slopes, with its E end in Tulse Hill while to the W is a mixture of big mid-Victorian detached houses (mostly flats), 1920s terraced homes and council blocks. Tree-lined **Athlone Rd**, which runs off to the E, has 1920s and '30s terraces, square-bayed (one 3-bed here, £335,000). The neat, cared-for atmosphere is maintained in **Elm Park**, where some flat-fronted mid-Victorian houses look smart in stock-brick and stucco. **Claverdale Rd** is more Edwardian/'30s: a 3-bed, £260,000. Elm Park meets **Brixton Hill** opposite the prison entrance. On the Hill here is Tudor Close, a large block of '30s flats (including studios: c. £96–112,000), with its own swimming pool. Some inter-war houses, such as those in **Mackie Rd**, punctuate the Victoriana.

There are several blocks of mansion flats along the length of **Brixton Hill**, varying in price and status. Christchurch House, a 1930s block, is a landmark; it, and the similar Effra Court and Brixton Hill Court, have relatively high service charges – and watch for length of lease. A 1-bed flat was on at £155,000 last autumn.

Somers Rd leads, somewhat unpromisingly at first, into the unexpected, hidden corner of **Archbishop's Place** and **Merredene St** with their pretty little early Victorian cottages: semi-detached, 2/3-bed. The Place is a cul-de-sac, with a few of the cottages tucked down paths at the end: a secretive corner, very popular with journalists, apparently. . . . These come on the market but rarely; sales are often by word of mouth. **Brading Rd** has more ordinary Victorian houses (and some flats). **Upper Tulse Hill** nearby, at the junction with **Ostade Rd**, has pairs of pretty early-Victorian villas facing mock-Tudor inter-war terraced homes.

Central Brixton

Central Brixton is mostly shops, offices, high-level railways and council-built flats. There are pockets of private housing, though. South of **Coldharbour Lane** to **Morval Rd** and between **Effra Rd**, W, and **Railton Rd**, E, are streets of 2- and 3-storey Victorian housing – including, in **Rushcroft Rd**, some mansion blocks recently refurbished. Couldn't be more central than this street – which is a lot more attractive since the blocks were done up. Search for bargains, though: an unmodernised 3-bed flat was £195,000 last autumn; in equally central **St Matthew's Rd**, a 2-bed ex-council, £129,000. In **Atlantic Rd** (right in the thick of it) a new, low-rise development has 1-bed flats for £165–175,000. Going on S, **Rattray Rd** forms the spine of a small grid of Victorian terraces in varying states of repair – a 4-bed house, £360,000, but a 3-bed, £390,000; one 2-bed flat, £250,000. **Kellet Rd**, a pretty street just to the S, is 'much requested' in agent-speak by buyers who want to be at the heart of things and can pay £160,000 and more for a 1-bed flat. **Dalberg Rd** gained a new house, two flats and workshop/studios on the corner with **Morval Rd**.

North of the railway that divides Brixton in two are some streets of 3- to 4-storey Victoriana between **Dalyell Rd** and busy **Stockwell Rd**. Here, on the shores of Stockwell Park, is Bellway's successful 'Drayman's Place' in **Combermere Rd:** 2-, 3- and 4-bed houses sharing a gym and a porter. These are popular, especially with women buyers, as they have good security. Nearby, Garrick Place is Bellway again: 1-, 2- and 3-bed flats.

Between **Stockwell Rd** and **Brixton Rd** stretches a triangle of council homes; **Brixton Rd** was once lined with solid early Victorian houses, and some still survive, though most are in commercial use. Converted flats in the old houses can be large.

East Brixton

Even **Coldharbour Lane** has been showing tentative signs of regeneration, with one or two of the large double-fronted old houses rescued from near-dereliction, plus some of the area's best known clubs and pubs. Here, E of the centre, are neighbourhoods that have been changed most by Brixton's unruly past: railways, the Blitz and the council between them destroyed what were once two smart Victorian suburbs, Loughborough Park and Angell Town. **Loughborough Park**, the road, survives in part; wide and leafy, with pairs of Victorian villas of varying sizes. There is a small park, then a modern low-rise council estate off **Moorland Rd**. Here, too, there are some cream stucco Victorian villas that would be worth a couple of million each in St John's Wood. The giant reversed-ziggurat council slab of **Clarewood Walk**, S of **Coldharbour Lane**, makes sense when you realize it was designed to turn its back on an eight-lane highway, planned but never built.

North of the railway, the curving street pattern is that of the mid-19th-century Angell Town estate, but most of today's buildings are '60s council-built flats, plus some far-superior, award-winning '90s mews-style ones. Some new houses appeared last year, looking a little out of place, on **Fyfield Rd**. An exception, though, is the rather grand 1880s complex on **Barrington Rd** that is now the loft apartments of 'College Green' – though it was built as the Brixton Orphanage for Fatherless Girls. Being a Brixton loft complex, there is a shared bicycle store. A few Victorian homes survive in **Villa Rd**, a tall terrace, now tidied, and Lambeth Council restored some more original Angell Town detached double-fronted houses in **St John's Crescent**. And in **Canterbury Crescent**, a 4-bed home in a redevelopment of a 1850s school building was £450,000 last autumn.

Many of the individual houses in this part of Brixton were owned by, even if not built by, the council; but Lambeth have been selling off the vacant ones in recent years.

Despite hopeful noises, Loughborough Junction is still not a polite neighbourhood, nor even a safe one for incomers. Some say that tougher policing in central Brixton has pushed trouble down to Loughborough Junction. Those taking a long view might gamble that the station (Thameslink–City) will tip the balance toward gentrification. We will see.

Brixton/Herne Hill borders

Railton Rd's once notorious reputation is fading since the council stepped in, compulsorily purchasing and smartening up empty shops. At the N end, where it runs into Atlantic Rd, Railton to a large extent deserved its reputation – but further S there is a grid of pleasant streets between **Railton** and **Dulwich Rds**. With the inevitability of estate agents, these roads, each named after a literary giant, have been dubbed the Poets' estate (London has several others such). Despite its position, Poets' Corner, as the area is alternatively known, is highly desirable. Prices reflect this: a 2-bed flat on **Railton Rd**, £199,000; a 1-bed in **Milton Rd**, £210,000. Indeed one could be miles away from trouble of any sort in these tree-lined, well-cared for streets, a short walk from the town centre and bordering Brockwell Park. The Victorian houses are much sought-after: most are detached, 3-, 4- and 5-bed. A 4-bed, **Chaucer Rd** example, £465,000 – or save one hundred thousand and buy a modern 4-bed in **Effra Parade**, four streets N.

Most of the streets are short and homogeneous, but **Shakespeare Rd** runs on E beyond Railton Rd and the railway, to a series of 1990s council-built cul-de-sacs (a 1-bed flat, £155,000) which add contemporary writers – **Derek Walcott Close**, **James Joyce Walk**, **Alice Walker Close** – to the traditional poets (**Chaucer**, **Spenser**, **Milton Rds**. . .) across the tracks. Despite the change in atmosphere there has been plenty of renovation work at this end of **Shakespeare Rd** – and now, at last, the Cleanaway depot looks set to become a new, much-needed Academy comprehensive. Paralleling Railton, **Mayall Rd** is a pleasant street of pretty 2-storey Victorian terraces priced at up to £325,000 (a 2-bed cottage, £240,000), but bear in mind that houses on the E side back onto the railway. To the N, the poets run out at **Effra Parade**, where Goldcrest's plans to split the old school into 107 homes met with local protests. Bellway now own the site: watch this space. . .

B *Herne Hill and Tulse Hill*

South of Brixton are two more areas with subtly different personalities. Their boundaries with Brixton are hard to define, but once in the centres of either Herne Hill or Tulse Hill you will know you are in another place. The bustle of Brixton is lacking, and some streets, especially in Herne Hill, have a solidly suburban feel. Another difference is the lack of a tube. Both places have rail stations on the Thameslink line, with trains to Blackfriars, City Thameslink, Farringdon and King's Cross, and to Victoria. As family areas, they benefit from the clutch of schools in nearby Dulwich.

Both districts are close to Brockwell Park, though Tulse Hill (which is on the South Circular and in transport Zone 3, not 2), is less desirable than family-friendly Herne Hill – which has a proper centre and is nearer to Dulwich. 'Evolving into a cosmopolitan and desirable place to be', say agents – who have a regrettable tendency to annex part of it as the 'North Dulwich Triangle' (see below). The homes vary, too: smaller 2- and 3-bed Victorian houses and Edwardian maisonettes are largely concentrated in Tulse Hill, while bigger family houses of 4- and 5-bed-plus are more characteristic of Herne Hill.

Tulse Hill

Tulse Hill provides properties with better-sized gardens and a far more suburban feel than those further N. It has distinctive, Art Deco-style early 20th-century houses that have seen a marked an upturn in their desirability – and prices.

Along **Tulse Hill**, S from **Brixton Water Lane**, council-built housing gives way to private properties on the E side at **Craignair Rd** and the W side at **Trinity Rise**. Homes are a mixture of 4-bed inter-war semis, some with mock-Tudor fronts (and £400,000-ish price-tags), and smaller 3-bed Victorian houses. The site of Dick Shepherd girls' school – closed down by Lambeth – became Fairclough's 'Brockwell Gate': 65 handsome, 4-bed, Regency-balconied houses (currently c. £420–430,000), and 158 flats (2-beds, c. £200–220,000). The site backs onto Brockwell Park, but is set in a council-built estate.

Inter-war semis line **Craignair Rd** and **Claverdale Rd**, giving way to small 3-bed Victorian houses (c. £300,000) at the W end. **Trinity Rise** comprises 4- and 5-bed Edwardiana and more '30s semis, leading to very desirable **Brockwell Park Gardens** – 3-bed Victorian terraces overlooking the park. **Deronda Rd**, **Deerbrook Rd** and **Romola Rd** contain semi-detached 4, 5 – and even £500,000, 6 bed – Victorian houses. Many, unsurprisingly, were split into roomy flats (£190–215,000 for a 2-bed). Going W, **Upper Tulse Hill** is mostly council-built housing – among the more attractive in this part of London. These, and some on nearby **Tulse Hill**, now appear on the open market. Downhill to the S is Tulse Hill station, with a collection of small shops. Opposite runs **Perran Rd** with small 3-bed Victorian terraces; to the W lies West Norwood. The A205/ South Circular runs around this southern boundary.

Herne Hill

Feeling now a place rather than an adjunct to Brixton or Dulwich, Herne Hill is settling down to be a proper family-based community. Brockwell Park, a wide sweep of grassy hill surrounding a Victorian mansion, edges it to the W. To the NW is the 'poets' district on the borders with Brixton (see above). A railway line forms a barrier against Brixton. The ground rises to the E of this line, forming a pleasant, hilly quarter of solid red-brick houses between **Herne Hill**, **Milkwood Rd** and the railway. Predominantly Victorian and Edwardian, and 3- or 4-bedroomed, as in **Kestrel**, **Gubyon**, **Shardcroft** and **Woodquest Avenues**, with larger double-fronted versions from the same eras in **Rollscourt Avenue** and particularly desirable **Fawnbrake Avenue**. Some are handsome examples of their period; some – thanks to the quite steep hill slopes – have sweeping views. Prices for the big 4-beds push half a million; a top 'Avenue' house can approach £700,000. All the 'Avenues' are well placed for the station and shops; a little further off, but on the slopes up to the Ruskin Park neighbourhood of Dulwich, **Brantwood Rd** and **Dorchester Drive** are peaceful, and could be anywhere in suburban London with their '30s semis and rose gardens. **Dorchester Court**'s purpose-built '20s blocks have become popular. **Milkwood Rd**'s S end is close to Herne Hill station and has small 3-bed Victorian terraces; the N end, though, is less appealing, with industrial estates and more traffic, merging into Brixton around the multiple rail bridges of Loughborough Junction.

There is a mixture of homes strung along **Herne Hill** (the main through-route), from very large Victorian or Edwardian detached and semi-detached houses, plus some inter-war housing, to mansion blocks. To the SE of the central parades of shops around Herne Hill's station, the atmosphere becomes strongly suburban. Off **Half Moon Lane**, on the Dulwich borders and much sought-after, lie **Stradella Rd**, **Winterbrook Rd** and **Burbage Rd**. These are wide, tree-lined and quiet; again, mostly late-Victorian/Edwardian homes: terraced and semi-detached houses with 60ft back gardens. **Burbage Rd**, though, holds surprises, with several large detached houses boasting large gardens and driveways – and Dulwich prices. It is a very popular road because as the name suggests it crosses the tracks to form a direct link through to lovely, upmarket Dulwich Village (which chapter see).

There is, by the way, a determined attempt on the part of estate agents to disinvent Herne Hill: the area bounded by **Half Moon Lane** to the S, **Herne Hill** to the N and **Red Post Hill** to the E has been dubbed the 'North Dulwich Triangle', and those searching for a home here should look out for that term (and premium prices) in property details. It contains many delightful streets of family housing – a mixture of Victorian, Edwardian and more modern terraced, detached and semi-detached homes. **Holmdene** is a good example, with its wide roadway, trees and hedges and 3-storey Victorian houses, plus some modern semi-detacheds at the **Herne Hill** end. The solid Edwardian 3-bed terraced houses in streets like **Elfindale Rd** are popular (2-bed house in **Frankfurt Rd**, £350,000). Dulwich Mead, off **Half Moon Lane**, is an enclave of smart 1–3 bed retirement homes.

Beckwith Rd, **Ardbeg Rd** and **Elmwood Rd** are more exclusive and expensive. These streets are even quieter, and stand right on the Dulwich border close to North Dulwich station. Their very popular 3-bed Edwardian terraces with small front gardens are close to a charming, well-kept public park, Sunray Gardens, with duck pond, tennis courts and children's play-area.

To the S of the station, **Norwood Rd** runs down towards Tulse Hill, with Brockwell Park on the W side. Just behind **Norwood Rd**, and still well placed for Herne Hill station, lie **Guernsey Grove** and **Harwarden Grove**, next door to a small estate of Peabody Trust housing. Mainly small houses and flats on **Guernsey**; 4- to 5-bed houses on **Harwarden**. Rail lines bracket this corner, though. Facing Brockwell Park along **Norwood Rd** lie large 3-storey double-fronted Victorian houses, some 6-bed detached, some semis, some flats, with smaller 3- and 2-storey houses nearer to Herne Hill.

Tulse Hill borders

The roads on the Streatham/Norwood borders, bounded by, but cut off from, **Christchurch Rd** – the busy South Circular – to the N, and **Palace Rd** and its side streets to the S, are very pleasant: spacious, tidy and tree-lined.

Palace Rd is by far the most expensive, with large flats in huge Victorian and Edwardian properties. As single homes, these have 5, 6 or more beds and price tags of c. £800,000. **Christchurch Rd** has big 3- and 5-storey Victorian houses of 5-beds-plus, most split into flats, though there are some double-fronted 2-storey, 5-bed houses, and a large council estate in **Coburg Crescent**. The roads between, like **Probyn**

Rd and **Perran Rd**, have smallish 3-bed Victorian terraces. **Lanercost Rd** is the exception, having larger 5-bed Victorian houses that can fetch £550,000–plus (a 4-bed house here, £480,000 last winter).

B

Transport Tubes: Brixton (zone 2, Victoria), to Oxford Circus 15 min, City 15 min (1 change), Heathrow 1 hr 10 min (1 change). Trains: Brixton to Victoria 10 min; Herne Hill to Victoria, Blackfriars, Tulse Hill to London Bridge, Blackfriars. Both are on Thameslink.

Convenient for Victoria and West End, City, South Circular, A23/M23 for Gatwick Airport and Brighton. Miles from centre: 3.5

Schools Local Authority: St Martins-in-the-Fields C of E (g). Private: Streatham Hill & Clapham High School (g). See also Dulwich and Clapham chapters.

SALES

Flats	S	1B	2B	3B	4B	5B
Average prices	100–130+	145–200+	180–300+	200–350	270–350	–
Houses	2B	3B	4B	5B	6/7B	8B
Average prices	220–400	240–450	300–550	400–850	–	–

RENTAL

Flats	S	1B	2B	3B	4B	5B
Average prices	120–150	150–250	180–300	220–370	–	–
Houses	2B	3B	4B	5B	6/7B	8B
Average prices	180–330	230–390	330–550	390–600+	–	–

The properties Wide range in Brixton: rows of Victorian (and the odd Georgian) houses, some of real quality. Also lots of council-build – ditto. Flats are mostly conversions (some large and lovely); some '30s blocks, new homes carved out of old schools etc. Increasing amount of new-build – not as popular as period if undersized and overpriced. Tulse and Herne Hills have Victorian/'30s family homes, often in quiet streets. Council-built homes now appear on open market.

The market Fashion and good transport links drive a market in which younger (and increasingly middle-class) buyers predominate. They also move here to swap flats in pricier areas for roomy houses: cries for a secondary school betray growing family presence. Brixton prices are cheaper; gap widens as size increases. Herne/Tulse Hill houses range higher, especially for big houses and near stations, but Clapham/Kennington overspill, and growing fashion for the area, have driven Brixton prices up.

Among estate agents active in this area are:

- Haart
- Oliver Burn
- Winkworth
- Bushells
- Martin Barry
- Kinleigh Folkard & Hayward
- Morgan Berry
- Whites
- Charles Gordon
- Barnard Marcus
- Gordon & Keenes
- Foxtons

CAMBERWELL

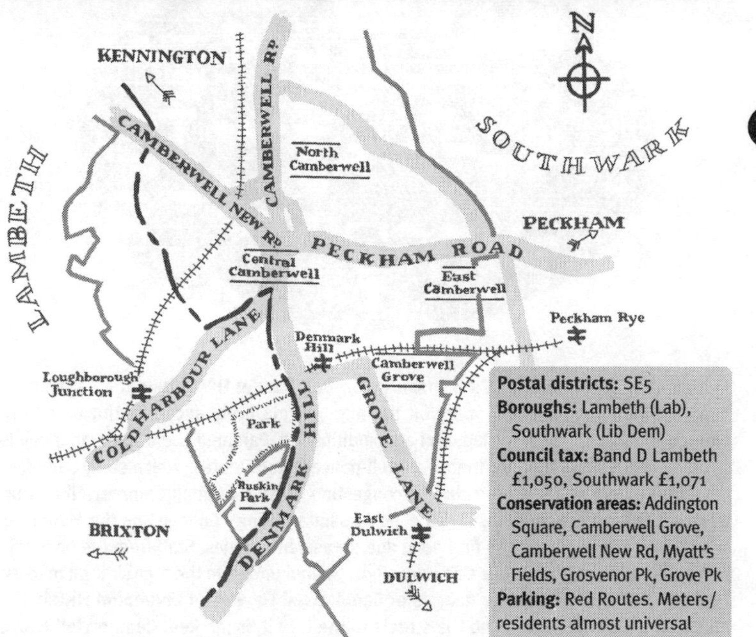

Postal districts: SE5
Boroughs: Lambeth (Lab), Southwark (Lib Dem)
Council tax: Band D Lambeth £1,050, Southwark £1,071
Conservation areas: Addington Square, Camberwell Grove, Camberwell New Rd, Myatt's Fields, Grosvenor Pk, Grove Pk
Parking: Red Routes. Meters/ residents almost universal

Thanks to the lack of a tube, Camberwell has stayed a bit of a secret. For decades, home-hunters who explore this crowded, mixed neighbourhood have been rounding corners from teeming main roads and discovering quiet, tree-lined streets of genuine Georgiana and handsome early Victorian homes left over from this former village's brief career as a health resort. Those who find it delight in the mixed, villagy atmosphere and the proximity to both City and West End.

A year back, Camberwell looked set to be on a new Metro service that would have linked the East London Line round via Denmark Hill station to Clapham Junction. Alas, this Guide's mantra ('Don't believe it till you see them digging') has yet again proved its worth, and the Croydon branch will get built first (see Transport chapter). Nevertheless, copious buses run from the Green to the West End in 15–20 minutes, on routes dramatically improved by bus lanes. Bikes are popular too, with much work done to tame pinch-points like the Elephant & Castle junction. And the trains from Denmark Hill provide satisfactory commuter links to Victoria, London Bridge and Blackfriars.

Camberwell Green clearly was once a village, but is now rather more of a traffic island surrounded by humdrum shops. Climb the gentle hill to the S to find streets like Georgian **Camberwell Grove** and homes with lovely unexpected views clear to the London Eye, or Canary Wharf. You can play the same trick in other directions: Camberwell is very much a place of enclaves – good and bad.

The Green lies at the junction of **Camberwell Church St, Camberwell Rd, Denmark Hill** and **Camberwell New Rd.** These busy streets define and divide the area's various neighbourhoods, and it is further split by two railway lines. The boundary with Brixton, along **Coldharbour Lane** to the W, is ill-defined, and Camberwell fades into Walworth to the N. On the whole, the SE5 postcode equals Camberwell.

The main shopping area is **Denmark Hill** (with **Walworth Rd** not far away). There is a

C

Morrisons with car park, and a Sainsbury's on **Dog Kennel Hill** (where, too, a dynamic head has put Dog Kennel Primary on the map). Some lively and colourful bars have emerged; restaurants are varied, and also multiplying. Parking in central Camberwell is virtually impossible, though: there's a (well-policed) Red Route – which sadly seems to have little effect so far on the chronic congestion. It runs through Camberwell and up **Denmark Hill**, where those visiting the local hospitals, King's College and the Maudsley, search for parking places and find none due to residents' zones. Staff from the hospitals and students from the famous Camberwell Art School underpin the area's rental market.

The contrast between the heights of **Camberwell Grove** and **Champion Hill**, half a mile to the S of the Green, and the streets to the N of it, is marked. **Camberwell Grove** has some of the handsomest Georgian houses S of the Thames. There are leafy, quiet streets of villas of every period from Regency onwards. Go a few blocks N and there are some of the nastiest of ex-GLC flats interspersed with some very ordinary late-Victorian terraces of the ubiquitous South London sort.

Prices vary as widely. Big ex-council flats in walk-up blocks can be c. £135–175,000, while a Victorian conversion can yield 2-bed flats ranging from £160–250,000. A standard little Victorian terraced house in a decent corner will be from just below the stamp-duty threshold at £250,000 to around £300,000, ranging up to the best big Victorian/Edwardiana, £650,000 plus, and top Georgian gems reaching up to seven figures. Prices rise once within the orbit of Oval tube, across to the NW in next-door Kennington, while Dulwich (which spells schools) pulls prices up to the SE.

Camberwell Grove

The area S and E of the Green, on the gentle slopes up towards Herne Hill and Dulwich, was the first to be developed as Camberwell began its expansion from village to suburb. **Camberwell Grove** survives virtually intact as a splendid street of late-Georgian houses. A lot have become flats; whole, the 5-bed-plus beauties hover c. £825–900,000 (£1.15 million is the top recorded price, some 18 months back). There are more modest-sized ones at c. £400–800,000. Some, at the N end, date from the 1770s; others further S (such as those that curve off to form **Grove Crescent**), are early 19th century. At the S end, 16 homes in two creamy terraces were restored in 1997: the 1830 row on the W side is 10 houses, while the E (1845) is split into 35 flats (1-beds c. £180,000, 2-beds, £270–300,000). **Lettsom St** runs E off the Grove with 1970s council-built flats (a 1-bed £118,000, 2-beds c. £150,000). In contrast, round the corner in **Graces Mews**, is a gated, 6-bed, 4-bath, roof-terraced home converted from a 1915 warehouse: £1.3 million.

The Georgian atmosphere continues on E into **Grove Park** and W into **Grove Lane**.

Grove Park, meandering round in a leafy, hilltop square, has a few Georgian homes but is largely lined with particularly peaceful, big, Arts-and-Craftsy Edwardian houses – which also share use of a large garden hidden away off one corner. Around £630–690,000, depending on condition, for a 5-bed example here.

Grove Lane – yes, *everything* hereabouts is 'Grove something' or 'something Grove' – is not as grand as Camberwell Grove, though it does have some lovely early 19th-century houses mixed with just about every 20th-century period – an Edwardian 4-bed here, £465,000 last winter – and also Camberwell Hall, the wonderful 1740s Assembly Rooms, scene of many a fashionable meeting and now a very unusual house. Railway land in the angle of Camberwell Grove and Grove Park yielded space for homes in the late '80s: **Grovelands Close**, off the Grove, has mews-style houses and maisonettes; **Linwood Close** , off the Park, has 137 studio, 1- or 2-bed flats (a studio, £120,000).

West of Grove Lane, **Champion Hill** and surrounding streets were developed in the 1840s. Some of these elegant stuccoed, pedimented villas still survive. The style continues, N of the railway and the Maudsley Hospital, in **De Crespigny Park**, though most houses here have been split into flats – and few of these come onto the market.

Back to the S, **Langford Green** is a popular 1968 enclave built in Regency style, and has large town-houses (and a few 3-bed, c. £350,000, ones) in pleasant stock brick. Round the corner **Champion Grove** has the genuine article: a pretty 3-bed Regency home (just done up, with big extended kitchen/family room) was £545,000 last autumn. **Ruskin Park House** is a pair of large blocks of '20s mansion flats: 1-, 2- (c. £180,000) and 3-beds. They have a good name: well-run and economical.

Ruskin Park

West across **Denmark Hill**, the bulk of King's College Hospital and the E–W railway line form a frontier cutting off the Ruskin Park corner in South Camberwell. The park is the centre of an enclave of 20th-century streets with a strongly, but pleasingly, suburban feel. Roads like **Deepdene** and **Sunset**, with their '20s/30s semis – not to mention a green-roofed, Spanish-style bungalow – slope peacefully down to Ruskin Park. **Ferndene Rd** lines the E side, its 1920s gabled and bay-windowed villas having fine views across it and the rooftops towards Central London. West of the park, **Finsen Rd** has handsome terraces built around 1914 (c. £270–340,000) looking out over the greenery from particularly pretty square-bayed windows. To the N, **Kemerton Rd** and surrounding streets have neat little Victorian cottages, some split into flats.

Denmark Hill itself is a busy but pleasant road. To the E are large brick council-built blocks, and further on lies a piece of London history: the **Sunray Avenue** estate of 1920s cottage homes on the borders of Herne Hill, built by the old Camberwell borough on Dulwich College land (they were 'encouraged' to grant a 200-year lease . . .) as part of the post-First World War 'Homes Fit for Heroes' campaign. The cottages are mostly in private hands now – a **Casino Avenue** 4-bed, £300,000 – but they rarely come onto the market.

East Camberwell

Between **Peckham Rd** and the railway line to the S, there are several streets of late-19th-century terraces such as **Maude Rd, Vestry Rd, Shenley Rd, Crofton Rd** and **Bushey Hill Rd**: a good source of 3- and 4-bed homes. A 3-bed, but '20s, bay-fronted house, £375,000; a 4-bed double-fronted in **Shenley** £420,000. **Vestry Mews** recently gained, courtesy of St George's, a gated courtyard of new houses, and a number of old ones were converted into flats; both are popular – so much so that they rarely appear for sale. The proximity of the respected art college also makes this a popular area for rentals.

A splendid old piano factory on **Peckham Rd** with vast windows received the loft treatment: as ever, these are the price of nearby houses: £425,000 for a big 2-bed loft.

To the E is Peckham, which is changing fast – see chapter – and Peckham Rye station.

Central Camberwell

You could drive through the area's traffic-filled heart every day without discovering Camberwell's most surprising corner. Off **Denmark Hill**, a tiny turning called **Love Walk** leads (only on foot) to the entrance to a tucked-away group of 3- and 4-storey brick blocks of flats, owned by the Orbit Housing Association. Walk on, and **Love Walk** reveals its surprise: Selbourne Village, a 1982 Wates estate of small, cottagy houses built – with great attention to materials and detailing – in the highest flight of village vernacular. Pleasant, peaceful, successfully human-scale, well-hidden corner – but an extraordinary stylistic jolt in so urban an environment. Cars can enter from the E end: garages are hidden in groups between the houses. One of these, needing work: £295,000 last winter.

On the other side of **Love Walk** are older – but equally unlikely – homes. First comes a little row of earlier, c. 1930s, versions of the country cottage: tile-hung, gabled and hidden behind an old wall, reached only through two arched gateways, seldom for sale. Further on are splendid small Regency houses – detached, double-fronted and (a real boon) with garages, that lead out onto **Grove Lane**: one, needing work, £795,000.

North Camberwell

This is the patch that will gain from Mayor Livingstone's Cross-River tram which – *if* it transpires, and even then not till 2011 – will provide a fast link to town. Most of the area E of **Camberwell Rd** and N of **Peckham Rd** is taken up by large council developments; a few older streets survive, however – notably just E of the road, around **Addington Square** (a conservation area). The square itself, which runs up to Burgess Park – Camberwell's northern frontier – is early 19th-century; it has irregular houses of the classic, tall, late-Georgian style (3-beds £400,000-plus, 4/5-beds £565,000-plus – a 7-bed, £765,000), plus a pair of low Regency villas. To the S is **Rust Square**, a pleasant Victorian corner.

South from here, where once omnibuses and horses were stabled, **Hopewell Yard** in **Hopewell St** harbours a distinctive, late-'80s homes development: an enclosed corner of flats (a studio here c. £100,000), maisonettes and offices around a central court-yard, with basement parking. **Vicarage Grove** has some large Victoriana. Other streets where private homes remain include **Havil St** (a 2-bed house, £300,000; a 4-bed Regency one, £500,000) and **Ada Rd** with its little flat-fronted or bayed cottages; the tower of an old workhouse was converted into cheese-wedge shaped flats in the 1980s: expect to pay £160–200,000 for one.

Off **Sedgmoor Place** is a surprise: **Pilgrims Cloisters**, the sensitive conversion of some 1837 almshouses into 1-bed flats and studios reached via a locked gate: cloisters (and chapel) survive. Their price (£130,000-plus) reflects their Grade II-listed status – which of course also means repairs/alterations must be in keeping. In another re-use, handsome, Edwardian St Giles Hospital off **St Giles** and **Peckham Rds** is now Peacock House: flats, now c. £150–240,000; a penthouse, £300,000 last autumn (but check service charges).

Activity here on the fringes of the vast North Peckham initiative (see Peckham chapter): Coleman Square off **Wells Way** gained 36 new homes in 2000: flats and 3-bed town-houses. Off **Southampton Way**, and right on the edge of SE5, Galliard's 'South City Court' has 80 open-market flats, 25 Affordable Homes and the conversion of a Georgian house into three flats, plus 10 new-build ones. And in **New Church Rd**, 'Admiral Point' has flats from a 1-bed, £205,000, to a 3-bed, duplex, terraced penthouse, £350,000.

Large Georgian houses – some intact, recently restored and used as single homes, while others are nowadays flats – line long stretches of both **Camberwell Rd** and **Camberwell New Rd.** Occasionally some of these come up for sale; many were owned by the council. Usually these large houses have lost all interior period features, though the shell is intact; expect to pay around £400–475,000. Along Camberwell New Rd, tucked in the angle of **Vassall Rd** and **Langton Rd**, is mewsy **Salisbury Place**: a pleasant and popular 1989 enclave within striking-distance of Oval tube.

South of **Camberwell New Rd,** Camberwell merges with Brixton. There are big council estates – but also the conservation area around the green space of **Myatt's Fields,** where the handsome, often 5- (and sometimes 6-) bedded villas of the 1890s Minet Estate, in roads such as **Knatchbull Rd**, always attract interest. Prices come down to earth somewhat in nearby roads like **Upstall St,** though a done-up and extended 5-bed here was £475,000 last autumn. **St Gabriel's Manor,** off **Cormont Rd,** is an 1899 seminary split into 50 mezzanined apartments. Towards **Coldharbour Lane** are cheaper homes in streets such as **Lilford Rd,** and new ones in **Empress Mews** off **Kenbury St**: a gated, industrial-chic scheme of 2- and 3-bed live/work units. 'Myatts View' in **Camberwell Station Rd** (a name of purely historic interest: trains stopped stopping in the 1970s) is a Buxton Homes scheme of five live/work units and 14 flats.

C

Transport Trains: Loughborough Junction to City via Thameslink 12 min; Denmark Hill to Blackfriars (10 min), London Bridge and Victoria (14 min). East Dulwich to London Bridge. Nearest tube, Oval. Also fast buses to centre.

Convenient for City, Westminster, Dulwich. Miles from centre: 3.

Schools Local Authority: Archbishop Michael Ramsey C of E, Sacred Heart RC; Lambeth Academy, Clapham. See also Dulwich chapter.

SALES

Flats	S	1B	2B	3B	4B	5B
Average prices	85–120	120–190	140–250	175–300	180+	–
Houses	2B	3B	4B	5B	6/7B	8B
Average prices	250–300	250–450	300–600	450–900	600–1M	–

RENTAL

Flats	S	1B	2B	3B	4B	5B
Average prices	115–145	140–200	165–250	200–280	230+	–
Houses	2B	3B	4B	5B	6/7B	8B
Average prices	200–270	230–370	275–400	400+	–	–

The properties Scruffy main roads conceal pockets of fine, hidden Georgiana and lovely examples of most periods since. Also ordinary terraces and converted flats. New developments appearing, adding town-houses and flats to an area that mixes some of the best and some of the worst of London homes.

The market Everyone mixes here – the less stinking-rich professions, plus art students, theatre, council tenants, hospital staff. . . . Not as well-known as it ought to be, the area has less bustle and street-cred than Brixton, but nicer houses: unconverted Georgian coveted. Price range reflects lack of tube and is dependent on location and architecture as much as size.

Among estate agents active in this area are:

- Andrews & Robertson
- Roy Brooks
- Ludlow Thompson
- Wooster & Stock
- Kinleigh Folkard & Hayward
- Hindwoods Hunter Payne
- Acorn
- First Property Sales
- Winkworth
- Reside

CAMDEN TOWN AND PRIMROSE HILL

Postal districts: NW1, NW3, NW5
Boroughs: Camden (Lab)
Council tax: Band D £1,200
Conservation areas: Widespread; include Camden Square, Jeffreys St, Camden Town, Primrose Hill
Parking: Residents/meters; permits not always granted to new developments

The spotlight this year is on the seedier end of Camden Town, as 'Just fifteen minutes from the Eurostar' becomes the local catchphrase (especially if you're selling). By spring 2007 – and it's on schedule – this will be true. The proximity of St Pancras and its attendant rail lines will become an asset to Camden Town, not the drawback it has been for 140 years.

Those who scoff that Camden Town cannot have a seedier end since it's all seedy, have not checked the house prices, or the air of affluence, west of the High St and (especially) over on next-door Primrose Hill. Here you have a neighbourhood which has sucessfully fought off Starbucks, where not to have written a book is death to your social life, and where money is in ample supply if always (so *very* British) in the background.

Indeed, Primrose Hill today is just what Earl Camden had in mind when he started to build Camden Town in 1791. But his attempts to create a sort of North London Belgravia were frustrated within a few years: the estate was invaded by the Grand Union Canal and the main railways from the N. These, and linked industry, lowered the tone. By the mid-19th century, though it had some claim to be a professional persons' suburb, it was never a smart one. In the course of the 20th, the by now ill-maintained homes went downhill, and the denizens of cheap boarding houses and tacky rented flat conversions outnumbered owner-occupiers.

A few enclaves apart, Camden Town remained cheap and cheerful, a haven for broke artists and struggling newcomers, until the start of the 1990s. Then bohemian London got rich. Writers became, or were replaced by, media stars. Warrens of bed-sits became carefully restored Victorian houses.

To buy in Camden now you need to be a pretty prosperous sort of bohemian. 'More blue-chip' is how local agents approvingly describe their current clients. Families are scarcer than well-heeled younger couples and singles.

Primrose Hill, an enclave of quiet streets beside the 110-acre open space of the Hill to the W, has a less eventful past. It has been known for handsome houses and spacious flats, both Victorian and modern, for several decades. Despite the property prices, Primrose Hill is still intellectual-smart – just about – rather than mere money-smart; more medicine, law, entertainment and media than City. Americans just love it.

Camden Town's southern frontier has been a disaster zone of semi-derelict railway land, enlivened only by the canal, for as long as memory goes back. Now, at last, it is changing. That new Eurostar station will indeed transform St Pancras; trains will run to Paris (as well as Derby) from 2007. After that date, the railway lands will become a new mini-city: see Bloomsbury & King's Cross chapter for details. The railway lines also mean excellent transport links, though Camden Town tube is in a sad state. London Transport promises a new station, with shops, flats and offices above it – but the proposed completion date has slipped back to 2011. Never mind, St Pancras will be the hottest hub in London well before then.

The lure of Eurostar and the billions that will flow in after it has unsettled the Camden Town property market. Homeowners are staying put, reasoning that all the investment will boost their property's value. Would-be buyers are less sanguine, leading to stand-offs where vendors stuck to higher prices than buyers would pay. After a brisk spring in 2004, prices – and activity – fell back in the autumn.

In the mid-20th century Camden Town was known for cheap housing, and Greek, Irish and Italian communities became established here. Most are now gone, displaced by a wave of designers, architects, writers – and, increasingly, media stars. Nevertheless, Camden retains its cosmopolitan, raffish atmosphere, with lots of excellent restaurants and specialist food shops. Lively clubs, pubs and other venues serve young people: the area is a tourist destination as well as a place to live – with, be warned, the downsides that such a hot-spot entails. The famous canalside markets at Camden Lock have been tidied up, as has the **High St**. The tidying can go too far, some say. The Electric Ballroom nightclub in the High Street is due for demolition as part of the tube station scheme: indignant locals reckon that closing the Electric and two markets (as the tube proposals imply) would mean that overcrowding at the station would indeed be solved – no-one would want to come to Camden Town any more. . . .

Living here often means having to put up with noisy main roads or the sound of tube or trains; as a result, each street commands a different price. Homes are nearly all

Victorian houses and conversions of these into flats, though the few, if high-profile, expensive new flats have their fans. The narrow-fronted Victorian houses give no more than a 1-, possibly 2-bed flat to a floor; bigger ones tend, therefore, to be maisonettes. The largest and smartest homes are in Primrose Hill (which is among London's top residential districts), around **Gloucester Crescent** and in the **Camden Square** neighbourhood.

The satellite areas, grouped around central Camden Town, are Chalk Farm, Mornington Crescent, Primrose Hill and, to the S, what little housing there is in Euston. Note that Camden (the borough) covers a much larger area than Camden Town.

Camden Town

The heart of Camden Town is a busy road junction with the tube station on its very busiest corner. **Camden High St**, running N from **Mornington Crescent**, is Camden's main shopping street, lively and never still. The best residential area of Camden Town is – perhaps surprisingly – in the narrow strip W of the **High St**. On the map it looks hemmed in by roads and railways (maps always distort the scale of roads), but the houses are good-period early Victorian and the streets both handsome and interesting.

On **Camden High St** there are flats and maisonettes above the shops in flat-fronted Victorian terraces at the S end, and red-brick mansion blocks near the tube station. **Delancey St**, also busy and wide, is one-way going W towards Regent's Park, and has youthful cafés and shops at the High St end, with flats above; thereafter terraces on either side. The narrow, flat-fronted Victorian buildings provide flats, maisonettes and houses, some with gardens; the W end overlooks the main line into Euston. Here it curves up to meet colourful, crowded **Parkway**, which is one-way back to the High St: a good range of shops and restaurants flank either side, and there's the Camden Odeon cinema, plus offices and shops (Gap, Starbucks: the usual suspects).

Wide **Albert St**, shielded from the rail line by Mornington Terrace, is one of Camden's most attractive and expensive roads. It boasts elegant and beautifully maintained terraces on both sides, set back behind gardens, a source of large 4-, 5- and 6-bed family houses. A 5-bed, 5-storey house here might be marketed now at c. £1.25–1.5 million (1971: £14,000; 1998: £625,000). **Arlington Rd**, parallel, has a similar middle section with terraced houses (smaller than Albert's) along either side, though prices are lower in this slightly less attractive street. Busy **Jamestown Rd** has both recent, if period-style, properties and older terraces, providing flats and maisonettes. On the corner with **Arlington Rd**, the 32-flat Piers Gough-designed Glass Building has also raised the tone of the road (unusually for central Camden these have secure parking). Part of the same development is a new canalside hotel, accessed from **Jamestown Rd**. This road also sports restaurants, a fashionable bar, and Gilbey House, a conversion of an 1890s canalside bottling plant to 76 flats (3-bed £650,000 last winter). Between the two is The Iceworks, with offices and 14 2- and 3-bed high-spec flats, developers Barratt.

At the N end of **Arlington Rd**, after the Delancey St junction, council housing is on the E side, more large, terraced Victorian homes opposite. An office development in **Carlow St** is crowned with 14 penthouse flats, ultra-smart, ultra-modern, with roof terraces. Twelve new houses appeared in **Beatty St** early in the 1990s.

Inverness St leads W off Arlington St to **Gloucester Crescent**. The Crescent is reckoned the best address in Camden Town (unless, like some agents, you swear that it's part of Primrose Hill across the tracks). Some of these big 1840s semi-detached houses are flats, some are enviable whole houses, and there is some later infill. Like the rest of Camden Town, Goucester Crescent failed to cling to the status intended for it, and by the 1960s many of the big villas were split into seedy lodging houses. Writer Alan Bennett has amusingly described how he and other young people, the first wave of 'gentrifiers', began to buy these houses in the '60s and return them to single homes. You'd need to be a lot more prosperous than the average young playwright to live there today, though the arts-

and-theatre mix remains. Prices are now comparable to those of (real) Primrose Hill.

Mornington Terrace is council in the S part; the N part has homes, in Victorian terraces, on the E side only; the W side overlooks the railway. Most are still single houses, both modernized and unmodernized. **Mornington Place** ditto.

In the triangle formed by **Camden High St**, **Hawley Crescent** and **Kentish Town Rd**, small new developments of town-houses and purpose-built flats rub shoulders with the vast TV studio complex and large, ugly commercial and office buildings. In the triangle on the other side of **Kentish Town Rd**, bounded by **Camden St**, is a large Sainsbury's supermarket. On the canal edge of the Sainsbury's site is a real surprise: ten high-tech houses (and some flats) by architect Nicholas Grimshaw, award-winning metal-clad pods with lofty galleried rooms behind vast, electrically operated windows. Now 16 years old, they are looking just a touch down-at-heel.

Camden St, the main southbound highway into the West End, has period terracing at the N end providing converted flats and maisonettes, plus a mix of council housing old and new. The Greek Orthodox church is on the E side. **Bayham St** is similar, with heavy traffic southbound, and has small workshops and council housing on E side; shops with flats above in period terracing opposite, and Victorian terraces. There are also some handsome former almshouses dating from 1818: these are occasionally for sale.

East of **Bayham St** is a relatively quiet, conveniently placed group of streets, which form the best place to live (Gloucester Crescent/Albert St excepted) in central Camden. **Greenland Rd** is a quiet street with flat-fronted London stock brick terraces; these are Victorian, 3-storeyed, with gardens both front and back, providing 3-bed houses and some converted flats. Some are privately owned, some housing association and some council, resulting in varying conditions of housing and a good mix of residents. **Carol St**, **St Martin's Close** and **Georgiana St** ditto (2-bed cottage in the latter £450,000). **Lyme St** has a pleasant row of early-Victorian terraces on the E side overlooking the canal: the S part is best. A 3-bed semi-detached house (S end) was £580,000 last winter, a 1-bed flat £220,000. Lyme Wharf, new in '03, has canal-side 2-bed flats in a smart new building by Berkeley. **Pratt St** has private housing between Bayham St and the High St, in flats and maisonettes above shops, plus some individual houses. **Plender St**, with a small fruit-and-veg market at its W end, is similar – though it also has some purpose-built blocks of flats.

Camden Town has many houses of mid-Victorian date, which feature sash windows such as this, often with vestigial 'balconies' in wrought iron. The window surrounds, of classically detailed stucco, form a pleasing contrast with the London stock brick. The large window panes contrast with the earlier Georgian small ones, which staged a reappearance late in the century.

The roads S of **Pratt St** through to **Crowndale Rd** are mainly council with the exception of **College Place**, which has large Victorian terraced houses in the N section only. **Royal College St** (a main through route, northbound only) has council housing at its S end; then terraces on both sides, some still single houses: two of these came onto the market in 2003, and the agent got 22 sealed bids. The King's Cross factor was cited.

East of the canal, **Baynes St** has a 1985 waterside development of mews houses and flats. **Rossendale Way** has conversions in the period terrace to the right, new mews houses beyond; it overlooks the canal at the rear. To the E is Elm Village, town-houses, maisonettes and flats built by Camden Council in the mid-1980s: the dinky name notwithstanding, some of the cheapest homes in Camden are to be found here. **Rousden St**, a narrow street running up to Camden Rd station (the tracks run on the S side), has a terrace of modern town-houses and flats plus converted flats in period houses. **St Pancras Way**, which runs S from **Camden Rd**, is a through-road with industrial and commercial buildings.

Tall Victorian terraced houses then reappear on the northern part of **St Pancras Way** and **Royal College St**. **Jeffreys St**, through to **St Pancras Way**, has 3- and 4-storey Victorian terraces on either side with basements, black railings in front and small balconies on the first floor. **Prowse Place**, closer to the railway line, has brick-fronted cottages and is still cobbled. **Ivor St** is a quiet, tree-lined street with brightly painted 2- and 3-storey houses. **Bonny St** is very mixed: some of its period houses yield converted flats; a clutch of town-houses dates from the 1980s. In **Jeffreys Place** are a further dozen big '80s town-houses with garages.

To the NE of St Pancras Way lie 'the Rochesters', a group of streets tucked in beneath the borders of NW5 and Kentish Town, which rank next in desirability and price to Gloucester Crescent/Albert St and Camden Square. **Rochester Rd**, a no-through-road, is part of an environmental area. It overlooks a small playground, which lies between it and **Rochester Terrace**. Here prices are slightly higher, thanks to S-facing gardens and larger, grander houses. **Rochester Place** is a very narrow street in which are council blocks, small workshops and a school. To the W, **Reed's Place** is a tiny, hidden-away street, blocked off to traffic at both ends. Small, square, stucco-fronted Victorian 2-bed houses set the tone; most have pretty front gardens. **Wilmot Place** has substantial pairs of brick-and-stucco-fronted houses, plus terraces. **Rochester Mews** has several little, white-painted mews houses in its E section, and a few 4-bed houses (one as £775,000 last winter). **Whitcher Place** is low, brick-built halls of residence for London University.

Camden Square

The area on the Kentish borders, bounded by **York Way** to the E, **Camden Rd** to the W and **Agar Grove** to the S, has some good houses in spacious streets and squares, and has become popular as a consequence. Camden School for Girls, with its tight catchment area, locks families into the area. The loom of King's Cross Central, to the S, is beginning to be felt. 'Walking distance King's Cross' is not something you'd have boasted about until recently, but now. . . .

Camden Square establishes the tone – an elegant, leafy cache of substantial 1850/60s houses, gazing out over the quiet, attractive square gardens; either still family homes (especially on the S side) or spacious flats and maisonettes in converted ones. A 7-bed house was £1.35 million late last year.

North Villas and **South Villas** run NE from Camden Square and have huge grey-brick 1860s villas on both sides. Garden flats are available in deep basements (2-bed £315,000). All these houses are now split into 1-, 2- and 3-bedroomed flats and maisonettes; **Camden Terrace** likewise. **St Augustine's Rd** – pleasant, wide, tree-lined and quiet – has large pairs of villas to either side in varying conditions of repair. Unmodernized examples are still sometimes available; conversions yield flats (a 2-bed £270,000 last winter). **Marquis Rd, Cantelowes Rd** (4-bed house £875,000) and **St Paul's Crescent** ditto. **St Paul's Mews**, 25 smart town-houses, dates from 1990.

Camden Mews runs parallel to Camden Square on the NW side: a group of seven new mews houses were added in 1998 to a street that has an eclectic mix of styles and sizes (and thus prices). 'It's had every architect you could name playing with them,' observes a local estate agent. The same can be said of **Murray Mews**, across on the other side of the Square (a smart if cramped modern 2-bed house-ette here, £450,000). Indeed Cherry & Pevsner's *Buildings of England: London North* comments 'architects' offices and homes . . . are thicker on the ground [in Camden Town] than anywhere else in England, squeezed, often with great ingenuity, into inexpensive plots along mews and back lanes behind the larger houses'. **Murray St** has a period terrace at its N end, a modern parade of shops on its W side with flats above. A 3-bed maisonette in the Camden School for Girls catchment area was £795,000 last autumn. The narrow 6ft-wide entrance from **Agar Grove** restricts heavy traffic. **Stratford Villas**, council at S end, thereafter has tall grey-brick-and-stucco fronted terraces, up to five storeys high, on both sides. Next-door **Rochester Square** (separated by Camden Rd from the rest of 'the Rochesters') has private homes on two sides: some in pairs of Edwardian-style villas with raised ground floors and semi-basements, some in Victorian terraces, many also flats.

C

Camden Rd is busy, but the Victorian houses on the E side, almost all converted into flats, are well shaded by trees and set well back. Some garden flats to be found – and one or two houses. On the Kentish Town side, the former Jews Free School (JFS) site is finally being developed by Crest Nicholson as 'North Point', with 109 homes, including 4-storey houses, in mock-Georgian style: 2-bed flats from £385,000, houses from £850,000. Over to the E, **Camden Park Rd**, **Cliff Rd** and **Cliff Villas** are a mix of council blocks, Victorian terraces mostly split into flats, and pairs of mid-Victorian cottages.

Agar Grove draws a line under the Camden Square corner, a busy E–W thoroughfare: noise from the road is augmented by noise from the railway lines. There is a mix of old and new council blocks on the S side particularly, interspersed with modern town-houses and tall Victorian terraces, which yield lots of converted flats. Historically, this has been the cheap bit of Camden, but the prospect of the King's Cross transformation is changing that. Three Victorian pubs have been sacrified to the mania for flats, including the City of London at the top of **York Way**. Running S, the continuation of **St Paul's Crescent** (a crescent no longer) has some Victoriana and leads to a low-level white-painted council estate. On either side are terraces of grey-brick houses, 2- and 3-storeys with basements. Council housing of an unfortunate mid-'70s sort continues S and E around **Maiden Lane**. South towards King's Cross is at present the domain of the tunnellers and bridge-builders as railways get disentangled and realigned to allow for the St Pancras Eurostar station. Then comes King's Cross Central: see Bloomsbury & King's Cross chapter.

Chalk Farm

Going N, **Camden High St** becomes **Chalk Farm Rd** as it reaches the canal and Camden Lock – across which the famous (but rather touristy) weekend market takes place. To the W is the splendid Roundhouse, a remarkable, circular former engine shed, built in 1847, saved from demolition and now a music/theatre venue (the RSC did a season here in 2002; further restoration is under way). Beyond, on former railway land, is a supermarket and housing-association flats. Opposite on Chalk Farm Rd is a new block of 1- and 2-bed flats above a Sainsbury's Local.

Hartland Rd's 2-storey, brick-and-stucco fronted, brightly painted late-Georgian terraces provide 3-bed houses on three floors, with small gardens. The railway line runs overhead at the end of the street. No private housing beyond the junction with **Clarence Way**. Similar 2-bed terraces are found in the N part of Clarence Way.

Pockets of good properties can be found in the streets around **Castle Rd** in the area S of **Prince of Wales Rd**, close to Kentish Town West rail station and on the borders of NW5 and Kentish Town. A good group of streets, part of the **Kelly St** conservation area, has cheerful and well-preserved 2-storey terraces. These include **Healey St**, **Grafton Crescent** and the northern end of **Hadley St**, which is pretty, tree-lined and not used by traffic; rows of brick-and-stucco-fronted 2- and 3-storey houses (£500,000 for a 4-bed) on both sides. Trains using Kentish Town West station pass behind; the street has a prosperous air. **Healey St** likewise, though houses here are slightly grander and taller. **Grafton Crescent** has large grey-brick-and-stucco-fronted terraced houses on both sides. The E end of **Prince of Wales Rd** is busy and noisy, but grey-brick-and-stucco houses, mostly flats, are set well back. For more on this corner see Kentish Town chapter.

C

Chalk Farm 'proper' lies W of **Harmood St**, taking in the area around the tube station. It is a small and highly convenient corner, with a good deal of council housing intermingled with homes that borrow some of the aura of Belsize Park and some of the trendiness of Kentish Town. Most of the homes here are in the huge blocks of mansion flats in **Eton College Rd**, or in small Edwardian villa-type houses in roads off **Chalk Farm Rd**. The area has seen some modern redevelopment, with new blocks on Chalk Farm Rd itself and on the corner of **Adelaide Rd.** These include the council-built **Beaumont Walk**, where resales offer good-value homes with gardens.

The S part of **Queen's Crescent** is worth a look: see Kentish Town chapter. In this part of **Prince of Wales Rd**, the N side has large blocks of red-brick council flats; on the S side are terraces of period houses, some in good condition, others run down. Best terrace of the three is Nos. 131–151. A converted college and a school offers loft-style flats at loft-style prices. **Crogsland Rd**, likewise, is council-build on one side; on the W side, a short terrace of 4-storey houses has been laterally split into flats. Further along **Prince of Wales Rd** going E there are terraces of period homes on both sides of the street; some single houses, some maisonettes, some flats. **Harmood St** has rows of low 2-storey Victorian/Edwardian terraces (2-bed house £485,000) and some council-built housing, including 4-storey Harmood House, where flats are often for sale. **Clarence Way**, a pretty street, has rows of brick terraced houses similar to Harmood St, though the North London Line passes over the middle of the street. **Chalk Farm Rd**, the busy main road, has some recent purpose-built flats and offices; flats over shops on E side.

Just to the W of the Chalk Farm tube station is **Eton College Rd**, a very pleasant, quiet road which has three huge mansion blocks known as The Etons. A major refurbishment programme went on through the 1990s: now comes work to upgrade heating systems, leading to service charges around £6,000 per annum. Prices have been stable for two years): 1-bed flat c. £220–235,000, a 2-bed c. £300–310,000. On the W side of the road, some large houses reach around £1.25 million for a 3-bed 2-bath. This end of **Adelaide Rd** is also regarded as part of Chalk Farm. Houses here are large, stucco-fronted terraces, split into flats. **Adelaide Rd** is busy, and houses overlook the railway.

Primrose Hill

Tucked away between St John's Wood, Regent's Park, Camden Town and Chalk Farm lies a small public park with soaring hilltop views over London. On its eastern slopes is a picturesque and prosperous enclave whose residents – many of whom are writers, photographers, actors, musicians – take great pride in the area. This is more of a family, settled area than Camden Town (with which it is somewhat uneasily linked: locals, and estate agents, like to think this is a place apart). The 'village' of Primrose Hill is tucked in between the curve of the main line railway to the E and the hill itself to the W. Quiet and secluded (due mainly to traffic controls on through-roads), it commands high prices. This is the most coveted part of the neighbourhood, mainly wide, tree-lined streets and elegant stucco-fronted houses. The quaint shopping street has a good selection of smart shops (and *no* Starbucks). There are very few small houses: the majority of homes are flats and maisonettes in converted period houses, and surviving un-split ones.

Regent's Park Rd, curving round past the Hill and back towards Chalk Farm (though only a footbridge links through), forms the W boundary of the 'village'. It is lined with substantial, semi-detached stucco homes (some with views over Primrose Hill, many still family houses) which are highly popular – and highly priced. A new, very smart, very designer 4-bed house behind a 'period' facade was £2 million last winter. So was the real thing: a Victorian 4-bed on the market for the first time in half a century.

Gloucester Avenue forms an eastern boundary: a wide, tree-lined street with the main-line railway (Euston-bound) behind the homes on the E side – this can lower prices on some houses by as much as 40 per cent, though the W side of the avenue is as smart (and pricey) as anywhere in the neighbourhood. Most of the period terraces on both sides have been converted into flats. There are also some modern blocks of flats. Unlike many Primrose Hill homes, these come on the market fairly frequently as young couples move on to bigger and better (and quieter) things.

C

The 'village' to the W is a maze of quiet streets, secluded, prosperous and sleepy. **Rothwell St**, **Chalcot Crescent** and **St Mark's Crescent** are among the most prestigious addresses: 4-storey stucco-fronted houses which can set you back £2 million or more. Even bigger and better are the mid-1850s stuccoed houses of **Chalcot Square**: the Square and **Chalcot Crescent** are the most sought-after streets in Primrose Hill. Last winter £1.4 million was being asked for 'the chance to create' (spend money on) a 5-bed maisonette in a house in the Square. **Chalcot Rd**, **Fitzroy Rd** and **Princess Rd** have rows of tall period terraces, now mostly flats. The canal, running between **St Mark's Crescent** and **Princess Rd**, makes for attractive gardens (W side of St Mark's, E side of Princess).

Off the N end of **Regent's Park Rd**, where prices are (slightly) lower, **Ainger Rd**, **Oppidans Rd** and **Meadowbank** form a quiet triangle. **Oppidans** and **Ainger** have large grey-brick terraces and semis divided into flats (a 2-bed garden flat, c. £450,000); **Meadowbank** has Primrose Hill Court (council), a well-maintained block, and some large modern town-houses. **Primrose Hill Rd** has two big modern blocks overlooking the hill, and the highly desirable period **St George's Terrace** at the bottom.

The E end of **King Henry's Rd** has strong links with Eton College – much of the land is still owned by the college: leasehold the norm here. Most of the elegant, tall grey-brick houses have been split into flats with well-proportioned rooms; garden flats available here (£570,000-ish for a 2-bed). On the N side, and in the roads leading up to **Adelaide Rd**, are groups of small, modern, 2-storey, white-painted houses.

Mornington Crescent

To the S of Camden Town lies another area centred on a convenient tube station. Mornington Crescent (the tube stop) is actually on the junction of busy Hampstead Rd and Eversholt St. **Mornington Crescent** (the street), a once-grand, semicircular terrace of tall stucco-fronted 1820s houses is nearly all split into flats (2-bed garden flat £385,000). This happened because, sadly, Mornington Crescent's garden was sold off in the 1930s and is now squatted on by a giant office block.

Crowndale Rd, E of Eversholt St, has tall brick-and-cream-stucco terraces on either side, mostly conversions: thereafter there is council housing and a small parade of shops. The N end of **Eversholt St** also has 4-storey terraces. Traffic-plagued **Oakley Square**'s S side is council; the N side is a pleasant if slightly scruffy terrace of Victorian houses. At the N end a rather grey, grim block of flats, St Matthew's Lodge, has flats of all sizes including studios. Both flats and houses face onto the leafy if small public garden. **Harrington Square** has a Victorian terrace, mostly flats, on the section which forms a busy one-way street carrying traffic to the West End. **Hurdwick Place**, off Hampstead Rd, has flats in period terraces: some garden flats.

Euston

The Euston area, bounded by **Euston Rd** to the S, **St Pancras Way** to the E, **Hampstead Rd** to the W and **Oakley Square** to the N, was (until Right to Buy) virtually all council-owned or charitable housing, except for some flats and maisonettes over shops on **Churchway** and **Chalton St**, which have the benefit of this very central location. Many of the council homes are handsomely restored period houses. There are some privately owned Victorian houses in the **Charrington St** area. To the S, the enormous red-brick British Library buildings have attracted attention to this neglected corner.

Similar homes, too, on the S part of **Eversholt St**, in **Starcross St**, **North Gower St** and **Drummond St** to the W, where there is privately-owned housing in Victorian terraces, well sheltered from the main road and centrally located. **Drummond St**'s exotic restaurants are well known. West of **Hampstead Rd** is a corner usually tacked onto Regent's Park, though with small streets of mixed council, housing-association and private homes – in great contrast to the Nash terraces.

C

Transport Tubes: Camden Town, Chalk Farm, Mornington Crescent, Euston (zone 1/2, Northern). From Camden Town: Oxford Circus 15 min (1 change), City 15 min, Heathrow 1 hr (1 change). Trains: Camden Rd to Liverpool St 20 min, Kentish Town West (Silverlink Metro).

Convenient for City & West End, stations, Regent's Park. Miles from centre: 2.5.

Schools Local Authority: Haverstock School, South Camden School, Maria Fidelis Convent (g), William Ellis (b), Camden School for Girls. Private: North Bridge House. See also Hampstead & Kentish Town.

SALES

Flats	S	1B	2B	3B	4B	5B
Average prices	130–200	145–450	200–650	240–1M	–	–
Houses	2B	3B	4B	5B	6/7B	8B
Average prices	350–600+	400–900+	450–1.2M+	550–2M+	–	–

RENTAL

Flats	S	1B	2B	3B	4B	5B
Average prices	160–220	200–350	250–600	300–600+	400–600+	–
Houses	2B	3B	4B	5B	6/7B	8B
Average prices	280–600	400–800+	500–1200+	550+	600–3000	–

The properties Victorian housing of all shapes and sizes, with wide variations in status and condition. Lots of converted flats. Quite a few modern homes and more on the way: flats and mews-style houses. Lots of council-built homes – some quite desirable.

The market Influx of prosperous, bohemian buyers 'discovering' good period homes has soaked up virtually all the untouched examples. The flats market centres on conversions plus a few split-up schools and new blocks. The few big family homes are in demand: once here, people stay. Primrose Hill, Gloucester Crescent are smartest. Look to E and S fringes (and Kentish Town) for cheaper homes.

Among estate agents active in this area are:

- Bairstow Eve
- Insignia Blenheim Bishop
- Stickley & Kent
- John D Wood
- Camden Bus
- Michael Charles
- Hotblack Desiato
- Dennis & Hayes
- Keith Cardale Groves
- McHugh & Co
- Winkworth
- Goldschmidt & Howland
- Anscombe & Ringland
- Compton Reeback
- Benham & Reeves
- Keatons
- Parkways

CHELSEA

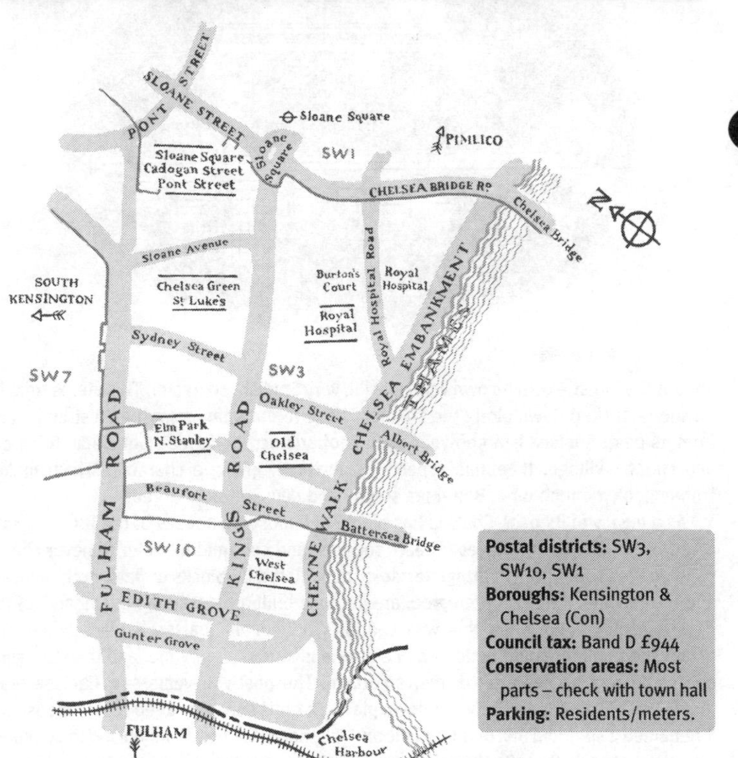

Postal districts: SW3, SW10, SW1
Boroughs: Kensington & Chelsea (Con)
Council tax: Band D £944
Conservation areas: Most parts – check with town hall
Parking: Residents/meters.

Whatever eight-star luxury is, and few of us by definition will ever find out, Chelsea is getting it. There must be a demand, for – we are told – 'a British financier' has paid £27 million (yes twenty-seven million) for a new flat in Manresa Rd. The 15 flats in the old Chelsea College of Art will be the area's smartest yet, offering '8-star' facilities, when ready in November next year. The quoted price is for shell finish, and doesn't include £100,000 a time for car-parking spaces, or the extra £5 million needed to complete the flat. Nine of these flats were sold by Christmas.

The fickle finger of football has turned the international spotlight on Chelsea. Billionaires around the world whose knowledge of London geography stopped at Park Lane now know where Chelsea is. All because a very rich Russian bought the soccer club. (Chelsea FC's ground isn't in Chelsea anyway, but Fulham.) Sporting money matters here: motor racing magnate Bernie Ecclestone owned the Art College site before selling it on to Candy & Candy, and he (and his dog) still live round the corner.

Back on the street, leaving the bodyguards and the '8-star fully automatic occupancy ventilation systems' behind, we find the King's Road. This is reverting to type as one of London's key shopping streets, boosted by the new Duke of York Square and the rebuilding of Peter Jones. Chelsea's moneyed inhabitants, new and old, have quietly reclaimed the King's Road from the young tourists.

This is one of London's prime residential areas; still – despite wave after wave of international and City money of which the Russians, the footballers and the financiers

C

are but the latest – with its own very special, very English, character. This stems from its location – tucked down along the Thames, close to but apart from the West End – and from its past: Chelsea is a 500-year-old mix of aristocratic retreat, bohemian hang-out and country village. It retains aspects of all three, giving a character which makes Fulham look monochrome, Battersea scruffy and Kensington bourgeois.

As a legacy of its past, Chelsea has plenty of handsome houses of the 18th and 19th centuries; most are in terraces or leafy squares, and set amid humbler (if never cheap) cobbled mews and pretty cottage terraces, punctuated by blocks of flats, both mansion and low-income. Here and there, too, are purpose-built artists' studios, remnants of the days a century ago when this was London's bohemian quarter, a place where the established painter could build or buy a spacious studio-cum-home, and the struggling one could rent a cheap flat or mews cottage. The post-war years saw Chelsea – as, indeed, all of London – a sadly run-down place. But this served to keep costs modest and it remained a splendid mix of the artistic and the theatrical, the dustman and the duchess – all short of cash. By 1980 the writing was on the studio wall. Chelsea was too pleasant, too close in, to survive on a mix of impoverished gentry, working- and art-classes.

The painters and sculptors have long gone, and their studios are owned by merchant bankers (or insolvency lawyers) rather than Royal Academicians. Chelsea has changed, and the clutch of recent and planned 'developments', with their several-million-pound flats and 'unobtrusive 24-hour security' are changing it yet further. The polite, artistic children of Chelsea – like the muddy aboriginals of some commuter village – have been priced out of their home. Seek them in Wandsworth or Tooting, not here.

All this said, that inimitable Chelsea flavour lives on in the garden squares, the white-stucco terraces, the pastel-painted cottages, the elaborate red mansion blocks, the occasional superb Georgian house. There is nowhere else in London quite like it.

The area was first made popular by Sir Thomas More, who bought a riverside estate in the early 16th century. The aristocracy followed, building more large country houses. They stayed and, as London expanded over the years, their rural retreats were replaced by their town-houses. To reach his country estate, Sir Thomas travelled by boat: the all-important King's Road, genuinely as royal as its name implies, came later when King Charles II had a farm track cleared so he could journey via Putney to Hampton Court (and, presumably, visit Nell Gwynn en route in Fulham).

The track became, literally, the **King's Rd**, later famous throughout the world as a symbol of the Swinging Sixties. It remains the main thoroughfare – the spine, running the entire length of Chelsea, from **Sloane Square** in the E to World's End in the W.

Strung along the King's Rd and the river, Chelsea has a self-contained air. It has its own department store (Peter Jones in **Sloane Square**), a shop which is a way of life as much as a source of supply. It has its own theatre, the Royal Court. Restaurants abound; shops sell most things, especially the ephemeral or expensive. The King's Rd is today richer than ever – if more ordinary. No longer the capital of cool, it serves the new, international, affluent Chelsea: supermarkets, fashion, restaurants, interior design. You must go a long way down the King's Rd before you find a butcher, baker or any of the other 'village' shops. The last of these were swept away in the early '80s. Ah well, let them eat cake: at least there's Pâtisserie Valerie in Duke of York Square.

Some may moan that Chelsea lacks a tube station apart from Sloane Square, and (off our map to the N) South Kensington. But there is the No. 11 bus, used by everyone, and the almost equally useful 19 and 22. And we have the testimony from 1834 of Thomas Carlyle that it took 'thirty-two minutes of my walking to Buckingham Gate' (just beside the palace). Carlyle lived in a house in **Cheyne Row**, for which he paid rent of £35 a year.

A factor when buying in Chelsea is that large parts of it, including a big chunk of the eastern, **Sloane St** side, are owned by the Cadogan Estate. The Cadogan, Sloane and Stanley families, all linked by marriage, gave their names to many streets and squares, and the Estate is still a big factor in the property scene in Chelsea. Many leases are short and the Estate, rejuvenated by a recent change in management (and inheritance by the current, 7th, Earl in 1997) is very businesslike in its dealings. When the Cadogan Estate grants new leases these can be for 125 years; however, those who qualify can buy the freehold or a 90-year extension of their existing lease.

Sloane Square, the Cadogans and Pont St

This is the neighbourhood bounded by **Pont St** and **Walton St** in the N, **King's Rd** and **Sloane Square** to the S, **Sloane Avenue** to the W, and the borough border in the E.

Unlike the rest of Chelsea's squares, **Sloane Square**, Chelsea's fulcrum, is a busy shopping area and junction, with traffic converging from Knightsbridge, the King's Rd and Pimlico. The paved square is thus a roundabout, with plane trees and a fountain. Lining it are hotels, the expensively rebuilt Peter Jones department store, the Royal Court Theatre and the tube station. Many of the commercial uses occupy lower floors of the 19th-century mansion blocks gazing down on the square. These flats are convenient, if noisy. **Lower Sloane St** and **Sloane Gardens** to the S are dominated by the tall red-brick and stone-gabled mansion blocks found in most of the E chunk of the neighbourhood.

Heading N, broad **Sloane St** is the main thoroughfare to Knightsbridge. It is lined by a jumble of modern and period buildings, mainly flats, with growing concentrations of fashion shops and some embassies. This is the heart of what was once called 'Hans Town', a complete estate built in the 1780s–90s. The developer was the architect Henry Holland. The name Hans Town has died out, and most of the area's buildings now date from after 1880 – though some of Holland's houses do survive, in **Sloane St** and **Cadogan Place**. The 'Hans' referred to Sir Hans Sloane, Lord of the Manor of Chelsea in the 18th century: his granddaughter and heiress married Lord Cadogan.

The private square gardens of **Cadogan Place** (car parking beneath), spread along most of the E side of **Sloane St**, are overlooked by terraces of period houses. Many have been split into big flats, with vast lateral converions much in demand. There has been a lot of renovating of 2- and 3-bed flats in Cadogan Place in the past few years. Houses are eagerly sought, and occasionally a building is returned to a single home from flats. An opulent late-'80s development, Royal Court House, takes up the S side.

Tucked away behind Cadogan Place, on the borders with Belgravia, is quiet **Cadogan Lane**, with its appealing mix of mews-type cottages and small houses. In **Sloane Terrace**, down towards Sloane Square, Cadogan has transformed an old Christian Science church into a 900-seat concert hall, the Cadogan Hall.

West of **Sloane St**, in **Pont St**, are classic examples of the late 19th-century red-brick, curly-gabled houses that Osbert Lancaster dubbed 'Pont Street Dutch'. They form the predominant style in most of the area from **Cadogan Square** with its leafy gardens W to **Lennox Gardens**, which curves round central greenery. Most of the houses have been split into flats, and many are on short leases. Lateral conversions provide very large flats. Hidden behind these tall buildings are occasional quiet, desirable mews (**Shafto Mews, Clabon Mews**). And running parallel, W of Sloane St is **Pavilion Rd**, where freehold mews houses mingle with commercial uses. **Cadogan Gardens** is a complex of century-old mansion blocks round shared gardens; the Estate did its own developing here in 2003, carving 28 new flats – for rent, not sale – out of one of the buildings.

West of Lennox Gardens, between Walton St and Cadogan St, lies an enclave of smaller houses: much sought-after, as estate agents say. **Ovington St, Hasker St, First St** – the most popular group – and **Moore St, Halsey St** and **Rawlings St** all have similar terraces of attractive, 2/3-storey plus basement, brick-and-stucco houses. The tube line runs beneath sections of Halsey and Rawlings Sts, which lowers prices – just a bit. Moore St houses were c. £2 million for 5-beds late last year, First St houses are typically £1 million for a 2-bed, £1.4 million with a mansard roof and another bedroom, £1.2 million for suit-deaf-trainspotter 4-beds in Halsey St. **Milner St** returns us to ornate, 5-storey stucco terraces.

Walton St is a narrow, busy little thoroughfare between South Kensington and Knightsbridge, given charm by its small-scale terraces that mix upmarket shops and restaurants with stretches of pretty houses. West of the cottage terraces are the Marlborough Buildings flats – the tall backs of which create a cul-de-sac in **Donne Place**, which has charming little mewsy houses at big prices (again, even higher if the tube were not beneath some). To the S, **Cadogan St** is a mix of late-Georgian terraced homes on the N side, with St Mary's Church, St Thomas More Secondary School, St Joseph's Catholic Primary School and the Guinness Trust Estate to the S. A 4-bed house rebuilt behind its late-Georgian facade was £2.3 million last winter. More red-bricks, and a pocket of smaller-scale 2/3-storey terraced Victoriana (**Coulson St, Lincoln St, Anderson St**), lie between Cadogan St, King's Rd and Sloane Avenue.

Royal Hospital

This area – classic Chelsea – stretches between King's Rd and the river, W of **Lower Sloane St/Chelsea Bridge Rd** and E of **Smith St/Tedworth Square/Tite St**.

The most coveted address in this neighbourhood is **St Leonard's Terrace**, which boasts some of the oldest houses in Chelsea (18th and early 19th century), which fetch from £3 million (up from under £1 million in 1993) to (exceptionally) £7 million. Most are listed, with leafy front gardens. But their main attraction, shared with the grand mansions in **Durham Place**, is their view over the green Burton's Court sports ground towards Wren's famous Royal Hospital. This imposing home for old soldiers forms the centrepiece of the area, with its extensive grounds (public tennis courts, handicapped-children's adventure playground) and the neighbouring leafy Ranelagh Gardens (the area's park), stretching towards the river. Residents of **Embankment Gardens** have the best of both worlds, with views of both the Royal Hospital and the Thames – the latter across the embankment traffic. Some unmodernized flats in this big old mansion block came on the market last winter, while a refurbished 44-year lease 1-bed was £270,000.

Dividing the neighbourhood in two is **Royal Hospital Rd**, lined at its W end by a mix of period and modern houses, flats, restaurants and shops. Here also stands the functional National Army Museum, by the drab concrete penance of St Wilfrid's Convent. **Tite St**, running down to the river, boasts studio houses (i.e. homes with proper, lofty artists' studios, not today's one-room flatlets) which recall Chelsea's bohemian past. Now their soaring two-storey windows stare glumly at the side of the convent. Some of these big studio houses change hands at sobering prices; others are flats. There are, too, some less stunning, but still £2 million, family houses. Across Royal Hospital Rd, tall red mansion blocks give way to the incongruous, once looked-down-on, now much-in-demand, 1930s mock-Tudor 5-bed houses in **Ormonde Gate** (leases can be fairly short). The 1980s redevelopment of curving Cheyne House at the river end of **Royal Hospital Rd** resulted in 11 smart flats – most with splendid views along the river.

In **Tedworth Square** the ungainly 1981 brick development on the N side (the Cadogan Estate demolished a handsome brick and stucco terrace to build this) contrasts sharply with the dignified, traditional 4/5-storey row of brick and stucco/red-brick £3 million houses on the other three sides of the central gardens. (Nearby **Christchurch St** survived the Estate's plans, and its pretty Georgian cottages, described by the late Earl Cadogan as 'nasty cheap little houses that were built a long time ago', survive and prosper.)

Head back E along St Leonard's Terrace to reach **Royal Avenue**. This tree-lined, gravelled parade is flanked on both sides by gracious terraces of early 19th-century houses – except for a post-war development at the King's Rd end. Its peace is guarded by the sensible barring of this end to traffic. Similarly, just a few steps back from the hustle and bustle of King's Rd stands **Wellington Square**, a fine group of 4-storey ornamental stucco Victorian houses. Despite its position, the terraces are set back from the road, and the tall trees in the central garden give an air of seclusion and privacy. Beyond the brick-and-stucco rows in **Walpole St** is the huge 1930s Whitelands House flats complex in **Cheltenham Terrace**, which dominates the terraces further along the W side of the street. Facing Cheltenham Terrace is the Duke of York's Headquarters with its new shops and some flats (let), S of which lie peaceful blocks of flats and modern town-houses. The mansion flats in the twin **Sloane Court East** and **West** complexes share expanses of communal gardens: ground-floor flats have direct access from graceful living rooms; those wanting a freehold can pay c. £4 million for the few 6-bed houses.

Whitehall has yet to make a decision on the Chelsea Barracks site, just around the corner along **Chelsea Bridge Rd**. The government has put it up for sale, with a result promised by early 2001... and still awaited. There are a number of listed buildings on the 11-acre site, and local conservationists are keeping a beady eye on plans. There could be 1,000 homes – making, in effect, a whole new Chelsea district (though, despite the name, the barracks lie not in Chelsea borough, but in Westminster) – with a big wall round it.

Old Chelsea

This area takes in the oldest parts of Chelsea and contains the most expensive and enviable homes. It is bounded on the N by **King's Rd**, by **Cheyne Walk/Embankment** in the S, **Beaufort St** to the W, and **Smith St/Tedworth Square/Tite St** to the E.

On the west of this tranche, **Beaufort St** is a main road leading down from King's Rd to Battersea Bridge. Most of its W side is lined by the red-brick and stone-gabled blocks of Beaufort Mansions – a block that, with its generous proportions, is perennially popular despite the heavy traffic. The Thomas More Estate opposite, built by the council in 1904, is now mostly private. More mansion blocks, with shops beneath, front the **King's Rd**.

Neighbouring **Paultons Square** is one of the best preserved of its type in the borough. Here handsome, 3-bed, £2.5 million terraces of the 1840s with decorative black iron balconies and railings are arranged on three sides of an elongated central garden square, a well-cared-for garden which benefits from the proceeds of a local resident's will. Terraces of a later date continue down **Danvers St**.

Crosby Hall, on the corner of **Danvers St** and **Cheyne Walk**, is a Chelsea curiosity. It is a late-medieval building (1466) which once stood in the City but was moved, stone by stone, to Chelsea in 1910. It became a student hall of residence, but is now the centre-piece of a vast riverside neo-Tudor mansion built, with detailing fit for Hampton Court Palace (which it strongly resembles), by businessman Christopher Moran after protracted planning battles. It's taken years, but is not finished yet: Mr Moran reckons on 2008....

Turn E along riverside **Cheyne Walk**, one of the most sought-after addresses in London, if not the most peaceful, with its fine 18th-century Georgian town-houses. Some are older still: one dates from 1686. Here you'll find a rich (in every sense) mix of homes: period gems in ample supply, like the Queen Anne £3.25 million affair on the market last winter. Cheyne Walk continues past Chelsea Old Church (much of which is new: it was badly bombed in 1941) into **Old Church St**, the oldest street in Chelsea. It now contains a hotchpotch of homes and commercial buildings in period and modern styles. It also holds the Old Rectory (1725), with its 2¼-acre garden, which sold in 1997 for £6 million and was rumoured to be on the market last winter – for £100 million. Artists'-studio houses here too: a lovely one, 6-bed, at £6 million last winter. A builders' merchant's survived until 1997, but was replaced by Painters Yard: 19 flats and four houses built at a super-smart standard.

Cut through the alleyway into **Justice Walk**, a delightful lane leading to the traditional heart and most exclusive part of Old Chelsea, **Lawrence St** and the Cheynes: quiet little streets with picturesque groups of houses and cottages, and fine brick-and-stucco terraces. Many houses here are dotted with blue plaques commemorating famous residents, from Rossetti and Isambard Kingdom Brunel to Thomas Carlyle. Rossetti left many memorials – the strangest being the clause in local Cadogan Estate by-laws which bans the keeping of peacocks. These noisy fowl were among a domestic zoo assembled by the artist at Tudor House, where to quote a local 'he kept a lot of poets and other wild beasts'. Today's **Cheyne Walk** houses are among Chelsea's most expensive, and house few poets and no peacocks (by order). The district has a real mix of houses of all sizes from cottages to splendid houses with their own studio and garden cottage.

The crossroads of **Cheyne Row/Upper Cheyne Row** and **Glebe Place** form one of the prettiest spots in the area. From here, **Glebe Place** winds through to **King's Rd**. On the W side of the first leg is West House: a Queen Anne Revival studio house and one of the landmarks of 19th-century British architecture. The W–E leg of the street has a mix of more highly individual studio houses, and the main N–S leg has purpose-built artists' studios (late 19th–early 20th century) facing a terrace of 3-storey Victorian houses to the W (large rear gardens). The £2-million-plus studios are now beyond the reach of most artists. Between **Lawrence St** and **Oakley St** lie more red-brick mansion blocks.

Oakley St is another major N–S through-route, leading to elegant Albert Bridge and Battersea Park, Chelsea's adopted open space. On the W corner of the bridge stands Pier House, a vast 1970s red-brick block stretching well up Oakley St to merge with older blocks. The E side of the street is lined with tall formal terraces of stucco, or stucco-and-brick houses (£2.2 million for a 6-bed, would gain from modernisation). Behind Oakley St we return to a prettier and smaller-scale corner in **Margaretta Terrace**; this leads to **Phene St** and horseshoe-shaped **Oakley Gardens**. Here charming, 3-storey brick-and-stucco terraces in leafy streets with pretty gardens convey a village character, but the prices are entirely metropolitan.

At the top of **Chelsea Manor St** stands the Old Chelsea Town Hall, housing the library and sports centre. Behind the town hall is the prestigious Swan Court apartment block, stretching through to Flood St: nine storeys enclosing a central courtyard (1-beds, £260–300,000). In **Flood St**, 3-storey brick houses hide behind tall hedges and flowery front gardens. There are more mansion blocks near the river and a striking 1986 town-house development in traditional style on the corner of **Alpha Place**.

The scene changes again E of Flood St, with a second enclave of smaller houses and cottages. Prettiest is once-threatened (see previous page) **Christchurch St** with its 1830–50s artisan cottages, some with flowery front gardens. Christ Church stands at the W end of the street near the infants' school. Between the gaily-painted cottages in **Smith Terrace** and the King's Rd, award-winning **Charles II Place**, 50 3/4-bed houses set around a cobbled courtyard, dates from the early '90s. The SE corner of the neighbourhood is covered by the famous Chelsea Physic Garden, founded in 1673. **Swan Walk** with its glorious, and rare, detached Georgian houses overlooking the Physic Garden, and **Dilke St** with its rows of mews and studio houses, lead to **Paradise Walk**. The W side is lined by a terrace of brick 2-storey town-houses (Wates 1986). The same firm built **Physic Place**, a mews of cottages through an arch off **Royal Hospital Rd**.

West Chelsea

C

West Chelsea, until recent years the area's poor relation, and beset by busy roads, has now come (well) up in the world. It is bounded by **Fulham Rd** to the N, the Thames to the S, the West London railway line to the W, and **Edith Grove/Beaufort St** to the E. The Chelsea Harbour development (see Fulham chapter) helped to push up prices in this previously neglected part of Chelsea. But its timing could hardly have been worse – no sooner was it finished than the recession of the early 1990s set in. Some of the buildings, particularly those near the **Lots Rd** power station, are looking a bit tired. The inhabitants also lost their battle to have the borough boundary line moved so that they were within the coveted Royal Borough of Kensington and Chelsea. They still pay their council tax to Hammersmith and Fulham, even if their postcode is SW10.

Lots Road Power Station is the last big development site at this end of Chelsea, and one of the last on the whole north bank of the Thames. Taylor Woodrow and Hong Kong investors Hutchinson Whampoa are working on a £350-million scheme – but the main products so far have been plans and rows. The latest (August 2003) scheme has two towers of 25 and 37 storeys, and a total of 817 homes, 47 per cent Affordable. This is an awful lot of people in a place with no tube, no train, and jam-ridden roads. The long-planned train station does seem likely to happen (2005?), but trains will be peak-hours only to start with on this overburdened line. Expect *much* more arguing before anything gets built at Lots Rd, the next stage being a public inquiry due to begin in mid-2005.

L-shaped **Lots Rd** itself comprises mainly commercial uses, ranging from auction rooms to interior designers to a car pound. The exception is a 1970s town-house development, **Poole's Lane**, walled off from the street on the E side. Turning the corner, the S leg of Lots Rd is dominated by the power station, with its tall chimneys and vast wall of arched glass windows. Next to it stands a refuse transfer station, water-pumping station and Chelsea Wharf – a complex of small businesses and studios. The homes lie along the E end of the leg. Most of the brick and painted houses (those from No. 28 down) overlook the public Cremorne Gardens fronting the Thames. This corner is well known for its villagey feel, and is smartening up with some new shops and cafés. The council plan to squeeze a new secondary school in Lots Rd, using the existing community group site and the design school.

Lying inside the L-shape is a network of small streets, lined with terraces of predominantly brick-and-stucco houses in varying styles and conditions. Some agents try to brand this corner 'Little Chelsea'. Cute. A number of the homes around here are owned by the council and Notting Hill Housing Trust. Many houses have been converted into flats/maisonettes.

Burnaby St, with its 3/4-bed Victorian terraced houses, is typical; **Stadium St** has 3-storey houses (the E end is smarter). Some new houses in **Tadema Rd** among the trad terraces, while **Uverdale Rd** has flats converted from the 3-storey houses (a 2-bed, £325,000 last winter). A park, West Field, is behind the World's End Health Centre in **King's Rd**. A handful of red-brick/stone mansion blocks, plus some intact Victorian houses, are found in **Ashburnham Rd**. Ashburnham Mansions is a popular block of flats: £500,000 for a 4-bed on a long lease. The N end of the street merges with **Cremorne Rd** to form the S end of the constantly busy West London one-way traffic system. The traffic runs N up **Gunter Grove**, S down **Edith Grove**. Plenty of converted flats here, a little cheaper than elsewhere (£260,000-plus for a 2-bed).

There is now an entire new tract of homes on the old King's College site, further W between King's Rd and Fulham Rd: 'Kings Chelsea' is a self-contained and security-conscious scheme set around a seven-acre park of which residents will have 'virtually exclusive' use. 'A world of its own' at World's End, in fact. The site, which also includes the William & Mary-era Stanley House (restored and sold in shell finish for £10 million to a Russian lady), has 300 homes in new and converted buildings, underground parking and 'luxurious leisure facilities', plus another, one-acre, public park. This large and pleasant scheme, home thanks to the ample car parking to several Chelsea footballers, also attracts empty-nesters due to its security. Sample prices: 3/4-bed garden-level flat £2.35 million, 2-bed 4th floor flat £600,000. But you do get an SW10 postcode.

The one-way system creates a dividing line between the **Lots Rd** area and World's End, dominated by the dramatic if rather crowded World's End council-built estate with its handsome, angular orange-brick towers (a 2-bed flat at the top of a tower can be c. £250,000). World's End Place, a piazza facing **King's Rd**, leads into the estate. East of the estate, behind the 1950s Cremorne parade of shops, lie modern low-rise council-built flats, also often for sale. Across **Milman's St** on the S-bend in **King's Rd** stands 355 King's Rd, an ex-council block which was reclad and converted into 50 luxury flats in the early 1990s. Nearby on the corner of **Milman's St** is Berkeley's 'the Quant Building' with a dozen 1-, 2- and 3-bed flats.

At the S end of the street, the houseboat colony moored on the river at **Cheyne Walk** comes into view. Houseboats offer a cheaper way of securing a smart Chelsea address (think £200,000-plus, and you'll need a marine surveyor). They lie in the lee of Chelsea Wharf – and yes, this old riverside flour mill has permission to become 11 top-flight flats.

Note that the Sydney St–World's End stretch of the King's Rd has been regaining some much-prized real shops: the butcher's and fishmonger's at World's End, the farmers' market at the foot of Sydney St, and even Sainsbury's 'market store' by the Gastrodome.

Elm Park/Chelsea Square

This prime neighbourhood between the Fulham Rd and King's Rd to the W of Sydney St includes some of the choicest streets and best squares in Chelsea. It also has Chelsea's general hospital – the Chelsea and Westminster. It gains from proximity to the fashionable shops-and-restaurants strip of the Fulham Rd W of the hospital, running to the cinema on the corner of Drayton Gardens. Some (including the Office of the Deputy Prime Minister) call this strip 'The Beach'. Others condemn it as the haunt of 'rugby boys and airheads'. Chelsea admits all sorts.

Sydney St, the broad and busy N–S link between South Kensington and King's Rd, has dignified terraces at its N end, plus the Brompton Hospital and the Royal Marsden cancer hospital. On the Fulham Rd, close to the main hospital, Ellesemere House will have 41 flats when complete next year: £350,000–£2 million-plus.

Tucked in behind the Marsden is **Chelsea Square**, one of the area's most expensive addresses. It started life in the 1830s as Trafalgar Square, but was rebuilt by the Cadogan Estate in the 1930s and nearly all the 3-storey brick houses are of that date or later. This is where you look for a modern house with parking behind tall gates. Foreign residents here are very security-conscious: count the bodyguards. The E leg of the square becomes **Manresa Rd** where the area's most expensive flats are being built behind the old Art College facade (see introduction); the SW leg leads into **Carlyle Square**: this is the jewel in the neighbourhood's crown, with its beautiful mid-19th-century brick and creamy stucco 6-bed houses overlooking the square gardens. This square is unique in that it is blocked off from the King's Rd by railings, trees and shrubs.

Turn W into Old Church St, a main through-route, and head N to **Queen's Elm Square**, where a group of mock-Tudor houses sit in a semi-circle off the street. The Chelsea Arts Club, haunt of writers and artists, is a short walk S along Old Church St.

Between here and Beaufort St many of the big houses have been split into flats over time: **Beaufort St**, **Elm Park Gardens** and **Elm Park Rd** are the main areas for conversions. A 2-bed flat on a 70-year lease in Elm Park Gardens might be £500,000. The more coveted **The Vale**, **Mulberry Walk** and **Mallord St** form a uniform colony of houses and flats, developed in the early years of the 20th century for artists, architects, musicians and writers 'of modest means'. They'll need to look elsewhere these days: a 5-bed house in **The Vale** was £4 million last winter.

At the S end of **Beaufort St** are the two parts of **Chelsea Park Gardens**, a development of 1920/30s 3-storey brick suburban villas. Those on the E side stand well back from the road behind a screen of trees and gardens. West-side ones have leafy front gardens, and the central section backs on to a communal garden. Some were once artists' studios: blue commemorative plaques dot the brick walls.

Park Walk is dominated by the huge **Elm Park Mansions**, where residents were among pioneers in buying the freehold. At the bottom of **Park Walk** is Park Walk Primary School, opposite the Man in the Moon pub on the **King's Rd** S-bend. Next to the school is a modern clutch of four mews houses and 10 flats.

Between **Park Walk** and **Edith Grove** can be found a popular residential corner of big mid-Victorian family houses with gardens (**Limerston St**, **Gertrude St**, **Hobury St**, **Shalcomb St** and **Langton St**) sometimes known as the 'Ten-Acre Estate'. The area is made up of surprisingly uniform, mostly 4-storey, brick-and-stucco terraces. Last winter prices of between £1.4 and £1.6 million were being asked for the 4-bed houses.

Chelsea Green/St Luke's

From **Sydney St** eastwards to **Sloane Avenue**, this neighbourhood N of **King's Rd** is characterized by big 1890s flats blocks to the N and a mix of bijou 'doll's-house' pastel-painted cottages and 1930s brick houses S of **Cale St/Elystan Place**.

Sloane Avenue, the main N–S through-route running between Chelsea and South Kensington, is lined by sprawling flats: 1930s blocks such as Nell Gwynn House (E), Cranmer Court and Chelsea Cloisters (W). The latter has been refurbished and converted into serviced pied-à-terre apartments: there are 747 flats (even more in Cranmer Court). This is a good place to look for studio flats: expect to pay £160–175,000 in Chelsea Cloisters; a good 1-bed might be £250,000. Nell Gwynn House commands higher prices (£180–235,000 last winter), but the subtle size differences between these diminutive homes – and varying lease lengths – make comparisons tricky. **Draycott Avenue**, which runs parallel, is similar, though the buildings are smaller and the street quieter.

Around the corner in **Lucan Place** (across the road from Chelsea police station) stands a 1989 Regalian development, Crown Lodge, set in an acre of landscaped gardens with fountains, waterfalls and pergolas. Covering the whole block, bounded on the other three sides by Petyward, Elystan St (the entrance) and Ixworth Place, it contains 130 1- to 3-bed flats with a pool and gym in the basement. Across **Elystan St**, the NW corner of the neighbourhood is dominated by rented flats: the Sutton Dwellings and Samuel Lewis Trust Buildings, with the exception of narrow lanes of cottages in **Pond Place** and **Bury Walk**.

At the S end of Elystan St, where it meets Elystan Place and Cale St, lies **Chelsea Green**, a corner which against the odds maintains a pleasant village atmosphere. The tiny green is encircled by upmarket food shops, restaurants, galleries and a surviving general store, among others. Between **Whitehead's Grove** and **Sprimont Place** is ivy-clad **The Gateways** – 1930s brick houses (some with gold-dust-like garages) set cloister-style around fountain courtyards.

South of the green lies a series of much-favoured small-scale streets – **Bywater St**, **Markham St** and **Godfrey St** in particular – with their colourfully painted 19th-century 3-storey houses, and around the corner **Burnsall St** is extremely striking with its painted, gabled houses. The little (some say pokey) pastel-coloured houses in **Bywater St**, one of the most popular streets in Chelsea, sell for over £1 million.

Caught up between these streets is 1830s **Markham Square**, one of the six formal squares facing the King's Rd, lined with terraces of 4-storey brick-and-stucco houses. In contrast are the 1930s brick houses in **Astell St** and **Jubilee Place** with their leafy front gardens: these offer more space than the nearby cottages and are popular with families. Different again is **St Luke's St**, lined with tidy terraces of 3-storey brick-and-stucco. The terraces on the W side of St Luke's St back on to the public St Luke's Gardens, the leafy 'lungs' of the area. They were once a graveyard for St Luke's Church on Sydney St. North of the church lies St Luke's public playground.

Transport Tubes: Sloane Sq (zone 1, District, Circle), South Kensington (zone 1, District, Circle, Piccadilly). From Sloane Sq: Oxford Circus 15 min (1 change), City 20 min, Heathrow 45 min (1 change).

Convenient for West End, Knightsbridge, Victoria & Waterloo stations, Thames, M4 to West. Miles from centre: 2.

Schools Local Authority: St Thomas More RC. Private: More House School. Many good prep schools. See also neighbouring areas.

SALES

Flats	S	1B	2B	3B	4B	5B
Average prices	140–240	200–400+	250–875+	400–1.9M	500–1.9M+	–
Houses	2B	3B	4B	5B	6/7B	8B
Average prices	635–1M+	675–1.8M+	800–3M+	1.3–5M	2.25–8M	–

RENTAL

Flats	S	1B	2B	3B	4B	5B
Average prices	200–380	250–500+	320–900	500–1500	600–2000+	–
Houses	2B	3B	4B	5B	6/7B	8B
Average prices	380–1000	600–1400+	1000–2000+	1900+	2400+	–

The properties Lovely Georgian/early-Victorian homes in garden squares, small streets of cottages and mews are the archetypal Chelsea properties. Also, N of King's Rd/Sloane Square, red-brick, Dutch-gabled mansion flats. Luxury flats increasing.

The market Buyers are now mostly City-based and prosperous: arty, upmarket locals mostly displaced by international bankers. Foreign buyers are Europeans and Americans, rather than Far East, with Russians etc. starting to appear. Young professionals colonize W Chelsea. Homes often 'stick' as rich vendors don't really need to sell. Best properties go for well over the mainstream averages above.

Among estate agents active in this area are:

- Beaney Pearce
- Jackson-Stops
- Aylesfords
- John D Wood
- Knight Frank
- W A Ellis
- Marsh & Parsons
- Savills
- Friend & Falcke
- Winkworth
- Hamptons
- Lane Fox
- Strutt & Parker
- Carter Jonas
- Faron Sutaria
- Russell Simpson
- Hobart Slater
- Humberts
- Douglas & Gordon
- Cluttons
- Farley & Co
- Farrar & Co
- Foxtons
- De Groot Collis

CHISWICK

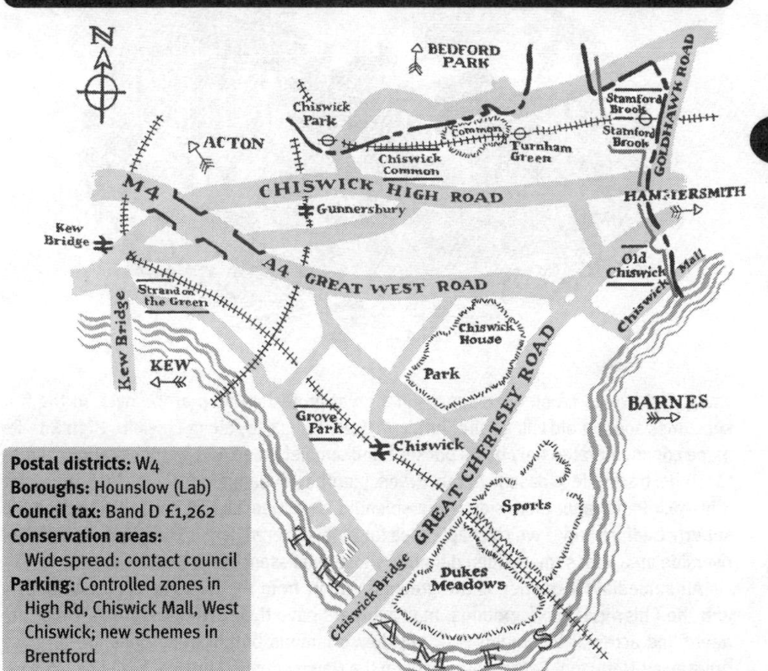

Postal districts: W4
Boroughs: Hounslow (Lab)
Council tax: Band D £1,262
Conservation areas:
Widespread: contact council
Parking: Controlled zones in High Rd, Chiswick Mall, West Chiswick; new schemes in Brentford

Three sentences say it all about Chiswick: It is the first big tract of family homes with gardens that you get to going west out of central London. Here are parks, schools and streets lined with trees and space for cars. Drive on west and you get to Heathrow. Its particular extra benefits are the river, which curls protectively round it to east, south and west, a lively high street and a wealth of homes from the most comfortable, if not the most distinguished, periods of English domestic architecture.

Downsides are traffic on the A4 and aircraft noise, both flip sides of being 20 minutes' drive from the world's busiest air hub. Busy enough, say council and residents, implacable in their opposition to the whispers of a third runway and/or more night flights. People power is to be reckoned with hereabouts: the residents of Chiswick and Bedford Park (which has its own chapter) have already seen off the Crossrail spur that would have chewed up a common and demolished some homes. The council's alternative proposal, for a new monorail to Heathrow with stops every kilometre, has gone quiet, however.

Back on the upside, Chiswick has acquired some attractive recent flats and houses and an important – even beautiful – new business park, smartening a derelict area. But despite flats both modern and converted, and a wide range of homes from tiny cottages upwards, this is family-home territory. Renters from glitzier areas come looking for a place to call their own – and once here they'll likely trade up within the area. Hence those fiercely vigilant residents' groups: there's a lot worth defending, and they intend to stay.

Old Chiswick began as a riverside village whose traces can still be seen in **Church St**, where St Nicholas Parish Church has parts dating back to the 15th century. Glorious Georgian (and some, behind those Georgian facades, considerably earlier) homes front the Thames here, and at Strand-on-the-Green – the corresponding hamlet at the Kew end of the river loop. Today's Chiswick covers everything between the two, sitting snugly (and

C

smugly) above its green open spaces in a great protecting loop of the river. To the N it subsumes another old village site, Turnham Green, which lay along **Chiswick High Rd** – its name commemorated only by its pocket-handkerchief green and its tube station. Across the tube tracks lie pleasant Acton Green (another endangered name: look, now, for 'Chiswick Park') and, alongside it the splendid, select enclave of London's first garden suburb, Bedford Park – which chapter see for both. Covered here is Brentford – a battered riverside area with some hidden delights whose renaissance is at last under way.

An immediate attraction is the greenery; apart from the riverside Dukes Meadows and the Chiswick House grounds, many corners have their own little green, while the deer-filled acres of Richmond Park and Kew's famous botanical gardens are an easy drive away. Note, too, Ravenscourt Park on the Hammersmith borders, prized by families.

The place is divided, as a community, by the A4/**Great West Rd**. Although the twain meet frequently, there is a slight difference of orientation between those who live between the A4 and the river, and those who dwell on the other, northern side. The river side uses South West Trains and looks for shopping as much towards Richmond and Sheen, while the other half has easier access to District Line tubes and to **Chiswick High Rd** – as its name suggests, the area's high street. (Go E and it leads, via Hammersmith, to Kensington's). But the A4 is boon as much as bane: lying on the direct route between London and Heathrow saves Chiswick from being a mere suburban backwater.

The resultant atmosphere is a combination of busy city and green suburb – even the High Rd is tree-lined and runs alongside Turnham Green. This is the main shopping street – though there are many little parades of shops scattered all round the area. There's an ever-growing number of bars and cafés, and restaurants from the everyday to the starry.

A number of small- to medium-sized developments have appeared, moving W along the High Rd: that end is moving up as the quality of the shops starts to improve, under influence not only of new and smart homes, but also of the most important change to the area – the emergence of Chiswick business park. This is turning the old Gunnersbury bus depot into a 'thoughtful and surprising workplace' for 7,000 souls; a 'happy campus' of Richard Rogers hi-tech (but mercifully low-level, 8-storey) office buildings – half of 12 complete – with health club, cafés and shoplets, set round lakes and feature waterfall.

Controversy still runs high, however, over the bid to increase the height of two of the unbuilt blocks; feisty locals are well practised in defending Chiswick's domestic scale. The futuristic 26-storey block which was to have loomed over the roundabout at the W end of the High Rd was slashed to 13 floors after strenuous protests; an application to turn it residential has been defeated; the offices have yet to appear. The battle then moved to Gunnersbury station, where 28 storeys of flats have likewise been scaled down – twice:

a public enquiry follows. . . . Next, St George proposed a high-density, 250-flat tower for the sensitive site at the N end of Kew Bridge, with predictable local reaction; the gateway to fast-changing Brentford (see below) deserves something more like St George's fine work on Kingston riverside. If the latest of many amendments they've made fails to get the scheme through – well, dates have already been set for a public enquiry for this site too.

All this area is worth defending. Although a few earlier houses survive, the Chiswick of today really began growing in the mid-19th century, the bulk of development happening between then and World War II. The result is a variety of choice from tiny early-Victorian cottages to huge Edwardian properties, from inter-war semis and vast mansion blocks to the odd infill of modern town-houses. Generally, the more recent the home, the smaller it is likely to be – even 1960s town-houses are positively roomy compared with the toy boxes of the '80s. Where this rule does not hold good (e.g. luxurious riverside developments or loft apartments), expect to pay dearly for the space.

Chiswick prices thus reflect the wide range of homes as well as their location. The biggest and most expensive houses are riverside ones – foremost among them those on **Chiswick Mall** (see below), but Grove Park, streets surrounding Chiswick House, and roads between the **High Rd** and A4, all hold good-sized houses with generous gardens. Despite locals' love of period homes, the most recent Thames-side developments are of a level of style and quality to command premium prices – very likely paid by 'outsiders'.

Higher-density housing – lots of flats, more conversions and rentals – is clustered round Turnham Green and Gunnersbury stations, along with the area by the Hogarth Roundabout and flyover. Council-built estates are small, scattered and low-rise, with a high percentage of owner-occupiers – and thus, nowadays, sales. In general terms, any home too close to the railway, A4 or **Great Chertsey Rd** loses some value. Certain parts are also prone to aircraft noise (the local paper even lists flight-path schedules).

Chiswick has attracted artists of all types ever since Hogarth bought a house (still standing, delightful, open to the public) in 1749, along with leading businessmen. The current mix remains much the same; it is popular with media people, City types, well-heeled executives, actors, architects. Young couples try to gain a foothold near the tubes, marry and move southwards into a flat or small house, then hope to progress to a larger one with garden. They contribute to various cultural and social activities and patronize the Riverside Studios and the Lyric Theatre in Hammersmith, the Watermans Arts Centre, Brentford, local pub theatres such as the Tabard, or the very professional amateur Questors Theatre in Ealing. They fought to save the local swimming pool (now with a gym). It is a predominantly middle-class family district (school league tables are obsessed over), where it still feels safe on the streets at night.

To begin, then, in the heart of Chiswick: just S of the **High Rd** lies the Glebe Estate (between **Duke** and **Devonshire Rds**): tiny 2- and 3-bed workmen's cottages, nowadays fashionable residences in the £380–490,000 bracket (1989: £120–200,000). Best to have a tiny car to match your tiny home here. There are other pockets of bijou homes, such as those round Chiswick Common, N of the High Rd, and many solid houses built just before and after World War I in neighbourhoods such as Stamford Brook on the Hammersmith borders. This corner gained some new homes, such as Barratt's Marlborough Court in **Marlborough Rd** (2- or 3-bed flats, basement parking), and Wates' popular Verona Court in **Chiswick Lane**: everything from 1-bed flats, through 2-bed houses (c. £450–550,000), to 4- (£800,000) and 5-beds (£850,000; one sold at £895,000 last spring).

One of the top older flats blocks is the 1930s **Watchfield Court**, a complex at the Turnham Green end of **Sutton Court Rd** that is large enough to be named on street maps (wide range of sizes, from c. £200–220,000). Running S from the High Rd, **Netheravon Rd N**, **Airedale Avenue** and **Homefield Rd** are desirable streets with larger houses, close to transport and Hammersmith. Look here for 4-, 5- or 6-bed homes –and the A4: a 4/5-bed can be £400,000 on top of it, £800,000 elsewhere; the best have touched a million.

Right on the Chiswick/Hammersmith borders, **British Grove** sprouted a clutch of 'executive homes' in 1997. West along the **High Rd**, down towards the Gunnersbury station end of the area, lie mansion blocks and houses of varying sizes, styles and periods. Here Galliard are completing 32 flats, all sold. Prices were from c. £250–420,000 for the 1-, 2- and 3-beds. A two-street enclave of terraced houses, **Silver Crescent** and **Thorney Hedge Rd**, forms a conservation area cheek-by-jowl with the new office park and opposite Gunnersbury station.

C

Adding to the mix are flats in ex-industrial or office buildings (this trend came early here). Bovis created **Devonhurst Place** in a splendid Victorian warehouse in the '80s, popular with renters. Near Chiswick Park tube, Chiswick Green Studios is more industrial space turned into loft apartments. Highly popular to buy or rent: apart from high ceilings and galleries, you're buying parking, porter, gym, security, views clear to the BT Tower if E-facing. Two-beds, c. £425,000 plus. And an ex-Army & Navy depot now has 51 flats round a spectacular central atrium, plus six penthouses perched above offices: porter, parking, communal roof terrace. That's in **Heathfield Terrace**, S of Turnham Green – which also boasts some Grade II listed Georgiana: a lovely 5-bed example, £1.65 million.

Grove Park

Grove Park is quintessentially Chiswick, with its wide, tree-lined roads (some specimen trees date back to the original Grove House gardens) and range of properties. It takes its name from Grove House, in the grounds of which the Duke of Devonshire built Chiswick's first large housing estate as a high-class area for wealthy merchants. The original estate was roughly bounded by the river, the **Great Chertsey Rd**, which leads up from Chiswick Bridge, the North London rail line, Silverlink, which marks the start of Strand-on-the-Green, and the Waterloo line. Estate agents today are insistent that Grove Park extends N of its railway and up to the A4. In terms of house style and price this is not unreasonable.

Some of the earliest houses are in **Grove Park Rd**; 4- and 5-beds can sport million-plus price tags. Grove House itself stood, until the 1920s, on the site of **Kinnaird Avenue**. Over the years further tracts were developed – and redeveloped in some cases, as war damage and demolition of bigger houses and gardens followed. Grove Park's leafy streets are particularly rich in Victorian and Edwardian architecture, from mid-19th-century terraces to Gothic, and from red-brick with hanging tiles to later brick and creamy stucco terraces. Typical prices are hard to sum up as homes vary a great deal, but 3-bed semis are c. £440–625,000; 4/5-beds c. £625–725,000; bigger 5-beds £850,000 plus.

The last big chunk of the estate was developed in the 1920s–30s with roomy semis, detached houses and the odd bungalow, while since 1960 there have been various small estates of town-houses and even the occasional striking example of modern brick- and-glass architecture. Flat-hunters can choose between gated Hartington Court – prestigious, balconied, 1930s, right on the river – or modern small-scale blocks. There is virtually no splitting of bigger houses into flats, apart from a clutch of homes at the Kew end.

Some of the best houses are in **Hartington Rd**, despite its busy rush-hour traffic, with a few having huge gardens that sweep down to the river. Three new 4-bed riverside town-houses are being inserted here. Between Hartington Rd and the river, too, are three earlier examples of the modern Thames-side developments:

Chiswick Quay: this is a 1970s development of 4- to 5-bedroomed town-houses set around a marina, designed to appeal to boat owners – tides here allow access to and from the river for two hours either side of high water, via the 12-year-old automated lock gates. A wide spread of prices, depending on size of home and whether it includes a view of the Thames: 5-bed examples without river view range from c. £700,000 inland to £800,000 with river view; the biggest houses can go up to £900,000. Despite their family size, these homes are unsuited to younger children because lack of garden and sheer marina sides make playing near the water highly dangerous. The CCTV signs are 'to deter . . . the public from walking around the marina'. You have been warned!

Chiswick Staithe: the word 'staithe' meant embankment, an appropriate name for these 69 3- and 4-bed houses, built in 1964 around a landscaped, traffic-free centre facing the Thames. There are stringent regulations concerning activities and development. The estate attracts couples (often both working), with older children, or retired couples, and appear for rent as well as to buy (a 4-bed, c. £550,000). No public access to the river here.

Thames Village: the peace of this low-density, 1955 estate is much appreciated by its residents; younger people are now joining this settled enclave. Two-bed maisonettes (c. £300–330,000, depending on river/off-river outlook) are set amid immaculate lawns and flowerbeds. The residents' association holds the freehold; strict covenants apply.

Back to the present, and at the W end of **Grove Park Rd**, almost in Strand-on-the Green, another riverside site has become **Redcliffe Gardens**: a dozen rather overbearing Millennium-neo-Georgian houses in a gated enclave.

Back across the railway, streets around Chiswick House, once the home of the Dukes of Devonshire, are spacious century-old dwellings, often with gardens to match. **Park Rd** is generally considered one of the best addresses in Chiswick, while **Staveley Rd** is famous for its avenue of flowering cherries. A development between Staveley Rd and **Burlington Lane** has flats and houses (all with parking space or garages) built around courts and crescents named, rather tenuously, after former famous Chiswickites: **Fitzroy Crescent, Huntingdon Gardens, Crofton Avenue.**

The Duke began selling off this part of his estate in 1884, but the charming little neo-Palladian Chiswick House remains in its 66-acre park, open to the public and a haven for urban wildlife and 20 bird species; hopes are high for a £7 million revamp of the site. It's Burlington Café serves, reputedly, the best park food in Britain. Extra green space – school grounds, allotments, playing fields – makes this a particularly low-density corner.

This whole district N of the Waterloo line between **Sutton Court Rd**, the A4 and the **Great Chertsey Rd/Burlington Lane** is a conservation area. In **Wolseley Gardens** and **Elmwood Rd**, the streets closest to the A4, expect to pay c. £425–600,000 for a 3- or 4-bed. Go south, away from the A4, and prices can rise quite markedly. This area also includes a corner between Chiswick House grounds and the Hogarth Roundabout – **Paxton Rd, Sutherland Rd** and **Short Rd** – of early Victorian 2- and 3-bed cottages built for the Chiswick House gardeners and Reckitt & Coleman employees: 3-beds c. £360–450,000.

Chiswick Mall/Old Chiswick

This riverside corner, where Chiswick began, is a paradox: it has remained a hidden time capsule, cut off and yet protected by the **Great West Rd**. Winding **Church St**, with its pretty houses and parish church, spans the centuries: the Hogarth Roundabout is at one end, the glorious Georgiana of **Chiswick Mall** looks tranquilly out over the Thames at the other. There is still very much a village feel to this tiny strip (and much local fury over the closing of the Post Office). Houses range from little add-on cottages to magnificent brick or stuccoed residences in a charming jumble of periods and styles facing onto the river. The facades indicate every century from the 17th to the 20th: some, though, are even older than they look, having been modernized 200 years or so ago. Wistaria House is one such, the lovely proportions of its Queen Anne, 1707, front concealing Tudor origins that sold for close on £1.5 million in 2003. Also in **Church St** The Guardship, an idiosyncratic compromise if you hanker for both warehouse loft and Georgian house, was snapped up for £1.2 million. Its basement retains the curved roof of its origins as a 1799 barrel warehouse; its upper floors were rebuilt, still in flat-fronted Georgian style, in 1860 and are now flooded with light and open to the pegged oak roof beams.

This remains a predominantly family area, where neighbours know each other and children play together. The houses are usually owned by big families and passed, if possible, down to the next generation. Several have vast gardens behind, while others have a garden patch across the road bordering the river; virtually none have been converted into flats. By way of comparison, one agent calculates that where Chiswick in general works out at £375–475 per square foot, **Chiswick Mall** costs £550–700.

The list of residents, past and present, is a roll-call of aristocratic, artistic and big-business names. Their community spirit is fostered by the shared fear of flooding: the river comes right over the road and there is a neighbourhood warning system so that cars are not marooned. Insurance premiums, one presumes, also run high. . . . Despite invasions from summer visitors strolling down the historic Mall, residents still love their pretty riverside pubs – not to mention the river life that passes their windows.

Space was found in this Elysium for one new house, 'The Cottage': modern in style but set well back. In recent decades there have been three smallish developments, with houses of up to 4 beds: **Eyot Green**, built 1960 round a green just off the Mall (a 3-bed, £600,000); **Millers Court**, a 1970s square leading to it; and **Chiswick Wharf**, 1980s brick town-houses (one sold at £760,000 in 2004) facing the river on the W side of **Church St**.

But Chiswick's most concentrated (and smartest) clutch of 1990s developments has transformed the once-industrial stretch of riverside S of Church St, along **Pumping Station Rd**. A peaceful corner: the road stops short of Church St, allowing access to the ancient village, but only by foot – and behind the inland side lies the church's cemetery.

A pleasing aspect of this stretch of Thames-side schemes is their mix of homes – from small flats to mansions – and prices. First come the electric gates (albeit handsome ones) that guard the landward privacy of Regency Quay, where McAlpine confused its monarchs and named one road **Gwynne Close**. The riverside path is open to all, however.

The long sweep of the pleasing **Corney Reach** scheme, by contrast, invites the public in, via its attractive piazza, to a splendid bit of planning gain: a deal with the developers, Persimmon, resulted in a new pier run by the Chiswick Pier Trust that anyone is welcome to use: one of the Thames lifeboats is based here. There's also a bar/restaurant with river views. Even smarter homes (sweeping curves, distinctive gables, decorative ironwork) at Barratt's **Thames Crescent** mark the S end of Pumping Station Rd: a 6-bed/4-bath/3 recep/garden/garage, £2 million in 2003; a smaller mid-terraced, £850,000. In contrast, **Edensor Gardens** inland is council-built: quiet, with lots of green space. **Edensor Rd** has Chiswick Pool & Gym, and nearby lie meadows, sports pitches, tennis courts.

Strand-on-the-Green

At the other, Kew end of Chiswick is Strand-on-the-Green, another ancient riverside village mirroring Chiswick Mall in the E. Where fishermen once caught eels and boatyards and breweries plied their trade, now tourists throng the popular towpath pubs. A working riverside village up to a generation ago, this is still a deliberately unpretentious community (despite the odd TV celebrity). Here, too, many houses are older than they look; the village dates back to the 15th century. Its medley of styles ranges from quite grand to a row of Arts-and-Crafts cottages, while little passages between the houses down to the towpath add to the informality. Artists (the most famous was Zoffany) were attracted to the area and some houses have studios at the back. Many desirable homes have humble origins, having once been shops, pubs, a post office or tea room. Gardens tend to be small. Like Chiswick Mall it's a conservation area, with many listed buildings along the river frontage. Flats are rare; the main inhabitants are families who stay for years, watching their children grow up messing around with boats on the river – the area's main hobby and focus. In short, a neighbourly community; a riverside address with charming, but slightly less large and grand homes than **Chiswick Mall**. That said, Georgian gems are, naturally, in the million-pound bracket. Oh well, there are little 2-bed off-river cottages, c. £340,000 – or perhaps a houseboat: one sold recently for £280,000.

Residents use Kew Bridge Waterloo Line, or take a 10-min walk under the Great West Rd for Chiswick High Rd buses, or Gunnersbury for the District Line tube and the N London

Line, Silverlink. Most riverside houses have garaging at the back as, unlike the Mall, which has a road alongside the river, they only have a towpath (which does get flooded). Parking is difficult at school-time as mums sweep up to collect from Strand-on-the-Green Primary, while **Thames Rd** with its shops can be a busy rat-run. A slightly less obvious drawback for the less-sociable riverside dweller can be bums and beer mugs on your windowsills during the summer: there are at least three good pubs.

Since homes still often pass to the kids (anyone with less than 10 years' residence is considered a newcomer), any new homes that can be sneaked in are popular. Barratts proved this with Rivers House: once a boring office block on the bridge approach, it's now a stylish 62-strong cache of 1-, 2- and 3-bed flats, with floor-to-ceiling windows and river views from higher floors. Last autumn a 1-bed was on at £235,000; a penthouse, £1.1 million. Others are shoehorned in where possible: e.g. **Bailey Mews**, off **Herbert Gardens**, off **Magnolia Rd**. . . Duke's Place, another small-scale scheme, added just a dozen 2-bed flats with parking to **Chiswick Village** (strange street name: neither half is accurate) tucked away in the backwater of little streets just N of the rail line. 'Quiet' might be too strong a word, given the tracks and the A4/M4 close by, but peaceful this cut-off corner is, and Gunnersbury tube/trains are handy; many homes are rented. Here, too, St James's Court's 3- and 4-bed town-houses are recent arrivals in **Brooks Rd**.

Nearer the river, **Chadwick Mews** appeared in 2001 on the site of the old Worth perfume factory in **Thames Rd**: six 3- and 4- (c. £470,000) bed town-houses. Industrial-strength double-glazing offsets noise from (very) adjacent trains. Across the road, Loretta Wharf has six new balconied riverside apartments. Even the old corner shop in Thames Rd has become a 4/5-bedroomed home with big rooms, on three floors. In fact, this corner, from Thames Rd on along to Hartington Rd in Grove Park, is a hive of activity.

Other caches of modernity squeezed in in the '80s: the tiny houses and flats of **Oliver Close**, again off Thames Rd; the favoured houses of **Magnolia Wharf**; 61 studio, 1- and 2-bed flats amid big double-fronted period houses in **Wellesley Rd**. The roads behind are Victorian working-class, 3-bed, red-bricks that now attract young middle-class families.

Borders: Brentford

Brentford, which begins where Chiswick ends, around Kew Bridge station, is just as much a Thames-side community as Chiswick or Kew, but it's only in the last four or five years that it has become noticed as a place to live. This is no surprise: the High Street's unredeemed '60s tattiness – in places dereliction – deterred anyone not in the know from even pausing. They thus missed first, an excellent, hidden Thames-side marina development, and second, London's best cache of Queen Anne houses.

These two enclaves apart, most land was taken up by council-built homes and industrial space (including boatyards). This has changed: big builders are cramming in waterside flats on brownfield land, and the entire town centre is set for an upheaval.

Those that do live here are real champions of its hidden attractions; they include actors, TV presenters, musicians, high-profile journalists in need of a discreet base. They are part of a real, settled community; check out the proper London pubs, though trendy bars and quasi-restaurant ones are adding to the mix. Brentford is extremely lucky in its position: across the Thames are the inviolate acres of Kew Gardens, giving an outlook reminiscent of Kingston's prospect of Hampton Court Park – and offering flat-buyers far better views than they'd get in Fulham (view of Wandsworth) or Wandsworth (view of Fulham). Here, too, a canal and two rivers add to the latent charms and possibilities.

New Brentford, N of the elevated M4, has suburban homes and some Victorian rows (2- and 3-beds, c. £240–280,000). In **Brook Rd South**, which passes the football ground, Crest's Watermark scheme has added 3/4-bed houses (sold c. £390–415,000), plus flats. Then areas of humdrum council-built housing, to the High Street's run-down '60s shops. The giant, glitzy international-HQ office blocks beside the M4 provide jobs – and demand for homes. GlaxoSmithKline's is one such; now Barratt wants permission to redevelop their old HQ by the Great West Rd with offices, over 1,000 flats, hotel, health club, shops and restaurants. Nearby, Berkeley plans a new campus for Thames Valley University, to include halls of residence and more flats – for key workers this time. When you add in the hundreds already built, plus yet another 1,000 that Isis want to build round a bus depot in **Commerce Rd**, by the canal, you could be forgiven for wondering if this isn't overkill...

C

It would be tragic if, having been wrecked once in the '60s, Brentford's remaining magic is to be overwhelmed. For this is the point of Brentford: here is the confluence of the Rivers Brent and Thames, and the Grand Union Canal. Two centuries ago, this was the vibrant gateway to the UK's main transport network. The legacy of locks, docks, basins and assorted bits of water has lain almost wholly derelict, though the canal is in use. In the last couple of years potential has become actual, with four big homes schemes under way, and Brentford's heart, the S side of the High St, set for complete transformation. But the latter is held up once again; the former already disappointingly messy.

In the town centre and along the river, big schemes have appeared. On the Thames, Ferry Quays by Fairview and Rialto added 190 flats off **Ferry Lane**; resales are from £240,000 (1-bed flat) to £500–600,000 for penthouses. Also a dock (moorings promised but unlikely), hotel, shops, three restaurants. Laing's 'Kew View' flats (**High St**) completed in 2003. But the best sites currently lie on the N side of the High St.

Between **The Butts** and the canal's confluence with the River Brent, is St George's 'Brentford Lock': flats and 3-bed work-homes in a scheme featuring 7-storey blocks. Heron View, the final phase, is completing: 2-, 3- and 4-bed flats, £235–765,000. Here, too, Charles Church (whose design is usually so good) and Nicholson have overloaded an enviable island encircled by canals with looming blocks of 173 flats, 20 town-houses and sizeable 'mill houses'; 1-bed flat, £269,000, 2-bed £299,000, town-houses c. £800,000.

Further E, Barratt's undistinguished 'Capital West', the big British Gas site at the of **North Rd**/High St junction, has 232 homes, some in 12-storey towers, plus a hotel and a rebuilt musical museum. It's on the N, inland, side of the High St, but some flats have river (and Kew Gardens) views: no buildings on the S side here. Barratt have gone on to build Temeraire Place: 39 1- and 2-bed flats from £185–300,000. This scheme is on **Green Dragon Lane**, which also holds a tidy, green encampment of council towers: 1-beds, c. £100,000, 2-beds c. £115,000 can be had, some with great views, but mortgages can be tricky.

Most vitally, there is the town-centre site, the S side of the **High St**, through to the river – including much of the surviving canal infrastructure: basins, weirs, locks and bridges. After a decade of planning rows, there is now approval for a cinema complex and big supermarket, plus car parks, with some homes, restaurants, offices. However, the developers need to acquire all the site before the legal agreements can be completed: they still lack two 'significant' land-holdings. Many details are still unclear, particularly how much of the waterside character – virtually the last of London's working boatyards are here – will survive the developers' attrition. Watch this space.

Finally, to those two existing, hidden enclaves of the first paragraph. That pioneer homes complex, Brentford Dock – a 21-acre land of flats and houses – is one of West London's best-kept secrets. Reached via **Augustus Close**, its equally classically-named blocks built by the GLC in 1972–80 have worn well, and trees and gardens have matured. Only a few of the 590 homes were let by the council (some 40 remain); most were sold on 98-year leases (999-year ones can now be had). Here is a very active (see its website) community: all owners share the freehold of the estate, which is grouped around a working marina (Brunel's old dock). It forms a triangular island: on one side is the Thames, another the River Brent and the mouth of the Grand Union Canal – and the third is the boundary wall of Syon Park (with a private gateway). Homes range from 1-bed flats (c. £175,000) through 2-beds (£235,000-ish) to 32 spacious 3/4-bed maisonettes and five town-houses (c. £400,000 plus); moorings available. The whole place is enormously well-kept and well-run: compare council-run estates such as Brent Lea across the canal.

And the jewel in Brentford's crown is **The Butts**, a square in the old town (of which little else remains). The Butts forms a large L-shaped enclave, centred on a gravelled square and with a wide avenue leading out E to the workaday world of Brentford proper. You reach it from the High St via **Market Place**, a paved alley alongside the magistrates' court. Suddenly you are in another world: one of late 17th- and early 18th-century houses with large walled gardens: look here for hen's-teeth rare, genuine Queen Anne with 4/5-bedrooms. Nearby streets offer less august, but still period, homes and there are some large late-Victorian ones (some are now flats) at the E end. **Upper Butts** leads on to **Somerset Rd**, with a mix of late-Victorian and earlier terraces and some '20s semis (a 4-bed, c. £500,000). **Brent Rd** is also mixed, with some bungalows rubbing shoulders with Georgian-style repro and a big 1900 villa. To the W is the River Brent. **Brentside** has 3-storey, tidy, 1960s council-built flats, while Orchard Rd has some pretty Victorian cottages close to the station.

C

Transport Tubes: Turnham Green (zone 2, District, restricted service Piccadilly); Stamford Brook (zone 2, District); Chiswick Park, Gunnersbury (zone 3, District). From Turnham Green: Oxford Circus 30 min (1 change), City 30 min, Heathrow 25 min (1 change). Trains: Chiswick & Brentford to Waterloo 30 min.

Convenient for Heathrow and M4. Kew Gardens. Miles from centre: 6.

Schools Hounslow: Chiswick Community School. Private: St Paul's (g), Godolphin & Latymer (g), Latymer (b), Arts Educational School.

SALES

Flats	S	1B	2B	3B	4B	5B
Average prices	100–180	130–300	185–500	240–500+	350–850	–
Houses	2B	3B	4B	5B	6/7B	8B
Average prices	250–450	300–600+	400–1M	500–2M+	600–3M	–

RENTAL

Flats	S	1B	2B	3B	4B	5B
Average prices	150–200	160–300	195–500	200–600	350–600+	–
Houses	2B	3B	4B	5B	6/7B	8B
Average prices	200–500	230–600	350–1000	400–2500	600–2500	–

The properties Solid family homes, mainly Victorian/Edwardian (though larger ones scarce); some smaller terraces; also popular '30s mansion blocks. New homes in all available pockets. Riverside has superb Georgiana, plus cottages and smart new schemes – some enviable.

The market Riverside and Grove Park are smart, with high prices for family homes; best period riverside rarely for sale (and in the millions). New developments too are pricey. The peaceful streets inland popular with families. Younger people cluster near underground.

Among estate agents active in this area are:

- Barnard Marcus
- Riverview
- Whitman & Co
- Winkworth
- Dexters
- Bellengers
- Chesterton
- Savills
- Kinleigh Folkard & Hayward
- Tyser Greenwood
- Fletcher Estates
- Quilliam
- Fitz-Gibbon
- Bushells
- Borthwicks

CITY AND FRINGES

Postal districts: EC1, EC2, EC3, EC4, E1, N1
Boroughs: City of London Corporation (apolitical), Hackney (Lab), Tower Hamlets (Lab)
Council tax: Band D City £773, Hackney £1,221, Tower Hamlets £1,008
Conservation areas: Widespread – check with Corporation/councils
Parking: Residents/meters/clamps

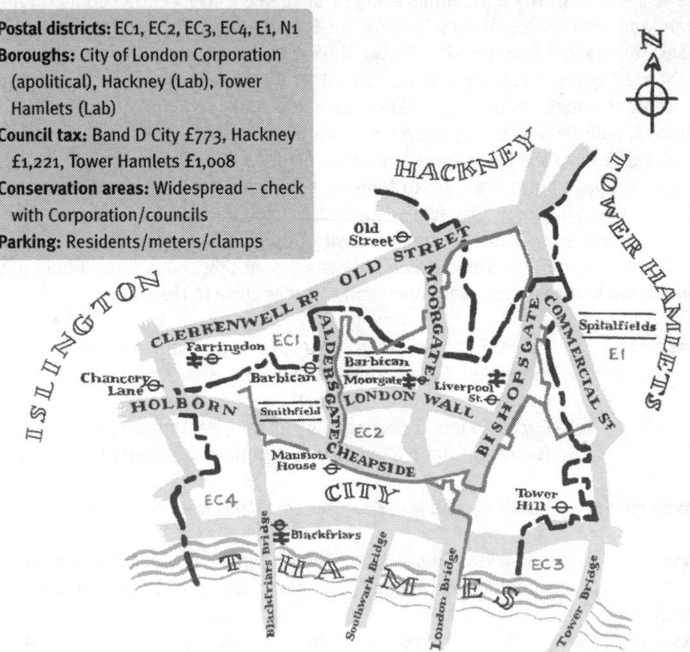

The City is different. In property market terms, as in virtually every other way, it is wholly unlike the rest of London. The rest of us fret over the mortgage rate, or the performance of our local schools, or the effects of a new road or tube. But here in the financial heart of Europe other things matter. Like the level of bonuses at merchant banks or hedge fund managers. With only 100 or so flats changing hands each quarter, it takes but a handful of fat-bonused bankers to perk up the market.

So it was no coincidence that prices in the City and its fringe, and its neighbour Clerkenwell, sank during 2003, which in restrospect was a very nasty year. Not only did the City's money machine (and its suppliers and services) shed 30,000 jobs. The big beasts at the top received far lower bonuses in '01 – '03 than in 2000. For these lumps of cash – some into seven figures – frequently get recycled into investment property.

Agents reported that City prices dropped ten per cent in the first half of '03 – not unreasonably, as turnover halved in the latter months of '02, and went on declining until the Iraq war (oh yes, there was a war on as well) was over in late spring 2003. Indeed, one agent spoke of a 'buyers' strike'. Last year, 2004, started off with a bit more cheer as bonuses returned. Prices were up 10 per cent by June. And then they slid back 10 per cent by December, as interest rate rises and doleful predictions sparked yet another 'buyers' strike'. Result: nil growth. However, rentals did improve, but only in activity: rents are broadly the same as they were in 1998 (yes, six years ago).

Whatever the ups and downs, plenty of people want to live close to where they work these days. And thanks to a ten-year boom in building and converting from 1992 on, there's now a choice. New supply is less than it was: most available sites have been used and current planning law discourages homes converted from commercial space. For new-build, look to Clerkenwell/Finsbury – or into Hackney borough (see those chapters).

The number of homes, measured against the number of workers, is still tiny. But there are far more than there were. The pre-1996 tally was basically the Barbican, plus a range of council homes (now increasingly open-market) and the familiar blocks of Guinness Trust and Peabody dwellings, far more rarely for sale or open-market rent. Add a few surviving Victorian and Georgian houses, often with shops on the ground floor, a couple of blocks of 1930s studios, and you had the City residential market: perhaps 2,500 homes in all within the 'Square Mile'. Now, there are well over 5,000: the late-'90s boom added whole blocks of new flats, a rash of 'loft' conversions (ex-offices, warehouses, factories) and the return to residential use of period buildings.

In the City's commercial heart (EC2 south of Broadgate, EC3, EC4 east of Blackfriars) homes are still few and far between – the Barbican estate aside. Indeed the City Corporation vetoes homes in the core banking area. Extend your search to EC4 and many more appear over the border in Clerkenwell and the area up round Old St (for both see Clerkenwell chapter), and in Smithfield. The less bankerly side of EC2 takes you across to ever-so-fashionable Shoreditch. Go east into E1 and E2 – the City's scruffier fringe – and there are yet more homes in historic Spitalfields, with a fast-growing cluster in hitherto unpromising but now terribly fashionable Hoxton, just across in N1.

There's an interesting City see-saw as sites and buildings can, depending on relative values, become either offices or homes. It made financial sense in the 1990s to develop valuable space as homes. The equation then swung back towards offices during 2000, and there was a marked slowdown in homes schemes. But 2002 saw the see-saw tilt again, and office-to-homes conversions have begun to reappear, though not at the same rate as in the 1990s.

The 'Square Mile' of the City of London runs E from **Chancery Lane** to **Aldgate**, from the Thames up to **Charterhouse St**, then on via (roughly) **Chiswell St/Sun St** in the N. In the City's heart, the banks' gleaming towers contrast with the narrow, twisting streets, unchanged in their alignment since medieval days. However, despite its moneyed image, the City contains scruffy streets as well as rich ones. Until the 1980s, industries – printing and graphics, leather, metal-working, textiles – dominated tracts on the edge.

The City's population reached a low in 1970 of about 4,500 people – compared to 30,000 at the start of the 20th century. Around 1995 the numbers began to increase seriously. Though this was in part due to a boundary change that brought the Golden Lane council estate into the City, it was also due to the building of new homes and the conversion of existing buildings. It is estimated that the population is now over 9,000 – up 51 per cent in a decade, making it the fastest-growing place in Britain. The City's workforce is just over 300,000.

The growth in the population – and the longer hours worked in the modern City – means shops, restaurants and bars have opened. Lion Plaza, in **Old Broad St**, is a new shops scheme. **Paternoster Square**, close to St Paul's, adds more shops, while the Royal Exchange has been revamped as a superior (and rather quiet) mall dedicated to high-status fashion. The House of Fraser department store close to the Monument adds to the two Marks & Spencer stores. Culture is provided by the Barbican Arts Centre.

The 'village' atmosphere of the City is prized by all its residents: the City is unique in that its local council, the City of London Corporation, is entirely independent and non-political – which contributes greatly to the area's feeling of detachment from the rest of London. There are some downsides: noise; lack of open space; few local services such as doctors and schools; cramped and overlooked homes; lack of daylight in some; extremely limited parking space. But the City is exciting – and still blessedly quiet at weekends.

The City proper

One hundred flats are promised when (and if: planners are *still* debating) offices by the river at **High Timber St** are converted. Hard times in the office market saw the swift conversion of a corner-site office block in **Pepys St**, close to Fenchurch Street station, into 89 flats during 2002, while winter '03/04 saw the revamping of a block in **Martin Lane**, off Cannon St, to yield 11 flats (still to be had are penthouses from £495,000). Recent large-scale developments include London House, St George's 2001 block of 81 flats in **Aldersgate St**, opposite the Museum of London (a 2-bed, £345,000 including parking space last autumn), and the 96 Berkeley finished in 2003 at the corner of **Queen St** and **St Thomas Apostle** – these were all sold off-plan in 2001.

Explore the City well; a hilly site and a medieval street pattern make for amazing corners away from the main arteries. The covetable address **Botolph Alley** could be yours (it's close to Monument, which is about as central as you can get), or **Trinity Square** over towards the Tower, with views of it and Tower Bridge: there are flats in both streets. Globe View – part new, part conversion off **High Timber St** – has some flats with views across the river to the new Globe Theatre, but most have to make do with a light well (or atrium as it is known in the trade); a river-view flat was £875,000 last winter. A converted tea warehouse in **St Ann's Hill** has 2-beds, 650-740sq ft, at c. £325,000.

A house in the City? You must be joking – but in fact they do exist. One, dating from the 1670s, was for sale in December for £3.2 million (it was £4 million a year earlier. . .). It is in **Laurence Pountney Hill** off Cannon St.

Barbican and its neighbours

For 20 years after the estate's completion in 1976, City living meant the Barbican. It had no competitors. With its 2,014 homes on 35 acres, it is still the largest residential district. The complex is bordered by **London Wall**, **Aldersgate St**, **Moorgate** and **Chiswell St**. It's described by the City Corporation, which controls it, as a 'city within a City' – and so it is. The fortress image is even more accurate: the whole thing turns inwards, looking down on the open space in front of the magnificent Barbican Arts Centre. Worryingly, there is no street level: walkways, stairs and lifts form a 3-D maze so cunning that yellow stripes had to be painted on the paving to guide bemused visitors to the arts centre (even Pevsner admits is is confusing). The key to orientation is the 'podium' level, two or three floors above the surrounding streets: some flats are below it, most above. The three soaring main towers – just some of the 21 residential blocks – dominate much of the Square Mile's skyline. To those expecting a world of penthouse flats and luxurious living, first impressions can disappoint. The complex looks rather drab, grey, concrete and uniform, and greenery on the balconies struggles to compete (the Corporation has just spent £12 million smartening the public areas, though).

But the inside of many Barbican flats tells a different story – they belie their outward appearance and provide some of the most exciting homes in Central London. There are over 140 different types of flat: you'll find 'type 59' on sales particulars (agents can advise). Some are split-level, others have L-shaped reception rooms. Biggest prices are paid for the 5-bed, 3-floor penthouses of Lauderdale, Cromwell (£1.45 million in 2002, some £100,000 less now – but a mere £600,000 in 1996) and Shakespeare Towers – the latter is Britain's tallest residential building. The view from it reaches right out to the bowl of hills surrounding London. The whole complex is now listed Grade II: this means any alterations, inside and out, require permission from the City's planners (will this preclude ripping out the now-iconic 1970s 'original Barbican kitchens' still found in some flats? See Golden Lane below).

Only a handful of the Barbican's homes are now rented from the City Corporation; the rest are leasehold. Local agents usually have a selection to buy or rent. Homes range from studios right through to a small number of town-houses: the majority, though, are 1- and 2-bed flats. As you'd expect, services such as estate cleaning and security are given a high priority and are excellent. The downsides are the under-floor heating, which is inflexible and expensive, and the service charges. Charges can vary quite widely: a 1-bed flat might attract £2,500 a year – or £5,000 in another block. Prices are up on last year, especially for the smaller flats: studio flats are c. £190–205,000, while 1-beds vary from £245,000 to £320,000. Two-beds start about £330,000, while the tower-block flats start at around £400,000. A 3/4-bed house might be £750,000. Demand is steady, with would-be buyers placing want-ads for the specific 'type' they covet.

The Barbican has a very strong and active residents' association, which presents a powerful voice at local council meetings. It has a strong community feel and many residents stay put for many years. Good security means low crime.

North of the Barbican is the well-regarded council-built (and Grade II*-listed) **Golden Lane** Estate, with over half the 557 homes now privately owned. Since 1994 this has actually been within the City boundary, though it has always been run by it. Typical prices are much as last year: £175–215,000 for a 1-bed, around £250,000 for a 2-bed and £295,000 for a 3-bed. Beware: the estate's listing means that bodies such as the 20th-Century Society will have a voice in how you arrange your flat: 'the wish of tenants to alter the carefully designed interior spaces to accommodate a personal preference . . . exemplifies a lack of understanding regarding the importance of the architectural environment in which they live.' One 'case' the Society 'investigated' involved (oh shock-horror) replacing the kitchen cabinets. You are also stuck with the thoroughly impractical, but architecturally interesting, sliding interior walls. Some people love all this: a flat was advertised last winter 'with original light swiches'.

On the E side of **Golden Lane** is a big Peabody Trust estate, with further council housing away E along **Banner St**, which also boasts a recent block by Croft Homes with 2-bed flats. Just N of the Barbican, **Bridgewater Square** has converted 2-bed flats. To the N, The Apex (formerly City Point) is a Berkeley conversion in **Bunhill Row**, on the fringes of the Old St area (see also Clerkenwell). On **Featherstone St**, Matisse Court is a new ('02) block; **Dufferin Avenue** and **Dufferin St** have lofts in ex-commercial buildings, and **Chequers St** some smart new whole houses. **Finsbury Square** has ten 1998 2-bed flats and a penthouse. In **Tabernacle St**, an old factory was split into 23 lofts in 1999: some live/work units, others penthouses; Galaxy House is a new loft conversion in the same street: £383,000 for 851 sq ft. In **Christina St** a warehouse became four flats in '03, and '04 saw three more in a former warehouse in **Tilney Court**, just S of Old St.

Smithfield

Smithfield, at the NW edge of the City and W of the Barbican, is dominated by the splendid Victorian wholesale meat-market buildings and historic Bart's Hospital. It is under the influence of Clerkenwell: see also that chapter. Smithfield is a great place for bars, restaurants and clubs – and for pubs which serve carnivorous breakfasts from 4am.

Contained by **Charterhouse St**, **Aldersgate St** and **Newgate St**, Smithfield has an increasing, if still small, clutch of homes amid the commercial buildings. This quarter, with its medieval bones still showing, is definitely one of the City's best residential areas.

One popular development is Florin Court, across in the welcome leafiness of **Charterhouse Square** to the N. One of London's last private, gated squares, Regalian refurbished the 9-storey, stylish 1936 building in the '80s to provide over 100 2-bed flats and studios: the latter go for c. £155–165,000. The square also has new, if small, flats – and a few Georgian houses dating from 1700–1775: nearly all offices; well over £1 million if homes. These, though, are new compared to the monastic buildings that form part of the Bart's Hospital medical college, behind: see Charterhouse in the Clerkenwell chapter.

An old bank in **West Smithfield**, which opens out in front of the meat market, has become little studios (£165,000–200,000) and 1-bed flats. In **Long Lane**, nine new flats date from 1999 and there are two schemes in **Carthusian St** on the Barbican borders.

One of the biggest schemes is 'the Hosier Suites' in **Hosier Lane**: 122 flats. 'The Spur' in Cock Lane (ouch) is new: 13 1- and 2-beds from £270,000. Ten flats in **Charterhouse St** date from the late '80s, as do ten mews-style homes in **Cloth Fair**, which hidden lane runs alongside the area's spiritual heart: reach St Bartholomew's church via the Tudor gateway off the circular square of West Smithfield, marvel at it, and read its history to find out just what makes this area tick, if you are thinking of living here. And if the thought grabs you, there's a £1.6 million house, with garage, opposite the church gate.

Spitalfields

Spitalfields is where the City merges with the East End. **Commercial St**, **Middlesex St** and **Bishopsgate** form the boundaries of this unique part of London, which is mostly in Tower Hamlets borough. The big wholesale fruit and vegetable market between **Lamb St** and **Brushfield St** moved out to Leyton a decade back: after a big row, redevelopment is now under way: about half the old market will remain. Delightful ad hoc markets and other events use the old halls. Just to the W, the handsome grandeur of the late-'80s Broadgate office development dominates the whole neighbourhood.

There are, however, older buildings in Spitalfields: some beautiful, *very* early Georgian houses, built by Huguenot silk merchants, with panelled interiors to make a classicist swoon. Some have been lovingly restored and will of course be retained in the area's renewal. These are found in **Fournier St**, **Folgate St**, **Princelet St**, **Elder St** – a 4-bed example here, with its original weaver's loft now supplying two of the bedrooms, was £935,000 last winter; it was last sold 30 years ago.

Conversions of old buildings provide nearly all the other homes. An early example was Pennybank Chambers, **Great Eastern St**, which has 65 small flats. The Cloisters, **Commercial St**, a purpose-built portered block, has 1-bed flats. Opposite, a recent conversion called The Xchange offers smart lofts and new, quirky, round-cornered flats. Just behind in **Calvin St**, Laing's Blue House offered nine 1- and 2-bed workspace flats and 13 ordinary ones. In what they reckon is called 'The Silk Quarter', St George built 16 1- and 2-bed flats in **Lamb St** behind a Georgian-style facade overlooking Elder Gardens. **Princelet St** has a few large lofts; a Grade II-listed Victorian pub opposite Broadgate is now ten flats. And the conversion of Tannery House in **Deal St** yielded seven floors of flats: a 2-bed duplex here, complete with roof-terrace views over London, £327,000 last winter. By comparison, the new Bishops Square development off **Folgate St** will have flats in Vanbrugh House: £350,000 for 750 sq ft.

Just off Middlesex St, in **Strype St**, are a clutch of 1-bed flats and penthouses, and the Wexner Building, a 1901 cigar warehouse, now flats – £340,000 for a 895 sq ft duplex – while round the corner in **Leyden St** St Clement's House is an Art-Deco style new-build block with 1- and 2-bed flats (a studio last winter £205,000, a 2-bed £365,000). There's a small row of new 2-bed houses in Georgian style in **Wilkes St**. A 1930s warehouse in **Commercial St** is now nine flats; **Brune St** has 12 new 1-beds in Esprit Court – and a listed soup kitchen, no less: now turned into a £1.2 million house with vaulted living room.

Further S, the **Leman St** area on the W edge of Whitechapel boasts a few homes. Four 3-bed town-houses in **Alie St** make an unusual contribution to this district of flats and lofts. Leybourne House is a modern block with swimming pool and that ever more vital City amenity, an underground car park. **Leman St** has a block of seven new flats. **Prescot St** has 'loft-style' apartments, and the 84-flat Prospect Tower is in the same street. There is Guinness Trust housing in **Mansell St**. Prospero House in **The Minories**, once a bank, has 14 flats. For more see Stepney and Whitechapel chapter.

C

Fleet St and Holborn

The newspapers having left, this area on the W edge of the City has found a new identity as a place to work (on a modest but upmarket scale: no vast towering blocks) and to live. Broad **Fleet St** runs from Temple Bar, the City boundary by the Royal Courts of Justice just past the Aldwych at the end of the Strand, all the way down to Ludgate Circus. In the 'Street of Shame' itself, St Bride House is a 1900 block converted into 2-bed flats in 2002 (now c. £335,000 for 635 sq ft), and there are similar flats in **St Bride St** round the corner. In **Poppin's Court**, which joins it to Fleet St, Sovereign House has 14 flats. **Wine Office Court** – an enviable address, and a charming paved courtyard – has six flats converted from a Victorian newspaper building. Pemberton House, again just off the Street, has 39: £440,000 for 1,020 sq ft.

Across Ludgate Circus, The Gallery on **Ludgate Hill** is sought-after. Evangelist House in nearby **Blackfriars Lane** is a new block of 16 2- and 3-bed serviced flats to rent.

Just to the S of **Fleet St**, don't miss the Temples – Inner and Middle – which house lawyers and a few favoured others in a very select live/work estate: London's oldest. In **Temple Lane**, an office building now has 60 flats, with 10 more off **Fetter Lane** in Greystoke Place, the conversion of a listed '60s office; £875,000 for a 2-bed penthouse. **Fetter Lane** also has flats in a portered block, Cliffords Inn (£350,000 for 600 sq ft), and will gain nine more this spring at No. 96: £240–300,000.

The Holborn area, however, has few homes, though **Red Lion Square** boasts some handsome houses, and there are a few small modern blocks. A 68-flat scheme at No. 7 **High Holborn** dates from 2002. In **Furnival St**, close to Chancery Lane tube, a six-floor 1995 block has 16 1- and 2-bed flats. Just off **Cursitor St**, Printers Inn Court is another old news building, now 19 flats. **Great Turnstile**, off Lincoln's Inn, is to gain 10 new flats.

Shoreditch and Hoxton

The triangle between **Old St**, **Great Eastern St** and **Shoreditch High St** has come from nowhere (or at least from a limbo-land of semi-dereliction) to become one of the buzziest places in London. It used to be all commercial/light industrial, with a few low-rent flats. Then all the businesses decamped. An influx of mid-'90s computer and new-media firms took advantage of the then-cheap office space . . . some have survived. But more important for the neighbourhood's renaissance was the live/work permissions policy adopted by Hackney Council, whose patch this is. Many 'work-homes' are conversions of existing factories or workshops. Another influence is the art/fashion scene: galleries, art-based businesses, The London College of Fashion in **Bateman's Row**. Now we have bars, galleries, restaurants, a flood of new homes.

Some period homes survive from earlier days of respectability: check out **Charlotte Rd** and **Cowper St**, and there are sizeable flats above some of the Victorian shops on **Shoreditch High St**. **Tabernacle St**'s City Lofts added 30 'shell' units in 2000. The 'Vetro' building in **Paul St** has 10 new flats. New this year are lofts and houses in 'The Mercer Building' converted from offices at the junction of **New Inn Yard** and **Curtain Rd** (nine flats, 15 live/work homes, from £295,000), plus two schemes in **Garden Walk**.

Hoxton, too, features in the style magazines – but the homes market here is limited, most property being still council-owned. The spotlight is on a small area round Hoxton Square, with a few more patches of interesting homes amid the well-intentioned post-war council monstrosities (would you believe a '60s block called Caliban Tower?). Hoxton manages to cling to the remnants of its vigorous past: the Victorian music-hall up in **Hoxton St** still stands as a thriving theatre/community centre. Hoxton St also has the new Hemsworth Building, with 17 flats, and now the pub next door has become four more.

C

Hoxton Square, once a very dangerous place to go without an entrée, has passed through the hip artists' hangout phase and is now more mainstream (the dread words 'bridge and tunnel' are being used about weekend visitors). The Square still boasts a highly fashionable gallery – and a circus school. Lots of action here: St George have built 36 new flats in the N of the square; at Nos. 48/49 is a new-build 11-flat live/work scheme, with nine more flats at No. 36. A dozen flats plus a good cache of 27 live/work units in **Drysdale St**, just off the Square, complete this spring. Hoxton Point is new-build on the **Rufus St/Old St** junction: four £250,000 live-work units.

Bankrupt Hackney Council is selling off property: the Victorian school in **Pitfield St** is now 27 flats, known as 'Arthouse', with 14 new-build flats complementing the new block at the corner of Pitfield St and **Fanshawe St**. This, called Lanesborough Court, has 2-bed flats. The Hoffman Buildings on **Pitfield St** are a conversion of grandiose 1820s almshouses, latterly a college, into flats by Copthorn. More 'proper houses' here if you look: try **Chart St**, **Buttesland St**, even busy **New North Rd**, where there's an attractive Georgian terrace and five flats carved out of the Edwardian Constitutional Club. **Fulwood Mews** is a stylish conversion: 2-bed houses; **Haberdasher St** has Victorian mansion blocks. More live-work units planned for the junction of **New North** and **East Rds**. A small new block of flats is under way at **Bevenden St**. A big site on the corner of **Nile St** and **Provost St** is being developed: yet more flats.

Shepherdess Walk has the best houses: 1830s terraces, many of which are in the hands of a housing co-op, but some do appear on the market. This road also has most of the loft schemes: The Factory and The Canal Building: 74 lofts and live/work units sold in shell finish. **Shepherdess Place** has a conversion of a 1920s building: The Chocolate Factory, now 24 live-work units. For more on this borderland see the Islington chapter. **Cropley St** has a pretty terrace of early-Victorian cottages; while by the canal, over on **Eagle Wharf Rd/New North Rd**, is Hitchcock's Gainsborough Studios: 210 flats (some live/work) in a five-block conversion plus new-build scheme. Just to the S, in **Britannia Walk**, 43 new flats by Goldcrest (£350,000-plus) joins a clutch of homes for key workers. A pub in **Rushton St** has been converted, and extended, into flats for rent.

This neighbourhood currently has a good supply of new homes (all those canal-view lofts) and a slight feeling of isolation. The two factors came together in 2003 and 2004 and made several developers rather nervous: £50,000 chunks were hacked off the prices of new flats. Some developers decided to let rather than sell, adding to the worries of earlier waves of buy-to-let investors.

Kingsland Rd, rapidly acquiring galleries, bars, cafés, is alleged by some enthusiasts to be the current decade's answer to the King's Road Chelsea. The old Roman road forms the frontier between Hoxton to the W and Haggerston to the E before heading, ruler-straight, via Dalston to Stoke Newington. Haggerston, a tract where the birthplace of the Kray Twins is still pointed out, is pioneer country. There's plenty going on around Kingsland Rd (see also Hackney chapter): just count the cranes – lofts plus penthouses at Union Central, warehouse canalside lofts at Quebec Wharf and Spice Wharf; Glassworks Studios in **Basing Place**, with live/work units and penthouses. Just N of the Geffrye Museum, Shoreditch Stables offers new homes, while on **Laburnum St**, nearly at the canal, yet more lofts have been carved out of a 1930s factory.

Optimists are banking on the extension of the East London Line, which will run alongside **Kingsland Rd** to bring metro-style transport to the area: stations to come at Shoreditch High St, behind Hoxton's Geffrye Musuem, and in Haggerston. The line will reach as far N as Highbury & Islington, and down through Docklands into South London. When? 'In time for the Olympics' (2012) is the latest guess, one made more plausible by the seizing of the project by Mayor Ken Livingstone, who has managed to borrow the cash – see Transport chapter.

Transport Tubes and main line, all zone 1, in profusion: see map. From Bank: Oxford Circus 10 min, Heathrow 1 hr 15 min (1 change).

Convenient for West End, Docklands & City Airport, Islington, Bankside. Miles from centre: 1.5.

Schools Local Authority: no secondary schools in City, see neighbouring areas. Private: City of London Schools (b) (g).

SALES

Flats	S	1B	2B	3B	4B	5B
Average prices	150–180	160–300	250–380	300–500+	–	–
Houses	2B	3B	4B	5B	6/7B	8B
Average prices	300–500	500–800	800–1.2M	1M+	–	–

RENTAL

Flats	S	1B	2B	3B	4B	5B
Average prices	180–220	225–300	280–400	350–500	–	–
Houses	2B	3B	4B	5B	6/7B	8B
Average prices	300–600	500+	600+	800+	–	–

The properties Homes at last reappearing in numbers both on fringes, including Fleet St and Holborn and especially Hoxton/Shoreditch, and among the offices. Barbican has 2,000 modern flats and a few houses. A very few period homes in fringe areas like Spitalfields and Smithfield, plus company flats, a few ex-council homes – and a fast-growing range of new flats and loft conversions.

The market Currently, quiet. Barbican homes, originally rented, can now be bought. Prices can be good value compared with West End — but watch service charges. Rare period homes joined by a rash of new flats and conversions. Prices here often quoted in £ per sq ft: £375–400-plus is a fair average, less on the fringes. Big, opulent flats hard to shift, but 1- and 2-beds sell fast. Plenty of choice in rentals; investors accepting gross yields in 6–7 per cent bracket.

Among estate agents active in this area are:

- Hurford Salvi Carr
- Frank Harris
- Hamptons
- Stirling Ackroyd
- Winkworth
- Spencer Thomas
- John D Wood
- Jarvis Keller
- Daniel Watney
- Phillips Residential
- Hamilton Brooks
- Carrington & Ptnrs
- DTZ Residential
- Keatons
- Scott City
- Lee Clements
- Currell
- Thompson Currie
- Bridge Estates
- Urban Spaces

CLAPHAM

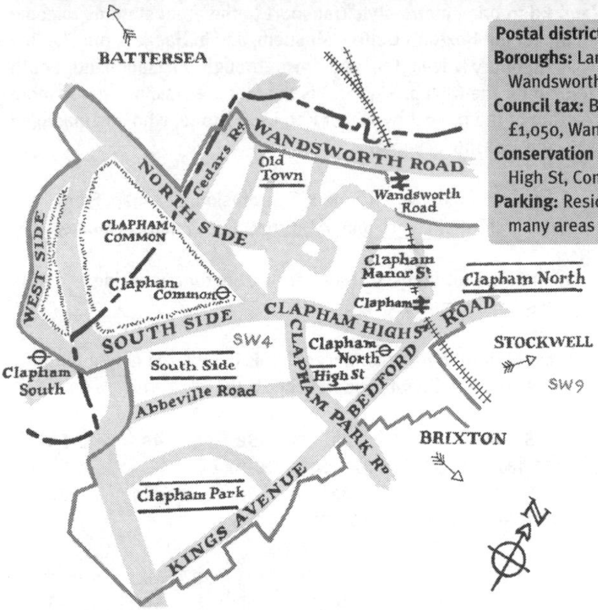

Postal districts: SW4, SW9
Boroughs: Lambeth (Lib Dem), Wandsworth (Con)
Council tax: Band D Lambeth £1,050, Wandsworth £597
Conservation areas: Old Town, High St, Common and others
Parking: Residents' zones in many areas

Two kinds of people flock to Clapham: young singles with City jobs who love the High Street's party-time buzz, and prosperous couples-with-kids who seek out ever-bigger and smarter family houses. Both groups appreciate the crowded but quick Northern Line commute, the proximity to Chelsea, Knightsbridge and the West End, and the wide open Common for Sunday morning football or a stroll with the kids.

To enrich the mix, and provide an alternative to the ubiquitous, and sometimes rather tired, flats carved out of Victorian houses, there are now quite a few smart, 21st-century flats, both new-build in odd corners and school conversions. These attract a third group, prosperous young media/arts workers who find Clapham's mix of architecture, homes and people enlivening. Families have the choice of standard-issue, but usually much-smartened, Victorian terraces in 'Abbeville Village' or more quirky, often older and bigger, houses in Old Town and N of the Common. Schools are a draw up to age 11/13, but families often move to find good secondary education: on to Wandsworth, or deep into Surrey.

Clapham's key assets are the tube, a billiard-table of a common and the fashionable (and convenient) cinema, bars, clubs, restaurants and shops of the High Street and Old Town. There's a gleaming modernist Sainsbury's (with a car park), a Holmes Place health club, and not one but two Starbucks. There are plans this year for a second Sainsbury's, a Local, to serve the N end of the High St.

Here, once, was a little hamlet surrounded by big mansions, where prosperous Londoners kept country retreats. Pepys, for instance, retired and died here. In early Victorian times more grand houses appeared as the energetic Thomas Cubitt, of Belgravia and Pimlico fame, built a whole suburb of them and called it Clapham Park. But as the century went on, and trams and later tubes made Clapham cheap and easy to get to, most of Cubitt's big, handsome villas were replaced by terraces for the modest City men of the day. By 1900, Clapham was a byword for ordinariness. 'The man on the

Clapham omnibus' became a judicial simile for all that was everyday and reasonable.

Clapham, unlike many a part of South London, has a direct tube to the City, West End and Waterloo (change there for Docklands or Paris). In the '80s, house-buyers began to discover that Clapham is as close to Sloane Square as Fulham is, and that the journey to Oxford Circus or Bank is a whole lot quicker. Clapham was on the up, after spending most of the 20th century in genteel decline. The tube, however, is now very overcrowded: it collects Balham and Tooting's commuters before Clapham's get a chance.

The old village of Clapham is still there, with a pleasant mix of buildings that includes at its heart a row of fine Queen Anne houses. From here the streets spread out, beginning with a handsome 1820s row and going on S to the site of Cubitt's 250 acres of 'capacious detached villas' (of which about six survive) in Clapham Park. Later Victorian times saw the growth of **Clapham High St** and a shift in Clapham's commercial centre of gravity from the **Old Town** eastwards. For once the postcode is a fairly accurate delineation: with a few bordering streets, Clapham is SW4. It divides into several distinct neighbourhoods radiating out from the **Old Town** – which is both a street name and the heart of the old village – and encompassing High St, Clapham Manor St, Clapham North to the E; Abbeville Village and Clapham Park to the S.

Across the common, the area to the W ('Between the Commons') and NW (down to Lavender Hill) is Battersea – see that chapter – as are the flat, low-lying streets N of **Wandsworth Rd**: Clapham is on a low but distinct hill. South of the foot of the Common, the first streets off Balham Hill are often called 'Clapham South' after Clapham South tube, but are in Balham (see Balham & Tooting chapter). East, beyond Clapham Park, is a zone debated with Brixton. Clapham Junction, by the way, is in Battersea (it was so-called since at the time Clapham was the classier area): a source of confusion for over a century.

The Common survived the Victorians, and is now a valuable green lung, meeting place (in more than one sense) and backdrop – and the source of some fine, open views from the handsome houses, flats and prep schools that gaze out over it.

Old Town

Strictly speaking, **Old Town** is a street, but the heart of old Clapham has annexed the name. As with all such desirable tags, estate agents try to stretch it as far as possible: it is usually reckoned to run N as far as **Wandsworth Rd**, E to **Clapham Manor St** and W to **Cedars Rd** and the borough boundary. **Old Town** proper has Clapham's oldest and handsomest houses, a row of three rare Queen Anne survivals, dating from 1705, looking out over the little triangle that marks the original village centre (now a bus halt). New homes here too: a 2-bed flat in a renovated building £335,000. More to come – one day:

C

the big, ex-police authority site on the corner with **Grafton Square** remains empty despite various plans. Grafton itself is Clapham's only garden square: a peaceful place, surrounded on three sides by tall, handsome white-stucco 1850s houses – shades of Cubitt's Pimlico, though one Captain Ross was responsible. There are also three very pretty 2-storey stucco houses; the humdrum block on the fourth side hardly detracts. One of the less handsome, later-Victorian houses was £1.3 million last winter. A row of modern (1990) 4-bed town-houses off the Square change hands for around £600,000.

North of the Square are streets of solid, 3- or 4-storey, £900,000-ish Victorian houses: **Offerton Rd** (particularly nice), **Fitzwilliam Rd** and **Liston Rd**. Some flat conversions amid the family houses: 2-beds are £320,000-plus. Fitzwilliam runs across Rectory Grove to North St: between the three, the triangular site of gated **Floris Place**, a 2002-vintage cache of 16 1- and 2-bed flats, 2/3-bed maisonettes and 2/3- or 4-bed houses by Persimmon. The new Holmes Place pool and gym is next door. The little terraced houses on busy **North St** are (as last year) around £375,000, 2-bed flats £300,000, though ex-council flats start around £195,000.

Rectory Grove, with some handsome houses (£750,0000-1 million) runs N from the Old Town to link with **Larkhall Rise.** The Rise has some lovely houses from Georgian days onwards (a 7-bed was £2.5 million last winter), and in contrast some council-built homes. **Rectory Gardens** is a row of tiny cottages, owned (and neglected) by Lambeth Council. **Turret Grove**, named after a feature of the Elizabethan manor that once stood here, has some pretty 1840s cottages as well as the Victorian terraces it shares with **Rozel** and **Iveley Rds** – the latter, which also has four 1999 4-bed houses, tucked away by the church. This is Clapham's most discreet and charming corner.

West of **Old Town** and its continuation **North St** is a quiet network of streets. Broad **Macaulay Rd** was built in late-Victorian times with very large, gabled, detached and semi-detached houses, many of which survive. Most are flats (1-bed £210,000-plus), but there are still a few vast, single homes, some smartened up to Chelsea level (these can prove hard to sell). **Macaulay Square** is a small council-built estate. Macaulay Court is a recently-refurbed block of '30s flats (2-bed c. £250,000), nicely positioned in the angle of **Macaulay Rd** and **Lillieshall Rd**. Lillieshall has some substantial Victorian terraces (4-bed £700,000-plus) with some pretty, very small cottages at the E end. Parallel **Broadhinton Rd** has some attractive early Victorian cottages and a few larger houses. Many of **Orlando Rd**'s big 3-storey Victorian houses are now flats; those that aren't start at around £800,000. Recent additions to this corner include **Redwood Mews**, off **Hannington Rd**: nine 1- and 2-bed houses around a courtyard, and **Sycamore Mews**, once the old royal laundry between North St and Orlando Rd and now a smart mews of flats (2-beds £350–400,000) and houses. More new flats on the corner of **Orlando Rd** and **Old Town**. Just across the street, a big period building next to the library has been refurbished as flats: here too is one of Clapham's two Starbucks.

Across **Macaulay Rd** to the E, **The Chase**, a parallel grand avenue, has similarly vast Victorian residences: where possible, the large houses of this corner of Clapham have been re-converted back to single homes. Some of the enormous double-fronted ones boast 6 or 7 bedrooms, and 120ft gardens. The smaller, 4- bed, houses are c. £650,000, with the bigger (5-bed) ones can ask anything from £975,000–1.2million. A third avenue, **Victoria Rise**, has gaunter and less kempt, but still huge, grey-brick-and-stucco houses: often now flats (e.g 2-bed £315,000) that share the equally huge gardens.

The **North Side** of Clapham Common has a succession of terraces of various eras, from 1695 through early Georgian to mid-Victorian, plus 1930s flats. It is now also (sign of the times) prep-school alley. Several of the enormous houses are flats, which have fine views across London to the N and the common to the S. You can still sometimes find a whole, unmodernized Georgian house here for the price of a Pooterish Victorian one across the Common in Abbeville – or you can stump up £3 million for a 5-storey affair with in-and-out drive. The two commanding blocks on either side of **Cedars Rd** are splendid examples of 1860s grandiose. Enviable flats occasionally come up for sale in the E block (e.g 2-bed £400,000); its twin is a hotel. Cedars Rd itself, once lined with villas, is now a main road lined with mostly set-back, council-built housing: resales are common (£200,000 for a 2-bed). Tiny **Wix's Lane**, to the W of **Cedars Rd**, marks the border of both Lambeth borough and SW4 (for the SW11 streets that run down from **North Side** to **Lavender Hill**, see Battersea chapter). The Lane now houses the latest private school, the Lycée Charles de Gaulle.

Back now towards the Old Town where **Clapham Common North Side, Old Town** and **The Pavement** meet to form the triangle that, though paved, irresistibly betrays its village-green origins; a curve of chi-chi shops along The Pavement face Holy Trinity Church on the common. There are some flats above the shops, and two inter-war blocks of flats: Trinity Close is well-run and popular with 3-beds c. £380,000. **The Polygon** is just that – an odd-shaped enclave on the common's edge; houses have smartened up, there's a very cool bar/restaurant, and eight modern 2-bed, 2-bath flats.

Clapham Manor St

The Old Town area is bounded to the E by a tract of modern council-built housing around **Cubitt Terrace**. These are nicely designed, brick-built, mainly 2-storey, and arranged in pleasant closes and green squares. Some appear on the market, a cheaper alternative to Cubitt's original 2/3-bed early-Victorian cottages, and can be priced at £400,000-plus. To the N of **Larkhall Rise** are some sloping streets of terraced houses: **Brayburne Avenue**, with 4-bed houses, is quieter since access to **Wandsworth Rd** was cut off at the N end. **Hesewall Close** has a dozen 3-bed 1995 family houses. **Netherford Rd** and, E of the railway, **Killyon Rd** are Victorian terraces. The little Wandsworth Rd station has a twice-hourly service to Victoria and London Bridge. The line is used by Channel Tunnel trains.

Clapham Manor St, especially at its N end, is handsome with 2- and 3-storey Cubitt terraces and a few detacheds, much in demand as family homes (houses £450–800,000 depending on size and sophistication). The S end, towards the **High St**, is more mixed. The little roads off Clapham Manor to the E, like **Navy St** and **Voltaire Rd**, have later Victorian terraces (many split into flats) while **Edgeley Rd** has rather looming 3-storey ones, again mostly flats, plus some cottagey-looking, 1920s 2-storey rows which are in fact tiny purpose-built 2-bed flats; the E side backs onto the railway. Twelve mews houses have been inserted behind a Victorian facade. Elmhurst Mansions is a purpose-built block: a 2-bed flat around here might be £250–275,000. The corner between Old Town and **Clapham Manor St** has some 3-storey purpose-built Victorian flats in **Bromells Rd** (plus a new-in-2003 gated mews with flats and five 3-bed houses); also some flats in smaller terraces in **Venn St**, two minutes from the tube. Wilberforce Mews, new last year, runs off **Stonhouse St**: its eight 3-bed houses are £488,000.

High St

One of Clapham's key assets is the **High St**'s profusion of bars and places to eat, reinforced by a modernistic Sainsbury's and, round the corner in Venn St, the Clapham Picture House cinema. There are night clubs, a health club, and of course Clapham Common tube at the top of the high street. The open-all-hours bustle makes many of the area's young singles feel safer on their trek home: Clapham North tube, at the bottom of the street, is less reassuring. There's a main-line station at this end, too: trains to Victoria and London Bridge. A new block over shops on the **High St**, between Stonhouse and Venn Sts, added 22 flats; now 14 smart 2- and 3-beds, £300-650,000, have appeared on the corner with **Aristotle Rd**: Gleeson's 'Arena' sits atop a new Sainsbury's Local.

South of the High St is a mixed area of Victorian terraces and council housing, a hot-spot for rented flats (locals call **Tremadoc Rd** 'rental road'). **Nelson's Row** with its dozen neat, flat-fronted 3-bed Victorian cottages (bigger than they look; a few split into £250,000 2-bed flats), and an art gallery, leads down to some smart new flats, then a much-tidied, '30s red-brick, council-built estate. **St Luke's Avenue** and roads to the E (**Tremadoc Rd, Kenwyn Rd, Cato Rd**) are mostly 3-storey Victorian, most now flats (1-beds c £265,000, 2-beds £250–280,000). **Aristotle Mews** is 17 houses (1999) by Fairview. The old school in **Aristotle Rd** is reborn as 'Grande Place', 35 1- and 2-bed loft-style flats.

C

The streets off the W side of broad **Clapham Park Rd**, which runs from the start of the High St down as far as **Abbeville Rd**, are largely council-built. Near the junction of the two, Belway's Cavendish Mews (2001) has 13 1- and 2-bed flats. **St Alphonsus Rd** has some Victorian terraces and 14 recent flats while **Northbourne Rd** boasts some well-preserved mid-Victoriana, detached and semis, on a handsome scale: £1.3–1.6 million has been asked for 5/6-bed semis. A rather sad office block on **Clapham Park Rd** gained a new floor and facade in the late '90s and became flats as St Paul's Court. Belway's Albert Mews added flats and mews houses. Smart houses and work-homes have been carved out of a clutch of old factory buildings round a courtyard. **Park Hill** runs down to Clapham Park (the area) with some '20s gabled terraces (dubbed 'Arts & Crafts' now: so £600,000 for a 4-bed), modern flats and a few large early 19th-century detached houses. Before we explore Clapham's southern 'suburbs', we look at the other, Stockwell, end of the High St.

Clapham North

East of Clapham North tube and N of the rail line (used by Channel Tunnel trains), and in the SW9 postcode, is a rather cut-off corner of Victorian terraces and council housing. The Southwestern Hospital forms the border with Brixton. Homes in this district were, until recently, cheaper than in other Clapham corners: it is furthest from the common and some streets were distinctly down-at-heel. However, the little network of roads N of **Landor Rd** – **Atherfold Rd**, **Hemberton Rd** and **Prideaux Rd** – is popular now that neighbouring Brixton is downright fashionable. Little houses, which were £80,000 in 1994/5, are now four times that – or more. **Landor Rd** itself is busy and unreconstructed: 2-bed flats £250,000. **Ferndale** and **Sandmere Rds** run E to Brixton: the little flat-fronted houses sell for £325–360,000 (2-bed flats £250–275,000), the gaunt 3-storey ones for £400,000-ish, plus a few smart developments. Along **Clapham Rd** towards Stockwell are some fine Georgian houses, most used as offices, but some reverting to homes. The old Savoy laundry site has been developed by Persimmon into 1- and 2-bed flats and 3-bed town-houses: ready autumn '05. By the tube in **Bedford Rd** – an otherwise uninspiring street – a clever new mews, **Coachmaker Mews**, has flats and houses (£430,000 for a 3-bed.

Things are on a larger scale W of Clapham Rd, where **Gauden, Bromfelde, Sibella** and **Chelsham Rds** have some big Victorian houses. Good flat conversions can be found – in **Gauden Rd** several adjoining houses have been split: all flats share the large garden and pool (1-bed flat c. £200,000). Some, though, are still single homes, including the very occasional spectacular 6- or 7-bedded, large-garden-to-match, £1.4 million example.

Clapham Park

South now, to Cubitt's elegant suburb of detached mansions: long vanished, but leaving a legacy of large trees, broad roads and the occasional, surviving square early 19th-century house, now flats. Centred on **King's Avenue**, this is furthest from the tube and is bounded to the S by the South Circular. King's Avenue itself has several flats blocks: Queenswood Court includes three of the original houses; Robins, Thorncliffe and Oakfield Courts are '30s blocks; Peters Court is '60s. A 2-bed in these is c. £210,000. Inter-war suburban-style detached homes punctuate the flats, here as on **Clarence Avenue.** There's a lions-on-pillars/in-and-out drive/porticoes tendency round here.

East of **King's Avenue** is in SW2, and is a border zone between Brixton and Clapham Park: there are several quiet streets of Victorian terraces. Brixton Prison dominates the eastern end of **Thornbury Rd. Kingswood Rd** has some larger, 3-storey houses. These streets are fairly evenly split between single houses and flats. A 2-bed garden flat here is still (as in 2002) c. £210,000. The S end of **King's Avenue** and west to **Clarence Avenue** is all council-built: houses and low blocks built in the 1930s and 1950s, set in a pleasant green space. Lambeth Council has ambitious plans for the whole area: watch your searches. Continuing N, the streets leading E off **Lyham Rd** are SW2, and have received a boost from the renaissance of Brixton (see Brixton, Herne Hill and Tulse Hill chapter).

South Side/Abbeville

This is the largest residential neighbourhood in Clapham and the most uniform, being almost entirely Victorian terraced housing. The grid of streets runs down a gentle slope from **Clapham Common South Side** to **Abbeville Rd**, then on up again towards Clapham Park. The clutch of shops at the junction of **Abbeville Rd** and **Narbonne Avenue** was dignified by '80s estate agents with the name 'Abbeville Village'. Here life has followed artifice, and what was a humdrum little suburban parade is now a neighbourhood, with its own night life, designer shops, restaurants and wine bar – even a village fair. It is a family area undergoing a positive baby boom: nursery schools abound. It is also impossible to park, though a residents' scheme is imminent. **Abbeville Rd** has some bigger than usual houses (5-bed, £600,000-plus), many now flats (2-bed c. £350,000). It is very busy (and now is speed-humped). There are flats above the shops in the parade and a few nice, (very) big purpose-built flats to buy or rent in Edwardian mansion blocks.

There is no way through from **Rodenhurst Rd**, which these days counts itself part of the Abbeville neighbourhood, to the next road E, Clarence Avenue in Clapham Park. This divide is architectural as well as physical: Rodenhurst Rd (except the S end) has large, popular pairs of Edwardian double-fronted houses set well back from the wide road: up to £1.25 million for these. It runs down to **Poynders Rd** – the South Circular. This has some rather depressed-looking inter-war flats (2-bed £205,000), modern town-houses and Edwardian terraces: but 12 new flats and two houses by Laing appeared in 2002. Poynders' equally busy continuation, **Cavendish Rd**, has big turn-of-the-20th-century houses.

West from **Rodenhurst Rd** is **Elms Crescent**, which is lined with late-19th-century bay-windowed terraced houses. From here to the Common stretch the uniform streets of Abbeville. Exceptions to the 2-storey-terraced rule include **Elms Rd**, which has some handsome, tall-gabled, wider-than-average, £1million-plus houses on the N side, and, up towards the common, some large 1880s houses, some detached and double-fronted. Five vast Victorian mansions at the W end are flats. The grid of parallel streets such as **Leppoc Rd** and **Narbonne Avenue** have mostly stolid, popular 4-bed family houses. The number of trees, width of road (and thus ease of parking) and distance from the tube and shops are the variables around here. The 4-bed terraceds, typical of the area, go for c. £600–650,000, but more will be asked for smarter/extended ones. **Hambalt** and **Mandalay Rds** are again mostly terraced, with quite a few purpose-built flats, which can be spotted by their pairs of front doors under a single arch. The streets S of **Narbonne Avenue** are mostly Victorian terraces, but with some post-war 3-storey flats. **Bonneville Gardens** has a few monster houses and an improving primary school.

Clapham Common South Side, by the junction with **Elms Rd**, is lined with big mid-Victorian terraces set back behind a strip of grass. These are South Kensington-like houses with pillared porches, all flats. **St Gerards Close** is a little estate of 1990s 4-storey flats. Next to **Elms Rd** is Brook House: 11 flats. Opposite, on the common itself, is the popular Windmill pub with a few tall houses behind it in **Windmill Drive**. Most are splendid flats, their turret roofs partially glazed to form big rooms with wide views, a 2-bed penthouse £450,000; though one is an entire, smart house.

Elms Rd now has a new secondary school, or rather Academy, courtesy of the Church Schools Company and Lambeth Council. Past **Crescent Lane** lies Clapham's premier street, the gated Regency enclave of **Crescent Grove.** The fine stucco crescent faces a row of grand semi-detached villas with linked coach houses: £1.5 million will buy you villa plus coach house. In the Lane itself, Laing's flats and town-houses round a gated court date from 2003. Older terraced 4-beds in the lane go for £700,000.

The old women's hospital at the S end of **South Side**, across from Clapham South tube, is becoming flats and a Tesco store, after an epic planning row. Marks & Spencer have just opened a food store, with five floors of flats above, at the top of **Balham Hill** by the tube. From here, running up the W side of the common, **Clapham Common West Side** scrapes into the SW4 postcode though its 'Between the Commons' hinterland is SW11 (see Battersea chapter). The tall, popular houses stand in their quiet road facing out over the common: traffic is deflected down **The Avenue**, part of the South Circular.

Transport Tubes: Clapham South, Clapham Common, Clapham North (zones 2/3, Northern); Oxford Circus 20 min (1 change), City 25 min, Heathrow 1 hr 10 min (2 changes). Trains: Wandsworth Rd, Clapham High St, to Victoria (9 min) and London Bridge.

Convenient for City, West End, Sloane Square. Miles from centre: 3.

Schools Local Authority: City Academy. See also Battersea, Dulwich and Streatham chapters.

SALES

Flats	S	1B	2B	3B	4B	5B
Average prices	110–165	170–260	220–400+	260–400+	–	–
Houses	2B	3B	4B	5B	6/7B	8B
Average prices	300–450+	350–650	425–650	475–1M+	700–1M+	❽

RENTAL

Flats	S	1B	2B	3B	4B	5B
Average prices	150–180	170–260	200–350	320–390	380–460	500+
Houses	2B	3B	4B	5B	6/7B	8B
Average prices	300–400	380–500	350–600	600+	–	–

The properties Many Victorian terraces. Some splendid Queen Anne, Georgian and Regency round Clapham Common, Old Town and in Crescent Grove, lots of converted flats (including good large ones) and some 20th-century flats blocks. A number of smart developments add up-scale flats and houses. Extra-large houses in The Chase, Macaulay Rd, Rodenhurst Avenue.

The market Old Town, South Side and Abbeville 'village' are well 'discovered'; latter pair attract families wanting space, Old Town has earlier properties with more character. Flat-hunters find smart new homes around fast-improving High St & Old Town. Prices drop (a bit) in N and E, but catching up fast due to 'Brixton effect'.

Among estate agents active in this area are:

- Barnard Marcus
- Bells
- Winkworth
- Hamptons
- Keatings
- Friend & Falcke
- Kinleigh Folkard & Hayward
- Bushells
- Armitage
- Haart
- Martin Barry
- John Hollingsworth
- Vanstons
- Savills

CLERKENWELL AND FINSBURY

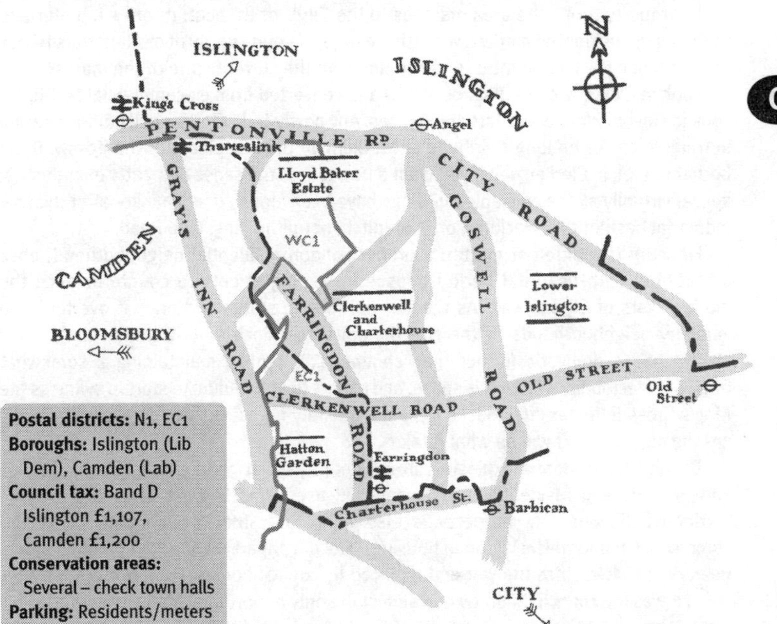

Postal districts: N1, EC1
Boroughs: Islington (Lib Dem), Camden (Lab)
Council tax: Band D Islington £1,107, Camden £1,200
Conservation areas: Several – check town halls
Parking: Residents/meters

Tell the young denizens of Clerkenwell's bars and apartments that this used to be an industrial quarter, and you will get a few quizzical looks. But the district was, until around 1990, the workplace of a good proportion of the City's 29,000-odd printers. Alongside the little print shops were metalworkers, clockmakers, warehouses. With startling suddeness they went, leaving a sad streetscape of industrial buildings no-one wanted: there are now just 2,000 people in the whole City of London working in printing. The light industries and crafts that had flourished over the previous two centuries departed as technology changed. The City offices expanded eastwards, into Docklands, not north as had been expected. Only the media business stayed put.

By that time Clerkenwell, like the City, had few residents; back in 1988 this Guide commented 'Clerkenwell and Finsbury have . . . enormous potential as a residential area: ideally situated, with a high proportion of Georgian buildings. . . .' Any homes that did appear in those days were snapped up; the problem was, very few did.

Then came the loft movement, taking its cue from similar districts in New York and transforming cold empty spaces into cool homes. The decade 1992–2002 saw around 2,500 new homes created in the areas covered by this chapter. Most homes in the first wave were carved out of those existing buildings; next, developers built afresh on derelict sites. The last two years have seen only a few new schemes, all on the fringes of the area. The catalyst for all this was a switch in planning policy. Islington Council finally acknowledged that the commercial space in the area was largely redundant; the planners at last relaxed the usage conditions.

Now, Clerkenwell is one of the smartest places to own a London flat, or (until the last year or two) to start a new restaurant. A once-proud London neighbourhood has been reborn and is a good place to live, work and relax once more. Its boundaries have been stretched by eager estate agents ever east and north, almost obliterating the old London borough of Finsbury and colonizing forgotten corners like St Luke's and the area round Old Street.

In property terms the area marches to the City's drum-beat. It forms a hinterland to the City's residential market, with (these days) a good supply of modern flats to buy and rent: see the City chapter for a run-down on the current state of the market.

Look in Clerkenwell for flats both new and converted from ex-commercial buildings. Look in Finsbury for period flats and houses. Any newly-built Clerkenwell homes now are in fringe areas or on long-moribund sites, filling in the last pieces of the jigsaw. Don't bother to look in Clerkenwell if you want a new loft, in the sense of a gritty ex-industrial space; virtually all the available buildings have been 'done'. If you hanker after the true industrial aesthetic try Hackney, or Shoreditch, or up the Kingsland Road.

Finsbury is a different matter: a proper London residential neighbourhood, once and future; with beautiful period houses in sloping streets to counterbalance the modern flats of Clerkenwell. As Clerkenwell rose in status and price it overtook the Finsbury neighbourhoods to the N – though these since early-Victorian times have always had a domestic (rather than commercial), profile, maintaining a somewhat fragile respectability. Watch this space, and expect the pendulum to start to swing as the King's Cross Eurostar effect kicks in; family-friendly infrastructure (good local schools are the obvious lack) will be what it takes. . . .

Despite the residential explosion, streets here are a rich mixture of architectural styles and periods, and residential and commercial uses: this is what gives the area its distinctive flavour. The property is also a mixture: there's Georgian, converted commercial, modern. The Victorian housing – Finsbury apart – was either bombed or has been demolished since the war and replaced by council homes. For four decades after 1945, it was the council that provided almost the only opportunity for living in this lovely, historic corner of London: most tenants lived there all their lives, often working in the printing trade; this led to a continuity in the population which has now, sadly, all but gone. Clerkenwell also had a name as London's 'Little Italy', with a population – largely devoted to the catering business – centred around St Peter's Church in **Saffron Hill**.

The real point about Clerkenwell is its history. It has been urban since the Middle Ages; monasteries, mansions, churches, almshouses, sober Georgian merchant homes, Victorian slums and distilleries succeeding one another. Some roads retain their medieval flavour still, twisting and turning like snakes and ladders on a board. Clerkenwell and its sub-zones Farringdon and Charterhouse are districts of narrow, dense streets, with concealed alleys and arches. There is a high percentage of Georgian; many other buildings have been given post-modern spruce-ups – some homes have had two renovations in a dozen years.

A quick guide to Clerkenwell lofts is their date: the first scheme came in 1992 with a real wave from 1994. The precedent was the Docklands warehouse boom of a decade before; but since the Docks had caught a bad cold when the market crashed in 1989, these new conversions looked to Manhattan's 'loft apartments' for a new gloss. But the point is that Clerkenwell values have risen so high that now so-called 'lofts' will really be smart, smallish flats with some exposed brickwork.The newest make only a passing stylistic reference to the loft aesthetic. 'Proper lofts' are much in demand and priced accordingly.

Would-be loft-dwellers now look E to the area between **Old St, Goswell Rd** and the **City Rd**: the live/work concept has caught on in this quarter. Photographers, designers, artists and the like all find it an attractive way of life. But they have to be successful ones.

One point: don't think bedrooms for all these flats, think square feet. Agents, and buyers, give prominence to the gross area of a flat, and monitor values in £ per sq ft (psf). Hurford Salvi Carr have tracked the market in EC1 since it began (which in real terms was 1994); they reckon that the December 2004 figure was £380 psf, against £425 psf in July 2002 (it started at £150 psf in '94).

So – to define the area: it lies N of the City and **Fleet St**, E of the **Gray's Inn Rd**, St Pancras and Bloomsbury, S of **City Rd** and the Angel – close to both West and East Ends, 5–10 min from the City, and close to major stations: convenient, then, for just about everywhere. Despite a scattering of squares and parks, it remains essentially urban. This is the place for restaurants – some of the best in London are here – bars and general buzz . . . the people who work here tend to party rather than go home to the family (just as well: this is not a schools area), and the loft-dwellers join them.

The area divides into four neighbourhoods. In the middle is Clerkenwell (which includes Farringdon and Charterhouse). Over to the E is Lower Islington, better known now as City Rd/Old St or – the latest coining – 'St Luke's'. In the W, towards Holborn, is Hatton Garden. Finally, to the N is Finsbury centred around the Lloyd Baker estate. These are all approximations; there are few definitive boundaries, and no clear consensus among inhabitants, much less estate agents, as to what to call where. Finsbury, once the accepted local name, is easily confused with Finsbury Park: it would be clearer to call that 'Finsbury's Park' – it was laid out for the people of Finsbury in what was then open land a couple of miles N. It was a separate borough from 1900 to 1965, when Islington took over (there is, too, a confusing tendency among agents and developers to use the name 'Islington' for everything in that borough). The EC1 postcode covers the area quite neatly.

Lower Islington, between the **City Rd** and **Goswell Rd**, holds almost exclusively council-built housing, with a large number of tall '60s-style tower blocks with 20-plus floors. Some lower-rise housing occurs towards the Clerkenwell border and in the N towards the Angel, and there is a lot of commercial property, some of which is being converted to residential, and university buildings.

On the N edge of the area lies the late-Georgian Lloyd Baker estate, the similar New River Estate and a swathe to the E of **Rosebery Avenue** and W of Lower Islington generally referred to as 'North Clerkenwell'. The architecture is mainly Georgian, mixed with some modern high-rises, a little commercial and a high proportion of council housing. Still not as fashionable as Islington proper, but getting there: this is the place to look for a family home. It's conveniently close to Sadler's Wells Theatre and the other amenities of Islington.

Hatton Garden is traditionally the centre of London's jewellery trade – especially diamonds. It's next door to Holborn, and so has a distinctly upmarket, big-business feel; streets are wider and less medieval in appearance. The surviving Georgian houses have been joined by a rash of new-build and converted apartments.

Clerkenwell has shot, since the late '80s, from cheapest to priciest neighbourhood, overtaking the Smithfield and Barbican borders and the Lloyd Baker estate. In the last-named, prices are still below those in Islington. If you want to buy more cheaply, try the King's Cross (see Bloomsbury chapter) borders – especially in the streets with heavy traffic such as **King's Cross Rd** or those near railway lines. Or search the Lower Islington quarter for ex-local authority flats (some blocks have been expensively spruced up) and homes in their shadows.

Clerkenwell and Charterhouse

New homes and new businesses replace the crafts and light industry of a generation ago. Design, media, computing and advertising businesses have migrated from Soho and the West End – though not all by any means survived the transplant. Restaurants, bars and cafés have opened (and in some cases closed). Fashion and jewellery are well in evidence, the latter continuing Clerkenwell's craft traditions, nurtured during lean years by dedicated locals who kept low-rent workshops going.

Clerkenwell centres around charming, if not green, **Clerkenwell Green** and the surrounding small streets. The very busy **Clerkenwell Rd** cuts straight through the neighbourhood from W–E, and **Farringdon Rd** runs N–S. To begin from the N, from the crossroads of **Rosebery Avenue** and **Farringdon Rd**, the area W up to **Calthorpe St** is on the NW boundary of central Clerkenwell and houses a variety of commercial buildings, including the old *Times* newspaper building in Coley St and Gough St, and the vast Mount Pleasant Post Office, which dominates Farringdon Rd and the top of Mount Pleasant. Continuing S down **Rosebery Avenue** there are Victorian commercial buildings and some mansion flats with shops beneath, followed by Rosebery Square Buildings, a large and refurbished Victorian working men's flats development that dominates both sides of the street as it goes to join the Clerkenwell Rd.

C

The triangle between **Clerkenwell Rd** and **Rosebery Avenue** is typical Clerkenwell, with a warren of narrow, densely-packed streets running higgledy piggledy, their names betraying their medieval trade origins: **Herbal Hill, Vine Hill, Baker's Row**. The architecture is in the main Georgian or early-Victorian, and uses have traditionally been largely commercial – though now four modern blocks in **Topham St** and **Warner St** provide some flats as well as shops and offices. The Herbal Hill apartments, 1–10 **Summers St** and the Warner Building were among the early conversions and provide some of the most expensive flats in the district. The Ziggurat Building in **Saffron Hill** has sought-after 'true' lofts, which seem to be holding their recent price at around the £440psf level. Next door at 55 Saffron Hill 20 new flats date from late 2002. Asking prices in **Summers St** last winter were around the £465psf mark.

This part of Clerkenwell ends at **Farringdon Rd**, which completes the triangle in the E: here a converted cheese factory is next in line for development (but not quite yet). On the corner with **Clerkenwell Rd** is a 1994 flats block that was planned as offices but which switched uses during construction.

Just E of the Farringdon Rd and the railway in its deep cutting is **Clerkenwell Green**. This is the centre of old Clerkenwell, gathering place for the Peasants' Revolt and now home to the Karl Marx Library. The heart of the area – a sloping, paved and tree'd square rather than a green – is a pleasant jumble of Victorian, Georgian and modern architecture, with its bars, upmarket restaurants, pubs and posh design studios. . . a decidedly prosperous atmosphere. Some homes too: distinctive No. 8 has flats, while next door is a modernist 6-storey, 3-bed, 1-garage house round a light-well: much swooned over by architects.

The two main streets of central Clerkenwell are **Clerkenwell Close**, running NW from the Green, and **Sekforde St** running NE. **Clerkenwell Close** retains some small Georgian terraced houses; to the left is a recent development by Islington Council, with shops below and 28 flats above, to the right is the imposing Georgian St James's Church, with its spire and surrounding small garden. At the end of the Close are the distinctive yellow-and-white-brick Peabody flats, which go on round into **Pear Tree Court**. No. 1 Pear Tree Court is a modern block of 18 flats, some with work-spaces. To the E, Clerkenwell Close twists round to meet **Bowling Green Lane** and **Corporation Row** – both mainly commercial with the odd flat; after this Clerkenwell Close becomes **Rosoman St**. Past Northampton Row is an adventure playground, followed by the gardens of **Rosoman Place** on the left; opposite is a high tower block.

Along Rosoman St the turning to the left is **Exmouth Market**, a pedestrian street smartened up with restaurants and cafés – even a designer jewellers – and a continental farmers' market at weekends. Exmouth Market is fast losing its Victorian pubs (the London Spa is now six 1-beds while the 1870s Penny Black is five 1- and 2-beds) but has gained a Starbucks and a Pizza Express. Is this progress? Back down on **Farringdon Rd**, there are 34 new flats at the junction with Bowling Green Lane. Opposite, also on Farringdon Rd, is a striking block of 10 new flats.

Sekforde St, one of Clerkenwell's finest streets, runs NE from **Clerkenwell Green.** It is made up of 2- and 3-storey Regency terraces, the middle portion of which have balconies. Some are flats, with a few still as whole houses. Residential and commercial uses mingle, with a former bank now stylishly changed into a single, 7,000sq ft, house.

Towards St John St, **Woodbridge St** to the N has 3-storey Georgian terraces currently overlooking a school building – which is about to be demolished and replaced with flats (Laing). Between **Sekforde** and **St John Sts** is Bellway's St Paul's Square: a big complex of flats behind a listed facade (of an old debtors' prison, actually). Forking to the N from Sekforde St is **St James's Walk**: on one side a mixture of Georgian homes and Victorian commercial buildings; on the other a children's playground and the garden surrounding St James's Church. The originally fine network of medieval streets that made up the middle of this area has now been obliterated, but it is still a very pleasing, gently sloping corner, bordered by **Sans Walk** in the N and **Clerkenwell Close** in the W. A big, peaceful walled square in **Sans Walk** is taken up by an old 1890s school (with the remains of an older prison in the basement. . .) which got the loft treatment in 2001: 46 flats by Persimmon – a lovely corner, but reconstruction work had to be undertaken after problems with the conversion. On **St John St**, the former Scholl shoe factory is now the Paramount Building: more flats (c. £500 psf being asked last winter).

East of St John St across to **Goswell Rd**, bounded on the S by **Clerkenwell Rd**, is an eight-acre block of property called the Clerkenwell Estate. This was owned by the Governors of Sutton Hospital for 350 years until 1995, when they sold to Bee Bee Developments. The new landlords, working with Islington Council, have drawn up a long-term plan to improve and develop the estate. Smart new homes and commercial spaces are appearing in roads like **Gee St**, **Goswell Rd** and **Great Sutton St**. A site on the corner of Great Sutton St and **Clerkenwell Rd** still awaits development.

An old print works at 9A **Dallington St** has been split into 10 flats, two large 2-storey live/work units – and a new 4th floor, which was to have been a pair of penthouses but which an interior designer snapped up before the ink was dry on the plans. No. 10 Dallington St is now another 14 flats: asking £540,000 for 1,000 sq ft. On the corner of **St John St** and **Compton St**, a small scheme of four flats and a live/work house dates from 2000. Compton St has 14 new-build flats.

Charterhouse and Farringdon

The area S of **Clerkenwell Rd** down to **Charterhouse St** and W to **Farringdon St** is also Clerkenwell, although the streets to the E of **St John St** across to **Aldersgate** are more commonly termed Charterhouse. There are virtually no houses, what homes there are being small flats and commercial conversions. The Charterhouse, which gives this corner its name, was a medieval Carthusian monastery: the site of it is located on the corner of St John St and Charterhouse St and stretches back to the Clerkenwell Rd. Used since 1933 by St Bart's Medical School, it is still a very special corner that mixes the Elizabethan with the utilitarian around a central park with plane trees, with tall commercial property in the W and down Charterhouse Mews.

Charterhouse Square – one of London's last private, gated squares – has some homes: see Smithfield, in the City chapter. To the E, Charterhouse Square becomes **Carthusian St**, with the occasional small flats block and a recent 10-flats scheme by Berkeley. Roads to the N off Aldersgate are solidly commercial.

To the W, off **St John St**, roads continue in a familiar Clerkenwell pattern, though a little more orderly. This is the site of the medieval Priory of St John, of which only the gatehouse survives. The lower end of **St John St** used to be largely commercial with many tall Victorian and Georgian buildings, some adapted in a post-modern style to provide posh office space close to the City, some concealing flats. Large chunks of the street have been or are being converted into homes, and quite a few of the ground floors have become restaurants. **St John Square** has an office building which is to be replaced by homes: Knight's Court is to provide 18 flats, with 1-beds (677 sq ft) at £360,000, 2-beds (1,033 sq ft) £540,000.

In what could well be Clerkenwell's last big homes scheme, the four-acre site of the old gin distillery (more recently a car park) on **St John St** has been developed by Berkeley Homes as 'The Edge'. It has 213 flats, seven houses and commercial/retail space which, it's hoped, will add to local amenities (a Sainsbury's has been promised for years, but there's still no sign of it). The first phase of 50 flats was sold off-plan to South African investors in 2001 at around £435 psf. No. 81 St John St was new in 2002: seven flats. Next-door is an empty site where permission is sought for a 7-storey block to hold 75 flats for sale plus Affordable Homes. Parallel to St John St is **St John's Lane**, which terminates in the N at St John's Gate, a stone arch dating from 1504 and the original entrance to the Grand Priory of St John of Jerusalem.

Britton St to the W runs parallel to St John's Lane, with mainly 4-storey Georgian and Victorian commercial, plus some recent flats. Next door is Persimmon's Clerkenwell Central: 20 warehouse apartments, five houses and 28 new-build flats (1-bed £280,000 last winter) on the **Turnmill St** frontage (facing the railway cutting). **Brisset St** has The Red House, converted into large, work-space flats. City Piazza by Fairbriar (2000) has 1- and 2-bed flats around a courtyard. On **Clerkenwell Rd** 'The Apartments' has nine architecty flats above the 3-floor Vitra furniture showroom.

Between **Benjamin St** and **Cowcross St** Exchange Place, a big hotel/offices/100 flats scheme completed in 2000, has short-let apartments in Zinc House. Further down, at the corner of Benjamin St is tiny St John's Garden; to the S is **Eagle Court** which joins Britton St to St John's Lane: this is mainly modern commercial, but has one 3-storey Georgian mews house. **Cowcross St**, which has been tidied up (Starbucks, Pizza Express, Books Etc. . .), holds Farringdon Station, the tube and train link for the area. It has been expanded, being on the N–S Thameslink rail line.

Charterhouse St runs E–W, forming the southernmost boundary of the area, passing behind Smithfield Market and across the Farringdon Rd divide on its way to Holborn Circus. The City's boundary runs along it: see also City and Fringes chapter.

Hatton Garden

The area to the N of **Holborn** and W of **Farringdon Rd** is Hatton Garden, traditionally (and still) the home of the diamond business. Its streets are wider, less densely packed and more logical in layout than Clerkenwell's. **Hatton Garden** itself leads N from **Holborn Circus**, and is a mixture of modern office blocks and smaller Georgian and Victorian terraces. It houses the best jewellers of the area (but, despite the verdant name, no greenery).

The district to the E has some smart recent flats, such as the Ziggurat and Da Vinci buildings in **Saffron Hill** (see above). **Viaduct Buildings**, a cul-de-sac (its entrance is at the corner of Charterhouse St and Saffron Hill), has a 4-storey flats block refurbished in post-modern style (including the De Beers Company's flats). Camden Council, whose patch this is, resists any further change of use to homes here.

To the W of Leather Lane, **Dorrington** and **Beauchamp Sts** form a quiet square with plane trees: mainly commercial but with a row of modern maisonettes at the end. **Leather Lane** itself is the site of the famous market, which runs down the length of the street between Georgian terraces with shops below. In **Baldwins Gardens** the Beeching Building is now lofts. Further W, off the **Gray's Inn Rd**, is Brookes Court, a 1980s 3-storey maisonette development in dark-brown brick, facing gardens. South of **Clerkenwell Rd** down to **Verulam St** is the council's Bourne Estate – quiet, '30s-style 5-storey flats entered by arches from the surrounding roads, in which many of the solid Victorian homes are now privately owned. Other good-quality council-built blocks are Vesage Court in **Leather Lane** and Jeygrove Court in **Hatton Garden**.

Old Street/Lower Islington (St Luke's)

The Old St roundabout is the most easterly point of this area; from it **City Rd** runs NW and **Old St** SW. The area in the fork between the two is sometimes dubbed 'Lower Islington' (the borough, not the area): this is almost exclusively modern council-built housing, mixed with some commercial and university property. Old commercial space is still to be found here, though it's mostly snapped up by developers moving E from Clerkenwell. There's a sensible move by some to revive the old name St Luke's for this quarter: this is the parish centred around the old Hawksmoor church on Old St – restored, at the cost of £18 million, as an education centre for the London Symphony Orchestra.

Bath St runs N–S: at the Old St end, modern low-rise maisonettes extend W towards **Lizard St**. Continuing N, you enter the council-built St Luke's Estate, a mix of tower blocks of between 16 and 20 storeys and low-rise, including roads to the E and W: **Peerless St**, **Galway St**, **Radnor St**, **Mora St** and the lower portion of **Lever St**. Some homes (especially in the later, 4-storey brick blocks) are now privately owned, with 2- and 3-bed flats frequently on the market. The old Lord Nelson pub in **Mora St** is now four live-work units and three flats. At the **City Rd/Bath St** junction, City Approach is a new flats scheme. Some years ago the Old St fire station was turned into studios and 1-bed flats: it also houses a restaurant. Turning W along **Lever St** (yet another pub gone, replaced by yet another 14 flats), roads to the N are mainly commercial. To the E of **Macclesfield Rd**, a successful development of derelict land has brought a business centre and several conversions, including the loft apartments of No. 1 **Dingley Place** carved out of a former coffee warehouse. Next door are 14 (surprising, that) rare shell-finish lofts in an old print works. Further W, **King Square** has 4- and 6-storey blocks, with a shopping precinct and a large rose garden. Note: in case you're wondering, 14 flats (or less) is the magic number that allows developers to avoid having to provide any social housing.

To the S of Lever St are 14(!) new lofts in among the commercial property in **Ironmonger Row**, followed by the Turkish baths and swimming pools, and more offices in **Europa Place**, at the back of which is a 5-storey tenement building. Further S past Norman St lies a park and the Finsbury Leisure Centre; this is bordered by **Mitchell St** which, together with **Bartholomew Square**, runs W–E. Both are commercial, although the streets at right angles to them off to Old St are residential, including the refurbished tenement block in **Anchor Yard** and the 3-storey Georgian terraces in **Helmet Row** (partly, including the old vicarage, offices). St Luke's View in **Bartholomew Square** has seven modern flats. Across Old St to the S, an old bedding factory in **Garrett St** is now 19 lofts. Close by is the 10ft wide, 7-storey 'Glasshouse' in **Golden Lane** which sold in 2002 for £875,000. On **Old St** itself, No. 68 has eight new 2-bed flats: £435,000 for 1,037sq ft.

Goswell Rd, a main through-route to the W, is changing, with new bars and restaurants appearing. There's been a string of blocks of 'loft-style' flats here in the last five years. Among the latest is 'Vantage', with six 1- and 2-beds (three left last winter, from £250,000). Other homes here include the Triangle development – 5-storeyed local authority-built homes on the corner of **Percival St**. The rest of the housing is mainly Victorian and Georgian terraces with a multitude of small shops – including some smart new ones – on the ground floor.

To the E of Goswell Rd, running like the rungs of a ladder, are **Seward St**, **Pear Tree St**, **Bastwick St** and **Gee St**, all of which have commercial premises of between three and five storeys and a growing number of homes. The Persimmon-built block in **Seward St** has 38 1- and 2-bed flats. **Gee St** also has Parmoor Court, a 12-floor tower block, plus a few houses and a large City University hall of residence. Fourteen new-build 'loft-style' flats, 'Pietra Lara' (since you ask, it's the limestone they used on the floor) in **Pear Tree St**, were priced at launch in mid-'02 at a startling £550 psf, but those still on offer last winter were around £465 psf. On Bastwick St, No. 26 has 12 smart modern flats, 1- and 2-bed, with a 2-bed offered at £425,000 (876 sq ft).

To the W of Goswell Rd, street patterns are a little more diverse. **Compton St** has a row of low Georgian terraced homes to the S, and an 8-storey tower block to the N. Running at a diagonal to Compton is **Cyrus St**, which has low '30s-style tenement

blocks at the Compton St end. The Percival Estate continues on the other side of **Percival St** with Harold Laski House, and tower blocks continue on both sides ending at College Heights on the corner of **St John St.**

The end of Goswell Rd forms an acute angle with City Rd. Several big commercial users have left this corner, to be slowly replaced by homes (see Islington chapter) and small office schemes. **Gard St** and **Masons Place** to the S, and **Pickard St** to the N, have large '60s tower blocks to flamboyant heights. Continuing N, **Hall St** has the 25-storey Peregrine House. The area to the W up to the Angel is mostly commercial. **City Rd**, the busy through-route, is mainly 3- and 4-storey Georgian terraces, set back from the road on both sides with shops and offices (though also with two new homes schemes just finished: one contemporary, one trad) down to Nelsons Terrace; from here the height drops dramatically, the standard becomes more uneven and begins to include modern developments. One such is a dozen flats on the N side at the junction with Haverstock St. Some of the **City Rd** Georgian terraced houses are reverting to homes.

Finsbury, the Lloyd Baker estate and North Clerkenwell

South across the **Pentonville Rd** from Islington, this neighbourhood lies between the top end of **St John St** and **Rosebery Avenue** to the E and S, and **King's Cross Rd** and **Penton Rise** in the W. It includes two distinctive enclaves of early 19th-century houses, the Lloyd Baker and New River estates, plus the **New River Head** complex where offices and other buildings have become expensive homes.

From the Angel tube, **St John St** runs N–S. Modern and Victorian commercial buildings soon give way to flat-fronted Georgian terraces on both sides. Past the Chadwell St junction is a row of little shops, early gentrified. More Georgiana in tiny **Owens Row**, where gracious houses have been painstakingly restored. Leafy **Rosebery Avenue**, which slopes SW taking traffic to and from the West End, has the rebuilt Sadler's Wells Theatre on the N side and some fine Georgian terraces on the S, which also command good prices.

Further down, past the theatre, is the imposing **New River Head Building.** This important (indeed, historic) building has now become an enviable enclave of flats by St James's Homes. The splendid boardroom makes a superb dining room – available to all the flats. Homes can be had in this big complex in a range of buildings, including the old offices, converted 1920s laboratories and stores, and new-build. Resale prices are static, as last year: around £245,000 for 1-beds, £315,000-plus for 2-beds.

Rosebery Avenue continues in a mixture of commercial buildings and Victorian workmen's flats; at the intersection with **Rosoman St** is the old Finsbury town hall with its distinctive stained-glass and wrought-iron porch: ambitious plans for a part-homes development are in limbo after developers Berkeley and the council could not agree terms. Near the Farringdon Rd junction, a large mixed development called Rosebery Court has light-industrial workshop space, offices and a modern block of 27 flats at the corner of Rosebery Avenue and **Coldbath Square.**

Chadwell St runs from St John St into the centre of the New River Estate, which dates from the 1820s. The street has a modern Georgian-style mews development through an arch on the right; the rest is genuine Georgian terraces that open out into the vast **Myddleton Square** with its central garden and church, surrounded on all sides by tall Georgian homes – one of the finest squares in North London. The roads running off to the W – **River St, Inglebert St** and **Mylne St** – are fine, wide streets with terraces of large houses (a 5-bed in Mylne was £1.2 million last winter). **Claremont Square**, which completes a right angle with **Amwell St**, is particularly imposing. It runs N–S to join **St John St**, and has Georgian terraces of varying sizes and states of repair, and a number of small shops.

Amwell St marks the boundary between the New River and Lloyd Baker estates. The Lloyd Baker estate was originally built by the eponymous family from 1819–25, and was partly sold to Islington Council on the death of Miss Lloyd Baker in 1975; Islington still owns a lot of the property. It consists mainly of handsome, Georgian flat-fronted brick terraces, retaining its charm with its fine squares with their central gardens. Streets are wider here and houses larger, generally 3/4-bed houses and 2-bed flats.

Three roads parallel each other W from Amwell St. First is **Great Percy St**: tall Georgian terraces, four storeys with first-floor balconies. The road is steep and drops sharply just before Percy Circus, giving a superb view to the W over London. **Percy Circus** is a fine square (or rather circle) with a park in the centre, two-thirds encircled by a long crescent of terraces. But it is sadly marred by the last third, which is a low-level flats block. One site, a car park for 50 years since the Blitz, has been redeveloped as homes in a partnership between Try Homes and Peabody Trust.

Parallel to Great Percy St, Wharton St and Lloyd Baker St converge at **Lloyd Square.** This is the heart of the estate, with a railed garden in the centre, a fine view across to the BT Tower and handsome Georgian houses – big double-fronted ones, measuring 2,500sq ft and priced (as one was last winter) at c. £1.5 million. The style continues down **Wharton St** (both sides) and **Lloyd Baker St**; then the estate peters out NW of Rosebery Avenue with a welter of large Victorian and Edwardian tenements and modern commercial and residential blocks – until **Wilmington Square** and **Tysoe St**, which border on Rosebery Avenue and mark the limit of the area. **Wilmington** is the last fine period square, with tall, 5-storey Georgian terraces behind a raised pavement and a large central garden. **Tysoe St** has smaller and slightly untidier terraces. A new block in **Margery St** offers 2-bed flats. Close by in **Amwell St** two warehouses are now 10 flats, while the 43 recent flats of 'West City One' are on the corner with **Margery St.**

The triangle E of **Rosebery Avenue** across to **Goswell Rd**, N of **Skinner** and **Percival Sts**, is not part of the Lloyd Baker estate but has some similar features. West of St John St is predominantly council tower blocks: **Gloucester Way** has Michael Cliffe House – 23-storeys – and it's on stilts. **Myddleton St** is the only period street, with neat Georgian houses and a handful of tidy shops at the bottom. Nine loft apartments, carved out of a Victorian warehouse, have appeared in **Whiskin St**: £838,000 for a 2-bed (865sq ft). **Lloyd's Row** has another large tower block. The point where it joins St John St also marks the end of the Georgian terraces; these are replaced to the S by more modern commercial and academic buildings. Ex-airline offices here are now 14 flats called St John's Point.

The last part of North Clerkenwell is enclosed by **St John St** and **Goswell Rd** as they diverge away from the Angel, making a triangle bounded by **Percival St** in the S. The whole of this area is very mixed. In the S, on the corner of **St John St** and **Percival St**, is the 4-storey College Heights development. Originally an old warehouse, it was stylishly refurbished in the late '80s into a 24-flat complex with gym and car park. More recent schemes include Pattern House, which is known as the Ingersoll Building.

Within the triangle, forming a circle with roads radiating off it, is **Northampton Square** and the central core of the City University. The quiet square, with a garden and folly in the centre, is bounded on the N by the 7-storey university complex and on the other side by a crescent of 4-storey Georgian terraces with first-floor balconies: one of these houses was £875,000 last winter. SW of the Square is the council-built Brunswick Close Estate, where 2-bed flats in Emberton Court, a recently-refurbished

13-storey slab block, represent the cheaper end of the flats market. The streets leading off to the E, **Ashby St** and **Sebastian St**, are also mainly Georgian terraces. Where Sebastian St meets **Northampton Square**, an ex-factory/warehouse has been converted into four 2-bed, 2-bath flats. **Spencer St** to the N has anonymous university buildings on one side and **Earlstoke St** council estate on the other.

Rawstorne St up to **Friend St** is a mixture of low modern mews developments, ex-council homes and late-Georgian, 3-bed, half-million-pound terraces. The last remaining streets up to the Angel, beyond which lies Islington, are mostly commercial, but with a couple of big new flats schemes detailed in the Islington chapter.

Transport Tubes: Angel (zone 1, Northern), Farringdon (zone 1, Circle, Metropolitan). From Angel: Oxford Circus 10 min (1 change), City 6 min, Heathrow 1 hr 10 min (1 change). Trains: Farringdon (Moorgate 10 min and Thameslink to Gatwick and Luton).

Convenient for The City and West End, stations. Miles from centre: 1.5.

Schools Local Authority: Central Foundation (b). Private: City of London Schools (b) (g).

SALES

Flats	S	1B	2B	3B	4B	5B
Average prices	160–180	200–310	280–400	420–900	–	–
Houses	2B	3B	4B	5B	6/7B	8B
Average prices	350–480	450–700	650–1.2M	800–1.3M	–	–

RENTAL

Flats	S	1B	2B	3B	4B	5B
Average prices	170–210	220–320	300–500	450–550	–	–
Houses	2B	3B	4B	5B	6/7B	8B
Average prices	375–500	400–800	800–1300	1000–1500	–	–

The properties In Finsbury, handsome Georgian, Regency and Victorian houses; everywhere, loft conversions of offices/factories/warehouses, new flats blocks (many apeing the lofts), a few mews houses and council- and housing trust-built flats.

The market Steady demand for the biggest (earliest) lofts, and new-build. Newer flats, increasingly stylish, have less space for the money. If priced out of the heart of Clerkenwell look E and N. Finsbury – traditional but solid – looks best value now. New-build prices look optimistic this year: compare with the local resale market and negotiate hard, but homes in this crowded corner still scarce.

Among estate agents active in this area are:

- Hurford Salvi Carr
- Urban Spaces
- Hamptons
- Stirling Ackroyd
- Daniel Watney
- Bridge Estates
- Frank Harris
- Currell
- Thomson Currie

CRICKLEWOOD

Postal districts: NW2
Boroughs: Barnet (Con), Brent (Lab)
Council tax: Band D Barnet £1,214, Brent £1,141
Conservation areas: Hermitage Terrace
Parking: residents' scheme either side of Broadway

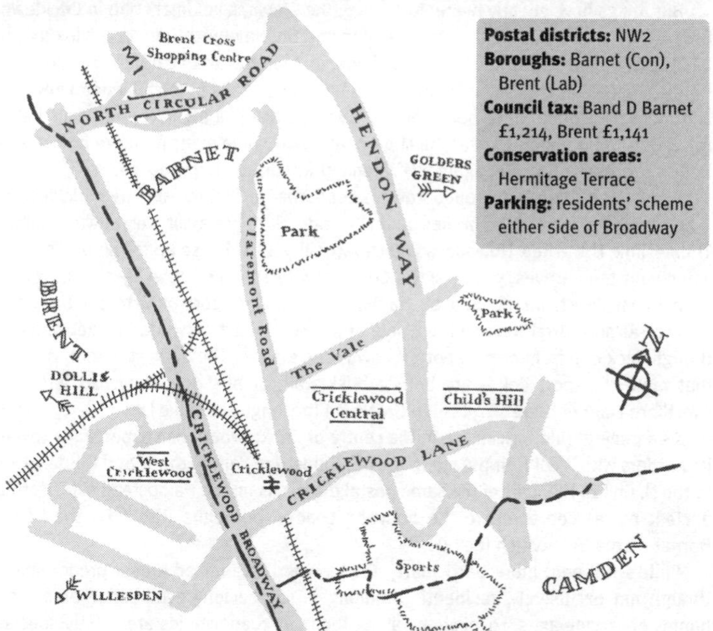

This is where people look when they've outgrown their West Hampstead flatlet or Queen's Park cottage and want more space for their money. Some move on when the kids grow to school age, others settle down to enjoy affordable family homes with a credible-sounding postcode just three and a half miles from Marble Arch.

Traditionally, Cricklewood's been that sort of place: a bit of a staging post, both geographically – rail, roads, motorways (the end of the M1 is nigh) and freight depots loom large in its history and topography – and as a roost for a few years. But there are settled communities here, some of them rather select and very discreet (just look at the Hocroft Estate). But there are also plenty of rented flats – and flats to buy a little more within the reach of ordinary incomes. Estate agents like to upgrade Cricklewood (and its property prices) to 'Hampstead borders', 'West Heath estate', even solidly respectable Golders Green or Willesden Green. Incomers tend not to admit to living in Cricklewood.

But one day . . . might the railway, the spread of which began the blurring of London's original hamlets, reinstate the name of Cricklewood? The broad framework is still being discussed for North London's most massive, 15-year scheme, which will encompass the railway and its adjoining land. The multimillion-pound development of the 'Cricklewood Brent Cross and West Hendon Development Area' will create a whole new town centre – and a new High St, to cross the North Circular via a bridge – out of the vast swathe of disused sidings W of **Claremont Rd**, and on N: 7,000 new homes, no less, about a third of them Affordable, plus offices, shops, hotels, squares, a park, leisure and its own train station – and a Rapid Transport System to run right through to Hendon Central tube, via the shopping mecca of Brent Cross. This most exciting scheme may make Cricklewood a destination, not a place that's merely easy to get out of to almost anywhere else.

The long shadow of the St Pancras/King's Cross transport hub – Eurostar's London terminus from 2007 – reaches as far out as West Hampstead station, which is only one stop away from Cricklewood. An amalgamation of the three West Hampstead stations will become a major hub, linking also to Heathrow and all the Thameslink destinations.

But things have already begun to change: the Crown, a landmark pub in **Cricklewood Broadway**, these days hosts comedy nights and Sunday-lunchtime jazz. A luxury hotel has just completed next door, with 200 beds, restaurants and health club to add to the Holmes Place outpost, shops, hairdressers and beauticians in **Cricklewood Lane**. More and more developers have been seen: **Draycott Close** is a big cache of smart flats by Fairview off **Claremont Rd** near the station. And now come plans for more homes at the Hendon Football Club site, again off Claremont Road: watch this space. . . .

Road access both in and out of town is good: the North Circular marks Cricklewood's N borders; Junction 1 of the M1 lies on the far side. But once again the railway, thanks to Thameslink, is the key. Nowadays you can wheel your suitcase up to the platform and, when your train arrives, get to King's Cross, or City Thameslink, in 15–16 min. You can even travel direct, unimpeded by traffic, N to Luton Airport or S to South London, Gatwick Airport, Brighton and the whole of the South-East network. Cricklewood does, though, lack one form of transport: its own tube station. The nearest – until they build that rapid transport link – are both a brisk walk or bus ride away: Golders Green (Northern Line) or there's Willesden Green, on the magical Jubilee Line.

As a general rule, prices sag in the centre of Cricklewood, rise expectantly towards its borders with West Hampstead to the SE, Gladstone Park to the W and Golders Green to the N. Child's Hill, part of the same postal district, is on the Hampstead side. Both are ancient places compared to the *nouveau* London boroughs (Brent on the W side, Barnet on the E) in which they lie.

Child's Hill and, more particularly, Cricklewood, are mixed areas: predominantly, though not exclusively, residential. Infilling in such a long-established area means homes of varying ages. Local shops along the main road arteries are mostly specialist and mini-markets: Brent Cross, conveniently a mile or so up the road, throws a large (and expanding) shadow. A shopping centre opened in **Cricklewood Lane** in 1991, which added a little more convenience.

The grip of the past lingers in the main roads, such as **Cricklewood Lane** (formerly Child's Hill Lane) and **Cricklewood Broadway**, part of Roman Watling St. Ancient rights of way are still here, but are now secluded footpaths between the houses. People have lived, and worked, here (often catering for their more prosperous neighbours in Hampstead or Central London) for centuries: traditionally running laundries, storing furniture, driving carriages and repairing cars. Many of these industries have gradually succumbed to development, as big builders have squeezed homes onto every available site. That said, there's still a good amount of open space – not only in gardens but also in local parks, playing fields, sports grounds and municipal playgrounds, offering breathing-space for relaxation and exercise. And Hampstead Heath is not far. . . .

The area developed in recognizable spurts. The opening of Cricklewood station in 1868 resulted in a rash of Victorian brick villas in **Claremont Rd** and **Cricklewood Lane** alongside, and in groups of streets opposite called, misleadingly, after the trees of the forest (to fit into the Wood of the Crickles?). **Hendon Way** to the E followed in the years between the wars: a bypass, precursor to the roads leading northwards – now the M1. Ribbon development spread alongside: semi-detached houses with garages for the new motor age. Council housing from those years, and post-1945, began to appear on the market as tenants cashed in on their 'Right to Buy' in the late '80s, broadening the spread of homes. (Some ex-council homes are now downright desirable – others well-nigh unmortgageable.) Then came the estates, large and small, by the mass-market builders in the '80s, '90s and onwards.

Churches of various denominations range from St Agnes' Catholic Church and Primary School in **Cricklewood Lane**, to a Mosque and Islamic Centre that stretches from **Chichele Rd** to **Howard Rd.** There are two local libraries, half a dozen primary schools, and Hampstead (comprehensive) School in **Westbere Rd.**

Child's Hill

On the electoral map, Child's Hill is a Barnet ward extending well into NW11. Not so in estate agents' descriptions, where it's usually defined as the NW2 area of Hampstead.

Semantics apart, the select Hocroft estate certainly includes some very prestigious and expensive houses, and residents to match. Hocroft houses are one-off brick-built neo-Georgian: detached in **Ranulf Rd,** leading down towards Fortune Green, detacheds and semis in **Hocroft Rd, Hocroft Avenue, Farm Avenue,** and **Harman Drive** (**Harman Close** is a surprise: it has some half-dozen architect-designed 1970s houses: individual, young and smart). Even the semis here are 4/5-bed, usually 2-bath, plus plenty of space for the cars. Prices for these roomy, comfortable houses, which are competing in the Hampstead market, range from around a million for the 4-beds to double that for the 6-bed detacheds in **Ranulf Rd**; close on £5 million was asked at one point for one of the grandest, a vast mansion in **Hocroft Rd.**

Most of the area's blocks of flats are also in Child's Hill; Vernon Court at the corner of **Finchley Rd** and **Hendon Way,** Wendover and Moreland Courts about 30 yards further on at the top of **Lyndale Avenue.** All three were built in the 1930s: mock-Tudor red-brick with 1-, 2- and 3-bed flats. Ground-floor ones have access to the garden. As original tenants slowly gave up the ghost (and their protected tenancies), flats were modernized and nowadays come onto the market with regularity. They're popular with the newly retired (some of whom may always have lived nearby, or have children living there), and with young couples whose pockets don't run to West Hampstead prices: here you can expect to pay up to around £320,000 for a 2-bed flat, from c. £300–350,000 for a 3-bed. **Finchley Rd** dwellers also have the option of a longer bus ride down to Finchley Rd tube. It's further away than Golders Green, but reckoned worth it for the Jubilee Line (direct to West End, Waterloo, Docklands. . .) and large Waitrose for shopping on the way home.

Further along the **Finchley Rd,** Orchard Mead, a former police barracks, was spruced up in the late '80s with porters, sauna, small garden to sit out in, parking – though the gym was reported to have been replaced by a snooker room. Owners share the freehold; 1-beds are c. £260,000, 2-beds c.£ 300–320,000. It is at least partly let for investment. Heathway, at the corner with **West Heath Rd,** has 54 flats; here, too, many were bought as buy-to-let. The 20 luxury 1-, 2- and 3-bedroom flats of 1989's Portman Heights, opposite, get the coveted NW3 postcode.

The former Child's Hill House, near the junction of **Hermitage Lane** and **Pattison Rd,** is still in single occupation, but most of the Victorian 3-floor houses in the latter street were converted into flats and/or maisonettes in the '80s. There's an intermingling of older houses with others built pre-1914, between the wars, and since, in these sought-after roads which lead up to Hampstead Heath. Often, as in **Hermitage Lane,** there has been a deliberate attempt to adapt to existing spacious pre-war houses with latticed windows and mock-antique touches, but there are also two terraces of newer, more frankly functional, houses for people who prefer streamlined living. More enthusiastic gardeners plump for the bungalows of **Hermitage Terrace,** a secluded place where children and/or grandchildren can play in safety; it is a conservation area.

Back across the Finchley Rd, there's concrete-jungle Sunnyside House above shops and car showrooms (a 2-bed flat, c. £190,000); flats here bring in rents of £225–240 pw. Opposite, **Crewys Rd** – sometimes known as Little Sicily – has small turn-of-the-century houses, c. £350–375,000: mostly terraced with gardens and lovingly spruced up by owners. Busy Hendon Way has just the sort of 1930s semis you'd expect along a busy road: their location holds prices down to £250–350,000.

There are also ex-council properties on the market here. In the '80s Barnet encouraged tenants to exercise their enterprise this way, and sold off close to a third of its housing stock. The range of these homes is, to say the least, wide. But the good ones are very popular: look for 2/3-bed houses, terraced, in **Garth** and **Cloister Rds** (c. £200,000 for a 2-bed needing work, up to c. £280,000) off Hendon Way; 2/3-bed flats in **Longberrys** (an unmod 2-bed, £175,000), **Cricklewood Lane** and 2-bed flats in Hermitage Court.

Cricklewood Central

This area covers a broad band each side of **Cricklewood Lane**, starting from Hendon Way to the NE, the Farm Avenue sports ground on its S side, and with its other two sides bordered by Cricklewood Broadway and the North Circular Rd. The railway runs right through the middle. It includes large areas of council-built housing in the **Claremont Rd** area (plus new developments: see introduction), also the Westcroft Estate in **Lichfield Rd**, which is Camden Council housing on land leased from Barnet; **Westcroft Close** runs beside the railway, S of Cricklewood station: a 1-bed, split-level, ex-council flat here, c. £125,000. Main kinds of homes to look for here: pre-1914 housing near the railway station and the semis built between the wars when the **Hendon Way** was being developed.

Often the two mix and mingle – 1930s 3-bedroom semis alongside and opposite Victorian villas (£450,000 for a 4-bed detached) in **Cricklewood Lane**, where some split into flats have been restored to single houses; solid homes with gabled entrance lobbies and steep-sided roofs, sometimes joined up in terraces of four and six as in **Somerton** and **Gillingham Rds**. Then there are stretches of widely-spaced semis and detached houses in **Greenfield Gardens**, **Purley** and **Sanderstead Avenues**, roads which are incongruously wider than the main thoroughfares. Most of the houses are owner-occupied (up to £450,000 for a 3-bed detached), although there's also a certain amount of letting. Some former bungalows in **The Vale** and nearby have had their roofs extended – indeed, much individual attention, money and ingenuity have gone into changing and adapting these houses and gardens (4/5-bed semis here can fetch £425–495,000).

But building land is scarce here now. Developers manage to find patches of land to transform, though: sandwiched in the angle between Brent Terrace and Claremont Rd is **Romney Row** – a smart terrace of 2-bed houses completed in the early '90s. Next door are 32 recent flats at **Dover Close** and **Rye Close**. These now fetch c. £170,000-plus for a 2-bed, up from £130,000 two years back and £90,000 five years ago.

Behind the other side of **Brent Terrace**, however, is the aforementioned vast waste-land of redundant railway sidings and depots. One day, the terrace should back onto the bright new land of housing, offices, shops – even parks – that figure in the ambitious regeneration outlined above. Whatever, the pretty little Victorian cottages here (2-bed, or 3- with bath downstairs) cost the gambling man, or woman, some £225,000 at present.

For something rather different, look to an inward-looking Shakespearean-fantasy (the street names, rather than the architecture) 1990s corner between **The Vale** and **Somerton Rd**. Boasting over 150 flats and houses, **Ophelia Gardens, Hamlet Square**, and **Elsinore Gardens** attract prices above average for the immediate area (£390–400,000 for a 3-bed town-house). Next door on the corner of **The Vale/Claremont Rd**, Wimpey's Compton Place, 21 town-houses, 3-storied 3-beds, appeared in 1998. Further S on Claremont Rd, on the dairy site, Fairview squeezed in **Draycott Close**: studios, 1- and 2-bed flats, definitely convenient: views over Cricklewood station. Prices now c. £145–180,000 for 1-beds, £230–240,000 for 2-beds; £260,000 for the bigger, 2-bath ones. To the N, across The Vale, once stood an aerodrome – now covered by stadium-shaped streets of neat, suburban 1930s, 3-bed, £300–325,000 semis which curve away from the central spine of **Pennine Drive**. North again are recreation ground and football club.

Quite a lot of industry remains in these residential streets, but rubs shoulders fairly unobtrusively with placid suburban semis in **Somerton Rd**; less so in **Dersingham Rd**, a 3-bed house here, c. £425,000. Many of the older houses in the Cricklewood Lane end of **Claremont Rd** are subdivided for letting, but when they come up for sale are attracting 'Hampstead overspill' young professionals. Round in **Cricklewood Lane** itself, flats above shops offer two bedrooms for up to £195,000; larger, 3-bed, £300,000 ones can be had in a purpose-built block.

It's a different, more crowded world on the other side of the railway bridge. It is more cosmopolitan: shops near and in **Cricklewood Broadway** include halal butchers, sari shops, jewellery stores and Oriental grocers, greengrocers and bakers.

Next, to what one wit dubbed 'the Tree of Groves', but is known more universally as just 'the Groves'. **Yew Grove, Ash Grove, Elm Grove** and **Oak Grove** are all Edwardian 2-storey terraces which seem to have been rebuilt, converted, improved and adapted as if to show just how many variations on the original could be achieved – dormer windows, balconies, teak and glass doors, cladding. These split into good, convenient (the station is just across Cricklewood Lane) 2-bed flats (c. £210–240,000), within three miles of Marble Arch. But there's simply not enough pavement and kerbside space for residents, shoppers and railway users to park their cars. They try, which helps to explain why the council doesn't seem to be able to keep these streets litter-free.

So far, so predictable. But the former railway cottages (know locally as just 'the Cottages') some 300 yards up **Cricklewood Broadway** on the E, Barnet, side are a surprise. Sold off to the then residents some 30 years ago, these are five parallel terraces of 2-bedroom (3-bed – if you move the bath downstairs) houses, some boasting pretty gardens, sometimes with one large communal lawn on one side and individual private patches on the other. Access by car is limited, but it's a cosy spot (if close to the tracks, it's also close to the station) where residents have shrugged off the original railway grime and coal dust. In the '90s it attracted an artistic if impecunious bunch (including actors and magicians); many got to love it and stuck, even starting families in accommodation where it might not be easy to swing a cat or a baby. Then these houses became viewed as collectors' pieces; the streets are now a conservation area. Prices have fallen back a bit, but 2-bed cottages still go for c. £225,000. Don't stop to think, as you sign the cheque, that as recently as 1996 they cost, on average, £80,000.

West Cricklewood

Streets named after trees to the E of **Cricklewood Broadway** are 'the Groves'; here, on the W (Brent) side, are 'the Roads' (often annexed to Willesden Green by wily agents). Most contain 2-storey houses built at the turn of the century, so there's been plenty of time for **Pine, Larch, Cedar, Olive, Ivy, Oaklands**, etc., **Rds** to have developed mature, leafy trees (not of appropriate species) and for conversions into flats, maisonettes and garden flats. A 4-bed terraced with a 70ft garden, c. £425–475,000 if it's a semi. In these streets, c. £200,000 gets you a 2-bed flat – £250,000 for a good garden one; houses get smaller, and cheaper, as you get closer to the Broadway.

Multi-occupation usually means parking problems in streets built before cars – or indeed bathrooms – were considered necessary, so it's worth noting the width of any road before deciding. Ashford Court is the only really large block: a 9-storey, Y-shaped one with 180 1-, 2- and 3-bed flats at fairly reasonable prices.

Between Sheldon Rd and Cricklewood Broadway, **Sylvan Grove**, a clutch of 33 flats and 21 houses, appeared in 1992 on the site of an old aircraft factory. The whole development has now been taken over by a housing association. There are also late-'80s Laing flats and houses in and off **Langton Rd**, not far from either the station or the park: again now mainly housing association. A row of little 1-bed houses in Langton Rd is popular. Purpose-built flats, two to each house, were built pre-1914 in **Wotton, Temple** and **Langton Rds**. Note the double front doors: one leads to the staircase for upstairs. A 3-bed garden flat might be £225,000.

The scene changes in the wide leafy roads near Gladstone Park, with their comfortable

4/5-bed houses in **Anson Rd, Oman Avenue** and in many of the roads running into the former. A 4-bed Victorian terraced house in **Heber Rd** was £450,000 last winter, while a 5-bed semi in Anson Rd was £675,000. There are also some large detached houses, prices for which have reached £975,000. Others have become flats; up to £330,000 for a big, 3-bed garden one with period details. Some streets – for example, **Oman Avenue** – also have blocks of flats (2-beds, £190–210,000) where elderly parents can live near the children.

C

These sights defy anyone who thinks that civilization stops at the boundary with Brent. It's true that there are still industrial buildings, as well as garages, workshops and even a street where casual workers still wait to be hired each morning. **Hassop Rd** is totally industrial. What happens is that the better roads are dubbed Willesden Green (see Willesden and Dollis Hill chapters). No wonder Cricklewood is said to be shrinking.

Transport Trains: Cricklewood, Thameslink to King's Cross, City, Gatwick and N to St Albans, Luton & Bedford (City 18 min).

Convenient for Gatwick and Luton Airports by train. Routes both into and out of town: M1 (Junction 1), Golders Green, Willesden Green, Kilburn tubes and roads to the West End. Ikea and Tesco superstores. Hampstead Heath. Miles from centre: 4.5.

Schools Local Authority: Hampstead School. See also Hampstead and adjoining areas.

SALES

Flats	S	1B	2B	3B	4B	5B
Average prices	100–130	145–200+	175–320	270–400	–	–
Houses	2B	3B	4B	5B	6/7B	8B
Average prices	220–280	250–450	360–500+	450+	–	–

RENTAL

Flats	S	1B	2B	3B	4B	5B
Average prices	125–140	150–190	200–250	275–350	350+	–
Houses	2B	3B	4B	5B	6/7B	8B
Average prices	250–300	275–400	300–450	400–500+	–	–

The properties Wide range, from large Hampstead-fringe detached houses and mansion flats, via '30s semis, to Victorian and Edwardian terraces, semis, railway cottages, converted flats. Prices for individual houses can rise into the millions towards Hampstead. Also pockets of new-build; much more to come on ex-sidings.

The market Good prospects for area with good links to everywhere else (Paris in '07). The smarter corners gained as a knock-on from Hampstead, etc., as prices rose. A place to hunt still for (relatively) affordable, unsmartened, cosmopolitan streets.

Among estate agents active in this area are:

- William Nelhams
- Rainbow Reid
- Hoopers
- Callaway & Co
- Gammell & Co
- Albert & Co
- Gladstones
- Ellis & Co
- Carltons
- McGowans

C

CROUCH END AND STROUD GREEN

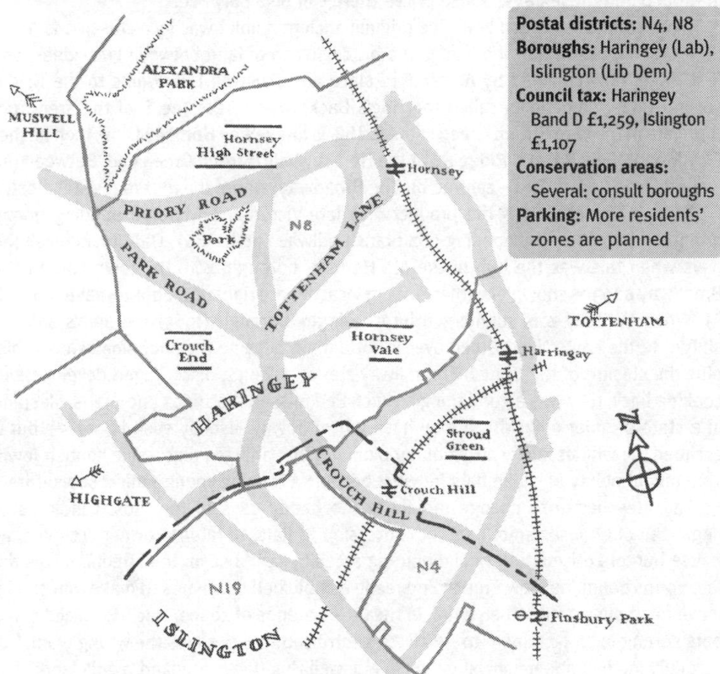

Postal districts: N4, N8
Boroughs: Haringey (Lab), Islington (Lib Dem)
Council tax: Haringey Band D £1,259, Islington £1,107
Conservation areas: Several: consult boroughs
Parking: More residents' zones are planned

The name 'Hornsey' is set for a revival. Once, Hornsey borough ruled Crouch End, but when both were subsumed into Haringey 40 years ago Hornsey lost its identity, while Crouch End became better known. Now, with the building of nearly 500 very smart flats on old waterworks land, and more to come next door, Hornsey High Street should become a place once again, not just a shadow.

The 'New River Village' scheme uses up just about the last bit of land in the wider area. Long-time locals already fret that workshops and small industrial sites are being replaced by flats and more flats, and opinion is divided as to whether a further influx of 'people who have got a few quid' (to quote the waterworks' unusually honest developer) will make the place more or less attractive to live in. There are already reports of bars and eateries in the 'new, aspirational' Hornsey High St, but also talk of a mini-glut of rental flats as buy-to-letters try to fill their properties: some selling out.

Smart new flats, for those who regard Crouch End/Hornsey as a desirably bohemian place to be young and well paid, are just one aspect of the area. There are plenty of family houses, providing customers for the well-regarded local primary schools, and an even larger supply of converted flats, carved out of the sometimes enormous Victorian/Edwardian houses at every optimistic moment in the past 30 years.

The mix of ages, types and tendencies is (at the moment) a happy one. Crouch End's arty, slightly radical, good pubs and quirky shops image has gained from the influx of the affluent: the café society of Crouch End is a reality. As the arty young begat families, so the kids' infrastructure blossomed: nurseries, playgroups, events in the parks. The influx of mini Crouch Enders, and especially their monster buggies, is ruining the cafés and bars, say some. 'Whatever happened to fish fingers at home for lunch?' grumbled one.

Stroud Green, long the poor(er) relation – if not as downtrodden as Hornsey – is on the up, with renewed confidence in the name: locals feel less need to pretend they live in Crouch End these days. House prices there can be a surprise.

What counts as Crouch End? The original ancient hamlet was by a crossroads (crux, then Crouch) where four roads met in a broad sweep of land between two ridges. The first ridge, now crowned by Alexandra Palace and Muswell Hill, looms to the N; the second ridge, sometimes called the Hog's Back, runs across the S of the area from Highgate in the W to Stroud Green in the E. This is marked by **Hornsey Lane**, then further E by **Mount View Rd**, and **Ridge Rd** at the Hornsey Vale/Stroud Green end. Between the two ridges is Crouch End – centred on **The Broadway**, where the four roads still meet.

Today's Crouch End is the product of a late-Victorian/Edwardian building boom, prompted in part by the opening of a branch railway line in 1867. Old-timers recall the days when this was the hub of the old Hornsey borough, with the town hall off the Broadway a 1930s showpiece (there's a big local debate right now about what to do with it). When Hornsey was submerged into Haringey borough (1965) the area's balance shifted to the east; Wood Green over in Tottenham became the shopping centre. This, plus the closure of the Crouch End railway station in 1954, discouraged development. Looking back, that was a good thing. Crouch End missed the 1960s and 1970s, sleeping in a state of quiet obscurity. It may have grown dowdy – seedy even in parts – but it escaped the wholescale destruction-by-planning that afflicted places like Kentish Town. That meant plenty of cheap flats for what became a thriving young-radical subculture.

The area began to change rapidly in the heady days of the '80s. Landlords of neglected old houses sold them for conversion to flats, or later to owner-occupiers as house-hunters priced out of neighbouring areas began to scour the streets. It was the late-1990s boom that saw Crouch End really established as an area to make that crucial move to a house, rather than a flat. In the little parades of shops, chic health clubs and bars sprung up, a testament to – well . . . gentrification is perhaps the wrong word, but certainly modish bohemianization. As in Muswell Hill, this is arts-and-media land – but more rock than opera here. Indeed, Crouch Hill boasts a recording studio in an old church, and a proliferation of cafés.

The inward flow of young professionals renting or buying here highlighted this area's convenience for both City and West End – although it lacks a tube station. There are, however, four within a mile (Finsbury Park, Highgate, Archway and Turnpike Lane), and buses to get you (slowly) to Finsbury Park tube and train station. Some say that a tube would change the ambience: they like the feeling of apartness.

The houses were largely designed with Victorian or Edwardian families in mind. In contrast to districts further in, such as Camden Town, most houses here are quite big. You have to hunt for the classic, compact late-Victorian 3-bed terrace, and 2-bed cottages are really scarce, but if you have a taste for ungainly gables and jutting bays, and can put up with lots of stairs, here you will find the home of your dreams. These solid houses also convert into good, roomy flats (and such conversions are still more common, and more desired, than purpose-built blocks).

Families are happy with schooling at nursery/primary level, but although Hornsey Secondary has been awarded Beacon status, there's still an exodus up to Muswell Hill – or a move out to the sticks – as soon as a 10th birthday arrives. However, the new Church of England Greig City Academy on Hornsey High St, with its just-complete £16-million revamp of the old St Katherine & St David school's buildings, may change things.

The villagy Broadway, with its clock tower, mingles smart clothes shops – for kids, too – with a great mix of shops and restaurants, thanks to the wider area's Greek, Afro-Caribbean and Asian communities. At its centre is the old Town Hall, focus of a yet to be settled spat between articulate and organised locals, who want it kept as a community focus (art house cinema, perhaps?) and the Council, which would like to sell it.

Green space is another plus. Even in the meaner streets, parkland, woods or playing fields are never far away – and the route of the old railway is now the Parkland Walk, which runs across the area from Highgate to Finsbury Park. Greenery and postcodes are the keys to prices: the more street trees, the better. As for postcodes, N8 carries a premium (though note it spreads E beyond Hornsey to take in part of Haringey). Although the divide is not as sharp as it was, N19 (to the SW, towards Upper Holloway) and N4 (Stroud Green and down towards Finsbury Park) are still reckoned less desirable.

Crouch End

Crouch End has been stretched, as the name has become more accepted, to take in virtually the entire N8 postcode. The smartest, and priciest, neighbourhood is the W side, towards Highgate, where green space, good houses and proximity to Highgate tube make a potent mix. The pleasant streets closer to Alexandra Park in the N of the area are increasingly prosperous, and the past few years have seen the E side smarten up, too (especially the ridge between Hornsey Vale and Stroud Green – rechristened, heaven help us, 'Crouch End Heights').

West of the Broadway

The most expensive homes in Crouch End are found to the W of **The Broadway** and **Crouch End Hill**. This area is particularly well off for open spaces, including Crouch End playing fields off **Park Rd**, Queen's Wood over towards Highgate and the ex-railway-line Parkland Walk. There's an upmarket tennis club, too. Parking is difficult, and the one-way road pattern in the streets close to the Broadway is complex. Many of the late-Victorian houses survive, though the biggest are split up; and there are several groups of late 20th-century houses, plus plenty of same-vintage blocks of flats.

Busy **Wolseley Rd** (a 2-bed flat here, £395,000) leads up to **Shepherd's Hill** with its blocks of modern flats (Highgate Heights, Panorama Court etc) which have replaced most of the rambling old houses. These flats are very popular: plenty of choice, long views (as the blocks' names suggest). Prices for a 2-bed can range up to £700,000, with close on a million asked for a really big apartment, though £400,000 for a 2-bed garden flat is more typical. With Highgate tube at the far end of the road, people living here tend to say they're in Highgate: the N6 postcode jinks to include the Hill and surrounding streets; **Stanhope Rd**, wide and elegant, sweeps down S to Hornsey Lane. Off it are **Hurst Avenue** and **Avenue Rd**, with large, seven-figure houses set well back behind neat lawns, playing fields adding to the verdant air. The area, these days, screams money.

Crouch Hall Rd is the spine of a district of 1880s-onwards houses, from **Glasslyn Rd** in the N to **Coleridge Rd**. The houses are Victorian-Gothic and Edwardian 3-storey terraces or semis of varying sizes, some double-fronted; many have been split into roomy flats (3-bed garden flat, £335,000). **Coolhurst Rd** has some modern flats (1-beds from £170,000), and some recent town-houses at the N end mingling with the Victorian monsters (6-bed £1.7 million) and a new 5-bed detached (£2 million). The old TUC building, previously Hornsey College of Art, may become a new primary school: there's pressure on school places locally. **Hornsey Lane** runs across to Highgate, with million-plus 6-bed houses at the W end but 2-bed flats too. **Crescent Rd**, with a few massive 1870s houses and smart modern blocks (the Standard Apartments, in gated grounds, are the latest) loops round to **Crouch End Hill**. On the Hill, Berkeley's 'The Exchange' has 51 smart flats above an M & S food store and gym: £325,000 for a 2-bed, top floor. Across in **Edison Rd**, Acorn Homes' 'Tara Mews' is a courtyard of modern 4-bed (but only 1-recep) houses.

Priory Park

North of the Broadway now, where 'Priory Park Village' is the rather stagey estate agents' name for the triangle between **Park Rd** and Priory Park up to Alexandra Park, with **Priory Rd** its spine and the greenery of Priory Park its heart. The junction of Priory and Park Rds offers a good clutch of shops: pâtisserie, coffee shop – even an organic mini-market – plus (especially in Park Rd) fashion. The cricket ground, tennis courts, swimming pool and local French bistro (in Park Rd) contribute to the genuine community feel. Both main roads have modest Victorian terraces; the side roads off **Priory Rd** are wide, tree-lined and packed with comfortable Edwardian 2- and 3-storey gabled homes (5-beds £625–700,000). **Redston Rd** has houses backing onto Alexandra Park; **Park Avenue North** has 5-bed terraces and semis (both streets up to £600,000); quiet **Linzee Rd**, cut off from the grid of Hornsey streets to the N, is also popular. To the E the 1950s–60s council Campsbourne Estate, E of **Nightingale Lane**, is less well regarded.

Hornsey

Many who live in Hornsey use the excuse of the N8 postcode – that comfort blanket, a local observer calls it – to say they live in Crouch End. However, while N8 continues E beyond the railway (see Tottenham chapter), only the tract to the W – either side of the old **High St Hornsey** – can lay any claim to Crouch End. Now, with a major flat development actually marketed as 'Hornsey', that name should see a renaissance.

The old waterworks site to the N of the High St at the railway end is now 'New River Village': 460 new homes, a third Affordable (at the N end, apparently), landscaping along the New River, a 2-ha park attached to the Alexandra Palace grounds, and – in an old Victorian pumping station – an art gallery, an outpost of the Royal College of Art. Last winter studio flats were c. £185,000, 1-beds £210,000, 2-beds £285,000. Plenty were bought off-plan and investors now compete for tenants. Check also on plans for the area of railway and gasworks just to the E across the tracks, which could include 1,000 new homes. Follow the High St E into Tottenham to find Turnpike Lane tube (Piccadilly Line).

East of, but cut off from, the Priory Park streets (see above), though close to Alexandra Park, lies the Campsbourne Conservation Area. Agents particularly tip streets between **Beechwood Rd** and **North View Rd**, immediately S of the park, as good places to look for smaller 3-bed Victorian houses around £350,000, while first-time buyers seek out 2-bed garden flats. **North View Rd** (buy on the N side for those views of Ally Pally) has some purpose-built late-Victorian/Edwardian maisonettes dating back to very early council-home building, while **Nightingale Lane** has tiny, £275,000-ish terraced houses. 'A real sense of community here,' says an inhabitant, citing the tidy (if small) gardens, local schools and shops. Nightingale Lane divides the district in two: however, **Rectory Gardens** aside – tipped by agents as a road worth looking at, with some mileage yet to come – roads to the E are mostly council-built, with some particularly unreconstructed, dismal blocks in the Campsbourne Estate. This is the cheapest corner of Crouch End; deservedly so, but should cheer up as the council spends the £11 million it has extracted from (sorry, negotiated with) the waterworks' developers.

Hornsey: Middle Lane/Rokesly Avenue

South of Hornsey High St is a triangle of streets with **Middle Lane** to the W and **Tottenham Lane** to the E. Here you'll find quiet roads lined with fairly large 2- and 3-storey houses. Rokesly Avenue Junior School is a big draw locally. To the NE – and close to Hornsey station (trains to King's Cross/Moorgate) – streets such as **Gisburn Rd**, **Temple Rd**, **Ferrestone Rd** and **Hillfield Avenue** are worth a look for a mix of whole houses (5-bed in some cases) and converted flats. Hillfield, which has ranks of big, ungainly but spacious 1880s houses, some double-fronted, is quite busy, and is the focus of energetic infill development. It is still a bit tatty at the N end. To the W, the L-shaped **Lightfoot Rd** encloses a low-rise council estate.

Rokesly Avenue has popular early 20th-century semis and rows (they extend from 3- to 4-beds: £480,000 if so). Closer to the Broadway are **Elmfield Avenue**, **Rosebery**

Gardens and **Elder Avenue.** Here are late-Victorian houses, most split into flats, plus some modern purpose-built ones; they get cheaper as you go N. On the W side of **Middle Lane** are some charming little streets which are blocked off to through-traffic: **Chestnut Avenue, New Rd** and **Lynton Rd** have that local rarity, 2- and 3-bed Victorian cottages. West again, in the tract between Priory Park and **Park Rd, The Grove** is a tranquil, well laid-out council-built estate. **Palace Rd** has some medium-sized Victorian houses. Behind the Broadway, off **Back Lane,** Topsfield Terrace is a treat: a row of early Victorian cottages.

Hornsey Vale: Ferme Park Road and 'Crouch End Heights'

Head S of Tottenham Lane into Hornsey Vale for a big tract of housing with the busy bus-route **Ferme Park Rd** running, spine-like, from N to S. Here is Barratt's 2002-vintage North Point – 50 1- and 2-bed flats (plus concierge and gym) in **Tottenham Lane**: £275,000-ish for a 2-bed. Social housing forms part of the scheme. Over on the E side, towards the railway, there are some industrial estates off **Cranford Way** (big row about a proposed concrete factory here), but most is streets of good, solid houses, improving as they catch up with the rest of Crouch End and justify their N8 postcode. **Mayfield Rd** has the little Stationers Park and a splendidly Gothic Victorian church split into flats.

Look in **Nelson Rd**, and some of its neighbours, for 6- and 7-bed homes, big even by Crouch End standards. The western end of **Weston Park** is a sought-after address (a 6-bed house, £875,000 late last year); so, too, is **Gladwell Rd** (5-bed £635,000).

In the wider neighbourhood, to the NE where Tottenham and Church Lanes meet, streets such as **Hillfield, Hermiston** and **Rathcoole Avenues** are reckoned worth a look, being close to Hornsey station. To the W, Gladwell Rd leads to **Cecile Park**, a well-regarded road with some spacious houses which mingle with shoehorned-in new homes. Nearby **Tregaron Avenue** and **Briston Grove** have later, Arts-and-Crafts-style houses. Busy **Crouch Hill** leads back to the Broadway; it has some Victorian mansion blocks with good-sized flats. The ground rises in the S along **Mount View Rd**: see Stroud Green, below.

Crouch End South

This corner is in Islington borough rather than Haringey, which some feel is a step up in prestige; however, N19 is not as popular as N8. It is within reach of Zone 2 tube fares at Finsbury Park, though (see chapter). The N8 postcode continues on S for a few more streets – for example, **Haslemere Rd**, which snakes between Crouch End Hill and Crouch Hill: it has enormous 6-bed houses, mostly split into flats (but £1 million-plus has been asked for a whole one). Here, too, are several purpose-built flats blocks, some overlooking the sylvan Parkland Walk (see above) and others the Parkland Recreation Centre. Victorian mansion blocks such as Albert Mansions, with its bulbous iron balconies, can offer roomy, 3-bed flats. The streets from **Warltersville Rd** to **Ashley Rd** offer a mix of more mansion flats, big old houses, council-built, and the mid-status, mid-Victorian, terraces of **Trinder Rd** and **Shaftesbury Rd** to the S. The Holly Park Estate (big, red-roofed council blocks) stands N of the main road (**Crouch Hill**). In **Beaumont Rise**, W off Hornsey Rise, The Citadel is 11 modern flats. **Hazelville Rd** mixes quiet, neat council-built blocks with porticoed late-Victorian houses; a good hunting ground for flats. South-west of here lies Upper Holloway, and St John's Way leads down to Archway tube.

Stroud Green

From the ridge (called 'Crouch End Heights' by some) defined on the map by **Ridge Rd** and **Mount View Rd,** the land slopes away to the S. The large covered reservoir S of Mount View Rd gives an open feel, justifying £1.1-million prices for whole houses. Houses predominate, such as the 5-beds in streets such as **Oakfield Rd** and **Quernmore Rd. Mount View Rd** is the top (in both senses) address hereabouts; better views, and more expensive, at the Crouch Hill end. The railway cuts across, with the rather useless

Crouch Hill station (trains to Gospel Oak and Barking. . .). **Mount Pleasant Crescent** to the S has popular, Gothic-windowed Victorian terraces, with plenty of pastel paint and an air of established gentrification. Prices can be surprisng, especially for the handful of handsome, double-fronted, 4-bed ones. One side of the street overlooks the railway – **Mount Pleasant Villas** leads N across the tracks, where cheaper prices indicate proximity to the Holly Lodge council estate.

C

Stapleton Hall Rd snakes right across the area. For so long the land of bedsits and small flats, it is now vastly improved: houses here split into flats are family homes once more. A footbridge at the E end leads to Haringey station. Nearby streets, such as the S end of **Ferme Park Rd,** are cheering up too. The grid of streets across from **Stroud Green Rd** to **Florence Rd** has good, neat, much-sought-after 3- and 4-bed Victorian houses (£580,000 for a 4-bed); some council blocks in **Osbourne** and **Marquis Rds.** Quick access to Finsbury Park tube is a plus here. The roads E of the Parkland Walk, **Lancaster Rd, Cornwall Rd** and **Connaught Rd,** contain 3-storey brick-and-stucco houses – good flat-hunting territory, though whole houses can be c. £850,000.

Transport Tubes: Finsbury Park (zone 2, Victoria, Piccadilly), to Oxford Circus 11 min, City 30 min, Heathrow 1 hr; Turnpike Lane (Piccadilly); Highgate & Archway (Northern) Trains: Hornsey, Harringay, Finsbury Park (Moorgate 13 min, King's Cross 8 min).

Convenient for Alexandra Park. Miles from centre: 5.

Schools Haringey Education Authority: Hornsey School, Greig City Academy, Alexandra Park. Private: see Highgate chapter.

SALES

Flats	S	1B	2B	3B	4B	5B
Average prices	110–150	160–220	170–350	280–400	320–500	–
Houses	2B	3B	4B	5B	6/7B	8B
Average prices	250–390	350–460	400–600	550–850	650–1M	800–1M+

RENTAL

Flats	S	1B	2B	3B	4B	5B
Average prices	150–190	175–230	200–280	250–360+	375–450	–
Houses	2B	3B	4B	5B	6/7B	8B
Average prices	200–300	280–400+	350–500+	450–650	600–800	–

The properties Big late 19th-century suburban houses, many converted to flats. Largest and smartest close to Highgate, though typically houses on the big side right across the area. Few Victorian cottages. Some p/b flats; new-build increasing. Also ex-council bargains.

The market Popular with young professional families – though pressure on secondary-school places lessens long-term appeal. Two-bed flats selling well, houses sticking. Central Crouch End sells best; more impecunious home-hunters head N and E; most of N8, however, is regarded as desirable. Meaner, cheaper streets, though better for transport, towards Finsbury Park.

Among estate agents active in this area are:

- Martyn Gerrard
- Hobarts
- Tatlers
- Castles
- Winkworth
- Prickett & Ellis
- Davies & Davies

CRYSTAL PALACE

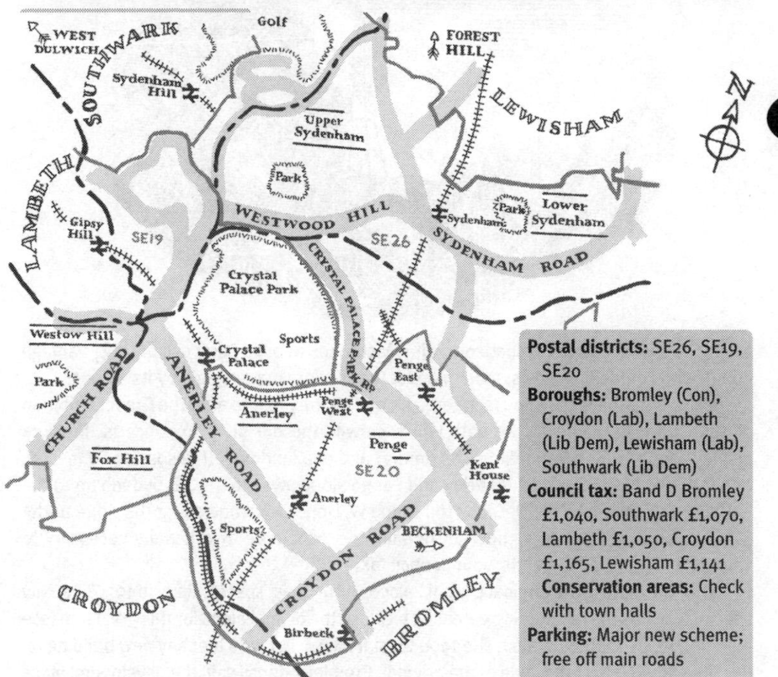

Postal districts: SE26, SE19, SE20
Boroughs: Bromley (Con), Croydon (Lab), Lambeth (Lib Dem), Lewisham (Lab), Southwark (Lib Dem)
Council tax: Band D Bromley £1,040, Southwark £1,070, Lambeth £1,050, Croydon £1,165, Lewisham £1,141
Conservation areas: Check with town halls
Parking: Major new scheme; free off main roads

Sometimes the underdog wins. Amid all the waffling about plans for new London tube lines/tram routes/metro services, Crystal Palace's plaintive cries could be heard. What about us? Stuck on our hill with just a train, and traffic-clogged buses . . .

Well, Good Fairy Ken looks like coming to the rescue. The only surviving segment of the East London tube extention (ELLX) plan includes a branch to Crystal Palace, and the only Croydon Tramlink addition to weather the financial storm is a link up the hill from Norwood Junction. The claims of Clapham, demands of Dulwich have been ignored: the other two ELLX lines are back on the back-burner. But the New Cross Gate–Croydon link, and its spur up the hill to Crystal Palace, is going ahead. Or so says Transport for London: see Transport chapter for more.

This news must aid plans to do something exciting with the Park and the palace site. Locals fought off a dire plan for a monster multiplex cinema on the site of Joseph Paxton's masterpiece, the wonderful glass palace that gave the area its name. Now we are in the first of six phases that should end up, in say 2006, with new and better plans. By that year too the London Development Agency, a GLA spin-off, will have taken control of the park's sports centre. But first, where is this hotbed of planning high anxiety?

Sydenham Hill rises greenly and abruptly southwards from Dulwich, offering long prospects, cleanish air and solace for those who get claustrophobia in the former marshlands closer to the heart of town. This South London eminence forms a distinct boundary between inner London, to the NW, and the essentially suburban borough of Bromley, which meanders off SE into Kent. London postal districts stop on the SE slopes.

The hills and valleys of this interesting landscape give character to the area, define the neighbourhoods and influence the type of property. Large houses and mansions (the

C

advent of Crystal Palace persuaded wealthy Victorians to build here) occupy lofty vantage points with compelling views; more modest terraces are made magic by its slopes.

Paxton's glorious glasshouse, re-erected on this lofty hilltop after the Great Exhibition of 1851, gave its name to the park which crowns the hill (host to concerts, firework displays and the '60s National Sports Centre) and of a landmark (the soaring TV masts), rather than a place. Round it, Anerley and Penge slope away to the SE, Sydenham to the E, Upper Sydenham to the N, Gipsy Hill to the W, Upper Norwood along the ridge to the SW. Five boroughs, no less, meet at the hilltop, so it's more than usually necessary to enquire who gets, and spends, your council tax.

What will replace the original Crystal Palace, burnt down spectacularly in 1936? Equally spectacular was the resounding defeat by locals of the dismal plans for this great site (see the 2002 *Guide* for the details). The 1990 Crystal Palace Act says that any new building on the site should reflect the style of the original. Bromley Council said the developers' plans did; campaigners disagreed (and even the architects quit). The plans were defeated.

A tangled saga of inquiries, inspectors, consultations and briefs began, and continues. A new player, the London Development Agency, is now involved, taking over the sports complex, and maybe the whole park (from 2009). This long-winded processs at least allows time to decide what might eventually fill the site: ideas include a reconstruction of the original Palace, filling it with attractions to include an Edwardian funfair and a virtual-reality zone; others want their Crystal modern, with a glass 'alien spaceship' teetering on spindly legs, from whose galleries the views would be amazing. We will see.

If homes are (relatively) affordable on the Hill, it is largely because of the difficulty in getting back off it. So the news that Crystal Palace will be on the East London Line Extension is significant. Meanwhile, the even spread of rail stations across the area makes for convenient commuting. Local journeys on congested roads are the problem, despite the new bus station, and despite the one-way system round the 'Triangle' with its villagy shops. There's a go-ahead, too, for a spur up to the Palace from the excellent Wimbledon–Croydon Tramlink, which runs to Birkbeck and Beckenham down the hill.

When all this has come to pass, and if, ultimately, the Palace – once a famous concert venue – is reborn, you will see a sharp upturn in the fortunes of some of these leafy, hilly, attractive but not yet spankingly smartened streets. The top schools of upmarket Dulwich are nearby, and amid the more humdrum roads are some really pleasant corners to explore.

Revolving around Crystal Palace Park, which crowns the hill, are first, Sydenham itself – today still with the feel of having strayed from an Edwardian novel, or Sherlock Holmes story. Houses of that period were lavishly spacious, and flats made from them can be as big, or bigger, than a house. Then there's Gipsy Hill; next, the villagy tip of Upper Norwood, the 'Triangle', between **Westow Hill/Church Rd** (see West Norwood chapter for

Gipsy Hill, Upper Norwood). Then premier **Fox Hill** and **Belvedere Rd** make their elegant descent SE from Church Rd. Finally Anerley and Penge sweep down the southern slopes.

Westow Hill and the Triangle

We begin at the pivotal junction at the start of **Crystal Palace Parade**, the wide, busy main road which runs along the hilltop next to the sad site of the Palace. From here **Westow Hill**, Victorian and villagy, though now part of a one-way system, runs W along the ridge; it has the reassuring feel of a traditional high street, with useful everyday shops interspersed with some better-than-average restaurants – one or two quite chic.

C

Jasper Rd and **Farquhar Rd** roll northwards from the Parade, down the flanks of the hill, across the tracks and the borough boundary into Southwark, towards the southernmost tip of West Dulwich. **Jasper Rd** has lofty Victorian terraces, still not all as tidy as they could be (the council own some); but these, and the sprucer, bay-fronted semis of **Farquhar Rd**, make for great roomy flats, into which they are largely split. Further down are homes old and new, including large, detached Tudor-timber-style in broad **Dulwich Wood Avenue**, 1960s flats (2-bed £195,000) and modern town-houses (4-beds, £350,000). These are peaceful residential streets.

Back to the hilltop roundabout, where on the plateau between **Westow Hill** and **Church Rd** lies the 'Upper Norwood Triangle', with **Westow St** joining the two to form its base. (For the record, you are now in Croydon's borough.) **St Aubyn's Rd** curves through with a mix of nice Victorian-gothic houses, tidied en masse, and modern flats (a 2-bed, £160,000); **Brunel Close** has 2/3-bed modern terraces and 3-bed mews houses (c. £215,000). **Westow St** continues the Hill's small shops: the likes of a (great) vegetarian café, a graphic designer/printer and an arty/crafty interiors shop face a supermarket-plus-community-centre complex across the often busy road. There are luxury retirement flats here; also a rather pedestrian development of flats squeezed in behind the shops. A glimpsed church tower in the distance was reincarnated as a 5-bed, million-plus 'des res' a few years back.

Church Rd, with the excellent local bookshop, is the Triangle's third side – and yet another boundary: Bromley's this time. Just past the Triangle, further S down Church Rd, is award-winning **Nesbitt Square**: 5-bed homes (£430–460,000) near Westow Park. Original Church Rd houses include handsome Victorian (but looks Regency) detached. Modern town-houses (3-bed, garage) in quiet **Fitzroy Gardens**; this leads into **Wakefield Gardens**: a cul-de-sac of modern homes with little Westow Park at the end of it.

Fox Hill

This leafy district slopes SE down from the hilltop, in the angle between **Church Rd** and **Anerley Hill**. Here, a conservation area protects **Belvedere Rd** and **Fox Hill**, this corner's premier streets; see, too, the odd survival in **Auckland Rd** for evidence of the grand mansions that once studded South London's answer to Hampstead. **Fox Hill** starts with small cottages and a modern development; it's steep (20 per cent gradient), with truly panoramic views: see Pissarro's picture in the National Gallery. It holds some beautiful old, well cared-for detached homes; Victoriana paired, single (some vast) or terraced (even the latter are 5-beds), plus '60s town-houses. Off it lies **Palace Grove**, a delightful little mews. (Look, too, at **Alma Place/Spring Grove**, off Church Rd.) Plenty of flats, new and converted, on this slope: £150,000 will buy a 1-bed, £185,000-plus a 2-bed.

A low stuccoed terrace of watermen's cottages that once backed on to the long-gone canal starts **Belvedere Rd** which, like Fox Hill has some vast Victorian semis: a 7-bedroom one, £725,000. 'The View' is a newbuild – but in mansion style – block of eight 1-, 2- and 3-bed flats: two still on the market last winter at £280,000.

Round the corner, **Waldegrave Rd** has smaller period homes (a bit untidy, and mainly flats: 2-beds here, £195,000-plus); also a Grade II-listed curiosity, the 1883

C

Swedenborgian Church was the first to be built of concrete (it merits an approving note in Pevsner). Now split into homes, it's known as New Church Court. A cache of town-houses hides behind homes in **Cintra Park**; off it, and not for the faint-hearted, is **Milestone Rd**: so steep, the gardens of the semis are terraced. **Patterson Rd** completes this corner: modest '30s 3-bed homes, immodest views. Trees shield the Victorian mansions in **Auckland Rd**, which curls all the way downhill to South Norwood: predominantly 4- to 7-bed Victoriana – (think £600,000 plus) – and a diversity of flats. Explore the pleasant cul-de-sacs – a hallmark of this area – that run off it: e.g. **Limekiln Place**, a modern gated clutch of 5-bed, £550,000, houses. Hilly **Sylvan Rd** has some modern detacheds (£320,000) as well as many a flat. Also here, a City Technology College and sports centre. **Maberley Rd** turns back N; some big 5-bed semis with 140ft gardens here. You're never far from a small green, park or open views – even, between the little closes that run off **Fox Hill** and quiet **Stambourne Way**, a small wood. Homes at the S end of **Auckland Rd** back onto playing fields; there's sailing on the lake.

Anerley

Busy **Anerley Hill** starts loftily at the junction with **Westow Hill** – commanding views of South London and beyond. Tall Victorian detached and terraced properties – most converted into flats – and '60s town-houses make the descent from Crystal Palace Park. Midway, there are a number of council-built estates. Homes for shared ownership have been built on two sites here. If you can find a sub-£150,000 home in SE20, you pay no stamp duty under a scheme to boost 'depressed' areas. Like Anerley and Penge.

Thicket Rd's larger-than-average detached Victoriana follow the SW edge of Crystal Palace Park (2-bed maisonette here, £250,000). Orchard Grove is a 'village-style' scheme of studios, 1- and 2-bed flats on a 5-acre former goods yard: the train line loops S of Thicket Rd. Across the tracks, long **Anerley Park** boasts a station close to either end; its big Victorian semis also yield many a flat (2-beds c. £185,000); also '30s flats, some large, in blocks like Anerley Court or Kelso Court. Charming terraced, 3-bed cottagy homes are found in peaceful, cut-off little **Trenholme Rd.** On **Anerley Rd** itself, where a few shops cluster round the station, seven newly-converted flats were £165–210,000 last autumn. In the angle between **Anerley Hill** and **Croydon Rd**, Betts Park holds the key to the Victorian development of Anerley and Penge: the remaining stretch of the Croydon Canal, which carried in all the building materials.

Penge

Modern shopping facilities in busy (and improving) **Penge High St**, with its clock tower and market, contrast with the quiet dignity of the King William IV Naval Asylum and the almshouses of **Watermen's Square.** The focal point of its four low-built rows is the chapel – nowadays the area's most unusual home, twin-towered and standing loftily above its flock. More almshouses in **King William IV Gardens** – fronted by a council-built block, recently renovated. A church hall on the corner of the High St and **Mosslea Rd** converted nicely to flats: a 2-bed here, c. £230–270,000. **Maple Rd** holds the library, and the street market at the High St end; Victorian cottages here, £200,000 plus for a 3-bed; 1-bed flats £135,000 plus. Beween it and **Oakfield Rd** lie 'the Groves', a clutch of streets all named after some plant or other. Early-Victorian 4-bed detacheds might be £340,000. A big scheme in **Chestnut/Woodbine Groves** added 27 flats and 20 2/3-bed houses in '03.

South of the A213 Croydon Rd, **Kenilworth Rd**'s bay-fronted 1930s terraces have wooden porches; narrow **Clevedon Rd** is similar. Quiet, popular roads are **Chesham Crescent** and **Rd** – '30s semis; **Ash Close** is a cul-de-sac of new homes. South across the little Pool River, **Ravenscroft, Birkbeck** (with new 2-bed flats at £250,000 last winter) and **Mackenzie Rds** are long, parallel streets: this convenient corner has two train lines – and the Wimbledon–Croydon Tramlink.

Back up the hill **Parish Lane**, near Penge East station, has cottagy rows (around £200–240,000) popular with first-time buyers – as do **Victor**, **Edward** and **Albert Rds**: little cul-de-sacs off it (a conservation area). Swallows Court is a recent cache of 2-bed flats in **Morland Rd**, also a cul-de-sac. **Green Lane** has taller Victorian terraces (4-bed £235,000); **Wordsworth Rd** bay-fronted ones. Larger houses in wide, busy **Lennard Rd** (Victoriana, £365,000 for a 4-bed semi; also mock-Tudor semis), **Woodbastwick Rd** and **Cator Rd** (Victorian detached: a 6-bed, £1 m). This is a leafy corner of parks and school – there are several – playing fields, leading N to Lower Sydenham.

Sydenham

Sydenham, to the N of Penge, is an elegant suburb which enjoys a good community spirit – the Sydenham Society is very active. Upper Sydenham historically had more lavish properties: surviving examples dot **Westwood Hill** and **Sydenham Hill**. Suddenly we're in million-plus territory (Georgian-style detached, 5-bed/3-bath, you know the type of thing); well, that *is* Dulwich at the foot of the slope. You can find good big homes for less – try the ample 1930s 4-bed semis at £400–450,000-ish – or more: £2.25 million was being asked last autumn for a 5-bed, 5-recep. Other hill-climbers here are **Wells Park Rd** and **Longton Avenue**, which bracket Sydenham Wells Park – this was a minor spa, an Elizabethan hamlet, and a desirable suburb in the early 19th century.

Wells Park Rd runs W from **Kirkdale**, starting modestly with Victorian rows and small shops. Off on the right, narrow **Halifax St** comes as a surprise – bright-painted terraced cottages with white wood fences. Council-built homes occupy the lower slopes; further up is green and hilly Wells Park. Halfway, modern flats with balconies and raised gardens. **Canonbury Mews** is mainly town-houses with neat lawns. Right at the top is large, modern St Clement's Heights estate with its white picket fences. Wide, hilly **Longton Avenue**, beside the Wells Park, has large 19th-century bay-fronted semis and modern terrace infills. Further up are '30s semis with sloping front gardens; higher still these become larger – occasionally detached. Delightful views of the park.

Sydenham Hill, also the borough boundary, skirts the NW edge of the neighbourhood. From the junction with **Kirkdale** (with 'Peak Hill View' – get the message?– new flats at £200,000), the wide, busy Hill runs SW with flats, detached houses – and its own woodland nature reserve, reached via **Crescent Wood Rd** (new conversion here: 21 flats £155–400,000). Also a walled-off, modern City of London Corporation estate. Lammas Green council estate has some stuccoed terraces. Smart 4-bed town-houses are set in a private square. More council-build appears – including high-rise. Victoriana mingles with '30s detacheds, modern terraces, town-houses – also the occasional, enchanted, wooded cul-de-sac: **Bluebell Close** is one, a covetable row of mock-Georgiana (4-bed town-house £270,000). Long, sweeping views of London are a joy. On the hilltop, near Westwood Hill roundabout, there are the **Wavel Place** flats: very popular, as is Bucklands Court, opposite (1-beds here, c. £140,000). The mini-Eiffel Tower of the TV mast soars into view.

Westwood Hill descends E towards central Sydenham, with modern town-houses on left (e.g. '90s **Westwood Place**), mansions on right. Torrington Court is a '30s mansion block (a 2-bed, c. £220,000). Sydenham High School is here; next, an imaginative flats scheme uses a tower motif. More town-houses are followed by retirement flats. Three-bed bungalows in **Hassocks Close**, while **Beaulieu Avenue**'s '60s town-houses (£270,000) have neat, pocket-handkerchief front lawns round two greens. In the triangle between the railway and Kirkdale, leafy **Sydenham Park Rd** is a mix: Victorian; some council; flats; six new semis plus detached house. Lovely **Sydenham Park** crosses it, mixing beautiful, flat-fronted stucco terraces, now flats, with '30s bay-fronted homes, some cottages, large semis. **Peak Hill** has an unusual terrace, Dutch-barn influenced.

To the S of Westwood Hill, the roads with **'Lawrie Park'** in their name – **Avenue**, **Gardens**, **Road** and **Crescent** – are popular. Lawrie Park Rd, wide, tree-lined and gently undulating, is a variety of Victoriana: mansions, detacheds, semis and bay-fronted terraces. Many flats conversions, and also modern flats and terraces. New flats and houses shelters behind high gates, while **Lyric Mews** is a recent cul-de-sac with 36 flats. **Crystal Palace Park Rd** is a conservation area; large Victorian red-brick mansions by the park – many now equally large (can be 4-bed) flats. Also mansion blocks – Ashley Court, '30s Park Court. **Sydenham Avenue** (mock-Georgian, big Victorian semis) has a rural air, with bench beneath tree on the green and views to St Bartholomews in Westwood Hill. Off it lies **Cobden Mews**, 3-bed/3-bath town-houses. **Lawrie Park Avenue** has Victorian mansions, '30s detacheds.

The N–S railway line divides Sydenham Park from Lower Sydenham to the E. **Sydenham Rd** leads past the station into Lower Sydenham. This Victorian red-brick street has useful shops (a 2-bed flat above one, £120,000) and station in the upper part. Behind lies the semis and terraces of the popular, Edwardian, Thorpe Estate (every street name ends in '-thorpe'): 3–6-bed semis and terraces from c. £330–575,000. On the N side of **Bishopsthorpe Rd**, houses back onto Mayow Park; some new 4- and 5-bed houses here. An office block in **Silverdale Rd**, near the station, became an imaginative conversion into 24 1- and 2-bed flats. The rest of the area ends modestly round **Bell Green** – where there's a monster Sainsbury's Savacentre.

Transport Trains: zone 3: Crystal Palace to Victoria/London Bridge; Anerley, Penge West, Sydenham to London Bridge/Charing X; Penge East, Sydenham Hill (zone 4) fast to Victoria. Gipsy Hill (zone 4) to Victoria.

Convenient for Dulwich; Tram to E Croydon for Gatwick. Miles from centre: 7.

Schools Local Authority: Westwood High (g), Cator Park (g), Kingsdale, Harris City Technology College. Private: see Dulwich chapter.

SALES

Flats	S	1B	2B	3B	4B	5B
Average prices	95–110	120–180	150–205	160–245	–	–
Houses	2B	3B	4B	5B	6/7B	8B
Average prices	175–250	200–320	220–400+	300–700+	850–1.3M	–

RENTAL

Flats	S	1B	2B	3B	4B	5B
Average prices	100–130	120–185	150–200	175–250	–	–
Houses	2B	3B	4B	5B	6/7B	8B
Average prices	175–250	185–300	230–450	300–600+	–	–

The properties Grand Victorian mansions, many now big flats; rows of smaller terraces, flats blocks and inter-war homes. Quite a lot of good new houses and flats. Greenery, gardens, long, long views.

The market Young professionals moving in. Larger houses great for families, especially conservation areas Fox Hill, Belvedere Rd. Plentiful 1- and 2-bed flats. Sydenham, Crystal Palace most 'up-and-come'.

Among estate agents active in this area are:

- Haart
- Wooster & Stock
- Cooper Giles
- Your Move
- Acorn
- Halifax
- Kinleigh Folkard & Hayward
- Wates
- Baxter Lambert
- Lynx
- Conrad Fox

DOCKLANDS

Chapter contents page

Docklands is different; so this chapter differs, too, from our normal format. 'Docklands' is the umbrella name for a vast riverside swathe of London. It was once the greatest port in the world – and is now a giant business and residential district.

For a map, turn to page 254: you will see the various districts in this big, six-mile-long strip. To get an idea of the scale, superimpose Docklands on 'traditional' London – west, instead of east, of Tower Bridge: it will cover the City, West End, Hyde Park and on through Hammersmith to Chiswick's Hogarth Roundabout *en route* to Heathrow.

Londoners have always looked west for fun and fashion, and it has taken quite a while to banish the thought that Docklands was the back of beyond. Then there's the awesome size of the place and its new-ness. In a city used to the small-scale, the villagey, Docklands is big. Now Londoners, having got used to Docklands, are having to adjust their horizons all over again. For Docklands is the gateway to the Thames Gateway, that brave new world of Olympic bids and vast new housing schemes.

So here we take a little time to run through the what, where and when of Docklands, its recent history (for those who'd like to know), its property market, its prospects. Then we go, as is more usual in this Guide, district by very different district through the area.

In 1964 this was the world's busiest port. And in 1981, nothing. Just miles of empty quays, and acres of still water in the great enclosed docks that lie parallel to the river. 'Docklands', an invented concept, was an attempt to find uses for all this and to come to the aid of the locals, whose *raison d' être* had ebbed away downstream with the ships to Tilbury. The attempt succeeded – way beyond the dreams of the cautious planners of 1981, who were at the time castigated for wild enthusiasm.

Today Docklands' centrepiece, the Isle of Dogs around Canary Wharf, is a business district on a world scale, with a workforce of 75,000. Around 30,000 new homes have brought new people, and money, to the Docklands districts. New tube and rail lines, new roads, a new airport, exhibition centre, university: all are in place. A new city, in the old.

Docklands as a place to live

It is magnificent – all gleaming marble and sparkling light bouncing off water – but it is not London. In truth Canary Wharf – and the rest of the Isle of Dogs and greater Docklands beyond – is an alternative London. It has more in common with downtown Chicago, or Sydney, or Singapore than with the City of London, or Fulham, or Highgate.

And the homes – are they all smart, expensive flats, or warehouse conversions? Once, that was about all you'd find. Today, the choice is much wider. There are whole districts of modern family houses with gardens, some of basic standard; others as good as anything you'll find in London. There are fairly everyday 'inland' flats, there are the riverside and dockside ones. Some blocks have every serviced luxury and compete easily in style with the grand apartments of West London. Others are very ordinary indeed.

The warehouse conversions range from vast airy spaces full of river-reflected light to cramped little dens looking out on stagnant, sunless docks or back streets. Even the bigger warehouse flats can have a lot of floor space relative to window area: check you get some sun. And, of course, there are new, shiny, straight-from-the-developer homes; others that go back 15 or 20 years. You might even find a flat or (even rarer) a house that pre-dates the '80s boom. People have lived round here since Shakespeare was a lad.

The Docklands property market

Docklands is a byword for boom and bust in property. So far, we've had two of the former and one of the latter. And now – well, it's quieter than most Docks-watchers are used to. Mid-2001 saw the end of the second Docklands boom. The first, of course, was 1986–89. The first bust was sudden: a combination of factors (history lessons available on request) turned the market off like a switch. From 1990 to 1994 the LDDC, the main source, found no buyers for building land. Some builders went bust, others spotted the signs and pulled out of Docklands entirely. The nadir was 1992. But the dawn came, and the market awoke, gaining momentum around 1996 – and regaining '89 price levels a decade later. (Yes, the 1990 slump was that deep. A decade in negative equity was not unusual here.) Conversely, those who bought in 1992 in some cases tripled their money in six years.

By 1999, people were camping out overnight to reserve as-yet unbuilt homes in the Royal Docks – the farthest-flung, eastern end of Docklands (so far-flung that its market is quite different: see its own, separate, chapter). One big bank in February 2002 restricted lending in the Royals as it feared speculation had become too heated. Then came the downturn in the City and the ferment cooled. Docklands prices, broad-brush, fell 10 per cent in 2003: rents and sales. Then 2004 saw a brisk spring rise – and gentle autumn fall. Result: prices back where they started. And the decline of speculation has led to a renewed role for the cautious owner-occupier, hitherto elbowed aside by the gung-ho, geared-to-the-nines speculator. Sales offices are having to work harder to convince buyers this year, though their rental colleagues are doing brisker business.

In 2002 and '03 Docklands discovered the hidden snag: all those flats, bought to let in the hope of capital gain (long-term or short), need tenants. And in the wake of the downturn in finance, tenants there were not. Anyone buying here is a captive of the world financial market. Elsewhere, a doctor, advertising man or oil executive may rent your flat; here it's a banker (or perhaps a lawyer) or no-one. This makes for a rather lumpy rentals market: if big firms move in to Canary Wharf (BP and Reuters being the latest) then rental agents are busy. But if a major player merges or moves on, it can leave a big hole.

The risk is also – in a district with a steady flow of new homes and a population which thinks itself financially astute – of speculation in 'off-plan' buys. When prices are rising the gearing effect can be irresistible. But with stagnation, an excess of gearing in the market can turn quiet times into a panic. It happened in 1989. It can happen again.

Prices quoted in this chapter are those being asked at the end of 2004/start of 2005. At that time, discounts of 10-15 per cent were widely available on new-build homes bought from the developers, and 'second-hand' values were responding to the competition. This is certainly a year to 'try an offer'. You might be surprised.

Of the Docklands areas, Bermondsey/Shad Thames achieves the highest prices, with Wapping close behind: £600 per sq ft is perhaps the ceiling. The place for value is still the Surrey Docks, though it shot up (from a low base) with the opening of its Jubilee Line station in 1999, with some of the more remote Isle of Dogs developments also keenly priced. As mentioned, see separate chapter for the Royal Docks.

Today: communities not masterplans

Twenty-five years of change have been led by big, visionary plans, plans that were – unusually for London – backed with real cash. Docklands is a different world, and so it should be: more money was spent here than anywhere else in the UK in the same period.

Around £11 billion of public and private cash has been sunk into Docklands.

Now, things are changing. Communities have grown up, and they – just like their counterparts in the rest of London – are active in defending their amenities. It's far harder for Docklands councils, or developers, to force through large schemes than it was.

This growth in community makes Docklands a better place to live. Overall, the population is made up of singles, childless couples and middle-aged empty-nesters – no Nappy Valleys here: they leave that to South-West London. And the large number of rented homes makes the population more transient. But there are emerging family quarters – Surrey Docks, inland Wapping – as well as established business-singles ones such as Wapping riverside, Rotherhithe village and Limehouse.

The maturity of some of these neighbourhoods can surprise outsiders. Wapping and Limehouse riversides, grim sinks of dereliction just 25 years ago, have settled down into being largely middle-class districts. The English have the ability to create a village idyll in the most unlikely surroundings – though not yet the village secondary school, hence the lack of kids. People who used to have a little place in SW7 now live in Wapping and talk of 'going down to the Village'. There – in Wapping Lane – they visit the excellent butcher (who sells *foie gras*), the post office, the pharmacy. Over in historic Bermondsey they can patronize top-flight restaurants in Shad Thames. On the Isle of Dogs they have a multi-cinema to stroll to, town-centre shops, dozens of places to eat and drink – and that's just Canary Wharf. However, take time to assess the 'step-out factor': would you feel happy leaving the building on foot, and if you do is there anywhere to buy a pint of milk and the Sunday papers? Some parts of the Isle of Dogs, Royals and Surrey Quays fail this test.

The what, where and when of Docklands

Here is a summary of Docklands' history – i.e., the last 22 years – to explain how and why it came about, and a few of the lessons learned, for those interested. Feel free to skip to Progress report below, if you prefer, which is followed by the detailed descriptions of the neighbourhoods and their homes.

No ships on the river: the sudden death of London's docks

Up to the late 1960s the river right up to Tower Bridge was crammed with ocean-going ships. Then, from 1967 to 1981, the vast docks closed one by one; the ships vanished. Containers for cargo made London's docks out of date. The legacies were great sheets of water, the surviving warehouses, the small, beleaguered communities of little houses built for dockworkers. And a virtually empty river.

London was faced with 5,000 acres of land, 20 miles of river bank and hundreds of buildings that suddenly had no function. The response was indecision, wrangling and piecemeal demolition as the docks closed, one by one. Reality dawned slowly: money was being spent on cranes and warehouses in the West India Docks (now the site of Canary Wharf) as late as 1976 – they closed in 1980 – and in the same year County Hall planners gave their aim as 'creating a flourishing and viable port in East London'. The City Corporation looked on the docks and their empty space as threat, not opportunity. London has never been a place for grand strategic plans, but the docks certainly needed one. Various wacky schemes were mooted: one that sticks in the mind was a plan for a linear park all the way from the Tower to the sea – in effect, grassing Docklands over.

After much talking and several abortive attempts at cooperation, in 1981 Mrs Thatcher's government imposed a new kind of body, a development corporation. Fierce rows arose, with the established communities, and more especially their politicians, opposing the centralized, undemocratic and virtually all-powerful London Docklands Development Corporation (LDDC), which ran Docklands until 1989. One key achievement was to get the rest of London to think of 'Docklands' as an entity. This is valid: it is a new place overlaying a clutch of old ones, and newness and the attitudes it engenders are common to places well apart in geography as well as character. But from the Docklands collective the individual neighbourhoods have now happily re-emerged.

The first dock to emerge from decline was St Katharine's, next door to Tower Bridge. In 1828 it cost £1,700,000 to build; in 1969 – nearly a century and a half later – the PIA sold it to Taylor Woodrow on a 125-year lease for £200,000 *less*. By the mid-'70s the marina, shops and homes complex had taken its basic, splendid shape. In 2004 Taylor Woodrow sold it, with its surrounding development, for more than £270 million.

Most of the London Docks, a little to the E, were filled in as if they had never existed: a few surviving bits of dock wall are their only legacy. The Surrey Docks closed in 1969; West India and Millwall Docks on the Isle of Dogs survived until 1980; and the last ship to unload in the Royals, the great down-river complex, steamed away in October 1981.

The transformation begins

No-one at the LDDC in 1981 knew they were starting a new business city; they thought they might with luck achieve an office and light-industrial park and a few new homes. In 1982, land in Wapping sold for £60,000 an acre. By 1987, the going rate was £4 million; by 2002 £10 million was reported.

The real, untold story of 1980s Docklands was the rocket-like rise in the area's expectations. After decades in which many hopeful plans dissolved on contact with reality, this time the problem was that the plans were far too timid. The growing pains – awful traffic congestion, lack of services – were the product of totally unpredicted success. The Docklands Light Railway (DLR) was only five years old when Canary Wharf came along: the DLR had to be virtually rebuilt to allow more people to use it than had ever been foreseen. Even the City Airport, now a steady success, was mocked.

Then came the 1990 recession. Developers went bust, owners of smart new flats found their blocks filled up with council tenants (yes, really) as despairing landlords and developers struck discount deals at Tower Hamlets Town Hall. Even Canary Wharf went under: negative equity on a £1.2-billion scale. It would have taken a brave speculator to buy into Docklands around 1992. But they would have been wise: Shad Thames and Bermondsey came second only to Kensington on a survey of price growth from 1992 to

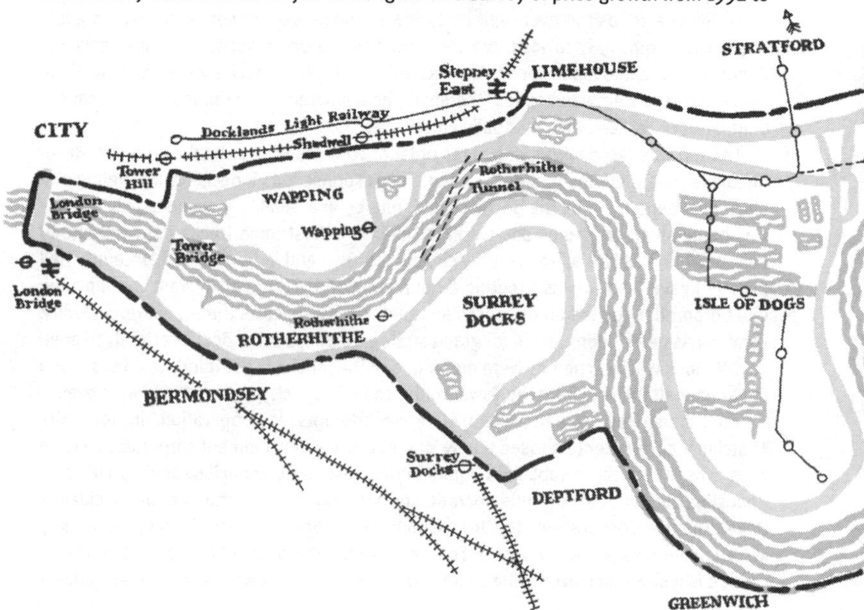

1997. In parallel came the explosion in offices. Led by Canary Wharf, Docklands has become a world-class business district and a serious rival to the City. No-one planned, or even dreamed, that in 1981. Or expected it in 1991.

Progress report

In many respects progress in Docklands can be judged by the number of cranes active around Canary Wharf. The tower was completed in November 1990; Olympia & York, the developers, went into receivership in May 1992 and re-emerged (owned by 11 banks) in 1993; in 1995 it was sold to a consortium led by Paul Reichman. After a brief career as a listed company, it was bought last year by a private consortium. Canary Wharf now has more than 6 million sq ft of high-quality offices and shops in a raft of buildings, with planning applications in for half a dozen more towers. The working population has grown to 63,000 from 8,000 a decade ago.

Big banks continue to dominate: HSBC tower alone houses 8,000 staff, Citigroup's 42-storey tower (one more floor than HSBC's) has joined its subsidiary Citibank's existing building. Barclay's is moving its HQ here in 2005, heading a blue-chip list of lawyers, yet more bankers, newspapers, even publishers. Plans for new towers come and go, but short of a seismic shift in the world of finance, Canary Wharf is now a permanent part of the global business jigsaw.

There are over 150 shops here, including the Tesco Metro that keeps the bankers in champagne, and a Waitrose (with an oyster bar, befitting its clientele). There are now some 50 bars, cafés, pubs and restaurants, including very smart ones in the Riverside complex – and now they stay open in the evenings. Back in

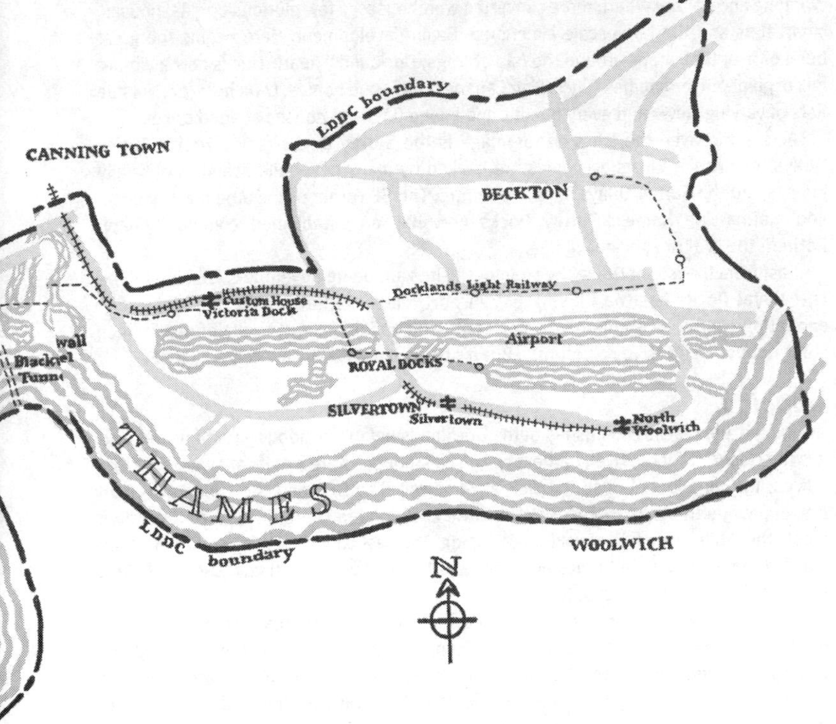

1992 the few bars used to shut at 8pm. Jubilee Park, around the five new towers south of the existing complex, is a green space on top of another shopping mall, Jubilee Place, with a Marks & Spencer's. Canary Riverside, to the W of the main complex, has its own four residential blocks, Four Seasons hotel, health/leisure club, bars and restaurants.

The Jubilee Line tube station at Canary Wharf connects Docklands to the West End in 15 minutes – and, perhaps more crucially, it links the area to London Bridge, Waterloo and their commuter trains. The Limehouse Link, a four-lane underground highway, links Tower Hill to Canary Wharf; it and a big network of fast (most of the time) roads now link to the City, West End, the City Airport and the M25, with the A13 the latest to be improved. Crossrail (if it ever happens: 2012? see Transport chapter) will have a station on North Quay. The DLR's extension to Greenwich and Lewisham added another swathe of London to Docklands' hinterland. Next comes a link to the City Airport (due this year). Money is being spent on yet longer trains and platforms to cope with the growth.

The shape of Docklands

First-time visitors start here for a whistle-stop tour. The most central areas are N and S of the Thames within view of Tower Bridge. North, downstream of the Tower, is **Wapping**, with the restored **St Katharine's Dock**, a mature, successful business/tourist/homes centre. The waterfront has the best warehouse conversions, with sunny river views, plus a large choice of new-build flats. Inland are new streets of well-placed houses and flats. The S bank, around **Shad Thames** and **Butler's Wharf**, has lovely converted and new flats in what is now a classy city neighbourhood with shops, restaurants and a museum.

Next E along on the north bank comes **Limehouse**, the favoured river strip between Wapping and Canary Wharf: more converted warehouses, a few glorious original houses, smart flats and the large-scale Limehouse Basin development. Here begins the great bend of river that wraps around the **Isle of Dogs**, Docklands' heart. This is now a vibrant mix of giant office schemes – including Canary Wharf – and homes. Look here for riverside flats of varying views and every quality, and inland flats and houses at good prices.

Across the river, the Isle's mirror-image is the **Surrey Docks** (some prefer **Surrey Quays**) peninsula. Riverside homes are backed by many new-build schemes of family houses and the Surrey Quays shopping centre. The SE corner of the area has the dock- and marina-side homes. **Surrey Docks** now has an established community feel; **Rotherhithe** is a true ancient village.

East from the Isle of Dogs, the Leamouth sites are being developed. East again, the vast **Royal Docks** has the thriving City Airport, plenty of new roads, the vast ExCeL exhibition centre, a complete new university and an increasing supply of new homes – but not yet a cohesive community. But it does have its own chapter, which see.

Wapping

Wapping is the oldest-established of the Docklands neighbourhoods – perhaps because it is the closest, N of the river, to the City. The western parts are a pleasant walk from City offices; further E people use the DLR at Shadwell. The DLR and the Limehouse road tunnel provide the links to Canary Wharf; the East London Line's Canada Water station meets the Jubilee Line two stops from Wapping. The East London Line's expansion posed a threat to the station, but it has been reprieved and by 2010 it will have far better links to N and S (see Transport chapter).

Local shopping is centred round the Safeway Compact on **Thomas More St**, but there is also Canary Wharf and the City shops via 'hoppa' buses. The useful little 'village' shops in **Wapping Lane** are fiercely championed by locals. There's culture, too: the enormous 1880s hydraulic pumping station at the S end of **Wapping Wall** has – after 20 years of dereliction – become an arts centre with an amazing post-industrial restaurant.

There are several sides to Wapping. St Katharine's Dock is a neighbourhood on its own. Then along the river to the E come the smart flats, in old warehouses or new-build, of **Wapping High St** and **Wapping Wall**. Inland, to the N, the tract once taken up by London Docks has 200 well-planned acres of mostly council-built housing, some 1,500 homes, plus some industry. At the E end is Shadwell, with the sole surviving dock basin (St K's apart) and some attractive waterside homes. The growth in places to live has been explosive: the Royal Mail lists 775 addresses, nearly all homes, on **Wapping High St**, which 20 years back was entirely lined by decaying warehouses. The LDDC years (1981–98) saw 4,000 new private-sector homes in Wapping.

Wapping starts, in the shadow of the Tower, with **St Katharine's Dock**. This is only just Docklands – more City-with-scenery: the two dock basins shelter yachts and provide an attractive outlook for homes and a hotel just a step from the City. (A step best taken, by the way, via the riverside walk between Tower and Thames.) It's reckoned a pleasant place to live, with a good community spirit (not that common in Docklands). Development began in 1971, and most of the buildings are 20th-century, with just one 19th-century warehouse left intact. There are 300 local authority homes around the E and N sides of the dock – most bought by tenants, and on the open market occasionally at sub-£300,000 prices. **Mews St** has 10 small cottages; **Marble Quay** has four flats in an office development. **The Ivory House**, a fine old converted warehouse, has 37 2-bed flats which have been let ever since conversion, but are now for sale on new 125-year leases, with current tenants having first refusal (from £310,000 for 460 sq ft up to £1.75 million). Spread over two sides of St Katharine's Dock, Taylor Woodrow's **City Quay** is an impressive complex, just completed, which offers 209 1-, 2- and 3-bed flats (1-beds £475,000, 2-beds £675,000) and 3- and 4-bed penthouses. **Tower Walk** is a crescent of seven 4/5-bed 'Nash' style stucco houses, reckoned to be worth c. £2 million each.

Barratt were responsible for the area with **Hermitage Waterside** around the little Hermitage Basin E of the dock – all that is left of the W end of the old London Docks complex. This features 53 1- and 2-bed flats and 20 3-bed houses. A detached Georgian house stands on the edge of the dock, a rare survival amid its 1980s neighbours.

Back on the river, **President's Quay** is a particularly stylish 1985-vintage block; the twin glass-roofed pyramids of its penthouses a riverside landmark; quality is high. Next door, **Miller's Wharf** has 22 homes in a handsome Terry Farrell-designed warehouse conversion. **Tower Bridge Wharf** is a 64-home 1990 development. One end is semi-circular, with a courtyard, which gives the opportunity for some unusual shapes and two differing, but enviable, penthouses at either end of the crescent. A spacious river walk runs along the front. On **St Katharine's Way** and next to the **Hermitage Wharf** block is **Riviera Court**, which has a dozen new-build riverside 2- and 3-bed flats.

Berkeley's **Capital Wharf** has 85 riverside flats. **Hermitage Wharf** (the developer's name – known to the postman as **Cinnabar Wharf**) is Berkeley's latest, big (2-plus acre) scheme. There are 95 flats in three stylish blocks; adjoining a new public park. Recent Cinnabar resales include a 1-bed at £375,000 and a 1,917 sq ft penthouse at £1.35 million. Opposite is the same firm's **Halcyon Wharf**, with 41 flats and three houses. Adjoining is **E1 Waterside**: 14 new-build flats (2003 vintage).

On the inland side of **Wapping High St** is **Hermitage Court**: 97 homes. Next comes the glorious **Wapping Pierhead**; the area's one remaining enclave of genuine Georgian houses. Some are split into flats, others remain as 3-bed, 3-recep houses. All share a half-acre garden between the two facing terraces running down to the river. Extending inland, local authority houses were built to match the Pierhead style. 'Victorian-style' **Pierhead Wharf** dates from 1997, and in 2003 gained four new penthouses.

Back on the Thames, **Oliver's Wharf** has about the most coveted flats in Docklands: bought in 1973 by a group of architects and artists – some of whom still live there – this is the one that started the whole conversion fever off. The group paid some £14,000 each for their industrial space. Today these remain some of the largest of Docklands (or, indeed, London) flats – a typical one has a 54 x 38ft galleried living room. An enormnous (4,200 sq ft) penthouse was £1.9 million last winter (having been £2.25 million a year earlier). Just inland, the old St John's School in **Scandrett St** is now a lovely 5-bed house, and a 3-bed house a few doors along (with a roof garden) was £895,000 last autumn.

Orient Wharf homes are let by a housing association; the Town of Ramsgate pub sits on a sliver of riverside real estate. On the inland side of the High St, **Dundee Court** has 48 1- to 3-bed flats in a 19th-century warehouse converted in 1986: a 2-bed might be c. £375,000. **The Sanctuary** is inland, but with some good river views. It boasts rooftop pool and gym, and basement parking. Also inland on **Brewhouse Lane** is warehouse-style **Chimney Court**, with 41 studios plus 1- and 2-bed flats. No. 78 **Wapping High St** was once a wine warehouse; now 16 homes. The spectacular white and cream stucco 1840s **Aberdeen Wharf** was probably the final warehouse conversion on the Wapping riverside. It was split into 17 flats in 1998. Those with river views gain from the wharf's location on the southern tip of the Wapping bend. No crime fears here: the River Police HQ is next door. The '60s apparition nearby, covered with abstract glass-fibre hieroglyphs (and bound to be listed one day), is the police's boathouse. **St John's Wharf** was turned into 22 large flats in 1984; resales are sought after. **King Henry's Wharves** are next, another warehouse conversion.

If you want a really memorable address look for a home in **Execution Dock House** (more prosaically No. 80 Wapping High St): a 1,547 sq ft flat in this converted warehouse was £645,000 last winter.

Barratt's **Gun Wharf** conversion provided 68 flats in 1985: they're spacious and have worn well; a 1,100 sq ft flat was £375,000 in November. The adjoining **Gun House,** by the same developer, eight flats plus a penthouse, is new-build. **Gun Place** is on the inland side of the High St and has 73 flats in a conversion. Alongside, **Bridewell Place** is also Barratt: this one is a gated, cobbled and positively quaint mews with 52 homes (houses and flats, some new, some old) completed in 1988. Also on the inland side – and close to Wapping tube station – is **The Carronade,** 42 flats, some double-height and galleried. **Towerside,** by Wates, straddles Wapping High St; the waterside part is new; the rest – **Prusom's Island** – award-winning refurbished warehouses (a decent-sized studio was £200,000 last winter). A total of 97 flats and new-build houses here; although not the most sophisticated of riverside schemes, it does provide among the least expensive: a 1-bed riverside flat might (this year as in the last two) be £220,000, a 2-bed £330,000, considered the best Thames-side value in Wapping. **St Hilda's Wharf** is a smart, late-1980s riverside scheme of 39 large – especially for new-build – flats.

New Crane Wharf is a warehouse conversion with a courtyard (**New Crane Court**), around which are grouped 143 homes plus some offices, shops and also restaurants. A very popular, good-quality development; a 3-bed, 2,193 sq ft flat was £800,000 last winter. **Great Jubilee Wharf**, refurbished and extended in 1996 by Galliard, created 30 flats. Further along, straddling **Wapping High St**, Persimmon's **Thorpe's Yard** is a group of three buildings – riverside warehouse conversion and new-build – dating from 1998. The riverside chunk is called **Merchant Court**. One part, **Spinnaker Mews**, is six 4-storey, 3-bed houses on **Wapping Wall** – the name for the riverside street from here on E. **Pelican Wharf**, next door to the famous Prospect of Whitby pub, has 13 large 1,700 sq ft apartments – each bigger than a normal modern house. Walkways round an atrium and a whole-floor penthouse with three roof gardens are among its attractions.

On the other side of the pub **Prospect Wharf** (a.k.a. **Trafalgar Court**) has 60 flats in a rather ungainly, gabled-roof 1980s warehouse style, built by Trafalgar House in an enviable position between the river and Shadwell Basin. Great views, therefore, on both sides, though some odd-shaped rooms. Another plus is the open courtyard between the river and the curve of the buildings; a rare commodity in crowded Wapping. The flats are 1- and 2-bed. **Prospect Place**, N of Wapping Wall, has 70 houses and flats in a successful

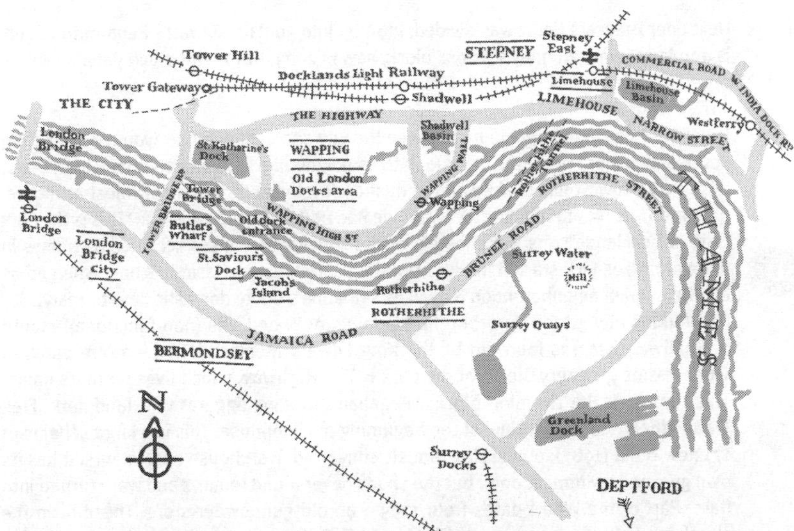

layout next to a Regalian refurb of a block of council flats, **Riverside Mansions** in **Milk Yard**, which were sold to waiting-list locals at a discount. These are 750 sq ft 2-bed maisonettes (this year, as in the last two, c. £215,000), many with views over Shadwell Basin. **Monza St**, which runs down to the river, has the **Monza Building**: Furlong Homes' 20-flat modern block. Some have Basin views: last winter a 1-bed (838 sq ft) was £295,000. House-hunters may like the big Victorian pumping station engineer's house on Wapping Wall, a survivor of the old hydraulic power system: 4 beds; yours for £1 million.

Shadwell Basin has 172 flats and houses – some with 5 beds – grouped round three sides of the dock, which is home to a youth watersports club. The gabled brick buildings of **Maynards Quay** with their distinctive semicircular windows and red detailing are popular – not surprising, given their attractive dockside position. **Peartree Lane** has 4-bed dockside houses to match those across at Maynards; **Newlands Quay** has 3-bed duplex flats. Head W to the junction of **Wapping Lane** and **Pennington St** to find Tobacco Dock, a lovely, listed warehouse, which started out as a 'themed' shopping centre around 1990, but now stands empty – except when it's used for post-film-premiere parties.

Wapping's inland quarter is mostly built on the site of the old, filled-in London Docks, but only Shadwell Basin and a shallow, ornamental, tree-lined canal remains to remind us. The canal provides an attractive environment for some good-value homes, now mature after 20-odd years. Industry such as News International's giant printworks S of **Pennington St** come rather close to some, though; there are plans to redevelop this site if News International moves, but think five to eight years. Meanwhile, plans are afoot to build shops and two tall office towers on the existing car park.

Among several 'inland' schemes, award-winning **East Quay** and **Waterman Quay** have 170 houses and flats grouped around the canal. **Portland Square** is a 1986 Barratt development with some (rare) large 3-storey houses grouped around a private square with fountain, and a range of other homes, including 2-beds which sell at c. £300,000, and 4-bed houses at c. £490,000. The gated, traffic-free square has proved very popular with families. Also on the old site of the London Docks are **Spirit Quay** – 182 low-cost (originally) homes by Broseley (some houses began as shared-ownership through a housing association), and **Quay 430**, a 300-home Regalian scheme.

Also inland are some ex-council homes which sell at lower prices than the local norm. On **The Highway**, Wapping's main road, **Telford's Yard** has 68 spacious warehouse flats.

Next door **Breezers Court** was divided, in 1985, into 30 flats. Barratt's **Pennington Court** is a 1987 scheme. Wimpey's **'Eluna'** block, new in 2003, has 1- and 2-bed flats: all sold.

Limehouse

Limehouse has a great position, between the City and Canary Wharf (you can walk from here), and is more domestic in scale than its neighbours Wapping and the Isle of Dogs. Villagey **Narrow St** has shaken off the dust of development and is now most attractive, perhaps on its way to fulfilling local heroine Rae Hoffenberg's prediction: 'This is the Park Lane of Docklands'. Mrs Hoffenberg's battles to get warehouses accepted as homes in the early 1970s kick-started modern Docklands. Limehouse Basin has now emerged as another marina neighbourhood to rival St Katharine's (more domestic, less touristy).

D

Working along the river from the Wapping, or W end, the (non-functional) mouth of Shadwell Basin is followed by the King Edward Memorial Park – a rare patch of Thames-side greenery. North of the park is **The Highway**, which lives up to its name. This runs N of the riverside blocks. Regalian's orange ziggurat of a landmark, **Free Trade Wharf**, stands sentinel at the beginning of Limehouse. This is a large scheme of 171 new-build (1987), and six luxuriously converted, warehouse apartments. It has its own gym and swimming pool, but the shops never found tenants and were turned into flats. Part of the Wharf dates from 1795 – an old gunpowder store. These form the chunk marketed in '99–2000 as **The Listed Building**: 37 riverview 1- and 2-bed flats. Regalian's rather gaunt **Atlantic Wharf**, 213 1-, 2- and 3-beds, most with Thames views, continues the riverside.

Keepier Wharf, a reclad warehouse with 24 spacious flats completed in 1987, signals the start of Limehouse's best-known address, **Narrow St**. This runs the length of the waterfront and is famous for its short surviving row of splendid riverside Georgian houses, as well as for the equally venerable Grapes pub. Narrow St's riverside blocks include: **Papermill Wharf** (1992); Barratt's 1997 **Victoria Wharf**, 66 2-bed flats – and a 3-bed, 3-terrace, £1.1-million duplex penthouse with 360° views – by the Limehouse Basin lock; **Chinnocks Wharf** by St George's; **Old Sun Wharf** (don't confuse with Sun Wharf, below), a 2002 block of 36 2- and 3-bed duplexes all with river views. Opposite Victoria Wharf is Fairclough's **Victoria Lock** – a mix of 1-, 2- and 3-bed flats plus 3- and 4-bed houses. Latest scheme is Angel's **Phoenix Wharf**, right at the W end: 11 large flats.

On the inland side, between Narrow St and The Highway, is **St George's Square**, a remarkable mix of architectural styles from neo-Docklands vernacular to mock-Tudor, executed in red brick: 41 houses and flats surround a small courtyard. **The Mosaic** is a very high-spec 2001 St James scheme, also on the N side of Narrow St, running through to **Horseferry Rd**: some of the top-floor flats out of the 195 here still get Thames views.

Along the riverside are several smaller conversions, including the heavily rebuilt 1930s **Ratcliffe Wharf**, and **London** and **Commercial Wharves**. The latter pair are by the hand of the unquenchable Mrs Rae Hoffenberg, the Docklands pioneer who started converting warehouses (and living in them) in the early 1970s when Tower Hamlets Council was insisting that they all still had an industrial future. Mrs Hoffenberg crusades to maintain the area's character. Adjacent **Roneo Wharf** has 2-bed flats. **Sun Wharf**, however, is just one vast 11,000 sq ft home: it used to belong to the film director David Lean. It is unique in Docklands in having a complete waterside garden – lawns, trees and all – with a 124ft frontage to the river. The whole place was carved out of four old warehouses in 1985: it changed hands for £3 million – and that was in 1995.

Across the road from Victoria Wharf sits the **Limehouse Basin**, a marina – and, delightfully, the entrance to the country's canal system. The Basin's development was held up not just by the 1990 recession, but also by the digging of the giant road tunnel which runs beneath it. Several developers have contributed: St George produced **Quayside** – a modern but classical-looking development of 1-, 2- and 3-bed apartments and duplexes around a courtyard; **Commercial Wharf** (yes, another one) is Barratt's scheme of low, brick terraces just back from the eastern side of the Basin.

Bellway are responsible for the W side: four rather dramatic blocks with canted roofs named **Marina Heights**, and a smart steel tower, **'The Pinnacle'**: 500 homes altogether, continuing round onto the N side of the dock, and there's six modernistic town-houses (one was £865,000 last winter). Bellway's 102 flats about to appear will be the last of the Basin schemes. The Basin houses a thriving marina and the HQ of the Cruising Association: you can access the canal network from here, or berth an ocean-going yacht.

Back on the river, **Blyth's Wharf** is a terrace of 4-bed houses: 16, over 2,000 sq ft, all with river views. It boasts an extensive pier, giving a promenade open to the public. Inland is **The Watergardens**, a stylish refurbishment of Roy Square, once as beige as its name; 1- and 2-bed flats. Past these two are the real thing: the Georgian waterside houses and the Grapes pub. **Duke Shore Wharf** is next: new-build, in a horseshoe shape.

Inland, opposite the Grapes pub on Ropemaker Fields, a small new park, is a row of large modern 4-bed houses attached to a pub, 'The House They Left Behind' (literally: the rest of the Victorian terrace was demolished). Between this and the Watergardens is Persimmon's **Sovereign Place**: 51 homes from 1- and 2-bed flats to 3-bed town-houses.

Narrow St curves on round the N side of Limekiln Dock, an inlet off the river. A footbridge across the dock gives access to the Wharf complex. The N side of the dock has 109 flats, including a split-level penthouse, all under the banner **Dunbar Wharf**. The existing old warehouse was converted in 1999, and three new buildings added. A 3-bed, 1,700 sq ft riverside flat in Dunbar was £750,000 last winter. **Limehouse Wharf** is a small 1840 warehouse, an early conversion into flats: large, with unusually high ceilings. **Limekiln Wharf** at the head of the inlet has six flats in a renovated building, and 23 new ones in an L-shaped block. Next door are two new houses, while a small dockside warehouse has, unusually, been converted to a single, 3,400 sq ft, 3-bed house. Next door on **Three Colts St** is **Dundee Wharf**, a 10-storey block on the Dock's corner variously described as 'futuristic' and 'imposing', with spidery balconies and a tower that looks like a post-functional crane. There are 112 flats, 21 penthouses and five houses. Most have splendid views upriver to the City or across to Canary Wharf.

London Bridge

South of the river now, to where the westernmost tongue of Docklands intrudes right into the heart of London, facing the City, between London and Tower Bridges. **London Bridge City** has a million sq ft of offices, plus shops and restaurants, in the handsome Hay's Galleria with its soaring atrium, flats to rent, health club and a private hospital. A riverside walkway continues the promenade which runs W as far as Vauxhall.

The 13-acre site to the E, stretching to Tower Bridge, is marketed as 'More London Bridge' and has 500,000 sq ft of offices – including the futuristic newt's-eye-shaped City Hall for the Greater London Authority and Mayor of London. No homes are envisaged – though the demolition of several blocks of council flats just to the S is, to the fury of residents, who justifiably feel that they are being tidied out of the way.

New homes are appearing in the area; a 1901 Aston Webb-designed dock office building in **Tooley St** has become 14 2- and 3-bed flats (one 2-bed here, £450,000), and 14 new-build flats in the same street were on the market last winter from £315,000. The Jubilee Line links London Bridge to Waterloo, the West End and Canary Wharf – though the 17,000 workers in the whole complex will stretch the infrastructure, as will the planned 66-floor 'Shard of Glass' tower above London Bridge station: an amazingly elegant design – if it is ever built.

For homes, look to the area S of London Bridge and around newly fashionable **Bermondsey St** – see the South Bank chapter – a good hunting ground for warehouse conversions and new-build homes. There is a lot of activity on all fronts here.

Shad Thames/Tower Bridge and Bermondsey

Not all that long ago, Shad Thames was of interest only to TV companies looking for seedy, derelict locations. The dripping brickwork of the abandoned warehouses, the sinister iron walkways spanning the narrow streets, the weed-grown cobbles . . . it's a bit different now. This is the most successful, established and generally expensive Docklands neighbourhood, known both for its flats (few houses here) and its four Conran restaurants. It could be said to have moved out of Docklands and into Central London, except for its concentration on warehouse conversions and modern copies of them. In price terms it has now overtaken longer-established Wapping, with the exception of top St Katharine's and Hermitage Wharf homes.

Shad Thames is the name of the atmospheric, narrow street which runs behind the riverside wall of warehouses, curves behind the Design Museum and turns inland to run parallel to St Saviour's Dock up to **Jamaica Rd**. It has given its name to the neighbourhood (though those with no feel for history prefer the classier-sounding Tower Bridge); **Butler's Wharf** – the biggest single warehouse complex – is a name also used as shorthand for this entire, distinct quarter.

This area, which stretches on the south bank downstream from Tower Bridge, starts with one of the river's most splendid buildings. Not another warehouse, but an old Courage brewery. The **Anchor Brewhouse** is a 10-storey edifice rising sheer from the river right next to the bridge. The interior has been totally rebuilt: the shell of the old 'Boilerhouse', with its towering landmark chimney, has 35 flats including the spectacular triple-decker penthouse. Another Brewhouse flat, as spectacular in a different way, is at river level, with inch-thick glass in the living room to keep the Thames out at high tide. Studios start at c. £225,000, biger flats command c. £500 per sq ft.

The Malt Mill, now managed as part of the Anchor Brewhouse, is nearest the bridge. It has more large flats, all with river views. Here, too, is an amazing penthouse: this time on four floors, and boasting the original cupola and belvedere gallery. Where the first was glass-walled modern, its main room like the deck of a '30s liner, this one would be more like owning a Georgian house – set high in the air. It even has a 'garden': a double-height conservatory. On a more mundane level, there are 1- and 2-bed flats. From here you see the Tower of London framed within Tower Bridge. To the E of the brewery buildings is **Butler's Wharf West**, with 14 flats.

Directly behind the brewery lies **Horselydown Square**, where unlovely derelict 1950/60s buildings were cleared to be replaced by shops, offices, workshops et al, around **Tower Bridge Plaza**, an open landscaped square: 178 homes, some conversion, some new-build, have been created (2-bed duplex £385,000). Names to look out for in this corner are **Eagle Wharf** (1-beds, with balcony and parking, c. £330,000), **Compass Court**, **The Cooperage**, **Crown Apartments** and **Horselydown Court**. **Tower Bridge Square**, on **Gainsford St**, was built for sale by the Nationwide Housing Trust: 1- and 2-bed flats and town-houses. On the E side of **Lafone St**, the **Cardamom Building** is a smart, well-regarded warehouse conversion fronting Shad Thames (2-bed £625,000). Behind it, moving away from the river, is Galliard's **Cayenne Court**, completed in 2001.

Next, back on the riverside, comes **Butler's Wharf**, a very large, long and handsome warehouse range dating from the 1870s. It fell out of use in 1971, and until 1980 was an artists' colony as all kinds of creative people occupied the vast, decaying spaces. They were displaced by the start of the Docklands warehouses-to-flats boom – but the surviving warehouses were declared a Conservation Area, and the resulting conversion to homes restored the original dignity to their cream-painted riverside facades. Nowadays Butler's is five blocks of apartments, which until 2000 were rented out. The current owners have refurbished the flats to a very high specification, creating in all around 80 1-, 2-, and 3-bed flats, duplexes, and penthouses. Examples on the market last winter ranged from a 900 sq ft 1-bed at £400,000 via a river-view 646 sq ft 1-bed at £475,000 to a 3-bed duplex at £1.65 million. On the ground floor three Terence Conran restaurants are housed: The Chop House, Pont de la Tour and Cantina del Ponto; it is to the long-term vision of Conran that the Shad Thames area owes a lot of its fortunes. This 'gastrodome' complex revived Conran's own fortunes after the Butler's Wharf Development Co. (in which he had a large interest) went into receivership in the early '90s.

Also beside the river is **Spice Quay**, a new-build block of 92 flats completed by Galliard in 1999. A river-view 2-bed here might be £650,000 or so. The ground floor has shops, bars and two restaurants. Next to this is the Design Museum, in which is the Blue Print Café (the fourth local Conran restaurant – but first to open). A 4-storey house – the only one on **Shad Thames** – was built here in 2000. Fairview's **Vanilla** and **Sesame Courts**, just behind Spice Quay, completed the following year: there are 124 1-, 2- and 3-bed flats over seven floors: expect to pay c. c. £285,000 here for a 1-bed, £365,000 for a smallish 2-bed. Next to Butler's Court and also behind Spice Quay is **Wheat Wharf** – a recently refurbished 18th-century grain store, now 25 flats.

D

The enviable Thames-side parade of homes between Shad Thames and the river ends E of the Design Museum with the long-derelict 1920s (not Victorian, whatever the developers say) Butler's Wharf Building No. 15. Only in 2003 was this developed as **Tea Trade Wharf**. Galliard have created 64 flats; a restaurant occupies the ground floor. It has a superb site at the mouth of **St Saviour's Dock**, a river inlet, now bridged.

Many warehouse conversions and new-build schemes crowd together along the narrow **St Saviour's** waterway. It is north-facing, so lack of light can be a drawback, especially on lower floors. On the W side of the Dock is **Cinnamon Wharf** – a stylish late '80s conversion of a former 1950s block into 66 flats. Next to the S is **Saffron Wharf** – an '80s office converted into 13 units by Berkeley Homes (3-bed £750,000).

(All these spicy names reflect the original trade from these warehouses. Spices were still ground in odd little workshops in **Gainsford St** up till 1995. This led to the first excited flat-buyers claiming that the very walls of their new homes were scented by the 'long-gone' spice trade. Had they walked just round the corner, they could have met the dusty, blue-overalled grinders in person.)

Next door to Saffron is **Java Wharf**, a listed warehouse with spacious 2-bed flats. **Christian's Warehouse** is a 1989 conversion/new-build scheme, with 87 flats overlooking St Saviour's Dock. (It takes in the old St Saviour's, St George's, St Christian's, Shuters, Dockhead and Jamaica wharves.)

Away from the Dock, on the corner of **Maguire St** and **Gainsford St**, is **Tamarind Court** – a warehouse carved into 62 flats by Galliard, where 2-beds are c. £380,000. On the other side of Gainsford St, on the corner with **Shad Thames**, Nicholson Estates has created a complex of homes located around a gated courtyard. The splendidly named Butler's Grinders & Operators buildings ('spice and gum grinders' in the old days) have been reborn as **Butler's and Colonial Wharf** (why wharf? It's well inland), with some new town-houses, flats (c. £420,000 for a 2-bed) and some live/work units. Across the road from Tamarind on the corner of Gainsford Street, and opposite Butler's and Colonial Wharf on **Maguire Street**, are the **Anise** and **Coriander Buildings** (that's enough spices, lads), a conversion of two Victorian warehouses by Maskell into 25 1- and 2-bed flats.

Next, something truly original: straddling **Queen Elizabeth St** is **The Circle** – a name from which you might have inferred its fluid circus shape, but not perhaps its bright blue-brick fascias, nor the splendid dray-horse statue at its hub. Dating from 1988 – the first Docklands boom – studios are c. £225,000, 1- and 2-bed flats are c. £245–500,000. Further along the street and at 16–19 **Lafone St** is **Raven Wharf**: 21 new-build 2- and 3-bed flats (2,500 sq ft £975,000) and two live/work units by Gleeson Homes (2003). **Boss House**, E of **Boss St**, is a 20th-century warehouse converted into spacious 2-bed flats.

The beautiful footbridge at the mouth of **St Saviour's Dock** links the Shad Thames quarter to the rest of the Bermondsey riverside. Inland,on the E side of the head of the creek is **Scott's Sufferance Wharf**: an attractive, Italianate courtyard of shops, offices and 93 flats of various sizes (2-beds £350–400,000). **Lloyd's Wharf** has 24 flats sold as shells in 1985 (for – this will make you sob – £30–60,000). Today, pay c. £600,000 for a split-level 2-bed. **Unity Wharf** has four gloriously large work/live flats.

Vogan's Mill sits on a big, deep dockside site: the conversion of this old flour mill yielded 64 2-, 3- and 4-bed flats plus penthouses in six buildings: some old, some new. Thanks to the existence of the mill's tall silo, the developer got the chance to replace that structure with an 18-storey high-tech tower – a quality development topped by an enviable 3-floor penthouse. Next door, the refurbishment of **St Saviour's Wharf** made 47 flats (going these days at c. £400 per sq ft) and offices.

D

And downstream, at the creek's mouth, is the award-winning **New Concordia Wharf**, a vast 1880s warehouse discovered on the point of demolition by young developer Andrew Wadsworth; his 1981–85 conversion sparked the revival of the entire Bermondsey bank. New Concordia is still the benchmark for Bermondsey quality, and is much requested by homeseekers. Note that some have Dock views, some river views, some look onto the courtyard. One of the latter was £500,000 for 1,400 sq ft last winter. Next door is Wadsworth's 1986 **China Wharf**: new-build, smaller rooms, glorious views, edgy architecture (by CZWG; more awards). **Reeds Wharf**, adjoining, has flats and offices. The residential barges at Reeds Wharf that add much charm to its views were saved last year despite a campaign by nearby flat-dwellers to have them 'tidied away.' Next to Reeds Wharf, a single 5-storey house appeared on a riverside plot.

Providence Square takes up most of **Jacob's Island** – the historic name (and why on earth is no developer using it?) for the tract E of **Mill St**: Berkeley's new-build scheme has eight blocks of 1- and 2-bed flats and penthouses, set round a water-garden. On the river front going along **Bermondsey Wall West**, first comes Berkeley's smart **Providence Tower** (a 2-bed, £775,000), then **Springalls Wharf,** a handsome new flats block (river view flats c. £650 per sq ft). Next is **River View Heights**, 1-, 2- and 3-bed flats: 62 of them, on eight floors (more like £510 per sq ft here). **St Saviour's House** is on the inland side of the street and not that close to the dock: 12 high-spec flats and two live/work units.

The smart conversions and new-builds of the riverside and Jacob's Island contrast, as you go E along **Bermondsey Wall**, with the Dickens Estate of 1930s council flats, which spreads S towards **Jamaica Rd.** Not beautiful, but quite a few are now in private hands and they're popular with both owner-occupiers and investment buyers. East again lies the last surviving, and empty, warehouse of **Chambers Wharf.** Next to it Berkeley are building 226 flats, new and converted, in the **Tempus Wharf** scheme. This runs in from the river to S of **Chambers St**, straddling **East Lane**. The first two blocks (of five) will be ready this spring: they had 15 flats still unsold in January, priced £240-390,000. More follow until 2006, the riverside blocks – but not all have car parking.

Next comes **Cherry Garden Pier**, with 64 nice, riverside, council-built houses (new and rehab) and five terraces of flats and town-houses built in the 1980s (typically, and as last year, 1-beds are £180,000, 2-beds £240,000, town-house £330,000). From here on E, you'll find the name 'Rotherhithe' creeping in to agents' descriptions, but we're not there yet. **Corbetts Wharf** was converted to flats back in 1984; **Angel Wharf** across the road in 1995. The semi-rural cottages around **Marigold St** are 1920s. Next to Corbetts and on the river is **National Terrace**, ten 4-storey, 4-bed houses with garages: popular and spacious. More council, and ex-council, flats and houses abound along **Bermondsey Wall East** and inland, including some in an incongruous 1920s rural-cottage style.

Rotherhithe

On eastwards, to the surviving waterside hamlet of Rotherhithe, dripping with history. It boasts a glorious 1715 parish church, St Mary's, the internal pillars of which are not stone but old ships' masts, plastered over. Surrounding church and churchyard, the wonderful old school, rectory and some of the warehouses also all date from at least Georgian days. Here, too, is the 16th-century Mayflower pub, heavily but cleverly rebuilt after war damage, so still looking much as it did. In 1620, then named the Spread Eagle Inn, it saw the Pilgrim Fathers set off from Rotherhithe on their way to America. On the W edge of the village **Elephant Lane/Mayflower Court** has 76 houses and flats, plus offices, built in 1984 in an avenue running from the river to the Rotherhithe Tunnel (which takes cars beneath the Thames to Shadwell) roundabout. **Pilgrim House**, off Elephant Lane, is a dramatic red, gabled block with loft-style flats, c. £230–350,000. Around the ancient village are several blocks of pre-war council-built flats: those on **Swan Rd** are particularly popular with buyers.

At the very beginning of **Rotherhithe St**, at King's Stairs Close, stands **Princes Tower,** an imposing 1930s-inspired white block with 2- and 3-bed flats which sell for £300–900,000. The historic, award-winning **Thames Tunnel Mills** is a riverside warehouse converted into fair-rent flats, while **Ronald Buckingham Court** is sheltered housing. The next development is **Bombay Wharf** in **St Marychurch St**, where Taylor Woodrow has converted two riverside warehouses – flats here last winter from £420,000 – while a third riverside building forms a single house. Inland, another warehouse plus two new blocks make up the total of 77 flats. The conversion of two warehouses and also the building of a new block at **Hope Sufferance Wharf** between the river, Rotherhithe St and St Marychurch St has created 32 homes: flats (c. £230,000 for 2-beds) and stylish 2-bed houses. This successful scheme has raised the profile of the village – though this very real community rather hopes to remain reasonably undiscovered. . . . Once a hidden, cut-off corner, its station is on the East London Line (extending – see Transport chapter), and Canada Water (Jubilee Line) is not far. **Isambard Place**, the name of which recalls the tunnel's builder, has 94 2- to 4-bed flats, plus 44 for a housing association. Distinctive **Tunnel Wharf**, dating from 2000 and designed by Piers Gough, has eight flats plus short-let apartments. Three on the market in the autumn were £395,000 each (£30,000 less than in March '03). Across the road, the **Atlas Reach** scheme adds a further 100 flats.

Surrey Quays

The river bends like the shape of an upside-down horseshoe as we travel downstream from Rotherhithe. On eastwards, round this great sweep, is the frontage of the old Surrey Docks. Nearly all the docks were filled in, and over the past 20 years large areas of new housing have been built on what was in effect a vast greenfield site. These homes thus differ markedly in character, if not in style, from the riverfront schemes: inland, houses with gardens predominate, rather than warehouse flats or flash new developments – though there are plenty of nice, popular examples of those, too, around the river margins and what is left of the docks – now a much-appreciated marina. There's a hotel, too. For families, there are thriving schools. Even a farm. Surrey Quays shopping centre has been joined by Surrey Quays Phase II and includes an 8-screen cinema, bingo, bowling and eateries. While restaurants and bars appear in the wake of all the young tenants, most locals still rely on Shad Thames, Canary Wharf or the West End for leisure: easily reached now, thanks to the Jubilee Line.

Inspired planning back in the LDDC days led to preservation of quite a bit of the dock infrastructure, and the creation of two new lakes: Canada Water and Surrey Water. The former is at the centre of a planned new development that will add 2,000 homes, a department store, a library and other amenities. The new, eco-friendly plan, by developer British Land working with Southwark Council, is a big advance on the idea mooted by the council in 2001 to fill in Canada Water – the focal point of the area, and a wildlife reserve – and build a 40-acre office/retail/homes complex. Residents, vowing to keep their 'waterside village' 'low, clean and green' started a campaign and forced Southwark to rewrite the plans. Southwark is working with British Land to come up with an agreed masterplan. There is already permission for a 224-flats block, plus an IT hosting centre and some shops, on the corner of **Canada St** and **Surrey Quays Rd.**

To the N of the lake, the splendid Canada Water tube station is the key to this area: this is where the Jubilee and East London Lines intersect. There are plans (see Transport chapter) to extend the East London both N and S. The river taxis across to Canary Wharf from Greenland Pier and the Hilton provide rapid alternatives to the tube.

D

The interior of the Surrey Quays neighbourhood has large areas of 'normal' – i.e. family-style – housing, put up by large builders: the result has a strong new-town flavour. No new town, however, has the dramatic view of the City towers offered by Stave Hill, the artificial mound at the centre of the area. **Dock Hill Avenue**, a tree-lined walk, flanked by new houses, leads from the hill to Surrey Water. The walkway is cleverly aligned to point straight at the City skyscape across the river. This is the affordable side of Docklands, with 4-bed houses still available for the sort of money which would barely buy you a 1-bed flat in some of the top-flight Docklands developments. There's further choice in resales of the Southwark Council-built family homes along and off **Salter Rd** that date from the 1970s, before yuppie flats were thought of. An Ecological Park, waterways and sports fields are further enticements for family buyers.

Starting right next to Canada Water tube station, a century-old hydraulic pumping station (**The Pump House**) was converted into 31 loft flats, with a further 23 new-build flats and houses in a courtyard. Small 1-bed flats start at £210,000; a 3/4-bed, 3-bath town-house here might be £420,000.

Rotherhithe St runs right round the peninsula. On from Isambard Place and to the E of **Brunel Rd,** Bellway Homes have built **Brunel Point**: 2- and 3-bed flats, some with river views (2-beds £220–240,000), and town-houses on the other side of **Rotherhithe St**. Two-beds here start from around £220,000. This part of Rotherhithe St has been permanently closed off to traffic. An inlet leads through a disused lock to Surrey Water, which is surrounded by homes.

From Surrey Water a canal (again, just to look at) called Albion Channel winds through various housing developments to Canada Water. Along the canal, amid now fully-grown trees, are pleasant groups of homes. These vary from social-housing flats up to **Wolfe Crescent**, built by Lovell in a red-brick semicircle curled around four pale-coloured, strikingly designed octagonal blocks: 1-, 2- and 3-bed flats and 3/4-bed houses. **Hithe Point** was built by Barratt: 1-, 2- and 3-bed flats (a 1-bed, c. £180,000), 2- and 3-bed houses. Opposite **Wolfe Crescent** and bordering **Surrey Quays Rd** is Persimmon's gated 1999 development **Woodland Crescent** (2- and 3-bed flats; 3-bed houses). These homes are close to the tube and are much in demand: 2-bed flats are currently from £280,000, 3-bed houses £420,000.

At Island Yard, by the lock, stands a large pub called Spice Island. Adjacent to Island Yard and on the corner of **Rotherhithe St** and the YMCA a new block of 18 flats is known as **Trade Winds. Pacific Wharf** by Fitzpatrick has 72 new flats. Next to this on **Rotherhithe St**, and before King & Queen Wharf, is **Prince's Riverside** – a large development (184 units) of 1- and 2-bed riverview flats and 3/4-bed houses, completed in 1997. Four-bed houses sell now for £420,000-plus. **King & Queen Wharf** is nicely detailed new-build by Fairclough, first marketed in 1990: 140 flats with porterage and swimming pool/leisure complex, the river view 2-beds going for £300,000 upwards.

Next to King & Queen Wharf is Berkeley's **Globe Wharf**, a sensitive and much-in-demand restoration of this former grain warehouse: you'll be asked £330,000 for a 2-bed with river view, £1.3 million for a really big flat. **Sovereign Crescent** – a large neo-Georgian development (including the refurbishment of the old fire station on Rotherhithe St) – was built by Barratt between 1991–93; units vary from 1- bed flats to 2- and 3-bed houses with garages built round six squares, most with river views. Pay c. £450,000 for a 3-bed town-house. Also facing the river is **Pageant Steps**, built by

Barratt in 1996. This consists of three blocks of 1- and 2-bed flats, some with river views, and 3-bed houses (c. £500,000) with conservatories and gardens and direct river views. Off **Sovereign Crescent** on the riverside are four squares of handsome brick houses and two blocks of flats. Two-bed houses here are £260–280,000, flats £220–280,000. Opposite Pageant Steps, and inland, is the 141-home Lavender Dock complex, now named **Admiral Place** and **Heron Place**. On Rotherhithe St is **3 Nine 2**: 34 smart new 1- and 2-bed flats.

Canada Wharf is the stark, modernist refurbishment of a former granary by Metropolis Developments. Homes are 1- to 3-bed flats (from 500–1,600 sq ft), several with high ceilings and bed decks. Next on the riverside is the 622-bed Holiday Inn Hotel. The original warehouse **Columbia Wharf**, with **Nelson Dock** and **Lawrence Wharf**, were all part of **Port Nelson**, a scheme developed by Islef. In the midst of the development Nelson House is a rare and charming Georgian survival: this, Columbia Wharf and Nelson Dock – where 18th-century warships were once built – now form part of the hotel, while the original Lawrence Wharf flats, after a chequered career in the '90s as a timeshare and then rented, have been refurbished and sold off. It has 156 flats: 1-, 2- and 3-beds with river views, in three blocks together with 30 3-bed garden flats and 1-bed ground-floor flats in a terrace on **Rotherhithe St**. Opposite, on the inland side, the **Amos Estate** has 131 housing association flats. Next comes **Lavender Dock North**, 51 1985 Wimpey houses, inland. **Lavender Green**, inland across **Salter Rd**, is 1981 low-cost (but not any more) housing by Lovell.

Opposite Lawrence Wharf is **Silver Walk**, an ex-local authority complex of flats and 21 stylish 3- and 4-bed houses (refurbished, gated, popular and now selling for £300,000-plus) and some new-build units (**Patina Walk**). Patina Walk was sold to the LSE for student housing in the early '90s. Rialto's 2002 **'South East One Six'** has 88 flats and two houses (resales from £240,000). A tiny, peaceful park (Durands Wharf) gives access to the riverside plus views to the Isle of Dogs and the Canary Wharf towers. Next to the park is **Trinity Wharf**, a Bellway development dating from 2000, with 2- and 3-bed flats. **Barnard's Wharf** and **Commercial Pier Wharf**, next to the splendid Surrey Docks Farm, have 139 homes built by housing associations. This is Downtown, for years a very depressed corner of council flats, now a thriving area after a £55-million rehabilitation of the flats blocks by a group of housing associations. Further down is the riverside **New Caledonian Wharf**, which has 104 luxurious flats and includes swimming pool and sports centre, extensively sold off-plan in 1987; expect to pay £250–350,000 for 2-beds, £350,000-plus for 3-beds; a nice scheme, but a bit far from transport (and check the service charges). Next door is **Custom House Reach**, a 1970s 9-storey block of un-special flats – many, however, have mooring rights and are well proportioned.

Greenland Dock in the SE corner of the Surrey Quays area is the main surviving, un-filled-in dock. It, plus adjoining (also original) **South Dock**, has provided waterside sites for a variety of builders, British and European, since 1982, and there are 1,500 homes. It is also a thriving marina, London's largest. **Greenland Passage** at the dock's mouth has 152 homes, many of family size. These flats and houses, built, like Port Nelson, by the Danish firm Islef in 1986, are some of the most expensive in the Surrey Docks and fulfil the early Docklands ideal of living in generous airy spaces with ashwood flooring, white walls and marbled bathrooms and kitchens. (Here 4-bed houses are now over £430,000). Next inland is **Rainbow Quay** in **Rope St**, two years old, with 144 1-, 2- and 3-bed flats, most having dock views. On the S side of **Plough Way** is **Iceland Wharf**, a new-build scheme which completed last winter: prices £185,000-plus for 1-beds, £265,000 for 2-beds. The S side of South Dock, between it and Plough Way, has several closes with good-value flats: studios from £140,000, 1-beds with a Dock view £180,000-plus.

Back on Greenland Dock, **Aland Court** has 1-, 2- and 3-bed flats and duplexes (Lovell). **Russell Place** (original development name **Russia Court East**) juts into the dock, with a circular 7-storey tower (**Tavistock Tower**) of flats on the point; the scheme includes further homes, shops, offices and a pub.

Finland Yard's 1- to 3-bed flats were new in 1999. **Greenland Quay** uses open courtyard layouts to give everyone water views. **Swedish Quays** on **Rope St** sits between **Greenland** and **South Docks**: 96 flats and houses (some very large) completed in 1990. At the tip of Greenland Dock, on a corner near the shopping centre and **Lower Rd**, are two blocks – **Howland Quay** (Fairclough, 1996; 2-beds, 240,000-plus) and **Lock Keepers Gate** (Redrow, 1997). **Brunswick Quay**, one of the earliest schemes, runs along the N side of the Dock with flats and town-houses (the latter, as since 2002, c. £290–380,000).

D

Just N of Greenland Dock is **The Lakes**, built on **Plover Way** on the site of Norway Dock (177 houses and flats around a shallow lake, with the largest villas actually on pontoons, by Ideal Homes). Water is pumped up from boreholes, and a complete eco-system has emerged, with top-flight dawn choruses. The Lakes was completed in 1995 after a long pause during the last recession. This is very popular: perhaps the best address in the area, with flats and large 3- and 4-bed semi-detached villa-style houses (c. £350–500,000 last winter).

Baltic Quay, in **Sweden Gate**, is on the S side of **South Dock**. A 13-storey tower has 24 flats and a 5-storey block another 133, with current prices of £270,000-plus for 2-beds. The scheme dates back to the '80s. The flats were let for a decade and done up for sale since 2000. The South Dock Marina, London's biggest working marina, opened in 1989. On the S side of the dock, Fairview completed a range of flats and houses in 1996: these have fantastic views of the marina and Canary Wharf. The marina has prompted a marine workshops building, and the Dock offices overlook the water. At the mouth of the dock stands **Dock Master's Quay**, a stylish terrace of 3-bed houses overlooking the dock and the river.

Canary Wharf/The Isle of Dogs

The Isle of Dogs is indeed an island, cut off by a great bend of the Thames and with its isthmus all but severed by the West India Docks. Unlike the Surrey Docks it has kept its water, providing vast lengths of quayside. The Isle is special in two other ways: it had the most cut-off indigenous community, for decades hardly part of London at all and only tenuously involved in the rest of Docklands, and it now has Canary Wharf, described in detail under Progress Report above.

By the end of the 1970s the Isle of Dogs had lost all its working docks and most of its other employers. Five hundred acres of land and water, and many buildings, were derelict. The housing, such as it was, was council-owned: these homes are still there, all on 'inland' sites away from river and docks. There were just 203 owner-occupiers – 4 per cent of the households – in 1981. Now, a quarter-century along, the Isle renaissance is old enough to have a history. The hesitant days of light industry, timidly built on land almost given away by the LDDC with no local taxes to pay thanks to the Enterprise Zone (the EZ, 1982–92), were succeeded by homes and taller, smarter, more self-confident commercial buildings. By the time the DLR arrived in 1987, early '80s buildings were already being torn down: they no longer earned their keep on the rapidly appreciating sites. Then the 1990 recession came and everything halted, to start up again with a bang in the mid-'90s (though no-one much noticed, so ingrained was the 'Docks Disaster' mind-set). Now the property world is eyeing the low-rise office buildings in the S half of the Isle, and on the margins of Canary Wharf, and planning their replacement with towers. The Isle of Dogs is now a city-centre location, not a business park.

By no means all the building sites are office blocks: homes have appeared apace, with around 5,500 built since 1981, around 500 being marketed now (some off-plan, some new-built) and any number you care to think of – 2,000, 4,000 – planned. The

Isle's riverside has a wide range, from modern social housing to glitzy apartment blocks with state-of-the-art features. Watch for the date of the development, as nobody could at first believe quite how smart the Isle would become and things built after 1985 tend to be a lot better quality, while post-'95 blocks are glitzier still (though often the newer flats are smaller).

Most Isle housing is new-build: there were no old riverside warehouses left to convert. Exceptions are the listed buildings of **Burrell's Wharf** and the dock-front flats at **West India Quay**. The riverside sites have now all been used up: any new schemes will be 'inland', probably along the Millwall Dock S of Canary Wharf if the offices don't get it all.

Coming onto the Isle from the NW, **Canary Wharf** dominates. This enormous 'city within a city' spreads from the river across the neck of the Isle between the two surviving West India Docks – one dock, the old middle section, has been built over. The complex is now expanding southwards across the E part of the **Heron Quays** site, and the two enormous bankers' towers on **Canada Square** now rival the original pyramid-topped skyscraper. And the Millennium Quarter, across the dock, will – if built as currently planned – in scale rival Canary Wharf itself.

West India Quay, to the N of Canary Wharf, has some of the finest warehouses to survive the bombs of the last war (and other, later, redevelopers). They date from 1802 and are Grade I listed, so the builders working on them had to number every one of the 6,000 paving slabs from the York stone floors – and put them back in the right order. Flats in the warehouse conversions offer plenty of bare brick, sturdy iron columns and oak beams. New oak and slate floors complement the old materials. There are also shops, restaurants, a 10-screen cinema and the Museum of Docklands – and, new this year, a hotel plus 158 £575,000-plus flats in a futuristic, bow-shaped 34-storey tower (No. 1 West India Quay) which also houses a Marriot hotel. Also on West India Quay, St George has the **Horizon Building**, a new-build 12-storey flats block.

In **Garford St**, in the shadow of Canary Wharf and close to Westferry DLR stop, is Regalians' **Premier Place**, with 1-, 2- and 3-bed flats. On **Westferry Rd** close to the station is a CZWG-designed building with 27 live/work units built by the Peabody Trust. The name 'Westferry' in 9-metre letters in the brickwork has become a landmark. A site on **Hertsmere Rd**, just on the edge of the Canary Wharf estate, has planning approval for a 63-storey edifice (also bow-shaped, doubtless iconic) dubbed 'Columbus Tower' which will (if built) be an hotel and offices.

On the river front is **Canary Riverside**, an enormous complex with the 5-star Four Seasons hotel, a health club, restaurants, 322 1-, 2-, 3- and 4-bed flats and double-height penthouses (ranging from 625–2,400 sq ft, eight available last winter from £1.75 million) and gardens. You can tell where they hoped buyers would come from: the four blocks (one a 22-storey tower) are named after West End honey-pots such as Berkeley and Belgrave (names also familiar in the Gulf and points E). Some resistance here to high prices and lack of parking. Next to the S comes an empty riverside site earmarked by Canary Wharf for two big office towers – to be built if and when tenants are lined up. **Cascades**, built 1988 but refurbished 2003, is just to the S, its stepped, 21-storey riverside tower of 171 flats a landmark (2-beds £300,000-plus). Equally well placed is **The Anchorage**, on **Suffrance Wharf**, which is next door, beside the river pier on **Cuba St**. Built of light-coloured brick, it is understated, chic and expensive; there are 123 homes in this block ranging from 1- to 3-bed flats to eight houses. Inland, **Manilla St** is gaining **Canary South**: 175 flats (1-beds from £240,000) and a new fire station.

Next to the Anchorage on **Westferry Rd** is Ballymore's **Millennium Harbour**, with 276 flats in a 10-storey tower, new in 1999: ex-rental flats were being marketed here last winter in quantity, at prices from £365,000. Next door, the two-acre **Seacon Wharf**, industrial throughout the Isle's booms and busts and the last riverside plot, has finally succumbed to development by St James: 179 flats in two buildings. Asking £510,000-

plus for a 2-bed. Architects are CZWG. Inland, on **Mastmaker Rd** and cheekily named **Canary Central** is a 406-flat scheme by Cathedral Group (1-beds from £240,000, 2-beds from £350,000). **Discovery Dock** is also here: 185 flats plus hotel, pool etc in three linked towers on **Marsh Wall,** 2-beds on for £335,000-plus for 2005 completion. Close by is Weston Homes' 352-flat **41 Millharbour** scheme, on the same schedule. Weston have plans for another 523 flats, in two 22-storey towers, on the site to the S. Here wre are in 'The Millenium Quarter' – the whole tract along **Marsh Wall** and **Millharbour.** Sites here can go either way, offices or homes, depending on demand. Just because it has a warehouse on it now doesn't mean it won't be 20 or 30 floors high by 2010.

D

Back on the Thames, **Hutchings Wharf** and **Ocean Wharf** have riverside flats by Furlong Homes in a smart circular tower. A welcome open riverside space, Sir John McDougal Gardens, will remain a park. Opposite, **Glengall Place** is an early inland estate by Barratt with 79 houses. **Arnhem Wharf** is 62 1989–'90 1- and 2-bed flats and 2-bed penthouses. Next to this and opposite the Docklands Sailing Club is **Old Bell Gate** by Galliard Homes – 61 flats, 1- and 2-beds.

Back on the river, and S of the park, Persimmon's **Icon Building** (formerly **Atlas Wharf**) has 151 high-spec flats new in 2003. **Cyclops Wharf** bravely kept the wonderful original name for this site, but is in fact a new-build late '80s development with 176 waterfront flats and 24 houses on the inland side, grouped around a square. Cyclops is showing its age, and prices are lower than on new schemes: c. £210,000 for a 1-bed. Inland along **Spindrift Avenue** Fairview completed 390 homes at **Mill Quay** in 1999. Bellway plan 36 flats at **St Edmunds,** on the corner of **Westferry Rd** and **Spindrift Avenue.** Broadway Malyan propose 275 homes on another Westferry Rd site, opposite Burrell's Wharf (see below). Other off-river sites are **Island Square, Cahir St,** which has 31 homes – 1-bed flats to 3-bed town-houses – by Laing. Cahir St also has a few Edwardian terraced cottages. **Clipper's Quay** is 256 homes around an old dock; **Quay West** comprises 127 homes, including some 4-bed town-houses, by Wimpey in surprisingly undistinguished style.

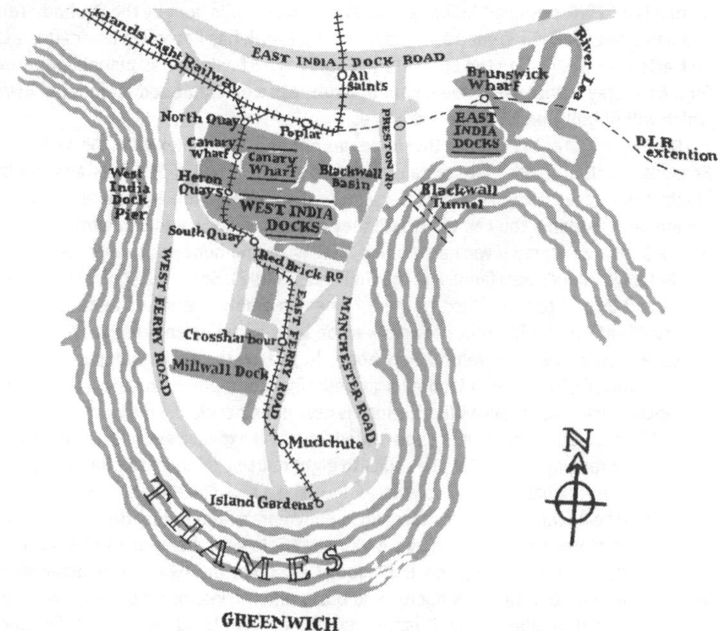

Riverside land at **Crews St** provides the site for Redrow's new **Odyssey** scheme (formerly Merchant's Point) which has 460 flats in five blocks up to 14 storeys high. Prices start at £210,000 for a 1-bed with no view. At **Napier Avenue,** N of Burrells Wharf, **Maritime Quay** is also by Redrow; 60 2-, 3- and 4-bed houses plus flats.

One of the few remaining historic sites in the Isle is **Burrell's Wharf**. Here the *Great Eastern*, the largest ship of its time, was built in the 1850s. The piles of its slipway can be seen, and remain on public view. Burrell's combines converted original with new buildings. **Machonochie's Wharf** is a self-build project, where local people planned and created their own houses.

On the southernmost site on the Isle, seven-acre **Lockes Wharf,** St George's 2003 scheme with 464 homes (including 3- and 4-storey houses, some with top-floor studio room onto roof terrace) and a leisure centre: **St David's Square** is the street name. Fairviews' **Westferry Quay** takes in **Clyde Wharf** and **Langbourne Wharf**. Homes here are superbly placed at the very tip of the Isle: 180 1- and 2-bed flats.

Felstead Wharf, a 1984 Wates scheme of 28 homes in an open square onto the river, also has great views across to Greenwich. Next to it is the 14-house **De Bruin Court. Horseshoe Court** has 80 homes, mostly flats, on an inland site. Also inland are terraces of pre-war cottage council-built houses, with large gardens. Back on the river, Barratt's **Luralda Gardens** scheme of 48 flats, which was their first Docklands venture, also shares views of the *Cutty Sark* and Greenwich. Just inland, and directly opposite Island Gardens DLR station, Telford Homes are building **Equinox:** 84 flats in two blocks (£245–390,000).

Cumberland Mills is architecturally one of the most pleasing new-build developments anywhere in Docklands. Its tiers of roof gardens step courteously down to the riverside from the high point of its four quarters without looming over its surroundings, which include a fine church. It's worth noting that riverside homes past Cumberland Mills on eastwards have views across to the Millennium Dome site at East Greenwich – and of the thousands of new homes planned around it. The award-winning **Caledonian Wharf** is an earlier 104-home scheme by Bates, the same developer as Cumberland Mills. Inland is Tower Hamlets' **Cubitt Town Estate**; on the riverside is **Plymouth Wharf,** a two-acre site with 62 homes around a square. Going N from **Mariners Mews,** Redrow Homes have added **Millennium Wharf** – 160 1- and 2-bed flats including some warehouse conversions, spread over 10 blocks.

Compass Point – again one of the best 1980s developments – has 134 houses and some flats, stretching inland across the road. Unusually, the riverside has 5-bed town-houses rather than flats. Two rows of houses reminiscent of early-Victorian brick villas run inland, facing each other across a central garden; across the road the square is completed by a white-rendered crescent of flats. **London Yard**, one of the earlier schemes on the eastern bank, consists of very large orangey-brick buildings grouped around ornamental water. Inland from this is **Friars Mead,** 72 houses built in 1986. The attractive 'pagoda' blocks of four houses are also unusual in having gardens.

From **London Yard** north for a long stretch is council-built housing. Barratt's **Pierhead Lock** at **Stewart St** is a white hi-tech development that includes a crescent and a 14-storey tower, giving a total of 91 2- and 3-bed flats. Nearby on **Preston's Rd,** Wates' **Vantage 2000** on either side of the Blackwall Lock has 132 1- and 2-bed apartments, duplexes and town-houses. Next comes **QTI,** 14 new 2-beds.

There are a few early 19th-century riverside houses along **Coldharbour**: the Isle's only answer to Limehouse. Rarely do homes in this attractive enclave come up for sale. The old dockers' boozer here is now a gastro-pub, and Weston Homes have built 26 flats and houses. **Crown Wharf** is 1970s houses, and even the old river police station has been split into homes. **Yabsley St** off **Preston Rd** has St James's 'the Lighthouse': three new blocks, in Art Deco style, up to 13 floors, with 85 flats: 2-beds from £310,000.

Inland, on the dock waterfront off **Marsh Wall** is **Meridian Place**, with 32 1-bed and 80 2-bed flats. On the same street is Galliard's **Antilles Bay**: 46 2-bed flats, all with watery views. On the E side of Millwall Dock, Epsom Homes' 6-storey glass and brick **City Harbour** has 2-beds with balconies and dock views. Crossharbour DLR station is close by. The London Arena, a giant ex-dock shed that's been a sports/concert venue for a couple of decades, is closed. In its place Balleymore plan 1,000 flats (some in a 53-floor tower) but plans are taking time to come to actuality. The ASDA site further S is also only 20 years old, but may be redeveloped at higher density with retail and homes.

D

At the entrance to and around **Blackwall Basin** is **Jamestown Harbour**, developed since 1982 by Wates; its latest phase, **Cotton's Landing**, has 101 homes. A picturesque site, making good use of the water – which offers private moorings as well as water-sports: fine views of Canary Wharf's towers. So, too, does Bellway's **The Boardwalk** between the W side of Poplar Dock (boats in plenty) and the N side of Blackwall Basin. There are over 300 homes in this stylish development. The W side is next to **Trafalgar Way** into Canary Wharf. Fairbriar are building 29 flats on **Poplar Dock** at £295–750,000.

British Waterways, of all people, emerged from the winding-down of the LDDC as landlord of a 20-acre tract between Blackwall Basin and South Dock. This is to be the **Wood Wharf** development, the masterplan for which calls for 1,500 homes plus commercial space – and a new canal to link the two docks. A developer should be chosen this year: the final shortlist has British Land fighting it out with a Canary Wharf/Manhattan Lofts/Ballymore consortium.

By now we are at the top NE corner of the Isle of Dogs, site of one of the biggest current schemes, **New Providence Wharf** on **Blackwall Way** (the old Charrington's site). Ballymore are building 735 homes, in a curving riverside arc rising to 18 storeys plus two inland blocks, and a 29-storey tower that was going to be a hotel, but is now being marketed as the Ontario Building, with 260 flats, 70 per cent studios of less than 400 sq ft. Prices start at £195,000. Prices at the first phase, now ready, start at c. £280,000

On round to the E, Barratt have built 700 homes, part named **Virginia Quay** and another **Meridian East**. The site borders the old East India Dock, now a nature reserve, to the E, with the Thames to the S and a big S-facing piazza with views down both sides of the river bend, and the Millennium Dome. The Greenwich Meridian runs through the site: it will be marked by an avenue. Next from Barratt comes the conversion of an inland 1930s electricity station on **Aspen Way** into a 10-storey, 200-flats tower, with 60 new-build flats next door.

Residents in **Virginia Quay** have had a spur to their neighbourly spirits: they have formed a residents' group to fight Reuters' plans to develop their riverside site just to the W. The latest plans are for six towers, 11 to 29 stories high, totalling 716 flats. One of the towers would be 105m high, and the Virginians grumble that it would block their views and their TV reception. However the Mayor of London has cleared the scheme.

For the next few miles east, the Royal Docks, see its own chapter. For the Isle of Dogs Mark Two across the river, the Greenwich peninsula, see the Greenwich chapter.

Among estate agents active in this area are:

- Carlton Smith
- Knight Frank
- Housemartin
- Michael Kalmar
- Living in London
- Kinleigh Folkard & Hayward
- Duncan Allen
- Hurford Salvi Carr
- Cluttons
- Savills
- Alex Neil
- Oliver Jaques
- Tower Property
- Winkworth
- Chesterton
- Hamptons
- Keatons
- Phoenix
- Roger Lewis
- John D Wood
- Burnet Ware & Graves
- Stirling Ackroyd
- Alan Selby
- Property Liaisons
- Felicity J Lord
- D P Seager

DOLLIS HILL AND NEASDEN

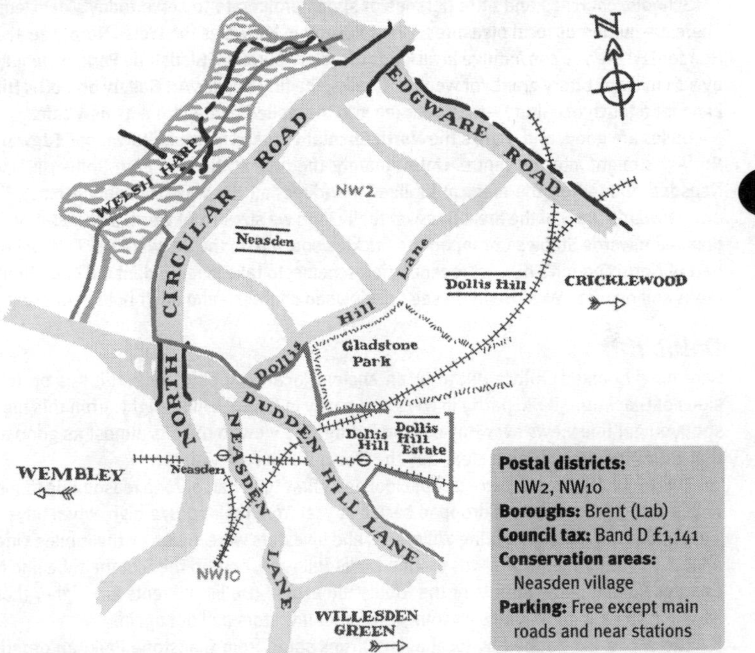

Postal districts: NW2, NW10
Boroughs: Brent (Lab)
Council tax: Band D £1,141
Conservation areas: Neasden village
Parking: Free except main roads and near stations

Comfortably tucked away in the angle of the North Circular and the Edgware Rd, Dollis Hill and Neasden denizens find these two great through-routes convenient for their own use – and for carrying others straight past their own peaceful streets. You might be forgiven for thinking that the road planners intended to prevent people from going to either of these suburban enclaves. Neasden (often first encountered by lost souls seeking Ikea) now looks to the massive plans for nearby Wembley to help put it on the map. Meanwhile people do live here. Very happily. According to one agent, every community of the globe has a representative somewhere among the local population. . . .

There's a strong family feel to this area – plus an influx of rather smarter young couples scouring the rather smarter streets of Dollis Hill. That said, here too groups of youthful sharers can find whole houses to rent affordably (some long-term residents have been heard to regret this, in the early hours). Homes come largely in the form of 3-bed semis, or terraces, with flats fewer and more often in purpose-built blocks. You won't find too many new developments – there's little, if any, space – but more houses have been split into flats that are a hunting-ground for first-time buyers.

Dollis Hill has, just once, strutted the stage of world history. It's been known since some inadvertently revealing memoirs in 1971 that a World War II command bunker sheltered Churchill's War Cabinet, but *where* was the 'Dollis Hill War Room'? Not, as Churchill wrote in his memoirs, 'near Hampstead'; nor, as local historians still assert, at Dollis Hill House itself. And no more was it beneath the putting green – this *Guide*, too, was for several years the victim of deliberate official misinformation on this point! Burrowing (literally) by enthusiasts has shown that the true underground citadel, code-named 'Paddock', lay (and lies still) beneath a Post Office research establishment round the corner, now flats. And that Churchill had, and used, a bolt-hole flat in a 1930s mansion block nearby. If things had gone otherwise, might the last action of World War II have been fought on these green suburban slopes?

Schools, churches and little parades of shops proliferate to serve today's denizens. There are numerous local pleasures: Brent Reservoir, known as the Welsh Harp (see also Hendon) where you can indulge in all kinds of watery pursuits; Gladstone Park, revamped by a £1 million Lottery grant, for weekend walks; the tiny Stables Art Gallery on **Dollis Hill Lane** for a touch of culture – take your tea into the walled garden from its new café.

Buses are good, and there's the **North Circular** to take you round town, the **Edgware Rd** (A5) straight into the centre. Unfortunately, the tube stations of both Dollis Hill and Neasden, though on the magical Jubilee Line (direct all the way to Canary Wharf), lie away towards the S of the area. But eventually (and we stress that word) a new station is planned towards Staples Corner on the Cricklewood side of the Edgware Rd. This will be part of North London's biggest regeneration scheme, to take in redundant rail land, Brent Cross and on up to West Hendon: see Cricklewood chapter – and don't hold your breath.

Dollis Hill

Charmingly named Dolly's Hill after an ancient local resident, Dollis Hill lies on two sides of Gladstone Park, partly in NW2 and partly in NW10. 'Hill' is right: from this high spot you get fine views over Harrow and Ealing. The view to the S is almost as good as that from Hampstead; on a clear day the North Downs are visible.

This is still the sort of place people look for a first-time flat, or for a reasonable family house with a garden. Prices dropped back last year from their 2001/2 high, when buyers were priced out of neighbouring Willesden, and investors were drawn by the Jubilee Line. A lot of the buy-to-let action was around Dollis Hill tube, both to the S of the tube line in **Chapter Rd** and in the streets of the 'Dollis Hill estate' (Dollis Hill rents are higher than Neasden's): look for bargains as some latecomer investors bail out again.

The estate (so-dubbed by local agents) runs south from Gladstone Park: an orderly grid marching down from park to tube line that forms a clearly-defined neighbourhood. While most of Dollis Hill is inter-war, this enclave of gracious Edwardian houses, close to the tube – streets such as **Fleetwood Rd**, **Ellesmere Rd**, **Dewsbury Rd** and (busier) **Burnley Rd** – commands a premium. Here, a 3-bed house might be £340,000-plus for a terraced, £400,000-plus for a semi. Buyers hunt for the houses with a balcony off the largest bedroom: a done-up 3/4-bed one went for £460,000. Flat-hunters crossing the tracks from pricier areas to the S find more for their money: first-time buyers can still find 1-bed flats in the £120,000-plus bracket. **Cornmow Drive**, off **Aberdeen Rd**, is one source of recent purpose-built, rather than converted, flats (1-bed, c. £160,000; 2-bed, £200,000) but is tucked away by the rail line. (Don't, by the way, confuse the agents' 'estate' with the Dollis Hill Estate on **Brook Rd**, council-built and on the other side of the park.)

Next, cross to the NE side of the park to find **Dollis Hill Avenue** and **Gladstone Park Gardens** (small, neat semis: a 3-bed, £330,000; some bigger detached). Again, agents report 'yuppie types move into these streets because they've kept their original features and have lovely views over the park'. These roads lead away from the busy **Edgware Rd** towards the park where Prime Minister Gladstone often stayed with Lord and Lady Aberdeen in the late 19th century. In 1995 their Regency mansion, Dollis Hill House – by then owned by the council – suffered a great fire. Sadly a spirited campaign lost the battle to raise funds to resurrect it, and the council (having pocketed the insurance) voted to demolish. Luckily the GLA intervened, and now the local health-care trust hopes to restore it as a medical/community centre. The campaigners hope to have an input into the plans and will continue to run their fundraising 'Gladstonebury Festival' – enjoyed by all in June.

Brook Rd runs N from opposite Dollis Hill House. Off it to the W, the handsome 1930s building that started life as the Post Office Research Establishment is nowadays the hilltop 'Chartwell Court': flats here go for c. £160–185,000 for 1-beds, £195–230,000 for 2-

beds. Converted in 1998 by a housing trust, it is sometimes possible to buy a shared-ownership flat. Beneath the research building, locals were startled to learn, is further accommodation for 200: the 'Paddock' bunker mentioned in the introduction above.

More history round the corner in **Dollis Hill Lane**, the busy thoroughfare linking Dollis Hill and Neasden, which skirts the ridge at the top of Gladstone Park. As well as houses (a 3-bed semi, £310,000-plus; 4-beds, £385,000-plus; a detached, c. £425,000) and bungalows, this is the place to look for purpose-built blocks of flats. In particular, look at Dollis Heights – and at **Nevilles Court**, the 1935 block where, in 1940, two flats were knocked into one to provide a home for Churchill should the Paddock bunker be activated: today, a 3-bed flat with S-facing balcony would cost the PM £240–250,000. Off **Parkside**, the E side of the park, the old school site was converted into **Campbell Gordon Way** in 1995 – a Wimpey scheme of 1- and 2-bed (c. £150–180,000) flats.

D

Coles Green Rd runs all the way from the stores at Staples Corner to Dollis Hill Lane. Here there are purpose-built blocks such as Coles Green Court; also bay-fronted terraces (a smartened 3-bed, £275,000). To the E, smaller terraced houses scattered amid the little industrial pockets: 3-bed houses go for upwards of £210,000. Along what was a country lane is the Ox and Gate pub by **Oxgate Lane**, and a delightful surprise: a little ivy-covered cottage called Oxgate Farm, last remnant of a more rural, Tudor Dollis Hill.

Neasden

Neasden is on the map at last. One agent reckons that most people discover it when lost on the way to the vast Ikea store on the **North Circular Rd**. Neasden also boasts one of Tesco's largest superstores (24 hours, six days a week) at Brent Park, while across it to the E streets around **Neasden Lane North** get the Welsh Harp Reservoir and the drive-in McDonald's on **Blackbird Hill**. What more could you possibly want?

Neasden may not be smart – it's decidedly scruffy at the edges and the pubs are lively, too – but affordable it is, and convenient: it lies just S, across the **North Circular/Edgware Rd** junction, from the foot of the M1. And its tube stop is on the Jubilee Line.

Now locals look towards the soaring arch that signals the new Wembley Stadium – and a decade's-worth of regeneration round it to include 3,800 homes in a hitherto derelict corner – and hope that this will bring benefits across the area. Meanwhile the council has revamped the town centre, removing the unsuccessful pedestrianized part. There's lively, if not smart, shopping on Neasden Lane: stores sell food from around the world here. More spectacularly, the biggest Hindu temple outside India, hand-carved from white marble, rises above the rooftops of the semis on **Brentfield Rd**.

The first homes in Neasden were 2-bed cottages built for workers on the Metropolitan Railway in 1882–3 and 1904–5, and there was further development in the late 1920s and '30s when the North Circular Rd, which bisects the area, arrived.

The majority of Neasden homes are 3-bed terraced (c. £270,000-plus) or semi-detached houses in roads such as hilly **Tanfield** and **Cairnfield Avenues**, (£310,000-plus for a 3-bed '30s semi; some spacious 4-beds in **Randall Avenue**, c. £370,000). There are also some flats: in the heady days of the late '80s, eager developers overestimated the need for 1-bed flats in this family-semi land – it's worth noting that it took until 2000 to mop up the final pockets of negative equity. **Hawarden Hill** off Brook Rd, down on the Neasden/Dollis Hill border, was one such: by Barratt, it's a red-brick block of 1- and 2-bed flats very near to Gladstone Park, but also the big Dollis Hill council estate. A 2-bed with views of park and London, c. £185,000. Nearby **Shepherds Walk** has 1988 Costain-built 1- and 2-bed flats (£150–180,000), and 2- and 3-bed terraces (£220–285,000).

A development on **Dog Lane** (look, naturally, for **Baskerville Gardens**) has added a cache of 2-bed flats (no 1-beds here) and 2-, 3- and 4-bedroom houses over the past few years, handy for the **North Circular** and also the Jubilee Line tube. These replaced – another sign of the times – the 200-year-old Spotted Dog pub.

Across Neasden Lane lies **Prout Grove,** whose handful of 4- and 5-bed Victoriana are a cut above Neasden's other homes: £450,000-plus for one of these, close to the tube if also to the busy Lane. Agents also talk about the pebble-dashed homes of the Brent Water estate to the N of Neasden, a good first-time buyers' hunting-ground that includes roads such as **Review Rd** (a terraced house here, £270,000), **Dawpool Rd** and **Warren Rds**. Close to bus routes but not the tube: rental prices, in particular, are thus cheaper. And the North Circular forms a barrier between these streets and the Welsh Harp lake. (For another first-time hot-spot, look at the 1- and 2-bed flats, c. £135,000 and £165,000 respectively, in **Harp Island Close** off Braemar Avenue across by the foot of the reservoir.)

D

What Neasden lacks in charm it makes up for with shops: Ikea, the Tesco superstore, the huge stores and multiplex cinema at Staples Corner, the North Circular/Edgware Rd junction. Over the junction lies Brent Cross shopping centre. More modern homes are found (to navigate by superstores) across the North Circular from Ikea, in the southernmost reaches of Neasden: here 1990s **Kestrel Close** has 1-beds c. £130,000. Brentfield Rd heads off towards Harlesden, and the old Neasden Hospital site gave way in the '80s to developments like the council/housing trust flats and studios of **Mitchellbrook Way.**

Transport Tubes: Dollis Hill, Neasden (zone 3, Jubilee). From Dollis Hill: Oxford Circus 25 min, City 30 min, Heathrow 1 hr 15 min.

Convenient for North Circular Rd, Brent Cross, Ikea. Miles from centre: 6.

Schools Local Authority: John Kelly Technology College (b), John Kelly Technology College (g). Private: The Swaminarayan School.

SALES

Flats	S	1B	2B	3B	4B	5B
Average prices	95–135	120–170+	160–240	200–280	–	–
Houses	2B	3B	4B	5B	6/7B	8B
Average prices	200–250	220–400	250–500	400–550	–	–

RENTAL

Flats	S	1B	2B	3B	4B	5B
Average prices	120–150	140–175	170–225	230–250	–	–
Houses	2B	3B	4B	5B	6/7B	8B
Average prices	190–240	230–350	275–400	300–600	–	–

The properties 1930s semis dominate in Neasden, plus smaller blocks of flats – private, council and housing association; the old fire station became flats, but such modern ideas are less common. Dollis Hill is more spacious: similar to Neasden plus a favoured grid of older Edwardiana S of the park, close to tube. A few early 20th-century terraces. Some expensive new-build and larger period houses. Both areas still a source of less-expensive homes to buy or rent.

The market Families buy here for gardens and open space; flat-buyers look to Dollis Hill if they can't find one in Willesden Green. Investors bought many flats, especially near tubes: some now selling out.

Among estate agents active in this area are:

- Camerons Stiff
- Hoopers
- Haart
- Peter Carrol
- Daniels
- Rainbow Reid
- Regal Estates
- McGowans
- Gladstones
- Carltons
- Gammell
- Ellis & Co

DULWICH

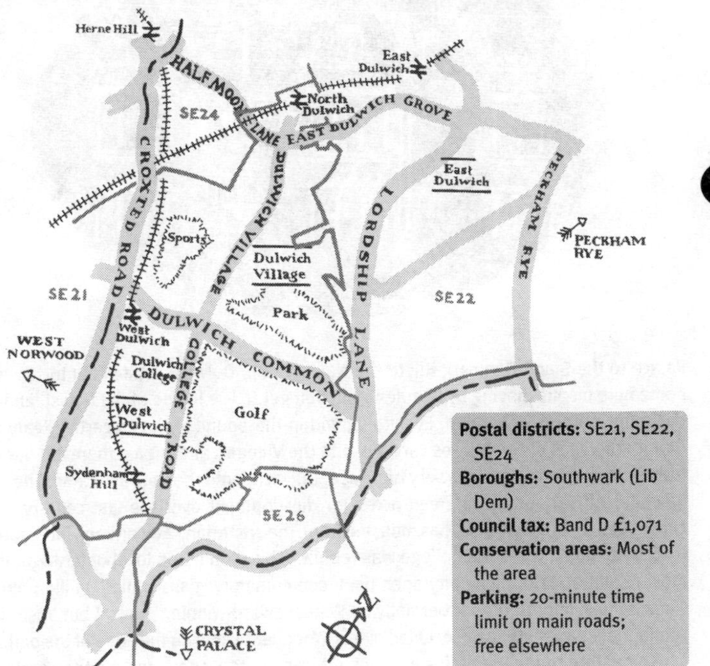

Postal districts: SE21, SE22, SE24
Boroughs: Southwark (Lib Dem)
Council tax: Band D £1,071
Conservation areas: Most of the area
Parking: 20-minute time limit on main roads; free elsewhere

Dulwich, that green island in the grey South London sprawl, is an anomaly of an area – a real village (not an estate agent's fabrication) within sight of the capital's major landmarks. 'The Village' boasts duck pond and cottages, finger-post road signs, picture gallery, a working tollgate, and is set in a wide-open sweep of green. 'Near, but yet so far' could be its motto.

The secret of its land-that-time-forgot air is that Dulwich proper was – and still is – one large estate: it gains its character, and its history, from the charitable foundation set up by Edward Alleyn, renowned actor-contemporary of Shakespeare, who prospered in the reign of James I. A successful businessman, Alleyn was a partner in the Rose Theatre, where Shakespeare also acted, around the corner from the Globe. He spent his money on the manor of Dulwich, leaving the 1,500-acre estate as an endowment for a school. Dulwich College still exists, and its playing fields are among several extensive open areas that surround the Village. The College (in the person of the estate governors) is a major landowner still: many Dulwich homes are on long estate leases.

The whole area relies on trains for commuting, with stations all round the outskirts. (The governors were reluctant to let the trains anywhere near; when forced to concede, they stipulated that all the bridges should be to their own architect's design).

There is more to Dulwich than the Village. East Dulwich – really NE of the old centre – is straightforward 1880s suburbia. There are fringe areas to the W and S too; as with any reputable area, bits of surrounding neighbourhoods try to edge into Dulwich. All of Dulwich *proper* is in SE21, with East Dulwich taking up part of SE22 – and what is dubbed by hopeful estate agents the 'North Dulwich Triangle' spilling into SE24.

But between **Croxted Rd** in the W and **Lordship Lane** in the E, the heights of Crystal

D

Palace to the S and Denmark Hill to the N, you are in Dulwich estate country. Owning a home here means playing by its rules – but you get to live in one of the tidiest, and most charming, corners of London. Everything within the boundary has a certain leafy unity, though the ages of the houses vary. Despite the Village's ancient air, there are not many truly old houses: it was not a very big place, Dulwich, until the railways came. The estate has sold off various of its green acres for development over the last century, and in consequence Dulwich also has houses from the Victorian, Edwardian, inter-war and modern periods. (Even the College was rebuilt.) This didn't stop local outcry against the most recent addition: nine airy open-plan, contemporary, glass-walled, million-plus Huf Haus homes, imported from Germany by Wates: award-winning, radical but upsetting to traditionalists despite their secluded site in **Woodyard Lane**, on the edge of the park.

The estate today maintains a strong interest in its 1,500 acres, be they built-on or open space. Leaseholders have to adhere to strict conditions. Over half of the 6,000 houses on estate land have now been bought under the Leasehold Reform Acts – but even then the estate keeps control: it has retained powers over the appearance of houses and (a major concern, this) the trees in their gardens. Touch a tree in Dulwich and the estate governors will have something to say about it.

Led by the College, the area is well served by good private schools: 95 per cent of buyers are families and/or professional people, say agents. First-time buyers and singles may look at fringe areas – which have better rail links – but the Village is family country. Clapham, Battersea and Wandsworth families migrate here for more greenery and more space, but above all for the schools. For those that haven't migrated yet, the (private) schools in Dulwich extend their catchment areas with a (private) school bus service, which brings in pupils from as far away as Clapham to the four prep schools that emerged in the 1990s to serve the three big independent schools (see below).

On the local authority front, 2000 saw the opening of The Charter School, a new co-ed secondary, up to age 18, in high-tech premises that boast a glass-roofed atrium. Five times oversubscribed, its intake comes from within a one-mile radius. Primaries like Dulwich Hamlet Junior in the Village and St Anthony's RC, East Dulwich, do well in SATs tests. Look out for code in estate agents' lists: 'in the parish of St Barnabas' translates as 'sporting chance of place at Dulwich Village C of E Infants, which feeds Dulwich Hamlet Junior, which sent *x* number of boys to Dulwich College last year. . . .'

Dulwich Village

First, outsiders should note that the main street in Dulwich Village is called . . . **Dulwich Village**, and that **Dulwich Common** (the road) is not an open space but a stretch of the South Circular. The Village (the neighbourhood) starts abruptly; a busy W–E suburban road, starting in Herne Hill as **Half Moon Lane**, becomes **Village Way**, then **East Dulwich Grove**, and skirts the village centre. Turn S into **Dulwich Village** (the road) and you are instantly in the old village. Houses are Georgian (or well-built 20th-century Georgian pastiche) and highly desirable. The larger mansions here will change hands for over £2 million; and if in the golden triangle 'between pub and Park' – the core of the Village – you can be asked double that.

Dulwich Village is about the most coveted street; also its continuation, **College Rd**. Others include **Pickwick, Aysgarth** and **Boxall Rds** – which also have about the only smaller terraces (popular, pretty Edwardiana here, in rows or in pairs: 3- or 4-bed in Pickwick, 2- or 3- in Aysgarth (c. £350–550,000). **Mitchell's Place**, off **Aysgarth Rd**, has 10 smart 1998 houses: in the £600,000 bracket. The 3- and 4- bed houses of Chapel Walk were added to **College Rd** by the same developer.

Turney Rd has open ground to the rear of the houses on both sides – a fairly common feature in Dulwich. Curving off it, **Roseway** features picturesque 1920s semis overlooking the sports ground: prices picturesque, too, at around £800,000. There is so much green space in Dulwich that many homes back onto parks, sports grounds, golf courses. . . . This includes Barratt's '80s development, **Hambleden Place**.

Desirability continues S and W past the lovely 1811 Picture Gallery and the College. **Alleyn Park**, with stately, £2.5 million-ish houses, runs close to the College and on down into West Dulwich near the station. **College Rd** runs S, harbouring such delights as a lovely low, white Regency mansion (coach house, parking for eight, set in two acres) but also crossing the South Circular – a regrettable intrusion. **Frank Dixon Way** adds modern 5/6-bed homes, say £1.2 million, and **Dulwich Oaks Place**, a cul-de-sac of '80s mansions (c. £900,000), runs off College Rd by Sydenham Hill station.

South, on the slopes of Sydenham Hill, you find a mixture of a few older properties plus big inter-war and modern detached homes, and now-coveted '60s Wates-built town-houses in green surroundings. The Wates houses of **Peckarman's Wood**, for example, are built on the southern, Sydenham, edge of the golf course. Views across much of London can be an extra bonus here.

To the E of the Village, roads of large, smart inter-war semis (a '30s 3-bed, £535,000) and Edwardian detached houses run as far as **Lordship Lane**. On the S side of **Court Lane** they overlook Dulwich Park. **Woodwarde Rd**, too, has open views behind its NE side. (A 4-bed Edwardian house, £640,000; a mock-Tudor monster, £675,000.)

East Dulwich

To the E and NE of the Village, there is SE22 and East Dulwich – the area that flanks **Lordship Lane**, spreading E of **Woodwarde Rd** across the Lane towards Peckham Rye. The Lane is the spine, with shops (flats above some), wine bars, cafés – and, at its S end, the South Circular. East Dulwich homes are largely Victorian: terraced or semis. Be aware, if buying in the Lane area, that the W (Dulwich) side thinks itself superior to the E (Peckham Rye) side. Since both sides are in E Dulwich, the distinction is lost on anyone else.

That said, the leafy eastern streets between the Lane and **Crystal Palace Rd** have become increasingly popular: here are the smaller, 2- or 3-bed terraces in, say, cherry-tree-lined **Nutfield Rd**, or in **Lacon, Felbrigg, Ulverscroft, Silvester Rds** – or **Crawthew Grove**, where a house that went for £325,000 last spring resold at £380,000 in the autumn. Smaller ones can still be had for £295–325,000. To the S and E (in for example **Friern** and **Upland Rds**) the houses are larger, 4- (c. £385,000) and 5-bed ones, while from **Barry Rd** (a big 5-bed, £595,000 last winter) on you can also find 6- to 8-bed monsters – but hunt for flats round here: many are converted.

The southern heights – round **Overhill, Underhill, Friern** and **Upland Rds** – have prices kept lower by lack of a station nearby: you can get a lot of space (a 4-bed, around

£420,000) for your money. Worth noting, though, that in this corner Honor Oak Park station can be just as close as East Dulwich's (and may one day be linked into the East London Line: see Transport chapter); neither is in strolling distance, however.

The last few years have seen many small schemes fon old garage sites, etc, such as 'The Mews', a gated cache of Regency-style town-houses on **Underhill Rd.** High up in **Overhill Rd** are late-'80s flats; at the Lordship Lane end, a terrace of six recent 3-bed houses (c. £350,000). New homes have also sprouted along **Lordship Lane** itself: at the Dulwich-proper end, Dukes Court is a big block of 1- and 2-bed flats; some get views over the Common. At the Underhill Rd junction, Streamline Mews is handsome, 3- and 4-bed red-brick-and-stucco houses (one here, £360,000), plus a couple of flats (a 2-bed, £225,000); Streamline Court has 2- and 3-bed flats that appear for rent. Then, N towards the station, the old Working Mens' Club site sprouted Lordship Mews (eight standard-issue little 3-bed semis). To come is 'High Wood', a Laing scheme on the TAVR Centre site at the Forest Hill end of the Lane. Nearby, Acorn's Levande is new flats: £175–285,000.

D

West of **Lordship Lane** and S of **East Dulwich Grove** is a cache of pleasant larger houses in a cut-off corner – Alleyn's School lies behind these 4-bed family homes in **Glengarry, Tarbert** and **Trossach Rds.** East Dulwich station is nearby – and is itself, naturally, a magnet for developers: Wimpey added 185 2- and 3-bed houses in **Burrow** (a 2-bed, £270,000), **Abbotswood, Shaw** and **Talbot Rds.** Behind is **St Barnabas Close,** 1998: 3- and 4-bed houses, reached from East Dulwich Grove. Off **Melbourne Grove** is cobbled Dudrich Mews: six stylish 3-bed modern homes, all curves and angles, plus two split-level flats: c. £265–375,000. And Fairclough added 88 flats and houses – 25 per cent Affordable Housing – in **Grove Vale.** A leafy, pedestrianized Dutch-sounding corner, with names like **Delft Way,** holds '70s council-built 2-bed houses: they now go for c. £220–250,000.

Goose Green is East Dulwich's northern border. The neighbourhood, round a small wedge-shaped park, stretches a good way E towards Peckham Rye, but the 1900s terraces to the N of the Green and **East Dulwich Rd** are considered Peckham Rye, not Dulwich. Large Victorian houses in **The Gardens,** off the Rye, are sought-after, though most are now flats. Altima, Laing's big scheme overlooking Goose Green, has 72 1- and 2-bed flats, from £150,000, plus 11 3-bed town- houses, from £370,000, just completing.

West Dulwich

West Dulwich is the SW tip of the area, running down to Sydenham. There are fewer homes here: the land is largely taken up by the golf course, allotments and the College's sports ground. **Alleyn Park** and **College Rd** lead from the Village S off **Dulwich Common**; there are some popular Edwardian houses and '60s flats at the top end of **College Rd.** Choice **Alleyn Park** is joined by **Alleyn Rd** as it crosses the tracks below West Dulwich station; the standard Alleyn 5-bed Victoriana can set you back a million. Between **Alleyn Park** and the railway, five detached houses 'in linear style' were squeezed in. As Dulwich rises to meet Sydenham, blocks of flats line the borders: these command superb views.

Dulwich Borders

The allure of Dulwich leads to a slow spread of the name into adjacent areas. One that has a good claim to the revered name is the patch W of **Croxted Rd,** centring around **Rosendale Rd:** this runs down from Brockwell Park and Herne Hill, and the railway bridge that crosses it perhaps marks the true Dulwich frontier. Its varied mix of homes includes some big Victoriana/Edwardiana; there are local shops plus some trendy (and good) stores and cafés, a sports ground with tennis, and attractive streets of mixed terraces. This patch is equidistant from West Dulwich and Herne Hill stations. Recent additions include a cobbled mews of 14 trad-style houses in the angle of **Croxted** and **Thurlow Park Rds** (a.k.a. the South Circular); also Thurlow Mews, again in period style: a mix of new/converted flats, maisonettes, bungalows. Flats – and three more bungalows – by West Dulwich station. . . And now – two *more* bungalows (£310,000 apiece), plus six flats (1-beds from £195,000; 2-bed £265,000 plus), in 'Hamlet Mews'.

In the N of the area, the two railway stations of North and East Dulwich confuse geography. They lie less than a mile apart – and East Dulwich station is N of North Dulwich station. Many now call the streets off **Half Moon Lane** 'North Dulwich'. Those E of **Beckwith Rd** perhaps qualify, but the other pleasant streets further W, such as **Stradella Rd, Winterbrook Rd** and **Burbage Rd** with their spacious family homes, are Herne Hill borders, and are dealt with under that area (see Brixton chapter). **Burbage Rd**, after crossing S of the railway, does indeed run down to Dulwich. The large, detached houses (a 6-bed, £1.3 million) have sports grounds (and Herne Hill stadium) behind.

There's a determined effort to disinvent Herne Hill; the tract bounded by **Half Moon Lane, Herne Hill** and **Red Post Hill** is now, in estate-agent-speak, the 'North Dulwich Triangle'; whether the people who live here think of it as Dulwich or Herne Hill (see Brixton chapter) probably depends on the station they use: Herne Hill for Victoria, North Dulwich for London Bridge. The latest move is to lay claim to the area across **Herne Hill** (the road) as far as **Milkwood Rd**: this is definitively Herne Hill; beyond Milkwood is Brixton.

Transport Trains: East Dulwich, North Dulwich (to London Bridge), West Dulwich, Sydenham Hill (to Victoria, some to Blackfriars), Herne Hill (Thameslink to King's Cross, Blackfriars, Cannon St). Average times to London terminals: 15–20 min.

Convenient for Parks, golf courses, schools, South Circular. Miles from centre: 5.

Secondary schools Local Authority: The Charter School, Kingsdale School. Private: Dulwich College (b), Alleyn's School, James Allen's Girls School.

SALES

Flats	S	1B	2B	3B	4B	5B
Average prices	100–140	125–220	150–300	280–400	–	–
Houses	2B	3B	4B	5B	6/7B	8B
Average prices	220–375	240–600	300–600	380–800	450–1M+	700–1.5M+

RENTAL

Flats	S	1B	2B	3B	4B	5B
Average prices	125–160	150–200	185–230	200–300	275–350	–
Houses	2B	3B	4B	5B	6/7B	8B
Average prices	190–275	275–325	300–450	325–500	350–500+	650+

The properties Dulwich has it all: the Village has carefully tended family homes from glorious Georgiana to cutting-edge modern, some 'country' cottages, some vast mansions; few flats. Fringe areas developed later: Victorian terraces, converted flats and increasing pockets of new homes. Lower prices above are E Dulwich and fringes.

The market Actors, artists. . . Families above all: large gardens, green acres, schools. Singles go to E Dulwich for flats, small terraces.

Among estate agents active in this area are:

- Kinleigh Folkard & Hayward
- Burnet Ware & Graves
- Winkworth
- Haart
- Harvey & Wheeler
- Wates
- Acorn
- Ludlow Thompson
- Spencer Kennedy
- Roy Brooks
- DVR

EALING

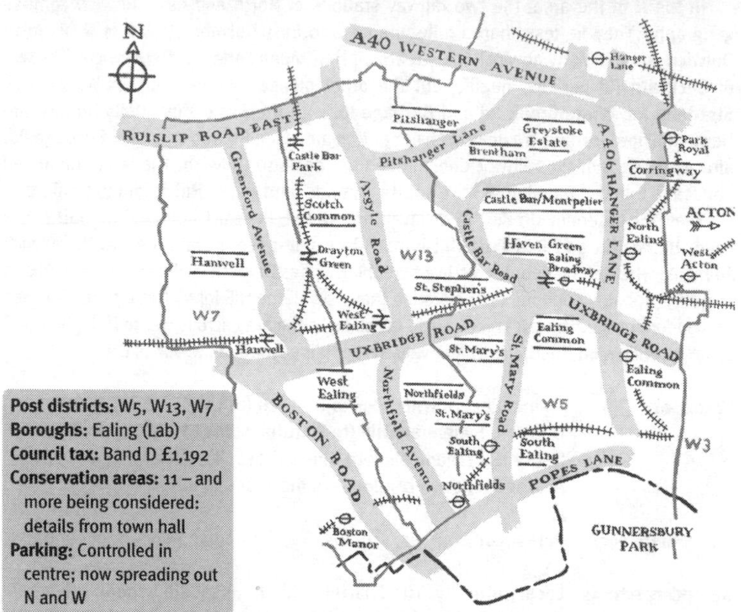

Post districts: W5, W13, W7
Boroughs: Ealing (Lab)
Council tax: Band D £1,192
Conservation areas: 11 – and more being considered: details from town hall
Parking: Controlled in centre; now spreading out N and W

Large and comfortable, leafy and respectable, Ealing branded itself the Queen of Suburbs in the 1880s, when being respectable was an aspiration not a matter for apology. While other areas have seen swings in fashion, status – and respectability – Ealing has remained stubbonly Ealing. Here is a place where families care about the schools, join residents' associations and hold summer fairs in the parks. Where single people, both young and old, are conscious of the merits of a well-run block of flats with tidy common parts and set in green space. All appreciate the fast links with central London and Heathrow, most are mildy in favour of the town centre, with its shops (though they deprecate the cluster of bars whose patrons may make loud noises).

What would really cement Ealing's fortunes – though maybe change its character – would be Crossrail. Which, if built, would make Ealing four stops from Heathrow, three from the West End and eight through to Canary Wharf. . . . One day.

Meanwhile, there's a surprising variety of distinct, villagey – one positively rural – corners to discover here. If Ealing has a slight complex about not being considered quite as stylish as Richmond, its homes can be a good deal more peaceful. At its heart there's a good shopping centre (mainly high-street chains), the Common, a pretty green, a gothic-style town hall, a station. Trees line the spacious streets. It feels a world away from gritty Acton next door. Back in the 1880s Ealing only allowed the building of solid homes for the professional classes. Which is why you have to travel to the edges of Ealing to find the late-Victorian terraces so common elsewhere in London.

Ealing's old guard of middle-class families and their heirs are still holding strong, particularly in the favoured Castlebar/Montpelier area. They are joined by couples and singles who like Ealing's pretty streets and good facilities. Lecturers, advertising executives and middle management are being joined by City workers, according to estate agents – and workers from Heathrow and the vast BBC complex at White City. Both Central and Piccadilly Lines serve the area, and 19 bus routes converge at the

Broadway. Traffic (there's the North Circular, Hanger Lane) and parking are hot issues, as is the mooted tram – arousing the ire of those who fear extra traffic in their leafy streets.

Ealing borough has a rich cultural mix, which includes Irish and Asian families, Japanese and Arabs – and is also the centre of London's large Polish community: it is twinned with a Warsaw suburb. The town centre has an attractive 'mall', an outdoor precinct with coffee shops and sculpture, a large M&S and Beales department store. There are ambitious plans to expand the shopping centre: Ealing is aware of the giant White City development. The big stores and mall are complemented by interesting and individual shops. Central Ealing also has good restaurants, plus pubs, cafés, wine bars. The cinema is soon to have a £20 million revamp: 12 screens behind the old facade.

The **Broadway** lives up to its name: a spacious and wide processional route, with prosperous shops giving way, W of the Gothic town hall, to ranks of office blocks; one, re-clad in gleaming greeny glass, is now 11 storeys of flats courtesy of Comer Homes. The prices at Cavalier House (complete this spring) run from £261,500 up to £976,000 for a penthouse, and include use of pool and health club. As you go west, the **Broadway/Uxbridge Rd** swaps names frequently and becomes less smart.

E

Ealing Common

Green views, big Victorian houses and comfortable flats are the attractions of this prime neighbourhood. Traffic – the North Circular crosses the Common's E side – is a drawback; on the other hand, there's a riding school. . . . It's convenient for the shopping centre, the A40 and the stations at Ealing Common and Ealing Broadway. Local shops round the former include a Japanese bookshop, hairdresser, deli and sushi restaurant, thanks to the Japanese community settled here and in West Acton. Other assets are a Polish/Lithuanian deli, a violin-maker and a splendid fish shop.

Overlooking and near the Common are large family homes, such as those on **Creffield Rd** which snakes off E towards Acton. The nearby Ealing Lawn Tennis Club is another draw: surrounding roads such as **Western Gardens** have a decidedly family feel, as do **Fordhook Avenue** and **Byron Rd**, opposite Ealing Common tube station. To the S, a street back from the North Circular, lies **Tring Avenue**, with some very large 7-bed Victorian houses, which can tip over the million mark, plus 1920s and '30s detacheds and semis (half a million upwards for the semis).

South of the Common, the **Delamere Rd** estate has an enclave of smaller 3- and 4-bed Art Deco semis. **Warwick Dene** is in a different league: the big Victorian houses look across the Common and can fetch £1.4 million. A step away, close to the Grange pub, are tiny 1-bed 19th-century farmworkers' cottages in **St Mark's Rd** and **St Matthew's Rd** that nudge £250,000, while 2-bed versions nearer the tube are c. £325,000. **North Common Road** has more big houses with spacious gardens and a gated enclave of 11 recent flats; **Hamilton Rd** (railway behind the N side) has more, plus mansion flats in Hamilton Court. This street, and **Northcote Avenue** across the Uxbridge Rd, are handy for the Broadway; nine new flats are appearing in Northcote: all are 2-beds, prices from £280–420,000.

St Mary's

St Mary's is real village Ealing, the oldest part of the area. The streets around the parish church on **St Mary's Rd** hold Victorian terraces and detacheds, close to the Broadway; the Grange schools are popular. The homes nearest Lammas Park top the bill, but all the streets are pretty, tree-lined – and pricey. This favoured little spot offers a mishmash of styles from Victorian to Art Deco. **Coningsby Rd**'s 3-bed houses are popular, despite being small and having, generally, downstairs bathrooms. **Clovelly Rd** runs beside Lammas Park: many of its Victorian/Edwardian homes have loft conversions.

Clutches of newish town-houses add to the mix, such as the five in gated **Soane Close** off **Warwick Rd**. Flats are arriving too: the latest include 'The Curve', 14 flats on St Mary's

Rd: the penthouses sold at £695,000-plus; the 10 flats are £395–465,000. A further 14 flats are on the market at £495,000-plus in **Grange Rd**, joining Common and Green.

At some odds with the old-world feel of St Mary's is the redevelopment of the famous film studios in **Ealing Green** into a 'leading media centre': three buildings house new stages and studios, plus smart offices; more to come to facilitate complete productions for film, TV and new technologies. Not all locals are star-struck, however, and notices abound reminding the builders to respect the neighbours and keep it quiet.

Further S, around the Piccadilly Line station of South Ealing, the streets are less rarified but still popular: 4-bed homes fetch c. £400,000. This corner is brightened by the Ealing Park Tavern – a draw for its food, beers and al fresco summer dining.

Haven Green/Castlebar/Montpelier

E

Some would call this Ealing's best area – it is certainly the home of the 'old guard' of middle-class Ealing residents, whose families have often lived in the borough for generations. Haven Green is a pretty, if traffic-beset parkland patch just N of **Ealing Broadway**; the Castlebar/Montpelier area lies N of the green, leading up the hill to Hanger Hill Park. Haven Green has the Broadway mainline station and tube, the taxi rank and bus terminals. Homes overlooking the green are mostly in luxury purpose-built blocks or, to the E along **Madeley Rd**, in large red-brick detached houses – mostly split into flats. **Haven Lane**, leading N from the Green, is a charming street of terraced cottage-style homes, each with pretty gardens. The lane is tight for parking, but also has two nice pubs: it is one of Ealing's most popular roads. It leads to the cricket ground, on the corner of **Woodville Gardens** and **Corfton Rd**, where a new Conservation Area has been declared. N from the Green, **Mount Park Rd**, **Park Hill** and **Mount Park Crescent** all boast big, tall, late Victorian, up to £2 million houses in large gardens, and fewer 20th-century infills than other neighbourhoods.

In the **Montpelier Rd** area, N again, the houses are large, Edwardian and detached, with some flat conversions and 1920s/30s mansion blocks. A 2-bed mansion flat might be £280,000-plus. Modern town-houses are tucked into odd corners. Roads such as **Charlbury Grove** have big 1900-ish houses. Berkeley added a smart development in 2001: town-houses and 2-bed flats. To the W **Castlebar Park**, a wide attractive road, winds down from **Castlebar Hill** into Pitshanger Village. At the top of the hill is Sovereign Close, a clutch of nine modern 4-bed houses with garages. Montpelier Primary School in **Helena Rd** is a definite draw for house-hunting families.

Don't confuse **Castlebar Park** with the branch-line rail station of Castle Bar Park – at least half a mile separates them and in terms of status they're worlds apart: the station serves the unfortunate Copley Close council estate (see under Hanwell below).

Greystoke/Brentham

Homes on the Art Deco Greystoke estate, S of the **Western Avenue** and just W of the **Hanger Lane** junction, are also popular with families thanks to Montpelier and North Ealing primary schools (both with very confined catchments). The '30s 3/4-bed semis are not as imposing as the older homes further S, but they are spacious, with large gardens and easy access to major roads, Ealing Golf Club, Helena Park and the pretty Hanger Hill Park. The atmosphere is rather 'villagey', and very family-orientated. You can spend up to £400,000 on a 3-bed house in **Brunswick Rd** – the busy road closest to Western Avenue – but streets such as **Kingfield Rd**, **Ainsdale Rd** or **Brookfield Avenue** command a good 10 per cent more, with extended 5-bed homes at c. £500,000. Going up the scale, **Lynwood Rd**'s 4-bed homes are more pricey, while the 4- to 5-bed double-fronted **Birkdale Rd** houses, near to the Montpelier neighbourhood, can fetch £750–850,000, depending on level of renovation/extension.

The Brentham Garden Estate, around **Brentham Way**, is for anyone who yearns for a romantic rose-covered cottage. Its 60 acres have 600 houses in the garden-suburb ethos, in the manner of (but preceding in date) Hampstead Garden Suburb. Work began in 1901 with the formation of Ealing Tenants, six local men who joined together to build nine houses in **Woodfield Rd**. The early houses were in terraces, with semis following as architects Raymond and Parker were brought in. The original plan was for residents to own shares in the estate, but not their specific home. However, a change of mood in the inter-war years led to the selling of homes and they are now bought and sold as normal. Demand is brisk for these little houses, such as the small, c. £300,000, 2-bed cottages of **Ludlow Rd**, **Fowler's Walk**, **Denison Rd** and **Neville Rd** and the 3-bed, £380,000 ones (semis up to £425,000) in **Brentham Way** (wider, a prime street). The estate is a conservation area (with its own fiercely active protection association). Locals often belong to the Brentham Club, a sports and social centre, which evolved from the original high-minded, educational (and teetotal till 1936) Institute. There are neat allotments. A recent book about Brentham gained the accolade of a foreword by Prince Charles.

Hanger Hill

Hill this is, with great views from the summit. For those who live on the Hanger Hill estate it is '*the* Estate of Ealing': large 1930s houses, with spacious gardens and garages – now a conservation area. Park Royal and North Ealing tubes bracket this corner, and the tracks wall it off from West Acton. It lies just E of **Hanger Lane**, and its concentric rings of roads include **Corringway**, **Audley Rd**, **Beaufort Rd**, **Chatsworth Rd**, **The Ridings** and **Ashbourne Rd**. For those who do not live on the estate, Hanger Hill is laughed at slightly for a certain ostentation: a place of stone lions roaring on pillars. The homes, created by builders Haymills in the late '30s, are quite varied in style and fetch from £600,000 up to a million. **Corringway** and **Ashbourne Rds** are a bit of a rat-run, but traffic-calming has helped. **Beaufort** and **Audley Rd**s are quieter, with some of the best 5-bed houses; **Chatsworth Rd** has some really big (7-bed) ones. Across in Acton, the smaller, 3/4-bed mock-Tudors of the Hanger Hill Garden Estate are c. £400,000. The sale in 2000 of the 22-acre Barclay's Bank sports ground, back to the W of **Hanger Lane**, to a reclusive buyer started gossip about development (and a degree of panic in the big houses on adjoining **Park View Rd**), but nearly all the land is Metropolitan Open Land and cannot be built on.

Pitshanger and Scotch Common

The northernmost area of Ealing, just W of the Brentham Estate and S of the A40, is a lively neighbourhood dubbed by estate agents 'Pitshanger Village'. Indeed, for once they're right: the genteel shops and atmosphere remind one irresistibly of a small market town of 30 years back. Everything you need is here: doctor, dentist, optician, library, delis, bakeries – even a small furniture and carpet shop, centred on its bustling 'high street', **Pitshanger Lane**. The shops are bracketed by a pair of 'village inns': one a free-house for real ale fans, the other with garden for the family trade. Talking of which, there's naturally both park (tennis courts, meandering River Brent, Community Association village fair . . .) and school: popular North Ealing Primary adds £50,000 to house prices. The streets leading down to Pitshanger Park are nearly all Edwardian 3-bed terraced homes, £350,000-plus – £60,000 more with loft/rear extensions. For recreation, the village also lies close to Ealing golf course, Trailfinders sports centre and the Brentham sports club.

To the W is Scotch Common, where a large 1970s development provides a variety of homes from small studios through to 4/5-bed town-houses. Among the purpose-built blocks of the Cleveland Estate, some are decidedly better built than others. **Argyle Rd** has some big 1920s detached houses: 6 beds from c. £700,000. West of Argyle there are '30s-style houses in the £320,000-plus bracket for 3-beds. On **Ruislip Rd East**, housing-association homes for rent adjoin Bellway's **Pelham Place** 2-bed flats scheme. New this year are Fitzmor's five 3-bed houses at **Woodbury Park Rd**, starting at £475,000.

St Stephen's and Drayton Green

South from Scotch Common, this large area forms the bulk of middle-class Ealing. It was once a solid tract of big Victorian villas, but many have been replaced with homes of various vintages, including some smart 1960s and '70s town-houses and flats. An appropriately cross-shaped conservation area centres around St Stephen's Church, a landmark of 1875 converted into plush and expensive flats, which caused quite a stir when they appeared on the property market in 1987. More typical are the 5-bed detached Victorian houses in leafy **St Stephen's Avenue.** Off **St Stephen's Rd** are **Whiteledges, Heronsforde, The Cedars** and **Lakeside**: smart modern town-house/flats enclaves. **Wimborne Gardens** is 1920s bay-windowed terraces. **The Avenue** leads grandly down the hill, graced by enormous though attractive 2-storey Edwardian houses, which lead to tall South-Ken-style 1880s terraces, with shops and hotel, opposite West Ealing station. Expect to pay around a million here for a 6-bed, double-fronted Victorian detached – or £260–280,000 for a 2-bed flat in a similar house. There are plenty of 5-bed period houses: £600–800,000 is the norm.

To the W are The Draytons, with some streets of terraced railway cottages and others with larger, grander homes. Houses vary in size and status, with both increasing as you move further from the tracks: **Manor Rd** has the smallest (£275–300,000 3-beds) with bigger and better homes in **Drayton Avenue**, **Gardens**, **Grove** and **Rd** (a 3-bed, £350,000). The attractive green at the W end of the neighbourhood is overlooked by some 5-bed, half-a-million terraced and semi-detached houses, while roads like **Courtfield Gardens** have £700,000 detacheds. Just to the N, off **Cavendish Avenue**, Barratt added a gated cache of 23 4-bed houses, named **Chelsea Gardens.**

West Ealing

This neighbourhood, with its W13 postcode, is reckoned less smart than W5, though prices and respectability rise as you go E. North of the Uxbridge Rd up to the railway the area is dominated by the Green Man council estate of grey concrete system-built blocks. There are a few streets of owner-occupied homes to the N and W – **Ecclestone Rd, Endsleigh Rd** and **Felix Rd**, where flats are the norm. To the E, the 'five roads' between **Drayton Green Rd** and **St Leonard's Rd** have become a 'home zone', with pedestrian priority over traffic. A new controlled parking zone covers the whole of West Ealing.

The Broadway has BHS and Sainsbury's, and there's a Waitrose on **Alexandria Rd,** near West Ealing station. A good hunting place, now, for new flats: on the M&S site Barratt are building 'Iconica': 80 open-market and 51 Affordable 1- and 2-beds (completion autumn '05). Waitrose is building a new store complex which will have 100 flats, while the Gosai Cinema site is also to be 34 flats. And the Daniel store is to be redeveloped by Crest Nicholson with 137 flats (62 Affordable).

South of The Broadway, things are more up-and-coming – particularly in the streets nearest **Northfield Avenue.** The terraces in the parallel streets E of **Grosvenor Rd** have a more suburban feel: the pebbledashers have done their worst here and in many cases the Victorian and Edwardian character has been smothered by faddish renovation. Here £250–300,000 can buy a little 2-bed house. However, streets such as **Coldershaw Rd** can yield attractive and sizeable semis from c. £325–380,000: a good one sold for £380,000 last winter. **Mattock Lane,** just N of Walpole Park, has big, Victorian £650,000-plus semis.

Northfields

Northfields boasts a popular shopping street, **Northfield Avenue**, bustling with interesting and useful independent shops. It is an area scoured by families attracted by road upon road of solid, 1900 houses, the successful Fielding Primary School in **Wyndham Rd,** the spacious Lammas Park – and the Piccadilly Line tube. A 2-bed Edwardian house (in the Fielding School area) costs up to £340,000: there is plenty of choice. New flats have appeared by the tube, and gated 'Gunnersbury Mews', opposite, is a year old: 15 2-bed flats plus nine 3-bed, 3-floor houses. To the E of Northfield Avenue, houses get bigger and pricier as you approach Lammas Park, and then on E towards Walpole Park and central Ealing (see St Mary's). **Elers Rd** is busy but popular: its imposing 4- and 5-bed houses are stable at up to £800,000 for a 4-bed. Moving E towards Walpole Park are yet more big houses, many split into flats.

Hanwell

Canalside walks, city farm and a church amid a golf course give a real village atmosphere (if you ignore the rather down-at-heel, urban Broadway) to Hanwell, the district that borders the River Brent in the W of the borough. It has its upmarket enclaves, but also terraces and traditional semis for those who can't quite afford Ealing proper – yet.

To the S the area around Boston Manor Piccadilly Line station is popular with commuters and office workers from the Great West Rd towers. There are '30s semis in the roads off **Clitherow Avenue** boasting that prized commodity – a garage – and some come into the Fielding School area. Three-bed houses here are c. £325,000. Houses in **Haslemere Avenue** are mostly Edwardian.

Further N along **Boston Rd** is 'Old Hanwell' (as the estate agents like to term it), a series of streets leading off SW down to the Grand Union Canal. This little corner has no through-traffic, a charming (and successful) small primary school in St Mark's and a country-style pub, The Fox, the garden of which is a magnet for families in the summer: much to the relief of all, a family buy-out saved it from redevelopment as flats. Century-old cottages, in **Green Lane**, **St Dunstan's Rd** and **Rosebank Rd** in particular, are popular, with 2-beds c. £260,000, 2/3-beds £275,000 3-beds £285,000. The Fox pub, **Oak Cottages** and **Fox Cottages** form a delightfully rural corner flanked by allotments, a family of goats and a Shetland pony (occasional pony rides!). Only the cigarette-pack council block on the horizon reminds you of Hanwell. Half a million will buy you the old lock-keeper's cottage (2 beds, with heated pool), on an island between locks and canal. **Billets Hart Close** leads on to **Mallard Close**, forming a neat group of canalside red-brick houses and flats built in 1996 by Laing: 2- and 3-bed houses from c. £270,000. Things peter out at the S end of this corner: **Hume Avenue** is humdrum 1920s homes; **Trumpers Way** leads to the industrial estate across the canal. Another villagey (if less hidden) spot, however, lies back up across **Lower Boston Rd**, where **The Heath** edges a small green, complete with the Dolphin pub.

East of **Boston Manor Rd**, a group of quiet streets (**Deans Rd, Montague Rd**) offer modest 1920s houses. Heading N you come to **Hanwell Broadway**, which the council hopes will smarten up. Some new restaurants may be the first signs of change. Near the cemetary, on the Uxbridge Rd, Ealing Gate – a gated clutch of 1-, 2- and 3-bed flats – is all sold bar the penthouses, which are £380,000.

North of the Broadway is a nice, tree'd clutch of Edwardian houses – **Laurel Gardens, Myrtle Gardens, Connolly Rd** and **Lawn Gardens** – leading to the railway viaduct, which shelters a pretty sunken garden with lake. Three-bed houses fetch c. £310,000. The 2-bed terraces of **Half Acre Rd** have long gardens sloping down to the River Brent: one sold for £300,000 at the start of '04 (their neighbours across the street, with small gardens and no river, go for c. £285,000). These homes are close to the Brent Lodge Park.

Backing onto the park, NW of Hanwell railway station (direct line to Paddington), is the aptly named Golden Manor estate – the jewel in Hanwell's crown. The gardens are beautiful and the houses large and well maintained. A modest 4-bed semi here might be £500,000. Among the best streets is **Manor Court Rd.** In the less popular **Campbell Rd**, which has the railway station, a 3/4-bed house might be £350–500,000. On the S side of the tracks, in **York Rd**, Fairclough added 3-bed town-houses.

Church Rd, a cul-de-sac which leads into the midst of a park, is the heart of the old village of Hanwell, complete with said church, a few old houses and even a thatched cottage. Most homes are standard-issue spacious 1930s–1960s suburban. To the NE of Hanwell station, across the busy **Greenford Avenue**, is a leafy 'Poets' Corner' – **Shakespeare, Milton, Cowper, Tennyson** and **Dryden Rds** – of Victorian/Edwardian semis. Choose your poet with care: a 4-bed house in **Cowper**, £340–400,000 – but expect up to £650,000 for 5-beds in **Shakespeare**. They also make roomy 2-bed flats.

As you go further N up the hill along **Greenford Avenue**, standard 1900s terraces give way to the E to the big 1930s cottage-council Cuckoo Estate, with unexpected views from its hilly site. **Cuckoo Avenue**, its spine, follows the double avenue that once led to the Victorian poor-law school (it now houses a community centre). To the W of **Greenford Avenue** are streets of 1920s private-built semis and terraces. Homes on the Cuckoo estate are mostly private now: the 3-bed 1930s 'suntrap' homes now sell for £230–275,000. To the E is the '60s Copley Close Estate – one of Ealing's least desirable areas.

E

Transport Tubes: Ealing Broadway (zone 3, Central, District), Ealing Common (zone 3, District, Piccadilly). Others see map. From Ealing Common: Oxford Circus 40 min (1 change), City 1 hr 10 min (1 change), Heathrow 25 min. Trains: Ealing Broadway to Paddington 10 min.

Convenient for Heathrow, M4/M40, North Circular Rd. Miles from centre: 8.

Schools Local Authority: Brentside High, Drayton Manor High, Ellen Wilkinson (g), Elthorne Park High. Private: Ealing College Upper, King Fahad Academy, Japanese School, St Benedict's School (b), St Augustine's Priory (g), Notting Hill & Ealing High School (g).

SALES

Flats	S	1B	2B	3B	4B	5B
Average prices	120–160	150–250	170–350	220–450	375–500	–
Houses	2B	3B	4B	5B	6/7B	8B
Average prices	200–350	260–450	300–700	450–1M	700–1.5M	1–1.8M

RENTAL

Flats	S	1B	2B	3B	4B	5B
Average prices	100–185	150–250	180–300	200–400	300–400	450+
Houses	2B	3B	4B	5B	6/7B	8B
Average prices	200–300	250–450	300–600	400–700	650+	–

The properties Late-Victorian and turn-of-the-20th-century houses, some large; terraces in outer areas. Thirties semis and modern flats. Lots of converted flats, a few mansion blocks. Hanger Hill, Castlebar, Montpelier most favoured areas. New homes on every spare plot.

The market Families queue to move here for ample houses and good schools (checking catchments with care), then stay for green environs, local services, good transport. Younger buyers/renters find choice and convenience.

Among estate agents active in this area are:

- Sinton Andrews
- John Martin
- Bairstow Eves
- Barnard Marcus
- Grimshaw
- Brendons
- Winkworth
- Kinleigh Folkard & Hayward
- Northfields
- Robertson Smith & Kempson
- JAC Strattons
- Russell Collins
- Townends
- Tuffin & Wren
- Adams
- Colin Bibra
- Oak Tree

FINCHLEY

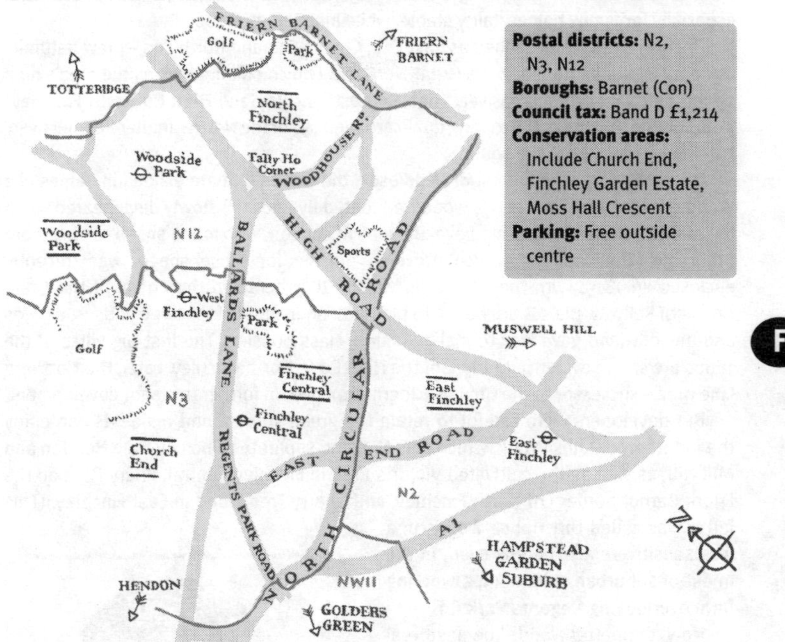

Postal districts: N2, N3, N12
Boroughs: Barnet (Con)
Council tax: Band D £1,214
Conservation areas: Include Church End, Finchley Garden Estate, Moss Hall Crescent
Parking: Free outside centre

'It was an offer we could not refuse' said the owner of Finchley's famous music pub The Torrington as he sold it to an unknown buyer. He added that despite a track record dating from 1967 its days as a music pub, indeed as a pub of any sort, were past. So, locals surmise, it will become flats – along with the building next door on the High Road, where permission for a dozen is already in place. Is there no end to the demand for flats in this dormitory area on the northern fringes of London?

There is more to Finchley than commuters, though, even if music fans will have to look elsewhere. Some pin their hopes on the brand-new £38 million centre, the 'artsdepot', just built at Tally Ho Corner. It boasts two theatres plus shops, restaurants, a health centre – and 158 luxury duplex apartments, many bought off-plan before a brick was laid.

Finchley residents are adept at protecting their suburb, and last year won a six-year battle with Barnet Council over the Long Lane pasture-land. Now the Finchley Society plan a statue of their late and long-serving President, Spike Milligan, who will be portrayed in bronze sitting on a park bench in the area where he lived for 20 years. It's hoped people will come from near and far to be photographed with Spike.

Finchley has been convenient commuting country since the 1820s, when a special stage-coach travelled each morning to the City. A year or two later the building of the Finchley Road, bypassing hilly Hampstead, made the journey faster and smoother. The area never looked back, with the railway and later the tube forging closer and closer links with central London. Today this is a prosperous suburb, replete with houses and flats in surroundings calm and green enough to soothe the savage commuters as they return in the evening.

But if people travel in to work, they are travelling out to live: the past two or three years has seen a steady flow of 'price refugees' from inner areas such as Camden and Kentish Town seeking something a touch larger for their money. This kept prices here, especially for family homes, fairly stable, while inner areas drooped.

Finchley – originally defined as East End, Church End and North End – grew naturally as hamlets sprang up along the Great North Rd (which still doubles as the area's high street: here labelled successively **High Rd East Finchley** and **High Rd North Finchley**) from London. But today the roaring dual-carriageways of the North Circular Rd effectively cut off East Finchley to the south.

Originally part of the forest of Middlesex, the woods that are echoed in names like Woodside Park and Finchley ('a wood frequented by finches') slowly disappeared when the manor belonged to the medieval Bishops of London, who found sheep-raising more profitable. The common, which provided grazing for those sheep, was 'recently enclosed' in 1815. With the 1872 train whistle that heralded the arrival of the Great Northern Railway, the suburb began to blossom; soon most of the large houses, estates and meadowland gave way to mainly middle-class housing. The first big villas of the 1860s are still in evidence to the E of the High Rd in North Finchley. Later, the Northern Line tube – successor to the Great Northern – opened up further tracts for development.

But developers were careful to retain the green spaces, and residents can enjoy the untethered Dollis Brook, which cuts N–S and separates Finchley from Hendon and Mill Hill, as well as the cultivated Victoria Park in Finchley Central, Friary Park on the Friern Barnet borders of North Finchley, and Cherry Tree Wood in East Finchley. (This latter was called Dirt House Woods in a less sensitive era.) There is even, in the midst of suburban splendour, a working farm overlooking **Regents Park Rd**.

Now Coppetts Wood, the last real vestiges of the original woods of Finchley, forms part of a green area sandwiched between the **High Rd**, **Summers Lane**, **Colney Hatch Lane** and the North Circular.

The wood (which also serves to mask the 24-hour Tesco superstore at the North Circular and Colney Hatch Lane junction) adjoins allotments and a nature reserve that run almost as far as the sports fields on Summers Lane and, at the High Rd end, the Finchley Lido sports complex with its open-air swimming pool. Then there's the bowling alley, tennis, multi-screen cinema and an increasing number of cafés and restaurants; at the Summers Lane end of this stretch is a David Lloyd sports centre. On the S side of the North Circular, more green 'lungs' are provided by the two big 19th-century cemeteries serving Central London parishes (St Marylebone, St Pancras & Islington), a golf course and numerous playing fields.

Finchley boasts some fine surviving Georgiana – including the original manor house off **East End Rd**, a listed building

Finchley suburban style makes constant references to rural models in its streets and buildings and, thanks to generous gardens and plentiful trees, goes a good way towards achieving the idyll. Mock-Tudor touches, such as half-timbering, leaded-light windows and tile hanging, add to the charm. Such houses are more appreciated today than they were and purists deplore the excesses of DIY improvers.

dating back to 1793. Renamed the Sternberg Centre, it is now used as a private Jewish teaching centre, museum and school. Further along East End Rd stands Avenue House, once the home of 'Inky' Stephens, the philanthropist MP and pioneering ink manufacturer. He left his estate to Finchley, and the house now shelters a museum and is run by a trust for meetings, 'weddings, birthdays and bar mitzvahs'. Its remaining grounds – now public – still hold a collection of rare trees. Also here is the listed, neglected 1860s mansion Hertford Lodge: the Finchley Society is concerned about its future following its sale (Barnet Council again) to developers; it may become flats.

And flats are what Finchley is good at: those, and the abundance of 3-bedroom, semi-detached respectable, family suburbia spread across the area. (There are strong Jewish and Asian communities.) Houses are larger, more spacious in Woodside Park; terraced and more cosy in the 'county' roads of East Finchley. Otherwise the area is bursting with flats. Many of the old suburban villas were converted in the '80s, and more and more luxurious (and pricey) apartment blocks have sprung up. There are 1930s blocks between the Finchley Central and Tally Ho Corner shopping areas, and beyond North Finchley along the High Rd to Whetstone. Plenty of homes, and generally plenty of demand too – both for buying and, thanks to the recent buy-to-let mania, renting.

Local shopping is concentrated along Finchley's spine, the **High Rd**, and **Ballards Lane**, which meet at Tally Ho Corner. For long depressed by the vast Brent Cross shopping centre, 10 minutes away by car or bus, individual shops are seeing a revival along the High Roads in both Finchley Central and East Finchley. New businesses have moved in, followed by coffee-shops and eateries – now cemented by the Tally Ho's 'artsdepot'.

East Finchley

Row upon row of terraced houses give a distinct flavour to what was traditionally called East End (changed by sensitive residents in 1886 lest they be confused with the Cockneys). Today the area is wider than the site of the original hamlet, with its weekly hog market, within the triangle made by **East End Rd**, the North Circular and **East Finchley High Rd**, and is fertile hunting ground for flats, too. Barnet Council erected a sign welcoming you to 'East Finchley Village' – not entirely without justification: it does indeed have that feel, with local shops that still include a butcher, baker, fishmonger and greengrocer. (Not so villagey, though, is the High Rd's congestion.)

This is home to those who balk at Highgate prices, and (unlike Muswell Hill to the E) it has the tube. It also has its own red-brick 'university' by the tube station – the hamburger training centre that forms part of McDonald's British HQ. Behind this academy, and a common sight elsewhere to the W of the High Rd, are purpose-built maisonettes and blocks of flats, some exclusively for retired people.

On the E side of the High Rd, **Fortis Green** is busy but picturesque: here large houses accompanied by their attached cottages (originally staff quarters), lie along a tree-lined route to Muswell Hill (see chapter). Prices are underpinned in this corner by the draw of good schools. There are firemen's cottages and Grade II-listed farmworkers' cottages from the early part of the 20th century, an '80s mews and modern and mansion flats.

South of Fortis Green, homes in the roads that run down to pleasant Cherry Tree Wood, one of East Finchley's few open spaces, have the benefit of being close to the tube as well. Here **Summerlee Avenue** has terraces of 3-bed white-painted 1930s homes; neighbouring streets such as **Park Hall Rd** have older and more varied terraces. Nearby, in **Southern Rd**, a clutch of 1996 houses in a gated close by the archery club.

North of Fortis Green are the so-called 'county' roads – **Hertford, Bedford, Huntingdon, Leicester, Lincoln** and **Durham Rds** – ever popular with 30-something professionals and minor soap celebrities who can afford the premium (up to c. £395,000) attracted for the best of these rows of cottagey little 2- and 3-bed Victorian/Edwardian homes.

The further away from the High Rd, and the nearer to Muswell Hill, the larger and more detached the houses in roads like **Creighton Avenue**, just N of the 'county' roads, with the luxury of their own drives and garages – and prices to match. At the W end of Creighton Avenue is Ashlar Court, a conversion of a church into 10 smart flats.

Across to the W of the High Rd, popular streets include pleasant **Leslie Rd**, which has a cache of 2-bed maisonettes and backs onto the Northern Line, but with the buffer of reasonably sized gardens. This road also features the flats of Parkgate Mansions, a little more modest than their name. North of the Bald Faced Stag junction, the **High Rd** is steadily improving, constant traffic aside. The huge public library is one of the highlights. Marcham Court nearby has increased the stock of purpose-built flats in this corner.

At the SE end of **Long Lane**, where it meets **Church Lane**, a tightly-packed mix of old cottages and maisonettes cluster in lanes like **Trinity Rd**. The old pasture by **Long Lane** has been saved from the developers, and a group has been formed to help tidy up the scrubland a bit, preserving it as a nature reserve.

F

Church Lane leads across the rail line to **East End Rd**, which though busy is pleasant round the small green, and has quiet cul-de-sacs like **Stanley Gardens**. South of East End Rd, and W of the tube station, is a different ball game: this is the Hampstead Garden Suburb and Highgate borders (see chapters), with prices as large as the houses in **Abbots Gardens**, the top end of **Deans Way**, **Bancroft Avenue** and the northern stretch of 'Millionaire's Row', the **Bishop's Avenue.**

Returning northwards, the North Circular end of the **High Rd** is flanked by two strongly contrasting council-built estates: Barnet's own Grange Estate, an older-style, modest complex, runs back from the High Rd in small tree-surrounded blocks. Almost opposite is the **Strawberry Vale** Estate, a Camden Council-controlled complex on Barnet land. Outside, this estate looks like a prison with its semi-circular wall shielding the noise of the North Circular traffic from the '70s mix of flats and houses inside.

North Finchley

Beyond the complex fly-over system of the North Circular, the terraces begin to disappear and the suburban 3-bedroom semis spring up in roads like **Squires Lane** and **Queens Avenue**. This is far more family-homes territory. Finchley's favourite son, Spike Milligan, lived here for many years. New flats appear where there's space. Across on the E side of the High Rd, **Summers Lane** skirts Finchley's green heart (see introduction), with playing fields, sport facilities both private and public including the Lido, the nature reserve, allotments and the leafy oasis of Coppetts Wood. Prices are lower close to the North Circular: a 3-bed terrace off **Squires Lane** can be had for under £300,000.

North from Tally Ho Corner, **Friern Park** and **Torrington Park** are typical of the roads E of the High Rd: at this end a mix of late-Victorian terraces, purpose-built flats and conversions. For families, house numbers are everything: the school catchment areas are different at each end of Torrington Park. The E end is a wide avenue, tree-lined and peaceful, while the W end is busier. A typical semi will be £500,000-plus.

As you continue northwards the mood changes, with streets to the E becoming blissful suburbia: grass verges appear in roads such as **Ravensdale Avenue** (it may start by Sainsbury's superstore, but it ends down the road from the golf course), and quiet, tree-lined, traffic-calmed streets such as **Mayfield Avenue**, where uniform rows of white-fronted, 3-bedded homes have gardens fore and aft (£300,000-plus); the older 4-bed, 3-recep. semis on **Finchley Park**, £425,000. On E, towards Friern Barnet, in the tract bordered by **Woodhouse Rd** to the S and **Friern Barnet Lane** to the E, the '30s suburbia is in full blossom, with many mock-Tudor and modern town-houses overlooking Friary Park.

West of the High Rd lies a mix of large villas, split into attractive and spacious flats, and rows of 1920s terraces, many of them holding two maisonettes. **Lodge Lane** might be even more attractive without lorries from the bakery and the sorting office, and the ugly, if essential, shoppers' car park. It has rows of tiny cottages, all beautifully spruced up.

It is in North Finchley in particular that agents have seen an influx of 'price refugees' from grittier parts further in, seeking greenery and schools as well as affordability. From here incomers can view their old haunts from the top-floor duplexes on Bryant's 16-storey tower that tops the new arts complex by Tally Ho Corner: £600,000 gives you views clear to the City and Canary Wharf.

Woodside Park

Pleasant streets between the High Rd and the tube line lead across to Woodside Park – many have 'Woodside' in their names. Streets near the tube reflect the popularity of this side of Finchley as a place to settle into a comfortable and convenient flat – perhaps after the children have left home. Large houses mingle with modern schemes both deeply basic and (more recent developments) downright sybaritic. But above all, flats spring up wherever sufficient square-footage can be found. The mix is thus eclectic: alongside a 1998 block of luxury flats in **Woodside Lane** stands a magnificent late-Victorian mansion, all intricate plasterwork and turreted roofline. Look in these streets for big semis, £800,000-plus when whole, that yield roomy, high-ceilinged garden flats at £250,000 and up. Large tracts of land belong to institutions like Finchley Catholic High School, Woodside International School, North London Hospice.

F

Across on the W side of the tube tracks, there is an air of affluence to Woodside Park proper. Houses are larger (and much coveted), the cars are BMWs and Mercedes, the roads are wide, the gardens longer. **Holden Rd** has changed its character in the last 30 years: what was once an avenue of enormous houses with gardens tumbling down the banks to Dollis Brook has been transformed. A section of the road is devoted to a mid-'70s development of square town-houses facing late-'80s flats and the remaining original houses. Next door is another outbreak of rows of early '70s houses – entirely council-built, but nicely done – on the corner of **Holden Rd** and **Laurel View**. The tube station – which with its surrounding trees looks and feels more like a country halt than a stop on the Northern Line – is a big asset.

Across Dollis Brook, in the angle between it and the delightfully named Folly Brook, **Southover** and **Northiam** (*just* Southover and Northiam, note: nothing so common as 'Road' or 'Street') are leafy boulevards of posh detacheds or semis, with driveways, columns and roof extensions. Below Folly Brook, the streets with South Downs names – **Lullington Garth, Walmington Fold, Chanctonbury Way, Cissbury Ring North** and **South**, etc – are ideal for families whose purse strings are a little less elastic. This is Woodside Park Garden Suburb, developed in the 1930s by one Fred Ingram, who had advanced ideas about housing density, peace and quiet and green space, and it is still a well-defined community. The 4-bed semis go for £400,000-plus, a 3-bed flat for £380,000.

Church End

The home of Finchley's largest houses, most picturesque avenues and most historic buildings: the Christ's College building, St Mary's school house and, on **East End Rd**, Avenue House and the original manor house. This is the area most often depicted in paintings and sketches representing old Finchley.

East End Rd, linking the High Rd of East Finchley with Regents Park Rd and Church End, crosses the North Circular to streets such as **Thomas More Way** and **Hamilton Rd.** Here attractive, 2- and 3-storey yellow-brick flats and houses, with low walls and cottage gardens, cluster in a neighbourly way.

Church End itself, around St Mary's Church in **Hendon Lane**, is the heart of the old village, and site of the turnpike on the old road from Marylebone. At the apex of Hendon Lane and Regents Park Rd, it is Finchley's most visible (and congested) conservation area, close to the shops and Finchley Central tube. Plans for an 83-room Holiday Inn on the site of the Golden Eagle pub aroused plenty of indignant opposition.

To the W down prestigious (around a million upwards) **Hendon Avenue** – one of the widest roads in North London, with a North American air – is a more peaceful idyll, and another conservation area. **Village Rd** is the core of Finchley Garden Village, 54 semi-detached houses built around a rectangular green in the early 1900s. It was the brainwave of architect Frank Stratton who lived there himself. Equally attractive, and with its own 'village green', is the peaceful and wonderfully-named **Crooked Usage**.

But the immediate triangle of Old England at Church End, around the cottages of **College Terrace**, has become a virtual island – surrounded by tasteful, luxury flats developments down **Hendon Lane** and a vast outbreak of red-brick flats and office blocks in **Regents Park Rd**. More flats across the road, including the 1980s Embassy Lodge for retired people. **College Terrace** is a tiny row of handily-placed cottages facing the old Christ's College building, a Gothic showpiece that has spent a decade awaiting restoration. Further down Hendon Lane several new flats schemes have recently added to the local stock. The luxury developments run down to Henly's Corner and the hectic North Circular, punctuated by the fields of the picturesque, but currently closed, College Farm. English Heritage money should see its revival soon.

Around the side streets like **Tillingbourne Gardens** the houses are impressive, detached and dear. The Kinloss Gardens Synagogue stands at the corner of the uninspiring-looking but popular Chessington Estate, next to the North Circular.

Road experts at Barnet Council have turned the streets to the east of Regents Park Rd – **Mountfield Rd, Stanhope Avenue, Cavendish Avenue, Holly Park** and **Holly Park Gardens** – into a maze of one-ways and no-through roads to stop rat-running. The older houses here have gradually been converted into flats. St Luke's Court, a 1980s development in **Mountfield Rd**, however, went for exclusivity with a private courtyard behind remote-control gates. It has as its star the refurbished, 6-bed old vicarage (the developers built the vicar a new one), two new houses, flats and penthouses. Some handsome pairs of stock-brick and stucco semis in **Lichfield Grove**, a street back from the underground station. Four new 3-bed town-houses in **Holly Park** are £775,000.

Church End extends N as far as the impressive railway viaduct in **Dollis Rd**, built in 1867 and marking the highest point of the London Underground. The Dollis Valley green walk is a key asset for locals. Several homes back onto Dollis Brook.

Finchley Central

What's in a name? Finchley Central is really just the name of the tube and belt of shops along **Ballards Lane**, but estate agents seized on it in the '80s to describe the area N of the railway line on either side of Ballards Lane before you come to the postal district of N12 and Woodside Park. Barnet Council have attempted to reverse the trend with a sign near the tube firmly labelling this end of Ballards Lane as 'Church End Town Centre'.

If many of the streets have neither the leafy charm of Woodside Park or the cosy trendiness of East Finchley, there are good local shops, pubs and restaurants, and the Finchley hallmark of homes of all shapes, ages, sizes and convenience, for which you pay: a small 1-bed flat near the tube will be £160,000 or more, while a 4-bed house will be over £350,000. Further N is the equally nebulous West Finchley which, again, covers the few streets around the tube station of the same name.

The overwhelming appearance in the residential streets on either side of **Ballards Lane** is of overcrowding – largely due to commuters' cars. Again there are lots of flats converted from houses in the '80s, although the further away from Ballards Lane you go, the more the 3-bedroomed semi dominates.

Victoria Park is the outstanding feature of Finchley Central – a small but pretty park with tennis courts and bowling green, it's an oasis in suburbia's sprawl of large bay-fronted detached houses (large gardens, but no garages) and purpose-built flats such as those of **Etchingham Park Rd**. Almost opposite the park is Finchley Court: spacious, well-maintained '30s flats, complete with stunningly blue roof and still one of Finchley's most attractive. Latest is Ward Homes' Victoria Heights: park views, and prices in the final phase from £300,000.

West of Ballards Lane, **Alexandra Grove** covers the whole spectrum of styles – from larger, detached mock-Tudor homes through medium-sized semis and a few '70s town-houses, to purpose-built flats of all ages: dull, everyday but sturdy '30s blocks to far more appealing recent luxury schemes. It ends with Philipson House, a curious yellow purpose-built block at the junction with **Nether St.**

Moss Hall Crescent, just off Ballards Lane, is a parade of attractive mansions. Nether St joins Finchley Central to North Finchley and runs beside West Finchley tube station. Traffic has always been a problem here though, particularly by Moss Hall Schools (junction with Moss Hall Grove) and by the tube station.

Transport Tubes, Northern Line: E Finchley (zone 3); Finchley Central, W Finchley, Woodside Park (zone 4). From Finchley Central: Oxford Circus 32 min (1 change), City 40 min, Heathrow 90 min (1 change).

Convenient for Brent Cross shopping centre, M1 & A1 to the North, M25, North Circular Rd. Miles from centre: 7.

Schools Barnet Education Authority: Christ Church C of E, Woodhouse 6th-form College, Christ's College (b), Compton School, Finchley Catholic High School, St Michael's Catholic Grammar (g). Private: Woodside International School

SALES

Flats	S	1B	2B	3B	4B	5B
Average prices	120–150	145–200	180–325	225–400	–	–
Houses	2B	3B	4B	5B	6/7B	8B
Average prices	230–350	275–475	350–650	450–800	–	–

RENTAL

Flats	S	1B	2B	3B	4B	5B
Average prices	130–160	160–210	175–300	225–325	400+	–
Houses	2B	3B	4B	5B	6/7B	8B
Average prices	250–325	275–400	325–600	500–850	–	–

The properties Quintessential suburbia: typical home is the 3-bed inter-war semi. Also Victorian/Edwardian terraced and larger homes, and modern flats in smart blocks, plus larger houses in select streets. Higher flat prices in recent luxury blocks.

The market A settled family community, strong but changing as newcomers move in: young singles and professional couples who rent or buy. Older couples swap family-sized homes for luxury flats after the kids move out. Strong Jewish and Asian communities.

Among estate agents active in this area are:

- Anscombe & Ringland
- Arthur Benabo
- Ellis & Co
- Jeremy Leaf & Co
- Copping Joyce
- Stevens & Son
- Addisons
- Winkworth
- Bernard Tomkins
- Martyn Gerrard
- Bairstow Eves
- Capital Estates
- Jac Strattons
- Spicer McColl
- Barnard Marcus

FOREST HILL

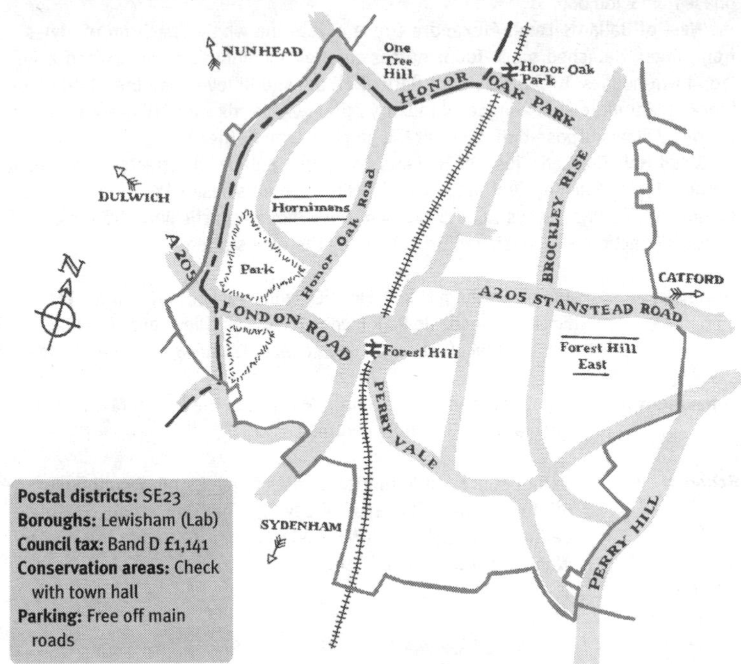

Postal districts: SE23
Boroughs: Lewisham (Lab)
Council tax: Band D £1,141
Conservation areas: Check with town hall
Parking: Free off main roads

If 'Forest' is overstating it, 'Hill' it certainly is, and there are plenty of wooded areas and quiet, tree-lined roads that continue to give the name meaning. This South London eminence rises to the east of Dulwich, north of Sydenham, and west of Catford and Lewisham. Like Sydenham, the area owes its development to the railway, which reached here in 1836; some impressive 19th-century villas have survived. And this is a canny time to consider the Hill, with transport once more the key: the East London Line is to be extended S from New Cross Gate via Forest Hill to Croydon – if mayor Ken Livingstone gets his way, and his chances are better than they were (see Transport chapter). Already, London Bridge is under 15 minutes via the fast and frequent trains – and from there the super-fast, super-smart Jubilee Line reaches the West End or Canary Wharf in another 10. Neighbouring Lewisham, the area's main shopping centre, is on the Docklands Light Railway. Lots of buses, too.

The hilly land gives Forest Hill its character (and views), but its unlikely hero is a tea merchant, who gave it a 21-acre park and museum. FJ Horniman amassed a vast natural history and anthropological collection from his world travels. This he made a gift to the people, along with the museum he had built (1897–1901). This splendid local asset has been transformed and extended, thanks to a £10-million lottery grant. There's the Living Water aquarium, the African Worlds gallery and the Natural History gallery; a café overlooks the delightful gardens with their pleasing views and free – indeed, the whole place is free – summer concerts. The Hill's best homes lie around this focal point.

The area, which is essentially the SE23 postal district, divides roughly into two parts – the high ground in the W (between **Honor Oak Park** to N, **Thorpewood Avenue** to S, the railway line to E, **Wood Vale/Sydenham Hill** to W), and the lower-lying ground to the E of the railway line. The centre, and principal area for shops, restaurants, etc, **London Rd/Dartmouth Rd,** meets basic needs but is not exactly picturesque – unless you count the new monthly farmers' market. There are plans to smarten things up, but nothing firm yet. The fact that **London Rd/Waldram Park Rd** doubles as both local High Street and the South Circular lessens the centre's appeal. It is, though, tidying: Sainsbury's is extending (adding 11 smart flats above, plus four Affordable Homes – 2-bed flats – round the back in **Pearcefield Avenue**). Cobbled **Havelock Walk,** tucked behind the shops, has an interesting mix of artists's studios, craft workshops and live/work units, one of which – all 4,000 sq ft of it – was on for £655,000 last winter. Barratt's 2002 gated, industrial-modern Century Yard, opposite the station, has 1- and 2-bed flats (c. £190,000) plus 3-bed mews houses. Or there are the 1-bed flats in a converted, and extended, listed public loo nearby. . . .

Away from the centre, the most elevated neighbourhood – in price and geography – is Hornimans: the estate-agent shorthand for the roads N of the Horniman Museum and Gardens. On the other side of the area the south-eastern quarter, across the tracks and between **Waldram Park Rd, Stanstead Rd** and **Perry Vale/Perry Rise,** is generally flatter and has a mix of property – detached and semis, terraced, Victorian/turn-of-the-century and '30s/modern as well as council blocks. To the N, the streets off **Honor Oak Park** near Honor Oak station (also due for tube services – in 2010?) have modest terraces.

The largest properties are usually found on the high ground, but few roads are homogeneous – you'll find Victorian houses next to bay-fronted '30s semis. Victorian homes predominate, though, and top the popularity list. Although many of the larger ones were split into flats in the '80s, in the '90s the tide swung back the other way and this is still a hunting ground for a bigger home at a (relatively) affordable level.

Forest Hill's leafiness and quiet tend to belie its inner-suburban location. It has a good share of gardens and parks, and Dulwich's park and golf course are nearby; there are no real pockets of deprivation. One point, though: the steepness of the hills demands fitness (some have 18 per cent gradients) and in ice or snow, can leave cars immobilized.

Hornimans

One approach to the Hornimans corner is up popular, if busy, **Honor Oak Rd,** which runs N from London Rd. Honor Oak Rd has vast surviving 1900s Italianate villas, which have largely become roomy (if sometimes scruffy) flats: an example, a 2-bed, was £180,000 last autumn. The road is a mixture, but not jarringly so – modern-box developments, a council estate, '30s semis, Victorian homes. One block of flats, Angela Court, has been twinned; next to Katherine Court, a modern white, 3-storey house roosts behind its gated entrance. Honor Heights is an interesting family-home addition. Then suddenly dainty Ashberry Cottage speaks of a more rural past: a Regency cottage once home to the Duke of Clarence, later William IV, and his actress-mistress Mrs Jordan.

Trailing hillward off Honor Oak Rd are **Westwood Park** and **Horniman Drive**. Horniman Drive has '30s detached homes with pretty front gardens (get your 4-bed detached Art Deco gem for £600,000-ish), a primary school, some low, 3-storey flats (2-beds c. £170,000), and ends, by an entrance to Horniman Gardens, with modern town-house cul-de-sacs. It also has breathtaking views over London – which gazes back at a towering, unsightly mobile phone transmitter recently added to the top of the hill. Large, detached '30s are also in demand in **Ringmore Rise**. The Drive and the Rise meet at a quaint, triangular communal garden, with **Liphook Crescent** and **Rocombe Crescent** curving round the other sides. Baxter House, a modern development, sits comfortably in the area, but is next to that transmitter. (At the top of **Ringmore Rise**, a '40s-style house, unexpected and out of keeping, adds a sense of light relief to this very proper corner.)

Steep **Westwood Park** starts with some large Victorian semis and follows round the hillside with '30s bay-fronted detacheds and semis (3-bed £290,000). Smaller '30s semis in **Tewkesbury Avenue** (watch for subsidence in these very hilly roads). A church hall is nowadays seven 2-bed flats and a 3-bed detached house. For spectacular views of the City and a mix of Victorian/turn-of-the-century/'30s semis (c. £275,000) there's **Canonbie Rd.** Canary Wharf, Big Ben, St Paul's, the Telecom Tower . . . all the capital's landmarks are there – earn the view by climbing the slope. Lovell's 2003 'Manor' has 13 new flats, and another new scheme by McNite offers 11 flats, 1- , 2 and 3-bed from £155,000. **Netherby Rd** (bay-fronted semis; some large Victorian ones) looks to wooded One Tree Hill.

Wood Vale marks the area's W boundary. It has seen some conversions, with names like Beech Court and Woodlands Court; also some new-build, but in trad brick-and-white-stucco style (£180,000 for a 2-bed). A redundant pub, too, became flats (closing-time never comes. . .). Nearby, however, large and hitherto neglected Victorian houses have been lovingly restored and sold as grand, £400,000-plus, family homes, with views out over the Hornimans nature trail. Where converted, they make big flats.

Across **Honor Oak Rd**, **Manor Mount**'s period homes mingle with flats. Worth investigation is **Devonshire Rd**, running parallel to the railway line, and thus blessed with a station at either end: Victorian semis, detacheds, terraced – large and stately ones – Edwardiana, 1930s. Plenty of renovation has gone on (1-bed flats c. £165,000, 2-beds about £180,000), and speed humps slow those late for a train; untidier, though, at the Honor Oak end, where the Boveney Rd Estate has at last had a partial face-lift. A small nature reserve comes as a pleasant surprise; in short, a very central corner. Several small blocks of flats, too – not always harmonious: Leyton Court's garish yellow brick, for instance; but then the '30s Postmen's Office (red-brick, sculptures on roof) is not exactly retiring, either. **Ewelme Rd** has some vast, 7/8-bed, 4-storey detached Victoriana.

Busy **London Rd** in its western stages near the museum has council blocks, but also brightly painted terraces – now flats – further down. On the N side is Horniman Grange, a 1988 redevelopment of some wrecked Victoriana: studios, 1- and 2-bed flats. South lies **Sydenham Rise**, an outlier of the Dulwich Estate (see chapter), with small, leafy private closes of modern 3-storey houses, and a 9-storey block with fabulous views. A cool white '30s block in well-kept grounds in Taymount Rise rubs shoulders with 1970s town houses (4-beds £250–270,000), detached 19th-century cottages and council-built homes. Off **Dartmouth Rd** are some more tucked-away homes, in little unmade-up roads. **Thorpewood Avenue** – here '30s semis outnumber the occasional Victorian houses – holds Holy Trinity School and the library, and marks the S boundary of this side of Forest Hill.

Forest Hill East

East of the local station, **Honor Oak Park** (the road) is more mundane. Shops line both sides – a small gallery, a good music shop. Small roads such as **Ballina St** and **Gabriel St** (now a well kept cul-de-sac) have stolid, uniform Edwardian terraces; **Grierson Rd** also has some '60s town-houses; plus Victorian semis and some post-war infill (the streets between Honor Oak Park and Brockley Rise have a fiendishly confusing traffic system). Busy **Honor Oak Park** itself has some large, 5/6-bed houses and some shops. Tucked behind the **Waldram Park Rd/Stanstead Rd** stretch of the South Circular, **Rockbourne Rd** has some handsome early 1900s terraces and a clutch of smart 2- and 3-bed flats; also five new houses. Large Victorian houses on **Waldram Park Rd** make for excellent flat conversions, close to Forest Hill station and buses. **Stanstead Rd** has big 3-storey Victorian detacheds and semis; also Victorian terraces (a 4-bed £445,000) and 'The Enclave' a gated clutch of new town-houses (£230–325,000). The streets leading off both sides of **Vancouver Rd** are quieter, period terraces; also some 1930s and modern infills.

Busy **Perry Vale**, which runs SE from Forest Hill station, starts with Christchurch C of E Primary, and a belt of unattractive walkway-access council estates, their impact lessened by surrounding trees. Large Edwardian semis follow (half a million asked for one last year), with a parade of shops in the curve. Running S from Perry Vale, a council-built estate, Forest Hill School and a town-house development make up leafy **Dacres Rd** until the right turn.

Then come detached, 5/6-bed Victoriana, leaf-obscured modern town-houses and a modern mansion block. Off **Mayow Rd**, which leads back up to Perry Vale, **Acorn Way** is a small cul-de-sac of modern homes where children play in the street. A real mixture of styles in this corner: **Mayow Rd** holds 3-bed town-houses backing onto a nature reserve, 5-bed 1910 semis, some boring flats, some new social housing. **Wynell Rd** has council-built estates and 3-storey red-brick houses, but by the time it joins Perry Vale these give way to larger, brick-and-stucco houses and gardens that would not look out of place in Notting Hill.

Wide **Sunderland Rd** has a primary school, large Victorian/turn-of-the-century detacheds, '30s semis. Some of the big 19th-century mansions remain; some are flats. A church conversion has yielded 13 £230,000-plus flats and £500,0000 4-bed houses. Tree-lined **Woolstone Rd** starts with terraces and neat 1930s semis; some big Victorian detacheds .

Perry Rise continues Perry Vale's snake across the neighbourhood (a 3-bed 1930s semi, £225,000). Off it, pleasant **Allenby Rd** is quiet and leafy: large, detached Victoriana. Peaceful **Garlies Rd** mixes in some 1930s semis with more handsome period villas. **Paxton Rd** saw one of the area's biggest developments: more than 150 flats made pretty by balconies and gardens, in 3-storey blocks. More, 4-storey, behind. **Queenswood Rd** is terraced turn-of-the-century and '30s semis plus some recent 3-bed houses. **Perry Rise** itself adds some 1950s homes; also bay-fronted Victorian semis, before giving way to small terraces near **Bell Green**, on the Lower Sydenham borders, with its hypermarket.

F

Transport Train: Forest Hill to London Bridge (for Jubilee Line) 14 min, Victoria 30 min, Charing Cross. Also to Croydon (for Gatwick).

Convenient for Dulwich golf course and park, Crystal Palace park and National Sports Centre, Lewisham shops and DLR. Miles from centre: 6.

Schools Local Authority: Forest Hill School (b), Sydenham School (g). Private: Sydenham High (g). (See also Dulwich, Catford).

SALES

Flats	S	1B	2B	3B	4B	5B
Average prices	80–120	100–170	130–230	140–260	–	–
Houses	2B	3B	4B	5B	6/7B	8B
Average prices	180–230	180–350	240–450	250–600	300–600	–

RENTAL

Flats	S	1B	2B	3B	4B	5B
Average prices	100–150	125–175	150–200	175–300	230–350	325–370
Houses	2B	3B	4B	5B	6/7B	8B
Average prices	175–220	210–275	260–350+	300–370	350–400	350–450

The properties Respectable Victoriana, plus examples of all periods since. Larger homes to W of area, smaller terraces to the E. Three-bed houses most common; larger houses have often become flats; some now converting back. Little 2-bed houses a popular alternative to flats.

The market First-time buyers after 1/2-bed flats join families seeking space and greenery. They, and agents, reckon area is still good value.

Among estate agents active in this area are:

- Acorn
- Oak Estates
- Robert Stanford & Hayward
- Kinleigh Folkard
- Sebastian Roche
- Winkworth
- Wates

FULHAM

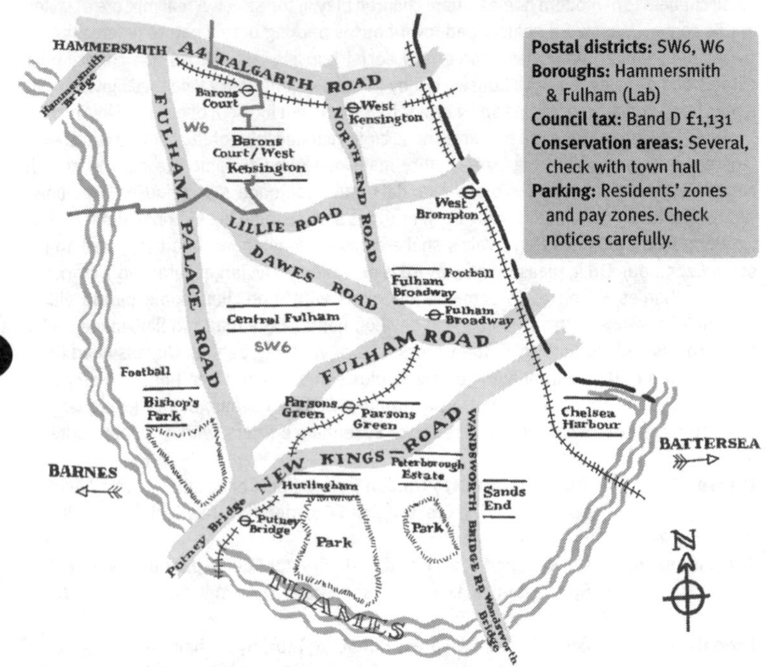

Postal districts: SW6, W6
Boroughs: Hammersmith & Fulham (Lab)
Council tax: Band D £1,131
Conservation areas: Several, check with town hall
Parking: Residents' zones and pay zones. Check notices carefully.

While London becomes ever more a world city, Fulham stays resolutely British: the residential quarter for the City of London. People from all corners of the world settle here, of course, but they adopt a British lifestyle: family-centred, friends for dinner, gossip at the school gate. Life is lived in century-old terraced houses masquerading as country vicarages, and cosy flats that are certainly not lofts.

Local estate agents contrast Fulham's Britishness with the edgy cosmopolitanism of neighbouring Chelsea and South Kensington. Some may find this exciting, but to a certain kind of Fulhamite it just means that those places are full of foreigners.

Fulham has a seemingly unlimited supply of fussily detailed, late-Victorian terraces, much smartened, even rebuilt, at great expense over the last three prosperous decades. It has all the shops, bars, cafés, health clubs its denizens expect. It has sparse but just-about-possible public transport, and just-about-bearable driving and parking (as long as you have a residents' permit: in some streets, non-locals are banned till 8pm). Heathrow is within reach. Above all, it is predictable. People-like-us will be living next door.

What Fulham lacks is a central focus, being an amalgamation of several old hamlets; Fulham Broadway is the nearest thing, with its new complex round the tube. This added bigger shops (Virgin, Books Etc, Pizza Express, Sainsbury's), offices and cinema to its complement of little ones selling every kind of designy, interiory or gastronomic delight.

The downside is transport. The District Line badly needs supplementing by a new rail service along the West London Line, which forms Fulham's frontier with Chelsea. The only station on this line is at West Brompton, and at present the trains run at the rate of two an hour. Ideas about boosting the service have been around for years, but have foundered on the line's restricted capacity: it's heavily used by freight trains.

However, a condition of planning permission for Imperial Wharf is the building of a new station. It is needed: this vast development, virtually a new suburb, adds 1,665 new homes to this cut-off river bend (flats mostly; half open-market sale, half Affordable Housing of various sorts). St George have indeed put up the money, and the station is now promised to open in summer 2005. Transport for London will subsidize a shuttle service between Clapham Junction and Olympia – but at peak times only, with four trains an hour.

The station will also serve Chelsea Harbour (in Fulham despite the name), plus the planned Lots Road Power Station scheme just across the borough border (yet another 800-odd homes: see Chelsea chapter). The SW London to Hackney tube (re-branded Crossrail 2) would be even better, linking Fulham direct to the heart of town. But that plan goes back to 1948, and may collect its pension (as a plan. . .) before it gets built. Meanwhile, the District Line will have to cope: it is the most congested part of the tube network, and stops nowhere near these riverside schemes.

Glitzy new developments notwithstanding, families dominate the market here. Some people never leave Fulham, except to go to work. They cluster here for the District Line to the City, the schools, the networking: gym, nanny, nursery, shopping.

Until 1880 almost all of this deep, cut-off pocket of the Thames was market gardens. With the completion of the District Line, an enormous tide of development flooded over Fulham – the bulk between 1880 and 1900, but extending up to World War I in various corners. These houses – almost entirely terraced, with only a few detached and semi-detached in areas such as Hurlingham and Bishop's Park – cover most of Fulham. There still exist a very few 18th-century buildings, mainly associated with the original villages of Walham Green (now Fulham Broadway) and Fulham itself (right down by what is now Putney Bridge), and extending along the New King's Rd.

After the pre-1914 building boom, Fulham relapsed into a condition of quiet working-class respectability (except for definitely dodgy Sand's End). As late as 1971, more than 40 per cent of the homes in most of Fulham were privately let. It was a stable community, with strong local loyalties and a tendency to stay put: three generations of the same family would live in the same group of streets. This pattern was shattered by the closure of the many firms that provided work for the locals, and by the property boom of the early '70s. Demand from would-be owner-occupiers began to spill over from Chelsea and Kensington, and the first quiet Fulham streets were 'discovered'. Landlords, beset by the Rent Acts then in force, hurried to sell their tenanted homes (many, even at this date, still with outside lavatories) as soon as the residents could be persuaded to leave.

The early '80s cemented the trend, which spread across the whole area. In came the young, middle-class professionals, out went the skilled workers and their families to new estates on the fringes of London. By 1990 the transformation was all but complete.

In a few frantic years, the face of Fulham changed . . . and set, as face-lifted faces do, into a rigid new pattern. In 21st century Fulham, if your neighbours are not bankers or lawyers you are pretty unusual.

Fulham has a fair sprinkling of council estates, though they have been gradually changing as residents exercised their 'Right to Buy', and as modernization has taken place. The biggest is Clem Attlee Court in the N of the area, off **Lillie Rd**. These large blocks, named after Socialist luminaries of the 1940s, form a community of their own and provide a source of good-value housing. Two have been demolished to make room for low-rise housing-association homes. Sand's End has more council blocks in a fast-changing area. Smaller clusters of council-built and housing-association homes occur across the borough; some, such as those by the river off **Stevenage Rd**, are very attractive. The council has just won £78 million to spend on council homes across the borough over the next couple of years, so expect existing enclaves to smarten.

The wide sweep of the Thames forms Fulham's southern and western boundaries. The river is crossed at two points to the S, by Putney (the oldest and lowest fording point on the Thames, as used by the Romans) and Wandsworth Bridges. The eastern boundary is the main N–S railway line, running down from Kensington Olympia to cross the river alongside Chelsea Harbour: only three roads cross this line. Closing off the northern approaches is the barrier of the A4/Hammersmith Flyover and Cromwell Rd Extension/Talgarth Rd, leading westwards to the M4 motorway. Three roads cross this. There are thus only eight roads into or out of Fulham – something that often becomes painfully obvious to drivers.

The E–W roads define neighbourhoods. Going northwards, they are **New King's Rd**, **Fulham Rd**, **Dawes Rd** and **Lillie Rd**. There are two main N–S routes: **Fulham Palace Rd**, leading to Putney Bridge; and **North End Rd/Wandsworth Bridge Rd**, leading to Wandsworth Bridge. Again these routes are neighbourhood demarcation lines.

New King's Rd and **Fulham Rd** have changed a lot in the last 20 years, acquiring fashionable shops selling antique furniture, clothing and specialist delicatessen, plus restaurants and bars. **Lillie Rd** and **Dawes Rd** still maintain many of the old-style small local shops, selling a wide range of goods, but they are changing fast. Lillie's shops are less junk, more antique these days. To the amazement of those who knew it just a few years back, **Munster Rd** boasts street cafés, bars and restaurants. **Fulham Palace Rd**, especially S of **Lillie Rd**, is predominantly residential. **North End Rd** has a colourful street fruit-and-veg market operating side by side with a Waitrose supermarket, while **Wandsworth Bridge Rd** is a mix of homes and trendy shopping – it has been the stripped-pine capital of West London for years, and has recently widened its scope. The Sainsbury's on **Townmead Rd** is a hub of life for the S of the area.

Fulham has a number of open spaces and parks. In the S is Hurlingham Park with its sports ground. The Hurlingham Club, which adjoins it and has all the river frontage, is (very) private. It has a swimming pool and tennis courts and is centred around the 18th-century Hurlingham House. Nearby, little South Park has children's play-areas, cricket pitch, tennis courts. Parson's Green and Eel Brook Common are small, tree-lined open spaces overlooked by many attractive homes. To the W, Bishop's Park, originally the gardens of the 16th-century bishop's palace, borders the river above Putney Bridge. To the N is little Normand Park and, up at Baron's Court, the Queens Club private tennis club.

Tree-planting along the streets has also helped to mitigate the main difference between Fulham and Chelsea: the lack of the general leafy impression provided by Chelsea's square gardens. Fulham, built later, has dense rows of streets, not squares.

Fulham also boasts two football grounds, which attract considerable traffic. To the W is Fulham's riverside ground, while on the Kensington/Chelsea borders is Stamford Bridge, home of Chelsea FC. Both grounds have for years been the focus of plans, rows and more plans. Chelsea's ground, now called 'Chelsea Village', has seen the biggest changes. It has acquired a hotel, 9-storey block of flats (including clutch of loft-style flats calling itself 'The Italian Village'), three restaurants and more. The stadium has grown from a capacity of 28,000 to 43,000, and gone are the days when it was used only twice a week in winter. Fulham FC last year abandoned plans for a big flats scheme and refurbished the **Stevenage Rd** ground to Premiership standard.

The three District Line tube stations are augmented by two Piccadilly Line stops just N of the area, at Barons Court and West Kensington: these give direct links to Heathrow. However, large tracts of Fulham are quite a distance from a tube station. Roads take you out of London to the W along the M4 to Heathrow and the M25, to the S over Putney or Wandsworth Bridges to join the South Circular or A3, and to the N through Shepherd's Bush. However, the traffic saturation on these routes means incalculable journey times (particularly if Chelsea are playing at home).

Parking in the residential streets is an ever more desperate problem, as many owners of the narrow-fronted terraced houses have two cars (at least); overnight double parking is common. All the residential roads now have controlled parking. A parking space is the first asset an agent will mention: single garages sell at around £50,000.

As far as most inhabitants and estate agents are concerned, Fulham ends at **Lillie Rd**, the SW6 border. The W14 area to the N between **Lillie Rd** and **Talgarth Rd** has a very different character, centred around Barons Court and West Kensington tube stations. It is largely made up of big, late-Victorian houses and mansion blocks, and until recently rented homes dominated. One major agent has tried to dub this tract 'Fulham Cross'; however, it has more in common with Hammersmith (which chapter see).

The neighbourhoods of Fulham can be divided into the expensive, the established and the up-and-coming, and are dealt with here in that order:

Peterborough Estate

Perhaps the best-known part of Fulham is the ever-popular, ever-so-pricey Peterborough Estate, a conservation area between Parson's Green, on the **New King's Rd**, and South Park. These were always a cut above, and known as the 'lion houses': terracotta lions (trademark of J Nicholls, the builder) prance the party walls at roof level. This is where the Fulham renaissance began. Incoming owner-occupiers started buying, gutting and remodelling them in the early 1970s (and referred to their neighbourhood as 'Hurlingham': no-one in Chelsea thought Fulham was an OK address in those days).

F

By the end of the 1970s these houses, smartened up, were the first in Fulham to break the £100,000 barrier. Now prices soar well past the million. Prices can be deceptive as there's an astounding range of interior configurations behind the monotonous facades: most have been extended up, back and down ('just look what we've done to the basement!' is a local catchphrase). Many have been virtually rebuilt, some more than once. A 3-bed example in **Coniger Rd**, £1.25 million last winter; a 5-bed in **Chiddingstone St**, £1.8 million. Un-done-up houses are increasingly rare, though a **Quarrendon St** property was £875,000 in the autumn. The estate, which lies W of Wandsworth Bridge Rd, forms a series of streets running N–S from the Parson's Green stretch of New King's Rd down to **Studdridge St**: **Perrymead**, **Chipstead**, **Quarrendon**, **Chiddingstone** and **Bradbourne Sts**, and **Coniger Rd**. These matching terraces of substantial houses are handsome, red-brick, gabled, flat-fronted late-Victoriana (c. 1895), 3-, 4- or 5-beds. Back gardens are small; the streetscapes distinctive, with attractive mullioned windows and those lions. The majority are still single-family houses, though a few flats can be found.

Fulham, at first sight a district of uniform terraces, has some unusual domestic buildings such as this splendidly ornate turret house near Hurlingham. The slate-capped turret, the Romanesque detailing around its eaves, the handsome sash windows and the iron railings make up an attractive whole.

Similar architecture is found E of Wandsworth Bridge Rd (see below), and in **Broomhouse Rd** the lion motifs have been copied in 'King Henry Row': five new houses named after Henry VIII's spouses: Seymour House was on the market for £1.5 million last winter (4-bed, 4-bath, garage). Others include Boleyn and Parr. . . but which of the queens is missing?

Hurlingham/High St

The appeal of this corner, also S of **New King's Rd**, is its leafiness – Hurlingham Park is here, and South Park and Bishop's

Park are nearby – the river, and the convenience of Putney Bridge tube. It also holds most of Fulham's small stock of larger houses (that is, large to start with – not modest ones extended up, down and backwards).

Fulham High St, down by Putney Bridge, marks the site of the original village of Fulham, but today is a bit of a misnomer. It has a few shops, but is mostly tall blocks of mansion flats on the W side; a mix of uses on the E. Parkview Court is one such mansion block: 124 flats that back onto Fulham Palace grounds – as does **Steeple Close**, enviably tucked away off **Church Gate** by the parish church: 3- and 4-bed town-houses with (rare assets in Fulham) garages. Across the road, 3- to 5-bed houses in **Burlington Rd** can top a million (1978: £19,000; 1984: £98,000. . .).

But for the nicest (and priciest) homes look to Hurlingham's conservation area, consisting of **Napier Avenue, Ranelagh Avenue, Ranelagh Gardens, Edenhurst Avenue** and **Hurlingham Gardens**, close to the tube and bounded to the N by **Hurlingham Rd**, which skirts Hurlingham Park. This, and the private grounds of the Hurlingham Club, which continues the park's greenery right down to the river bank, are the remains of the grounds of Hurlingham House: the Georgian mansion is still there, and serves as the clubhouse. Hurlingham Lodge (as opposed to House), 'a country house in London', sold in 2000 for a vast but undisclosed (thought to be £12 million-ish) sum. Predominantly, though, this enclave has imposing late-19th-century detached and semi-detached 5- or 6-bedroom houses set back from tree-lined streets, each with its own character and – unlike the uniform Peterborough homes – architectural style, with drives and off-street parking. A **Hurlingham Rd** detached needing modernisation, but with a flower room (how nice) and a double garage (how necessary), was £2.9 million last winter. Round in **Edenhurst Avenue**, £1.3 million buys a 6-bed (with wine cellar).

In **Ranelagh Gardens** there are two much-sought-after '60s apartment blocks (1-bed c. £280,000, 2-bed c. £425,000, 3-bed c. £625,000), plus a late-'80s riverside development, **Carrara Wharf**: a private enclave of 20 houses and 69 flats. Vast mansion flats in **Rivermead Court**, tucked beside the club grounds and river, reach well above a million for 5-beds (remember Fulham is short of large homes). In secluded **Hurlingham Gardens** is a large inter-war luxury apartment block. On Hurlingham Rd, **Melbray Mews** is a group of live/work units, unusual for this part of town. **Napier Avenue** has imposing 6-bedroomed houses.

On the far (E) side of Hurlingham Park, Barratt added a new square to the area in the late '80s: **Hurlingham Square**, in the angle of Peterborough and Sulivan Rds, has 50 4/5-bed homes in an enclave reached via electric gates; a 4-bed example, asking £650,000 last winter. Further N off **Peterborough Rd** the neat, pleasant Sulivan Court estate of council-built homes runs through to **Broomhouse Lane**, which bounds Hurlingham Park.

Skirting South Park, **Clancarty Rd**'s N side can provide larger-than-usual Fulham gardens between it and the Peterborough Estate's Studdridge St. Riverside **Carnwath Rd** has seen big changes as industry and commerce are replaced by homes. Here a '50s office block, the former British Gas research HQ, was sold as 'The Piper Building' (artist John Piper was commissioned by the Gas people to adorn the outside with a big abstract mural), transformed into fashionable shell-finish 'loft' apartments in 1997/98 (a 3-bed, £750,000 last autumn). Keep an eye on this street as more land gets developed.

Bishop's Park

Another small conservation area, Bishop's Park takes in the pleasant tree-lined streets that are the first few of a ladder of alphabetically-named roads, **Bishop's Park Rd, Cloncurry St, Doneraile St, Ellerby St** and **Finlay St**, running from **Fulham Palace Rd** to **Stevenage Rd** which here borders Bishop's Park. Here the Fulham style changes: you find terraced or semi-detached houses that were built at the end of the 19th century or later, and have four or five bedrooms. Many have been extended upwards with loft conversions (not always sympathetically), and to the rear with back extensions and conservatories. Most (untypically for Fulham) also have substantial gardens. The later date of these houses celebrates the stubborn hold-out against the developers of the last major market gardener in what was once known as 'London's kitchen-garden'.

This orderly grid of roads marches on, past Fulham Football Club at the W end of **Finlay St**, up to **Niton St** (though the alphabet gets jumbled after **Inglethorpe**). Here you will find more flat conversions (2-beds, c. £350,000), and more modest houses. The small, 3-bed houses are often extended to give an extra bedroom (such 4-beds, if smart, £700,000-ish). Along the river-bank are a string of apartment blocks built in the '70s, with fine views across the river to the old Barnes water meadows, now a wildlife sanctuary, and (the N part) the exclusive '90s Barnes Waterside homes. River Gardens, which has pool and sauna, has 2/3-bed flats with spectacular terracing and balconies; Rosebank is a conventional high-rise block with 2/3-bed flats. **Eternity Walk**, which leads down to the river, now has Waters Edge, a Thirlstone development, where £1.1 million was being asked last autumn for a 4-bed house with off-street parking and two balconies.

F

At **Crabtree Lane**, SW6 gives way to W6. The grid running on N between the Lane, Fulham Palace Rd and the river is the 1911 Crabtree estate (see Hammersmith chapter).

Chelsea Harbour

On the Fulham/Chelsea borders, Chelsea Harbour was until now the area's biggest clutch of modern apartments and houses. But many more are being added next door in the Imperial Wharf scheme (see Sand's End), not to mention the Lot's Road scheme (currently stalled at planning stage) on the other, Chelsea, side.

Chelsea Harbour is a parable of our times: only in the 1980s could a developer take a triangular site bounded by a busy railway and a muddy creek and present these as advantages – even if the third side is, as here, river frontage. But this inconvenient and cut-off corner was thus able to offer that goal of every really top-flight development: complete security. Chelsea Harbour was the W side of town's answer to Docklands: a gated community of 310 homes in blocks, terraces, crescents and the landmark tower, plus starry health club, hotel, restaurant, plentiful interior-design shops (but not much else), a deli, offices – all of it alongside (if not part of) Chelsea, not the Isle of Dogs.

The centrepiece is the reopened harbour. This marina provides the neighbourhood with a much-needed tranquil spot to relax by the bobbing boats (a public walkway runs along the Thames). Homes vary widely in size and price; check position, condition – and sound insulation: some back onto the increasingly busy rail line. You can pay c. £385,000 for a 1-bed (but at least you get underground parking), £950,000 for a Thames-view 2-bed; there are 4/5-bed town-houses and the really swanky flats in the Belvedere Tower.

What will make Chelsea Harbour is better public transport. There is a river bus, peak hours only, to Blackfriars, and a 'hoppa' bus to Clapham Junction/Earl's Court. The long-hoped-for rail station (see introduction, above) will make it less of a backwater. For the big scheme to develop the next-door power station see the Chelsea chapter.

Moore Park Rd

A cache of large mid-Victorian stucco terraced houses and later-Victorian detached and semi-detached ones lies on the Fulham/Chelsea borders, between **Fulham Rd** and **King's Rd**. This was one of the first bits of Fulham to become respectable – 'almost Chelsea, actually' – and it is a stable, established corner. The proximity to busy Chelsea football ground is mitigated because the streets (**Moore Park Rd, Waterford Rd, Britannia Rd, Maxwell Rd, Holmead Rd, Rumbold Rd**) are barricaded off to through-traffic. The bigger, 4- or 5-bed houses are £800,000–£1.2 million numbers; some have been converted into flats.

Parson's Green

In estate agents' terms, this covers an ever-growing area, bounded by streets either side of **Fulham Rd** to the N (up as far as **Bishop's Rd**) and either side of **New King's Rd** to the S, extending as far as Eel Brook Common to the E and **Munster Road** to the W. Anything, in fact, that can be defined as 'within easy walking distance of' pretty, triangular Parson's Green (another ancient hamlet) with its pubs, restaurants – and tube. The most popular area after Hurlingham and the Peterborough Estate, the bit of the Fulham Rd that falls within the neighbourhood became a hot-spot of yuppy bars in the 1980s (agents talk sagely of the seminal importance of Pitcher & Piano opening in 1986) and it's about to gain that other mark of distinction, a Tesco Metro.

The big 3-storey houses overlooking the actual, rather charming, Green are coveted and priced accordingly. There are a *very* few Georgian houses on New Kings's Rd opposite the green (one was £1.1 million last autumn). Mostly the streets round here are lined with 1890s bay-windowed terraces, many of which have been extended upwards with loft conversions to provide a fourth bedroom. Favourite streets include **Delvino Rd, Linver Rd, Guion Rd, Crondace Rd, Felden St, Mimosa St, Chesilton Rd.** Houses can be anywhere between £750,000 and a million-plus depending on smartness and clever space manipulation. More substantial houses, different in style and up to 6-beds, in **Whittingstall, St Maur, Winchendon** (a 4-bed, £850,000), **Lillyville** and **Clonmel Rds,** and **Cloncurry St** (4- to 6-beds, £1.1–1.2 million). Flats are now rare in these streets: there's an observable 25-year cycle whereby flats are turned into houses and back again.

Mustow Place, small homes in attractive mews style, has been squeezed in between the railway and Munster Rd. Another new mews, **Claridge Court**, has 10 town-houses and two flats. And 35 homes appeared on the Courtaulds site, also in Munster Rd: now the Coda Centre. Busy Munster Rd itself has slightly cheaper flats, plus some new ones to let. Attempts to brand this bit as 'Munster Village' seem a bit much, even for Fulham.

On the fringes of Parson's Green are two small neighbourhoods. To the E is **Eel Brook Common,** with the large, late-19th-century terraced houses that overlook the pretty park with its tennis courts from flanking **Musgrave Crescent** and **Favart Rd** being particularly popular. Five new 2- and 3-bed houses have squeezed in on a corner site: secure parking is a big plus. To the W, curving **Fulham Park Gardens** is a small conservation area of very distinctive, substantial red-brick houses of 5/6 bedrooms and considerable character; those on the E side of the road's 'elbow' are close to the tube line.

Fulham Broadway

This old but now submerged village was known as Walham Green – the green in question now goes under the name of Eel Brook Common – until London Transport renamed its station **Fulham Broadway** in 1948. Conservation areas include **Walham Grove**, which is a street of 1860s semi-detached villas, and **Barclay Rd**, mid-Victorian terraced houses (some split into flats: 1-bed £200,000).

The Broadway which, with its tube and town hall, should be the hub of modern Fulham, stayed resolutely down-at-heel as the area climbed socially around it. At last, action: the station has been rebuilt, with new bookshop, health club, supermarket, nine-screen cinema etc. And Manhattan Lofts have added another complex, 'Fulham Island', over the road in **Vanston Place**: designed by Piers Gough, the shops here include an M&S food-only store, a Conran bar and grill, offices, 34 flats and a rooftop tropical garden. Despite the makeover, The Broadway still lacks the villagey charm of, say, Parson's Green, but locals are hopeful that the upturn will continue.

Homes exist in the gaps between roads and shops. To the S of the Broadway, Harwood Mews is a cache of town-houses in **Harwood Rd**. Pleasantly-named **Farm Lane**, where there are plans for a new homes development 'soon', curves round behind the big Samuel Lewis Trust housing estate N of the Broadway. **North End Rd** is the scene of a thriving street market. The Council is spending money to cut traffic, widen pavements and generally tidy up the market, and bars, etc, are cautiously opening. Berkeley Homes added six town-houses and five 2-bed flats, plus offices, at 'Crowther Market' off North End Rd. To the E, a fairly cut-off corner of streets runs through to **Seagrave Rd**, off which is leafy **Brompton Park Crescent**: a cul-de-sac of flats (1-bed £200,000, 2-bed £270,000) and houses, complete with central greenery, pool, health club and parking. West Brompton station (and hence the tracks) are close; to the S lies Chelsea's football ground.

Central Fulham

To the N of **Bishop's Rd**, the street pattern changes; the N–S roads running off Fulham Rd give way to later, tight-packed E–W rows running up to **Lillie Rd**. These hold similar 3/4-bedroom terraced houses, all built between 1890 and 1910; many were converted into flats in the '80s. There are several pockets of pretty streets – **Marville Rd**, **Brookville Rd**, **Rosaville Rd**, **Parkville Rd**, **Orbain Rd**, **St Olafs Rd** – with occasional streets of unusual mansion blocks in yellow London brick. Agents reckon the 'ville' roads offer value, at least compared to streets closer to Parson's Green. Even **Dawes Rd**, once a byword for dowdiness, is cheering up, though it's still a busy bus route (and knowledgeable Fulhamites have the area's measure: shops and restaurants are opening, but an attempt to coin the term 'Dawes Village' met with much laughter). There are some big, older-style flats, though many around here are above shops. North of Dawes Rd is less desirable, so cheaper; streets like **Fabian Rd** offer an SW6 toe-hold to the impecunious.

F

Sand's End/Riverside

Sandy End, Addison called it, when he stayed here in 1708. The house survives as Sandford Manor, but its surroundings went downhill from then on, attracting a monster gasworks in 1824 and gaining a name for slums and later for (very) dodgy council estates. Meanwhile, the riverside was lined with factories, warehouses and (in 1936) a coal-fired power station. Sand's End became a pretty grim place.

Its revival began when it was declared a Housing Action Area in the '70s. Owner-occupiers dipped tentative toes into the little terraces in the '80s, reasoning that the Peterborough Estate was not *that* far away. Chelsea Harbour and a large Sainsbury's in **Townmead Rd** furthered Sand's End's rehabilitation – though it is still scruffy in parts. Imperial Wharf has given it another boost.

St George's monster **Imperial Wharf** scheme includes a 10-acre riverside park, hotel, health club, M&S food store etc. A boulevard runs – through security gates, of course – from **Townmead Rd** down to the river, replacing the S part of **Imperial Rd**. The big blocks, with their coloured panels, plus the planting and paving, are reminiscent of a Spanish *urbanización* – albeit an expensive one. Homes are still building, and selling off-plan, though several blocks are occupied. Acton Housing Association's Affordable Homes, at the N end, are now finished, and occupied by what in Fulham counts as the struggling classes: web designers, data analysts, marketing consultants (a row about this). A penthouse starts at £1 million; for traditionalists a crescent of very large, high-spec mock-Georgian town-houses lines the W side. The river walk leads to Chelsea Harbour's pleasant enclave. The new station (see introduction) will help the access problems.

Tucked behind the giant site are the delightful, restored Victorian cottages of **Imperial Square**. Sandford Manor is in there somewhere, used as the gasworks manager's house for decades. Further W, along Sand's End's river frontage, on the site of the former Fulham power station, is a modern complex of 250 flats, all with a river view. They range from 1-bed to 4-bed penthouses, and the name changed from Sand's Wharf to 'Regent on the River' and **Sailmakers Court**, Ferrymans Quay etc: a 2-bed flat, c. £480,000. A leisure centre (the Harbour Club) offers squash, tennis and pool. Barratt contributed a further two schemes off **Harwood Terrace** in the N corner of Sand's End. Chelsea Walk and Chelsea Lodge – named to stress proximity to the borough border – total 20 4-bed £850,000 houses. More new homes are coming on the corner of Wandsworth Bridge.

There are also pockets of council housing and a large area of typical Fulham-style late-Victorian terraces not yet completely smartened, and cheaper than the rest of Fulham: **Stephendale Rd, Broughton Rd** (3-bed house, c. £500,000; 4-bed c. £540,000), **Lindrop St, Glenrosa St, Byam St.** The exception is a small area E of **Wandsworth Bridge Rd**, where **Rosebury Rd, Oakbury Rd, Cranbury Rd, Haslebury Rd** are smaller Peterborough Estate-type houses, converted to flats. The area's 'come up' to make an attractive corner. They even have an estate-agent name: 'the Bury Triangle' (as in the traditional Chelsea divorcée's cry 'don't bury me in Fulham'?). Up to £600,000 for a 4-bed here now. Busy **Wandsworth Bridge Rd** has many flat conversions (2-bed £285,000) and a few big houses: the N end is the priciest.

Transport Tubes: Parsons Green, Fulham Broadway, Putney Bridge (zone 2, District). From Fulham Broadway: Oxford Circus 30 min (1 change), City 45 min (1 change), Heathrow 45 min (1 change).

Convenient for A4, M4, Sloane Square and King's Rd shops. Miles from centre: 4.

Schools Local Authority: Fulham Cross (g), Hurlingham & Chelsea, London Oratory RC (b), St Edmunds RC, St Marks C of E, Lady Margaret C of E (g).

SALES

Flats	S	1B	2B	3B	4B	5B
Average prices	150–220	180–250	230–350	300–450	375–1.2M	→2M
Houses	2B	3B	4B	5B	6/7B	8B
Average prices	350–425	400–500	500–750+	600–1.2M	–	–

RENTAL

Flats	S	1B	2B	3B	4B	5B
Average prices	150–250	200–325	230–425	320–500	375–800	400+
Houses	2B	3B	4B	5B	6/7B	8B
Average prices	350+	370–550	525–850	700–1200	–	–

The properties Row after row of solid, late-19th-century family houses. Also some Victorian/Edwardian/'30s p/b flats and many flat conversions. After two decades of energetic renovation, many houses boast top-flight interiors. Much recent new-build and conversions on infill and river sites, including Imperial Wharf.

The market Fulham is the City of London's residential quarter, favoured by the more traditional kind of banker and lawyer. Buyers and renters are 'young professionals' and families.

Among estate agents active in this area are:

- Hamptons
- Douglas & Gordon
- Winkworth
- John D Wood
- Friend & Falcke
- Chard
- Chesterfields
- Savills
- Peter Woods
- Sebastian Estates
- Kinleigh Folkard & Hayward
- Lawson & Daughters
- Foxtons
- Wellington

GOLDERS GREEN

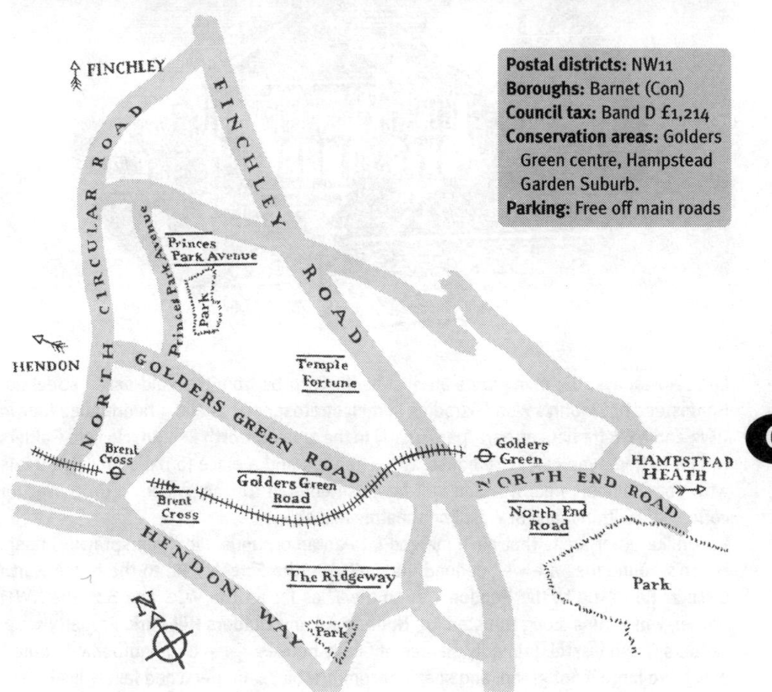

Postal districts: NW11
Boroughs: Barnet (Con)
Council tax: Band D £1,214
Conservation areas: Golders Green centre, Hampstead Garden Suburb.
Parking: Free off main roads

It will soon be a century since the tube bored its way beneath Hampstead Heath, turning Golders Green from farmland to suburbia in a few short years. The crossroads at Golders Green once stood in the middle of open fields, with a signpost pointing south 'To London'. The farmland is gone – but the signpost remains, resolutely pointing down the Finchley Rd as if 'London' is a place with which it would really rather not be associated. . . .

The arrival of the tube in 1907 sparked a fury of development here and in neighbouring fields: next door, Hampstead Garden Suburb (which chapter see) was built by that idealistic philanthropist, Dame Henrietta Barnett.

Many were seduced by 'Sanctuary', the famous 1908 Underground poster, exhorting them to hear the roar of the 'great Babel' at a safe distance – from a bright new, turn-of-the-century, stockbroker-Tudory, Arts-and-Craftsy, Golders Green home. The Green's advent was also nicely timed to attract some first- and second-generation immigrants, notably the Jewish community, which was then ready to move on from the East End to more congenial surroundings. And few places could be more congenial than Golders Green.

From a property point of view, this is one of those cohesive, local markets: people decide to live in Golders Green, and nowhere else will do. And once here, they stay, migrating to a bigger house perhaps, or downsizing to a smart flat. Locals are constantly on the look-out for properties for their children and relations, say estate agents. Prices have risen here as they have all over London, but Golders Green is still, as one estate agent put it, 'the first affordable suburb you get to when you drive north from the West

G

End'. Nowadays, the immigrants are just as likely to be from the gold-paved streets of Hampstead or St John's Wood – trading in their stratospheric 2- and 3-bedroomed flats in NW3 and NW8 for houses here, particularly in the area off **North End Rd**, close to Golders Hill Park. Here, you can get a house with a garden, and a place to park, in leafy streets with good schools nearby – and still be close enough to Hampstead to drop over for coffee, still within reach of West End theatres and shops.

Unlike other areas that have merged into an amorphous suburban sprawl, Golders Green's boundaries are well-defined. Its limits are the **Finchley Rd** to the E, the **North Circular Rd** to the N, the **Hendon Way** to the W as far as **The Vale**, and S to the NW11 border, which runs along **Dunstan Rd**, **Hodford Rd** and **Golders Hill Park**. Property-wise, Golders Green is, still, primarily an area of family houses: 3-, 4- or 5-bedroomed homes, which are large if not grand, and speak of comfortable, semi-detached family life. These are Edwardian villas, the area having been developed too late for the usual tide of Victorian terraces – though there are some patches of '20s and '30s ones. There are also many purpose-built blocks (along **Golders Green** and **Finchley Rds** and in the area around **Woodlands**) and the '80s saw a lot of flats conversions around Temple Fortune. Here, too, is a fair amount of rented accommodation, so there are lots of young single people: Golders Green is very convenient for several of the London University colleges.

The bustling **Golders Green Rd**, which runs through the centre from the tube up to the **North Circular Rd** and Hendon, boasts a lively, cosmopolitan atmosphere and a selection of interesting shops and eateries. Near the tube wall-to-wall coffee shops offer café culture for young locals – you need to leave the area for any other form of culture though, even a pub or a cinema. . . unless you count the 24-hour Tesco as night life.

Residents point out that this makes for a friendly, neighbourhood feel, though. People swear by Carmelli's Bakery, get fit at the gym, head for Blooms, an offshoot of the famous East End restaurant. Still home for many of London's Jews, Golders Green is awash with delicatessens, kosher bakeries and takeaways. At festival times you'll see people in their holiday clothes strolling the streets, and during Chanukah (December's festival of lights) the tube station houses a huge candelabrum which is lit every evening. There are also Asian and Far Eastern communities – plus a floating population of young Aussies, New Zealanders and South Africans – and these too are reflected in the area's shops and restaurants.

Golders Green is blessed with churches of every denomination and synagogues, official and unofficial, of every shade of orthodoxy. Estate agents know the synagogues in detail, since purchasers will often only consider properties in roads near to a particular one. The same goes for the schools . . . . There's plenty of open space too, if you'd rather commune with the Almighty in less formal surroundings; and the Hampstead Heath Extension is nearby – not to mention the Golders Green cemetery and crematorium in **Hoop Lane**, regularly on TV when a star departs.

If godliness is its first name, convenience in the form of transport is its second. The Northern Line provides great links to West End and City, direct to Tottenham Court Rd, Leicester Square and Bank. Buses are very good, too.

After a positively Biblical 12 years of argument, poles were finally installed to mark the North London 'eruv' – an area within which Sabbath laws are relaxed for Orthodox Jews. The largely notional boundary is defined by existing features (for example, the M1), but gaps or 'gateways' are bridged by wires strung between 84 poles. Planning permission was granted back in 1998, but then came a succession of further disputes about the exact siting of poles. At the public inquiry, local estate agents were scolded for talking up the effect on house prices: they predicted (hoped?) it would prompt an influx of the Orthodox. No such effect has been noted. It comes as no surprise that the eruv is still causing controversy, with cases of alleged criminal damage to the poles and, conversely, the lopping of tree-branches to repair a section of the boundary wire incurring the wrath of the Superintendent of Hampstead Heath.

The Ridgeway

Some of the best houses in Golders Green are found in the area to the W of the **Golders Green Rd**, off **The Ridgeway**. In roads such as **Ridge Hill, Gresham Gardens, Armitage Rd, Basing Hill, Hodford Rd** and **Dunstan Rd** you'll find 4- and 5-bedroom houses, detacheds and semis, with large gardens. A 4-bed semi c. £650,000 – but prices here regularly exceed £800,000, and flats don't come cheap: a 2-bed garden flat in **Woodstock Avenue** was £300,000 recently. Little Basing Hill Park, the nearby tube station, cinema and shops are all attractions, though parking can be a problem in **Rodborough Rd** and **Helenslea Avenue.** Jewish residents have often chosen to live here because of the proximity to synagogues in **Dunstan Rd** and **The Riding**. The busy **Hendon Way** runs past the bottom of **Wessex Gardens** and **Ridge Hill**, so prices are lower at that end: a typical 3-bed example – if you can tolerate the roar of the traffic – can still be had for around £300,000. Cheaper, too, as you go towards Cricklewood.

Brent Cross

Brent Cross does not really constitute a neighbourhood by itself, though it houses the famous shopping centre and has a tube station (the two aren't as near to each other as you might think). **Highfield Avenue**, with the tube station, is one of the nicest roads in Golders Green and **Highfield Gardens** is where you'll find one of Golders Green's most popular purpose-built blocks, Windsor Court. In **Hamilton Rd** prices may be more modest since the street runs parallel to the **Hendon Way**; houses on the **Sandringham Rd** side won't suffer from noise as much as those right by the main road, but will still be relatively less-expensive for the area. Also look out among the 3-bed terraces and semis in **Woodville Rd** and **Elmcroft Crescent** for homes at the lower end of the price scale.

Recent moves to expand the Brent Cross shopping complex have little effect on Golders Green, apart from increasing the traffic on the North Circular yet further.

Golders Green Rd

This runs northwards like a main artery through the area from the station and the Hippodrome – first a music hall, then a theatre, now a BBC studio. Shopping, much of it now seven days a week, causes parking problems; triple-parking (and generally eccentric driving habits) in Golders Green are legendary. Busy residents can buy a suit on Sunday and toiletries until midnight every day, but the local shopping centre has long suffered from the competition from Brent Cross. Heading towards Hendon, the flats above the shops give way to large family houses around **Ravenscroft Avenue** and across to the E in **Rotherwick Rd**. Here, prices equate to those of the favoured streets of the Ridgeway neighbourhood.

Golders Green isn't usually noted for exceptionally pretty houses, but there are some surprises in **Brookside Rd.** You'll find flat conversions and family houses in streets off **Golders Green Rd, Gainsborough** and **Powis Gardens** to the W, **Beechcroft** and **Elmcroft Avenues** to the E, where there are also a couple of blocks of flats and small hotels. The Vale is nearby, and boasts roomy, comfortable-looking family homes. A typical 4-bed in this sought-after corner would have set you back c. £465,000 in late 2004.

There are larger, purpose-built blocks of flats along the main road – Gloucester Court and Eagle Lodge, for example. The popular 1930s block in **Golders Green Rd**, luxurious **Riverside Drive**, is big enough to be named on the A–Z – though the river in question, Dollis Brook, is marooned on the far side of the North Circular.

Princes Park Avenue

As with the streets around The Ridgeway, there are some very large houses to be found in the vicinity of Princes Park: look for them in the **Princes Park Avenue/Leeside Crescent/Bridge Lane** triangle. Princes Park, in the triangle's centre, makes houses here particularly desirable; on Saturday afternoons the little park is full of children. Again, agents mention the synagogue factor; Jewish people who live here have often chosen the neighbourhood specifically. Coveted bungalows, some with extra rooms in the roof, are to be found in **Decoy Avenue** across **Bridge Lane**. Popular if unlovely purpose-built blocks include Dolphin Court in **Woodlands**, and James Close, where a 3-bed penthouse was £600,000 last winter. This corner is not as convenient as the Ridgeway area, though buses to Golders Green run, numerous and frequent, along the main road.

Temple Fortune

This area brackets the **Finchley Rd** northwards from **Hoop Lane/Wentworth Rd** up to the **North Circular**. The neighbourhood takes its name from the **Temple Fortune Parade** of shops (among them the police station), which is slightly less frantic than the chic **Golders Green Rd**, but is improving: witness the cafés and esoteric food outlets. There's also a tennis club for sporty types and a major Marks & Spencer food hall.

Roads between **Hoop Lane** and **Temple Fortune Lane** have small houses and some conversions, cheaper even though they are nearer the prestigious Hampstead Garden Suburb because they back onto the cemetery. (Family homes in the Suburb – which chapter see – are highly sought-after, and the chance to live close to showbiz types in the Bishops Avenue direction can cost you well into the millions.) Further up on that side of the **Finchley Rd** you find purpose-built blocks like Belmont Court.

Roads on the other (W) side of the Finchley Rd – **Templars Avenue, St Johns Rd, Portsdown Avenue, St George's Rd** and further up, **Hallswelle Rd** and **Monkville Avenue** – have smaller family houses and some conversions. **Elmcroft Avenue** has some larger homes: a 6-bed house was £750,000 last autumn.

At the N of the neighbourhood is Henly's Corner, the incredibly busy and complex junction of the North Circular, Finchley Rd and the A1. The London Mayor has scrapped the long-debated plans for a flyover or underpass, which pleases locals, if not North Circular users, and improvements will be small-scale and aimed at making life more bearable for pedestrians and cyclists.

Back southwards now – but pause en route to the North End Rd quarter to note an enclave of larger, comfortable family houses in and around **Corringham, Middleton** and **Rotherwick Rds**. Cut off from Hampstead Garden Suburb (and often claimed by agents as 'borders') by the green spaces of the crematorium and the heath extension, houses here can range from £500,000–1 million. A 2-bed flat in one, £350,000 last autumn.

North End Rd

The neighbourhood to the S of the tube station, nestling in the angle between **North End Rd** and the **Finchley Rd**, sports Golders Hill Park (look out for the flamingos and wallabies in the zoo).

Enviable roads like **West Heath Avenue** and **The Park** triangle have lovely views of the park, which merges into West Heath. Flat conversions and blocks are gathered along **North End Rd** itself. **Chandos Way**, very close to the station and the Heath, has some 2-bed modern flats.

New homes are rare in Golders Green. However, the former Manor House Hospital in **North End Rd**, opposite Golders Hill Park, made way for 60 new homes, from flats to town-houses, courtesy of elite builders Octagon. Close by, the famous Bull & Bush pub thrives, but the Hare & Hounds is now 'Manor Heights', a smart gated enclave.

Transport Tubes: Golders Green, Brent Cross (zone 3, Northern). From Golders Green: Oxford Circus 20 min (1 change), City 30 min, Heathrow 1 hr 25 min (1 change).

Convenient for Brent Cross shopping centre, Hampstead, Hampstead Heath, North Circular Rd. Miles from centre: 6.

Schools Barnet Education Authority: Henrietta Barnett (g), Whitefield School, Hendon School. Private: King Alfred, Menorah GS (b). See also Hendon, Hampstead, Highgate chapters.

G

SALES

Flats	S	1B	2B	3B	4B	5B
Average prices	130–175	150–225	190–310	225–400	325–500	–
Houses	2B	3B	4B	5B	6/7B	8B
Average prices	250–350	325–500	380–750	450–1M	700–1M+	–

RENTAL

Flats	S	1B	2B	3B	4B	5B
Average prices	125–180	175–225	200–320	280–420	350–500	–
Houses	2B	3B	4B	5B	6/7B	8B
Average prices	280–375	350–500	375–750	450–1000	750–1000+	900+

The properties Mock-Tudor suburban homes, large and comfortable, mix with prosperous blocks of flats and some flat conversions. These are now supplemented by some luxury flats schemes. Less pricey suburbia, and some good value ex-local authority (the lower end of our price guide) towards Hendon Way and Brent Cross.

The market Primarily family; long-established community (largely Jewish; also Japanese) now joined by house-hunters from Hampstead and St John's Wood. Good transport links and solid, peaceful family homes ensure its position.

Among estate agents active in this area are:

- Ellis & Co
- Winkworth
- Goldschmidt & Howland
- Alexander Ross
- Moreland
- Glentree Estates
- Kinleigh Folkard & Hayward
- Kingsleys
- Alan Goldin
- Litchfields
- Jac Stratton
- Claridges
- Hausman & Holmes

GREENWICH AND BLACKHEATH

Postal districts: SE10, SE3
Boroughs: Greenwich (Lab), Lewisham (Lab)
Council tax: Band D
Greenwich £1,140
Lewisham £1,141
Conservation areas: Several, check with town hall
Parking: Residents/meters

The bankers have landed. At first it was a trickle, then a big slice of Canary Wharf's finest found elegant Georgian Greenwich, and serene Regency Blackheath, and have bought up the big houses. It was the DLR that did it, that and the Jubilee Line and its £5 a day car park next to North Greenwich station, which is one stop to Canary Wharf.

Greenwich used to be both an affordable and a bearable place to live, a slice of riverside, green-framed sanity in the traffic-plagued, council-block ridden wastes of SE London. You did not need to be a master of the universe to afford a lovely house. Classic, Grade II 1840s terraces in **Burney St** were £400,000 in 1999, now they're £830,000 (down by some £70,000 from 2003, mind you). Six-bed Victorian monsters around the Heath and Westcombe Park started at £360,000 in '99: now you'll nudge a million, twice that for a Heath view, more still if it's Georgian.

Luckily, the two areas between them offer homes of all sizes, ages and prices, and those hunting for terraced cottages, modern flats, or eco-homes can join the idyll too.

The Georgiana is set around the parkland that is the backdrop for the glories of the former Royal Hospital, Queen's House and Observatory. In complete contrast are the high-tech homes appearing a mile or so – and another world – away in the revitalized industrial wasteland of the Greenwich Peninsula, beside The Dome. The innovative homes of the Millennium Village, so far as successful as the Dome was disastrous, offer an alternative to period property. And this is just the start – the new owners of the Dome have been given the land around it as well as the structure itself, and plan a complete new 10,000-home community (see below).

The charms of historic riverside Greenwich have long been muted by the equally historic difficulty of getting there. This changed with the coming of the two new rail links. From most of Greenwich you can see Canary Wharf across the Thames, with its ranks of

gleaming office towers. And now, thanks to the Jubilee Line tube and the extended Docklands Light Railway (DLR), you can get to them. Now, too, you can get to the City and Canary Wharf by river: a refurbished river pier allows conmmuter boats – only a sparse service as yet, but a start. There are problems still with the amount of traffic trying to get out to the Channel Tunnel road – though heavy trucks are now barred, and have to trundle instead up the road across the Heath. However, there's new concern about the effect of this heavy traffic on old chalk pits: one road descended into a cavern in 2002.

So much for the present outlook for this gracious old naval town. The past is around every corner in Greenwich; every age since the Romans has made its contribution. As far as the streetscape goes, however, the period that has stuck is the Georgian/Regency one: glorious examples that encouraged some of the better exponents of Victorian building in their wake. Gathered around the royal park by the Thames, Greenwich centre, for long rather neglected, still has the bustle and air of a slightly down-at-heel seaside, more than riverside, town. Trippers flock to the Cutty Sark, the National Maritime Museum, the Observatory. The growing number of students adds to the bustle.

On the plateau at the top of Shooters Hill, Blackheath – at heart a country hamlet – considers itself a cut above. Those with money can choose 18th-century restrained elegance or even, tucked away, Marbella-level opulence.

Greenwich itself divides neatly into two: the boundary is the superb sweep of park from hill to river. East Greenwich still retains a working identity and some riverside industry, starting to give way to flats, while the inland Victorian cottages are nowadays snapped up by young buyers. Westcombe Park, sloping up the hill S of the railway, is grander and greener, full of family houses, though still (comparatively) affordable.

West Greenwich – the historic, if not yet smartened, centre – boasts 17th-century masterpieces such as Wren's Royal Hospital, now home to Greenwich University and Trinity College of Music, the re-vamped National Maritime Museum and the Royal Observatory. It also has street after street of superb 18th-century and later houses. At weekends crafts and food markets add an air of fashionable bohemia.

West Greenwich

To the W of the set-piece buildings and the great sweep of the park lies the heart of Greenwich, with its generous mix of Georgian and Regency style. Homes here often change hands privately, to the frustration of estate agents. **Croom's Hill**, with its huge, high-ceilinged Georgian and Victorian houses overlooking the park, is the most enviable address in Greenwich (£1.5 million for a 5-bed house here last winter). Near the bottom of the hill lies one of the prettiest streets in South London – **Crooms Hill Grove.**

Thousands pass by its tiny entrance, not realizing that a beautiful row of 2- and 3-storey terraced homes lies yards from the park's entrance. Developers Laing are copying the Georgian style with some panache in their 'Feathers Place' scheme of seven 4-bed houses (£795,000–1.5 million). Also off Croom's Hill, near to Greenwich Theatre, lies the late-18th-century crescent of **Gloucester Circus**, with its 2-storey houses and fenced garden to the front. The perfect proportion of the Circus is, however, spoiled by the block of brick-built council flats opposite. **Burney St**'s handsome 1840 terraced houses, complete with wrought-iron balconies, are in demand. **Luton Place**'s early-Victorian brick-faced semis face new town-houses.

From the Circus, cross over Royal Hill and Circus St to the **Brand St** area, where the Georgiana gives way to 3-storey Victorian terraces (a 2-bed house, £350,000). A council estate at the foot of **Royal Hill** is medium-rise and not too intrusive. Go up the hill, passing marvellous **Hamilton Terrace**: 3-storeyed, with garden flats. Six 1930s semis make a sudden appearance near the hill top. **Hyde Vale** has some 20th-century neo-Georgian houses to compete with the (£1.1 million) real thing – and the pretty, terraced flat-fronted early-Victorian homes which raise almost as much. Back down Royal Hill you arrive in **Greenwich South St**, a busy thoroughfare, but with some lovely late-Georgian/early Victoriana – plus a charming row of almshouses.

Between South St and **Greenwich High Rd**, the Ashburnham Triangle conservation area's streets are lined with 2/3-storey, flat-fronted early-Victorian homes (£450,000-plus). Off Guildford Grove is **Admiral's Gate**, a neo-Georgian close; **Catherine Grove** has a school conversion by Durkan: £350,000 for a 2-bed flat here. West of the High Road is Mumford's Mill, a big, listed creek-side industrial building converted, at great trouble and expense and with some controversy, into flats: £290,000–1.2 million. Developers CYZ had to carve windows out of the blank walls of the 1897 mill buildings.

Going N, the rail line marks a change to less smart streets. In **Straightsmouth**, six new houses (three with work-space) in a modern-style terrace are minutes from trains and DLR. Period stuff, here, too: terraces include 4-storey houses for c. £480,000. **Traves Way**'s big 1960s council estate, no ornament, is to be razed: 256 new flats for sale, plus 85 for shared ownership and 169 for rent will replace it in a £90 million partnership between Bellway, the council and housing associations. **King William Walk** has the new 'Clipper Apartments', with £700,000 3-bed penthouses.

The waterfront has seen much work – and there's more to come. There's a new plaza round the Cutty Sark, the famous tea clipper in dry dock by the riverboat pier, with new shops, flats and eateries to tidy up the approach from the DLR station. From here, a major site stretches W along the river to the mouth of Deptford Creek: the eight acres of Greenwich Reach East, the 'Gateway to Greenwich', is currently in limbo, with no news for a year now on the 'awaited' revised, 600-home, planning application.

Westcombe Park

This is the name for the rectangle of residential streets E of Maze Hill and the park, S of the railway and across to the A102 motorway. South of Westcombe Park station lies a cluster of tree-lined streets of small terraced family houses. **Westcombe Hill** is a busy road, with terraced houses (larger at the top end). Climbing up the slopes are the 3- and 4-bed houses of peaceful **Mycenae Rd** and **Beaconsfield Rd** (Victorian-gothic and '30s, all with large gardens). **Hardy Rd** has 5-bed houses (as does **Humber**), but this is a good hunting-ground for all sorts and sizes of homes. The spine of this corner is **Westcombe Park Rd**, which snakes E–W with delightful, ornate 2- and 3-storey Edwardian/Victorian houses and 1930s homes. It ends at **Maze Hill**, with its large Victorian and turn-of-the-century homes that gaze out over Greenwich Park. Behind Maze Hill station, 'Woodland Heights' off **Restell Close** has 42 1-, 2-, and 3-bed flats (£210–410,000) in a refurbished nurses' home. The top of Maze Hill and streets up to **Shooters Hill** look to Blackheath.

East Greenwich

North of the railway (and thus in SE10, not Westcombe Park's SE3) and E of the Royal Naval College is East Greenwich. The riverside has some enviable homes: Georgian houses (£600,000-plus) on charming **Ballast Quay**, 1999 3-bed houses by Berkeley on **Highbridge Wharf**. Further riverside sites (there are still plenty) are slowly being claimed for homes: nearby, Berkeley's Anchor and Iron Wharf, along **Lassel St** beside the power station, has 90 flats in two buildings, one seven storeys, one four. One-beds start at £250,000, and there are some shared-ownership flats. There will also be a restaurant, a new public space and a new stretch of riverside walk.

Around **Trafalgar Rd** and the former Greenwich District Hospital (state of the art in the 1960s, now closed, an eyesore, plans inconclusive), typical East Greenwich homes – terraced cottages – quickly reassert themselves. Land N of the hospital is largely filled by well kept, low-rise council-built homes, but to the S and W 2- and 3-bed terraces abound. These little houses lacked inside toilets and bathrooms until the '80s, but have been converted by waves of young buyers. Today (as a year ago) a smart 2-bed cottage goes for c. £280,000; (less for roomier ex-council houses, or for those in streets E of the motorway). Durkan have two schools-into-loft-flats conversions hereabouts: **Maze Hill** (2004), and the **Annandale Rd** School (launching this spring) following Catherine Grove's.

Prices are highest to the W: the 1920s 2/3-bed cottages in **Greenwich Park St** are popular. In contrast, the old Granada cinema on **Trafalgar Rd** is now 37 1- and 2-bed flats, and in the same road 'Oxford Mansions' has smart 2-bed flats at £269,000. Vanbrugh Mews is a recent scheme off **Woodland Grove**, with 3-storey town-houses.

G

West along **Trafalgar Rd** the recent Vista Apartments scheme at the corner of **Maze Hill** has 22 1- and 2-bed flats. East on Trafalgar Rd the picture is largely the same, although there is some low-rise council housing. Most cottages are 2-bedroom, with signs of recent renovation. Many were formerly rented from the Morden College estate, but owner-occupying young City types are increasingly common.

North Greenwich Peninsula

Here on a windy riverside tract you have a tube station – beautiful; a Sainsbury's, ditto, and a Dome (to be a 22,000-seat arena by Christmas 2006 – two years later than at first announced). The blank canvas of this ex-industrial landscape also holds the first homes of the Greenwich Millennium Village (which is E of **John Harrison Way**, and nowhere near the Dome). Along with the first 1,377 homes come the new Millennium School, health centre and so on in a 'template for urban living' with lots of eco-awareness, public transport, hi-tech cabling, bike routes and so on. Combined heat and power systems plus energy-efficient building aim to make the homes deep-green and economical. Next batch due 2006; a recent resale price £410,000 for a 3-bed house. A fifth are Affordable Homes; also some live/work. Lots of buy-to-letting of the early phase. Developers are Taylor Woodrow and Countryside.

With the fate of the Dome at last set – 26,000-seat sports/entertainment arena, with a role in the Olympics if London gets the 2012 games – the rest of the Peninsula can settle down to 20 years' worth of building an entire new community in addition to the Millennium Village: 10,000 new (including 4,000 Affordable) homes, school, transport links, park, shops, hotel, leisure, businesses are planned. . . .

Blackheath

Most of Blackheath is in the borough of Lewisham, not Greenwich. The busy A2, **Shooters Hill**, forms the boundary and carries the traffic from Central London to Dover, as it has done for two millennia. Blackheath grew up in Georgian times as a select suburb, and the heart of the neighbourhood so remains. Elegant terraces line the wind-blown heath, and Blackheath Village is a good facsimile of a rural one – only the shops are smarter. The wider area is defined to the N by the heath, by **Lewisham Rd** in the W, by **Lee High Rd** to the S, and by an upwardly curving arc which excludes the unfortunate Ferrier council estate before joining with **Kidbrooke Park Rd** in the E.

The best way to approach Blackheath must be from the W up the steep **Blackheath Hill**. Taking a right turn into **Dartmouth Hill**, you are rewarded with a breathtaking view of the heath and the Village. In **Dartmouth Row**, many of the early 18th-century houses are now smart flats: £750,000 for a 2/3 bed late last year. A double-fronted Edwardian house, 7 beds, 4 baths and three-quarters of an acre, was £2.5 million. Crossing the heath into **Hare and Billet Rd**, you first pass a small '60s development of box-shaped houses with flat roofs, and then some typical terraced 2- and 3-storey houses in a dip in the ground which appear from a distance to stand just a few feet tall. **Aberdeen Terrace** has grand mid-Victorian houses. Other splendidly confident terraces and mansions – in roads like **The Pagoda, Eliot Hill, The Paragon, South Row** – gaze across the heath all the way to the Village and beyond. Many have been split into flats: a lateral-conversion, top-floor 3-bed in **West Grove**, loooking over Blackheath, was £475,000 last winter. Tucked behind the Georgiana in **Fulthorpe Rd** is one of the poshest council-built estates in Britain, dating from the 1950s.

G

Across N of the heath, streets round **Vanbrugh Park** and **St John's Park** are Victorian and blend into Westcombe Park. Prices are lower here than in Blackheath proper and some modern flats widen the choice available. The new Stratheden Mews off **Langton Way** added 15 town-houses. Victoriana yields 2-bed flats, or a whole 5-bed house (rather run-down) at £550,000.

Blackheath Park

Go down **Pond Rd** and into Blackheath's surprise package – the exclusive Blackheath Park or Cator Estate. This incredible array of homes, begun by developer John Cator at the start of the 19th century, now has every conceivable architectural style. Some are very opulent; many homes here have swimming pools. The estate spreads E from **Lee Rd** and S to **Manor Way**; gates at the five entrances are closed during rush hours, though the lodge keepers have long gone. There are Victorian and Edwardian mansions, mock-Tudor 1930s detached houses and a sprinkling of 14 small 1960s Span estates, highly praised by architects: one estate is listed. In contrast, the SE corner has the ugly Ferrier Estate of brutal GLC public housing. Plans to rebuild it with mixed public/private homes may have some effect on the Cator streets. Prices here vary widely as homes are so individual. The Span homes can be good value (3-bed houses, c. £310,000). There's a wide range of other, modern, houses (a 5-bed, £1.2 million last autumn) plus flats converted from the 19th-century Cator Estate houses.

SW of Blackheath Village, **Lee Terrace** marks the N edge of a district of pleasant streets such as **Belmont Park** and **Dacre Park**, with Georgian and Victorian family homes and flats. A 2-bed conversion on **Lee Terrace** is c £315,000. This W edge of Blackheath, towards Lewisham (see chapter), has good transport links via the DLR. **Belmont Hill** has a dozen smart flats newly converted from The Cedars, a fine 1860s mansion. North of the rail line, roads like **Granville Park** offer big flats in solid 19th-century houses.

Borders

Along **Lee High Rd**, properties are a jumble of council-built and terraced homes with the quality generally declining as you leave the heath behind. On the steep slopes just to the N is a fair sprinkling of 1- and 2-bed conversion flats, where incomers replace fireplaces ripped out in the 1970s. Homes here are cheaper than those with a heath view. S of **Lee High Rd** the Manor conservation area has streets with big Edwardian houses.

Kidbrooke is the next district E from Blackheath and shares the SE3 postcode (beware: ignorant agents call everything in SE3 'Blackheath'). It is split by the A2/A102 highway, and the parts to the W, around **Kidbrooke Grove** and **Kidbrooke Park Rd**, are thought best (though still divorced from Blackheath). Look here for 6-bed Victorian houses in large gardens – or flats carved from them. Kidbrooke station is just to the S – but the streets close to the station are less special.

Go E of the A102 and you come to Charlton, where Charlton Village has Victorian streets of some charm – and at less-than-Greenwich prices. East again is Woolwich, with a major, 700-homes scheme at the 70-acre Woolwich Arsenal site, 70 per cent in lovely listed buildings. This corner, next-door to Thamesmead, should eventually (2008?) get a DLR link across the river; renewed plans, too, for a major new road bridge.

Transport Trains: Greenwich to London Bridge 15 min, Charing Cross 20 min; Blackheath to London Bridge 12 min. DLR from Cutty Sark and Greenwich station to Docklands and City; Jubilee Line links North Greenwich to Canary Wharf & West End. See also map.

Convenient for Docklands, A2 to Dover/Channel Tunnel. Miles from centre: 5.5.

Schools Local Authority: St Ursulas' Convent RC (g), John Roan School, Blackheath Bluecoat C of E, St Joseph's Academy RC (b), Thomas Tallis, Haberdashers Askes, Hatcham College. Private: Blackheath High School (g), Colte's, Eltham College, St Dunstan's College.

G

SALES

Flats	S	1B	2B	3B	4B	5B
Average prices	120–180	140–220	180–290	220–400+	–	–
Houses	2B	3B	4B	5B	6/7B	8B
Average prices	250–450	320–600	500–800+	600–1M+	700–1.5M	1.5–2M

RENTAL

Flats	S	1B	2B	3B	4B	5B
Average prices	150–180	160–250	170–285	260–450	300–400+	–
Houses	2B	3B	4B	5B	6/7B	8B
Average prices	200–450	250–500	400–600	500–600+	→1000	–

The properties Superb Georgian in Greenwich and Blackheath, mid-Victorian in Blackheath Park and Westcombe Park, plus more ordinary period and modern homes in E Greenwich and other fringe areas, modern waterfront flats coming in West Greenwich (eventually), hi-tech ones on N Greenwich Peninsula near the Dome.

The market Prices vary dramatically from East Greenwich (still cheaper) to heath views and period homes in top roads, eg Croom's Hill. Nearest established residential areas to Docklands – now linked by tube from the Greenwich Peninsula and by the DLR – means Wharfers with West End mind-sets drive up top-property prices.

Among estate agents active in this area are:

- John Payne
- Meridian
- Winkworth
- Kinleigh Folkard & Hayward
- Humphreys Skitt & Co
- James Johnston
- Peter James
- Oliver Bond
- Hamilton Kershaw
- Your Move
- Haart
- Harrison Ingram
- Comber & Co
- Paragon

HACKNEY

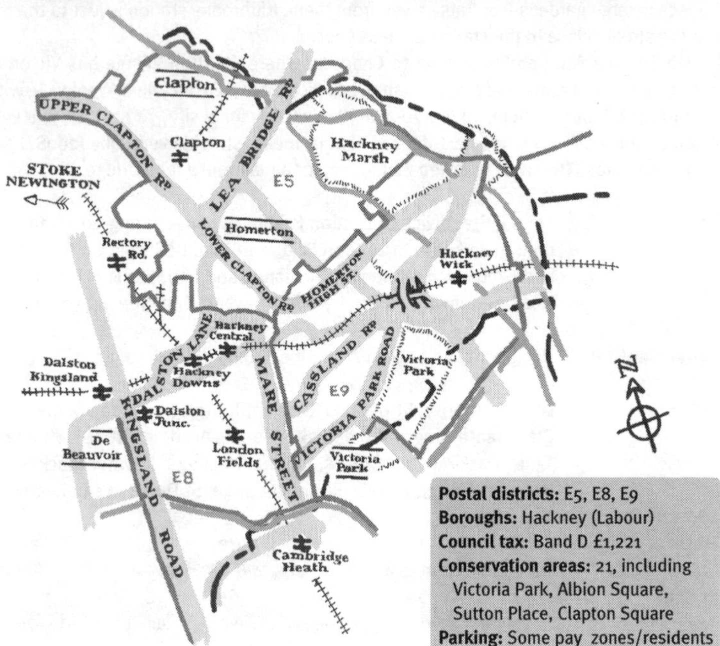

Postal districts: E5, E8, E9
Boroughs: Hackney (Labour)
Council tax: Band D £1,221
Conservation areas: 21, including Victoria Park, Albion Square, Sutton Place, Clapton Square
Parking: Some pay zones/residents

As a borough, Hackney ranks high as one of London's most schizophrenic. There are just four neighbourhoods that escape a listing among the capital's most deprived. On the other hand, parts of the borough house some of the City's richest companies, and even in the area's heart beautiful Georgian houses (and luxury lofts) can change hands for well over half a million.

This has been, is now in parts, and has copper-bottomed reason to be again, a great place to live. But incomers must be prepared to assist in the process, not expect it to arrive a week on Monday. The borough has its pockets of pleasantly gentrified Victorian villas; some districts – such as Stoke Newington (see chapter) – have escaped the all-embracing poverty and belong to Hackney only by virtue of their council-tax bills. Smart flats and mews houses are emerging on long-derelict sites and in converted ex-schools.

In 20 years, owner-occupation in Hackney has nearly doubled, from 16 to 29 per cent of households. Yet owners are still a minority – in some wards hardly figuring on the graph. This will not, cannot (indeed, should not) become Fulham overnight: poor people cannot be uninvented or tidied away. Yet some incomers, particularly ill-informed buy-to-letters, have been acting on the assumption that today's E5 equals tomorrow's SW6.

The area's membership of the bottom-fifth club – the list of council wards which fail every test, from poverty through health to housing – is one factor to bear in mind when moving here. But look at the map to see some other, countervailing, facts: the proximity of Islington, the City and the transport hub at Stratford, the Zone 2 status of the bus and train links (though no tube as yet); the life, the street markets, the Hackney Empire . . . a better chance (though nowhere in Inner London can be called cheap) to buy a home.

Hackney's problem is that its people – people with jobs and prospects – have been leaving to find better homes and secondary schools. They have no choice: homes are expensive to buy, yet unavailable to rent. Their place is taken by the poorest of the poor, whose poverty qualifies them for social housing. 'Consequently,' concludes a council analysis 'Hackney's place in the economy of London has been to sustain deprivation.'

Alongside this process (an escalator of opportunity, say the optimists; or a cycle of despair, to the pessimists) runs a strong counter-trend, the arrival of a second sort of incomer: owner-occupiers who have chosen Hackney for its (to them) affordable homes and who import a strong interest in upgrading their new neighbourhoods. Which trend will win? The optimists have had a boost from the decision to bid for the 2012 Olympics: Hackney borders the Lea Valley sites which would host the games, and can only gain from the spotlight even a failed bid will shine on some of its darkest corners. Hackney Wick needs all the help it can get. Even without the Games, the East London Line Extension – see Transport chapter for details – will arrive: its effects are already being felt in Dalston, now bursting with developments both under-way and planned.

The borough of Hackney takes in Clapton, Homerton, Dalston, Stoke Newington and half a dozen other former hamlets. Hackney abuts the City to the S, Islington to the W and ends in the E with the Hackney Marshes in the Lea Valley. (Stoke Newington has its own chapter; the borough's southernmost rim is described in the City chapter.)

Newcomers have rediscovered Hackney's proximity to the City. They find surprisingly usable communications (if no tube) and that some local amenities are improving, especially on the cultural side. The town square at the north end of **Mare St** has been smartened: it's designated as a cultural centre. The famous Hackney Empire music hall is triumphantly open at last, following a major rebuild. Then there's the Technology and Learning Centre – hi-tech library, museum, gym and shops – but sadly the splendid Ocean Music Venue with its auditorium, rehearsal rooms, bars and cafés, has now closed.

Hackney's young population, and ample (if no longer noticeably cheap) warehouse/ living space, lends credence to the borough's claim to be home to the biggest concentration of working artists in Europe. They started in the south of the area, in Hoxton, Shoreditch and the City fringes (see City chapter), but are being driven out by rising prices and loft-dwellers. Hackney Wick, with its plethora of decaying industrial space, is the new artists' quarter (see also Deptford), but the Olympic bid looks set to tidy this corner, too. Agents routinely list live/work units as well as flats and houses, but the council is now cautious about permission for these: too many live/works have turned out to be flats or houses with a computer in one corner, thus providing no new jobs.

Just as in the last boom in the 1980s, the buyers are young City and media/ fashion/arts types, the sellers (in many cases) long-term residents who are moving out to Essex or Suffolk. So despite strenuous – and successful – efforts to revive Hackney's wide areas of public housing, the gap between the prosperous and the poor is growing. A tenacious left-wing pressure group irritates the Labour-run council, and while Labour supplied Hackney's first elected mayor, the Socialist Alliance candidate came within half a per cent of the Tory. Also on the local scene are the Socialist Party (Hackney) and the Independent Working Class Association, which gained 30 per cent of the vote in a council by-election in Haggerston. Fulham it ain't.

Some Hackney neighbourhoods are becoming known as young-family (up to secondary-school age) places, not just bolt-holes for radical singles. Round London Fields and large, lovely Victoria Park – the East End's answer to Hyde Park – among the regulation terraces some grander Victorian houses and even some Georgian corners survive. The De Beauvoir area too, W of the busy **Kingsland Rd**, carries a premium as it borders Islington and Stoke Newington (which chapters see) and is just in coveted N1 .

Victoria Park, a conservation area, is divided between Hackney and the neighbouring borough of Tower Hamlets. Hackney Marshes, along the Lea Valley, is marshland no more, but is another large area of welcome green open space – its flat expanse makes for excellent football pitches. Then there's London Fields towards Dalston, Hackney

Downs, a handful of recreation grounds; and further north is picturesque Springfield Park, an attractive, hilly area with Springfield Marina and a rowing club on the River Lea.

Hackney council's well-aired problems centre on its schools, but areas as diverse as street cleaning and council tax administration have attracted government scrutiny. The council relies on asset sales (buildings, land) to close its deficit. This has led to school conversions and other homes developments, but is not popular with some locals.

Homeowners discover Hackney's failings after the kids arrive, and this dampens the family-house sector of the property market. Schools are now run not by the council, but by the Hackney Learning Trust, which has raised the GCSE pass-rate to a little closer to, but still below, the London average. Primary schools can be good – Lauriston, Culverstone Crescent, Rushmore, London Fields, Gayhurst, Mapledene are all singled out (kids who can't get into Lauriston often cross the park to the private Gatehouse School). But after that, parents vote with their feet. 'People move to places like Brighton or Suffolk once their children get to secondary-school age' observes a local estate agent. That said, the new Mossbourne Community Academy, which replaced Hackney Downs, is now open. Three time oversubscribed, it will hold 900 pupils by 2008; a 6th Form is planned. Another Academy is proposed for the site of the Kingsland School, for next year.

Hackney missed out on the tube. None of the existing lines enters the borough, which boast not a single station. Hopes rest on a northward extension of the East London Line to Dalston and across to the Victoria Line at Highbury & Islington. This has at last been voted some real, hard cash, so this should finally go ahead: see Transport chapter.

Like most of North London, all was sylvan peace here once, interspersed with country seats and pleasure gardens. The late Georgian era saw houses spread along the main roads – look above the shops and you'll see them still. Hackney became smart for a while, as its few surviving Georgian squares indicate. Then came the railways and the Victorian housing boom. The City clerks and respectable working men who rented the endless terraced homes found their way to work by foot, by horse-bus or by train into Liverpool St, and they formed the heart of Hackney. Outright slums and filthy factories intruded into the SE corner, around Hackney Wick, but the bulk of the place was a suburb for the great army of London's East Enders, both indigenous and immigrant.

And so it remains today – with respectable areas, corners of fair deprivation, and the ones that are downright dangerous. Yet the average E8 terraced house now costs £330,000 – some £120,000 more than the figure across the River Lea in E7. Social housing – which shelters the majority of Hackney households – has seen much change, with several council estates redeemed by enlightened housing-association and town-hall activity (those that have not been dynamited – 19 blocks have gone since 1986, and the last two Clapton towers were blown up at the end of 2003) and replaced by better-planned homes. One tower block in Lower Clapton was smartened up for private sale – mostly to investors for renting out. The developer is said to have broken even – just. And the price rises have pushed ex-council 3-bed flats – which could be had for under £100,000 three years ago – up to £175–200,000. Investors have been buying these, but only on the small, relatively peaceful estates.

So, a schizophrenic area; one that shot up the London house-price ladder in this last boom. Neighbourhoods such as Victoria Park and City-convenient Dalston led the way, with the big Victorian homes in the former stabilizing at above half a million. Clapton and Homerton lagged behind the rest, but have also made gains, while Hackney Wick, always the cheapest corner, gained from a big estate refurbishment programme and is now in the spotlight as the Eurostar/Olympics effects boost next-door Stratford. Right across Hackney, the larger, more expensive houses, having escalated first, have seen the smallest percentage price rises since 2000; but 2004 has been Dalston's year: with transport and regeneration plans for its town centre, 1-bed flats hit £200,000.

In truth, Hackney had a lot of catching up to do: the area fared just as well in the late-

'80s boom but, like many non-blue-chip neighbourhoods, fell back hard when it came to the bust. Home prices here dipped deep into negative-equity land around 1990–92 – and for the most part remained under water for a decade: buying in Hackney is not a one-way bet. And incomers need to be streetwise about this impoverished borough, where, despite the improvements above, many services remain uncomfortably close to collapse. If some neighbourhoods are great places to live – especially for those who've come to join a community, not just to make a fast buck – it's undeniable that other parts not only feature on every index of urban deprivation, but also star on the TV news due to their levels of gun- and drug-related crime. Clapton's 'murder mile' – the Upper Clapton Rd – earned its name, with eight fatal shootings in two years. Things are improving, but incidents continue.

Hackney Central

The central spine of Hackney is the N–S road variously named **Mare St** and **Lower Clapton Rd.** Here are the town hall, the famous Russian Baths – now refurbished as the King's Hall Leisure Centre – and Hackney Central station (N London Line). Hackney Downs station (10 min Liverpool St) is close. Off Lower Clapton Rd is lovely **Clapton Square**, a garden square surrounded by fine Georgian terraces, some 5-storeyed, and the heart of a conservation area. Furlong have added 29 flats, 1- and 2-beds (the last is £190,000), plus 10 for shared ownership, in a gated enclave fronted by a Georgian-style facade. **Clarence Mews**, behind the Square, has a row of five modern, mewsy town-houses. The square leads on to **Clarence Place** and **Clapton Passage**, which both have a charming villagey feel and coveted homes: impressive 3-storey terraced Georgian houses graced with entrance steps, railings and tiny wrought-iron balconies. This whole network of streets forms a green oasis in the midst of Hackney. A house in the Square might cost £580,000.

On **Lower Clapton Rd**, an Art Deco factory became The Strand Building: 1- and 2-bed (1-bed, c. £150,000) flats. On the E side of Lower Clapton Rd, opposite Clapton Passage, more 2- and 3-storey Victorian houses can be found in **Powerscroft Rd** and **Glenarm Rd**, close to Hackney police station. West of the road – and in marked contrast to polite Clapton Square – is the Pembury council estate, which stretches from **Hindrey Rd** N to **Downs Park Rd** and the brand-new Mossbourne Community Academy (see introduction, above). From the S edge of the estate **Amhurst Rd**, a busy bus route, leads back SE to the Mare St shopping centre. The Aspland council estate lies along part of Amhurst Rd. The Peabody Trust's new mixed-tenure scheme in **Clarence Rd** has six flats and five houses.

On the junction of Dalston Lane and Amhurst Rd is Eastside, a 1998 conversion of an Edwardian college, now 57 flats including some big 3-beds for which up to £350,000 has been asked. Also in Amhurst Rd is Berkeley's refurbishment for sale of the old Samuel Lewis flats. The Ujama Housing Association is active locally, most recently adding four new homes to **Bodney Rd** and a flats block to **Elsdale Rd**.

Next to Hackney Downs station is **Spurstone Crescent**, where Wimpey's 'Junction 67' scheme has 67 flats with 1- to 3-beds: current releases are 2- and 3-beds from £285,000. A former synagogue near the station is now 11 flats (1-beds, c. £200,000). To the S of the railway line serving Hackney Central, **Graham Rd**, a busy main road, has 3-storey terraced houses, some now flats. **Navarino Grove** has neat flat-fronted cottages (£300,000 for a 3-bed flat here) in a corner near both stations (it crosses the tracks).

Another notable central Hackney street is **Sutton Place**, backing onto the grounds of St John's Church, S of Lower Clapton Rd – which has this year won lottery and local money to restore its churchyard. A conservation area, Sutton Place boasts grand, listed, Georgian terraced houses complete with front steps, railings and basements. Several were bought as wrecks in the mid-'80s by intrepid DIY converters and turned into superb homes. Now, people pay around £580,000 for one. Behind is **Sutton Square**, a late '80s development curved round central gardens: 2-bed houses around £235,000. Attractive streets S of Sutton Place include **Mehetabel Rd** and **Isabella Rd**: the former has well-preserved flat-fronted cottages, while the houses in the latter are grander in scale.

Lots of new homes in this busy area, both social and private, conversions and new-build. Latest are six housing-trust flats now being created in an ex-pub in **Chatham Place**, off Morning Lane with its Tesco superstore. An old school provided 30 flats in **Chelmer Rd**, near Homerton Hospital. Just N of the hospital is **Clifden Rd**, where Galliard have found a cut-off corner for a mews of 13 houses hiding behind electric gates. (A Victorian 3-bed nearby, c. £275,000). Leading back down to **Homerton High St** is **Brooksby's Walk**, with a 14-flat Furlong scheme from 2002. Ujama housing trust have an attractive contemporary mixed scheme here: business units and Affordable 1-bed flats. **Wick Rd** has Lovell's recent 32-flat block: 18 for sale, the rest housing trust.

Near London Fields **Reading Lane**, just off Mare St, has 'The Style Building' – an old garment factory now eight 2-bed flats. **Mare St** itself has Barratt's big new 159-flat 'East Central E8': resales are asking around £190,000 for 1-beds, 2-beds c. £250,000, 3-beds £320,000. The current release is the 16-storey 'Martello Tower', which completes this spring: 1- and 2-beds, £200–314,000. The penthouse sold for £750,000.

London Fields

West of **Mare St**, the streets around the 26 acres of London Fields – successively sheep pasture and cricket pitch – form a neighbourhood coming up, agents say, as nearby Dalston rises. Here are streets of solid, readily-modernized, 2-, 3- or 4-storey Victoriana popular with young couples. Impressive 4-storey terraces, some split into flats, are found in **Lansdowne Drive**, W of the Fields, and **Navarino Rd** (c. £500,000-plus). **Gayhurst Rd**, **Mapledene Rd** and **Lavender Grove** have 2-storey, 3-bed attractive mid-Victoriana from c. £380,000 – £458,000 was asked for a Lavender one last autumn. The conversion of a Victorian-Gothic parsonage beside the Fields added lavish flats with period features. Yet another school conversion where **Lansdowne Drive** meets **Wilton Way**, marketed in 2002 as 'East Eight', sprouted 14 new flats in the grounds last year.

Middleton Rd (en route to Dalston), **Albion Drive** and **Shrubland Rd** abut the well-located Fields council estate (2-bed duplex, £175,000). These roads, too, have handsome 2- or 3-storey (c. £400,000-ish) flat-fronted Victoriana – some with 120ft gardens. The E side of London Fields, behind busy Mare St and with the rail line bisecting it, is less smart but improving, with new houses in **Ellingfort Rd** and a new arts centre, The Hothouse, between the park and the rail line to the E. **Martello St** borders the Fields and has new loft-style homes and flats plus housing-association flats (33 for shared ownership). More to come in **Sidworth St**: 36, atop new offices. On S towards Haggerston, **Broadway Market** now boasts art galleries, shops and cafés; also a clutch of studios, flats and a new pub, the Cat & Mutton. **Andrews Rd**, off the Market, overlooks the canal (the border with E2) and boasts some recent canalside homes: live/work units are £395–485,000.

Victoria Park

The park, laid out in 1845, is one of London's largest. The neighbourhood to the N has some of the biggest, most expensive houses in Hackney, but in this vicinity you can find humble homes, Victorian grandeur, modern loft-living. . . . The rocketing prices of the top houses in recent years reflect the enormous restoration and improvements undertaken; this is now factored in, and agents anticipate no further leaps for the moment.

Much of the housing is on land owned by the Crown Estate, so some residents can claim to have Crown leases just like their grander counterparts in Regent's Park. The Crown has some 593 homes, most dating from the 1840s. Some 500 are let at fair rents: these have been expensively smartened up in the past few years. Key workers are given priority for (rare) new tenancies, but many residents are long term. Purpose-built flats in roads near the park offer good value, while conversions of the big old houses yield flats with plenty of space – many with lovely views of the park and its several lakes. The disadvantage around here is lack of communications. Bethnal Green tube station is a mile or so to the S, though Cambridge Heath and London Fields have trains to Liverpool St (c. 10 min). But look E: just across the Lea Valley lies Stratford – soon to be the major communications hub for East London (see Transport chapter).

Another green space, Well Street Common, adjoins Victoria Park and provides open views for the Victorian and '30s-mock-Tudor houses of **Meynell Rd** and **Crescent**. **Lauriston Rd**, to the W of the Common, forms the hub of what estate agents began to promote as 'Lauriston Village'; they've now decided on the better-known park name, so this is where they mean when you see 'Victoria Park Village' on property details. Whatever; there's a well-regarded primary school, good shops and a smart wine bar/pub. Some of the most popular homes in Hackney are here: a 5-bed house overlooking the Common goes for over half a million (back in 1988 the benchmark was £250,000, but £275,000 was reached in 1989). Streets such as **Penshurst Rd** have 3-bed, 3-recep Victorian terraceds that can command half a million. Royal Park Lofts in **Lauriston Rd** is a Victorian school conversion, and in nearby **Connor St** is Lauriston Studios, with open-plan live/work units: 900 sq ft, from c. £230,000. Victoria Park Lofts in **Rutland Rd**, by Bexwell Homes, has 12 flats and two houses: c. £335,000 for 1,200 sq ft. Gerard Place (marketed by Lovell as Victoria Park Mews), off **Groombidge Rd**, has five 3-bed town-houses plus two 3-bed cottages. Other recent homes – new-build, conversions (a pub is the current victim) and some smartly refurbished Victorian ones – will be found in **Victoria Park Rd**, and in **Cassland** and **Bramshaw Rds**. Just off Cassland Rd, School Lodge is a conversion of a modern school building. **Cassland Crescent**, though, is the real thing – a beautiful Georgian terrace with walled gardens. Some of its early-Victorian neighbours are almost as fine: **Queen Anne Rd** has 3-storey, 4-bed terraces that fetch some £400,000.

H

Gore Rd, overlooking Victoria Park, has more of the area's most desirable homes, imposing 3- and 4-storey terraced houses presenting a dignified front to the large and pleasant park. There are also some modern Crown Estate homes. Gore Rd leads back W into **Victoria Park Rd**; where this meets **Mare St**, a modern development in **Earlston Grove** and **Northam St** has flats and houses blessed with private garages. A little to the N, the conservation area of **Fremont St** and **Warneford St** provides fine 2- and 3-storey mid-19th-century terraced houses with basements. By contrast, nearby **Sharon Gardens** (said to have been built by Jewish immigrants) offers some of the few 1930s semis in the area. **Beck Rd** is also popular. In nearby **King Edward's Rd** are recent live/work units in a 1930s industrial building, plus three large Victorian blocks of flats.

East of the park in Hackney Wick, in a cut-off corner E of the East Cross motorway, the site of the old Trowbridge Estate is now St Mary's Village, with 240 new homes: 89 on the open market, the rest shared ownership. You choose your home – then the style of tenure: no-one can tell which is which. Close by, a riverside site off Berkshire Rd has become **Leabank Square**: flats and houses. Back on the W side of the highway, Victoria Mews, off **Swinnerton St**, is a 1980s scheme with flats and houses.

Dalston

It's been Dalston's year. Look here for new flats – and plenty more sites that have been just waiting for the advent of the East London Line Extension (see Transport chapter), now at last with funding. Not to mention a fountain-filled, pedestrianized new heart for Dalston: by December Gillett Square will emerge N of Dalston Kingsland rail station, with, apart from 46 flats, shops and offices, a library, a new home for the famous Vortex jazz club – and a Culture House. Given its position next to Stoke Newington and Islington, W of the London Fields neighbourhood, Dalston should have come up years ago.

For now, the existing Dalston Cross shopping centre lies off **Dalston Lane/Kingsland Rd**, and there's the bustling **Ridley Rd** street market, long one of Hackney's landmarks.

Further shops along busy Kingsland High St and nearby streets reflect the area's cosmopolitan image. **Colvestone Crescent** curves N from Ridley Rd to a clutch of streets round St Mark's Church, with massive 4-storey Victorian houses. More big 3- and 4-storey Victorian terraces with steps up to their doors can be found in popular **Sandringham, Cecilia** and **Montague Rds**. Chester Gate, modern 3-storey houses off **Ridley Rd**, provides some contrast. Between Cecilia Rd, Sandringham Rd and **Downs Park Rd**, which fringes Hackney Downs, lies part of the Mountford council estate.

Recent new-build includes Furlong Homes' dozen houses in **Speechley Mews**, off **Alvington Crescent**; Independent Place is a work/homes complex off **Shacklewell Lane**; opposite is **Gateway Mews**, an enclave of 3–5-bed modern mews houses. Long-derelict Kingsland Library is also now flats: 17, with 10 at low rents. To the S, Centenary Place is a Laing development in **Middleton Rd**, from 1-bed flats to 4-bed houses, which in part replace the notorious Holly Lodge Estate towers.

Victorian terraces in Middleton Rd can be large (6-bed) and expensive (c. £750,000), and just to the S is **Albion Square**, one of the finest garden squares in Hackney. Its early 19th-century paired and detached houses with pretty gardens lie tucked away.

But look up and down **Kingsland Rd** for many a flat a-building: circling the Dalston Cross end, where the new East London Line tube station will be, 'Strada' is 14 1- and 2-beds by Higgins; similar-sized schemes are also planned for **Ramsgate St**, **Dalston Lane** and **Sandringham Rd**; 'The Sanctuary' adds some 2- and 3-bed houses, £279–335,000, to **Queensbridge Rd**. And the semi-derelict area beside the tube site should eventually hold a cinema and an 8-storey block of 280 flats, 53 per cent Affordable; while yet another plan foresees 550 homes, no less, across on the opposite corner by **Ashwin St**.

At the Haggerston end of Kingsland Rd, and close to **Lee St**, where *its* new tube station will be, Ability Plaza is a new 16-storey tower with 101 flats, 1- to 3-beds; Haggerston Studios is 45 flats (from £205,000) and live/works £250–280,000). Benyon Wharf, across the road by the canal basin, is a clutch of 53 live/works: £280–535,000.

Clapton

Clapton is the remaining area, to the N and E of Hackney's centre, on ground rising up from the Lea Valley. This is still one of the cheapest parts of the borough in which to buy a home: it holds more rows of Victorian and Edwardian housing, modern council estates and, in the far N of the area, attractive Springfield Park by the River Lea. The price divide between Lower and Upper Clapton has eroded: if **Upper Clapton Rd** earned the soubriquet 'Murder Mile', **Lower** more recently saw a well-reported rise in crime between gangs. Nevertheless Lower Clapton has if anything rather overtaken Upper, with 3-bed terraceds typically costing £250–325,000 in Lower Clapton, £250–300,000 in Upper. And now developers have their eye on this corner too.

South of the junction of **Lea Bridge Rd** and **Lower Clapton Rd**, two of the area's busiest thoroughfares, lie **Thistlewaite Rd, Thornby Rd, Newick Rd** and **Fletching Rd**: a cache of large 2- and 3-storey Victorian terraces in tree-lined streets. The Millfields green open space provides a focus for this district. Across on **Charnock Rd** there's a conversion of a brush factory into flats, and some adjacent mews houses. Among other corners worth noting is attractive **Ashenden Rd** in the SE of the area, near Clapton Park. This includes Tower Mews: once a warehouse, now flats.

Across in Linscott Rd, old meets new as a landmark gets a new life: the Clapton Portico, a grand pillared and pedimented hall, is all that is left of a vast Regency orphanage. Now it's to house the latest digital equipment as part of the Clapton Girls' Technology College.

Going N, **Mount Pleasant Hill** has Riverside Walk, 1- and 2-bed flats by Wimpey. And so to Upper Clapton. Overlooking little Clapton Common is **Clapton Terrace**, where large, handsome Georgian terraced houses with basements and gardens give respite from the prevailing 19th-century rows. Homes in the hilly Springfield Park neighbourhood, E of the Clapton Common conservation area, have the added attraction of the nearby River Lea and the open spaces of the Walthamstow Marshes. North of the park is **Watermint Quay**, on the river and reached via **Craven Walk**. This is a facing pair of 1980s terraces set end-on to the river towpath (c. £400,000). Just to the S, rows of 2-storey Victorian terraces in **Spring Hill** lead directly to the Lea with its Springfield Marina and City Orient Rowing Club. Similar homes in **Lingwood Rd** and **Overlea Rd**. In **Theydon Rd**, a 1930s factory is now the 'de Havilland Building', with loft apartments.

By contrast, some of Clapton's cheaper (and smaller) properties are found to the S beside Hackney Marshes, which again border the River Lea. South of Clapton Park is the massive Kingsmead council estate, encircled by **Kingsmead Way**. This has seen a remarkable turnaround, with tenants now in charge of the estate, the worst system-built homes razed and replaced, and crime plummeting. New homes on the sites of four unloved and now demolished tower blocks are for open-market sale and low-cost/shared ownership. The surviving tower, which stands N of the main estate across the park on **Daubeney Rd**, was refurbished by a developer and has become 'Landmark Heights', with 114 flats (a 2-bed last winter was £178,000).

Convenient for Stratford, the City, Docklands, Miles from centre: 4.

Schools Local Authority: Mossbourne Academy, Cardinal Pole RC, Homerton Coll of Tech (b), Clapton Tech Coll (g), Haggerston (g), Hackney Free & Parochial C of E, Private: Tayyibah (g), Yesodey Hatorah, Lubavitch, Beis Malka (g), Beis Chinuh (g), Beis Rochel (g).

H

Transport Trains (Zone 2): Hackney Central, Hackney Wick, Homerton (N London Line); London Fields, Hackney Downs (Liverpool St).

SALES

Flats	S	1B	2B	3B	4B	5B
Average prices	100–135	130–200	170–270	200–300	220–330	–
Houses	2B	3B	4B	5B	6/7B	8B
Average prices	210–325	240–450	240–500	350–700+	–	–

RENTAL

Flats	S	1B	2B	3B	4B	5B
Average prices	120–140	160–200	200–250	250–320	300–450	350–550
Houses	2B	3B	4B	5B	6/7B	8B
Average prices	180–250	250–350	320–475	450–550	–	–

The properties Many Victorian houses, some early; a few Georgian. Victoria Park established; Dalston, London Fields rising; other parts mixed: widespread council housing and gentrified pockets. Smart new-build; converted schools/factories now flats and live/work lofts.

The market Owner-occupation rising: people took advantage of Hackney's lower prices; now eyeing homes old and new near proposed new tube stops. Agents prefer to keep quiet about Hackney's schools.

Among estate agents active in this area are:

- Winkworth
- Shaw & Co
- Douglas Allen Spiro
- Spicer McColl
- Keatons
- Robert Alan
- Sovereign House
- City Lettings
- Strettons
- Felicity Lord
- Bunch & Duke
- Bennett Walden

HAMMERSMITH

Postal districts: W6, W14
Boroughs: Hammersmith & Fulham (Lab)
Council tax: Band D £1,131
Conservation areas: Several
Parking: Residents/meters everywhere; zones altered incessantly.

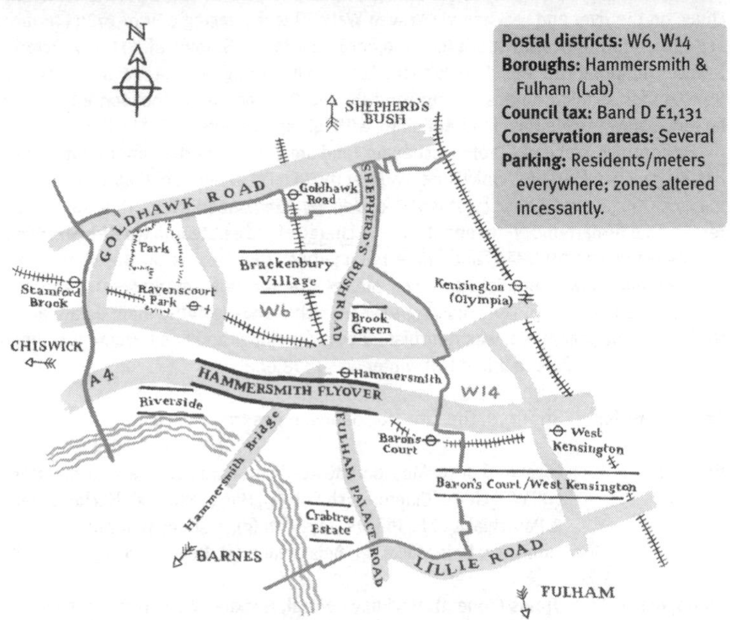

On the direct route from Heathrow to the West End, the point about Hammersmith is convenience. If both places are important in your life, a Hammersmith home will be a good idea. Plenty of people have worked this out for themselves, which is why prices in, and the reputation of, this part of town have moved up steadily. Rentals, too: its position has attracted some state-of-the-art new office blocks to Hammersmith – and workers in them, plus hospital and BBC staff, swell the local renting market. Recent buyers, comments one agent, include Fulhamites who have worked out that the time spent queuing to get up to Hammersmith Broadway can be saved by just moving to Hammersmith instead.

Hammersmith would be a large square on the map if it were not for the curving Thames, which bites off the SW corner. As it is, the boundaries are the protective arm of the Goldhawk Rd to the W and N, the river and Lillie Rd to the S, and to the E the boundary with Kensington – reinforced by the much more physical barrier of the railway, which runs N–S. Within this square lies Hammersmith proper (essentially the W6 postal district), Baron's Court and West Kensington – the latter, with Kensington's name but in Hammersmith's borough and the W14 postcode, always good for confusing outsiders.

This is about as close in as you can get in West London and still find a choice of family homes and (relatively) affordable flats. You sense that buyers here use their own money, not multinational corporate funds or a big inheritance. Even so, agents report that first-time buyers tend to be polite, dual-income young couples with some family backing. Or people buying a flat for their student/just-married kids to use initially, which may be kept on to rent out later. The family homes harbour many an infant: there are good primary schools, and some excellent private secondaries – but a move out to Richmond or Ealing for better state secondaries can take place as eleven looms.

Hammersmith's prestigious arts scene gives the West End a run for its money: the Lyric

Theatre, the vast Hammersmith Apollo and the Riverside Studios contribute to the 'buzz' which attracts and keeps affluent young people. But there are downsides: the Great West Road charges through, cutting off the river end, and King Street, which is Hammersmith's high street, has never quite taken off in the way that Chiswick's has. And the tidying effect of the gleaming redevelopment of Hammersmith Broadway (shops, restaurants, new tube and bus stations, Coca-Cola's European HQ offices), immured on its roundabout, does not seem to have spilled out into the area as a whole. The council is on the case, though: they plan a revamp of Lyric Square – complete with 'water feature'.

Nevertheless, there are several characterful enclaves of family homes to explore. In pole position is some gorgeous Georgiana (and even earlier) by the riverside; then there are the unexpected delights of pretty, tucked-away villas and rows off spacious Brook Green and the leafy, well-established and popular terraces of corners like Ravenscourt Park and Brackenbury 'village'. For the rest, by and large, the streets are a little too narrow, the houses rather too tall (often split up into the most common homes in the area, small 1- and 2-bed flats), the ways through too confined. A built-up borough – but, largely thanks to the river and the plentiful tube stations, not that claustrophobic.

Next door, in Shepherd's Bush, is the BBC's vast White City HQ. The area attracts media workers: apart from the BBC, there's EMI in Brook Green, Disney in Hammersmith. City types come for the airport and the tube links into town.

Now, just over its borders, comes the vast, 40-acre, £700-million, futuristic White City shopping and leisure centre (see Shepherd's Bush chapter). Will this be an asset? Or will it presage the final clogging of already choked roads in and out of Hammersmith? And how will the local shops fare with such competition up the road?

H

Hammersmith has a low-key cosmopolitan character; all social classes and most races are represented here, with small, well-established Polish, Irish and Afro-Caribbean communities; however, there are no high concentrations of individual groups.

Barons Court/West Kensington

Fulham Palace Rd is the boundary of this neighbourhood to the W; **Hammersmith Rd** to the N; **Lillie Rd** to the S; the West London railway line to the E. The whole district is bisected by the A4 **Talgarth Rd** running E–W and by **North End Rd** running N–S.

'North End' is the name of the original Tudor hamlet here; agents have, however, attempted to hitch the southern swathe of the area to Fulham's star by calling it 'Fulham Cross'. But most residents prefer the albeit-tenuous link to respectability that the 'Kensington' name confers. The name of West Kensington tube station – sited where **North End Rd** crosses **Talgarth Rd** – cements that connection. This section of the North End Rd lacks charm, and cafés, and restaurants, and is hardly a destination.

Most homes in this neatly defined square are those tall Victorian houses that convert well to flats – and flat-land it is: it's estimated that they outnumber houses by 10:1, if not more. These streets are truly a hotchpotch, with buildings running the gamut from done-up to eyesore, though council-build is patchy, not sprawling. There are also many unkempt flats in need of a lick of paint – a sign, perhaps, of the large number of rented homes in the area. Greenery, apart from Normand Park to the S and the little garden off **Greyhound Rd**, is supplied by the quiet, well-kept gardens of Hammersmith Cemetery. Normand Park has a leisure centre run jointly by Holmes Place and the council.

So flats prevail. But floor space is limited and little 2-bed apartments are the norm: usually one large bedroom and a much smaller one – fine if you only need a spare room; less so for sharing renters (and thus investors). Three-bedroomed flats are rare, but occasionally they can be carved out of the top two floors since, in these tall, thin houses (pity the Victorian servants), one floor more often than not simply won't yield more than a couple of rooms. North of the **Talgarth Rd**/A4, the streets such as **Gunterstone Rd** are wider and pleasanter, lined with roomier late 19th-century houses:

the 2-bed flats get more spacious, but 3-bedroomed places are still scarce. An intact Gunterstone Rd house, if you can find one, would be a million plus.

A particularly popular segment is the grid bordered by **Gledstanes Rd**, **North End Rd**, **Baron's Court Rd** and **Perham Rd** – the original Barons Court estate. This corner is close to both Barons Court (District and Piccadilly) and West Kensington tube stations, where you'll find a scattering of shops. Young, as yet childless, couples in their 20s and 30s discovered the Barons Court grid in a big way in the 1980s – and in the last few years their successors (and their children) had to compete with investors looking for buy-to-lets, and developers wanting yet more properties to convert. . . . A 1-bed flat on **Baron's Court Rd** might be £200–220,000. Note, as you drive westwards along the **Talgarth Rd** highway past this corner, the splendid, soaring, idiosyncratic windows of the high-Victorian St Paul's artists' studios: it's a sad irony that such windows should have inherited such a view. Despite the traffic, arty types still covet these, and prices aspire towards the million mark.

The most popular homes in Barons Court are flats in the substantial 1890s red-brick mansion blocks in **Queen's Club Gardens**, just south of the famous tennis and sports club itself. Queen's Club Gardens, a conservation area, has a small central park with tennis courts for residents – but not, now, for their barbecues or parties after some unfortunate incidents. This, and its aura of affluence and gentility, makes it something of an oasis. The portered complex is run by its residents, who all have a stake in the freehold. These flats are the price barometers for the neighbourood, and prices have cooled over the past year: a 1-bed flat might be £240–250,000; a 2-bed, £290–350,000.

For more mansion flats cross the Talgarth Rd to **Fitzgeorge** and **Fitzjames Avenues**, where the mansion blocks were built around 1910. Prices in these vary widely to reflect their differing ages and conditions: some still rejoice in original kitchen and bathroom fittings. They can, though, be large – 3-beds range from £450–625,000, while 4-beds are not uncommon: £550–850,000 for one of these; 1- and 2-beds are c. £240–450,000. Many inhabitants of these commodious flats are from overseas: Russians, Middle-East and French families, admixed with corporate lets. The trick, say agents, is to aim high: the lower flats can be a little dark. Other mansion blocks – late-Victorian and 1920s/30s – occur in the **North End Rd** area (Talgarth Mansions, West Kensington Mansions). St Paul's Court, between **Hammersmith** and **Talgarth Rds**, is a 1980-vintage complex with ample communal green space (1-bed, c. £210–230,000). A few whole houses survive amid the converted flats in the Victorian terraced streets.

The pastel-coloured Dutch-gabled 1930s villas on and around **Palliser Rd** are in great demand. The triangle enclosed by **Palliser**, **Baron's Court** and **Barton Rds** consists of about three-quarters of an acre of communal greenery. These 4-bed villas are rarely sold – well, they also have something rarer than hens' teeth: their own garages. Prices are c. £700–750,000. At the end of Barton Rd is a tall archway that leads into **Comeragh Mews** – two attractive rows of 3-storey mews houses (2/3-bed, c. £400,000). Another arch leads out to **Comeragh Rd**, which has the Baron's Court Theatre fringe venue. **Palliser Rd** has on its W side big, 4-storey, just-below-£1 million houses, overlooking the green of the cemetery.

The cheaper part of this neighbourhood is in the W: the rows of smaller terraced houses leading E off **Fulham Palace Rd** in the shadow of the big Charing Cross Hospital. Streets such as **Greyhound Rd** and **St Dunstan's Rd** have 1-bed flats c. £200–240,000, with c. £300,000 for a 2-bed; 3-bed houses close to the Broadway are c. £450–500,000.

Riverside

The thin strip of river bank bounded – and protectively cut off by – the roaring traffic of the **Great West Rd**/A4 to the N, **Hammersmith Bridge Rd** to the E and by the borough boundary to the W is an eastward continuation of **Chiswick Mall.** The river, suddenly smaller-looking and more rural here than in central London, is to the S. In summer, the small patches of grass and trees fill with locals enjoying the rowing on the river – there are several clubs. Their wants are supplied by a clutch of pubs, among them one of the nicest, oldest riverside pubs in London: The Dove, originally a Georgian coffee house.

Some of London's rarer surviving Georgian homes are here, strung along **Hammersmith Terrace** (dating from the 1750s) and **Upper** and **Lower Malls** which run on to **Chiswick Mall**. The homes on **Hammersmith Terrace** have no road separating them from the river, but the two Malls are a little more public than the corresponding Chiswick stretch. Still, this most affluent and desirable corner has estate agents reaching for words like 'ambassadorial'. When the riverside houses do come up for sale (which is hardly ever), expect to pay well into the millions: sales between £3–4.5 million have been clocked up in the last few years, though a 5-bed with 60ft riverside garden did go for a positively modest-seeming £2.3 million.

Some modern homes here, too: **Lord Napier Place** is a peaceful enclave of town-houses (3/4-beds) just off **Upper Mall**; while down on the Fulham borders **King Henry's Reach**, a 1996 block of 83 flats set among fountains and gardens behind a gated entrance, yields a wide range of sizes and prices: a 2-bed that might be £350,000 can put on £100–150,000 if it has river views. Many flats are owned by foreign investors and let.

North from the riverside and Great West Rd/A4, just S of King St (Hammersmith's high street, with stores and small shopping mall), is **St Peter's Square**, a conservation area full of unusually large (for Hammersmith), handsome, 5/6-bed stucco-fronted houses. These were built 1825–30 in sub-Belgravia mode, around one of Hammersmith's rare garden squares: a 5-bedroom example was £1,675,000, while a 6-bed asked £2.1 million last winter. The surrounding streets of more modest houses and 2-bed cottages are plainly of the same date. In this area there are also several red-brick, Art Deco blocks of mansion flats such as Digby Mansions: roomy, 3-bed flats can be found here; or there are the modern town-houses of gated **Black Lion Mews**, just S of King St.

Brackenbury Village

Across to the N of King St, this corner is bounded by **Paddenswick Rd**, **Hammersmith Grove**, **Glenthorne Rd** and **Goldhawk Rd**. Since the 1980s it has moved from newly discovered, through up-and-coming, to firmly established. Riverside Georgiana apart this, along with Brook Green, is Hammersmith's best neighbourhood. It still has a delightful villagey atmosphere, though the shops are increasingly smart rather than useful. Young professional couples planning children, moving from Notting Hill and Kensington in search of family homes (and places in the well-regarded John Betts primary school, or the much-improved Brackenbury primary), have spent money on their houses and tidied the neighbourhood up. To serve them, smart restaurants have joined (sometimes replaced) the attractive local pubs. There is little through-traffic.

Generally the homes are small, 2- and 3-bed early Victorian terraced cottages and small villas, especially on the W side of the area (for example, **Carthew Rd**, **Cardross St** and **Dalling Rd**), while larger houses, sometimes split into flats, can be found towards the E in the streets leading to **Hammersmith Grove**. The little 2-bed cottages generally change hands at c. £400,000 plus (though a little one straight off the street went for £350,000 in **Banim St**); the bigger 3- or 4-bed houses go for around £450–650,000 and £550,000 plus respectively. On the village's northern border, the 4-bed, 3-storey houses in **Brackenbury Gardens** can be more.

In the NW, **Wingate Rd**, **Wellesley Avenue** and **Dorville Crescent** fringe the Ravenscourt Park conservation area and are seen by their residents as being part of Ravenscourt Park: these pretty streets contain early-Victorian terraced houses or villas. Buyers, especially young couples, are still willing to pay a premium for 2-bed cottagey homes, with larger houses and those in the conservation area going for considerably more. Demand from the BBC in Shepherd's Bush underscores the popularity of this area.

Ravenscourt Park

To the west of Brackenbury, on the Chiswick border, this neighbourhood is bounded by **Goldhawk Rd, King St** and **Paddenswick Rd**. It has a laid-back, suburban feel, more reminiscent of neighbouring Chiswick's wide-open spaces than of densely packed Hammersmith. Look here for bigger houses – including some detacheds – and gardens. Most of it falls within a conservation area centred on Ravenscourt Park itself, formerly the grounds of a fine 18th-century house which was bombed during the war. All that is left now are delightful gardens and formal lake, a pretty coach house (used as very popular tea rooms), tennis courts and rather splendid gates.

Queen Charlotte's maternity hospital, a landmark on the W side of the park, has moved to a new site in Du Cane Rd in Shepherd's Bush. Its big, leafy **Goldhawk Rd** site has now filled up with hundreds of new homes, including some sheltered housing and many housing-association ones for shared ownership or letting at fair rents. Regrettably, the architecture fails to live up to the ideals: a wasted opportunity. Those for sale were by Crest Nicholson: six 4-bed town houses, some re-using old buildings, plus 2- and 3-bed flats in a gated complex. The white, Victorian-Gothic admin building is now eight large flats: a 2-bed resale here, £500,000. The vast Royal Masonic Hospital site, alongside Queen Charlotte's, re-emerged as a clutch of 2-bed/2-bath flats in 1998.

Look to this leafy corner of Hammersmith for pockets of charming 18th- and 19th-century villas and terraces (**Ravenscourt Park, Ravenscourt Gardens, Hamlet Gardens**), and a rather pretty square (**Ravenscourt Square**) which has some lovely houses on three sides – the fourth side opens to the park. There are also homes backing onto the park – for example, along **Goldhawk Rd** and **Ravenscourt Rd** – with prices that can sail over a million (a 5-bed sold for £1.1 million last year), though £600,000-plus for the 4-bed Victorian houses is more usual. Note, too, the clutch of smart, white-stucco, semi-detached mid-Victorian villas with gardens and driveways at the park end of **Ravenscourt Gardens**. The choice of flats around here includes mansion blocks in **Hamlet Gardens** and the well-run Stamford Court next to the Queen Charlotte's development.

On the fringes of Ravenscourt Park, it is worth looking at **Wingate Rd, Dorvill Crescent** and **Wellesley Avenue**; and to the N, on the other side of the **Goldhawk Rd** (but still in the conservation area), **Ashchurch Park Villas, Rylett Rd** and **Ashchurch Grove, Binden Rd** and **Ashchurch Terrace** (see also Shepherd's Bush chapter). Further towards Chiswick on **Stamford Brook Rd**, St Mary's Court is a converted church, where original stonework meets parking-space-and-entryphone; a 1-bed here, £275,000.

Brook Green

Strictly speaking 'Brook Green' consists only of pretty **Brook Green** itself (a conservation area), plus the small network of streets leading immediately off either side of it – **Blythe Rd** is the obvious divide to the E. But the term is often used to describe an entire area that stretches as far N as **Minford Gardens/Sinclair Gardens** and as far E as **Sinclair Rd**, which runs alongside the railway line down to Olympia.

Brook Green *proper*, despite its rather smaller houses and location just off the busy but tidying **Shepherd's Bush Rd**, is even more popular than Ravenscourt Park. Indeed it's perhaps the most sought-after neighbourhood in Hammersmith, especially popular with City workers with families: St. Paul's, Godolphin & Latymer and Sacred Heart schools are draws. It has an international dimension: the French school, and the Chinese Church in London (both on the Green), attract foreign families. ('People like the proximity to Holland Park and Kensington High St – without their prices' says an agent.)

The scattered family houses in **Brook Green** (the road) overlooking the green itself are splendid, often leafily secluded and highly prized – and priced: c. £1–1.6 million. They also get access to the green's tennis courts. (In the streets off the Green, the homes are

c. £850,000–1.3 million, though two 5-beds, in **Girdlers Rd** and **Luxembourg Gardens**, went for £1.5 and £1.6 million respectively.) Then there's a mansion block, Queen's Mansions, plus flats of later periods including the 1980s **Mercers Place**, an enclave which also includes some town-houses. Two smart modern developments are tucked in off the **Hammersmith Rd** end of **Brook Green** (the road): **Windsor Way** is a group of 200 smart houses and flats behind electric gates and popular with overseas investors and tenants. Prices are c. £350–425,000 for a 2-bed/2-bath; 3-beds from £575,000; £700,000 plus for a 4-bed town-house – up to £1 million for the most opulent ones.

Look next at the peaceful network of little streets to the S, tucked into the triangle between the Green, **Shepherd's Bush Rd** and **Hammersmith Rd**. A closer inspection of the pretty, low-rise homes in streets such as **Rowan Rd** and **Bute Gardens** shows them to be deceptive: they are wider than average and particularly pleasant, though those on the E side of Rowan Rd are smaller. **Rowan Terrace**, off Bute Gardens, is a tiny close of hidden cottages. A one-way system protects this enclave from through-traffic.

Back across the green, the streets running off to the N have tall red-brick-and-stucco terraces – a good hunting-ground for flats – interspersed with some smaller Victoriana. **Blythe Rd**, which curls through from Shepherd's Bush Rd to Hammersmith Rd to enclose the Brook Green enclave, has a mix of Victorian and later houses (a 1980s terrace of 4-bed houses boast 3 baths plus garages, but also gables in a graceful nod to 19th-century neighbours). Prices for the period homes vary with their position on this long road: west is best. At the Hammersmith Rd end stands Kensington West, an 8-storey, luxury 1989 apartment block with its own sports complex. Lots to rent in the 1- to 4-bed flats of big, 1930s Latymer Court mansion block (complete with porter and ornate cage lift) on **Hammersmith Rd**; plenty for sale, too: 1-beds c. £170–220,000, 2-beds £200–300,000. The good security makes it a favourite with overseas buyers and single women.

The Brook Green borders area between **Blythe** and **Sinclair Rds** (we recall 'Blythe Village' being touted as a name for it in the '80s . . .) is a great hunting-ground for BBC staff: it, too, contains many larger terraces, frequently split into 1- and 2-bed flats. They often have semi-basement/garden-level flats that can boast Victorian-sized back gardens with mature trees. In some cases, semi-basement and ground floors together make good maisonettes (a 2/3-bed, £410,000). Ground-floor rooms can be high-ceilinged, with ornate plasterwork. Look out for homes in **Addison Gardens, Bolingbroke Rd, Lakeside Rd, Irving Rd, Hofland Rd, Milson Rd** and **Masbro Rds**, for 3-bed houses at c. £525–650,000; Addison has 5-beds that can top £800,000. **Ceylon Rd** has some modern town-houses: 4-bed, 2-bath, garage. Homes on the E side of **Sinclair Rd**, which back onto the tracks, are not so popular with insomniac buyers; a plan to build flats in the car park by the line has stalled due to ecological concerns. This tract does have a particular atmosphere – villagey to some, claustrophobic to others, certainly a community. It also has well-patronized pubs, corner shops, health centre and Addison Primary.

Crabtree

This neighbourhood takes its name from the 1911 Crabtree estate, a small grid of neat and peaceful streets running N from **Crabtree Lane** on the Fulham/SW6 borders, between the river and **Fulham Palace Rd** up to **Hammersmith Bridge Rd**. Apart from the estate itself, this corner – particularly the riverside – used to be predominantly industrial, but more and more homes have appeared (some in exceedingly smart new developments). If it says 'works' on your street map you should probably amend it to read 'posh flats – or offices'. Leading the new-build is Richard Rogers-designed 1988 Thames Reach complex of three 5-storey blocks off **Rainville Rd**: living rooms, with floor-to-ceiling glass, get wide views across to Barnes Waterside (the nature reserve and upmarket housing estate), and picturesque Harrods Depository building, now also flats. Rogers' architecture practice has its offices here, and the famed River Café is next door. . . .

This corner also holds the splendid Riverside Studios arts and performance centre. Another Thames-side scheme is next door: Chancellor's Wharf, 1990, is eight 5-storey town-houses and 32 flats, just downstream from the bridge. Further down, **Crisp Rd** has the Hammersmith Embankment Office Park, partly built and blocking the riverside. Locals are campaigning for the path to be opened. Going on S, the Crabtree estate houses are unassuming late-Victorian, 2-storey terraces, made pleasant by no-through-traffic schemes. Many have been split into flats over the years. The riverside to the S, into Fulham, is mostly low-rise council-built homes. A path runs along the riverside.

Transport Tubes: Hammersmith (zone 2, Piccadilly, Hammersmith & City, District), West Kensington (zone 2, District), Barons Court (zone 2, Piccadilly, District). See also map. From Hammersmith: Oxford Circus 25 min (1 change), City 35 min (1 change), Heathrow 40 min.

Convenient for Heathrow via M4, roads to the West. Miles from centre: 4.

Schools Local Authority: Phoenix High, Sacred Heart High (g), Cardinal Vaughan. Private: St Paul's (g), Godolphin & Latymer (g), Latymer Upper (b), Ecole Française, Holborn College.

H

SALES

Flats	S	1B	2B	3B	4B	5B
Average prices	120–180	130–275	200–400	300–500	400–700	600+
Houses	2B	3B	4B	5B	6/7B	8B
Average prices	330–600	390–750	450–1M	700–1.5M	850–2M	–

RENTAL

Flats	S	1B	2B	3B	4B	5B
Average prices	150–200	180–300	240–450	300–500	400–750	–
Houses	2B	3B	4B	5B	6/7B	8B
Average prices	300–400	400–700	450–800+	500–1200	1000–2000	–

The properties Close-packed Victorian terraces predominate – but also pockets of beautiful earlier riverside homes, handsome houses in leafy corners, mansion blocks, some smart new flats and houses. Many converted flats. Thames-side industrial swept away by luxury new developments towards Fulham border.

The market Globetrotters, BBC workforce and other busy couples and families, and City commuters look for homes here. Riverside houses scarce and expensive. Good location (tubes, M4 to airport) and BBC HQ in nearby Shepherd's Bush make this a hunting ground for both flats and family houses. Schools dictate market in Brackenbury and Brook Green.

Among estate agents active in this area are:

- Finlay Brewer
- Bushells
- Shaws
- Cavanagh Smith
- Barnard Marcus
- Marsh & Parsons
- Hamptons
- Royston
- Savills
- Leslie Marsh
- Ravenscourt
- Wilmotts
- Foxtons
- Winkworth
- Lansdowne
- Quintons
- Kinleigh Folkard & Hayward
- Faron Sutaria
- Townsends
- Tates
- Coutts de Lisle
- James Anthony
- Chiltons
- Northfields
- Sebastian
- Brook Green

HAMPSTEAD

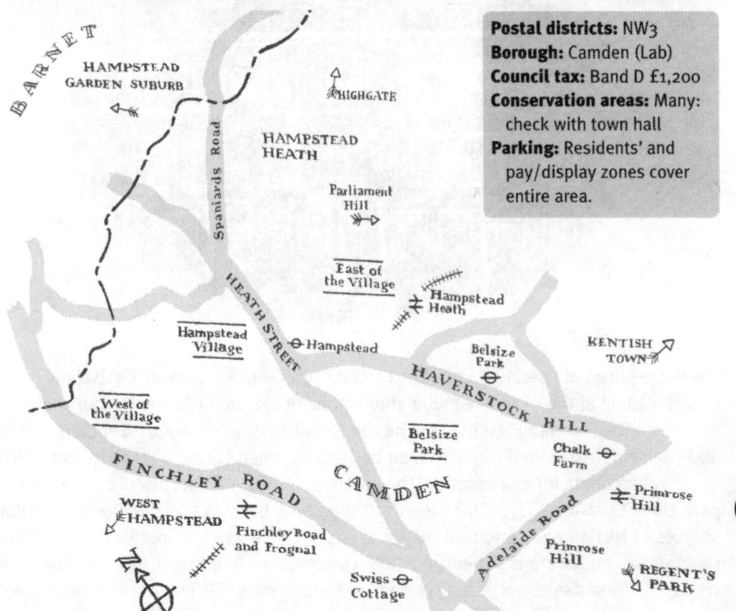

Postal districts: NW3
Borough: Camden (Lab)
Council tax: Band D £1,200
Conservation areas: Many: check with town hall
Parking: Residents' and pay/display zones cover entire area.

H

Hampstead, steeply sited on its commanding hill to the north of London, has been a fashionable choice for three centuries, ever since the allegedly health-giving spring-water 'wells' began to be exploited. The ancient village gained a clutch of smart houses in the early 18th century, and every age since has added its own versions. The latest grand homes are flats with seven-figure prices carved out of opulent mansions or recycled public buildings.

Early on in its vogue, Hampstead acquired a name for prosperous intellectualism. It was the summer retreat for writers and artists, politicians and plutocrats eager for country air not too far from Town. It was this community, self-conscious about itself and its surroundings, that saved Hampstead Heath – that glorious 800 acres of sandy, hilly *rus in urbe* – from being built upon. Since their victory over the lord of the manor in 1871 the Heath has been public land, run these days by the City of London Corporation. There were plans in Victorian times to lay the land out as a 'proper' park – but luckily for Hampstead, none of the public custodians have ever been inclined to spend money on the Heath, and its scruffy, bushy appearance is maintained unmanicured.

The green space grew as Parliament Hill to the S, West Heath, the Heath Extension to the NW, and later (the crowning glory) Kenwood and its stately-home park to the NE, were successively added. The result is that Hampstead's close-packed Georgian village centre is bordered by great, rolling tracts of open land on two sides.

Unlike other London suburbs, Hampstead has never really been out of fashion. It thus retains glorious houses of every period from Queen Anne to today. Its latest fashionable phase has introduced international wealth: as a result, since around 1985 it has gained more than its fair share of London's lavish new flats and security-conscious, multi-bathroomed houses. Their inhabitants add to a community that is today a mix of money and intellect. The archetypical Hampstead Man (or Woman) is no longer an academic –

they were priced out decades ago – but a TV presenter with a sideline in bestselling books, or an architect at the head of a multinational firm, or the boss of an American bank.

They bring their families: the area has an astonishing 32 schools, 20 of them private; and congestion at school-run time is so bad that Camden Council reckoned that driving to school accounts for 23 per cent of the borough's traffic. Parents have to get permits to park close to schools for 15 minutes. Traffic, parking permits and the like are constant sources of friction and complaint, which is unsurprising when a population armed with German saloon cars and American MPVs confronts a streetscape made for Georgian carriages and sedan chairs. As one controlled parking zone (CPZ) starts, next-door streets feel the knock-on effect and demand their own. There are now 16 CPZs in Camden borough (and two more are planned, for North End and Highgate), and that's not counting Hamsptead's many private roads, which are free to set their own rules. Says our spy, 'you can spend half your life in your car, waiting in some narrow street for oncoming traffic. . . '

Hampstead today is up in the top handful of London residential areas: as an agent put it, quizzed on where was best, 'Hampstead is good roads surrounded by better roads.' If the last two or three years have been, in common with the rest of Town, much quieter in the property market, this followed a run of years that left prices probably unmatched in any but the most exclusive areas of Very Central London. Many buyers pay cash – even for million-plus properties: when rising mortgage rates are mentioned in the papers as a potential problem, agents here smile.

Families may favour Hampstead, but they need to be well-heeled ones: a family house in NW3 under a million is hard to find. Good-sized houses are well over, and you can double, treble, quadruple that million with ease; but you can find a little Georgian cottage and still stay in six figures. At the top of the scale, two houses in the Village and environs were on the market for £15 million and £20 million last year, prices which worked out at about £1,000 per sq ft (Mayfair prices), and a mere flat was advertised at 9.5 million. But 2004's shortage of really good properties on the market betrayed the fact that selling your Hampstead home is for most a discretionary matter, to be put off when top prices are unlikely to be achieved.

It is also a popular area to rent in (the New Year '05 market opened briskly, and rents are up for the first time in four years), with the majority of the tenants – and not a few of the landlords – foreign. The American School down the hill in St John's Wood generates a regular flow of families, while international business people fly in to fill up the 2-bedroomed flats.

Hampstead has everything the modern affluent want: the Heath, glorious architecture, smart shops, good restaurants, reasonable transport – Northern Line to City and West

BARGAINS!
REPOSSESSIONS
Rental Investments
Properties in need of work
or reduced for quick sale
Capital Property Lists
"The London Specialists"
Open 7 days: 10am – 10pm
020 7288 0288

W rth

LONDON CENTRAL

Clerkenwell & City	020 7405 1288
Kensington	020 7727 1500
Knightsbridge & Chelsea	020 7589 6616
Notting Hill	020 7727 3227
Paddington & Bayswater	020 7262 2900
Pimlico	020 7828 1786
South Kensington	020 7373 5052
St John's Wood	020 7586 7001
West End	020 7240 3322

LONDON WEST

Chiswick	020 8994 7096
Ealing & Acton	020 8896 0123
Fulham Parson's Green	020 7731 3388
Fulham Barons Court	020 7385 1115
Hammersmith	020 7371 4466
Ladbroke Grove	020 7792 5000
Shepherd's Bush	020 8735 3266

LONDON SOUTH of the RIVER

Balham	020 8675 9696
Barnes	020 8255 0088
Battersea	020 7228 9265
Blackheath & Greenwich	020 8852 0999
Clapham	020 7498 8600
Croydon	020 8686 6667
Crystal Palace	020 8655 9530
Dulwich	020 8299 2722
Herne Hill	020 7501 8950
Kennington	020 7587 0600
New Cross	020 7277 7298
Putney	020 8788 9295
Richmond	020 8940 9986
Streatham	020 8769 6699
Surrey Quays	020 7237 9119
Tooting	020 8767 5221
Wimbledon	020 8946 2930

LONDON EAST

Bow	020 8981 6776
Hackney	020 8986 4216
Shoreditch	020 7749 7650
Stratford	020 8519 0006

LONDON NORTH

Crouch End	020 8342 9999
Edgware	020 8621 4000
Finchley	020 8349 3388
Golders Green	020 8458 8313
Hampstead	020 7794 1155
Hendon	020 8202 1031
Highgate	020 8341 1988
Islington	020 7354 2480
Kentish Town	020 7485 9210
Stoke Newington	020 7923 3332
Tottenham	020 8808 9200
Totteridge	020 8492 2399
Wembley	020 8904 8822
Willesden	020 8451 1000

HAMPSHIRE

Winchester	01962 866 777

KENT

Tunbridge Wells	01892 519600

LINCOLNSHIRE

Lincoln	01522 531 321
Sleaford	01529 303 377

YORKSHIRE

Sheffield City Centre	0114 276 5715
Chapeltown	0114 245 9696
Dronfield	01246 291 555
Hillsborough	0114 234 9204
Woodseats	0114 255 7873
York	01904 676 154

PORTUGAL

Largos	+351 282 769341
Praia da Luz	+351 282 789787
Boliqueime	+351 289 362173
Carvoeiro	+351 282 356952
Albufeira	+351 289 585700

SPECIALIST SERVICES

London Surveyors	020 7874 1075
Sheffield Surveyors	0114 249 7770

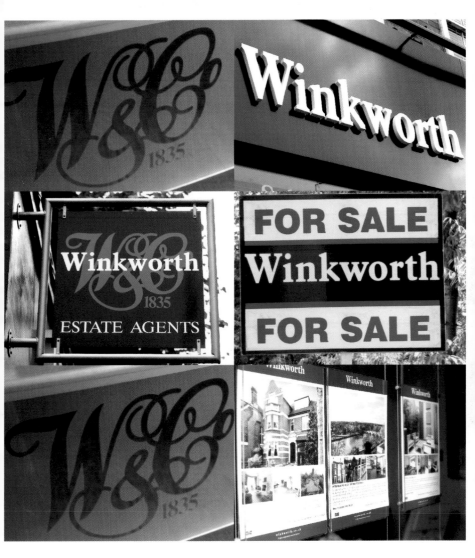

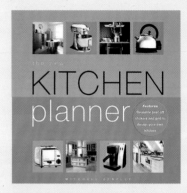

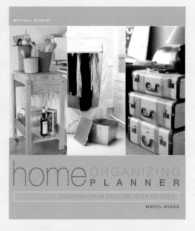

End – excellent schools and smart, characterful, high-specification homes. The fast Heathrow train to Paddington – a cab-ride – has made the airport an hour away, encouraging international buyers who used to stick to Kensington to investigate Hampstead. 'When they see Hampstead,' said one local agent 'they want to live here.'

Hampstead Village

Few visit Hampstead Village without wanting to stay, the only constraint being the failure of the lottery numbers to come up. The choice ranges from wide, leafy avenues with imposing detached mansions to picturesque, almost medieval lanes, squares and cul-de-sacs. The place is packed with a fascinating variety of homes dating back 300 years and more – many with historical and literary connections. The population still contains a remarkably high proportion of artists, writers, actors, musicians (many of whom got here before prices went stratospheric), diplomats and other professionals, and the centre reflects the cosmopolitan flavour of the area with many a fashion store, specialist food shops, bookshops, restaurants of all descriptions and some celebrated pubs like the Flask and the Hollybush. Difficult to buy a needle and thread here, though.

From **Hampstead High St**, beautiful little streets like **Gayton Rd** and **Flask Walk** lead to the old spa area where roads named **Well Rd** and **Well Walk** reflect the history. Here, too, is Burgh House, the Grade I-listed mansion built in 1702, now a community centre, art gallery and local history museum. The Everyman cinema in **Holly Bush Vale** has been done up by new owners and is happily back in action. Houses in this area are mainly Georgian, Edwardian and Victorian terraces, many of which have been split into flats. Cottages abound, ranging upwards in size from tiny 1-bed ones. But penetrate the maze of little streets and paths and you'll find suprisingly large houses in secluded corners like **New End**, **Cannon Place** and **Christchurch Hill**, home of the New End Theatre. **Flask Walk** offers all periods from Queen Anne to Edwardian, with a 4-bed Queen Anne house at £1.4 million last winter, or an early-Victorian 5-bed for the same price.

Particularly attractive is the **Gainsborough Gardens** private estate, off Well Walk, a ring of houses on its own circular road: large, late-Victorian semis and terraces. Mansion block flats in The Pryors and Bell Moor, literally overlooking the heath, are also popular: both blocks have been smartened up, and 2-beds go for c.£450,000 – though one vast 5-bed one in **Bell Moor** sold for £1.35 million. Look out, too, for terraced houses and flats in the **Vale of Health**, an exclusive enclave built out onto the heath itself. Once known, less scenically, as Hatche's Bottom, the land was drained in 1777 – a few houses are indeed Georgian. It lies off East Heath Rd, where the traffic scheme introduced five years back has dramatically reduced rat-running and infuriated car-borne commuters.

Heath St is the other main road through the village – leading, on the W side, to the upper part of the old town, with beautiful houses in tightly packed squares such as **Golden Yard** and **The Mount Square**, or in delightful secluded streets: these include **Windmill Hill**, **Hampstead Grove** with its larger semi- or detached homes, and **Admiral's Walk** with its unusually shaped houses – one has a quarterdeck – with naval names. Some date back to as early as 1700. Prices in this part stray readily into the £2 million and upwards bracket, but the little cottages in corners like **Golden Yard** can be under a million.

The potential for new developments of any size in Hampstead is limited by the extreme scarcity of available land, with nearly all the new homes of the last 15 years resulting from the conversion or replacement of redundant public buildings such as hospitals and colleges. The old New End Hospital in **Heath St** became flats in 1998; 2001 saw the marketing of 60 flats and penthouses converted from the old Mount Vernon Hospital in **Frognal Rise**, in the heart of the Village. Mount Vernon is reckoned the smartest recent block, popular with pop stars, etc, and a good flat can make £1,000 per sq ft: a 2-bed was £825,000 last winter – though a penthouse was £9.5 million.

Heath St leads, at the S end, to the splendid terraces (some Queen Anne, the rest Georgian) plus some late-Victorian mansion flats, of **Church Row**, and on past the ancient St John's Parish Church and **Frognal Gardens**, to **Frognal** – one of the oldest roads in Hampstead, and the site of University College School. Frognal was a hamlet in its own right under the Stuarts, and most ages have added something enviable since: a 1920s 9-bed detached was £3.5 million in December.

Further S are the very large houses in **Fitzjohns Avenue**, many of which have been converted into schools, hotels and clinics. **Maresfield Gardens** also has large (£2-million-plus) homes, the Freud Museum in the house where the great man died in 1939, and UCS's sister school South Hampstead High. Homes here are popular; there's something for everyone: old, new, flats, houses – and traffic not *quite* so bad as the village centre's.

West of the Village

These are the quiet, spacious tree-lined avenues, bounded by **West Heath Rd, Platts Lane, Finchley Rd** and **Arkwright Rd**, where the large Victorian mansions are disputed between affluent families and developers eager to split them into flats. Homes here, part of the estate laid out by Sir Thomas Maryon Wilson, Lord of the Manor of Hampstead (see also West Hampstead) are within the magic 10-minute walk from the tube. Luxury flat conversions began to flow in a steady stream in this area in the mid-'80s, and quite a few new homes – houses and flats – have either replaced earlier mansions, or been squeezed in between surviving ones. Some gated enclaves occupy the former mansions' large gardens: these can give the streets a crowded air, but no-one likes gates (electric of course) more than the householders of Hampstead. Latest is a group of five new houses off **Oak Hill Park**, priced between £1.8–2.1 million.

H

At the top of the heath, right on the NW3/NW11 border in **North End Way**, the enormous Inverforth House, rebuilt 90 years ago for a soap tycoon as a single mansion (originally called The Hill), is now homes once more after a career as a hospital. The nine flats sold in 2003 at an average of £1.5 million, with penthouses at twice that. Security is tight, service charges high.

Also cresting the heath is the famous, idiosyncratic, clapboarded Jack Straw's Castle pub, now (sadly) turned into yet more flats (2-beds £565–695,000) and houses by Albany Homes. Albany will next deal similarly with the adjacent, Georgian, Old Court House.

Examples of the upper-tier apartment blocks around this high point of Hampstead include Heath Park Gardens, 13 flats overlooking the heath on the corner of **Templewood Avenue** and **West Heath Rd.** These unusual homes – split-levels and duplexes – are just starting to show their age, by Hampstead standards (they go back to 1988). Similarly luxurious, but also just a mite faded, is Summit Lodge next to Whitestone Pond in **Upper Terrace** which, at 440ft above sea level, is the highest point in London. Not surprisingly, its 12 large flats rarely change hands: the top ones have unbeatable 360-degree views of the capital from the roof. The big Westfield College scheme, 149 flats in 2.5 acres of land on **Kidderpore Avenue,** dates from 2001.

When it comes to Hampstead houses the biggest – some positively ambassadorial – are the ones in **West Heath Rd** that are opposite West Heath: these merit price tags of £2 million and go up from there: a new 8-bed was £2.85 million last winter, a mock-Tudor 6-bed detached was £3.5 million. Prices fall gently as you go downhill – you might get closer to £1 million – towards the **Finchley Rd**. Half a dozen private closes off **West Heath Rd** offer detached houses in even more privacy and with yet more electric gates.

But there are also houses of all sizes and in all conditions (but most verging on the opulent) in roads such as **Redington Gardens, Heath Drive, Hollycroft Avenue, Ferncroft Avenue, Templewood Avenue** and **Greenaway Gardens** – some with very large gardens. Once again you must budget for £2–3 million for a house here. **Chesterford Gardens** has a particularly fine terrace of houses, as does **Redington**

Rd, an extremely graceful curving street, which links West Heath Rd with Frognal. **Hollycroft Avenue** and **Platts Lane** have good family houses, with the latter offering 3- and 4-bed Victorian terraces which might be less than £1 million. The award-winning 1980s Firecrest development, between **West Heath Rd** and **Templewood Avenue**, added exciting contemporary-styled houses and flats cleverly fitted into a beautiful, wooded site. The two largest houses have their own basement pools.

These roads have easy access to **Finchley Rd**, which runs N to connect with the M1 and A1, and S through St John's Wood and Regent's Park to the West End. Bus services along the **Finchley Rd** are good, and it's a short hop to Golders Green or Finchley Rd tubes – and to the O2 shopping/cinema complex on the Finchley Rd. Plenty of mansion flats along here: a 4-bed in an Edwardian lock is reckoned 'a steal' at £500,000, or you can cross to the West Hampstead side of the street for 'The Pulse': 55 new 2- and 3-bed flats around a courtyard.

East of the Village

South of **Willow Rd** is a district of pleasant Victorian terraced roads, now almost exclusively converted into flats and maisonettes (a very large, laterally converted 3-bed one, £3 million late last year), though the odd entire house does come up. Down the hill is what is sometimes known as the Downshire Hill triangle, comprising **Downshire Hill, Keats Grove** and **South End Rd**. This is one of the most elegant (and sought-after) areas in Hampstead. **Downshire Hill** has a number of handsome Regency stucco-and-brick houses, most of which have remained as single-family homes. They are nearly all listed, and as a group they are listed Grade II as being of 'considerable merit'. One of these houses will cost you £2 million – £3.5 million for the detached ones in **Keats Grove**, near lovely Keats House, now a museum and library. More modest homes in the form of flats at the Rosslyn Hill end of **Downshire Hill**.

Further down the hill is villagey **South End Green**, with its shops and cafés and Hampstead Heath station (North London Line/Silverlink). The cinema has succumbed: it is replaced by a Marks & Spencer store and 'Panoramic': 36 flats (2-beds £495–795,000), plus 11 flats for nurses. It took three years of planning negotiations to get the scheme through to approval. Locals fret that the village character is being eroded: besides M&S, there's a new Starbucks. . . . Nearby in **Pond St** is the giant, modern, Royal Free Hospital, which mixes it with the odd 5-bedroomed, large-gardened Georgian house and the new flats behind a Victorian facade that sold fast in 2001.

Also off South End Green is the attractive enclave of streets, reached only via **South Hill Park**, which juts out into the Heath at the foot of Parliament Hill. It holds a mixture of family houses, flat conversions and modern, individual houses. There are a few post-war blocks of flats in **Parliament Hill** (the road). The great attractions here are the lack of through-traffic and the instant access to the Heath and Hill. Most coveted are the houses on the N side of **South Hill Park** that overlook the Hampstead Ponds (a 5-bed house here was £2.65 million last winter), though those on **Tanza Rd**, which also back onto the Hill, get pricey too: these rarely come up for sale.

There's a very attractive group of streets bounded by **Constantine Rd, Savernake Rd, Fleet Rd** and **Mansfield Rd** known as the Mansfield Road Conservation Area. The last remnant of Victorian Gospel Oak, it is very popular because it has direct access to Hampstead Heath via a footbridge over the tracks. These streets were used for years as the unofficial parking area for the Royal Free Hospital, but five years ago residents' parking was introduced and this led to a dramatic rise in prices. 'The last area in NW3 with a good choice of family homes under a million,' one agent said. Hurry while stocks last, as they say . . . the best price so far is £920,000, though £950,000 was being asked for a house in **Roderick Rd** that needed work. Flats split from the Victorian houses are c. £280–295,000 for a 2-bed. **Byron Mews**' cache of recent homes leads off Fleet Rd.

Also interesting are **Parkhill Rd, Upper Park Rd** and **Lawn Rd**, which meander southwards from Fleet Rd down to Haverstock Hill: a mixture of flat conversions, family houses and some modern council estates. A large Victorian semi in **Parkhill Rd** sold for £1.5 million in 2001, despite being split into four flats, while a showbiz couple bought here for £2 million. Lesser mortals seeking a family house pay anything from £1–2 million.

The architecturally famous, Grade I-listed 1930s Isokon block in **Lawn Rd** became seriously run down over the years. Built in the Bauhaus style, it was designed as an experiment in socialist living, complete with communal areas, for broke-but-creative artists and musicians. The council had owned it since 1972, and at last over the past two years an Isokon Trust/Notting Hill Housing Trust partnership has been restoring it, true to the ideal: now 25 flats for key workers, plus 11 open-market ones, are ready. Live in an architectural statement for £270-525,000. Apparently the shared-ownership deals on the key-worker flats are not proving that attractive to their target market: £180,000 for a studio is perhaps the reason why.

Belsize Park

Belsize Park was once regarded as the less desirable end of Hampstead, replete with bedsits and studios. In the last decade it has come to life, with larger flats (and even whole houses) reinstated: it now has a character and atmosphere all its own – and prices not far off Hampstead's. It has two shopping centres, around the Belsize Park underground station in **Haverstock Hill**, and in what has become known as 'Belsize Village' in **Belsize Lane**, which has some attractive mews. The population density is high, the streets are very congested; but the architecture is charming and the typical Belsize Park flat will have generous-sized rooms and gloriously high ceilings.

H

Haverstock Hill is busy, but with the tube and shops its plentiful flats are popular: pay around £350–400,000 for a 2-bed in one of the big blocks here. Two million has been asked for the surviving big Victorian semis. The dominant road in Belsize Village is **Belsize Avenue**, which runs from Haverstock Hill across to the Swiss Cottage end of the suburb. On the N side are the roads that lead up to the graceful, tree-lined **Lyndhurst Gardens** and **Wedderburn Rd**. On the S side are **Belsize Park, Belsize Park Gardens** (pretty mews houses), and **Belsize Square**. In the latter a large house, only recently a warren of bedsits, has become a £5 million 'minimalist statement property' (it says here). More extravagance in **Lancaster Stables**, one of the local mews, where two £2.25 million houses have been added, one boasting an indoor waterfall in its 4-floor atrium (as a light-well is known in expensive properties). Also interesting, if small, are houses in 'The Glens' – **Glenloch Rd, Glenilla Rd** and **Glenmore Rd**, only a minute or two's walk from the tube. The bigger 5-bed terraced Victoriana in Glenmore Rd broke through the million-pound barrier in summer 2001: typical asking prices are now up to £1.5 million, though £1 million will buy an un-smartened one.

Englands Lane has a very useful clutch of shops and restaurants, convenient to the large houses in **Steeles Rd** (home of several film stars, house prices rise from one million to beyond three. . .). Flats above the shops in **Englands Lane** – an address to boast of, surely – sell for c.£250,000 for a 2-bed. There are interesting terraces in secluded **Primrose Gardens**, and some modern town-houses in **Antrim Rd**, most of which is, however, taken up by the flats of Antrim Mansions.

Swiss Cottage

Elderly Central-European residents wistfully remember the days when Swiss Cottage was known as Schweizerhof, and they whiled away the hours drinking coffee and eating pastries in Viennese cafés like Louis. But the street market disappeared, they built a business complex, and the area lost most of its student-party atmosphere and became a sharply contrasting area divided between those who use the community centre and the City/estate-agent types. Conservation-area status has enhanced the appeal to outsiders.

Swiss Cottage took its name from the original Regency chalet-style tavern: this architectural oddity has been perpetuated by a more recent pub and restaurant complex opposite the tube station (Jubilee Line). It also has one of the best libraries in the country, a hotel, a six-screen cinema and close proximity to the thriving **Finchley Rd** shopping and the O2 complex.

After about 30 years of dithering, something has finally been done with the Swiss Cottage civic-centre site: the sorely outdated sports centre and a desultory park have been replaced by a 16-storey flats block that funds a new state-of-the-art sports and fitness centre, plus a new park. The 135 Barratt flats ('Visage') are selling briskly at prices from £400,000 all the way up to £1.3 million, and there are 42 Affordable Homes. ('The designs are looking quite horrible' commented an escaped local, 'but I'm sure the new sports centre will be fantastic'). The Grade II-listed library, by Sir Basil Spence, has been refurbished at a cost of £8 million (including the £1.5 million it ran over budget). The new £15 million Lottery-funded Hampstead Theatre at the **Eton Avenue** end of the site is open, as is the outdoor market: the new park is being planted this year.

Much of the wider area – some 243 acres – was once owned by Eton College, which was also responsible for a great deal of the housing development. The estate still owns large swathes of property in the area, particularly in roads like **Eton Avenue**, **Fellows Rd**, **Provost Rd** and **King Henry's Rd**. There are still large detached 1880s–1900s houses here, but most are subdivided into flats. The area gained over 100 modern flats and town-houses in the Quadrangles development, between **Adelaide** and **Fellows Rds**. In **Eton Avenue** houses sell for £3 million, indeed £4.25 million was being asked last winter for an 1890 monster still split into flats.

In parallel **Fellows Rd**, which has 1860s houses, prices drop slightly (to a mere £2.5 million for an 8-bed) due to the council tower blocks; the district is also characterized by a number of council estates and tower block developments, as well as some large blocks of mansion flats, including Regency Lodge in **Avenue Rd**, and Northways in **College Crescent**. Pay c. £450,000 for a 2-bed flat hereabouts.

There are some beautiful houses in the broad sweep of **Elsworthy Rd**, at scenic prices like the £3.45 million asked for a 5-bed detached last autumn, but the street does suffer a little from being an unofficial through-route from Primrose Hill to St John's Wood. However, some of the houses on the N side share a magnificent communal garden with houses in **Wadham Gardens**. Flats in **Elsworthy** – 2- and 3-beds – go for around £500–600,000. Big, double-fronted houses in both streets are popular, being close to St John's Wood and Primrose Hill.

Transport	Tubes: Hampstead (zone 2/3) Belsize Park (2): Northern Line to Oxford Circus 20 min (1 change), Bank 25 min, Heathrow 70 min (1 change). Trains: Hampstead Heath, Primrose Hill: North London Line/Silverlink to Liverpool St 20 min. (Also on to Stratford, City Airport)
Convenient for	Hampstead Heath, Kenwood; M1, A1 to North. Miles from centre: 4.
Schools	Local Authority: Hampstead School, Haverstock School. Private: University College School (b), South Hampstead High School (g), Royal School (g), Fine Art College, St Margaret's (g). See also neighbouring areas.

SALES

Flats	S	1B	2B	3B	4B	5B
Average prices	160–200	240–320	340–1M+	450–1M+	650+	–
Houses	2B	3B	4B	5B	6/7B	8B
Average prices	450–600+	650–1M	850–3M	1–3M+	1.5M+	1.7M+

RENTAL

Flats	S	1B	2B	3B	4B	5B
Average prices	175–220	220–350	300–650	350–850	750+	–
Houses	2B	3B	4B	5B	6/7B	8B
Average prices	285–750	350–1000	1000–3000	1500–5000	→	–

The properties Georgian gems in heart of Village and scattered among the surrounding gracious streets. Victorian and later homes, many now flats, further out. More good modern houses than anywhere else in London. New developments, generally towards the Heath, are luxury level: some innovative, some merely opulent. Conversions of grand old hospitals, colleges etc provide yet more sybaritic pads (or statement homes, as they are called locally).

H **The market** Everyone wants to live here. Prices rise, with the hill, to ultra-luxury level homes around the Heath: figures above reflect the wide spread of quality: houses (and even flats) inclined to sprout swimming pools etc. It's getting hard to find a choice of family homes in Hampstead under £1 million.

Among estate agents active in this area are:

- Anscombe & Ringland
- Knight Frank
- Foxtons
- Behr & Butchoff
- Day Morris
- Kinleigh Folkard & Hayward
- TK International
- Goldschmidt & Howland
- Benham & Reeves
- John D Wood
- Faron Sutaria
- Chesterton
- Naylius McKenzie
- Glentree
- In London
- Savills
- Hamptons
- Parkheath
- Alan Charles
- Heywoods
- Keith Cardale
- Keatons
- Abbey

HAMPSTEAD GARDEN SUBURB

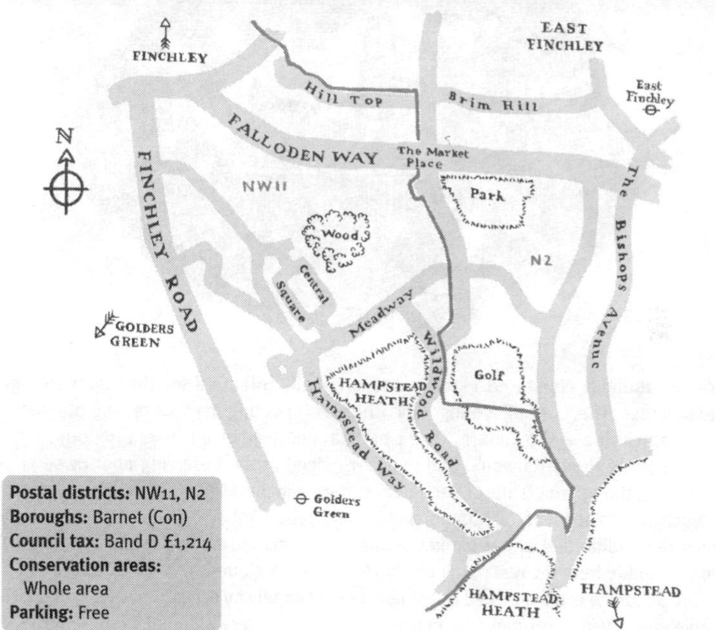

Postal districts: NW11, N2
Boroughs: Barnet (Con)
Council tax: Band D £1,214
Conservation areas: Whole area
Parking: Free

New homes for 'The Suburb'? To anyone who knows this place apart, the thought is (almost) as startling as the news that its pride and joy, the Institute – which is as old as the Suburb itself – is moving from Central Square across the border into East Finchley.

Leafy, picturesque and pleasing to the eye, Hampstead Garden Suburb was the philanthropic vision of Dame Henrietta Barnett, cosmetics heiress and reformer, at the start of the 20th century. The result was a model village, the embodiment of her dream of social cohesion and artistic sensibility, and it has been scrupulously preserved all these years. She planned her ideal suburb as a place where people of all classes, conditions and ages would co-exist happily in beautiful, tree-lined streets, with woods and open spaces available to all. The Trust she set up still controls every aspect – well, every visual aspect – of life here.

'The Suburb', as it is universally known, is grouped at the head of its own extension of Hampstead Heath. It lies just to the north of the Extension and golf course, and across the **Finchley Rd** from Golders Green. The Trust provides a map with the boundaries of the area clearly marked, though less punctilious estate agents happily claim swathes of Golders Green and East Finchley as 'HGS borders'.

Hampstead Garden Suburb was carefully designed by architects Parker & Unwin (Raymond Unwin planned the estate) and Lutyens (who didn't last long: he fell out with Dame H and was fired), but the inspiration was Dame Henrietta Barnett's.

The founder's ideals ensure you find a great variety of type and harmonious style of housing in the area, from the terraced cottages around **Erskine Hill** and **Hampstead Way** (where 'artisans' were to live, benefiting from 'the contagion of refinement') to the double-fronted mansions of **Winnington Rd**, built later for those who, well, didn't need to work quite so hard. Baillie Scott's Waterlow Court in **Heath Close**, a delightful cross between almshouses and stable-doored country cottages grouped round a cloistered garden, was originally intended for that then-strange phenomenon, the working 'young lady' ('homes for young men' were also planned – on the other side of the suburb). The 1-bed flats here now sell for c. £195,000.

Alas, Dame Henrietta would find that few indeed of the deserving poor dwell here these days, though the fabric of her model suburb remains virtually unchanged – so far.

Such is the appeal of the Suburb, and its small size, that even in quiet times scarcity keeps the middle and upper market stable. It is regarded by the estate agents as a separate entity from the rest of the capital, 'due to the uniqueness of the area'.

The Suburb was once viewed as being inhabited largely by eccentrics – 'crazy, freakish people', observed *The Times*, not mincing matters. It is very different from Hampstead itself – and it was designed to be. (When a careless journalist accorded Peter Mandelson a Hampstead childhood, his old teacher from the Suburb's Infants' School was careful to set the record straight in a letter to the *Telegraph*.) Today the Suburb's residents are much like those in the rest of North West London – though probably rather richer. There are many Jewish inhabitants; also Americans and South Africans who love the feeling of space. Most of the old founding families are now gone and a younger age-group has been moving in – though it's known that the average age of the Suburb's 13,000 residents is on the high side. Living here means you're close to Kenwood and the Heath for summer walks and concerts, yet just five miles from the centre of London. This is for those who like to feel in touch with the metropolis, but to dwell amid green space – and good schools.

Today's residents tend to stay once they've lived here for a while, and there are always others looking to move in. It's an estate agent's dream – the houses, particularly those in the Old Suburb, or NW11, area really are 'full of character': the major roads are wide and tree-lined, and hedges rather than fences or walls divide the plots. Little secluded closes (the Suburb pioneered this layout) suit those who prefer more privacy. It can be though – well, a bit 'like living in a goldfish bowl', confides one agent.

The North London 'eruv' – a notional boundary within which Sabbath laws are relaxed for Orthodox Jews – includes much of the Suburb. Recently completed, it's not universally popular and hit a snag when Suburbites said that they wanted wood, not metal, poles in **Wildwood Rd**. Prosecutions ensue if anyone damages this religious boundary.

Market Place – along the **Falloden Way**, also known as the A1 – provides some (expensive) shopping and a welter of estate agents, but you'll have to go down to Golders Green/Temple Fortune or up to East Finchley for most necessities. The original plan envisaged shops in the Square, but they were never built (Lutyens left them out). Nor have they been allowed since: the ban, to the regret of some incomers, extends to cafés, pubs and any other signs of frivolity.

There is, though, a well-concealed post office along **Lyttelton Rd**, and on **Central Square** a library, schools, churches, a synagogue – and, for the moment, the Institute. Founded, with the Suburb, in the spirit of self-improvement, it's where you can take courses in everything from photography to pottery and where your au pair (this is very much au pair country) can learn English. Now, however, plans are for the Henrietta Barnett School to take over the building, and the Institute itself to move to new quarters on the site of the old Neurological Hospital on the Suburb's eastern extremity, near East Finchley tube. And it is this redevelopment that will – if it ever gets approved – also add two new blocks of flats to the sum of Suburb homes.

When it comes to disadvantages the major one (apart from the price of property), is transport. Neither Golders Green nor East Finchley stations are really close by, and those who don't drive or have access to a car are apt to feel stranded. There are no amenities for teenagers in the Suburb itself, though the area is great for small children. The Suburb mini-buses, the H2 and H3 'hoppas', run a circular tour from Golders Green station – prospective buyers might invest in a round trip to see the area. Ask the driver to stop when you see a house you like the look of; he'll halt anywhere along his route. When Suburb dweller needs to get out, the 102 bus connects to shopping therapy at Brent Cross.

Parking in the Old Suburb, which is full of closes and cul-de-sacs, can be problematic – particularly as few of the houses were built with garages. Agents highlight off-street parking if a property can boast it. Residents were not intended to have carriages or cars – especially the 'contented artisans' the founders hoped would populate the Suburb alongside the middle classes. Today, those in **Willifield Way** often resort to parking on the pavement, to the fury of Barnet Council. A number of traffic-calming measures have been introduced, in busy **Meadway** among others.

The whole Suburb is a conservation area, and you have to apply to both the Trust (hgs.org.uk) and to Barnet borough before making any alterations to your property right down to painting the front door – there's a list of approved colours – even if you own the freehold. Wily residents in need of extra living space have been known to develop very luxurious 'garages'. Matters like 'illegal summerhouses', satellite dishes (a 5-year licence may be granted on certain conditions), etc, command the attention of the Trust Committee – of which you cannot be a member till you've lived here at least three years.

Many of the houses are listed Grade II as being of significant architectural and historical importance – and many are 'starred' listings at that. In 1997 there was a mass listing of a further batch of more than 500 houses in the Suburb that had not been so designated before, and more already listed were given a star. This was the result of years of pressure by the Hampstead Garden Suburb Trust on English Heritage and the government. Most residents were delighted by the decision. In 2002, a photographer was appointed to record all 3,500 homes in the Suburb for the Trust's archive.

The Old Suburb

The area around **Central Square** and **Meadway**, and N up to **Addison Way**, is known as the Old Suburb – although it is actually not that much older than the New. Purists regard the Old Suburb as being just the tract W of Big Wood and N of the Heath Extension. Generally, the term 'old' is used for the NW11 part. The founders placed the 'artisans' cottages' to the N, and the middle-class housing to the S, with the really grand homes beside the Heath Extension.

Central Square, designed by Lutyens, is the heart of the suburb; a very green and peaceful centre, where you'll find neo-Georgian terraced houses and flats. Here, too, you'll find the parish church of St Jude, the Free Church for Non-Conformist worshippers, and (for now) the Institute, with its neighbour the Henrietta Barnett School for Girls. In the corner of **North Square** is a Society of Friends' Meeting House and a clutch of 3-storeyed, terraced town-houses that command around £1–1.5 million. In **South Square**, opposite St Jude's Church, is a block of 3- and 4-bed flats (£500,000-plus). Also some detached or semi-detached houses here; semis fetch over £1.5 million, while a 6-bed detached can be more than £2 million. . . . There's a memorial to Dame Henrietta on the fourth side of the square, and one of the Suburb's many passageways (the aim was to keep pedestrian and motor traffic separate) leads down to **Willifield Way.**

This is possibly the most charming road in the area, with a village green which is overlooked by Fellowship House, where the over-60s meet. A 3-bed terraced cottage on Willifield Way was £470,000 last winter. Many of the Suburb's younger residents attend the Garden Suburb School, also here – which means, however, that the Temple Fortune Hill end can be made hideous twice daily by 4x4-wielding school-run mums and nannies.

If your taste is for a cottage with roses round the door, then the roads around Willifield Way are where you should look. The first cottages to be built in the Suburb were at Nos. 140 and 142 **Hampstead Way** in 1907. They were designed by Parker and Unwin, who were strongly influenced by the Arts and Crafts movement – hence the traditional East Anglian cottages with medieval German vernacular gable, dormers and wooden window frames. Particularly charming are **Erskine Hill, Asmuns Hill** and **Asmuns Place** where you'll find 3-bed cottages with pretty gardens at up to half a million. **Erskine Hill** also has 3-beds, and larger terraceds and semis towards the North Square end.

The Orchard, nearby, is still inhabited by elderly residents, just as Dame Henrietta intended – though the original homes have been rebuilt. **Addison Way**, where the cottages and purpose-built maisonettes have slightly less character, leads into **Falloden Way**, the busy A1: 2-bed maisonettes backing onto the A1 can be had for around £220,000. Still, if you're immune to traffic or want to save money, houses here can have lovely views over Northway Gardens, where there are tennis courts. **Market Place** has flats on the two floors above the shops; there are also some purpose-built maisonettes (2-, 3- or 4-beds) tucked away on the **Ossulton Way** side, but these can be noisy, too.

Cross over the **Falloden Way** and you're on the 'wrong' side of the Suburb, although the roads are just as pretty and cottages in **Westholm**, **Midholm** and **Eastholm** (the names indicate how carefully planned the Suburb was) and in **Brookland Rise** and **Hill** are decidedly desirable – £400,000 for a 3-bed – and in 'the popular Brookland Primary catchment area'. **Hill Top, Maurice Walk** and **Midholm Close** all have purpose-built maisonettes, usually with their own gardens; **Brim Hill** has some £1 million houses.

Back in the main part of the Suburb, **Oakwood Rd** links **Addison Way** with **Northway** and the New Suburb. The road used to be something of a rat-run until traffic-calming was installed to dissuade motorists from using it as a short cut: this worked well.

South of **Central Square** is **Meadway**, the Suburb's main thoroughfare, which leads from **Hoop Lane** and Golders Green. Meadway Court, a mansion block, lies on the N side of the road, and leading off on the S side are the prestigious Closes, some of them private roads, where the 6- and 7-bed houses are the largest in this part of the Suburb. The three prime ones are **Meadway Close**, **Linnell Close** and **Constable Close**, their exclusivity added to by their location on the S side of the Suburb. Here 4–6 bed family houses can fetch anything up to £3 million. Unless you knew they were there, you'd never come across them; royalty have been known to lurk here. The same applies to **Linnell** and **Turner Drives** which both have terrific views over the Hampstead Heath extension: more top locations, along with **Turner Close**. Their detached homes are £2 million plus – if you can get one: these are 'nod-and-a-wink properties', say agents, though a 7-bed **Linnell Drive** house, with lots of car space, did appear on the market at £3.65 million last winter.

For splendid views – and splendid 6-bedroomed houses – look in **Wildwood Rd**, where an outlook over the Heath and Hampstead Golf Course commands top prices. At the Meadway end of Wildwood your budget might be around £700,000, but go S and you have to find over £4 million, while a home off Wildwood, in **Wildwood Rise**, went for £13 million a year or two back (it does have its own lake). **Heathgate**, just S of Central Square, has some 6-bed houses; it also gets richer as you go S. On the other side of the Heath extension runs **Hampstead Way** where you'll find Heathcroft, a large 1920s block not far from Golders Green station. Hampstead Way also boasts some splendid 5-bed houses that share coveted access to the HGS Trust-run tennis courts.

Towards the S end of Hampstead Way, near **North End Rd**, elite builders Octagon's Manor Heights development has added 16 houses and 35 flats.

The New Suburb

Suburb snobs are rather patronizing about the 'New Suburb', generally reckoned the N2 area, which lies E of **Ossulton Way** and **Kingsley Way**, plus **Northway**, **Southway** and **Middleway** back in NW11. It's true that the architecture is less interesting and the area is more densely planned, but the houses are large (and expensive), with grand gardens and plenty of space. Parking – difficult in the Old Suburb – is not such a problem here (though curbs around East Finchley tube have pushed commuter parking into **Brim Hill** and **Vivian Way**). Cars were considered a normal adjunct to life when the New Suburb was laid out in the 1920s/30s and were catered for (if not necessarily approved of) by the architects.

Holne Chase is the continuation of **Meadway**, and off it run the elegant **Spencer Close** and **Neville Drive.** Houses on the 'right' side of Neville Drive have a splendid view of the golf course: the architecture of the Drive houses is a mix of Art Deco and Cape Dutch, which does not stop prices rising to around the £3.5 million mark for the very best. Prices in **Kingsley Way** are not quite so eye-watering, though the favoured 'closed' end of the cul-de-sac can still ratchet up to £2 million. **Linden Lea** and **Norrice Lea** (where you find the Suburb synagogue) both have large family houses; often these are detached, and are always very much in demand.

North of the noisy A1 or **Lyttelton Rd** – where popular and good-value purpose-built blocks of flats include Widecombe Court, set back from the road – are roads like **Gurney Drive, Widecombe Way** and **Edmund's Walk**: all quiet, pretty and with the advantage of being nearer East Finchley station. Edmund's Walk has a convenient footpath through to the tube station, which means its pretty houses range up to a million – but check, this year, the plans for the redevelopment of the Neurological Hospital site, which may affect some homes. Westwards, at the top of **Ossulton Way, Neale Close** has purpose-built 2-bedroomed maisonettes kept private by hedges. Across the road, **Denison Close** has a popular block set around a pretty garden square. The 'Holm' roads (**Eastholm, Midholm, Westholm**) have smaller, villagy houses. This northern district is reckoned better for schools than the Surburb's heart: Brooklands Infant & Junior has a good name.

Fanning out from **Central Square** and counted as the New Suburb despite their NW11 postcodes, are **Northway**, **Middleway** and **Southway,** which are joined by **Thornton** and **Litchfield Ways.** Here you'll find large family houses with gardens to match in spacious hedge-lined roads at prices around the million mark.

The most expensive roads in the Suburb are **Ingram Avenue** and **Winnington Rd**, where prices outdo telephone numbers and the detached houses are huge and (particularly in **Winnington Rd**) rather ostentatious. The Sultan of Brunei owned at least three. The same kind of home can be found in corners like **Spaniards Close**, off **Ingram Avenue**, where your starting point is likely to be about £2 million.

Agents in the area also lay claim to the famous **The Bishops Avenue**, known with reason as 'Millionaires' Row' (though the Suburb Trust disclaims anything S of **Lyttleton Rd**). It is favoured by the ultra-rich international set as much for the privacy and security that the vast (for London) 2- and 3-acre plots afford as for the houses themselves, which are imposing, but undistinguished, mainly 1950s mansions (though most 20th-century decades are represented). There are more Middle-Eastern royals here than in Marbella. 'In the Middle East,' observes a knowledgeable estate agent, '**The Bishops Avenue** is probably the best-known road in London.' In 1991 King Fahd bought five more homes opposite his family's existing mansion – to house his guests. Recent prices range from £2.5–12 million, though you can spend more if you want to; the odds are no-one will ever know. There are sundry closes and private roads off it: prices much the same. Last winter's offerings included an 8-bed, 8-bath affair for £8 million – and a mansion boasting, among other things, an underground driveway for £35 million.

The roads E of the Avenue count as Highgate, which chapter see.

Transport No trains or tube, but Golders Green and East Finchley tubes are nearby. H2 and H3 buses do circular routes via Golders Green.

Convenient for Hampstead, Hampstead Heath. Miles from centre: 7.

Schools Barnet Education Authority: Henrietta Barnett (g), Whitefield School. See also Highgate and Hampstead chapters.

H

SALES

Flats	S	1B	2B	3B	4B	5B
Average prices	130–160	170–225	200–400	250–500+	350–500+	–
Houses	2B	3B	4B	5B	6/7B	8B
Average prices	250–450	350–650	510–850	700–2M	800–4M	2M+

RENTAL

Flats	S	1B	2B	3B	4B	5B
Average prices	150–200	175–250	225–400	350–650	475–700	–
Houses	2B	3B	4B	5B	6/7B	8B
Average prices	250–375	350–575	550–1000	750–1500	1000+	2000+

The properties Purpose-built century-old suburb mixing picturesque cottages with houses of all sizes including mansion scale. A few flats. 'Old Suburb' is smaller-scale, distinguished English-picturesque. 'New' (mostly in N2) has less special, more ostentatious larger, later houses. The Bishops Avenue sets hemisphere records for bad taste and high prices.

The market Inhabitants include international and Jewish families; many families long-established. Radical, doctrinaire even arty-crafty past is now a memory. Multi-million properties found on fringes of area – principally in The Bishops Avenue. These attract princes, showbiz stars and tycoons.

Among estate agents active in this area are:

- Glentree Estates
- Ellis & Co
- Kinleigh, Folkard & Hayward
- Godfrey & Barr
- Litchfields
- Goldschmidt & Howland
- Anscombe & Ringland
- Benham & Reeves
- Savills
- Foxtons
- Knight Frank
- Chesterton
- Felicity J Lord
- Hotblack Desiato
- Winkworth

HENDON AND MILL HILL

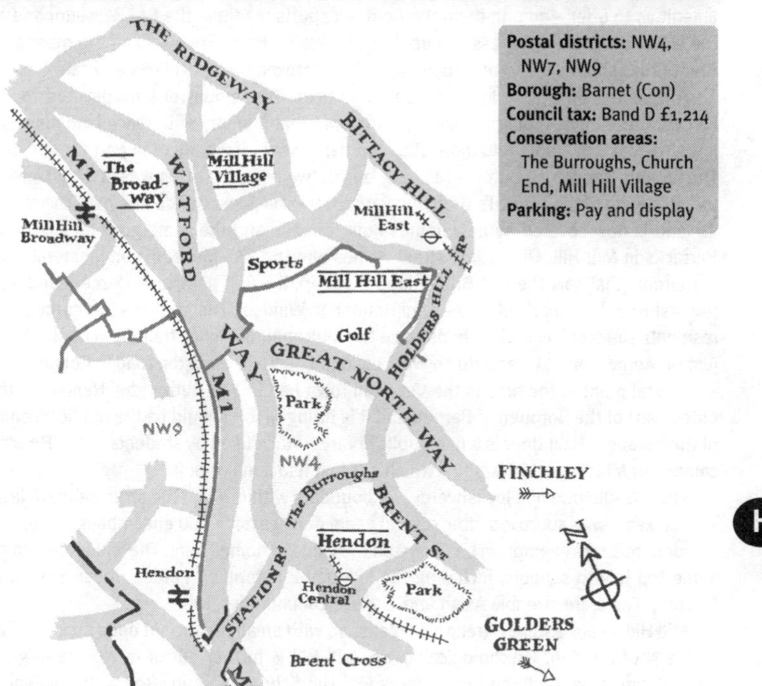

Postal districts: NW4, NW7, NW9
Borough: Barnet (Con)
Council tax: Band D £1,214
Conservation areas: The Burroughs, Church End, Mill Hill Village
Parking: Pay and display

All ways lead to Hendon – or at least through it. The Hendon Way, the Watford Way, the A1 Great North Way and the M1 motorway – not to mention the Edgware Rd, and the North Circular Rd which forms an eastern boundary. The area is a crossroads for all roads that lead somewhere else. Consequently, this suburb still divides into several old-style hamlets, each with its own identity.

If this means that there's no real centre, it also means that Hendon and neighbouring Mill Hill offer a wide variety of corners, never far from parks and playing fields – and Brent Cross shopping – including those where first-time buyers and/or those of limited means may get to scramble onto, or up, the homeowning ladder at prices they might (just) afford.

That said, the range has broadened perceptibly hereabouts, with the advent of a shoal of luxury-level developments. The homes market is a local one, with firm local reasons to buy undepinning it. Home to a sizeable Jewish community, the area gained from the introduction of the eruv (see below); it also basks in the growing realization that the Thameslink line to King's Cross will mean, in a couple of years, one change for Paris.

When Hendon Central tube station opened in 1923 it was surrounded by open fields – as witnessed by the 17th-century Church Farm House, still standing and today a museum. Hendon Hall in **Ashley Lane**, too, stands here still – complete with the famous but incongruous brick columns which the renowned 18th-century actor David Garrick reputedly won in a card game. He became Lord of the Manor in 1796 and set about rebuilding the Hall, these days a select hotel.

Such rural tranquillity is hard to imagine in the busy and congested suburb today; the 1930s saw a rash of speculative development – one of the biggest architects of this suburban sprawl being John Laing, whose headquarters were, and are, in Mill Hill's

Pursley Rd. (One of Laing's award-winning designs was first used to build the Sunnyfield site, off **Lawrence St** in Mill Hill.) Nevertheless, the area today has a wide range of amenities to offer – among them the Copthall sports stadium, the RAF Museum and all the water-sport activities associated with the Welsh Harp. Then there's the mammoth Brent Cross shopping centre: expanding, with improved transport links and cafés.

A reminder of a more spacious past has been the amount of land devoted to the Forces. These days, though, it pays to remember that Ministry of Defence land may well not stay that way: more and more sites are being sold off wholly or in part for housing. The famous Hendon aerodrome (actually one of two here; the other was in **Stag Lane**) is today the site of the council's Grahame Park Estate (see West Hendon below). The rest of its land is now covered by new homes built for sale, and the same goes for the Inglis Barracks in Mill Hill. Only some street names and the RAF Museum commemorate the aerodrome that saw the first British loop-the-loop, the first parachute descent and also the first British air-mail delivery – from Hendon to Windsor. The law likes this corner, too: residents sleep safely in their beds since the Metropolitan Police training school is here, just off **Aerodrome Rd** – and North West London Police HQ is up the road in Colindale.

A focal point in the area is the Victorian town hall in **The Burroughs**. Hendon is the oldest part of the Borough of Barnet, and it is fitting that it should be the political centre of the borough. Next door is a fine public library – much used by students at the Hendon campus of Middlesex University – which has just had a major refit.

H

The introduction of a Jewish 'eruv' – a boundary within which the strict Sabbath laws are relaxed – was approved after several years of discussion and encompasses much of Hendon: this rare exemption has boosted the value of homes here. The wider area holds some top Jewish schools, including the league-table-topping Pardes House School in Finchley. There are sizeable Asian and Chinese communities, too.

Mill Hill – contrastingly green and pleasant, with an abundance of open spaces – lies to the N of Hendon. Psychologically, too, Mill Hill is further out of town. The original village stands on a hill, and close by is Mill Hill School, built in 1807 with a splendid classical frontage. It was here that James Murray, a master at the school, edited much of the *Oxford English Dictionary*. Established for the sons of Protestant Dissenters, the school was originally known as 'an island of nonconformity in a sea of Roman Catholicism' – there are still several Roman Catholic institutions here, led by St Joseph's College in **Lawrence St**. Mill Hill is also home to the Medical Research Laboratory.

Cut off from the rest of Mill Hill by the roaring Watford Way is **The Broadway**, a busy shopping parade with bars, health-food shops, an M&S and buses both local and into town. The train station (15 min to King's Cross via Thameslink), is here, too; bear in mind that, around 2007, you should be able to change there for Paris (see Transport chapter.)

In fact, there's a good range of travel options spread across this sweep of North London. Apart from the road and motorway links – it's no coincidence that many a taxi driver hails from Hendon – both areas have a Thameslink mainline station, and are served by a scattering of tube stops. The Northern Line gets split ends here, with the Edgware and High Barnet branches running down to Euston and the centre of town.

Hendon

If you take a detour from the speeding roads, Hendon has homes to suit every taste: large detached houses in tree-lined **Brampton Grove, The Downage, Cedars Close**; retirement flats in **Church Rd**; rows of suburban terraces round **Montague Rd**, West Hendon; quaint cottages in picturesque **The Burroughs**; large and pricey new developments throughout.

Turning into **The Burroughs** from the **Watford Way** is a surprise. Immediately the grey commercial buildings, which match the busy road, make way for cottages and larger old houses converted into spacious modern flats. The old bus garage has become a luxury office block, changing the appearance of the street. **Brampton Grove**, the first on the right, is probably Hendon's most exclusive road – £3 million has been suggested for a top price here, with £1–1.5 million for a 'more regular' house. A 2-bed/2-bath flat in the Grove, £440,000. Just along the road from the imposing town hall, flanked by a modern library and fire station, is the beautiful corner of Church End, which has the Norman St Mary's Church in **Greyhound Hill** as a focal point. Next door, dating from the 17th century, Church Farm House is the borough's museum. It twice escaped the post-war bulldozers.

Between museum and church stands the Greyhound Inn, originally the Church House and used for parish meetings. Opposite the museum, the back of Middlesex University campus includes a fitness centre, which is open to residents. Further down **Greyhound Hill** the suburban semis are neat and tidy, just as the planners of the '30s imagined them: many with lovely green views, though the road is used as a cut-through from the Watford Way to The Burroughs/Church Rd and not as tranquil as it once was. One of those semis will be around £500,000, and a 5-bed detached was £600,000 last winter. Roads like **Sunny Hill** and **St Mary's Crescent**, with less traffic, are popular with students renting; c. £330,000 for a 3-bed semi here. Modern homes – flats and small houses – appeared in the late '80s W of **The Burroughs** on a large site, originally school playing fields.

Heading down Church Rd (permanently congested), **Sunningfields Crescent** and **Rd** are to your left: both pretty, both with plenty of flat conversions and more under way. Smart new flats grace **Sunningfields Rd**: c. £260,000 for a 2-bed with garden, while a 2-bed conversion flat was £235,000 last winter, and a 2-bed/2-bath/2-balcony flat sold for £299,950. **Sunny Gardens Rd** – one could be forgiven for thinking that Hendonites are sun-worshippers – runs N to a footbridge that leads across the A1 highway to the sports fields and golf course. It attracts buyers after big Edwardian semis and house-sized flats converted from them. This corner has its own pleasant Sunny Hill Park – and also a private hospital (4-bed semi, suit hypochondriac, c. £480,000); a school, too, which underpins house prices – though not, apparently, for those homes closest. . . .

Florence St, just off The Quadrant, is a real find: not as cut off as the Sunningfields roads, it has charming little houses set along a narrow street (a 3-bed sold for £340,000 last autumn. The corner of **The Quadrant**, once the local cinema, is now sheltered housing (the area is well supplied with homes and housing for the elderly). Quadrant Close is a 4-storey block of '30s mansion flats: short leases here – buyers take the likely costs of renewal (c. £20–100,000) into account. The Quadrant becomes **Finchley Lane**, which leads to the A1, where Nos. 133-135 now hold a new, turreted flats block.

Now turn N from The Quadrant down **Parson St**: this brings you to some of the premier streets in Hendon – **Downage** (a 4-bed house, £1.2 million), **Ashley Lane** and **Cedars Close** with its mock-Tudor houses set in a circle around little private gardens. **Tenterden Gardens, Tenterden Close** and **Tenterden Grove** are also nice (a 5-bed detached, £1.25 million), though homes at either end of **Tenterden Drive** may suffer a little from noise from the A1 – hence 4-bed semis range from £400–600,000. **Westchester Drive**, at the Parson St/Great North Way junction, is surprisingly unaffected by proximity to the main roads, and has small houses and the Westchester Court flats. Hendon Hall Court, next to the old Hall, has smart flats; several recent schemes in and around busy **Parson St** mean that while most 2-beds here cost £250–260,000, you can pay £325,000 – or £415,000: pick your luxury level. The market not being quite what it was, though, the stated price on new schemes can disguise a discount: a roomy 2-bed/2-bath in Christopher Court, views A1, comes with mortgage subsidy worth £12,000. Across the A1 divide, ever grander flats sprouted in leafy **Holders Hill Rd**, which runs up past the golf course to Mill Hill.

If Hendon could be said to have a high street, then **Brent St** is probably it. Here you'll find the mini-shopping centre at **Sentinel Square**, with its Tesco's and pay-and-display parking. Also many eateries – including one of only two kosher Chinese restaurants in the UK. New developments in progress here, and permission sought for another 160 1- and 2-bed flats. At the Golders Green end, a recent block dubbed 'The Carltons' by its developers has prices that rise, with the storeys, to half-million-plus penthouses. Or there's 1- to 3-bed flats, c. £135–185,000, in ex-council tower blocks nearby.

Bell Lane – with 2-bed conversion flats at c. £225,000 – leads down towards the **North Circular**; to the left, roads like **Alexandra** and **Albert Rds** have smaller semis and terraces (c. £300,000 for a 3-bed). Albert Rd is the site of Jew's College with its fine library. **Green Lane** and the roads around have large family houses and a number of synagogues. Local estate agents, when drawing up property details, list 'proximity to places of worship' as an asset second only to being close to the tube. The **Brent St** shops give way to a number of attractive '30s semis. South lies the Shirehall estate, where many of the detached (5-beds, £775,000–1 million) and semi-detached (a 3-bed, £550,000) houses have delightful views over Hendon Park. **Shirehall Lane**, which runs through the middle, is, however, used as a short cut by Hendon's shoppers on the Brent Cross trail.

Queen's Rd runs alongside the park down to Hendon Central tube – not to mention the health club (**Queen's Gardens** has the benefit of the park without the commuter-traffic drawback: some big, c. £800,000, detacheds with garages here). **Queen's Rd** itself has been the target for developers, both for new-build (two flats blocks have been added in recent years) and for luxury-level conversions: look in this street for spacious, expensive, bathroom-per-bedroom apartments and expect to pay accordingly.

To the N of Queen's Rd lie more of Hendon's best streets. **Brampton Grove, Wykeham Rd** and **Raleigh Close** have large family houses. They are particularly popular with Jewish residents due to the proximity of synagogues in **Egerton Gardens** (the Yakar centre) and in **Raleigh Close** itself, which is now gaining a new apartment block.

Station Rd runs down from The Burroughs to Hendon rail station and provides a link between Watford Way and Edgware Rd (crossing the M1 to do so). Here you'll find the popular High Mount block: good 2-beds from c. £235,000 – and a new scheme with 2-beds at over £300,000. Beside the hugely busy **Watford Way** is a recent Rialto scheme, The Harlequin: 2-bed flats resell for c. £220,000; 3-bed houses in 'this well-known location' as the agent has it (i.e., beside a six-lane highway) can nevertheless reach up to £380,000. The grid of roads off **Vivian Avenue** have 4-bed semis, less expensive as you near the M1 motorway. To the S of them lies Brent Cross shopping centre.

West Hendon, on the far side of the M1, is the cheaper end of Hendon. Shopping is not very good (the locals use Brent Cross) and the area, with its terraces and small semis, has a somewhat run-down air. However, it is convenient for the **Edgware Rd**, leading all the way to Marble Arch, and for the facilities of the Welsh Harp. Welsh Harp Village, entered via **Goldsmith Avenue** at the N tip of the Welsh Harp Reservoir, is one of this area's most popular developments. Its wide range of homes and prices – from studio flats to 3-bed houses – attract first-time buyers: a 2- or 3-bed terraced, c. £200–235,000). Beyond the police training centre, N, the problem-ridden Grahame Park council estate is late 1960s and looks like it – but massive, long-term rebuilding begins this year. The grim towers will go, replacing 1,314 flats and houses with 2,977 human-scale homes round a central boulevard. It's to be self-funding, with homes for sale funding the 36 per cent social. And across the way St George's plan a mixed-use scheme that will add another 2,800 homes.

Mill Hill

A trip to Mill Hill is in order for London house-hunters who would prefer to be in the country. It lies to the N of Hendon, from which it is cut off by the **Great North Way** (the A1) and a swathe of green open space that holds golf course, cemetery and playing fields. The link between the two is **Holders Hill Rd**, a major hunting ground for luxurious new homes – mainly flats, to take advantage of the views of the golf course. Look not only in the **Road**, but also in the **Crescent, Gardens** and **Drive**. Holders Hill Road sprouted a clutch of blocks in the '80s, more in the past few years; 14 2- and 3-beds are building now; two further schemes to come. One 2-bed example, £260,000, but depending on luxury level they can range on up to £300–400,000 – on a par with the 3-bed semis that this corner holds. Three of Rochester Court's six house-sized, 3-bed, £525–685,000 apartments are still available (we noted last year that £775,000 would buy you a 5-bed detached house in nearby **Manor Hall Avenue**, where drives hold many a Jag, Merc or BMW). Indeed, the key to Mill Hill is its range (in size, price, vintage) of homes, from humdrum flats to luxurious, Surrey-style new-build, and from everyday semis to large detached double-fronted period residences that lurk down drives in leafy locations.

Holders Hill Rd leads on up towards Mill Hill East. Mill Hill has a Thameslink station at The Broadway, but the tube line ends here at the bottom of **Bittacy Hill** – the cheaper end of Mill Hill: it doesn't venture up to the dizzy heights (in terms of both altitude and price) of **Uphill Rd**. Here the prices start high – say around £800,000 – and keep climbing till you've added a million. The E edge of Mill Hill has a popular riding school in **Frith Lane** that seems to take in every little North London girl – and quite a few showbiz types. And, indeed, **Bittacy Hill** now boasts French pâtisserie, organic butcher, fitness studio.

Mill Hill East is an attractive belt of suburbia with a carefully-planned grid of roads. Here the semis each have their own identity with a variety of modern windows and extensions. The main avenue, **Devonshire Rd/Sanders Lane**, radiates out relatively peacefully from **Holders Hill Circus**, overlooking Hendon golf course and Copthall playing fields. At the foot of **Devonshire Rd**, formerly overshadowed by huge gasometers behind **Bittacy Hill**, residents' prayers were answered: they've gone at last, leaving a major redevelopment site. This is to include a Waitrose supermarket and a Holmes Place gym, while Crest Nicholson are building avenues and squares of flats and houses, big and small; prices so far have been in the order of 2-bed flats from £240,000; 2-bed houses £285,000, 3-beds from £315,000. Retirement homes, too, here.

H

The former Inglis Barracks on **Bittacy Hill** is another tranche of MOD land that has been transforming into some 360 new homes – beginning with mainly 2-bed flats. Moving W, you come to **Pursley Rd**, **Page St** and **Wise Lane**. Houses here are fairly ordinary semis but, set in green open spaces, they are very pleasant. In 1998 John Laing added new 2- and 3-bed/2-bath houses (from c. £280,000), in roads such as **Colenso Drive** and **Ladysmith Close**, on the site of its former headquarters.

From there, climb **Milespit Hill** to **The Ridgeway**. Here, Mill Hill Village stands quiet and glorious, still with its village pond, overlooking the green fields. Not all the houses are old: a handful are 'modern architect-designed', as the estate agents say, but all are very des. res. In the village, **Hollies End** is a cul-de-sac just off the Ridgeway: a modern 3-bed here, £425,000.The **High St** belies its name: the nearest main shops are in Mill Hill Broadway. At The Ridgeway end, **Wills Grove**, which branches off to the left just before Mill Hill School, is charming, with larger houses and plenty of trees.

In the angle of **Daws Lane** and **Hammers Lane** lies Mill Hill's 'poets' corner'. This one is a surprise, with pleasant 4- and 5-bed houses (some now flats: 1-beds c. £170,000, 2-beds c. £210,000) in roads such as **Tennyson**, **Milton** and **Shakespeare**. Further along The Ridgeway at **Holcombe Hill**, where the Old Forge stands, lies **Lawrence St**, off which is Mill Hill's premier **Uphill Rd**. Houses in neighbouring **Sunnyfield, The Reddings, Uphill Grove** and the **Tretawn** roads have been extended in all directions; on gently undulating ground, they boast spacious gardens and views over of St Joseph's College grounds. Hill View is a recent flats block in **Victoria Rd**. But across it, and between the 'poets' and **Lawrence St**, the outpost of Green Belt land is the lower field of St Joseph's College. A furore has broken out: the missionaries want to sell it off for 400 houses, and to build 44 luxury flats in their grounds, to fund renovations. A public enquiry ensues. . . .

Flanking **Hammers Lane**, three little cottagy clusters are the Drapers', or Retail Trust, charitable homes started by Mr Marshall and Mr Snelgrove, of department-store fame.

Highwood Hill has larger-than-average old cottages along just one side – thus with splendid views – plus some 5-bed Tudor-style surburbia in the £800,000-and-up bracket;

off it, the very exclusive (reputedly haunted) **Nan Clarke's Lane**: a home here can cost £2 million plus – indeed, up to £5 million. Roads to the N of picturesque **Marsh Lane** such as **Hankins Lane** and **Glenwood Rd**, are equally pleasant upmarket residential turnings.

Back across **Watford Way** lies the area's high street: the shops and restaurants of **The Broadway**. A convenient corner, flanked by roads (A1, M1) and rail. Nearby Butlers Square added 24 new flats, and **Flower Lane** has seen several developments in recent years; here you can find £400,000-ish 3-bed, 2-bath town-houses, a handsome Georgian-style estate with 5-bed detacheds that can be over £700,000 – or there's the million-pound homes that appeared on the old tennis club site. **Russell Grove** and **Weymouth Avenue** are good roads with detached houses; **Newcombe Park** is popular too. West of the M1 are recent 2-bed flats, c. £220,000, in roads like **Grenville Place.**

Transport Tubes: Mill Hill East, Hendon Central (zone 3, Northern). From Hendon Central: Oxford Circus 30 min (1 change), City 30 min, Heathrow 1 hr 30 min (1 change). Trains: Mill Hill Broadway (King's Cross Thameslink 15–18 min).

Convenient for Brent Cross shopping centre, 24-hr superstores, Copthall Sports/Swimming Centre, Welsh Harp/Brent Reservoir. A1, M1, North Circular Rd. Miles from centre: 7.

H

Schools Barnet Education Authority: Copthall (g), Hendon School, Hasmonean (Orthodox Jewish) Schools (b) & (g), Mill Hill County High, St James's High RC, St Mary's C of E. Private: Mill Hill, The Mount (g).

SALES

Flats	S	1B	2B	3B	4B	5B
Average prices	120–150	150–200	180–400	200–400+	–	–
Houses	2B	3B	4B	5B	6/7B	8B
Average prices	200–270+	280–500	340–600	400–1.5M	500–2.5M	–

RENTAL

Flats	S	1B	2B	3B	4B	5B
Average prices	100–170	160–210	200–400	240–300+	–	–
Houses	2B	3B	4B	5B	6/7B	8B
Average prices	200–400	300–500	400–600	600+	–	–

The properties The 3-bed semi of inter-war vintage is most common; some larger prestige homes. A burgeoning number of new developments join flat conversions, plus smaller houses, including some ex-council. More space for your money here.

The market Popular for family homes: sizeable Jewish plus Asian and Chinese communities. Also commuting flat-dwellers, students renting and first-time buyers. Look to West Hendon for value, to Mill Hill Village to spend serious money.

Among estate agents active in this area are:

- Ellis & Co
- Winkworth
- Alexander Jay
- Martyn Gerrard
- Sole Estates
- Warren Bradley
- Jayson Russell
- Philip Phillips
- Bairstow Eves
- Douglas Martin
- Seymours
- Gerald Linke
- Culwick Lerner
- Talbots
- Caulfields
- Ashmore

Highgate

Postal districts: N6
Boroughs: Haringey (Lab), Camden (Lab), Islington (Lib Dem)
Council tax: Band D Haringey £1,259, Camden £1,200, Islington £1,107
Conservation areas: Highgate Village
Parking: Free so far, but threat of pay-zones. Congested in village and near tube

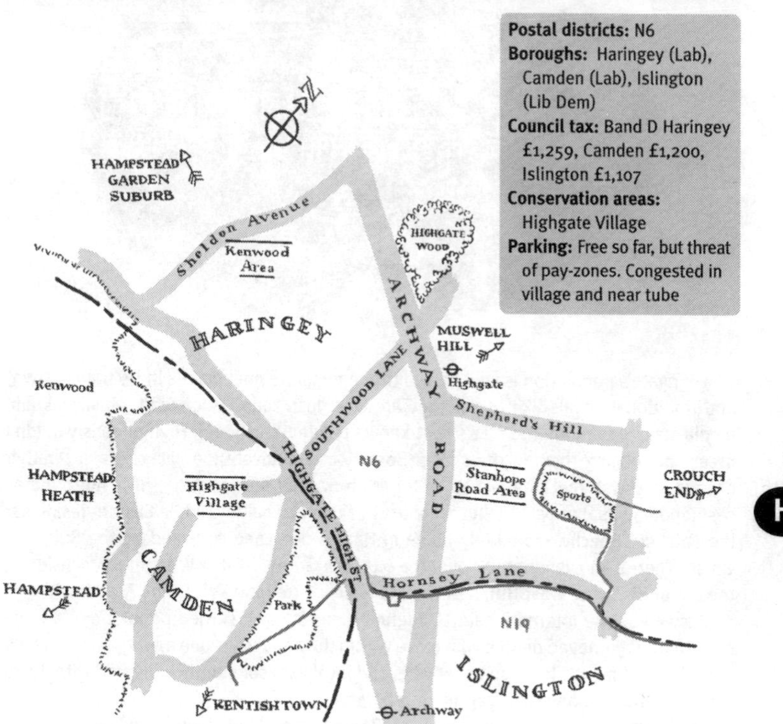

One of the old villages that command the 'northern heights' around London, Highgate has plenty of history and considerable charm. It was on Highgate Hill that the disillusioned young Dick Whittington heard the sound of Bow Bells and was persuaded to 'turn again' to resume his progress towards becoming 'thrice Mayor of London'. The alleged spot is marked with a stone and a statue of his famous cat.

Highgate lies just across the Heath from Hampstead, but its residents' claim that their village is just as nice – but without the noise, congestion and overinflated property prices – is wearing a little thin. Those prices have been steadily catching up with NW3: indeed, £3-million mansions with grounds and security gates are now as much part of Highgate as gentlemanly Georgian gems. Taking the wider area, Victorian and Edwardian is more common than Georgian, which is found only in the heart of the village. The 20th century added blocks of flats and suburban houses of every level from modest to opulent, plus a surprising selection of the sort of modernist homes which excite architects. Little new building goes on here: look to Hampstead for new flats.

A Highgate home has long been the dream of many a North London resident. Recently, prosperous families have been deserting Camden Town and Islington in search of schools and gardens. The increasing buying pressure in Highgate created its own overflow into the rest of N6 (especially the section E of Archway Rd), Muswell Hill and Crouch End – areas that, until the '80s and '90s, were fairly sleepy enclaves with relatively stable property prices.

Highgate's population is well heeled (there are more millionaires in N6 than in NW3) and traditional: locals like to say they are less flash than Hampstead. Musicians and media stars are among the area's best-known residents – though Highgateans wouldn't dream of noticing them in the shops. Some locals cultivate the village air in a rather exaggerated way (hacking jackets in the High St, that sort of thing). It is not quite as cosmopolitan as Hampstead, but there are pockets of wealthy Middle Eastern residents: the splendid Beechwood stately home in Hampstead Lane is owned by the Sultan of Oman. There's an even grander pile: the 64-room Grade II-listed Witanhurst mansion at the top of **Highgate West Hill**, now a conference centre (and TV's 'Fame Academy').

As well as the international set, Highgate has its own settled population: 'a huge base of local moneyed people who move within the area,' says one agent: estate agents hate this as it means few homes for sale, and locals are constantly badgered with flyers asserting that 'we have a buyer for your home. . . .'

Highgate shares with Hampstead the 800 acres of fields, woods and ponds of the Heath – owned and managed by the City of London Corporation – plus the grounds of Kenwood, where wonderful open-air concerts are held during the summer. Kenwood, a beautiful Adam mansion, houses the Iveagh Bequest, a notable collection of old masters. The W side of the village, towards Kenwood, is amazingly rural: **Merton Lane** even has a farm. This, with a scattering of cottages and the winding, wooded lanes, makes this a corner more like Hampshire than Hampstead Heath – all that's missing is the slow tractor ahead of you (school-run mummies in gas-guzzlers are N6's equivalent).

Transport is less than ideal, however: Highgate tube is well N of the village off **Archway Rd.** Its escalators periodically break down – a daunting problem given that it is one of the deepest stations in London. The 'hoppa' bus from Parliament Hill makes slow but useful progress to Regent's Park and on across to Liverpool Street, and the new Muswell Hill to Hamsptead bus has made a real difference. Archway Rd is a red route leading to the A1 and is busier than ever: its congestion spills up into the village.

Highgate village

This is what residents reckon is Highgate proper: the old village, still recognizable as such, with its accretion of lovely homes that have offered fresh air and sylvan views to prosperous Londoners from the time of Elizabeth I onwards. It is bisected by **Highgate High St**, with its smart shops ('wicker-basket and bulging-wallet' ones, says our spy) and restaurants. Locals use Muswell Hill for everyday shopping – though a Tesco Express has opened on the High St, leaving many locals appalled ('It hits the corner shops and it's *ugly*!'). The High St is the boundary between Camden Borough in the S and Haringey in the N. The main residential section of the village is on the Camden side, including the marvellous **Pond Square** with its 18th-century houses, late-Victorian mansion flats and the headquarters of both the Highgate Society and the Highgate Literary and Scientific Institution, side by side in **South Grove** at one end of the square. South Grove House, standing opposite Witanhurst and the internationally famous Flask pub, is still one of the most desirable blocks of flats in the village, or you can pay £895,000 (though no-one was queuing to do so last winter) for 'the *tiniest* cottage'. Houses in **Highgate West Hill** range from cottages through 4- and 5-bed houses to a handful of 17th-and 18th-century gems and some amazing £3-million modern houses. The premier address in the village is, however, **The Grove**: a row of houses of which some date back to the 1680s, set back from the road behind an avenue of trees. Grove residents have included pop icons and film stars (it's noticeable that brasher celebs like footballers and pop girls choose Hampstead, Highgateans sniff). Houses in The Grove command £3.5–6 million. **North Grove,** just across Hampstead Lane, has some modern neo-Georgian houses.

Off The Grove is **Fitzroy Park**, an exclusive, gated private road that leads to several sumptuous and secluded homes, plus the 24 luxury houses in **Highfields Grove**, an enclave in seven acres of the Witanhurst grounds. This 1988 estate is very popular, though gardens are small. Near the bottom of **Fitzroy Park**, which leads directly to the Heath, is a splendid 15th-century house called Fitzroy Farm, set in well over an acre of land adjoining the Heath. Here, too, is newly built Birch House: it and next door Moate House are on the site long owned by the Soviet Embassy. If you prefer Regency, The Elms (1838, 3.5 acres) is being virtually rebuilt and may be back on the market soon. H

Back at the village, the terraced houses in **Bisham Gardens** are almost all converted into flats which, on the S side, have stunning views towards the City over Waterlow Park (one of London's most delightful parks) and the extraordinary Highgate Cemetery which, apart from being the last resting place of Karl Marx, is a major tourist attraction – guided tours are given (but at a price: £20). **Highgate West Hill** starts in the Village with some superb Georgian houses, some Edwardian ones (a large, newly smartened one was £1.8 million last winter) and ends, on the N6 border, with some well-regarded, spacious Victorian mansion flats (a 2-bed, c. £400,000).

Swain's Lane with its Victorian homes – many split into flats – leads down from the village to enclose, with **Highgate West Hill**, the cemetery and the Holly Lodge Estate. This enclave on the site of Baroness Burdett-Coutts' estate has a mixture of houses and blocks of flats (the flats became council-owned, but most are now private once more) built in the 1920s in a mainly mock-Tudor style which is either smashing or vulgar, depending on your point of view. **Hillway** forms the spine of the estate. A Holly Lodge 2-bed flat was £285,000 last winter; a 5-bed house, £1.3 million. Next door on **Swain's Lane** is **Holly Village**, a delightfully eccentric group of Gothicky cottages built in 1865 around a 'village green'. Also popular is **West Hill Park**, an award-winning estate of flats and houses built in the 1970s in **Merton Lane**, overlooking the Highgate Ponds.

The Haringey side of the village, N of the **High St**, is slightly less dramatic, but has some lovely leafy and secluded streets holding a mixture of semi-detached houses and converted flats – and even a few large post-war blocks of flats such as Southwood Hall, Cholmeley Lodge and Northwood Hall. Particularly popular are the spacious Victorian houses in **Southwood Lawn Rd**, **Cholmeley Park** and **Crescent** (a good range of 3-bed flats here, 1930s–2000s, £450–600,000), and **Cromwell Avenue** with some fascinating flats in a converted church (a 1-bed, £250,000). Note, too, the modern houses set around a communal garden in the triangle between **Hillside Gardens**, **Jacksons Lane** and **Southwood Lane**. The latter has a new terrace of half a dozen 5-bed houses, converted from an old hospital. They sold last year for £1.25–1.65 million. Opposite, the old sorting office will become a health club. Parking can be difficult: tube-bound commuters use these streets, though a CPZ will be introduced soon on nine roads near the station.

Kenwood

Hampstead Lane leads from the village around the N end of Hampstead Heath to the grounds of Kenwood House. Directly opposite Kenwood are expensive roads lined with mini-mansions such as **Courtenay Avenue, Compton Avenue** (a well-thought-of, gated private road), **Sheldon Avenue** and **Stormont Rd** – all a stone's throw from **The Bishops Avenue** (better known as Millionaires' Row) in the borough of Barnet. These streets lead to Highgate Golf Club in **Denewood Rd.** Prices of £6 million are normal, and sums regularly go well over £10 million. For more see the Hampstead Garden Suburb chapter.

Other roads in the area encircle the spacious grounds of Highgate School (which also owns a lot of property in the vicinity), such as **Bishopswood Rd, Broadlands Rd** and **View Rd.** Mostly traditional large houses, but a sprinkling of new properties as well. On the corner of **View Rd** and **North Hill** stands a clutch of recent (2002) 5-bed, 4-bath houses, plus a dozen mews-style homes. Some smart new flats too, in a converted drill hall. **North Rd** and **North Hill** have some Georgian houses, (one, which was a prep school, sold for £2.5 million last year) and also large mansion blocks, including the architecturally renowned 1938 Highpoint, which has the distinction of the highest rooftop in the whole of London (flats from c. £375,000) and a swimming pool to boot. Also worth a look are the mixed homes in **Talbot Rd, Bishops Rd, Bloomfield Rd** and **The Park.** Note that the **Archway Rd** ends of these streets suffer from the heavy traffic.

Stanhope

East of **Archway Rd** is a clearly defined area bounded in the N by **Shepherds Hill** and **Priory Gardens** (a sought-after cul-de-sac leading to Highgate tube – which, however, brings parking problems), in the E by **Coolhurst Rd,** and in the S by **Hornsey Lane.**

Shepherds Hill, with modern blocks of flats replacing the semis, has great views to the N over Muswell Hill and Alexandra Palace and Park for those homes whose outlook is not obscured, and dramatic views to the S for others. Blocks like Panorama Court and Highgate Heights are well named, though Stanhope House is the most popular. Two-bed flats along here start (as last year) around £350–400,000.

The area is bisected N–S by **Stanhope Rd** which carries most of the traffic, leaving other streets relatively free. The prime road is **Hurst Avenue** which has very large houses overlooking the playing fields of nearby St Aloysius Catholic Boys' High School. **Avenue Rd,** at the bottom of the dip, has a row of blocks of flats on the S side (built in the '80s much to the disgust of the house- and flat-owners across the street). The main drawback of this area is its distance from public transport – it's a stiff walk in either direction to Archway or Highgate tube stations, although there are buses along **Archway Rd** to the City and West End. An important feature of this area is the Parkland Walk, formerly the route of the old railway that ran from Finsbury Park to Alexandra Palace, turned by Haringey Council into a nature trail and wildlife reserve that's very popular with walkers and joggers. Houses alongside, or with access to, the Parkland Walk are much in demand.

'The Miltons' is an enclave made up of **Avenue Rd, Stanhope Rd, Hornsey Lane, Milton Park** (large houses, mostly split into flats), **Orchard Rd** and **Claremont Rd. Parkgate Mews** is a 1997 development of 16 flats and four houses in **Stanhope Rd. Milton Park Avenue** and **Milton Park Rd** have a good selection of smaller flats and houses which get less expensive the closer they are to **Archway Rd.** Miltons houses are £500–600,000; you can find spacious 2-bed flats from £230–300,000. Lots of purpose-built flats in **Avenue Rd** and **Hornsey Lane,** including the huge Northwood Hall block.

Borders

South of Hornsey Lane is an attractive group of streets called the Whitehall Park Conservation Area (in Islington borough), with well-preserved Victorian terraces in **Whitehall Park, Gladsmuir Rd, Parolles Rd, Miranda Rd** and **Harberton Rd.** The lure is a decent family house for around £500,000, and a short walk to Archway (zone 2) tube.

The boundary with Muswell Hill has some interesting streets, including **Lanchester Rd** with its 5-bed houses and **Woodside Avenue** (now a no-through-road and thus up in price) behind Highgate Wood; and the group of streets surrounding Queen's Wood, including **Onslow Gardens, Connaught Gardens, Summersby Rd** and **Wood Lane.**

On the Kentish Town border, St Peter's Church in **Dartmouth Park Hill** has become nine distinctive flats, most boasting amazing stained-glass windows. Less-fashionable **Beaumont Rise** has new 2-bed flats in 'The Citadel', while at the bottom of **Highgate Hill** The Academy, once a Victorian school, has 1- and 2-bed flats (£300–330,000). St Christopher's Court in **Junction Rd,** just S of Archway, has expensive flats. **Archway** itself, with its '60s shopping mall and traffic intersection, is best avoided.

Transport Tubes: Highgate, Archway (zones 2/3, Northern). Highgate: Oxford Circus 25 min (1 change), City 18 min, Heathrow 1 hr (1 change).

Convenient for Hampstead Heath, Kenwood. A1/M1, City. Miles from centre: 5.

Schools Local authority: William Ellis (b), Acland Burghley, Parliament Hill (g), Highgate Wood. Private: Highgate (now mixed), Highfield, Channing (g), St Aloysius (b). See also Hampstead.

H

SALES

Flats	S	1B	2B	3B	4B	5B
Average prices	120–175	190–250	220–600+	280–600+	500+	–
Houses	2B	3B	4B	5B	6/7B	8B
Average prices	350–500	400–700+	550–1M+	500–1.2M	→2M+	–

RENTAL

Flats	S	1B	2B	3B	4B	5B
Average prices	150–230	180–250	200–550	300–700	350–500+	–
Houses	2B	3B	4B	5B	6/7B	8B
Average prices	250–450	350–575	400–1000+	500–2000+	600–5000	–

The properties The roads around this ancient hill village hold not only 18th-century houses, but some 1680s ones. Victorian terraces and converted and purpose-built flats have been added, plus large and ever-more-opulent mansions, town-houses and coveted private estates, from 1930s to present-day.

The market The thinking star's Hampstead, say locals: musicians, media folk and the professions buy here, joined by exalted foreign potentates for the large mansions in vast grounds. Flat-buyers get glorious views. Prices and range of homes vary widely.

Among estate agents active in this area are:

- Anscombe & Ringland
- Prickett & Ellis
- Winkworth
- Kinleigh Folkard & Hayward
- Day Morris
- Sturt & Tivendale
- Stonebridge
- Benham & Reeves
- Mendoza
- Taylor Gibbs
- Fitzroys
- Goldschmidt & Howland
- Hamptons
- Heathgate
- Knight Frank
- Savills
- TMD
- Barnard Marcus
- Litchfields

HOLLAND PARK

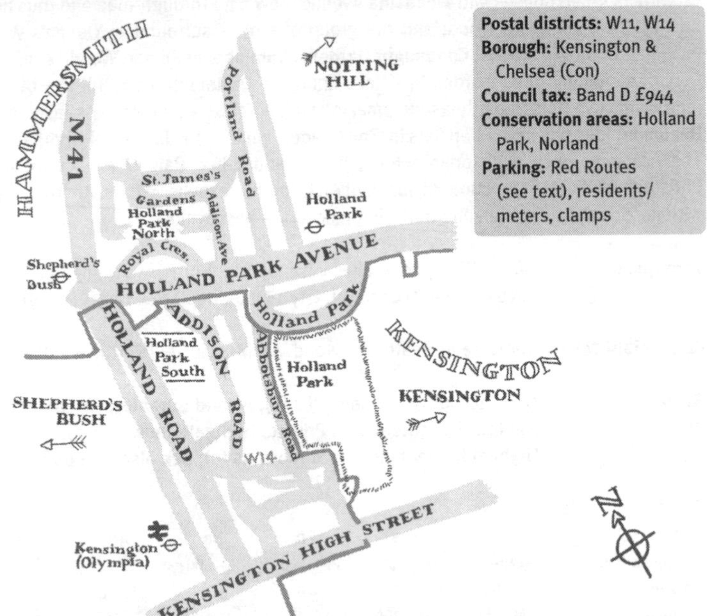

Postal districts: W11, W14
Borough: Kensington & Chelsea (Con)
Council tax: Band D £944
Conservation areas: Holland Park, Norland
Parking: Red Routes (see text), residents/ meters, clamps

Holland Park is one of the luckier parts of London. Lucky to have been in the right place at the wrong time. Or with the wrong homes. Perhaps because Notting Hill, with its then-raffish connotations, was a little close, most of Holland Park escaped the knock-down-and-build-flats boom of the 1960s and '70s. Its early-Victorian elegance remained intact, if seedy. In the 1940s and early '50s the grand old monsters were hardly saleable; you will, should you look back at the figures, be mortified that your grandfather didn't buy a detached 9-bed mansion for the family for £8,000 in 1954. By 2000 they commanded £12–15 million, having reached £3.5 million by the late 1980s.

The past few years – since mid-2001 – have been quiet, with the word 'cautious' used to describe market sentiment, and a commensurate drop in prices across the board. But the sense of solidity prevails. There are still buyers for the gracious white mansions, and they can still reach top prices – but now condition is all, and one of these can take three years for a serious modernization job. But a lot of people who live here – and who want to live here – are really, truly rich. If you want a rather startling example, three old garages in a muddy half-acre of land were due to become a super-sized, 22,000 sq-ft mansion for an oil sheikh – until the three householders whose homes backed onto it clubbed together and bought the plot, for £8.8 million.

Green and spacious, the area known as Holland Park covers the western flanks of Campden Hill and boasts the biggest concentration of large houses in the Royal Borough. 'The area known as' is said with care, since there's Holland Park (the park) and also **Holland Park** (the road – which isn't exactly: it's more a sort of square, in the middle of which is sandwiched **Holland Park Mews**); the grandest, largest, ambassadorial residences – some *are* embassies – are here. On the S side is the park, on the N side, the busy **Holland Park Avenue**, which runs westwards to even busier Shepherd's Bush roundabout. 'The area known as' fans leafily out on either side of the broad, tree-lined

Avenue: southwards it runs between the park and **Holland Rd**, down towards the W end of **Kensington High St**. Here there is further confusion in the shape of **Holland Park Rd**, which is right at the S of the area. Northwards the area has, over the years, been pushed upwards into Notting Hill and Notting Dale to take in the pleasant corners between **Portland Rd**, **St James's Gardens** and **Royal Crescent**.

H

The big Victorian mansions make wonderful flats, if split, and also have their fans as stand-alone houses. Add to these a number of late-20th-century flats/town-house developments, usually set in their own landscaped grounds, some big apparment blocks, and the small mews cottages with their garages that are the legacy of the horse-drawn age, and you have a neighbourhood with a very good range of home sizes and styles – though not of prices. Nothing is cheap. This variety has attracted families (schools, the park, communal square and crescent gardens), City people (the Central Line goes straight there) and Hampstead-style politicians, actors and media people (the BBC mega-HQ is down the road at Shepherd's Bush). And now ambassador-level personages and international millionaires, plus a sprinkling of stars, have completed the circle and reinhabited the ambassadorial-sized homes, reclaimed after years as rented flats.

Today, the pleasant, community feel is added to by small, villagey shops and good restaurants. Thanks to the neighbouring areas' amenities, there's been no incentive to clutter up the place with big supermarkets, etc – some locals are up in arms at the arrival of a modest Tesco Metro near the tube, deeming its bright facade too brash. Most streets are within strolling distance of **Kensington High St** or **Notting Hill Gate** for cinemas, clubs, pubs, restaurants, shops; several leading stores line Kensington High St. By 2007, when the monster White City development is ready over on the far side of the M41 West Cross Route (see Shepherd's Bush chapter), Holland Park will have West London's answer to Brent Cross to hand – though locals fret about the traffic it will generate. As it is, **Holland Rd**, **Addison Crescent** and the S part of **Addison Rd** are a Red Route.

Another attraction is the amount of green space in the shape of Holland Park itself and nearby Kensington Gardens. The Park covers 55 acres of woodlands and formal gardens, sports, adventure play park, ecology centre, the Orangery and Ice House for art exhibitions and private events – and an open-air theatre for popular summer plays and concerts.

Because of the embassies in the area, this has long been a favoured place for top-flight renting. The big blocks of flats in Holland Park South, and the converted mansions in the heart of the area, offer apartments of enormously varying sizes and characters. There is usually a choice of family houses with gardens and parking: plenty of these, too, are being revamped – and the quality on offer rises yearly.

Holland Park South

Tree-lined **Holland Park Avenue** sets the tone for this choice neighbourhood made up of large houses and leafy gardens. Vast stucco, or brick-and-stucco, mansions set back from the road behind sloping front gardens spread along the southern side of the busy avenue. Some have been hotels; indeed, one pair are about to be turned back into 14 flats. More pairs of large brick-and-stucco houses split into flats lie to the W, beyond the smart shops and restaurants clustered around Holland Park underground station. You can pay £2 million-plus for one of the few undivided houses or, at the other end of the scale, anything from £210,000 (a basement) to c. £380,000 for 1-bed flats.

But the most coveted of imposing Victorian mansions are found in **Holland Park** (the road). Many of these double-fronted, detached, creamy stucco houses still have their decorative, highly ornate cast-iron and glass entrance canopies. (This delightfully idiosyncratic feature sits strangely, to be honest, on the dignified, pillared entrances: they date from a little later than the houses, which were built 1860–80, and look for all the world as if they were sketched in as an afterthought by Ronald Searle.) Many have been divided into sybaritic flats that are particularly popular with the diplomatic community – security video cameras are a regular feature of the area. Some mansions are indeed used as full-blown embassies, but the council's Unitary Development Plan states that planning permission to convert houses into embassies will now be granted less readily.

H

As for the whole houses, it just depends who's in the market, and to what level the place has been done up. Recent sales have attracted £10.25 million, £12.5 million; one, 'beautifully restored and backing onto the park' (which adds a couple of million), was on for £15 million last winter; another was reputed to have changed hands privately for £17 million. Prices for the flats in converted villas vary as widely, with size, individuality, condition, lease length and proximity to the park all affecting the price. Examples last winter ranged from a 1-bed at £380,000, 3-beds for £900–1,295,000, a 2-bed at £1.8 million, to house-sized garden maisonettes – a 4-bed with 50ft drawing room for £3 million and a 2-suite, 3 reception room one with self-contained studio at £4.5 million.

Lying between the N and S arms of the street, through a stone arch, is **Holland Park Mews**, lined by 2-storey cottages with garages. Note that **Holland Park** (the road) and its mews take the W11 postcode, together with the streets N of **Holland Park Avenue.**

Holland Park merges with **Abbotsbury Rd**, which runs southwards along the W side of the park itself: the postcode changes to W14. Abbotsbury has humps in a bid to slow traffic down, but it's still a popular route from **Holland Park** to **Kensington High St.** Most of the homes on the W side of the street are from the second half of the 20th century, from the 10-storey flats block, Abbotsbury House, at the NW end to the series of select, private, neatly landscaped 1960s cul-de-sacs, some with garages, which make up **Abbotsbury Close** (4-bed houses, c. £1.2 million). This is the deepest, most secluded part of Holland Park, select even for Kensington. Urban grime seems a world away.

One of the most consistently popular places to buy in Holland Park is **Oakwood Court**, a complex of 7-storey red-brick Victorian mansion-flat blocks which together form the street of the same name. A strip of lawn, trees and shrubs divides the blocks on each side of the street. The mansions were refurbished a few years back, and prices start around £300,000 for a 1-bed flat and go up to £800,000-plus for a 4-bed, depending on lease and condition: a vast, 2,950 sq-ft one was £1.9 million. On the corner is a modern development of 3-storey red-brick homes and some matching red-brick flats called Manderley. **Ilchester Place** opposite is leafy and salubrious: the big, low-built houses, some with gardens backing onto Holland Park (the park), can be 8-bedroomed: one such, needing work, sold for £4.75 million recently.

Melbury Rd to the S is noted for its vast, artist's-studio houses designed by the likes of Norman Shaw and Halsey Ricardo. An outstanding example is the eccentric red-brick Tower House, a copy of the Welsh Castell Coch. Built in the 1870s, it was renovated in the 1960s by actor Richard Harris. The houses are a legacy of the days when **Melbury Rd** and parallel **Holland Park Rd** formed a 19th-century artists' quarter. There are several more big, red-brick detached studio houses, including Leighton House, once the home of painter Lord Leighton, now a gallery and museum: it's a temple to high-Victorian living – and a superb venue for chamber music, attracting all the top names. The size of these mansions, built on the scale of country houses, merit price tags such as the £13.5 million asked for one with 19 bedrooms.

Needless to say, this sort of scale makes for spectacular flats in those that are converted. These include the erstwhile home of pre-Raphaelite artist Holman ('Light of the World') Hunt, and a pair designed by architect Halsey Ricardo for his father-in-law and his patron, respectively. They are nowadays six huge apartments of which the smallest is a mere 1,723 sq ft (3-bed, 3-bath, 3-recep) and the most impressive the vast 4-bed/4-bath/3-reception room one of 3,036 sq ft – excluding its two terraces, conservatory and 76ft private garden. Another spectacular conversion, of sculptor Sir Hamo Thorneycroft's 1870s studio, produced three flats. There are also less extreme houses, many divided into flats.

To the S of **Melbury Rd**, near the **Kensington High St** end, grand houses are punctuated by exclusive modern flats. Woodsford is a 5-storey red-brick development, Stavordale Lodge a 5-storey slate-coloured block, just refurbished and with private parking, while **Park Close**'s nine storeys of flats overlook both the park and the Commonwealth Institute grounds.

H

The S side of **Holland Park Rd** forms **St Mary Abbots Terrace**, a modern development of neo-Georgian town-houses. The 3-storey, near-a-million houses are set around a series of three cul-de-sacs. Some are turned sideways on to the street, their rear gardens adding to its leafy look. At the end of this terrace, facing Addison Rd, lies a 9-storey apartment block. Opposite is a private road, **Strangeway Terrace**, with its water sculpture and the attractive flats of Monckton Court. It is closed to through-traffic from Holland Park Rd to Melbury Rd.

This S end of **Addison Rd**, up to Addison Crescent, forms part of the southbound one-way traffic system, which detracts from the character of an otherwise exclusive road – it contains, among others, one of London's grandest homes, built in 1905 for millionaire draper Ernest Debenham and designed by Ricardo (see Melbury Rd above). It is now listed Grade I and, having been vacated by the charitable Richmond Fellowship, is currently the setting for a reality TV show with an 'upstairs/downstairs' theme. Detached and semi-detached stucco and brick-and-stucco villas, and a terrace of gothic-style houses, line the road's W side. Opposite them are two large modern blocks, 10-storey Monckton Court and 6-storey Farley Court: both are set in landscaped grounds off the road. The S curve of **Addison Crescent** forms the link in the Red Route one-way system between Addison Rd and Holland Rd. This short stretch of, again, detached and paired villas consequently suffers from heavy traffic and noise, which does not stop people spending extravagant sums on them. The N curve, with its big 2/3-storey detached brick-and-stucco villas with walled front gardens is noticeably quieter and more desirable. Traffic or not, these enormous villas make enviable homes.

Grander white stucco-fronted detached villas line the W side of the more peaceful, N stretch of **Addison Rd**, set back behind securely walled gardens and small sweeping driveways. On the opposite side of the road is a group of detached and semi-detached houses, including the intriguing glazed brick-and-tile Richmond House. Selby Court, a 9-storey block of flats, lies between **Somerset Square**, a modern development of red-brick town-houses and flats, and **Woodsford Square**, a 1970s development of large town-houses c. £850,000–1.3 million. Both are set in landscaped grounds walled off from the road behind a shield of trees. Homes at the N end of Woodsford Square overlook the Holland Park tennis club, tucked in behind **Holland Park Gardens.** Holland Park Mansions, a 4-storey red-and-white block on the E side of the Gardens, also overlooks the courts. There's always a choice of rental flats here.

At the N end of **Addison Rd** next to Cardinal Vaughan School stands Addisland Court, an 8-storey brick-and-stone 1930s block, which stretches around the corner into wide, exclusive, Victorian-streetlamp-lined **Holland Villas Rd.** Opposite this stands the 4-storey modern Parkland flats. The large brick-and-stucco detached villas in this quiet, leafy street require a budget of £6–8 million (one, with eight bedrooms and swimming pool, sold at £7.95 million last year). Off the NW end of **Holland Villas Rd** are **Upper** and **Lower Addison Gardens,** both tree-lined streets of 3-storey terraced houses. At the top end, near Holland Park Rd, Fitzclarence House is a modern development of 27 flats.

Holland Park North

Enter **Holland Park Avenue** from the Shepherd's Bush roundabout end, and you find, on its N side, beautiful **Royal Crescent.** Two curving terraces of white-painted, 5-storey homes sweep around a tree-lined semicircular garden with ornate iron railings. Each of the end houses has graceful circular pavilions to finish the row, and the whole crescent appears to have been transported from Regency Brighton. Alas, it gazes out on the unfortunate 1970s Kensington Hilton rather than the English Channel. Expect, nevertheless, to pay c. £2 million for a house, c. £300,000 for a 2-bed flat. Tucked in behind the W side is the curve of **Royal Crescent Mews,** with a few period homes, but also a 1980s terrace of 2-storey brick-and-stucco cottages with their own garages.

St Ann's Villas, which leads off **Royal Crescent,** is a relatively busy local road much improved by residents' parking. It has a mix of houses and flats – notably a group of Victorian Gothic detached brown-brick gabled houses. Cutting W–E through this street is **Queensdale Rd,** a pleasant and very popular street of Victorian terraced houses. Boundary changes here brought **Queensdale Crescent, Norland Rd** and **Kingsdale Gardens** into the Royal Borough rather than Hammersmith. At the end of **Norland Rd,** facing onto Queensdale Rd, stands a splendid Sikh temple with a roof adorned with gold. Norland Rd is made up of pastel-painted stucco-and-brick houses with railings, and is closed to traffic: the resulting mini-plaza had a pub and shops – but the shops have gone, making way for offices with flat and a pair of 2-bed mews cottages behind. Across from the houses a large Victorian house has become social housing, with next to it another development of Affordable Homes. Norland House, set behind these, is a 22-storey council block: still Hammersmith's baby despite the boundary change.

The best stretch of **Queensdale Rd,** E of St Ann's Villas, has 3/4-storey, with basement, brick and pastel-painted stucco houses. Three-bed houses here command up to £1.3 million. Off it, **Queensdale Place** is a pleasant little cul-de-sac of 2-storey stock-brick-and-stucco terraces, to which was added a spectacular trio of new homes, one with indoor pool. **St Ann's Rd,** the northern continuation of St Ann's Villas, has some pleasant 4-storey houses, giving way to smaller ones, then modern flats. There's a small shopping complex with flats above, forming part of the council-built Edward Woods Estate with its three tower blocks. Work is ongoing to smarten the estate: one low-rise block has been replaced by 122 new homes, half housing-trust ones to rent, the rest sold from c. £190,000 for 1-beds. Flats in the low-rise blocks can be 3-beds, which have attracted buy-to-let buyers at c. £285,000 when they appear for sale.

Addison Place, off the opposite side of Queensdale Rd, is lined by a variety of period and modern 2-storey mews cottages (c. £500,000 for a modern one, £650,000 for period) and ends in cobbles. It curls round behind the E parade of Royal Crescent, debouching into **Addison Avenue,** the showpiece of the area with handsome 2-storey houses and a few incongruous stockbroker-Tudor ones. The best stretch of this wide tree-lined avenue with its splendid vista of St James Norlands Church lies N of Queensdale Rd. Elegant paired stucco houses painted in pastel shades line both sides. The smaller pairs S of Queensdale Rd give way to an attractive parade of shops and offices: permission is awaited to turn one building into flats and to build a new mews house behind. Green Victorian street lamps add to the avenue's period character. Opposite is **Taverners Close**, with a row of mews houses and five red-brick detached houses.

St James Church sits in the central garden of **St James's Gardens** – another of the neighbourhood's choicest addresses – which also has the Spanish and Portuguese Synagogue. Pairs of attractive, £2-million-plus, 3-storey-plus-basement houses linked by paired entrances surround the communal gardens (one was £2.6 million last autumn). The lower floors of these handsome houses are painted in pastel shades.

Return down Addison Avenue to Queensdale Rd and turn S into **Queensdale Walk**, a tranquil cul-de-sac of 2-storey painted cottages, E, facing a long garden wall with overhanging trees. North into **Princes Place** are three 2-storey homes, plus a 3-storey block of housing trust flats. One street away is **Norland Square**, which opens out at the S end onto Holland Park Avenue. The three terraces of 4-storey-plus-basement stucco-fronted houses (c. £2–2.5 million) stand around their large, tree-filled central garden with tennis court. Parallel to the square runs **Princes Yard**, with modern flats. Off the square runs **Norland Place**, a cobbled mews of 2-storey painted cottages (one with a newly-added modernist frontage), which stretches through to **Princedale Rd**. Princedale Rd has mainly Victorian terraces, a mix of houses (£1–1.7 million for the 4- and 5-beds) and flats, plus speciality shops and popular pub near the junction with **Penzance Place**. Here the homes are individually coloured. More brick-and-stucco terraces, too, next to St Clements & St James primary school, and there's a modern 6-storey flats block.

Penzance Place with its flat-fronted Victorian rows leads into **Portland Rd**, another popular street of Victorian terraced houses, many converted into flats. Homes on the E side are more expensive (over the million; a 6-bed was £2.5 m last summer), being wider and with larger gardens. The road is sealed off to traffic at **Clarendon Cross** – a smart villagy enclave of posh shops, galleries, antique shops and restaurants/wine bars.

Lying behind the NW side of Portland Rd, across the road from Avondale Park with its tennis courts, is award-winning **Hippodrome Mews**. Two terraces of 3-storey brown-brick town-houses face each other across a narrow cobbled mews in this private cul-de-sac (1970s). The pleasingly bulbous shape of an old kiln, as high as the houses, is preserved among them, and no doubt accounts for the name of **Pottery Lane**, which, running S from here, has an attractive group of 3-storey painted brick-and-stucco terraced houses at its junction with Penzance Place. The top end of **Pottery Lane**, and part of **Princedale Rd**, are now in the Norland conservation area.

Clarendon Rd, which parallels Portland Rd to the E, marks the start of the climb up Notting Hill (which chapter see). Many of the big Victorian semis and detacheds are now flats; of those that remain whole, some have changed hands at starry prices – you can pay anything from one million to five here. . . .

Borders

Holland Rd is a major traffic artery running down to Kensington High St from the M41, which ends at Shepherd's Bush roundabout. Its S end is one-way: the traffic flows N, while the S stream dives down the bottom half of **Addison Crescent** into **Addison Rd**. A series of small hotels clusters around the S end of **Holland Rd**. The rest is lined by mainly stucco, or brick-and-stucco, terraced houses of varying quality. Those not in hotel use are split into flats. Double-glazing is cited in sales details: you'll need it. This is where you look if prices in Holland Park proper make you go as white as the stucco: a 1-bed flat might be £200–250,000. **Napier Place** is a contrast – a wide, peaceful cobbled mews only yards from the traffic: a 3-bed cottage here sold at £625,000. **Russell Rd** to the W has more hotels and flats in the 3-storey-plus-basement terraces (1-bed flats, c. £240,000) overlooking the increasingly busy West London railway line and the glass facade of the Olympia Exhibition Centre.

Russell Gardens has small local shops and restaurants, plus a pub and flats. **Russell Gardens Mews** has working garages at its S entrance, giving way to 2-storey cottages towards the rear. Properties at the NW end of tree-lined **Elsham Rd** also back onto the railway. Here a 2-bed flat might cost £250,000, with ones with garden c. £290–350,000 – while a large 3-bed asked £550,000. Beside the railway is a development of new homes by Barratt, which has boosted the neighbourhood.

Transport Tubes: Holland Park, Shepherd's Bush (zone 2, Central); Kensington Olympia. To Oxford Circus 12 min, City 22 min, Heathrow 50 min (2 changes). Trains: Kensington Olympia.

Convenient for BBC TV Centre at Shepherd's Bush, M4/M40 to Heathrow and the West. Direct tube line to West End, City. Miles from centre: 3.5.

Schools Local Authority/Foundation: Holland Park School, Cardinal 6th-Form College, Cardinal Vaughan School (b). Private: Norland Place School, Notting Hill & Ealing High (g).

H

SALES

Flats	S	1B	2B	3B	4B	5B
Average prices	150–250	215–500	280–800	450–1.3M	650–2M	900–2M+
Houses	2B	3B	4B	5B	6/7B	8B
Average prices	400–900	550–2M	750–3M	1.1–5M	3.5–10M+	8–15M+

RENTAL

Flats	S	1B	2B	3B	4B	5B
Average prices	150–300	250–600	300–800+	450–1500	750–4000	1500–4000
Houses	2B	3B	4B	5B	6/7B	8B
Average prices	350–850	500–1500	700–4000	1300–5000	3000–5000	–

The properties Vast, snowy-white villas and terraces, imposing Victorian red brick, smaller-scale squares, modern town-houses – all gather round Holland Park and Avenue. Rich source of family homes, flats converted and mansion, ambassador-level grandeur, in leafy streets. Some new conversions and mews houses to be found.

The market Firmly in the top bracket: prices reflect that it is N of Kensington, rather than next door to North Kensington. The embassy-sized houses have reverted to multimillion-pound status after years as tatty flats. International and City jitters felt at top end here.

Among estate agents active in this area are:

- John Wilcox
- Cluttons
- Anthony Sharp
- Cavanagh Smith
- Marsh & Parsons
- John D Wood
- Winkworth
- Savills
- Hamptons
- Anscombe & Ringland
- Chesterton
- Faron Sutaria
- Foxtons
- Scotts
- Jackson-Stops & Staff
- Chesterfield
- Aylesford
- Tates
- Barnard Marcus

Islington and Highbury

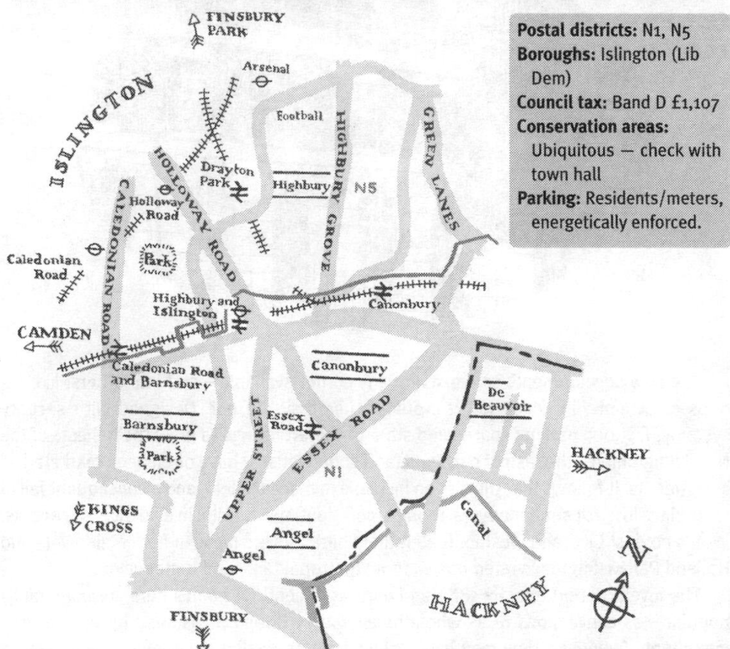

Postal districts: N1, N5
Boroughs: Islington (Lib Dem)
Council tax: Band D £1,107
Conservation areas: Ubiquitous – check with town hall
Parking: Residents/meters, energetically enforced.

Football, until now just something Islingtonians talked about over supper to display their streed cred, is the catalyst for the big developments here. Arsenal FC's well-advanced plans to build an enormous new stadium, and the knock-on schemes for the use of its old one and related sites, will – say opponents – fatally overcrowd an already claustrophobic corner of London. Supporters are equally vehement about the 2,000 new homes, the new shops, the leisure facilities.

All this seems a world away from the serene terraces of Canonbury and the elegantly raffish bustle of Upper Street. But the opponents of 'VizionN7' (not a misprint but the tag for the homes phase of the Arsenal development) have a point. Traffic gridlock is only a Volvo's-length away in much of the area, much of the time (especially during school terms). The tubes stagger to cope already, the cross-town North London Line – so useful on the map, so prone to disruption in actuality – must await a successful Olympic bid (!) before it can be properly upgraded.

The fuss over the Highbury end of the area distracts attention from perhaps a more important trend, the adding of a 'new Islington' to the old. The new takes the form of smart flats, in secure complexes over underground parking. These homes attract a rather different kind of inhabitant from the traditional Islington terraces.

Fast transport to the City by the much-improved Northern Line tube, and on to Docklands via the DLR from Bank, as well as easy access to the West End, brought the new breed of well-heeled buyers to Islington. It never quite made it in the '80s, the area as a whole staying cheerfully scruffy – though decidedly 'up-and-coming' throughout – while individually its Georgian terraces were fought over. Then came the boom years of City bonuses. . . . Now **Upper St** is one of London's smarter locations, with designer-chic and coffee shops from the Angel up to Highbury Corner.

The new developments squeeze into any corner available – and into others, like ex-pubs or schools, in which locals would rather they did not. Designed with security systems, £35,000 parking spaces and state-of-the-art fittings to meet the behests of the New Islingtonians, the rash of new flats (and some houses) have often been marketed as investments. It follows that there is an increase in places to let – and a consequent fall in rents since '01. Investment buyers, though more cautious, are still in evidence, say agents.

It's not just City (and West End) high-fliers here. Buyers move in from Maida Vale and Holland Park: Islington is rated busier, more metropolitan – and better value.

I

The lovely, period (mostly 18th- and early 19th-century) homes here are perennially popular – as conversions or as whole houses. Very British pleasures, these; and their inhabitants (wherever they may have hailed from originally) are somehow very British folk. The international jet-set do not appreciate, as do we, the inconvenience of the tucked-away, charming – but often narrow-gutted, many-staired – houses, however Georgian the terraces. ('The madness of King George is explained,' claimed one owner.)

But for all its inhabitants, old or new, city-slickers, lawyers or middle-class radicals in 'the Arts', Islington, with Highbury to the N, is a most satisfactory place. Due N from the City, the area lies E of **Caledonian Rd** and King's Cross, W of **Green Lanes** and thus Hackney/Stoke Newington, and S of Finsbury Park (**Gillespie/Mountgrove Rds**). It has a definite shape, which starts from the southern baseline of **Pentonville Rd/City Rd**, unfurls on either side of the central spine of **Upper St**, and is neatly capped by Highbury with its green, open fields. Then, too, it is set on pleasantly hilly ground for variety; it boasts a village green to offset the commercialism of the S end; also theatres (the internationally renowned Almeida, the King's Head and the Union Chapel), clubs, galleries, a canal – and real gems of residential corners, which are made all the more pleasing by the fact that through-traffic struggles along the main routes without suspecting their existence.

The area divides into four neighbourhoods: the Angel, Canonbury and Barnsbury make up Islington; to the N lies Highbury around the green open spaces of its Fields. The southern fringes, around Sadler's Wells theatre and S of the City Rd, is outside N1 and is disputed with Clerkenwell, which has its own chapter. The **Pentonville Rd/City Rd** shoreline is now even more of a Great Divide, since this is the northern boundary of mayor Livingstone's congestion-charge zone.

As with other London boroughs (Camden, Wandsworth), be aware of the distinction between Islington the place and Islington the borough, ruled (if that's the right word: they'd prefer guided) from its town hall. The borough is by far the bigger. Islington – the place – is reckoned to encompass most of N1, while Highbury is fairly neatly N5.

Follow **Essex Rd** as it forks off along the E side of **Islington Green** to reach Canonbury, Islington's heart, and its most pricey neighbourhood. A popular spot since the days of Elizabeth I, it thrived under the Georges and still has fine terraces from that period in its leafy roads. Mainly family-sized terraces, but flats and some larger houses, too.

Barnsbury, to the W of **Upper St**, is just a little later: a stock-brick-and-stucco land laid out by Cubitt (see Belgravia) in the 1820s. This is almost exclusively family housing, more completely residential in character, arranged in pretty streets around half a dozen garden squares. However, its fiendishly maze-like traffic scheme is no longer stemming the tide, and has been made more complex still, with chicanes and a 20mph speed limit. There have been complaints that the combined effect of street closures in Barnsbury and humps on Liverpool Rd have made Upper St more congested than ever.

The Angel corner, aside from offices, has some glorious flat-fronted Georgian and early-Victorian rows tucked away to the E of **Islington High St**. Front gardens are rare, but some streets have central greenery – or water: the Grand Union Canal runs here, with new 'loft-style' homes round its basins. Roads tend to be narrower, widening towards the N, where streets in the angle of **New North Rd/Essex Rd** have larger houses and more flats.

By contrast, Highbury is virtually all Victorian, aside from roads bordering Highbury Fields. Generally you'll find more ornate, late-Victorian houses with broader avenues and gardens, split between flats and family homes. Some large properties in **Highbury New Park** and **Highbury Hill** – if you can find one that has not been chopped up into flats.

Once here, people tend to stay. Families, though, have to consider schooling. Even Tony Blair balked at sending his kids to the local state schools; many families move out once offspring reach secondary age (Muswell Hill is a favourite). A ray of light is the plan for a new Church of England 'Academy' secondary school in Liverpool Rd, planned for 2006, and more funds for the others announced by the aforementioned T. Blair.

The Angel

The Angel is the gateway to Islington, spreading northwards from the baseline of **Pentonville Rd/City Rd** at the junction with **Islington High St**, where Angel Square, a big office complex over the tube, provided a new entrance to the underground with London's longest escalators. **Islington High St**, **Upper St** and adjacent roads are Islington's main shopping streets. From the High St westwards to **Penton St** there's a mix of offices and flats, with several recent developments. One such runs N from **Pentonville Rd** to **White Lion St**, which also gained a further cache of live/work and flats a year back.

Running W–E is **Chapel Market**: it still has one, for fruit and veg. High-street stores are in **Liverpool Rd** – now joined by the £25 million Parkside shopping mall, with all the big names, inevitable (though welcome) multiplex cinema (but the revived Marquee Club didn't last). Curving around a new, open square in the angle of Liverpool Rd and **Parkfield St**, its advent swallowed up some favourite little shops, restaurants and an entire street, Layton Rd. On the site of the Angel School, which locals fought to save, are 50 new flats (1-beds £270–415,000, 2-beds £335–440,000) and four houses (£560,000).

Back across **Upper St**, on the E side just before the Green, is the distinctive Mall antiques arcade; behind this, and parallel, are **Islington High St** (a surprise: it's more of a charming lane) and **Camden Passage** (an equally confusing name), a great centre for antiques. There's also a farmers' market on Sundays in the Mall. Antiques and small, old-fashioned shops continue down **Essex Rd**, mixed with new bars and designer stores. Homes here, too, including Georgian houses and new flats squeezed into vacant corners.

To the S and E of the Angel junction, in the busy and once rather run-down corner between and around **City Rd** and **Goswell Rd**, smart new flats are appearing. 'Angel Southside' has 98 flats by Grove Manor Homes between Goswell Rd and **St John St**. The scheme, completed in 2002, has a 'Virgin Active' gym. A 2-bed resale here was £415,000 last autumn (same as a year before). Along the **City Rd**, 'Angel Central' is a smaller (23-flat) scheme, while **Goswell Rd** has Delph Property's 14-flat scheme (£425,000–1 million).

Back N of City Rd, the area to the E of **Upper St** and **Essex Rd** is by contrast quiet and residential, and almost exclusively glorious flat-fronted Georgian terraces. Streets are narrow; parking is restricted. When the graceful rows of **Duncan Terrace** and **Colebrooke Row** first faced each other in 1768, what separated them was not today's strip of greenery but the New River – the first attempt to supply London with clean water. A 4-bed house in **Duncan Terrace** 'in need of refurbsihment' was at £1.85 million last winter. Off Colebrooke Row's later, N, end, **Bridel Mews** is a rare new mews: 3-storey homes, all contemporary curves in designer-industrial style. **Colebrook Place** just opposite gained a similar scheme in 2002: three loft-style apartments and nine houses around a private garden.

Vincent Terrace has fine Georgian houses with lovely views onto the Grand Union Canal; across it, on the N bank, **Noel Rd**'s houses turn their back on the water, and thus have sunny raised gardens that stop at – or rather, above – the towpath: the Hanging Gardens of Islington. South of **Vincent Terrace** and W of the City Rd Canal Basin, houses tend to be smaller, streets narrower and more mixed towards the City Rd: **Elia St** has low Georgian terraces on one side, low council-built blocks on the other. There's now a cache of 80 flats to rent – thus the fate of the old St Marks Hospital in **City Rd**. Between the two canal basins, **Wharf Rd** marks the borough boundary.

If you want a waterside home, City Road Basin on the Islington side, and Wenlock Basin on the Hackney side – see also City chapter – are the current building hot-spots ('The Canal Quarter' in property-speak). On the completed and lived-in list are the 90 'lofts' of the Royle Building, and 49 loft-style, galleried live/work units in the Wenlock Building, **Wenlock Rd**. The W side of **Graham St** has (would you believe, but this is N1) 'The Angelis', Goldcrest's latest offering: 24 1- and 2-bed flats (about half with water views), at £395,000-plus for the 30 per cent as yet unsold. Off Graham St, Grove Manor's striking 'Angel Waterside' late last year still had two flats in the first phase, 'Palazzo', for £395–595,000 – *sans* water view. Next comes phase 2 'Crystal Wharf' where a 2-bed waterside flat is £500,000. Persimmon's Wenlock Works added another clutch in 2003. For more canalside homes see the City & Fringes chapter.

Back N of the canal, at the corner of **Packington St** and **Prebend St** is the Packington Square Estate, which may be demolished due to gas safety fears. From here, across E to **Southgate Rd** and the borough boundary, are some fine period terraces (mainly family houses) known to estate agents as The Arlingtons. Streets are wider, squares and trees more common, parking easier, prices higher. **Arlington Avenue** and **Square**, with tucked-away **Clock Tower Mews** (pioneer of modern mews re-creations, a 3-bed house £500,000 last winter), are typical. **Wilton Square** is also particularly quiet and fine; the Victorian terraces E of **New North Rd**, around **Baring St**, are an improving corner. Union Wharf, a 2001 mews of seven canalside houses off **Arlington Square**, includes the old Lock House: high specs include garages/parking, rooftop conservatories.

Essex Road

The streets that lie NE of the **New North Rd**, between **Essex Rd** and the borough boundary at **Southgate Rd**, are more mixed, with different periods appearing in the same road (witness the 8-storey tower block in **Elizabeth Avenue**). The neighbourhood has predominantly flat-fronted, substantial terraces, and some houses are double-fronted. Other streets are later, such as **Elmore St** and **Northchurch Rd**. Dover Court council estate is just beneath the **Essex Rd/Balls Pond Rd** junction.

This corner attracts developers, too: The Pinnacle's 19 flats, complete with rooftop terrace and Japanese garden, appeared in 1999. Nearby, off Ockendon Rd, **Ockendon Mews** is a cobbled courtyard redevelopment of ex-industrial buildings. The Royal George on **Essex Rd** has succumbed and is reborn as a town-house and three 1-bed flats, and the old cinema on **New North Rd** is now 14 new flats. On the corner of **Englefield Rd** and **Southgate Rd** is Croft Homes' clutch of 1- and 2-bed flats, while 'OneNI" brings more flats to Southgate Rd (1-beds from £200,000).

Islington Green and Canonbury

Upper St is the main artery of Islington, running N into its heart – where **Essex Rd** forks off to the NE, at **Islington Green.** The leafy triangle of the Green has seen a blossoming of new homes: the key site on the N side, in the sharp angle between the two roads, now holds 'The Angel on the Green' by Grove Manor Homes: 1- to 3-bed flats and penthouses round a courtyard with angel sculpture. Then LondonTown added seven roomy flats plus house-sized 3-bed penthouse, next door to the Slug & Lettuce pub. More new flats on the adjoining site behind Waterstone's, too, in a Piers Gough-designed scheme that is supposed to be adding a new theatre to Islington on the site of the 19th-century Collins Music Hall. The scheme has shops, restaurants too, and the 74 flats called, would you believe, 'N1rvana', are all sold. Details of the theatre are sadly elusive, with a Shakespearian replica now firmly off the agenda and a 300-seat studio on it. Nearby, Sager's '8 Islington Green' has 21 flats, with curving copper roof, set around a zen garden. Little passageways and courtyards (like **Dagmar Passage**, with a 2-bed cottage £575,000 last winter) continue N up to the period terraces of **Florence St** and **Cross St.** Beyond these are the red-brick mansion flats of **Halton Rd** and **Canonbury Villas.**

Running NW and intersecting with the Essex Rd is **Canonbury Rd**: the heartland of Canonbury lies in the triangle between these two, with **St Paul's Rd** at the top. At the Essex Rd/Canonbury Rd junction is **Essex Rd** station, with a service into Moorgate on weekdays; the 66 flats of Melville Place are just opposite. Georgian flat-fronted rows on either side of **Canonbury Rd** give way to modern council blocks just before **Canonbury Square**, a superb Regency square with terraces of tall, thin houses round the central garden. One of Canonbury's most prized corners – but not as peaceful as you'd expect, since busy Canonbury Rd cuts across. A 5-bed house was £1.4 million last winter.

I

Round the corner we rejoin the main Upper St where **Compton Terrace**, a fine, lofty Regency row, is set back from the road behind a sheltering line of trees and a garden. Houses here are marketed at c. £2 million. Just to the N, Upper St and Canonbury Rd meet at Highbury Corner, the busy junction beyond which Highbury begins. Eastwards from Canonbury Square, **Compton Rd** has tall Georgian terraces that give way to double-fronted houses where it joins **Alwyne Villas**' broader-fronted rows. On the corner with the Georgian **Canonbury Place** you'll find Canonbury Tower, a romantic 16th-century Tudor relic: this is a last remnant of the monastic manor house.

To the N along **St Mary's Grove** are a whole series of neo-Georgian homes, low flat-fronted terraces culminating in **John Spencer Square** (a house here – with a garage – £575,000 last autumn). At the end of Canonbury Place, the road splits into **Grange Grove** and **Canonbury Park North** and **South**. The area is very mixed: modern semis nestle with mock-Georgian ones, which rub shoulders with the real thing – and a few even older survivals. Grove Manor Homes squeezed nine neo-Georgian houses and 25 flats into **Canonbury Park South** to such good effect that they received a 1998 Civic Trust award. At its corner with **Willow Bridge Rd** is an imposing red-brick Victorian mansion, which sets the tone for the rest of that street – quiet, spacious, covetable early-Victorian semis (c. £1.8 million) . This, along with **Canonbury Park North** and **Alwyne Place, Rd** and **Villas,** holds Canonbury's Victoriana: particularly large and grand in **Alwyne Rd.** A 4-bed Canonbury Park South house was £1.4 million last autumn. Houses in **Alwyne Villas** share a communal 'secret garden', a survivor from the old Canonbury manor that included the tower (see above).

Between **Alwyne Rd**'s back gardens and those of **Canonbury Grove** to the S, ran the New River – built in the 17th century as London's first proper water supply. It now ends in

Stoke Newington, but a replica channel runs through a small, linear park from St Paul's Rd down to Canonbury Rd – the charming New River Walk. Willow Bridge Rd crosses this, leading to **Canonbury St**, where two new flats blocks offer a contrast to the big houses.

Across the New River, in the angle of **Essex Rd** and **St Paul's Rd**, are the quiet, low-rise council houses, maisonettes and walkways of the (former) Marquess Estate, which is centred around **Clephane Rd**. Unmanageably large, it is now being carved up and remodelled (and renamed New River Green) in a £57 million partnership between council, Housing Corporation and private developers Copthorne and its parent Countryside. The transformation – well under way, Phase 5 now completing – is yielding 308 new homes and 845 refurbished ones.

You'll have to cross to the Highbury side of the **St Paul's Rd** highway to find Canonbury's little station (North London Line), and a handful of shops. **Wallace Rd**, which leads to it, has fine, tall, flat-fronted terraces on the right, on the left later ones with good front gardens – and in 2002 gained 'Terrazza', Laing's new, curved terrace of 3-bed town-houses. To the E are the fine terraces of **St Paul's Place** and **Northampton Park**. Much of the area W towards Highbury is large period houses, cheaper (comparatively) near the tracks or along busy **St Paul's Rd**.

Barnsbury

Liverpool Rd, running N from the Angel, is the main avenue of the Barnsbury side, and is typically composed of flat-fronted brick terraces. The streets to the E of it, across to **Upper St**, are not strictly Barnsbury but may well be referred to as such by estate agents. Eight little mews houses have been squeezed in here (£525–665,000). **Barford St** has the smart Business Design Centre, with its glass arches. North is **Old Royal Free Square**: early-90s flats and houses converted from a hospital. Next, the fine **Gibson Square**, and above this **Milner Square**, an 1840s creation completely restored by the council in the 1970s. A modern development around the corner mimics its rather eccentric, vertical style. East lies **Almeida St**, home of the renowned Almeida Theatre and of the latest Terence Conran restaurant. Small period terraces continue up to **Islington Park St**. An old pub at this end of **Liverpool Rd** was recently transformed into 10 smart 2-bed flats. Looming over the Almeida corner is the proposal for a 4-acre complex of shops, offices and flats, taking in the redundant Post Office depot and running across to **Gibson Square**. Islington Council has vetoed the scheme, amid much local opposition, but the developers have vowed to appeal.

Barnsbury *proper*, a tract of homogeneous residential groves laid out – by Cubitt, among others – in the 1820–40s, stretches westwards from **Liverpool Rd** across to the **Caledonian Rd**. In the best Islington traditions, this stock-brick-and-stucco land is a secretive corner. Its peace is unassailable, courtesy of an outsider-proof one-way system – just beefed-up still further with several road closures: maps are issued to friends. To the S **Ritchie St** and **Bachelor St**, with their neat terraces and first-floor balconies, border on the Angel and end in Culpeper community garden. Continue W along **Tolpuddle** (Culpeper St, if your A–Z is an old one) **St**, which intersects with **Barnsbury Rd** and **Penton St** running S–N. To the W **Copenhagen St** crosses Barnsbury Rd and curves round to meet the **Caledonian Rd**; S of here are the Pentonville council estates.

Cloudesley Rd runs N from Culpeper Gardens, and to the W is Barnard Park – a rare open space for the Islington area, it boasts tennis courts. To the E is **Cloudesley St** with its wide avenues and dignified double-fronted houses, leading into the superb **Cloudesley Square** – 1820s Regency, with the Celestial Church of Christ in the centre, and seven-figure price tags for 4-storeyed, 4-bedroomed homes here, if anyone will sell. Richmond Avenue runs W from Liverpool Rd, and connects with the Caledonian Rd; off it is **Richmond Crescent** (former home of T & C Blair), with larger, 6-bed houses. Also off the Avenue is the secluded **Lonsdale Square**, substantial terraces of – a sudden shock –

heavily Gothic styling: the only high-Victorian square in the area, and one of the first corners to be 'gentrified' in the early-1970s rediscovery of Islington. Nowadays the 5-bed houses are £1.5 million or so; in 1970 they were £15,000; in 1966 £8,000.

North of this is the ivy-clad **Morland Mews**, one of the few modern developments; this corner, taking in **Lonsdale Place, Barnsbury St, Gissing Walk**, saw some rebuilding around 1970. Then we regain 1820's terraces in **Brooksby St** and **Bewdley St**, which lead into **Barnsbury Square**: sadly this has not survived intact, though it is the site of the original monastic moated farmhouse and grange. It boasts some large (7-bed) homes. Back S lies delightful, hilly **Ripplevale Grove** – small, tidy cottage terraces and gardens – and, to the W, **Thornhill Square**, a fine Regency cache of substantial homes; its curved end mirrors **Thornhill Crescent** (where a 5-bed house was £1.375 million in December). **Matilda St** runs S, with the 1995-built **Bramwell Mews**. **Thornhill Rd** has some double-fronted, £2 million-plus, houses. Barnsbury ends with the Caledonian Rd: mostly small, old shops, cheerfully and irredeemably scruffy, though tidying. **Offord Rd** marks the N limit of Barnsbury. Close to the tracks (and station), lined with Georgian houses, it runs E to join Liverpool Rd by the 1910 Samuel Lewis red-brick flats.

Highbury

From the fulcrum of Highbury & Islington station at Highbury Corner, **Holloway Rd** runs off to the N, and the E–W **St Paul's Rd** neatly divides Georgian Islington from Victorian Highbury. In the angle of these two roads Highbury unfurls around its Fields, with **Highbury Grove/Park** neatly bisecting the area. The open expanse of the Fields lives up to its name, a breath-of-fresh-air common with swimming pool, tennis courts and adventure playground. As you'd expect, the streets immediately bordering the Fields – **Highbury Place, Crescent** and **Terrace** – are the poshest part of Highbury, not only thanks to the green acres, but because here is the area's Georgiana, with some vast, detached mansions and tall, flat-fronted terraces dating back to the 1770s. If you prefer new, 'Viewpoint' by Crest Nicholson offers 29 flats overloking the Fields from £430,000.

Otherwise homes are mostly Victorian rows with bay windows in wide streets – though as elsewhere in the area modern homes are being squeezed in. **Highbury Terrace Mews** is a modern outcrop of 3-bed houses; the old Central Hall in **Ronalds Rd**, too, has been split into 10 flats, and a new mews, **De Barowe Mews**, appeared a few years back in Leigh Rd. The latest development is in **Highbury Grove**: 29 flats, again by Crest Nicholson (£325–625,000). Between **Highbury Grove** and the Fields, **Corsica St** and **Baalbec Rd** mark an area of 1889 terraces, large million-pound family houses with elaborate facades. At the junction of **Corsica** and **Calabria Rds** are 15 modern houses – three of them 6-bedders overlooking the Fields. A house here was £960,000 last winter.

To the N of the Fields is **Highbury Hill** – a pretty corner with St John's Church to the E and a clock tower at the centre. Another coveted location, this: houses are large Victorian double-fronted, decreasing in size and becoming terraced towards Arsenal. Roads to the N of Highbury Hill and W of **Highbury Park** hold later Victorian terraces, again reducing in size and quality (and price) towards **Gillespie Rd**. New homes have appeared: 100 **Drayton Park**, a vast office-block, is now 84 Art Deco-inspired flats.

Arsenal will soon move to its new stadium on former industrial land at **Ashburton Grove**, W across the tracks. New homes will replace the old stadium in a vast scheme – a total, with other sites involved, of 2,300, no less: 25–35 per cent of them Affordable Housing. However, this means moving a waste depot to **Lough Rd** – and building a clutch of Affordable Homes right next to it. The complex scheme is sprouting new homes in **Drayton Park**, at the existing Highbury Stadium, beside the new **Ashburton Grove** stadium, in Lough Rd (close to the depot) and in **Hornsey St**, next to Hollway Rd tube. You can buy 2-bed, 2-bath flats at the latter from £289,000.

NE of Highbury Park and **Riversdale Rd** to **Mountgrove Rd**, Victoriana continues. Off

I

Mountgrove the flats of 'Old Stable Mews' surround a cobbled yard. The Highbury Quadrant Estate covers the area from here down to **Green Lanes**: housing is low-rise blocks. South from **Sotheby Rd** to **Highbury New Park** in the SE is late Victoriana: large, ornate terraces and quiet tree-lined streets. Exceptions are **Kelross Rd**, off Highbury Park, with some modest 1930s semis, and **Fountain Mews** off **Highbury Grange**, an extensive development of post-modernist and tower blocks.

Across the road are a series of large mansion flats, **Taverner Square** and **Peckett Square**, with interconnecting courtyards. **Aberdeen Rd** runs S to **Aberdeen Park**, the most secluded corner in the district: styles range from 1960s flats through 1930s semis to spacious Victorian mansions.

Highbury New Park skirts the area to the E, broad and long, with Quadrant Estate in the N and Spring Gardens Estate in the S. Vast Victorian mansions here are mainly now flats, such as sophisticated Belmont Court on the corner of **Balfour Rd**. To the E runs **Petherton Rd**,with 4-storey Victorian terraces in a wide avenue, a grassy shoulder down its middle. A grid of roads crosses W–E to **Newington Green Rd**, made up of Victorian terraces decreasing in size from **Poets Rd** to **Green Lanes**.

De Beauvoir

'The De Beauvoirs' are in N1, but not in Islington borough: they pay council tax to Hackney. The pleasant cache of wide streets around **De Beauvoir Square/Rd** came up rapidly in the '80s, and its denizens think and act as Islingtonians, though recently they have looked too to the hot-spots of Hoxton to the S. Another sign of evolution is the way the place has changed its name: you'll find it labelled 'Kingsland' on maps, but that has long dropped out of general use. The part S of **Downham Rd** maps show as 'De Beauvoir Town' is now largely the modern blocks of the De Beauvoir council estate.

De Beauvoir's modest-sized, unfussy villas come in ones, twos and threes as well as the more usual rows, offering a rare chance to buy half a house rather than a slice of terrace. Even rarer is the size of garden these 2/3-bed homes enjoy: 75–100 ft or more is not uncommon – and some get garages. A fourth bedroom often betokens roof or back extensions. **De Beauvoir Square** is a 1840s Gothic square of smart paired 4-storey villas with bay windows and ornate gables, around a central garden. Some of the houses are semis, others are in terraces, with odd arrangements of front doors which can signal flying freeholds (ask your solicitor and see his eyes light up). The square is the hub of a network of streets – similar homes can be found in streets like **Mortimer Rd**, **De Beauvoir Rd** (a busy thoroughfare), **Hertford Rd** and **Englefield Rd**. Those closest to **De Beauvoir Square** tend to be best; quality frays a little towards the edges, eg **Southgate Grove**. In **Culford Rd** the recent Eagle Court added 30 flats and houses to the area, while **Orchard Mews**, off Southgate Grove, is an individualistic 1980s addition complete with corner towers. **Southgate Rd** has recent homes; more on the way in 'Park Place' (flats and houses £200-750,000) and at 'OneN1'. On **Kingsland Rd**, the E edge of the neighbourhood, 'De Beauvoir Place' is a conversion of listed Georgian terraces into 1- and 2-bed flats and 2- and 3-bed duplexes. In **Tottenham Rd** the Victorian De Beauvoir Primary School now has 23 conversions plus 14 new-build flats.

Borders

Lower Holloway, to the N of Barnsbury, lies N of the railway line and W of the Holloway Rd. Property is mostly modern council-built, radiating off **Paradise Passage** (where, however, some new £750,000 houses look out across Paradise Park). Other exceptions include **Arundel Place** and **Arundel Square**: spacious flat-fronted terraces surrounding a central garden and playground, and **Ellington St**, which has lower-level Georgian terraces, rising to the substantial. Look, too, at **Furlong Rd** which, with **Orleston Rd**, runs E from Liverpool Rd: both have large semi-detached period houses.

North along **Liverpool Rd** are a few small Victorian terraces, **Morgan Rd**, **Ringcroft St** and **Sheringham Rd** – quality uneven. Liverpool Rd itself has some handsome, flat-fronted early 19th-century houses. Over on the **Caledonian Rd**, there's a Piccadilly Line tube. Some recent developments around here, for example in **Stock Orchard Crescent** and **Frederica St**, and the old police station opposite the tube.

The area towards King's Cross, between the **Caledonian Rd** and **York Way**, N of **Wharfdale Rd**, is also mainly low-level council homes, of various periods. The main interest here is around the canal: see Bloomsbury & King's Cross chapter.

Transport Tubes: Highbury & Islington (zone 2, Victoria), Angel (zone 1, Northern). From Highbury & Islington: Oxford Circus 8 min, City 18 min (1 change), Heathrow 1 hr 10 min (1 change). Trains: Highbury & Islington (Liverpool St 10 min and N London Line/Silverlink); Drayton Park, Essex Road, Caledonian Rd, Canonbury.

Convenient for City, Docklands and West End; King's Cross, St Pancras and Euston. Miles from centre: 2.5.

Schools Local Authority: Islington Green School, Highbury Fields (g), Highbury Grove (b), Elizabeth Garrett Anderson School (g), St Aloysius College, Arts & Media School.

SALES

Flats	S	1B	2B	3B	4B	5B
Average prices	140–220+	175–250	210–400+	250–400+	500+	–
Houses	2B	3B	4B	5B	6/7B	8B
Average prices	300–600	350–600+	450–1M	650–1M+	1.5M+	–

RENTAL

Flats	S	1B	2B	3B	4B	5B
Average prices	175–200+	200–300+	250–400+	300+	450+	–
Houses	2B	3B	4B	5B	6/7B	8B
Average prices	350+	450+	500+	700+	900+	–

The properties Good choice of early- and mid-Victorian houses in attractive areas such as Barnsbury and Canonbury (latter also some stunning Georgian). Highbury has smaller houses plus some lovely Georgian ones. Two-bed converted flats in good supply. New developments, increasingly classy, appear where space allows: particularly round the canal basin and the Angel.

The market Character period homes in interesting area attract City workers, media types, lawyers. Influx of those priced out of West London, and/or looking to invest/live in smart new flats.

Among estate agents active in this area are:

- Bairstow Eves
- Holden Matthews
- Evans Baker
- Hotblack Desiato
- Brooks & Co
- Hugh Grover Associates
- Healey, Graham & Co
- Copping Joyce
- Thomson Currie
- Kinleigh, Folkard & Hayward
- Hamptons
- Winkworth
- Thompson Currie
- Anthony Garfield & Co

KENNINGTON, VAUXHALL AND STOCKWELL

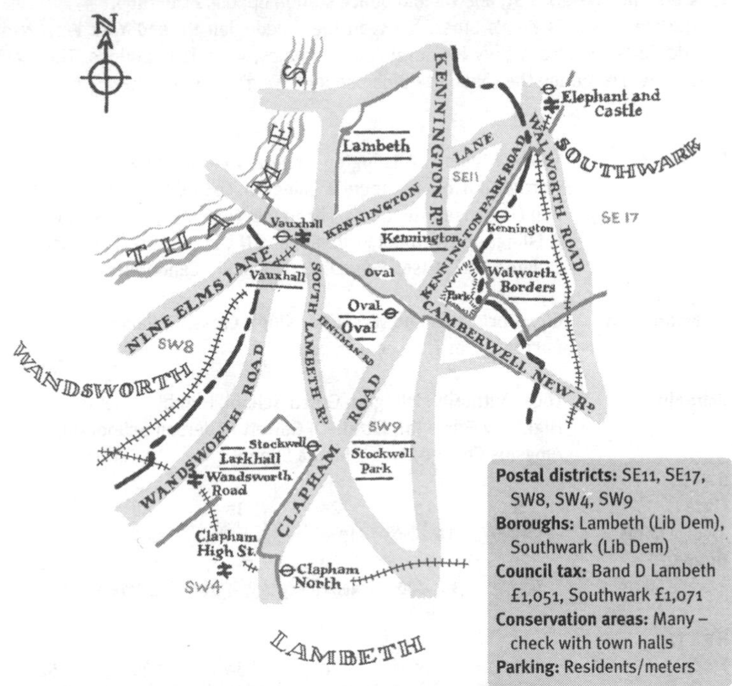

Postal districts: SE11, SE17, SW8, SW4, SW9
Boroughs: Lambeth (Lib Dem), Southwark (Lib Dem)
Council tax: Band D Lambeth £1,051, Southwark £1,071
Conservation areas: Many – check with town halls
Parking: Residents/meters

Stand well back from a wall-map of London and the point of these three areas becomes plain. Only the broad blue Thames divides them from Pimlico and Westminster, the City is a brief bike-ride away, the West End a bus-journey; Waterloo – most international of London transport hubs – is at the heart of the place.

So why isn't *everyone* living here? The answer comes from another look at the map. That position along the river – but on the opposite side from London's magnets, the City and West End – means that Kennington and Vauxhall are cut about by rail lines and eternally busy roads. Everyone in London, it sometimes seems, needs to pass through here to get to the bridges. This means noise, dirt, and the dislocation that comes from roaring roads dividing up districts. Slowly, the damage is being repaired as re-designed junctions, traffic calming and residents' parking schemes reclaim the streets for those who live there.

There is a steady flow of new developments, of which the most obvious, the giant flats and the new bus/tube/rail interchange by the bridge at Vauxhall, have done a lot to raise the profile of the area. It's hard if you're a Londoner not to drive through Vauxhall Cross, and all those who do so spot the changes.

London icons like Big Ben and the Eye break the skyline of large parts of the area, reminding locals that they really, truly live in London, not an urban village that wishes it was in Surrey. That said, a bit more village spirit would not come amiss. There are few obvious centres here, the main roads being what they are. Kennington Cross, where **Kennington Lane** intersects with **Kennington Rd**, has slowly gathered to itself a group of useful shops, restaurants and bars. But the natural hub, the Elephant and Castle, is a disaster area unlikely to be redeemed for a decade at least. Stockwell and the Oval have lost their 'village' centres, and Vauxhall never really had one.

For all that, there are some lovely homes here: Georgian houses set in peaceful squares and terraces. But these occur in patches amid tracts of Victoriana and 20th-century council-built housing, some of it pretty dire. For several decades, the radical/adventurous/broke sought out these Georgian gems, ignoring the rest of the housing, which was mostly rented (though some was – and in places still is – squatted) and mostly in poor condition. But as the demand for London property has grown, so incomers have bought the Victorian homes, developers have raised towers of flats on sites often empty since the Blitz, and Right to Buy has moved many of the council homes into the private sector (and their original inhabitants out of the area). All this means this is an area on the move, experiencing more social change in the last few years than the previous fifty.

There is much still to do. Glitzy towers rise on the river-front, but the Elephant scheme has stalled: the promising partnership between Southwark Council and some of the biggest names in the property industry collapsed in '02. The puce monstrosity will be with us a while as planners pick up the pieces: for the latest plans see South Bank chapter.

The monster new flats complex at Vauxhall Cross, and the even more massive tower proposed for the site next to it, show optimism in triumph. This is a place where development on a grand scale is possible, if the will and the money can be brought together. The giant New Covent Garden Market site, off **Nine Elms Lane**, may be redeveloped – or it may be expanded to become an even bigger food market. Renewal of the monolithic council estates on the E side of the area is a bigger challenge yet.

The neighbourhoods are ill-defined. Kennington is the northernmost and closest to the centre: its postcode is SE11. Vauxhall is less enticing than its riverside position might suggest: it has shrunk to be little more than a giant traffic intersection – and the Victoria Line tube/SW Trains/buses station complex.

The Oval, to the E, centres round its tube station at a busy crossroads and, of course, the world-famous cricket stadium. It shares the SW8 postcode with Stockwell. Stockwell, to the S, is a mix of lovely houses and grim council-built estates, and lacks a focus apart from its tube station and a rather down-rent parade of shops on busy **Clapham Road**. Stockwell received a boost 30 years ago when the Victoria Line brought it within minutes of the West End; it has some enclaves of real character, but does not seem to have kept up the momentum of improvement begun in the 1970s.

Over to the E, a few pockets of interesting housing are also to be found on the SE17 borders with Walworth and Camberwell. There are no tubes here, so distance from Kennington's station becomes an important factor. To the N, Waterloo and the Lambeth area (the site of the old village, not the sprawling borough) have moved into the residential frame (see South Bank chapter).

People looking to buy here are often young, always busy. Government ministers base their families in Kennington's Georgian houses, and MPs favour the area as being about the closest place to Westminster where you can find a choice of family houses; but most couples with kids look to Clapham and further southwest: schools are often the deciding factor in a move away, though the new £20 million Lilian Baylis comprehensive in Kennington Lane may swing the balance back a bit. Much of Vauxhall and Kennington is in the Division Bell zone, and – partly because of the MPs, judges and other notables who live here – the area is considered to belong to Inner London by cabbies.

Of the three areas in this chapter, Kennington is the most sought-after. Prices rise as you get nearer the river. Buyers who want to find a house but stay in the area, or who cannot afford what they want in Clapham or Wandsworth, look at the southern and eastern fringes, towards Clapham and Brixton. The neighbourhood served by Clapham

North tube is now, according to agents, 'young, affluent and single'. Stockwell's lovely houses suit families, and the market has been brisk here, too.

The area falls into no less than three boroughs – Wandsworth illogically sticks a finger into the W corner. Their council tax, education and other policies differ a lot, so look hard at the map. Transport is good, with Northern and Victoria Line tubes and Waterloo trains (including Eurostar, plus the Jubilee tube to Docklands, West End etc) just up the road. For vital shopping, there is a big Sainsbury's at Vauxhall, and a Tesco in Kennington Lane.

Kennington

The heart of the area, Kennington, gains much of its character from its historical association with the Duchy of Cornwall Estate. The Princes of Wales have owned land here since the Black Prince had his palace in Kennington. In the last 15 years, however, that influence has waned as most of the Duchy's homes have been passed on to housing associations or sold. Street names, and architecture, remain as a legacy.

The road names around here are very confusing: it is hard to recall which is **Kennington Park Rd**, which is **Kennington Rd** and which is **Kennington Lane.** The first-named is the main road, following the line of the old Roman Stane Street and linking the Elephant and Castle in the N with the Oval and Stockwell, passing Kennington and Oval tubes. **Kennington Rd** runs due N from near the Oval to the Imperial War Museum at Waterloo. The area now called 'Kennington Cross', at the junction of **Kennington Rd** and **Kennington Lane,** is the nearest thing to a villagey bit, boasting tapas bars, deli, etc – not to mention a plethora of estate agents. There's a Pizza Express, a French restaurant with a name for seafood. Lambeth Council has plans for an 'arts space' in the old underground gents' WC in the middle of the Cross. It's hoped recent work will improve the road pattern and streetscape, making the Cross more friendly for pedestrians.

To the W of Kennington Rd is the old heart of the neighbourhood, the 45-acre Duchy of Cornwall Estate. A chunk stands NW of Kennington Lane – S of the site of the Black Prince's palace, which lay between **Black Prince Rd** and **Sandcroft St. Courtney Square, Cardigan St** and **Courtney St** have Duchy-built homes in neo-Georgian style: however authentic they look, they were built in 1913. Ex-Duchy cottages remain around £350–450,000. **Woodstock Court** is an attractive enclosed square of homes, which the Duchy rents to elderly tenants.

Kennington Rd owes its existence to the building in 1750 of Westminster Bridge, and its regular rows of Georgian terraced houses are still largely in place. Many are flats, some offices – but some remain as large, potentially grand, houses. Some have had their potential realized: a 4-bed Georgian house in good order will be over £600,000, while 5-bed ones can be c. £800,000, and it's rumoured that the biggest and grandest house sold for £1.6 million. To the E of the road, in the angle formed by its intersection with **Kennington Lane**, is another part of the Duchy Estate. Pretty **Denny Crescent, Denny St** and **Chester Way** are, again, all 20th-century Georgian; they are reckoned among Kennington's best streets. Like other Duchy homes, the 2/3-bed cottages and flats have come onto the open market.

Kennington Rd has at its N end the park that surrounds the Imperial War Museum. Just S of the museum is **Walcot Square**, which dates from the 1830s. The charitable Walcot Estate occasionally sells unmodernized houses: expect to pay up to £500,000 for a 4-bed. **West Square**, which is in truth to the E, has houses from three decades earlier, as does **St George's Rd** on the N edge of the area – but this road carries heavy traffic from the Elephant. **West Square** and the surrounding streets are by contrast peaceful. These Georgian homes, some still unmodernised, overlook a garden square and sell for £800,000–£1 million, top price £1.5 million for a 7-bed. Those with smaller budgets look in streets such as nearby **Hayles St**, with its 2-bed, flat-fronted £350,000 cottages. **Brook Drive** offers plenty of flats, and some houses, all late-Victorian 3-storey.

Off Brook Drive in **Monkton St** Bellway's 31 3/4-bed houses at 'Kennington Place' started out from £400,000 in 2001, but Bellway were being generous: they now change hands at £500,000 minimum, with the best ones into the 700,000s. Nearby **Oswin St** has solid 4-storey Victorian houses. Lovely Georgian houses in **Walnut Tree Walk** were offered unmodernized in 1989, and those who bought did well: their homes are now Grade II listed and half a million. . . .

Much of the rest of the district to the E of **Kennington Rd** and W of **Kennington Park Rd** is council-built housing. One mid-1970s flats development is private, however: Vanbrugh Court on **Wincott St**. This popular complex has communal gardens and an underground garage. South of the hospital, a 1980s mews development was slotted into the angle between Gilbert Rd and Renfrew Rd: **Heralds Place** has underground parking for its compact 3-bed houses and flats (1-bed flat here, c. £190,000). **Renfrew Rd** itself has some ex-council houses. Round the corner is 'Parliament Terrace', off **Gilbert Rd**: 1997 houses in neo-Georgian style, which now sell for £350,000 plus. **Renfrew Rd** also boasts the old Kennington fire station, now converted into smart flats: £250,000 for a 1-bed.

Tucked to the E of the Kennington Lane/Kennington Rd junction is **Cleaver Square**, one of the best places to live in the area and the first to be 'discovered' – allegedly by a '60s barrister trying to find his way back to civilization from a court hearing at Newington Causeway. This urban-feeling square has a mixture of houses, but all are extremely attractive. Those 1960s barristers were scandalized when houses in the square reached £20,000 in 1971; today, their sons and daughters would have to find £1.2 million for the biggest, a 6-bed, and £650,000-plus for a 3-bed cottage.

Round the corner in **Bowden St**, 'City Lights' is a three-floor block of 14 flats. Going S, in the angle of **Kennington Rd** and **Kennington Park Rd** is a neighbourhood of smaller terraced Victorian homes of unusual design, with spacious semi-basements. **Stannary St's** name makes clear the connection with Cornwall and thus the Duchy. **Ravensdon St, Methley St** and **Radcot St** are similar. **Kennington Green**, a small widening of Kennington Rd, has a few pleasant old houses. **Montford Place** adjoins the site of the local Tesco. The flat-fronted Georgian 3-bed houses here are still, as last year, around £350–400,000.

Kennington is best known for its Georgian terraces, but the area also has some interesting survivals from other periods, including these almshouses with their Gothic porches and windows. Other distinctive architecture can be found on the Duchy of Cornwall Estate, where small houses in Georgian style were built before World War I.

The loft boom has had its effects on Kennington. The old college situated on **Kennington Rd**, close to Stannary St, is now 'The Lycée' loft apartments: a vast (5-bed, 4-floor) one is around £795,000; a more normal 2-bed £360,000 – prices static over the last year or two: they started high when new. Trumping these is a former pub in **Stannary St**, now a house: £2 million was asked last autumn. Over towards the river in **Vauxhall Walk**, Spring Gardens Court has 1- to 3-bed flats. In **Kennington Lane** Imperial Court, an old military building with its fine 1836 portico, is flats which share a spa, gym etc: a 1-bed might be £200,000, a 3-bed £350,000.

The other big trend is to exploit the river: on **Albert Embankment**, the riverside office block long graced by Lord Archer's penthouse is now flats, and Berkeley have turned No. 9, another former office block, into 95 more. The same firm has just finished the even bigger block ('Salamanca Square') next door with 270 flats. Yet more building work next door presages an hotel and more flats. At the N end of the Embankment, across from Lambeth Palace, curvy 'Parliament View' is a well-named new block of 190 flats with £3 million penthouses.

The Oval

Partly because of heavy traffic, and also owing to the depressing influence of some pre-war council estates, the Oval neighbourhood has less charm than Kennington. Cricket fanatics might consider the period houses on the S side of the **Oval** itself, although the new stands now restrict their view of the pitch. The other sides of the Oval, and the streets to the N, are lined with 1940s and '50s council blocks. Ex-council flats here start at around £145,000 for 1-beds. One former council block, Kilner House on Clayton St, is now in private hands and boasts a smart garden courtyard where there was once a car park (1-beds £180–190,000). New stands at the W end of the cricket ground annoyed locals who say they block their light (and view?). South of the Oval, and sealed off from the traffic, **Ashmole St** and **Claylands Rd** have small terraced houses, rather overwhelmed by the large council developments (a Claylands 3-bed house was £595,000 last winter; a 2-bed flat £250,000). **Meadow Rd** has flat-fronted terraces.

The main road S from the Oval intersection and tube station is the wide, busy **Clapham Rd**. This forms a clear divide: most of the best streets are to the W. The prime street is **Fentiman Rd**, a terrace of dignified, well-discovered (largely by MPs wanting to be in reach of Westminster) mid-Victorian houses (some split into flats: 2-beds £200,000-plus, though a 5-bed house might be £500–800,000). Most lack Kennington's Georgian charm, but are large and conveniently between Oval and Vauxhall tubes. Periods vary between Regency and mid-Victorian. Higher odd numbers overlook Vauxhall Park.

K

Off neighbouring **Rita Rd**, with its 3-storey terraced houses, most now spacious flats, is the gated entrance to a walled enclave, **Regent's Bridge Gardens** – often called 'the Vinegar Works' (better, and more accurate). This is an expensive, still smart, 1986 conversion of the Regency/early Victorian Sarson's works, the manager's house and his splendid ballroom. There are lofts, flats and town-houses; some conversions, some skilfully matched new-build. All have use of a pool complex.

Between **Fentiman Rd** and **Richborne Terrace** is 1980s **Usborne Mews. Richborne Terrace** has early-Victorian houses in an area once scruffy, now smartened up. **Palfrey Place** runs behind the W side of **Clapham Rd**: here, seven new 2-bed, 2-bath town-houses sold in late '99 from £365,000; local agents now price them at £375,000-plus. The Victorian 3-bed houses in the same street are around £410,000.

Close to Oval tube, pretty **Hanover Gardens** is a surprise: this popular pocket of little early-Victorian houses and cottages is tucked away in a cul-de-sac that opens out at its end to enclose a circular pocket-handkerchief of grass. Across to the E of Clapham Rd, a few convenient streets such as **Handforth Rd** have 3-storey Victorian houses, which convert into pleasant flats that sell for a steady £190,000-ish for a 1-bed. A few survive as single homes. Round the corner, **Offley Rd** is well placed for the tube and park – but also close to the big road junction. Plenty of converted flats: 2-beds up to £300,000. **Caldwell St**, to the S, is off the E side of Clapham Rd: here Laing in 2000 built Caldwell Place; flats and town-houses.

To the E again, in **Langton Rd** off the **Camberwell New Rd**, is 1980s **Salisbury Place**: 100 homes from studio flats to 4-bed houses. **Vassall Rd** has big, classic

Georgian houses – £675,000 has been asked ('a crazy figure' say knowledgeable agents) for a done-up 5-bed detached, but a more normal price would be £450–500,000. Families find this neighbourhood challenging, though flat-buyers may be happier, paying £200,000-ish for a 2-bed. Further S in **Lothian Rd**, close to Camberwell New Rd, is a recent development of 2-bed flats and 2- and 3-bed houses.

Vauxhall

Roads, railways and the New Covent Garden Market take up much of the floor space in Vauxhall, and council-built homes dominate the rest. The shadow of the vast (*still* as yet only planned: see Battersea chapter) Battersea Power Station scheme falls over the S of the area. Another shadow is now cast by the giant St George's Wharf towers, which are filling the horizon between the traffic and the river, providing offices, an hotel, a Conran restaurant and 618 flats in a positive cliff of six riverside towers plus linking blocks. Current prices for 1-beds £350,000-plus, 2-beds start at £430,000, with a 3-bed with roof terrace £1.5 million. There's direct access into the complex from the tube station and new bus station.

The 72-metre high blocks will be dwarfed by the 180-metre, 49-storey tower with 167 flats which will round off the scheme to the S. A big wind turbine on the top will power common-parts lighting (when and if it is built). The Mayor of London is (predictably) pro the scheme, but wrangles about Affordable Housing, parking and the design of the garden (!) led Lambeth to turn it down. Verdict of an inquiry is awaited.

On the opposite, northern, corner of the bridge approach is the Hollywood-Babylonian biscuit-coloured lair of spymasters MI6, forced out of Mayfair by rising rents. A terrorist rocket attack on it back in 2000 reflects one downside of inner-city living, though people who watch James Bond films will at least know where you live.

Back at Vauxhall Cross, **Vauxhall Grove** looks promising on the map: a square tucked in off the Vauxhall Cross junction. The Grove was partly squatted for some 20 years (the old GLC let the houses to eco-groups on a short-term basis – and then forgot it owned them) and wholly scruffy: 3-storey Victoriana looms over too-narrow streets. Now, however, Lambeth has regained control and the Grove is smartening up. Round in **Bonnington Square**, a housing association has improved some similar 3-storey flats buildings. Much of this attractive, secluded square seems to be inhabited by young people in a sort of post-hippie time warp ('eco-left-fieldish' was how one visitor put it); there's a community garden, a café, an annual street parade. Locals fear extra rat-run traffic and are angry they have not been included in the traffic-calming scheme. Join the party for c. £300,000 for a 2-bed flat, though you've missed the rare intact (if deeply shabby) house which a developer snapped up last summer for £500,000.

At the junction of **Langley Lane** and **South Lambeth Rd** is a turn-of-the-20th-century mansion block, Park Mansions, which has a steady turnover of flats for sale. In **Langley Lane** itself, a neat clutch of two houses and five flats has been squeezed in. At the end of **Lawn Lane** is a council estate around **Ebbisham Drive**: 2-storey houses and two tower blocks. An old school in **Lawn Lane** is becoming 'The Academy' with 33 2- and 3-bed homes, converted and new-build, by Copthorne: prices from £400–665,000.

To the S – in what used to be called 'South Lambeth', but is now a fringe area between Vauxhall and Lambeth – roads such as **Tradescant Rd** have a lot of flats carved out of 3-storey Victorian terraces. **Meadow Place**, nearby, has some 3- and 4-bed Victorian houses still intact which can reach around £470,000. There are some recent mews houses in **Dorset Rd**. From here on S is considered Stockwell.

A tract to the W of **Wandsworth Rd**, towards Battersea, is attached to Vauxhall – mostly because railway lines shut it off from anywhere else. Most of it is the council-built 28-block Patmore Estate. North of the railway, off **Stewart's Rd**, is a 1980s clutch of studio and 2-bed flats with a fine view of the Eurostar trains on their roof-level viaduct.

Back up Wandsworth Rd, an interesting enclave entered from **Cowthorpe Rd**, including **Crimsworth Rd**, has cheerfully scruffy but well-loved late-Victorian cottages, some purpose-built flats (including the Victorian two-from-a-terrace sort), and 40-odd new ones. Flats here are £190,000-plus for a 1-bed, £250,000 for a 2-bed; 3- and 4-bed houses from £350,000. Round the corner in **Thorpatch Rd**, a clutch of town-houses and flats dates from 1988. Along the river towards Battersea Power Station are some new blocks of flats with good views of Pimlico (better views, in fact, than the other way round). Riverside 'Elm Quay' in **Nine Elms Lane**, also late-'80s, has 1-, 2- and 3-bed flats and penthouses (a 1-bed river-view flat, £280,000), with their own sports and leisure complex. This was Regalian's first try at new-build: everyone has to start somewhere.

Stockwell

Stockwell struck lucky in the early 19th century, with an expansive estate of Regency villas. Just enough survives to provide some gracious streets and architecturally interesting homes, but not enough to make Stockwell a fully-fledged gentrified suburb. The select streets have an air of being marooned in an ordinary patch of South London. Indeed, Lambeth Council reckons Stockwell ward is the 12th most deprived ward in England – due to the big council-built estates. Locals report recent improvement, in part due to the overspill of affluent buyers from Brixton, in part to improved policing, in part to painstaking improvement of the estates.

West of Clapham Rd is **Albert Square** and its associated streets. The giant mid-Victorian houses in the square loom over the central gardens, and are in turn dominated by the nearby tower blocks of the Mursell Estate. Houses in the square – a popular, villagey enclave – have been selling, when they come up, at around £700,000, though one sale of £1.2 million was reported in 2003; some have been split into flats (a 1-bed, £200,000). The Mursell Estate council towers offer a cheaper option: £130,000 for a 2-bed on the 18th floor. **Wilkinson St** and **Aldebert Terrace** have a more human scale; the former is the smarter. **St Stephen's Terrace** has pretty early-Victorian houses which have reached up to £650,000. Just off **South Lambeth Rd** is **Saddlers Mews**, recent 2-bed houses. Down the street, Wingfield House, a former masonic banqueting hall, is now flats.

West of South Lambeth Rd is a mixed neighbourhood of pleasant new council-built houses and surviving Regency villas. Most of the period homes are clustered around **Lansdowne Gardens**, which opens up in the middle into a perfect circus. The 1840s houses are double-fronted, detached and boast big pillared porches. Prices here have 'gone mad' to quote a local agent: where £650,000 was a good price five years back, a 6-bed was on the market for £1.2 million last autumn, with a 7-bed at £1.2 million and a 4-bed at £800,000. **Guildford Rd, Thorne Rd** and linking roads are similar in style, though cheaper. **Lansdowne Way** is a busy E–W road with a mix of properties, some Georgian. A church hall has recently been carved into five smart 3-bed houses, ultra-modern in style. West of **Hartington Rd** is the big council-built Lansdowne estate, recently much improved, with 3-bed flats at c. £185,000.

East of Clapham Rd comes Stockwell Park, the surviving Regency suburb and now a conservation area. Over the last few years it has become – to quote another local agent – 'dead posh'. Many of the houses are good-sized family homes, often inhabited by parents with young children. This encourages more sense of community, with the sharing of school runs etc. The Stockwell Park Estate, to the S, is much better than it was, benefitting from steady Council investment and the renaissance of nearby Brixton. **Stockwell Terrace** overlooks the roundabout and tube station: tall early 19th-century houses. There are similar homes – many split into flats – in adjoining **South Lambeth Rd** and **Clapham Rd. Stockwell Park Rd** runs E with a mix of homes from small Regency to '20s gabled villas. Again, plenty of flats conversions amid surviving 4-bed Victorian semis which command £450–550,000 (some new houses were slotted in in '02). Goldcrest added eight new 2-bed maisonettes in 2003. At the junction with **Groveway** and **Stockwell Park Crescent**, the road opens out. All these streets have a mix of 1830s villas and terraces, with lots of trees and gardens. (Ignore the street atlas's label 'Angell Town' on this bit. It is not here but half a mile SE in Brixton – which chapter see.)

Durand Gardens, hidden away to the N, is a surprise: a pear-shaped square with big Victorian houses, mostly semi- and detached. The 5- and 6-bed houses have been known to top £1 million in late 1999. A little Gothic villa and an enormous detached house add variety. A few Arts-and-Craftsy 1898 gabled terraces stand on the way out to Clapham Rd. **Hillyard St** to the E has some modern town-houses: 3 beds, £350,000.

West of Stockwell Park Crescent, **St Michael's Rd** and **St Martin's Rd** have 3-storey mid-Victorian brick terraces. Flats converted from these are £250,000 for a 2-bed. Cranworth Gardens is a red-brick block of ex-Peabody flats smartened up to mansion-block status ('would not look out of place in Barnes' remarks a local) and selling for £250–280,000. A little to the E, **Hackford Rd** has some handsome flat-fronted early-Victorian houses, some split into spacious flats (a 1-bed £180–200,000).

South of Stockwell tube is a mixed district dominated by council blocks but with some routine Victorian terraces. **Landor Rd** marks the border with Clapham North and Brixton. Agents now point out that this side of Stockwell is close to Brixton: this used to be kept very quiet, but Brixton is buzzing these days – and Stockwellites frequent its bars, cinemas and night life as well as that of Clapham High St. Thus little houses off **Landor Rd** that were £80,000 in 1994–95 are now selling – if close enough to Clapham and with original features intact – for £350–400,000.

Larkhall Lane becomes **Larkhall Rise** as it runs through to Clapham, a little less of a rat-run now the railway bridge is one way. The housing off it is mostly council, though there are a few good corners. The Lane itself has some early-Victorian houses, much interrupted by car-sales yards and council blocks, though new homes are appearing.

West of the Lane, **Priory Grove**, overlooking the recently-created Larkhall Park, has some pretty, small houses and 'The Studios', a converted school (2-bed flats). From **Larkhall Lane** E to Stockwell tube is council.

To the S of the area lies a grid of wide streets on the Clapham borders (which chapter see): **Chelsham Rd** and **Bromfelde Rd** have big houses, mostly now flats. A few are still large (up to 6-bed, can be 7-figure sum) family homes, though most are 4-bed and go for £750,000. **Gauden Rd** is similar, with some extensive flat conversions and family houses.

Walworth Borders

East from Kennington tube is mostly council housing. Some period stuff, indeed, is also council-owned but no one knew (or was saying): a whole 14-house terrace in **St Agnes Place** was discovered in 1999 to be squatted, as it had been for 20 years. Lambeth asked for it back, confessing that the previous administration had forgotten that it owned the place. The inhabitants claimed that they had become owners, but lost the court case, raising Lambeth's hopes. To no avail: the squatters have not budged – an eviction last October was thwarted by a 100-strong posse of squatters and sympathizers. The town hall also, by the way, asked locals to inform them about any more council-owned homes they'd lost track of.

This is a tract unloved by estate egents, who venture here with reluctance – which could be good news for buyers brave enough to make their own judgments. There are some known gems: the best of the lot is **Sutherland Square** which has some handsome 4-bed, 4-storey early-Victorian houses: these are popular (£425,000–500,000, depending on done-up-ness) despite the proximity of the railway line just beyond the E side of the square. Nearby streets such as **Fielding St** and (to the N) **Berryfield Rd** have

Victorian terraced houses that can reach £300,000 (2-bed flats £185,000). **Lorrimore Square** has a mix of Victorian terraces and new houses. All the streets S of here are part of, or are dominated by, a vast council estate. The mostly post-war flats and houses are interspersed with now-restored Victorian terraces.

A few handsome early-Victorian houses survive to the W in the aforementioned **St Agnes Place**, by Kennington Park. This area also has several streets of rather run-down purpose-built Edwardian flats. **Surrey Square**, over towards the **Old Kent Rd**, has some Georgiana, some split into flats – see South Bank chapter.

This is a good hunting ground for cheap, mostly ex-council, homes. A 2-bed flat in a tower block can be around £100–120,000, though you'll pay £50,000 more in a favoured, low-rise block – but ask about service charges. These prices are a fifth of those asked for new flats by the river: how much do you really need that concierege?.

Transport Tubes: Kennington, Elephant & Castle, Oval, Clapham North (zones 1/2, Northern), Stockwell (zone 2, Victoria, Northern), Vauxhall (zones 1/2, Victoria). From Stockwell: Oxford Circus 10 min, City 20 min, Heathrow 1 hr 15 min (2 changes). Trains: Elephant & Castle (Thameslink), Vauxhall (to Waterloo).

Convenient for City, Westminster, Waterloo, South Bank. Miles from centre: 2.

Schools Local Authority: Lilian Baylis, Stockwell Park, Archbishop Tenison's C of E (b), Charles Edward Brooke (g).

SALES

Flats	S	1B	2B	3B	4B	5B
Average prices	100–150	140–200	225–350+	170–400	–	–
Houses	2B	3B	4B	5B	6/7B	8B
Average prices	220–400	250–500	400–600+	400–1M	500–1M	800–1.5M

K

RENTAL

Flats	S	1B	2B	3B	4B	5B
Average prices	155–220	190–300	210–400	290–500	400–675	–
Houses	2B	3B	4B	5B	6/7B	8B
Average prices	230–400	300–500	400–625	400–600	450–700	570–1300

The properties Enclaves of handsome Georgian amid Victorian houses and flats; some modern mews and flats, pretty repro-Georgian on Duchy of Cornwall Estate. Smart new flats on riverside. Widespread council-built housing – some good, some dire. Old schools and factories fast becoming loft apartments.

The market Good communications attract professionals, City people, MPs, lawyers and doctors. Location matters: select period enclaves are close to run-down inner-city. Houses in family enclaves, eg parts (see text) of Stockwell, in demand; in fringe areas less so.

Among estate agents active in this area are:

- Ludlow Thomson
- Barnard Marcus
- Murray Estates
- Movingspace
- Halifax
- Winkworth
- Field & Sons
- Kinleigh Folkard & Hayward
- Foxtons
- Burne & Shield
- Alan Fraser
- Greenacre & Co

KENSINGTON

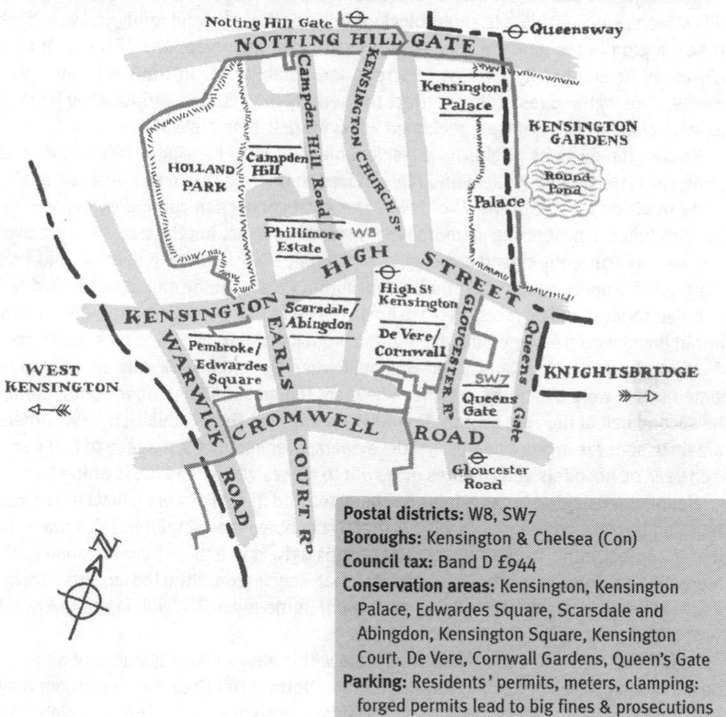

Postal districts: W8, SW7
Boroughs: Kensington & Chelsea (Con)
Council tax: Band D £944
Conservation areas: Kensington, Kensington Palace, Edwardes Square, Scarsdale and Abingdon, Kensington Square, Kensington Court, De Vere, Cornwall Gardens, Queen's Gate
Parking: Residents' permits, meters, clamping: forged permits lead to big fines & prosecutions

Should you wish to spend £25 million on a property in Kensington, you have a choice. There's an entire Edwardian mansion block with 45 flats, let on the short tenancies that this very central, very cosmopolitan area demands. Or there's a family-sized detached mansion with a pool, garage for four and bedrooms for seven.

The two properties – the one, in **Allen St**, a hard-working investment and the other, in **Upper Phillimore Gardens**, a London HQ for a don't-need-to-worry type – exemplify the two faces of Kensington. It is a transitory home to thousands of people from around the globe who stay any length of time from a night – still plenty of hotels here – to a three-year work assignment. And it is, as it was intended to be by its Victorian builders, the location of choice for the rich and the powerful.

Estate agents here cling on tight to their benchmarks. It's £1,000-per-sq-ft territory, they aver. So it is, at the top end, though even up in the heights (or the mid slopes, if you are a Top Agent), stuff between say £1 million and £3 million is down. Down, that is, on mid-2001, which looking back was clearly the local peak of this particular house-price cycle. And even at the very top, properties can 'stick' – that £25 million house mentioned above has been on the market for three years.

Fall there has been, no-one denies. Down by 10 per cent in 2002, and by another 10 for a lot of homes in '03 – though the autumn months arrested the slide, and values began to climb again. Last year, 2004, overall saw a neat reversal of the '03 pattern: prices went up in the spring – and back down in the autumn. The top end, that £3-million-plus market, however, has been brisk here recently, primed by Russian and

Middle Eastern money. Get above £5 million, and only one buyer in four is British, though they form a big majority in the 'normal' sector (£1–2 million).

Kensington is often touted as a safe haven. Its solid virtues – lovely houses in leafy, hilly streets, spacious flats in smart blocks – bring both native and foreign buyers back to Kensington in the end. For this is, as a local agent observed, one of the very best addresses in Europe. It is classy, discreet and established. In troubled times, say agents, Kensington does at least attract the serious buyers. And serious they have to be, when flats at £385,000 are reckoned 'ideal for first-time buyers'.

Kensington owes its origins as a fashionable suburb to Kensington Palace, a royal home since 1689 when William and Mary moved their court out to the fresh air of this pretty roadside hamlet to the W of town. The royal connection continues; Kensington Gardens holds a most fitting memorial to Princess Diana: no, not the water feature over in Hyde Park (currently closed once again for 'modifications'), but a delightful children's playground. Sundry royals still inhabit Kensington Palace, many embassies crowd the dignified squares and terraces. Here we are in the heart of a Royal Borough – one of only four in the kingdom – something dyed-in-the-wool Kensingtonians don't let you forget.

Most of present-day Kensington was built when Queen Victoria was alive. Though some houses were a century old when she died, the main building boom came during the second half of the 19th century, immediately after the Great Exhibition. Few corners remain to squeeze in more homes; yet developers, ever ingenious, manage to find some each year, as hospitals and colleges move out to places where land costs rather less.

Happily, Kensington today retains its character, and its rich mix of leafy Victorian and Georgian terraces, grand stucco villas, attractive cobbled mews, tall red-brick mansion blocks and eccentric studio houses. Not surprisingly, this is blue-plaque country. It's interesting to note, wandering the streets, that Kensington attracted an arty crowd: Siegfried Sassoon, Dame Marie Rambert, Edward Burne-Jones, TS Eliot, James Joyce and Turner, who painted in Campden Hill Square.

Today's residents find that most streets are within easy walking distance of either of the two main centres of **Kensington High St** and **Notting Hill Gate**. Between them they boast cinemas, clubs, pubs, high street stores and designer shops. The shopping area has the big high-street names and is thronged with tourists, but it retains its character and the tiny lanes and streets off the traffic-filled High St and **Kensington Church St** are still quiet. The council decided that Kensington lacks a grand piazza, so it has spent £5 million revamping the High Street: widening pavements, reinstating the York stone paving, de-cluttering (and replacing in stainless steel) the street furniture.

Restaurants crowd the affluent streets, and every service is on offer for those with money, but no time. And not the least of the area's attractions is the vast amount of public open space in the shape of Kensington Gardens and Holland Park.

This chapter deals with Kensington proper: Holland Park has its own chapter, as do South Kensington, and Notting Hill and North Kensington.

Campden Hill

Campden Hill Rd climbs sedately upwards from **Kensington High St** and down again to **Notting Hill Gate**. A through-route between two main shopping streets, it is lined by a range of homes both period and modern, merging with pubs, shops and restaurants at its N end. Off this street are some of the most charming, private and unexpectedly peaceful places to live in inner London. And the grandest, too: in 2002 someone (discretion rules at this level) bought the Uruguayan Embassy at No. 1 **Campden Hill** for £16 million. It has a gated acre of privacy, 12 bedrooms and (most vital) security.

Hidden away behind a tall brick wall and trees on the corner with the **Duchess of Bedford's Walk**, former college buildings recently became 'The Phillimores', a (very) secure, gated complex of 67 flats: 2-, 3-, 4-, and 5-bed ones (prices were £1.65–6.95

million, plus an extra £75,000 for a parking space). Last winter a 3-bed, 3-bath, 3-recep, 2 parking-space flat was £3.8 million: its selling agents made a point of the 16-ft ceilings; not all the flats are that airy. As well as the now-complete conversion of the main college, there will be another 68 homes on the site of the Atkins Building.

Opposite stands Campden Hill Court, a red-brick and stone gabled mansion block with elaborate towers, turrets and domes. A short distance away in **Airlie Gardens** is Holland Park Comprehensive School. A series of large modern flat blocks extends between **Airlie Gardens** and **Notting Hill Gate**. Many have superb views E across London.

Turn W into **Aubrey Walk**, sitting on the hilltop: a surprisingly quiet, leafy backwater – before the builders arrived. Brick-and-stucco terraces, 20th-century Dutch-gabled houses and some highly individual studio houses line the S side, facing out over the former waterworks opposite. However, the site of the underground reservoir has been redeveloped by St James with 12 new covered and open tennis courts (Campden Hill Tennis Club has been here for decades) and of course homes: 19 large new houses with gardens and 30 2- and 3-bed flats. Aubrey Walk's existing residents fought the plans and lament that their backwater will be quiet no longer. The Royal Borough has plumped for **Wycombe Square** as the postal address: it was marketed originally as Aubrey Square. Despite (or because of?) a steady stream of celebrity sightings, viewings did not speedily convert into sales. In January, after three years-plus of marketing, just a handful of flats (1- and 2-bed) were on offer at £895–995,000, but half the houses were still available (£6.95–11 million).

Around the corner **Aubrey Rd**, lined with large houses, slopes downhill to **Holland Park Avenue**. Halfway down Aubrey Rd is the entrance to **Campden Hill Square**: the main terrace of this three-sided Regency square perches near the brow of the hill above its private, tree-lined central gardens. The remaining two terraces step down the slope on either side, lined with big, handsome houses: some with 6/7 bedrooms. The houses have leafy front gardens, and street trees add to the summer canopy of greenery.

The houses and painted cottages in **Hillsleigh Rd**, E of the square, also tumble down to Holland Park Avenue. This corner also hides two enormous houses, which crown the Hill. One, Hill Lodge, a virtual country mansion, boasts 60ft of reception rooms and has a separate cottage within its walled grounds. Another, 18th-century Aubrey House, in **Aubrey Rd,** sold in 1999 for around £20 million after being the home of the same family since 1873. Its gardens extend to two acres. Last winter one-twentieth of that would buy you a more normal-sized 4-bedroomed house in the road.

East across **Campden Hill Rd** is 'Hillgate Village', a charmed, small-scale enclave of pretty painted little 1850s cottages, with a pub and a few shops. It has been popular since the early 1950s, when it was one of the first clutches of artisan cottages in London to be 'discovered' by the middle classes, who now pay c. £750–950,000 for these once-humble homes. The village lies between **Notting Hill Gate** (N), **Campden St** (S), **Campden Hill Rd** (W) and **Kensington Church St** (E). Best examples of the gaily coloured, all-cottage lanes are **Jameson St, Calcott St, Farmer St, Hillgate Place** and tree-lined **Farm Place.** Last year saw seven warehouse flats (in W8?!) converted from a building on the corner of **Uxbridge** and **Farmer Sts.** The surprising figure of £4.3 million was being asked last winter for a 4,700 sq ft Uxbridge St penthouse.

Kensington Place has terraces of attractive 2-storey plus basement stucco/brick cottages on the N side. Opposite are Fox Primary School and a 1970s red-brick cache of 3-storey town-houses, lying between two tall blocks of flats set back from the road. **Peel St** and **Campden St** are more mixed. Last winter the former had one of W8's freeholds on the market, a little sliver of a 1-bed terraced cottage at £425,000. The latter has terraces of 2/3-storey cottages and houses – some 1820s, some modern – and also Byam Shaw House: now flats, but once the studio and art school of the famous Pre-Raphaelite artist. A smartly modernised 3-bed/2-bath house with a big studio room was £1.65 million last winter. More painted brick-and-stucco cottages are found in **Peel St**, where half of the N side is taken up by the tall red- and grey-brick blocks of Campden Houses. **Bedford Gardens** to the S is a leafy street with taller, mainly 4-storey, houses – including one with a 2-bed cottage in the garden.

Terraces of mainly 3-storey creamy-white houses and some big villas stand on the N side of **Sheffield Terrace** (poet and novelist GK Chesterton lived at No. 32). By contrast, most of the S side is lined by a long row of matching tall, red-brick gabled buildings with white-stucco striped entrances. The flats of Campden House Chambers were an 1894 take on the Queen Anne style, and much admired at the time. This street also has modern blocks of flats. And hidden away behind the S side of Sheffield Terrace is a 2½-acre private garden, shared with the residents of **Hornton St** and **Gloucester Walk.** Gloucester Walk has a mix of modern flats and more red-brick gabled mansions, as well as 3/4-storey houses. **Campden Grove** has houses (a 5-bed, £1.9 million) and flats.

Tucked away off the NW end of Hornton St opposite Gloucester Walk is **Campden House Close**: a narrow lane leads to a group of 2-storey cottages set around a pleasant, spacious courtyard. Varying styles of houses and flats stretch down **Hornton St**, including some large pairs of stucco homes. An eye-catching terrace of brown-brick-and-white-striped Victorian buildings with elaborate stucco decoration steps down the W side as far as Holland St. The style continues into **Observatory Gardens** with its red-brick-and-stone striped 3-storey houses. An attractive terrace of 20th-century Dutch-gabled houses extends down **Hornton St** opposite the town hall.

Cutting across Hornton St is **Holland St**, a popular, narrow road where detached stucco houses and Georgian-style terraces are interspersed with a handful of speciality shops and restaurants plus a local pub – this corner of Holland St/Gordon Place, just yards from Kensington Church St, has a nice villagey atmosphere. An undistinguished terrace of 20th-century houses lies on the S side. Halfway along Holland St is **Gordon Place**, where the 3-bed houses go for just over a million. The S end forms a pretty, overgrown walkway, set back from the road and looking like a country lane. Hidden behind the trees and mature front gardens are two terraces of Georgian-style houses turned sideways on to Holland St. Going N up **Kensington Church St** is Bullingham Mansions. This Dutch-style, yellow- and red-brick and stone block is built around a landscaped fountain courtyard guarded by some impressive stone lions.

Dominating the SE corner of the neighbourhood is Kensington's parish church, St Mary Abbot's, with its dramatic 250ft spire – the tallest in London.

Kensington Palace

The focal point of the neighbourhood is the palace, rebuilt in the late 17th century by Sir Christopher Wren, and set in beautiful Kensington Gardens. It was here in 1837 that the young Princess Victoria was awakened to be told that she was queen.

The second most exclusive address here is a long, tree-lined, gated avenue running N–S alongside the palace and gardens. The N end is called **Kensington Palace Gardens**, the S end (it's the same road) **Palace Green.** Stately mansions with sweeping driveways line this wide, *very* private road. Although known as 'Millionaires' Row', most of the homes are now embassies. The Crown Estate owns 54 of the houses, most of which have been sold on long leases. Twenty or so are private homes; they command c. £2,000 a square foot (double the price of 'ordinary' Kensington streets). The Crown Estate announces primly that they prefer families: what are they worried about – groups of rowdy Ozzie sharers? Both ends are guarded by gatekeepers, there's an elaborate chicane to slow what traffic they allow through, and the police's Diplomatic Protection Corps takes an interest, which reassures the nervous among the incoming rich.

Time to talk telephone numbers: No. 10 sold in 2002 for over £14 million, despite being only half renovated. No. 16 went for £20 million plus. And then there are Nos. 18

and 19: converted from former embassies, and dripping with marble, they were bought by Formula One king Bernie Ecclestone for £50 million in 2001. But despite amenities that include a hair-dressing salon, a Turkish bath, underground parking for 20, when he sold in 2004 it was for not much more than £57 million – and he had agreed to split the profit with the previous owner. Not surprising, then, when all the costs are taken into account, that he told the *Telegraph* it was 'a bad investment, as it happened'. At the SW end, overlooking the Palace, is 3A Palace Green. These vast flats launched in 1990 (just in time for the last crash) at prices of up to £10 million. A 2,700 sq ft one (including staff flat, of course) was on the market last winter for £4.3 million.

Alongside 3A Palace Green is **York House Place**, a narrow passageway leading to the two blocks of York House, soberly smart Victorian mansion flats. The 7-storey red-brick and stone blocks with red-and-white striped gables stand in a relatively quiet cul-de-sac with an ornamental water garden in the middle, creating a courtyard.

The passageway emerges on **Kensington Church St** opposite the Lancer Square shopping precinct. From here the streets wend their way gradually uphill to Notting Hill Gate. **Church Close**, opposite the Carmelite Church in Kensington Church St, is a 3-storey red-brick-and-stone Tudor-style complex, set around a garden courtyard.

The scale suddenly changes where **Vicarage Gate** branches off Kensington Church St. Two 8-storey 1930s flat blocks, Winchester Court (W) and Vicarage Court (E), spread along each side of the street. A studio in the latter is about as cheap as Kensington gets; they start at c. £150,000, while a 3-bed in the former at £415,000 (needing work, share of freehold) is perhaps more typical. A Victorian brick-and-stucco terrace with polished marble porch columns stands on the N side: one of these, needing work, was £3.95 million last winter, with the option of splitting it into flats or keeping it as a 6,500 sq ft house. Vicarage Gate House, until 2003 a home for elderly gentlefolk (how Kensington), is soon to be developed by Northacre, the company behind The Phillimores. St Mary Abbot's modern vicarage is set in a private courtyard at the end of the street, forming a cul-de-sac. **Vicarage Gate** N has a jumble of tall houses in varying styles. It leads to **Vicarage Gardens**, lined with terraces of white stucco at the N end, plus brick-and-stucco versions. A barrier of trees separates Vicarage Gate from **Inverness Gardens**, a snowy, semicircular sweep of 3-storey stucco houses. More stucco terraces, some split into flats, line **Brunswick Gardens** and **Berkeley Gardens**.

The white paint continues in tree-lined **Palace Gardens Terrace** – 3-storey basement terraces on the E side and 4-storey basement houses with elaborate Greek-style columned porches on the W. This is a 'hot-spot', say estate agents, with more modest-sized (say 5-bed, perhaps £3.5 million) homes for more modest-sized millionaires who can't quite aspire to next-door Kensington Palace Gardens. **Strathmore Gardens**, lying off the W side of the street, is a short cul-de-sac of 4-storey-and-basement stucco terraces. Hidden behind them is an enviable studio house. Just beyond here, **Palace Gardens Terrace** becomes part of a one-way traffic system, linking Notting Hill Gate with **Kensington Church St**. Church St, a residential/shopping street lined by pubs, antique shops, galleries, restaurants and jewellers, retains a lot of charm, but is also a main N–S traffic route, running down the hill from Notting Hill Gate to Kensington High St.

Queen's Gate

Queen's Gate is a busy, sweeping boulevard – the right word: this is more Paris than London – tree-lined and wide enough for parking down the centre. It is flanked by the grand stucco terraces that are a feature of this neighbourhood. The majority were built between 1850 and 1870, and have since been converted into vast grand flats, hotels, embassies and ambassadorial homes. East of here is considered Knightsbridge. Most houses are smart, but a few retain the slightly seedy air of a stucco building that has not had quite enough spent on it. These usually turn out to have been split into flats 25 or more years back, before the money really started to flow Kensington-wards.

More long stretches of 4/5-storey Victorian terraces, with columned porches, stand on both sides of **Queen's Gate Terrace** (white and cream stucco) and **Elvaston Place** (brick and stucco). Both are wide streets and, like Queen's Gate, have extra parking space in the middle. In **Queen's Gate Gardens**, the imposing 5/6-storey stucco terraces are set around three sides of a large central garden screened by trees. A 1960s flats block, Campbell Court, which fronts **Gloucester Rd**, backs on to the W side of the garden.

Dotted around this network of streets is a series of small-scale mews, which once served as stables and staff quarters for the large houses behind which they lie. Most have mixtures of groups of 2-storey brick/painted cottages, some still with working garages or car showrooms. **Queen's Gate Mews**, lying just off **Queen's Gate Terrace**, has the added attraction of its own pub, the Queen's Arms. A new 3-bed house here sold for around £1.5 million in 2001, though 1960s houses in the same mews have established a level at around £850,000. Impressive classical stone arches lead into **Elvaston Mews** (which still has a working stables) and **Queen's Gate Place Mews**. The latter sits behind more stately, 5-storey terraces in **Queen's Gate Place**. It is wider than the other mews, leaving room for cobbled forecourts in front of the modern and period cottages.

The tall brick-and-stucco terraces reappear in **Gloucester Rd**, a busy through-road and shopping centre. They have been turned into hotels, offices or flats, usually with shops on the ground floor. **Gloucester Rd** merges into **Palace Gate**, which is lined mainly by stone, or red-brick-and-stone, buildings: offices, flats and embassies.

Exclusive **Kensington Gate** lies to the E at the point where Palace Gate and Gloucester Rd meet. Two grand terraces of richly ornamented white stucco houses stretch along a narrow strip of garden with trees and flower beds. At each end of the terraces stand paired 'tower' houses, looking like iced wedding cakes. Kensington Gate and **Hyde Park Gate** to the N still have high proportions of single-family houses.

The E leg of **Hyde Park Gate** contains a mix of period and modern houses and flats, plus some large 'one-off' houses – such as No. 28, where Sir Winston Churchill lived and died. Tall red-brick-and-stone mansions and the 11-storey, 1960s red-brick flats block, Broadwalk House, flank the entrance to the more exclusive W leg of the street. Beyond here, the street opens out into a circle with a central garden. A handful of elegant detached villas with their own large gardens (one big enough for a tennis court) sit around the circle. Halfway along the street off to the W is **Reston Place**, a charming little enclave of 2-storey white-painted cottages set around a secluded courtyard.

The **Kensington Rd** frontage of the neighbourhood is dominated by the huge modern 11-storey red-brick Thorney Court flats block (see Knightsbridge), and the flank of Broadwalk House, which gaze out over Kensington Gardens. In common with the other period/modern properties lining the N boundary (flats, embassies and offices), they are set back from the road behind driveways and screens of trees.

De Vere/Cornwall

West of **Gloucester Rd** is a neighbourhood that in many ways is the heart of Kensington. The area runs southwards from the centuries-old **Kensington Square** in a series of quiet, leafy streets. On the E side of the neighbourhood **Gloucester Rd** is a busy thoroughfare lined by a mix of homes and offices and shops. It also has a tube station; the main group of homes is the 4/5-storey Edwardian red-brick and stone mansion block of St George's Court, which has a row of shops on the ground floor.

Behind St Stephen's Church (now a health centre and kindergarten) at the SW end of Gloucester Rd is **Emperor's Gate**. This almost triangular-shaped street has a tiny patch of green in the middle and a central block of stucco terraced houses sitting on a similarly shaped site. A row of late-Victorian, red-brick-and-stucco buildings with ornate columned porches stands on the W side, a terrace of 5-storey plus basement buildings on the E: not surprisingly, most are split into flats. A new offices/flats block stands at the S entrance. Concealed behind a red-brick and stone arch in the NE corner of the street is **Osten Mews**, a looped, cobbled mews of little 2-storey painted cottages.

The view here is dominated by the towering Point West – an apartment block converted from the former West London Air Terminal fronting **Cromwell Rd.** This huge scheme was on hold for a decade after the owners ran out of money in 1987, but in 1997 a consortium led by Regalian restarted the scheme. It has 350 flats, from studios up to 3-beds. Prices start with studios at c. £235,000. At the top the 'Sky Apartments' – houses in the air – boast their own high-up lobby and concierge. Also in the block are offices, a health club, shops – and there's a smart Sainsbury's next door, plus Waitrose just up the road.

It may look 18th-century – but it is modern. A clever pastiche of the Kensington town-house style, with 'Georgian' fanlight, panelled door with windows either side – even the ivy is authentic. For the real thing in Kensington, visit Kensington Square, which grew up as homes for Palace courtiers and has some beautiful Queen Anne and early-Georgian houses.

Off **Grenville Place**'s brick/stucco rows lies **Cornwall Mews South**, a pretty corner with its mix of 2-storey period and modern painted brick cottages. The scale changes dramatically just up the road in **Cornwall Gardens**, with its tall cliffs of white and cream stucco. Terraces of mid-Victorian Italianate houses with columned porches stretch along both sides of three large private gardens. The trees match the height of the 5-storey plus basement homes, long split into flats of various sizes and conditions.

Launceston Place to the N signals the beginning of an enclave of highly desirable, quiet streets lying at the neighbourhood's heart. The group is bounded by Launceston Place itself, **Victoria Grove** (E), **Stanford Rd** (W), **Albert Place** (N) and **Kynance Mews** (S). **Canning Place** is in the same style: the whole enclave dates from around 1840.

Picturesque **Kynance Mews** must rate as the most attractive mews in the whole of the Kensington and Chelsea area. Divided by **Launceston Place**, the shorter, eastern, leg is lined by 2/3-storey white or cream-painted cottages with a splendid view of Queen's Tower. The W, and most delightful, section has a mix of charming, vine-covered, 2-storey cottages. A profusion of flowers and shrubs spreads along the mews in tubs and urns. Part of the N side backs on to the walled gardens of the houses in **Eldon Rd** and the prize-winning gardens of Christ Church in Victoria Rd, giving the mews a particularly leafy look.

Halfway along the mews, a set of steps leads to **Victoria Rd**. Many a household name has been attracted to the elegant homes in this 1840s street known, in former days, as 'Love Walk'. Small groups of semi-detached stucco or brick-and-stucco villas with leafy front gardens line the most desirable stretch of the street S of Cambridge Place: expect to pay £2 million or so for a 4-bedroomed house here. To the N, the road is flanked by the backs of hotels fronting adjoining streets. Victoria Rd continues N to meet Kensington Rd and Kensington Gardens.

More 2-storey, semi-detached early-Victorian villas are found in **Launceston Place**, running parallel. The black-and-white colour scheme is accentuated by the black window canopies remaining on the houses on the W side of the street. **Eldon Rd** is a particularly attractive street with terraces of pastel-painted 3-storey stucco houses adjoining Christ Church. Groups of highly individual brick/stucco houses stand on the N side. Tree-lined **Cottesmore Gardens** to the N has paired 3-storey stucco villas and more big individual houses, some of which have been split into equally spacious flats.

The W end of the street runs into **Stanford Rd**, lined by detached brick-and-stucco villas, with some paired houses and simple brick-and-stucco terraces. Standing in their midst is Cottesmore Court, a tall 1930s brown-brick mansion flats block, which spreads around the corner into **Kelso Place**. The S arm of this T-shaped street has rows of 2/3-storey, brick terraced houses (£1.275 million for a 4-bed last winter) which back onto the Kensington Green development on the W side (see below). A cache of modern brown brick town-houses lies in a private cul-de-sac at the end of the W arm of Kelso Place, which flanks the Circle & District tube line (running above-ground at this point).

Running across the N end of Stanford Rd is **St Alban's Grove**. More brick-and-stucco detached and paired houses can be found on the S side opposite Richmond College, the American international college of London. Next to it is the red-brick and stucco cliff of St Alban's Mansions. The W end of the street culminates in a small local shopping centre, a feature of which is the famous Leith School of Food and Wine. A bunch of grapes and a knife and fork have been wittily worked into the brickwork of the gabled building. To the W are the private grounds of the Maria Assumpta Centre, housing a convent and the LAMDA drama college. Hidden around the corner to the S are the vine-covered St Alban's Studios, set around a neo-Tudor courtyard.

The E end of the street also forms a pleasant, villagey centre at its junction with **Victoria Rd**. A terrace of 1840s stucco houses with the Regency's style hallmark of a continuous black first-floor canopy and decorative ironwork columns stretches along the N side. It joins up with more shops spilling around the corner from **Gloucester Rd**.

Canning Place just to the N is a pleasant, leafy street with pairs of linked stucco villas and a terrace of 2/3-storey-plus-basement stucco houses. On the N side are the entrances to two converted mews developments, **De Vere Cottages** and **De Vere Mews**. **De Vere Gardens** off to the N is lined mainly by tall terraces converted into flats, with hotels at its N end.

Canning Passage, a pedestrian walkway, runs through to Victoria Rd. Off this road is a series of three leafy cul-de-sacs – **Albert Place**, **Cambridge Place** and **Douro Place**. The first two have early-Victorian stucco villas; much of **Douro Place** was completely rebuilt following war damage, resulting in modern and period houses standing side by side. The cul-de-sac here is created by the back of the flats in Kensington Court.

Kensington Court is both the name of the street and of the red-brick Jacobean-style complex which dominates this 7-acre triangular site S of Kensington High St. A series of mansion blocks and terraces of gabled houses of differing heights and degrees of ornamentation make up the complex. Built 1880–1900, Kensington Court was the first group of buildings in London to be lit by electricity. You will be asked c. £1.6 million here for a 4-bed, 2,000 sq ft, long-lease flat. At the S end of the Court is **Kensington Court Mews**, an unusual late-Victorian multi-storey stable block, which now has two tiers of flats above ground-floor garages. Another 5/6-storey red-brick block, Kensington Court Gardens, stands on the E side of **Kensington Court Place**, dwarfing the terrace of 1840s 3-storey cottages opposite (c. £1.25 million for one of these).

Beyond **Thackeray St** with its parade of shops is **Kensington Square**. This is one of London's oldest squares, dating back to 1685, when it was built to house Palace courtiers. Some of the houses, which range from Jacobean and Georgian to 1905, remain as homes (a very smart Georgian one with 7 beds was £6.5 million last winter), while others are offices. Blue plaques dotted around the square with its large central gardens recall former distinguished residents, including Edward Burne-Jones, Mrs Patrick Campbell and John Stuart Mill.

Scarsdale/Abingdon

The Circle Line in its deep cutting and the Kensington Green development divide this neighbourhood from **Kensington Square** to the E. **Wrights Lane** is the entry point from Kensington High St; a short way down it is a 1990s development of 119 1-, 2- and 3-bed flats with underground parking and fitness centre (marketed as 'Royal Gate' – but both council and Palace vetoed this, and the blocks are now called Consort, Regent and Sovereign Courts). Its 1-, 2- and 3-bed flats go for between £325–800,000.

Wrights Lane leads on to the big London Copthorne Tara and Kensington Close hotels. On the W side of the lane, not far from its junction with Kensington High St, stand two of the late-Victorian mansions blocks that make up **Iverna Court**, a set-piece complex of 5-/7-/8-storey-and-basement red-brick and stone mansion blocks with elaborate entrances and black cast-iron balconies. The blocks spread around the corner into **Iverna Gardens**, stretching almost to its junction with Abingdon Villas. Some modern dark-brick blocks here have just been expensively revamped, with 17 garden-square-view flats on the market (1-beds from £425,000, 2-beds from £495,000). Flats in the square at the N end of the street overlook the unusual white marble St Sarkis Armenian Church, which sits in the middle, behind a screen of trees and shrubs.

More tall brick-and-stone mansion blocks, including the popular Zetland House, line the E side of busy **Marloes Rd**. House-sized – 2,500 sq ft – flats in this block have sold for some £2 million. Off Marloes Rd, on the site that was once the local workhouse and then the hospital, is 'Kensington Green', a 1991 complex of 1- to 4-bed houses and flats. The only access is via **St Mary's Gate**. The rest of **Marloes Rd** has 3/4-storey-plus-basement brick-and-stucco terraces, some with shops and offices on the ground floors. The large grey concrete and blue-glass building at the S junction with **Cromwell Rd** is the private Cromwell Hospital. **Pennant Mews** runs behind the hospital.

Lexham Gardens stretches across the neighbourhood, changing in character as it goes. The S crescent, which curves N from Cromwell Rd, contains mainly hotels, presumably remnants from the days when the West London Air Terminal stood behind the street. The rest of the brick-and-stucco terraced properties here have been converted into flats. This is perhaps the cheapest corner of Kensington, with a brisk turnover of homes and 2-bed flats in the £400,000 bracket. Leading off the N end of the crescent is **Lexham Walk**, a pleasant passageway lined by painted 2-storey cottages. It crosses into the De Vere/Cornwall neighbourhood to the E.

East of Marloes Rd, **Lexham Gardens** is made up of 4/5-storey plus basement brick-and-stucco terraced houses of varying quality, set around narrow central gardens. The houses in the W arm, across Marloes Rd, are built in the same style, but are generally of better quality. As in the E arm, most have been split into flats.

Tucked away behind the W end of Lexham Gardens are **Lexham Mews** and **Radley Mews**, which join together at the S end of Allen St. The long cobbled mews has mostly 2-storey period/rebuilt brick/painted cottages, with garages and other commercial uses. Emerge from the mews into **Stratford Rd** with its upmarket 'village' shops and terraces of 3-storey and basement brick-and-stucco houses, some with small front gardens and forecourt parking.

Lying off the N side of Stratford Rd, around the corner from the parade of shops, is **Blithfield St**, an appealing tree-lined cul-de-sac of colourfully painted 3-storey 1860s terraces. **Sunningdale Gardens** stands on the S side of Stratford Rd at the junction with Abingdon Rd: here the terraces turn sideways on to form an attractive cache of brick-and-stucco houses flanking a small central garden with trees in the middle.

Well hidden behind the houses on the N side of Stratford Rd near its junction with Earls Court Rd is **Shaftesbury Mews**, a development of modern 4-storey brown-brick houses with garages. **Scarsdale Studios**, off Stratford Rd, is a unique enclave of nine artists' studios built in the 1890s around a private courtyard. These are much desired, and the 3,000 sq ft houses sell for over £2 million. Tree-lined **Scarsdale Villas** has Victorian terraces of 3-storey-and-basement stucco, or brick-and-stucco, houses up to Allen St. Going E they become paired villas on the N side, with groups of four on the S.

In tree-lined **Abingdon Villas**, a mix of 3-storey Victorian terraces stand next to tall red-brick and stone mansion blocks. **Abingdon Court**, N, which stretches from Iverna Gardens to Allen St, is late-Victorian; **Abingdon Gardens** to the S is Edwardian.

Allen St and **Abingdon Rd**, which run N–S from Kensington High St to Stratford Rd, combine a mix of homes and commercial uses. Shops and restaurants spill around the corner from the High St into both. A short distance S of the High St in Allen St is **Wynnstay Gardens**, a massive cache of 4-/5-storey, red-brick and stucco mansion-flats blocks. One group fronts Allen St, while further blocks are tucked away behind, lining a private road. There was a choice of 3-and 4-bed flats here for c. £1.6 million last winter. Allen House, a red-brick gabled block of 45 time-share and short-lease flats, stands on the opposite side of the street: yours, last winter, for £25 million. More mansion flats and 3-storey brick-and-stucco terraces lie to the S.

Beside the chapel is one of two entrances to **Adam and Eve Mews**. (The other is in Kensington High St.) The mews has 2- and 3-storey modern and period houses, some garages and offices. **Eden Close** at the NW end is a modern red-brick development, where a mews has been created within a mews. Mews flats are very popular, with 2-beds in this neighbourhood averaging £575,000. A 3-bed cottage will go for around a million.

Abingdon Rd is lined with 2/3-storey terraced houses of varying styles. Off to the E, Octagon in 2001 created **Vantage Place**, a peaceful, sloping courtyard surrounded by four imaginative houses, a flat and the refurbished 'gatehouse'. This mews is where the first Aston Martin cars were made in the 1920s. The brown- and red-brick late-Victorian flats in **Pater St** to the W spread around the corner into the N end of Abingdon Rd, merging with the shops and restaurants that lead to the High St.

Earls Court Rd on the W boundary of the neighbourhood is a two-way street as far as Stratford Rd, where it joins the notorious West London one-way traffic system, now a Red Route. The most attractive residential section – a terrace of 4-storey-and-basement stucco-fronted houses – lies between Stratford Rd and Scarsdale Villas. The modern building at the junction of Earls Court Rd and Kensington High St is flats and offices, topped by a penthouse overlooking Holland Park. Monarch House has luxury flats to let, aimed at businessmen and expatriates, with hotel-style amenities.

Pembrokes/Edwardes Square

Although bounded by some of the busiest and noisiest roads in the borough, this neighbourhood contains some of the earliest and choicest properties in Kensington. The first surprise lies at the end of an unpromising lane off the N end of bustling Earls Court Rd, behind the Odeon Cinema. Turn the corner to find **Pembroke Place**, an oasis of pretty, painted 3-storey Victorian houses set around a courtyard with trees in the middle. The 3-storey brick-and-stucco terrace on the E side is a modern rebuild.

Tucked away behind Kensington police station immediately to the S is **Pembroke Mews**. The mostly 2-storey brick or painted cottages in this secluded corner mingle with offices (design companies etc.) and a primary school (St Phillip & St Barnabas C of E).

Within yards of busy **Earls Court Rd** with its mix of residential/commercial properties is **Pembroke Square**. This Georgian square is neatly shielded from the main road by Rassells garden centre and the flower-bedecked Hansom Cab pub. Two terraces of 4-storey yellow-brick terraced houses with stucco-faced ground floors line a long private central garden. The garden has its own tennis court and even a daily weather chart posted on the gate. The W end of Pembroke Square becomes **Pembroke Villas** to the S, an attractive colony of 3-storey paired stucco or brick-and-stucco villas set in gardens with tall trees overhanging the street.

Pembroke Walk, an easily missed cul-de-sac tucked away off the E side of the street, is a narrow lane with unusual, nay, eccentric, 2-/3-storey period and modern houses/studios. North of Pembroke Square, past the pretty Scarsdale pub with its profusion of hanging baskets, stands **Edwardes Square**, the neighbourhood's gem. This fine Regency square was built 1811–20. Immaculate terraces of beautiful 3-storey-and-basement brick houses with stucco ground floors stretch along the W and E sides of mature central gardens. Front gardens, wisteria-covered houses, hedges and overhanging trees contribute to the leafy look of the spacious square, only a short walk from the shops and restaurants of Kensington High St. Green and gold Victorian street lamps, original cast-iron fanlights and black cast-iron railings with unusual pineapple kingheads add to the period character of the area. The pineapple, our sources say, is a traditional symbol of welcome.

The N side of the square is bounded by a long brick wall and a mass of trees in the rear gardens of **Earls Terrace**, which fronts Kensington High St. Here a long, uniform Regency terrace, set back from the main road behind a private carriageway, with iron gates, Victorian lamp posts (green this time) and trees, was at the turn of the millennium the talking-point of Kensington. Its high-security, 6-bedroomed houses were renovated to superstar status: buyers were offered the choice of a cinema, a pool or a games room in the basement. All were sold after a *very* long marketing campaign and many sightings of elusive superstars (this is one of the many places in London where Madonna did *not* buy). A recent price asked was £4.5 million, with £3.75 million for one the year before – though asking prices of £5 million, the alleged top figure in 2001, met with resistance.

The S arm of **Edwardes Square** feels like a separate street, being a complete contrast to the Georgian terraces. It has mostly century-old studio houses (Annigoni lived here), an art gallery, and 1930s Pembroke Court, a 5-storey brick-and-stone flats block. These buildings face the white 'Temple' – a listed gardener's cottage in the square garden, designed to look like a Grecian temple. Lying just to the S of the square at its W end is **Pembroke Gardens Close**, a private landscaped cul-de-sac of 2-storey brick houses. This exceptional enclave has the peaceful air of a village green.

Pembroke Gardens (the name derives from the Welsh estates of Lord Kensington's family) is split into two arms. On the corner with **Warwick Gardens** a modern house, No. 12A, is built round a central swimming pool: it sold in 2003 for £12.5 million. A feature of the N arm is **Pembroke Studios**, 2-storey brick Victorian houses, looking like a group of 19th-century almshouses, set round a courtyard, and separated from the street by a garden and cast-iron gates. The rest of the street has a mix of brick-and-stucco paired houses, 1920s Dutch-gabled houses, modern brick terraces and Victorian terraces.

Pembroke Rd is cut in two by Earls Court's heavily trafficked one-way system, which runs southbound along the E stretch to join Earls Court Rd. Two large

1930s flats blocks – Marlborough and Chatsworth (a 1-bed, £250–320,000) Courts – dominate the S side of the E arm. Painted brick or stucco/brick houses, detached and paired, line the rest of the S and N sides. A recent red-brick block, Huntsmore House (formerly Pembroke Heights), stands at the Pembroke Rd/Cromwell Crescent junction. The block of 79 1- to 3-bed flats stretches to the council's central works depot on the corner with **Warwick Rd**, W. It encloses a large garden and boasts both pool and gym.

Although **Warwick Gardens** forms the S-bound section of the Earls Court one-way system, it is a relatively pleasant, if busy, tree-lined street. Pairs of large, white stucco houses with columned porches, and terraces of 3-storey-plus-basement brick-and-stucco ones predominate. St Mary Abbot's Court is a group of three large 7-storey brick flats blocks, grouped at the NW end of Warwick Gardens.

Warwick Rd is a major route on the N-bound section of the one-way system. The council's central works depot with a modern housing estate perched on top dominates the E side of the road. On the W side, public car and lorry parks, a petrol station, a Sainsbury's Homebase DIY centre, a smart modernist Tesco superstore (with Affordable Homes above) lie between the road and railway line. St George's 'Kensington Westside' just N of here, on the other side of the High St, has 294 flats including 59 Affordable Homes; penthouses aspire towards a million.

Phillimore Estate

Substantial Victorian houses and villas predominate in this leafy, smart neighbourhood. The streets climb gently uphill and are remarkably peaceful, considering their proximity to busy Kensington High St, just to the S. Most of the big, white-stucco detached villas and 4-/5-storey stucco or brick-and-stucco terraced homes on the W side of **Phillimore Gardens** have the splendid added advantage of rear gardens that back onto Holland Park. More large detached mansions are on the E side, alongside 4-storey semi-detached houses. Some have front gardens, others patios with flower-filled tubs.

A path leads into Holland Park from the N side of the street where it joins **Duchess of Bedford's Walk** at the top of the hill. Plane Tree House, an award-winning 7-storey 1960s flats development, is in the N corner overlooking the park. Edwardian flats blocks, including the well-regarded Duchess of Bedford House, spread along the rest of this tree-lined street, adjoining The Phillimores (see Campden Hill, above) on the E corner. The 7-storey blocks stand in landscaped grounds, set back behind neat hedges.

They overlook the walled back gardens of houses in **Upper Phillimore Gardens**. This street is lined by large, white-stucco linked houses and smaller brick-and-stucco terraced homes – all front gardens, hedges and doorstep urns full of roses, shrubs and bushes. Tall trees add to the street's charm. One of the largest houses, a 7-bed complete with indoor pool, was on the market for a suggested price of £25 million last winter – as it had been for three years. **Phillimore Place**, a one-way street, and **Essex Villas** have mainly 3-storey and basement brick-and-stucco rows – the rather startling exception is a sudden group of Tudor-Gothicky houses in the former. Back to taller, if more ornate, brick-and-stucco terraces **Stafford Terrace.**

The scene then changes completely in **Phillimore Walk**, which is overshadowed by the back of Stafford Court, a big early 20th-century brown-brick and stone flats block. It fronts Kensington High St and takes up the whole block between Phillimore Gardens and Argyll Rd. Shortish leases here, as elsewhere on the Estate, did not deter buyers who looked to the recent law change (see Buying and Selling chapter) to justify their investment. More very big semi-detached houses and white stucco terraces with front gardens line **Argyll Rd**: £3 million for 3,000 sq ft is the general benchmark.

The S end of **Campden Hill Rd**, which forms the neighbourhood's eastern boundary, also has large white houses and brick-and-stucco terraces. They look across to the modern red-brick Kensington Town Hall in the E side of the street, which adjoins the slightly older library complex; both buildings fill the block across to **Hornton St** to the E and down to little **Phillimore Walk**, just behind the High St.

Transport Tubes: Notting Hill Gate (zone 1/2, District, Circle, Central), Queensway (zone 1, Central), High St Kensington (zone 1, District, Circle), Gloucester Rd (zone 1, Piccadilly, District, Circle). From High St Kensington: Oxford Circus 15 min (1 change), City 25 min (1 change), Heathrow 40 min (1 change).

Convenient for Hyde Park, West End, Heathrow, the West. Miles from centre: 3.

Schools Local Authority: Holland Park, Cardinal Vaughan RC (b), Sion Manning RC (g). Private: St James' (g), Colegio Espanol Vicente Canada Blanch, Queen's Gate School (g), Ashbourne College, David Game College, Duff Miller College, Mander Portman Woodward School, Southbank International School.

SALES

Flats	S	1B	2B	3B	4B	5B
Average prices	165–285	250–350	350–1M+	420–1.5M+	1.2–3M+	–
Houses	2B	3B	4B	5B	6/7B	8B
Average prices	600+	600–1.5M+	1–3M	1.5–3.5M+	1.5–5M+	–

RENTAL

Flats	S	1B	2B	3B	4B	5B
Average prices	250–350	300–550	350–800	600–1500	800–1600	–
Houses	2B	3B	4B	5B	6/7B	8B
Average prices	500–700+	750–900	900–1000	1000–4500	3500+	–

The properties Heart of desirable, residential London: good choice of handsome Victorian family houses, some earlier ones; legions of flats, mansion and converted; plus mews cottages and some new-build flats in smart, secure complexes. Hardly a bad street in the place.

The market Kensington has never been unfashionable. Today, the settled, prosperous population is joined by international buyers/renters – but the market is very sensitive to the US economy. More domestic than Knightsbridge, more respectable than Notting Hill, smarter than South Ken. Some glorious, if multi-millions, homes.

Among estate agents active in this area are:

- Hamptons
- Beaney Pearce
- Winkworth
- John D Wood
- Knight Frank
- Foxtons
- Douglas & Gordon
- Farley & Co
- W A Ellis
- Bective Leslie Marsh
- Lane Fox
- Marsh & Parsons
- Strutt & Parker
- Aylesford
- Friend & Falcke
- Scotts
- Savills
- Chesterton
- Finlay Brewer
- Faron Sutaria
- Kensington Property Services
- Anscombe & Ringland
- Harpers
- Jackson-Stops & Staff
- Farrar & Co

KENTISH TOWN AND TUFNELL PARK

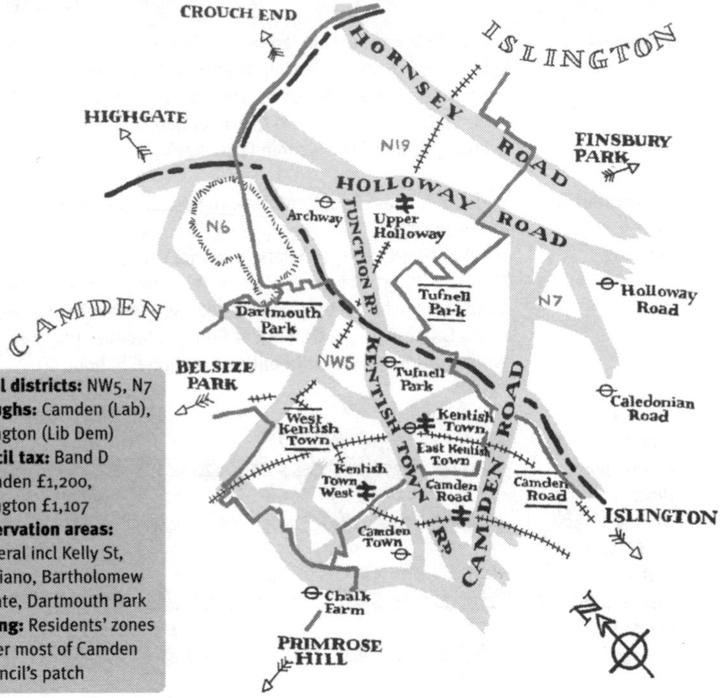

Postal districts: NW5, N7
Boroughs: Camden (Lab), Islington (Lib Dem)
Council tax: Band D Camden £1,200, Islington £1,107
Conservation areas: Several incl Kelly St, Torriano, Bartholomew Estate, Dartmouth Park
Parking: Residents' zones cover most of Camden Council's patch

There are some really interesting homes to discover in Kentish Town and in Tufnell Park, its eastern neighbour – if you can find your way in through the confusion of railway lines, main roads, fiendish one-way systems and formless council estates. Worth finding, too: they are still cheaper than Camden Town, to the S; and Hampstead and Highgate, round the lovely Heath, lie to the N. People take the trouble to search here because the schools are relatively good, and it's close to town and the Heath.

Value is relative, however: the grander, larger houses of Dartmouth Park are cheap only in comparison to these lofty neighbours. Indeed, Dartmouth Park has come up in the world to such an extent that it has left the rest of Kentish Town behind and would be Highgate if it could (and if it were not for the postcode).

In Kentish Town proper, the handsome early-Victorian terraces that survive in a somewhat mixed area are now 'riddled with trendy property' according to local agents, who pray that, given its neighbours and its convenience, it's only a matter of time before it catches up with Camden Town. But like Camden, there are gritty bits and downright uneasy ones, with big pressure from locals for more street lights and CCTV.

To explore this area, get off the main roads. These workaday, run-down thoroughfares are starting to show signs of tidying – new furnishing stores and the Phoenicia Mediterranean Food Hall (an epic deli) at the S end of Kentish Town Rd to add to the well-respected Owl bookshop, music shops and Sainsbury's Local in Fortess Rd. 'It's trying to be villagey,' comments a local agent, 'but it'll never be Hampstead'. But the main drags still do little to betray that behind them are worth-exploring pockets of attractive Victorian homes. There are also rather larger zones of post-war council-built housing, ranging from the acceptable to the lamentable. These developments quite often disrupted the Victorian street plan, imposing a random mess of blocked-off streets, paths, car parks, odd green patches and service roads.

The original village was around the present-day stations, where **Kentish Town Rd**, **Highgate Rd** and **Fortess Rd** meet. It was on one of the main roads to the north, and was favoured as a pleasure resort for Londoners out for a day at a country inn. **Angler's Lane** may seem a meaningless name today, but the Fleet River used to run above-ground here. . . . The village grew as the area around became important farmland (explore **Grove Terrace, Little Green St**), but the real population explosion came in the 1840s, when large-scale development began – catering for middle-class families with servants. Kentish Town was respectable, but not able to compete with its illustrious northern neighbours, Hampstead and Highgate, for really wealthy inhabitants.

The area passed through ups and downs, becoming at first a rather pretty and fashionable place, but then (as the railways carved the area up) falling into a long and steady decline that lasted until the 1960s, when two important things happened. The first was the dramatic acceleration of large and mostly unattractive housing schemes started by St Pancras Council and continued, with more vigour, by the newly formed larger borough of Camden; this changed the face of Kentish Town, particularly the W.

The second was that Kentish Town – in particular its jewel, leafy Dartmouth Park – began to benefit as an overflow area into which trickled those who just couldn't quite afford to buy in Hampstead or Highgate. This is still the dominant feature of the property market in the area – only now people moving in are those who just can't quite afford Belsize Park or Camden. . . . Here they find pockets of substantial family houses, a good supply of small- and medium-sized homes, and plenty of converted flats, particularly 1- and 2-bed ones – though the conversion frenzy of the '80s assumed nothing like the proportions here that it did in, for example, West Hampstead.

The entire area suffers from parking overload: residents' schemes cover the whole Camden Council part except Dartmouth Park.

Dartmouth Park

This is the corner where people first realized that Kentish Town had streets to offer that were every bit as nice as in Hampstead, *and* just as close to Hampstead Heath *and* within reach of a tube (Tufnell Park) *and* close to the West End *and* with large, 6/7-bed houses – but where prices were, and still are, a bit lower – though the gap has narrowed.

As prices have risen, so the enclave feels increasingly removed from Kentish Town. Estate agents record a steady influx of families from Hampstead and Islington, attracted by the nearby Heath and the good local schools. Two of the local comprehensives, William Ellis (boys) and Acland Burghley (mixed) have tight catchment areas – and they overlap in Dartmouth Park. Parliament Hill girls' school is right on the doorstep, as is La Sainte Union convent school. There's a strong community atmosphere: 'affluent without being flash' was a local's summing up. The neighbourhood's rising fortunes can be tracked in the pubs: a steady change from spit'n'sawdust to gastro-chic.

Owned and developed by the Earl of Dartmouth in the 1870s, the area lies between **Dartmouth Park Hill** to the E and **Highgate Rd** in the W; from Highgate's Holly Lodge Estate and the famous cemetery in the N down to busy (and narrow) **Chetwynd Rd**. Generally, the homes get grander as you move SW across this hilly neighbourhood.

Spectacular speed humps and one-way streets attempt to deter through-traffic, with limited success as motorists desperately search for alternative ways through the Kentish Town bottleneck. However, there are also hidden delights, such as the sports ground, tennis courts and bowling club tucked away off **Croftdown Rd**, and the sudden views W and S from some of the houses in the loftier streets.

Particularly popular are **Dartmouth Park Rd** (a 1-bed garden flat here, £275,000) and

Dartmouth Park Avenue, where the grand double-fronted 5-bed detacheds go (as they did last year) for up to £1.5 million; and also peaceful **Boscastle Rd**, round the corner from the heath (4/5-bed houses c. £1.2 million). There are some smaller, more cottagey houses in **St Alban's Rd**, and mansion blocks and older-style council-built homes in St Alban's and **Croftdown Rd**, contrasting in the latter with 6-bed terraced houses which nudge £1 million.

Kentish Town's most elegant (and pricey) homes are also here – pre-dating Dartmouth Park, the splendid row of late Georgiana in **Grove Terrace** off **Highgate Rd**: these are deceptively large houses. Look, too, just to the S, parallel with and E of Highgate Rd, for hidden **College Lane**, a treasure-trove of 2-storey Victorian cottages and larger 3-storey houses; it really is a lane, too, lit by old-fashioned gas-style street lamps. And it gets better: **Little Green St**, just off it, has bow-windowed Regency cottages. And **Lady Somerset Rd**, away at the lane's southern end, has handsome 1860s houses.

West Kentish Town

This neighbourhood, W of the busy **Kentish Town Rd** shopping centre, is Kentish Town in a nutshell: streets of desirable Victorian houses right next to huge, and in places intimidating, council estates. These estates swallowed up dozens of Victorian streets. They range from the worst of municipal mistakes to shining showpieces of successful urban development. But, in among the estates and tower blocks, there are pleasant streets where bargain-hunters search for unmodernized homes in handsome, early-Victorian terraces. Their arrival, and the efforts of the council, have improved the area markedly. Local agents admit, though, that the estates still put some buyers off.

There are interesting terraces towards Maitland Park, on the W edge of the neighbourhood, though the streets just over in NW3 with **Maitland Park** in their name (**Villas**, **Rd**) are council housing, and on the rough side at that. Look, though, at attractive **St Leonard's Square**, and also at the SW end of **Queen's Crescent**, off which quiet, leafy little cul-de-sacs hold colourful terraces of pastel-painted homes: **St Thomas's Gardens**, **Baptist Gardens**, **Modbury Gardens** and **St Ann's Gardens**. A 3-bed maisonette in Queen's Crescent was £395,000 last winter, while ex-council 1970s houses are around £260,000 for a 3-bed. The NE end of **Queen's Crescent** is more run down, albeit with bustling street market. **Grafton Rd**, which is quite busy, has a mix: some flat-fronted mid-Victorian terraces and – just two years old this year – nine flats carved out of the old Mitre pub. The Peabody Trust are, unusually, selling off some 1-bed flats in **Spring Place** and **Arctic St** as they come vacant: £160,000 for a 1-bed.

The N part of the neighbourhood, still marked on maps as **Gospel Oak**, was standard-issue 1860s houses in a network of streets set around a circus (**Lismore Circus**). Sadly, this district was zapped in the 1960s by council planners. Today you'll find 20-storey towers, aimless groups of low-rise council-built housing and a street plan to baffle a maze designer. A few 19th-century homes survive (try the **Grafton Terrace** area in the W, and **Basset St/Coity Rd**), but all that now remains of Victorian Gospel Oak is the pleasant cache of NW3 streets running N of **Mansfield Rd** up to the heath (see Hampstead chapter) and the 'Oak Village' corner just to the S of Mansfield Rd (and in NW5), where **Elaine Grove** holds some 3-bed Victorian cottages. In the same corner, and in contrast, ex-local authority flats offer views, and value, from the upper floors of the big blocks: 1-bed flats from c. £160,000, 2-beds in lower-rise blocks £200–230,000, a 3-bed maisonette £270,000.

Just W of Kentish Town Rd, **Inkerman Rd**, **Alma St**, **Cathcart St** and **Willes Rd** offer flat-fronted Victorian brick-and-stucco houses almost as smart as those to the E in the Bartholomew conservation area. A 3-bed house might be £465,000.

While Victorian terraces are patchy in Kentish Town West, there are big old public buildings to split into loft flats. The 1920s ex-college building at 1, **Prince of Wales Rd**, was transformed by Dorrington into 65 galleried flats, some with terraces, in 1999: a 2-bed was £415,000 last winter. In the same street, an 1850 school building next to Kentish Town West station, bought from Camden for £3.6 million, has become luxury flats. This is called 'Hampstead Gates' and gated parking (if not a Hamstead address) is one of the selling points; others are high-spec interiors and Italian-influenced detailing (the developer is Italian). Most of the 14 2- and 3-bedroom flats were still available last December, prices £420–800,000.

East Kentish Town

The triangle bounded by **Kentish Town Rd**, **Camden Rd** and **Brecknock Rd** contains the heartland of Kentish Town. It escaped the attention of council planners, with the exception of some crumbling pre-war estates around **Islip St**, near the station (watch for the rail line, which slices across the area). Otherwise this is a grid of handsome mid-Victorian family houses and converted flats called the Bartholomew Estate, a conservation area (**Islip St** in the N, **Bartholomew Rd** in the S are the borders). Here we come under the influence of the Camden School for Girls catchment area: the school is in **Sandall Rd**.

There is a great deal of charm and elegance – particularly in the Dartmouth Estate section, **Bartholomew Rd, Lawford Rd** and **Bartholomew Villas**, which has semis rather than terraces, with pleasing architectural features such as cast-iron balconies. These rather narrow streets date from just prior to 1870: in Bartholomew Rd, a 4-bed house was £750,000 last winter, while a 2-bed garden flat was £275,000. **Patshull** (4-bed house £650,000) is reckoned one of the best streets because, unlike most of the others, there are no council homes. ('But' says a local 'it is 150 metres from **Oseney Crescent** where there are lots'.) To be fair to Oseney Crescent, the Victorian homes survive at the S end. And the ex-council homes provide the chance to buy a 2-bed flat for under £200,000. Closer to the tube, and a little older, is a group of streets with a more spacious air – the Christ Church estate: **Gaisford St** and **Caversham Rd** are the major streets.

North of the narrow and busy **Leighton Rd**, where a 4-bed house was £695,000 last winter, there are more rewards and surprises. The main surprise is **Lady Margaret Rd**, built in the early 1860s, which lives up to its name: it is almost twice as wide and gracious as any other street in the area. Some of its houses have attractive glass porches. You can be asked £900,000 for one of the big Victorian semis. Leading off it are the rewards: traditionally narrow streets that rank amongst the most intensively gentrified in North London. These include **Falkland Rd**, **Ascham St**, **Dunollie Rd**, **Leverton St**, **Ravely St**, **Countess Rd** and **Montpelier Grove**, all with 2- and 3-storey terraces and semi-detached rows: Countess and Montpelier are reckoned the best. Pretty pastel-coloured stucco facades and interesting cobbled mews add to the charm. Think c. £400,000 for a 3-bed house here.

Off **Leighton Grove**, **Leighton Crescent** boasts a mix of handsome pilaster-and-balcony houses, some overlooking a private square garden, some a little unkempt, some split into flats, plus some council-build. **Leighton Place** is a cul-de-sac: an old warehouse here is now big loft flats, and there are some 1930s suburban-style 3-bed houses (one smart example was £485,000 last winter).

Tufnell Park

Over the border to the E in the borough of Islington, this area, bounded by **Camden Rd**, **Brecknock Rd** and **Holloway Rd**, was almost completely ignored by buyers and even estate agents until the last couple of decades. These days it is giving Kentish Town a run for its money, though it's still a good place to look for space at a saner price. Its pleasant streets, although bordered by busy trunk roads, are themselves quiet, wide, tree-lined and relatively free of traffic. In Tufnell Park, the rule of thumb is: avoid **Holloway Rd** – though it does have decent shopping as well as the constant traffic.

The neighbourhood is split between two postcodes: N19 for the N and a corner of the W side, near Tufnell Park tube; N7 for the S side. The W side of Tufnell Park is within reach of the Northern Line tube, while on the E and S sides the option is the Piccadilly Line at Caledonian Road and Holloway Road stations.

This is a district of wide streets and occasional huge, mid-Victorian houses. **Tufnell Park Rd** runs W–E, dividing the neighbourhood in half. To the S are some large council estates (between **Brecknock Rd** and the famous Holloway Prison for women). **Tabley Rd**, E of the prison, has 4-bed houses in a recent, gated mews. **Carleton Rd** and **Anson Rd** have some surviving 1860s houses: large, ornate, gothicky. Most of the big semis and detached houses (some rather unkempt) are split into flats (a choice of 2-beds at well under the magic £250,000). On tree-lined **Anson Rd** three of the monster houses are still B & Bs. There are a few mid-20th-century smaller terraced houses here and in **Huddleston Rd**, which runs N–S. It, like next-door **Dalmeny Rd**, is divided off to stop through-traffic, and is wide, pleasant and tree-lined. A 3-bed house in Huddleston was asking £535,000 last winter, while in Dalmeny a 5-bed was £700,000.

Closer to the tube in the W there are popular streets: **Hugo** and **Corinne Rds** with attractive 2- and 3-storey terraces (the S end is better in **Corinne**). Leafy **St George's Avenue**, S of Tufnell Park Rd, has spacious flats and the occasional whole house. Big flats can be found, split from even bigger houses. Along the tracks W of the tube station, **Ingestre Rd** is the centre of a late-'60s low-rise council estate.

North of **Tufnell Park Rd** the end of **Huddleston Rd** forms an attractive cul-de-sac. Also worth a look are the mostly late-Victorian houses in the group of roads around **Tytherton Rd**, which include **Mercers Rd, Yerbury Rd, Beversbrook Rd, Campdale Rd** and **Foxham Rd** with its unusually pleasing development of modern council houses, some 5-bed Victoriana (and flats split from them), communal gardens and children's playground. The E end of **Tufnell Park Rd**, over towards **Holloway Rd**, has some early 19th-century terraces. Wedmore Place, off **Wedmore St**, is a modern scheme with 3-bed houses.

Camden Road Borders

Camden Rd – a busy through-route – has some surviving early 19th-century terraced houses, though most are either hotels or flats. **Middleton Grove** has some big detached Victorian villas. Across York Way and NE of a large council estate, there are roads off **Hillmarton Rd** which have grand houses, now mostly flats. These streets, too, are blocked off to traffic and are convenient for Caledonian Rd tube (Piccadilly Line). On the Islington side, off Stock Orchard St, **Heddington Grove** is a street of 134 flats and town-houses dating from the late '80s.

Archway Borders

Between Junction Rd and Dartmouth Park Hill roads like **Bickerton Rd** (mix of new flats and 3-storey Victorian houses) and **Tremlett Grove** adjoin a quiet unnamed park around a covered reservoir. Ex-council flats have also proved to be good buys in this area, which has gained from its proximity to Dartmouth Park. **Hargrave Park** has some pretty Gothic-style houses amid the council-built homes. New homes here tend to come from imaginative conversions: a recent one is a redundant church in **Junction Rd**, which three years back became St Christopher's Court: 18 interesting flats plus two big penthouses. Go N up Junction Rd to reach the Archway junction – a traffic hell but home to a Zone 2 tube station (Northern Line). On the Islington side, and E of busy Archway Rd, is a surprisingly secluded and popular set of roads. North of the huge council estate blocks in **St John's Way**, these streets include the Whitehall Park conservation area, comprising **Whitehall Park, Gladsmuir Rd** and **Harberton Rd** – a well-preserved Victorian estate ranging from grand semis to modest 2-storey terraces. The land slopes quite steeply, adding to their attractiveness and giving splendid views.

Transport Tubes: Kentish Town, Tufnell Park (zone 2, Northern). From Tufnell Park: Oxford Circus 20 min (1 change), City 15 min, Heathrow 55 min (1 change). Trains: Kentish Town (Thameslink); Gospel Oak, Kentish Town West, Camden Rd (North London Line/Silverlink). Proposed new station at Junction Rd on Gospel Oak–Barking line.

Convenient for Hampstead Heath, Islington, roads to North. Miles from centre: 3.

Schools Local Authority: Acland Burghley, Parliament Hill (g), Camden School for Girls, William Ellis (b), La Sainte Union Convent (g).

SALES

Flats	S	1B	2B	3B	4B	5B
Average prices	120–175	160–250	200–400	230–450	350–450	–
Houses	2B	3B	4B	5B	6/7B	8B
Average prices	300–450	400–600	450–850	550–1.4M	1.2M+	–

RENTAL

Flats	S	1B	2B	3B	4B	5B
Average prices	150–200	180–250	220–475	300–600	380–600	–
Houses	2B	3B	4B	5B	6/7B	8B
Average prices	320–400	375–500	450–650	500–850	–	–

The properties Victorian terraces appeared early – 1840s onwards – so those remaining can be handsome; many houses now flats. Some streets of Hampstead quality, others disrupted by council building good and bad. Grandest and priciest in Dartmouth Park and Camden borders. Some big houses in unlikely places, some interesting modern ones too. Svelte school conversions at unlikely prices.

The market First-time buyers still cope here, just; and families find this a good spot between expensive areas. Schools increasingly important. Incomers are moving the place up-market, but it's still mixed. Many homes have been spruced up or turned into flats, and many vendors are former council tenants taking the profit from Right to Buy. The closer to tubes and the further from main through-routes, the higher the price.

Among estate agents active in this area are:

- Olivers
- Winkworth
- Salter Rex
- Capital Sales
- Matthew James
- Benham & Reeves
- Day Morris
- Barnard Marcus
- Keatons
- Dennis & Hayes
- Hotblack Desiato
- Drivers & Norris

KILBURN, KENSAL GREEN AND QUEEN'S PARK

Postal districts: NW6, NW10, W10, W9
Boroughs: Brent (Lab), Westminster (Con)
Council tax: Band D Brent £1,141, Westminster £605
Conservation areas: Queen's Park, Queen's Park Estate, Kilburn, N Kilburn, S Kilburn, Kensal Rise
Parking: Controlled zones have spread to take in most of area

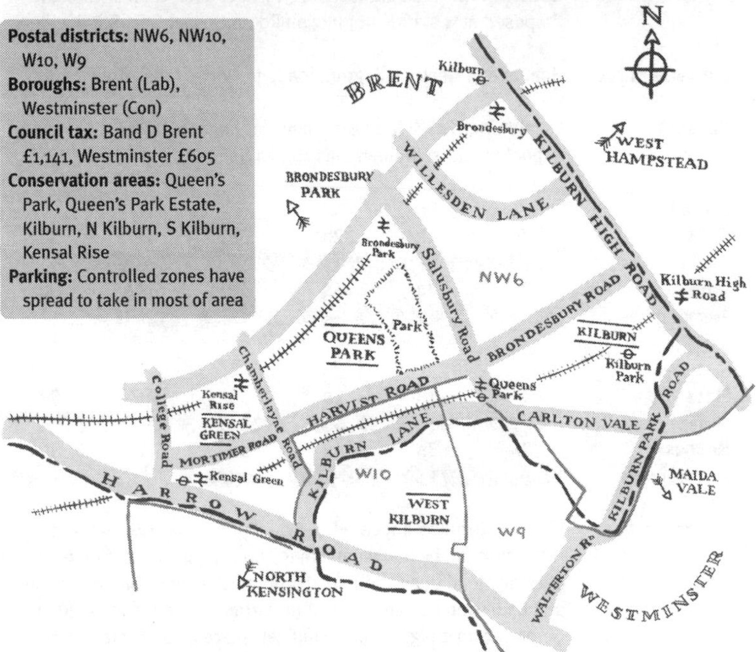

Save the name of Kilburn! Caught between creeping West Hampstead to the E, expansionist Maida Vale to the S and a swollen Queen's Park (which has conveniently forgotten that it's part of it), 'Kilburn' seems in danger of extinction. Confusion over tube station names and postal districts further erodes Kilburn as a known residential area. This year a development on the far side of West Kilburn is being blatantly sold as 'in the heart of North Kensington' – Heart? It's not *in* North Ken – nor even the borough!

Whatever you call this tract, it has several things in its favour: the first being location. It's just up Ladbroke Grove from stratospheric Notting Hill, straight up Edgware Rd from Marble Arch ('I used to walk in: it's just over 2 miles, and the straight road gives you a sense of closeness'), just as near to the centre as North Kensington – closer than, say, Hammersmith, let alone Shepherd's Bush. Second, transport: the Bakerloo and Jubilee Lines have splendid connections, not least with Paddington and its Heathrow link. Postcodes do *not* delineate an area, but for those reassured by them, Kilburn and Kensal Rise share NW6 with West Hampstead; the Kensal Green bit is in NW10; West Kilburn shares W10 with North Ken (see above), and there's even a corner with Maida Vale's W9.

And here you'll find a good choice of (mostly converted) flats of a decent size, and a range of family houses from artisan's cottage to spacious Edwardian villa. All kinds of homes can be had at prices still a fair bit lower than in starry nearby areas – though those of Kilburn's two most charming neighbourhoods, the big family houses set round Queen's Park and the bijou cottages of the Queen's Park Estate (an interesting yardstick), raced ahead of the surrounding streets. Two-bed cottages in the Estate started 1999 at around £145,000, added £20,000 from January–March, another £15,000 by July; began 2000 at £205,000, ended it at £220–255,000. On up we went in 2001: c. £240–290,000

– or double the number you first thought of – since when first-timers have mostly had to rely on parental aid. Things then settled back a bit post-September 11. But not for long. By autumn 2002 these dear little cottages – vertical flats, more like – had reached £270,000 for the smaller, with downstairs bathrooms, while those with upstairs bath sailed past the '£300K' barrier up to £325,000. Two years on, this is still the ceiling for the biggest; the tiniest are £250–260,000; the rest make £285–300,000, depending on those baths.

Much of the present-day Kilburn was built up between 1860 and 1890, as what was a rural hamlet on the **Edgware Rd** became organized urban sprawl – following the railway lines that cross the area. The many little stations drew more and more new inhabitants, and **Kilburn High Rd** grew into a flourishing centre for shopping. Another wave of building spread up from Paddington along the canal, likewise expanding early-Victorian Kensal Town and Kensal Green into today's neighbourhoods.

Up to 1890, most of the housing (and presumably many of the residents) ended at Kensal Rise Cemetery. Next (1895–1905), and to the N, came the larger houses and wider avenues of Queen's Park. There is much confusion over the name 'Queen's Park', because there are two of them: parks (or green spaces) as well as suburbs (streets around said spaces). The name was first used for the estate of Gothicky little terraced cottages that are to be found across to the S of the railway line in W10 – hereafter referred to more properly as Queen's Park Estate. These were built for renting to respectable artisans in the 1870s–'80s. However, the lovely 33-acre park N of **Harvist Rd**, laid out in 1886, was given the same name, and Queen's Park (no 'estate') as a neighbourhood now signifies the big villas and rather grander NW6 streets round the park itself.

Kensal Green, W from Queen's Park across **Chamberlayne Rd** and in NW10, is less assuming. Built up in 1880–1900 and run down by 1920, it is now reasserting itself on the market, increasingly popular thanks to its proximity to the Sainsbury's superstore and the top end of terribly fash **Ladbroke Grove** (minus Notting Hill prices). Its high-density terraces, now mixed in with some dull council houses, are arranged (by means of barriers and no-entry signs) into curious little groups of roads that those house-hunting by car may never find their way inside.

Another neighbourhood that must be treated separately is West Kilburn, S of **Kilburn Lane** – not least because it is in Westminster, rather than in Brent (return to information box at top of chapter, and note respective council-tax levels), and in W9 not NW6. Apart from the unspoilt Queen's Park Estate (which is in W10 . . .), it is an area undergoing much change, with new flats fitted snugly into Victorian terraces.

More news this year of the £600 million regeneration of the council lands S of the railway, in the area roughly between Kilburn Park and Queen's Park stations, stretching S towards Maida Vale. The master plan has now been approved (details below) and by 2019 1,534 homes should have been demolished and rebuilt to a normal streetscape, instead of locked away in high-rise estates; another 775 will be refurbished, and 1,419 new homes added for private sale. We are assured there'll be enough room for all these. . . .

Rail and tube station names seem designed to further confuse the local geography. Kilburn tube (Jubilee Line) is on **Shoot Up Hill** in the far N of the area, just in NW6 but outside Kilburn by most definitions. It serves the select Mapesbury estate neighbourhood, between Willesden Green and Brondesbury Park; locals want the station name changed to Mapesbury. Kilburn Park tube (Bakerloo), to the S, is closer to **Kilburn High Rd.** Queen's Park and Kensal Green stations (also Bakerloo) are sensibly placed, as is Kensal Rise (N London/Silverlink), though Brondesbury station is on **Kilburn High Rd** – as is Kilburn High Rd station (trains to Euston). Confused? Blame the Victorians.

Kilburn lives, however! Its street-cred as an area in its own right was kickstarted by the rebuilding of the famous Tricycle Theatre, with its art-house cinema; there are some well-regarded bars on the **Harrow Rd**, while hitherto down-at-heel **Salusbury Rd** (now boasting an organic eatery, a health club and more) is developing something of a café society. This reflects the influx of media types (the BBC drift north) and Notting Hill-ites cashing in flats for family homes: just count the kids in Queen's Park's playground. Salusbury Rd's nursery and primary schools are a popular draw, and there's a cache of the good-size houses so lacking in other areas. Young professional couples scour the surrounding neighbourhoods like Kensal Green, and the tinier cottages of the Queen's Park Estate make a freehold alternative to a flat – for singles with cash.

Kilburn

The **High Rd**, with its shops, Sainsbury's, chain stores, pubs and stations (from N to S, Kilburn tube, then Brondesbury and Kilburn High Rd rail stations), is the main artery rather than the heart of Kilburn. That said, even this traditionally scruffy through-route now boasts its handful of smarter cafés, sitting amid reflections of its Irish heritage from post-war days as the preserve of hard-working (and hard-drinking) immigrant workers. It will take a while yet, though, before the pound shops and charity stores give way – and LOOT's ex-offices, squatted last year, may become retail space plus a 52-bed hostel. . . . An antidote to spiralling homes prices, 22 fair-rent flats appeared thanks to the Peabody Trust, along with a health centre, plus facilities for the Tricycle Theatre next door. More new flats by the station: 43 of them, atop the new library and café opening this spring. Across the High Road, a new hotel will replace a tired parade of shops.

The junction of **Kilburn High Rd** and, at its S end, **Kilburn Priory** marks the centre of the old village – virtually nothing of which survives. Note that the little Priory that gave the area its name lay E of the High Rd, on the site of St Mary's Church, just across **Abbey Rd** – in what has long been firmly known as West Hampstead. Four Georgian (if in the shadow of a tower block) houses on **Springfield Lane** stand out from their surroundings, sole relic of Kilburn's 1770s heyday as a fashionable spa; less distinguished corners include the Abbey Estate – council-built on the NW8 border towards **Abbey Rd** – and Kilburn Vale Estate to the S of **Quex Rd**, which includes 1980s town-houses with garages on **Mutrix Rd** and **Bransdale Close** that now come up for sale.

K

Away from the council-build, just about every other residential street to the E of Kilburn High Rd (which is the border between Westminster and Camden), is claimed by West Hampstead. **West End Lane** here has some purpose-built flats blocks, both private and council; **Birchington Rd** has 4-storey terraces with imposing porches. Off Quex Rd, gated **Quex Mews** holds ten 1- and 2-bed flats and five mews houses. North of here near the enormous Catholic church are the ornate terraces of **Mazenod Avenue**, while **Kingsgate Rd** has a mixture of terraces, council blocks and flats over shops. The terraces of **Messina Avenue** stand opposite little Kilburn Grange Park, which boasts tennis courts, a local-authority nursery and a children's play area. N of the park is more council-built housing up to the railway.

Back to the W, across the High Rd and N of Willesden Lane, quiet **Dyne Rd** has some large square-fronted houses, not all split into flats, that look at a first glance like semis but are linked at the back. (The N side of the road backs onto the railway). **Torbay Rd** has smaller rows, while **Plympton Rd**, **Buckley Rd** and **Dunster Gardens** have larger ones: bright and cheerful houses on quiet streets (a conservation area). Good-sized houses here appeal to families: 3/4 bed homes can fetch c. £450,000; a 5-bed, un-done-up, from c. £500, 000 up to c. £650,000. In less-tidied **Burton Rd** you may find a 6-bed house.

Willesden Lane, with its small shops, mansion blocks and junior school, is the N border of a tract of more modest rows running S to **Priory Park Rd**. In this grid, **Tennyson Rd** has an unbroken terrace along the W side incorporating a dozen minor variations on, and later amendments to, its Victorian artisan theme. These back onto Willesden Lane Cemetery, as does the N side of **Lonsdale Rd**. In **Kimberley Rd**, across the cemetery, the live/work flats of Kimberly Lofts have been slow to sell: 1,000–1,200 sq ft of open-plan space, £320–360,000. **Willesden Lane** flats get pricier as they go W: 2-bed mansion flats at the High Rd end rise from c. £220,000 to £250,000; a 2-bed Victorian conversion from £240,000 to £280,000.

Brondesbury Rd runs the gamut from council tower blocks at **Kilburn Square** in the E, through large red-brick 3-storey terraces – some ornate, some Italianate, nearly all flats – to some very suburban semis near Queen's Park station. Homes range from 1-bed flats c. £185,000, which can be spacious if in the vast Victorian houses, through normal-sized 2-beds to elegant ones that can be small-house-sized: a 'huge' one, with huge garden too, £430,000. **Brondesbury Villas**, also a popular address, runs parallel; it echoes its namesake for much of its length, but has some particularly ornate houses, now mostly flats (a 2-bed 'needing work', £225,000); some homes back onto the railway. Both roads, together with **Honiton** and **Lynton Rds**, form a conservation area. Houses on **Donaldson**, **Victoria** and **Hartland Rds**, many nowadays flats, display a touching homogeneity: nearly all highlight the decorative panels on the 2-storey bays. Buyers look here for c. £260,000 2-bed conversions, and 3/4-bed houses from around £550,000 upwards.

South of the railway are largely sprawling council estates on either side of **Carlton Vale** – about to be transformed, as detailed in the introduction. First, 20 new homes in **Granville Rd** will be 'test-driven' by guinea-pig tenants; more residents are already working with the architects and planners to help build the right homes and a new community. The council sprawl surrounds the 1860s James Bailey villas of **Cambridge Avenue**, **Chichester Rd**, **Cambridge Rd** and **Oxford Rd**: a conservation area near Kilburn Park tube. These villas were restored by the Paddington Churches Housing Association; some now come up for sale. The PCHA also added flats and houses between the Vale and **Stafford Rd**. **Malvern Rd** has shops, with some flats above; just off it is **Malvern Mews**: mainly homes, with some commercial. Visible just to the S of **Kilburn Park Rd**, across the Paddington Recreation Ground, are the mansion blocks of Maida Vale.

West Kilburn

West Kilburn lies between **Harrow Rd** in the S and **Kilburn Lane** in the N. Ten large live/work homes have been added to the Lane itself, while its continuation, **Banister Rd**, holds 'NoKo', erroneously being sold as 'the heart of North Kensington' (see intro). It is not. K

The E boundary is the modest terraces of the **Fernhead Rd**/**Saltram Crescent**/ **Walterton Rd** area, often marketed as Maida Hill (cross **Shirland Rd** and you are in Maida Vale proper). Former council tenants of these 1860s–1880s terraces – after epic battles with Westminster Council and developers – banded together to form a housing trust, take over their own homes and carry out a major programme of repairs. Their successful initiative is widely praised but, sadly, rarely emulated: see Maida Vale chapter.

A modern estate separates these streets from the terraces of **Bravington Rd**, **Portnall Rd** and **Ashmore Rd**: there are many rented flats here. Once a good hunting ground for first-time buyers, the past few years saw prices spiral away from them as buy-to-let investors piled into this convenient (and low council-tax) corner, despite some unlovely council estates. Some have since piled back out: check out the number of 'for sale' signs. . . c. £170–190,000 for a 1-bed. Next comes the deceptively named Mozart Estate: a discordant jumble of red-brick blocks at last starting to look better thanks to ongoing rebuilding: nevertheless its reputation is still poor. **Beethoven St**, to the N of it, has seen a lot of the refurb, a few private houses, some light industry and schools. Beyond it and the Mozart, however, is a different story:

The Queen's Park Estate

Just follow **Ladbroke Grove** northwards, dears; you'll still be in W10. . . . And here, just across the canal and the **Harrow Rd**, you will find the placid Queen's Park Estate, happily sheltering all those who can't afford W11 and who prefer a (freehold) cottage of one's own to a grotty North Ken leasehold flat. There are 2,000 charming terraced brick 2- or 2/3-bed cottages, many with Gothicky porches suggesting benign ecclesiastical origins, despite the rationalism of the **First** to **Sixth Avenue** names. The 'Avenues' run N–S; between them, the E–W 'Streets' work down the alphabet from **Alperton St** to **Peach St**.

The Estate was built in the 1870s–80s by the Artisans, Labourers and General Dwelling Co., which ran an orderly grid of streets across farmland at the Kensal Green/West Kilburn borders and built homes for rent. The aim of the 'five per cent philanthropists', as they were called, was to 'provide the labouring man with an increase of the comforts and convenience of life', with (a true Victorian touch, this) 'full compensation for the capitalist'.

Now a conservation area, the Estate passed through council hands, but today some 85–90 per cent of the houses are privately owned. They are a popular buy: a W10 postcode, neat, cut-off streets without through-traffic, plenty of charm: patterned brickwork, Gothicky detailing, porches, turreted corner houses. Buyers of these bijou 2-storey houses – more vertical flats – should note that the conservation area rules are very strict (and some in the main boulevard, **Fifth Avenue**, are listed). Roofs must be of Welsh slate; replacement windows must be wood, conservatories, once banned, must be in scale.

The tree-lined streets are uncluttered and pleasingly domestic in scale: the lack of through-traffic means children can still play ball in the streets at the weekends, as well as in the little park. Inhabitants are a good mixture: locals whose families have been there for years, media-but-broke types who found the place before the prices rose, and now younger, still-single professionals – often women – who like the small-scale homes. They can expect to pay between £250–325,000: see introduction for details. **Oliphant** and **Peach** are indeed peachy streets, while the ABC corner is less favoured, being close to the hard-red-brick '70s Mozart council estate. Controlled parking has helped.

From the E, the boundary of the busy **Harrow Rd** has shops and pubs near the **Great Western Rd** junction, then modern council-build below Queen's Park Estate opposite the canal, up to **Ladbroke Grove**. Housing associations are very active in this area, offering shared ownership deals and putting up new developments such as the complex off the **Harrow Rd** that incorporates flats for rent, the ultra-modern London Print Studios (which is both a commercial studio and also runs courses) and a free public gallery featuring artists specializing in printmaking. Illuminated displays (and occasionally music) enliven the street at night. Up the road is a canalside café with waterside seating.

Kensal Green

The triangle bounded by **Chamberlayne Rd**, **Harrow Rd** and the rail line N of **Purves Rd**, is little Kensal Green: the 'green' is provided by the cemetery (rather bigger) across the Harrow Rd. Concealed behind the shops and offices are 3-storey terraces giving way to smaller ones in a tiny, quiet triangle W of the Queen's Park Estate: popular **Wakeman, Rainham, Pember, Buller Rds.** Flat-dwellers from pricier parts congregate here in search of 3/4-bed houses at up to c. £420,000. Last year added Artisan Quarter to **Warfield/ Wellington Rds**: 25 town-houses (four left: £425–495,000), flats and live/work units.The deeply trendy William IV on the Harrow Rd, and the Paradise Bar, put the spotlight on this corner. . . but if some agents call it 'the new Notting Hill' – well, it is not, yet.

Next, cross the tracks via **College Rd**, which runs N past Kensal Green station (rail/tube), dividing larger, E–W terraces of **Ashburnam, Burrows** – a 3-bed here cleared £520,000 – and **Mortimer Rds** from smaller N–S rows (including some council) S of **Purves Rd**.The similar terraces of **Napier Rd** and **Victor Rd**, tucked away in the angle of road and rail, are shaking off a once-poor ('notorious') image: 3-beds, £280–310,000. Easy to miss from **Harrow Rd**, which here has shops and some flats above; note terraced cottages next to **Alma Place. Purves Rd**, running back E, leads to the shops of **Station Terrace** below Kensal Rise station, and a mansion block. Here, too, are the shops of busy and steep **Chamberlayne Rd**, hoping to emulate Salusbury's now-trendy image: is the smart shoe-shop a harbinger? The pleasant name 'Kensal Rise' for this corner seems to have been eclipsed (save for the station) by that of Queen's Park.

Queen's Park

Across **Chamberlayne Rd** are the putative beginnings of desirable Queen's Park, marked by the monkey puzzle trees of **Chevening Rd**; this runs E with its huge, leafy-gardened semis, some flats and large terraces – those N of **Dunmore Rd** having garages at rear. But Queen's Park *proper*, the conservation area with its rich mixture of late-Victorian and Edwardian styles, begins only at **Peploe Rd** (and continues between the rail lines as far as **Salusbury Rd**). On roads that cross this W border, such as **Kempe** and **Keslake Rds**, both house prices and flights of architectural fancy can soar as one nears the park: up to £600–700,000 for a 3- or 4-bed house, a million for the biggest and best, over it for the top **Kingswood Avenue** homes. Smaller **Milman Rd** houses across the park also sought-after.

The smaller terraces of streets behind **Kingswood Avenue** are popular, but **Montrose** and **Hopefield Avenues** have some drab modern houses that detract from the essentially gracious tone of Queen's Park. **Harvist Rd** has a variety of 3-storey terraces (note the Dutch touches of Nos. 10–16) following the rail line to **Salusbury Rd** – which, between Brondesbury Park and Queen's Park stations, furnishes locals with popular schools, shops (books and boutiques the latest), churches, library, police station – and organic café, wine bar, art centre, health club. Modern flats include Vicarage Place, 1995, and '98 St Anne's Court. The award-winning park is a joy: a rolling site with open views, splendid playground, wooded nature trail, café with outdoor chess tables: the heart of the area.

Transport Tubes: Kilburn (zone 2, Jubilee); Queen's Park, Kensal Green, Kilburn Park (zone 2, Bakerloo). From Kilburn: Oxford Circus 20 min (1 change), City 25 min (1 change), Heathrow 50 min (1 change). Trains: Kilburn High Rd 8 min to Euston.

Convenient for West End, M1, Notting Hill. A40. Miles from centre: 4.

Schools Local Authority: Queen's Park Community, St Augustine's C of E, St George's RC. Private: Islamia High (g), Al-Sadiq (b) & Al-Zahra (g)

K

SALES

Flats	S	1B	2B	3B	4B	5B
Average prices	120–160	160–220	220–400	250–450	300+	–
Houses	2B	3B	4B	5B	6/7B	8B
Average prices	260–400	340–550	400–800	600–1M	–	–

RENTAL

Flats	S	1B	2B	3B	4B	5B
Average prices	100–200	160–250	210–350	275–400	275–500	–
Houses	2B	3B	4B	5B	6/7B	8B
Average prices	275–300	350–600	375–700	500–750	–	–

The properties Terraces of small Victorian homes, some delightful, give way, round Queen's Park, to large Edwardian ones in broader streets.

The market Locals upgrading; families; flat-dwellers from pricier areas after a house. Queen's Park's family homes command a premium.

Among estate agents active in this area are:

- Brondesbury Estates
- Noé Glasman
- Harris & Co
- Queen's Park Partnership
- Camerons Stiff
- Westminster Property
- Wenlock & Taylor
- Margo's
- Brian Lack & Co
- Gladstones
- Rainbow Reid
- Lewis Estates

KNIGHTSBRIDGE

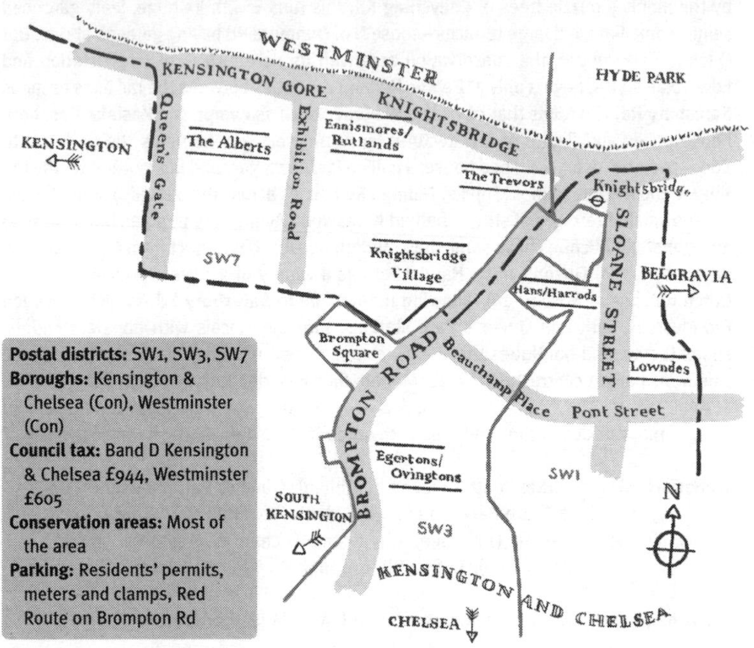

Postal districts: SW1, SW3, SW7
Boroughs: Kensington & Chelsea (Con), Westminster (Con)
Council tax: Band D Kensington & Chelsea £944, Westminster £605
Conservation areas: Most of the area
Parking: Residents' permits, meters and clamps, Red Route on Brompton Rd

Edwardian at heart, Victorian and Regency by inheritance, Knightsbridge seems unchanging. Yet the Sixties and Seventies intruded, amid the stately brick and stucco, a clutch of concrete office buildings unloved from birth. As they reach the end of their lives – and as their owners see ways of profiting from their sites – they are being replaced with developments equally commercial but a little more friendly and a lot more residential. The least loved of the lot, the Bowater building which looms between Hyde Park and the Brompton Rd/Sloane St junction – is now on the demolition list.

All this activity will do little for the calm of Knightbridge, but will probably only enhance its image as the heart of wealthy London. The recent and planned developments boost yet further the number of 'top-level' homes (a price bracket which starts at £4 million or £5 million, depending on who you ask).

What brings the world's wealthy to Knightsbridge? First, location. The area straddles the main routes between the centre and Heathrow and lies beside 600 acres of Royal parkland. Second, habit. Knightsbridge has been wealthy since Victorian times, and the cluster of smart shops and grand hotels it shelters has grown yet smarter and grander in the decades since the airport became Britain's gateway. Third, choice of property. The area is a dense cluster of grand apartment buildings (period and contemporary), elegant terraced houses and pretty mews cottages. Fourth, continuity. Foreign and British buyers look to Knightsbridge as the best London area in which to invest for the long term. Like Harrods, the Royal Albert Hall and the embassies and foreign cultural centres located here, Knightsbridge is itself an institution.

Knightbridge has spent the past four years adjusting to another big change – the lack of Americans. Traditionally it was US bankers, corporate chiefs, diplomats and the like who propped up the rental market. These have been thinner on the ground since

mid-2000 than Knightbridge is accustomed to. However an encouraging new source of wealth, Russia, came to the rescue, augmented by Europeans. The former are keen to buy (and pay cash, to the embarassment of money-laundering-conscious agents), the latter to rent. Whatever the ups and downs Knightbridge is prepared to take the long view: what's the odd stock market dive to the Old Money of Knightsbridge? This was borne out in the 1989/90 crash when Knightsbridge was one of the only areas in London where asking prices were routinely achieved.

To define the area: Knightsbridge lies beside Hyde Park, which is hemmed behind the busy road variously named **Kensington Gore/Kensington Rd/Knightsbridge**. To the S the boundary with Chelsea is **Walton St/Pont St**. In the W, a complex of museums and colleges cuts Knightsbridge off from Kensington, while Belgravia lies to the E. The old hamlet of Knightsbridge was originally part of a large forest around London – of which Hyde Park and Kensington Gardens are surviving open remnants. The parks are the area's biggest asset, providing a 600-acre playground, a green lung in the middle of the city, and some fine views. Within them you can go boating, riding and visit a royal palace.

The other big draw is the cluster of top shops and department stores, with ever more smart new shops being developed. Harrods' monster century-old store in **Brompton Rd**, with its green-and-gold canopies, gold-braided commissionaires and gawping tourists by day and lit up like a liner by night, is one facet. Harvey Nichols and the clutch of designer stores in **Sloane St** offer the alternative dimension: high-value, cutting-edge, international-name designer fashion.

Now the biggest development in Knightsbridge since the building of Harrods is taking place just across the Brompton Rd from its front doors. The 4½-acre Knightsbridge Green development has three components: the Prudential owned the site, and has built the main commercial section, with new shops and offices. The main residential part of the scheme, the 1.7-acre north site fronting **Knightsbridge**, is now owned by Hong Kong investors New World – and re-christened 'The Knightsbridge'. This is providing the area with 205 very expensive new homes (completion during 2005). The Pru also sold on the final, SW section: there will be 50 more flats here, plus offices and shops, in the **Lancelot Place** corner nearest Harrods. This was still just a hole in the ground last winter. Meanwhile, round the corner in **Trevor Square** (see The Trevors, below), yet another scheme – called, with restraint, Trevor Square – has converted the old Harrods depot into yet another clutch of 48 homes.

If and when the Bowater House office blocks go, two towers of flats will replace them, clad in red sandstone to better blend in with the Edwardiana around them. The current plan envisages moving the road link to Hyde Park to the W, between the Bowater site and Wellington Court. The existing road would become a pedestrian piazza. Many years usually elapse between the mooting and building of these big schemes.

Apart from all this new-build, traditional Knightsbridge caters for every urban taste in homes – from the tall late-Victorian, red-brick, gabled apartment buildings in the **Hans Gardens/Egerton Gardens** neighbourhoods to the grand Portland stone blocks in **Ennismore Gardens.** Mews cottages and classic London terraces, large and small, are spread throughout the area in some particularly pretty streets and cobbled mews.

Most homes, though, are flats, and leases are often short – though longer leases are gradually appearing. Strict maintenance conditions are imposed in many, to keep up the tone of the area by preventing properties slipping into disrepair. Service charges can vary widely, but you usually get what you pay for, according to local estate agents. Leasehold reform has changed the game in some streets, finally allowing leaseholders to buy the freeholds. Both the Cadogan and Wellcome Estates (the latter took over the Smith's Charity estate) have property in this area – and both enforce estate management agreements even on homes they no longer own.

A peculiarity of the area is that it falls within two boroughs. All of the area N of Brompton Rd (with the exception of **Brompton Square**, **Cottage Place**, the Oratory, Holy Trinity Brompton Church, **Cheval Place**, **Rutland St**, **Fairholt St** and **Rutland Mews South**) is in the City of Westminster; the rest is in Kensington & Chelsea. The confusion of the two boroughs within Knightsbridge leads to chaos with residents' parking. Where the boundaries run through the middle of the streets (as in **Lowndes St**) or squares (as in **Rutland Gate**) neighbourly coexistence can be strained.

Brompton Rd is the main shopping street, lined by a jumble of period and modern flats, blocks and offices with shops beneath. These range from fashion and shoe shops to jewellers, antique shops, galleries, banks, restaurants, smart cafés and bars. **Knightsbridge** and its continuation **Kensington Rd** form a busy main through-route running alongside the park westwards to Kensington and eastwards to the West End. It is flanked by a combination of tall apartment buildings and various embassies and institutions – punctuated by the enormous circular bulk of the Albert Hall.

Lowndes

Lowndes Square forms the heart of a neighbourhood bounded to the W by **Sloane St** and to the E by the Duke of Westminster's Belgravia estate. It differs from other garden squares in Kensington and Chelsea in that it is dominated by huge 1930s flat blocks. The 6/7-storey brown-brick buildings spread along whole blocks of the square and loom over its narrow central garden. Lowndes Court looks older but is newer: an ultra-luxurious 25-flat block completely rebuilt behind the period facade in 1989; one garden duplex here, for instance, has more bathrooms than bedrooms (his'n'hers ensuites. . .). Some 19th-century houses do remain – mostly 5-storey-plus-basement stucco terraces, many split into flats; overall, however, the atmosphere is of a square of hotels. This impression is heightened by the Sheraton Park Tower Hotel at the N end of the square, fronting **Knightsbridge** (the road). **Lowndes Square** is very popular, though, especially with foreign buyers: Octagon's 2003 eight-flat scheme managed to cling on to the £1,400 per sq ft prices it aspired to. Also in the Square, an expensively done-up 3,000 sq ft flat on a 53-year lease was £4.25 million in early '04. More normal-sized flats recently were asking just under £1,000 per sq ft for 56/57-year leases. The prettily named **Harriet Walk**, between Square and Sloane St, gained seven new mews houses and two studios in 1990.

Lowndes St runs off southwards from the Square's E leg, with more flats, shops, galleries and banks giving way, at the S end, to terraces of 4-storey stucco-fronted houses. Another 1900s flat block, Chelsea House, provides visual interest as it curves around the corner of Lowndes St into **Cadogan Place.** A collection of period and modern houses and flats at the N end of Cadogan Place overlooks its large tree-lined gardens.

Sloane St on the neighbourhood's W boundary serves as both the main road to Chelsea and an ever-smarter shopping street, encouraged in its ascent up-market by the Cadogan Estate, yet another long-term landlord. Flats – including some enviable Art Deco mansion blocks – line the street between the embassies and hotels.

Hans/Harrods

This neighbourhood is dominated by Harrods: the vast store covers 4½ acres. It is surrounded by tall red-brick and stone-gabled blocks of flats in **Hans Crescent**, **Hans Rd** and **Basil St**. The most ornate blocks are in Basil St, alongside a mix of hotels, restaurants, shops and the Knightsbridge fire station. **Hans Crescent** is another shopping street, but with flats too (including a clutch of 34 converted from what was the Hans Crescent Hotel). One flat in the Crescent went in 2003 for £6 million – it had eight bedrooms and took up a whole floor of one of the turreted red-brick blocks. The latest scheme in this much-recycled corner is the conversion of Nos. 10/12, two adjoining houses now remodelled as 11 flats.

Next is **Herbert Crescent**, where a group of large mock-Tudor houses stands out incongruously among the prevailing ornate red-brick mansions. The crescent leads into **Hans Place**, a garden square where largely red-brick, Dutch-gabled, buildings, converted into flats, encircle the private central gardens. Hill House preparatory school stands in the SE corner of this relatively quiet (for Knightsbridge) square.

Just beyond the NW entrance to the square, the red-bricks are replaced by orderly terraces of mid-19th-century white stucco houses in **Walton Place**. At the S end of this attractive street is the brick Gothic-style St Saviour's Church, providing a striking contrast to the white stucco. Half of it now also provides a rather worldly contrast to the holiness next door: it has been converted into a sybaritic £10 million, 5-bed house with interior pool complex. Two million less will buy you a 6-bed, 5-floor, large-garden affair created by knocking two Walton Place houses into one.

Knightsbridge has several enticing corners of mews cottages, which have evolved a long way from their earthy origins to become a style of home all their own. Many are in cul-de-sacs, tucked away from the busy streets. Mansard roof extensions are popular, as are shutters and flower tubs beside the doors. Roof gardens a draw, but most prized are homes with surviving garage: parking around here is impossible.

To the E of Walton Place, through a pointed red-brick arch and an automatic barrier lies **Pont St Mews**, a clutch of 2-bed, gabled, freehold cottages. **Beaufort Gardens** used to be lined by small hotels, but most of the tall brick-and-stucco Victorian terraces are now flats. An unusual feature of this wide street is the line of trees down the middle with car parking on each side. The street is closed off at its S end by a stucco balustrade and the backs of the houses in Walton St.

Beauchamp Place at the W edge of the neighbourhood is a high-class but pretty, small-scale shopping street, a charming lane containing some of the area's top shops and restaurants, with flats above. Back up towards Harrods, **Brompton Place** is a narrow street of little cottages leading to the store's car park.

K

Egertons/Ovingtons

This corner, enclosed by **Brompton Rd** to the N and W, holds several streets and squares of handsome houses. **Ovington Square** contains good examples of the 'Kensington Italianate' style – tall, narrow, white-stucco terraced houses with rich detailing. The 4-storey-plus-a-basement rows, built in the 1840/50s, are set around narrow private gardens. **Ovington Gardens** has 3/4-storey white stucco, or brick-and-stucco, terraces. Tucked away at right angles to the eastern side of the street is **Ovington Mews**: pretty 2-storey painted cottages line this pleasant little backwater. Tubs of flowers and window boxes add extra colour. **Yeoman's Row**, situated just one street away, is different again. A short terrace of 2-storey mid-Georgian cottages remain on the eastern side of this small-scale street, along with some 1960s equivalents: an attractive group of paired brick-houses with stucco entrances and leafy front gardens. Another handful of cottages is to be found in **Egerton Garden Mews** through a red-brick arch. And so to the Egertons. . .

Rows of late-Victorian red-brick gabled buildings congregate around rear communal gardens in **Egerton Gardens, Egerton Place** and the northern end of **Egerton Terrace**. The mansion blocks, built during the 1880s/90s, form the main concentration of flats. Leases are often short: less than 20 years in some cases. However, recently Wellcome has been granting new 105-year leases. As a rule of thumb, expect to pay approaching £1,000 per sq ft to live in a smartened-up flat here.

Now cross the road to the two most exclusive streets in Knightsbridge – **Egerton Crescent** and the S end of **Egerton Terrace**. A curved terrace of elegant, early-Victorian white stucco houses sweeps around **Egerton Crescent**, reckoned the grandest location in Knightsbridge. The 3/4-storey houses (over £5 million has been paid for a freehold) are screened from the road by their semicircular private garden. One house also has two enormous gardens tucked behind the crescent. Victorian lamps line the curve, and tubs of trees and shrubs on the first-floor balconies emphasize the green and white colour scheme. In **Egerton Terrace**, pairs of mid-19th-century white stucco houses have large, leafy front gardens. The street is closed off at its S end by a balustrade and trees.

Brompton Square

Brompton Square, to the N of Brompton Rd, is a very distinct little neighbourhood in itself. Terraces of 3/4-storey late Georgian houses stretch along narrow central gardens. Virtually all the houses in the square, built 1824–39, are Grade II listed. Houses here are enormously popular: standard-sized ones are £2.75–3 million, and the large ones at the end of the Square can be double that or more. Reason: they are much bigger than they look, taking up cake-slice shaped plots which run from the curved end of the Square back to Ennismore Gardens. One sold for £8.5 million in the late 1990s. Another, with 5 beds, 6 receps, was £10 million last year. A few houses are now flats. Oh, and the square's gardens are also listed as being of architectural or historic interest.

To the W is one of Knightsbridge's most important landmarks, the Oratory Catholic church. This Renaissance-style church with its impressive white stone facade and dome is the focal point of this end of **Brompton Rd**. Behind the Oratory sits Holy Trinity Brompton (C of E): its large, tree-lined churchyard provides welcome fresh air and a leafy open space and outlook for adjoining properties in the Ennismores – and a playground for inner-city squirrels. To the W the renowned Victoria & Albert decorative arts museum (the 'V&A') forms the boundary with South Kensington.

Ennismore/Rutlands

Northwest of Brompton Square as far as Hyde Park stretches a quiet, cut-off corner of mews and squares. L-shaped **Ennismore Gardens Mews** is a delightful long cobbled mews lined by gaily coloured 2-storey cottages: c. £1.3 million for a long lease or freehold. Tubs of flowers and window boxes add a picturesque touch. Cottages in the S leg of the mews gaze out over peaceful, tree-lined Holy Trinity Brompton graveyard. An imposing stone arch of Greek-style columns at the entrance to the mews is a hint of things to come in **Ennismore Gardens.** Unusual Portland stone terraces – grand, 5-storeyed, graced with double-columned porches, ornate black iron balconies and set round a large private garden – are much sought-after. The majority are now divided into flats, some (the lateral, across-two-houses, sort) themselves house-sized. Many short leases – though those on the white-stucco side have longer ones. Now, since the law has changed, flats can be had with share of freehold. The more traditional stucco-fronted terraces are in the E arm of the square, and more can be found in **Prince's Gardens.** The S and E sides of Prince's Gardens are taken up by looming mid-20th-century blocks housing Imperial College students: these are soon to be demolished and rebuilt with lower, more sympathetic modern terraces (though still with 902 students).

Spreading along the W–E section of **Ennismore Gardens** is the highly-rated 1930s Kingston House flats complex, which stretches right back to **Kensington Rd.** The big apartments are very popular with foreign buyers including Americans, Italians and Spanish: a 1,350 sq ft share-of-freehold flat was £895,000 last autumn. Around the corner, on the W side of the N leg of **Ennismore Gardens** and facing the gardens behind the Princes Gate block, is **Bolney Gate,** a row of seven 1960s 5-storey brick town-houses with handsome stone porches. These are neighbours to a larger clutch, **Moncorvo Close,** round the corner off Ennismore Gardens' N side. On the E side of the road stand, in quirky juxtaposition, the Russian Orthodox Church and the Omani Embassy. Just to the N is Princes Gate Court, a 1930s mansion block on **Kensington Rd,** which looks N across the Park and S over its own spacious gardens: a 3-bed, 2-bath £1.25 million.

South of the church is **Ennismore Mews,** an exceptional example of its type: 2-storey painted/brick cottages, often big for mews houses. Pay between £1.2 and £2 million-plus for a 3-bed. Window boxes, flower tubs, Victorian street lamps abound, though the Ennismore Arms pub at the corner with Ennismore St has been demolished: another pub lost to residential. Ennismore St leads into **Rutland Gate,** which is made up of two separate garden squares. Terraces of brick-and-stucco houses line the N square, just off **Knightsbridge,** and cream and white stucco-fronted houses are set around the more desirable S square. The homes have mostly been converted into flats or house foreign cultural institutes and other organizations – though one, which held an Italian institute, has just been restored as a single house, as has the monster stucco detached once owned by the Mitford family. Next, it's rumoured, the very run-down pair owned by the Sudanese Embassy will be restored. A large brick mansion block – Eresby House – stands where the two squares meet.

Rutland Gardens and its tiny mews contain a mix of interesting houses, cottages and flats of very different sizes and styles, but the dominant view here is of the tower of Knightsbridge Barracks, home of the Household Cavalry – but consistently voted one of London's biggest eyesores in public opinion polls. The horses are currently in temporary homes in Hyde Park, as their permanent stables in the barracks is upgraded (with a horse solarium, no less) to meet health and safety stipulations.

South of Rutland Gate lie more small mews, including **Rutland Mews West**: no more than a tiny group of white-stucco cottages clustered around a cobbled courtyard. **Rutland St** and **Fairholt St** are two more small-scale streets. Some of these cottages date from the 1820s, when Knightsbridge was still a farming village.

Knightsbridge Village

Exclusive **Montpelier Square** is the centrepiece of this small-scale neighbourhood of predominantly single family houses. The 19th-century brick-and-stucco/painted stucco houses in the square face onto mature private gardens. Narrow **Montpelier**

Walk is a mix of little painted brick/stucco houses. It leads to **Cheval Place**, where the 2/3-storey painted cottages stand alongside modern flats blocks, smart shops and restaurants. **Montpelier Place** is a pleasant street of 3-storey stucco or brick/stucco houses with two flower-bedecked pubs, one right next to the German Evangelist church. **Montpelier St** to the E is the main street of the 'village', lined with 3/4-storey brick-and-stucco terraced houses, pubs, restaurants, shops, galleries. Montpelier Mews has the usual mix of mews homes, some relatively new – and very smart.

A footpath through a gap in an old brick wall in **Rutland St** (this amenity dates from 1948, when the wall was rebuilt after bomb damage, and locals asked the council for a right of way to link two neighbourhoods) leads through to **Rutland Mews.** Pass through a grand archway, along **Ennismore Gardens Mews** to **Prince's Gate Mews** and you reach the museum/university quarter of South Kensington; one of the most charming walks in central London. Take a right turn from the Mews and go on through the 1960s brutalist Imperial College building for one of the most striking architectural contrasts the capital can offer: on the N side are the elegant if somewhat down-at-heel remnants of the old mid-Victorian **Prince's Gardens**, also owned by the College.

The Trevors/Knightsbridge Green

East of Knightsbridge Village come pleasant streets dominated by 3/4-storey early 19th-century terraces – until now. Flanking 'the Trevors' (**Place, Street** and **Square**), the gleaming ramparts of Knightsbridge's latest development now loom. In **Trevor Square** itself, those original houses, set on two sides of a long narrow private garden, go for £1.5–2 million. At the S end of the Square, what was Harrods' despatch depot S of the Square is now Crown Dilmun's 'Trevor Square' – 40 flats. The handful left unsold ranged from £2.1 million to £4.25 million (well over £1,000 per sq ft). Plus, of course, £75,000 for a parking space. The four 3-bed mews houses squeezed in at the E end were £2.3 million. As part of the planning deal the Square gained smart new garden railings.

K

Stretching westwards along **Knightsbridge** from the N end of **Trevor Place,** a 1.7-acre site marketed as 'The Knightsbridge' and developed by a Hong Kong company boasts a further 205 homes, completing this year. There are seven mews houses, plus two large blocks of 'unusually spacious' flats (starting at £400,000 for a studio, or maid's room to you and me), with prices working up from £1,350 per sq ft. The blocks are topped with seven state-of-the-art penthouses (up to £20 million) rejoicing in the marketing soubriquet the 'Crown Jewels'. Full '6-star' hotel services will be on tap, and marketing has been most active in Moscow and St Petersburg.

Across **Raphael St** and running S to **Brompton Rd** down the E side of **Lancelot Place** (noted until now for a row of little brick cottages), yet another 53 flats and a large store are to come. **Knightsbridge Green** is a paved lane, more a passageway, lined with small shops, cafés, restaurants. To the E is Park Mansions, a large red-brick block fronting **Knightsbridge** and stretching to Scotch Corner, where **Knightsbridge** and **Brompton Rd** converge. The Knight's Arcade of shops runs beneath the mansions.

The Alberts

The Royal Albert Hall is the focal point of the neighbourhood from which the main residential complexes take their names. They are Albert Hall Mansions – five large blocks of flats (London's first such) on the E side of the famous concert hall – and Albert Court to the rear in **Prince Consort Rd**. The tall red-brick and stone Norman Shaw blocks, also the very first to be built in the Dutch style, contain 80 flats each, including some of the largest family apartments left in Knightsbridge. They were built in the 1880s/90s by the Commissioners for the Great Exhibition of 1851 – who remain the freeholders to this day. The flats are popular with wealthy overseas, as well as established British, buyers; and are also used as a base for international companies – and make a secure celebrity hideaway. Very few are let out. Some have been modernized, others still have the original panelled walls, staff quarters – even wine cellars. Prices, too, can be on an ample, even Victorian, scale: £4.25 million was asked last winter for a 4-bed, 4,900 sq ft affair. All is not placid in this prosperous corner: controversially, the Royal College of Art plans a big new block, 'The Ellipse', on the W side of the Hall: a decision is expected late in 2005.

Transport Tubes, both zone 1: Knightsbridge (Piccadilly), South Kensington (Piccadilly, Circle, District). From Knightsbridge: Oxford Circus 10 min (1 change), City 22 min (1 change), Heathrow 42 min.

Convenient for Hyde Park, fashionable shopping, West End, Heathrow (via taxi, tube or Paddington). Miles from centre: 1.5.

Schools Local Authority: St Thomas More RC. Private: Hellenic College, Francis Holland (g), More House RC (g).

SALES

Flats	S	1B	2B	3B	4B	5B
Average prices	290–400	350–1M+	550–1.7M+	800–2.6M+	1.5–5M+	2–13M+
Houses	2B	3B	4B	5B	6/7B	8B
Average prices	800–1.7M	1–2.5M+	1.5–3M+	2–10M	3.5–10M+	5–10M+

RENTAL

Flats	S	1B	2B	3B	4B	5B
Average prices	180–300	280–500+	370–950	650–1500	800–2300+	–
Houses	2B	3B	4B	5B	6/7B	8B
Average prices	475–1000+	700–2000	1150–2000	2300+	2500–4500	–

K

The properties The scale ranges from tiny mews via elegant 18th- and 19th-century squares and terraces, to lofty apartment blocks in stone or the red-brick, gabled style widely known as 'Pont Street Dutch' to modern and expensively-serviced flats. And, building now, developments that add a further 300 top-of-the-range homes in the Trevor Square–Knightsbridge Green neighbourhood.

The market The wealthy market for these coveted homes, whether true-blue British or international jet-set, are as one in considering this the hub of London. Large houses are scarce and at a premium. Flats reign, with companies buying the short-lease ones as London bases. Prices vary widely according to degree of luxury/lease-length/views: a quiet square is more desirable than a park view, as this can mean traffic noise. International renters and buyers still make up 80 per cent of the market.

Among estate agents active in this area are:

- Strutt & Parker
- Beaney Pearce
- De Groot Collis
- Knight Frank
- Allsop & Co
- Winkworth
- Savills
- Foxtons
- Hobart Slater
- Harrods Estates
- Druce
- Hamptons
- W A Ellis
- Douglas & Gordon
- Lane Fox
- Aylesfords
- Anscombe & Ringland
- Cluttons
- Kinleigh Folkard & Hayward
- John D Wood

LEWISHAM AND CATFORD

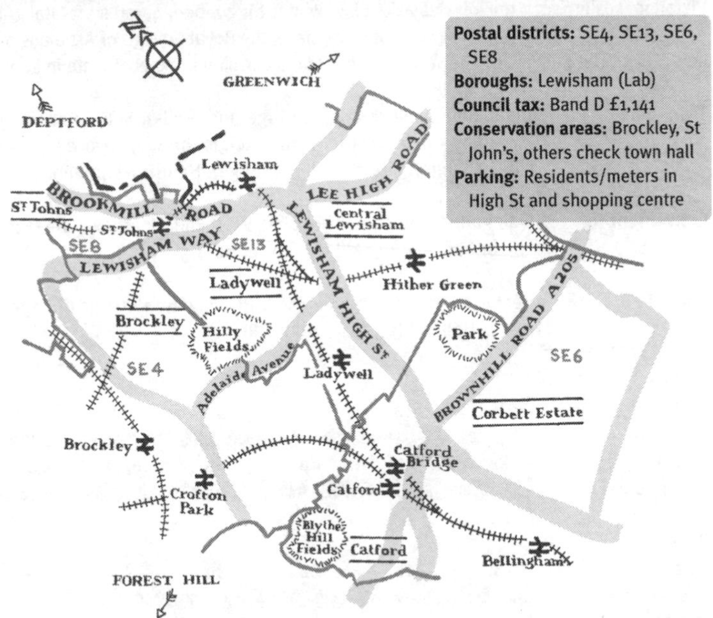

Postal districts: SE4, SE13, SE6, SE8
Boroughs: Lewisham (Lab)
Council tax: Band D £1,141
Conservation areas: Brockley, St John's, others check town hall
Parking: Residents/meters in High St and shopping centre

The influx of newcomers to Lewisham flows in two directions. Young business and professional people, often working in the City or Docklands, follow the DLR down from the Isle of Dogs. And growing families, priced out of Greenwich and Blackheath and Dulwich, seek out big old Victorian houses in Lewisham's conservation areas. However the typical impecunious first-time buyers are being pushed ever south – to Hither Green – by the incoming young bankers.

Banker or not, it is well worth taking a look at Lewisham and its encircling neighbourhoods. For so long marooned in traffic-clogged, tube-starved South-East London, it now has a link to Docklands and Canary Wharf: the arrival of the Docklands Light Railway (DLR) in 1999 began the image change from humdrum hub for local shopping to up-and-coming residential area. Now comes a big investment in a transport interchange to better link the DLR to the main-line station and buses.

Next, the tube, in the shape of the East London Line Extension, will be at hand. New Cross, just up the road, already acts as the terminus of the East London, which joins you to the Jubilee Line at Canada Water. With its extension (due 2010: see Transport chapter) the line will be much more use. Before then, in 2007, three-car trains will be introduced to the DLR. And locals point out that Lewisham has Zone Two fare status.

The transport interchange is part of a big renaissance of the area: in particular the centre, where the council, AMEC and Taylor Woodrow and the London Development Agency plan big things – including 1,000 new homes. Renaissance plans also include a Debenhams department store by '07. For now, the centre offers an excellent daily market rather than lifestyle emporia or trendy restaurants (and still has its run-down, yet-to-be-tidied corners). But around the centre are a surprising number of small parks and open spaces – between which lie neat little clutches of interesting streets. Beyond, north-eastwards up the hill, the neighbours are lovely Blackheath and historic Greenwich, while in the opposite direction lie Peckham Rye, Honor Oak, Forest Hill, Dulwich.

So now families and young professionals find more for their money here: along with the ubiquitous little terraces and the '30s infill, the area has caches of large-scale (and large-gardened) Victoriana: 6/7-bed houses, some intact; some split into flats. Close by, away from the tracks and the busy roads, there's usually a leafy space. Some, like Ladywell, have tennis courts or running-track; health clubs have appeared.

The area is ringed with convenient little stations (and therefore criss-crossed with rather less-than-convenient – should you be driving or living near to them – rail lines, which carry fast through-trains as well as local traffic up to London Bridge).

All this transport talk brings Lewisham full circle: it hardly grew from the large village already established by the Ravensbourne river in Domesday times, until the 1840s when the railway arrived and turned it into a new centre for commuting. By the start of the 20th century much of the available land had been built over – but there are clues to its gentler past in names like 'Silk Mills Passage'. Indeed, the last water-mill survives, complete with wheel, though (sign of the times) it is subsumed these days into Citibank's headquarters.

Central Lewisham

The best bits of Lewisham are those closest to the southern tip of Blackheath. From Blackheath Village turn W into **Lee Terrace** and explore the roads to your left bearing the SE13 postcode. Some of Lewisham's best buildings were destroyed by the heavy bombing from which the borough suffered in World War II, but happily streets such as **Quentin Rd**, **Dacre Park**, **Eton Grove** and surrounding roads escaped untouched. Here are 4-storey mansions with grand sash windows and huge back gardens: they would not be out of place in Kensington. Most are now flats, but some remain as superb family homes. The nearby parish church of St Margaret's, and little backstreet pubs, all add to the quiet country feel – until this illusion gives way to the modern, low-rise council-built housing, much now private, off busy **Lee High Rd**. Newbuild is slipped in wherever there's a space. A modern 2-bed flat around **Dacre Park** might be £215,000; a 2-bed ex-council £140,000.

Belmont Hill, the continuation of Lee Terrace, has seen a lot of the recent redevelopment in the area. Cedars Court's ten apartments are housed in a Grade II-listed mansion, while newbuild ones occupy the site in front of Our Lady of Lourdes School. Then there's Belmont Court: 15 2-bed flats, and off the Hill there are 2-bed flats at £205,000. Edwardian semis in Belmont Hill are eyed with interest by Greenwich and Blackheath families outgrowing flats; a 6-bed might be £500,000 – the same price asked for a 4-bed town-house in one of the more exclusive new schemes. Nearby, a 4-storey block appeared on the corner of **Brandram** and **Blessington Rds**. Yet more new flats, too, N of the tracks in William Close off **Granville Park**, curving from **Lewisham Rd** back up to Blackheath. Some homes in this area – on **Morden Hill**, for example – boast views right across London.

Lewisham High St has a massive indoor shopping complex and most well-known stores. The High Street has been turned into a well-managed, traffic-free shopping area: the pedestrianization has encouraged the wonderful (daily) market, and shopping is an altogether more pleasant experience. The clock tower has been moved back to its original Victorian site, and there's now also a large modern library. The centre has gained new pubs and a rash of eateries. A new, hi-tech police station too, with room for 24 police horses and the Serious Crimes Squad. And Citibank have built yet more offices in the area, behind the centre. W of the centre, between **Loampit Vale**, **Elmira St** and the river, is River Mill Park, on the site of the demolished Sundermead council estate: a mix of rented, shared-ownership and private homes – the first 98 released last autumn – and a new park down to the river. The shared-ownership homes, 1- and 2-bed flats and 2-bed houses, are £145–220,000, with buyers able to purchase shares from 40 per cent up. For straight purchase, try the modern 2-bed town-houses in **Algernon Rd** at c. £235,000. **Loampit Hill**, off towards St John's, has new Angel Court, nine 1- and 2-bed flats round a gated courtyard: £155,000-plus.

Roads to the E mostly contain Victorian homes, many of which have undergone conversion work after years of neglect. **Limes Grove** with its 4-storey pitched roofs and sash windows is a prime example (a 2-bed flat in one, c. £150,000), as are **Gilmore Rd** and **Clarendon Rise**, which sport terraces with steps to the front door and black wrought-iron balustrades. Between these two roads stands a 20-year-old group of red-brick terraces set round a small park. These were council-built, but not surprisingly tenants gave rein to their Right to Buy and these homes now regularly come up for sale (recently a 2-bed flat, £180,000; 4-bed house, £250,000). To the W of Gilmore Rd runs the delightfully-named Quaggy River; across it off **Weardale Rd** is Waterside, a clutch of 16 flats, one restored house and a live/work home.

North of the town centre, in the area along the river and DLR line (streets like **Crosslet Vale, Armoury Rd** and **Connington Rd)**, you will find a lot of Lewisham's latest homes, joining some existing 2-storey ones around **Connington Rd**. The latest scheme, by Barratt, brought new houses (from £370,000) to **Franklin Close**, which, with Crosslet Vale, is by the Quaggy River. This is where the young incomers want to be, report local agents: near the stations. This ex-industrial corner also holds a Tesco superstore, and is close to Deptford's burgeoning cultural quarter (see New Cross & Deptford chapter).

St John's

Next, explore St John's – which you'll find by following road signs for Deptford. It shares Deptford's SE8 postcode, but this conservation area is well worth discovering. Small-scale and villagey, it is bordered by **St John's Vale, Albyn Rd, Lewisham Way** and **Tanner's Hill**. Some streets are sealed to traffic by ornamental bollards, and the rows of neat stock-brick terraces, shops and pubs remain quiet. It has its own train station – an erstwhile patchy service now boasts eight trains an hour – and the DLR is close, too.

There's a variety of homes here: **Tanner's Hill** has red-brick council blocks (recently done up) plus some recent flats and houses, and a recent development of four 3-bed town-houses and 2-bed maisonette; then small shops, pubs and restaurant at the top end – and views to Canary Wharf. **St John's Vale** starts with little 2-storey, 3-bed terraces, gains basements halfway up and ends with 3-storey basemented semis past the station. (Lewisham College is also near, so parking is at a premium.) The homes in **Lucas St** have a park area for the kids to play in. The top end of **Friendly St** is made up of pretty little, neatly kept, close-packed, 2-bed workmen's cottages, many of which are listed; likewise **Admiral St**. Where these are 3-bed, it's thanks to a downstairs bathroom. **Ashmead Rd**, by contrast, has 2/3-storey Victoriana: some enormous, some still whole family homes – their coach-houses nowadays making separate ones.

Leaving St John's, travel back along **Lewisham Way** uphill to **Loampit Vale** (MFI, Matalan, etc, here). The small 2-up/2-downs are replaced by grander 4-storey homes; now flats, but still neatly kept with window boxes in evidence. Pause to check out **Somerset Gardens**: a small untouched oasis of pairs of Victorian homes, many with wrought-iron verandas, enclosing a central green. Back across the Vale turn into **Shell Rd**, which winds its way towards Hilly Fields and Brockley: this, and surrounding streets, are dominated by 2- and 3-storey houses with exuberant Gothicky turrets, ornate porches, high-pitched roofs. Look for fine examples of decorative plasterwork – often a shell motif echoes the street name; 4-bed homes here, while cut-off **Halesworth Rd** has handsome 6-bed ones, some split into flats (1-bed £155,000). By contrast, **Embleton Rd** has 3-bed '30s semis.

Brockley

On reaching the Hilly Fields park area, where '30s-style semis are dotted among the Victorian conversions, turn back towards New Cross and the popular – and charming – Brockley conservation area. By the end of the '80s these quiet tree-lined avenues had already been discovered by young, upwardly mobile commuters – and when the longed-for East London Line extension comes to pass, this will be two stops from Canada Water and the Jubilee Line. Four-bed homes here, in handsome, flat-fronted, semi-basemented terraces; but also many vast, 5-, 6- or 7-bedroomed houses; conversions thus make large, spacious, sought-after flats (some the size, and price, of nearby '30s semis). Note, though, that Brockley's charms lie almost exclusively within its conservation area: W of **Brockley Rd** is still seen as the wrong side of the tracks, though the '90s **Croftongate Way** breaks away from this stigma. Its private road of 38 homes – some with glass balconies and modern designs – is a breath of fresh air: 1-bed flats here command £145,000.

So, first check out the conservation area boundary: **Tyrwhitt Rd** to the E, **Lewisham Way** to the N, **Upper Brockley Rd/Brockley Rd** to the W, down to the **Adelaide Avenue** junction. These streets are largely 3- and 4-storey houses, mostly – but not entirely – converted into flats. Some have huge 150ft gardens and there are panoramic views across to St Paul's for people with attic bedrooms. Inside the grand yellow-brick mansions the rooms are large, the ceilings high. A decent-sized, 5-storey Victorian house starts at c. £425,000; a 7-bed monster might make £750,000. Flats in **Manor Avenue, Breakspears Rd** and **Tressillian Rd** are popular (a 1-bed may be £140,000). Look out, too, for some original mews and coach houses: for example the un-tarmaced **Wickham Mews; Tressillian Rd** (1-bed flat £175,000). **Breakspears Mews**, however, is a 1997/8 addition: flat and houses. Off Wickham Rd is **Wickham Gardens**, a delightful crescent set round a small woodland area, with a mix of Gothicky 2-storey homes at one end, '70s-style council blocks at the other. The big tracts of council property in Brockley are gaining from a £44 million refurb, covering 2,000 homes.

Ladywell

From Brockley travel on to Hilly Fields park, mostly surrounded by post-war 2-storey family homes, some with balconies. Parents with daughters cluster round Prendergast secondary school, in its smart new buildings next to the Fields. From **Vicars Hill**, with its big late-Victorian semis, look out for **Adelaide Avenue**'s ornate terrace fronting the park (2-bed flat £250,000). Next, head down the hill into Ladywell 'village', perhaps more of an invention of local estate agents than a real village, but getting smarter. There is a good selection of shops in the 'village' centre on **Ladywell Rd** – and yet another station within a few minutes' walk. The huge, impressive Ladywell Leisure Centre is also just round the corner. Village homes are largely Victorian conversions of 2- and 3-storeys – some with huge gardens; though there are some '30s semis to provide a contrast, notably in **Veda Rd** and **Ermine Rd. Peppermead Square** is a modern infill of 2-bed houses.

Catford and the Corbett Estate

Catford will never be quaint. The centre, graced by the Catford Island shops/leisure complex, suffers from being a junction on the South Circular. However, now the wider area is on the move, Catford (despite being Zone 3) may well prove estate agents' assertions that the long-sighted will find they've bought a bargain.

Catford owes much of its housing character to a single man – Archibald Corbett. This canny Scot bought nearly 300 acres of then-virgin land in the late 19th century and proceeded to build thousands of houses, laying out the roads in a strict grid pattern. Many of the street names have a Scottish flavour – **Arngask** and **Glenfarg Rds**, for example. The boundary roads are **Wellmeadow** to the E, **Hazelbank** to the S, **Muirkirk** to the W, up to **Brownhill Rd** (otherwise known as the South Circular). The estate is known for its distinct lack of pubs – Archibald was teetotal.

Homes here range from 3- to 6-bedroomed houses, all solidly built, with spacious rooms. Many of the bigger properties were split into flats (a trend now reversed), but the estate still retains its prim-and-proper identity. All the houses have front gardens, and most have 80ft rear ones. The smaller, single-fronted Corbett houses are almost exactly half the size of the double-fronted ones, which are slightly more ornate – and a lot more pricey. Prices for a 3-bed vary from around £190,000 (small, with downstairs bath) to c. £250,000; a terraced 5 beds, £300,000; a double-fronted 5-bed, £500,000. The area remains very quiet, very respectable – very desirable: doctors, solicitors and the like. But be warned: visitors will need a map: every road really does look the same.

Another popular enclave (in part a conservation area) is made up of '30s-style semis and is bounded by **Bellingham Rd** to the S, **Thornsbeach** to the E, **Bromley Rd** to the W and **Culverley Rd** to the N. Wide roads here: 3- and 4-bed homes boast large gardens. Look to **Culverley Rd** for flats: some big houses here were split in the '80s, and there's a recent red-brick, 4-storey block. Some down-market streets near the stations, but popular St Dunstan's College lies on **Stanstead Rd** backed by green space, and attractive 3-storey Victorian homes line streets such as **Ravensbourne** and **Montem Rds**. To the E lies **Hither Green**, its flats and terraces a hunting-ground for first-time buyers. Now, though, Bellway are building a whole new village at 'Meridian South' on the old hospital site: 1-3 bed flats round a piazza of shops and cafés.

Transport Trains: St John's, Lewisham (London Bridge 14 min, Charing Cross 18 min), Ladywell, Brockley, Catford, Catford Bridge. Docklands Light Railway to Canary Wharf & City.

Convenient for Docklands, West End, City, Greenwich, Kent. Miles from centre: 6.

Schools Local Authority: Catford, Crofton, Prendergast (g), Addey & Stanhope, Deptford Green, St Joseph's RC. Private: St Dunstan's .

SALES

Flats	S	1B	2B	3B	4B	5B
Average prices	85–115	100–140	125–170	145–200	165–280	–
Houses	2B	3B	4B	5B	6/7B	8B
Average prices	200–230	210–260	250–300	300–450	400–500+	500–800+

RENTAL

Flats	S	1B	2B	3B	4B	5B
Average prices	115–140	140–175	160–210	185–230	210–250	–
Houses	2B	3B	4B	5B	6/7B	8B
Average prices	175–220	200–275	230–400	250–450	275–475	–

The properties Mainly Victorian, from tiny workers' homes (some listed) through larger terraces to grand 7-bed villas with conservatories. Some '20s/'30s suburbia intersperses, and increasing new-build. Catford has a well-preserved and popular estate of 3/6-bed 1880s houses, many now flats, plus '30s semis in large gardens.

The market Once hardly considered London; now on the Central London workers' list of possibles – large (up to 7-bed) houses have reverted from flats to family homes. Prices rose thanks to DLR and tube plans, but still modest given City/Docklands proximity. First-home hunters now forced S to Hither Green and beyond.

Among estate agents active in this area are:

- Oakleys
- Acorn
- Mark Beaumont
- Kinleigh Folkard Hayward
- Robinson Perkins Jackson
- Oak Estates
- Mann
- Winkworth
- Mark Beaumont

LEYTON AND WALTHAMSTOW

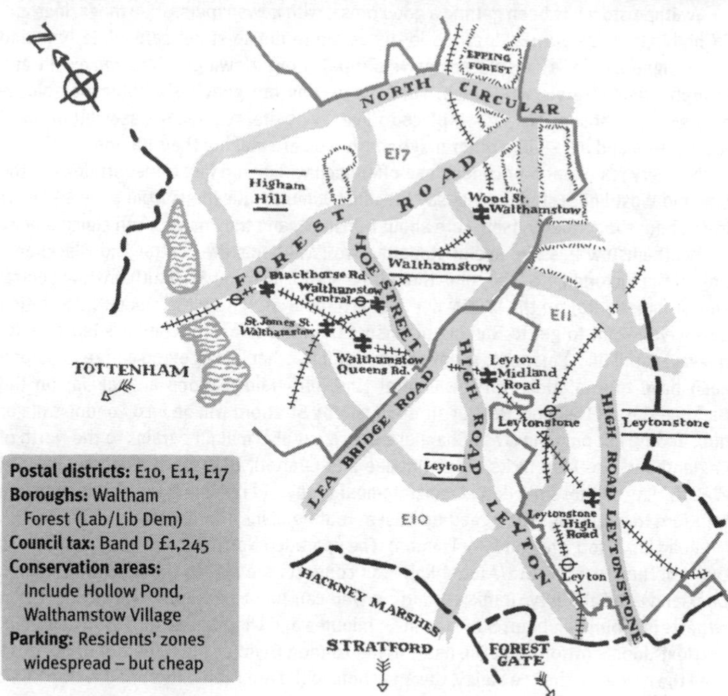

Postal districts: E10, E11, E17
Boroughs: Waltham Forest (Lab/Lib Dem)
Council tax: Band D £1,245
Conservation areas: Include Hollow Pond, Walthamstow Village
Parking: Residents' zones widespread – but cheap

'Wilcumestou' may, or may not, have meant 'the welcome place', but Walthamstow with its village has certainly re-established itself in London's consciousness. First-time buyers for long viewed Leyton and Walthamstow as a staging-post – the bottom rung on the ladder that lead to somewhere else. Now, they are likely to stay on. Second-time buyers, and couples making the leap from flat to family home, search here: in particular, Walthamstow. They find things a little easier now competition from investors – who at one point made up over a third of the local market – has ceased. Indeed, a number of buy-to-lets have been coming back onto the market as renters, finding they could afford trendier areas, became scarcer. Prices finally levelled off after the barnstorming rises of 25–30 per cent in 2002 alone; sellers are accepting offers.

Stratford, just to the S, is part of the reason for the spotlight swinging back Leyton and Walthamstow way: Olympic bid notwithstanding, the train due to arrive (and it's on time) in 2007 will be the Eurostar from Paris. And if much demand in the past few years was generated by those priced out of other places, increasingly incomers buy into the area for its own virtues. And, crucially, those existing owner-occupiers are making their next move within the area, comforted by improving primary schools, nearby green space and regeneration plans. Advocates of the wider area praise the diverse but tolerant community, the friendly shops and markets, the good transport, affordable homes – and hope that in being 'discovered', Walthamstow and Leyton are not ruined.

Waltham Forest – the borough that covers both areas – is taking a pro-active approach, figuring that if owner-occupiers stay their spending-power stays, too. Money has been conjured out of Europe and Whitehall; Leyton is an 'Area for Regeneration' in the London Plan – an Opportunity Area is how the council put it. Leyton and parts of Leytonstone are still marginally cheaper – and sometimes deservedly so – but here, too, there are well-defined enclaves of solid and sensibly priced Victorian homes.

Walthamstow has been getting a good press, with newspapers, style magazines and TV highlighting its virtues. Startled locals began to notice street cafés, late bars and other signs of life, as displaced (or would-be) Stoke Newingtonians moved in and brought their lifestyle with them. The Village, tiny but genuinely Domesday-old, is now well-established as a good place to live – website, residents' association, local restaurants and all – while other neighbourhoods are making their names.

Not very many parts of London can offer such varied and fast transport links to the City and West End. Estate agents say the most common questions from buyers – apart from about the property itself – are about transport, and the answers can clinch a deal.

Walthamstow has five useful stations: two (Walthamstow Central and Blackhorse Rd) on the Victoria Line tube, plus three train stations (Wood St, Walthamstow Central and St James's Rd) on the WAGN line into Liverpool St. Ignore the Queen's Rd station unless you want to get to Barking or Gospel Oak: this is one of London's least useful railways, until (if. . .) money is spent connecting it to other lines. Leyton and Leytonstone each have tube stations on the Central Line, but train stations are, again, on the Barking–Gospel Oak line. Best of all, soon nearby Stratford will be East London's major hub, adding not only the cross-Channel express but also mainline trains to the North of England and Scotland to its tubes (Jubilee and Central), DLR, North London Line and WAGN. Now all that's needed is reinstatement of the old rail link from Walthamstow to Stratford to augment the clogged-up buses – but no plans at present.

Road links, too, are good (for London). The upgraded North Circular Road runs across the N of the area; the A12/A102M link road connects the M11 to the Blackwall Tunnel, Docklands and the City. Traffic permitting, you can be at Heathrow, Gatwick or Luton airports in around an hour; Stansted in 35 minutes and London City Airport in about 20.

Next-door Stratford is at the heart of the London Olympic bid. Whether or not 2012 sees the games in the Lea Valley, the attention on the area can only spur development.

Walthamstow

This may not be one of London's most elegant corners, but it is probably one of its liveliest – and will be livelier if the council gets its way. What it has lacked – but is now gaining – are some good bars and restaurants. The café scene is improving, locals report. The town centre is undergoing a badly needed facelift which the council hopes will activate 'an evening economy' – at present, nearly everything shuts down except a few eateries. Sadly, a few of the plans have been modified/dropped since last year – notably the major new library planned for the **Hoe St/High St** corner: the site will go for retail and flats, though the Grade II-listed EMD Cinema will be kept. The existing library will now be expanded, instead of becoming the much-hyped arts centre.

At least there's the bus station – new, landscaped and much more attractive; a link to the tube is under way. The town centre enjoys excellent transport: it has a tube/overland rail link and good buses centred on the new station.

The **Selborne Walk** shopping mall, also awaiting expansion to include cinemas etc., has been set back by a recent fire; however the famous Walthamstow market along the High Street, its 400 stalls grown shabby over the years, is to be smartened and renewed, with a wider variety of stalls and possibly – a persistent rumour – a farmers' market. Shopfronts in the High Street, too, are getting a facelift.

Most of the homes are terraced houses (or flats converted from them) built in late-Victorian and Edwardian times, but there are also purpose-built blocks of flats, small cottages in Walthamstow Village and large detached houses in the area to the E known as Upper Walthamstow. You can find 3-bed terraced houses in some of the less regarded corners for £200,000, with plenty of viable choices at around £225,000 –

£250,000 if in Upper Walthamstow; while in the heart of the Village you'll pay up to £270,000 – likewise in corners near parks or tubes, or both.

The Village/Walthamstow Central neighbourhood is steadily the most desirable, and most expensive, corner for home-hunters. The Village, which is E of the stations, is a little area gathered ecclesiastically round St Mary's Church, with quaint, narrow streets and alleys, old houses (some extremely old, and listed), two rows of almshouses, the Vestry museum, cafés, bakery, ironmonger's – and of course village pub. Here, too, is popular Walthamstow Girls: known locally as 'the green school' after both uniform and now, we're told, ethos; it boasts an open-air Greek theatre. Look out for **Church Path**, with its 2-bed cottages, **Church Lane** (a 2-bed house c. £220–230,000; a 3-bed £250–270,000) **Beulah, Orford** and **Vestry Rds**, and bordering **Eden** and **Church Hill Rds.** To balance the old, 16 flats are being carved from an industrial building at the start of **Church Path.**

Beware, though, of attempts to expand 'the Village': strictly speaking it's the conservation area (which only includes part of many of the above streets), and one local agent got into trouble for redefining its borders a little too freely. The looser local rule-of-thumb is, unless you can hear the church bells, you're not in it.

West of the Village is the town centre, where **Hoe St** meets the **High St.** The Victorian terraces off both roads are great for commuters: the stations (tube and overground) are here. Some of the biggest and priciest homes are in the **Cedars Avenue** corner S of the centre, where the 5-bed houses are c. £400,000; but the popular streets here include a range of homes: **Albert Rd** (3-bed terraced, c. £235,000), **Chelmsford Rd, Belgrave Rd** (2 bed house, c. £210,000), **Landsdowne Rd** and **Boundary Rd**, where a good 2 bed flat recently sold for £170,000.

The Higham Hill neighbourhood, lying N of **Forest Rd** and W of the **Chingford Rd**, has a mix of smaller, terraced houses and council or ex-council homes. This is a quiet corner, with pleasant Lloyd Park on the E side and allotments adding to the greenery. There's a tube/train station at the SW end of the neighbourhood at **Blackhorse Rd**, but the N side, around **Billet Rd**, can feel a bit remote. Most of the Victorian houses are to the E, towards Lloyd Park. The whole neighbourhood has a mixture of 2- and 3-bed houses and purpose-built 2-bed flats. The flats start at c. £140,000 (more if closer to stations or in especially nice streets). Look out for homes described as 'Warner': these were built by local landowners of that name at various periods from late-Victorian to 1950s. Their standards were high, and these homes are sought-after (a few still sport a proud 'W' on their facades). A Warner 3-bed terraced house in the Lloyd Park area might be £230,000, with a choice of 1890s and 1950s vintages usually on offer; a 2-bed flat in, say, **Mersey** or **Diana Rds** c. £160,000. Just off Forest Rd, **William Morris Close** recalls Walthamstow's most famous resident, who as a child lived in Water House on **Forest Rd.** There's a museum which is dedicated to his work – and his typography graces the 'W' symbol used to 'brand' the town centre.

L

More terraced houses are to be found to the S, in the **St James St** corner of Walthamstow: although a bit further from centre, and again quieter and slightly cheaper, this does have its own railway station into Liverpool St. Places to look include the St James's Park estate and the Markhouse Road estate. Three-bed terraced houses are around £220–250,000, though ex-council 3-beds can be under £200,000. **Markhouse Avenue** leads through to the industrial sites and 'civic amenity site' (tip) in the Lea Valley, so it can be busy at times. The tip is set for redevelopment, but the industry will stay.

The **Coppermill Lane** area, to the W of **Blackhorse Rd**, is becoming popular due to its Warner homes (£160,000 for a 2-bed flat), nearby tube and primary school. There's also the attractive green space, nature reserve and open water of this part of the Lea Valley. The Victoria Line tube at the junction of Blackhorse/Forest Rds boosts prices: recent flats, just opposite the station, are around £130,000 for a 1-bed. Nearby, 'The Edge' is a new scheme overlooking the reservoirs: 2-bed flats (from £182,950), duplexes and 3-bed houses.

The east side of Walthamstow is in many ways the smartest (Village excluded), with the influence of the Epping Forest affluent lifestyle beginning to be felt (see Chingford, Woodford etc. for the heartland). This is Upper Walthamstow, where tree-lined roads sport large detached Victoriana, often with five or more bedrooms, plus more modest 1930s semis. **Wood St** – a road with its own station – marks the frontier; soon you start to leave the tiny terraces behind. **Forest Rise** (5-bed houses, £400,000-plus) marks the apogee, with views across the green spaces towards South Woodford.

New homes are scarce: there's little undeveloped space. Recent additions have been near the **High St** and off **Hale End Rd.** In **Willow Walk**, just off the High St, The Willows is a Rialto scheme of 1- and 2-bed flats; another recent housing development appeared in **Westbury Rd**, also close to the market. Up on **Billet Rd** in the N of the area, Weston's flats scheme was completed in 2000. On **Mansfield Rd**, 'Tudor Mews' is a group of six 3- and 4-bed houses with garages, dating from 2002. Most developments are by housing associations, which are building low-rise homes for residents moving out of grim '60s tower blocks that are being demolished. Circle 33, one of the biggest North London housing associations, has bought some rented homes from the Warner Estate.

Leyton and Leytonstone

Leyton and Leytonstone lie between the green open expanses of Hackney Marsh and Wanstead Flats, their postcodes being (broadly) E10 and E11. Though they boast a direct tube – the Central Line – to the City and West End, they have historically been cheap places to buy and rent, with a rich, friendly, ethnically diverse community though suffering from traffic and poor facilities; things are changing, and the London Plan identifies this as an Area for Regeneration. Many buyers, often teaming up with friends, find their first homes here – and are mopping up ex-buy-to-let properties. Cheap rents now attract quite a lot of foreign workers, many working on the new developments.

A key change for the area was the opening, in 2001, of **Orient Way**, the Leyton Relief Road, which has taken a lot of the heavy, industrial traffic away from local streets such as **Church Rd** and **Leyton High Rd** and straight onto the M11 Link Road. The new, six-acre Langthorne Park in Leytonstone – London's first new park for many years – has also opened. Tesco (who pulled out of Waltham Forest in the early 1990s) has returned with a superstore at the Green Man roundabout, and Asda has arrived at Leyton Mills (off the Relief Road) to provide some competition. Around Leytonstone tube, the range of restaurants (if not yet many smart bars) is slowly increasing. A new shopping complex on **Leyton High Rd** opposite the tube opened, with a nursery, a health club (the area's first) plus Asda, TK Maxx, Currys, B&Q, etc. Next to it, 25 new 2-bed/2-bath flats above shops are completing – and for footie fans, more are planned in the revamp of Leyton Orient.

Secondary schools have been patchy, but the new Lammas School in **Seymour Rd**, purpose-built and open in 2002, is already doubly oversubscribed: its catchment thus currently covers a circle of less than a mile radius.

The best corners of Leytonstone include the leafy Bushwood estate, near the golf course, while in Leyton the Barclay estate is very popular. Flats close to the stations are naturally in demand. Three-bed houses in Leyton, which could be found for £63,000 at the start of 1998, are now £200,000 minimum, with smarter roads attracting prices of £240–270,000; up to £400,000 in the best enclaves such as Leytonstone's **Bushwood**.

The area features a good mix of century-old houses in wide streets. Most of the homes here are in terraces built in the early 1900s, though some date back to the 1880s. Three-bed terraced houses are the most common, though there are a few with four, possibly five, beds. Many converted flats here; developers have been quietly adding to the stock (small, so far) of purpose-built ones – though the Whipps Cross Hospital site, E of **Peterborough Rd**, is to gain 200 key-worker and 200 social homes as part of a big revamp of the hospital. Look, here, for the terraces of small houses built as two flats

('Abrahams flats' in local parlance). These provide an interesting phenomenon: 1st-floor flats with outside steps down to their own back gardens. Pay c. £160,000 for a 2-bed.

On the borders with Upper Leytonstone is the area known as the Barclay estate, which contains some of the best houses in Leyton, both Victorian and 1930s. These lie behind Leyton Midland Rd station: the roads here are quieter and more pleasant in appearance, with more trees than is common in the area. Prices in the estate start around £260,000 for a 3-bed house. Nearby, a cache of good-value, and equally convenient, terraces include **Colchester, Nottingham, Canterbury, Ely, Epsom, Cromer, Essex, Sandringham Rds**: a 1-bed flat conversion here, c. £140,000. **Grove Green Rd** stretches from Leyton to Leytonstone, and the streets which lie off it have steadily been tidied; again, plenty of terraced houses and flat conversions. Roads round Leyton Orient football club (revamping, with some new flats to come) also have reasonably-priced terraces in reach of the tube.

Francis Rd is the spine of a small neighbourhood of pleasant streets: a 3-bed house in, say, **Newport** or **Twickenham Rds**, c. £265,000. And away on the W side of the area the Clementina estate (off **Clementina Rd**) has Warner-built (see Walthamstow) purpose-built 1900s flats at around £160,000 – close to the new Lammas School: see above.

While **Leytonstone High Rd** still has some way to go, it is certainly now less bleak – especially at the N end, which is seeing a rash of new homes: that's the vast Stratford International station taking shape (another two years of construction traffic) at the far, S, end. Bellway are building 61 1- and 2-bed flats, launching this spring, on the Hills Garage site, while across the road Centro is another, 20-flat, scheme: 2-beds from £189,950. And in **Kirkdale Rd** by the tube (Stratford two stops),Wimpey are adding flats and live/works.

Upper Leytonstone, though divided by the new M11 Link Road, contains some of the largest and most desirable homes, and has the advantage of being close to public transport (Central Line tube). **Forest Drive East, Forest Drive West** and the surrounding roads have big – up to half a million – houses in tree-lined streets: the 'forest' in question is Epping, which extends a final open green swathe, with boating lake, just across Whipps Cross Rd – a defining bulwark to the area.

There are some blocks of flats in the area, in addition to council-build, though the majority of flats are conversions. Flats blocks include **Brockway Close, Silks Court** and **Chessington Mansions** (which is not council-built even though it looks like it). There are new studio and 1-bed flats on **Holly Rd** close to the Green Man roundabout. The area along **High Rd Leyton** is residential, and purpose-built flats are a feature here, though local agents say most buyers prefer conversions, particularly near the station. Those that like new-build can try the new flats in **Norlington Rd**, next to the Midland Rd station, opposite the leisure centre in **Cathall Rd** and in **Leytonstone High Rd.**

East of **Leytonstone High Rd**, almost in Wanstead, lies the popular Bushwood estate. Here are some of the area's largest homes: c. £325–350,000. Curving **Bushwood**, the street that gives it its name, overlooks the open ground of Wanstead Flats and boasts sought after, grand, late-Victorian 4-bed terraced houses (c. £400,000). **Browning Rd** is a pretty conservation area of little Victorian cottages (£240–260,000 for 3-beds). **Barclay, Leybourne** and **Leyspring Rds** have solidly built 3-bed terraced houses. A well-planned one-way system leaves this estate free from all but residential traffic.

Borders: Chingford

The northern end of the borough holds the spacious streets of Chingford, its origins as a cluster of rural hamlets showing in the old village names like Chingford Green and Chingford Hatch. Airier streets and larger, roomier houses characterize this area, with the occasional earlier building still to be found amid the Victorian and (the majority) 1930s houses. Select North Chingford, based around the **Ridgeway** area, holds the premier streets, restaurants and bars. Three-bed houses here are now £330–420,000 plus (though ex-council on **Friday Hill** or **Yardley Lane** can be had for £190–230,000).

At Chingford Green the streets peter out on the edge of Epping Forest – all bordering homes much prized. On **Forest View**, pricey new 2- and 3-bed flats plus 3-bed houses start at £325,000 for a 2-bed flat.

Among the less expensive, but equally spacious, streets of South Chingford, the Palace View estate, which lies close to beautiful Larkswood, has turn-of-the-century semis and is considered to be one of the most desirable corners. Other streets to watch for include **Leadale Avenue, Priory Avenue** and **St Catherine's Rd**.

Some of the best Victorian/Edwardian and 1930s houses are in Highams Park, just to the N of – and across the North Circular from – Walthamstow's Higham Hill. Top streets are on a par with North Chingford: a 4-bed house, c. £350,000. Some homes display the 'W' of the Warner family estate: coveted due to the high building standards. Highams Park has its own station on the Liverpool St line, and a variety of parks and open spaces.

Transport Tubes: Leyton, Leytonstone (zone 3, Central); Walthamstow Central, Blackhorse Rd (zone 3, Victoria). From Walthamstow Central: Oxford Circus 25 min, City 40 min (1 change), Heathrow 1 hr 20 min (1 change). Trains: Walthamstow Central, Wood St and St James' St: to Liverpool St 15–20 min.

Convenient for City, West End; Epping Forest, Lea Valley, M11 to Cambridge, M25, City Airport, Stansted Airport. Miles to centre: 6–7.

Schools Local Authority: Leytonstone School, Aveling Park, Lammas, McEntee, Walthamstow (g), Warwick (b), Willowfield School, Connaught (g), George Mitchell, McEntee, Holy Family College (RC), Kelsmcott, Norlington (b). Private: Forest School.

L

SALES

Flats	S	1B	2B	3B	4B	5B
Average prices	100–115	120–150	135–190	180–220	–	–
Houses	2B	3B	4B	5B	6/7B	8B
Average prices	170–230	200–300	260–400	300–500	–	–

RENTAL

Flats	S	1B	2B	3B	4B	5B
Average prices	100–130	150–170	165–200	190–280	–	–
Houses	2B	3B	4B	5B	6/7B	8B
Average prices	180–220	200–260	240–300	280–340	–	–

The properties Largely 1900s terraces of 2/3-bed homes and p/b flats. Upper Walthamstow boasts some large detached houses; bigger ones, too, in Leyton's Barclay estate. Flats, mainly converted but a growing number of purpose-built, abound.

The market Good transport links; a hunting-ground for first-time buyers. Second-timers and local families starting to stay put rather than treating area as a stepping-stone to politer climes.

Among those estate agents active in this area are:

- Churchill
- Outlook
- Next Move
- Trading Places
- Douglas Allen Spiro
- Bairstow Eves
- James William
- Century 21
- Adam Kennedy
- Allen Davies
- Theydon
- Henley
- Haart
- Central
- Haart

Maida Vale and Little Venice

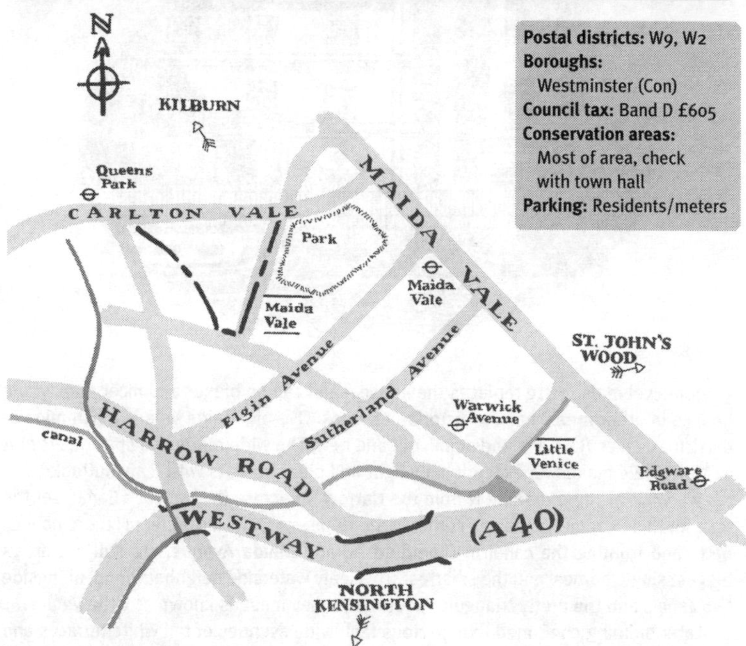

Postal districts: W9, W2
Boroughs:
Westminster (Con)
Council tax: Band D £605
Conservation areas:
Most of area, check with town hall
Parking: Residents/meters

Parisians would feel at home here. Maida Vale and Little Venice form a wholly residential district centred on wide boulevards of flats, rather than houses – carved out of the sort of creamy, dignified terraces that typify Belgravia: spacious, well placed, leafy, elegant and decidedly popular. This corner lies in the angle to the north of the **Harrow Rd** and west of the **Edgware Rd/Maida Vale** (the road). Strategically placed for the main routes west and north out of town, its position was confirmed by the Paddington–Heathrow 15-minute express: you can check in for nine airlines at the station. And now there's the new business quarter of Paddington Basin, kept at arm's length by the Westway but a new and growing source of home-hunters. They join buyers and renters both indigenous and international, with not a few celebrities thrown in. Nevertheless, it's a good hunting-ground: prices have softened here as they have across the capital – the asking price may not look that different, but sellers are accepting offers, and the difficulty of making rents cover mortgages now means some buy-to-let landlords are selling.

Next-door neighbour to St John's Wood, Maida Vale's slower rise to full-throttle desirability was only because, until the mid-1980s, hardly any of Maida Vale's homes were for sale. Its character was largely determined by the district's long-time ownership by the Church Commissioners, who planned, built, maintained, laid down the rules for and also let the property. This meant very little buying and selling: nearly all homes were rented. Only in the 1980s did this begin to change. Those tenants who could afford to do so bought their homes at preferential rates; developers moved in wholesale. The snowy terraces were converted, the hitherto run-down – and, it must be said, decidedly seedy – area was transformed; prices soared. The steady progress of leasehold reform has helped cement the area's status, allowing flat-dwellers to buy shares in freeholds.

What you *won't* find here are the usual London rows of small terraced houses, although there is a scattering of new and refurbished mews houses. In this area the

garden-level maisonette replaces the house – and can be bigger and nicer than whole houses in other areas' narrow Victorian terraces. Overall, Maida Vale is a rich mine of particularly nice flats, big and small, old and new. The wide roads and spacious layout of Maida Vale makes for exceptionally light and pleasant flats with leafy outlooks.

Warwick Avenue, running N from the **Harrow Rd** across the Regent's Canal, set the tone for this extremely pleasant corner in the 1840s–50s. The large cream stucco houses here, and fronting the canal in **Blomfield Rd** and **Maida Avenue**, are still the area's biggest single homes, and the smartest. This leafy waterside neighbourhood, alongside two canals and the pretty triangular pool where they meet, is known as Little Venice.

Later building confirmed the spacious feel: wide avenues of tall white terraces and red-brick mansion blocks, behind whose ramparts are often concealed large (some vast) shared gardens – a secret unsuspected by passers-by. These delightful 'inverted square gardens', the area's hidden bonus, can include tennis courts, and ground-floor flats with direct access via gates at the end of their own back gardens: a boon for those with kids.

The most coveted homes, however, are those nearest to or overlooking the canal: truly a 'Little Venice' – though beware those estate agents who spread the use of this more picturesque name for all Maida Vale's most desirable white stucco streets. These snowy rows form the heart of the area, and are succeeded further N and W by streets of red-brick mansion flats: these can provide a lot of space for your money. The church land ends in the W at **Shirland Rd**. Next come smaller-scale Victorian terraces, fast improving, but quite different in character: you are back to ordinary inner London now.

It is now common for flats to appear for sale with a share of the freehold. Many leaseholders jointly bought the freehold to their blocks after 1993, when the law changed to make this easier. This accelerated in the mid-'90s when some faced five-figure bills for major refurbishments to their mansion blocks. Take advice, if buying, about whether the (frequently high) service charges contribute to an adequate sinking fund to guard against enormous extra outlay when, say, the roof needs replacing. Accessibility also makes renting popular, with multinational companies, embassies and, especially, Americans.

Little Venice

Blomfield Rd and **Maida Avenue** residents have homes made magic (and even more expensive) by the presence of water. The canal runs between the two, widening by the **Warwick Rd** bridge – where it branches – into a young lake with willow-pattern islet and waterside public gardens and walk. The canal ends of adjoining roads also get called Little Venice; non-natives can be startled by narrowboats apparently gliding across the top of the street. A charming, prized corner of London.

Starting from **Paddington Green** to the S of the canal (today marooned between the Westway flyover and '60s college blocks, council towers, drug-addict centre), **St Mary's Terrace** runs away towards the canal: No. 1, in classic double-fronted stucco, sets the tone. Across the street is Fleming Court (council-built), then the stately red-brick mansion blocks of Osborne House and **St Mary's Mansions** – the latter several blocks around a courtyard: popular, family-sized flats. Porteus Rd, opposite, leads to 1980s **Hogan Mews**, close to the Westway. The opposite side has council-built flats.

St Mary's Terrace becomes **Park Place Villas** (some little 2/3-bed cottages here, at less than modest prices), which runs to the canal – and Little Venice proper. On the corner with Maida Avenue, an enormous Italianate villa has prime position: a 9-bed, 9-bath, indoor-pool mansion. Both **Maida Avenue** and **Blomfield Rd** have vast, very handsome white stucco villas facing over the water – one recently, £3.5 million; but expect anything between £3–5 million. These give way, towards the Edgware Rd end, to later Victoriana; mansion blocks that can provide flats the size of young houses, and as various: prices depend on the block and the view. At the other, W end of Blomfield is a row of handsome terraced homes, all now flats. These are council-run, as is the S side of **Bristol Gardens** behind (a communal garden runs between them); not surprisingly, many are now private. To the W, along the canal past the Waterway pub/restaurant, is council-built Amberley Estate: pleasant 1970s low-rise through to **Shirland Rd/Sutherland Avenue.**

From the Harrow Rd Bridge westwards, the S bank of the canal is Westminster City's Warwick Estate; pleasant '60s low-rise plus two tower blocks, now increasingly in private hands – particularly the smart, cream canalside homes in **Warwick Crescent**: a studio, £200,000. The canal then dips below the Harrow Rd, and between the two on the N bank is the Vale's biggest new-build area: on **Admiral Walk**, Carlton Gate, Swift and Swallow Courts are 1995 studios, 1- and 2-bed flats – a 2-bed here, £295,000; a 3-bed penthouse, £499,950. Note: those who opt for canalside flats here ironically also get fine views of the Westway elevated section and the North Ken tower blocks, while the ex-council Warwick Estate flats opposite gaze tranquilly across to Little Venice. . . .

Behind Blomfield Rd, to the W of Warwick Avenue lies pretty, villagey **Warwick Place**: (small-scale, with pub, a little shop or two – a 4-bed house, redesigned and Grade II listed, £1.693 million last winter. **Bristol Mews**, off Bristol Gardens, was reborn in 1995 as 25 smart new stock-brick, 2-storey homes in an unusually wide cobbled mews. That year also saw the refurbishment of the 44 homes of **Elnathan Mews.** These two add a cache of small houses – otherwise a rarity here, as are their garages. **Clifton Villas** lives up to its name: beautiful big 5/6-bed whole houses here. East of Warwick Avenue, streets between the canal and Clifton Gardens also enjoy the Little Venice premium.

Maida Vale central

The name really applies to the old church estate, from Little Venice northwards, with **Maida Vale** (the eponymous road) forming the E boundary. **Warwick Avenue**, which is the Vale's boulevard, runs NW from Little Venice into the heart of the district with the clean, striking lines of the modern St Saviour's Church (junction with Clifton Gardens) as its focal point. The church has matching flats, Manor House Court, behind. The Avenue is a delight – lined with classical white early 1850s mansions, many of which escaped being subdivided and are still single homes, particularly on the E side. However, a terrace of the tall stucco houses on the W side opposite the church is very dilapidated: watch this space. . . . **Formosa St**'s E end forms a little dog-leg of still-local shops (launderette and newsagent with Post Office counter) and cafés/restaurants.

Clifton Gardens, a wide and desirable street of 1860s stucco terraces, runs NE from St Saviour's (and the tube station) to **Maida Vale**. Top-class conversions into luxury flats back, on the N side, onto vast communal gardens. Cumberland House, on the junction with Warwick Avenue, is quite new (1987), despite its handsome 'period' appearance:

top-of-the-market apartments (£600,000 for a 2-bed here last winter). Another such is Europa House in **Randolph Avenue** (a street that saw several luxurious developments in the '80s): this has underground parking, and its flats are rented as short lets. This long road runs from top to bottom of the area – from the shores of Kilburn in the N to the Little Venice canal and the land of big stucco terraces in the S. Here you can buy a 1-bed flat for £249,950 (just under the Stamp-Duty threshold), a 2-bed flat, £350,000 – or look for house-sized flats or maisonettes. The 3-bed (or 2-big-suite) apartment can vary in size/style/ position/lease as much as houses do elsewhere – from around half a million to one and a half. Some even boast more outside space than most whole houses: look for top-floor ones with perhaps two roof terraces plus access to communal gardens. The Avenue also now boasts a Starbucks. Other Avenue homes are flats carved out of some very large pairs of Victorian brick-and-stucco houses, though a few do remain as single homes – with price tags, when they appear, of £2.5 million or so. At the S end of **Lanark Rd**, too, are neat pairs of little 19th-century 2-storey-plus-basement villas: rare in the area, and around a million. Both streets run S down to the canal to rejoin Little Venice.

Off that S end of Randolph Avenue are three closes of 1960s town-houses: **Elizabeth**, **Robert** and **Browning Closes.** Across in hidden **Randolph Mews**, through an archway, smaller '60s mews cottages with deep eaves and bays enjoy lots of parking space and garages. Also a red-brick electricity substation, transformed into a house in 1988 to become one of the most enviable in the area: there are other 4/5-bed, 3-bath homes hereabouts, but few with gym, wine store, conservatory, courtyard garden, balcony, terrace, carport – and off-street parking for four.

Clifton Gardens becomes, at the E end, **Clifton Rd** – the Vale's 'high street', with useful, individual shops (including a butcher) joined by the odd smart restaurant, wine bar, etc. Enviable **Warrington Crescent** curves N from Clifton Gardens to Sutherland Avenue: communal gardens behind both sides of its massed flats – reckoned to be some of the area's best. Similar style and price in **Randolph Crescent**, which curves a parallel course – though homes with access to the 3-acre triangular gardens that the E side shares with stretches of Clifton Gardens/Randolph Avenue are even more highly rated.

Castellain Rd, parallel to (and converging with) Warwick Avenue on the E, is a long street which crosses Sutherland Avenue to reach Elgin Avenue. Between these two lies Castellain Mansions, a large block of red- and grey-brick mansion flats. A roomy 2-bed flat here on a long lease might be c. £330–360,000. Behind, to the E, are communal gardens; to the W, Paddington Bowling and Sports Club offering 'bowls, tennis, squash, social'. In the angle behind Castellain and Sutherland, the communal gardens boast tennis courts. **Castellain Rd** also has modern Katherine Court, the style of which handsomely acknowledges that of its neighbours. Across the road in **Warrington Gardens** more than 50 flats and penthouses, with parking, were built at No. 1 in 1995: a 2-bed, 2-balconied flat here, £485,000 last winter).

Sutherland Avenue is classic Maida Vale, a wide, tree-lined boulevard – the area's second-largest – with parking down the centre, its vista stopped to the E by the '60s Stuart Tower. At the western end (W of Shirland Rd) stand ornate stucco houses, with wrought-iron balustrades at the first floor. Then come slightly smaller models, then vast Victorian red-bricks. A useful Tesco Metro here has added to the area's shopping. **Shirland Rd** marks a price, as well as a physical, divide: W of it, **Sutherland Avenue** runs down to the Harrow Rd; a 2-bed flat, c. £250,000, in this more humdrum stretch could cost another £100,000 if located across the Shirland divide, on the E leg that runs up to Maida Vale (the road); indeed, one 2-bed was £465,000 at the favoured end last winter. Back in **Shirland Rd**, you could double the bedrooms and take a third off the price: a 4-bed ex-council maisonette, £320,000. Nevertheless, a few smart new 2-bed flats, and the odd trendy café, have appeared in **Marylands Rd**, to the W. **Lauderdale Rd**, running westwards from the E end of Sutherland Rd to Elgin Rd, has more mansion flats – large gardens behind those of the S side. **Elgin Avenue**, lined with comfortable red-brick mansion blocks, starts in the E at Maida Vale tube and shops, runs W to cross Shirland Rd and on into western Maida Vale (see below). Elgin Mansions is a vast flats block with access to communal gardens. Compared with Sutherland Avenue, Elgin is both busier and more anonymous, its homes hitherto less coveted and thus somewhat cheaper (a studio, £208,000; a 2-bed maisonette, £285,000); the better ones have, however, done some fairly definitive catching-up. On the **Elgin Avenue /Morshead Rd** corner, a trad-style red-brick block of 2- and 3-bed flats was built in 1995.

Elgin Mews, North and **South**, are tucked behind the shops around Maida Vale tube. Mews North has been rebuilt: smart town-houses. Mews South is original: pretty, painted brick, half-million-ish homes. **Ashworth Rd** and **Biddulph Rd** hold a surprise: the stretch S of Elgin suddenly becomes Surrey: low-built, between-the-wars pairs of houses joined by garages – the nearest semis to Marble Arch? Low eaves, deep porches, stockbroker-Tudor Arts-and-Craftsy – and nowadays a million and over. . . .

But red-brick mansion blocks are the leitmotif for this end of Maida Vale. Once thought dowdy by contrast with the southern stucco, they have nearly all been restored. New balconies, street railings, exterior lights, paintwork – they are now as their architects intended: dignified, uniform, smart. This holds good for the whole tract between Elgin Avenue and the Paddington Recreation Ground which divides Maida Vale from the shores of Kilburn: green and open, and much smartened-up. A quiet corner, but close to the tube, its streets include **Essendine Rd**, **Morshead Rd**, **Grantully Rd**, **Wymering Rd** (which also has a few 4-bed, c. £800,000, infill houses) and **Widley Rd**, plus the N ends of **Ashworth** and **Biddulph Rds**. Two-bed flats in, say, Wymering Mansions start around £300–365,000. Views from the **Morshead** ones (Nos. 25 onwards) are across the recreation ground (a 2-bed, £400,000), likewise the balconied homes (Nos. 171 on) at the N end of **Randolph Avenue**. From the tube, Randolph Avenue and **Lanark Rd** turn back S to run parallel to Maida Vale (the road). The N end of Lanark Rd is the Maida Vale council estate with tower blocks, now renovating, but further S the smart villa-style blocks of flats, designed by Jeremy Dixon, were built by Westminster Council in 1983 as starter homes; these now appear for sale. Back S of Elgin Avenue, **Delaware Rd** holds the BBC rehearsal/recording studios with mansion flats opposite. Behind these is a sports club.

Maida Vale, a major road, bounds the district: across it is St John's Wood. At the far N end, almost in Kilburn, is Regent's Plaza, a big and smart hotel/flats complex; 2- and 3-bed flats can be had here on long leases. Other homes on this busy through-route are council-built or '30s mansion flats – then the local landmark of '60s, Y-shaped, Stuart Tower: council-built, but now a private, portered block. Enjoy fine views from upper floors (these £210,000-ish 1-bed flats are described as 'bachelor apartments': appropriate, given the Tower's erstwhile reputation). South of Sutherland Avenue come big 1890s blocks such as Blomfield and Sandringham Courts (a 3-bed flat, £650,000). Look here for spacious flats, but without the charm of those in the 'hidden gardens' roads. Clarendon Court is the rebuilding two years back, by Galliard, of the old Clarendon Hotel: the 97 flats, then c. £625–925,000 for 2-beds, struggled to compete with existing homes. Once over the canal bridge, **Maida Vale** becomes **Edgware Rd** with scruffy but lively shops.

Borders

Having converted everything in sight in Maida Vale proper, the developers moved W of the **Shirland Rd** divide into a zone which is somewhat of a no-man's-land of council estates and small terraces, many now split into flats. The S part, N of **Harrow Rd** and up towards Queen's Park station, is in Westminster's patch. The NE corner is in Brent.

The N part of the borders district is largely sprawling council estates on either side of **Carlton Vale**. South, the modest terraces of the **Fernhead Rd/Saltram Crescent** area are a good-value corner in a mixed council/private area. **Saltram** was discovered early by converters; check out the church, now flats, here. The Westminster frontier runs from the S end of **Kilburn Park Rd** up behind **Saltram Crescent**. The streets between **Walterton Rd** and **Fernhead Rd** became a bitter battleground between Westminster Council and local tenants in the 1980s. The tenants eventually formed Walterton and Elgin Community Homes and bought their homes *en masse* from Westminster (which had been set on selling to developers) and set about major renovations. These are now a source of less-pricey flats to buy/rent of all sizes from studios to 3-beds. A modern estate separates these streets from the private terraces of **Bravington** (where 'Octavia Mews' adds eight new houses), **Portnall** and **Ashmore Rd**: another hunting-ground (2-beds c. £250–260,000, 3-bed c. £330,000). Across the **Harrow Rd** lie **Hormead** and **Fermoy Rds**: Victorian rows, many now flats, near the canal.

To the W (see Kilburn, Kensal Green and Queen's Park chapter) are the council's Mozart Estate and then the placid Queen's Park Estate of charming terraced cottages.

Transport Tubes: Maida Vale, Warwick Avenue (zone 2, Bakerloo); Oxford Circus 15 min, City 25 min (1 change), Heathrow 30 min (1 change).

Convenient for Paddington station (for Heathrow Airport), roads to W and N, West End. Miles from centre: 3.

Schools Local Authority: St George's RC, North Westminster. Private: American School. See also St John's Wood.

SALES

Flats	S	1B	2B	3B	4B	5B
Average prices	150–240	190–320+	250–650+	350–1M+	450–1M+	1M+
Houses	2B	3B	4B	5B	6/7B	8B
Average prices	340–1M	600–1.5M+	800–1.5M+	→	1–2.5M+	–

RENTAL

Flats	S	1B	2B	3B	4B	5B
Average prices	150–250	200–400	280–600	300–700+	700–1000+	1000+
Houses	2B	3B	4B	5B	6/7B	8B
Average prices	350–500	400–800+	800–2500	1000–4000	2000–5000	–

M

The properties Gracious white stucco terraces and villas, rows of neat red-brick mansion flats, some modern mews/town-houses. Flats reign: mainly mansion blocks or period conversions – many luxurious and recent. Flats can also be large – the garden maisonette replaces small houses here – and lovely. Of the few houses the best are the canalside ones of Little Venice.

The market The range of flats, rather than houses, attracts buyers and renters, native and international. The Vale's location makes it a good long-term bet. Its 'hidden gardens' and wide, leafy avenues are its best assets; American love the trad, not glitzy, style.

Among estate agents active in this area are:

- Greene & Co
- Anscombe & Ringland
- Pembertons
- Fraser & Co
- Chesterton
- Marsh & Parsons
- Foxtons
- Cohen & Pride
- Brian Lack
- Central London
- Clifton
- Goldschmidt & Howland
- Winkworth
- Vickers
- Howard Estates
- Homeview
- Londonwide

Marylebone and Fitzrovia

Postal districts: W1, NW1, NW8
Boroughs: Westminster (Con), Camden (Lab)
Council tax: Band D Westminster £605, Camden £1,200
Conservation areas: Most of area
Parking: Residents/meters/clamps

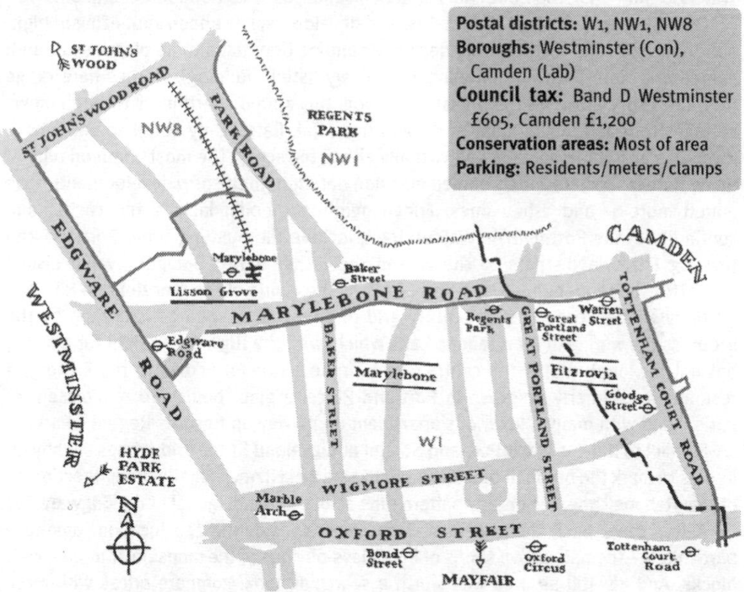

Urban villages are the new craze in the sober world of W1. Respectable estate landlords, with ownership dating from Shakespeare's time, are flirting with flighty fashion retailers, cutting-edge café proprietors and smart supermarkets. 'Come to be part of Marylebone Village', said the Howard de Walden Estate (family-owned since 1611). It worked, too. Marylebone High Street, which does have claims to historical village-dom (see Domesday Book) has been successfuly reinvented, and now boasts every urban amenity from several book stores to a farmers' market ('and more French patisseries than is good for anyone' to quote a resident).

Now the Portman Estate (family-owned since 1553) is trying the same trick. Lacking a high street to start from, it has identified the corner just N of Marble Arch, around the W end of Seymour St and New Quebec St, as Portman Village. The Estate wants to encourage useful shops: butcher, baker, fishmonger; and they hope to start a farm shop selling produce from the estate's farms in Hertfordshire. A Swedish antique clock dealer, a fashionable florist and a *couturier* have already been enticed.

With Regent's Park as its back garden, the West End at its feet, this area could hardly be more central – or more varied. Yet only in the past few years has it begun to be rediscovered by the home-hunter. It is closer to the hub than Mayfair, Belgravia, and Kensington. But this tract is a diverse one: many original homes were appropriated for shops or offices, its through-routes are busy. People think first of its landmarks: the BBC's Broadcasting House, the Courtauld Institute, the Wallace Collection – and of course Harley St, heart of the medical profession. But 'Marylebone Village' is no estate agents' (or aristocratic landlord's) conceit, it is the reflection of reality. There is a community here, hidden to all but locals and taxi drivers, between the roaring six-lane highway of the Marylebone Rd and tourist-thronged Oxford St. Away from the bustle of Selfridges, John Lewis and the like lie corners of surprising residential peace and tranquillity, plus others which hum with ever-more-stylish life.

Nearby Paddington has the Heathrow Express, making for swift exits and entrances. Baker St tube, always a useful hub, now includes the Jubilee Line to Westminster, Waterloo (for Paris), the South Bank and Docklands, as does Bond Street station.

Over the past few years the estates, and developers, have been squeezing in high-spec new flats, and resuscitating decaying genuine Georgiana (blue plaques abound: sometimes more than one on each, very likely listed, building). Homes here range from the 18th century to the present day, from tiny studio apartments through mews cottages to grand family mansions – and flats, flat, flats. (Only about 10 per cent of dwellings are whole houses; and virtually all are terraced). The most common type of home here is the 3- or 4-bedroomed mansion flat, though the new developments have added more 1- and 2-bed ones. Fringe neighbourhoods, lacking the cachet and continuity of the Portman/de Walden tract, include the bustling Great Portland and reviving Fitzrovia districts to the E, and the rather mixed but good-value Lisson Grove/North Marylebone tract N and E, across the divide of the **Marylebone Rd**.

Marylebone's orderly 18th-century grid of streets and squares is broken by the irrepressible wiggle of **Marylebone Lane** which, with the **High St** (straight for a while, but not for long), marks the centre of the original village. Across to the E the grid resumes its soldierly progress to **Portland Place**, a giant boulevard reminiscent of Paris, lined with many a luxurious apartment on its way up towards Regent's Park.

Parallel to the E is **Great Portland St**, and at **Cleveland St** the grid swings slightly on its axis to mark the borough boundary and the start of Fitzrovia. In the other direction, W of **Marylebone Lane**, the orderly pattern runs across to the diagonal of the **Edgware Rd**.

A few years back there were real bargains, considering the location, among – particularly – the flats above shops or in the less-obvious of the mansion or more recent blocks. And it's still an area well worth a searching look: compare prices with more obvious places: Clerkenwell, say, or Notting Hill. It best suits single people – professionals/City workers who want to be in zone 1 – and couples unburdened with young children. Although many happy families do live N of **Oxford St**, they are not typical; proof from estate agents in the area, many of whom say they have never been asked by anxious parents for advice on schools. Renters include the international business set, attending the London Business School; also students at the LSE or UCL. Americans, especially lawyers and military men assigned to the embassy, also rent here.

M

The continuing ownership by major landlords such as the de Walden and Portman Estates means few freeholds and, frequently, short leaseholds. But leasehold reform now allows leaseholders to extend leases, or to buy their freeholds: even the most reluctant estates have to comply (see Buying and Selling chapter). So differences in property prices (one flat can cost double what a seemingly similar one costs) depend not just upon its quality and location, but also upon the length of the lease. Also on the service charge (can be huge), a parking space (add £30,000), any outside dimension (gardens are rare: add £100,000), the presence of a porter. Medical licences – granted by the landlords and allowing doctors to practise – inflate prices considerably.

Know your landlord: Howard de Walden owns 90 acres, mostly to the E of the area, around **Marylebone High St** and **Harley St**. The Portman Estate (110 acres) is dominant in the SW corner, from **Oxford St** and **Edgware Rd** up to just N of **Bryanston** and **Montagu Squares**, with **Manchester St** marking the eastern edge. Both estates rent homes directly: see their websites. A fair amount of land here is also owned by the Crown Estate (for example, parts of **Harley St** and **Park Crescent Mews West**).

Marylebone

Marylebone has always been synonymous with medical excellence, for it is here that the cream of the British medical profession is gathered, crammed into **Harley St** and its immediate environs (**Wimpole St**, for example). This district, which is bordered by the southern margins of Regent's Park, as well as **Edgware Rd** and **Great Portland St**, encompasses street-by-street variations in architecture, general character – and price.

If landlords such as the de Walden Estate mean few freeholds as yet, they also make for continuity – thus the unchanging nature of the medical groves. They are responsible for the lovely Georgian doorways, staircases and rooflines still so much in evidence. These older buildings are supplemented by the red-brick blocks built at the start of the 20th century and some modern apartments that replaced wartime damage (a purpose-built block in **Wimpole St** has underground parking). Doctors must still get permission from the estate in order to mount their brass plate upon the door – qualifications and status are strictly vetted. About 1,500 doctors have premises here.

The Howard de Walden estate has successfully revived the retail heart of its patch. Smart shops – books, fashion, design, cafés – now cluster on **Marylebone High St**, which even its landlords admit had sunk into decline: there were 51 empty shops in the mid-1990s. The estate, pleasingly, intends to use its ownership to ensure that useful and interesting shops (several with a French flavour) stay amid the glitzy ones. A branch of renowned Pâtisserie Valerie is especially welcome – as is Waitrose; Cecil House above it is flats. A Sunday farmers' market is a recent hit, adding to the quality food shops and restaurants that the area has attracted (and the Cordon Bleu cookery school). The new Tesco Metro is viewed by the Estate with a little well-bred alarm: they are negotiating with the supermarket firm to see if it can tone down its 'bright colours'.

In addition to the sophisticated charm of Marylebone Village, there is the cheerfully commercial (busy but not unpleasant) **Baker St** – home of Sherlock Holmes, sleuth of legend – stretching from Regent's Park to the upmarket Selfridges department store on Oxford St, and **Wigmore St** with its concert hall and smart shops.

Then there is **Portland Place**, the grand, wide-avenued home to the BBC's Broadcasting House, the Royal Institute of British Architects and a clutch of embassies. Homes are likely to be luxurious flats (discreet luxury, or dripping-gilt-and-marble luxury – but decidedly luxury) in conversions or – more likely – the modern buildings that have superseded Robert Adam's original elegance. Many blocks have uniformed porters; a large and smart one in nearby **Mansfield St** runs to maid service and its own restaurant. At the N end of **Portland Place** is a delight: instead of debouching straight onto roaring Marylebone Rd, the street divides into the two curving arms of Nash's **Park Crescent**, its lovely homes (most are flats) sheltering behind the protective half-moon of its gardens. The rare family home with garage is occasionally to be had in its two mews behind.

Indeed, one of the area's special delights is the many and varied mews tucked away behind its main streets. These compact little homes – mainly modernized, but some unrefurbished – are dotted across the area, though many are concentrated in the **Harley St** environs. Prices start around £600,000 for modern houses in the less central, less picturesque mews – and go right on up (bear in mind that many are leasehold). These, of course, are often the extremely proud possessors of (sometimes rather small) garages, thanks to their original function as stables – some still have rings for tethering horses. Though if you don't care for history, look for the modern version to **Richardson's Mews**, just off Warren St, **Duchess Mews**, **Jacob's Well Mews** or **Weymouth Mews**.

Then there is the discreet elegance of the various squares: at the western, Marble Arch, slice of Marylebone – between **Edgware Rd** and **Gloucester Place** – lie **Bryanston Square** and **Montagu Square**, with their communal gardens at their hearts. These well-kept and railed patches of green are accessible only to residents: not to be sniffed at in a district where private gardens are almost non-existent, or barely bigger than a suburban household's window box. A 2-bed maisonette in **Montagu Square** was £935,000 last winter, while a whole house will be over £2 million. The mews E and W of the square offer houses in a range of sizes, degrees of smartness and prices.

There is always a good supply of mansion flats, of every standard from down-at-heel to palatial. Century-old buildings such as Bickenhall Mansions are popular, with high ceilings and coved fireplaces to their house-sized, long-lease flats. There are even occasional vast 9-bed flats in blocks such as Orchard Court in **Portman Square**. **Harley St** is, as you might expect, another prized address, but is mostly medical consulting rooms with a scattering of mansion blocks (Harmont House, for instance) offering occasional unmodernized flats such as a 1-bed on a long lease for £325,000. Edwardian Montagu Mansions, S of **York St** in the Baker St direction, has flats on share-of-freehold basis: a large 2-bed, 2-recep, £900,000. A 1980s scheme in **Marylebone St**, Maybury Court, has 80 1- to 3-bed flats. Welbeck House, a stone block on the corner of **Wigmore St**, has vast apartments; Harley House on **Marylebone Rd** has some new ones on the roof at £4.2 million. See also the Glentworth St blocks under Lisson Grove, below. In **George St**, Bryanston Court is a well-regarded '30s block where security is a priority (3-bed £875,000); the same goes for Portman Towers, built 1969 (3-bed, 2-bath flat £795,000).

The 'Portman Village' corner (see introduction) has a major refurb (rebuild, really) of Georgian houses in **George St** resulting in 37 flats. The old synagogue in **Seymour Place**, too, is now 21 flats. The Portman Estate's revival of **New Quebec St** will yield some flats as well as smart shops. Busy **Gloucester Place** is gaining 55 flats in restored Georgian buildings – for rent, not sale. The first 29 are now available at £325–570 per week.

Modern flats can be found in the SW corner, around **Great Cumberland Place**, and along **Baker St**; Bilton Towers, on Great Cumberland Place, usually has a range of flats on sale with leases around 45–50 years. The fashion for turning ex-commercial premises into homes crops up here and there – converting a big former store on the corner of **Welbeck St** resulted in some very smart new flats. For those who appreciate 1960s commercial architecture and want a room with a view there is Marathon House, once an office tower, now 107 flats, up on **Marylebone Rd**. Then there are flats in another old office building in **Nottingham St**; and large flats (sold as shell finish: design your own space) behind a retained facade on the corner of **Welbeck Way** and **Wimpole St**. New-build includes Galliard's 2001 Bourne House in **Old Marylebone Rd**, over in the area's NW corner, which has Paddington (and thus Heathrow, and the rest of the world) round the corner. The old juvenile court nearby in **Seymour Place** is now 'The Courthouse': nine flats (from £450,000 for 1-beds) and five mews houses (from £850,000). In contrast, flats can be had in the big old red-brick mansion blocks along the W edge of the area, such as Hyde Park Mansions (a 3-bed needing work, £525,000) and Oxford & Cambridge Mansions.

A recent **High St** addition is smart Copperfield House, a 20-flat block with underground parking. In **Devonshire Place**, ten flats were created in the conversion of two Georgian terraced houses, but if you want a whole house a wide, 4-floor affair was £3 million last winter (partly because three of the floors had medical use). To the S, very close to Bond St tube, The Phoenix in **Bird St** is a new-build block with 2-bed flats on a 996-year lease. Heron Place, on the corner of the High St and **George St**, has 2-bed flats in a modern block.

Some Georgian terraced houses in **Molyneux St**, in the NW corner of Marylebone, have been recently refurbished, and this district has several streets of such houses, in varying condition, plus a handful of modern, neo-Georgian ones. For something smarter, try **Marylebone High St**: one or two 3-bed houses here, and a giant 6-bed on the corner of **Upper Wimpole St**, much smartened, was £3.5 million a year ago.

Great Portland St

The area E of Portland Place has a style of its own. It has been, and to a large extent still is, the centre of the London wholesale fashion trade. However, here, too, quite a few warehouses and offices are being converted into homes. On the new-build side, in **Wells St** Berkeley's big West One House recently added 73 new homes: 1- to 3-bed flats and

3-bed town-houses. Nearby, enticingly named **Market Place** is now a mini-piazza with shops, café and bars. The new flats join mansion blocks around **Mortimer St**, **Riding House St** and **Foley St**. There are mews – many still commercial – and odd corners such as **Booth's Place**, where 2-bed flats have their own garages. **Berners St**, just N of Oxford St, has Berkeley's restoration of York House into flats. Between Riding House St and Foley St there are modern houses in **Middleton Buildings**.

Lisson Grove & Dorset Square

The area around **Lisson Grove** (over in NW8) remains the least fashionable part of Marylebone. The Regent's Canal runs through the area, conveying hints of neighbouring Little Venice and Regent's Park – and, where the Grove crosses it, a big mooring of narrow boats. Despite these assets, and NW1 or NW8 in the address, Lisson Grove has yet to really take off, only taking a turn for the better as it reaches the borders of St John's Wood N of the Lilestone Estate. The Lisson Green and **Church St** Estates are not a plus (the Lilestone estate is less obvious than the others in its origins: a 2 bed ex-authority flat here, £275,000, while a 2-bed in a new scheme nearby in Frampton St, £320,000). The Georgian facades at the Marylebone end of **Bell St**, which runs from Edgware Rd to Lisson St, have attracted attention. **Broadley St**, just to the N, has similar homes plus a corner pub now turned into two 4-bed houses; cobbled **Ranston St** has a mix of Victorian houses, gabled Edwardian cottages and modern infill. There are ex-local authority flats of 1980s vintage at Bolero Place, **Gateforth St**, and similar blocks in **Broadley St**. **Cosway St** has a couple of rather unprepossessing Edwardian 4-storey flats blocks at the N end.

Gradually, though, rafts of new homes have been appearing. Barratt's 2001-vintage 'Prince Regent's Gate' (street address **Palgrave Gardens**) is 400 homes on reclaimed railway land W of **Park Rd**: a NW1 postcode and proximity to Regent's Park – plus pool, gym, porters, parking – make these popular, especially with London Business School students, who rent; to buy, 2-bed, 2-bath flats are c. £600,000. In the same scheme are 97 housing-trust homes. Portman Gate in **Lisson Grove** is a 1980s development of 114 houses, flats and penthouses: it, too, has pool, gym and 24-hour porters; new this year in **Bell St** is the Sanctuary: modern-styled flats and houses, £415,000–1.4 million. The Wallis Building in **Penfold St** has 22 lofts in a neo-Art Deco factory (a 2-bed was £475,000 last autumn). **Plympton St** has eight smart new mews houses, and also a 'warehouse-style' conversion on last autumn at £600,000.

And E of Marylebone station, which is faced by the superbly restored 1900 Landmark Hotel, is a quiet district of Georgian, mid-19th-century and modern houses, part of the Portman estate until 1948. **Gloucester Place** is a roaring highway, but **Dorset Square** and **Balcombe St** and nearby roads are pleasant, low-key and mostly residential. This is another place to look for a house (3-bed needing work in **Linhope St**, £725,000 freehold) rather than a flat. **Glentworth St** has some period mansion blocks, well located for the Baker Street tube and Regent's Park; among them is Berkeley Court, which boasts a 1¼-acre roof garden to complement its carriage-drive entrance, featuring golden nymphs leading to marble halls – a large 3 bed flat at £850,000 last winter.

Fitzrovia

Fitzrovia is the rectangle enclosed by **Euston Rd** to the N, **Oxford St** to the S, **Great Portland St** to the W and **Tottenham Court Rd** to the E. Presiding over the northern end of the neighbourhood named after it is handsome **Fitzroy Square**, lined by offices and embassies, but also by private homes. Fitzrovia is a quiet, quirky London village with a bohemian flavour and history – William Blake lived in the Square and the area has long attracted artists, writers and aesthetes. It is a centre for advertising and TV companies – which take up some of the nicest Georgian buildings. There's a push from some to re-brand Fitzrovia as 'Noho' – North of Soho – but locals reckon Fitzrovia is good enough.

Fitzrovia divides into two sections: there is the **Charlotte St/Tottenham Court Rd** slice – a 'fun' area with pedestrian walkways. Then there is the grandeur of **Fitzroy Square** and its surroundings. Modernized mansion blocks house hundreds of studio and 1-bed flats. Look for these on the W side of the neighbourhood. In **Charlotte Place,** interesting old houses have been done up by a housing association.

Modern homes include a clutch of flats and mews houses in **Whitfield St** (1988) and new houses with garages in **Fitzroy Court**. The 3-bed and garage houses in **Whitfield St** date from 1990: some 4-bed ones in **Whitfield Place** from 1987. In **Fitzroy Square** itself three superb Georgian houses were renovated in 2002, and two Adam houses, ex-NHS, were for sale last winter at £1.75 million apiece. Search avidly and you might find a whole house: try charming, paved **Colville Place.** Or for a smart modern flat there's **Nassau St**, where a block with nine such was converted in 2003.

Transport Tubes, all zone 1: Baker Street (Jubilee, Circle, Hammersmith & City, Bakerloo), Oxford Circus (Bakerloo, Victoria, Central), Marylebone (Bakerloo), Marble Arch (Central). Others see map. Trains: Marylebone, Euston, Paddington (Heathrow 17 mins). From Oxford Circus: City 15 min, Heathrow 52 min (1 change).

Convenient for West End, Regent's Park, City. Miles from centre: 1.5.

Schools Local Authority: St Marylebone (g), North Westminster School. Private: Queen's College (g), Francis Holland (g), Portland Place.

SALES

Flats	S	1B	2B	3B	4B	5B
Average prices	140–220	175–350	300–600+	380–1M+	700+	850–3M
Houses	2B	3B	4B	5B	6/7B	8B
Average prices	450–750+	700+	800–1M+	1M+	→1.3M+	2–3M+

RENTAL

Flats	S	1B	2B	3B	4B	5B
Average prices	150–400	250–475	350–650	450–800	600–1200	850–3000
Houses	2B	3B	4B	5B	6/7B	8B
Average prices	500–700	600–1000	750–2000	1200–1800+	–	–

The properties Mostly flats, from tiny studios to company luxury. Cheaper ones above shops; red-brick mansion blocks; conversions of the gracious period homes; now more new-build. Also mews; a few surviving family homes. Parking atrocious, garages at a premium, most (S of Marylebone Rd) is inside congestion charge zone.

The market Marylebone is long-established, especially the medical district. Fitzrovia is more bohemian but changing. Whole area is mixed residential/commercial, therefore cheaper than other central areas. Better value than many would expect, despite W1 postcode.

Among estate agents active in this area are:

- Egertons
- York Estates
- Chesterton
- John D Wood
- Kay & Co
- Oakleys
- Winkworth
- Alexanders
- Park Estates
- James Anthony
- Jeremy James
- Richard James
- Robert Irving & Burns
- Elliot Son & Boyton

MAYFAIR AND ST JAMES'S

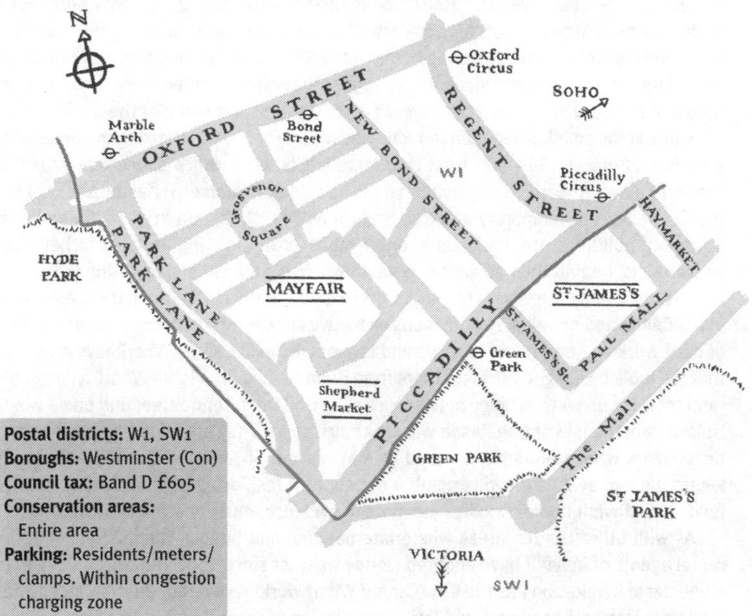

Postal districts: W1, SW1
Boroughs: Westminster (Con)
Council tax: Band D £605
Conservation areas: Entire area
Parking: Residents/meters/clamps. Within congestion charging zone

Mayfair has reclaimed its status as London's rich quarter. It never really lost the money, but its grandeur and glamour faded as the 20th century faded likewise. It was beset by tawdry commerce in the shape of indifferent shops and a sea of offices instead of homes – and by time, as its remaining flats and houses became tired and faded. Other areas took up the baton and became the talking points of fashionable London. But what was for three centuries the capital's premier residential district has staged a remarkable comeback.

Mayfair's renaissance has a lot to do with foreign money. Natives may see the charm of Chelsea, the novelty of Notting Hill, but if you use your London home for just a month or so a year, then you like to be close to the shops. And the restaurants. And the private bankers and blue-chip financial managers and lawyers.

A glance at Bond St's shops spells the way Mayfair is going. Not long ago, the surviving purveyors of traditional class to the gentry mingled uneasily with some pretty moderate operators. Now the place heaves with multi-floor temples to fashion, to the latest labels, to the names rich people – international rich people – know.

Mayfair is the place to look if you need a mansion – and not just a mansion flat. It is one of the very few places in Central London where the really rich can find a really large house, with servants' quarters and a grand suite of reception rooms and somewhere to garage a Rolls or seven (though for a garden as well, try Regent's Park). Luckily for the merely well-heeled, there are plenty of less opulent homes, too, including flats of every size and mews houses. And Mayfair is a cab ride, or a walk, from just about everything London has to offer: theatres, parks, culture – and all those lovely shops.

Mayfair homes date from every period from 1680 to 2005. They have one thing in common: they were built for the rich, or at least their servants. The upper echelons of society congregated here, first in St James's to be close to palace and court and then, as the aristocracy got richer still, in palaces of their own on land between Piccadilly and Park Lane – Mayfair. Most, though not all, have gone, to be replaced by great blocks of flats and hotels – even the **Bruton St** mansion where the Queen was born. For a perfect taste of Mayfair past, look to Crewe House in **Curzon St**, built 1730, an oasis of cream stucco amid green lawns and home to the Saudi ambassador. Some of the dukes and other magnates down-sized in the 1890s, though the replacement town-houses they had built seem like palaces to most of us (**Park St** has some of these).

Many of the smaller Georgian terraced houses live on, some reverting to homes after a period as offices. Business took over large tracts when office space was scarce in London following World War II bombing, but the tide of commerce has turned over the past 15 years: the temporary office persmissions (TOPs) expired in 1990. Some lovely Georgian buildings on Park Lane once more have drawing rooms, rather than boardrooms, behind their elegant bow windows. Mayfair has been reverting to type.

So now, among the expensive shops, offices, hotels and restaurants, there are plenty of residents, and not all are anonymous executives or country-hopping potentates. Lots of hard-working, long-hours bankers and lawyers down in Canary Wharf have reasoned that the Jubilee Line goes straight there from Bond St. And for a lot of Wharf-type people (and their spouses) the choice between a flat a stroll from Bond Street and one a windy trudge from the Isle of Dogs Asda was no choice at all. They are joined by bankers and dealmakers whose firms have moved to Mayfair and St James's because, well, that's where the money is. A growing number of people in fashion, design and other creative fields call Mayfair home. Families are more in evidence: nursery schools thrive.

As with other London areas where international and finance clients dominate, the rental agents of Mayfair have endured cloudy weather since 2001. But the sun began to shine again in mid-2003 as the City/Canary Wharf world recovered. Russian money has made a splash at the top end, and European a bit lower down, but it is American bankers that the rental companies look to for sheer volume of deals. And they are still scarcer than they were.

The past decade has seen a noticeable uplift in the level of properties here. Luxury is an over-used word, but an increasing number of Mayfair homes, large and small, are now almost impossibly smart, even grand. Mayfair residents view homes from an international perspective, and each year new must-have amenities appear in the estate agents' lists: security systems are the latest – though some maintain that *too* heavily fortified is offputting, and welcome the swing back to sheer, understated class.

Mayfair is bounded to the N by the great shopping parade of **Oxford St**, in the E by **Regent St**, to the S by **Piccadilly** – across which royal St James's slopes gracefully down to its Park – and in the W by **Park Lane**, the eight-lane highway that separates Hyde Park from Mayfair's western rampart of hotels and car showrooms.

The NW part, about half the total, from Marble Arch down to **Berkeley Square**, belongs to the Grosvenor Estate, as does Belgravia. The rest is divided among several landlords and, until the advent of the Leasehold Reform Acts, freeholds were rare. Now this is changing, as residents exercise their right to buy (not that you 'buy' in Grosvenor terminology, you enfranchise). See the Buying & Selling chapter for the latest on this complicated business.

The other important change began in 1990, when the 'temporary' planning permission granted for office use of many Mayfair sites – including some very fine Georgian houses – finally expired, allowing a small but significant increase in the number of people actually living here. The split is now fairly even, with approximately one-third residential, one-third offices; galleries, restaurants, hotels accounting for the final third. About 80 office buildings have reverted to homes, some 20 of them to single houses – mansion is sometimes a better word: one in **Park St** totals 25,000sq ft plus swimming pool. Nor is this the largest abode: one is reckoned to be twice that size. Another trend is the return to single homes of houses that have long been flats: a Charles St house is whole again, having been 14 flatlets.

Recently the Grosvenor Estate has been developing properties and keeping the flats to let, making it the largest Assured Shorthold tenancy landlord in the area

Sales prices in Mayfair at present hover either side of £1,000 per sq ft (psf). Park Lane and similar 'top addresses' have seen £1,500 psf, with a penthouse in Davies St reaching £1,750. Most homes change hands in the £850–1,350 psf bracket, with mews houses having topped £1,000 psf quite recently. In real money, the 'entry level' to life in a Grosvenor Square flat is around £1.25 million.

Mayfair

Mayfair is big, and has its quiet corners and its districts of bustle. As a broad generalization, the further W, the quieter and smarter and more residential. In general, the E and S are older than the N and W. Local experts distinguish the 'international' addresses – like Park Lane or Grosvenor Square, which everyone has head of – from the 'village' around Mount St which has a more local reputation (but much more charm). The SW corner, Shepherd Market, has an air entirely its own and is covered later in this chapter.

The NE corner, around **Hanover Square**, although among the oldest parts of Mayfair – the square dates from 1715 – is today mostly commercial, with offices and shops spilling out from Oxford St. It is hard to find much to live in E of Bond St, though occasional flats can be found above shops. **New Bond St**, Mayfair's main shopping street (and light years away in style from Oxford St's tourists and department stores), divides this area from the fashion quarter centred around pedestrianized **South Molton St**. Keep an eye on the Hanover Square district, as developments in the offing will include flats.

Davies St, running N–S and dead straight as so many Mayfair streets are, forms the edge of a more residential district to the W. The crowds of Oxford St are a moment away, but here is a more peaceful world of mansion blocks and converted period houses. **Gilbert St**, **Binney St** and **Duke St**, running parallel N–S, contain some attractive red-brick mansion blocks with gabled skylines, and (in Binney) housing trust homes. Many apartments sit above shops. Whole houses are rare, though the (very) occasional large one does come up, with a few in **Gilbert St**. Grosvenor have redeveloped buildings (formerly the Estate's offices) on **Davies St** to provide flats to let: 11 of these in Erskine House on Davies St, another 18, contemporary but behind Georgian facades, are round the corner in **Mount Row**. Just three of the 14 flats in 'The 21st' on **Davies St**, Mayfair's smartest block yet, are still on the market (from £2,350,000, for 1,730sq ft).

Few realize that this N part of Mayfair includes not only grand houses and flats, but also a wide area of fair-rent housing. These enviable flats are tucked away between Grosvenor Square and Oxford St and are owned by the Grosvenor Estate, and run by it in partnership with housing associations and the Peabody Trust.

Off **Duke St** is a neglected square with a pavilion, raised on a plinth over an electricity station. This awaits restoration: structural work is going on. Hereabouts are mansion blocks in what Pevsner calls 'typical Northwest Mayfair style – red-brick and pink terracotta, gables and much smaller Renaissance detail'. This is Grosvenor Estate country.

Busy **Brook St** runs through from Grosvenor Square to the shopping mecca of New Bond St, passing Claridges en route. Look round corners to discover **Avery Row**, a narrow lane with attractive 3-storey terraces of flats above shops. This corner has been neatened up and branded 'Avery Village': there are signposts to prove it. A peaceful, unexpected, classy enclave of small-scale shops and restaurants and bars: **Lancashire Court**, with its open-air restaurant in a cobbled square – and the back entrance to the Bond St Versace – could on a sunny day be in Italy. (Some splendid names hereabouts: across Brook St lie **Haunch of Venison** and **Globe Yards.**) Behind Claridges is **Brook's Mews**, its flat-fronted brick cottages facing an unattractive modern block providing five floors of flats. These achieve high prices as pieds-à-terre.

To the S, in another discreet corner above **Berkeley Square**, **Bourdon St** has big, mewsy, tall, Dutch-gabled buildings, some residential: a modern 3-bed mews house behind a Victorian facade was £1.3 million last winter (101-year lease). The 1900 Grosvenor Buildings is refurbed walk-up flats. At the E end is Bloomfield Court, a handsome modern interpretation of the traditional red-brick mansion block built in 1989 by the Grosvenor Estate. Savile House is a smart refurbishment of 2-bed flats in **Berkeley St**. Flats in the grey concrete Grosvenor Hill Court are popular London bases.

Mount St boasts mansion flats above some of London's premier antique shops, and is considered to be Mayfair's 'village high street'; here, though, the local bed-and-breakfast is the Connaught, and the local fish and chip shop is Scott's. The nicest flats are on the S side, overlooking the gardens: a studio, rare locally, was £395,000 last winter (132 years). Again, there are human-scale side streets away from the main parades: **Carpenter St** turns off, leading through to **Mount Row** and its brick mews houses, with leaded glass in their casement windows and mansard roofs, mingling with Edwardian and 1960s flats and offices. Also off Mount St and part of the 'village' is **Balfour Place** with yet more mansion flats. **Carlos Place** is lined with red-brick, terracotta'd, Dutch-gabled blocks above galleries and restaurants. Crown Dilmun's 2001 renovation of a big block added 1- and 3-bed flats.

Vast **Berkeley Square** is the centrepiece of a 10-acre estate sold in 2001 by the BP pension fund to a Middle East consortium. The new owners intend 'more active management', and want to turn **Bruton St**, known as the Queen's birthplace and the present-day home of art dealers and car showrooms, into a mini-Bond Street. Stella McCartney has set up shop here, just to show the way it is going, and more traditional tenants are moving on. The **Square** itself has everything from beautiful early Georgiana, via '30s, to a modern office block. There are handsome stucco-and-brick houses – all offices – along the W side. And there's one block of up-to-£3-million flats. **Bruton Lane** is just the back access to office blocks, but **Bruton Place** is mewsy, with galleries and other commere – though two or three galleries have relocated – and some homes.

M

On **Curzon St** is the Christian Science Church, behind which a courtyard of flats and offices was cunningly inserted. Smart modern blocks such as Glendore House punctuate the houses of **Clarges St** and **Half Moon St** – or, if you prefer a mews, there is **Clarges Mews.** In **Half Moon St** dignified red-brick gabled houses line the SW side.

Chesterfield Hill contains an attractive row of 5-storey stucco-and-brick period houses with handsome railings at the front, its decorative, cast-iron balconies bedecked with window boxes. This small area of **Hill St** and **Hays Mews** contains some of the most charming mews and traditional homes, hidden away in relative peace and quiet. Approaching from **Charles St** (where a freehold period house, with garden, pool and mews house was £15 million last autumn), you pass plaques commemorating the former residence of King William IV, the sailor king who lived there in 1826, before his accession. Dartmouth House is stunning, with its splendid facade (cream stucco, of course) and its splendid ironwork. **Hays Mews** is a wide, sloping street with charming mews cottages of brick (some bare, some painted) with garages below. Curled around the top of the mews is **Red Lion Yard**, with a pretty pub giving it an 'out of London' atmosphere. Cobblestones lead to more 3-storey brick 1960s town-houses in Red Lion Yard itself. The E end of **Hay's Mews** on the opposite side of Chesterfield Hill has a mixture of modern houses and little mews cottages, and a 5-storey block of modern brick-built flats, Rosebery Court (main entrance **Charles St**).

Farm St has gained some new houses (real rarities in Mayfair) in the past 20 years.

South St is residential, and dominated by 6-storey 1920s Aberconway House (which was rented last year for £30,000 a week). There are also red-brick flats, St George's Primary School and a number of attractive smaller houses, for which you will nevertheless need a million or three. Some flats overlook the Mount St gardens, a public space which is also used by the children of St George's school. A garden view boosts flat prices in this crowded neighbourhood (£2 million for a 4-bed flat, share of freehold, last autumn).

Waverton St's houses (but not the flats) share a hidden garden with **South St/South Audley St/Waverton St** and **Hill St**. Travelling up **South Audley St** there are dignified cream stucco houses and gabled red-brick and terracotta mansion flats above pleasant shops. Purdey's, the famous gun shop, is on the corner of Mount St and South Audley St, with spectacular refurbished flats above. Mayfair Library, built in 1894, stands in a cul-de-sac alongside the Grosvenor Chapel (where the local mother-and-toddler group meets). To the W is **Balfour Mews**, where the red brick hides flats above the garages. **Reeves Mews** has brown-brick and stone flats opposite its row of mews cottages.

Grosvenor Square, at six acres the largest square in the district, is best known as the site of the vast American Embassy. The other sides have some smart flats, reckoned the most luxurious cache in Mayfair: 99-year leases can be had here now. One block of flats has a ballroom for residents' use: £1.25 million for a 1,100sq ft flat here. Oh, and there's the Italian ambassador's residence, grandeur on the scale Trollope had in mind for Augustus Melmotte, the great swindler (though his house was on the S side, not the E). **Upper Brook St**, which runs W from the square towards Hyde Park, has some very large and expensive houses (£13 million for one last year) and a collection of 18 flats, with hotel-type amenities, next door to the Gavroche. **Upper Grosvenor St** also has large houses, plus flats, including four in a listed building last autumn at £2.5–3.7 million.

Culross St, behind the American Embassy, has terraces of traditional town-houses. Shutters and tiny steps up to the front doors on some homes give this road a village feel. There is vastly increased security here and in **Blackburne's Mews** since September 2001: residents have to have ID cards, and all visitors are checked. Some locals complain that 'the embassy has exceeded its international boundaries'. The row continues, which may well be why three of the terraced houses were for sale last winter (£1.9–3.4 million).

Green St's tall houses, many now flats, hide another concealed garden which is shared with **Park St, Dunraven St** and **Woods Mews**. A Dunraven St flat was £795,000 for 1,500sq ft last winter.

Park St, the main spine of this NW corner of Mayfair, has some large red-brick and stone flats blocks with colonnaded facades and balconies. It also has some splendid late-19th-century houses built as London mansions by those who had not had the luck to inherit a Park Lane palace – or who found the family palace too big, a problem faced by several magnates in the early 20th century. Now they are reverting to homes after 50 years as offices. Some of these buildings have become flats. New Hereford House, built in 2000 behind a Lutyens facade, has six penthouses and 34 other flats. In **North Row**, at the Marble Arch corner of Mayfair, a late 1980s conversion yielded 15 house-sized apartments: the penthouses have 5 bedrooms, conservatory, roof terraces – and a summer house. For a welcome contrast in scale, turn off **Park St** into **Lees Place**: this, together with pedestrianized **Shepherd's Place**, has the most eclectic mix of styles so far: mewsy houses stand opposite grandiose late-Victorian, next door to a mock-Tudor cottage. . . . Right on Marble Arch, 'Park Lane Place' has 18 new flats above an hotel.

'Big is beautiful' is the motto (in terms of both money and square footage) in the far from aptly named **Park Lane**, with its eight roaring lanes of traffic that separate Mayfair from Hyde Park. Only a handful of its grand original homes survive, having been replaced by monolithic hotels and car showrooms. The recent new block Brook House was sold to an Arab group. One restored Georgian house, complete with conservatory and garden, is on the market as six flats (£4 million each) or as a single home.

Then there are the new penthouses on the 9th and 10th floors of Fountain House. These two floors were added specially in 1997 to create these super-apartments: 4-bedroomed, double-garaged, lofty views over Hyde Park or Mayfair. These are, says a local agent, 'proper penthouses' – his definition demanding balconies all round. One of the two large blocks of the Grosvenor House Hotel is in fact short-rent flats – with the bonus of all the hotel's facilities on hand, should you so desire. Next door to the Hilton, a big commercial/homes scheme on a site running back to **Curzon St** has new flats set around a piazza (Curzon Square): £1.4 million for 1,230sq ft. Also in Curzon St, there's the redevelopment of the cinema with offices, four £3.65 million-plus flats and a 2-storey penthouse. **Brick St**, just to the S, has modern flats in tall Park Towers. On Piccadilly a corner building has become Latymer House, with 12 2- and 3-bed flats. **Hill St**, running E towards Berkeley Square, has some big remaining houses.

The SE corner of Mayfair, towards **Piccadilly Circus**, has fewer homes. **Albany**, the famous warren of prestige 'chambers' off **Piccadilly** – the original bachelor pads – is very exclusive and inhabited by the great, the good and the long-term rich. There are flats above shops, a few mews, and some blocks in streets such as **Hay Hill**.

Shepherd Market

Shepherd Market is a surprise: an unexpected village of narrow Georgian streets and small-scale buildings, charmingly and incongruously tucked away behind Mayfair's grandeur. Not long ago it was frowned upon as being seedy and the haunt of prostitutes. Today the area's image has greatly changed; more streets have been pedestrianized and it is seen as Mayfair's restaurant quarter, and there are homes ranging from modern apartments through period mansion blocks to tiny town houses and mews cottages. Despite the upgrading, homes in the district tend to have the note 'private residence' in big letters by the door-bell, which suggests that the original trade still flourishes. . . .

The Shepherds Tavern sports bow windows and a jaunty, flower-hung exterior which sets the tone for the pretty village that scatters down **Shepherd St** and round into **Shepherd Market**. Shepherd St has flats over shops; **Shepherd Place** small, 2-bed houses (£1.1 million for a freehold here last winter). Larger 3-storey brick-and-stucco buildings line the continuation of **Hertford St**; cobblestones lead you on towards 3-storey mewsy houses.

Approaching from **Hertford St**, there are mansion flats in brick-and-stucco blocks and some handsome old houses. A massive 7-storey block, Carrington House, occupies the corner site of **Hertford St**, **Shepherd St** and **Carrington St**, where 1- and 2-bed flats come up for sale; until recently the flats were rented on short lets and had a high turnover of residents. A long-neglected block in the heart of the market, real small-scale Georgiana and the subject of protracted planning rows, may soon be rescued: at last there are plans, which will include flats. **Shepherd St** has some attractive old cream-painted little 2-storey cottages. Across the street is a modern red-brick block, May Fayre House, the flats of which are available to rent. **Market Mews** has red lights still above some of its mews cottages' front doors.

St James's

The best homes in St James's are palaces, and are unlikely to be for sale. Non-royals have to hunt hard for a flat, harder for a house. **Cleveland Row**, next door to St James's Palace, is mostly offices, though there is at least one house. **Little St James's St** has some old houses in mixed use, and there are some exclusive flats in **St James's Place** – the best with wonderful views over Green Park. This is the plushest address in St James's. This area is much favoured by English buyers (and by Italians), but spurned by some of the more serious shopping nations (notably the Middle East) because it's too far from the shops. More flats line the park itself, reached from **Arlington St**, which also has the 1936-built Arlington House with some vast ambassadorial-sized flats.

Busy **St James's St** itself has a mere handful of homes. Some flats are in a corner block next to **Little St James's St**. Further E is **St James's Square**, which was once a dignified assembly of town-houses, but by 1990 had only one residential building. However, developers Berkeley Homes in 2001 converted a house on the corner with **King St**: this added ten very smart 2- and 3-bed flats. **Bury St** has some flats in tall buildings, often above shops and offices, as does **Duke of York St**. **Duke St** and **Ryder St** both have some mansion blocks, such as St James's Chambers. The best source of flats is **Jermyn St**, where a 2-bed on a long lease was was £795,000 last winter. **Carlton Gardens** has a cache of six flats including two penthouses in a modern (Sir James Sterling-designed) building, while round in **Pall Mall** a few studios gaze across at the clubs, and there are flats with views of Nelson's Column in the old Norway House.

Transport Tubes, all zone 1: Marble Arch, Bond St (Central, Jubilee); Oxford Circus (Victoria, Bakerloo, Central); Piccadilly Circus (Bakerloo, Piccadilly); Green Park (Victoria, Piccadilly, Jubilee). From Green Park: Oxford Circus 2 min, City 10 min (1 change), Heathrow 1 hr.

Convenient for Everywhere. Miles from centre: 1.

Schools Local Authority: Westminster City C of E & see neighbouring areas.

SALES

Flats	S	1B	2B	3B	4B	5B
Average prices	200–300+	300–750	400–900+	750–2.5M+	1.5–3.5M	1.5M+
Houses	2B	3B	4B	5B	6/7B	8B
Average prices	800–1.6M+	1–2M+	1.5–3M+	2.5–5M+	3–8M+	→15M

RENTAL

Flats	S	1B	2B	3B	4B	5B
Average prices	200–350	250–600	400–1200	600–2000	1000–3000	–
Houses	2B	3B	4B	5B	6/7B	8B
Average prices	500–1200	800–2000	1000–2500+	2000–4000	2500–5000	–

M

The properties Mostly flats and mostly grand ones, in mansion blocks or conversions of period homes, a few new-build. Mews cottages and lovely Georgian and Victorian houses. Degree of luxury ranges from the ordinary mansion flat to the super-opulent. St James's has fewer homes, but some with lovely park views.

The market A vast range of homes from £200,000 all the way to £40 million. Freeholds/new leases becoming more common. Flat prices vary wildly: length of lease and degree of opulence key factors. Check service charges in big blocks. 'Locals' highly international, plus old-established and/or very rich British.

Among estate agents active in this area are:

- Wetherell
- W A Ellis
- Carter Jonas
- DTZ Residential
- Knight Frank
- Savills
- Hamptons
- Blenheim Bishop
- Beaney Pearce
- Chesterton
- John C Vaughan
- Beauchamp Estates

MORDEN, MITCHAM AND COLLIERS WOOD

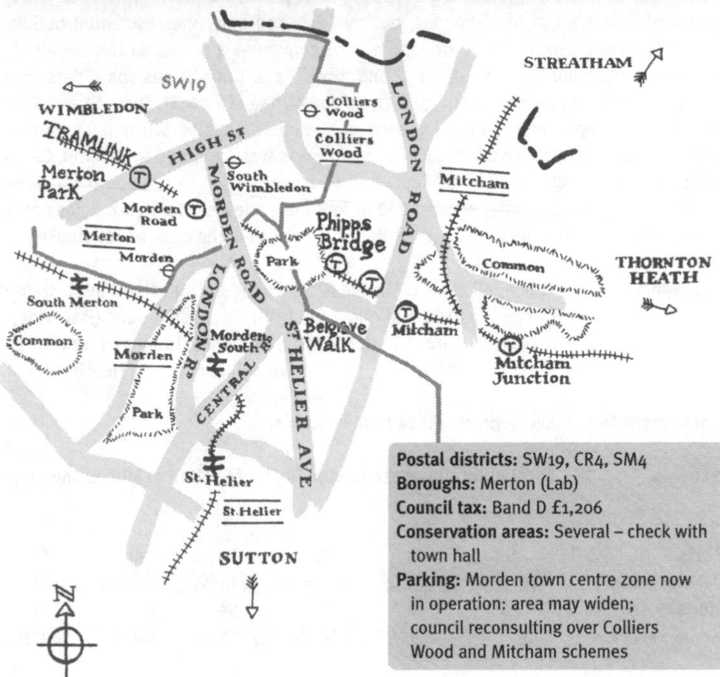

Postal districts: SW19, CR4, SM4
Boroughs: Merton (Lab)
Council tax: Band D £1,206
Conservation areas: Several – check with town hall
Parking: Morden town centre zone now in operation: area may widen; council reconsulting over Colliers Wood and Mitcham schemes

This is where Victorian London's southward sprawl came to a reluctant halt among the villages, fields and woodlands of Surrey. Here the ubiquitous London terrace peters out, to be succeeded by leafy, semi-detached suburbia. Urban expansion last received a major boost in 1926, when the Northern Line made it to Morden.

Now transport is once more the spur to a new chapter: the area (tubeless Mitcham in particular) has seen a renaissance as the Tramlink has proved such a success. Journey times across crowded South London have been cut dramatically: the trams run direct into Wimbledon's mainline train/District Line tube station, and in the other direction stop outside East Croydon's station, for trains to Gatwick Airport. The modern, quiet trams, with their tidy little halts, are a morale-boosting addition. Also a property-boosting one: the tram provides links that just did not exist before, making some rather remote corners commutable by public transport.

The borough of Merton, which takes in all this area, shelters a wide spread of suburbia of every 20th-century vintage lapping around the remnants of the past, and punctuated with increasing amounts of new housing. Wimbledon, on its hill, commands the W of the borough. To the SE is Croydon (the tram's final destination). The area between centres on the valley of the Wandle, which flows N from here to the Thames at Wandsworth. Merton itself is ancient, but little survives except the parish church and a road called **Merton High St**. Merton Priory, which for some reason the borough decided to elevate to an abbey (it wasn't), was the medieval focus for the villages of Morden, Mitcham and especially next-door Colliers Wood. Much of Merton has been annexed by South Wimbledon – the name of the tube station. Marooned across the tracks on that W side is the interesting century-old enclave that still carries Merton's name, Merton Park (see Wimbledon, Raynes Park and Merton Park chapter).

Morden also clings to what's left of the rural charm: there is a church dating from 1636, and behind the church a pub with 16th-century foundations. Morden Hall Park belongs to the National Trust; through it wanders the River Wandle, dividing and rejoining to form lake and islands – but its Georgian buildings such as Morden Hall itself and a 'gentleman's villa' have found new occupations (pub/restaurant, etc. etc.). The snuff mill and stables are craft shops; there is a garden centre and (free) city farm.

Mitcham is an old place, too, with a few survivors of its rural days – notably its village greens and common – and one of the largest caches of recently-built homes in South London. Of Colliers Wood, the only notable landmark is the underground station – or was, until the advent, at the Merton end, of the vast grey flanks of the Savacentre hypermarket, where Merton Priory once stood and the young Thomas à Becket was educated.

The **Merantun Way** relief road and the Savacentre transformed **Merton High St.** It forms the start of a tract of fast roads and retail sheds which sets the tone for the whole area: suddenly, the South London small-scale shops are left behind and you are in retail city, or rather edge-of-city. The Savacentre forms part of the River Wandle development area, alongside **Christchurch Rd** behind **Merton High St.** Then came the Tandem Centre, by the **Merantun Way/Christchurch Rd** roundabout (Boots, Holiday Hypermarket, Next, Comet . . .); next, between the two, The Priory (PC World, Currys, Burger King . . .).

Cross **Merantun Way for** something altogether more attractive – and the scene of a major new development. Merton Abbey Mills is a pleasant corner of craft shops, bookshops, pubs, restaurants and museum down by the Wandle, where Liberty's once printed its famous silks and William Morris had workshops. Cloth-working and dyeing here date back to the Huguenots in the first Elizabeth's reign. And now nearly 300 new homes are a-building here too: see Colliers Wood below.

Mitcham and Morden mushroomed in the 1920s and 1930s, after the extension of the Northern Line tube speeded commuting into the City. The result was wide areas of neat, semi-detached homes. Mock-Tudor detailing was popular – this is quite a restrained example. The tile-roofed porch-cum-bay is also typical. After a period of disdain, these houses are now fashionable.

The Morden/Mitcham/Colliers Wood area appeals strongly to those who prefer the charms of suburbia to cramped inner-city living. Homes for all here: a wide range of styles and prices, from ex-council to new-build (1-bed starter homes are a freehold alternative to flats); from city terraces to semi-detached suburbs. Look here for vast caches of – for London – relatively inexpensive homes: the sum asked for 2-bed Clapham flats will, five stops down the Northern Line, buy a 3-double-bed house with 85ft garden. Lots of Mitcham terraces in the £170–220,000 bracket, with ex-council homes at the lower end. Morden Park's well-thought-of 'Crouch'-built mock-Tudor terraces (c. £220–235,000) and semis (up to £280,000-ish). Or look for a (rarer) 4-bed home, perhaps by one of the area's little parks, Ravensbury for instance; or down by the River Wandle.

The Morden tube does, in a definite way, tie the area into London, and E–W links have been transformed by the

Wimbledon/Croydon Tramlink, with stops at Dundonald Road, Merton Park, Morden Rd, Phipps Bridge, Belgrave Walk, Mitcham and Mitcham Junction.

Morden

Morden lies at the southern extremity of the Northern Line tube. Atop the terminus is a large, modern office complex, with Civic Centre and library. The tram stops here, too, just to the N, at Morden Road. Until the mid-1920s this was a small, agricultural community; the landscape was dramatically changed by a high-concentration council house-building programme and today can be described as '1930s-semi suburbia'.

Generally, Morden is a green, leafy, residential area and includes three large open spaces: Morden Hall Park (more than 50 acres of National Trust parkland, with craft centre, city farm etc.), Morden Park (swimming baths, playing fields) and, to the W, Cannon Hill Common. Houses facing, or with views of, park areas are naturally the great favourites. Premier roads include the leafy **Lower Morden Lane**, and **Hillcross Avenue** and streets off it (mainly 1930s 3-bed solid semis, with front and rear gardens and garages: £230–270,000). **Central Rd** has Park View, 14 good-sized (i.e. 4-bed) town-houses. Flats are in short supply, though the **Birchwood Close** scheme, off **Bordesley Rd** and *very* convenient for both tube and trains, has 75 1- and 2-bed flats, some with bay windows, in landscaped gardens; from c. £150,000. And in **Reigate Avenue**, 48 more new 2- and 3-bed flats, plus the odd starter home, appeared. On the banks of the Wandle, flats in the 1990s Ravensbury Mill development are c. £180,000 for a 2-bed. This year 'Aragon Place', flats and houses by Kingsoak Homes, is appearing on the edge of the King George's Field sports ground off **Aragon Rd**: £180–320,000; the top price buys a 3-bed town-house. The same developer's 'Hamilton Gate' in **Malmesbury Rd** has homes in the same price bracket.

The St Helier Estate, built by London County Council in the 1920s–1930s and advanced for its time, is a large area of wide, well-planned roads (**Blanchland Rd** is typical) of 2/3-bed red-brick terraces with gardens fore and aft: a 2-bed, c. £195,000. These pleasant pre-war houses, of high quality and popular with first-time buyers, account for some 25 per cent of sales in the district. Many new owners have added imaginative (if sometimes misplaced) exterior features. St Helier has its own train station, too.

Mitcham

Mitcham, once renowned for its lavender fields and watercress beds, is an odd blend of bustling town, light industry and country village. Though it, like Morden, has a Surrey postal address, it comes under Merton Council.

Determined to retain its rural atmosphere, Mitcham resisted efforts to link it to London's Underground. For years, commuters were faced with a goodish walk or a bus ride to the nearest tube stations (Colliers Wood or Tooting Broadway); now there are three tram stops: Phipps Bridge, Belgrave Walk and Mitcham, and another at Mitcham Junction train station, which serves Victoria (18 min). Plans for a new rail station at Eastfields Road have been around since 1930, but no-one ever seems to have the money. There is good road access to the M23 (Gatwick) and M25 (Heathrow), but the centre of town is busy and often clogged with through-traffic. Like most of the capital's satellites, it divides into the good, the bad and the definitely ugly – but strenuous efforts have gone to reduce the latter. Privatized ex-council homes, on much-improved estates, allow for a low start to the wide range of prices and can provide a great deal of space for your money.

Georgian cottages, manor houses, 18th-century houses and Eagle House (a superb example of Queen Anne architecture) are reminders of Mitcham's rural past. **Commonside East**, looking out over Mitcham's Common and pond, has a row of pretty 2-bed Victorian terraced cottages, c. £190,000. These, like homes facing Fair Green and

Mitcham Park, are the streets people aspire to – a waiting list has been known to develop for homes in the **Cricket Green** conservation area, at the heart of Mitcham (the game in question is reputed to have been played here for over 300 years.) Other desirable streets include **Gorringe Park Avenue** (a 3-bed semi with garage here, c. £230,000) and **The Close.**

Quite a few modern homes developments appeared in Mitcham in the 1980s and 1990s – caches include the popular **Chatsworth Place**: flats (2-beds £165,000) and 4-bed semis, just off **London Rd**; 20 mock-Victorian 1- and 2-bed flats and 2/3-bed houses in **Chestnut Grove**, which leads down towards the common; Mitcham Village Studios – a Georgian schoolhouse, now studios and apartments – at **Lower Green West**. More 1990s homes in **Crossways Rd** on the edge of Streatham Park, while in **Church Rd**, the spine of a popular corner between **Western Rd** and the Wandle/Merton Abbey Mills borders, Cannons Place has 2/3/4-bed houses with private gardens and garages/parking. New developments also sprouted in the **Western Rd** area: Laings got busy here, building every size from studio flats (about £105,000) to 3-bedroom, £230,000-odd houses; look, too, in the **Mount Rd/Lewis Rd** corner, across **Western Rd**, for older-style, reasonably priced homes.

The biggest recent tract by far is on the former King's College playing fields off **Lavender Avenue.** A thousand homes, private and housing association, appeared here in the '90s, as a street map (with its squiggly closes and little squares) clearly shows. Some grumble that the housing association homes are too numerous.

Cross the common into the spider's web of humdrum streets S of Manor Rd to find the Pollard's Hill estate, a council-built 1970s tract run now by a housing association and far better for it. Of more interest, and really more accessible from the Norbury side, is **Pollard's Hill** proper: a splendid eminence crowned by a little park, hidden in an enclave of curling roads with individualistic houses laid out in the 1920s/1930s (a 5-bed here c. £425,000). **Ena Rd**, one of the few ways in, has a gradient that's 1 in 4 steep at one point (a 4-bed semi £375,000). This tract is in Croydon borough and SE19.

For something really exciting and innovative, follow **Beddington Lane** S from the common to discover what was a sewage works and is now, thanks to the Peabody Trust, 'BedZED' – the Beddington Zero Energy Development: despite gruesome acronym, this is an amazing scheme of 88 eco-friendly, energy-efficient homes (1-bed flats to 4-bed houses, plus 20 workspaces). There's even a car pool. It's a mix of tenures: you can buy outright (a 2-bed resale, £215,000), rent affordably or part-own/part-rent. Go to see.

Colliers Wood

Colliers Wood is sandwiched between **Merton** and **Tooting High Sts**. Somewhat overshadowed by a large, grey tower of offices, it was dismissed for years as a 'depressed' area. It perked up in the late 1980s, and has been making the effort again now that the neighbours are going up in the world: the welcome green space of Wandle Park (part-owned by the National Trust) has been spruced up along the river bank.

A plentiful hunting-ground, especially for first-time homeowners, and more of a known name than formerly, though some bits get 'moved' to South Wimbledon or even Tooting by estate agents and developers. Astute vendors sell their homes through Wimbledon estate agents to harvest price refugees from 'up the hill.' By way of revenge, Colliers Wood has annexed the eastern part of Merton, so counts the Savacentre, the two newer shopping centres and the Merton Abbey Mills, a pleasant corner with its craft centre, cafés etc, down by the Wandle as part of its patch. Here local outcry led to the redrawing of plans for Countrywide's 288 1-, 2- and 3-bed flats (76 Affordable Homes) in eight blocks; prices for those blocks released so far, with central glass atrium and 'open-plan, flexible layout', are: 1-beds (500 sq ft) from £190,000, 2-beds/2-baths from £278,000. There's a Virgin Active health club (a restaurant and hotel to come, too). The

Nook, off **Brangwyn Crescent**, is a 9-flat block on a nearby islet in the Wandle.

With direct access to Central London from Colliers Wood tube station, it's good commuter territory. Homes here are a pleasant mix of 1880s, 1930s and 1960s houses with pretty stucco/stock-brick Edwardian villas, many Victorian terraces and some conversion flats; bargain-hunters search out pockets of un-'improved' Victoriana: a 1-bed flat on the High St might be £150,000. The better roads, some closed to through-traffic, are bordered by **Cavendish Rd** and include **Marlborough**, **Clive** and **Warren Rds**, **Daniel** and **Defoe Closes**, **Norfolk** and **Harewood Rds**.

The other side of **Colliers Wood High St**, round **Boundary** and **Acre Rds**, is popular with staff from St George's Hospital Tooting, just across the tracks via a footbridge. Mead Park, in the Wandle Valley NW of the High St, added 160 homes, from studios to town-houses, on ex-sewage-works land. The tube and Haydons Rd Thameslink station are handy.

Transport Tubes: Colliers Wood, S Wimbledon, Morden (zone 3, Northern). From Morden: Oxford Circus 35 min (1 change), City 40 min, Heathrow 90 min (2 changes). Trains: Mitcham Junction to Victoria, London Bridge. Tramlink: to Wimbledon (for District Line and rail links), East Croydon (for Gatwick and Brighton).

Convenient for Wimbledon, Gatwick, routes South, Ikea.

Schools Local Authority: Raynes Park High, Rutlish (b), Ricards Lodge (g), Tamworth Manor, Ursuline Convent (g), Bishopsford, Wimbledon College (b). Private: see Wimbledon.

SALES

Flats	S	1B	2B	3B	4B	5B
Average prices	100–120	125–160	130–225	165–250	–	–
Houses	2B	3B	4B	5B	6/7B	8B
Average prices	165–220	185–300	250–375	300–350+	–	–

RENTAL

Flats	S	1B	2B	3B	4B	5B
Average prices	115–140	140–175	165–225	185–250	265–375	390
Houses	2B	3B	4B	5B	6/7B	8B
Average prices	185–225	210–260	275–350	350–400	–	–

The properties Victoriana peters out after Colliers Wood, replaced by semis. All three areas have large estates of 1930s terraces: the most common source of converted flats or 2/3-bed homes. Larger, 4+ beds scarce. Top houses are alongside Mitcham's parks. New and recent homes plentiful. Lots of cheaper ex-council homes.

The market First-time buyers find good-size, good-value homes here. Mitcham prices, long held back by lack of tube except for best family homes (see above), climbed thanks to Tramlink.

Among estate agents active in this area are:

- Andrews
- Goodfellows
- Ellisons
- Tarrant & Co
- Winkworth
- James Alexander
- Townends
- Christopher St James
- Andrew Purnell & Co
- Bairstow Eves
- Drury & Cole
- Greenes
- C James & Co
- Finch & Co
- Barnard Marcus

MUSWELL HILL

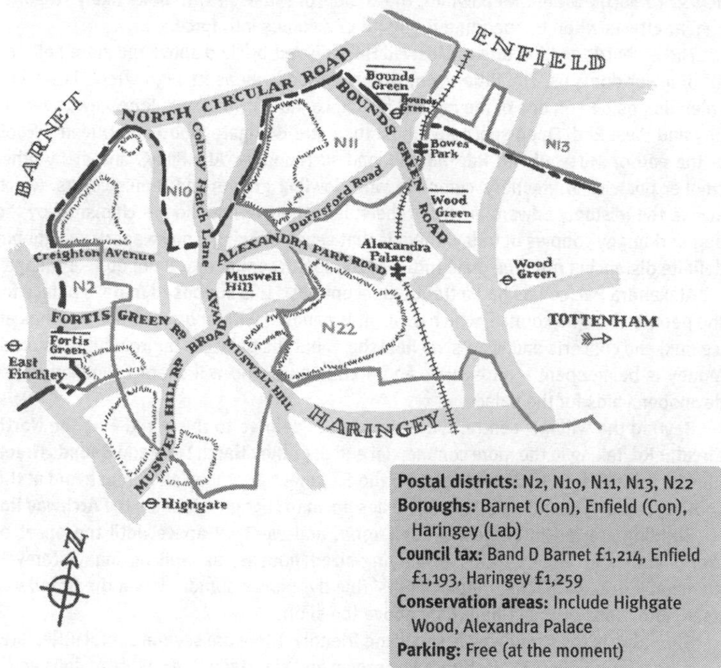

Postal districts: N2, N10, N11, N13, N22
Boroughs: Barnet (Con), Enfield (Con), Haringey (Lab)
Council tax: Band D Barnet £1,214, Enfield £1,193, Haringey £1,259
Conservation areas: Include Highgate Wood, Alexandra Palace
Parking: Free (at the moment)

This is where people move to when they discover that Islington is a bit too funky for bringing up the family. Here they find good – if over-subscribed – schools, family-sized houses, gardens and green space, distant views. . . even a lively collection of pubs and bars to spice the Edwardian elegance of the centre. The only thing missing is a tube.

The other great asset of Muswell is that Hill – or rather a string of them, culminating in Alexandra Park where the looming great 'palace' commands views right across London. Incomers from grittier tracts down the hill find fresh air, Edwardian homes with a quirky charm to do up (not much need to extend, they're often enormous) and the network of amenities that make up a family-centred community.

The problem is that many of these families want to drive across to Hampstead and Highgate – where all the private schools are – and term-time traffic gets worse and worse. Indeed, with the North Circular running across the N of the area, through-traffic is a constant problem. It has grown busier yet since a lorry-drivers' website offered Rosebery Rd and Dukes Avenue, high-status residential roads at the heart of Muswell Hill, as a useful cut-through. Haringey Council and locals have worked out a traffic-calming plan – the first of several – for the Dukes Avenue area. A long-promised bus service to Highgate and Hampstead is now running, but in school-run hours only.

Parking is also the source of acrimony on the Hill as a planned controlled parking zone (CPZ) has been blocked by the eloquent local middle-class. Now, as a compromise, only the centre of Muswell Hill is to have a mini-CPZ (but when? no action yet). The local consensus is that the present truce is not the end and that possession of a garage or off-street parking could be useful insurance: the resultant rash of block-paved off-street parking in front gardens is upsetting local conservationists.

Perhaps to the relief of the town hall, residents in Fortis Green have *asked* for a CPZ: next-door Barnet Council put one in East Finchley, which drove commuter parking across to Fortis Green. Meanwhile, the S side of Muswell Hill looks likely to suffer similar effects when the pending Highgate CPZ comes into force.

The eccentric architecture of Muswell Hill sails red-bricked above the more polluted air of lower domains. The little town, with the **Broadway** as its high street, is set in a splendid position on one of the highest hills in London, giving long, long views over the City and West End. Open space abounds: there are Highgate Wood and Queen's Wood at the end of **Muswell Hill Rd**, the parkland surrounding 'Ally Pally', and many other smaller pockets of greenery, complete with bowling greens and tennis courts, which invoke the leisurely Edwardian era of the suburb's flowering and are cherished by the dog-and-buggy couples of today. There is that sense of being a place apart, a slight but definite distancing from the main thrust of London. A community, if not quite a 'village'.

Alexandra Palace has had a troubled recent past. It is supposed to be 'a palace for the people', but the council, which owns it, is saddled with enormous debts. It has an ice rink, and concerts and events are held there, but the palace is far from fully restored. Money is being spent – on lawyers and accountants who will share £1 million to vet developers' bids for the palace.

Beyond the 'village' centre, the wider area is defined to the N and E by the **North Circular Rd**, taking in the more commercial end of **Colney Hatch Lane** and **Bounds Green** plus its tube, across to Wood Green. To the S, it meets Hornsey and Crouch End at the southern tip of Alexandra Park, and reaches down to Highgate tube on the **Archway Rd**.

Building started in earnest around 1900, and went on apace until the onset of World War I, in large estates of varying-sized houses, as well as many-storeyed mansion blocks of 'bachelor apartments' (big by today's standards) on the **Broadway** itself, and those purpose-built flats above the shops.

Shopping in the **Broadway** is small and friendly: there are several useful little, late-opening supermarkets (Sainsbury's has grown and smartened), a couple of delis and a Marks & Spencer food hall. There has been a flowering of cafés, art shops, coffee houses and other independent shops and restaurants. The necessary chain- and department-store shopping is supplied by nearby Brent Cross or the more humdrum centre at Wood Green. Closer to home, there's a 24-hr Tesco superstore on the North Circular (junction with **Colney Hatch Lane**). There are a cinema and swimming pool in the area, as well as the golf course and Alexandra Palace. Interestingly, as the main estates were built on Methodist Church land, there are few original pubs; this, however, has been rectified of late with a continuing stream of newcomers (some converted churches), plus bars and restaurants, on the **Broadway** drag. Muswell Hill night life has a distinctly youthful and sometimes raucous air, if not as rock'n'roll as Crouch End.

The greatest drawback (or blessing, according to some) is the lack of a nearby tube. Highgate and Bounds Green are a 5-min bus ride away, and Finsbury Park's a good 20 (though speeded recently by a cashless bus). There are several bus routes to the West End and to the City, which is also served by a good train service from Alexandra Palace to Moorgate. Nevertheless, this is a car driver's area and many households have two. Streets tend to be wide and parking is not the nightmare it is in denser-packed suburbs, though double-parking makes some journeys rather like a slalom.

So, on the whole, the sort of people buying in this area are families: middle-class, dual-income ones, many in the media industries or smart, high-income professionals. Stemming from this, most local schools have a good reputation as they are well supported by parents, who donate not only money, but also a great deal of time and energy to their children's education. Thus house-hunters' (and agents') emphasis on the 'right' catchment areas. Stress levels, and prices for strategically placed homes, can be high. Last year saw a very well-organised campaign by parents to get more primary classes, perhaps a new school, after 45 kids were left with no local reception-class place. The campaign's website shows maps with catchment areas – and big gaps between them.

Prices here are below their peaks, reached perhaps at the Millennium, and agents describe present levels as 'realistic' (they would say that, wouldn't they, and they said it last year, since when top-level prices have gone down another 5–7 per cent). Homes above the £650,000 level are far harder to sell than of yore, but at every level schools underpin prices. Fortismere, reckoned the best secondary, is to be expanded, as will Alexandra. It is a big draw, as are private schools Highgate (soon to be co-ed) and Channing (girls).

Muswell Hill

Muswell Hill has always had a genteel air. Its homes are mostly ranged in grandiose Edwardian terraces or set in wide, leafy roads. Double-fronted or single, detached or semi, they are big. They boast almost bizarre architectural features including spires and balconies, heavily ornamented gables, pillastered bays. About 25 years back, many houses were divided into flats or maisonettes. Restoration, not conversion, is the watchword these days, with the demand for family homes making it more cost-effective to keep the big houses intact – or to restore them to splendid family homes of up to six bedrooms. Those short of bedrooms follow the nanny-loft option to magic the fifth out of the attic – though, as agents point out, the spell often won't enhance value if the house is left with more bedrooms than the living space allows. The last year has seen a ratcheting up of extension fever in Muswell Hill: count the skips, dodge the scaffolding.

There are three covetable enclaves that ring **Muswell Hill Broadway**: one to the E of the Broadway across to **The Avenue**, N of the park; another, the grid of streets at the W end of the Broadway between **Fortis Green Rd**, **Grand Avenue** and **Midhurst Avenue**; a third in the angle of Highgate Wood and Queen's Wood, to the E of **Muswell Hill Rd.**

This last enclave holds some of Muswell Hill's choicest homes. These select streets to the S, in the angle of **Cranley Gardens** and **Wood Vale**, also lie nearest to Highgate tube. Prestigious **Onslow Gardens** (perhaps the most coveted street), **Woodland Rise, Woodlands Gardens, Connaught Gardens, Wood Vale**, as well as the main **Muswell Hill Rd**, are lined with very large houses, sometimes with balconies and basements which are definite assets. Often set further back, or higher up, from the road, these houses command high prices for the most luxurious – anything from £850–£1 million-plus. But those backing onto the woods may have rather small gardens. The large 6-bed houses in **Church Crescent**, close to the Broadway, sell for c. £1.25 million. The Rookfield Estate (or 'Garden Village') developed by the Collins family off **Muswell Hill** has neat 1900–1920s Arts & Crafts-style houses on hilly (watch your survey) private roads – with five barriers to bar through-traffic. The huge detacheds go for £1 million-plus. Five new million-plus houses are due this year at Cranley Dene, E of Muswell Hill Rd.

Popular **Fortis Green**'s conservation area, to the W, has a grid of Edwardian roads, more convenient for East Finchley tube, spreading out from the top of **Muswell Hill Rd** westwards to **Midhurst Rd** (on the corner of which is the area's prime butcher). The monster flats in the century-old mansion blocks excite lovers of Arts & Crafts architecture. **Grand Avenue** matches its name: one of the prime streets, it also has no through-traffic and 120-foot gardens on the S side: £1.4 million has been paid for a 6-bed house. **Collingwood Avenue, Leaside Avenue, Fortismere Avenue** and **Birchwood Avenue** are almost as popular – but expensive. Prices here start at £600,000, though some 1920s 3-beds are cheaper and Birchwood's houses can be nearly £800,000.

Modern 1980s developments here include the 4-bed town-houses of **Alexandra Mews** and the 3-bed flats of **The Copse**, a refurbishment of ex-police flats – both on **Fortis Green**, both very nice. Cheaper but not so large and grand are the streets off nearby **East Finchley High Rd** itself – smaller-scale versions of the Muswell Hill style intermingled with 1930s semis; much more everyday roads, but highly convenient for the tube journey to town. Look for the 'county' roads: pleasant, grey-brick Victorian terraces with names such as **Lincoln Rd, Leicester Rd**, etc.; a small 3-bed house in one of these can be found for £400–500,000. To the S across this end of Fortis Green, the streets down to Cherry Tree Wood get dearer again (and closer to East Finchley tube). **Eastern Rd** and its neighbours have some attractive Edwardian-vintage houses, including pretty cottage-style and £800,000-ish Arts & Crafts monsters. Big Edwardian mansion flats in **Fortis Green Rd** share communal gardens and are increasingly in favour: c. £220,000 for a 2-bed.

The third coveted enclave lies off **Dukes Avenue** behind The Broadway, stretching north-eastwards across to encircling Alexandra Park Rd. The peaceful streets are tree-lined and wide enough to take four cars abreast. No parking restrictions – yet – but problems with rat-running should soon be eased (see introduction above). Dukes Avenue is especially afflicted. The houses are mostly large – anything from 3- to 6-bed, some double-fronted – with longish gardens and festoons of the 'original features' so beloved of estate agents. The really big double-fronted (5-bed, 5-recep) ones aspire to £1.25 million, but there's a range of sizes and prices, all in the same happy Edwardian style. The Park end of **Dukes Avenue** has the best views and gardens, and the W side of **Curzon Rd** is reckoned the better. A group of four modern town-houses (**Parham Way**) has been squeezed in off **Rosebery Rd.**

Somewhat plainer Edwardian streets stretch from the far side of **Alexandra Park Rd** across to Colney Hatch Lane. The district has the new secondary school off Albert Rd (well equipped, oversubscribed and so far doing well) and Rhodes Avenue Primary – the school people fight to get their kids into. The 'lake' roads – **Windermere Rd, Grasmere Rd** (very popular, close to the golf course) – are popular, with houses at c. £650,000. The 3-bed Tudor-style semis, which take over from the Edwardian here up towards the golf course, command lesser prices, though the schools underpin values.

West of Colney Hatch Lane the houses in **Sutton Rd**, **Wilton Rd** and **Greenham Rd** do not have quite the same dignified air as the mainstream Edwardiana. However, they still have plenty of space, are close to Coldfall Wood and are still not far away from the main shopping area. These homes are narrower than the Muswell Hill 'classics' and are consequently rather deep, and dark, front to back.

M

Just N of the centre is **Queens Avenue**, laid out in 1900 as Muswell Hill's smartest street, which however went down in the world after many of its grand houses became hotels. Now, aided by conservation-area status and grants, its gracious 5-bed houses are back in favour. The 1930s bay-fronted hilltop homes of **Creighton Avenue** have fine views (those on the N side also back onto Coldfall Woods, a prized dog-walking tract soon to be tided up) and are well provided with garages and parking space. **Pages Lane** has three smart, recent houses carved out of an old convent.

To the N up towards the North Circular Rd are neighbourhoods offering cheaper prices and smaller houses. Streets around the lower end of **Colney Hatch Lane**, with their ex-council and smaller terraced houses, are seen as a way in to N10 and Muswell Hill for the younger buyers. The tenor gets decidedly more commercial (small industry and even a thriving tattoo shop are to be found here), but this corner, though mixed, is certainly improving. Edwardian homes jostle with smaller Victoriana, 1920s and 1950s blocks, and recent schemes: detached 4-bed houses in **Pembroke Mews**; **Cambridge Gardens,** a cul-de-sac of new homes; retirement flats in **Wetherill Rd**.

Houses off **Coppetts Rd** to the W, although in leafy streets, are generally less popular, thanks to a 1960s block of flats and a fairly large council estate of indifferent architectural value. A big tract of flats and houses, both housing association and private, has been built on land sold off by Coppetts Wood (tropical diseases) Hospital. This big development has attracted a lot of speculative buying, and letting: resale 4-bed houses to be had for c. £400,000. Rialto and Laing have been active here: the latter's offerings are deemed to be better finished, and thus more popular.

South of the hospital development is a group of roads in green surroundings: **Hill Rd** and **Steedes Rd** are rated among the best streets. The local primary school, Coldfall, has won high praise from Ofsted and its intake is being increased.

Look E of **Colney Hatch Lane** for the area's most affordable homes: the houses are smaller, with ex-council 3-bed 'cottage-style' houses around £300,000: this, again, is reckoned a good place in which to gain a foothold in Muswell Hill. A converted pub in **Sydney Rd** has 2-bed flats. To the SE, where **Park** and **Priory Rds** meet is dubbed 'Park Village' by hopeful agents. This corner, including the pleasant streets round Priory Park, is regarded as Crouch End (which chapter see).

Bounds Green and Wood Green

Look north and east if Muswell Hill's prices appal: you can save £100–150,000 buying a house here in N11. Bounds Green to the E has the same sort of good-quality, solid houses – not such elegant roads, but close to the tube (Piccadilly Line: a straight run to West End and Heathrow). 'Great place to move after an N10 divorce' says a local; 'same size house, same friends, less money'. Start thinking around £300,000-plus for a 3-bed semi, a little less on busy **Durnsford Rd.** More neat semis with garages, set back from quiet, more suburban roads, lie to the W between Muswell Hill golf course, **Bounds Green Rd** and **Durnsford Rd.**

Some smaller Victorian (1870s to be precise) 'artisan dwellings' around Bowes Park are still affordable: agents tip this corner, with its villagey atmosphere, close to the tube (Bounds Green is the last stop in Zone 3) and with own rail station. A 2-bed cottage in **Highworth Rd** was £300,000 last winter, and pleasant flats are around £200,000. This also goes for the small, quiet roads E of Alexandra Palace station in Wood Green, which hold purpose-built maisonettes, as well as houses. A few monster Victorian houses lurk in Bowes Park: one in **Palmerston Rd**, with gardens running down to the New River, was £1.5 million last winter

Back on the Muswell Hill side of the tracks, but N22, not N10, the triangle between **Durnsford/Albert Rds**, **Victoria Rd** and the rail line is leafy and popular: it is likely to figure in estate agents' details as 'Alexandra Park', or just N22, rather than referring to Wood Green. **Clifton Rd** and **Clyde Rd** are the best streets, and the W, Muswell Hill, end of **Victoria Rd**: these are in the Rhodes Avenue school area (whereas parts of N10 are not). More flats here, and solid houses: 3-bed Edwardian terraces £450–475,000, though a Clifton Rd house might make £100,000 more. Where **Albert Rd** meets **Alexandra Park Rd**, a church conversion ('The Chantry') offers flats at £300–395,000. In **Albert Close**, eight 2-bed flats are due on the site of existing garages.

Most of **Alexandra Park Rd** backs, on the S side, onto the deer park behind the palace: greenery and nature in abundance. A set-back group of late 1990s houses and flats, **St Saviour's Court**, offers some imaginative layouts and deer over the garden fence. Its 5-bed town-houses are popular and go for £600,000-plus. The E sides of **Crescent Rise** and **Dagmar Rd** back onto the tracks. The E side of this district, towards the railway, is typically £50–75,000 per house cheaper than the Muswell Hill end.

Over this rail line to Wood Green desirability definitely lessens, but **Truro** and **Nightingale Rds** offer good value (new flats, 21 of them, due in the latter). The pocket between **Park Avenue** and **Station Rd**, N of Wood Green Common, has little 2-bed Victorian cottages in leafy no-through-road streets. To the N lies a little cache of pretty railway cottages, between **Bridge Rd** and the station. Fast trains to Moorgate suck in City types. Wood Green may have its Shopping City, but is less select – a very much more urban, edgy, bustling, multi-cultural atmosphere – than tranquil Muswell Hill. However, the **High Rd** has smartened up somewhat with the addition of Hollywood Green (cinema, bars, cafés, all tinted glass and burgers).

Transport Tubes: Bounds Green, Wood Green (zone 3, Piccadilly – direct to Heathrow); East Finchley, Highgate (zone 3, Northern). From Highgate: Oxford Circus 20 min (1 change), City 25 min, Heathrow 1 hr 15 min (1 change). Trains: Alexandra Palace to City 12 min.

Convenient for Brent Cross shopping centre, Ikea, Wood Green Shopping City. North Circular Rd, A1/M1. Miles from centre: 6.

Schools Barnet, Haringey Education Authority: Fortismere School, Alexandra Park School. Private: see Highgate.

SALES

Flats	S	1B	2B	3B	4B	5B
Average prices	120–140	130–240	160–350	245–450	360–500	–
Houses	2B	3B	4B	5B	6/7B	8B
Average prices	220–350	260–475+	330–575+	430–900+	625–1.5M	–

RENTAL

Flats	S	1B	2B	3B	4B	5B
Average prices	140+	175–200	190–300	250–400+	400–700	–
Houses	2B	3B	4B	5B	6/7B	8B
Average prices	250–350	300–450	400–600+	450–800	6000–1300	–

The properties Solid, superior Edwardian houses, some very large and charmingly quirky, provide roomy conversions as well as excellent family homes. Also some mansion flats – which can offer good value. Smaller houses 1920s/1930s, but smallest are modern or little Victorian terraces in less-exalted fringe areas. New homes in Coppetts Wood area.

The market Spacious houses attract families – many of media/professional/liberal persuasion – who find value in this green, well-schooled area. Big jump in quality (and prices) from 3- to 4-plus bed homes, with the best – in terms of size and school catchment – exceeding £1 million. Homes get less expensive towards edgy, urban Wood Green.

M

Among estate agents active in this area:

- Sturt & Tivendale
- Keats
- Delemere
- Kinleigh Folkard & Hayward
- Prickett & Ellis Underhill
- Winkworth
- Anscombe & Ringland
- Bairstow Eves
- Barnard Marcus
- Martyn Gerrard
- Tatlers
- Holden Matthews
- Keatons

NEW CROSS AND DEPTFORD

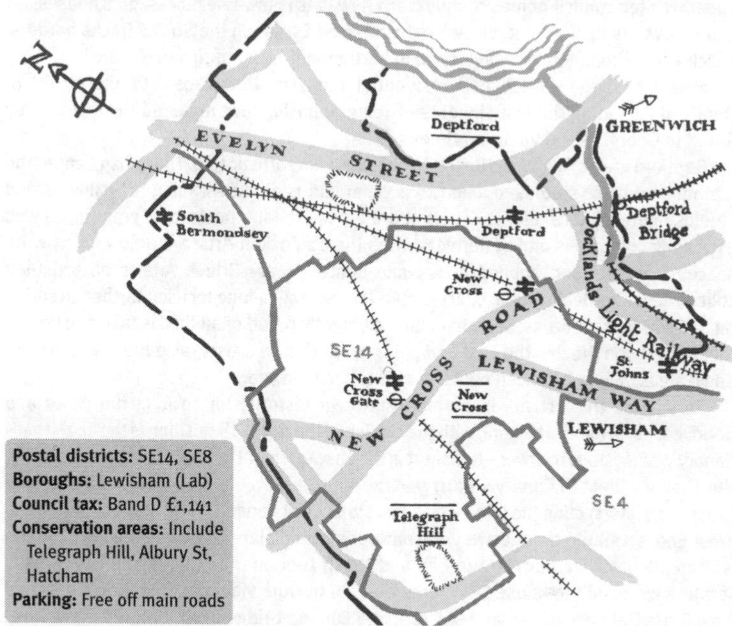

Postal districts: SE14, SE8
Boroughs: Lewisham (Lab)
Council tax: Band D £1,141
Conservation areas: Include Telegraph Hill, Albury St, Hatcham
Parking: Free off main roads

At long last the trend is very slowly upwards for one of London's most historic – and most neglected – waterfronts: a hidden quarter could receive a Cinderella-style transformation. Lacking fairy dust, however, this is coming about in frustratingly slow motion. Council officials' desks groan with the weight of planning proposals; the Deptford Creek zone, from the mouth of the Ravensbourne to the Thames, has more than 1,500 new homes built, building or planned – but meanwhile on the river itself Convoy's Wharf, a site of Londonwide importance, lies hidden behind high walls.

This most sensitive site (and large: nearly 40 acres) was Henry VIII's Royal Dockyard, no less. Dream, now, of arriving here by cruise liner, maybe going on into town by riverbus – or to your home in one of three gleaming new skyscrapers in what the Mayor's office fondly hopes will be a 'dramatic new urban quarter'. Dream on . . . and pray that reality will match the plans. But when? With schemes this big, a glacier might be quicker. A year on from the application, and we are no nearer a decision, let alone a schedule.

The outline draft, designed by Sir Richard Rogers and submitted by site owners News International, is for a mixed scheme with 3,514 homes (35 per cent Affordable), a warehouse transformed into exhibition/performance space, job space in the shape of artists' and designers' studios, film/stage set-making, etc. Plus cafés, bars, parking, that liner-sized wharf – and a boat repair yard. Will the *Times* and the *Sun* berate their owners if the eventual outcome fails to live up to a site where – maybe, just maybe – the remains of Francis Drake's Golden Hind lie buried?

If some of the above seems to fly off into the realms of wishful thinking (especially the boat-repair yard), there is one aspect that could prove central to Deptford: the exciting plan to extend **Deptford High St**, which now stops dead at **Evelyn Rd**, right through the site, opening it to all. This reclaiming of the riverside would give Deptford back its focus and allow its true resurrection in a way that no security-gated, flash-flats ghetto will.

That said, the renaissance already taking place in this long-neglected corner is not just of plush new schemes. Work is under way on the Thames-side Pepys Estate, a superbly sited council-homes complex: 261 new flats in low-rise blocks, plus houses, for shared ownership/fair rent. Likewise the Silwood Estate on the Surrey Docks borders, which will be completely redeveloped in partnership with Southwark Council.

Meanwhile, the established residential areas of New Cross, to the S/SW of Deptford, including the leafy heights of Telegraph Hill, have regained the favour they found in Georgian and Victorian times.

Deptford is also following Hoxton to become a new artistic hub. The Laban Centre, the £22-million dance studios, opened to acclaim and is abuzz with life; art galleries and studios figure in plans. Pioneering Deptford Albany Theatre hosts local projects, as well as visiting companies and performers. Then there's Cockpit Arts: a studio with 75 work spaces for crafts and applied arts, while Contemporary British Arts is an artist-led collective of affordable studio space . . . An arts festival in June focused further attention on SE8's artistic denizens. Lewisham Council, rightly proud of all this, is taking action so that things won't follow the East End pattern, which saw artists raise the status of run-down areas only to be priced out as gentrification followed.

So why all this activity in an area (however historic) for so long run down and deprived, its *raison d' être* gone with the closing of the docks? If position is the key – that's Canary Wharf across the river – transport is the answer. The DLR, which now trundles under the Thames direct to Canary Wharf, was the spur; there's the East London Line to New Cross, now intersecting the Jubilee Line two stops on at Canada Water station: at last the West End is a single change away. Recently confirmed plans to extend the East London will greatly improve links to the City and North London. And there's rail: New Cross's terraces were built to house City clerks who got to work via trains from New Cross and New Cross Gate which ran, and still run, into London Bridge in six minutes. New Cross station also has a useful link to Gatwick. And all stations are in zone 2.

All this has focused minds and wallets on the waterfront of Deptford Creek and the surviving historic buildings of the old centre. Many Deptford homes are council-built and (still) owned, but the stock of houses here includes inexpensive, unmessed-about, unmodernized Victoriana. And think flats, flats, flats – ex-council, conversion, new – lots of studios around c. £110,000, 1-beds c. £130,000, 2-beds from c. £145,000. Agents (you'll find most still cover it from New Cross or Greenwich) report much interest in ex-council flats – especially 2-beds. These have attracted the buy-to-let brigade as well as first-time buyers: the 10,000 students of nearby Goldsmiths' College underpin rental values.

The scene changes in New Cross, where the larger, once-grand South Kensington-style terraces make for good flat conversions. The Telegraph Hill area at the S end is a pleasant and surprising eminence (long discovered by property writers). It is one of several conservation areas: prices in these can be a good jump higher than elsewhere. A local agent reckons that a 2-bed flat in one costs the same as a 3-bed elsewhere. Among the New Cross terraces developers have inserted small blocks of flats.

It is certainly this area's turn. Back in Tudor times Deptford was to London what Heathrow is now: the launching pad for trade and adventure, a place full of bustle, business (and thieving) and well-paid work. Times change . . . Henry VIII's naval yard finally closed in 1869; the Victualling Yard just upriver, which Pepys knew, was all but razed in the 1960s to make way for a council estate. World War II's bombs had already blasted great gaps in the area. The death of the Surrey Docks in the 1970s did the rest. Now, at last, the resurgence of Docklands is having a real effect south of the river.

Deptford

This untidy, unkempt corner of town, cheerfully grimy in some parts – still plain grim in others – nonetheless feels like a proper place, unlike many a politer but more faceless tract. Deptford lies on the river, between Greenwich and the Surrey Docks. Deptford Strand was the scene of historic events as disparate as Peter the Great's apprenticeship in shipbuilding and the murder of Shakespeare's rival Marlowe in a riverside tavern.

Deptford's industrial and seafaring past is still in evidence, with streets such as **Mechanics Path**, **Shipwrights Rd**, **Frigate Mews** and **Bronze St**, not to mention the statues of famous admirals which adorn the town hall. The **High St** was long a byword for scruffiness: in 1550 it was 'so noisome and full of filth that the King's Majesty might not pass to and fro to see the building of His Majesty's ships'. St Paul's Church, another pointer to Deptford's past status, lies between the High St and Church St. This magnificent baroque building was erected for the people of Deptford in the 1720s, after they requested a 'grand church' – they got it. Over on Griffin St/Church St is the Wavelength Leisure Centre, with swimming pool and library. Deptford market is useful (and cheap): best days are Wednesday and Saturday, when the High St is closed to traffic.

Deptford Creek is now the epicentre for new schemes, housing and cultural. It runs S from the Thames and at its mouth, on both creek and river, sits Fairview's Millennium Quay, Deptford's first major development: 600 flats and houses, now a real community (check out their web site). Prices vary with size, specification and views: 3-bed house £300,000, 2-bed flat £250,000, 2-bed river view flats £280–340,000. Next door, and actually on the Thames rather than the Creek, is Paynes and Borthwick's Wharf, where 257 flats are planned in a mix of an 18-storey tower and the restoration of a dramatic 1860s Itailainate boiler-works.

Going S along the Creek, Meridian Gateway is a big scheme between main road and creek around **Copperas St**. Planning granted here (but no action yet): 630 flats (178 social, 10 live/work) in 12- to 16-storey blocks, plus offices, leisure, health etc. Incomers will be warned that the gravel wharf is staying. . . . Beyond the neighbouring Laban dance complex, Kent Wharf, **Creekside**, is still on paper: offices plus 70 new-build flats; some live/work. Across the road, Mumford's Mill, a vast Grade II-listed flour mill, will be 36 more flats (see Greenwich chapter). Fairview's flats on **Creek Rd** already exist: from £172,000.

South again, close to Deptford Bridge DLR and still in the borough but on the Greenwich bank, is OneSE8, St James's *very* self-contained flats complex: nearly 500 homes and other uses. Reached via **Deal's Gateway**, it's targeted at 25–35-year-olds: the stress is on Canary Wharf's closeness. Just scuttle to the DLR: no need to step out into Deptford. At OneSE8 you've pool, gym, restaurant – just about everything else, from dry cleaning to hot meals, can be delivered to your door by the concierge service. Shop via the Internet: it'll be stored till your return. Oh, and there's a car-hire system (few parking places provided). Studios c. £165,000; 1-bed flats £165–220,000; 2-beds c. £250–290,000; a penthouse £395,000; also live/work units. Immediately across the creek lies the big Seager's Distillery site, on **Brook Mill Rd**. This, too, is earmarked for homes – 219, with social and live/work: a 26-storey tower, art gallery, restaurant. Completion due 2006. Its present role is as temporary arts studios.

Back in Deptford's centre, modern flats appeared on the **High St** near the station, and other houses (one for sale last autumn: £400,000 for a 3-bed) have been added in **Mary Ann Gardens**. **Albury St**, a cobbled Georgian street that escaped the bombing, is the site of a new if Georgian-style 4-bed house: £400,000. Around the back of Albury St, facing onto **Creek Rd**, are some new houses and flats. In **Deptford Green**, alongside the fine medieval church, some council-built flats have been renovated. Off **Deptford Broadway** and **Harton St**, St John's Lodge is now award-winning apartments. On the Broadway itself old listed buildings have been converted to fair-rent flats. **Watson's St** and nearby streets W of the High Rd have pretty little cottages: £240,000 for 2-beds.

Heading up towards Surrey Docks along **Evelyn St** you pass large Victorian houses, many with semi-basements. There are small Victorian terraces in **Gosterwood St** – a quiet, domestic-scale road with a pleasant feel (a 2-bed flat in one, c. £175,000) – and

Etta St (a 3-bed house, £255,000), and more 3-bed houses in **Trundleys Rd**, **Alloa Rd** – and in **Scawen Rd**, where the houses can look out over Deptford Park. At the other end of **Trundleys Rd**, near the one-way system leading to Surrey Docks, is 1990-vintage Chester Circus: 30 handsome homes ranging from studios to 3-bed houses (£350,000). Opposite here, on the corner of **Evelyn St** and **Sayes Court**, is Sayes Hall Court: 55 flats and houses built in 1989 around a courtyard.

Between **Evelyn St** and the river lies the Pepys Estate, a 1960s council scheme: multi-storey concrete towers and low-rise blocks built on the site of bombed Georgian merchants' terraces . . . but look in your A–Z for **Deptford Strand**; at right angles to it lies The Terrace, along **Longshore.** Here are the remains of that Georgian heritage: houses and waterside warehouses are now converted into flats – some private, some social (an ex-housing association 2-bed in a period building: £210,000, wth river views). The Pepys was a model estate in the 1960s (lots of design awards) and is recovering from its former dangerous reputation. Aragon Tower, the largest, has stunning views over the river: Berkeley have smartened it up and they're selling duplexes at £230,000. These blocks have split-level flats with the sort of layout that gets architects excited. Council homes are giving way to 261 new shared-ownership/fair rent homes: 1- to 3-bed flats and 4-bed houses. These should be very popular; the same cannot be said of the grimmer blocks of Milton Court, another council estate to the S between **Milton Court Rd** and **Sanford St**, in the angle between two rail lines: not the place for your evening stroll. Even here, new housing-association homes have appeared opposite attractive Berwick Gardens park. Between **Sanford St** and the railway are the 1980s houses of **Southerngate Way** and **Sterling Gardens**, with New Cross station nearby.

New Cross

New Cross apparently used to be a pretty village until its high street evolved into the main Dover road, effectively slicing the place in half. New Cross thus has once-grand, early- (some very early) Victorian terraces, the potential of which depends on distance from the road: great for trains, tube and buses, but somewhat transient in feel, compared to Deptford's far more villagey air. However, from time to time a new restaurant or a smarter shop appears. Much recent development is squeezed in close to busy rail lines.

Buyers and renters will find plenty of best-period Victorian terraces, and flats converted from them, plus a good sprinkling of 1980s/1990s blocks. Central New Cross is unlovely – but big, beautiful houses can be found tucked away: look to the leafy enclave of Telegraph Hill, the mid-19th-century homes of **Florence Rd**; the conservation area of St John's (see Lewisham chapter). Most of the tall, handsome, 5-storey houses along busy **New Cross Rd** and **Lewisham Way** have been split into flats (a studio £120,000, 2-bed £150,000-plus). There are also some 3-bed flats – mostly over shops. Goldsmiths' College has invested in new student housing, but flats to rent are still in demand. Just to the N of the main road, near New Cross station, **Glenville Grove** has a newish small estate of flats (a 1-bed, £140,000) and older council homes, many now private. Near the other station, New Cross Gate, there's recent housing from studio flats to small 3-bed houses.

N

Go S from the station, past the 1930s terraces and 4-bed Victorian mansion flats on **New Cross Rd**, and you come to a neighbourhood with an identity all its own. These are the pleasant boulevards, lined by trees and flanked by roomy (and some huge) Victorian homes, built by the Haberdashers' Company, which run up and around Telegraph Hill and its park. The eponymous telegraph station passed the news of Waterloo. The houses in this pleasant, quiet and very popular area are big, 4- to 6-bed family homes, or split into roomy flats. 'Hill' this is: **Kitto Rd**, **Vesta Rd** and the top of adjoining streets have magnificent, panoramic views over central London. **Jerningham Rd** has 3-storey, 4/5-bed Victoriana, including semis – bigger, 6-bed/4-recep houses have reached c. £675,000. **Erlanger** and **Waller Rds** have 5-bed houses. Later houses in **Troutbeck Rd.** You'll pay

£160,000-plus for a 1-bed flat, £180,000-plus for a 2-bed, though spacious 2-beds can be £230,000 and 3-beds £250,000-plus. Houses start around £450,000 for a 4/5 bed and go on up. Some houses at the lower ends of the streets have suffered from subsidence: watch your survey. South of the park, **Drakefell Rd** has Victorian terraces, some flats. Across the tracks, **Shardeloes Rd** has some handsome 3-storey Victoriana, most now flats.

North of Telegraph Hill, across New Cross Rd, is the Hatcham Park conservation area: more Victoriana courtesy of the Haberdashers' estate. Streets include **Brocklehurst St** (3-bed cottages), **Billington Rd** (4/5-bed terraces), **Camplin St** (2-bed terraces), **Hunsdon Rd**, **Hatcham Park Rd** (3-bed, 3-storey houses) and **Hatcham Park Mews** – with ten new industrial-chic live/work units: £245,000. **Hunsdon Rd** has a well-regarded school. Off **Avonley Rd** is Barratt's 1990 Avonley Village: studios, flats and houses; next, Rialto, 2001 onwards, added **John Williams Close**: 3- and 4-bed houses, 1- and 2-bed flats off **Cold Blow Lane**; then more of 2002 vintage, including 3-bed, 2-bath £275,000 houses, in **Joseph Hardcastle Close**.

Transport Tubes: New Cross, New Cross Gate (zone 2; East London Line) Oxford Circus 25 min (2 changes), City 20 min (2 changes), Heathrow 70 min (2 changes). Trains: New Cross, New Cross Gate, Deptford (London Bridge 6 min, Cannon St 12 min). DLR from Deptford Bridge to Canary Wharf (12 min), City etc.

Convenient for Docklands, City, Greenwich. Miles from centre: 4.5.

Schools Local Authority: Haberdashers' Aske's Hatcham, Deptford Green School, Addey & Stanhope School.

SALES

Flats	S	1B	2B	3B	4B	5B
Average prices	80–120	110–130	120–220+	145–250+	–	–
Houses	2B	3B	4B	5B	6/7B	8B
Average prices	175–250	190–325	240–450	350–550	400–600+	–

RENTAL

Flats	S	1B	2B	3B	4B	5B
Average prices	115–150	140–175	175–240	210–325	275–350	–
Houses	2B	3B	4B	5B	6/7B	8B
Average prices	180–280	200–325	275–350	350–400	375–550	–

N

The properties Deptford: 3-bed Victorian and older terraces (much council housing being improved). New flats massing along Deptford Creek. New Cross: 19th-century terraces, many split into flats; stately streets of flats, 4/5-bed houses on Telegraph Hill; run-down terraces on the main roads, cottagey in conservation areas.

The market Good-value, convenient (only tubes for miles) homes attract first-time buyers. Families head for the enclave of Telegraph Hill. The DLR links Deptford to Docklands and is attracting new buyers.

Among estate agents active in this area are:

- Peter James
- Your Move
- Burnet, Ware & Graves
- Oak Estates
- Cannon Kallar
- Wilson Rogers
- Meridian Estates
- Winkworth
- Bairstow Eves
- Burwood Marsh
- First Property Sales
- Utopia

NOTTING HILL AND NORTH KENSINGTON

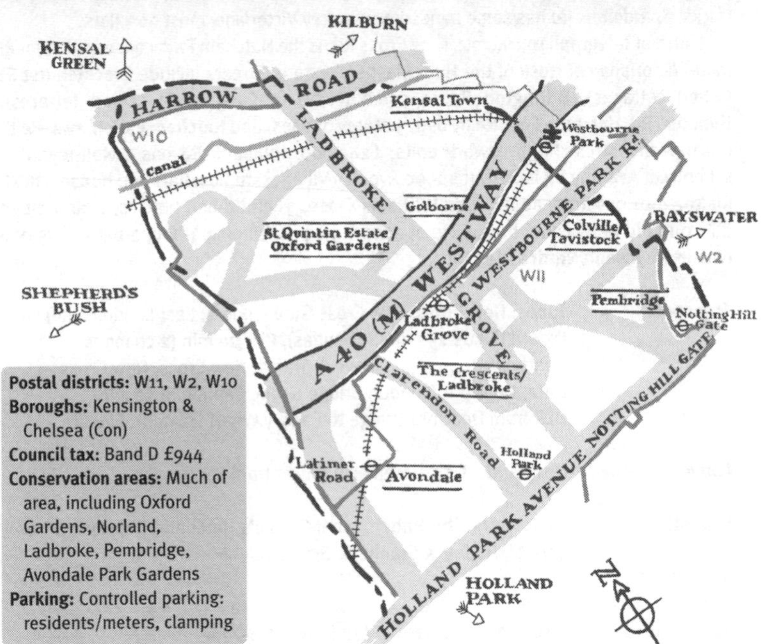

Postal districts: W11, W2, W10
Boroughs: Kensington & Chelsea (Con)
Council tax: Band D £944
Conservation areas: Much of area, including Oxford Gardens, Norland, Ladbroke, Pembridge, Avondale Park Gardens
Parking: Controlled parking: residents/meters, clamping

As the stars moving to Notting Hill become ever more bankable and less raffish, is it not time to reassess the area's image as London's rich-bohemian quarter? With houses now costing up to £6 million, it has, perhaps, become the New Kensington.

A generation has gone by since Notting Hill was truly scruffy (though some of the inhabitants still are, and proud of it). Portobello Road Market and the annual eruption of Carnival are now internationally famous events rather than central to the local fabric. North Kensington ('North Ken' to everyone), though a lot more expensive than it was – £4 million houses here now – remains delightfully mixed in every sense: more than 100 languages are spoken by its denizens, whose cultures, shops and cafés are ever present on the streets.

Notting Hill sits on a gentle rise just NW of Kensington Gardens. From its summit, the ground drops away to the N, in a small but (for this far into London) steep slope. To generalize, for over a century the wealthy and respectable have lived on the top of the hill, their big family houses backing directly onto acres of delightful communal gardens – some of the biggest tracts of exclusive greenery in London. The poor and the unconventional (two quite different types, divided by cash) have lived at the bottom. Poverty made serious inroads into the respectable bit in the years 1930–1980. Much of the area became a warren of bedsits and seemingly terminal dilapidation. The past 25 years have seen prosperity regain its ground, returning the big houses to single use or redividing them into ever-smarter flats. With each year, the poor and raffish are driven ever further north, with virtually the entire zone S of the Westway – except for some pockets of council and housing-association flats – now smartened.

The areas' borders retain a certain subtlety: all of Notting Hill is in W11, but not all of

W11 is Notting Hill. The corner to the NW, in the angle of the M40 and the M41, is not Notting Hill. Once called Notting Dale – and a notorious slum – it is now quieter, more respectable 'Avondale', and the southern end has aspirations to be Holland Park. All of W10 lying S of the **Harrow Rd** is North Ken; N of it, a small part of W10 forms Kilburn's Queen's Park Estate neighbourhood (see Kilburn, Kensal Green & Queen's Park chapter).

One should not overstate the changes; despite the influx of celebrities, bankers and industrialists, North Kensington in particular still gains character from a wide mix of social classes and races: this is a cosmopolitan and lively place to live. The streets are busy at midnight, and there is a distinct inner-city feel to the whole area. This character in recent years has attracted first art galleries then fashion stores, cafés, bars and restaurants to Notting Hill, which rivals Soho or Shoreditch. It deters some home-hunters who shy away from the 24-hour party atmosphere. Agents redirect them to Fulham.

Notting Hill gives homeseekers plenty of choice, especially in flats, mews cottages and grander houses, and North Kensington offers yet more flats – plus, to the surprise of those who only know the grittier bits, family homes with gardens. A recent trend is live/work units, which attract the likes of fashion and jewellery designers.

Amid the stucco, a sprinkling of daringly modern houses and flats are appearing, some from the drawing-boards of distinguished architects. Another recent move is towards international-level luxury, with no-expense-spared makeovers of houses and flats on a scale to rival Mayfair. Notting Hill is now a sensible place to spend unreal sums of money on a home, agents aver, as there's always someone richer than you who will love it . . .

Other assets include the (sometimes well-hidden) communal gardens of Notting Hill, and the direct underground links to the West End and City. The area gains, too, from its position on the 'right' side of London for Heathrow, a big plus for relocating foreigners.

One unusual feature of the housing scene here is the domination by housing trusts and associations. These own large amounts of property – usually homes they have bought up and converted, though some are new-build. For instance, Kensington Housing Trust owns over 500 homes in the Golborne ward alone. Unlike council housing, many of the trusts' homes are dotted around in otherwise owner-occupied streets. And once in association hands they generally stay that way, rarely being resold. This preserves the social mix, but also 'freezes' whole sections of streets, cutting the number of homes on the market.

When prospecting for a home, beware the ubiquity of local street names: Ladbroke Square is indeed posh, but it's a mistake to expect Ladbroke Crescent to be smart too. It isn't. Even roads known to be smart have the odd house long ago converted into flats and with a freeholder who cannot see the point of paint.

Two major street events also inform the character of the area – the weekly draw of the renowned **Portobello Rd** market (Saturday is the busy day) and the annual Notting Hill Carnival, Europe's biggest street festival. It draws up to 2 million people every August Bank Holiday weekend. Festivities are generally concentrated in the Colville/Tavistock and Golborne neighbourhoods: for two days, the streets are alive with pulsating rhythms and superbly colourful floats. Residents either love it or hate it. It is regularly proposed to re-route the Carnival through Hyde Park, where there is more space than in the little streets of W11 and W10. However, these plans have so far come to nothing. Another event is the Portobello Festival, which brings two weeks of music, film, literature and arts to the area in late July.

Portobello Rd has had a market since the 1860s, when it was known as The Lane. Antiques, bric-à-brac, fruit-and-vegetable and clothing stalls spread for two-thirds of a mile along the road from **Simon Close** to **Golborne Rd**, with the antiques concentrated at the S end. The market is a major tourist attraction, drawing thousands of visitors every Saturday. Council proposals to tidy it up brought protests from locals, who like it the way it is: scruffy and lively. Antiques traders have colonised many side roads, too.

The social N–S divide in the area is accentuated by the physical barrier of the **Westway** elevated motorway. Built in the mid-1960s, it chops across the area just S of **Cambridge Gardens**. The space under the Westway has been put to good use by the Westway Development Trust: the Gipsies and their ponies (at the W end) have been joined by a vibrant mix of commercial ventures and community uses. Small charities, a fitness centre, a centre for the elderly and an information point can variously be found in the archways. There's a huge, two-floor bar/restaurant close to Ladbroke Grove tube, a nightclub and the Portobello Green arcade of small, specialist fashion shops – with the Saturday stalls at this end of the market, this is a jumping-off point for young designers. Further W, the Trust has a massive sports centre, with tennis, climbing, riding (!), football – all taking place under the motorway. A converted warehouse provides work-space for 140 artists and creative businesses.

Ladbroke Grove is the area's main traffic artery, stretching from the desirable, leafy southern boundary of the neighbourhood right through to the unkempt northern border. The main shopping centre for the area is **Notting Hill Gate** to the S: the windy legacy of a 1960s road-widening scheme, the gate has been humanized by a steady programme of tree planting and public art. Notting Hill Gate boasts two cinemas and a number of popular restaurants, cafés and pubs. It also prides itself in the avant-garde Gate Theatre, above a smart pub. The refurbished Electric Cinema in **Portobello Rd** has an outpost of the members-only Soho House club and a glass-fronted brasserie. Oh, and leather armchairs in the cinema.

Shopping – fashion, interiors, antiques, anything 'designer' from handbags to herbs – is excellent, though bohemian locals complain that chain stores and identikit coffee bars are driving out more characterful individual shops. On a more prosaic level, the big canalside Sainsbury's at the N end of **Ladbroke Grove** is a local bus destination (the No. 23) in itself.

Rising property prices and general prosperity have led residents to spend money on their homes, and there has been a rash of painting, decorating and modernizing. Few of the truly picturesque, peeling-stucco slums survive – at least S of the Westway. However, the council's planners are tightening controls, making it harder to extend homes upwards (loss of light is feared) and downwards into basements. They do, however, encourage the splitting of neglected little terraced houses in W10 into flats, and the return to family homes of bedsit properties.

N *Notting Hill*

This is the smarter half of the area, but even here the contrasts can be great: serene mansions to the S, stimulating street life to the N. Notting Hill's west side, centred on the N–S boulevard of **Ladbroke Grove**, has a spacious air stemming from the laying out of the Ladbroke Estate from the 1820s. The sweeping crescents of dignified creamy terraces betray not just the curve of the hill but the site of the short-lived race course that crowned the hilltop in the 1830s. Many of the houses date from later, though: the estate was a graveyard of developers' fortunes, and building followed a stop-start course through to the 1860s. The streets further E are on a less grand scale, with **Portobello Rd**, the ghost of a farm lane, wriggling through to break their regular pattern.

Pembridge

Pembridge stretches N from Notting Hill Gate as far as **Westbourne Grove**, bounded on the W by **Kensington Park Rd** and on the E by **Chepstow Place** and **Ossington St**. The E part is in W2. **Pembridge Rd**, the main route between the Gate and Westbourne Grove, leads into the heart of this sedate and leafy neighbourhood. To the E lies

Pembridge Square, the only one in the borough lined by large detached villas – grand terraces and paired houses reign supreme in Notting Hill. The 4-storey stucco houses look out over their narrow, shared central garden. Some remain as family homes, but many have been converted: some into spacious flats, a few into hotels and schools. One of the big, detached cream-painted villas has just been split into five 2,000 sq ft flats: £1.9–2.6 million each. The E side of the square is across the borough boundary in Westminster.

South of the square are the cul-de-sacs of **Linden** and **Clanricarde Gardens.** Tall, ornate stucco terraces and paired houses characterize both streets. In **Clanricarde Gardens**, the large houses of bedsits have mostly now been converted into flats. In **Linden Gardens** is The Limes, a 6-storey modern development with private parking. There is also the private, gated **Linden Mews** with its quaint brick houses, and **Garden Mews**, where four recent houses can be found.

The scale changes in **Ossington St** on the E edge of the neighbourhood. Here terraces of smaller (but still close to £2 million) stucco houses face the backs of buildings fronting **Palace Court**. At the end of the street is little **Victoria Grove Mews.** More large houses are found N of Pembridge Square in leafy **Pembridge Place** and **Dawson Place.** Both are lined by paired stucco villas with front gardens. Dawson Place has detached villas, some with the same decorative cast-iron and glass entrance canopies as the imposing mega-mansions of Holland Park down the road. Prices are not dissimilar. Groups and pairs of substantial houses curve around **Pembridge Villas,** the N half of the main route through the neighbourhood. Leading off to the NW, **Pembridge Crescent** has stucco villas. These contrast with the 2-storey painted cottages in **Pembridge Mews. Chepstow Crescent,** which has mainly 3/4-storey brick-and-stucco terraces with wrought-iron balconies – and a couple of hideous post-war flats blocks – leads into tree-lined **Chepstow Villas**, considered the best address in the neighbourhood. About half of the elegant paired villas remain as family houses; the rest are flats: a 2-bed one with roof terrace was £675,000 last autumn.

Leading N from here into the Colville/Tavistock neighbourhood is **Ledbury Rd**, a pleasant, smart street of stucco houses with antique and designer-clothes shops, galleries and bars. (As recently as 1972 an architectural author warned his readers not to walk down this street alone: now a 2-bed flat is £400,000.) A recent addition is the **Ledbury Mews East** development. Behind the Walmer Castle pub is a clutch of workshops, and Westbourne Grove Church hides tiny **St John's Mews** with more. The church itself has shrunk in size but has sprouted a collection of smart flats on the roof, thanks to a clever scheme by Manhatten Lofts. **Denbigh Rd** has a mix of properties ranging from Longlands Court council estate to low-rise modern brick homes and trad, painted stucco houses. **West Hill Court** is a modern mews of 2/3-bed flats reached via an archway opposite the council estate. A winged stucco arch halfway along the E side leads through to **Pencombe Mews**, a group of 3-storey town-houses.

The W side of the neighbourhood is dominated by Portobello Rd. S of **Chepstow Villas** stands a row of charming, painted 2-storey stucco cottages with front gardens. Street trees add to the leafy look. These face the backs of the big red-brick and stone 1890s flats blocks fronting **Kensington Park Rd**. At the rear of the cottages is **Simon Close**, a small cul-de-sac of modern 2-storey town-houses. Although this stretch of Portobello Rd is quiet during the week, on Saturdays it is invaded by thousands of tourists from all over the world heading for the market. Antique stalls spread along both sides of the street, spilling around into **Denbigh Close**, a pleasant, cobbled cul-de-sac of cottages, some with roof terraces. **Denbigh Terrace**, one street away, has an attractive pastel-shaded stucco row of 2/3-storey-plus-basement family houses on the southern side, looking across to Longlands Court council estate. **Vernon Yard**, a cobbled mews off Portobello Rd further N, has a few houses.

The Crescents/Ladbroke

This is the most prosperous and elegant part of the area, set on the highest ground at the top of the hill, and delightfully laid out in an expansive, curving street plan of crescents and gardens. The homes date from the mid-Victorian age and many large houses, echoing those of Belgravia and South Ken, survive undivided. It is here that people apply for planning permission for underground swimming pools beneath a conservatory in their back garden and double car-lifts in place of the front one.

Clarendon Rd on the W edge of the neighbourhood sets the tone, with period houses at £3 million-plus and some (slightly) cheaper modern ones. The best stretch, between Lansdowne Walk and the smart Clarendon Cross shops, has big, paired, 1840s brick-and-stucco villas with front gardens. South of here are terraces of 3-storey-plus-basement mid-Victorian houses, modern town-houses and flats. North of the junction with Elgin Crescent the street becomes more mixed, with the appearance of council blocks and a parade of shops. However, a terrace of 4-storey pastel houses on the E side backs onto the beautiful communal gardens between **Elgin Crescent** and **Blenheim Crescent.**

Leafy **Elgin Crescent** has terraces of mainly 3-storey, painted stucco houses with basements and attic windows. Huge communal gardens lie at the rear on both sides of the street. Many houses have been converted into flats.

Terraces of 3-storey-plus-semi-basement houses, many split into flats, at first line both sides of tree-filled **Blenheim Crescent**: those on the S back onto the communal gardens. But the Crescent becomes a different street as it travels eastwards across Ladbroke Grove: here a mix of private (S), council and housing trust (N) properties merges into the shops, pubs and cafés in the stretch between Kensington Park Rd and Portobello Rd. Artisan House, a block of Victorian studios, has been revamped to provide six double-height shell-finish units: one, arranged as a 2-bed, was £975,000 last autumn. Tucked away here is **Codrington Mews**, with a clutch of contemporary-style houses.

Heading back south of Elgin Crescent, the streets climb uphill. **Arundel Gardens** has mainly 4-storey brick-and-stucco terraces with small ornate iron balconies on the first floor. **Ladbroke Gardens** is lined by ornate stucco terraces. A garden flat with 3 beds and all-important communal garden access was £1.275 million last autumn, while a 3rd-floor 2-bed, which just overlooks the gardens, was £375,000. This street leads into **Stanley Crescent** with its huge, 6-storey, brick-and-stucco paired villas at the bottom of the hill, and a terrace of 4- and 5-storey ornate painted stucco houses at the top (£6.75 million was being asked for one of these last autumn). Interesting gaps and intriguing arches between the houses give glimpses of the sky, trees and the lovely communal gardens between the Crescent and Kensington Park Gardens. **Stanley Gardens** runs off the Crescent between two patches of these hidden gardens.

N

The summit of the hill was laid out in the form of an oval, sliced in two by Ladbroke Grove. **Stanley Crescent** forms one half of the oval – originally a Regency racecourse – and across the Grove to the W is the complementary **Lansdowne Crescent**. An elegant white 'iced wedding cake' terrace curves halfway round the semicircle to the N. The richly decorated houses have distinctive rounded facades, Corinthian-columned entrance porches and £3-million-plus price tags. Big, paired brick-and-stucco villas, stone-gabled houses and some modern brick town-houses spread around the rest of the crescent. Lansdowne Lodge, on the corner with Ladbroke Grove, is a modernist new block designed by John Pawson with five flats – one per floor – at £2.4–2.95 million each.

Yet more big communal gardens lie behind Lansdowne Crescent and **Lansdowne Rd**: another choice street. Terraces of 3-storey-plus-basement painted stucco houses, some gabled, wind around the hill, merging with pairs of villas where the street drops down again to Holland Park Avenue. South along Lansdowne Rd, at the junction of St John's Gardens, the road becomes 'No Entry'. You are now entering a complex series of one-way streets aimed at reducing traffic speed and flow: it can be very confusing. **Lansdowne Walk** has groups of handsome stucco and brick-and-stucco houses. On the NE corner of the street, set back from Ladbroke Grove, is Bartok House, considered one of the best blocks of flats in the Notting Hill area. The modern brown-brick development with its own communal gardens joins up with a terrace of brick-and-stucco houses (split into flats) and another modern flats block. These flats face **Ladbroke Grove,** but are separated from the road by a private driveway and a screen of trees and lawns. Tall trees in the gardens surrounding St John's Church on the hilltop add to the leafy outlook. The church spire can be seen from miles around, rising above the treetops. This stretch of Ladbroke Grove and the leg between Ladbroke Square and Ladbroke Rd (attractive 4-storey, wide-fronted painted stucco houses) are the best sections of this long, very varied, road.

Lying between the houses in **Kensington Park Gardens** and **Ladbroke Square** are the largest private gardens in the borough – indeed, at seven acres, some of the largest in London – and only accessible to subscribers. Despite its name, **Ladbroke Square** is made up of a long terrace of 4- and 5-storey brick-and-stucco houses on one side of the street, facing the gardens. Most are divided into spacious flats. The gardens are enclosed by tall trees and hedges, and street trees stretch along adjoining roads as far as the eye can see.

Ladbroke Rd, a relatively busy but pleasant local road, has a mix of smaller terraced houses, plus a tall-gabled red-brick one, next to the pub, which was to be had for £1.3 million last autumn. Also here is Bonham House, a 4-storey block of flats, plus big detached houses and a 5-storey, 1900s flats block. Traffic is slowed by a roundabout at the junction with Ladbroke Terrace. Notting Hill police station stands on the corner with Ladbroke Grove and the Kensington Temple (Nonconformist) at the E junction with Pembridge Rd. Leading off here are a series of small streets and pretty little cobbled mews, including **Wilby Mews**: this, tucked in behind the flower-bedecked Ladbroke Arms pub, has a mix of little 2- and 3-storey cottages and a few new houses set around an unusually wide courtyard. More low, painted Victorian cottages in **Horbury Mews. Horbury Crescent** has curving rows of larger brick-and-stucco homes, many now flats. Hidden away behind houses at the SE end of Ladbroke Rd and the shops in Pembridge Rd and Notting Hill Gate is **Bulmer Mews**: 1980s 2-storey brick houses with garages.

The E border of the neighbourhood is **Kensington Park Rd**, a busy bus route. Three-storey terraces with restaurants, shops and bars on the lower floors line the N end of the street. They give way to terraces on the W side, broken up by

Stucco is the trademark of the Ladbroke area. The pillared porch, the rusticated stucco around the ground-floor window, the steps, the railings, the balcony – all are typical of these large houses. Some are now flats, which benefit from the lofty rooms. Many of the houses back onto communal gardens: the area was planned as one estate, though built over quite a lengthy period.

N

stretches of the area's splendid shared gardens and Kelvin Court, a 5-storey flats block. Princes House and Buckingham and Matlock Court, impeccably kept 1930s mansion blocks, stand opposite Kensington Temple: a 1-bed might be £335,000-plus. Really grand houses in this road sell for well into the millions; some famous names have homes here.

Notting Dale/Avondale

Victorian terraces and newly-created private squares and mews stand amid large council estates and housing-association schemes in this very mixed, confusingly laid-out but increasingly fashionable neighbourhood of Notting Dale (its original name), curving round the N and W foot of Notting Hill and enclosed by the Westway and the West Cross Route.

The W end of **Lancaster Rd**, a short walk from Ladbroke Grove station and the shops ckustered round it, mixes homes, education, health and light-industrial uses. A terrace of 3-storey-plus-basement brick-and-stucco houses, many split into flats, lines the NE arm of the street. Opposite is the Royalty Studios, a complex of studios/workshops; next door to this is the London Lighthouse HIV/AIDS hospice and support centre. Standing alongside is Notting Hill's Holmes Place health club, housed in a converted school.

Ruston Mews, in the shadow of the Westway, is a recently modernized gated mews. **St Mark's Rd** leads under the Westway to North Ken. **Bartle Rd** runs between Lancaster Rd and the Westway; off it are **St Andrew's Square** and **Wesley Square**, with their modern 3-storey brick houses boasting off-street parking and pleasant communal gardens. Homes are shielded from Lancaster Rd by a high wall, adding to the sense of enclosure and privacy. Opposite is part of the large Lancaster West council estate. Lancaster Rd becomes **Silchester Rd** beyond the Methodist Church, and you cross into W10. At the **Bramley Rd** junction is modern Arthurs Court. Opposite is 4-storey Goodrich Court, on Bramley Rd at the junction of **Darfield Way**: a dead-end road which leads onto the Silchester West Estate and **Waynflete Square** and **Shalfleet Drive**. Eleven modern flats make up **Charlotte Mews**. The estate with its tower blocks spreads through **Verity Close** where it becomes a cul-de-sac of modern 2/3-storey red-brick terraced houses with small gardens. The remainder of the estate stretches along the N side of **Cornwall Crescent**. A Victorian terrace lines the S side.

More Victorian terraces are found to the N in **Ladbroke Crescent** – tall painted stucco houses converted into flats. At the NW end of Walmer Rd is Kensington Sports Centre, with swimming and many other sports. More brick council blocks extend S along the street, leading to smart **Hippodrome Mews**. Here 3-storey brown-brick town-houses line two private mews overlooking Avondale Park (3-bed houses, £650–750,000). Terraces of modern brick, low-rise, housing-association properties are found in **Wilsham St** and **Kenley Walk** S of the park, and **Runcorn Place** and **Hesketh Place** to the N. Beside Kenley Walk, and at the top of **Wilsham St**, lies a group of 2/3-storey town-houses. Wilsham St has tiny flat-fronted pastel-coloured cottages – like a Chelsea backstreet. There is no way through for cars, but pedestrians can walk to Walmer Rd.

N

Private homes in the SW corner of the neighbourhood are concentrated in **Avondale Park Rd**, **Mary Place**, **Sirdar Rd**, **Stoneleigh Place** and **St**, **Treadgold St** and **Grenfell Rd**. Sirdar Rd is leafy, with prettyish cottages. **Avondale Park Rd** has been cut off to form a cul-de-sac. Many of the 2/3-storey terraced houses found here are still split into flats. Tucked away in the middle of this group is **Avondale Park Gardens**, a pleasant square of 2-storey brick artisan cottages with walled front gardens set around a small central green with trees. The cottages, built by the former LCC after World War I, were passed on to the local council, which gradually sold them off. Avondale Park Primary School is also here. Bordering this chunk of private property is the big Henry Dickens council estate (a 2-bed flat, c. £250,000), fronting **St Ann's Rd**, which also has flats and houses of varying vintages (a 3-bed Victorian terraced house here, £600,000-plus). Just N of

Avondale Park, **Mary Place** has small 1-bed flats at under £200,000.

Boundary changes in 1996 extended the Borough of Kensington & Chelsea in this area, removing an anomaly so that both W11 postcode and borough border now follow the physical barrier of the M41 West Cross Route. Thus a clutch of streets W of Henry Dickens Court on St Ann's Rd, once in Hammersmith & Fulham, are now in the Royal Borough. **Rifle Place** has a 1990s group of 3-storey flats in light brown brick, set around gardens; new homes are under way on a big site across to **Olaf St. Mortimer Square** with its low stucco-and-brick homes is another recent addition. The Designers Guild building in **Olaf St** houses a collection of media companies: five houses have been built in front of it. At the top end are residential blocks and other small business units. Worth noting that this corner will have access via a footbridge to the vast, ongoing White City development just W of the motorway, which will boast acres of shops plus new transport links (see Shepherd's Bush chapter).

Colville/Tavistock

This is the heart of the 'other' Notting Hill, down the slope and a world away from the snowy crescents of Ladbroke. Things have changed in the past decade: traditionally poorer, it's now rather funkier. **Westbourne Grove** with its proliferation of smart antique shops, galleries, fashion stores and other ways of spending money is a main W–E route between Notting Hill and Bayswater. (Ever inventive, the area's criminal element has found that snatch-and-grab raids on the rails of the fashion stores can net useful sums . . .)

Where **Westbourne Grove** meets Denbigh Rd is a little group of shops, graced by a modernist public loo and flower stall which has won architectural prizes. On Saturdays antique and bric-a-brac stalls spill around the corner into the street from the Portobello Rd market. Stucco/brick terraces line this end of Westbourne Grove, many of which have shops on the ground floor. **Lambton Mews**, with its health club and business premises, is tucked away to the S. Around the corner on the E side of **Kensington Park Rd** is an attractive terrace of painted 3-storey houses. More antique shops at the S end of **Ledbury Rd**, beneath the 3/4-storey brick-and-stucco which stretches along the W side (a 1-bed flat, £270,000). The E side is in Westminster.

Off to the W runs tree-lined **Lonsdale Rd** – probably the nicest street in the neighbourhood together with the southern end of **Colville Rd**. Hidden between the two are **Colville Mews** and **Lonsdale Mews**, with businesses and homes, including five very modern new houses in Colville Mews (2-bed, £1.5 million; a million more asked for a very smart one). Attractive terraces of 3-storey painted houses stand in **Lonsdale Rd**, E of the brown-brick Portobello Court council estate (some private these days), which spreads back to **Westbourne Grove.** Taller stucco terraces line the E side of **Colville Rd** and 4-storey semi-detached villas the W. **Colville Terrace** has 4/5-storey stucco houses, mostly converted into flats. On the corner of **Westbourne Grove** and **Colville Rd**, a former petrol station site has become 16 new flats over a fashion store.

Powis Square to the N has a mix of private 4-storey stucco terraced houses to the W (most have been split into flats) and a long modern row of 4-storey brick council-built flats to the E. They lie on either side of a public garden with a children's playground in the middle: suddenly, in contrast to streets to the S, this is a much more family area. At the N end of the square is the Tabernacle Community Centre.

Another public garden and playground lies to the W in **Colville Square**. Backing onto the E side of the garden is the 5-storey Pinehurst Court flats block, which actually fronts **Colville Gardens.** It is set back off the road behind railings, lawn and trees. The N end of Colville Gardens is a pedestrianized cul-de-sac leading to the attractive paved square opposite All Saints' neo-Gothic church. Overlooking the W side of **Colville Square** are more 4-storey terraces. Lining the **Talbot Rd** side are blocks of tall modern red-brick, housing-trust flats. Some 2003 homes in **Colville Square Mews**: four flats and eight mews houses.

Westbourne Park Rd, another busy W–E road (the E end is the smarter), has mainly brick-and-stucco terraces with clusters of shops on the ground floor. The council's Convent Gardens Estate and a modern housing-trust scheme take up the S side of the street from Ladbroke Grove to Kensington Park Rd. Off to the N is **All Saints' Rd** – once notorious only for drug dealing and street robberies, but now home to fashionable restaurants, clubs and smart shops (and expensive flats).

Crossing All Saint's Rd and running parallel to Westbourne Park Rd is **St Luke's Mews**, with one end housing an interesting blue building of small offices, and some modern mews houses. On the opposite side of All Saints' Rd, the mews continues with older more characteristic homes. **McGregor Rd**, off the E side of All Saints' Rd, is lined by 3-storey Victorian terraces – and is a play street from 8am to sunset.

Long, stepped terraces of modern yellow-brick housing-trust co-ownership flats stretch along **Tavistock Crescent**. It runs into **Tavistock Rd** (3-storey brick-and-stucco terraces), which is pedestrianized at its W junctions with Portobello Rd. **Tavistock Gardens** has a sculpture garden and play landscape for children. **Basing St** has smaller, 2-storey stucco-and-brick. This stretch of **Portobello Rd** takes in the heart of the market: antique and bric-à-brac stalls line the section between Westbourne Grove and Elgin Crescent (Saturdays only); fruit-and-veg stalls (Monday–Saturday) take over between here and the covered market under the Westway – bric-a-brac, funky fashion from young designers and second-hand clothing (Fridays and Saturdays). From Acklam Rd to Golborne Rd, a junk market on Friday morning and Saturday. Several small mews off the E side of Portobello Rd are used by market traders to store their barrows and stock; **Alba Place**, a short cul-de-sac between Lancaster and Westbourne Park Rds, also has brightly painted 2/3-storey cottages, some with roof terraces, at its E end (and a smart modern named-architect 2-bed house, £750,000-ish). Opposite is **Hayden's Place**, with the Portobello Studios.

New homes in **Dunworth Mews**, between Westbourne Park Rd and Talbot Rd: a dozen contemporary-styled flats and mews houses forming the 'Portobello Collection' – a 3-bed house was £595,000 last autumn.

Lancaster Rd, which leads W to Ladbroke Grove, has mainly 3-storey terraces and paired villas, these days split into flats. The Serbian Orthodox Church and community centre stands near the junction with the Grove facing the Lancaster Youth Club, with the council library on the corner of Ladbroke Grove and Lancaster Rd.

North Kensington

From here on we are N of the motorway, in the W10 postcode. Historically, the area was poor, with quite a lot of substandard housing; as a result, a lot of council and government cash has been spent. North Ken (as it's commonly known) has its gritty streets (especially, still, in Golborne and Kensal), but it also has surprises: family homes amid greenery, near suburban in atmosphere, yet a stroll from the bright lights of W11. It is also losing its last industry and gaining new homes, some at affordable prices.

A council-led initiative is involving locals and businesses to develop a 'cleaner, greener' North Ken: grafitti, litter and street cleaning are priorities.

Golborne

Golborne is tucked into the NE corner of the area, bounded by the railway line to the N and E and the Westway to the S. Most of the Golborne area is dominated by council and housing-trust/association homes, mainly brick low-rise. These cluster in **Bevington**, **Swinbrook**, **Acklam**, **Wornington** and **St Ervan's Rds**, though there are still some Victorian terraces in Bevington Rd. The early 1960s Wornington Green estate, owned by Kensington Housing Trust, is typical: a 539-home neighbourhood much improved by a 'greening the estate' scheme and by anti-crime measures.

The northern ends of **Portobello Rd** and **Ladbroke Grove**, and **Golborne Rd**, have some conversion flats, often above shops. These used to be the cheapest homes in the area – except for ex-local authority flats – but with current asking prices such as £260,000 for a 1-bed flat above a shop in **Golborne Rd**, or £450,000 for a tiny mews cottage, cheapness is decidedly relative. This end of the **Portobello Rd**, on the fringe of the famous market, traditionally sold mainly second-hand clothing and household goods, but this is changing as the money filters north. Stalls spread along **Golborne Rd**, a bustling shopping centre in its own right, with a strong North African ambience. Upmarket restaurants and specialist shops – French bistros and little fashion stores – jostle with stalls to souk-like effect.

Kensal Town

In the far N of the area, and about as far in atmosphere from the lush Kensington heartlands, is Kensal Town. Crossing **Golborne Rd** railway bridge is like entering another world. Grim concrete council blocks scar the landscape on the E side of this deprived neighbourhood, lying between the railway in the S and the Grand Union Canal in the N. You're still in the Royal Borough, though it's hard to tell. Dominating the skyline at the gateway to Kensal Town is 30-storey Trellick Tower. This grey concrete 1970s block is regularly singled out in opinion polls as one of the capital's biggest eyesores – from the outside. But residents enjoy spacious flats and stunning views, and modernist architects revere it: it was listed Grade II in 1999. Pevsner calls it 'unforgettable'. You either love these flats or hate 'em: agents say they sell readily. A 3-bed on the top floor was £330,000 last autumn – as it was the autumn before. However, most are still owned by the council or housing trusts.

The rest of Kensal is taken up by trading estates, workshops and industrial uses, mainly concentrated in **Kensal Rd**, with only a handful of private homes scattered about the neighbourhood – though there are signs of new flats developments being built. In **Southern Row**, just N of the railway, a big old Victorian corner boozer is now two vast flats and ground-floor offices. This corner is home to two splendid (and wonderfully-named) community gardens: Meanwhile Gardens and Emslie Horniman's Pleasance. On the W side of **Ladbroke Grove** alongside the railway line is the 1930s Kensal House complex. A big Sainsbury's just to the N.

However, the best news for this area is taking shape between railway and canal, on the 10-acre gas works site. Here the excellent Peabody Trust is building Ladbroke Green, a 'hi-tech urban village' of 308 homes (95 Affordable Homes, 109 for private sale, 104 shared-ownership, some in a 15-storey tower), plus live/work units and workshops, to a master plan by star architect Piers Gough. A restored canal basin will allow waterbus services through to Little Venice, and there will be residential moorings on the canal. Completion is set for 2005.

St Quintin Estate/Oxford Gardens

This neighbourhood, cut off to the S by the **Westway**, is as distinct in its way as Golborne to the E. Immediately N of the motorway lies the main concentration of family homes. Hundreds of 2- and 3-storey, red-brick terraced houses, built between 1890 and 1925, dominate the SW corner, in **Oxford Gardens, Highlever Rd, Balliol Rd, Finstock Rd, Kingsbridge Rd, Kelfield Gardens, St Helen's Gardens, Wallingford Avenue** and the W end of **Barlby Rd**. Most have reasonably sized front and rear gardens, and many of the streets are lined with trees. A 4-bed in Wallingford was £860,000 last autumn, the larger 5-beds can approach £1 million. Homes are cheaper towards the less-accessible north, and at the western end of **Oxford Gardens**, where they back onto the flyover.

Cutting through this enclave is **St Quintin Avenue**, a pleasant tree-lined street, popular despite being a main through-route between Scrubs Lane and Ladbroke Grove. Semi-detached houses stretch along the Avenue from the local shops in North Pole Rd. Halfway up on the N side is St Quintin Health Centre and Princess Louise Hospital for the Elderly. Behind the hospital lies Kensington Memorial Park: five acres of welcome public open space. **Oakworth Rd, Hill Farm Rd** and **Methwold Rd,** N of the park, have inter-war council homes: 2-storey brick houses and flats. Late-Victorian 3-storey brick-and-stucco terraces and 2-storey brick or painted pebbledash houses with timber porches appear at the N end of tree-lined **Highlever Rd.** More 2-floor/pebbledash homes stretch along the W end of **Barlby Rd** into **Dalgarno Gardens** (some split into flats) and **Pangbourne Avenue,** where homes on the W side back onto the West London Bowling Club (a smart 3-bed house here, £750,000). At this junction is modern **Blakes Close,** with Affordable Homes. To the W, but close to the motorway, **Bracewell Rd** has 4-bed houses.

An 11-acre site on the N side of **Barlby Rd** is now a massive council and housing-association estate of shared-ownership and rented low-rise flats and houses. The NW corner of the neighbourhood is dominated by the Peabody Trust flat blocks in **Dalgarno Way** and the Sutton Dwellings in **Sutton Way.** The latter flanks Little Wormwood Scrubs, a 22-acre recreation ground. Also along the N boundary are Barlby Rd railway sidings. At the NE end of Barlby Rd is **Barlby Gardens,** a small enclave of 2-storey houses set back off the road around a tiny green. Also here is Barlby Primary School. Between **Ladbroke Grove** and **Exmoor St** are the council's Treverton and Balfour/ Burleigh Estates – built to house returning servicemen from World War II. The estate is one of the most popular in North Kensington, with a long-standing, close-knit community. **Exmoor St** and **Hewer St,** between the two estates, have 2-storey, late-Victorian houses, mainly 3-bed. Hewer St boasts the Milk Studios, an open-plan office where freelances rent desk space: tenants range from novelists to property developers, and it's so popular that Milk Studios 2 is opening in Ladbroke Grove.

The main entrance to St Charles Hospital is in **St Charles Square,** which is half private homes and half housing association: 3-storey-and-basement brick-and-stucco semi-detacheds split into flats. Around the square are a Carmelite Monastery, the RC Sion-Manning Girls' School and St Charles 6th-Form College plus St Pius X Church.

The most sought-after homes in the neighbourhood lie S of the square in **Chesterton Rd, Bassett Rd** and **Oxford Gardens** (between St Helen's Gardens and Ladbroke Grove). They were designed for the first commuters when the Hammersmith and City line opened up North Kensington in the 1860s, linking it to the City.

N

Chesterton Rd has 4-storey Victorian terraced houses (an example was £1.3 million last autumn). The more expensive, leafier **Bassett Rd** has big 4-storey paired or detached brick-and-stucco houses with front gardens (£4 million was being asked for a 7-bed detached last winter). Many have been split into flats, some large: c. £700,000 for 2-bed, 2-bath, 2-floors; more ordinary 2-beds in these streets £450,000-plus. More large paired houses are found in **Oxford Gardens** and **Cambridge Gardens.** Properties here have front gardens and cherry trees line the former, bursting into a cascade of white blossom in spring. This is the best stretch of **Oxford Gardens,** with big flats and whole houses on offer. The E arms of both streets across Ladbroke Grove are more mixed, with council and housing-trust properties, and Cambridge Gardens as a whole is a bit close to the Westway for most tastes (it runs to the S). Off Cambridge Gardens is **Trinity Mews,** a 1988 clutch of live/work studios.

A handful of streets across to the E of Ladbroke Grove links architecturally with the neighbourhood, but these have little garden space. **Bonchurch St** and **St Michael's Gardens** S are both lined by 3-storey houses converted into flats. **St Lawrence Terrace** features high-Victorian rows, notably 3-storey brick houses with bands of stucco to give a striped effect.

Transport Tubes, all zone 2: Notting Hill Gate (Central, District, Circle); Holland Park (Central); Latimer Road, Ladbroke Grove, Westbourne Park (Hammersmith & City). From Notting Hill Gate: Oxford Circus 10 min, City 20 min, Heathrow 42 min (1 change).

Convenient for Kensington Gardens, West End, City, A40 to West, Paddington Station (Heathrow Express). BBC Centre. Miles from centre: 3.5.

Schools Local Authority: Holland Park, Sion Manning RC (g). Independent: Davies Laing & Dick, Colegio Español, St James (g), Southbank International.

SALES

Flats	S	1B	2B	3B	4B	5B
Average prices	175–250	190–450+	250–750+	300–1.3M+	700–1.4M	–
Houses	2B	3B	4B	5B	6/7B	8B
Average prices	450–1M+	575–1.9M+	650–2.75M	1–.254M	3M+	→

RENTAL

Flats	S	1B	2B	3B	4B	5B
Average prices	150–270	200–470	230–750	350–1000+	450–1400	550–1500+
Houses	2B	3B	4B	5B	6/7B	8B
Average prices	450–950	500–1400	600–1600	800–1900+	1500–2500	→

The properties Handsome Victorian terraces and paired villas characterize the area – as houses or split into flats – from the grand white crescents and rows at the Hill's top, through smaller brick/stucco streets, to the newly fashionable (and occasionally undone-up) roads down the Hill and in North Kensington, punctuated by council blocks. Mews cottages and ex-council homes add to the mix, and the price range. Note prices blurring as what was, say, 5-bed houses are now made 3-bed/3-bath.

The market Inhabitants are as mixed as the area: young people (rich and not-so-rich) buying the profusion of small flats; Far East investors, media millionaires, stars of screen and stadium, the more raffish kind of banker, diplomats. Affluent families are now well established in W11 (and the politer bits of W10). Cheapest homes in the NE part of North Kensington.

N

Among estate agents active in this area are:

- John Wilcox
- Savills
- Marsh & Parsons
- Bective Leslie Marsh
- John D Wood
- Townends
- Foxtons
- Faron Sutaria
- Winkworth
- Knight Frank
- Chesterton
- Granvilles
- De Groot Collis
- Jackson-Stops & Staff
- Bushells
- F W Gapp
- Barnard Marcus
- Property Fair
- Austin d'Arcy
- Boulle
- Bairstow Eves
- Brutens
- Anscombe & Ringland
- Powis Properties

PECKHAM

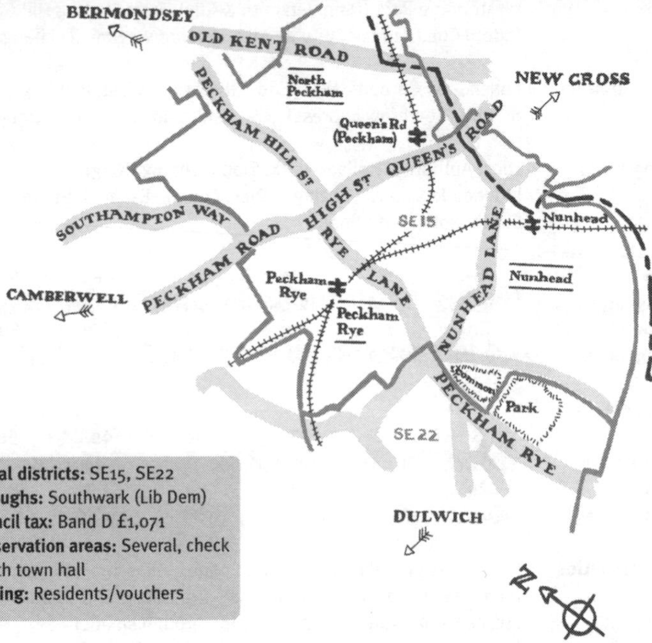

Postal districts: SE15, SE22
Boroughs: Southwark (Lib Dem)
Council tax: Band D £1,071
Conservation areas: Several, check with town hall
Parking: Residents/vouchers

Peckham could soon be the junction of two exciting new transport links – or it could remain, buses apart, one of the worst-served parts of inner London. All rests on Mayor Ken, or rather the state of his coffers. Will he raise the cash to get started on the Cross River Tram, which would run from Peckham to King's Cross, and the extension to the East London tube line (ELLX), which would link Peckham to Docklands?

As ever with transport schemes there is much talk but little certainty. The ELLX project has looked more firm since the govenment's deal on loan funding (see Transport chapter) but – there is always a but – the Peckham branch seems to be shunted into a siding in favour of the Croydon spur. As for the tram, who knows? As for timing, both would (of course) be ready in time for the London Olympics in 2012, should Paris be hit by a plague of giant snails.

Meanwhile there are buses, plenty of buses, headed by the No. 12 which trundles, briskly at that, through to the West End. And the trains are there if you look, though many people have a blind spot about the frequent 'Overground' services.

The congested and scruffy main road – Peckham Rd/High St/Queen's Rd – gives no hint of the two Peckhams. To the south, the original Georgian bone-structure of the Rye, its swathe of open green land shading off peacefully towards Dulwich. To the north, the brave new, brand-new world of enviable, attractive homes – to buy or rent – courtesy of a vast regeneration of what was once London's largest and grimmest council estate.

The late-Georgian village of Peckham bloomed into one of the original suburbs for rail-commuting clerks: the area was quickly carpeted by small streets of Victorian terraces. War damage and slum clearance lie at the root of the sharp contrast between north and south: the southern bit, Peckham Rye, survived. The north was rebuilt.

Sadly, North Peckham's towering 20th-century reincarnation proved an expensive mistake. By 1994, Southwark council had had enough. No cosmetic makeover here: at a cost of £290 million, they're in the final phase of knocking down 3,000 flats, replacing the grimmest blocks with 2,200 traditional houses and flats in good, old-fashioned London streetscapes. North Peckham's rejuvenation, now completing under the aegis of the Greater Peckham Alliance, is the largest urban renewal project in the UK and, it's been claimed, in Europe. Those few Victorian streets that had escaped the planners have seen their surroundings improve, and their position – just down the road from City and Docklands – reinforced. The local sink school has become a gleaming new City Academy.

Back to where we came in: older locals remember well the neat old terraced homes (called 'slums' then) that were razed. In place of the slabs and towers of the benighted council monoliths look for new, good-value homes to buy or to rent – and more, via housing associations, for shared ownership or at fair rents. The main seven-year programme is complete, and tree-lined new streets still remain graffiti-free in their neat, flowery front gardens. The last couple of tower blocks are staying: their makeover has won awards. They hold some of 1,500 homes being totally refurbished. This is not to deny the serious and stubborn problems, social and environmental, left by years of deprivation and mishandling here; but the will is there for things to change – and they are.

Next, turn southwards. Peckham Rye, across the high street and S of the railway, is a surprise: a mature, Georgian-rooted suburb opens up, sloping away round either side of a pleasant and picturesque common and park. Its pretty and spacious houses are sought by refugees from pricier tracts. Behind, respectable streets of solid homes set in green surroundings (more green spaces than many a more well-thought-of area) have more in common with Dulwich and Forest Hill, their neighbours to the W and SE, than they do with Peckham proper north of the tracks. Indeed, neighbourhood creep, whereby streets migrate silently into snazzier districts, is rife here: your Peckham Rye may well be the estate agents' East Dulwich, a confusion compounded by their shared postcode, SE22.

Prices here are held in a straightjacket by the Stamp Duty bands: the £250,000 ceiling has proved to be reinforced concrete in many a Peckham street, and it must be considered when assessing 'un-done-up' property.

Peckham

The traffic grumbles along uninspiring **Peckham Rd/High St/Queen's Rd** in a vain attempt to reach the A2 Dover Road. On either side, the north and central Peckham area extends to the **Old Kent Rd** in the NE, **Pomeroy St** to the E and **Southampton Way** to the W. The railway bridging **Rye Lane** forms the frontier with Peckham Rye to the S.

The northern border, along the route of the old canal, is the unexpected amenity of Burgess Park: a large green space, complete with lake, carved out of the slum streets over the last 35 years. **Trafalgar Avenue**'s big, handsome, flat-fronted, raised ground floor early-Victorian houses back onto the park's E end; £550,000 is a recent asking price for a 5-bed. **Glengall Rd** too has pairs of 1840s villas: upwards of £450,000 to c. £500,000 for 4- or 5-beds; £285–320,000 for smaller 3-beds, £180,000 for 2-bed converted flats.

These houses, worthy of Chelsea, and a few more modest parts of North Peckham, escaped both the Blitz and the post-war clearance: **Friary Rd** boasts some surviving late-Georgiana (pay c. £325,000 for a Grade II-listed double-fronted). **Kings Grove** has some roomy 3-storey flat-fronted houses for a bit less. Little Victorian terraces between the **Old Kent Rd** and **Queen's Rd** can be good value: 3-bed homes in **Elcot Avenue** are about £230,000 if tatty, £250,000 when smart. Streets between **Asylum Rd** and **Meeting House Lane** are similar, with houses and flat conversions; but **Clifton Crescent**'s listed homes sell for c. £230–350,000. **Asylum Rd** also holds some tiny old 1-bed almshouses, built for retired licensed victuallers (almshouses, especially with alcoholic connections, are a feature of Peckham). Very rarely, one appears for sale.

Newer homes include 2002-vintage Old Canal Mews, a gated corner by the park off **Nile Terrace** (a 2-bed, 2-bath flat, c. £250,000), a Victorian school converted to flats in

Gervase St, and six flats in an ex-pub in **Bird in Bush Rd** (1-bed, £145,000).

Homes for sale are now also to be found in the regenerating former municipal desert of North Peckham: 'Peckham Village' by developers including Laing and Copthorne has attractive houses and flats (resale 1-bed £155,000). On **Southampton Way**, Galliard's warehouse conversion 'South City Court' has 1–3 bed flats. Copthorne's 'South Quarter', across the way in **Blake's Rd** is now onto Phase Three: 23 1- and 2-bed flats, £160–265,000. The same street has Granville Square, with 2-bed flats at c. £160,000. And overlooking Burgess Park, by their award-winning housing association scheme, Laing's 'Renaissance' is 35 flats and houses with secure parking on **St George's Rd** (3-bed town-house £325,000). The same firm's 'Evolution' has 1- and 2-bed flats (£145,000-plus and £165,000-plus) and 3-bed town-houses from £260,000.

The E borders of Peckham, beyond Queen's Rd station, have some quiet if unexciting streets of Victorian terraces such as **Dayton Grove** and **Astbury Rd**: useful properties in a convenient and improving corner: an un-done-up house will be £210–230,000, a smart one up to £250,000. In **York Grove**, 'The Assembly' is a Victorian schoolhouse, now 40-odd 1- and 2-bed flats: 1-beds c. £180,000, 2-beds £230,000. To the S of Queen's Rd, and close to the station, in **Woods Rd** Kendrick Court is a pleasing modern block of 1- and 2-bed flats; Maple Mews has modern terraced houses. Running through to Evelina Rd, and thus close to Nunhead station as well, **St Mary's Rd** has early Victorian 3-bed houses on one side and larger Victoriana on the other; some have been split into flats (expect to pay £180,000 for a decent 2-bed).

Peckham High St, at its junction with **Rye Lane**, holds humdrum local shops and a mall, the revamped Aylsham Centre. The gleaming 'Peckham Pulse' (two pools and a leisure/fitness centre) is just across in **Melon Rd**. Alongside is the splendid new library in **Peckham Hill St**: this 'building to make you smile', as the judges put it, beat the London Eye and Canary Wharf's tube station to the top architecture award, the Stirling Prize. Now Peckham Town Square even boasts a Sunday-morning Farmers' Market. Plans for a development on the site of the timber yard in **Peckham Hill St**, dubbed 'Peckham Wharf', are on hold until the tram decision emerges.

Turn now S of the high street and W of **Rye Lane**, to the most interesting (and pricey) corner in this district. Check out the early-Victorian (estate agents, misled by the sober flat-fronted style, dub them Georgian) terraces and large detached houses in the conservation area centred on **Bellenden Rd**. The N end of Bellenden has handsome cottages, while in **Lyndhurst Way** some big 5- and 6-bed houses nudge £700,000; more for Grade II-listed homes (£950,000 has been asked, but that was some time back. . .), found here and in **Lyndhurst Square**. **Holly Grove**, too, has some fascinating early-Victorian houses: 4-beds for c. £420,000, while **Elm Grove** offers 5-bed double-fronted early-Victorian semis, and a terrace of 4-storey, 4-bed, c. £450,000, homes.

Highshore Rd has more large houses, plus gated **Oliver Mews**; also access, from here and **Elm Grove**, to the new flats that replaced the old market on **Rye Lane**. **Lyndhurst Square** is an interesting 1840s cul-de-sac of large-gardened houses (with half-million price-tags, as high as their gables) on Camberwell's borders. **Denman** , **Talfourd** and **Bushey Hill Rd**s, to the W, share the same leafy environment but have later-Victorian purpose-built maisonettes and large Victorian houses split into flats. As well as the nearby park and common, green spaces include Warwick Gardens, behind **Lyndhurst Grove**, the gardens in **Holly Grove** and in **Elm Grove**.

Peckham Rye

South of the station you move into Peckham Rye. First, discover **Choumert Square**, tucked away W of **Rye Lane**, for immaculate trellised rose gardens and tiny 1-bed houses: some of the smallest, but most desirable, in Peckham – often selling by word of mouth. Quantock Mews, 12 3-bed, 2-bath houses, has just been squeezed in behind: no gardens but close to station, £300,000 apiece (£25,000 less than last year' list price). **Choumert Rd** boasts almshouses, a vibrant street market at the E end, handsome mid-Victorian terraces, and now 'Choumert Mews', six attractive live/work units. **Choumert Grove** has gained a mosque with two modernistic minarets. **Blenheim Grove**, close to the station, has some converted 1-bed flats. The charming early-Victorian 2-bed cottages at this end of **Chadwick Rd** are £250,000-plus. New live/work houses by the surgery boast 4 beds.

Bellenden Rd curves S, enclosing a cache of small Victorian terraces W of the Rye and N of East Dulwich Rd. These include **Nutbrook St**, **Maxted Rd**, **Amott Rd** and **Ady's Rd** (where some are bigger than they look: good-value 5-beds). The houses in **Fenwick Rd** are larger still, 3-storey 1890s with big bays, 6-bed if whole – but many are flats. **Bellenden** has developed a little café culture: pavement tables, lively bars, coffee shops, deli and a new restaurant. In this corner, too, streets like **Nigel**, **Relf** and **Anstey Rds** benefited from a clear-sighted 1999 council-aided scheme to help renew roofs, windows, garden walls, fascia details: a smart Victorian streetscape re-emerged from scruffy, ill-maintained houses. Some mid-20th century terraces too amid the Victorian. New-build includes the popular Austins scheme on the Rye: 2-beds c. £225,000. Just up the road, the old Co-op is to go, with new housing and shops planned for the site.

Now to the heart of the area. As it goes S, **Rye Lane** suddenly widens and there – for all the world like some little market town – is a green (the Rye itself) surrounded by a cluster of shops and cafés. Then across East Dulwich Rd, Peckham Rye Common and Park open out in a sylvan, 18th-century sweep uphill to the S. **Peckham Rye** (the road) divides to run down either side of the common; the E side has some of the area's very few 1930s purpose-built flats (including ex-local authority ones). Here, too, some Georgiana has survived intact – with 100ft gardens to supplement the sweeping expanse of common they overlook. The 1930 'Jet' building has planning permission for conversion into 50 flats. Adjoining the common to the S is Peckham Rye Park, with gardens, playing fields, a bowling green and duck pond. Lottery money is financing an ongoing facelift for the park.

At its southern foot is the Park estate: first, streets of 1920/30s homes in **Colyton** and **Shelbury Rds** (these form the true Park estate, say local experts) with 3-beds going for c. £325–375,000. To the S, wonderfully named streets like **Mundania**, **Therapia** and **Marmora Rds** boast Victorian semis and a few detacheds with up to 7 beds: prices from £450–700,000 plus: a 7-bed, with a rumoured colourful past, was £750,000 last autumnn. Others have been split into spacious flats. Inhabitants cite their SE22 postcode and say that they're in (East) Dulwich, *really*. . . . This enclave is surrounded by greenery – walk over One Tree Hill and you're at Honor Oak Park station (tube extension here – eventually).

East of common and park, towards Nunhead, there are neat flat-fronted terraced houses in streets such as **Somerton Rd** and **Waveney Avenue**. Prices here are lower than on the W side of the common: £290–300,000 for a 3-bed house. Nearby **Carden Rd** and **Tresco Rd** offer early 19th-century 4-bed semis. Further N and further from the common – but closer to the station – **Consort Rd** has 3-bed ones. The Rye Hill Estate, originally council, is much privatized: for example 3-bed maisonettes in leafy grounds at c. £155,000. Streets in this corner include **Torridge Gardens** and adjoining **Limes Walk** with their roomy, low-rise houses and big 4-bed flats (c. £210,000). The Nunhead Estate of council-built flats (1930s brick blocks) also overlooks the common.

Nunhead

To the E of Peckham Rye is a quiet, tucked-away corner that spreads around the hilly slopes of romantic, overgrown Nunhead Cemetery and the adjacent park. Little 2- and 3-bed Victoriana run south off **Nunhead Lane** and **Evelina Rd**, which provide the busy main shopping streets. Nunhead has its own rail station – and nearby Queens Rd station may one day be on the extended tube; the 'villagey' local shops are an oft-cited asset – good bakery and famous fish shop included. The better properties are found to the S of **Evelina**

Rd on the Rye borders (see above). **Machell Rd** has tidy, flat-fronted, 19th-century cottages which fetch £180–220,000. Farriers Mews has modern town-houses: £325,000 for a 3-bed. The listed, 1930s Health Centre is nowadays 'The Pioneer Building': flats, town-houses with health club/pool (2-bed £250,000). Nunhead also has a fair turnover of ex-council houses. **Seldon Rd**, for instance, has unpretentious '60s 3-bed terraces. Ex-council 2-bed houses in **Daniels Rd** have magical views across to Westminster at the front, out over the leafy cemetery behind. The Linden council estate (**Linden Rd**) is being replaced by 121 flats and terraced houses, for council and housing-association tenants, some on shared-ownership. The old Camberwell Workhouse off **Gordon Rd** became flats in 1996. More modern flats – and a smart new gastro-pub – in **Nunhead Lane.**

The cemetery and allotments blanket the slopes of a little hill. Off **Borland Rd** at their foot is St James' 'Borland', 67 1-, 2- and 3-bed flats in contemporary style (from £200,000) in the peaceful triangle that spreads E from **Stuart Rd** towards Brockley. Streets like **Limesford** and **Harlescott Rds** have late-Victorian cottages; **Surrey Rd** added a new row of four 4-bed houses. **Lanbury Rd** has '30s cottage-style ex-council; the **Ivydale Rd/Kelvington Rd** corner has more (plus 3-bed period houses at c. £285,000). Here, too, are waterworks and a golf course. **Brenchley Gardens** bounds the area, from One Tree Hill up towards Brockley, with more council-built, and Victorian, homes in a green setting. Leafy **Brockley Mews**, well above the railway, is 1998 mews houses.

Transport Trains: Queen's Rd Peckham, Peckham Rye to London Bridge, Blackfriars, Victoria; Nunhead to Blackfriars, Victoria.

Convenient for Dulwich, Docklands, Miles from centre: 3.

Schools Local Authority: The Academy at Peckham, St Thomas the Apostle RC (b), Waverley (g), Private: see Dulwich chapter.

SALES

Flats	S	1B	2B	3B	4B	5B
Average prices	90–110	125–185	155–230	170–250	–	–
Houses	2B	3B	4B	5B	6/7B	8B
Average prices	200–270	200–300	220–330	300–550	500–800	–

RENTAL

Flats	S	1B	2B	3B	4B	5B
Average prices	120–150	140–195	175–250	195–275	–	–
Houses	2B	3B	4B	5B	6/7B	8B
Average prices	195–230	230–275	275–370	345–400	350–500+	–

The properties Peckham Rye has pleasant enclaves of Victorian/Edwardian (a few earlier) terraces and larger family homes – some Georgian. New flats join conversions and some '30s blocks. North Peckham is more mixed: new houses for sale and to let; some older terraces.

The market Young buyers discover new Peckham homes at sane (compared to Dulwich) prices. Nunhead coming up fast as buyers discover small, good ex-council houses and neat Victorian terraces.

Among estate agents active in this area are:

- Wooster & Stock
- Kinleigh Folkard Hayward
- Andrews & Robertson
- Winkworth
- Roy Brooks
- Burnet Ware & Graves
- Acorn
- Ludlow Thompson
- Bairstow Eves

PIMLICO AND WESTMINSTER

Postal districts: SW1
Boroughs: Westminster (Con)
Council tax: Band D £605
Conservation areas: Several covering most of area, check with town hall
Parking: Residents/meters everywhere; charging zone divides area

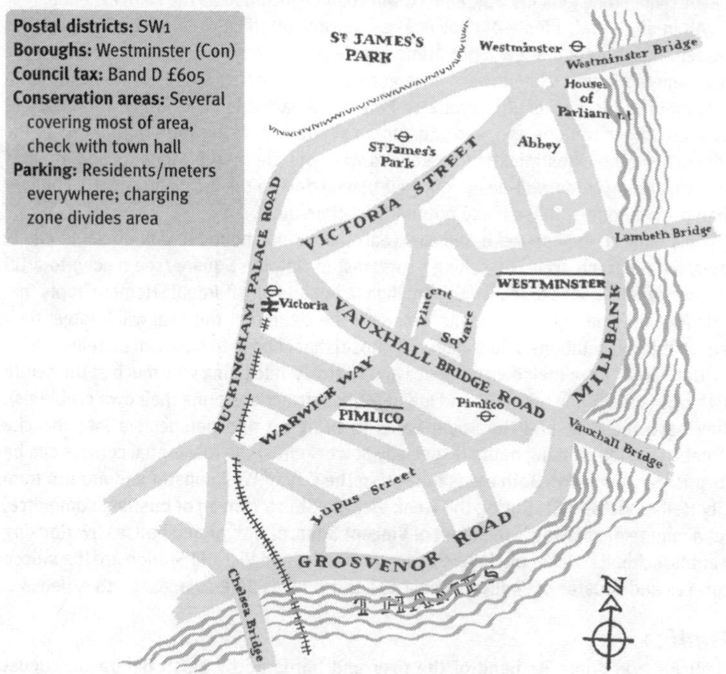

Pimlico can now be said to have finished its 30-year journey from joke (remember *Passport to Pimlico*? Roy Brooks's *Brothel in . . .* ?) to deep desirability. Its riverside is now lined with smart flats; inland, its peace is guarded by traffic management; its snowy stucco terraces – Belgravia, but cheaper – never (well, hardly ever) deserve the modifier 'peeling'. The new Sainsbury's adds the crucial retail, and Pimlico is a mine of really central flats or (and there's a few more of these than you'd think) family houses. There's scant space left for major new schemes – but how about a marina in Pimlico, with no fewer than 600 posh flats around it? St James Homes is providing just that, on the old council depot on the Grosvenor Canal in its SW corner, between Chelsea Bridge and the railway, just across the Embankment from the river. It's right on Chelsea's borders (though not, despite the marketing, in it: still, that *is* Chelsea – the Flower Show site – over the road). Work is under way: see below. Next in line will be Chelsea Barracks: its even bigger site also earmarked for homes – eventually.

Westminster, by contrast, has been a hive of activity in the past decade. It's still known far more for its grand institutional buildings than its homes, although a few Georgian gems remain (the glossy front door of its most famous residence, in Downing Street, gets more TV coverage than most. . .). However, the last time so many new homes were built here was during the Edwardian and '30s mansion-flats boom. Now many a block has been refurbished, others have moved from rental to sale. Much more scope here, too, for new developments: as the London market softened, the weight of new and refurbished units resulted in everything from price reductions to cashback deals, rental guarantees – and free scooters – by the end of last year: make 'em an offer. . . .

Those scooters were a response to the congestion-charge zone, which divides

P

Pimlico (out) from Westminster (in) along the Vauxhall Bridge Rd. It makes very little difference to prices: many, living so centrally, don't bother with a car – and in any case, if Mayor Livingstone gets his way, Pimlico will soon be included as the zone expands.

All in all, there's plenty of choice. The big wave of office-to-home conversions has passed, but there are a few more prime sites – particularly in **Marsham St**, where the government's brutal triple towers have gone at last. Another source of homes in both neighbourhoods is ex-council property. Pimlico, in particular, was firmly working class a couple of generations ago, and wide areas of public housing were built. Most of the homes owned by Westminster City Council were bought by their tenants and are now private, adding some well-designed, well-placed flats to the local choice. Still cheaper than period homes, these make popular first-time buys.

This balance may be redressed this year: the council hopes to pull off some equity release on a grand scale. By selling its interest in **Dolphin Square** (see below) to a US pension fund, it hopes to realise £130 million to put into an Affordable Homes charity that it will set up. The Square's tenants wonder if the claim that the deal will 'protect their reasonable expectations' and 'safeguard [those] that choose to stay' can be relied on.

Both areas have their own presence and charm. While being very much at the centre of things (a main-line terminus and major tourist attractions bring their own problems), they have the river and the Royal Parks to bring air and perspective into the city streets. Outside working hours (especially at weekends) the residential corners can be surprisingly peaceful. Both areas fall within the City of Westminster and are run from City Hall in **Victoria St**. During the week Victoria St is a canyon of bustling commerce, yet a minute or so away is the quiet of **Vincent Square**, with period houses overlooking a public school's cricket pitch. And a few streets beyond Victoria Station are the stucco terraces and squares of Pimlico. Almost as handsome as Belgravia; a lot less expensive.

Pimlico

Pimlico, tucked into its bend of the river and bordered by plush Belgravia, august Westminster and smart Chelsea, remained for a long time remarkably unknown. The social mix of the community changed as, in the course of the 1980s, a nearly all tenanted, rather run-down district became a place of converted flats and the first few smart developments. The latest rash of new homes – building and planned – has put the seal on the transformation.

This is MP land, full of politicians' pieds-à-terre or main homes within the division bell boundary – the zone close enough to the House for them to rush from dinner, or whatever, when there's a vote. **Cambridge St** is a typical 'little Westminster': at one count, 25 MPs had homes there (a studio flat, £195,000; a 2-bed, £325,000). They are joined by City people who love the central location and good transport: there's Victoria, and you're never more than ten minutes' walk from one of the tube stations.

Pimlico used to be part of the Grosvenor Estate, like Belgravia. Thomas Cubitt, the estate's architect and builder, laid out the handsome terraces, wide, straight streets and regular squares. The land was open, marshy and used for market gardens and pasture. In order to raise the level above Thames floods Cubitt, with typical ingenuity, brought thousands of tons of gravel and earth up by barge from St Katharine's Dock, which he happened to be excavating at the same time. If your Pimlico cellar is damp, remember that it's sitting at original marsh level.

Pimlico may look superficially like Belgravia – lots of snowy Regency stucco, classical detailing and regularity – but it was never *quite* as smart. Even in its first flush of youth, it was second-rank: one of Trollope's heroines is advised by a worldly friend to avoid 'anywhere beyond Eccleston Square'. During most of the 20th century its tall terraces were the province of the house clumsily divided into bedsits, the shared bathroom, the small hotel. The Grosvenor Estate sold off the whole area in the

1950s, preferring to concentrate on Belgravia and Mayfair (it was said this was to pay death duties, but some maintain that the Duke of Westminster was fed up with his name coming up in court cases about brothels – another use the enterprising had found for these big houses). It was only in the 1972/3 property boom, which coincided with the opening of Pimlico's Victoria Line tube station, that Pimlico began to be 'discovered'. The tall old homes began to convert into smarter flats, and Pimlico slowly started to change. The process was helped (some would claim hindered) by the council's pioneering scheme to ban through-traffic. The place is a maze of one-way streets, blocked-off cul-de-sacs and residents' parking bays, and thus remains remarkably peaceful – a place apart, despite being so central.

An average Pimlico property today is a big, stucco terraced house split into flats of varying sizes and sophistication, but usefully including some small, pied-à-terre-sized ones. Family houses exist – well-informed local agents reckon families are 30 per cent of the market – but this is primarily apartment land. The network of streets at Pimlico's heart ('The Grid') are predominantly Cubitt terraces: **Clarendon**, **Cambridge**, **Alderney** and **Sutherland Sts**, for example, and **Gloucester**, **Winchester**, **Sussex**, the **Moretons** and the **Westmorelands**; here you can pay £300,000-plus for, say, a 2-bed garden flat, £950,000 plus for a 4/5-bed house (in **Alderney St**, £1.35 million for 'the finest for sale for some years'). Even here there are gaps in the stucco and brick, often caused by wartime bombs, filled at various times by small and often ugly flats blocks. These are less admired ('quite unpleasant' remarked one agent) than period conversions.

Other exceptions are the mews cottages both behind the squares and terraces, and, occasionally, on the main roads: **Clarendon St** has a few such. Look for the cobbled, sloping charm of **Warwick Square Mews**; **St George's Square** also has its mews, and **Moreton Terrace** boasts two: **North** and **South**. Modern mews houses in **Charlotte Place**, off **Wilton Rd**: a 2-bed one in this gated scheme, £700,000.

Some houses survived the mania for conversion: try **Cambridge** and **Alderney Sts** – or **Westmoreland Terrace**, where prices last winter indicate condition/luxury level far more than size: one, unmodernized, £695,000; another, newly refurbished, £1.375 million.

For new-build, turn to **Buckingham Palace Rd**, 'only 600 metres from Sloane Square' (but also the multi-lane highway from Victoria Station), which bounds the area to the N, where Berkeley has added Consort Rise: 93 1- to 3-bed flats – plus gym, business centre and parking; a 3-bed, £625,000 last winter. On **Wilton Rd**, the new Sainsbury's (very upmarket) brought flats, completed last year, in its wake: 79 for sale, plus 81 Affordable Housing ones for rent/shared ownership, known collectively as Pimlico Place.

Pimlico is short of open space, though there's Ranelagh Gardens over on the Chelsea side and the splendid (if rather more public) St James's Park on the other. So the three large garden squares have long been its most desirable addresses – apart from the riverside flats. The big houses in the squares convert readily into spacious flats. The elegant stucco terraces surrounding the gardens make **Eccleston Square**, **Warwick Square** and **St George's Square** hugely attractive – in that order. A 2-bed flat in Eccleston, 'in need of complete modernization', was £465,000 last winter. While the first two squares have private gardens, those of St George's and of **Bessborough Gardens** are both open to the public. **St George's Square** has some interesting recent conversions, and lots of tiny flats and maisonettes; prices vary widely – one 2-bed, £325,000, but you can pay double. Look, too, for houses in cobbled **St George's Square Mews**, tucked behind.

The first new London square to be created since the war, **Bessborough Gardens** is part of the Crown's Millbank Estate. The gardens (locked at night) have a fountain in honour of the Queen Mother's 80th birthday. The L-shaped terrace surrounding the garden on two sides is classic Cubitt: the smooth stucco finish, decorative iron-work balconies, the mouldings of windows and pillared doorways . . . or so you might think: but these rows didn't exist until the late 1980s. The Wimpey-built replacements of war- and flood-damaged terraces for the Crown provided a great cache of new flats, from studio to 3-bed penthouses (a 2-bed, £450,000 last winter). The detailing inside matches the exterior, and on occasion the sales team had trouble convincing buyers that the apartments really were just built.

Much more development has since followed on the Crown Estate: next door to Bessborough Gardens, and sharing its entrance in **Drummond Gate**, is **Lindsay Square** which has 29 smart town-houses (life here can give you a 4-bed/3-bath/garage/patio house, with 24-hour porterage and communal gardens to boot). In **Balvaird Place**, just opposite the tube, are another 40 town-houses with garages.

The main road along the riverside is **Grosvenor Rd**; it does not hug the embankment, and wherever it bends slightly away a smart waterside development has been squeezed in. Imaginative, 1980s Crown Reach, with its cleverly staggered, balconied riverside and, inland, sweeping gull's-wing roofs, lies just W of Vauxhall Bridge: a 2-bed with roof terrace was £650,000 last winter. The 22-storey office tower at the corner by the bridge is now The Panoramic – accurate enough as a name. It now holds 88 flats ranging in size from studios right through to a glorious 2-storey penthouse (a 5th-floor 2-bed, £685,000).

Other plush and pricey waterfront blocks include River Lodge, parked on a narrow site almost in front of Dolphin Square, and St George's Wharf (not the current Vauxhall one), which appeared in 1990. These have been joined by the Belvederes, with 43 flats and penthouses. The list goes on: another 40 at Eagle Wharf – plus a 4-bed-and-home-cinema, 4,250 sq ft house: 'the ultimate bachelor pad', apparently, for which someone wants £4.25 million. The very stylish Icon has just 14 very large flats, completed 2001.

Further W, the new Grosvenor Waterside site: 600 1- to 4- bed homes gathered around the old dock – the first phase was launched late in 2003 with 1-beds from £350,000, 2-beds from £450,000, and completes this spring (2005); the latest release ranges from £365–2,200,000. St James christened all this Grosvenor Dock (ducal connections do no harm), then rechristened it Grosvenor Waterside (it promises not to change the name again) though 'Chelsea's new quarter' sure is new – in the sense that it, er, isn't in Chelsea at all. Well, it worked for Chelsea Harbour (in Fulham). Behind that, and even bigger, Chelsea Barracks will become a whole new neighbourhood – one day. Between the two sites, locals in Peabody's Ebury Bridge flats hope for a supermarket to compensate for the years of disruption to come.

Inland, **Lupus St** runs E–W, a wide, busy road paralleling **Warwick Way**, the other main cross-route to the N. At the W end of Lupus St is the **Churchill Gardens** Estate, a tidy, modern square of well-built blocks (many with splendid river views) built by Westminster City Council, but now mostly in private hands and popular first-time buys or rental investment: a 2-bed flat in Blackstone House, £240,000. Here, too, are local shops (and estate agents). At the E end, the splendidly uncompromising modern lines of Pimlico School are reticent in one respect only: the mass of the 'glass school', as it is known, stands amid its playground considerably below the level of the surrounding streets. A plan to redevelop the site with a new school plus flats was defeated, but at time of writing the school is closed temporarily due to worries over some of the glass.

Beyond rises the red-brick mass of **Dolphin Square** – an extraordinary institution. A huge 1930s flats scheme, (the biggest in Europe when built), its 1,200 flats set round a 3-acre garden are half rented, half privately owned. The non-profit-making Dolphin Square Trust holds a long lease (from Westminster Council) and can decide who rents there and for how much – resulting in a splendid community of those working anti-social hours: from chefs and waiters via the entertainment world to MPs. You must own no other home in London, must make the Square your main home and work in Central London. Fit the bill and you will pay between £241–398 a week for a 1- or 2-bed (larger flats, and studios, have a waiting list), including heating, hot water, service charge. It has its own shops, garage, pool and restaurant. All this is under threat, though: see introduction, above.

To the E along **Vauxhall Bridge Rd** are the low-built, dark-red-brick steps of **Lillington** and **Longmoore Gardens**, with their roof gardens, third-storey trees and green-edged terraces: council-built; better looking (and better built) than many a private development. Lots are now privately owned and are popular investments: a 2-bed, £275,000. On **Peabody Avenue** and the wonderfully named **Turpentine Lane**, and further E towards Vauxhall Bridge Rd, are two Peabody Trust estates of rented flats.

Behind Lillington Gardens the irregular meander taken by **Tachbrook St**, which contrasts with Cubitt's orderly grid, betrays its earlier origins. This is Pimlico's village high street, complete with not only shops, but also a thriving, much-prized street market. To its W lies **Belgrave Rd**, a main through-route to Victoria: still full of cheap hotels, slowly changing as more of these are converted to flats – and hotel consent is not being renewed when leases expire. To the N it joins **Warwick Way** (once a track through the marshes); across it, work has begun on new shops and flats in the **Upper Tachbrook St/Vauxhall Bridge Rd** triangle. North again, by Victoria Station, Laing's new Pimlico Place is 79 flats and duplexes (a 2-bed here, £490,000; another, £625,000) atop Sainsbury's in **Wilton Rd**; the sale of these subsidised the building of the 81 social homes for sale or rent in Pimlico Village, a £55 million mixed development by Network Housing Group. These much-needed affordable homes became available in September.

Westminster

Westminster is first and foremost the seat of Parliament and the Civil Service. However, the choice has widened remarkably in this surprisingly overlooked area, with homes new, refurbished or converted: take 'The View', in **Palace St**, a 40-year-old tower block becoming 123 large flats, completing autumn 05, from £310–1,200,000 .

Tucked away in side roads there are homes that can be peaceful, considering their centre-hub position; the most plentiful are the mansion blocks whose brickwork echoes the Roman Catholic cathedral. But there are also, by contrast, modern flats, a few neat terraced homes and a little cache of unsuspected Georgiana. And the past few years have seen **Vincent Square** re-emerge as a residential neighbourhood, its houses catching up, even passing, those of Pimlico's Grid.

Westminster the place – as opposed to the borough – starts across the **Vauxhall Bridge Rd** from Pimlico, and runs up to St James's Park in the N. The stretch between the park and the river is home mainly to the ministries of this or that along Whitehall. **Downing St** boasts only temporary accommodation: sheltering, strictly for their terms of office, the Prime Minister and the Chancellor of the Exchequer. You can, though, now live in **Whitehall** without being elected: recent 2-bed flats at No. 25. Between the riverside and Whitehall is the only other exception: the fantastical turrets of **Whitehall Court**, built 1884, where you can pay a very long price for a very short lease; views of river and the Changing of the Guard. Some flats are enormous – up to five bedrooms.

Mansion flats (and again, some can be house-sized) are the staple form of the homes that lie between the main through-road, **Victoria St**, and St James's Park. Vandon Court's in **Petty France**, for example, range from studios upwards. Berkeley's 2003 refurb of a 52-flat Edwardian block in **Matthew Parker St**, 'The Parliamentarian', had 2-bed resales for £390,000 and £450,000 last winter. Half of Artillery Mansions, on **Victoria St**, was extensively done up in 1999 to create 174 flats around fountained courtyards: Phase 2 is under way. Gladstone Court in **Regency St** is four red-brick blocks round a courtyard: Regalian's 1988 conversion. Regency Court is a modern 6-storey block; two other small schemes added flats and houses (a 2-bed, £645,000) in the same street.

This corner has hidden delights, though: glorious **Queen Anne's Gate**, where the stately houses date from the reign of that monarch and are steadily reverting from offices to homes, and **Old Queen St** – what an address – where a 7-storey house was £4.65 million last winter. Near Victoria lies tiny, hidden **Victoria Square**: its homes date from

1838. And a stone's throw from the Palace, **Strafford Place** has a couple of 1800 houses.

But the bulk of Westminster's homes lie S of **Victoria St.** Again, at the end nearest the station Edwardian mansion flats are the norm, though the first ultra-smart 1980s block was built in **Artillery Row. Morpeth Terrace** and **Carlisle Place** are typical of this corner, both lined with similar red-brick mansion blocks. Inside, the flats are impressive: large rooms, high ceilings; entrance halls with shining wood panelling and crusty uniformed porters. Winston Churchill lived in Morpeth Mansions in the '30s; now you can: his two-floor apartment, with 3 beds, 3 receptions – and Winston's study – are yours for £2 million. In **Ashley Gardens** 32 flats in one mansion block were refurbished and sold to 'traditional British buyers' – perhaps the great-grandsons of the Empire types who originally rented these flats to be near the Army & Navy Stores and their clubs (a big 3-bed/2-bath, £1.25 million; a 2-bed needing work, £520,000). Past Strutton Ground's street market is a cache of recent homes with, enviably hereabouts, garaging: the Crown Estate's 1- and 2-bed flats and penthouses in **Old Pye** and **Abbey Orchard Sts**. Here, too, within a mitre's toss of Westminster Abbey are 1900s yellow-brick blocks of Peabody flats. In **Marsham St**, Marsham Court is one of the best-known of the 1930s blocks: a short walk from the House means that MPs queue for these convenient mansion flats.

At last **Marsham St**'s three grotesquely hideous government towers that used, unbelievably, to house the Department of Environment are gone, reinstating the scale in the heart of residential Westminster. Accessed from **Monck St** behind, Galliard's New Palace Place adds 98 new 1- to 3-bed flats to the area, in a row of blocks with parking: 75 per cent sold by Christmas 2003; a year on, 3-beds still left are from £695,000 (plus cashback, rent guarantees. . .). Completing May. Opposite will be the new Home Office (lower, if not beautiful). Similar deals on the **Marsham St** side, where Galliard have refurbished the mansion flats of Romney House: £350–795,000.

St John's Gardens, in the angle of Marsham St and Horseferry Rd, has seen many new flats. Westminster Green, just completing, adds another 176 (2-beds from £420,000, penthouses £825–2,600,000), while Berkeley's Neville House has 71 1–3-bed flats, 2–4-bed duplexes, from £346,000). In nearby **Page St** is the chequerboard frontage of the listed, Luytens-designed Grosvenor Estate flats, built as affordable housing between the wars: some flats are rented, others leased. The whole estate, which includes the Edwardian red-brick Regency Estate, is well run by a Grosvenor team.

Albeit tree-lined, street succeeds street until, crossing Rochester Row, the vast green rectangle of **Vincent Square** surprisingly opens up. Some houses are lucky enough to overlook this open space – larger than Belgrave Square – used as a playing field by the boys of Westminster School. Watching the summer cricket is an increased population of square-dwellers – many new homes have been added here over the past few years, and the original houses can reach £2 million. In **Vincent St** Barratt's The Regency has added a further 155 flats and three 3-bed houses; a classic, pretty 3-bed brick-and stucco house in this street, £1.2 million. Next, the old Rochester Row police station is to become yet another 70 homes – 21 for key workers – courtesy of Fairbriar.

Between Vincent Square and Horseferry Rd is **Maunsel St**, a pretty terrace of brick cottages with gardens. **Greycoat St** has several flats blocks. Barratt's The Exchange adds 40 flats, studios to 3-beds with parking and concierge, on the congestion-zone side of **Vauxhall Bridge Rd**; here, too, Charles Church has built yet more, from £310,000 – marketed, despite being in Westminster, as Pimlico Apartments.

It is towards Westminster Abbey that the oldest buildings are found. These include the Georgian gems of **Smith Square, Lord North St** and surrounding streets. Some have been lost, some serve other purposes (i.e. the Conservative Central Office), but a few are still enviable homes. **Barton St** and **Cowley St**, for instance, have houses (one or two with garages . . .), and there's a row of little Victorian cottages, plus larger homes, in **Gayfere St**. You feel secure round here: always plenty of police on patrol.

The other source of Westminster homes can be found in the corner towards Vauxhall Bridge. En route, in **John Islip St**, are Millbank Court's convenient 1960s flats: high ones get river views; prices from c. £220,000 for a 1-bed. The far end of **John Islip St**, and the streets round it in the angle of the river and **Vauxhall Bridge Rd**, form the Westminster side of the Crown's Millbank Estate. Neat terraced houses line **Ponsonby Place** and **Ponsonby Terrace**; with beautiful converted flats in the river-facing white stucco **Millbank** terraces. They are a mixture of fair-rent homes and others available, when they come up, on long leases.

Transport Tubes, all zone 1: Pimlico (Victoria); Victoria (Victoria, District, Circle); Westminster (Jubilee, Circle, District), St James's Park (Circle, District). From Victoria: Oxford Circus (5 min), City (20 min), Heathrow 1 hr (1 change). Trains: Victoria to Gatwick.

Convenient for West End and City; South Bank, government, airports. Docklands via Jubilee Line. Miles from centre: 1.5.

Schools Local Authority: Pimlico School, Grey Coat Hospital C of E (g). Private: Francis Holland (g), Westminster School (b), The American International School.

SALES

Flats	S	1B	2B	3B	4B	5B
Average prices	130–200	180–350	240–500	300–1M	→1M	–
Houses	2B	3B	4B	5B	6/7B	8B
Average prices	420–700	500–900	650–1M	800+	1M+	–

RENTAL

Flats	S	1B	2B	3B	4B	5B
Average prices	170–250	250–400	250–500+	500+	→1000	–
Houses	2B	3B	4B	5B	6/7B	8B
Average prices	500–800	600–900	800+	800+	–	–

The properties Pimlico has snowy Regency stucco terraces, now mainly flats; mews cottages; p/b flats in ultra-mod or repro schemes, and ex-council. Westminster has mainly mansion flats (some very large), plus a few 19th-century and Georgian houses: look here for new schemes and conversions. Quality, though, varies widely depending on vintage: Pimlico's rise from down-at-heel bedsit land to high fashion began back in the 1970s.

P

The market Young professionals can buy or rent here; also MPs and pied-à-terre seekers. Prices have fallen, and seem good value compared to SW London suburbs and other central areas. Investors favour good-quality ex-council homes in Pimlico, and new flats. Surprising number of family buyers in Pimlico: 30 per cent of the market.

Among estate agents active in this area are:

- Tuckerman
- Dauntons
- Knight Frank
- Bensons
- John D Wood
- Winkworth
- Hamptons
- Chesterton
- Savills
- Jackson Stops & Staff
- Douglas & Gordon
- Moretons
- Best Gapp & Cassells
- Barringtons
- DTZ Residential

POPLAR

Postal districts: E14
Boroughs: Tower Hamlets (Lab)
Council tax: Band D £1,008
Conservation areas: Include York Square, Naval Row
Parking: Restricted

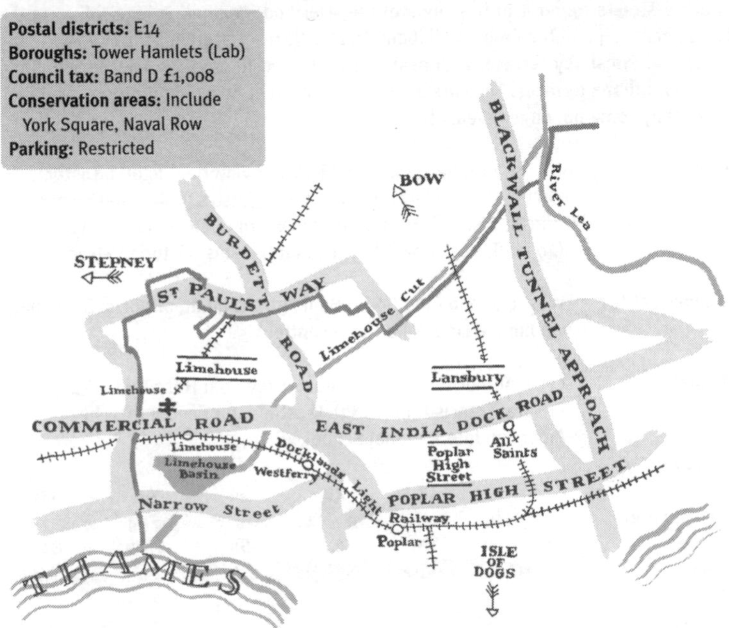

As Docklands becomes a historical episode rather than a place, the old neighbourhoods re-emerge – and Poplar is an area once more, back to its roots as a village around its inland High Street. Once a hamlet, Poplar grew in 1817 into a parish and took in the Isle of Dogs and Blackwall. The docks came, and with them tens of thousands of workers. From 1900 to 1964 Poplar blossomed as a proud, if prickly, borough – although World War II and its savage East End bombings left but half the population and few indeed of the buildings.

Then came the 1980s, London Docklands Development Corporation and the Isle of Dogs Enterprise Zone. The Docklands revolution changed more than the economy and population of London's East End. It changed the names, too. Much of Poplar's territory was lost: its own name became little used as the incoming residents of the mushrooming new Docklands developments (see Docklands chapter) said that they lived 'on the Isle of Dogs' or 'at Limehouse'. The West India Docks once formed a boundary to the S; today the frontier is the new highway of Aspen Way, which funnels traffic in and out from the City via the Limehouse Tunnel. South of Aspen Way the ever-expanding Canary Wharf fills the skyline with its towers.

Although the greater proportion of homes in traditional Poplar and Limehouse, N of 'Docklands', were built by the council at a less-than-lovely point in architectural history, now the place is a-buzz with construction – and this time it's not smart schemes for City whizz-kids. The refurbishment since 1997 of the many blocks of flats is spreading through the area, under the HARCA (Housing and Regeneration and Community Association) Estate Renewal Challenge Fund. Poplar HARCA has done excellent work on the estates: this makes quite a difference to the feel of the place, especially in areas like **Selsey St** and **Thomas Rd** (see below). Quite a few flats have been bought by their tenants in the last decade, and these now appear on the market, offering bargain alternatives to the gleaming new world to the S (dealt with fully in the Docklands chapter.)

Attention is now turning to the Lea Valley to the E, where there's plenty of land, plus canal- and riverside sites. And Stratford, East London's important new hub, is just to the N.

Poplar and Limehouse are within two miles of the City of London. With no tube station in the vicinity – Bromley-by-Bow and Mile End are the nearest – the area relies on the Docklands Light Railway (DLR). Limehouse, Westferry, Poplar and All Saints stations provide a regular service to Stratford (interchanges with trains and tube – and soon Eurostar), Bank, and the Royal Docks (plus, late this year, the City Airport) to the E. And the DLR also connects, at Canary Wharf, with the Jubilee Line, offering a fast route to Waterloo and the West End.

Poplar is the cheapest part of the East End to fall within transport zone 2. Watch out, though, when looking at property details, for the E14 postcode: it covers both Poplar and the Isle of Dogs. Poplar and Limehouse are bordered by Bow to the N, the Isle of Dogs to the S and Stepney to the W. To the E of Poplar is the Blackwall Tunnel Northern Approach road (now the A12, a motorway no more). East India Dock Rd is the area's main thoroughfare. The enormous (and expensive) road-building programme linked to the Docklands regeneration has given the area several new roads: ensure your street map is up to date. The main highway is the Aspen Way E–W dual carriageway from the City via Limehouse Tunnel, on across the S edge of Poplar, then over a new bridge across the River Lea to the Royal Docks; N–S is the Blackwall Tunnel Approach Rd, and a fast link out of town via the M11. This lot has eased the chaos on the East India Dock Rd.

The docks were the main source of employment, Poplar's *raison d' etre*, until the 1960s, and a large part of the fascinating history of Poplar and Limehouse. The area includes six conservation areas – **York Square** close to the border with Stepney, St Anne's Church, St Matthias Church, All Saints Church, **Naval Row** and **Narrow St**. One of Poplar's attractions is lively **Chrisp St** market, which is part of the Lansbury Estate. It is one of the more appealing parts of Poplar, with a true small-town atmosphere. Sadly the restaurants of Chinatown are now for the most part a distant memory.

Taken as a whole Poplar stills feels poor: there is a big contrast between marble-clad Canary Wharf on the skyline and the scruffy shops and council flats of Poplar.

Poplar

The Lansbury Estate, which includes **Chrisp St** market, constitutes Poplar's commercial centre. The Estate, built in the early '50s, comprises much of the district to the N of the busy East India Dock Rd. Apart from the market and shopping area, there's a good health centre, a contemporary-styled new library ('The Ideas Store') and the Emery Theatre. **Duff St**, **Grundy St**, **Susannah St** and **Ida St** have much-improved terraced ex-council houses. Houses in **Bygrove St**, N of Grundy St, are split into maisonettes and flats with roof gardens. Some of the newer town-houses and terraced homes in **Brabazon St**, **Carmen St** and at the N end of **Chrisp St** have been bought by their owners and improved. So, too, have flats in 4-storey blocks and terraced houses with attractive small gardens in **Giraud St**, and flats and maisonettes in **Hobday** and **Cordelia Sts**. Tower block ex-council flats can offer a lot for your money: a 4-bed split level flat was £185,000 last winter.

Quite a lot is happening on the Lansbury Estate: houses and flats in **Broomfield St** have been refurbished; Swan Housing Association has built 35 flats opposite **Market Square**; Busbridge House in **Brabazon St** has been modernized. In total contrast to all the social housing, **Fawe St** has 2,500 sq ft flats in an old factory, complete with 20ft ceilings, two bathrooms and exposed brickwork (£350,000 for a penthouse last winter).

To the W of the Lansbury Estate, the towering St Mary's & St Michael's Roman Catholic Church, opposite Mayflower Primary School, is flanked by more terraced ex-council houses in **Canton St** and **Pekin St**: these take their names from the nearby area once known as Chinatown. North, close to the canal, is Bartlett Park, a rare stretch of greenery and the heart of a 'Regeneration Area' with over a dozen homes schemes building or planned. Here you'll find Abbotts Wharf, off **Stainsby Rd**, a big development by Telford Homes set – a nice idea – around a canal-boat marina. One-bed flats from £180,000 here. In the same street new 2-bed flats, views over the park to Canary Wharf, are c. £225,000. Just to the W, new flats in **Pelling St** are now complete. Here, too, a newly completed school conversion, Old School Mews. Next comes Wimpey's 78 1- and 2-bed flats at Lockson's Wharf on **Broomfield St**.

Down at the S end of Chrisp St, on the S side of East India Dock Rd, is the DLR's All Saints station. The station sits between the two conservation areas of All Saints Church and St Matthias Church. The grounds of All Saints are overlooked by some of Poplar's most desirable, and priciest, private homes: imposing 3- and 4-storey Victorian terraced houses in **Newby Place** and **Mountague Place**. Similar (but cheaper: £400,000-ish) houses can be found to the W in **Woodstock Terrace**, which also has 2-bed Victorian cottages. These face the very well-tended, and well-used, Poplar recreation ground, which houses Poplar Bowls Club's green, and the entrance to St Matthias. In **Hale St**, overlooking the recreation ground, the 1890s Mission to Seamen – a splendid piece of neo-Jacobean red-brick – has become 'York House': a dozen smart flats. On **East India Dock Rd** itself All Saints Apartments is a new block by Westray Homes, while more flats are under way by Furlong Homes: 'Fusion' at **Susannah St** has 86 flats (1-and 2-beds).

South of Woodstock Terrace and Newby Place lies **Poplar High St**, with council flats on each side. The area along the High St has gained from the road-building to the S: it is quieter, and an increasingly desirable place to be. The refurbished council flats of the Will Crooks Estate and the new Tower Hamlets College (very high standards) are among local successes. Next to the college is the Workhouse Leisure Centre, opened in 1999. The Church Housing Association owns much of the S side of the street, but there are 24 new flats in a gated scheme in **Stoneyard Lane**, close to Poplar DLR station. One-beds, ex-council, start at £160,000; two-beds here are around £205,000.

On eastwards, beyond the Blackwall Tunnel highway in its cutting, is **Naval Row**, another conservation area. Pre-war flats here have been modernized: 2-beds go for c. £185,000 (same as a year ago). Near the Blackwall Tunnel entrance, Copthorn Homes added some flats and houses.

The grim slabs of the Stalinist 1968-vintage **Robin Hood Lane** flats loom over the Tunnel approach, unloved by all but a few modernist architects (though even the Editor of the RIBA Journal, to her credit, said it's cruel to ask people to live in them). They do offer a cheap flat within a stroll of Canary Wharf: £100–120,000 for a 2-bed. Further N, the motorway is flanked to the W by the still-run-down Teviot Estate: some of the blocks have been demolished, to be replaced by new Housing Association homes. Of the survivors **Daniel Bolt Close**, with its '60s-built 3-storey terraced houses, is popular with buyers. Another survivor is **Balforn Tower**, one of Mr Goldfinger's (the architect, not the villain) monsters, a twin to his Trellick Tower, North Kensington, where 2-bed split-level flats are c. £120,000. **Bright St**, **Byron St**, **Burcham St** and **Hay Currie St** are dominated by Langdon Park School and a sports centre and social club. A new DLR station, Langdon Park, is planned (but not yet scheduled) to serve this area and the new scheme E of the motorway (see below).

A redundant church in **St Leonard's Rd** has become St Michael's Court, a clutch of 34 smart flats – including a very desirable one in the church tower. A 1-bed flat here was £155,000 late last year. Opposite, on the edge of Langdon Park, are a dozen new houses. Further up St Leonard's Rd a pub has become six flats. These, together with the former church conversion, form what could be a pleasant group. East of St Leonard's Rd, **Mills Grove** has modern 2-bed terraced houses.

'Poplar Riverside' has a smart, even romantic, ring to it – but perhaps less so when the river in question is the Lea, not the Thames. This is the name for a 350-homes, hotel and commercial scheme E of the motorway, organized by the Leaside Regeneration Partnership. So far, the only result is the restoration of the Victorian Poplar Library, in **Gillender St**, which is now business units with six live/work-homes round a courtyard. Next (by the end of 2005) comes a new foot/cycle bridge across the Lea which will link the neighbourhood to Canning Town station (Jubilee Line/DLR). The reclassification of the motorway as the A12 means that pedestrian crossings can be added, letting people avoid the much-detested subways. This area certainly needs help: around here are some of Poplar's worst properties, and one recent visitor described the tract as 'desperately bleak'. However there's progress: the flats in Oban House, **Oban St**, have been refurbished, and there's a development of 14 1-, 2- and 3-bed flats for shared ownership in **Blair St**. Both streets also have open-market terraced houses, and in **Athol Square** Wharf View Court, a modern development, has 2-bed flats and 2-bed houses. South of the East India Dock Rd, the area round Saffron Avenue has been comprehensively redeveloped, with a Travelodge hotel and a big cinema.

In the N of the area, **St Paul's Way** provides the boundary with Bow. The steady work on local council-built homes continues on the Burdett Estate, which stretches S to Limehouse Cut through **Wallwood St, Burgess St, Selsey St** and **Thomas Rd.**

Limehouse

Limehouse, to the W of the area, is the corner that has seen the greatest renaissance as the Limehouse Basin became part of 'Docklands', and is now surrounded by enviable new waterside homes (see Docklands chapter for these). Limehouse has not only kept hold of its romantic name but is indeed expanding somewhat. The Limehouse Cut, the canal which runs from Limehouse up between Poplar and Bow to the River Lea, has seen several smart waterside developments following the Docklands example. Although these are now thought of as Limehouse, the original area lies largely to the W of **Burdett Rd/West India Dock Rd.**

The N end of West India Dock Rd is flanked by the Barley Mow council estate, and there is a stark contrast as the estate sweeps down to very expensive, fashionable **Narrow St**, whose riverside houses were among the first to be 'discovered' by West End artists and politicians. This is a conservation area and is covered in detail in the Docklands chapter. Westwards leads to The Highway and the Tower of London.

West India Dock Rd continues to the N across East India Dock Rd into **Burdett Rd**, where some of the larger properties on either side have been converted into split-level flats. West of Burdett Rd are the council homes of **Turners Rd, Clemence St, Dora St** and **Norbiton Rd** (more of those spacious 4-bed maisonettes: c £195,000) which all lead into **Salmon Lane** – where some delightful Victorian houses, the Mercers Estate, can be found on either side at its W end. In **Matlock St**, N of Salmon Lane, the flat-fronted Victorian cottages command c. £280,000; 4-bed Victorian houses c. £375,000.

This corner, too, is seeing a lot of redevelopment. At the top of **Turners Rd** two large housing schemes have emerged between Turners Rd and **Clemence St**. A new block of 31 flats, Denmark Wharf by Higgins Homes, is in **Copenhagen Place**, off Salmon Lane. Copenhagen Place, by the Limehouse Cut, also has some attractive 2-storey Victorian houses. Attractive Victoriana is also found S of Salmon Lane in **Barnes St** and **York Square**, a conservation area, as well as **Flamborough St**. **York Square** is the most favoured address, with its 3-bed houses c. £325,000 (unchanged since 2002). The Grade II-listed houses in **Barnes St** command about ten per cent less.

The southern end of Barnes St leads into busy **Commercial Rd**, almost opposite the Limehouse DLR station. The Mission is a conversion into flats of a striking corner building. There's porterage, gym and a roof garden. Further E along Commercial Rd is

St Anne's Church, which is the centre of another conservation area: within the area is **Newell St**, where c. £600,000 will buy a Georgian house, or go ultra-modern at Swallow Place, a small scheme of 2- and 3-bed houses (all sold).

Mile End Park runs N from **Rhodeswell Rd.** Where Limehouse Cut canal passes under Burdett Rd is Limehouse Court, a 1990 canalside development in **Dod St** with 50 homes and 50 commercial units. Further along the canal, **Cotall St** has some local-authority built flats. Enterprise Works in **Hawgood St** uses the Limehouse name (despite being N of the canal, in E3) for work-homes, ranging from 4-storey houses to 1-bed flats. And further E at the **Morris Rd** bridge, 'The Limehouse Cut' is a big 1980s conversion of warehouses into work-homes, featuring spacious open-plan lofts.

Further S, there is lots happening around the Westferry DLR station on the edge of the Isle of Dogs. **Grenade St** has Compass Point with 1- and 2-bed flats. In **West India Dock Rd** is a new Peabody Trust block; Peabody also have some new 1- and 2-bed flats for rent on **West India Dock Rd/Gill St**. Existing ex-council homes in **Three Colt St** are c. £185,000 for a 2-bed, or there are 18 new flats carved out of an old mission hall.

Transport Docklands Light Railway: Limehouse, Westferry, Poplar, All Saints. Trains: Limehouse.

Convenient for Docklands, City, rail interchange at Stratford, Fenchurch St. Routes East. Blackwall Tunnel to South. Miles from centre: 4.5.

Schools Local Authority: Langton Park, St Paul's Way, Morpeth.

SALES

Flats	S	1B	2B	3B	4B	5B
Average prices	90–130	115–190	130–250	140–200	–	–
Houses	2B	3B	4B	5B	6/7B	8B
Average prices	190–270	230–350	250–450	–	–	–

RENTAL

Flats	S	1B	2B	3B	4B	5B
Average prices	120–150	140–200	170–250	230–350	–	–
Houses	2B	3B	4B	5B	6/7B	8B
Average prices	200–250	250–350	250–400	–	–	–

The properties Warehouse conversions and live/work homes plus new flats schemes: prices below Docklands, but well above existing local homes, which are largely 2/3-bed flats and maisonettes, most of them ex-council. Studios and big houses are scarce. A few fine old houses – some Georgian – in conservation areas.

P

The market The lower end of the flats price scale represents ex-council sales; exceptions at top end are the new canalside schemes, and the occasional listed home in conservation areas such as Salmon St. Riverside Narrow St and Limehouse Basin, annexed by Docklands (see Docklands chapter), are not included here.

Among estate agents active in this areaare:

- Alex Neil
- W J Meade
- Savills
- McDowalls
- Keatons
- Adam Kennedy
- Globe Estates
- Land & Co
- Look
- Hamilton Fox

PUTNEY AND ROEHAMPTON

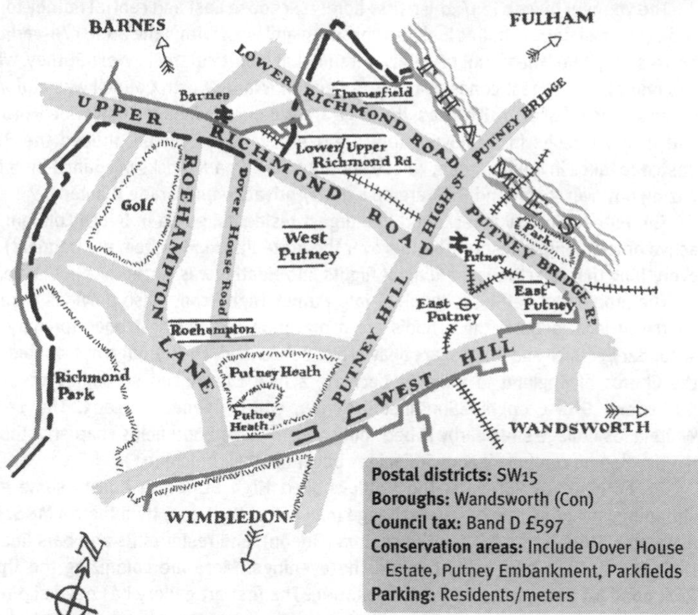

Postal districts: SW15
Boroughs: Wandsworth (Con)
Council tax: Band D £597
Conservation areas: Include Dover House Estate, Putney Embankment, Parkfields
Parking: Residents/meters

It is convenient, it's green – and it's by the river. Thus the *raison d'être* for lovely, leafy Putney, its streets lined with family homes and pleasant flats. It is not glitzy smart – except in odd spots along the riverside. When East Putney gained one apartment tower of the svelte riverview-concierge-and-car-park kind, this was a polite covering-up of the area's sole dreary 1960s office block; now another stylish office reworking, up by the tube this time, entices the younger and (very) well-heeled. But by and large Putney is leafy rather than louche, its useful High Street in full working order, but not yet the acme of cool. For most, the main point is that here one can espouse quasi-country living – plenty of Putney Common for one's dogs and horse-riding, and even a 100-acre country club with golf course – while living 12 minutes by train from Waterloo.

Flat-dwellers (rich and not-so) aside, prosperous families dominate the Putney property market. Apart from the trains and the District Line tube, its own heath and common are a gateway to acres more greensward: from the heath, Wimbledon Common and Richmond Park; from the common, Barnes Common and Wetlands Centre. Then there's Kew Gardens, plus some excellent schools . . . Who needs the country, ask the child-owning classes (and if you do, the A3 offers a speedy exit). As a consequence, million-pound houses are unremarkable in Putney, and you can pay three times that for six or seven bedrooms and all the trimmings.

Traditional Putney homes are substantial late-Victorian and Edwardian houses built for the middle classes and those who aspired to that status. The social mix, by and large, is back where it started. The 20th century added flats, flats, flats – in blocks of all kinds, Edwardian onwards, or carved with varying degrees of success from the big old houses.

Roehampton is the place to look if you feel priced out of Putney proper, with a good choice now of ex-council and other homes, and Richmond Park on your doorstep. It has no tube, but nearby Barnes station is on the Waterloo line. But it, too, is now beginning to attract the developers' eyes . . . see below. Richmond Park, which marks the borough

P

boundary, is glorious for walking and cycling, with riding stables at Roehampton and Robin Hood Gate and a public golf course on the Roehampton side.

The younger buyers (25/30-ish first-homers) choose East and central Putney for the wide choice of flats. Families look further south and west within the area: 5/6-bedroom houses are, if not the norm, certainly not unusual – particularly in West Putney, which has one of the biggest concentrations in London. Wandsworth Council was a pioneer of the selling off of council homes: the large areas it once owned are now widely private, and in most cases far removed from the 'council estate' image. Indeed the SW15 postcode takes in Roehampton, whose enormous landmark blocks of council-built flats gazing out over Richmond Park are now partly private – and Grade II listed.

The Putney Society is reckoned the largest residents' group in South London: it is active on planning, transport (battles over the maze-like road system are frequent) and everything that affects the area: night flights into Heathrow is currently a hot issue.

The problem of getting a daughter into Putney High School also provides a fruitful source of local debate: the schools are a big draw, but the best ones (primary and secondary, council and private) are heavily oversubscribed. The borough has worked with the Church of England to build St Cecilia's, a new £12 million secondary school in **Sutherland Grove**, on the Southfields border, which opened in 2003. The 17-acre Whitelands College site nearby is becoming housing (see Southfields chapter) – though the developers carefully ignore St Cecilia's advent in their brochure.

At the heart of Putney is the traffic-choked **High St**, which boasts some good shopping, including the Putney Exchange mall with a Waitrose; then there's M&S, Pret à Manger, Starbuck's . . . There's a cinema (Odeon), and restaurants and bars line the High St, which is noticeably busy in the evenings. More are colonizing the **Upper Richmond Rd** along towards the tube station. The first art gallery has been sighted.

The High St sweeps down the hill to Putney Bridge, with its handsome lamp posts and the riverside parish church, St Mary's. Putney Wharf, the office-block-turned-flats tower (see below), also has a new riverside square taking shape as part of the scheme.

Traffic congestion is a big local problem. **Putney Bridge** and **Upper Richmond Rd** act as a magnet for commuters from across the whole of South and West London (anything to avoid the Wandsworth one-way system), and the result is monumental traffic jams during rush hours. More 'traffic-calming' measures, parking restrictions, mini-roundabouts and one-way streets are brought in every year. Indeed, traffic – including school-run 4x4s – and parking are, according to partisan locals, the sole serpents in what they firmly believe to be Eden. The controlled-parking zone covers everywhere from (working clockwise) **Point Pleasant**, via **West Hill Rd** and **West Hill** to **Tibbetts Corner** and **Putney Park Lane** and on down to the borough border at Putney Lower Common.

Freeholders on or near the greenery, by the way, pay a small Commons Rate as an extra to the standard council tax: this goes towards the maintenance of common, heath and Wimbledon Common. Each of these has its own special character: Putney Heath is wild and much is heavily wooded; Putney Lower Common is old watermeadow land with a few spinneys, and hosts the 'country' Putney Show every third summer. We start there.

Lower West Putney: the river roads

This little wedge-shaped neighbourhood lies between the river and the **Lower Richmond Rd**, running W from the bridge to the common. Here the predominant house type is a 2-storey, cottage-style, late-Victorian terrace, for which you'll be asked c. £400,000. There are, though, pockets of older Regency and early-Victorian villas – and a few exceptionally large houses around Putney Lower Common.

Lower Richmond Rd leaves the High St, and soon the river, behind, swinging off inland till it meets the common, the borough border and Barnes. En route are small parades of shops, as well as a leavening of restaurants, bars, antique shops and Putney's first art gallery. Estate agents cluster. The road carries through-traffic from Richmond and Barnes, but does not suffer as severely as **Upper Richmond Rd** – both a Red Route and a pseudonym for the South Circular (one-way streets and other barriers curb rat-running).

West from **Putney High St** are three large, late-Victorian mansion blocks – Star and Garter Mansions, Kenilworth Court and University Mansions. Most but not all of the flats have river views, although you may need to crane your neck. Some flats in Star and Garter Mansions and Kenilworth Court hear noise from the nearby pubs at weekends. You can pay £350–450,000 for a 3-bed in Kenilworth – but £230,000 buys a 3-bed council-built flat round the corner in **The Platt**: a good location at reasonable cost: 'much better inside than out, and great value', reckon agents.

There are mainly terraced houses between the clutches of shops on **Lower Richmond Rd**, although there are some Victorian detached and semi-detached villas set well back. The roads leading off Lower Richmond Rd towards the river tend, in the main, to be smaller mid- and late-Victorian terraced cottages, with some purpose-built maisonettes and flats. **Ruvigny Gardens**, which loops off Lower Richmond Rd, features larger 3-storey Victorian terraced houses; some converted to flats – and some backing onto the **Embankment**, with gates at the end of the garden for launching your boat. Don't skimp on surveys close to the river: settlement can be a problem.

Festing Rd is one of the most popular streets in this area, with 4-bed, c. £600,000 houses; some of its homes are purpose-built Victorian flats and maisonettes. It runs down to Putney Embankment and its boathouses. By the river, too, is Leader's Gardens, a small, attractive park with tennis courts and play area. Popular **Ashlone Rd** is a street of mid-Victorian terraces; at its foot is **Stockhurst Close**, a small development of council-built flats, some with river views. Off **Danemere St** an infill development, **Waters Place**, has a dozen 3- and 4-bed town-houses, which now ask some half a million. All this group of streets and closes also runs down to Leader's Gardens and the riverside path.

Next, **Pentlow St** features attractive Victorian homes; mainly 3-bed houses, some semi-detached; and here Bewley Homes has just added, well, *neo*-Victorian, 3-bed semis (with garages), plus some 2-bed flats. **Sefton St** has 3-bed Victorian terraces (c. £450,000) leading to **Horne Way**, a cul-de-sac where well-kept gardens surround a group of inter-war council-built flats blocks backing onto (but cut off from) sports grounds. This leafy corner ends by the Common with **Commondale**, a row of 2-bed cottages, some flat-fronted. The prettiest ones were built in the 1870s to house the 'deserving poor' with money provided by Putney Pest House (the local fever hospital) and wealthy benefactors. The cottages overlook the common and the old Putney Hospital, still (as for some years) awaiting redevelopment: this must, apparently, include a medical component – perhaps a big new doctors' surgery, plus flats.

Lower Richmond Rd itself has plenty of flats above shops; the Putney **Embankment**, though, has few homes available – they are generally tied to the boathouses and rowing clubs which line the river. Should the rare 4/5-bed house appear on the market, reckon on some £1.5 million on its price tag. Ruvigny Mansions, a small Victorian block, has spacious flats, most with river views. It is inadvisable to leave cars parked on the Embankment, given the tide's unfortunate habit of rising above road level.

Lower Richmond Rd to Upper Richmond Rd

Cross now to the S side of Lower Richmond Rd, where another tract of streets spreads out, neatly ruled off from the South Circular (the Upper Richmond Rd) by the railway line. First, across from **Commondale**, is **Putney Common**, a tiny no-through-road used as a turnaround point for the No. 22 bus, which terminates here. Past the pub on the corner of **Lower Richmond Rd** are three cottages, then late 1960s flats (Commonview), then All Saints' primary school and church. The school is very popular, with a tight catchment area. A footpath leads through into **Egliston Mews** and to **Egliston Rd**, which boasts vast, mid- and late-Victorian detached houses with a handful of almost-as-large semi-detached Edwardiana; virtually all have substantial off-street parking and very large gardens. **Egliston Mews**, at the junction of Egliston Rd and Lower Common South, is a smart 1990 development of flat-fronted 4-bed, 2-bath town-houses, in 'developers' Georgian' style. These go for £550,000 and up (1990: £265,000-plus).

Lower Common South is a road of huge detached houses, mainly 1870s–1880s, mainly red-brick and wonderfully ornate, set well back from the road and overlooking Putney Common – this is one of the very rare common views not to be spoiled by heavy traffic. These homes are very, very, very rarely for sale – when they do come up, they are likely to start at £2.5 million. **Chester Close** and **Sherwood Court**, off Lower Common South, have small, attractive, late 1970s 'traditional' 3-bed town-houses.

Red-brick Dryburgh Mansions is on the corner of **Erpingham Rd** and **Egliston Rd**. A huge, late-Victorian mansion, Dryburgh Court, is split into seven flats. The main part of **Dryburgh Rd** is parallel to the railway and has late-Victorian/Edwardian houses: mainly paired, some detached. Odd numbers back onto the railway, but have decent-sized gardens as barriers. New homes here at 'Dryburgh Gardens', launching this March: 1- to 3-bed flats £250,000–600,000. Hidden at the end of the road is tiny **Beauchamp Terrace** with Victorian cottages; here low numbers are nearer the railway.

Erpingham Rd runs between Dryburgh Rd and Lower Richmond Rd, with 3-storey Edwardian semis and terraces – many extended, and some split into unusually large conversion flats. A clutch of new houses and flats has been squeezed in at the junction with Lower Richmond Rd. Rat-running is still a problem, although **Dryburgh Rd** is closed to traffic at the Upper Richmond Rd junction during the morning rush hour. **Felsham Rd**, with its late-Victorian terraced houses, and a few early-Victorian and larger ones, runs from Erpingham Rd through to Putney High St – but not for cars. The same is true for **Hotham Rd**. Roads running off are generally mundane (but very popular) South London late-Victorian/Edwardian terraces. Seven new contemporary flats are under way at St Mary Hall on the cormer of **Felsham Rd** and **Charlwood Rd.**

Stanbridge Rd, which runs off Felsham Rd, has some pleasant semi-basement, flat-fronted mid-Victorian houses on the W side: 4-beds c. £600,000 (this year as last). Houses across the road, E, are ex-council, and half the price. Homes in **Roskell Rd** are slightly larger 2- and 3-storey Victoriana, some semi-detached. By the mid-100s **Felsham Rd** houses are bigger, mainly 3-storeys. In **Henry Jackson Rd** is a council-built infill of low-rise homes. Thereafter more small council-built blocks and St Mary's C of E Primary School (successful but small). **Bemish Rd** includes some flat-fronted Victorian cottages and larger Edwardian houses. This road is one-way S-bound.

P

Charlwood Rd provides a welcome release from red-brick Edwardiana, with pairs of Georgian/Regency flat-fronted cottages, and larger detached houses set well back from the little lane running from Felsham Rd across Hotham Rd to Clarendon Drive. Perhaps the prettiest houses are between **Felsham Rd** and **Hotham Rd**: this is rightly a conservation area. **Redgrave Rd** also has pretty, smart mid-Victorian homes. An old pub on Charlwood has been replaced by 'The Quill' – 3-bed houses at £800,000 and 2-bed flats at £400,000, ready summer 05.

The High St end of **Lacy Rd** is dominated by the Putney Exchange shopping centre; otherwise it includes 2- and 3-storey Victorian terraces, some smaller cottages, a pub, some shops and some council infill. **Modder Place** has nice, plain flat-fronted 2-bed cottages on one side only, looking directly onto unprepossessing 1960s council-built flats, Crown Court Estate, which is why these can be less expensive than neighbouring roads. A group of cul-de-sacs – pedestrian-only **Quill Lane**, **Lifford St** and **Stratford Grove** – lies between the red-brick walls of the shopping centre and the 1960s estate. For all that, the flat-fronted 2-storey cottages retain their charm. Ex-council flats in Crown Court may not be scenic to look at, but are another cache of relatively inexpensive but brilliantly placed homes: 1-beds c. £200–220,000; 2-beds £260–270,000; the rare 3-beds c. £280,000. Good rental investments, local agents reckon.

West from Lacy Rd, **Hotham Rd** is mainly Edwardian 2- and 3-storey houses, most semi-detached (just); also top-scoring Hotham Primary at the **Charlwood Rd** junction. Most houses have 4-plus beds: you can pay £1.5 million now for one in Charlwood, or £600,000 for a 2-bed, 2-bath flat in a school conversion.

Clarendon Drive features more big 2- and 3-storey late-Edwardian and 1920s semis. Houses on the S side of the road back onto the railway line, but have gardens of up to 100ft to keep it at bay. This road also has Our Lady of Victories Catholic Primary School (very much in demand: the kids keep scoring 100 per cent in SATs tests) and thus £850,000-ish price tags. Then there's the RSPCA animal hospital (as seen on TV) . . .

From **Clarendon Drive** a road barrier blocks access to **Norroy Rd** which, along with **Chelverton Rd** with its good-sized late-Victorian houses, is handy for Putney station. **Spencer Walk**, W off Charlwood Rd, has pretty, flat-fronted, early-Victorian 3-storeys with semi-basements, and modern town-houses. Some train noise possible here.

Upper Richmond Rd is a major trunk road (the South Circular) and is choked at all times, despite Red Route status. However, the majority of houses are set well back. The W section of Upper Richmond Rd, towards Sheen, holds many blocks of flats from early 1920s to fairly new. Brittany House gained new penthouses in a total refurb in the 1980s.

Around **Upper Richmond Rd**'s junction with **Putney Hill/High St** are many commercial buildings, but also an increasing number of flats developments. The old police station site gained a 7-storey block of 32 flats above a restaurant; plus the section house, which has grown two floors and is now 46 flats with basement parking. Flats that sold new a couple of years ago for £320,000 are now £400,000. Among the best-known blocks close to Putney High St are old-style Ormonde Court and 1930s-built Belvedere Court, overlooking Putney Leisure Centre and thus handy for early-morning swims. All homes on this N side of **Upper Richmond Rd** back onto rail lines, though most have long gardens. Harwood Court (opposite **Colinette Rd**) is another 1930s-style block, while **Isis Close** is a 1960s-built development. Wellwood Court is next, then **Breasley Close** a council-built infill: houses and flats. Then a slightly cheaper corner: **Fairdale Gardens** is a small town-house scheme; **Dyers Lane** (a cul-de-sac), has Northumberland Row's mid-Victorian cottages, overlooking modern council-build.

Elaborate Edwardian is the hallmark of suburban Putney. These homes, solid and spacious, are eclectic in style. This one has copious 'Tudor' detailing in the heavy gable, the stuck-on 'timbers' and the tall chimneys. Other styles to be found, frequently in the same house, are Queen Anne and Gothic. However mongrel their architecture, they find favour with families.

The most enviable homes in **Upper Richmond Rd** are the 'Nelson' or 'Captains' Houses, a row of half a dozen lovely, late-Georgian/early-Victorian villas supposedly (though without much evidence: why would they all want to live in Putney?) built for Nelson's captains. Set well back from the road, they boast gravel sweeps and Regency ironwork canopies. You pay over a million for one of these: £1.6 million has been known.

East Putney

Prices for the late-Victorian/Edwardian terraced houses here are generally below those in the River Roads, above, and West Putney, even though transport (District Line tube here, as well as the train) and shopping are better. The difference is not as marked as it was, though, and houses are often bigger.

But here, Putney has gained a whole new riverside quarter. Unlike so many other such (including some of their own), St George's scheme opens up the riverside to the town, rather than walling it off. Putney Wharf stretches along the riverside from just E of Putney Bridge to **Deodar Rd.** It begins just behind the church with the old ICL tower, which St George has wrapped up in curvy glass with new, stepped roofline: this holds the three-floor (15th–17th) penthouse (4-bed/4-bath, £3 million asked, but no takers so it's let), a further 66 flats (a 2-bed, £450,000) and some offices. But on along the riverside, accessed via **Brewhouse Lane**, Putney Wharf also adds two new public squares to the Putney scene: another 75 flats (some 'loft-style'), a fitness club, bar, restaurant, parking etc; St George has kept one original building, for flats and bar/cafés. There's Carluccio's, Tootsie's, the Boathouse pub, the Rocket riverside restaurant. A proportion of the flats, run by a housing trust, are shared-ownership.

As a final flourish to this scheme, there are five big 5-bed houses (one left, at £1 million last year, £875,000 now) in **Deodar Rd** – the most popular (and expensive: up to c. £2 million) street in East Putney. The odd numbers among its big, 3-storey semi-detached houses gaze out over the river – and are the last houses before Central London to have private moorings at the end of their large gardens (although actual boats are, sadly, scarce). Two were for sale last autumn, each needing a complete re-do. There are drawbacks of course – the District Line bisects **Deodar Rd** (at roof level). The Blades development gets river views: three stucco-fronted houses plus 3-bed flats, backed by a commercial development of workshops with studios above.

Oakhill Rd links Putney Bridge Rd back up to Upper Richmond Rd. The street has, first, Victorian and later mansion flats, then detached double-fronted mid-Victoriana, then smaller red-brick terraces. Streets running between **Oakhill Rd** and **West Hill** – **Chubert Rd**, **Galveston Rd**, **Mexfield Rd**, **Cromford Rd**, **Santos Rd** – are generally substantial Edwardian terraces, with quite a few converted to flats, causing pressure on parking space, but all convenient for East Putney tube. Off Upper Richmond Rd is **Wood Close**, a modern development of small town-houses complete with garages.

Along **Upper Richmond Rd** (a.k.a. the South Circular) close by the tube station, is the latest swanky development – or rather, 'SW15H' ('swish' – geddit?). Laing has gone for a 1930s, ocean-liner feel to this curving, balconied reworking of office premises: shops, restaurant and 66 flats, in eight styles from 1-beds to duplexes and penthouses. The one-bed resales last winter started at £275,000. Each flat has a balcony or terrace, there are gardens, parking, glass atrium . . .

Eastwards, towards Wandsworth, growing numbers of 1930s-onwards mansion-flat blocks appear; off-street parking is an essential. Also more recent schemes: next to the tube station, Esprit House has 23 1- and 2-bed flats (with parking): most were bought-to-let, so look out for resales. In **Kendall Place**, near the tube station, one scheme of 14 flats and 26 houses boasts an indoor swimming pool: town-houses here £550,000, 1-bed flats £250,000, penthouses £750,000. **Cavalry Gardens**, too, is a recent, sybaritic complex of houses and flats, both new and converted, with its own pool and sauna.

Putney Bridge Rd runs parallel to the river from Putney High St to Wandsworth. It may be busy, but Wandsworth Park runs most of the length of Putney Bridge Rd, so many of the late-Victorian terraces of 2- and 3-storey houses and purpose-built flats have views across its greenery to the river and the lawns of the exclusive Hurlingham Club beyond. The latest scheme – now expected to be ready this year, and just into SW18 – is Vista: 27 flats with views, parking, 2 beds/2 baths apiece and price tags from £320,000.

Fawe Park Rd, with its Edwardian terraces, runs parallel to the S, and even numbers back onto the railway line. Trains notwithstanding, 4-bed houses still approach half a million, and there are some sizeable converted flats. Terraced houses in **Skelgill Rd** look out on Brandlehow Primary's playground, while **Brandlehow Rd's** attractive, £420,000-plus 3-bed houses overlook the front of the school. **Bective Rd** is a popular mix of flat-fronted mid-Victorian cottages and bay-windowed late 19th-century terraces (3/4-bed £530,000); where it meets **Fawe Park Rd**, Disraeli Gardens, a large Victorian mansion block, stands sentinel. **Wadham Rd** has a very popular mix of small, pretty, flat-fronted, late-Victorian cottages, many 2-bed, 2-storey; some 3-storey. But the tube runs at roof level behind.

Oxford Rd runs between Upper Richmond and Putney Bridge Rds. So do rat-running motorists, but there are some massive detached mid-Victorian houses with porticoed entrances; the remainder are Edwardian semi-detached with some modern (council) infill. Some flats here, too. **Montserrat Rd, Werter Rd** (with its Sainsbury's) and **Disraeli Rd** (with the local library) run between Oxford Rd and Putney High St with a range of large Victoriana, most of which are now converted into flats (whole houses c. £630,000). The roads are all one-way, either to or from **Putney High St**, and suffer from more frustrated, hopelessly lost rat-runners.

Numbers of new riverside flats building/planned across in SW18, E of Wandsworth Park: see Wandsworth chapter. These are not in Putney, whatever the brochures say.

Putney Heath and Putney Hill

Putney Heath is wild and heavily wooded, and walkers can get to the neighbouring expanse of Wimbledon Common via an underpass beneath the A3. A small, villagey neighbourhood at the junction of **Telegraph Rd** and **Portsmouth Rd** lies isolated in the midst of the heath: a lovely spot, if not best for transport (though a new community bus links to the stations). Approached via **Wildcroft Rd**, it includes the Telegraph pub and the unusual 1930s Wildcroft Manor mansion flats, built in mock-Tudor style with exposed beams – large 3- and 4-bed (up to £500,000) flats here. Many go to older overseas buyers, very unworried by hefty service charges. Then comes Highlands Heath, also 1930s mansion flats: slightly smaller homes, lower service charges, tennis and squash courts. Both blocks back onto the heath. Prices start at around £180,000 for a 1-bed (only four of these), rising towards £500,000 for a 4-bed.

Heathview Gardens and **Bristol Gardens** have among the most popular – and pricey – houses in this enclave and indeed in the area: vast 6-, 7- and 8-bed Edwardian detached houses in quiet tree-lined roads with gardens to match, some running out onto the heath. Virtually all remain in single occupation; one sold last year at £4.2 million, but was reckoned to need another £1.5 million spent on it. **Bensbury Close** has small, flat-fronted 2- to 4-bed mews cottages. **Portsmouth Rd** has small (in comparison with Heathview Gardens) detached houses overlooking the heath – including Bowling Green Cottage, a flat-fronted, whitewashed country cottage thought to date back to the early 18th century. And now also 'Fenetre', Bowling Green Paddock: four contemporary houses, all glass, galleries and jutting flat roofs: these struggled, 'too modern' opined agents. **Bowling Green Close** is a private development of extraordinary large 1930s Art Deco detached houses, very rarely on the market and over £2 million when they are. **Lynden Gate** is 1980s Developers' Regency: 3-storey, semi-basement stuccoed town-houses, 2- and 3-bedroomed (some rooms small), £550–600,000, in a high-security enclave with heath and woodland on three sides; 1990 prices: £300,000-plus.

Putney Heath (the road) runs from Roehampton to Putney Hill. It's mainly council-built (though increasingly owner-occupied) developments along the heath, then Exeter House, a large 1930s mansion block in its own large grounds. Many, but not all, the flats have magnificent views over the heath. Prices on this road vary a lot: 2-bed ex-council flats can be good value at below £200,000, with equivalents in private blocks costing up to £350,000. **Manorfields** is a huge 1930s mansion-flat complex of 9-plus acres on the corner site between **Putney Heath** and **Westleigh Avenue**. Prices for these flats are higher than at Highlands Heath (see above) because public transport is closer. The various blocks have 2-, 3- and 4-bed flats, most with good views of beautifully-kept landscaped grounds with specimen trees and ponds. The service charges are high, but full-time gardeners and porterage explain why.

The triangle enclosed by **Putney Hill, West Hill** and **Upper Richmond Rd** offers the largest choice of modern purpose-built flats in Putney, although there is also a wide selection of older Victorian and Edwardian houses. One of the grandest of these, a vast pile erected by a sugar magnate, has become 'Lyle Park', yielding 21 flats with a tendency to 20ft bedrooms, set in an acre of gardens, plus a row of three houses. **Putney Hill** is a choked through-road taking traffic to and from the A3, but flats in the (mainly 1930s and 1950s) blocks on either side of the road remain popular: most are set well back. They are interspersed with some substantial double-fronted mid-Victoriana, some also now flats. Here, too, is the mecca for families with girls: Putney High School and its prep. branch Lytton House.

At the top of the hill, a cut-off spur of **Putney Hill** holds two mansion blocks including Ross Court, popular for its large, roomy flats; these also rent well.

On down the hill, **Putney Heath Lane** has a mix of good-sized 2- and 3-storey Edwardian semis and terraceds (and a few detached – just), and yet more flats: modern mansion blocks. Off it, **Van Dyke Close** is town-houses and flats. Behind is **Lavington Stables** – a tiny mews too small to find in the *A–Z*, but where houses cost £1 million-plus. **Rusholme Rd** has flats at the junction with Putney Heath Lane, thereafter late-Victorian red-brick detached and semi-detached houses, some converted into flats, though whole houses are touted as cheaper than West Putney at a mere £1.2–1.6 million. Attractive modern flats at the junction with **Holmbush Rd** overlook a grassy triangle.

Kersfield Rd is mainly early 1960s blocks, with some late 1930s flats (private), although **Littleton Close** is council-built. Flats blocks include Heath Royal, Garden Royal, Heath Rise, a series of modern-style blocks close to Putney Hill with well-kept gardens. A wide range, from 1- to 4-bed. Council blocks in the area are reasonable, built during the same period and in similar style to many of the private blocks – spot the difference.

Radcliffe Square, between Kersfield Rd and Lytton Grove, is 1970s flats. **Lytton Grove** itself is a mixture of good-sized, late-Victorian detached (5-bed £1.2 million) and semi-detached houses with some 1930s and modern infill. Some of the houses are now (fairly spacious) flats: 1-beds £230–250,000, 2-beds £280–420,000. Houses on the N side of the road between Clock House Place and Rusholme Rd back onto the tube line, but again sidings cut some of the noise. Kersfield Estate by the junction with Putney Hill is 1960s council-built flats and houses. **Tintern** and **Arlesey Closes** feature quite small modern town-houses, then a mix of late-Victorian/Edwardian detached and semi-detached. **Chepstow Close** is a good modern town-house development (flat-fronted, 3-storey, garages); **Clock House Place** a red-brick cluster of Victorian-style homes (4/5-beds £600–650,000), with a way across the tracks into Keswick Rd for a quick route to East Putney tube.

P

Across the tracks, leafy **Keswick Rd** runs between Upper Richmond Rd and West Hill. Some buyers may be put off by the (above-ground) tube line behind, but gardens and large grassy sidings cut noise levels – and East Putney station is just round the corner. There are also some exceptional, large early-Victorian houses, typically 5-bed, with long gardens and some £750,000 price tags. It's an eclectic mix: big mock-Tudor mansions, hideous blocks and imitation cottages. Some of the monster houses are still family homes, others now flats. **Portinscale Rd** features some large detached Victorian houses and 1920s and 1930s infill of Tudor-style herringbone brick. By the junction with **West Hill** is the ADT City Technology College (getting good results) and Portinscale Estate (modern houses/low-rise flats). Opposite are large 1970s flats.

But **St John's Avenue**, crossing from West to East Putney, is the premier road for (older, well-heeled) flat buyers, with some of the top modern blocks: Claremont, Marlin House, Downside: all well maintained, with indoor swimming pools – and (from the E end) a three-minute walk to East Putney tube and the shops. Prices rise as the walk shortens. **Carlton Drive** is end-to-end 1960s blocks of flats: slightly less popular. There's just one 1990s version at No. 38: 2-bed flats in a big garden – but now there's approval for a new 5-storey block of 22 flats next to '60s Evenwood Close. Despite the classy names, however, neither road is the prettiest in Putney. **Rayner's Rd**, between the two, has a mix of decidedly everyday flats opposite huge, 6-bed, grand detached houses.

West Hill – a continuation of the A3 – is exceptionally busy, if not stationary, at all times. Close to Tibbett's Corner underpass, **Colebrook Close** runs off West Hill, an extraordinary 'Spanish Hacienda' style outbreak of expensive houses and maisonettes, built in the 1930s by a film company for stars and starlets on location in Britain. On down the hill are vast, mainly late-Victorian mansions – check the flamboyant detailing as you crawl down the Hill. Most, fortunately, are set well back with off-street parking; for the most part they have become spacious flats. Some purpose-built blocks, too. And Barratt turned an old college into Crown Mansions, flats and duplexes, in 1999. These are popular buys: prices for 1-beds are £220–250,000, 2-beds £280–285,000.

West Putney

Next, cross **Putney Hill** to West Putney. This is where you live when you have made it in life and have chosen not to commute each day from Berkshire or Hampshire. There are some small houses, flats, even council estates – but the vast, detached, late-Victorian houses in wide tree-lined avenues are the Putney properties of popular imagination. Five bedrooms is reckoned cramped: six, or even eight, is more common. Prices start at a million and go right on rising, with some roads having homes at £2.5–3.5 million. Indeed, one top agent reckons to have set a new record for a house in Putney last autumn at £747 per sq ft (and houses of 3,000 sq ft are not unusual). Demand is so great that those split into flats in the 1970s are bought for restoration to single units.

West Putney unfolds from **Putney Hill** westwards to **Putney Park Lane**, running downhill from Putney Hill to the **Upper Richmond Rd**. It is a wholly residential area save for the shops and offices on Upper Richmond Rd and is a conservation area.

The area is laid out on a grid pattern, with four long roads – **Westleigh Avenue**, **Chartfield Avenue**, **Hazlewell Rd** and **Howard's Lane** – making parallel E–W slices across it. Cutting N–S between them are shorter streets such as **Larpent**, **Castello** and **St Simon's Avenues**. Major building started in the 1870s, and houses range from vast detached Victorian and Edwardian through to mid-1920s architect-designed flights of fancy, with some 1950s/early 1960s infill. The number of large detached or generous semis is exceptional – a glance at a map shows the spacious street plan.

Westleigh Avenue running W from Putney Hill starts with low-rise council homes; then the mix of Victorian, Edwardian and newer detached houses, all set well back from the road, takes over. From the Pullman Gardens junction, council homes and small blocks of flats back onto a 1950s/1960s council-built estate (the mainly low-rise flats, houses and maisonettes of **Cortis Rd, Pullman Rd** and **Heyward Gardens**): these can make a good, cheap alternative to the Victoriana. Some houses on the S side of **Westleigh Avenue** back onto popular Elliot comprehensive school in **Pullman Gardens**. Granard Primary is by **Granard Avenue**, with its small, neat council houses then substantial detached – many 1920s, 1930s and 1950s double-fronted. **Genoa Avenue** is mainly late-Victorian 3-storey semis, plus some big 1920s detacheds and small council infill. **Solna Avenue** has small modern council houses, most now private.

Chartfield Avenue mixes detached late-Victorian/Edwardiana, set back from the road, with some substantial inter-war stockbroker-Tudor homes. Here, too, is the council-built Ashburton Estate, between **Putney Hill** and **Genoa Avenue** – now the scene of much buy-to-letting, with the area's student population providing the tenants: £250 a week for a 2-bed. Some of the largest Victorian detached double-fronteds are now converted to equally vast flats; 3-bed/garden/2-recep ones are not unusual. At the Putney Hill end are **Chartfield Square** and **Cherryfield Drive**: undistinguished modern town-houses, the former overlooked by the South Thames College block. Late 1960s council-built flats (low-rise) and houses opposite in **Winchelsea Close**.

The local estate agents call **Gwendolen Avenue** Millionaire's Row, and for once they do not exaggerate (though you'll need at least two million to buy these large, 1880s detached and semi-detached houses); the 1980s added more sizeable 5-bed semis in similar style. On the corner with Upper Richmond Rd a big old house is now six flats, plus a house carved out of the coach-house. The developers moved on to the house next door (10 flats), and the Victorian church: 10 duplexes (a 2-bed, £450,000).

St Simons Avenue features more very large detacheds ('seven beds are common'), and a church at the junction with Hazlewell Rd. **Genoa** and **Castello Avenues** are smaller (but big by any other standards) 2/3-storey semi or detached red-brick houses. **Larpent Avenue** has some modern infill amid the substantial 2- and 3-storey late Victoriana – but some of these (low even numbers) have extraordinary domes on the front elevations – Turkish architect perhaps? **Luttrell Avenue** is back to the late-Victorian/Edwardian semis and detacheds (£750,000–1 million).

The pattern continues in **Hazlewell Rd** – some with 6 bedrooms: £1–2.5 million. There are some smaller modern infill houses (also detached). **Coalecroft Rd** is a conservation area: even numbers are very pretty flat-fronted early-Victorian cottages, mainly 3-beds; odd numbers are good-sized Edwardian semis. **Holroyd Rd** is Edwardian 2- and 3-storey semis. Well-heeled **Tideswell Rd** has 3-storey Edwardian semi-detacheds, one of which, unmodernized, sold for £300,000 in 1994: think in terms of not much change from a million now.

St John's Avenue runs on to straddle Putney Hill: this side of it has very large 1880s 3-storey homes, both semi and detached (up to £1.8 million). **Ravenna Rd** and **Burston Rd** continue the pattern down to Upper Richmond Rd: handy for Putney station.

Howard's Lane is a wonderfully esoteric blend of house styles ranging from vast Victoriana and Edwardian to stunning, early 1920s architect-designed – with a few terraces, ancient and modern, thrown in for good measure. And here, too, is one of the most desirable houses in Putney: No. 115 is a fabulous, detached Art Deco flight of fancy with a vast red dragon weather vane. Nos. 50–60 is a nice-looking development of town-houses with integral garages. The Lane can get busy with school-run traffic. Where it ends at Woodborough Rd, **Kingslawn Close** is an attractive town-house and flat enclave with communal gardens that include tennis courts.

Leading off Howard's Lane to the N are **Carmalt Gardens** and **Balmuir Gardens**, 1900-vintage, 4-bed semi-detached (just) houses. **Tideswell** and **Enmore Rds** are similar but slightly larger. An attractive 14-house cul-de-sac by St George, **Fairfax Mews** (1999), was squeezed in off Upper Richmond Rd. **Parkfields** is a narrow, hidden lane concealing some enchanting Georgian/early-Victorian cottages and larger Georgian houses (prices £600,000–1 million depending on size). The street is one way, and convenient for a small parade of similar-period shops in Upper Richmond Rd. **Dealtry Rd, Colinette Rd** and **Campion Rd** all have 3-storey Edwardian terraced and semi-detached homes and some 1960s town-houses. **Pettiward Close** is a modern cul-de-sac of 3/4-bed houses. No. 22 **Colinette Rd** has been imaginatively split into eight 1- and 2-bed flats and duplexes.

The area between **Woodborough Rd, Malbrook Rd** and **Upper Richmond Rd** boasts some of the biggest and most popular houses in Putney: 2- and 3-storey, ornate mid-

and late-Victorian detacheds with 4, 5 or 6 beds, huge gardens and seven-figure prices. There is a small council block halfway up **Woodborough Rd**. Laing's 2000 development at 307 **Upper Richmond Rd** has added 16 flats (2-beds, 2-baths c. £360,000).

At the junction of **Woodborough Rd** and **Upper Richmond Rd** are private flats: The Briars, Somerset Lodge and also modern flats at the junction with **Briar Walk** – a road which in late 1998 saw the first £2-million house sale in Putney. Pear Tree Court, also modern flats, is at the junction of **Malbrook Rd** with **Upper Richmond Rd.**

West of here is considered to be Roehampton, though the transformation is subtle. The boundary is **Putney Park Lane** – not a road, but rather a woodland track marooned in suburbia, running N–S between the houses and past the bottoms of gardens.

Roehampton

Drive up the A3 **Kingston Rd** towards Putney and to your left you will see what anywhere else in the world would be a series of luxury blocks of flats overlooking the green acres of Richmond Park. They are, in fact, the 'point' and 'slab' blocks of the vast Alton Estate, built between 1951 and 1966 by the old London County Council and now owned and managed by Wandsworth Council. The views from them must be terrific – and the views of them, when seen across the park, give an inkling of what was in the minds of tower-block architects. A swing in architectural fashion has made the estate a talking-point once again: parts are Grade II-listed and it is now a conservation area. Large sums are being spent on regeneration here.

Roehampton is bordered by Richmond Park and Richmond Park Golf Course to the S and W, **Upper Richmond Rd** to the N and by enchanting, rural **Putney Park Lane** to the E. Surrounding the old village centre, large areas are taken up by the grounds of grand 18th-century mansions, now all schools or colleges; developers are beginning to quarter the place. . . . One big site, Queen Mary's Hospital, is set for development (see below). It is an area of contrasts – it is just a 5-minute walk from the modern towers of the Alton Estate to the small Victorian terraces of **Medfield St** or to the top-of-the-range houses of **Roedean Crescent.** And it offers keener prices than Putney.

It has thus, not surprisingly, been seeing a lot of buy-to-let investment: ex-council homes are cheaper to buy and the student population provides the renters. The 130-acre tract between Richmond Park, **Clarence Lane**, **Roehampton Lane** and the A3/**Kingston Rd** is mainly council-built homes – known under the generic name of Alton, but in fact a number of different estates. Low-rise blocks and houses are increasingly owner-occupied, and tower flats with views over the park are becoming popular. Recent Alton prices had 1-beds at £120–125,000, 2-bed flats (£140–165,000), maisonettes (£180,000). Compare that with a Putney studio at £155–170,000. **Holybourne Avenue** and **Laverstoke Gardens** back onto listed Manresa House – now Greenwich University's Roehampton outpost. As usual with these big estates the planners forgot about the transport and shopping needs of inhabitants: the only shops of note are in one handy but humdrum parade (chemist, optician, baker, Co-op, newsagent) in **Danebury Avenue**. Heading out of Roehampton along the A3, however, there is the Asda superstore.

Roehampton village, just across **Roehampton Lane**, could not be more different. **Roehampton High St** has charming early- and mid-Victorian houses and small, bay-windowed 'village' shops, plus post office and two pubs. **Angel Mews** added a dozen 2-, 3- and 4-bed houses off the High St in 1999. Most, but not all, of **Medfield St** overlooks Putney Heath and holds 2- and 3-bed mid-Victorian terraced cottages and a row of later, larger, red-brick Victoriana with tall chimneys; the road is a bus route and busy during rush hours. **Ponsonby Rd**, running S off Medfield St back to Roehampton Lane, has small, flat-fronted pairs of Georgian cottages overlooking the heath, then beautiful Roehampton Church and Roehampton Church School (primary). Part of Queen Mary's Hospital has closed, and the outline plan forsees a mix of homes, offices and a hotel on

11 acres of the site, and a smaller hospital on the rest. Listed Roehampton House, which dates from 1710 and forms the heart of the present hospital, will be restored and may be sold off separately. So far, plans are in for 241 flats and houses, just to the S, and a further 46 on the SW corner of the site.

South of the hospital, **Nepean St, Akehurst St** and **Umbria St** form a quiet enclave of semi- and detached houses ranging from million-plus 6-bed Edwardian semis through to £600,000 early-1930s (with some modern infill), many now flat conversions. They have large gardens and are generally very quiet, tree-lined roads. **Rodway Rd** is a little less so: it curves between High St and Roehampton Vale, but its pleasant houses and gardens thus have good transport links.

From Putney Heath, **Dover House Rd** leads N to the Upper Richmond Rd and passes through the Dover House estate with its pretty gardens: this was built in the 1920s by the LCC – like the popular Magdalen Park estate in Earlsfield – as a 'cottage' estate. It runs from **Crestway** down to **Upper Richmond Rd**, with **Huntingfield** and **Swinburne Rds** to the W, and peaceful **Putney Park Lane** to the E. The houses are a mix of inter-war semi-detached and terraced with steeply inclined roofs and dormer windows, and pretty flat-fronted terraces and semis. The estate is now a conservation area (too late for some houses, where new owners pebbledashed, rendered or fake-stoneclad) and is a quiet, family area, with 'village' greens and open spaces: £240,000-plus for 2-bed flats, £270,000-plus for the 2-bed houses; £275–380,000 for a 3-bedroomed one. Only a few are still in council hands: in one street there are only two council tenants left.

Roads leading down to the estate from Putney Heath such as **Dover Park Drive** and **Longwood Drive** feature large, mainly detached, family houses, most built in traditional styles in the 1930s and 1950s. Prices here are lower than in Putney proper, though still up to £2 million for the biggest houses – and, point out agents, you get bigger gardens. Among the homes most in demand in Dover Park Drive are those that back onto Putney Park Lane, the unmade-up, tree-lined track running right down from Putney Heath to the Upper Richmond Rd, forming the border between Putney and Roehampton. **Coppice Drive** backs onto playing fields behind Queen Mary's Hospital. Off **Upper Richmond Rd** are mainly late-Edwardian and early-1920s homes, with some modern developments. **Putney Park Avenue** is again a private, unmade-up, tree-lined road which features ferocious speed humps, plenty of 'private road' signs and a mix of Edwardian and newer houses with a small modern flats development at its head: a very quiet road. **Marrick Close** has a small clutch of modern town-houses. **Dungarvan Avenue** and **Langside Avenue**, with their substantial 1920s semi-detached houses, are one-way streets to counter rat-running. Cornerways is modern flats on the corner of **Daylesford Avenue** and **Upper Richmond Rd**. A small parade of useful shops at the **Dover House Rd** junction.

Roehampton Lane (A306) is the route from Hammersmith Bridge and the South Circular to the A3 and Kingston. The best houses are set back from the road behind high walls or in private closes: some are exceptionally large; there are also a number of 1960s low-rise blocks of flats. Prices here rise as you get closer to Barnes station. **Roehampton Close** has 1920s and 1930s mansion blocks well back in large private grounds; **Eliot Gardens**, modern 3-storey town-houses with garages, is also set back. Upper numbers of the lane, towards Roehampton proper, are mainly 1930s terraced and semi-detached homes set rather close to the road and with views of the Alton Estate.

On the edge of Richmond Park and bordered by playing fields and Roehampton Golf Course, **Roedean Crescent** could be renamed Portico Place: it features large, detached double-fronted houses, mainly 1930s and 1950s, built in traditional styles with vast gardens – most with in-and-out drives and with a scattering of truly vulgar add-on porticoes. Expect to pay £2 million-plus. Neighbouring **Roehampton Gate** has (relatively) smaller, detached pre-war houses.

Prices of the big 1930s detached houses in **Priory Lane** by Roehampton Gate also tend to be lower due to traffic – if you consider around £1.2 million low. It's convenient for the private Priory Hospital (celebrity-spotting popular) and the vast, opulent Bank of England Sports Ground.

At the northern (Barnes Common) end of **Priory Lane** is the 1970s brick-and-concrete Lennox council estate to the W, usually with some properties for sale, and Rosslyn Park rugby football club to the E.

Transport Tubes: East Putney (zones 2/3, District), Putney Bridge (zone 2, District). To Oxford Circus 25 min (1 change), City 25 min, Heathrow 50 min (1 change). Trains: Putney, Barnes to Waterloo.

Convenient for Putney Common and Heath, Richmond Park, the Thames. Routes to the SW and W. Miles from centre: 5.

Schools Local Authority: ADT City Technology College, Elliott, Sheen , St Cecilia's Church of England. Private: Ibstock Place, Putney High (g), Putney Park (g), Hurlingham, Prospect House.

SALES						
Flats	S	1B	2B	3B	4B	5B
Average prices	100–160	150–280+	180–450+	200–500+	400–650+	–
Houses	2B 3B	4B	5B	6/7B	8B	
Average prices	250–450+	300–650+	400–1M+	500–2M+	1.5–2.5M	1.5–3.5M+
RENTAL						
Flats	S	1B	2B	3B	4B	5B
Average prices	150–210	190–300	200–500	250–600	450+	600+
Houses	2B	3B	4B	5B	6/7B	8B
Average prices	300–500	350–600	450–900	600–1300	725–1800+	900+

The properties Family houses, some vast. Enormous range of flats: p/b, mansion flats and conversions, and new mews squeezed into the corners. Smaller Victorian cottages near centre and river. Ex-council homes, many in leafy streets. Riverside, heath and common locations attract prices in millions. Putney Hill is E–W divide: west is best.

The market East Putney is very slightly cheaper: flats, small terraces. Roehampton, too, is good value, especially for ex-council homes. Then in price order come smarter cottages W of the High St, smart inter-war and modern flats on Putney Hill and spacious family homes near the heath. Riverview flats add a new luxury layer. Big West Putney houses start at a million and go up to four. Families tend to stay put: schools are good and gardens large.

Among estate agents active in this area are:

- Winkworth
- Savills
- Bradford & Bingley
- Allen Briegel
- Allan Fuller
- Barnard Marcus
- Foxtons
- Andrews
- Townends
- Warren
- Scotts
- Kinleigh Folkard & Hayward
- Douglas & Gordon
- Bairstow Eves
- Hugh Henry
- Geoffrey Jardine
- Chesterton
- James Anderton
- Featherstone Leigh
- Hamptons
- Rolfe East

REGENT'S PARK

Postal districts: NW1
Boroughs: Westminster (Con), Camden (Lab)
Council tax: Band D Westminster £605, Camden £1,200
Conservation areas: All Crown Estate
Parking: Restricted in park, controlled everywhere else

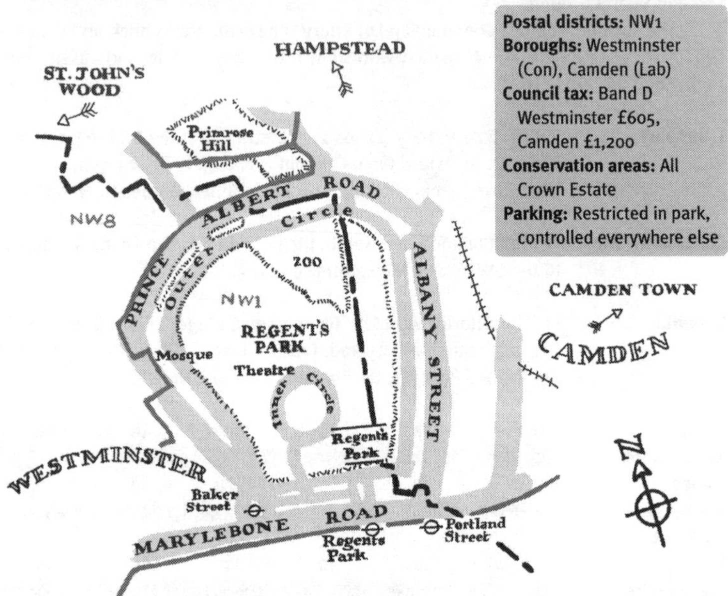

The three new villas (mansions to you and me) on the Outer Circle, all sold at £10 million each, add to the stock of the most select of the five types of homes in Regent's Park. These are the dozen stand-alone houses, with the carriage drives, the high walls, the space to park all your cars, that certain sorts of rich people seek. The top homes of this ilk are the original vast, scattered 1820s villas: Hanover Lodge, Grove Lodge, The Holme, St John's Lodge and – the biggest – neo-Georgian Winfield House, home to the US Ambassador.

Other rich persons here seem content with terraced houses: very grand, stucco-fronted, unified to give the impression of a palace frontage – often with mews house at the back and pool in the basement. Type three is the period flat, carved (often with great skill and flair) from one of those grand terraces: these can cost as much as a house almost anywhere else in London. Type four is the mews cottage, detached from its parent mansion, and offering garage and bijou living to the almost-as-well-off. Last, outside the park altogether, are the mansion flats, of every period over the past century, that line the park's northern and western rims.

R

Get to the small print in the opulent brochures that solicit your interest in the Regent's Park palaces and you will find the words 'Crown Estate lease of XX years'. Yes, you are being asked to pay prices like £18 million (a real asking price, in 2002) and you will not even own the land it sits on. The freeholds are all ultimately held by the Crown, and the area benefits from the Crown Estate's careful management and long-term planning, which has led to the restoration of all the great terraces since 1945. (Regent's Park survived serious plans to demolish half the terraces in the late 1940s: this was understandable as wartime bombing, dry rot and neglect had left most uninhabitable.)

Up to now, leases have been short, and extensions to these leases carefully rationed, if obtainable at all. Being royal and all that, the estate does not have to play by the rules which govern lesser landlords. Now, however, the Crown Estate has announced that it will grant (for a price) new leases of up to 90 years to those eligible under the law (see Buying & Selling chapter) – though it sets its face against selling freeholds, as the law insists other landlords must do.

Crown leases may now be extendable, but they are still tough. A common policy has been to sell houses in the terraces on relatively (for the Crown) long leases – 60 years was typical – on the condition that the leaseholder completely restores the house. The estate stipulates the architect, has a veto over the plans and retains control over the exterior. When a lease on one of the splendid individual villas came up for sale, the estate told would-be buyers that it, the Crown, would also choose the interior decorator and the landscape designer. All the buyer had to do, of course, was to pay their fees.

Buying a lease of one of the 880 Crown Estate homes means paying a good chunk of ground rent each year: £2,000 is typical, rising during the lease: it usually doubles at a certain point, then doubles again. A flat attracts service charges, too: these can be as high as £18,000 a year for a family-sized flat. And then there's the Crown Estate paving rate which can add another £4,000 . . . And even when a sale is agreed, completion can take six months, what with all the messing about with Crown leases.

Regent's Park is the one major exception to London's careful avoidance of large-scale civic planning. John Nash, with the backing of the Prince Regent, conceived the startling scheme in 1811, making each terrace of houses appear a single, classical palace, set in a sylvan landscape – thus accentuating the difference between London's town streets and this idealized countryside. There are 374 houses, many now split into flats, arranged in a great ring circling the park – the **Outer Circle** – or reached via the little **Inner Circle**, which also holds the Park's very own theatre. Any other form of vulgar commerce (shops, pubs), though, necessitates a trip into the workaday world beyond this charmed world.

The grand sweep of **Portland Place** leads triumphantly up to the park from Oxford Circus, dividing at the end into the graceful double curve of **Park Crescent**. The six-lane Marylebone Rd is decently shielded from view by the curve of its garden. North of the main road is more greenery, **Park Square**, with its two facing rows of Nash houses forming an entrance to the park. The clever trick Nash pulled was to design uniform facades and then give lease-buyers a free hand to design the homes and other buildings behind them. Thus **Park Square East**'s central three houses are not homes at all: they concealed the Diorama, a sort of 1820s proto-cinema, now converted into an arts centre, and owned by the Prince's Trust.

Clockwise around the **Outer Circle**, terrace succeeds snow-white terrace, each with a distinguishing feature within the overall classical style. Turn from **Park Square West** into short **Ulster Terrace**, which boasts pairs of bow-fronted windows at either end (behind these windows unmodernized flats have been on offer recently – a 2-bed for just under £1 million); the ground floor is offices. Next come the gardens of **York Terrace East** and **West**, flanking **York Gate**: these houses face onto their own private roads, while their backs look N over the park. The East terrace is original (offices and apartments): it is considered the more exclusive. The West was rebuilt behind the facade and has good, popular flats, complete with underground garage and security. Off here lies **Nottingham Terrace**, security-conscious flats tight against the rear wall of Madame Tussaud's.

Next, **Cornwall Terrace** is the earliest of all the park terraces, designed by Decimus Burton and dating from 1820. Again, there are bow windows at either end and three great, full-height porticoes with classical columns. Some of its 19 houses are offices. No. 1, truly 'of ambassadorial proportions' and with two houses along the mews (staff, relatives?), turned heads in 2002 when marketed at £18 million for a 74-year lease. A more normal-sized (but still 8-bed) one, unmodernized, was £6.5 million last winter (125-year lease).

Most of the terraces have mews, some of which are still linked to the grand houses so you can buy one of each. Or you can choose a mews house on its own – perhaps in **Park Square Mews**, tucked into the corner behind Ulster Terrace and Park Square West.

Clarence Gate leads out to the top of Baker St. Small, elegant **Clarence Terrace,** with 2- to 4-bed flats, and studios in the basement, is next in line, backing onto busy **Park Rd.**

Then comes **Sussex Place,** curving round behind its own garden and served by a private road. Its astonishing row of five pairs of Saracen's-helmet-shaped cupolas gives it a unique, exotic air. The graceful facade is original, but behind it lies a modern rebuilding carried out for the London Business School – the principal of which has a particularly enviable private residence.

The next building along, **Hanover Terrace,** is set back from the road behind a garden, its insubstantial-looking statues still adorning its blue-painted portico. This sweep has been completely restored following the Crown's sale of refurbishment leases. These enviable homes have private, 60ft, west-facing gardens and their own mews houses.

The grandeur of the London Central Mosque with its gold dome stands on the western edge of the park: a splendid building, the outlines of which somehow marry well with Nash's classical facades. From here on, the Grand Union Canal curves around the northern edge of the park. Between it and the Outer Circle is **Hanover Lodge,** the fourth of the splendid park 'villas' to revert from an institution to a home. Three detached villas – Ionic, Veneto and Gothic – by architect Quinlan Terry were built in the grounds in the early 1990s: one sold a couple of years ago for £10 million. Opposite, within the park, is vast **Winfield House,** the American ambassadorial residence. London Zoo takes up the N corner of the park, its muted cries and roars (alas, trumpetings no longer, the elephants have moved to Whipsnade) carried on the summer nights' breezes.

On the E side the terraces take up the tale once more: seven of **Gloucester Gate's** houses underwent no-expense-spared refurbishment in 1989. All seven of them boast mews houses with garages. There are also flats in the terrace. Next comes **St Katherine's Precinct,** with much-in-demand, c. £3.5 million, 4-storey houses – Gothic not classical – which leads to the Danish Church.

Cumberland Terrace was rebuilt behind its splendid, pedimented facade after World War II as houses (about £3 million) and flats (£800,000 for a long lease 2-bed). **Cumberland Place** boasts a lovely, large classical villa, bow-windowed at either end. Crown leases of 150 years on the rest of the row 'suitable for reinstatement into three houses' were bought by classy developer Octagon: two sold for £4 million apiece; the largest, some 9,000 sq ft, was £10 million. **Chester Terrace** is a long row of 42 more normal-sized houses, which remain as individual homes. They were rebuilt behind the facade 35 years ago, so allied to their lovely Regency proportions are such modern facilities as lifts and integral garages. You will need £3–4.5 million for one of these. The mews behind, **Chester Close North,** was rebuilt at the same time – but alas in mid-1960s style. The self-contained wings (gate-houses, some call them: they make 5-bed homes) set forward at either end are linked to the main terrace by flying-buttress-like archways. **Chester Place** has medium-sized (4-bed) Nash houses.

Cambridge Terrace, with its Georgian curved-top windows, nowadays contains flats, maisonettes and houses plus 30,000 sq ft of offices after a 1980s programme of modernization (a 3-bed flat, £2.2 million). Behind, **Cambridge Terrace Mews** is a group of 4-bed, 3-bath modern houses (c. £1.35 million) which share a communal garden.

The next block, **Cambridge Gate,** was built half a century later than its Regency neighbours in sandy stone, and has an ornate and overdecorated air beside their white stucco. A flat here, a 3-bed lateral conversion, was £3.6 million last winter. Nos. 1–9 Cambridge Gate are the latest Regent's Park houses to have been modernized and converted: homes include a 3-floor, 6-bed maisonette – and a vast, 16,500 sq ft house.

On past the uncompromising modern lines of the Royal College of Physicians, and then the little Regency cul-de-sac of **St Andrew's Place,** you return to **Park Square,** overlooking its private square gardens (tennis courts, and space to erect a marquee should you so desire), having completed the circuit.

Within the park, around the **Inner Circle**, are the enchanted Open Air Theatre and that handful of scattered 'villas'. Most dwindled into institutional use during the mid-20th century, but now have become homes again. These glorious original mansions, where the lucky owner can easily imagine himself to be in a country house, are among London's very finest. New Crown leases have been sold in the past 20 years on **The Holme, Grove Lodge** and **St John's Lodge** – with stringent clauses about renovation and upkeep.

Back in the (relatively) normal world, **Albany St** runs parallel with, but outside, the E edge of the park. Handsome terraced Georgiana here yields 3-bed homes, including flats at (relatively) more normal prices. At the S end, **Prince Regent's Terrace**, a row of flat-fronted brick houses, was remodelled into enviable duplexes in 1988: they could be bought singly or as pairs to make a house. At the same time five mews houses were added to **Peto Place** behind. Further N, several rows of mews belonging to the park terraces open off **Albany Rd**. There is also some recent housing in brick-and-stucco style. On the E side is the **Cumberland Market** estate, a complex of serviceable brick buildings let by the Crown Estate as fair-rent housing. The 500 flats were all renovated a decade ago. In **Redhill St** 1999 saw a new gated courtyard of 2- and 3-bed houses partially rebuilt behind a period facade.

Park Village West is a delightful oddity, a curving lane off **Albany Rd** where the Regency style reappears laced with Gothic in a surprising collection of little Nash 'country cottages' (though some have 6 bedrooms, and even the 3-beds are £1.6 million or so). **Park Village East**, which lies behind, has some of the best gardens in the whole area. It suffered when the houses on the E side were demolished to widen the Euston railway here and at the E end of **Prince Albert Rd**. Park Village East also has some pleasant modern town-houses and flats.

Prince Albert Rd runs in a sweep above the N bank of the canal, its grand parade of flats, from 1900 to 2000-luxurious, attracting top prices with their splendid park views across its traffic. It was here, during the early 1980s, that London first acquired a stock of international-standard flats – for jet-set buyers for whom 'Georgian' meant merely 'secondhand'. At the E end, by the canal, are some surviving pairs of 1850s villas. Nos. 6–15, which are in pairs, were expensively reconstructed in 1989: these are vast, 6-bedroomed homes, some with swimming pools, with long Crown leases.

St Mark's Square has mid-19th-century houses and links with the Primrose Hill neighbourhood (see Camden Town chapter). The green sweep of the hill rises up to the right, then the blocks of mansion flats for which **Prince Albert Rd** is famous begin. Prince Albert Court is dark, purply-grey brick, St James's Close is red-brick 1930s. Park St James, set back on **St James's Terrace**, was the first new block for some 15 years when built in 1984. Stockleigh Hall is 1920s, stucco and red-brick. Viceroy Court is also 1920s with inset balconies and curving ends. **Bentinck Close** is more 1930s, 3-beds; then comes 1920s Oslo Court. These blocks are a good hunting ground for a decent-sized 3/4-bed flat, and there are a few 5-bed ones.

Avenue Rd runs down to meet **Prince Albert Rd** from the heart of St John's Wood. On the corner, luxurious No. 2 Avenue Rd has large projecting balconies; facing it is a white stone balconied block, Imperial Court. The pair are well-established, modern blocks, 20–25 years old: flats here command premium prices (and rents). Then comes Edwardian splendour: the red and white mansion blocks of Northgate which stand on the corner of **Prince Albert Rd** and **St John's Wood High St** (which provides the shops for this side of the park). These are elegant, well-thought-of flats, some of family size (5-bed, 3-bath).

Busy **Park Rd** runs along the W, Lisson Grove, edge of the park; busy, and not quite 'prime' (sniff the posher agents), but a fertile ground for ever more flats schemes. Except at the extreme N end, blocks in this road lack the park views – penthouses may be an exception. The 13-year-old Beverly House is a U-shaped block (called the U Building by agents) on a rather cramped site. The place to live here is in one of the truly vast penthouses: 6,000 sq ft over two floors. The best flats are c. £1.3 million; £750,000-plus for something more ordinary. They are popular among 'rich folks' kids' say agents.

Crown Court (1980s) has just 23 flats of from one to five bedrooms in its seven floors. Abbey Lodge, 1920s mansion blocks, is on the W side of the road and backs onto the Nash Terraces, which resume with **Kent Terrace**. This, being tucked behind **Hanover Terrace**, is one of the few not to overlook the park, which means houses drop in price to £2 million or so. At the S end of **Park Rd** are some pretty early 19th-century houses, not part of the Nash ensemble.

There is scant space for new homes here, but Barratt discovered a plot in an old rail yard 'only 250 yards' from the park. Here, off Rossmore Rd and in NW1, **Prince Regent's Gate** has 400 flats (see Marylebone chapter). Marylebone station is handy.

Transport Tubes (all zone 1): Regent's Park (Bakerloo), Baker Street (Circle, Metropolitan, Bakerloo, Jubilee). From Regent's Park: Oxford Circus 3 min, City 20 min (1 change), Heathrow 55 min (1 change).

Convenient for West End, City. Miles from centre: 1.5.

Schools Local Authority: Haverstock School, Maria Fidelis Convent RC, St Marylebone C of E. Private: Cavendish (g), Francis Holland (g).

SALES

Flats	S	1B	2B	3B	4B	5B
Average prices	170–200+	240–700	400–1M+	525–3.5M	650–3.5M	1.3–4M+
Houses	2B	3B	4B	5B	6/7B	8B
Average prices	575–1M+	850–3M+	1.25M+	3–9M	→	6.5–18M

RENTAL

Flats	S	1B	2B	3B	4B	5B
Average prices	240–290	275–450	280–700	425–1400	550–1500	2000+
Houses	2B	3B	4B	5B	6/7B	8B
Average prices	500–1000	650–1000+	950–1250+	1900–3000+	3000–6000+	–

The properties Charmed circle of top-quality homes gaze out over the park: the lovely, snowy Regency terraces hold houses and apartments, many of them no-expense-spared rebuilds behind the dignified facades. Also a handful of London's finest mansions scattered within the park. Luxury 20th-century flats on Prince Albert and Park Rds, and mews cottages behind the terraces.

The market Crown Estate rethink on leases opens up market. Tall, thin houses (all those stairs . . .) put some buyers off. Always demand from foreign and British buyers for some of London's smartest (and priciest) homes. Think £800–1,000 per sq ft.

R

Among estate agents active in this area are:

- Aston Chase
- Anscombe & Ringland
- John D Wood
- Savills
- Keith Cardale Groves
- Knight Frank
- Hamptons
- Oakleys
- Regent's Park Property
- Winkworth
- Goldschmidt & Howland
- Foxtons
- Brian Lack
- Bargets
- Alexanders
- Behr & Butchoff
- Allsops
- Chestertons

Richmond and Kew

Postal districts: TW9, TW10
Boroughs: Richmond upon Thames (Con)
Council tax: Band D £1,339
Conservation areas: Include Richmond town, riverside and Green, Kew Green
Parking: Residents/meters in centre

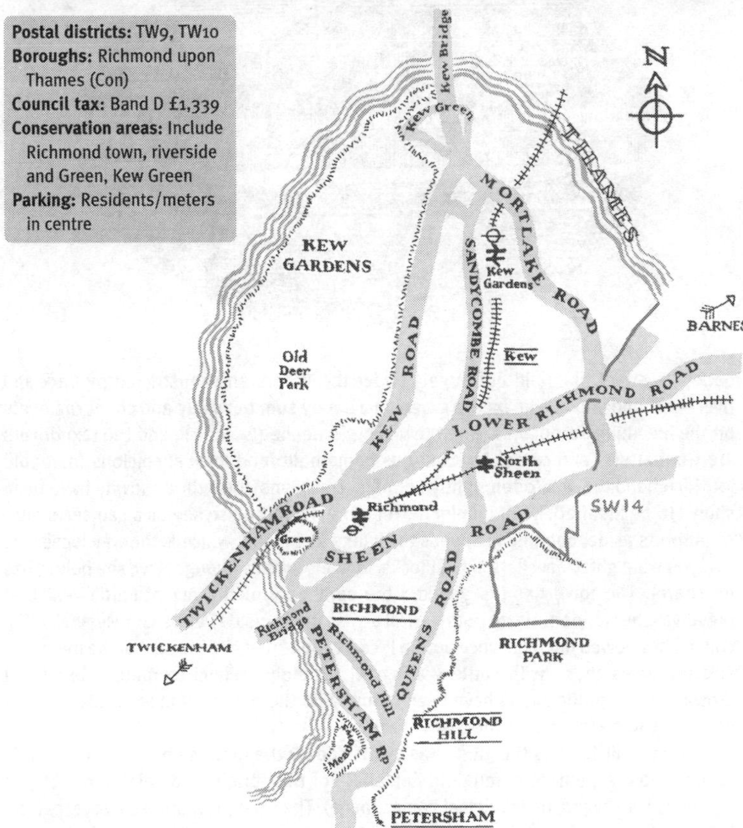

Richmond residents are Londoners who get to have their cake and eat it. A Georgian Thames-side town that the city flowed westwards to meet, this is in no real sense a suburb: on the landward side it is cut off by its own enormous royal park and gets Kew Gardens, just to the north, to boot. The people who live here see themselves, perhaps more than any other inhabitants of areas in this guide, as citizens of Richmond, Surrey, rather than the wider metropolis. *And* as 'virtually inner London' in terms of convenience, thanks to the tube. Vulgar commerce may take Richmond people by this, or by mainline train, into Town, and they claim smugly that the West End theatres are just as accessible as their own little gem; but their heart remains in the borough.

And who can blame them for keeping the place to themselves? It has a river promenade, a lovely green, a superb prospect from its Hill, a historic past, 2,500 acres of primeval English landscape – oaks and deer-dotted rolling grassland – in its park, and beautiful, beautiful buildings. People from elsewhere come to Richmond to eat out, to be entertained, to visit the pubs and bars, to stroll by the river. In the affluent reaches of South-West London, it's Kingston for shopping and Richmond for leisure.

So where is the snake in this demi-Eden? Transport, again. You can reach central London by tube, train (even riverboat, in summer); Heathrow is at hand; but traffic jams

R

bedevil a street plan laid out largely under the Tudors and constricted by park and river – oh, and you can lie on the green on a sunny summer's day and count the rivets on the incoming aeroplanes. Heathrow is both lifeline ('*so* quick, and the taxi drivers are wonderful!') and curse. Terminal 5 is being built; and local suspicions (paranoid lot, Richmondites, and often rightly so) of 'secret plans' for a third runway have been shown to be justified, if not imminent. Yet more aircraft noise seems a sad certainty.

Airports aside, not much happens to change Richmond, which is the way locals like it. If you want glitzy new flats in big blocks, look elsewhere (though Kew, see below, has its share). The town has just marked the centenary of the Act of Parliament that preserves the wonderful vista from the Hill across the riverside Petersham Meadows. The council has bowed out, and since 2001 a Preservation Trust has the care of the meadows and preserves them 'with cattle grazing in perpetuity'. Plans to route a branch of Crossrail through Richmond have been dropped, to the delight of most locals (and the council) who prefer to keep the District Line.

However, little dims the glory – as evidenced by the dizzying house prices in this second most expensive borough in England – of this 'bright and shining place' (the meaning, it's alleged, of its original name, Shene). The town grew around a royal palace, between the green and the river, and really took off when Henry VII rebuilt it (on a par with his son's later Hampton Court), and renamed it and the town – 500 years or so back, in 1501 – after his earldom in Richmond, Yorkshire. It remained a fashionable resort until Charles II moved to Windsor and the palace fell into disrepair.

But the area continued to attract the nobility (as is evident from the Georgian mansions here and along **Petersham Rd**), artists and writers. Today's equivalent are the rock'n'roll/Hollywood/media contingent on the Hill, who profess to love Richmond life despite the tug of their other homes in California and the Caribbean (you won't spot them on the tube, mind: they may not even know it exists . . .). The green peace of the Old Deer Park, Kew Gardens, Richmond Park and Thames-side walks still draw families and frazzled commuters who can shake off the city dust (Waterloo 20 min). There's a wealth of good prep, public, state secondary and church schools, while the borough's primaries regularly top the national league tables. The German School at Ham, the Swedish one in Barnes attract foreign diplomats and City people. Australian and American expats like the quintessential Englishness; the Japanese come for golf courses (Old Deer Park, Fulwell, Sudbrook Park) and the reasonable proximity to the Japanese School in Acton. They all like being a fast drive from Heathrow – and from the M4 corridor.

These buyers, of course, along with the City moguls (more Rupert than Alex) are just those that were hit first and hardest by the economic downturn that we can now see, with hindsight, began in summer 2001 and was only ameliorated, if not ended, by the stock market's climb in mid- to late 2003 and through 2004. Prices here dropped by quite chunky percentages, especially over £1 million. Top-end prices are now described as 'stable'. But most sales at that level are discretionary: many owners will simply decide not to sell if there's a lack of buyers, rather than accept any very large reduction. Even very covetable homes can take a long time to sell. This is *par excellence* a place for families – and once they get established, they stay put. Sometimes they trade down, more often they (try to) trade up. Winter 04/05 saw more property on the market than Richmond agents have been used to – one said supply was at its highest for five years – but, in the right brackets, there were 'still not enough' homes to satisfy demand.

Richmond and its satellites have an unfair number of wonderful period houses, from Queen Anne through all stages of Georgian to the most opulent of Victorian. The real period gems, family houses on the Hill and the mansions of Ham and Petersham, can cost anything between £1.5 and £6.5 million, depending on size, era, degree of dignity and position. It is easy to spend between £1 and £2 million on the Hill and come away with a fairly ordinary-looking, even terraced, house, or a 1930s detached of a distinctly suburban mien. Those seeking relatively more affordable but still roomy family homes look to Kew, cross the river to St Margarets or Teddington; or consider North Kingston.

There is a fair supply of 1-bed flats, but in really prime areas near the river, hill and green they can approach £300,000, given good views and a roof terrace. Two-beds encompass both mansion blocks (most are 1930s, in the centre, Richmond Hill and towards Sheen) and conversions of the big Victorian houses. Most 3-bed flats are found in mansion blocks, several of which also offer studios.

Richmond town

Richmond is squeezed between the river, its park, the Old Deer Park and the open fields of Petersham. Most of it dates from Georgian and Victorian times: there is very little modern housing. Shopping is pleasant around **George St**, the town's busy high street. There's a full-blown if rather tired department store (Dickins & Jones) and all the more tasteful high street chains, plus a Tesco Metro, Waitrose and Marks & Spencer. The smart shops extend S along **Hill St** towards the bridge, and on up **Hill Rise** (antiques, designer clothes). Restaurants and bars are plentiful. Little alleyways lead off **George St** down to the green, with delicatessens, coffee shops, antique shops, bookshops, jewellers. Traffic is the only problem: there's no way round Richmond (except over equally congested Richmond Hill) and delivery trucks and buses fight shoppers for foot space.

Richmond Green's lovely open space is surrounded by homes ranging from the 17th to 20th centuries. Most of the beautiful Georgian houses along its SE edge (the address is simply **The Green**) are still, sadly, offices. Its continuation, **Little Green**, holds a few houses and the endearing, cupola'd late-Victorian theatre (it's by Matcham); the redundant United Reformed Church close by now provides nine new 2- and 3-bedroomed opportunities to live here, courtesy of St George. On the NW side of the green are some splendid large Victorian villas; on the NE side **Portland Terrace** has some handsome 1970s houses (approaching £1 million). A busy railway line passing behind **Pembroke Villas** (the NW side of the green) and charming **Old Palace Lane** makes little difference to prices, as the substantial houses and the early 19th-century cottages in the Lane have such lovely outlooks. You can pay £500,000 for a 2-bed cottage, £1.6m for a 6-bed house.

Maids of Honour Row (1724: it was built for the maids of George II's queen), gazes out from the SW side of the Green. Behind, between it and the river, is the site of Henry VII's palace: look for names like **Old Palace Terrace**, where seven houses built in 1692 were among the earliest on the cleared site (£1.5 million for one of these, this winter as last), **Old Palace Yard** and **The Wardrobe** – three houses here are said to be palace remains. Trumpeters House (originally known, simply, as 'the Old Palace') is a perfect piece of riverside early Georgian, now four flats; its two lodge houses share the acre of gardens with them, and one has a further acre of its own, too. More neo-Georgian houses in **Trumpeter's Inn** and **Garrick Close**. **Retreat Rd** has lovely Regency 5-bed houses. **Friars Lane** curves down to the Thames where, past Queensbury House (neat 1930s flats) and a row of pretty Georgian houses, it joins riverside **Cholmondeley Walk**. The fine, restored Palladian villa, Asgill House, is at the N end of the Walk. Commanding spectacular views of bridge and river is the early-19th century **St Helena's Terrace**, a row of handsome houses built high above their own boathouses. Ignore no-parking signs in front of the adjacent White Cross, and you may return to find a car full of Thames: tides rise swiftly. A clutch of smart homes is tucked behind, off narrow, cobbled **Water Lane**.

Alongside the riverside promenade which leads to Richmond Bridge is Quinlan Terry's 1980s Thames-side complex of offices, flats, shops and restaurants. Unrivalled views of the river are a plus for the homes: studios, 1- and 2-bed flats, maisonettes, a couple of houses and a penthouse. This was one of the most argued-over pieces of architecture of the day, pitting Neo-Classicists against Modernists in a bitter professional spat. Terry used a variety of classical genres to produce this Georgian townscape (much new; some original facades) behind which the commercial elements are hidden. Whether or not you find this a cop-out, it works splendidly, the riverside face with its public gardens being the focus of the town's much-used Thames-side promenade: here pubs and cafés rub shouders with a working boat-builder's. South of the bridge, some **Petersham Rd** houses have gardens down to the riverside. The curving roofs of Blade House, a very successful new building beside a long-derelict riverside pub, the Three Pigeons, shelter enviable £1-million flats. They'll be joined soon by more in the restored pub itself: £700,000 flats above a restaurant, due summer '05.

On the other side of town, past the station, a church in **Kew Rd** has been split into 15 flats, from studios to 3-beds. The roads between **Kew Rd** and the Old Deer Park are pretty, if congested (5-bed terraced £600,000-plus). You could sell the car: one can live very centrally in Richmond. Explore the caches of tiny terraced cottages tucked away behind the shopping streets, or there are big 1930s mansion blocks near Waitrose in **Sheen Rd**; but for central Richmond's premier quarter, raise your eyes unto the Hill . . .

Richmond Hill

Richmond Hill rises S and SE of the town towards Richmond Park. The oldest homes are nearest the town: **Ormond Rd** has some Queen Anne houses (£1.5 million paid for a 4-bed), some of **The Vineyard** is Georgian or Regency, but further up towards the Park most homes are Victorian or later. There are favourite roads, but all Hill locations are desirable. For roomy, family 5-bed Victoriana, look to **Mount Ararat Rd, Grosvenor Rd, Dynevor Rd** and **Montague Rd** and budget for £1.3 million or so. To gain Hill cachet at a lower budget, try **Halford Rd**, where 4-bed Victorian terraced houses can be had for £700,000. **Lancaster Park** is a street of contrasts: Vine House, a very high-spec fake-Regency villa, 5,000 sq ft, is but four years old, while opposite are the minute, charming (but still c. £300,000) 1850 **Lancaster Cottages**, reached by a paved path. Behind Vine House are four new town-houses. **Lancaster Park** continues on up the hill, meeting **Ellerker Gardens**, both with big late-Victorian terraced houses – and a Regency fake-gothic cream-painted 'castle'.

R

All of these roads lie E of **Richmond Hill**, the street which begins at Hill Rise with a clutch of smart shops (Georgian houses behind and between them) and rises to the hilltop and **Downe Terrace**, a handsome row of very, very expensive homes, with just about London's finest sylvan view: out over the public Terrace Gardens and down to the winding Thames and the cow-grazed (in perpetuity, mind) Petersham water meadows.

Church Rd is fairly busy but big houses, some split into flats but £1.4 million for a whole 5-bed. **The Vineyard**, which crosses Mount Ararat Rd, is one of the prettiest streets on the Hill. It shelters houses from late-17th to early-19th centuries – including several clutches of almshouses from 1767 onwards. Last winter £2.75 million was being asked for a Georgian 5/6 bed house. **Onslow Avenue** has Edwardian 5-bed houses; pretty, secluded **Chislehurst Rd** has smaller mid-Victorian ones. On **Mount Ararat Rd** the smaller houses are to the N: higher street numbers are smartest.

The crown of **Richmond Hill** is lined with a mixture of prized 18th- and 19th-century houses (some split into flats) which enjoy that wonderful sweeping view of the Thames, painted by Turner and Reynolds. **Richmond Hill Court** is a big U-shaped complex of 1930s flats (£375,000 for a 2-bed). At the summit stands the huge, handsome Royal Star & Garter Home (to be sold in about 2007: a hotel? flats? If flats, they'll be hard to beat for location and views). The Georgiana opposite, by the park entrance, belongs to it too. Turn E down **Queen's Rd,** which hugs the park, go past the American University buildings and on the left is a range of enormous houses of various Edwardian and Victorian styles, many split into flats. As whole houses, done-up, these can be between £1.3 and £3 million; here, too, are 1930s mansion flats (2-bed c. £270,000) and 1930s detached houses. On the E side are houses and flats of the 1970s, 1980s and 1990s – and some side roads that lead to a hidden corner towards the park: **Cambrian Rd,** with its charming period houses, leads to a foot-gate into the park. **King George Square** is a gated clutch of 1980s homes set around a Georgian workhouse, forming a group with **Manning Rd.**

West of Queen's Rd are some pretty streets, such as **Park Rd,** with a blend of early-Victorian 3-storey houses and 2-bed cottages. **Marchmont Rd** and **Denbigh Gardens** have Edwardian, 1920s/1930s and 1950s detached houses; **Chester Avenue** some 1930s flats. **King's Rd,** with large Victorian-Gothic detacheds, a terrace of 1850s 4/5-storey ones and a group of four new ones, runs up to the prominent church at the junction with **Friars Stile Rd,** which has a few smart shops, some 5-bed period houses and 1960s flats.

At the N, lower, end of of **Queen's Rd** is Barratt's Queens Richmond: big houses (a 7-bed at £1.8 million), flats and a new primary school. Across the road Christ's School, an over-subscribed C of E secondary, has just spent £3 million on new buildings.

Back towards the town, sandwiched between **Albert Rd** and **Princes Rd** is a hidden corner of tiny 2- or 3-bed cottages known as **The Alberts.** These have been popular for years, and they have nearly all been tidied up. You can pay well over £300,000 for a 2-bed, up to £450,000 for a 3-bed.

North of busy **Sheen Rd,** in **Dunstable Rd, Sheen Park, Townshend Terrace** and **St Mary's Grove,** there is a mix of Edwardian, Victorian and Regency cottages and large 3-storey houses, some split into flats. Residents in **Sheen Park, Townshend Terrace** and the N end of **St Mary's Grove** have had the threat of Crossrail lifted. A 5-bed Victorian semi in Sheen Park is c. £900,000. Across the rail line, between it and **Lower Mortlake Rd** a grid of streets harbours 2/3-bed period cottages. **Cedar Terrace,** off Lower Mortlake Rd, has 90 modern homes: 2-bed maisonettes and 2-bed terraced houses. **Sheendale Rd** has beautiful (if cramped and gardenless) Regency cottages. **St George's Rd, Bardolph Rd** and **Trinity Cottages** are pretty.

East of **Manor Rd,** which joins Sheen Rd and Lower Richmond Rd via a constantly busy railway level crossing, there are council-built houses (tipped as worth a look) on **Kings Farm Avenue** and **Carrington Rd.** Roads S of and including **Tangier Rd** offer 1930s-built 3/4-bed houses. South of **Upper Richmond Rd** post-war houses are to be found, particularly on **Berwyn Rd, Orchard Rise, Sheen Common Drive.** Proximity to park and common (the excellent primary school helps, too) pushes top prices here well beyond a million. **Courtlands** is a large 1930s complex of mansion flats (2-beds c. £270,000).

Petersham and Ham Common

These villages on the borders of Richmond offer rural living to people who cannot bear to be more than half an hour by car from Hyde Park Corner. They have served this umbilical function for 300 years, as the dignified Georgian homes testify. That speed of journey may now only be possible at, say, two o'clock in the morning, but Richmond does well as a substitute for the West End for most purposes, and Kingston's large array of shops and stores (and schools) is just down the road in the other direction.

Petersham is glorious: a place that appears to reverse the natural village order, with more manor houses than small cottages. It is enclosed on nearly every side by green expanses: deer-grazed Richmond Park rears to the E, cattle-dotted water meadows by the Thames to the N, the dignified Ham House grounds to the W. Its only snag is the endless traffic that creeps along the narrow, twisting lane past the high brick walls that shut off the – truly grand – mansions. Mansions do occasionally come up for sale: a Georgian 6-bed one was £4 million last winter (it's been on for a year at this price), but for just a taste of fine living try the flats into which Rutland Lodge, one of the grandest, was split. Even the Victoriana can be on a magnified scale: for example the old vicarage, a 9-bed pile with 2.8 acres of garden adjoining the park. Its 1907 church, also redundant, was converted into one vast home three years ago. A Tudor house – moved here, beam by beam, from Kent some 80 years ago – sold for £4 million last summer.

There *are* some smaller houses in Petersham, including 20th-century ones in a more suburban setting over towards Ham, where **Sandy Lane** and nearby streets have Surrey-style detached houses (5-bed £850,000). For a contrast £4 million will buy the last of three Terry Farrell modern houses, all glass, steel and limestone, in **River Lane**. The German School and the excellent primary school attract families to Petersham.

Ham Common, to the S, is a splendid, large triangle of manicured rural England, with the gates to ducal Ham House to add class. There are more gracious Georgian homes here on the Petersham scale; a few charming cottages. Away from the Common, much of Ham is suburbia, including a tract of Wates-built 1970s housing and a big council-built estate bordering the woods and open spaces of Ham Lands towards the Thames. Here a Wates 2-bed maisonette will be c. £195,000, while on the well-regarded, Grade II-listed 1960s Span-built Parkleys estate on the Richmond Park side 2-bed flats are £175–220,000. Modern private-developer houses edging open, riverside Ham Lands are attractively sited. Ham Parade on **Richmond Rd** serves as the high street (good shops).

Towards Ham's Richmond Park gate, woodland takes over; leading through it, **Church Rd** has some 20th-century houses, mostly big and grand. A dozen more modest ones sold fast in 1998, despite being next door to the (very polite) Latchmere House prison.

Kew

To the N of Richmond, Kew also has a villagey feel, set round a green complete with cricket pitch – though the constant South Circular traffic, coupled with the Heathrow planes, dispels any rural illusions. It also has a village property market, with one agent finding that 75 per cent of his business is with locals moving around the area. However, some new blood – locals say a 25 per cent jump in population – is arriving thanks to the major redevelopments to the E of the area, off the **Mortlake Rd** – see below.

Kew is a peninsula bounded by the Thames, with Richmond to the S and Mortlake to the SE. The world-famous botanical gardens, together with the Old Deer Park, take up half the area. Despite this, Kew is plagued by main roads, with Kew Bridge linking the South Circular with the M4/North Circular junction. From the green, **Mortlake Rd**, (the South Circular) forks SE and **Kew Road** leads SW to Richmond. Between these roads is the bulk of the area's housing. The roads on the Kew Gardens side of **Sandycombe Rd** and the railway line are primarily Victorian, and are most sought-after, with the mostly 20th-century E side (sometimes called North Sheen) increasing in desirability. The ever-growing demand for spacious houses near open space and good schools has seen an influx of families, from Chiswick and areas further in; as with Richmond, once here, they stay.

Kew Green and the riverside

The most prestigious homes line **Kew Green**, where the gracious Georgian houses and cottages, surrounded by mature trees and decked with wisteria, back onto the river/botanic gardens and/or face the green. A rush of properties came up for sale here last winter, in a location where little usually changes hands: Kew's oldest house, dating from 1670, was on offer for £2.1 million. The Kew Park Estate (**Bush Rd** is the entrance), just W of the bridge, has pleasant dark-brick 1970s houses and flats in a leafy, gated enclave: a bit less than a million for a 4-bed town-house.

Hidden E of the bridge, between green and river, **Thetis Terrace**, **Cambridge** and **Watcombe Cottages** have charming old (mostly 2-bed) rows in a network of lanes and closes. Some overlook the Thames, others (in Thetis, and **Willow Cottages**) a little park. Think £600,000 for a 2-bed cottage, though a 5-bed riverside house was £1.65 million last winter. Also in this corner: some sizeable 1970s town-houses on the green, and **Old Dock Close** with attractive, tucked-away modern houses. In an enclave bounded by river, green and railway, leafy **Bushwood Rd**, **Priory Rd** (which gives its name to the neighbourhood, a conservation area), and **Maze Rd** have Victorian/Edwardian 3-bed terraces (£650,000-plus) and 4/5-bed semis (£850,000-plus).

The enormous modern Public Record Office, by the river, is a Kew landmark. Now, on the nine-acre riverside site next door, comes St George's 'Kew Riverside Park'. (Not to be confused with Kew *Retail* Park: some rather upmarket retail sheds sheltering M&S, Boots etc. – and lots of useful car parking, nor indeed with 'Kew Riverside', see below. . .) St George offers 200 1- to 4-bed flats in 6-plus-storey blocks (list prices last autumn, from £300,000 for 1-beds). Just downriver, the 26-acre former sewage works has been replaced with Kew Riverside, 534 plush homes 'in the classical style' by St James Homes, completing this spring. Over 100 of the homes are Affordable Housing. There are six acres of open space, surrounding some very large (4- to 6-bed) detached houses (from £1.3 million), and the usual mix of flats (in six buildings, from £2375,000) and town-houses (£925,000-plus). A concierge service (like having a communal butler) and 24-hour security are among selling points. St James has paid a million towards a new school (Riverside Primary in **Townmead Rd**). But harmony in this plush enclave was disturbed after developers and council failed to agree on plans to move the refuse dump ('recycling centre' in developer-speak) next door. So residents will have to get used to sharing an access road with the dump (*and* the crematorium). Next door, Barratt's 'Kew Meadows': 5-bed houses and flats opposite the crematorium on **Kew Meadows Path** are all sold.

Kew Gardens

Between **Sandycombe Rd** and Kew Gardens is a tract of prosperous, leafy streets that forms the heart of Family Kew. Here, little private schools disgorge uniformed mites to be packed into enormous people-movers to be ferried home a couple of streets. Local estate agents will helpfully provide maps showing the million-plus belt: the grid of streets from **Broomfield Rd** down to **Lion Gate Gardens**. The bigger houses are to the N: **Lichfield Rd**, **Homesdale Rd** and **Ennerdale Rd** have some enormous Victorian detacheds, some double-fronted (think £1.75 million for a 6-bed). Go S, to roads such as **The Avenue**, **Walpole Avenue**, **Fitzwilliam Avenue**, and there are some later, smaller (but still family-sized, still £850,000) houses, lots of converted flats (can be lovely) and groups of 1960s–1980s town-houses and flats. To the S is **Stanmore Gardens** where the Victorian houses mingle with solid 1930s styles (£725,000 for a 5-bed). Turning E into **Gainsborough Rd** there is a recent group of neo-Georgian houses (2-bed £440,000); opposite are some little council houses, part of a group that reaches to Sandycombe Rd.

Station Approach and Station Parade meet rather prettily at Kew Gardens station (District Line and North London Line). Here small shops (plus new Tesco Metro), a clutch of good restaurants and cafés cater for visitors to the gardens – a steady stream in summer – and the locals. **Layton Place,** a clutch of 2-bed mews houses at £445,000, has been squeezed in behind Station Approach. Busy, narrow **Sandycombe Rd,** which has a few useful shops amid smartening cottages (3-bed c. £325,000). The E side backs (odd numbers) onto the tube line. On **Kew Rd,** between Lichfield and Hatherley Rds, are recent blocks of studio, 1- and 2-bed flats as well as the remaining large houses. To the W of Sandycombe Rd there are **Victoria Cottages** and **Elizabeth Cottages** (2-beds £370,000). **Alexandra Rd** and **Windsor Rd** have terraced 2-bed cottages (£430,000-plus).

East of the railway **West Park Rd** has £850,000 houses. **Atwood Avenue, Marksbury Avenue** and **Chelwood Gardens** have large 1930s houses providing solid family homes. Gardens on this side of Kew are more spacious. For cheaper 3-bed houses and flats (Victorian/Edwardian, a few modern) look to **North Rd, Dancer Rd, Darell Rd** and **Raleigh Rd,** although these streets do run down to the **Lower Richmond Rd,** the direct link to the M3. **Chaucer Avenue** and **Marksbury Avenue** have more modest 3-bed houses which can be £430,000. This end of Kew is within walking distance of North Sheen station.

Transport Tubes: Kew Gardens, Richmond (zone 4, District). To Oxford Circus 35 min (1 change), City 40 min, Heathrow 45 min (1 change). Trains: Richmond, North Sheen to Waterloo; N London Line from Richmond and Kew Gardens.

Convenient for Heathrow, M3/M4 for South and West, River Thames, Richmond Park, Kew Gardens. Miles from centre: 8.

Schools Local Authority: Christ's School, Grey Court, Shene School. Private: German School. See also Barnes & Twickenham.

SALES

Flats	S	1B	2B	3B	4B	5B
Average prices	110–200	180–300	220–500	300–600	500–1M	1M+
Houses	2B	3B	4B	5B	6/7B	8B
Average prices	225–500	350–650	400–1M	600–2M	1M+	–

RENTAL

Flats	S	1B	2B	3B	4B	5B
Average prices	145–200	185–300	200–500	200–800	700+	1000+
Houses	2B	3B	4B	5B	6/7B	8B
Average prices	250–450	300–700	300–900	350–1000+	1300+	1500+

The properties Wide range of covetable houses from Queen Anne through Georgian, mid-Victorian (the majority) to modern, plus mansion flats and conversions. Family houses from suburban to starry. Two-bed flats are most popular; cottages in The Alberts.

R

The market More on the market than for some years. Big premiums paid for best locations on riverside, Hill, Kew Green. English (especially City/media) and foreign (German, Scandinavian, American) families find area a happy mix of London and country.

Among estate agents active in this area are:

- Featherstone Leigh
- Victor Lown
- Savills
- Corporate Letting Co
- Geoffrey Jardine
- Chancellors
- Phillip Hodges
- Dexters
- Fitzgibbon
- Dixon Porter
- Hamptons
- Bairstow Eves

Royal Docks and South Newham

Postal districts: E13, E6, E16
Boroughs: Newham (Lab)
Council tax: Band D £1,059
Conservation areas: consult Town hall
Parking: Controlled parking zones in West Ham and Canning Town – more planned

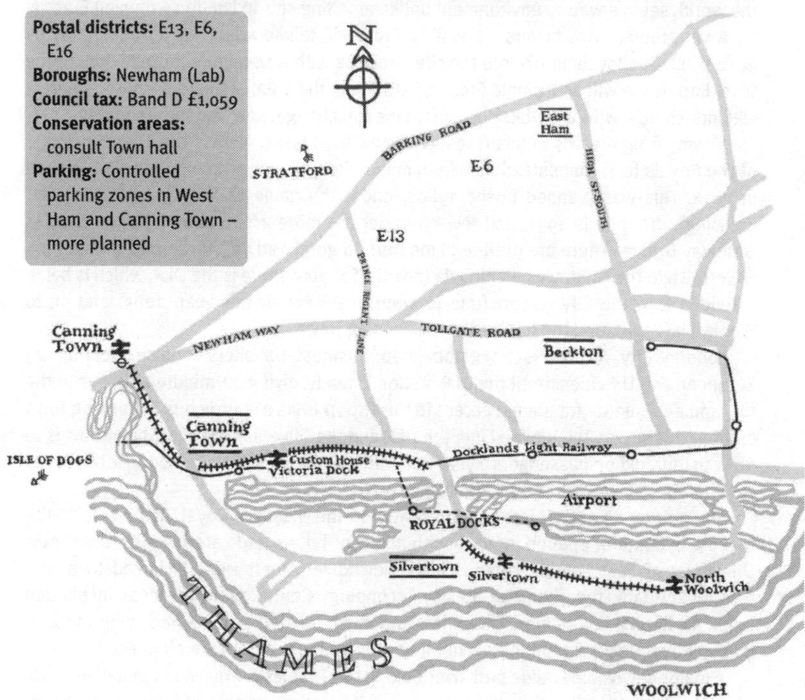

'A property theme park' was the verdict on the Royals by a recent first-time visitor. Look at the developers' websites and brochures, and you find a world of sun on sailboats, tree-lined boulevards and smiling blondes in acre-sized flats. Walk or take the DLR – don't drive – around the actuality and you find a bizarre mix of the derelict past and the shiny future, a place where every novelty in the architects' toy-box has been tried out, where roads are constantly being dug up and realigned, where a home is old if it is past its tenth birthday.

The contrast between the two halves of Newham could not be greater. Stratford (which chapter see) and the northern tract have classic Victorian London housing, some ponderously respectable, as in Woodgrange Park, some still not far removed from the slums which the area was notorious for a century ago.

Come south, and you find the vast, watery landscape of the Royal Docks, empty a decade ago of anything except decaying industrial sheds but now a burgeoning quarter of new flats, a new university and new schools, Britain's largest exhibition centre and (for 15 years now) London's innermost airport. It also has some depressing council estates only now receiving the investment they have lacked for up to 50 years.

South Newham encompasses the Royals – with both the new homes and the original dockside communities such as Silvertown, North Woolwich and Custom House – plus West Ham, Canning Town, Beckton and part of Plaistow.

When the Boat Show switches venue to Newham from Kensington's Earls Court, something must be going on out east. The prosperous visitors who now travel out east to view the yachts and gin palaces at the ExCeL Centre each January get a surprise. First, it's easier for many out-of-towners to get to ExCel than to Earl's Court (far easier, by car). Secondly, they find one of the largest and most sophisticated exhibition complexes in the world, set in a watery environment unlike anything else in London – or even Europe.

A yet greater prize hovers – possibly. Crossrail, talked about for decades, may by 2012 stitch the Royals firmly into the city structure with a 14-minute journey time to the West End. There will be a single Crossrail station in the area, at Custom House, where it will interchange with the DLR. However plans can change: see Transport chapter.

Moving from dreams to (near) reality, a new road bridge across the Thames from E of the Royals to Thamesmead has £200 million from the government, and should open in 2012. This was planned in the 1980s, under the name ELRIC (East London River Crossing), dropped in 1991, and revived under the more acceptable moniker Thames Gateway Bridge. There are outline plans (but no go-ahead yet) for a road tunnel from Silvertown to the Greenwich Peninsula (2015?). For now, there is the DLR, which is being extended E to the City Airport (due to open in December this year, 2005) and on to Woolwich (2008), and the Jubilee Line at Canning Town.

London City Airport is an established business-travellers' choice, serving 23 European and UK cities. Until the DLR station is ready, giving 22-minute journeys to the City and a 10-minute frequency, access to the airport is via a shuttle bus to Canning Town station: this serves the Jubilee Line, the DLR and the Silverlink service. The airport is to grow to four million passengers a year from the current 1.7 million (the 2004 total, 14 per cent up on '03), with up to 240 flights a day.

The 90,000 sq m ExCeL exhibition centre on the N side of Royal Victoria Dock, the biggest in London, opened in 2000 with adjacent hotels and catering. The smart new University of East London campus alongside Royal Albert Dock is linked to a new technology park, the Thames Gateway Technology Centre, with 'business incubation units' for hi-tech companies. Three new and much-needed schools, including the £17-million Royal Docks Community School, have been built; others are planned.

A major new Thames-side park overlooking the Thames Barrier was opened in 2000. An addition to the changing skyline is a regatta centre capable of handling Olympic-scale events (though it's not intended as the 2012 venue, should London get lucky), with its own leisure facilities and restaurant.

Excited by all this activity, buyers – residents, investors and out-and-out speculators – have been snapping up the hundreds of new, and desirable, homes which stand in dockside settings. The evangelism of developers and investors is exciting and, to some, convincing. But this is a district of scattered, often inward-looking blocks and developments. With the possible exception of Britannia Village, neighbourhoods they are not. The contrast between them and Canning Town could not be more marked. A community does not exist – yet. There is a lot of space to fill, both literally and figuratively.

Canning Town and Custom House

R

The Docklands boom and the Jubilee Line are attracting developers and private homebuyers to areas which until the mid-1990s were totally outside the property market. But now City Airport and Canary Wharf are five minutes away, the West End just 20.

But good transport does not change a place on its own, and Canning Town needs change as badly as anywhere in London. Newham Council has backed away from radical plans intending to raze 1,600 homes here and in neighbouring Custom House and replace them with new housing. Locals – this is the sort of community the papers call close-knit – were not all impressed, alleging that rocketing property values in the wake of the Jubilee Line are, in effect, pricing them out of their homes. Now the plan is to refurbish, and in some cases replace, 7,000 homes in the neighbourhood, and to revive the local centre – all on a 10-year timescale and using a PFI (private money) structure.

Canning Town was built in the 1850s and rated a slum by 1855. It was outside the old London County Council area of 1888, meaning lax planning laws, and so instant slums continued to be built. The devastation caused by bombing in World War II gave the opportunity for the building of enormous tracts of municipal housing, including the Kier Hardie Estate and the clutch of tower blocks that included the fated Ronan Point – destroyed by a gas explosion in the late '60s. Then the docks closed, and the sprawling estates lost their economic mainspring.

A decade ago respectable people from West Ham would avoid Canning Town after nightfall: today things are improving, but the denizens of the new flats along the dock still don't go there: can't think of any reason to, said one. Homes are, so far, mainly council-built: tower blocks and terraces. Two-bed ex-council houses now change hands (as rental investments, mainly) for around £180–200,000 (1998: £40,000). Older pockets of Victorian homes remain N of the Barking Rd in **Durham** and **Exning Rds**. Similar houses exist in the area between **Newham Way** and **Barking Rd** in roads such as **Alexandra St** and **Kildare Rd**. A 2-bed house here might be £170–180,000. The main street, **Barking Rd,** is typical tatty Victorian inner-London high street. The council hope for better things, in particular a better link with the tube/DLR station.

A sign of the changing times is the Crown Wharf plan, a proposal (in early stages) for 767 flats in towers up to 23 storeys between the River Lea, the A13 and **Bidder St,** on the edge of the proposed Canning Town civic centre area. The last time ayone built a tower block in Canning Town it blew up: better luck this time.

Silvertown and the Royals

Silvertown is a sliver of land between the Royal Victoria Dock and the Thames. Some 19th-century terraces survive, such as N of **Albert Rd,** but most homes here are new, a product of the Docklands boom – and thousands more are planned. The DLR serves the N side of the docks, and the new extension running along the S side and direct to the airport opens in December 2005, with stations at (from W to E) West Silvertown (**Knights Rd**), Pontoon Dock (on **N Woolwich Rd**), the airport and King George V Dock (N end of **Pier Rd**).

And it is here on the S side that the old Pontoon Dock will – if plans are followed through – become a marina at the heart of 'Silvertown Quays'. This vast, mixed-use scheme envisages 4,500 homes, no less (including lofts in the old Millennium Mill), as well as the Terry Farrell-designed aquarium. This will become the 'town centre' for this slice of the Royals.

All of a sudden, you are in the Docklands price belt. Britannia Urban Village, or West Silvertown as it is also known, is a big Wimpey development between the S shore of the Royal Victoria Dock and **North Woolwich Rd,** with a total of 940 homes, 800 on the open market. This has settled down into a proper community, with low-rise homes of all sizes and tenures. The main streets are **Wesley Avenue** and **Mill Rd**: 2-bed flats are around £200,000. A smarter Wimpey scheme, sited at the W end of the dock and called Western Beach (!), has 2-beds/2-baths reselling for c. £330,000, 1-beds £250,000. This includes a 13-floor block with 119 flats. **Eastern Quay,** on the S side and opposite ExCeL exhibition centre, is also Wimpey: 73 waterside 1-, 2- and 3-bed flats (now complete). A footbridge (high, but with lifts) links the village with ExCeL: it makes a great viewpoint on a fine day. R

Barratt's giant Capital East scheme at the W end of the Victoria Dock, close to Royal Victoria DLR, will have 700 dockside flats in ten buildings when complete in 2006. One-beds start at £215,000. Just to the E, on the N side of the dock before you come to ExCeL, old warehouses are being transformed into flats (Warehouse K had 12 on the market last year at £227,500-plus, Warehouse W had studios starting at £240,000; 1-beds from £290,000), restaurants and a pub, while 'WE5', a new block, sold out during 2004. The Grain Store, another warehouse, is becoming 70 1-, 2- and 3-bed flats in a development marketed in Dubai: completion autumn 2005, prices £230–700,000.

Barrier Point, on **Silvertown Way** overlooking the river and the Thames Barrier, was by Barratt, with 250 flats in a shiny, round landmark tower and stepped blocks, most with fine views along the river and across the adjoining new, and very handsome, 23-acre 'Parisian-style' park. Across the park at Wards Wharf, Barratt's Trade Winds scheme has another 250 flats, overlooking the Barrier and the river, in three stepped blocks and a 19-storey riverside tower; the last few were selling last winter at £460,000. Minoco Wharf, a 26-acre riverside site, has been bought by Ballymore and will be homes plus offices. There is quite a lot of industry on the river to the E, including the Tate & Lyle sugar works – which makes a fascinating smell.

North Woolwich has London's only vehicle ferry, linking the North and South Circular Roads. A few Victorian/1920s and 1980s homes cluster around the terminal, and further E, Fairview has completed 712 homes on riverside land at Galleons Lock (access via **Felixstowe Way**). These are popular, say agents: prices are £230–250,000 for a 2-bed flat with a view of the lock, with 1-beds at c. £170–200,000. To the N, land N of the old Albert Basin – now a marina – is being developed as **Royal Quay** by Furlong City. The old Gallions Hotel is being retained as a restaurant and health spa, with 446 flats in new blocks beside boat moorings. Prices start at £200,000.

Beckton

Beckton saw some early, and successful, Docklands-inspired housing. The new estates were Docklands' first concentration of cheap new homes – with 700 for rent and thousands to buy – and a runaway success. Beckton is now well established with a brisk resale market in its modern homes (none much over 18 years old), and a steady trickle of new-build. These are traditional homes with gardens and room to park the car – none of your Docklands warehouses here, thank you. Local agents produce special Beckton property lists: 1-bed flats are around £120–130,000, while £185–230,000 buys you a 3-bed house with a garage and a good garden and £300–325,000 gets a 4-bed. Recent homes include Fairview's Alpine Court off **Woolwich Manor Way**, with 1-beds at c. £145,000. At Gallions Reach in Beckton a £20 million, 24-hour Tesco store provides the anchor for over 30 shops and leisure facilities.

West Ham

To the NW lies West Ham – industrial, terraced and cheap. The map shows the differences between the two Hams: East (see Stratford chapter) is newer, with regular grids of terraced houses dating from 1880–1914; West Ham is older, less rigidly laid out, with a mix of homes – some very basic – and prices to match.

West Ham can seem like an industrial wasteland to the uninitiated. Don't be fooled by the *A–Z* map – West Ham, to locals, is considered to be the area around the tube station, nowhere near West Ham Park, Stratford (see above). This confusion arises from the days before Newham when East Ham and West Ham were not only places, but also wider, separate boroughs. West Ham Town Hall, for example, is in the middle of Stratford.

R

West Ham is still the cheapest end of the borough to live and, in proximity to the City, it is the innermost. Note that West Ham station has been upgraded and now connects the Fenchurch–Tilbury, Jubilee and District Lines. Much of West Ham's housing is owned by Newham Council: the rest is small and terraced: a typical 2-bed house can be had for c. £150–180,000, but don't expect designer decor and be prepared, a local agent warns, for a few surprises.

West Ham *proper*, then, is a small area roughly consisting of the terraced streets off **Manor Rd**, where a 3-bed house can be c. £250,000. In the late 1980s Barratt beautifully modernized the old council estate – now retitled Woodlands, the flats are huge and today very smart. To the W of **Manor Rd**, Gainsborough Park is a big, 1990-vintage tract of developer-built homes between West Ham and Canning Town.

The Lower Lea Valley to the W figures large in regeneration projects, never mind the London Olympic bid, and will be a 'linear park' plus lots of new amenities if plans are fulfilled. This is, after all, the Thames Gateway, upon which many hopes are built, and (courtesy of Newham Council), the Arc of Opportunity. Note, too, that West Ham may lose its North London Line station and gain a DLR service, linking to Stratford International, on the same tracks. A new station at Stratford market (**Bridge Rd**) is included in this plan, but 2008 is the earliest opening date.

Transport Tubes (all zone 3): Canning Town (Jubilee), West Ham (Central & Jubilee); Plaistow, (District – and Hammersmith & City during peak hours), Canning Town (Jubilee). From Canning Town: Oxford Circus 25 min, City 15 min, Heathrow 90 min (1 change). DLR: Royal Docks to Tower, Canary Wharf, Stratford, extending to Silvertown & City Airport 2005. Trains: North London Line.

Convenient for City, Docklands, City Airport; Epping Forest, M11; A12, A13 for M25. Miles from centre: 7.

Schools Local Authority: Brampton Manor, Cumberland, Eastlea, Forest Gate, Langdon, Royal Docks Community School. Private: Jamia Ramania Islamic Institute (b).

SALES

Flats	S	1B	2B	3B	4B	5B
Average prices	130–220	145–230+	200–400	250–525+	→	–
Houses	2B	3B	4B	5B	6/7B	8B
Average prices	150–220	185–250+	270–350	–	–	–

RENTAL

Flats	S	1B	2B	3B	4B	5B
Average prices	130–150	150–200	170–225	210–260	300+	–
Houses	2B	3B	4B	5B	6/7B	8B
Average prices	200–400	240–290	260–320	300–450	–	–

The properties Mostly modern: apart from a few Victorian terraces (in North Woolwich and parts of Canning Town, plus West Ham). Rest is either ex-council (some dire, some good), modern spec-built semi-suburban (Beckton) or Docklands-style, from basic to (most recent) rather smart. River views command a premium, dock views ten-a-penny.

The market Brisk trade in new and nearly new river- and dockside flats, including plenty to rent. Also family homes in Beckton, ex-council in Canning Town and elsewhere, and standard-issue Victorian terraces in West Ham. Watch for new DLR stations (see text).

R

Among estate agents active in this area are:

- Mark Murray
- Taylor Simpson
- Bryant
- McDowells
- James William
- Halifax
- Alex Neil
- Icon Estates
- Citiquays
- Rubicon
- Keiller Collins
- L & D Property
- Moreland
- Phoenix
- Dockside Property

SHEPHERD'S BUSH

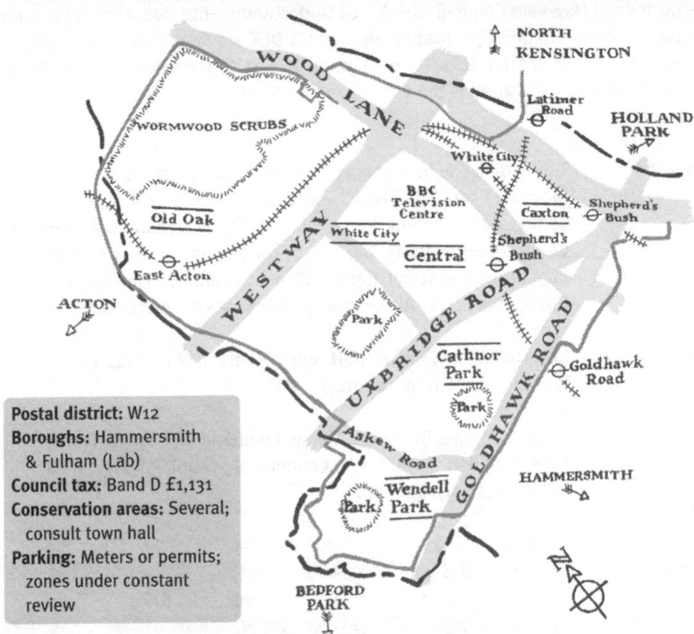

Postal district: W12
Boroughs: Hammersmith & Fulham (Lab)
Council tax: Band D £1,131
Conservation areas: Several; consult town hall
Parking: Meters or permits; zones under constant review

At long last the wind of change is being felt in Shepherd's Bush. This rather dowdy, very busy part of West London is finally looking up under the impetus of two fairy godmothers – though the slow-motion nature of the transformation has led to a pervasive air of unreality. 'To be fair, there is a different atmoshere about the Bush already – I'm starting to believe in it' says our hitherto sceptical mole. The sea-change began with the BBC's decision to build its new HQ here – and now, an even bigger 'media village' just to the north of it. And then came the plans, slowly, slowly turning into reality, for the vast White City scheme: 40 acres of retail therapy on a huge site north of the Green – with a second phase to come north of that. True, West London's answer to Brent Cross and Bluewater will take till 2007 to complete, but on the back of it come major transport improvements, starting now, with new homes and businesses to follow. And the council is intent on turning the heart of the Bush, the Green – at present a large and dismal island in the sea of traffic – into a proper, user-friendly focus for the place.

About time too: over the M41 West Cross Route and the railway, which rule a neat eastern edge to Shepherd's Bush, lie Holland Park and Notting Hill, no less. But it's still awaiting a bit of sparkle and decent shops (some great delis, but not much else). True, cafés and bars are opening round the green, which the council has been working hard to clean up – and to keep it so with street wardens. True, too, that £150 million is going on upgrading public transport because of White City, in an area famous for its bottlenecks. Locals hope all this will help counter-balance TV's Nigella Lawson, who described the Bush, her home for some years, as 'not especially nice' as she left – for Eaton Square.

But the Nigellas of this part of town are not entirely alone: the label 'passing-through area' may be unkind to the families who settle in Shepherd's Bush, but it is accurate. For many, this is still where you rent or buy a flat or small house before children force gardens, extra bedrooms and schools up the priority scale. Next stop, south or west to Hammersmith, Chiswick, Ealing . . . or beyond the M25.

Much of the personality of today's Bush derives from the heavy presence of the BBC. Its vast HQ up **Wood Lane** now shelters nearly all the programme-making staff, and it has been adding a 'media village': more buildings (plus shops, wine bars, juice bars, pampering parlour. . .) to house thousands more. This has changed the area's restaurant profile; while not Notting Hill or Soho, it has steadily gained a rash of upmarket 'dining pubs' and other interesting eateries certainly kept going by the media people – also the source of hopeful 'Bush now trendy' property stories that regularly dot the newspapers.

The BBC tribe joins the cheerful cosmopolitan mix of Asians, Irish, West Indians, Lebanese, Africans, Poles and representatives of most other ethnic groups; each brings its own specialist shops, fantastic delis ('It's where I come to stock up on Argentinian tea'), restaurants and cafés – and there's the traditional, colourful and very diverse market off the **Uxbridge Rd** under the railway bridge. Everybody, estate agents included, hopes very much that the area will retain its 'melting-pot' image.

Traditionally a good first-time buyer's hunting ground, the Bush is also scouted by those priced out of surrounding areas. Brook Green, Hammersmith and Fulham lie to the S; Holland Park, then deeply trendy Notting Hill, across the roundabout to the E. The Bush, even pre-improvements, is also extremely well placed for public transport and for major routes in and out of town. It is midway between the A40 and the M4 – gateway to Heathrow and the West. Buses run direct to the West End and Westminster. Plans for a tram link right through to Ealing, however, that would congest existing roads, force traffic into the side streets and involve some compulsory purchase have so far met with strong local opposition spearheaded by journalist Virginia Ironside.

Until the end of the 18th century Shepherd's Bush, as the name implies, was just another area of countryside around London. But buildings shot up during the 19th as the capital expanded rapidly, and the Bush, well placed on a main route from the W, soon became a centre. Its triangular green became a focus for travelling traders on their way to market. The origins of that quirky name remain a mystery: theories abound, but by far the most likely explanation springs from its position on a major droving route: here shepherds rested their flocks on the green before the final hike up to Smithfield Market.

Most houses here are of the solid, 2- or 3-storey, workaday terraced variety, built in the late 19th century, and Shepherd's Bush changed very little until the second half of the 20th, when council blocks, motorways and shopping precincts arrived.

Apart from the major traffic roundabout near the green, which links with the M41, the character of Shepherd's Bush has survived relatively unscathed, and much of the dominant Victorian and Edwardian architecture is still intact after a century.

Despite its name, what Shepherd's Bush really lacks is open spaces; there is a shortage of trees, greenery – take the bus to Kensington Gardens – and also of family houses with large gardens. General shopping is humdrum and will remain so until the White City scheme emerges, though there's the market, and a small mall (with cinemas) on the S side of the green, off the **Uxbridge Rd**. The Bush Theatre is a well-respected fringe venue; likewise the Bush Hall, a restored Edwardian dance hall that's now a venue for acoustic music, be it classical, folk, jazz or contemporary. The Shepherd's Bush Empire on the green attracts leading-edge music acts. And, as the council observes, the area has 'a high density of licensed premises'. Happily there's news that the imposing but run-down old cinema building on the west side is to become an 182-bed hotel.

The White City site is that of the 1908 Franco-British Exhibition (later a tube depot) along the M41/railway corridor, across to **Wood Lane** and S of **Ariel Way** – handy for the BBC. A few streets of homes divide it from the Green, but there will be access to the new shopping world – a giant complex under one roof – from its E corner by the tube (the Central Line: the station is to be rebuilt). Intergrated with this will be a brand-new train station for the West London Line; bus routes will be linked in, too. There'll also be a new

An essentially Victorian area, Shepherd's Bush shows every variation of the Victorian pattern-book builder's craft. Builders took house plans and details 'off the shelf', resulting in ornamentation like this bay, with its sash windows, stone, or perhaps stucco, parapet and decoration around the tops of the pillars. The house is built of London stock-brick, which when clean contrasts well with the stucco.

Hammersmith & City Line tube stop near the BBC. None of this can happen until a subterranean tube-train depot replaces the existing one: this too is under way.

The heart of this 40-acre complex, the 'wintergarden' – one of West London's largest public spaces, we're told – will have a translucent roof; under this 'indoor sky', events and performances will take place. There are three department stores to come, of which one should be a giant M&S. In between, shops, shops, shops, the wintergarden, restaurants, cafés, multi-screen cinema, library . . . .

But all this must wait till Christmas 2007; for now, the exciting new signs of the Bush transforming into a 'happening' place are the new Sainsbury's Local, Tesco Express and, yes, Starbucks (talk of other coffee chains to follow).

And so to the homes. Many of the taller Victorian terraces were split into 1- or 2-bedroom flats in the 1980s, but this was checked by local planning policy; some of the bigger houses have been turned back into family homes. There's still a lot of rented property (the BBC, recent job cuts notwithstanding, means there's lots of demand for it) and, though there are scaffolding and skips everywhere, some streets remain relatively undeveloped. The boom in flats conversions brought parking problems to many a street; residents pay for permits, and tow-away trucks prowl.

Good big family houses, still in the minority, are most common near the **Goldhawk Rd**, which marks the boundary with Hammersmith: look W of **Askew Rd**, around **Rylett Rd** and **Ashchurch Park Villas** (the latter about the lordliest road in Shepherd's Bush) and Wendell Park; prices here reflect those across the border round Ravenscourt Park.

Shepherd's Bush does not have enclaves as recognizably self-contained as Bedford Park or Brook Green, but homes of a similar type do tend to form neighbourhoods. The most popular lie between the **Uxbridge** and **Goldhawk Rds**; later, 1914–1930s style, houses can be found near Wendell Park, while the district N of **Cobbold Rd**, really East Acton (see that chapter), is a mix of purpose-built Edwardian maisonettes and Victorian terraces. Moving E, Cathnor Park has a village atmosphere that disappears at **Boscombe Rd**, known for its 4-storey Victorian terraces: largely flats; c. a million if still whole houses.

North of the **Uxbridge Rd** homes are generally smaller, although tall houses are found between **Wood Lane** and **Loftus Rd**. West, to **Wormholt Rd**, is a mix of purpose-built Edwardian maisonettes and rows of solid 2-storey Victorian terraces. Streets of larger 1930s semis border the Cleverley and Flower estates, which lie to the E of **Old Oak Rd**. North of **Sawley Rd** council-built property is the norm, although much of the stock W of **Bloemfontein Rd** is now privately owned. Out eastwards, towards **Wood Lane**, lies the sprawling White City Estate – far fewer owner-occupied flats here: it is not an aesthetic gem. Council-built homes, in the form of the Old Oak Estate, continue N of the **Westway** near East Acton tube station. These, by contrast, are pleasant cottage-style homes and are in a conservation area. They often now appear for sale.

Two small but very distinct neighbourhoods complete the picture. The first, just N of the **Westway**, offers a mix of Edwardian terraces and purpose-built maisonettes. The second is 'Caxton Village', off the green; a quaint network of Victorian terraces.

Wendell Park

This is the farthest W and most sylvan bit of W12. Beyond peaceful, residential, semi-lined **Emlyn Rd**, and across the borough border, lies Bedford Park – the 1914 terraced homes that overlook little Wendell Park also have an Arts-and-Crafts air. The tree-lined streets round about hold 3- or 4-bed late-Victorian family homes as well. The delightful, secluded little park and nearby tennis courts give this quiet, prosperous area a sense of space. Go N along **Emlyn Rd** and the semis give way to Edwardian flats and the local-authority built Emlyn Gardens Estate.

To the S of Wendell Park there is a favoured district of wide, leafy roads with some of the most expensive homes in the Bush. These include **Rylett Rd** and **Crescent, Ashchurch Park Villas** and **Ashchurch Grove.** Many of the large family houses here are still intact despite the 1980s conversion blitz. Some are double-fronted, well-proportioned homes, others 3- or 4-storey Victorian terraces; they ooze classic style with their ornate pillars, regal front steps – and price tags that can hover around a million. There are even some (would you believe) bungalows with garages on **Rylett Crescent**. Note, too, the private mews of **Balmoral Mews** and **Cosmur Close** off the Crescent. Some houses have garages, gardens can be huge and much is spent on their upkeep. Along **Goldhawk Rd**, the section that runs E–W rather than N–S is the more desirable; some pleasant 3-storey 1850s villas have attractive raised ground floors. Stamford Brook tube is a walkable distance. This corner used to be called **Starch Green**, a name that's happily now showing signs of renaissance (residents and agents tended to refer instead to 'Ravenscourt Park': the large and welcome green space across on the Hammersmith side of the busy Goldhawk Rd). Much money has been lavished in these streets, and the price range is wide: c. £275,000 for a 2-bed garden flat, £450–470,000 for a 3-bed terraced house; after that it depends on degree of renovation/extension. In **Wendell Rd**, 4-bed (i.e. loft converted) terraces are c. £525–600,000; if overlooking the park, expect to pay up to £650,000.

Going N of Wendell Park, purpose-built Edwardian maisonettes can be found W of **Askew Rd** towards the **Uxbridge Rd**. Attractive red-brick Victorian houses are particularly plentiful in **Cobbold Rd**: smaller homes in this speed-humped street. A 3-bed house sold last autumn for £433,000. Further N, in **St Elmo Rd**, Victorian terraces dominate. Many have been converted into flats – a 2-bed, up to £250,000 – but it's still possible to buy a whole house (still around £450,000) in this popular area.

Over to the W, just across the borough boundary and in W3, is a group of streets around **Valetta Rd** that agents dub 'Little Malta'; again, a good source of flats. This district abuts the Wendell Park area, and homes are similar, but it looks to Acton for shops and leisure, and tubes are a fair way off. Between Valetta and Cobbold Rds, in **Holley** and **Mayfield Rds,** is the private Wellington Court complex, consisting of several modern blocks of flats in neat, landscaped gardens.

Cathnor Park

Similar style continues E of **Askew Rd**, though the houses are not as grand as in the Wendell Park neighbourhood. Most homes are 2-storey, although elegant 3-storey versions, in **Westville Rd**, make roomy flats if split. Here you also find modern blocks.

Wedged between two bustling districts is little Cathnor Park. A particularly pretty corner of this villagy area, **Melina Rd**, has some of the rare cottage-style houses in the Bush, plus 3-storey-and-basement terraces and flats converted from them. A child-friendly street, with car-free end and a (very) bright blue under-fives centre. **Goodwin Rd** boasts well-recommended Greenside primary school. Check the **Percy Rd** area for other pleasant cottagey homes, as well as 2- and 3-storey, 4/5-beds, c. £550–650,000. Hidden between **Becklow** and **Vespan Rds**, a Victorian school is nowadays housing-trust flats. **Askew Rd** itself is smartening – new shops (including organic food), restaurants and bars – and, to local surprise, the Eagle has been done up as a gastro-pub.

Central Shepherd's Bush

Moving E beyond **Coningham Rd** the houses are taller and mostly divided: this is the heart of flat-land. The seven or so roads W of the green are among the most popular in Shepherd's Bush; they are ideally placed for two Hammersmith & City Line tube stations as well as regular buses on **Goldhawk** and **Uxbridge Rds** (most streets have been blocked off to stop through-traffic between these two main roads).

Coningham Rd is busy, but traffic-calmed. For a quieter life try **St Stephen's Avenue, Hetley Rd** or **Godolphin Rd**; a tiny park links Hetley and Godolphin. Roads are relatively wide, light and tree-lined, and the flats have classic elegance, sash windows and high ceilings: 'they get their price', say agents. From c. £200,000 for a 1-bed flat, £240,000 and up for a 2-bed. Unmodernised whole houses can be found: one went for £615,000; another, 4-storey, for £630,000, recently. Between £700–800,000 once done up.

North of the **Uxbridge Rd**, on the corner with **Oaklands Grove** (see below), Ealing Housing Trust have built 33 homes for rent. This side of the Uxbridge Rd divide, houses are generally smaller, the neighbourhood generally less well regarded. Exceptions, though, lie W of Wood Lane, where **Frithville Gardens** and **Stanlake Rd** have some very pleasant 5-bed houses amid the smaller terraces: good prices for these good-sized family homes with Hammersmith Park and the BBC at the top, the tube at the bottom. An even bigger, 6-bed end-of-terrace with permission for off-street parking, £725,000 last winter.

Nearby **Tunis Rd** has a completely different character; its Victorian terraces have attracted many flats conversions, and the gardens here are tiny. Hammersmith Park has an interesting history: it is the only remnant of the Franco–British Exhibition of 1908, an oasis of ornamental gardens, pavilions and pools. Recent improvements added an 'interactive water feature' and the restoration of a Japanese garden.

Loftus Rd – an attractive tree-lined street and conservation area – also holds the football stadium, home to Queen's Park Rangers. This normally quiet road turns into a sea of fans at weekends. This area has a mix of flats and houses (a typical 5-bed terraced, £550–750,000; a 2-bed flat, £225,000; with garden, £250,000), and a strong residents' committee is vigilant over the stadium and the proposed tram.

West of Loftus Rd lies an area of Victorian terraces and purpose-built Edwardian maisonettes. **Bloemfontein Rd** runs straight through the neighbourhood and can be busy: drivers are inclined to use it as a cut-through from the Westway in the N to the Uxbridge Rd. More peaceful streets to the W; **Oaklands Grove** is popular (though a little far from the tube and a shade too close to as-yet unreconstructed White City Estate for some). Larger, £500–600,000 houses hereabouts, and first-time buyers comb **Galloway** and **Thorpebank Rds**, to the W for flats and smaller, un-done-up houses: a 3-bed Edwardian one, £290,000 last autumn; a 'done' 3-bed/2-bath, £365,000. All these streets lead up towards little Wormholt Park – beyond which, near the Phoenix high school, a new sports and fitness centre and, soon, swimming pool replace the ones in the park.

S

West of **Wormholt Rd**, to busy **Old Oak Rd** and the borough boundary, the houses are newer – 1930s semi-detacheds mostly. A pleasant neighbourhood; it borders the Cleverley and the cottagey 'Flower' estates to the N. This model village, originally council-built (and officially the Wormholt Estate), is universally known as the 'Flower' since street names include **Wallflower, Orchid, Clematis, Lilac** . . . and **Hemlock**. Oh, and **Pansy Gardens**. Much is nowadays privately owned, and it's very well tended. Streets like **Sundew Avenue** have red-brick houses grouped round small greens. The 'ex-council' stigma is fast receding, and the 2- and 3-bed houses in the appealing estate are, say agents, highly saleable. Prices for the 3-bed houses typically hover round £300,000 (one in **Wallflower** did go for £340,000: a 'blip', most think). The contrasting homes of Peabody's Cleverley Estate are grouped round **Sawley Rd**: dignified, flat-fronted, grey-with-red-brick 3-storey blocks with nice detailing such as arched doors and round windows.

The cosy village atmosphere of the 'Flower' changes dramatically E of **Bloemfontein Rd**, where we swap horticultural hyperbole for Commonwealth country names for the streets of the White City Estate: a grid of roads that house council tenants in huge blocks of oppressive red-brick flats. **South Africa Rd**, to the S, runs alongside to Queen's Park Rangers FC; 20 new-build housing-trust homes have added to the stock here. The road can be used as a cut-through to **Wood Lane** and the BBC stronghold. West of Wood Lane, a vast expanse of sheds lies just above the White City site – this will be Phase II: a masterplan is being formulated. With the White City tube and a spur off the A40(M), what's the betting that the gleaming towers of 'Notting Hill West' will arise here one day?

Caxton Village

Back S now, to Shepherd's Bush Green and 'Caxton Village'. Undeniably the most convenient spot in the whole of Shepherd's Bush, it will become more useful still when the giant White City mall is built behind it. Off the N, **Uxbridge Rd**, side of the green, this select, relatively tucked-away neighbourhood of little Victorian terraces in roads such as **Tadmor, Sterne, Bulwer** and **Aldine Sts**, and **Aldine Place**, is in walking distance of three tube stations: two on the Hammersmith & City Line and Shepherd's Bush on the Central (a 3-bed house, £400,000 upwards; a 5-bed £500–550,000). **Caxton Rd** itself will one day regain its peace: its bus terminus will disappear off into the White City shopping complex. Better still, the plan for the complex buries the car parks that previously loomed over these streets. However, the denizens of **Shepherd's Bush Place**, a tiny cul-de-sac of little listed Georgiana, are resisting a plan to site some off-street parking here for the tube station when it's rebuilt.

Old Oak

Finally N of the **Westway** is once again council-built housing. Busy **Du Cane Rd** runs between **Scrubs Lane** and **Old Oak Lane** in Acton, past Hammersmith Hospital and Wormwood Scrubs Prison. The area is dominated by the huge prison compound, which looks out over the common towards Willesden Junction and Brent in the distance.

The eastern edge of this no-man's-land area (often annexed to East Acton), is depressing and lacks identity. But a little farther W down **Du Cane Rd** between East Acton tube and the common is the Old Oak Estate, with a strong community atmosphere. The 1909–1920s estate consists of houses grouped around greens, very much in the garden-suburb ethos. So far, it is less 'tidied up' than the similar Flower Estate to the S, but with its tube station and pleasant architecture it has a future. To the NE is the open space of Old Oak Common/Wormwood Scrubs; to the E lies the eponymous prison. The estate crosses the rail line and is bounded to the S by the major six-lane Westway (A40). It merges in the W with the 1920s estate centred on **The Fairway** (see Acton chapter). Its E edge is speed-humped **Braybrook St**, by Old Oak Common, with attractive, flat-fronted brick terraces with sash windows. It is surprisingly 'countrified'; sadly, though, the village feel dissipates towards the road's E end with views of imposing prison walls, bright floodlights and watch-towers. Ah well, the Scrubs has the Linford Christie sports stadium and athletics track – and it's now a nature reserve, which should help to raise the profile of Shepherd's Bush's forgotten green lung.

It's possible that a very large commercial development may take place one day on the 'Old Oak Triangle', a big tract of railway land N of Wormwood Scrubs. It keeps being mentioned in strategic plans, but that's for the future. . . .

Borders

Just N of the **Westway**, between **Wood Lane** and the tracks, is a quaint collection of roads on the Kensington/Chelsea border. The streets running off **Eynham Rd** are a mix of purpose-built Edwardian maisonettes and tall terraces split into flats. The roads here are surprisingly quiet considering their proximity to the Westway junction with the M41. As neighbouring North Ken becomes ever more expensive, these are combed by buyers priced out of the St Quintin estate. The area is popular with BBC people who rent.

Transport Tubes, all zone 2: Shepherd's Bush (Central, Hammersmith & City); White City, East Acton (Central); Goldhawk Rd (Hammersmith & City). From Shepherd's Bush: Oxford Circus 15 min, City 25 min, Heathrow 1 hr. Trains: station planned on West London Line, part (eventually...) of the proposed round-London metro.

Convenient for BBC Centre, West End, Notting Hill, Heathrow, M4/M40 to West. Miles from centre: 4.5.

Schools Local Authority: Burlington Danes C of E, Phoenix High (g); London Oratory (b); Lady Margaret (g). Private: Latymer (b) (g); Godolphin (g). See also Chiswick and Ealing chapters.

SALES						
Flats	S	1B	2B	3B	4B	5B
Average prices	130–160	130–250	190–350	210–400	220–400	–
Houses	2B	3B	4B	5B	6/7B	8B
Average prices	250–400	275–550	370–700	450–750	700–1M	–

RENTAL						
Flats	S	1B	2B	3B	4B	5B
Average prices	140–160	170–250	230–400	260–500	400–450	→500
Houses	2B	3B	4B	5B	6/7B	8B
Average prices	300–400	325–400+	380–650	500–750	–	–

The properties Victorian terraces are the staple: smaller 2-storey ones as single homes, taller ones often converted to satisfy demand for 1/2-bed flats. Some larger family homes, mainly near Hammersmith borders, now command large sums. Also pockets of Edwardian p/b maisonettes; some roomier inter-war houses. Cheaper: ex-council; cottages, e.g. 'Flower' Estate, especially popular.

The market The BBC's White City HQ set seal on the Bush renaissance. Young buyers find it convenient, with good transport to town for those who don't work for the Beeb. Those who do shell out for the small stock of big family houses. For the rest, singles in studios become couples in flats, but children presage move to more family areas.

Among estate agents active in this area are:

- Willmotts
- James Anthony
- Bushells
- Barnard Marcus
- Collingwoods
- Finlay Brewer
- Northfields
- Winkworth
- Whitman
- Scotts
- Townends
- Faron Sutaria
- Bellengers
- Kinleigh Folkard & Hayward
- Marsh & Parsons
- Foxtons
- Ravenscourt

SOHO AND COVENT GARDEN

Postal districts: W1, WC2
Boroughs: Westminster (Con), Camden (Lab)
Council tax: Band D Westminster £605, Camden £1,200
Conservation areas: Whole area
Parking: Don't even think about it

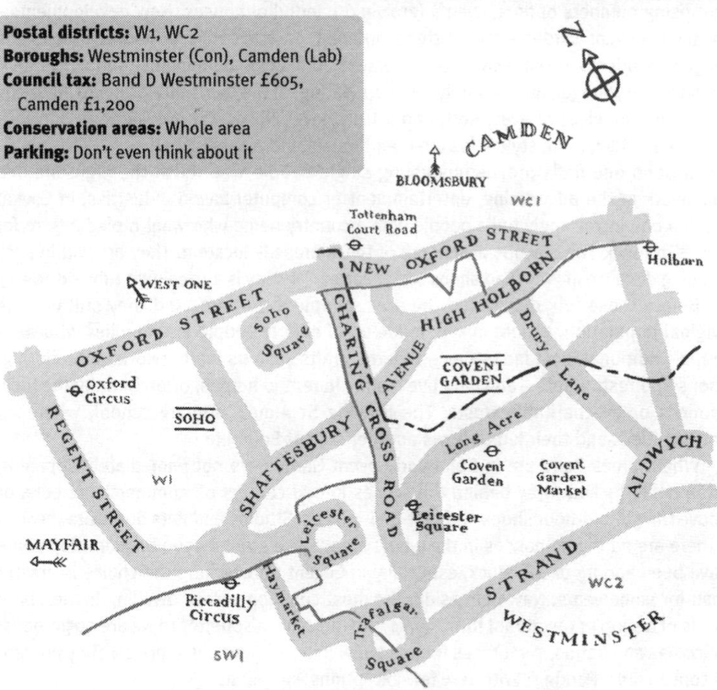

To use the words smart, flat and Soho in the same sentence used to be oxymoronic. Only 15 years back what homes existed were either characterful (which could mean scruffy or downright sordid) or rented from the council. Now we can have our choice of a few deeply gorgeous restored 18th-century houses, or startlingly modernist lofts, or luxury serviced apartments. Even the scruffy flats have been smartened, and broke bohemians will have to look elsewhere. When a laundry room in a block of flats (a potential studio) is a quarter of a million, you know the money has arrived.

These close but very different areas manages to combine culture and debauchery, shopping and sex, in a remarkably successful way. Covent Garden's the more public: a meeting place, alive with the excitement of theatre and opera, and with the equal showmanship of its market-place. Soho is edgier, ruder and drunker; it has long been London's 'foreign' quarter, the place where daring Englishmen ventured for a little Continental naughtiness and a good meal. It's still true, though the food may equally now be Chinese or Indonesian. Between them, Soho and Covent Garden have some wonderful shops, some touristy-tat ones, every kind of eating and drinking – and entertainment. This is the place in London to watch people.

S

The tension here – a very creative tension, naturally – is between smartness and sleaze. The smart money wants to graft five-star hotels and loft apartments onto Soho's grainy lifestyle, while existing denizens – many either making money out of, or enjoying, various doubtfully legal pursuits – want it left the way it is. Will the whole area get so rowdy and noisy that the theatre-goers stay away? Will shop rents rise and drive away the individual, creative businesses? Will mass tourism turn Covent Garden into a theme park? Will the mega-bars outweigh the very real village-community atmosphere of

Soho? The debate goes on, and despite (because of?) the tensions, both places thrive.

In the gaps between all this excitement, people live. There are quiet corners, a surprising numbers of flats, even a (growing) handful of houses. New developments – mainly in Covent Garden – attract steady interest. An active rentals market attracts City singles, students (from rich, often overseas, families), bohemians. Today, Soho is perhaps the younger, and certainly the more daring, of the two, more prone to inner-city pleasures and vices of every sort, and it truly never closes. Covent Garden's denizens tend to be older, more stylish (as are their homes), more established.

In Soho one finds prosperous young single people who relish the night life and may work in the advertising, entertainment or computer-based industries. In Covent Garden one increasingly finds people with a country home who want a pied-à-terre for nights in town. The obvious advantage of these areas is location. They are within easy strolling distance of West End shops and theatres. The City is a 10-minute tube ride away.

Before these folk discovered the area, people lived here. And they still do. The original population is more mixed, made up of elderly people and families who work in the traditional local industries – theatre, crafts such as leatherwork and tailoring, shops and restaurants – and who live mainly in rented homes, often built by the local councils or by charitable trusts. The thriving St Anne's primary school, where 20 nationalities send their kids, shows another side of Soho life.

What homes there are in Soho and Covent Garden are not immediately apparent, often being tucked away behind the scenes in odd corners off commercial streets, or above the ground-floor shops and first-floor offices. Studios and flats dominate the lists – there are hardly 20 houses in the whole area. Since around 1990 new developments have been adding to the stock, especially in Covent Garden, and the choice is greater than for some years. New flats aside, the most common sort of dwelling is the upper floors of a shop or restaurant forming a 2/3-bedroom maisonette. There are no gardens; balconies and patios, sometimes found in new flats, add greatly to prices. They are rare in conversions. Parking? With very few exceptions – forget it.

There's a new determination by police and council to clean up Soho; it needs it. Homelessness and drugs have placed heavy burdens on both districts: they attract every lost teenager in Britain, and quite a few from further afield. Some streets are gritty to the point of threatening after dark. The sex trade, which has attracted gangsters of a dozen nationalities over the years, is now the province of some dangerous Albanians. But Westminster's clean-up policy includes a general refusal for all-night or even late licences for clubs and bars. On the other hand, they smile on the turning of offices (often in Georgian buildings) back into homes, thus increasing the numbers of people living here.

Fringe areas include Fitzrovia to the N – dubbed NoHo by would-be trend-setters – which is covered in the Marylebone & Fitzrovia chapter. Bloomsbury, to the NE, is another place to look if your Covent Garden search proves fruitless (again, see chapter).

Soho

S

Soho is the area S of **Oxford St**, N of **Leicester Square** and E of **Regent St. Charing Cross Rd** divides it from Covent Garden to the E. In the 16th century Soho was a royal park where hunting took place – 'So-ho!', an ancient hunting cry, being the presumed origin of the name. It was developed with grand houses in the 17th century, and later settled by the Huguenots: they gave the area its abiding Continental character. By 1711 there were 600 French householders in Soho and 3,000 foreign lodgers, again mostly French. The population increased rapidly in the overcrowded houses until a serious outbreak of cholera in 1854 – after which its aristocratic residents moved out and prostitutes and other dubious characters moved in. At the start of the 20th century new theatres were built along **Shaftesbury Avenue** and **Charing Cross Rd**. Restaurants, invariably started by foreigners, gave the area a gastronomic reputation. One famous restaurant was opened by a French family in answer to desperate pleas by visiting compatriots for something decent to eat. . . . After World War II, strip clubs and clip joints increased in this area and the population declined rapidly. This exodus of residents has now reversed and, thanks to the clean-up campaign mounted by Westminster Council after pressure from the Soho Society, the number of sex clubs has been reduced from more than 100 to a mere couple of dozen. The sex trade is being coralled into **Rupert St** and **Peter St**. However, locals say that the vogue for huge megabars (and thus equally huge numbers of drunks disgorging late at night) is now as much, if not more, disruptive of life here.

Sadly, the French connection, three centuries old, is now all but broken: the last truly French grocer, Roche, closed in the early 1980s, though two great pâtisseries survive. Still, there's the Italians – and it's the best place in London to buy foreign newspapers.

Soho is still a maze of narrow streets and alleys. Many 18th-century and early 19th-century houses remain (though most are still offices), interspersed with later buildings including offices and warehouses – some now homes. Council and housing-association homes have been squeezed in, and re-sales offer cheaper flats to buy or rent.

Head S of Shaftesbury Avenue, where **Wardour St**, **Gerrard St** (pedestrianized) and **Lisle St** form the core of Chinatown, a tightly-knit neighbourhood which sits just to the north of Leicester Square. It is characterized by the many excellent Chinese restaurants, supermarkets and bakeries, and the Chinese New Year is marked by colourful celebrations in January. Property here is largely owned by the Chinese community and the stock of homes is under great pressure.

North of Shaftesbury Avenue, the area where **Brewer St**, **Berwick St**, **Wardour St** and **Old Compton St** meet is the scruffier part of Soho (not that this affects demand, or prices, for its homes). These streets, including **Archer St**, **Great Windmill St**, **Tisbury Court** and **Walkers Court**, traditionally had the largest share of the sex industry – though this is changing. Several renowned Italian delis and Italian and French cafés are also found here; and along **Old Compton St**, now much improved due to the council clean-up, there are one or two small infill developments: 'Greek Court' is new this year, with three 1-bed flats (£250–275,000). You can still find 1-bed flats above the shops for c. £240–300,000 – but you do need to be both nocturnal and broad-minded.

Behind the shopfronts and the neon, much of Soho is old. It was a fashionable suburb in the 17th and 18th centuries, and some houses still survive from these periods. These, in Meard St, were restored after years in disrepair. Door, elaborate doorcase and railings are all perfect examples of their period.

Golden Square and the surrounding roads, **Upper** and **Lower St James St**, **John St** and **Great Pulteney St** are much more 'respectable', and quieter. Again, though, this is more a business district – though one ex-hospital in **Golden Square** is now 14 flats. Four covetable Georgian houses in Lower St James St and John St have been done up: yours for £975,000–1.65 million. Golden Square is a desirable bolt-hole – Soho's only green oasis now that **Soho Square** has become somewhat notorious . . . especially after dark.

S

On the W fringe of Soho, towards Regent St, **Kingly St**, the famous **Carnaby**

St and **Fouberts Place** are largely shopping areas – rather self-consciously calling themselves 'West Soho' – though the occasional flat does appear on the market. In **Marshall St**, Marshall House is a 1989 block of 21 1-bed and 2-bed flats (the penthouse £895,000 last winter). At the other end of the street, Stirling Court is a 1970s ten-storey flats block (c. £280,000 for a 1-bed). Sandringham Court in **Dufours Place**, off Broadwick St, is a popular development completed by Barratt in 1987 – £450,000 for a 2-bed recently. There's a council-built block in the same street. Flats may also occasionally be had in the Georgian terraced houses of **Lexington St**; a 2-bed might be £450,000.

Great Marlborough St, **Noel St** and N of here is unlikely to be fruitful for homes, being more of a business/office area. **Poland St**, **Broadwick St** with its Georgian terraces and **D'Arblay St** are more popular, and more expensive. There are flats blocks in all three streets and in **Hollen St**: recent prices include studios at £280,000-plus and 1-beds at £280–500,000. **Berwick St**, S of Broadwick St, houses the well-known fruit-and-vegetable market and is therefore very noisy and delightfully messy during the day, which keeps prices down a little. Ingestre Court in **Ingestre Place** – Soho's solitary, 15-storey, tower block – has 1-bed flats which go for c. £325,000.

Meard St is unique, having a splendid terrace of early 18th-century houses (Grade II listed): a few of these Georgian delights are still in single occupation; most have been split into flats. Tenanted until 1987, the near-derelict estate was then auctioned and split up. Rarely for sale – and prices tend to be high to reflect the scarcity of this kind of period home: one 4-bed house has that Soho rarity, a garden.

The next street along, **Bourchier St**, is back in the heart of 24-hr Soho and is worth a care at night. It has 17 recent flats with parking spaces in a smart (and secure) Wates-built scheme: 2-beds are stable at c. £545–550,000. **Wardour St** is mostly ofices, but planning permission has been granted to redevelop a big site on the corner with **St Anne's Court** in a 6-storey office scheme that would include Peabody flats. There are homes in atmospheric St Anne's Court already: £650,000 has been asked for a 3-bed triplex in a Georgian building here. The old NCP car park between **Wardour** and **Dean Sts** has been replaced by the ever-so-smart Soho Hotel.

The streets leading N from Shaftesbury Avenue to Soho Square are grander than the Berwick St district. **Dean St**, **Frith St** and **Greek St** are prestige addresses: flats will be pricey and, in the square itself, the most expensive of all. Agents say that Greek St prices are 40 per cent above those of flats around **Great Windmill St**. There are several fine restaurants and famous/notorious clubs. At the northern ends of these streets, another one or two Georgian houses may be found intact. There are some in **Frith St**, for instance: one has become a hotel, another has been expensively restored as home or office. Kings House, a modern block in the NE corner of **Soho Square**, has 10 flats; Townsend House in **Dean St** is a 1950s block. The big Mezzo restaurant has some flats above it in 'Soho Lofts', a Manhattan Lofts development accessed via **Richmond Mews**: this caused great excitement as 'Soho's first lofts' when launched in the '90s, but is now described by some as passé.

On the N edge of Soho is Centrepoint House, an 8-storey block next to the famous office tower on **St Giles High St**. It became 36 2-bed maisonettes in 1990; these are now sold on short (19-year) leases: pay upwards of £350,000. The little streets round **Denmark St**, London's 'Tin Pan Alley', are both a conservation area and the target for redevelopment, with an eye to the possibility of a Crossrail station (though see Transport chapter) round the corner at Tottenham Court Rd. **Denmark St** is, in fact, thought to be the last street in London with original 17th-century terraces surviving on both sides. The whole corner is on the up residentially. South of Denmark St, the new Phoenix Apartmnts, behind the Phoenix Theatre, has 10 new flats 'in modern, industrial style' for £585–995,000.

Covent Garden

The area S of **High Holborn**, E of **Kingsway** and N of **Strand** takes its name from the development, in the early 17th century, of a former convent garden to form an Italian-style piazza laid out to an Inigo Jones design. The original fashionable residents soon moved further W, and by the middle of the century a fruit-and-vegetable market had started and grew rapidly. In the 18th century it became an area of seedy lodging houses and brothels. By the early 19th century the neighbourhood had been transformed by the market, which had expanded and been taken over by traders in all manner of goods.

In 1830, the Duke of Bedford organized the construction of the market buildings in an attempt to restore order. The market remained, in greater or lesser degrees of picturesque confusion, until 1974. Londoners grew to love the fruit, vegetable and flower stalls, the ribaldry of the market traders – and the pubs which opened at four in the morning to cater for them. Covent Garden became a unique community of market traders and actors, banana wholesalers, down-and-outs and ballet dancers.

When the market finally moved out, an epic row began about the area's fate. A giant scheme to knock most of it down was thwarted by an energetic local campaign – the first of its kind – and the GLC converted the central market building into a specialist shopping centre which has become a hugely successful tourist attraction. This started the transformation of the area around the market. Warehouses have been converted into flats, many small shops stayed and more, plus cafés and bars, have opened, while the marketplace and many courts and alleys have been pedestrianized.

Covent Garden is now a very popular area to live, and a steady flow of new developments and conversions of fine old buildings is widening the choice. Houses are extremely scarce, a few remaining around **Mercer St** and **Shorts Gardens**; agents reckon there are in fact only a dozen freehold houses in the Garden. Most available homes are flats above shops and restaurants, or in a selection of enviable, purpose-built developments – mainly recent, and again usually with commercial uses at ground level. The E side of the area has some blocks of flats belonging to housing associations and charities such as the Peabody Estate. The Mercers' Company has owned its Covent Garden estate for 470 years: it includes 90 flats north of Long Acre which are let on Assured Shorthold tenancies. These add to the number of residents, but not to the market for homes. The Mercers are careful to let their shops to interesting, individual concerns, reasoning that the mutliples have plenty of other opportunities. That said, the M&S in **Long Acre**, Tesco Metro in **Garrick St** and Sainsbury's in **Southampton St** mean that shopping is now useful as well as pleasurable.

The borough boundary between Camden and Westminster runs along **Shelton St**. To the N lies Seven Dials, where **Monmouth St**, **Upper St Martin's Lane**, **Shorts Gardens**, **Earlham St** and **Mercer St** converge. In 1990 the Seven Dials monument was restored to its position at the meeting point. The slender column of this faithful copy, adorned with its six sundials, itself forms the seventh. Seven Dials is an enormously popular place to live – as evidenced by the £650,000 paid for a large, lovely, light – but only 1-bed – flat in the Thomas Neal Centre, **Shorts Gardens**, in 2003. So, too, are **Neal St** and **Neal's Yard**, now both pedestrianized – the latter packed with wholefood cafés and organic farm produce – and with lots of interesting shops. One coveted address is Seven Dials Court (a duplex £650,000 last autumn), built around an attractive landscaped courtyard at first-floor level; it's approached from **Shorts Gardens** leading through to **Neal's Yard**. Also in Neal's Yard is an enormous duplex carved out of an old warehouse by Rick Mather; new this spring are three flats, all sold but available for rent. At 19 **Mercer St** is the Terry Farrell-designed development in the Comyn Ching triangle (named after an iron foundary that grew up there). There are seven enviable, tucked away flats with balconies or roof terraces (a studio £260,000 last year) and a rare, 17th-century house, on the market last year for £1.5 million. At the N end of Monmouth St, where it meets **Shaftesbury Avenue**, 'the Glasshouse' has 14 1-, 2- and 3-bed flats priced at £365–705,000.

Matthews Yard off **Shorts Gardens** is a 1989 development of three houses, three 1/2-bed flats and three 4-bed maisonettes. Georgian conversions in **Monmouth St** are popular, while 15 flats in Fielding Court date from 1990: two knocked into one were on the market last winter for £1.5 million. **Tower Court**, a footway, has a few of the rare, seven-figure freehold houses.

Moving across to **Endell St** (still in Camden), you'll find a noisier, so somewhat cheaper, corner. Only relatively, though: smart new flats cluster round a courtyard in the Ventana development. In this street, too, the old St Paul's Hospital has become 'The Hospital', a sort of workspace-cum-club for creative types, with serviced apartments – and a recording studio: the Eurythmics' Dave Stewart was behind this. As part of the deal the developers have built 13 new housing-trust flats in **Drury Lane** and **Newton St** – and double-glazed flats in earshot of the sound studio. **Odhams Walk**, off Endell St, has ex-council homes which offer 1-, 2- and 3-beds at c. £300–650,000 – popular because they have parking.

Drury Lane is also a rather busy street – especially around theatre-time – but a number of developments have been appearing. Garden Court, on the corner with Broad Court, is well regarded; lushest is Taylor Woodrow's 145 Drury Lane – a 42-flat office conversion: porterage, parking, 'like a hotel without the food': c. £400,000 for a 1-bed; 2-bed/2-baths £650,000. Over in **Macklin St**, N towards Holborn, there are ex-council flats in the Winter Garden block, and coming soon are seven 'funky apartments' in an old theatre costume laundry, no less. Barratt's block in **Newton St**, completed in 1999, has 2- and 3-bed flats. Round in **Bow St**, five new flats in 'Covent Garden Central' are from £425–850,000. **Kean St** (again) has 25 2003 flats in a Taylor Woodrow conversion of a splendid 19th-century warehouse, and ten more 'warehouse style' flats by McCabe are due early this year (called 'Debut': £425,000–£1m).

On the corner of **Upper St Martin's Lane** and **West St** a reclad office tower has 12 flats in a smart Art Deco-style low-rise section, Meridian Place. Garrick House in **St Martin's Lane** was a major refurb in 2000: 24 flats (a 2-bed, £615,000 recently) and a penthouse. Otherwise, theatres, clubs, restaurants and offices occupy this street. **Long Acre** is largely shops and offices, but gains three big new £1–2 million flats this year in 'Balletica', a former ballet school. Quieter **Floral St** has a couple of extremely popular mid-1980s developments and the 2003 conversion of an old art-college building.

All streets close to the Piazza are much coveted, although most of the buildings which overlook the market – and the buskers in front of the portico of St Paul's Church – are in commercial use. But views over the churchyard can be had from some superb flats: from St Paul's Court, a 1974 conversion; also from a vast modernist-luxury, balconied 4-bed duplex, £2.5 million, in **Henrietta St** – and now from **King St**, where the latest offering is 1717 Russell House, split into six flats (£425,000–2.5 million) which do overlook the piazza. Period flats occasionally appear, too, in **Maiden Lane** and **New Row**. Henrietta St has a £4.5 million, 6,700 sq ft house-cum-recording studio.

Off **Bedford St**, behind the Coliseum in **Bedford Court**, is clutch of ten flats, plus Edwardian Bedford Court Mansions (£700,000 for a 3-bed); **Hanover Place** has some converted warehouses. More period conversions occasionally crop up in **Russell**, **Tavistock** and **Wellington Sts**. On the corner of Wellington St, Eden is a 2001 development of 15 flats. The biggest recent scheme is Harlequin Court, just round the corner in **Tavistock St**, where the Strand Palace Hotel staff annexe has been gutted behind its ornate century-old facade, and a Japanese-gardened atrium inserted: expect to pay £600–800,000.

Council-flat resales are now relatively common in Covent Garden: in some blocks, virtually all the flats are privately owned. The walk-up 5-storey blocks around **Tavistock**

St and further N off **Drury Lane** yield flats for the young and fit. There is usually a choice of studios, 1-beds at £250–265,000, and 2-beds at up to £325,000.

Strand

Just beyond Covent Garden, between **Strand** and the Embankment gardens, one or two houses (like the £1.9 million 1688 gem in **York Buildings**), and some flats, survive in an unexpected, tucked-away corner. York Buildings also has flats; **Buckingham St** a handsome Georgian house that gained six flats on the upper floors. Little Adelphi in **John Adam St** boasts 66 flats with 24-hr porterage: mostly to rent, but think £500,000-plus for a 2-bed (with garage space). In the same street Durham House has 2-beds at £575,000. And of course there are the splendid serviced apartments next to the Savoy Hotel. If you have to ask the price (or service charge) – you can't afford them.

Craven St and Northumberland Avenue lie the far side of Charing Cross. A number of refurbished houses here: a 1730-vintage mansion in Craven St has proved slow to sell at £2 million-plus after the owner's French wife, who hated the place, moved back to Paris. Period 1-bed flats here are around £350,000, and there are 20 2-beds in a 1980s block at c. £350,000.

Transport Tubes, all zone 1: Leicester Square (Piccadilly, Northern), Covent Garden (Piccadilly), Oxford Circus (Victoria, Central, Bakerloo), Tottenham Court Road (Central, Northern). From Leicester Square: Oxford Circus 10 min (1 change), City 15 min (1 change), Heathrow 1 hr. Trains: Charing Cross.

Convenient for Everywhere: West End entertainment and shopping, City.

Schools Local Authority: Westminster City C of E (b), Grey Coat Hospital C of E (g). Private: Portland Place School.

SALES

Flats	S	1B	2B	3B	4B	5B
Average prices	175–250	220–500	300–1M+	400–1.5M	–	–
Houses	2B	3B	4B	5B	6/7B	8B
Average prices	900–1M	900–2M	1.5–3M	2–3M	–	–

RENTAL

Flats	S	1B	2B	3B	4B	5B
Average prices	200–300	250–600	325–1000	450–2000	–	–
Houses	2B	3B	4B	5B	6/7B	8B
Average prices	500–1000	800–2000	1300–3000	2500+	–	–

The properties More homes than there used to be: rare, lovely pre-Victorian houses, flats above shops, conversions of warehouses, etc., some cheaper ex-council, and corners are found for stylish new-build. An exciting, historic (if noisy) place to live.

The market More choice these days, with increasingly smart homes. Brisk rental market and steady rents.

S

Among estate agents active in this area are:

- E A Shaw
- Copping Joyce
- Barnard Marcus
- Winkworth
- Hallmark Estates
- LDG
- Frank Harris

THE SOUTH BANK

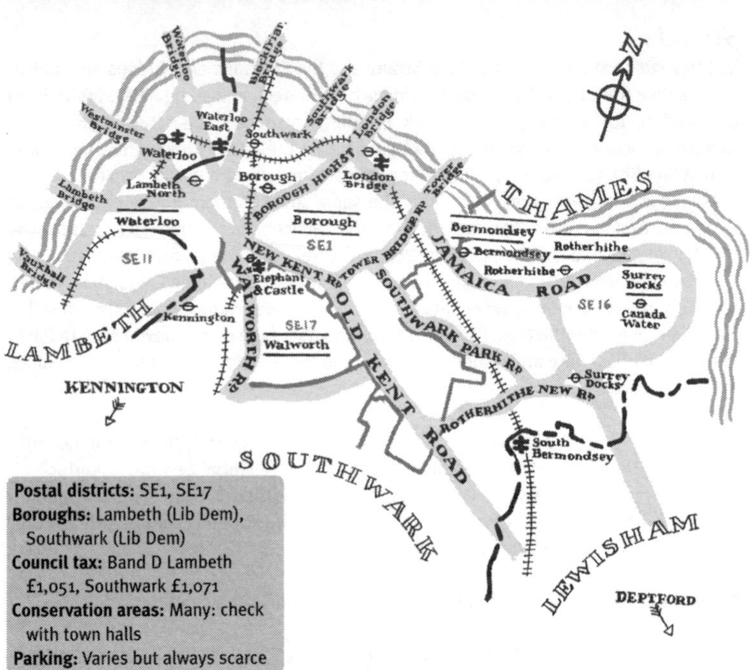

Postal districts: SE1, SE17
Boroughs: Lambeth (Lib Dem), Southwark (Lib Dem)
Council tax: Band D Lambeth £1,051, Southwark £1,071
Conservation areas: Many: check with town halls
Parking: Varies but always scarce

Soon it will seem extraordinary to everybody (not just to those who, to declare an interest, have loved the place for years) that this part of London was overlooked for so long. So central that it gets into the large-scale pages of the A–Z, it takes in a great sweep of London S of the Thames from Waterloo, via Borough and Bermondsey, across to Rotherhithe, bang opposite the West End and the City. Wander its gritty back streets – it extends S to the Elephant and Castle, and Walworth – stroll the splendid waterfront promenade and you will see more life, more innovation, more money being spent (and with more flair) than anywhere else in town. Call it the South Bank (the most accurate), or Bankside, or Southwark, or 'London's Fourth Quarter' or even (heaven forbid) 'South Central': no one name is quite right – the area is too big and diverse – but this is among London's most exciting places.

This is not one amorphous stretch: it has distinct neighbourhoods – and distinct neighbours. Its feisty denizens, whether long-term local or recent resident, do not lie down to be walked over – as many a developer, also the council, also Mayor Livingstone, have discovered to their cost. This tradition began with the local community rising up and fighting would-be developers off **Coin Street** (see below). But people power is not always triumphant: locals seem likely to be saddled with an ill-mannered tube of a building that would overshadow Tate Modern (no mean feat) and block the light and views from existing homes in and around **Hopton St**. The planning inspectorate approved this – to the utter disbelief of the locals, who petitioned the High Court for a judicial review, which they were denied. Next stop the House of Lords. . .

A lot of hope is being pinned on the great improvements planned for the Elephant and Castle, which would give this quarter the one thing it lacks: a central focus, largely traffic-free, instead of a vast, roaring double roundabout. Plans includes a new civic square, new town park, new market square, more greenery at an improved St Mary's Churchyard, a new square for Walworth. This would be achieved primarily by removing the well past its sell-by Heygate council estate, replacing it with 1,000 new homes in four smaller, mixed private/social developments. Much more for local people, too, such as the millions being spent on the stark Aylesbury estate – another instance where residents defeated the original plans, to transfer the estate's ownership to a housing association. All this is planned, if not financed; but Southwark Council has learned from its previous failure and the plans are specific, cogent and attractive. However, back in the 1950s it was boasted that the Elephant as it now exists would 'put Trafalgar Square in the shade and become one of the traffic spectacles of the world.' Worryingly, the Council's publicity for the new scheme desribes the proposed Walworth square as 'similar in size to Trafalgar Square. . . . '

Bankside is the new cultural heart of London. There's Tate Modern in the massive old Bankside power station, the new/old Globe Theatre and its fine museum, the Oxo Tower, colonized by artists, the redoubtable Coin St community, Zandra Rhodes's fashion museum. All this in an area already boasting the National Theatre, the Old Vic and the South Bank cultural centre around the Festival Hall. And circling above is the London Eye, raising spirits right along the Thames as it comes into view at unexpected places, while the equally beautiful Millennium Bridge spears across the Thames straight into the City. There are, too, the two new Hungerford footbridges, making Waterloo and the South Bank centre a scenic stroll away from the West End.

Thanks to an amazing expenditure of energy and vision, more and more people are living in this new district of London. New, of course, only in the sense of a place where they can choose to live and enjoy themselves (rather than merely work in or struggle through). The South Bank hadn't been that for a century or more, but go back and you find Chaucer, Shakespeare – just about everyone back to, and including, the Romans.

Incomers tend to be young and broke, or young and well-heeled: renters or buyers without, as yet, kids (schools are not the strong point, and a local comments 'no kids north of the Elephant'. . .). They look to Waterloo and the County Hall end of the South Bank for smart international flats (next stop Paris); Bankside for even smarter ones with a cultural bent (Tate Modern, Globe Theatre). Bermondsey St for bohemians and *fashionistas*, Borough for foodies, the Elephant and its environs for the daring urban pioneers – and those whose pockets do not stretch to the riverside: 'SOBO' – South of Borough – is one attempt to rebrand the frontier district around the Bricklayer's Arms flyover down the Old Kent Road. The area ends triumphantly with the Shad Thames/ Butler's Wharf corner of Bermondsey – arguably the most atmospheric (despite the makeover) and successful quarter of Docklands: see Docklands chapter for details of this, Rotherhithe and the Surrey Docks.

This is a very, very mixed area: it contains public and commercial buildings of every kind. There are theatres and railway stations, office blocks, university and hospitals. High-level rail lines and busy roads, plus the concentration of commerce and industry, have until very recently forced homes into small pockets – albeit sometimes surprising, Georgian ones. Traditionally this is an area of poverty and overcrowding. Big new council estates were shoehorned in in the 1960s and '70s, but these proved a false dawn. Now at last enlightened, detailed work, and money money money, are improving the estates – in many cases beyond recognition. Ally this process to the spate of commercial buildings becoming homes and it's clear why streets, and reputations, are changing fast.

The Jubilee Line Extension gave this area its real boost, making Canary Wharf accessible in one direction, and offering a fast link to Westminster and the West End in the other. To this has been added the Riverside Bus service, linking all the communities and cultural attractions at street level, from Covent Garden right round to County Hall. There's also an excellent Cross-London Tramlink planned (but don't hold your breath), which would stitch through the area via the Elephant and Castle and Waterloo.

The big excitement, in terms of new homes supply and price rises, took place in 1995–97. Things went quiet for a while, with another burst in late 1999–early 2000 (the millennium effect?). Then London's growing prosperity made offices attractive again, and developers began to switch sites back to commercial instead of residential. Recently, a slowdown in office schemes (though more are planned) has turned attention back to homes. Most of the action since 2000 has been in the 'fringe' areas such as Bermondsey St/Long Lane. East again, the Bermondsey Spa area is due a revival, if council plans mature. And then there's the Elephant . . . .

Add everything up, and around 8,600 private-sector homes have been completed in SE1 (including the Tower Bridge district) since 1994: a rash of conversions of old schools, offices and factories; new-builds in odd inland corners, riverside warehouse flats, ex-council resales. New social housing (but never enough) adds shared-ownership and fair-rent homes for locals and key workers that are a world away from the grim '60s estates – themselves already improving: the target of multi-million pound renewal or replacement.

The catalysts for change have been the City, with its earning power and need for easy access; the Jubilee Line tube, the river. The riverside strip is alive: restaurants, shops, bars, designer workshops, cafés jostle the cultural showplaces. Inland, new homes crop up amid the offices, and amenities arrive to serve them.

Our sketch map covers perhaps a dozen neighbourhoods, each very different. The riverside strip from County Hall downstream to Tower Bridge has a certain unity: a string of monuments tied together by the Queen's Walk, but stray a block S and you are in Waterloo – Bankside – Borough – Bermondsey. Go further S to find Lambeth and Southwark (the old parishes, not the sprawling modern boroughs), the north edge of Kennington, the Elephant and Castle, Walworth and the Old Kent Road.

The best place to start an exploration is – as it has always been – the river:

Waterloo, South Bank and Bankside

County Hall, once the giant riverside home of the old Greater London Council and across Westminster Bridge from the Houses of Parliament, is now a hotel, aquarium, gallery, health club – and flats (see below). The South Bank cultural complex lines the river from County Hall round past Waterloo Bridge to the National Theatre. Expensive plans to revamp the '50s complex come and go: the latest 'masterplan' includes flats. Wait and see: so far the only gainers have been the architects, to the tune of £6 million in fees.

To the S, Waterloo Station has grown to embrace Waterloo International, the Eurostar terminal, and the vital Jubilee extension. North of the station, **Theed St**, **Whittesley St** and **Roupell St** are quiet roads of little flat-fronted, early Victorian terraces on a human scale, which are popular buys: 2-beds have topped half a million since the Jubilee Line joined the transport hub of Waterloo. Off **Theed St** is the 'Royal Millennium Village' development (never use one buzzword when three will do) with 2-bed/2-bath flats and mews houses (2-bed house £675,000 last autumn). South of Waterloo East station are some '30s council flats in **Wootton St**.

Coin St, to the N, was the centre of a big early-'80s redevelopment row, in essence pitching office-block developers against community activists supported by Lambeth Council. The activists won and formed Coin Street Community Builders: this unique set-up has resulted in the area gaining rented homes for 1,300 locals, some in restored 1829 terraces. Their latest £40-million scheme created a superb hollow square, with big family houses and some flats overlooking a private garden above a car park. Next up are more flats (for sale and rent) plus a swimming pool and indoor sports centre on the site behind the National Theatre. Coin Street runs the homes through housing associations, with all tenants being members of a cooperative. A terrific idea – though friction within one co-op, the **Oxo Tower** one, led to a rather public spat last summer.

Also in this corner, flanking **Stamford St**, are **Duchy St** and **Aquinas St** (with its 1911 cottages); these were until 1949 part of the Duchy of Cornwall Estate, then local authority, now mostly private since Right to Buy.

Behind Waterloo station, **Lower Marsh** with its cheerful street market also holds some recent 1- and 2-bed flats (a 1-bed looking out at the rail tracks went for £180,000 last year). The Lower Marsh residents' group, 'Marsh People', has plans, and cash from Lambeth, to smarten up the street. Cobbled **Launcelot St**, off Lower Marsh, has a handful of cottages. Smart flats in a concierged block in nearby **Westminster Bridge Rd** are, the developers insisted (wrongly and outrageously), in 'South Westminster'.

East of **Baylis Rd** is a large council-built estate with some attractive homes. A new open space, Waterloo Millennium Green, was created by local people opposite the famous Old Vic Theatre. **The Cut**, which holds the Old Vic, has a block of new flats and some more traditional ones – which can be big 3-beds – above shops. Further S, **Mead Row** has some flats run as a housing cooperative. **Hercules Rd** has a mix of small 19th-century cottages (on the site of William Blake's), some 3-storey houses and council blocks. Busy **Lambeth Rd** is on the fringe of Kennington, and has some similar large, early 19th-century terraces.

The source of many South Bank flats during the 1990s was the conversion of offices. **County Hall**'s inland blocks, just across the street from Waterloo International, hold flats nowadays: up to £370,000 for a 1-bed; £450,000 for a 2-bed, £550,000 plus for 3-beds – apart from the usual health club, comprehensive room service can be had here. Or you could choose to buy a room in an 'aparthotel' (an 'investment opportunity', we are assured. . .) that caused much excitement in mid-2004. The old Shell building, the downstream block next to Waterloo Bridge, also became 'The White House' flats in 1996 amid much hype. These make popular rentals: from £310 a week for a 1-bed, £450 2-beds, £750 3-beds; to buy, from around £280,000/£450,000/£250,000 respectively.

Next to it, the dramatic drum of the Imax cinema replaced the former seedy 'bullring' at the S end of Waterloo Bridge. Even Century House in **Westminster Bridge Road**, once the lair of spymasters MI6, is nowadays The Perspective building, a redevelopment by Nicholson. The 180 ensuing flats were mostly sold off-plan; re-sales now c. £375,000 for a 2-bed, £1.3 million for a penthouse. They feature 'secure parking' for the Aston Martin.

To the E the borough of Southwark (not to be confused with The Borough) begins. The landmark **Oxo Tower**, with its high-profile restaurant and artists' shops and studios, graces the riverside here. There are also some Coin Street housing co-op flats (see above) in the building. Worth noting, too, that the Coin St crew are also responsible for the heart of this corner, **Gabriel's Wharf**, which serves as the riverside's village square: individual, idiosyncratic, human-scale shops and cafés in what has been a 'temporary' complex since 1988. Happily it shows no sign of stopping. And as well there's the colourful and well-established Coin Street festival, which enlivens the riverside over summer weekends.

Apart from the Oxo flats, there is little Thames-side housing along the **Upper Ground** stretch to the E of the London Television Centre tower except for some council-built homes, the odd block (**River Court** and, inland, rather tired **Rennie Court**: 1-beds c. £250,000, £335,000 for 2-beds), and some smart flats in part of the **King's Reach** development. More homes, though, E of Blackfriars Bridge, where the enormous brick-built Bankside Power Station is now the enormously successful Tate Modern. Nearby, a commercial building is now 'The Gallery' loft apartments; close to the bridge in **Hopton St** is **Falcon Point**: riverside Southwark Council flats, many now private (1-beds £300,000-plus). Also here are Bankside Lofts, Manhattan Loft Co's Piers Gough-designed flats which have commanded premium prices. However, both these and some Falcon homes may suffer loss of views (and value) if an unmannerly 20-storey tower block is permitted on the actual riverside right by Blackfriars Bridge. As noted in the introduction – see above – the final legal challenge by locals is ongoing.

Bankside (which we should point out is not, as some imagine, an invention of the

Tate's, but the ancient name for this riverside way) also has one of London's most historic houses, Cardinal's Wharf: the house was already old when Christopher Wren lived there while building St Paul's. Alongside it, the late Sam Wanamaker's reconstruction of Shakespeare's Globe Theatre is a triumphant success: a magnet for the whole neighbourhood. Flanking it on **New Globe Walk**, Berkeley's Benbow House, 71 flats, sold out in hours in 1999. This is now just about the prime development on the South Bank, and last year saw its penthouse on the market at £3.25 million – a record for this area (note, though, that it was for sale a year before that, at the same price). Next door, a warehouse has become Globe Walk: 34 more flats, 2-bed £320,000.

Inland, past the sites of the rediscovered Elizabethan theatres, the Rose and the Globe, some new homes have enviable positions. On **Southwark Bridge Rd** a handsome Georgian row, Anchor Terrace, has been restored as 29 flats known as **Red Lion Court**: it sits across the site of the original Globe Theatre. A block away on **Great Guildford St**, Peabody added 17 fair-rent homes and four shops. The Tate/Globe hinterland is a hotspot for commercial property developers, with big players like Chelsfield accumulating land S of Tate Modern and Land Securities starting work on a 750,000 sq ft office complex on Bankside, due for completion 2006.

One of the new Jubilee Line underground stations (Southwark) is on **Blackfriars Rd**, just where it meets **The Cut**, which street is the focus of a council re-hab scheme. There are plenty of council properties here; **Nelson Square** and nearby streets have restored early 19th-century houses and council flats, both low-rise and in towers. **Short St** has 14 new 'boutique apartments', 2-beds £435,000-plus. **Surrey Row** has live/work homes in a gated complex called 'La Gare' (it's over the railway line). **Blackfriars Rd**, like all the main streets in the area, has a few surviving earlier houses, some Georgian. Most of these are offices, but one or two are reverting: one is now eight flats. Off Blackfriars Rd are modern houses in **Scoresby St** and 1980s **Bridge House Court**, with 28 mews-style houses and flats built around a garden and over a car park. **Davidge St** has a pub conversion: it's now three 2-bed flats and a live/work unit. **Southwark Bridge Rd** has some Victorian houses, now flats. For the streets S of **St George's Circus**, see Kennington chapter.

Back on the river, the renovated **St Mary Overie Dock**, which contains a replica of Sir Francis Drake's 'Golden Hind', is the centrepiece of a range of modern riverside offices and flats. This successful development sweeps back to form a precinct round glorious Southwark Cathedral. Another reminder of past glories, the rose window of Winchester Palace, still stands, lending its name to **Winchester Square** and Winchester Wharf with its flats. Several new flats blocks, mostly small, have been cleverly squeezed in, and the view of the rose window opened up. South of the Cathedral, **Green Dragon Court** has some 4-storey homes – but the sound of bells is supplemented by that of passing trains (never very far away in this corner – and a possible threat: see below). **Clink St** already boasts Horseshoe Wharf (14 flats, some with river-view balconies, and Clink Wharf (11 more), sold at 'shell' stage with one back on the market, all smart, at £2.9 million. . . . Now comes Victor Wharf, on the **Stoney St** (see below) corner. Built where the Palace kitchens once stood, its 14 flats include a 3-bed penthouse with circular 'glass curtain' reception: four unsold last autumn, from £440,000. On **Montague Close** between river and cathedral, Minerva House has new 1-, 2 and 4-bed flats: £750,000 for a 4-bed.

S *The Borough and Bermondsey Street*

Borough High St meanders southwards from London Bridge, and is the centre of the oldest part of South London (check out The George, a galleried 16th-century inn). Just S of the cathedral is **Borough Market**, an atmospheric survival of Victorian London much used as a film set. Progress is about to overtake it: a big new railway viaduct, part of Thameslink 2000 (sic), may go through at high level: the public inquiry gave the all-clear, but several homes and other properties would have to be demolished (round the cathedral in **Stoney St**, **Green Dragon Court** and **Borough High St**). Latest news in this epic is that Network Rail put in new plans last June: Southwark is considering.

Meanwhile, the market itself is a centre for fine foods – wholesale most of the time (early mornings are busiest), and thronged with foodies when the retail fine food market runs on Fridays (from noon) and Saturdays. A £4 million upgrading scheme has just finished, including the reconstruction of the beautiful old Covent Garden Floral Hall, moved here to provide a restaurant. With the Vinopolis wine exhibition, and a rash of new restaurants, The Borough is becoming a gourmet's paradise.

London Bridge station will be redeveloped – but not until 2010 on the present schedule; last winter plans for the 'Shard of Glass', a beautiful, church-spire-shaped, 66-storey tower on top of it, were in some doubt as the biggest commercial tenant backed out. The Shard, which would add considerable open space as well as offices and flats, and reinstate a proper streetscape to two roads, has been given the go-ahead by John Prescott's office. On the E side of the High St, **St Thomas St**, behind London Bridge station, boasts some Georgian houses. **Snowfields**, behind Guys Hospital, has some good old houses, nearly all split into flats, and is a popular location: the doctors provide a ready public for these convenient homes, and local agents say they very rarely appear on the market. Off **Newcomen St** Bellway's **Bowling Green Place** scheme added more 2-bed flats. West of the High St, **Union St** has some working-men's cottages built late in the 19th century; also **Maidstone Buildings**: once a hop warehouse, now 52 loft-style flats. On **Borough High St** itself Bank Hall Chambers is now 10 flats, and 14 more have been added at no. 210. Bridegate House is new flats; the 2-bed penthouse £550,000.

To the S, as far as **Lant St**, there is a little neighbourhood of mostly 19th-century housing, all built by various philanthropists and public bodies. As such they are rarely for sale, though roomy 3-bed ex-council flats sometimes come up. Wimpey have built 70 new flats at 54 Lant St: prices from £290,000. Homes in this street also include an ex-pub, now six 2-bed flats, and warehouse conversions: look for lofts here and in **Redcross Way**, **Marshalsea Rd** and adjoining streets. In **Swan St**, E of the High St and near Borough tube, 106-flat Berwick Court has large (some 4-bed) new flats.

Long Lane is a busy street running E–W and its residue of industrial/commercial buildings means it is the focus of much development. The Borough (W) end has most going for it, both in ambience and convenience (the tube station), but the E end joins **Bermondsey St** and hopes to gain some overspill from that hot spot. Galliard's Royal Oak Yard scheme is just to the N, with four live/work units and 22 flats; nearby 2003 saw six new town-houses and 37 flats in a smart new corner building.

Berkeley are building a big scheme at the junction of **Long Lane** and **Tabard St** called 'Tabard Square': three blocks, one a tower, with 519 flats (162 of them Affordable Homes) plus a new public square. The square was prescient planning: archaeologists have just discovered a Roman temple precinct beneath the site, complete with paved square, column and statues (they found a bronze foot). Nearby Borough tube station is being smartened up. South of Long Lane on **Great Dover St**, Bellway's recent scheme has 2- and 3-bed flats from £280,000-ish.

Borough High St runs down towards the Elephant and is less characterful at this S end. But turn down **Trinity St** to discover a surprising enclave: the Trinity estate, on land owned by Trinity House. **Trinity St** and **Trinity Church Square** have handsome early 19th-century houses belonging to the Seamen's Widows' Housing Trust; **Merrick Square** (1850s) and **Cole St** are similar. Houses and flats are occasionally sold – 2-bed flats c. £285,000; 4-bed houses, c £850,000 – others are available at charitably cheap rents. New loft-style houses were built here in 1997, and Georgian-style 4-bed houses round in **Brockham St** in 2000 (c. £650,000). Fairclough's Frazer Court round in **Harper St** has 2-bed flats and 4-bed houses; Bellway's Chadwick Square brought 140 flats. **Bath Terrace** has some Victorian flats in a large, rather dour block, but at good-value prices.

Bermondsey Square is in truth only a corner of handsome old houses overlooking the antiques market and the busy road N to Tower Bridge. There are plans to 'regenerate' the Square, at a cost of £36 million: it will include – apart from new homes – 'enhanced facilities' for the market, an arthouse cinema, film production premises – and open-air film or theatre shows at night. All due by '06.

East of here is **Grange Rd**, with several buildings converted to homes. Three houses in **Grange Walk** have medieval origins, the last relics of the great Bermondsey Abbey, which stood where **Abbey St** now runs. There are some Victorian houses, too, and at the **Jamaica Rd** end a warehouse conversion, Neckinger Mill. Neckinger Cottages has neat 2-bed houses. A **Grange Walk** school was an early, and clever, 1980s conversion: galleried studio houses and characterful flats. The 165-home Grange Park scheme, by **Rouel Rd**, was done by Laing in 1988. The 1930s industrial **Alaska Building** is 150 1- and 2-bed flats.

Off **Grange Rd/Spa Rd** to the E, check out the **Bermondsey Spa** area, a neglected corner where 11 sites are earmarked for homes for sale, rent and shared ownership: among the first is a scheme from Blueprint. This is a corner well worth watching.

Bermondsey St, which leads back up to London Bridge station, is the old village centre. It has some surviving old houses, Zandra Rhodes' new orange and pink fashion museum, plus attendant flats – and is the best address in the 'new' Bermondsey. Recent homes schemes include several by pioneer Bermondsey developer Acorn Homes, flats and live/work units, and Bellway's 54-flat block Magdalen Mews. Several houses in Bermondsey St have been expensively smartened up: £1.3 million was being asked last winter for a 3,400 sq ft, 5-storey house; £585,000 for a 3-bed house. Acorn has also built in **Tower Bridge Rd** and **Weston St**. **White's Grounds**, which leads off to the N, has some large flats in a converted Victorian building. **Pages Walk** has a school conversion from 1995. **Tyers Gate** has warehouse conversions (1,900 sq ft £875,000).

Leathermarket St has a big block of 1994-built flats around a courtyard. In **Tanner St**, opposite a little park, is a converted Victorian print works and five new-build houses. Even Hartley's old jam factory in **Green Walk**, off the S end of Tower Bridge Rd, has succumbed to Acorn Homes' conversion into 154 flats and some live/work spaces: a popular scheme (2,000 sq ft £785,000). The same street has some little Georgian cottages.

The Docklands chapter covers in detail the exciting Butler's Wharf/Shad Thames quarter by Tower Bridge, between Tooley St and the river, and ancient Rotherhithe village.

Inland, the Docklands effect has been encouraging interest in the pockets of housing between the river strip and the **Old Kent Rd**. This district has a surprising number of homes, including some of the oldest in London, in what is still a very mixed environment. **Leroy St** has some Victorian flats in a 4-storey terrace and has just gained 'SEBO', a Rialto scheme with 14 flats. A small row of Georgian survivals on the N side of the **New Kent Rd** change hands for c. £500,000. The Bricklayers Arms site, E of **Dunton Rd**, has 600 homes, half now owned by housing associations, built in the late 1980s. Likewise the Abbey development nearby: pleasant cottage-style 1- to 3-beds. To the E, the district S of **Southwark Park Rd** has some nice streets of small-scale Victorian terraces. **Lynton**, **Esmerelda**, **Strathnairn** and **Simms Rds** have flat-fronted cottages, mostly well-kept and attractive (c. £300,000). Further S, **Avondale Square** has 3-storey mid-Victorian terraces. To the N, **Yalding Rd** boasts some pretty, flat-fronted houses.

S

Walworth and The Elephant

The big plans (see Introduction above) for the Elephant are cited by property bulls as a plus for the whole area – as indeed they will be, when and if. But even Southwark Council are talking about a completion date of 2011, and they have yet to 'choose' a housing partner, or a commercial partner, for the scheme.

Homes in 3-D rather than on paper at the Elephant include 'Metro Central', the 'brutalist aesthetic' office-block turned into 413 flats by St George five years ago. In

Steedman St the 'South Central' scheme's 100 flats, designed by Piers Gough (also architect of the Bankside Lofts development), sold fast off-plan last year. The 110 live/work units go on the market this January.

From the Elephant, the **Walworth Rd** runs S towards Camberwell. Once it was lined with handsome houses, but few survive. **Albany Rd** runs off to the E, forming the boundary between Burgess Park to the S and the enormous and notorious Aylesbury Estate, built to house more than 8,000 people on 64 acres. The triangle between **Walworth Rd**, the Elephant and the **New Kent Rd** has equally little to recommend it, though a few corners of 19th-century housing survive amid the council slabs. Some such occur in and around **Brandon St** and **Chatham St**, many now flats. However, if it's a low price you seek, ex-council flats can be had. Just check the Elephant plans first . . .

Surrey Square boasts some 1790s houses – also some 1970s ones: naturally cheaper. **East St** is another place to look, although the area is busy on street market days. Some purpose-built Edwardian maisonettes in **Aylesbury Rd** and **Wooler St**; 3-bed Victorian houses in nearby **Searles Rd** have been joined by a school conversion, 'The Pepperpot': 1,000 sq ft around £340,000. Just N of the Old Kent Rd, **Marcia St** has been 'recreated': Galliard built 68 Victorian-style 4-bed houses where the originals once stood. **Bartholomew St**, a little closer to town, has a row of original Georgian houses.

Transport Tubes (all zone 1): Many – see map. From Elephant & Castle: Oxford Circus 22 min (1 change), City 7 min, Heathrow 1 hr (2 changes). Trains: Waterloo, London Bridge, Elephant & Castle.

Convenient for City, West End, Docklands. Miles from centre: 1.

Schools Local Authority: London Nautical (b), Notre Dame RC (g), Alwyn (g), Geoffrey Chaucer, St Saviour's & St Olave's C of E.

SALES

Flats	S	1B	2B	3B	4B	5B
Average prices	160–200	180–300	220–400	250–450+	–	–
Houses	2B	3B	4B	5B	6/7B	8B
Average prices	200–300	250–450	350–500	–	–	–

RENTAL

Flats	S	1B	2B	3B	4B	5B
Average prices	170–250	190–350	230–450+	325–800	–	–
Houses	2B	3B	4B	5B	6/7B	8B
Average prices	195–450	300–550	350+	–	–	–

The properties Wider choice as warehouse and office conversions, plus new-build, join ex-council homes. Whole houses scarce, flats plentiful. Locations vary from riverside smart to very inner-city.

The market Once a place for bargains, now becoming mainstream. Lofts and conversions, some very smart, attract international buyers. Grittier lofts and new flats attract the designing classes. New tube and cultural schemes have raised area's profile.

Among estate agents active in this area are:

- Acorn
- Cluttons
- Frank Harris
- Winkworth
- Williams Lynch
- Daniel Cobb
- Field & Sons
- Stirling Ackroyd
- Felicity J Lord
- Burnet Ware & Graves

SOUTH KENSINGTON, EARL'S COURT AND WEST BROMPTON

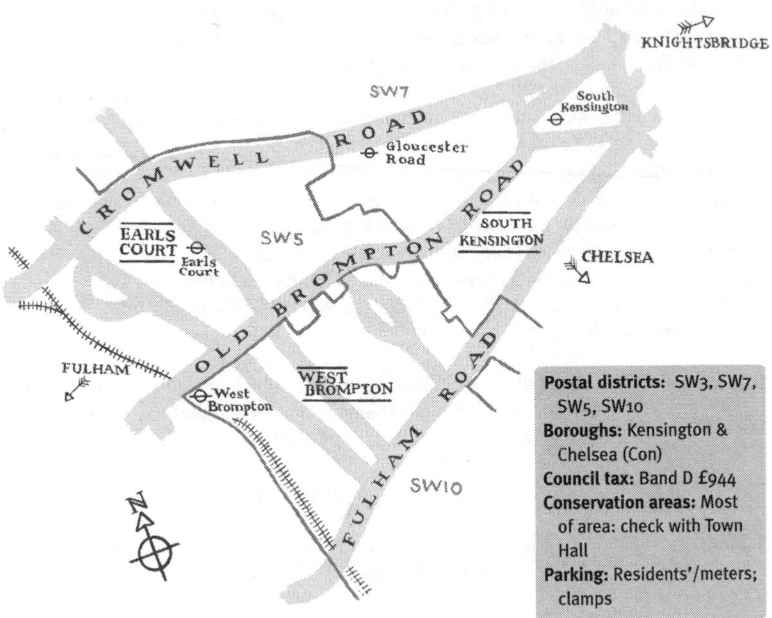

Postal districts: SW3, SW7, SW5, SW10
Boroughs: Kensington & Chelsea (Con)
Council tax: Band D £944
Conservation areas: Most of area: check with Town Hall
Parking: Residents'/meters; clamps

We think we have property booms, but they are nothing compared to the 20-year frenzy of speculation that erased the fields of Brompton. Between 1855 and 1875 came the towering terraced houses in snowy stucco, followed late in the century by a second wave of red-brick blocks of a new fashion in homes: the mansion flat.

A steady revival over the past 25 years has returned these three areas to the state of bourgeois respectability intended by their Victorian developers. The difference now is that nearly all the enormous, dignified houses are split into flats.

As houses, they had a short run of luck. The demise of domestic servants made them unviable and so most spent much of the 20th century as hotels or cheap but seedy rented flats and bedsits. But no longer. The area is still dotted with hotels, be they smart South Kensington ones or the fast-vanishing number of Earl's Court B&Bs; but the rocketing values of the 1980s and late 1990s finally made it worthwhile to expend care and attention on the tall decaying terraces. Skips, scaffolding and designers moved in *en masse* as the classier developers set to work. Clever – indeed, state-of-the-art – conversions transformed Evelyn Gardens, the Onslows, the Cranleys, the Courtfields in the 1980s. Then the 1990s saw conversions mop up most of the lingering South Ken hotels and in the new century they have spread into Earl's Court. Amid the ever-smarter flats, a few houses even survive as single homes.

So now this heart-of-London tract heaves with the sort of seriously wealthy people that its original developers dreamed of; what they would never have foreseen was that the well-heeled businessmen and their families who congregate here, buying or renting, would have come from all corners of the earth. Its through-routes may be congested, but there are calm corners and leafy, peaceful squares; schools, museums and the vast green tract of Hyde Park and Kensington Gardens for the kids. 'You can eat well, shop, even buy a car – as long as it's a Ferrari', comments a local. The clientele that attracts a Ferrari dealer kept the property market ticking over when other parts – neighbouring, even posher, old-money Kensington proper included – went soft last year. Foreign corporate rentals kept the lettings scene lively. Balancing the international – and again unlike Kensington – there is more choice, in Earl's Court especially, at the lower end of the price scales, and home-grown (especially City) workers are more important.

The three diverse districts covered by this chapter form a largely residential triangle between Chelsea and Kensington proper. The area lies between **West Cromwell Rd/ Cromwell Rd** to the N, **Fulham Rd** to the S, the West London railway line in the W and **Brompton Rd** up to The Oratory church in the E. It contains some of the most expensive houses in London – the ponderously handsome, enormous, £10-million-or-so, Italianate villas in **The Boltons** – some pleasant little mews and a seemingly endless supply of converted and purpose-built flats, flats and more flats.

Two major factors influenced the development of an area previously covered with nursery and market gardens. The first was the Great Exhibition of 1851 in Hyde Park, profits from which were used to build the major museums complex on the border with Knightsbridge and the two main routes along which they stand, **Cromwell Rd** and **Exhibition Rd.** The second and most important influence was the arrival of the Metropolitan and District railways during the 1860s, which allowed speedy access to Central London. Ease of access remains one of the biggest attractions of the area.

Every neighbourhood except West Brompton has tube stations within walking distance. West Brompton station on the District Line is W of the Brompton Cemetery and is convenient for a few streets in Earl's Court; its usefulness has increased since a linked station has been added to the West London Line, which has three trains an hour to Clapham Junction and Willesden Junction.

The Piccadilly Line calls at all three of the other local tube stations and runs straight to Heathrow Airport: a big plus for this international area. **Cromwell Rd** also links directly with the M4 to Heathrow, drawing tourists to the hotels in the area.

The most cosmopolitan corner of the already various Royal Borough, Earl's Court was once known as the 'Polish Corridor', then 'Kangaroo Valley', after successive waves of transients. It is now home to an increasingly affluent mini-United Nations, has been discovered by young City types and is also a favourite haunt of London's gay community. Some Middle-Eastern families still remain in neighbouring South Ken, as it is known, but it is no longer the 'Saudi Ken' of the 1970s. The French have colonized the area around the Lycée Français near the tube. They are but one community among many: it would be hard not to feel at home in South Kensington, whichever corner of the world you hail from.

One thing all the neighbourhoods have in common is garden squares, although there is only one public garden – in **Redcliffe Square**, West Brompton – unless you count Brompton Cemetery, adopted as a de facto park by the locals. You are never far from Kensington Gardens, though.

The most densely populated part of the area lies to the N of **Old Brompton Rd**, where red-brick mansion blocks abound and the majority of houses have been converted to flats. The most desirable chunk lies between here and the **Fulham Rd**. Many of the terraces of big brick-and-stucco houses have been converted into flats, but there are still enclaves of single-family houses in small-scale villagey streets, charming cobbled mews and peaceful cul-de-sacs. Shops are generally clustered around the tube stations and restricted to the main roads.

Old Brompton Rd, a busy boulevard running E–W, cuts through the middle of the area. Here the shops, pubs and cliffs of big brick mansion-blocks tend to congregate in groups, the shops near main junctions such as **Earl's Court Rd** and around South Ken station. A string of smart emporia, restaurants, bars and antique shops stretch along most of **Fulham Rd** with a concentration of deeply fashionable stores at Brompton Cross (the junction with **Sloane Avenue**). **Cromwell Rd**, a wide, noisy six-lane route to the M4, has hotels standing side by side with tall terraced houses divided into flats.

Many homes in this area are leasehold (see, for example, Wellcome and Thurlow, below). However, the legislation on leasehold reform, giving rights to extend the lease or buy the freehold has radically changed the market: see Buying and Selling chapter.

Wellcome Trust and Thurloe Estates

This strip between **Old Brompton Rd** to the N and **Fulham Rd** to the S, extending W to **Drayton Gardens**, is the heart of residential South Kensington. Until 1995 most of this district was owned by the Henry Smith's Charity, landowners here since the 17th century. Smith's Charity sold its estate to the Wellcome Trust in 1995. A number of leaseholders have bought their freeholds, but they are still a minority. More people have extended their leases to 105 years. However, short leases are still common, and this is a neighbourhood where the workings of the latest law changes are being eagerly watched.

All householders – and that includes freeholders – are still subject to strict controls on how they maintain their properties under an estate management scheme imposed by Wellcome: no pink front doors here, please. The trust's holding is concentrated around **Onslow Gardens**, **Cranley Gardens**, **Evelyn Gardens** and the **Pelhams**. A degree of estate control also applies to the Thurloe Estate (lying between **Pelham St** S, **Thurloe Place** N and **Brompton Rd** E). The Thurloe Estate has sold off the freehold of a number of properties, but here, too, all residents are subject to an estate management scheme.

One of the gems of the Wellcome Estate is **Pelham Crescent**. Elegant, white-stucco terraced houses sweep in a Regency (in style – it's 1833, but poor William IV never gets anything named after him) semicircle around leafy private gardens, which screen the crescent from the Brompton Cross end of Fulham Rd. Stretches of black iron railings, columned porches and green Victorian street lamps complete the scene. Most of the houses are still in single-family occupation: prices of over £4 million have been achieved for a long lease (last winter one was £3.95 million, another £4.45 million). The white stucco continues into **Pelham Place**, which curves across **Pelham St**, a feeder road between South Kensington, Knightsbridge and the Fulham Rd.

Pelham Place leads to 1840s **Thurloe Square**, one of the area's most exclusive garden squares. Here 4-storey plus basement brick-and-stucco houses (mainly split into flats) stand on three sides of an elongated private garden. An unmodernised freehold house here, 4,700 sq ft, was £2.8 million last winter, while a 1-bed flat on a 48-year lease was £350,000. Residents in the SE corner of the square enjoy an exceptional view of the entrance to the Victoria & Albert Museum at the top of **Thurloe Place**, with its imposing crown-shaped stone tower. Houses on the S side of **Thurloe St** back onto the tube line, as do those at the S end of **Thurloe Square** and in **South Terrace** (houses here c. £2.4 million, add another £300,000 for the quieter side of the street). Tucked to the W of Exhibition Rd, and just S of the Cromwell Rd, is **Thurloe Place Mews**. To the E of the square lies a group of late-Georgian terraced houses in **Alexander Square** and neighbouring streets; despite its name, Alexander Square is a single street of 1830-vintage 3/4-storey brick-and-stucco houses, overlooking small private gardens. The gardens act as a barrier between the houses and Brompton Rd as it winds from Knightsbridge to Fulham Rd.

Returning westwards, where **Brompton Rd** merges with **Fulham Rd** is the fashionable Brompton Cross, with its cluster of ultra-smart shops and restaurants and the Art-Nouveau Michelin Building. Passing Pelham Crescent again, **Sydney Place** combines with the E leg of **Onslow Square** to form a main through-route to Chelsea. The big 1930s block here has underground parking, which adds to its appeal, but leases can be on the short side. Onslow Square proper stretches westwards, its immaculate terraces of 4-storey 1846 houses with their columned porches overlook award-winning gardens in this choice square. The houses were split into flats during a major conversion programme in the 1960s. 'The Onslows' form the most popular clutch of properties in South Kensington, agents report. Prices vary considerably, depending on size, condition and crucially, the length of the lease: 3-bed flats run from just under, to a good bit above, a million. An example is the 2-bed, 3-level, long-lease affair, with direct access to the communal gardens, for which £2 million was being asked last autumn. White stucco and brick-and-stucco terraces of varying sizes, with the same columned porches, are the dominant style in **Onslow Gardens** (these enormous houses back onto tree-lined communal gardens, and ground-floor flats with direct access are much in demand: again, 3-bed maisonettes replace small houses here) and in **Sumner Place, Cranley Place** and the N arm of **Cranley Gardens.**

Stucco and the term 'cottage' do not often go together, but they coexist happily in this house in Elvaston Place, called a cottage despite its classical rusticated stucco and elegant door surround. Trees hide the lower pair of windows: there are six, set symmetrically in the facade. The six-panel door echoes the windows. These features recur on the larger homes.

Most of these were converted into flats, many at top-of-the-market levels – but wherever possible they have been refurbished and turned back into single houses: one, in Cranley Place, was £5.5 million last winter for 7 beds, lift, mahogany panelled wine cellar and air-conditioning. The spacious houses in **Sumner Place** have leases of c. 50 years. Nearby **Neville Terrace**, and **Neville St**, next along, have smaller, 4/5-bed, houses: most have been expensively done up in recent years. A smart 5-bed house in the terrace was £1.95 million last winter.

In **Onslow Mews East**, what looks like a row of cottages is in fact two handsome, 3-bedroom, 1980s-built houses. Parallel to the W side of Cranley Gardens is **Cranley Mews,** where the range of both sizes and prices is large: one example, a 2-bed, 1,017 sq ft house, freehold, was £745,000 last winter. At the S end of **Cranley Gardens** and **Evelyn Gardens,** stucco gives way to Victorian red-brick flat blocks. The most attractive are the renovated Dutch-style ones with unusual brick and white-stucco porches that line the S arm of **Evelyn Gardens.** Few buildings around here have not been converted and smartened up over the past 25 years.

In contrast to this densely-populated area is a network of small streets just off Fulham Rd, N of **Elm Place** and outside the Wellcome Estate. Elm Place itself (2-storey, late-Georgian cottages with tiny front gardens) and **Selwood Place** (fine Georgian terrace on the N side) are charming, leafy streets. Selwood Place is blocked off at its W end by the back of St Peter's Armenian Church in **Cranley Gardens.**

On the corner of **Foulis Terrace** and **Fulham Rd** stands The Bromptons, a very-high-security, very expensive complex of 73 very-high-spec flats of 1- to 5-beds. Behind the carefully retained high-Victorian style facade, pool, gym and underground parking are also provided. A boundary quirk gives The Bromptons an SW3 (Chelsea) postcode.

An arched brick entrance and steps on the E side of **Elm Place** leads up to **Regency Terrace**, a group of 3-storey brick-and-stucco terraced maisonettes above the rear of shops fronting Fulham Rd. As the name suggests, the houses line a Regency-style terrace at first-floor level, complete with black iron railings and street lamps. They look down on **Lecky Street**, a quiet little private cul-de-sac of white 2-storey houses with columned porches. A number of mews streets are spread throughout the area, by far the most picturesque being **Roland Way**, tucked away off **Roland Gardens** (itself a street of much-desired semi-detached houses). Pretty painted cottages decorated with hanging baskets and colourful window boxes give cobbled, private **Roland Way** its charm: these little homes rarely come up for sale, but tend to go for over a million and a half when they do. A row of 27 3/4-bedroom terraced houses appeared in the late 1980s in **Eagle Place** and in **Roland Way** itself. These prove harder to sell than the nearby period homes, agents say, though buyers appreciate the security barriers placed at either end of the street.

The S end of Roland Way leads into **Thistle Grove**, a shady pedestrian walkway lined with green Victorian lanterns and trees overhanging the rear walls of Evelyn Gardens. Small houses and cottages of varying styles merge with tall brick and stone mansion blocks. **Drayton Gardens**, which forms the W boundary of the area, combines a mix of styles from brick-and-stucco terraced houses with front gardens (NW side, a 5-floor house was £2.25 million unmodernised last winter) to Dutch-style brick-and-stone mansion blocks and modern flats. At the S junction with **Fulham Rd** stands the cinema, and a modern building with 14 flats completed in 2002.

The Fulham Rd from here back E to Brompton Cross has many expensive shops and restaurants: hard to recall the down-at-heel state of 15 years or so back. It is now far smarter (and a bit quieter) than King's Rd. This stretch forms a clear boundary between South Ken and Chelsea, although a few homes N of Fulham Rd are in the SW3 postcode.

Museum/Lycée Area

As its name suggests, the area is dominated by the major museums standing along **Exhibition/Cromwell Rds**. The Science, Natural History, Geological and Victoria & Albert Museums were built following the Great Exhibition of 1851. The museum developments and improved transport links attracted wealthy residents to the area. Nowadays, the neighbourhood is particularly popular with the French, who have established their own colony – with excellent bookshops and cafés – near the Lycée Français. The school, together with the French Institute, covers a whole block stretching from **Cromwell Rd** through to **Harrington Rd**. The area also attracts other Europeans and Americans who like its atmosphere.

South Kensington underground station and a number of busy main roads have attracted a mix of shops, hotels and other uses, ranging from the College of Psychic Studies to Cancer Research, both in **Queensberry Place**. The Aga Khan's gleaming cultural centre for Ismaili Muslims stands in **Thurloe Place** opposite the V&A Museum.

Amid all the hustle and bustle, **Bute St**, with its cluster of small shops, manages to keep a delightfully village-like atmosphere. Away from the museums smaller-scale terraces and street trees make the heart of the area, centring on the Grade II-listed underground station, an appealing corner despite the busy, five-road junction by the tube, dominated by the curving, red-brick inter-war Melrose Court flats opposite. Hence the outraged local reaction to the plans for the complete redevelopment of the station with a scheme for an office tower, shopping mall and 125 flats. It was hastily withdrawn, and the station smartly listed. An appealing alternative with airy glass roof and domes has been drawn up by the Brompton Association, but the (would-be) developers are considering returning to the plan that got permission in 1999: at the time, they decided it was 'unviable' (too pricey). Watch this (expensive) space . . .

Reece Mews is another pleasant, small-scale corner: a little cobbled street running N–S between **Harrington Rd** and **Old Brompton Rd.** An attractive group of recent 2-storey brick mews houses fits in well with the older 3-storey painted cottages, one of which was for sale last autumn, much smartened, at £1.5 million (1,560 sq ft). Beyond, **Manson Place** is a wide cul-de-sac of tall terraces, much improved in recent years.

Back to the monumental with broad **Queen's Gate.** Many of the houses around it and on E are truly vast, and have nearly all been divided into flats at various periods – and at various levels of quality behind the stucco. Most have lifts – lacking in many other conversions – which enhances their appeal. A house of this style in **Queensbury Place**, a block away, was on the market freehold last winter at £2.95 million: it's currently nine flats but there is permission to revert to a house. Expect to pay £320,000-plus for a 1-bed, £400,000 up for a 2-bed, though some very smart rooftop and garden-level duplex conversions are priced at over a million, and a 2,500 sq ft penthouse was £2.5 million last autumn.

Courtfield

Between **Cromwell Rd** in the N and **Old Brompton Rd** in the S is a varied district which looks to Gloucester Rd tube, rather than South Kensington's, as its transport hub. **Queen's Gate**, running N–S, is a wide tree-lined boulevard – wide enough for central parking – flanked by tall brick-and-stucco apartment buildings and hotels (see also Kensington). To the W lies **Stanhope Gardens** with its three companion mews to the W, E and S, where a number of small-scale development schemes and quality conversions have taken place. Stanhope Gardens itself is one of a series of garden squares in the neighbourhood. Four-storey brick-and-stucco terraces of 5-bed houses (c. £2 million) line the private gardens, the E arm forming the most attractive stretch. Developers LCR transformed the W side of Stanhope Gardens into flats behind the original creamy Victorian facade. These are in two blocks known as Stanhope Court and Charlesworth House, which between them have 83 1- to 3-bed flats (a 2-bed £595,000 last winter). The mews behind, **Stanhope Mews East**, is a cache of 2/3-storey brick cottages: some painted, some with roof terraces and most with their own garages: a 3-bed house was £895,000 last autumn (1,046 sq ft, freehold).

Popular **Clareville St** to the S branches off busy Gloucester Rd: painted houses and cottages stand alongside a handful of offices, the Chanticleer Theatre and the Webber Douglas Academy of Dramatic Art. The street becomes a lane as it wends its way towards Old Brompton Rd. Two hi-tech modernist £3 million houses date from 2000.

Parallel is tree-lined **Clareville Grove**, a peaceful oasis within walking distance of both Gloucester Rd and South Ken tube stations. This is easily the most highly regarded street in the neighbourhood with its variety of attractive period houses, front gardens and hedges. The street becomes more mixed to the S with Clareville Court, a modern brick flats block near the junction with Old Brompton Rd. Across Gloucester Rd, **Hereford Square** is one of the best-preserved garden squares in Kensington, its three symmetrical terraces of 3/4-storey, £2-million, white-stucco houses built in 1848 remain unaltered, except where some parts were rebuilt following war damage.

Between the square and Bolton Gardens to the W, the streets are dominated by concentrations of red-brick, late-Victorian mansion flats: in **Gledhow Gardens** and **Bina Gardens**, these overlook private gardens. **Wetherby Gardens**, a popular street, has probably the most attractive gardens in the district and homes in a mix of styles ranging from brick-and-stucco paired villas to late 19th-century Dutch-style red-brick. Exceptional examples of this 'South Ken Dutch' look, with its steep gables, riot of terracotta decoration and tall chimneys, are found in **Harrington Gardens** – where lived

Gilbert of the Gilbert and Sullivan opera partnership – and in **Collingham Gardens.** Most houses have since been split into smaller units; they share rear communal gardens, and properties on the E arm of the square also pleasantly overlook private back-gardens behind the homes of Wetherby Gardens. One or two of these big old houses survive as single homes, some still complete with mews house: £10.5 million was asked late last year for an 11-bed affair in Ashburn Place, which runs N–S across the end of **Harrington Gardens.** Smaller-scale homes in **Rosary Gardens** tend to sell by word of mouth, comment agents; the street also has a complex of 54 short-let studio apartments (for sale, if you want to go into the renting business: £6 million).

To the N lies **Courtfield Gardens**, another garden square lined with tall Victorian brick-and-stucco rows of varying quality. This square has been transformed by the conversion of hotels into smart flats. As a result, values have risen, though there's a big variation depending on quality and size: a 1-bed was £295,000 last winter; 2-beds £350–525,000 while a 3-bed was £650,000 – and you can pay far more. The E side is the most popular: the other end is a bit close to the busy **Earl's Court Rd.** There are still hotels in the streets between here and **Cromwell Rd**, with the big towering ones clustering around Gloucester Rd tube station to the E. A 12-storey block of mainly 1- and 2-bed short-let flats looms behind the station. Dotted among the tall terraces and mansion blocks is a series of mews, mostly residential, such as **Laverton Mews** – a tiny cobbled cul-de-sac, with homes rarely for sale – and **Gaspar Mews** with its white-painted cottages.

Earl's Court

When Earl's Court was built, between 1865 and 1885, it was intended to be, and was regarded as, a select suburb. The well-to-do moved into the substantial terraced houses which sprang up around the original Georgian gardeners' village. The surviving market gardeners, and the service workers, lived on alongside in modest little cottages. Ironically, by the latter third of the 20th century the situation had reversed: the poor set up home in the run-down big houses, divided into seedy flats and bedsits; the prosperous paid high prices to live in the remaining cottages.

With the new century there is a reversion to plan here: hotels, bedsits and hostels are retreating fast in the face of smart flat conversions. Backpackers arriving at Earl's Court station find the choice of cheapish hotels and hostels much diminished as grants from the council allowed these to upgrade. There is, however, still a youth hostel in **Bolton Gardens.**

The price gap between Earl's Court and the rest of the South Ken area continues to narrow. Since the mid-1990s cheaper prices in Earl's Court – at least compared with the rest of the Royal Borough – have attracted aspirational young professionals who are making their presence felt as much as the gay community and the surviving antipodeans of 'Kangaroo Valley'. Gay pubs with their windows blocked out sit near decorators' shops and coffee bars, and a sparkling new Langans Coq d'Or stands where **Old Brompton** and **Lillie Rds** meet. More new restaurants and wine bars appear: locals say they are 'getting rid of the sleaze'. But whatever happens to the social mix, the elegant Edwardian interiors of Coleherne Court, where Princess Diana lived before her marriage, ensure that it remains one of the prestigious addresses of London. Budget for £800,000-plus for a smart 3-bed flat here (share of freehold).

S

The quaint colour-washed cottages live on, tucked away in a now-exclusive triangle behind busy **Cromwell Rd** and **Earl's Court Rd** known as 'Earl's Court Village' (calling it Kenway Village upsets the locals). Although only a few minutes' walk from the hubbub of Earl's Court Rd, this pocket of freehold family homes retains its villagey character, in sharp contrast to the rest of the area. Properties here are among the most sought-after in Earl's Court. The enclave formed the heart of the original hamlet, the earliest homes in **Kenway Rd** dating back to the 1820s. Tree-lined **Wallgrave Rd** is the quietest and most popular street, pleasant and leafy with 2-storey-plus-basement brick cottages fronted by black wrought-iron railings: last winter £895,000 was being asked for a 3-bed house. There's a small communal garden, owned by the residents. **Child's Place** and **Child's St** are cul-de-sacs running parallel to each other, but noisier because they lie directly off Earl's Court Rd. The former has mainly 3-storey brick houses and the latter 2-storey cottages with small, flowery front gardens (one, with a good-sized garden, was £575,000 last winter). A black wrought-iron gate in Child's St leads into **Child's Walk**, a charming private passageway of 2-storey cottages lying no more than 10ft apart. Tubs of flowers, window boxes and benches line the short alleyway, giving the impression of a single patio garden. **Kenway Rd** itself is a mix of 2- and 3-storey houses (ranging from c. £600,000 up towards £2 million: some have been elaborately rebuilt and are ultra-smart), rubbing shoulders with shops and restaurants. At the top of the road, a traffic-free corner holds the entrance to 171 **Cromwell Rd**, a handsome, 1980s block of 12 flats with garaging.

North of the village, at the busy junction of Cromwell Rd with **Earl's Court Rd**, are two 1980s apartment blocks. The flats have not worn well – due mainly to a succession of short lets. Across Cromwell Rd, the Edwardian Moscow Mansions, now refurbished and much sought-after, has house-sized penthouses. South of the village, **Hogarth Rd** marks the N boundary of the area's fast-eroding hotel land. With **Earl's Court Gardens** (family-sized houses with 70ft gardens – the side that overlooks the tube is cheapest), it forms a buffer of Victorian terraced buildings between Earl's Court Village and the red-brick, gabled mansion blocks which dominate the rest of the area off Earl's Court Rd.

Barkston Gardens, a group of smart red-brick mansion blocks, overlooks a large, private tree-lined garden enclosed by hedges and iron railings. A top-scale redevelopment into flats last year achieved £900 per sq ft – thought to be an Earl's Court record. The popular **Bramham Gardens** blocks are also built around a leafy garden square. **Earl's Court Gardens,** despite the name, has no garden.

Earl's Court Rd itself is dirty, noisy and battered by heavy traffic. It forms the southbound leg of the Earl's Court one-way system, nicknamed 'Juggernaut Alley'. Several attempts to devise relief road schemes – the latest in 1989 – have all come to nothing, but a Red Route is now in place and takes in Warwick Rd and Earl's Court Rd. Despite the traffic people pay about £330,000 for a 2-bed flat here. **Warwick Rd** is lined with late-Victorian mansion blocks and undistinguished terraces.

West of Earl's Court Rd, the streets of terraces lying between **Warwick Rd** to the W and **Penywern Rd** S, make up the last remains of hotel-land. **Nevern Square** with its red- and brown-brick buildings fronting its gardens is primarily residential, with only a single, new interior-designed hotel. Nevern Square holds a wide choice of flats, with more added since Barratt converted an old nurses' home into Nevern Mansions: 27 1-, 2- and 3-bed flats. These mostly front Warwick Rd, not the square. One block S, at the junction of **Trebovir Rd** and **Warwick Rd**, sits Kensington Mansions, a 5-storey 1880s block (2-bed flats c. £380,000). **Trebovir** and **Penywern Rd**s, which bracket Earl's Court tube station, are new hot-spots, with old hotels being split into flats at a brisk pace.

Lying to the W is a series of crescents – **Philbeach Gardens, Eardley Crescent** and **Kempsford Gardens**. The condition of properties here varies. Many developments have taken place recently, such as the conversion of an **Eardley Crescent** house into 10 flats. Tree-lined **Philbeach Gardens** enjoys the advantage of 2.5 acres of exceptional landscaped grounds, forming a huge rear communal garden for the homes that sweep around the E curve of the crescent. Properties at the mid-point of the W curve back onto the railway line. Styles vary considerably from the heavy brown- and red-brick buildings at the N entrance of the crescent to the earlier and more desirable brick-and-stucco houses, with columned porches, at its mid-point.

All three streets suffer from traffic from the Earl's Court Exhibition Centre immediately behind, and the council has imposed a special residents' parking scheme which runs until mid-evening during exhibitions.

West Brompton

Brompton is one of those London villages which has effectively ceased to exist. Few people, nowadays, would describe themselves as living in Brompton, and this part of SW10, bounded by **Old Brompton Rd** to the N, **Fulham Rd** to the S, and running W from **Drayton Gardens**, is known either as Chelsea or Kensington, depending on your predilection. Or, indeed, as straightforward 'Fulham Road' – though straight may be the wrong word for the clutch of lively bars, restaurants and clubs (known to some as 'The Beach') between **Hollywood Rd** and **Drayton Gardens.**

West Brompton gained improved transport links in 1999 when a station opened on the West London Line, which links Clapham Junction with Olympia, Willesden Junction and points north. This is next to the District Line tube station. There are plans to improve services on the West London Line by linking it up with others as part of an orbital metro – but see the Transport chapter, and don't hold your breath.

The residential, as opposed to recreational, focal point of the neighbourhood is **The Boltons,** the centrepiece of the Gunter Estate – at its high point one of London's biggest landowners, but reduced to a remnant of around 40 properties by leasehold enfranchisement. The last members of the Gunter family sold out in late 2001, after several generations of ownership – and some enlightened restoration and conservation work over the past 40 years.

The Boltons – the street as opposed to the district – consists of a mere 30 handsome, vast, white-stucco, Italianate villas set around an eye-shaped oval garden – unique in London. In the middle of the central gardens (key access only; apply The Boltons Association) is St Mary's Church, with its angel-bedecked spire rising high above the treetops. The enormous paired mansions, with their columned porches and rich ornamentation, were built in the 1850s–60s to attract the wealthy to the area. They still do: a very select clutch of international royalty and business magnates. They were originally sold for £1,350 each; today it rather depends on the level of luxury, but £10 million is a reasonable figure. Some have staff accommodation in the grounds, or are still linked to their original mews houses behind. One pair of houses has been joined together by a vast basement, which includes staff quarters, a pool and a garage. A few were split into flats in the dowdy days of the 1930s–50s, but several have become single homes again.

The Boltons also gives its name to a network of salubrious streets of big stucco-fronted houses with the same 'villas-in-gardens' character. Leafy **Gilston Rd,** too, has some fine examples with high-walled front gardens: in its different way – a younger, more show-biz crowd – as exclusive as the Boltons. A music star put his on the market early in 2003 for £7.25 million (it was £1 million in 1988, but has been done up three times since). **Milbourne Grove** and **Harley Gardens** are desirable small streets with a mix of paired stucco villas and brick-and-stucco 3- or 4-storey terraces (a mere £3 million or so). Houses on the E side of **Harley Gardens** overlook the walled back gardens of those in **Gilston Rd,** as do the pastel-painted terraces in **Priory Walk.** Vast paired villas predominate in **Tregunter Rd** (£4 million-plus). **The Little Boltons,** forming the W boundary of the neighbourhood, has more brick-and-stucco semi-detached houses, but on a (slightly) less grand scale (they still sell for c. £3.5 million). **Bolton Gardens,** where some houses have been split into flats, but where the intact ones (later, even bigger) can be even pricier, is just across Brompton Rd to the N.

Caught up in this sea of stucco is cobbled **Cresswell Place,** a charming backwater of 2/3-storey £750,000 brick cottages, while S lies **Cavaye Place,** a cul-de-sac of colourful cottages. At the N end of **The Boltons**, a defunct telephone exchange on the corner is now Bladon Lodge; a dozen flats, porter, lift and parking.

Redcliffe Rd, off Fulham Rd, is lined with cherry trees and is ablaze with blossom in the spring: a 4-bed house here was £1.95 million last winter. **Seymour Walk**, one street to the W, is one of the earliest in the area. The oldest terrace in this exclusive, characterful cul-de-sac of 2/3-storey houses dates back to 1797. A kink in the road at the S end of the street hides it from Fulham Rd and a tree-lined terrace seals off its N end, creating a sense of peaceful seclusion.

Hollywood Rd to the W introduces a commercial note into this predominantly residential area: smart restaurants, galleries, antique shops and bars creep around the corner from Fulham Rd into the S end of the street. A new gated mews of 18 town-houses and eight flats appeared at the start of the 1990s on the W side. Further N, across the street, is **Hollywood Mews**, entered through an arch. Modern 2-storey white painted cottages sit around a tiny courtyard with trees in the middle. **Hollywood Rd**, with its mix of brick-and-stucco £1 million-plus houses and red-brick flats, merges with **Harcourt Terrace**, a pleasant, leafy street, its rows of houses divided into flats.

A surprise lies in store in **Redcliffe Mews**, lying at right angles to **Harcourt Terrace**. The mews was rebuilt in 1987 in traditional style: attractive 2-storey brick cottages with gaily coloured garages and entrances. Despite its proximity to noisy **Redcliffe Gardens**, the mews is surprisingly quiet thanks to a barrier of big houses separating the two. A short walk away lies **Redcliffe Square**, divided in half by Redcliffe Gardens, the southbound stretch of the one-way traffic system running between Earl's Court and Chelsea. The square is lined by tall ornate brick-and-stucco terraces, nearly all flats, with French Renaissance-style dormers and polished marble columns flanking the porches. Homes on the W side of the square overlook the tree-lined gardens occupied by St Luke's Church and those on the E side face the only public gardens in West Brompton. An oddity is the 3-bed house set back from the street (£875,000).

Cathcart Rd, Fawcett St, Redcliffe Place, Redcliffe St, Westgate Terrace and **Ifield Rd** form another network of streets dominated by 3/4-storey brick-and-stucco terraced houses split into flats (typical prices for 2-beds, £400–480,000). Cutting a swathe through the area is **Finborough Rd**, the northbound leg of the one-way system. A short distance from the noise and fumes of the main road lies the tranquil haven of Brompton Cemetery, which doubles as a local park. The cemetery provides a leafy backdrop for the enclave of pretty artisan 2-storey, £500,000-plus cottages in The Billings, just off the Fulham Rd: **Billing Place, Billing St** and **Billing Rd** form a series of three private cul-de-sacs on the shores of Fulham: they go back to the days (in the mid-19th century) when the Kensington canal, not the road and railway, was the N–S artery here.

Transport	Tubes: South Kensington, Gloucester Rd (zone 1, District, Circle, Piccadilly); Earl's Court (zone 1, District, Piccadilly); West Brompton (zone 2, District). Trains: West Brompton links to Clapham Junction/Willesden. From South Ken: Oxford Circus 12 min (1 change), City 21 min (1 change), Heathrow 41 min.
Convenient for	West End. Heathrow by tube or M4. Miles from centre: 2.
Schools	Local Authority: St Thomas More's RC, Holland Park School. Private: Collingham, Duff Miller, Hellenic, Lycée Français Charles de Gaulle, Mander Portman Woodward, More House (g) Queen's Gate (g), St James Independent School (g).

SALES

Flats	S	1B	2B	3B	4B	5B
Average prices	180–270+	220–650	285–1M	450–1.5M	750–1.5M	–
Houses	2B	3B	4B	5B	6/7B	8B
Average prices	445–1.1M	700–2M	1–2M+	1.5–2.2M+	3M+	4–12M

RENTAL

Flats	S	1B	2B	3B	4B	5B
Average prices	200–400	280–500+	350–1400	575–1600	750–1550	850+
Houses	2B	3B	4B	5B	6/7B	8B
Average prices	400–650	500–1200+	1000–3000	1700–5000+	2000–5000	–

The properties The peaceful, leafy streets and squares hold large brick-and-stucco terraces, target of much conversion into luxury flats. Flats, converted or p/b (mansion and 20th century), reign, but there are enclaves of mewsy cottages, artists' studios and large villas.

The market South Kensington is elegant, expensive, international, with a wide choice of homes to rent and buy, rising to luxury level. Its stucco streets gleam with fresh paint after 25 years of hectic refurbishment. The huge villas of The Boltons account for the top 'houses' figure above. This is one of London's money-no-object enclaves. Earl's Court is fast catching up to its more established neighbours. New leasehold laws have shaken up the market: take qualified advice on enfranchising and extending.

Among estate agents active in this area are:

- Ruck & Ruck
- Tylden-Lofts & Calvert
- Farrar & Co
- Farley & Co
- Winkworth
- Lane Fox
- Cluttons
- Marsh & Parsons
- Hobart Slater
- W A Ellis
- Jackson-Stops & Staff
- Russell Simpson
- Beaney Pearce
- Hamptons
- Humberts
- Druce
- John D Wood
- Foxtons
- Blenheim Bishop
- Douglas & Gordon
- Savills
- Friend & Falcke
- Faron Sutaria
- Chesterton
- Anscombe & Ringland
- Scotts
- Strutt & Parker

SOUTHFIELDS AND EARLSFIELD

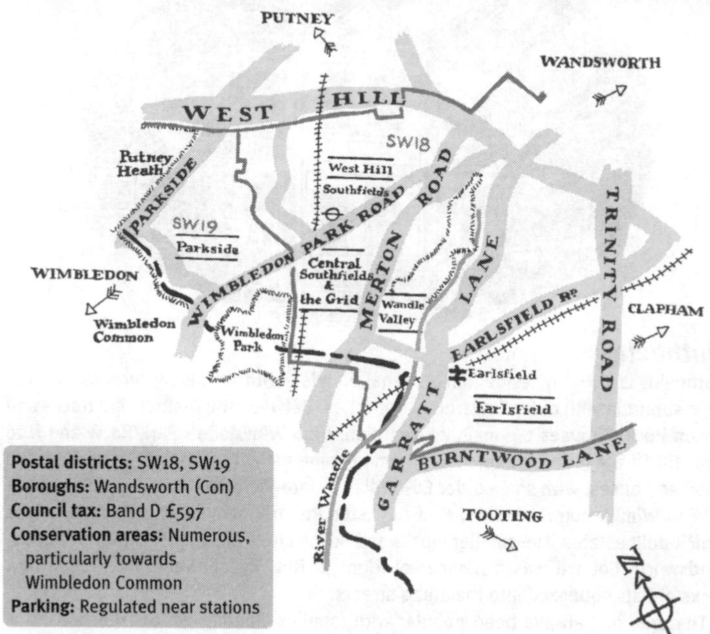

Postal districts: SW18, SW19
Boroughs: Wandsworth (Con)
Council tax: Band D £597
Conservation areas: Numerous, particularly towards Wimbledon Common
Parking: Regulated near stations

Squashed between solidly bourgeois Southfields and Wandsworth Common and sharing a postcode with Wandsworth, Earlsfield had it coming. Smart young persons crowd onto the trains on their way in to the City, Canary Wharf and the West End. A decade ago, the only passengers were a few schoolkids and railwaymen on their way to Clapham Junction. At that point, there seemed more separating these two enclaves, set on opposite banks of the Wandle valley, than the little river that runs between them.

What kept Earlsfield from modishness was the lack of a tube, a concentration of council-built housing, and a hard-to-eradicate air of South London scruffiness along the main roads. Its borderlands with Wandsworth Common have seen some surprising prices for big family homes since the early 1990s, but the rest of it only started to take off in the second half of the decade. In 2002–3, the price gap with Southfields narrowed; 2004 saw it disappear. Given the cost of even the humblest home in nearby Wimbledon – the area's hub for shops, leisure, entertainment and transport – it had to come.

Southfields, to the W, still thinks of its neighbour as *arriviste*. Here the change began back in the 1980s, and the neat Edwardian streets of the 'Grid' with their tube-station security blanket are well established. Southfields is only one stop further out on the District Line than East Putney (and with more chance of a seat in the mornings); here incomers find plenty of 3/4-bed terraced houses, and flats, in quiet streets; also semis (some quite large) in leafy ones. Apart from the Grid, a rash of ex-council homes – some with fabulous views from lovely, green hillsides – and some warehouse, school (and even laundry) conversions have boosted the range of homes to buy or rent.

South from Wandsworth, the Wandle valley is best known as a barrier to E–W traffic. The valley has parks and playing fields, depots and factories – but only two bridges linking Earlsfield, to the E, with Southfields to the W. With the busy A3 and the notorious Wandsworth one-way bottleneck to the N, the two stations are the key to this area.

S

Southfields

Southfields is a wholly residential area that blends – with surprising success – classic 1930s suburbia with older Edwardian properties. Between the District Line tracks and **Merton Rd** the houses are mainly Edwardian; from **Wimbledon Park Rd** W and N to **West Hill** (the A3) and Wimbledon Common come typical 1930s semi-detached and detached houses, with some older Edwardian or late-Victorian ones. From **Beaumont Rd** W to **Wimbledon Park Side**, N of **Augustus Rd**, are many large 1960s/early '70s council-built estates. The smaller blocks and houses here are largely owner-occupied: Wandsworth Council was a pioneer of Right to Buy. Recent years have seen new blocks of flats squeezed into the area's streets.

The area has always been popular with families wanting good-sized houses in generally quiet roads. They are joined (particularly in 'the Grid') by young couples, especially second-time buyers thinking of kids . . . once here, families tend to stay put, trading up within the area. But the most notable influx in recent years has been of young, professional South Africans. They discovered an area where they first rented, then bought: gardens – for barbecues – are a big draw. Many stay for four years, then go back, but increasing numbers are applying for citizenship and opting to stay.

Replingham Rd, near the tube station, is a pleasant street that provides the main shops of any note in Southfields, and a couple of new-style pubs and cafés; otherwise there's the major shopping centre of Wimbledon, and Putney or Wandsworth's. You'll find the occasional corner shop, but there are virtually no pubs in the Grid area because of covenant restrictions laid down when the land was sold for building. The area suffers somewhat from hordes of tennis fans during Wimbledon fortnight, but enterprising locals can let their homes out for considerable sums.

Central Southfields and The Grid

S

The Southfields Grid, bordered by **Astonville St**, **Elsenham Rd**, **Revelstoke Rd** and **Replingham Rd**, takes its nickname from the orderly layout of the streets (these run N–S) and roads (E–W). The Grid was begun with the opening of Southfields station in 1889, but was not completed until 1905. Homes are mainly spacious 3- and 4-bed terraced houses, although a few have been split into flats. Typical prices are now around £190–220,000 for a 1-bed flat, £230–270,000 for a 2-bed, while 3-bed houses command £350–450,000 and 4-beds £420–500,000. A number of the houses in **Trentham St**, **Replingham Rd** and **Revelstoke Rd** are actually purpose-built maisonettes; the supply of newly converted flats on the Grid dried up some years back after Wandsworth Council banned any more such splitting. However, the old snooker hall opposite the tube did become smart flats: balconies, high ceilings, high prices (c. £300,000 for a 1-bed). There are some small council infill blocks in **Elsenham St**, and even-numbered houses back onto the District Line to Wimbledon – but have long gardens as compensation. Between **Merton Rd** and **Astonville St** there are some recent 2/3-bed houses in **Handford Close**. By the station, **Crowthorne Close** is one of the few modern non-council developments in the area, with 2- and 3-storey blocks of flats, some backing onto the tracks.

The triangle bordered by **Granville Rd**, **Pulborough Rd** and **Merton Rd** features generally Edwardian houses in tree-lined roads slightly narrower than in the Grid. Odd-numbered houses in **Pulborough Rd** back onto the tube line, but benefit from exceptionally long gardens and the large railway landholding as a buffer. Prices have levelled at around £420,000 for a 3-bed terrace, £460,000 for a specially large one. The streets between **Pirbright Rd** and **Smeaton Rd** are mainly late Victorian/Edwardian terraces, while **Longfield St** and **Smeaton Rd** itself are smaller, 2-bed, Victorian versions. However, in 1999 **Standen Rd** saw a fashionable warehouse-style conversion yielding 1- and 2- flats and 2/3-bed penthouses. Those braving the name to live here may be amused to know that 'Tiffany Heights' is an old pea-canning factory. The largest split-level units get price tags of half a million or so.

West of the tube line, the land rises quite steeply up towards Wimbledon Common and Putney Heath. **Gartmoor Gardens** has attractive large £530–600,000 Edwardian houses with ornate metalwork balconies on the first floor, a number now converted to flats. Proximity to Southfields station compensates for some noise from trains: some recent 3/4-bed town-houses in a gated scheme by Berkeley sold for £410–420,000, despite backing onto the tracks. Houses on the S side of **Southdean Gardens** back onto Wimbledon Park: very popular but, unsurprisingly, rarely on the market. Prices are c. £500–600,000 for good 4-bed/2-bath houses, though ones backing onto the park fetch quite a bit more, as do the 5-bed houses: around £600–650,000 for these.

For new homes, look to **Sutherland Grove**, running alongside the tracks from the station to West Hill. Here an ex-college and an old boys' school have yielded an enormous tract of homes, both newbuild and converted from the original buildings, with at their foot St Cecilia's, Wandsworth's brand-new Church of England secondary school, opened in 2003 with high hopes. Next to it is Berkeley's 'Arcadian Place': 50 houses and flats in four phases. Phase One was four Arts-&-Craftsy semis, with garages; Phase Two was a new street ('The Avenue') of 12 large neo-Edwardian semis (four remain, c. £850,000); in Phase Three flats, some with own gardens, in the old Boys' School (a 1-bed, £350,000) complete this spring (2005); Phase Four, four mews houses, are building now, from £395,000. A complete contrast, 'Viridian' is ultra-contemporary: paired villas by Crest Nicholson (3-bed/3-bath, £700,000); these are part of Whitelands Park: 13 leafy acres of new houses and flats, plus the refurbishment of the listed Gilbert Scott Whitelands College building by Westcity. The remaining original homes in Sutherland Grove are '30s semis (mainly 3-bed) with off-street parking: c. £375–400,000 for one with decent garden. Also a few vast (6-bed-plus) Edwardian houses – not all of which have been split into (very popular) flats.

The tube line (District) is above-ground here and runs E of Sutherland Grove, crossing **Granville Rd** and then going into a tunnel by the junction with **Melrose Rd** and **Cromer Villas**. **Gressenhall Rd** has Edwardian-style houses and a mosque. The roads leading off Sutherland Grove, notably **Skeena Hill**, **Cromer Villas** and **Girdwood Rd**, are larger 1930s: mainly Tudor-style, with integral garages: internally, these vary enormously. Most – notably in **Coombemartin Rd** – are set well back (a 5-bed here might be £700,000); a 5-bed in **Skeena Hill**, £650,000 last winter. There are also small modern blocks of council-built flats, and the W side of Coombemartin Rd backs onto a (low-rise) estate.

Parkside

The area bordered by **Beaumont Rd** in the E, Wimbledon Common to the W, **Queensmere**

Rd (the border with Wimbledon) to the S and **West Hill** is a complex mixture of council-built estates (high- and low-rise flats, some houses) and private detached houses – some very large, which fetch equally large prices. The area is green and hilly, with some splendid views eastwards towards central London, and there are plenty of trees. Don't let the council-built housing deter you from a good look around this interesting corner.

The heaviest concentrations of council estates are between **Wimbledon Park Rd** and **Albert Drive**, **Augustus Rd** and **Whitlock Drive** – the area between **Beaumont Rd** and **Princes Way** from **Augustus Rd** to **West Hill** is almost exclusively so. But all the estates are well landscaped, a lot of the flats are now owner-occupied, and there are a few small housing-association schemes. Resales of council-built properties offer the cheaper homes: 1-bed flats up to c. £160,000, 3-bed houses with garage £250–270,000.

Beaumont Rd, running between West Hill and Wimbledon Park Rd, has modern council-built homes on either side and a small parade of shops by **Keevil Drive. Albert Drive** runs between Augustus Rd and Victoria Drive: again there is a mix of council and private blocks and good-sized private houses (mainly detached). Between Albert Drive and Wimbledon Park Rd are mid- and late 1960s council-built blocks. On the other side of the street are some red-brick, detached, modern infill houses, set well back from the road, then stockbroker-Tudor, again red brick, detached, but larger. Midway down Albert Drive, former '50s police flats were revamped in the late '80s as 'Southfields Village': 2-bed flats (Augustus Court off **Augustus Rd** is a similar scheme by the same developer).

Augustus Rd has everything from ancient to modern, from council-build to Georgian mansion. It runs leafily W up the hill from Southfields station to Inner Park Rd, mixing 1930s and large, older detached houses (a 5-bed can fetch a million here); late Georgiana with 6 beds (*very* occasionally for sale). A number of flat developments are grouped close to Inner Park Rd, including The Acorns (red-brick modern) and Doradus Court. Then there are modern houses and flats, brick-built: mainly 1960s and early 1970s. Increasingly, from the junction with Albert Drive, large detached houses appear, usually stockbroker-Tudor but also older mansions – including the late-Georgian-style 'White House'. Some 1950s infill, too, but all set well back with large front gardens and off-street parking. Just off is John Paul II Catholic School; its buildings are followed by more mainly council-built property on either side of the road. And **Augustus Rd** has three caches of new homes this year. One council block has vanished, and 2-bed flats are a-building on the site: c. £300–325,000. Next, an Edwardian office-block up at the Inner Park Rd end is transforming into 1- and 2-bed flats, £325–410,000, ready this year. Lastly, 'Chalfont Mews' adds four large new houses to the road, with 1- and 2-bed flats behind.

Princes Way tumbles roughly N–S from up by the Tibbet's Corner roundabout right down to Wimbledon Park Rd. At the N end is the **Fleur Gate** development of attractive, Victorian-style terraced town-houses (a 4-bed here, c. £425,000), and some new flats (c. £350,000 for a 2-bed). Opposite the junction with Castlecombe Drive (council housing) is a small row of detached Tudor-style 1930s houses. Further on is Linden Lodge School for the Blind, set leafily in large grounds, then private flats and **King Charles Walk**, an attractive town-house development. **Weydown Close** is modern low-rise council-built.

Tree-lined **Victoria Drive** parallels Princes Way, similar in its hilly mix of council-built and private; a 1-bed flat with patio in a pretty, low-built coach house here, £210,000. Pines Court, a modern block, has studio flats; **Oak Park Gardens** is a small and attractive development of town-houses, after which it's back to larger 1930s-Tudor homes.

S

Inner Park Rd runs in a half-circle from Wimbledon Park Side to meet Augustus Rd and then back to the common, featuring a similar mix of modern and older-style blocks of flats, council and private. **Pilsdon Close**, with small town-houses and flats, is set back; then comes **Holly Tree Close**, with private flats. Some remaining enormous Victorian mansions have mainly been split into flats.

Opposite **Inner Park Rd**'s junction with Augustus Rd is the Argyll Estate, a mix of high- and low-rise flats. Three tall council blocks here were demolished in the 1980s to be replaced with flats and houses. **Limpsfield Avenue**, with 1930s-style houses, detached and semi-detached, some mock-Tudor, backs onto council-built. **Kingsmere Rd** has detached mainly 1930s houses. A spur off **Inner Park Rd** (easy to miss), close to Wimbledon Park Side, marks the entrance to **Roundacres**, a small, pleasant, curved terrace of early 1960s houses and flats set in communal gardens. The entrance is masked by big traditional-style red-brick 1950s houses.

Queensmere Rd, marking the borough border, is very much Wimbledon rather than Southfields in feel and price: fairly steep and tree-lined, its homes mainly big, detached, modern, set well back from the road; **Queensmere Close**, though, is a clutch of bungalows. The vast former college site on the corner with **Wimbledon Park Side** has been developed with an extensive (and expensive) tract of new houses and flats (see Wimbledon chapter.)

Wimbledon Park Rd, by the common, suffers traffic at rush hour, though calming measures have helped. North past Bathgate Rd's junction come blocks of flats: modern council-built and older-style private. Lakeview Court flats are reputedly comfortable and well run, looking over Wimbledon Park and its lake. Thereafter large detached pre- and post-war family homes are set well back off the road towards Southfields station, where Edwardian semi-detached and then terraced houses take over.

West Hill

The little triangle between the West Hill junction with **Sutherland Grove, West Hill Rd** and **Granville Rd** likes to consider itself Putney, not Southfields, and has good access to East Putney tube. It is a mix of large Edwardian semi-detached houses and 1930s semis with some modern infill, plus some early and mid-Victorian detached houses (some reaching seven-figure prices) on **West Hill Rd**. Among the most popular roads is the 1930s **Sispara Gardens** (large semi-detached houses with integral garages) while **Cromer Villas** again mixes 1930s and Edwardian semis (a 4-bed can reach a million). **Coldstream Gardens** has 1960s-style town-houses and flats; **Valonia Gardens** is neat 1930s semis, with some 1950s infill built 1930s-style. **Melrose Rd,** as it meets West Hill Rd, has big terraced and semi-detached Edwardian homes. **West Hill** itself is stationary much of the time, though: it leads inexorably to the dreaded Wandsworth one-way system.

Merton Rd to the E is a very busy through-road carrying traffic between Wimbledon and Wandsworth, and is also a commuter cut-through from the A24 to the Wandsworth one-way system. Large detacheds and semis (some creamily stuccoed) appear between **West Hill Rd** and **Wimbledon Park Rd.** Thereafter, going S, the houses are 3/4-bed late Victorian semis, set well back from the road. New in 2003 was Lion Gate Mews: 4-bed town-houses, c. £425,000. A primary school stands at the junction with **Standen Rd.** Then come late Edwardian mansion flats, originally council, now owner-occupied. At the junction of **Burr Rd** and **Kimber Rd** is Coleman Court, a 1930s block with views over King George's Park, but heavy traffic restricts prices (1-beds from c. £130,000).

Wandle Valley

Between **Merton Rd** and **Garratt Lane** lie a handful of early Edwardian terraces, S of King George's Park, which are the no-man's-land between Earlsfield and Southfields. Agents are unable to agree as to which these roads belong. **Penwith Rd,** being one of the few to cross the Wandle, suffers heavy traffic; thus prices for its purpose-built late Victorian 2-bed maisonettes are a bit lower than the rest of the area at £220–245,000. **Acuba Rd** (Edwardian) and **Bodmin St** are quieter, as is **Strathville Rd** (3-bed house c. £425,000) despite a small industrial development. **Dounsforth Gardens**, a corner of modern town-houses off **Strathville Rd,** backs onto the Wandle. Acuba House, an Edwardian block, was council; now it's mainly owner-occupied. It borders King George's Park, which has gained a health club. The playing fields N of **Bodmin St** have in part been replaced with homes.

Earlsfield

Earlsfield climbs E up the hill from the banks of the River Wandle towards Wandsworth Common, running northwards from **Burntwood Lane** to **Allfarthing Lane**, with **Garratt Lane** as its spine. Earlsfield, like Battersea, is apt to expand as it becomes fashionable, to take in areas that have been Tooting or Wandsworth since they were built. Popularity first rose in the heady days of the late '80s, but the area (unlike Southfields) didn't quite make it into respectability before the 1990 crash. Now once again many a buyer outpriced in Battersea, Clapham and Wandsworth Common is heading down **Earlsfield Rd**. They seek streets close to the station and parks, and prefer private to council-built homes – though the gap has narrowed. The best homes have even overtaken Southfield's.

First evidence was a rash of estate agents' and the turning of old boozers into new bars, ex-petrol stations into blocks of flats. Now come St James, with a new **Garratt Lane/ Furmage St** development of 25 1-bed flats, around £200–220,000, near the Wandle.

Between **Magdalen Rd** and **Burntwood Lane** is the large, very pleasant, council-built (but now nearly all private) Magdalen Park 'cottage' estate, running from **Swaby Rd** in the W to **Tilehurst Rd** in the E (streets beyond are Wandsworth Common: see chapter). The homes are a mix of simple 1920s and 1930s terraced and semi-detacheds, plus maisonettes on the E side of the neighbourhood. Most have large gardens (50–80ft is not unusual). Streets and pavements are wide and there are plenty of trees: the atmosphere is of deepest Surrey, not inner London. A double front door reveals houses that were built as two separate flats. The far-sighted bought 3-bed estate houses (freehold) for the price of a 3-bed Victorian flat – and close to Earlsfield station in **Magdalen Rd**.

Charmingly named, charming (and high-scoring – check catchment area carefully) Beatrix Potter Primary School is sited at the N end of the band of greenery – playing fields and allotments – that traverses the estate. **Openview** and **Fieldview** overlook the playing fields: 3-bed houses, £330–340,000. **Tilehurst Rd**, marking the E end, suffers some rat-running; **Magdalen Rd** and **Burntwood Lane** have serious traffic at peak hours. Most of the mainly 1930s semis in Burntwood Lane enjoy open views over the school, golf course and grounds of Springfield University Hospital. **Swaby Rd**, running N towards the station, has late Victorian small terraced houses and some purpose-built Edwardian maisonettes (a 3-bed, £315,000) in a quiet, pleasant street that marks the end of the estate.

Running between **Tranmere Rd** (late Victorian terraces, some maisonettes) and **Garratt Lane** are the well-regarded trio **Quinton St**, **Isis St** and **Littleton St**: these have spacious (for Earlsfield) 3-bed Edwardian terraces, increasingly popular – especially **Littleton St**; third beds elsewhere in Earlsfield tend to be very small. These can fetch £430–440,000. More maisonettes, too, also roomy: 2-bed with garden, **Isis St**, £310,000.

More new homes are appearing hereabouts: the large Victorian ex-primary school that stands at the junction of **Tranmere Rd** and **Waynflete St** has been 'lofted'; **Victoria Mews** (half-million pound 4-bed houses) appeared off **Magdalen Rd**. A big cache of new Affordable Housing, too. **Garratt Lane** itself has some flats, cheaper than their neighbours due to the busy road: £150,000-plus for a 1-bed, but £235,000-plus for recent 2-bed/2-bath flats. **Burmester Rd** has the conversion of the Anglo-American Laundry into smart galleried flats (2-beds c. £320.000), plus Harper Mews: 2-bed town houses c. £270,000. **Weybourne St**, W of Garratt Lane, has a nicely detailed gated scheme of Victorian-lookalike houses built in 2000 by Crest Homes. Copper Court is redeveloped ex-council at the corner of **Garratt Lane** and **Burntwood Lane**: 2-bed flats run at c.£220,000, while 3-bed houses are around £320–340,000.

S

To the N of the railway that slices diagonally through Earlsfield, homes between **Allfarthing Lane**, the N limit of the area, and **Earlsfield Rd** are generally small late Victorian or early Edwardian terraces with some council-built infill blocks. In **Earlsfield Rd**, high numbers (Garratt Lane end) are small Victorian rows set close to the road (no off-street parking). Then comes modern council infill by **Inman St**. From **Dingwall St** houses are set back and grow from two- to three-storeyed: many now flats with off-street parking.

Odd numbers of **Earlsfield Rd** back onto the railway line, but generally have large gardens. Houses near the **Heathfield Rd** junction enjoy a view across the tracks of Wandsworth Prison (you could always pretend it's a castle). Here there are some larger 3-storey, 5-bedroomed late Edwardian semis to be found (at Wandsworth Common prices). **Bassingham Rd, Bucharest Rd** and **Brocklebank Rd,** leading off Earlsfield Rd to Swaffield Rd, have 3-bed early Edwardian/late Victorian terraced houses, with ornate door surrounds and windows. In **Swaffield Rd** a handsome Edwardian school conversion makes for roomy flats (but high service charges): a 1-bed here, £215,000.

Aslett St, Treport St, Delia St and **Daphne St** are all late Victorian terraces – some maisonettes: c. £270,000. Spencer Walk in **Aslett St** is a new clutch of 3- and 4-bed houses. **Barmouth Rd, Swanage Rd** and **Cader Rd** E of **St Ann's Hill** are more Wandsworth Common than Earlsfield; 3- and 4-bed late Victorian/Edwardian rows.

Transport Tubes: Southfields (zone 3, District). To Oxford Circus 30 min (1 change), City 30 min, Heathrow 55 min (1 change). Trains: Earlsfield to Clapham Junction and Waterloo (12 min).

Convenient for Wimbledon Common and tennis. Tube to town via Fulham and Sloane Square, trains to Waterloo. Miles from centre: 5.

Schools Local Authority: ADT College, Southfields Community, Ernest Bevin College (b), Burntwood School (g), John Paul II RC, St Cecilia's C of E. Private: Emanuel.

SALES

Flats	S	1B	2B	3B	4B	5B
Average prices	125–160	145–250	180–300	200–350	210–350	–
Houses	2B	3B	4B	5B	6/7B	8B
Average prices	230–350	250–450	315–500	450–1M	600–1M+	750–1.5M

RENTAL

Flats	S	1B	2B	3B	4B	5B
Average prices	140–225	165–280	210–320	250–350	275–400	–
Houses	2B	3B	4B	5B	6/7B	8B
Average prices	200–350	240–350	275–500	450–600	600+	–

The properties Mainly Edwardian terraced homes, including many p/b and some converted flats, plus some larger houses towards Putney and Wandsworth Common and ex-council homes from 1920s cottages to 1970s tower flats. New flats appearing on infill sites. Cheaper buys in ex-council can still be well under averages above.

The market Southfields, with its tube, is more established, especially for flats: 2-beds popular with young sharers. Earlsfield has caught up fast: hunting-ground for first-time buyers and refugees from pricier areas. Families too, following new Cof E school.

S

Among estate agents active in this area are:

- Bells
- Haart
- Townends
- Douglas & Gordon
- Jacksons
- Jackson-Stops
- Barnard Marcus
- Ellisons
- Kinleigh Folkard & Hayward
- Savills
- homelondon
- McKenzie
- Maalems
- Desouza
- Craigie & Co

SOUTHGATE AND PALMERS GREEN

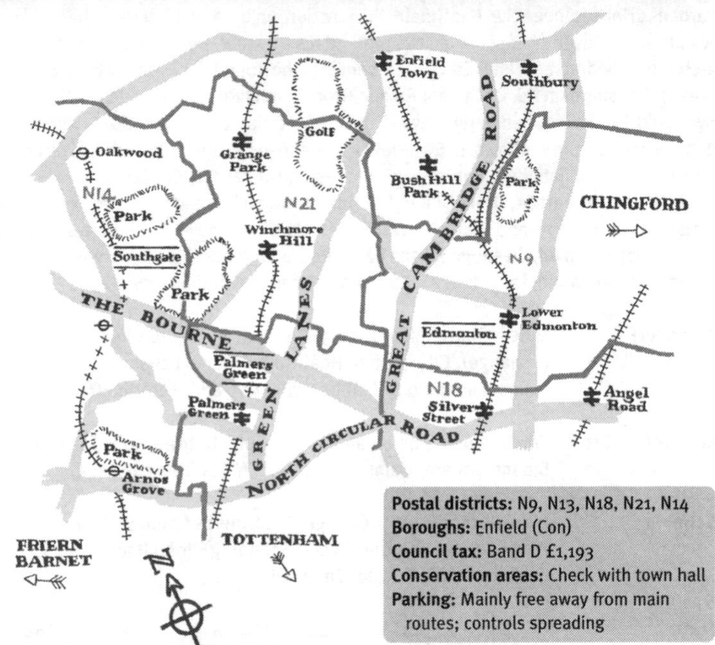

Postal districts: N9, N13, N18, N21, N14
Boroughs: Enfield (Con)
Council tax: Band D £1,193
Conservation areas: Check with town hall
Parking: Mainly free away from main routes; controls spreading

That part of the North Circular Rd which runs between the Lea Valley in the east and Arnos Grove tube in the west separates two remarkably different areas. Below this dividing line the northern parts of Tottenham and Wood Green have petered out into a rather colourless hinterland, but head northwards and, as soon as you cross the North Circular Rd, the atmosphere immediately begins to change.

The large suburban tract beyond the North Circular which consists of Southgate (N14), Palmers Green (N13), Winchmore Hill (N21), and Upper (N18) and Lower (N9) Edmonton lies far enough from the centre of London to lead a life independent of City and West End business, but still suits the commuter – inwards or outwards. While the train journey to the City generally takes 20–30 minutes, the M25, M1, M11 and the A10 (**Great Cambridge Rd**) are also all within reach – if more often than not congested. Live here, and you can work anywhere north of London.

Edmonton and the parts of Palmers Green lying closest to the North Circular are at first similar in style to North Tottenham and Wood Green, with fairly similar shopping serving similar humdrum inter-war homes; however, already the *feel* of the place is different. Down the wind comes the first whiff of the Alpine North – or, at least, the fresh air from the Green Belt, blowing via a thousand alpine-planted rock gardens.

Indeed, this area changes quite dramatically the further north one travels into it, becoming more and more green, leafy, suburban – and prosperous: golf clubs, parks, horse riding, wide tree-lined streets, huge modern detacheds, outbreaks of 1980s-onwards developments. It is populated largely by well-off middle-class families – now being joined by Crouch Enders questing for family homes and schools, Tottenham/Wood Greeners looking for a better quality of life. Here, too, is a large Greek Cypriot community and a smaller Asian one in Palmers Green. The 1980s rush to split large houses into flats aimed at the outwards march of the young professional classes soon subsided: this is still predominantly a family area, though that encircling motorway bracket just over the horizon makes it a good base for a household with one partner tied to a local, or Central London, job and the other who travels out of town. Otherwise, youth is represented by the rentals market for Middlesex University students.

Among the neat, untroubled streets of comfortable inter-war houses, however, new developments have been inserted – carefully. But these, and further flat conversions, are kept in check by Enfield Borough's disinclination to let parking get any more congested. Homes values here took till 1998 to regain the ground lost in the early 1990s crash; prices in Southgate, Winchmore Hill and parts of Bush Hill Park then rose fast. On average, though, they still show good value compared to homes across the North Circular. A 4-bed house, Edwardian, with garden and perhaps garage can still save you a hundred thousand or more on the price of its equivalent in Crouch End or Muswell Hill.

Edmonton is very different in feel, and still a mainly local market. The most humdrum swathe of the area – but regeneration is under way, new homes are appearing – as are first-time buyers and buy-to-let investors priced out of more southerly parts.

Southgate, Winchmore Hill, Bush Hill Park

This well-off, salubrious area, perched up between the Lea Valley and Barnet, holds in the main a wealth of large semis and detached houses set in broad, tree-lined streets. Proximity to Enfield Town and surrounding Green Belt is an added advantage. It's served by Enfield Town and Bush Hill stations (Liverpool St 30 min); Enfield Chase, Grange Park and Winchmore Hill stations for King's Cross and Moorgate; plus Oakwood and Southgate tubes (Piccadilly Line to King's Cross, the West End – and, of course, Heathrow). Schools are a big draw, with a clutch of excellent primaries cited by estate agents.

Southgate is a prosperous, leafy suburb that divides into three areas: Old Southgate, New Southgate and Winchmore Hill with its village atmosphere. Its centre may revolve (literally) around the hub of **Southgate Circus**, but close by are playing fields, tennis courts, cricket club and parks – in particular Grovelands Park, with its large boating lake, in the grounds of which stands a sports centre and Grovelands Priory Hospital.

In these days of car-borne foraging, shopping is not the *raison d'être* of this area, despite the M&S foodstore in Winchmore Hill, near the leisure centre. The sons and daughters of Southgate do not feel that a Thai and an Italian restaurant can really add up to an exotic nightlife. It lacks the trendy shops, bars and cafés of nearby Crouch End or Muswell Hill, unless you count the family-friendly Pizza Express.

The tube station, on the Circus, is Southgate's most surprising landmark. A spirited bit of 1930s design, the circular building looks like a spaceship heading skywards for Mars rather than leading down to the underground; it is in fact a listed building. **Bourneside Crescent** curves round the Circus, a big block of 1- and 2-bed flats whose convenience makes for price tags of c. £160–165,000 for 1-beds, £220,000 for the 2-beds. New schemes are adding more homes within reach of the tube. On the **High St**, which leads S, Fontaine Court is 22 recent 1- and 2-bed flats, with communal gardens and parking, where a smart 2-bed costs around £249,000. Fairview (much in evidence hereabouts) added more 2-beds (£240,000-plus), again with parking, in The Chase, its gated development in **Chase Rd**. Latest is Bellway's gated block of 1- to 3-bed flats with parking: again, off the Circus on **Tudor Way/Winchmore Hill**. The first released, 16 2- and 3-beds, are £285–335,000. In an older, 1990s scheme, a 2-bed with garage, £190,000.

The **High St** and its continuation, **Cannon Hill**, also hold a college and a variety of attractive properties, including little mewsy cottages. Tucked away behind a high wall off **Cannon Hill** in this old part of Southgate is the old Legal & General building. This had enveloped what was an 18th-century mansion, Arnos Grove (thus the tube station's name), and was converted into homes in 1997. Now known as Lulworth Court, it holds exclusive, original-featured 2/3-bed flats: a 2-bed, when and if for sale, £350–450,000 here. Newbuild houses were also added; and sharing the site is the Beaumont Nursing Care Centre: retirement flats with care on hand. This was the most important of a number of stately houses; several more survive as college or hospital buildings.

Southgate has three popular enclaves: the Meadway estate, in the angle between **High St** and **The Bourne** (the most expensive: an unmodernized 4-bed here was £550,000 last winter); the Monkfrith estate (a 3-bed, £400,000); and the Minchenden estate: a semicircle of closes and conifered gardens enclosed by **Morton Way**, **Powys Lane/Cannon Hill** and **Waterfall Rd** (the latter also holds a number of bungalows). Its well-proportioned houses and wide, quiet streets are arguably the best value. Its spine is **Arnos Grove** (the road): the estate is built on the grounds of the 18th-century manor; Arnos Park is what remains. Good primaries (e.g. Osidge, Monkfrith) are a big draw round here, with a 20 per cent premium in the small catchment area of the Hillel Jewish school.

Off **Fox Lane**, Corrib Court is an interesting conversion of an old schoolhouse into 1- and 2-bed flats which reflects the policy of preserving the original environs. Nowadays developments include houses as well as flats: witness the large homes in **Crothall Close**.

It is, however, the village atmosphere of Winchmore Hill, with its neat streets, quaint houses, tidy gardens, attractive pubs, that suggests the prosperity of the area. Follow **Hoppers Rd** up from Southgate to the delightful village green, with older houses (and a clutch of neo-Georgian town-houses) clustered picturesquely; the sweet cottages of **Compton Terrace**, rarely for sale (though a 2-bed on **Hoppers Rd**, £228,000). Coffee shops, deli, florist, boutique run from the green round to the station (agents reckon proximity adds up to £80,000). Wide, leafy **Compton Rd** has commodious Edwardiana dripping period features: a family area (4-beds c. £550–650,000-plus). Contrasting **Broad Walk**, leading back towards Southgate off **The Green**, is the Beverly Hills of the area (count the beauty salons). Rock stars and celebrities lurk in these vast modern houses with drives holding equally vast cars : over a million, and they can reach closer to two.

The Bourne borders pleasant Grovelands Park, as do streets such as **Seaforth Gardens** (and **Queen Elizabeth's Drive** on the Southgate side); some homes have gates directly into it. **Church Hill** leads past from the station to leafy **Eversley Park Rd**; pretty **Eversley Crescent** is nearby. Carrington Court, **Green Dragon Lane** and Broadfield Court, **Wades Hill** are good examples of recent flats developments. **Eversley Park Rd** leads N to popular Highlands Village: on the site of an old hospital, its cul-de-sacs of '90s homes (£250–450,000) sell to families drawn by Grange Park Primary, in the park itself, Eversley Primary and the new secondary, Highlands. Old hospital buildings made interesting flats: one has own belfry. New or converted, c. £135–240,000 for 1-/2-beds.

Across Winchmore Hill to the E, wide-spaced streets of suburbia thread between sports grounds and playing fields. Off **Church St**, which winds down to the A10, Rowan Gate – ten 3- and 4-bed semis – was added to **Rowantree Rd.**

Head N now, up **Village Rd** towards Bush Hill Park. The roads grow wider and more tree-lined, with solid 3- (c. £425,000) and 4-bed semis. Through the centre marches **Wellington Rd**, the streets off which hold surprisingly large family houses with big gardens, and small 'courts' of neo-Georgian homes. **Abbey Rd** is counted among the nicest streets. Just off **Park Avenue**, Croft Mews's modern 2-bed flats and houses border a tennis club. Large, impressively suburban houses round the golf course.

Agents refer to the streets E across the tracks between the Bush Hill Park–Enfield Town rail line, **Southbury Rd** and the **Great Cambridge Rd** as the 'Triangle'. They reckon these streets, which contain the Bush Hill Park recreation ground, more desirable than comparably priced ones in Edmonton, and a good corner for home-hunters.

Palmers Green

To the S lies Palmers Green: away from the shops and cafés of bustling **Green Lanes**, this boasts large homes and good primaries: an influx of families from areas such as Crouch

End here. In its heyday it was a bastion of Edwardian respectability, the 3- and 4-bed houses of which, replete with original features, are set along leafy roads – the best closest to Southgate: a grand, 5-bed corner mansion in **Amberley Rd**, for example. Many of these were converted into 1980s flats – particularly in the 'Lakes' estate, the **Ulleswater Rd, Derwent Rd, Lakeside Rd, Grovelands Rd** and **Old Park Rd** ladder – but that trend has been reversed. Large Victorian houses boast original features and stained-glass windows. This is counted among the best corners: a 4-bed here, £475,000-plus.

Palmers Green is still a good place to look for larger homes: 5-bed period houses now run from about £475–500,000 upwards – but these can be matched and surpassed by the occasional atypical, top-flight new development: looking out over Broomfield Park, with its lakes, sports and leisure, from **Aldermans Hill** is Willowcroft Lodge, six new (2002) 2-bed flats where the penthouse sold for £695,000.

Agents – and developers – look fondly on the area south of the park, too, bounded by **Powis Lane/Broomfield Lane, Green Lanes, Wilmer Way** and **Bowes Rd** (North Circular) to the S. As well as the park this is a hilly corner, which makes for far horizons.

Across Green Lanes and S of Hedge Lane, **Osborne Rd, Windsor Rd, Park Avenue** and **New River Crescent** sport Edwardian and '30s houses – and nearby is well-regarded Hazelwood Primary; new 2-bed/2-bath flats in **Hazelwood Lane**, £250–300,000. Homes then become slightly more humdrum, the roads busier: full of mainly '30s rows – but tipped as 'good value', 'up-and-coming' by agents. Big period houses yield popular flats.

Cheaper homes are found on the New Park estate; a 3-bed terraced in **Briar Close**, £245,000. And look just S of the **North Circular** for new homes (many by Fairview). Chequers Green in **Chequers Way** added 30 houses and 100 flats – now comes Phase 2. **Cherry Blossom Close** has good-value flats (a 2-bed £150,000) by the allotments; in Westminster Gardens, **Westminster Drive**, 3-bed/2-bath/garage houses: c. £340,000.

Edmonton

Edmonton – Lower (N9, somewhat greener) and Upper (N18, more 'inner-city') – lies between the A10 in the W and the Lea Valley reservoirs to the E, straddling the **North Circular**. There's sailing on the reservoir, and sport at Picketts Lock Leisure Centre; an affordable area increasingly attracting first-time buyers and buy-to-let investors.

Traditionally the least 'desirable', in estate agents' terms, of the four areas, things will improve as some unsightly high-rise council blocks are gradually replaced with new, street-scale social housing, and the 1960s concrete 'wartime bunker' shopping centre is made over. Developers in evidence, too: Laing's successful North Nine is a large scheme of solar-electric homes (resales: studio flats c. £95,000, up to 4-bed houses, c. £250,000) off **Montagu Rd**, near the Lock, leisure centre, golf course – and filter beds; next door, Valley View is a shared-ownership scheme for local first-time buyers, part of the council's regeneration. More recent flats in **Swaythling Close**: studios to 2-beds, c. £85–140,000.

'Angel Square' is Laing again: 'funky' town-houses and flats, c. £160–200,000, on ex-gasworks land off **Dysons Rd**. This Upper Edmonton corner is on the S, Tottenham side of the North Circular, which looks to **Fore St** for its shopping (and estate agents).

Lower Edmonton's green lies a mile to the N: home to the bus station and above-mentioned 1960s shopping centre rather than anything verdant and villagey. Edmonton's little flat-fronted 2/3-bed Victorian/Edwardian terraceds start modestly around £160,000 unmodernized, while a 4-bed sold for £230,000. These and inter-war semis (around **Granham Gardens**; some now flats) are standard here, though styles are certainly varied, stone cladding ubiquitous. A 1930s terraced in reasonable order, c. £190,000. Homes are mixed with council-build (a lot now ex-council, especially around **Northern Avenue**), plus industrial corners – but also the odd football pitch or recreation ground; some, too, get open views towards Essex. For Edmonton's best, look to the Huxley, Galliard, Midland, Westerham and Latymer estates: mainly 3-bed houses from c. £220,000. Also **Charlton**

Rd: some late 1980s flats; **Nightingale Rd** and **Oxford Rd**, leafy and neat. A scheme in **Scotland Green Rd** has 1-bed flats up to 3-bed houses set round communal gardens.

Near the North Circular lies Pymmes Park, complete with bowling green, lake, tennis. These much more appealing, leafy streets, such as **Sweet Briar Walk** which skirts the park, and round **Silver St** (not-yet-tidied Victorian semis), are also close to Latymer, one of the best state grammars. Buy-to-lets find tenants in hospital and university students.

Park Lane has a clutch of 4-bed town-houses: from c. £260,000. Just off **Church St** in **Lion Rd**, 1- and 2-bed flats are convenient for Edmonton Green station. Moving W along **Church St** (inter-war semis) the area becomes increasingly attractive with playing fields and sports grounds providing pleasant backdrops. Here the A10, bustling importantly off towards Cambridge, runs for a while with allotments bordering both sides of the road. Homes get bigger and pricier towards the Palmers Green, N18, borders.

Transport Tubes: Southgate, Arnos Grove, Oakwood (zone 4, Piccadilly). From Southgate: Oxford Circus 35 min (1 change), City 30 min (1 change), Heathrow 1 hr 15 min. Trains: Palmers Green, Winchmore Hill to Moorgate, King's Cross; Bush Hill Park, Lower Edmonton to Liverpool St.

Convenient for North Circular, M25, M1, M11, A10. Parks and sports/leisure; water sports. Miles from centre: 8.

Schools Local Authority: Highlands, Chace, Kingsmead, Latymer, Alyward, Winchmore, Southgate, Edmonton, Enfield Grammar (b), Broomfield, Enfield County (g), St Anne's RC (g). Private: Palmers Green High (g).

SALES

Flats	S	1B	2B	3B	4B	5B
Average prices	80–120	100–180	120–280	250–350	–	–
Houses	2B	3B	4B	5B	6/7B	8B
Average prices	165–340	180–350	280–600	550–1.8M	–	–

RENTAL

Flats	S	1B	2B	3B	4B	5B
Average prices	100–140	135–185	160–210	200–350	–	–
Houses	2B	3B	4B	5B	6/7B	8B
Average prices	185–230	205–320	250–415	300–580	–	–

The properties Leafy, suburban homes in Southgate and Winchmore Hill including some large expensive ones. Many modern houses, flats. Palmers Green has Edwardian 3/4-bed homes, some 1930s, some Victorian, and flats. Cheaper Edmonton, smaller terraces, inter-war homes.

The market Commuter country: trains to City and good access to motorways to attract executives. Junior ranks buy converted flats and terraces in cheaper areas; some expensive new-build. High rental demand from students. Edmonton forms lower end of price scale above.

S

Among estate agents active in this area are:

- Bairstow Eves
- Castles
- Havillands
- Haart
- Mckenzie & Co
- Anthony Webb
- Adam Kennedy
- Peter Graff
- Property Bureau
- Kinleigh, Folkard & Hayward
- Meadway Estates
- Cousins
- Lanes
- WJ Meade

ST JOHN'S WOOD

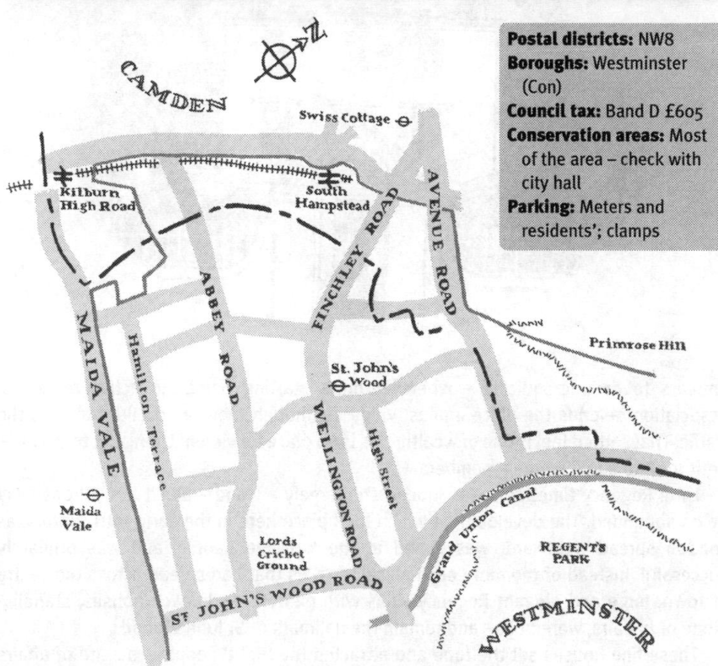

Postal districts: NW8
Boroughs: Westminster (Con)
Council tax: Band D £605
Conservation areas: Most of the area – check with city hall
Parking: Meters and residents'; clamps

London's 'first suburb' – both in the sense of being just about the earliest and just about the closest in – is now also its best connected. Geographically it is set in the angle of the green, open tracts of Regent's Park and Primrose Hill, yet just across that park lies the West End. And now in terms of communications, the area has got it made. The Jubilee Line tube means that Canary Wharf can be reached direct in 20 minutes, and it's one change – at Waterloo, a mere 10 minutes away – to Paris. The 15-minute Paddington–Heathrow Express, opened in 1998, is handy for the rest of the world. And of course the West End is a short cab ride away.

Despite thus being pretty well the centre of the universe, and despite the many modern apartment blocks which have replaced earlier mansions, the pace and the style of these select streets are still set, it seems, by the lazy, summer sound of leather on willow that drifts across the high, enclosing walls of Lord's Cricket Ground. Away from the busy artery of **Wellington Rd** and the hustle and bustle of the **High St**, The Wood's life is conducted at strolling pace – and a very pleasant place to stroll it is. Other reasons for the area's appeal include shopping, with the High St boutiques supplemented by the good range along the **Finchley Rd**; the American School in **Loudoun Rd** – always cited by agents as paramount; and religion – the London Central Mosque in Regent's Park, several synagogues, Lord's Cricket Ground.

The international set that St John's Wood attracts means a high number of renters as well as buyers. The size of the rental market, and its international nature, also means that uncertainties in, say, the American economy quickly get translated into quiet times for landlords. This was the case in 2001–3, and the Americans are still scarcer than they were in the heady late-'90s. Their place has been taken by Australians, Chinese, Europeans. But there is also a very settled backbone here, and a sense of belonging

appears to develop quickly – wherever one's starting point. An active residents' association defends the place against vulgarity, though they can do little to curb the traffic. That settled feel is one of wealth; this is no place for violent change. It took Lord's until 1998 to admit women members.

Until Regency times this was indeed still largely a wood – albeit a royal one. Hay fields abounded. The development which took place here in the early 19th century, as London spread westward, was aimed at the 'carriage people' and was brilliantly successful. Instead of the more economical terraces that had spread across the centre of town, large and elegant Regency villas with gardens and coach houses, standing alone or in pairs, were built – and remain the hallmark of St John's Wood.

These fine houses set the tone and attracted the 'right' people – a state of affairs which has largely persisted. Its inhabitants are well-established men and women who see a home in St John's Wood as fair reward for their hard work; globe-trotting business people; diplomatic staff. Ambassadors find the area sympathetic. While flat-dwellers move on quite quickly, house-buyers tend to stay put – or trade up within the area. Buyers are likely to be people in arts and media, or lawyers, with a good sprinkling of City (or rather Canary Wharf) types, and well-heeled foreign students: the London Business School is close by, the American School means quite a few families know the area already.

During the 1990s overseas investment buying, particularly from Singapore and other parts of the Far East, drove the market up. New schemes were bought off-plan – The Pavilion Apartments in **St John's Wood Rd**, which overlooks Lord's, entirely so. More recently Chinese investors have appeared. Now uncertainty about Leasehold Reform is over, buyers are seeking out enfranchisable homes (see Buying & Selling chapter).

As various as the St John's Wood dwellers are the St John's Wood homes. Every size, from pied-à-terre flatlets to vast and splendid mansions; every period, from those Regency villas (and a few rare Regency-Gothic cottages) via stock-brick terraces, high Victoriana, artists'-studio houses, substantial between-the-wars mansion blocks, bomb-damage infill, 1960s town-houses (garages!), small outbreaks of excellent recent houses – and flats, flats and more flats up to the super-luxury models which come with share of porter and pool at the cost of the average West Country manor.

The earlier history of the area still has a bearing on buying homes here today. After the Priors of St John lost the land at the Reformation it was split up; a long, narrow strip (lying along the **Edgware Rd**) became, eventually, part of the Harrow School Estate. A larger section belonged to the Crown: Charles II used some of it to settle a debt. In 1720, 200 acres of this was bought (for £20,000) by Henry Eyre, a prosperous merchant, whose estate remains largely intact today and is remembered in the name of Eyre Court, a popular 1930s block on the corner of the **Finchley Rd** and **Grove End Rd**. Thus many freeholds in the area have, historically, been owned by Harrow School, the Eyre Estate (usually shorter leases) and (a few) Eton College, and most property is leasehold. Paradoxically, some of the best houses are on these short leases. There are roads where one side has, say, 45-year leases, the other side 70; which explains strange price discrepancies – though freeholds are growing as leaseholders enfranchise their homes.

It's a neat area: its wide and leafy roads lie mainly in Westminster (which stops at the aptly-named **Boundary Rd**, though a more tangible frontier is the railway line that separates this area from South Hampstead to the N), and encompass most of NW8. Pencil-straight **Maida Vale** (the road) rules it off to the W, with Regent's Park and Primrose Hill lapping round the eastern periphery. Its internal geography is split – neatly, of course – by the main through-route of **Wellington Rd/Finchley Rd** into two distinct halves: the Lord's side and the Park side.

The Lord's side

The Lord's side refers, of course, to St John's Wood's most sacred shrine – the cricket ground. On this, western, side of the **Wellington Rd/Finchley Rd** divide also lie most of the area's other religious institutions: churches, synagogues, etc.

The neighbourhood's southernmost boundary is **St John's Wood Rd**, the busy road that divides Lord's and St John's Wood from Lisson Grove and Marylebone. Across the cricket ground, **Cavendish Avenue** holds some of the largest houses and gardens. This is a good corner for hypochondriacs: at one end of the avenue is **Wellington Place**, at the end of which stands one of London's most expensive private hospitals, Humana's Wellington Hospital (South). At the other end is **Circus Rd** (the name of which reflects an early, thwarted, plan to develop St John's Wood around a large circus with streets and squares containing pairs of houses); across this is the back of the Catholic St John and St Elizabeth Hospital. Circus Lodge is a mansion block here, with 2- and 3-bed flats (a 5-bed penthouse, £795,000).

For grand mansions of varying vintages and styles try **Hamilton Terrace**, which runs the length of the area: this is the Wood's premier boulevard. Wide, tree-lined, prestigious, it stretches about three-quarters of a mile. Begun in 1820, its variety of homes include semi- and detached mansions so large that some have been split into house-sized flats. When intact, however, houses here range from modest (i.e. a mere £2–3 million or so) through the merely big (£5 million for 6 beds last winter) to ambassador-class (the one in our drawing boasts 10 bedrooms, 5 receptions, drive, garage, swimming pool . . .).

Flats around here (or apartments, maisonettes, duplexes, penthouses: terms escalate along with the size and price) can have great views out over greenery – the most coveted being the 22-yard strip with the Test Match being played on it. The Pavilion Apartments, a well-regarded block on nine floors in **St John's Wood Rd**, has parking, 24hr porterage; some flats have a terrace and, yes, view of Lord's (£420,000 for a 1-bed). For a contrast in styles look to **Hall Rd**, where the old telephone exchange was in 2001 converted by Yoo – John 'Manhattan Lofts' Hitchcox and design guru Philippe Starck. A 2-bed here was £720,000 last winter.

In the surrounding streets, a jumble of ages and styles provide flats for all requirements: 1900s ones in the big, recently modernized, council-run **Scott Ellis Gardens** (a good choice for a flat at what counts locally as low prices); 1930s ones in **Hall Rd**; while **Abbey Rd** and **Abercorn Place** have good examples built just after the war. On the corner of Abbey Rd, 38 **Abercorn Place** is a 1988-built block of smart apartments. Under its raised roof, a penthouse enjoys the entire top floor. Next door to it is a delight: a Regency artists'-studio house designed by Decimus Burton. Across the road, 29 Abercorn Place has studios (still c. £165–175,000) and 1-bed flats, while imposing, Edwardian Abercorn mansions has 2-beds at c. £475,000.

Grove End Rd, which runs N from **St John's Wood Rd**, is a pleasant if busy street with a mixture of flats in blocks from mansion to modern – and enormous houses such as magnificent Tadema Lodge, with swimming pool complex and ballroom, designed by the artist James Tissot and later owned by Sir Lawrence Alma-Tadema. More everyday houses in the street (i.e. merely detached and double-fronted period/20th-century copies) come up occasionally for £3 million or so. The St John and St Elizabeth Hospital, founded by colleagues of Florence Nightingale, stands opposite St John's Wood United Synagogue, one of three well-known synagogues in the area. **Grove End Rd** joins **Wellington Rd** just opposite **Acacia Rd**, on the corner of which is the St John's Wood tube station, and here, too, is the big Eyre Court mansion block. Off Acacia Rd, on the site of an old dairy, is Tatham Place, a rare clutch of 12 modern houses (a 3-bed £875,000).

Running N from **Grove End Rd** is **Loudoun Rd**, where you'll find the famous American School – a magnet for US families – and, opposite it, the boys' prep school Arnold House. Traffic jams at school times are legendary – as are the eagle-eyed security men who watch over Mom as she packs the kids into the people-carrier. To save getting the car out, Mom could buy a small 3-bed semi-detached in Loudoun Rd itself for £1.2 million.

Parallel to **Loudoun Rd** is **Abbey Rd**, made famous by the Beatles, who cut their records here (today, spot tomorrow's stars at the studios). It, too, has sprouted stylish new developments: the 1990 complex of eight houses and 100 apartments at No. 20 was among the first to be marketed extensively in Hong Kong, helped by a Beatles-linked promotion. A block called The Galleries by Persimmon added 20-odd 2-bed flats in 2001 – think half a million for a 2-bed here; also many for rent. With so many flats **Abbey Rd**, busy but wide and leafy, is very popular on the rentals, as well as the sales, market – as is **Abercorn Place**, where a 3-bed flat in a stucco-fronted peiod house was £750,000 last autumn.

Off Abbey Rd lies one of the prettiest corners of St John's Wood. Roads such as **Blenheim Terrace**, **Carlton Terrace**, **Boundary Rd** have a smaller-scale, villagey atmosphere. There you'll find little shops, boutiques, galleries in pretty **Nugent Terrace**, and little parks like the one in **Violet Hill**, where the 4-bed flat-fonted Victorian houses are c. £850,000. In **Clifton Hill** is the Clifton pub, a country pub in atmosphere, alongside houses which can change hands for around a million, while across the road up to £3 million has been paid for detached ones. Some big ones, too, in **Carlton Hill**: the 5-bed 19th-century houses here go for c. £2.8 million, and there are modern ones at perhaps a million less. The 4-floor, 5/6-bedroomed terraced 1850s houses round pretty **Alma Square** share its gardens.

To the N of this corner runs **Marlborough Place**, where Galliard's three neo-Georgian, 4-bed/4-bath/3-recep/covered-parking houses were £3–4 million last year (though a Victorian 7-bed was just £2.2 million), and a 2-bed flat in 'Le Residence', a modern block, was £450,000.

Back on busy **Finchley Rd** the 1930s Apsley House was crowned in 1990 with six luxurious new penthouse flats. This became a popular trend for blocks in the area – Clive Court on **Maida Vale** is another example – popular except, of course, with the erstwhile top-floor dwellers, whose penthouses are now merely penultimate.

The Park side

East of the **Wellington Rd/Finchley Rd** divide – which connects St John's Wood with Swiss Cottage – the Park side not only laps up to the shores of Primrose Hill and Regent's Park, but also boasts the **High St**, and some peaceful corners to live. **Queen's Grove**, with its terraced houses boasting large Ionic and Corinthian columns, is a leafy road leading (as many cars discover) to Primrose Hill; round the corner in **Queen's**

Terrace, Nos. 4–7 plus the former pub are now shops, offices and nine new flats. **Norfolk** and **Acacia Rds** are both pretty streets with brick-and-stucco houses, sought after – even fought over – by those who prefer older-style homes (for example, a 7-bed detached with double garage and staff cottage) in the £3-million bracket. Lilly Langtry, Edward VII's actress mistress, dwelt in Acacia Rd. Cul-de-sac **Acacia Gardens** is a new addition.

In the middle of this corner, off **Ordnance Hill**, lie the barracks of the King's Troop Royal Horse Artillery – a splendid sight to see in the early morning when the horses are exercised: this can involve 60 horses with gun carriages. It also boasts classic white-stucco terraced homes, as well as those of 1995, gated **Rosetti Mews**. A good cache of flats to let in Ordnance Hill, too.

Woronzow Rd, where learner drivers practise their three-point turns, contains the (comparatively) less expensive terraced houses. Since you ask, the Woronzow in question was a Russian count who left £500 to build almshouses: they were erected in **St John's Wood Terrace** in 1827, but were rebuilt in the 1960s.

Newer houses in St John's Wood can be seen further towards Swiss Cottage. **Queensmead** is an estate of 17 town-houses and three blocks of flats owned by the Eyre Estate, built in the late 1960s. They were let until 1990, when some were refurbished and sold: around £500,000 buys a 2-bed flat. **The Marlowes** is another sought-after clutch of town-houses; they look, comments a local, like flats tipped on their sides, but are desirable because of their location. **St John's Wood Park** also has modern houses, in a portered enclave handy for Swiss Cottage tube.

Running between Circus Rd and Prince Albert Rd is **St John's Wood High St** with its boutiques, bistros, wine merchants, smart fashion stores and a well-regarded Oxfam shop. Round the corner is Panzers, St John's Wood's most upmarket grocer, and the post office. There are 1-bed flats above the shops – some up four flights of stairs.

Council-built flats (select ones, to match the area) lie behind the **High St**. Some in **Barrow Hill, Allitsen Rd** and **Townshend Rd** now appear for sale, having been bought by the tenants (and subsequently by buy-to-letters): a 2-bed in Townshend Court was £340,000 last autumn. **St John's Wood Terrace/Charlbert St** junction has some of the area's only run-down buildings.

At the end of the **High St** is the roundabout presided over by St John's Wood Church, a large, elegant building. The broad and busy ribbon of **Prince Albert Rd** curves around the N side of Regent's Park (see that chapter), cutting it off from the Wood. The Pavilions at 24–26 **Avenue Rd**, a luxurious development of six flats, sumptuous penthouse and swimming pool, was built in 1988. Avenue Rd is a grand thoroughfare, highly desirable to the international set: ambassadors from many nations make their homes in the large mansions with landscaped gardens; overseas business people buy flats, such as those in the century-old Northgate building with their views across Regent's Park.

Borders

Across **Avenue Rd**, a small clutch of streets run E to Primrose Hill. Look for flats, and modern town-houses, in streets such as **St Edmund's Terrace, Ormonde Terrace**. An old electricity building in St Edmund's has been replaced by four new houses for the Notting Hill Housing Tust and a dozen flats for sale. For the homes of villagey Primrose Hill proper, across the 200ft-high hill, see the Camden chapter.

To the N of Primrose Hill lies a group of roads with huge, handsome Edwardian red-brick villas. Look for them in **Harley Rd, Wadham Gardens** and **Elsworthy Rd** – a street with big, wide 3- and 4-storey Hampstead-style houses. To the S, the giant modern blocks that form ramparts along **Prince Albert Rd** are in the Regent's Park chapter.

To the N, and still in NW8, a big swathe of council-built homes runs along **Boundary Rd**. On the S side of the street are some pleasant 1950s blocks, where a 2-bed flat might be £200,000-plus. Across the street you enter Camden borough, which in the 1970s redeveloped here on a vast scale, taking up the whole space between **Loudon Rd** and **Abbey Rd.** The upper flats, which have S-facing terraces, are worth a look. Just to the S, **Springfield Rd** has some (privately built) 1960s town-houses and some 1930s neo-Georgian ones (a 4-bed £1.75 million last year). These both offer a more suburban style than St John's Wood is used to, which may well be why, in cautious times, agents find them harder to sell than 'period' houses – despite their double garages.

Transport Tubes: St John's Wood, Swiss Cottage (zone 2, Jubilee); Maida Vale (zone 2, Bakerloo). From St John's Wood: Oxford Circus 15 min (1 change), City 30 min (1 change), Heathrow 30 min (1 change). Trains: South Hampstead (direct to Euston).

Convenient for West End, Regent's Park, Lord's Cricket Ground. Routes to North and West. Paris, Canary Wharf thanks to Jubilee Line Extension, Heathrow thanks to Paddington Express. Miles from centre: 3.5.

Schools Local Authority: Quintin Kynaston, St Augustine's C of E, St George's RC. Private: The American School, Francis Holland (g), International Community School, North Bridge House. See also: Hampstead, Kentish Town.

SALES

Flats	S	1B	2B	3B	4B	5B
Average prices	160–250	190–400	275–500	325–1M+	800–2M+	–
Houses	2B	3B	4B	5B	6/7B	8B
Average prices	450–700	500–1M+	900–4M	1.2–5M	1.5–4M+	–

RENTAL

Flats	S	1B	2B	3B	4B	5B
Average prices	180–250	250–400	350–800	300–1500	400–2500	–
Houses	2B	3B	4B	5B	6/7B	8B
Average prices	450–950	500–1500	900–2500	1000–5000	→	→

The properties Smartest of suburbs, with big, early 19th-century villas and an outstanding range of homes: virtually every size and style of house and flat from late-Georgian terraces through '30s mansion blocks to state-of-the-art modern. A good place to find that elusive inner-London parking space – and even electric gates to your in-and-out drive.

The market Cosmopolitan: diplomats, business folk, celebrities, all buy here for big family houses, and international-class apartments that can cost as much and more than whole houses. Much overseas investment/bolt-hole buying – so market here is

S

Among estate agents active in this area are:

- Anscombe & Ringland
- Knight Frank
- Bargets
- Winkworth
- Jeffersons
- Behr & Butchoff
- Goldschmidt
- Greenstone
- Daker Estates
- Arlington Residential
- Brian Lack
- Foxtons
- JAC Strattons
- Keith Cardale Groves
- Hamptons
- Savills
- Benham & Reeves

STEPNEY AND WHITECHAPEL

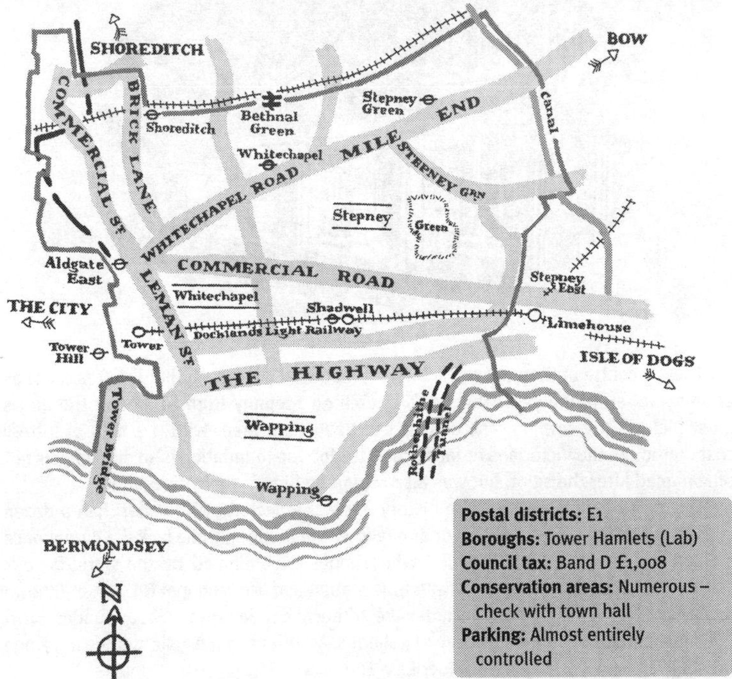

Postal districts: E1
Boroughs: Tower Hamlets (Lab)
Council tax: Band D £1,008
Conservation areas: Numerous – check with town hall
Parking: Almost entirely controlled

Stepney, Whitechapel and Wapping, an area defined quite precisely by the E1 postal district and immediately east of the City of London, is the heart of the old East End. The 20th century's traumas of war and slum clearance brought great changes, leaving it a curious mixture of some of London's best and worst housing. Now the ferment in its neighbouring areas brings more: the City's expansion has crossed the border into Stepney, while the Docklands boom has brought wealth to riverside Wapping (see Docklands chapter).

The most fundamental change here in the past decade is the resurgence of living in and around the City and its fringes – Spitalfields and Aldgate, on the Stepney side – which until around 1995 had a nocturnal population of more cats than humans: see also City chapter. The property market (a phrase still fairly new to this part of town) woke up as this trend rolled outwards, and those priced out of Islington, Clerkenwell and Docklands took a look at Stepney. West End estate agents now market Stepney homes.

Stepney is as convenient for the City as Docklands, and with more of a 'village' air; buyers, particularly the young, are finding it attractive. Unlike most of modern Docklands, Stepney's neighbourhoods have been around for a long time . . . the sense of history, of real life in an existing community, and of course the prices, are all more congenial to them.

S

The Stepney and Whitechapel area is shaped by three main roads running E–W: **The Highway, Commercial Rd** and **Whitechapel Rd**, which continues from **Mile End Rd**. All three lead to the City and are, therefore, perpetually busy. The Liverpool Street main line cuts Stepney off from Bethnal Green to the N, while the canal divides it from Poplar to the E. Wapping and the river underlines it to the S, and the City lies to the W.

The old centre of Stepney was a thriving medieval village. All that is left is Stepney Churchyard, surrounding St Dunstan's Church on **Stepney High St**: one of the area's most picturesque corners. The church has been renovated, with the help of lottery cash. Although the Victorians re-faced the exterior, the foundation is so old that it is not only named after the saint, but was also *rebuilt* by him, in the 10th century.

This part of London drips with history – a fact reflected by no fewer than a dozen conservation areas. The Tower of London falls within Stepney, while Jack the Ripper once stalked the streets of Whitechapel. Whitechapel is dominated by the world-famous London Hospital, directly opposite the tube station and **Whitechapel Rd** market (known locally as 'The Waste'). Culture includes the Whitechapel Gallery, the first (founded 1901) and most famous of numerous local art galleries. According to the gallery, there are 7,000 artists living and working in the wider East End.

The area used to be in parts strongly Jewish, and about 3,000 Jewish people still live in the inner East End; however, now a Bengali Muslim flavour predominates, especially around **Brick Lane** and the mosque in **Whitechapel High St**. This corner has over the centuries always been a haven for incomers: in 1900 Jewish, Irish, German, Scandinavian and Chinese people lived here.

Apart from the explosion of new housing developments in Wapping (described in the Docklands chapter), some of Stepney's most coveted homes are to be found in the **Albert Gardens/Arbour Square** conservation area, which includes Arbour Square police station. Less desirable – in terms of living – are the streets on either side of the W end of **Commercial Rd**. These are dominated by the East End 'rag trade' and scores of clothing manufacturers and wholesalers operate here.

Spitalfields is now firmly linked to the City, with much new development. It includes three conservation areas – **Elder St, Fournier St** and **Artillery Passage** – which still hold some beautiful, intact homes left by even earlier immigrants, the Huguenot silk merchants: these date from very early Georgian days. For details, see the City chapter.

S

Watney Market, S of **Commercial Rd**, is an as-yet unreconstructed corner, but it has the asset of the DLR's Shadwell station (and a tube station on the East London Line). **Middlesex St** holds the famous Petticoat Lane market on Sunday mornings, and there is also a daily market in nearby **Wentworth St**.

Stepney

At the eastern end of the neighbourhood, conveniently close to Stepney Green District Line tube, an enclave of streets is hidden in the angle between Globe and Mile End Rds. **Portelet Rd, Carlton Square, Holton St, Grantley St, Massingham St** and **Tollet St** are well placed near the Mile End annexe of the London Hospital. These delightful 2-storey Victorian terraced houses, some with semi-basements and steps up to the front door, are also near Tower Hamlets Central Library in Bancroft Rd and various Queen Mary College buildings. Bancroft Rd's amenities also include a music rehearsal space in the old railway arches. Back off the Mile End Rd itself, and a step from the tube, **Mile End Place** is a little cul-de-sac of 2-bed cottages behind blowsy front gardens: £270,000 remains a typical price here, with c. £335,000 asked for larger homes. In contrast, Green Court is a smart new block of flats on the Mile End Rd.

Residents in **Grand Walk**, at the E end of Mile End Rd, have modern terraced houses made magic by the Grand Union Canal, which also features anglers and the occasional houseboat. Across the canal, Canal Rd has disappeared in the massive, ongoing, splendid development of long, thin Mile End Park; however, in **Copperfield Rd**, also between park and canal, is a 1930s building that escaped the Blitz: Falcon Works, where the Queen's wedding dress was made, now holds 40 waterside flats. Here, too, is Clementina Court: 20 new 1- and 2-bed Affordable Housing flats for locals.

The Mile End Park is a major, lottery-financed, monument to the Millennium – and a lot more permanent than some. It runs N–S down the course of the canal, and where the busy **Mile End Rd** slices across it a 'green bridge' has been created, with trees and bushes growing above the road. **Grove Rd**, which bounds the park on the E, is being landscaped. New bridges over the canal give extra pedestrian routes to the park. There are all kinds of sports facilities in the park including a climbing wall.

Across to the S of Mile End Rd, down to **Ben Jonson Rd**, is the sprawling, hitherto run-down Ocean council estate, which takes in **Beaumont Square, White Horse Lane, Matlock St, Commodore St, Solebay St, Emmott St, Shandy St, Duckett St** and **Harford St**. Now, though, this is being extensively rebuilt – especially between Harford and Duckett Sts N of Ben Jonson Rd – with new access roads, the removal of three tower blocks and hundreds of new houses. Housing associations and the Central Stepney Regeneration Project have been active here, again for affordable renting to locals; Laing built 41 such new homes in a large estate on **Harford St**. Between Harford St and the canal, a big scheme by Bellway will eventually bring 300 homes for sale, and more homes for key workers, on the old gasworks site. This was held up by a long planning enquiry, but government go-ahead was finally given in May 2002. The slow process of decontamination is still under way.

White Horse Lane has 2-storey terraced houses, including some 1950s 2-beds which sell for up to £250,000 and, to the W, the green of **Beaumont Square**, which faces the London Independent private hospital. **Maria Terrace**, off Beaumont Square, has a row of ten 3-storey Victorian houses. Close by in **Louisa St**, nine 3-bed neo-period houses have been built. And in **Rectory Square**, behind Stepney Green, a converted synagogue is now Temple Court, a clutch of split-level flats.

Stepney Green – not the open, featureless expanse between Stepney Way/Redman's Rd, but the street of the same name just to the N – is an unexpected gem. Behind the narrow strip of green, enclosed by railings, stands a row of wonderful Queen Anne/early 18th-century houses, in what is reputed to be the only blue-cobbled street left in South-East England. The period houses do occasionally come onto the market; they are supplemented by some faithful modern copies. One of these is **Trinity Mews**, on Redman's Rd, a mix of homes and commercial, which includes town-houses with studio workspace. Beatrice House, which has 1-bed flats, is also modern, but period-style.

Also here is Foundry Place: 12 flats, 2 town-houses. Off the Green, **Roland Mews** is 1950s infill, round a courtyard. And **Hayfield Yard** is a gated mews development of flats and small houses between the Green and the Mile End Rd. In **White Horse Lane** is The Rosery, an old rectory now divided into nine smart flats. To the SE is Stepney Green Court: walk-up council flats. Close by are the ivy-fronted red-brick Cressy House (1- and

2-bed flats here) and Dunstan House – walk-up red-brick flats from 1899 by the East End Dwellings Co. Also another area of transformation – what was the Stifford Estate (council): this included **Tinsley Rd, Cressy Place, Redmans Rd, Jamaica St, Stepney Way** and **Smithy St.** On the site of some demolished tower blocks 106 homes – flats and houses, to rent, for sale, or shared ownership – have appeared courtesy of the Stifford Regeneration Project, another public/private partnership that includes Lovell Homes and Paddington Churches Housing Association. W of **Jamaica St,** though, is the still very run-down Clichy Estate.

Back to the **Mile End Rd** where, in the stretch between Globe Rd and Cambridge Heath Rd, **Cephas Avenue** has attractive 2- and 3-storey Victorian terraced houses, many with steps and railings and some with flat roofs, always in high demand. Now 18 houses (reserved for key workers, such as nurses) and a retail park (Currys, PC World) have emerged between Cephas Avenue and Nicholas Rd. In **Cephas St** is a 1999-vintage church conversion with 37 flats, and Durkan Homes has converted No. 95 next door. Nearby **Cooper's Close** has neat 4-storey modern flats from studios upwards. **Cleveland Way** has smart new housing-association flats and **Cleveland Place**, a 1998 development of 10 flats; a further enclave shelters behind electronic gates. The site of the old brewery on the corner of **Cambridge Heath Rd** and **Mile End Rd** is now the Chronos Buildings: a handsome new-build courtyard scheme with six town-houses, 10 penthouses and 49 flats – including eight semicircular ones in a rotunda. Next door are the 1695 Grade I-listed Trinity Almshouses. Some fine, large Georgian houses survive as single homes along the Mile End Rd. On the corner of **Cleveland Way** and Mile End Rd, new flats were converted from period buildings last year.

Close to Whitechapel tube and in stark contrast to its busy surroundings in Mile End Rd is **Trinity Green**, a small 1961 Civic Trust Award development with beautiful gardens enclosed by railings and wall.

Commercial Rd to the S, towards Wapping, lives up to its name with heavy traffic – this is also the A13, the main road out east from the City's Aldgate – and is dotted on either side with council estates such as Pitsea, Watney Market, Exmouth and Mountmorres. The garden square of **Albert Gardens** is a peaceful haven from the noise of the through-route. These desirable 4-storey Victorian terraced houses are part of a conservation area that also includes **Havering St,** where 3-storey versions with railings lead down to a railway arch. Viewed from the rear, the roofs of Havering St give an unusual wave effect. To the W, St Mary and St Michael's Roman Catholic Church and Primary School are next to the Watney Market council estate, which includes **Deancross St, Sidney St, Hainton Path, Hungerford St, Tarling St, Watney St, Dunch St, Timberland Rd, Bigland St** and **Burwell Close.** Berkeley is developing in Tarling St: mostly Affordable Housing. Across in **Sutton St,** Samuel Lewis Housing Trust has added fair-rent homes: 1-bed flats, 2- and 4-bed houses and a 6-bed one.

The Exmouth Estate, N of **Commercial Rd,** includes **Clark St, Musbury St, Cornwood Drive, Jubilee St, Exmouth St, Summercourt Rd, Jamaica St, Aylward St, Clovelly Way** and **Clearbrook Way.** A new development for this corner, too: Stepney City is 73 flats converted from a pair of Victorian school buildings by a painstaking developer, Roger Black: the last few 2-beds are around £250,000. To the E of the estate is the **Arbour Square** conservation area, where Arbour House council flats stand alongside 3-storey Victorian terraces, some of the houses with front steps up to the door, facing a garden square. These Grade II-listed homes sell for c. £350,000 (a stable price over the last two years). Houses on the S side of the square have a drawback as they back onto far less attractive 4-storey terraced houses in **Commercial Rd.**

S

Further E along Commercial Rd is **Bromley St,** where railings surround delightful 2-storey Victorian terraces, refurbished in 1986 and adjoining the Mountmorres council estate. Similar homes are to be found in **Belgrave St,** as are 74 homes added in 1999 by a housing trust on a rent or shared-ownership basis. A new road between the two streets leads to the homes of **Lighterman Mews.** Belgrave St leads back up to **Stepney High St** and picturesque St Dunstan's Church at the heart of old Stepney (see introduction, above), much favoured for local weddings. The church is surrounded by Stepney Churchyard, and facing the church land are **Mercers Cottages**, four beautiful terraced homes that share a communal front garden.

The **York Square** conservation area, to the SE of the green, is half in Stepney and half in Limehouse; the Stepney half includes **White Horse Rd** and **Barnes St.** Run-down 3- and 4-storey terraces in **White Horse Rd** face attractive 3-storey Victorian terraced properties with railings and hanging baskets of flowers. Similarly attractive 2-storey Victorian rows in **Barnes St**, on the opposite side of Commercial Rd to Limehouse rail and DLR stations. On **Cable St** Sceptre Court (1998) has underground parking; Cable St has an excellent cycle path that runs from the City to the Limehouse Link tunnel entrance. Reservoir Studios is a recent block of 30 flats and 18 live/work units. For riverside Limehouse and Wapping, see Docklands chapter.

Whitechapel

The world-famous London Hospital dominates the centre of Whitechapel. The front entrance of the hospital stands in **Whitechapel Rd**, opposite the tube station and Whitechapel Rd market. Some of the Victorian terraced houses at the back of the hospital are owned by the hospital itself, in **Philpott St** for example, and used for research. Other hospital buildings are to be found in **Newark St** – part of the **Sidney Square** conservation area, which also includes part of **Cavell St**, **Halcrow St**, **Ford Square**, **Ashfield St**, **Sidney Square** itself and the E end of **Varden St.**

Attractive **Sidney Square** boasts 3-storey Victorian terraced houses that have tiny wrought-iron balconies on the second floor; homes in the square have sold for up to £475,000. Just to the W, **Fordham St** has 3-bed terraced houses with basements. City Walk is a large, luxury-level flats scheme by Furlong Homes in **Raven Row,** to the W of the hospital. At the junction of **Cavell St**, named of course after Nurse Edith Cavell, and **Varden St** is a new development of 20 luxury flats. More 3- and 4-storey Victorian terraces, some converted into flats, are found in pretty **Ford Square**. Many of these are now occupied by the local student population. The area's cramped streets also include premises for many garment manufacturers and wholesalers: vans loading and unloading sometimes make access difficult.

The renowned Whitechapel Bell Foundry, established in 1570, is at the junction of **Fieldgate St** and **Plumbers Row**; this street, too, has sprouted new homes: Mulberry Court's 'spacious City apartments' date from 2001, and 2003 added 20 more at the Space Works; Fieldgate St has a 19th-century doss-house (reputed former client one Joe Stalin) which will soon be loft apartments. The Whitechapel Gallery in the High St is a world-famous art venue which balances the cultural with the practical: it's also a well-known local place to eat. The East London Mosque, on Whitechapel Rd, is a focal point for the Muslim community. To the N of Whitechapel Rd, the big Sainsbury's provides basic shopping, supplementing the excellent street markets. **Coventry Rd**, up towards Bethnal Green, has a church conversion, Steeple Court (2-bed triplex £289,000). Next door is new-build **Bartholomew Square.** Nearby in **Durward St** is Cityside, a conversion of an old school. Also situated on **Whitechapel Rd** is Albion Yard, the now-converted old Albion brewery.

From **New Rd** westwards, the nearer the City, the greater the concentration of developers' boards. Between **Whitechapel Rd**, **Commercial Rd** and **New Rd**, a vast 2002 development tried to reinvent the area as the 'Aldgate Triangle': a group of three buildings designed by architects CZWG, complete with 2-storey gym and gardens. The same developer, Ballymore, added 53 flats next door, in the Colefax Building. Next to it are 18 live-work units. Across the street, Albany Court has new penthouses (Galliard). Nearby, St George's Skyline Plaza on **Commercial Rd** has 130 flats sharing a roof garden with splendid views.

Streets from **Leman St**, which includes a police station, across to **Mansell St** are now generally accepted as part of the City itself (the City's boundary actually runs down Mansell St). Leman St is the site of a Berkeley scheme which will convert the old Co-Op HQ into 38 flats, adding 170 around it; more new homes (in the hundreds) are planned for **Alie St/Goodman's Yard. Prescot St** has a conversion of a 1930s office building into flats, and Berkeley Homes' Londinium Tower: 84 1-, 2- and 3-bed flats with parking below. **Henriques St** has 64 new studios and small flats carved out of a century-old children's refuge. On the fringes of Wapping, **Royal Mint St**, to the S, has a 2002 block of 1- and 2-bed flats, while in **Ensign St** Liberty House has 3-year-old 2-beds.

Transport Tubes (zones 1 and 2): Stepney Green, Whitechapel, Aldgate East (Hammersmith & City, District); Wapping (East London); Aldgate (Metropolitan, Circle); Tower Hill (Circle, District); Shadwell (East London). From Stepney Green: Oxford Circus 15 min (1 change), City 10 min (1 change), Heathrow 60 min (1 change).

Convenient for Docklands, City. Miles from centre: 3.5.

Schools Local Authority: Bishop Challoner RC (g), Bishop Challoner RC (b) Bow (b), Central Foundation (g), Mulberry (g), Sir John Cass, Stepney Green (b), Swanlea School. Private: Madani (g).

SALES

Flats	S	1B	2B	3B	4B	5B
Average prices	120–150	130–200	170–270	200–320	–	–
Houses	2B	3B	4B	5B	6/7B	8B
Average prices	230–280	275–350	330–500	–	–	–

RENTAL

Flats	S	1B	2B	3B	4B	5B
Average prices	130–160	160–220	230–280	270–350	–	–
Houses	2B	3B	4B	5B	6/7B	8B
Average prices	230–300	300–370	300–450	–	–	–

The properties Loft conversions and new-build flats appearing as City workers discover the area. Homes here range from ex-council to Grade II listed, from flats to new mews schemes, from Victorian rows and Edwardian red-brick to Georgiana on Stepney Green.

The market Prices reflect range, and closeness of City and Wapping. Small, everyday terraces rub shoulders with large, listed Georgiana. Investors weigh up ex-council flats, in demand as rentals, but at lower prices than private-sector homes.

S

Among estate agents active in this area are:

- Keatons
- Prevost
- Baker Allen
- Ludlow Thompson
- Alex Neil
- Carrington
- Look
- McDowalls
- W J Meade
- Tower
- Land & Co
- Atkinson McLeod
- Alan Selby
- Hamilton Fox
- Globe

STOKE NEWINGTON

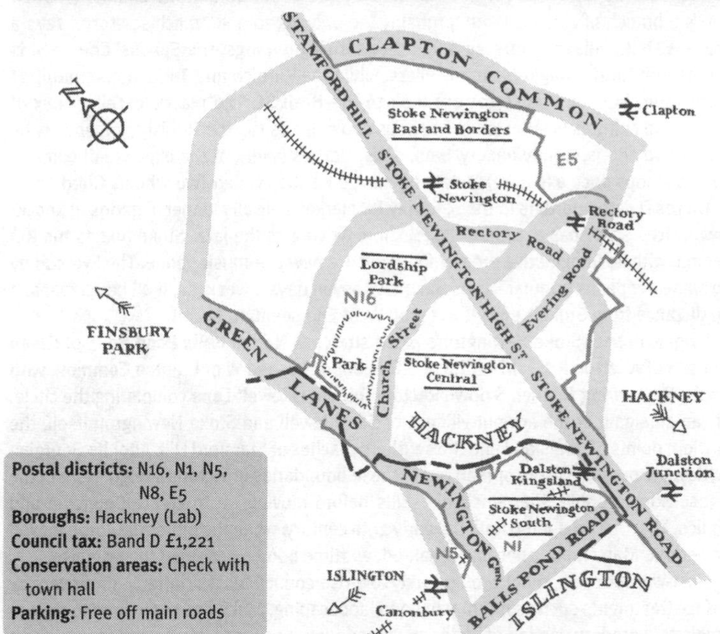

Postal districts: N16, N1, N5, N8, E5
Boroughs: Hackney (Lab)
Council tax: Band D £1,221
Conservation areas: Check with town hall
Parking: Free off main roads

It's easy to find Stoke Newington. Begin at London Bridge and go due north. Follow Bishopsgate (no mystery about *that* name) through the City, along Shoreditch High Street and up the Romans' road – the still almost ruler-straight A10. This, in its northwards charge, changes its name from Kingsland Rd to Kingsland High St, then Stoke Newington Rd and at last **Stoke Newington High St.**

Since the Saxons started the place – **Stoke Newington Church St**, running off westwards, marks the old village centre – many have made that journey. The village became a haven for dissenters; Daniel Defoe lived here for 20 years after his release from Newgate (his crime was seditious libel) and the Unitarian chapel, 1708, is the world's oldest. The place retains its air of a place apart, aided by some more early 18th-century survivals, the lack of tube, the ample parks – though housing, inhabitants and surroundings are cheerfully mixed across the area. Today's 'incomers' uphold the nonconformist tradition in a rather different way: thirty-something creative types come hunting here for their first flat, Islington flat-dwellers after their first family home – and better-than-Islington nurseries/primary schools – though they must now look north to the Stamford Hill fringes to get more space for their money. Everyone wants a 2-bed for under the £250,000 stamp duty point – but a nice garden flat in the centre is now £300,000.

Despite the now-high prices, there's still a definite air of alternative lifestyles: lots of musicians, in particular, drawn to the Vortex jazz club (moving to nearby Dalston). Even now the glossier *arrivistes* are drawn from the ranks of architecture, fashion, journalism, TV; but sadly prices have driven out the first-time buyers: agents comment that many a better-heeled resident moving on to a house failed to sell their flat, hanging on to it instead as an investment. Letting to buy, rather than buying to let, in effect.

The rather self-consciously right-on nature of Stoke Newington comes out in the shops, pubs and eateries along characterful, winding **Church St** – still the main street.

Here displaced Islingtonians find a good substitute for Upper St – better, in fact, as here the local stores have not yet been ousted by the usual ubiquitous chains. (Though there's a branch of Fresh & Wild: 'probably the only acceptable franchise store,' says a local.) With its village-centre air and 18th-century buildings, the Saxons' Church St is still the hub for the Anglo-Saxon dwellers, while the Kurdish and Turkish communities (great food, but they don't get on) look to the **High St**. The place's excellent mix of classes and cultures is reflected in its shops and eateries (try the Turkish), joined now by health-food shops, trendy bakery, bars, delis, clothes (sadly, at the expense of some of the bookshops once a feature), estate agents', bike shop called Two Wheels Good.

On the Dalston borders to the S, **Ridley Rd** market sells all manner of goods at knock-down prices – and has a 24-hour bagel shop. As well as the jazz, Stoke boasts the Rio Cinema, with its imaginative programming; now a new live-music venue, The Eye, run by the same people as popular Ryans Bar, plays seven days a week. . . . It all helps to make the distance from Stoke Newington to the West End seem irrelevant.

Largely in N16, Stoke Newington's patch stretches N from **Balls Pond Rd**, E of **Green Lanes**, S of **Allerton Rd**, **Fairholt Rd** and **Dunsmure Rd**, and W of **Clapton Common**, with **Brooke Rd/Evering Rd** then S down **Rectory Rd/Shacklewell Lane** completing the circle. It is an amalgam of the ancient villages of Shacklewell and Stoke Newington itself, the northern points of Kingsland and the southern reaches of Stamford Hill. After its Georgian heyday, the original village spread out to these boundaries in Victoria's reign. Here in the 1830s Thomas Cubitt sharpened his skills before moving on to create Belgravia and Pimlico. The area prospered until the early 20th century, when the more well-to-do moved further out. Many homes became tenanted; wartime bombs hastened their demise.

Post-war redevelopment brought ugly low-rise council blocks, latterly 'improved' by surface treatments such as bright paint and landscaping. Much has been done to restore streets to a modern version of Victorian splendour – by council, locals and the numbers of young middle-class families who have found homes here; conservation areas abound. It's an ongoing task. Next, the old Town Hall is to be returned to its former Art Deco glory.

Success has had unfortunate consequences, however. Stoke Newington's splendid Midsummer Festival nearly vanished: the area no longer qualifies for regeneration, and Hackney council (ah, yes, Hackney council) withdrew funding. Renamed 'Stokefest', it was promptly rescued by volunteers, who are fundraising to keep it going.

Although most of the length of the **High St** remains cheerfully scruffy, especially S of Church St, the stretch between Church St and Northwold Rd is smartening, with new restaurants and the restoration of long-empty premises: the old Vogue cinema is now smart flats, and the Kwik-Fit tyre centre has been demolished: watch this space . . .

New homes in the area often include live/work units, which appeared as developers latched on to the creative types who make a beeline for 'Stokey'. The largest, Red Square, led the way, and is being joined by several others: see below. Another trend, led by the Peabody Trust, mixes social and open-market homes. Their splendid landmark building on **Newington Green**, the rounded, balconied tower of Holland House, seemed at first glance yet another clutch of luxurious flats and penthouses – indeed, rather more distinguished than many. Gated parking, stripped-wood floors, state-of-the-art kitchens, even cable TV points . . . and a ban on buy-to-let purchasers. Peabody used profits from this scheme to fund yet more affordable homes for local people. Indeed, 24 of the Holland House flats were sold on a shared-ownership basis. Other developers, please note. Next, Peabody moved on to **Northwold Rd**. This is the second of their projects to use prefabricated units, delivered fully finished. Atop eight live/work places for sale are five storeys of 2-bed flats, with 3-bed family homes behind: 53 units for key workers or locals.

The state-of-the-art Clissold Leisure Centre finally opened in 2002: late, over budget, but 'magnificent' – and closed in '04 needing £5 millions of repairs: you can take the plunge again come 2006. Never mind; spacious Clissold Park also holds a truly eccentric 'zoo', praised café, bowling green, tennis courts, band stand for summer sonatas – and original Manor, now more open to the public. In wooded Abney Park Cemetery rests many an eminent Victorian, beneath wonderful Gothic tombs (we hear it livens up at night . . .). The area also boasts a major watersports centre and a climbing centre.

Lordship Park

The most northerly of Stoke's four neighbourhoods is Lordship Park – not a park but a road, though both Clissold Park and Abney Park Cemetery are in this leafy corner that runs N from **Stoke Newington Church St** to the reservoirs. **Lordship Park/Manor Rd**, the main thoroughfare, is an E–W bus and traffic route. At the W end are monumental 4-storey 1860s houses, set back from the road, making them quieter than might be assumed. These give way to smaller 2-storey bay-fronted houses as you go E; unlovely commercial/industrial by the time it meets the A10. A former woodyard in **Manor Rd**, however, sprouted **Abney View**, a gated mews of hi-tech houses and flats by the leafy cemetery.

North of **Lordship Park** is **Allerton Rd**, a great choice if you like outdoor pursuits. One end is overshadowed by a bizarre Gothicky water tower – now home to Britain's premier indoor climbing centre (a flats scheme next to it is graced with the name 'Castle View'). And homes on the N side of the street have gardens backing onto the reservoirs. No longer needed to store water, one has re-emerged as Stoke Newington West Reservoir Centre, the fine facilities of which include dinghy sailing, fishing, windsurfing, sub-aqua and dragon-boat racing, while the East is now a developing wildlife reserve. To the W of **Green Lanes**, the former filter beds hold a mix of housing-association and open-market homes; at the junction with **Portland Rise**, recent 2- and 3-bed flats, and 4-bed town-houses.

Allerton Rd leads into **Queen Elizabeth's Walk**: here you pay over half a million for a 4-bed house at the S end, where the houses overlook Clissold Park. The back gardens of these are in turn overlooked by council-built low-rise. Look out for the lovely double-fronted terraces in the Walk – rare beauties: one sold for £800,000 last winter. Tree-lined **Fairholt Rd** and (untrendy) shop-studded **Dunsmure Rd** complete Stoke's northern reaches. Both contain generous bay-fronted family houses, some flats, some council. Look hereabouts for large houses at (somewhat) lower prices. In **St Andrew's Mews** 53 flats appeared, set around a landscaped courtyard.

Running S, houses tend to be less tidied. **Bethune Rd, Heathland Rd, St Andrews Grove** and busy **Lordship Rd** are all edged by large, often done-up and split up, Victorian bay-fronted houses – Lordship in particular the scene of much renovation work. The E–W streets – **Paget Rd, St Kilda's Rd** and **Grangecourt Rd** – are smaller, with mainly 2-storey terraces: some very pretty, notably the S side of Grangecourt Rd and St Kilda's Rd between Bethune and Heathland Rds. The area, close to Stamford Hill, has a strong Hasidic Jewish community, and homes often do not appear on the open market.

South of Manor Rd the streets are noticeably smarter. Most of the renovation work here has already been done, with hardly a break now in the glistening paintwork and new planting. Here **Bouverie Rd** matches **Queen Elizabeth's Walk** in desirability. Homes with even numbers back onto the leafy cemetery, and there is light industry at the S end. Odd-numbered houses are either large, 4-storey and flat-fronted or charming 2-storey terraces. Low odd numbers have small gardens. This street, though, is used as a traffic shortcut; more peaceful are the pleasant homes in **Yoakley, Grayling** and **Grazebrook Rds**.

Yoakley Rd has a charming Victorian terrace in the E side, broken now and then by small, eccentric detached villas. Again, houses here rarely come on the market – and are snapped up if they do. Much of the W side is humdrum council low-rise. Running E–W, **Grayling Rd** has lovely 2-storey bay-fronted houses and **Grazebrook Rd** has 3-storey terraces on the W side overlooking the edge of a largish, modern council estate. **Fleetwood St** runs N off Church St, a short, one-sided, Victorian terrace running up to the cemetery and local fire station. Running parallel, **Summerhouse Rd**, too, has some beautiful Victoriana; **Wilmer Place** a development that includes commercial as well as 10 flats (resales are around £178,000 for 1-beds; £230,000, 2-beds) and 14 town-houses.

Stoke Newington central

Stoke Newington central – the old village of Shacklewell – lies S of **Church St**, W of the **High St**, and has as its W and S border **Green Lanes, Matthias Rd** and **Barrett's Grove.** It is this central area, with its mid-19th-century mix of 2-storey terraces interspersed with streets of bigger buildings, which saw the first ungentlemanly price leaps in the late 1980s, although the large houses to the NE have made the biggest jumps this time around.

The area is split in two by **Albion Rd**, a bus route and general N–S thoroughfare. Here 3-storey terraces (a 4-bed/3-recep, £455,000) give way to large, renovated Victorian blocks – the street's been just about completely tidied. As it goes S, the road narrows and is lined by 3-storey, bay-fronted Victoriana, split into flats by a housing trust and seldom for sale. At No. 147, however, a Grade II-listed house is now flats, with four new houses in the garden. These big, double-fronted 1820s houses ask c. £650,000 when whole.

West of **Albion Rd**, running to Clissold Park, lies what hopeful estate agents some years back dubbed the 'North Islington Overspill Quadrant', no less. Despite the hyperbole this patch is well worth a look, and friendly-trendies are so doing. **Winston Rd** has small 2-storey houses, and off it look out for **Reedholm Villas** – a wee gem of a cul-de-sac. **Springdale Rd** and **Aden Grove** have bigger homes; **Burma Rd**'s are 3- and 4-storey ones.

The twin curves of **Clissold Crescent** and **Carysfort Rd** also have larger, late-Victorian houses (a 4-bed, £500,000), many sporting original porch tiles or glass (also, in the latter, brickwork painted a variety of colours); most gardens are tiny, however. Here, too, is London's largest scheme of flexible live/work units, phased in over the past couple of years: Red Square by Ballymore has 120 units round a courtyard. The domed red blocks have deck access to encourage neighbourliness. These sold at from £175,000 (for 700 sq ft) to c. £330,000 (extra-large duplexes; 3-bed flats). Resales currently c. £210,000 for a 1-bed, £250,000 for 2-beds. A factory conversion, **Indigo Mews**, is also live/work.

Clissold Crescent, too, boasts recent developments: on the E side of the road is the hi-tech building of the ill-fated Clissold Leisure Centre (closed till 2006: see above). At the crescent's S end is a cache of housing-association and private flats. In **Hawksley Rd**, a Victorian school became 'Scholars Yard': 1-, 2- and 3-bed flats by Durkan, while Albion House on **Church St** now holds six roomy warehouse flats sold as shells.

To the E of **Albion Rd**, N of **Barbauld** and **Dynevor Rds** is a maze of charming little streets, lined mainly with 2- and 3-bedroomed houses. Though occasionally turned into tiny flats, for the most part these streets remain relatively unspoilt. Some houses are bigger, with a semi-basement floor as in the N side of **Dumont Rd**; light industry behind.

Defoe Rd has St Mary's, a church hall split into live/works and flats. Also Laing's Victorian-style The Point: 1–3 bed flats (from c. £235,000, all sold); now selling are the 14 4-bed/3-storey town-houses, from c. £400,000, plus five 4-bed/2-storey mews homes.

South of **Barbauld Rd** and the kink in **Nevill Rd** the area changes. The well-designed low-rise estate on Nevill's E side faces shops with flats above. From here a ladder of roads – **Beatty Rd** down to **Barrett's Grove** – hold some larger 3/4-storey houses. **Beatty, Walford** and **Brighton Rds** have houses with big gardens on their N sides. Many now flats.

S

The further S you go, the cheaper; but this less-tidy corner has been smartening – especially **Palatine** and **Brighton Rds**. Palatine has smaller 2-storey houses, but the W end finishes with a strange ziggurat configuration of buildings, recently tidied; between this street and Brighton Rd, a group of architects has squeezed in three houses. **Prince George Rd** enjoys open space halfway down, with tennis courts. **Belgrade** and **Princess May Rds** and **Barrett's Grove** are a mix of 2- and 3-storey houses. In this corner, too, are the Textile Building and Button Court: the former an industrial conversion into convincing live/work units and 4-bed house, the latter a contemporary balconied flats block.

North of **Allen Rd**, **Milton Grove** and **Shakspeare Walk** are 4-storey terraces, now often flats – narrowish streets given the heights of the buildings, but some get superb-sized gardens. Shakspeare Walk's handsome, half-million-plus houses are particularly popular. **Londesborough, Osterley** and **Clonbrook Rds** have 3-storey houses and many council flats.

South of **Allen Rd**, a new mews squeezed in between it and Butterfield Green; then the area gives way to a bleak 1950s estate, improved though by bright paint, trees, turf. Nearby streets hold friendly shops with a wide and interesting range of goods.

Stoke Newington South

This area lies S of **Green Lanes/Matthias Rd/Barrett's Grove**, N of **Balls Pond Rd**, W from **Wallace Rd/Petherton Rd** and follows King Henry's Walk back to **Stoke Newington Rd**. This stretch of Green Lanes has been much smartened in the past few years – and now, at its end, **Newington Green** is once more a focal point. It had dwindled into a dilapidated, traffic-marooned, wino-ridden scrub: now landscaping, playground, wide pavements, new crossings have reclaimed the Green for all, including families. Round it stand not only some Georgiana but four even earlier homes – these, amazingly, survive from the 1650s ('Cromwellian' is not a common architectural reference).

And great improvements, too, to the humdrum later surroundings: at the junction with **Albion Rd**, the charitable Peabody Trust built Holland House, its landmark round tower of flats, plus medical centre: see introduction. The council estate to the S is also renovating – and just finishing is the transformation of what was the China Inland Mission by Haworth Tompkins Architects: with a new-build block behind, now 191 student flats. (A scattering of recent houses on the Green were built and designed by architects for themselves.) Next, there's the old petrol station site on the Green's E side: watch this space. . . .

Starting in the NW of the neighbourhood, **Leconfield Rd** snakes southwards and is edged with 2-storey bay-fronted Victoriana with semi-basements. Light industry at the N end is the downside; large gardens the up. **Poet's Rd**, similar in size to the Leconfield Rd end, is first in a ladder of streets: **Ferntower Rd, Pyrland Rd, Beresford Rd** and the E end of **Grosvenor Avenue.** All have big 3- and 4-storey houses with good gardens, but the S side of **Grosvenor Avenue** backs onto the railway, as does the N side of **Northampton Grove,** where pretty 2-storey cottages are uncomfortably hemmed in by light industry. **Northampton Park** curves S to join the Balls Pond Rd and is a wide, tree-lined street of handsome Victorian villas, one agreeable low-rise scheme and one laughable modern attempt at Victorian proportions. Echoing its curve, but accessed from **Wallace Rd,** is Terrazza, Laing's sleek terrace of contemporary 3-bed houses. Canonbury station is round the corner – and note that it will be on the East London Line Extension: see Transport chapter – but Canonbury *proper* lies S across the roaring Balls Pond Rd.

Crowning this area is wide **St Paul's Place**, where the unspoilt 4-storey, flat-fronted terrace has gracious curved windows, its stucco-finished first storey painted uniformly grey. This street has an air of calm superiority, unlike anything nearby. Discreet **Bingham St** is lined with lovely double-fronted but modest-sized houses. It joins **Newington Green Rd**, an extension of Albion Rd, running S from the Green with buses and through-traffic. Lined with shops, pubs and eateries, it holds most of the neighbourhood's amenities. Some flats are found above shops, and well-maintained council-built terraces lead into a medium-sized high-rise estate, entered by **Mildmay St** and **Mildmay Avenue**.

This introduces the 'Mildmay' area, where prices are high – sometimes deservedly, sometimes not. Running E–W through the middle is **Mildmay Grove**, eccentrically not one but two streets, separated along their length by the railway line. The houses stand behind front gardens, and gaze at each other across the walls which separate the grand terraces from the trains (soon to include Eurostar in a tunnel beneath the tracks). Large back gardens help to hold prices. Now, through an arch in one terrace, a mews of four highly unusual 2-bed courtyard houses and live/work studios is appearing on some back-land:

the plans have already won a Housing Design Award for Peter Barber Architects.

Busy **Mildmay Park** runs N–S. It is bordered by 4-storey buildings, mostly flats, and a housing-association scheme which included some 14–17 flats for outright sale. **Mildmay Rd** runs E–W, with some charming 3- and 4-storey houses, a featureless 1960s block, and homes at the E end overlooking another bleak council high-rise. In between, wide **Wolsey Rd** and **Queen Margaret's Grove** are well worth a look, despite less-lovely council-build in the Grove. **King Henry's Walk** zigzags N–S and is a hotch-potch of mostly well-kept council-build to the N and Victorian shops sandwiched between less arresting structures. Continuing the Tudor theme, **Boleyn Rd** runs N–S: formerly grim, the estate here is now tidied. **Pellerin Rd** runs E, and has pretty 2-storey Victorian houses on one side.

Across **King Henry's Walk** Stoke meets Dalston and Kingsland by Dalston Cross, where Balls Pond Rd/Dalston Lane meet Kingsland Rd/High St. This corner holds Dalston Kingsland mainline – N of which, round **Bradbury St** and **Gillett St**, is emerging the splendid Gillett Square, a new heart for the area complete with new home for the Vortex Jazz Club (see Hackney chapter). Over the Cross will be the new East London Line station.

Look in this corner for many a small site, now empty, to be developed as all this emerges – not before time. The S end of **Boleyn Rd** and the streets off it were desolate for years; a place where houses once stood and others, boarded up, waited for the renewal which has taken place further N. **Bradbury St** saw the process begin and now boasts a bohemian jazz bar. At last two new developments, one Peabody Trust (by local architects Bernstein Levitt), one by Presentation Housing Association, made a big difference; more homes now, both social and open market, in **Boleyn Rd**. In another example of community spirit, locals transformed a disused playground into a 'millennium peace garden'.

Stoke Newington East and borders

North now, to the neighbourhood E of **Stoke Newington Rd/High St** and **Stamford Hill** and bordered to the N and E by the busy **Clapton Rd**. The SE border follows **Brooke Rd**, then S again down **Rectory Rd** and **Shacklewell Lane** back to Dalston (see Hackney). The further N, the larger the houses, interspersed by the large Stamford Hill and Broad Common Estates. This big area is split by main E–W through roads: **Cazenove Rd**, **Northwold Rd**, **Evering Rd** and **Manse Rd**.

Stoke Newington High St and its continuation, **Stamford Hill**, are themselves seeing new homes: a clutch of 1- and 2-bed flats appeared at No. 181 in the High St on a site that once housed a brewery and, later, a hosiery shop. The old bus garage gave way to housing-association flats and houses. Latest, next to the police station, is Durkan's mixed scheme: 41 1- and 2-beds, from £190,000, above a bar/café and some business units.

At the northernmost, Stamford Hill end, **Leweston Place** has Victorian terraces on one side of the road, 1930s semis on the even side. **Darenth Rd** has large Victorian bay-fronted houses, some with basements; at its S end **Lynemouth Rd** and **Lampard Grove**, blighted by an unlovely MFI store. A site in **Windus Rd** with planning for flats above a shop may signal the start of a move to residential for a down-at-heel corner just N of the station.

Popular **Alkham**, **Kyverdale**, **Osbaldeston**, **Forburg** and charming **Chardmore Rds**, however, have half-million-plus Victoriana (also stylish church-to-flats conversion). These quiet, tree-lined streets – skip-lined, too: their size (big basements) attract young families.

S

South of **Cazenove Rd** many houses are now flats and, although streets seem narrow for the size of houses, large gardens compensate in some. Streets get smaller again E of **Fountayne Rd**, with 2-storey/basement Victoriana, bordering Northwold council estate; **Northwold Rd** has local shops – and Peabody's big Raines Dairy scheme: see introduction.

Across it, to the S, **Jenner Rd**, **Benthal Rd**, **Maury Rd** and **Norcott Rd** are now quiet due to an eccentric traffic system. These Victorian houses (£350,000-plus for a 4-bed) enjoy generous gardens. Odd-numbered houses in **Jenner Rd** back onto the railway (Rectory Rd station is handy), but generally these are desirable streets. On eastwards

Alconbury, Geldeston, Narford and **Reighton Rds** have mostly well-maintained mid-sized Victoriana – but E from here is **Upper Clapton Rd**: see Hackney.

Between the **High St** and **Rectory Rd**, N of **Brooke Rd** with its organic farmers' market (the country's first), is the Brooke Rd Estate; this improves towards the E and is bordered on that side by a beautiful 4-storey flat-fronted terrace facing the remains of Stoke Newington Common. Running S, **Darville, Bayston** (the better pair; a big 4-bed £450,000), **Leswin** and **Tyssen Rds** have mainly smaller 2-storey houses, some with cellars (c. £375,000 for a done-up 3-bed). Tyssen is remarkably peaceful, despite the nearby High St.

South of **Evering Rd**, curving **Amhurst Rd** returns the homeseeker to larger houses, 3-storey with semi-basements. **Foulden Rd** and **Sydner Rd** are narrower and have smaller houses; again, closer to the **High St** commercial buildings impinge. The S side of **Farleigh Rd** (which has some big houses) backs onto the Somerford Grove Estate; the E end is overlooked by The Beckers, a bleak 1960s eyesore estate. This is the least expensive part of Stoke. Further S, the Somerford Estate is bordered by areas of light industry. What housing there is, is sandwiched between ugly factories and a 1930s council block, making this section less appealing than anywhere further north.

Transport Trains: Stoke Newington, Rectory Rd to Liverpool St. Dalston Junction, Canonbury will be on E London Line. Buses to West End.

Convenient for City. Buses to tube at Highbury & Islington (Victoria Line direct to West End). Miles from centre: 4.5.

Schools Local Authority: Stoke Newington, Kingsland, Our Lady's Convent RC, Skinners Senior (g). Good schools open to Orthodox Jews only, and also one Muslim school, in Stamford Hill.

SALES

Flats	S	1B	2B	3B	4B	5B
Average prices	120–160	150–230	190–290	260–335	300–350+	350–410
Houses	2B	3B	4B	5B	6/7B	8B
Average prices	250–330	300–420	400–500	450–600	525–670	–

RENTAL

Flats	S	1B	2B	3B	4B	5B
Average prices	120–160	150–210	210–270	250–330	330–400	430–500
Houses	2B	3B	4B	5B	6/7B	8B
Average prices	220–240	250–350	330–410	480–550	550–620	–

The properties Mid- to late-Victorian terraces, much done up, plus a few far earlier ones around the Green. Highest prices generally to W of High St. Some Victorian and 1930s flats blocks; much council-build; new homes, p/b and converted, live/work, etc. in all available corners.

The market Professionals/media people/Islington refugees move here. The area S of Church St is the most popular — and highly priced – but people now moving north to the better-value streets towards Stamford Hill (seen, too, as safer than venturing further east).

Among estate agents active in this area are:

- Philip Phillips
- Holden Matthews
- Michael Naik
- Brooks
- Next Move
- Patrick Joseph
- Oakwood
- Winkworth
- Foxtons
- Bairstow Eves
- Keatons

STRATFORD AND NORTH NEWHAM

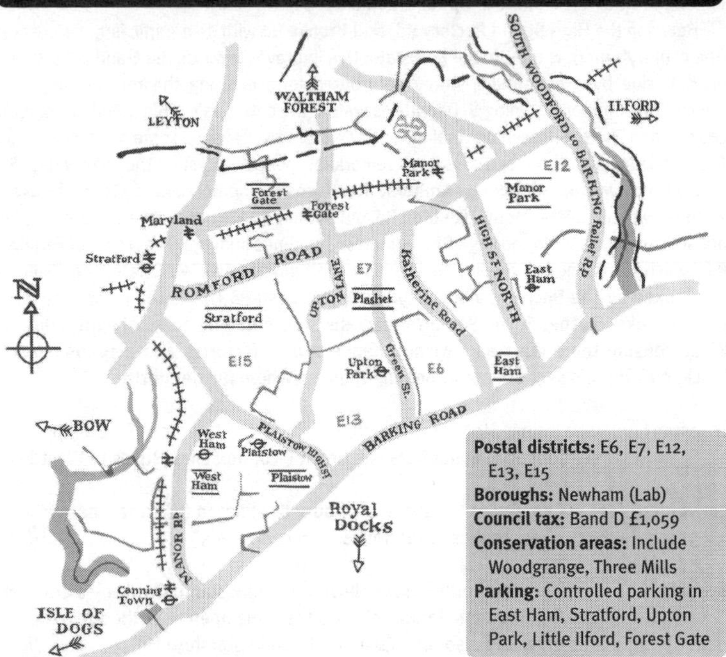

Postal districts: E6, E7, E12, E13, E15
Boroughs: Newham (Lab)
Council tax: Band D £1,059
Conservation areas: Include Woodgrange, Three Mills
Parking: Controlled parking in East Ham, Stratford, Upton Park, Little Ilford, Forest Gate

Anticipation became apprehension in the early weeks of 2005 as Stratford estate agents waited for the International Olympic Committee's visit. Hyping up the place to attract – what's the collective noun for lemmings – well, *lots* of buy-to-let investors in recent years was the easy part. The beady-eyed veterans of the IOC, immured by now to the charms of a hundred cities, were a tough audience.

But come Olympics, go Olympics – the Eurostar station is here, will be open soon (early in 2007) and has already propelled Stratford into the premier league of London investment locations. Those lemmings (sorry, investors) in evidence so far are just the beginning, say the estate agents, who have plenty to offer them up to and including 3-bed flats for £400,000. It's not that long – just back in 1998 – since the average 3-bed flat here was £40,000 and the most expensive homes in the borough were £150,000.

Stratford will soon be the hub of six, maybe eight, rail systems, with fast and modern links to the City, Docklands – and direct to Paris. A decade back, it was a tatty East London town centre, blighted by traffic and known in the rest of London only for its theatre – and its poverty.

The key is Stratford International, a giant new station connecting Channel Tunnel trains to local and tube trains, and to lines that will allow you to go direct to the north and east of England, and to Scotland. This is on schedule – and any cynic who doubts should climb to the top of Stratford's town-centre car park and look to the north. There they will see the enormous, kilometre-long station taking shape. The fast line to the Channel Tunnel is already complete and in use across Kent; the giant machines have finished the tunnels to St Pancras. Already in use, the splendid Jubilee tube station has links with the Central Line, the DLR, the Silverlink Metro (North London Line) and trains into Liverpool Street and out to Essex. It will link into the new International station, too, and via an extended DLR down to the Royal Docks.

A quick exit-route is one thing, but is there anything about Stratford, and its Newham hinterland, that makes it worth staying put, if you are not a native? Over the past few years, the centre has transformed. A spacious pedestrian square round the renowned Theatre Royal holds the new library and a smart cinema, and links through to the bustling, bright shopping centre. Stratford Circus, a superb new arts centre, exists but has had a troubled start in life. Barratt's re-use of a town-centre office block as flats in this precinct complements the culture.

Just N of the station square – itself a very handsome addition – is the entrance to the planned Stratford City site, all 180 acres of it around the International station.

Stratford is also the key to the Lea Valley regeneration zone, running S–N from Canary Wharf up to Leyton, and which is the centre of the London 2012 Olympics bid – guaranteed to trigger a range of development projects even without the Games.

Fore-knowledge of transport plans, plus some active promotion of the place, led to a positive craze to buy homes in Stratford. Smart flats have sprung up, old buildings have become loft apartments; little terraced houses have shot up in value. In 2003 Stratford was one of the few places in London where the buy-to-let fever continued unchecked as investors gambled on values rising when the infrastructure completes. Prices went on rising in the first half of 2004, but by December they were falling back.

It took the opening of the Jubilee Line in 2000 to really convince the rest of London that Newham was worth a second look. The swooping canopy over the Stratford station is a crucial contribution to the revival of the town centre – London Transport's architect cruelly but aptly called pre-Jubilee Line Stratford 'an abandoned city'. The post-War world was grim for the East End.

The next step is to finish the Eurostar station: it is on schedule (for once) for early 2007. Then comes Stratford City: developers Chelsfield and Stanhope speak of a new 'metropolitan centre' for East London, integrated with central Stratford. There is outline permission for some five million sq ft of offices (compare Canary Wharf: six million sq ft at present); a big-as-Bluewater retail centre; 4,500 new homes – with a 50-storey tower next to the station as the centrepiece. Some 35,000 jobs are expected to be created. The development should begin to the south of the new station from 2006, with completion in phases by 2020. Its site, prudently, is being raised five metres above the Lea Valley floodplain by the use of the soil dug out for the International station and tunnels.

Excitingly, the developers intend to remove all the unsightly pylons and power cables from the site. It's proposed that a high-capacity link of some sort will move passengers from the International station into the development. The existing centre will be linked to the new one by a 'living bridge' (wide, tree'd) over the railway just N of **Meridian Square**.

So much for the future. What of this area's present? Newham borough, which spreads E, S and N from Stratford, takes in what might be called the outer East End. The old boroughs of East Ham and West Ham, themselves successors to a dozen medieval hamlets, mushroomed in the second half of the 19th century. In 1965 they merged: hence 'Newham'. The borough also takes in the vast landscape of the Royal Docks. Decline was Newham's theme right from its inception, as East London lost both its industry and its docks in two decades. Docklands has been transformed (see that chapter – and the chapter on the Royal Docks & South Newham). Now, it might be said, it's Stratford's turn.

History still casts a long shadow. Over a quarter of Newham's houses were destroyed in the Blitz. This, plus the borough's legacy of poor housing, led to a programme of slum clearance and regeneration: the result was a legion of council-flat tower blocks (fewer now: the most notorious were blown up), post-war terraces, patchy gentrification of the remaining Victorian villas, and a general 1970s plastic-cladded tattiness. But the 1980s saw a renewal of private new-build, with the stress on low-rise developments. This continued through the 1990s, with smart flats appearing in Stratford centre of all places. Newham still has drab, seedy districts. Equally, most parts seem affordable to anyone with a West London perspective, though not as bargain-basement as they were.

The Jubilee Line Extension has received the limelight, but all of North Newham has long had reasonable tube and rail links into the City and West End, and has historically been a dormitory area for London's armies of clerks and shop-workers.

Today's Newham is a young borough, with a very high proportion of people below 25. Building on its East End heart, it is one of the most diverse places in London, if not the world, with large communities originating from the Indian subcontinent and elsewhere.

Stratford is the nerve centre, dominating the area. Newham, though, takes in a dozen other distinct neighbourhoods, each with their history. To the south (and with their own chapter) are the Royal Docks, with names such as Canning Town, Custom House, Silvertown. Covered here are cosmopolitan Manor Park, East Ham, Plashet, Plaistow and the respectable Victorian suburb of Forest Gate – historically the most expensive place to buy a home in Newham, until the Royals and (more recently) Stratford took off.

Stratford

Stratford's good transport and young and optimistic atmosphere attract home-buyers who work in the City or Docklands, and who need accessible housing. Stratford's status as a shopping and entertainment centre has been enhanced by the new 'Culture Quarter' (see Introduction). The existing (but smartened) Mall has been joined by a Morrrisons superstore in **The Grove** in a scheme that includes a new parade of shops, a library, hotel and parking. In **Burford Rd** to the S of the town centre is Hallings Wharf/Victoria Mills, a smart mixed-use scheme with business space and around 100 live/work units in a small town square. These offer flexible, hi-tech flats with moveable walls: 900 sq ft for £275,000. **Jupp Rd** has 24 new flats, some for sale, some shared-ownership. Along **Stratford High Street** to the SW, 78 new flats provide Affordable Housing, and a block of 200 more is planned. The former Co-op building has been converted from offices into 142 homes and two large shops.

New flats schemes are queuing up to be noticed: opposite the theatre and arts centre, Barratt turned a 9-storey office block into The Heights: 140 1- and 2-bed flats; resales in this so-central block now £260–300,000. Round in **The Grove**, also part of the centre, The Q Building completed in 2003: 3-bed flats sell for c. £300,000. Just N of the centre, and handy for the new station, Barratt's The Mill in **Windmill Lane** has 1- and 2-beds in a new (in 2003) block with a rooftop gym. On the **Romford Rd**, to the E, Barratt has split an old college into The Quadrangle – converted (and some new-build, called Stratford Square) 1 and 2-beds, and 4-bed town-houses, from £197,000 to £367,000. Barratt addressed the less affluent (or perhaps less location-savvy) with another flats block, New Central House, described honestly as 'just off the Bow Flyover, E15': current price for a 1-bed up to £200,000.

Not far away, and equally handy for the A11, is Fairview's Waterside Gardens in **Blaker Rd**, where 2-beds flats are c. £230,000; the 'water' is the City Mill River canal, and the 10-minute walk to Pudding Mill Lane DLR station is not yet pleasant. Up the Lea, on the border with Hackney Wick, is 'Fish Island', a newly coined name for a clutch of streets (**Roach Rd, Bream St** . . .) where a live/work scheme, with 57 units, completed last year. On **Warton Rd**, opposite one planned entrance to Stratford City, Telford Homes plan 249 flats in three blocks – one of 18 storeys – on the site of an old warehouse.

S

Existing homes around Stratford include rows of Victorian terraced houses, flats carved out of these with varying degrees of skill (remember, homes are still inexpensive here and recently were very cheap), ex-council housing and a few private flats.

East and north-east of the centre, the surroundings are grimmer – in part because the enormous rail construction site impinges. Nevertheless, 2-bed flats in **Louise Rd** were c. £135,000 last winter, while 2-bed terraced houses were c. £210,000. This is where you'll find the real **Albert Square**: an anticlimax of a road that doesn't resemble a square or 'The Square'. Neatly anonymous c. £240,000 terraced houses line this street – and, indeed, most of the area bounded by **Forest Lane** to the S and Forest Gate to the E. But new flats are also to be found there, and they are modestly priced. Closer to Stratford centre, **Windmill Lane** and **Carolina Close** are popular for their purpose-built flats, well placed for Stratford International station. **Manbey Park Rd** is the centre of a popular little enclave, with a choice of flats converted from Victorian houses (1-beds up to £170,000). Two local housing associations are responsible for the 11-storey tower with 105 flats at Maryland Point just opposite Maryland station. There are 41 shared ownership, 52 outright sale and 12 rented homes.

South from the centre, follow **West Ham Lane** past Queen Mary's Square, an enclave of 1980s 1- and 2-bed flats, part private and part housing association. It's convenient (and next to the police station). Nearby **Aldworth Rd** is popular; other good roads include **Tennyson** and **Vernon Rds** and **Pitchford St**: a 2-bed terrace c. £200–220,000.

Church St North has real character, a glimpse of what Stratford could be all about; a handful of Victorian 3-storey houses that have been marketed for over £300,000. Recently-built town-houses stand elegant in the privacy of this quiet turning. The **Portway** is a pleasure with its solid, gabled 3-storey Victorian houses (£320–380,000), and runs S of the surprisingly verdant West Ham Park. Off the Portway, **Evesham Rd**'s 3-bed houses are cheaper. Across to the N of the Park, **Mathews Park Avenue** was once optimistically dubbed the 'Little Hampstead of Stratford'. Hardly – but the grid it inhabits has quiet(ish) streets, with the green park at their foot. Happy householders here, with last winter's prices around £280,000 (1998: £80,000). **Ham Park Rd**, which faces the park, is a local favourite: here the houses are large, Victorian, some smart, lots of original features: a 5-bed could be over £300,000.

Plashet

Plashet is a rather ill-defined neighbourhood N of Upton Park and S of Manor Park. Here are some of Newham's more desirable homes ('a safe bet' say agents), and a highly regarded girls' school. Look in **Stopford Rd** for family homes: 3-bed and large 1930s houses at £190–220,000. Similar prices in the neighbourhood E along **Plashet Grove** as far as **High St North**, East Ham. The cluster of streets to the N of **Plashet Rd** is known as Upton: slightly smarter than Upton Park, and with the use of the latter's tube station.

Forest Gate

Forest Gate, on the edge of Epping Forest, has long been considered the jewel in Newham's crown. The area has kept much of its leafy village feel and Victorian character. It is perhaps the priciest part of Newham, particularly in Woodgrange Park with its large 19th-century houses. Here too is one of the best Victorian parks in London, at Wanstead Flats. It also has trains to the City via Stratford. Some areas of Forest Gate are in need of an uplift, however, and council funds have been allocated.

Capel Rd overlooks Wanstead Flats, the southernmost outpost of Epping Forest (hence 'Forest Gate'). There are some modern 4- and 5-bed houses which compete with the original family-sized late Victorian terraces: these are now £350–400,000, with smaller 3-beds at c. £280,000 (1-bed flats c. £170,000). Capel Manor, a Grade II-listed manor, was converted 15 years ago into luxury flats, with town-houses neatly attached.

'Woodgrange Village' (an estate agents' term for the gentrified Woodgrange estate, running up towards less-fashionable Manor Park) is a pleasant cache of streets. The conservation area instantly increases the price of houses in this part of Forest Gate, and even the nearby run-down council blocks have undergone a face-lift. A 2-bed terraced near the pretty little station (more ornament than use) wil be c. £180–210,000; but the estate's claim to fame is its handsome, low 1880s villas in orderly, leafy streets to the E of **Woodgrange Rd**. Wander down **Richmond Rd**, **Hampton Rd**, **Claremont Rd** or **Windsor**

Rd to view these regal-sounding residences – a 5-bed sold last autumn for £485,000. Some have front drives and distinctive, original glass porches extending across the width of the house, fringed with decorative wooden 'teeth' (think Victorian railway-station canopies). Over to the W, streets round **Earlham Grove** such as **Norwich Rd** have some larger, solid Edwardian houses which also aspire to £400,000-plus prices. In **Woodgrange Rd** itself, opposite Wanstead Park station, a new development of 177 homes is planned, with 57 for sale, the rest other tenures.

Manor Park

Manor Park is largely devoted to resting places. Lacquer-black horse-and-carriage Cockney funerals regularly plod to the huge City of London Cemetery or Manor Park's own smaller graveyard. But the area is far from dead: it's brash, cosmopolitan and bustling, especially in the area around the **Romford Rd,** and has good transport links.

The neighbourhood of Little Ilford, on the E side, is a quiet backwater, and the parks and playing fields in the W of Manor Park form a welcome break from the row upon row of terraced housing. Streets S of **Romford Rd** named **First** to **Seventh Avenues** offer 4-bed terraces for (much as last year) £220–250,000. The heart of Manor Park is a comparatively sleepy area to the S, off the High St, centring on poetic-sounding streets – **Browning Rd, Coleridge Avenue, Shakespeare Crescent** and **Shelley Avenue** reside here. Three-bed terraces in these ever-popular streets fetch £190–230,000 (for a large one), while c. £175,000 is the price to pay for a 2-bed Victorian terrace. Flat conversions abound: £140–170,000 buys a large 2-bed flat and £120–130,000 is the going rate for a 1-bed flat. Ex-council 1-beds, and those above shops, may be even less. Woodgrange Park House on Romford Rd – a former DHSS building – is now 'Lumiere', 60 flats.

Plaistow and West Ham

Plaistow is deceptively large, running from its District Line station in the N along the **High St,** down **Greengate St** and **Prince Regent Lane** to the A13. To the E it extends to the Abbey Arms pub on the **Barking Rd,** continuing along to **Green St** which marks the Boleyn neighbourhood of Upton Park. Scattered between the stock-brick terraces – rows and rows of them, varying widely in quality and location, c. £240,000 for a decent 3-bed – are new flats. One such Wimpey development lies tucked away behind the Memorial Recreation Ground (the birthplace of West Ham FC). Rowan Court in the **Broadway** and flats in **Plaistow Park Rd** offer a similar style. For something cheaper, larger and older look in **Balaam St** (pronounced Bale-am). A novelty hereabouts, a Victorian warehouse conversion: plenty of choice at the Spectacle Works, **Jedburgh Rd**, or a 2-bed flat in a Victorian boys' club on **Barking Rd.** A big tract of Post Office land SW of West Ham station will be developed soon with up to 2,300 homes, council planners intend.

One Plaistow neighbourhood has become very popular: the New City estate, a triangular grid of around 15 roads of terraced 20th-century houses centring on **New City Rd,** with **Boundary Rd** marking the E edge, **Barking Rd** (the A124) the N and **Tunmarsh Lane** to the S. This district abuts the well-regarded Central Park estate in East Ham (see below). For the S side of Plaistow, see the Royal Docks chapter.

S

Upton Park and East Ham

Upton Park is a fairly small neighbourhood, stretching from the tube station in **Green St** down to the Boleyn pub on the **Barking Rd** and extending E to **Katherine Rd. Green St** continues to prosper as a speciality Asian shopping (and restaurant) centre. Purpose-built flats and new terraces are scattered in the streets around the football ground.

East Ham is considered to be one of the best parts of Newham, and new flats and houses are being built, such as those in **Vicarage Lane.** Central Park is a popular inter-war terraced estate. **Cotswold Gardens** contains the only line of semis on the estate;

Lonsdale Rd, Henniker Gardens, Haldane Rd and most of the other streets have 2-bed 1930s terraces – some with ground-floor bathrooms. **Central Park Rd** and its offshoots contain larger, often pebbledashed, versions. Houses in this area boast three double bedrooms and go on the market for over £250,000. For convenience, investigate the streets on the E side of **High St North**. Streets such as **Lathom Rd, Caulfield Rd, Clements Rd** and **Skeffington Rd** are within easy reach of the tube.

Streets running E to **Burges Rd** are a quiet, respectable neighbourhood where 3-bed houses are c. £225,000; look here, too, for 4-bed houses. There's a big contrast between **High St South** and **High St North**: look to the E of High St South, and you'll see suburbs mirroring those in Central Park, but a fraction cheaper. The huge minareted town hall divides the 'posher' south and the less-well-favoured but still popular north of East Ham.

Transport Tubes (all zone 3): Stratford (Central & Jubilee); Plaistow, East Ham (District – and Hammersmith & City at peak hours). From Stratford: Oxford Circus 30 min, City 12 min, Heathrow 90 min (1 change). DLR: Stratford to Royals Docks, City, Isle of Dogs. Trains: Stratford (Liverpool St 8 min). More to come: see text.

Convenient for City, Docklands, Epping Forest, M11 for M25. Miles from centre: 7.

Schools Local Authority: Forest Gate, Lister, Little Ilford, Plashet, Rokeby, Sarah Bonnell, Stratford, Trinity, Royal Docks, St Angela's RC (g), St Bonaventures RC (b). New Newham VIth Form College (NewVic). Private: Jamia Ramania Islamic Institute (b).

SALES

Flats	S	1B	2B	3B	4B	5B
Average prices	100–105	120–190	140–250	→	200–350	–
Houses	2B	3B	4B	5B	6/7B	8B
Average prices	150–210	165–300	200–340	250–400	–	–

RENTAL

Flats	S	1B	2B	3B	4B	5B
Average prices	100–130	140–160	160–190	190–220	220–260	250–300+
Houses	2B	3B	4B	5B	6/7B	8B
Average prices	160–210	190–240	250–300	275–325	350+	–

The properties Largely 1900s terraces of 2/3-bed homes and p/b flats. Woodgrange Park has larger Victorian houses, as do a few other pockets. East Ham has some inter-war family homes. Stratford has smart new flats. Plenty of ex-council homes.

The market Still affordable compared to other areas, luring investors/ speculators and first-timers. Some districts have very local markets. Plenty of homes to rent.

S

Among estate agents active in this area are:

- Charles Living & Son
- Douglas Allen Spiro
- Haart
- Halifax
- Taylors
- W J Meade
- Winkworth
- Spicer McColl
- J Webb
- A J Scott
- Adam Kennedy
- Property Link
- McDowalls
- Bryants
- Glen Rose

STREATHAM

Postal districts: SW16, SW2
Boroughs: Lambeth (Lab), Wandsworth (Con)
Council tax: Band D Lambeth £1,051, Wandsworth £597
Conservation areas: Many, incl Streatham Village: check with councils
Parking: Residents' zones

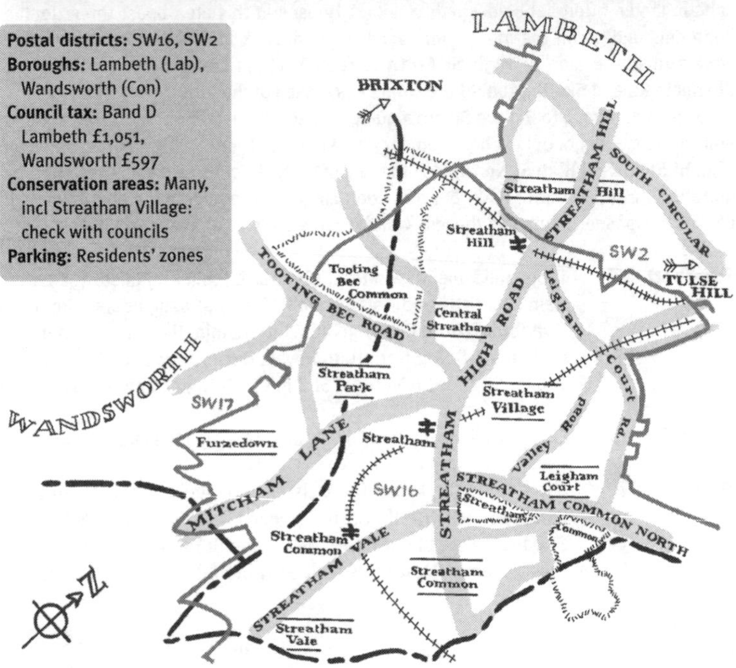

Key workers are in the vanguard of a steady flow of young Londoners discovering Streatham. The nurses, police persons, social workers and teachers who qualify for the government's £50,000 bounty have been seeking out the sub-£200,000 homes still to be had in this area. They join the private-sector 'young professionals' who have traditionally bought Streatham's 2-bed converted flats. Further up the market, families realize how close this area is to Dulwich's schools; they swap cramped terraces in Clapham or Balham, or a first-purchase Streatham flat, for garden-and-garage suburbia – 'it's not that much further out, really'. Making space for these incomers are families relocating beyond the M25 in search of schools.

Incomers are finding a smarter Streatham than of yore. Stung by the allegation that its High Road was Britain's scruffiest, council and business have combined to collect rubbish, wash pavements, increase policing. New bars and restaurants open and (to the applause of most locals) Caesars, the big nightclub on Streatham Hill, has closed. It will be replaced by a large Somerfields supermarket with flats above, according to the latest plans. One of the area's two cinemas has also become flats behind its listed facade.

Streatham's homes range from Victorian and Edwardian of all sizes from cottage to mansion, through '30s mansion blocks and semis to every variant on the modern – except perhaps the smart flats that Balham and Clapham have been gaining. Many older homes have been split over the years into flats of varying standards from the imaginative down through degrees of tiredness to grungy, though there's still a good selection of family houses (some *very* large) with gardens. Some neighbourhoods offer plenty of small houses, while the centre's mansion blocks, those great 1930s leviathans, offer value in £-per-sq-ft terms. Even so, agents report that the Streatham flat-buyer prefers 'period features' (Victorian twiddly bits) or smart modern to fading Art Deco.

What's missing is the transport. Driving north is a seriously bad idea, and there's no tube. The lack is in part psychological: Streatham boasts three rail stations – lines from Streatham Hill and Streatham Common converge one stop on at Balham (Northern Line tube interchange). Disappointing news on the tube front, though: Streatham will after all not gain a branch of the projected East London Line Extension (see Transport chapter).

Streatham's shape was defined when City merchants established magnificent estates here in the 18th/early 19th centuries. Modern Streatham splits into distinct neighbourhoods based to a large extent on these same estates: eager developers bought up their farmland following the coming of the railway in 1856. The last of the great mansions along the N side of the Common is Sir Henry Tate's, of sugar and Gallery fame: for long a convent, it's now homes – see below.

The neighbourhoods, radiating round the Common, hold great homes but currently lack a real heart. **Streatham High Rd** is hampered by its double duty as the area's high street and the relentlessly busy, six-lane, red-routed A23, one of the main arteries out of London and rated its second-busiest bus route. While smarter than it was, the High Rd decidedly lacks the charm of Dulwich or Bellevue, or the buzz of Clapham High Street.

Streatham Hill

At the top – in terms of geography, height, desirability and transport links – lies Streatham Hill: N of the station and wide, leafy **Leigham Court Rd,** E of **Rastell** and **King's Avenues,** S of **Atkins Rd/Christchurch Rd** (the South Circular), W of **Hillside Rd.** This increasingly popular area is in SW2 – which no longer has a stigma now that Brixton is so 'in'. As well as its own station, there's Brixton's Victoria Line tube a bus-ride away. The 'golden triangle' lies between **Kings/Thornton Avenues, Atkins Rd/Streatham Place** and **Streatham Hill:** the attractive period homes in **Killieser Avenue, Criffel Avenue** and **Kirkstall Rd** are very popular, with charming terraces and some larger houses. A 6-bed semi in Killieser was on the market for £785,000 last winter. **Criffel Avenue** also has some particularly nice maisonettes. There's a cache of respectable '30s semis in streets such as **Kirkstall Gardens.** There are also some purpose-built flats as well as conversions. Near parkland (we're on the Balham borders here), the large, idiosyncratic homes in the 1880s Telford Park estate N of **Sternhold Avenue** are highly regarded. Prices range up to £950,000. **Telford** and **Killieser Avenues** and **Montrell Rd** also have good converted flats.

The corner round the South Circular/**Streatham Hill** holds many a flat. **Palace Rd,** closed off at its junction with the South Circular, has a few surviving large 19th-century houses that make equally roomy flats (though a few are still single homes: £1 million has been asked, £800,000 is more realistic), and an ex-GLC estate in attractive grassy setting. At its far end **Leigham Vale,** down by the tracks and heading off for Tulse Hill, has some big (5-bed) Victorian terraces: the cheaper end of the market. Between **Leigham Court Rd** and Leigham Avenue is Leigham Lodge, last autumn's local hot spot as Galliard sold flats created from the 19th-century house, and refurbished single-storey, 350 sq ft 'cottages' in the lawned grounds. 'Atmosphere like a holiday village' commented an agent: these sell for £150,000-ish, rent for £650 a month.

Near Streatham Hill station are the curious 'ABCD' streets (**Amesbury, Barcombe, Cricklade** and **Downton Avenues**), with their red-brick terraced cottages and maisonettes built 1889–94 by the philanthropic Artisans & General Dwellings Company – these were the forerunners of council housing, many in Amesbury and Barcombe only becoming private under Right to Buy. There are few conversions (flats-to-houses ratio is about 1:4). Popularity runs in reverse (DCBA) order, with **Downton** (plus **Wavertree Rd**) and **Cricklade** having attractive later terraces, too: look for original stained glass in Cricklade, largest gardens in Downton. (In all four, gardens get smaller near the High Rd.) Four-beds are £365–385,000. Beneath the 'ABCDs' are largely '20s and stately red-brick, eg the leafy **Mount Nod Rd** (a 3-bed converted flat here, £225,000), but also note

Hitherfield – its Victorian cottage terraces lining a steep hill. The mansion flats along **Streatham Hill**, like those along **Streatham High Rd**, vary: some are good first-time buys – but check lease length; some have high service charges.

Central Streatham

Running E from **Garrad's Rd** to centre on **Streatham High Rd**, this neighbourhood contains some truly splendid houses. Well placed for the High Rd and the rail stations of Streatham and Streatham Hill, its leafy roads are popular. A noticeable feature of 'Central' is the epidemic of doctors' and dentists' name-plates; a good plus is that most houses have off-street parking – needed, due to the nearby High Rd.

Homes here are mainly attractive '20s and '30s detacheds and semis in a variety of styles – stucco and bay-windowed/tile-hung gables/mock-Tudor. There are large, impressive, 6-bed turn-of-the-20th-century houses in **Steep Hill**, **Woodbourne Avenue**, **Prentis Rd** (home to the South London Liberal Synagogue) and **Becmead Avenue**. Fewer homes have been split into flats here; survivors such as one 7-bed in **Ockley Rd** go for £600,000. Emsworth Court in the same road is flats with squash club adjoining; **Tarrington Close** has '70s houses. **Woodbourne Avenue** has some 5-bed '30s mock-Tudor semis; in **Kingscourt Rd** the 4-bed semis are Victorian. Modern homes on the corner of **Woodbourne Avenue** and **Garrad's Rd**: 3- and 4-bed houses, plus 18 flats in a converted Victorian building. Garrad's Rd itself has a few very large Edwardian mansions: these can be 5,000 sq ft. The roads to the N, running up to Streatham Hill station, have large period homes in varying states of repair. A number have been converted – particularly on the E side of the area near the High Rd. There are some spacious '30s houses in **Broadlands Avenue**. **Drewstead Rd**, next to Streatham Hill station, had a 5-bed house for £825,000 last autumn.

Search for flats and modern town-houses down near the other, Streatham, station: in **Gleneagle Rd**, for example, which runs along the tracks. On the corner with the High Rd is Barratt's new 'Eagle Heights': 48 1- to 3-bed flats by the station, starting at £155,000. **Conyer's Rd** has an '80s clutch of 1- and 2-bed flats and 1- and 3-bed houses, and new 4-bed town-houses.

Back W of the High Rd lies the Uttings estate, also known as Culverhouse: a quietly respectable area, its mix of Victoriana and smart chalet-style '20s/30s popular with locals. **Pendennis** and **Pinfold Rds** have '30s semis; the former with 60ft gardens, the latter large 5- or even 6-bed, £600,000, houses. Always in demand – especially the attractive 1930s ones. **Angles Rd** holds Peregrine Court, a courtyard scheme of 25 flats and houses.

Streatham Village

On S lies Streatham Village – which isn't as old as it sounds. The original nuclei of Streatham, around St Leonards Church and Streatham Common, date back to medieval times, whereas the 'Village' only appeared in the 19th century. Well located between Streatham and Streatham Hill stations, and near to the main shops, it is a conservation area. Houses are now very mixed in style, but rather appealing, especially the charming and much-in-demand 2- and 3-bed cottages in **Sunnyhill** and **Wellfield Rds**. Some newly-built 'cottages' compete with the originals. Period 2-beds are £235–250,000, 3-beds £250–300,000. There are also larger, early-Victorian villas in red brick (skilful conversions are to be found), some '30s houses and a few modern 2- and 3-bed homes.

The remaining streets, between **Gleneldon Rd**, **Valley Rd**, **Streatham Common North** and the High Rd, have a real assortment of homes from Victorian to early 20th-century and council-build. Increasingly desirable **Valley Rd** has some 3-bed/2-recep Edwardian maisonettes that are popular buys at c. £230–250,000. Impressive red-brick homes are found in **Gleneldon Rd**. Nearby, **Streatham High Rd** has flats both above shops and in 20th-century blocks: a 2-bed might be up to £155,000, but watch the service charges.

Leigham Court

Across Valley Rd to the E, leafy Leigham Court on its steep hill lies between **Valley Rd**, **Leigham Court Rd** and **Streatham Common North Side**. Basically council-built (though now mostly privately owned) to the N, with largeish, smart, '30s 4-bed semis and smaller, older houses to the S. New homes keep springing up here: the 1980s block of flats on the apex of **Valley** and **Leigham Court Rds** is popular, while **Fawcett Close**, off **Etherstone Rd**, is a pleasant 1998 Laing development. **Leigham Court Rd** was once lined with large detached Victorian mansions, standing in their own grounds – most have been turned into sought-after flats and commercial uses. The council has ambitious plans for already pleasant Leigham Court Estate, now a conservation area.

Streatham Common

One of the original nuclei of the town was here, the site of a spring that became a spa. This area, very popular with the professional classes, is filled with handsome Victorian and Edwardian houses with large gardens to the E side of the **High Rd** in roads such as **Heybridge Avenue**, **Fontaine Rd**, **Copley Park** and **Braxted Park** – pricey, highly desirable being near to the Common, with quiet leafy streets.

Above the Common, the **Hopton Rd/Polworth Rd** enclave is close to High Rd and station. East of the Common, 'much-requested' **Ryecroft Rd** loops round, with detached 3- to 5-bed houses (5-beds, 3 en-suites, gated drive £795,000) boasting large gardens. **Streatham Common North** has good Victorian/Edwardian 4- or 5-bed houses, mostly split into flats (a 2-bed, c. £195,000) – and the area's one remaining grand Regency mansion. Once owned by sugar magnate Sir Henry Tate, and the site of the original art gallery, it was for years a convent. Now it is homes. The rest of its two acres of land beside the common is 'Tate Gardens': Barratt's 2- to 5-bed neo-Regency town-houses: a 4-bed house re-sale, £450,000. Over on **Streatham Common South** a 5-bed house was £895,000.

Cheaper, if smaller, houses lie to the W of the High Rd (note, though, the attractive mock-Tudor of **Penistone Rd**). **Lewin** and **Barrow Rds** have many conversions (1-beds £175,000-plus); **Ferrers** and **Natal Rds** have smaller cottages, some of them split into flats and relatively cheap. **Green Lane**, on the very southern edge of the neighbourhood, has 4-bed detached homes.

Streatham Park

Streatham Park is bordered by **Tooting Bec Rd**, **Mitcham Lane**, **Thrale Rd** and the railway to the E. This was once the Thrale family's estate; visits by their friend Samuel Johnson are recalled by **Dr Johnson Avenue** (across Tooting Bec Common). Their mansion went in 1863 and the area now holds smart, well-maintained council-built blocks – notably the GLC-built Fayland Estate – most homes now private. A few stately villas from Streatham's late-18th-century heyday overlook the Common, a little noisy with the main road, mixed with modern infill (flats and houses). South of the council-built blocks, homes are small Edwardian, grand Victorian (some now flats) and quaint '30s whimsy. The area is leafy, quiet, attractive – look for **North Drive** and **Abbotsleigh Rd** – and taxed by Wandsworth.

The small patch to the E of the railway, towards the parish church, is possibly the oldest part of Streatham. **Pinkerton Place**, off **Tooting Bec Gardens**, has comfortable early '80s flats: small rooms, but well designed. Surrounding homes are mainly stately Victorian; sought-after roads with Lake District names (**Thirlmere Rd**, **Rydal Rd**, etc) have large 6/7-bed period houses, mostly flats; tree-lined **Riggindale Rd** has some good conversions of Victorian semis (a 3-bed flat, £250,000).

Furzedown

Furzedown lies N of the Tooting–Streatham railway, W of **Mitcham Lane/Thrale Rd** and E of **Rectory Lane**. Two-thirds is considered Streatham – roughly the roads N of **Southcroft**

Rd and E of **Freshwater Rd**; the rest is in Tooting (which chapter see). The whole lies in (cheaper) Wandsworth. This rather humdrum area is attracting families eager for a 4-bed house near good schools. It consists mainly of Edwardian terraces, 2- to 4-beds – and some bigger. The best are in **Clairview Rd,** off **Thrale Rd**: lovingly looked after, large, 6-bed homes. The rest of Furzedown has pockets of Victorian and '30s terraced houses. **Ribblesdale, Nimrod** and **Pretoria Rds** have 3- and 4-bed houses: £300–325,000. Things are cheaper to the E of **Mitcham Lane** as the transport is less good. **Rural Way**, off **Streatham Rd**, has a modern development of smart 3/4-bed houses.

Streatham Vale

The cheapest part of Streatham, offering cheaper homes to a still largely local market, the triangular Vale is bounded by converging rail lines to E and W, and by its small park and **Greyhound Terrace/Hassocks Rd** to the S. It's an area of very intensive housing with roads packed tightly together – more like Tooting than Streatham. Most was built by Wates in the '20s/'30s: rows of 2-storey terraces or semis; also a few flat conversions.

Transport Trains: Streatham Hill (Victoria 15 min); Streatham (London Bridge 18 min, Blackfriars 18 min); Streatham Common (Victoria 19 min, London Bridge 25 min).

Convenient for Routes to Gatwick Airport and South Coast. Miles from centre: 5.

Schools Local Authority: Dunraven School, Bishop Thomas Grant RC, La Retraite RC (g), Chestnut Grove, Graveney, St Martin in the Fields (g). Private: Streatham Hill & Clapham High (g); see also Dulwich.

SALES

Flats	S	1B	2B	3B	4B	5B
Average prices	100–130	130–165	160–240	190–250	200–275	–
Houses	2B	3B	4B	5B	6/7B	8B
Average prices	190–250	220–350	300–450	350–600	500–800	–

RENTAL

Flats	S	1B	2B	3B	4B	5B
Average prices	110–150	140–180	160–230	200–300	230–300	–
Houses	2B	3B	4B	5B	6/7B	8B
Average prices	200–230	250–300	375–415	325–450	400–500	–

The properties Some very large houses, Victorian and inter-war; finest overlook leafy commons. Roomy terraces of Victorian/Edwardiana, '20/30s semis, plus big blocks of mansion flats. Also useful ex-council flats (converted and p/b) and houses. Some pleasant new developments.

The market Here you still get more space and leafier surroundings for your money. Lack of tube (though trains, buses, plentiful) means lower prices in the more humdrum corners: a boon to first-timers. Look here for larger family homes with gardens, and good-value flats.

Among estate agents active in this area are:

- Charles Bartlay
- Winkworth
- Conways
- Haart
- Hooper & Jackson
- Kinleigh Folkard & Hayward
- Bushell
- Thomson Vale
- Townends
- Bonds
- Barnard Marcus

TOTTENHAM AND FINSBURY PARK

Postal districts: N22, N18, N17, N15, N4
Boroughs: Haringey (Lab), Islington (Lib Dem), Hackney (Lab)
COUNCIL TAX: BAND D
HARINGEY £1,259, ISLINGTON £1,107, HACKNEY £1,221
Conservation areas: Several: check with town hall
Parking: Controlled in Finsbury Park, Seven Sisters; extending

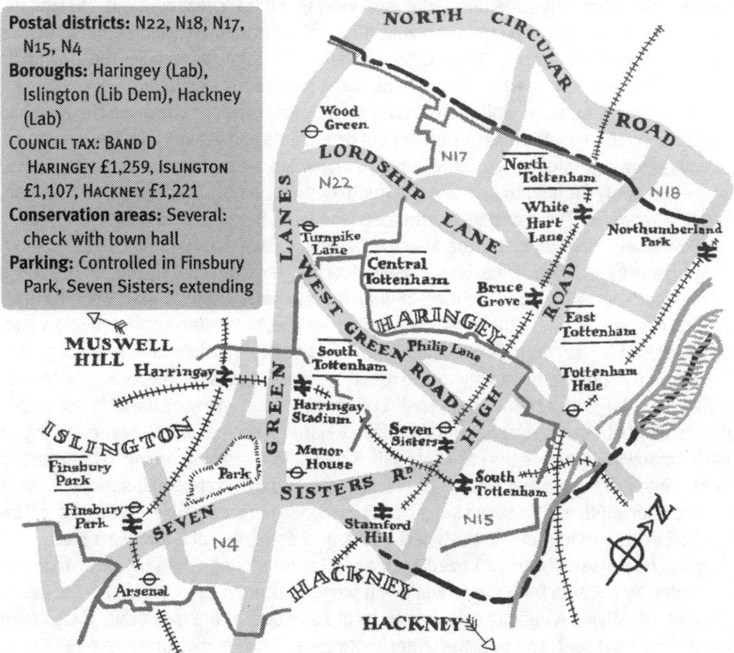

'Where else can you buy a nice 3-bed Victorian house for £250,000 and still be in the West End in 15 minutes?' ask the local agents hereabouts. The 'next to' effect has been working its magic on Tottenham, as prices in Stoke Newington and Crouch End moved beyond the reach of young buyers. What was an entirely local market has, over the past few years, seen the arrival of foot-soldiers in London's army of couples seeking that little terraced house in which to start a family. A good number of Tottenham's many rented homes, which were often of (very) low standard, have in consequence been either smartened up or sold. 'Key workers', especially teachers, have been finding homes here – and, apart from the terraces, new homes are being built to cater for them.

So what took this area so long? We're hardly talking edge-of-universe here – that's King's Cross three stops down the tube line (one change for Paris, soon). But this is one of those unfortunate corners on the edges of several boroughs and neglected by them all. Haringey council acknowledges that Tottenham is in the deprived half of its borough; indeed the contrast between Highgate in the W, and Tottenham Hale in the E, could scarcely be greater.

At last all of Finsbury Park and Tottenham are part of long-term (long-needed, long-awaited) regeneration strategies and considerable European Union funding. Numerous schemes exist, covering every aspect from the environment to education . . . And just north of Stoke Newington, in a bend of the New River and overlooking the reservoirs, the vast Woodberry Down Estate is to be transformed 'from an estate into a neighbourhood': early days, but there will be a net gain of 1,226 new social/key worker homes over the 2,500 existing, which will themselves be replaced/renewed over the coming years.

Meanwhile, new estate agencies have appeared in both Tottenham and Finsbury Park – with predictable results: fancy living in 'Brownswood Village'? Or 'Harringay Hills'?

These now follow 'Crouch End Heights' (of absurdity) onto the local scene: translations below. Owner-occupation has risen – with prices up, but rents not, there's less competition from buy-to-letters, who are moving off to cheaper areas. Residents' associations – always a sympton of 'gentrification' – have emerged in corners such as Tower Gardens and around Bruce Castle. Families pinpoint, especially, the Downhills Park/**Philip Lane** corner, where larger houses can reach £265–275,000.

It's a long-term thing: while some move on (after three years!) because the area has not instantly turned into Islington, others put down roots and get stuck in. The results are already showing; under a group repair scheme, whereby private owners in three key zones can apply for help to upgrade the fronts of their homes, **Black Boy Lane**, for one, is much improved. The areas are Northumberland Park, Seven Sisters and West Green.

Developers have dipped a toe into the Harringay Ladder (sorry 'Hills') close to the magic name Crouch End. Price rises and new schemes have not entirely eroded the area's advantage: it's still a good hunting-ground for teachers, hospital staff and the like. Streets may not be smart, the homes sometimes less so, but there's better transport than other parts of N-E London; it's becoming known as an affordable, identifiable place to live.

Tottenham homes are mainly 2- and 3-bed terraced houses: whole, or split into 1- or 2-bed flats (larger, ex-council flats too). Even modernized, many of these houses have downstairs bathrooms, but half retain original features such as fireplaces, cornicing or sash windows – these are the easiest to sell. A council-backed programme to bring empty homes into use means that owners can receive grants to renovate. Shell-shocked buyers from further south and west can still find the £160,000 terraced house – though it will be a 2-bed in tatty condition, not the smart 3-bed, now £250,000, of a few years back.

Flats have risen faster: you need £140,000-plus for a good 2-bed flat now. This was prompted by a Stamp Duty exemption on all properties under £150,000 which applies to most of Tottenham. A definite price bar exists at £250,000: at that point duty jumps from one to three per cent, and only the larger/more exceptional homes break through.

Tottenham is a fairly clear square on the map, lying N of Stoke Newington in the right-angle between the **North Circular** and the Lea Valley's reservoirs, and bounded to the W by **Green Lanes**. Officially at least, its N border is the Enfield borough boundary, though in practice the North Circular is a much more tangible divide with next-door Edmonton. Tottenham was a small village, boasting several fine houses, right up till the late 19th century. Today only one or two of these remain, such as Bruce Castle, now the local history museum. With the advent of the railways (and especially cheap fares for workmen), street after street of small terraces were built between 1890 and 1920. Not all the terraces survived the Blitz and the council bulldozers – though in some cases the brave new tower blocks that replaced them are themselves being demolished.

Expansion continued between the wars, particularly in the Dowsett Estate region on the E side. This was followed in the 1960s by much council housing in the N of the area – including monolithic Broadwater Farm Estate to the E of Lordship Recreation Ground, now happily rehabilitated as a place to live after a grim past. Light industry and warehouse depots bordering Hackney Marshes declined, with new homes starting to replace industry. The wider picture today focuses on the Lea Valley, running down to Stratford and Docklands: London's last major cache of unbuilt land. And Stratford (which chapter see) is about to become the major transport hub for this side of town – Olympics or no.

Tottenham already has excellent transport links, with quick access by rail and tube to the West End and the City, and by road to the North Circular, M25, M1 and M11. Buses are frequent, and particularly good for local travel. Transport, especially proximity to tubes, is what decides prices here. The area is truly cosmopolitan – Haringey council reckon 193 languages are spoken – with great diversity in the shops and leisure activities available. Wood Green is the place to go for cinemas and shops, though new bars and restaurants keep appearing in Tottenham's various centres.

Finsbury Park, a green spur to the SW, makes up for Tottenham's lack of more distinctive, family-sized homes; again, it's a bit of a mystery why this area has not tidied up more or received more attention from the gentrifying brigades than it has: it's on both the Piccadilly (for Heathrow) and Victoria Lines, and the train takes 12 mins to the City.

South Tottenham (N15)

The tract stretching northwards from the **Seven Sisters Rd/Amhurst Park** boundary up to **West Green Rd/Philip Lane**, and eastwards from **Green Lanes** to the **High Rd**, holds Tottenham's most popular streets: this is N15 territory, bordering the up-and-come areas of Stamford Hill and Stoke Newington. Prices rose sharply here last year, with buyers coming up the Roman road from Stamford Hill – indeed, you'll need to watch out for more 'estate agents creep' here: suddenly, Stamford Hill has glisséd across the borough boundary and according to some only stops at the railway (and the uncompromisingly named South Tottenham station). The proximity of Seven Sisters tube (Victoria Line) also sends prices above those in N17. Most homes in this neighbourhood are 2- and 3-bed terraces, built during the later 19th and early 20th centuries; many of the larger houses are now split into flats. Popular roads bordering Stamford Hill include **Wargrave Avenue**, **St John's Rd**, **Norfolk Avenue** and **Vartry Rd**, with large Victorian maisonettes close to the station: £165,000 for a 2-bed is typical. **Crowland Rd**, alongside the tracks, is cheaper.

Work is starting on exciting plans for the heart of the area: along **High Rd/Town Hall Approach**, opposite Tottenham Green, the old town hall and the swimming pool will form part of the frontage for the (long-awaited, as is the funding) arts/theatre/cinema complex: landscaping the Green has begun, and Town Hall Approach is to be pedestrianized.

The triangle behind, bounded by **Philip Lane, West Green Rd** and the railway – an area that includes several small garment factories centred on **Lawrence Rd** – holds a series of roughly parallel streets of 2- and 3-bed terraces, dating from the 1900s. These are broken by the popular **Clyde Circus**, with its attractive double-fronted, bay-windowed houses (a big 3-bed here, £265,000), and **Clyde Rd** (the depot site is included in the theatre plans). There are also larger, Victorian, 5/7-bed homes on **Bedford Rd**, some of which have escaped becoming flats and kept their original features; **Beaconsfield Rd**, though a notorious traffic cut-through, has much gentrified larger 3-bed terraces. A popular corner, with the Seven Sisters (Victoria Line tube/City trains) at the E end of **West Green Rd**, and Turnpike Lane (Piccadilly) reachable at the W end. Across the tracks to the E, a pleasant modern ex-council corner on **Pelham** and **Portland Rds** has small rows of 2-bed homes.

The traditional terraces resume S of **West Green Rd** in the rectangle formed with **Green Lanes**, **St Ann's Rd** and the **High Rd** – with **Seaford Rd**, **Roslyn Rd** and **Greenfield Rd** particularly good. Houses in this corner become increasingly pricey towards **Green Lanes** and **Turnpike Lane** (the tube is here), with **Cranleigh Rd** and **Conway Rd** typical examples of the higher price range of 2- and 3-bed houses.

The region S of **St Ann's Rd/Seven Sisters Rd** is bisected by **Hermitage Rd** (eight new 3-bed houses here, £339–350) and includes 'The Gardens', a block of neat Victorian streets including **Kimberley**, **Chesterfield** and **Roseberry Gardens** that link up to **Warwick Gardens**. Traffic-calming has stopped rat-running here: kids can play cricket in the street, and the homes are much more in demand; prices (a typical house, c. £280,000) have now risen towards those of the (busier) 'Ladder' roads to the E (c. £300,000; see below). St Ann's Hospital lies behind **Warwick Gardens**, with the railway to the S of it. The nearby Harringay Green Lanes station is not much use: trains to Gospel Oak one way and Leyton and Barking the other – and no useful tube connections in between.

On the other side of the tracks, there's a large Sainsbury's plus McAlpine's 220 1998–9 homes, from 1-bed flats to 4-bed houses, in streets such as **Wiltshire Gardens** and **Surrey Gardens**. Prices are comparable with the surrounding Victorian terraces in **Vale Rd**, **Eade Rd** and **Finsbury Park Avenue**, though the latter are larger.

Central Tottenham (N17)

... Or 'Downhills Park', 'Bruce Grove', 'West Green': families moving into the 2-, 3- and some 4-bed terraces of this next-most-popular tract, N of **West Green Rd/Philip Lane,** from **Westbury Avenue** across to the **High Rd**, prefer the particular to plain Tottenham. The S side has prices comparable to N15: £240–275,000 for a smartened up 3-bed house. Further N is the (improved) Broadwater Farm Estate; on towards the football ground prices fall 5–10 per cent. Again, both tube lines plus City trains are reachable.

Green, family-friendly open spaces – Downhills Park, Belmont and Lordship recreation grounds – boost house prices. This corner is establishing as a solid family area, with some good primaries (Downhills, Belmont); secondaries, though, are still a problem. Look here for larger houses in leafy streets near the park, such as **Keston, Kirkstall** (a 3-bed/3-recep, £275,000) and **Clonmell Rds. Downhills Park Rd** and **Dongola Rd** have some sizeable, 4-bed terraced houses, which have now risen to c. £280,000. To the N some of the worst of the Broadwater Farm council estate has happily been demolished, which should lift the shadow over nearby streets (**Higham Rd, The Avenue,** N end of **Mount Pleasant Rd**). The W4 bus from Wood Green improves accessibility.

To the E, roads off **Philip Lane** are priced at N15 levels. Characteristic mid-range early 20th-century 2/3-bed (and a few 4-bed: many a loft converting here) terraces, some split into flats, cluster in streets such as **Napier Rd, Steele Rd, Morrison Avenue** (a little 3-bed £225,00). **Mount Pleasant Rd** has 3-bed '30s rows (£235–240,000) and bay-windowed, bigger Edwardiana. The 4-bed houses in this street saw much division into flats – no longer: the council is keen to keep this a family area, with traffic blocking or calming. Streets round **Napier Rd** have a 20 mph speed limit. Those off **Broadwater Rd** (not to be confused with the estate) are sought after, with roomy, wider-than-average 3- and 4-bed houses, some double-fronted: these can tip over the £300,000 mark. Other roads in the Bruce Grove area include **Whitley Rd, Lordsmead Rd, Woodside Garden**; these have good-sized 3/4-bed 3-recep homes in quiet streets: very popular with families.

North Tottenham (N17)

Tottenham officially ends where N17 becomes N18 and the borough boundary also runs, some half-mile S of the North Circular Rd – a more tangible divide. This neighbourhood runs from **Lordship Lane,** with the A10 to the W, the **High Rd** to the E. Inter-war semis start to appear – also some Georgian relics, not to mention a castle. Nevertheless considerably lower prices here (comparable with Edmonton, to N) with a 2-bed house from c. £140,000.

Brand new homes here: Ambleside Close is 46 smart, 2-bed shared-ownership flats by Landmark housing trust on the **High Rd.** Resales, from c. £160,000, appearing in Old School Court, **Drapers Rd,** the gated, gardened conversion of a splendid Victorian school. Don't miss the dense grid of little streets in the Tower Gardens conservation area, one of the first garden suburbs. Enclosed by **Lordship Lane** and **The Roundway** and bisected by **Risley Avenue,** it is, says the town hall proudly 'recognized as one of the most important council estates in the country'. These Arts & Craftsy brick, tile and pebble-dash cottages date from 1903–14: spaciously laid out, well built, and popular buys (some are housing trust, others privately owned). Just don't think about changing the paint on your doors without permission. Pay c. £185,000 for a smartened 2-bed; £210,000 for a 3-bed.

Eastwards, **Church Lane** – also a conservation area – has pretty, Grade II-listed, 2-bed mewsy cottages (£200,000-ish). It borders Bruce Castle Park: the Elizabethan castle has museums of local history and inventions; the park, with its lido, hosts the carnival and numerous family events This corner also has most of Tottenham's Georgian buildings, including the 1826 Bruce Terrace in **Lordship Lane** – these are very rarely for sale. There's also a clutch of attractive late 19th-century cottages in the **Kings Rd/Church Rd** corner.

Just N of the Cemetery and White Hart Lane station, Rialto tucked in **Somerset**

Gardens off Creighton Rd, 356 flats – so always some for sale – that are popular first-time buys. Good-sized studios (from c. £105,000), 1- and 2-beds around £130,000 upwards.

East Tottenham (N15 and N17)

The eastern slice of Tottenham runs between the **High Rd** and the River Lea, down to the Hackney border. South of the **Monument Way/Ferry Lane** divide, running W–E beneath Tottenham Hale station and the retail park, N17 becomes N15.

Prices to the E of the **High Rd** are generally 10–20 per cent cheaper than to the W, and streets are less smart. The Northumberland Park Estate area is cheaper than further S due to the Spurs stadium (called, but not on, White Hart Lane). **Park Lane** in particular, which borders it, fails to live up to its name. Mainly 2-bed terraces here, and some conversions into flats. Hopes that a new tube station would accompany the regeneration funds poured into the Estate have faded; locals pray Spurs will move to Picketts Lock – eventually. Off **Hampden Rd**, Croudace squeezed 19 2- and 3-bed houses and some flats.

South of **Lansdowne Rd** is the Dowsett Rd estate, with **Sherringham, Seymour** and **Thackeray Avenues** popular with families who pay c. £210,000 for a typical 1930s 3-bed house within striking distance of the tube/rail station. This is a more down-at-heel part of Tottenham – so it attracts every sort of project and scheme to entice new businesses. And other factors help: Tottenham Hale station, modernized, offers Victoria Line tube, rail (including the Stansted Express) and buses. Middlesex University has bought a big site E of the station, which is to be its main campus plus student flats. This will not only boost this corner, but also allow better access to the reservoirs, nature reserve and Lea Valley greenery. Leisure facilities are planned upriver at Stonebridge Lock. South again, a mix of inter-war homes and Victorian rows in streets like **Carew Rd** (a 3-bed, c. £220,000) share the convenience of the Hale and the retail park.

Enclosed by **High Rd** and one-way system (**Chesnut Rd/Broad Lane**) is a strange combination of older, gentrified homes and rather shabby ones. **Tynemouth Rd** is still good value (4-bed house £225,000), with **Talbot** and **Springfield Rds** (a 4-bed, £250,000) slightly more upmarket versions. South of this area things tend to decline.

Fairview built 250 homes on **Bream Close**, S of **Ferry Lane**, in 1995. This patch of land has arms of the River Lea on two sides, justifying its name. There are light, airy river views. Local agents praise these homes for room size and layout, as well as views and location: a studio, £100,000, a 2-bed, £155,000. To the E is the nature reserve.

South of **Broad Lane** and the railway, towards Stamford Hill, is dubbed 'Tottenham Village' by locals and estate agents. Centring on **Wargrave Avenue, Grovelands Rd** and **Page Green Terrace**, sizes and prices are higher here (a loft-extended 4-bed, £310,000). **Wakefield Rd**, just N of the railway, is worth a look for its larger houses.

Borders: the Harringay ladder

Very popular 3- and 4-bed terraces – with much evidence of gentrification – throng the grid of streets marching up from **Endymion Rd** to **Turnpike Lane** on the W side of **Green Lanes** – just across the tracks from trendy Crouch End. The Harringay Ladder (or 'Harringay Hills', as agents tried to dub it!) is ever popular, especially the lower half (**Warham Rd** and on S: you're in N4, stations are in zone 2). Crouch End/Stoke Newington overspill also boosts demand: many Ladder children go to Crouch End primary schools.

Some houses were split into 1-/2-bed flats, but none were allowed after 1988. So these are mostly family 3- or 4-bed homes – a typical 3-bed is c. £310–320,000; a 4-bed needing work went for £325,000 on **Mattison Rd. Green Lanes** and **Wightman Rd** – the Ladder 'uprights' – are busy traffic routes. Traffic calming has, however, eased things in the 'rungs' between the two. Developers have dipped a toe in here: recent 1-, 2- and 3-bed flats on **Wightman Rd** (2-beds c. £250,000). And in **Effingham Rd**: a row of £400,000-plus houses: 2-bed/2-bath but all get big 'attic rooms' and some, studies.

Finsbury Park

Finsbury Park has been nobody's baby. It ought to be a hotspot: it has excellent transport: tube (Piccadilly, Victoria) and rail station (quick access to West End and City), good buses. It dips down to the N shores of Highbury. It has interesting houses of varying sizes. But three boroughs meet here, and the place has been neglected by all. Crime has been a problem (three police districts meet here, too). But at last things are looking up, families are moving in. Money is being spent: the station is having a multi-million rebuild – including a manned cycle park; also on the parkland and the housing, on CCTV, policing. The area has £25 million of Government cash: this is managed by the Finsbury Park project (www.finsburypark.org.uk), which produces excellent information. There are now signs of gentrification. At this rate people will soon admit to living here.

Haringey borough takes in the park and some of its surrounding streets – **Stroud Green Rd** marks the border with Islington, **Seven Sisters Rd** with Hackney. The name 'Finsbury Park' is not so much used (except when talking about the tube or the park itself): agents have tended to annexe its streets to more 'up-and-come' neighbours. Likewise incomers from Crouch End and Islington, attracted by large houses and cheaper prices, say they 'live in Islington' because that's where they pay council tax.

The big difference between Finsbury Park and Tottenham is in the size and quality of the houses – here is a much greater number of large, attractive 3- and 4-storey houses. Also more variety, with some big double-fronted, semi-detached properties, but the whole area is mixed, with several council estates. The larger houses – originally 5- and 6-bed – are ideal for splitting into flats, something that developers exploited to the full.

Seven Sisters Rd leading down from Manor House is bordered on its W side by the park and on the E by a series of hotels (quite a few are DSS/temporary accommodation). Behind, in the triangle formed with **Portland Rise** and **Gloucester Drive**, are some very attractive homes, including detached double-fronted houses which make roomy flats.

Next is the area's hot-spot: the rectangle formed by **Seven Sisters Rd**, **Queens Drive**, **Blackstock Rd**, **Brownswood Rd**. 'Brownswood Village' is perhaps over-egging it, but these are relatively quiet, tree-lined streets of large, mid-Victorian houses. **Finsbury Park Rd** is reckoned the best street: Victorian houses with handsome porches, big windows, 5- or 6-beds: a 5-bed sold for £590,000 last winter. Homes in **Queens Drive** have long gardens (and prices: c. £700,000); **Wilberforce Rd**'s have bigger than average rooms.

Improvements here include the replacement of the tower blocks of King's Crescent Estate, S of **Brownswood Rd**, by St Mary's Village, a tract of Affordable Housing: the rented homes are run by Peabody, while others were for sale. The old filter beds, too, E of **Queens Drive**, have given way to a large number of new houses.

But the greatest excitement here has been the news that at last, Arsenal is to relocate. This especially affects the triangle formed by **Blackstock**, **St Thomas's** and **Gillespie Rds**: smaller, 2-storey, rows, with a few 3-storey pockets. An increasingly popular corner, with the N5 postcode: the 'Highbury effect'. Look for **Plimsoll**, **Prah** and **Ambler Rds**; here you can find 3-bed houses for c. £450,000; a 4-bed (needs work) sold for £500,000. Some new homes in tucked-away corners. **Blackstock Rd**, not the smartest, is boosted by a new college and library. People look to Highbury as the centre of their world; for them the stadium's replacement with smart flats and cafés (see Islington) can't come soon enough.

Cross the park, and the tract SW of **Stroud Green Rd** and N of **Seven Sisters Rd** has attractive streets such as **Charteris Rd**, with many 4-storey houses now flats (a 1-bed £160–170,000). **Alexander Grove** has larger houses. Further S is a large council estate in the **Durham Rd**, **Seven Sisters Rd**, **Birnam Rd**/**Moray Rd** and **Hornsey Rd** rectangle; lower prices in this corner; however, agents pinpoint **Playford**, **Moray** and **Lennox Rds** as 'up and coming'. Nearby is the excellent Sobell Sports Centre. Three-bed, c. £350,000, houses in the **Corbyn St**/**Thorpedale Rd** area are popular; the next step up is the 3-storey houses hereabouts, now running at c. £450,000.

North of **Stroud Green Rd**, some streets of Victorian 3-storey houses are a short step to the tube. Most are flats, but a few houses survive: try **Woodstock Rd, Perth Rd, Woods Rd, Ennis Rd, Scarborough Rd.** Despite traffic, this corner of solid 3/4-bed Victorian houses is tidying: 'relatively good value', think agents. Just to the N, on the Stroud Green borders, Bellway's Regents Quarter in **Tollington Way** added new flats and town-houses. East of Stroud Green Rd, **Stapleton Hall Rd, Florence Rd** and **Upper Tollington Park** are popular. New bars and cafés sprout for a younger clientele, and (much to local amusement) agents try to re-brand the area 'Crouch End Heights' or 'South Crouch End'.

Back up in the Tottenham direction, some spacious, green streets close to Manor House tube are uneasily split between the Woodberry Down council-built estate and a surviving clutch of large single-occupant houses.

Transport Tubes: Finsbury Park (zone 2, Piccadilly, Victoria); Arsenal, Manor House, Turnpike Lane, Wood Green (zones 2/3, Piccadilly); Tottenham Hale, Seven Sisters (zone 3, Victoria). From Seven Sisters: Oxford Circus 20 min, City 25 min (1 change), Heathrow 1 hr (1 change). Rail: 12–16 min to Liverpool St. Good buses.

Convenient for North Circular, A10, Wood Green Shopping City, Alexandra Park.

Schools Local Authority: Greig City Academy, The Drayton, Gladesmore Community School, High Cross, Northumberland Park.

SALES

Flats	S	1B	2B	3B	4B	5B
Average prices	90–120	125–170	150–210	160–325	300–350	–
Houses	2B	3B	4B	5B	6/7B	8B
Average prices	185–250	220–350	250–400+	350–600+	→	–

RENTAL

Flats	S	1B	2B	3B	4B	5B
Average prices	120–150	170–220	180–250	200–400	–	–
Houses	2B	3B	4B	5B	6/7B	8B
Average prices	185–300	210–400	230–450	280–450	–	–

The properties Two-storey terraces (2/3-beds) built 1890–1920 are most common. Fair number of inter-war houses. Many flats: small conversions, bigger ex-council. New-build, school/commercial conversions appearing. Bigger, smarter, pricier homes in Finsbury Park, in roads nearest Highbury; also Stroud Green side, 'Ladders' roads, Downhills for young families. N17 least expensive: far from tube, close to council estates and football.

The market Affordable ground for first-time buyers: flats and original-details terraces. Young families moving in. Many wards get Stamp Duty exemption below £150,000: check Inland Revenue website.

Among estate agents active in this area are:

- Cousins
- Winkworth
- Adam Kennedy
- Bairstow Eves
- Castles
- Michael Morris
- Bridges
- Drivers & Norris
- Paul Simon
- Varosi
- Davies & Davies
- 1st Class Estates
- Gelb & Co
- Brian Thomas
- Haart

TOTTERIDGE AND WHETSTONE

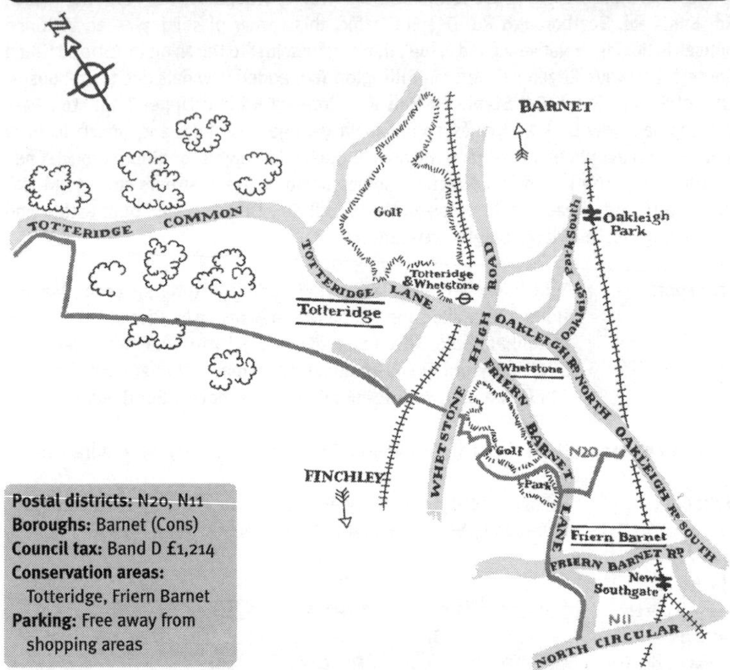

Postal districts: N20, N11
Boroughs: Barnet (Cons)
Council tax: Band D £1,214
Conservation areas: Totteridge, Friern Barnet
Parking: Free away from shopping areas

Take The Bishops Avenue – Hampstead Garden Suburb's 'Millionaire's Row' – move its mansions to the northern fringes of London and dot them along a meandering country lane, add ponies and paddocks and even a working farm. . . there you have Totteridge.

This foretaste of open countryside and its attendant areas of Whetstone, with its busy shopping parade and the Northern Line tube, and Friern Barnet, are still London – just. To the north lies Barnet proper, out of the London postal area and suddenly, indefinably, Hertfordshire. Southwards lies Finchley and the metropolis. A sign that these areas have joined London proper is the interest taken in them by West End estate agents, as people look further out for almost-country, very-much-luxury homes.

Friern Barnet is the scene of an explosion of smart flats and town-houses on the land freed by the closure of the famous Colney Hatch lunatic asylum, among Europe's biggest buildings when it was erected (it took 10 million bricks) a century and a half ago.

Totteridge

Totteridge, despite its London postcode (N20), is to all intents and purposes a country village – albeit one largely consisting of houses all pillared, porticoed and swimming pooled. To the N of **Totteridge Common/Village/Lane** and the roads off them lie the golf course and wide-open spaces, with the village itself as a pretty focal point.

Totteridge is not a big place, and while the mini-palaces see a regular ebb and flow of well-known faces (half of London's premiership footballers, generally); at the 4/5-bed family-home level people know each other: their children attend the village school, or they are active in the residents' association. Not, probably, over the garden fence, though: houses tend to be set in large, secluded plots of land. On Sundays Totteridge folk can drop in to the Orange Tree pub for a drink, then head down to Laurel Farm to feed the ducks. This is not Hampstead where people go to be seen; here remarkable faces go by relatively unremarked-upon. Its professionals or media/showbiz denizens relish the privacy that a home here affords (the local post office displays neatly-written ads appealing for au pairs and cleaners). Ongoing concerns to the residents' association are intrusive mobile-phone masts, cars speeding in Totteridge Lane and the closure of the local library – though as the locals are among London's most active mobile phone and prestige car users, the association may have a fight on its hands over the first two. Good news on one local issue: lovely 18th-century Darlands Lake, fed by the Folly Brook, is to be saved after Barnet Council came up with the cash to repair the dam.

Totteridge lies in the borough of Barnet – which, by the way, has one of the best local authority education records in the country – but after primary (St Andrews; Woodridge) most of Totteridge's residents prefer to send their offspring to the many fee-paying schools in the surrounding areas. For communications, the A1, M1, M25 are not far.

However, for those *sans* chauffeur transport is more difficult: the bus service is poor, though the Northern Line does come out to Totteridge & Whetstone. No shops to speak of; but The Spires, Barnet's shopping centre, adds major stores to the **Whetstone High Rd** selection, and a 'hoppa' bus goes to Brent Cross. **Totteridge Lane** is a long, winding, wooded road: a daunting walk from the tube on dark evenings. Most households seem, however, to have enough cars to make walking a sport rather than a necessity: 'parking for several cars' is a constant refrain in property details.

There are few small (and fewer discreet) houses in Totteridge. It's known for its 4- or 5-, or indeed 6- or 7- or 8-bedroomed, homes complete with tennis court, sauna and hi-tech security systems. The term 'over the top' is unknown in Totteridge: interiors flaunt marble and chandeliers plus a feature staircase; exteriors are set behind electric-gated drives, indoor pools have neat little bridges over them leading to the private gym. **Totteridge Lane** and any of the turnings off it are prime locations: many of the roads are private and have views over the golf course or acres of Green Belt land. Think mainly in millions for houses – Georgian or 20th/21st-century – in the best roads, which include, as well as **Totteridge Lane**, **Village** and **Common**, **Pine Grove**, **Grange Avenue** and homes in and around **The Green**. Another is **Northcliffe Drive** which, along with **Harmsworth Way**, recalls the great press barons who once lived here.

And they keep coming: a 'modernist mansion' (a usage that will give architects the vapours) with pool, gym, billiard-room, indoor *and* outdoor Jacuzzis, stables, was £6.5 million last year (there was no rush). It joins a recent clutch of 6-bed/6-bath mansions in **Hadar Close**; more 6-bedders that hit the market in 2001 in **Barnet Lane**; yet another imposing gated development of detached homes in **Elder Close** completed 2002. Totteridge has been the place to live for a century: in 1895 T E Collcutt, architect to the stars of the Naughty Nineties, built himself a Tudorbethan mansion, The Croft, on **Totteridge Green**. It was for sale in 2003 at £6.5 million: 6-beds, self-contained flat, cottage, pool, paddock. Nearby, in peaceful **Horeshoe Lane**, £3.25 million was asked last autumn for a huge place behind gates, with its own detached guest cottage. At the other end of the scale, a tiny, if listed, 2-bed cottage hidden down a path went for c. £350,000.

Not a few properties in the estate agents' windows in N20 bear a polite note to would-be buyers, 'price available on application': if you need to ask. . . . Much depends upon luxury level: homes which look quite ordinary and suburban conceal Premier League interiors with prices to match. Whether these prices will survive the inevitable ageing of the high-fashion fixtures and fittings remains to be seen.

Normality reasserts itself as you travel eastwards (which also takes you towards the tube station); 3/4-bed semis and flats begin to appear in roads like **Southway** and **Lynton Mead**, or there's 1930s 3-bed detached houses in **Coppice Walk** and **Greenway** (c.£550,000). In **Southway**, £2 million was asked last winter for a 2000-vintage 6-bedder, but the 5-bed house virtually next door was 'just' £800,000 a year or so back.

Generally speaking, this is not the place to look for flats – unless you're thinking of converted mansions like The Grange, or the listed Totteridge House in the village. You might capture a 2-bed in Totteridge Park – a much tidied but fundamentally 18th-century manor house, now 10 flats; but generally agents point to Friern Barnet (see below) or Woodside Park (see Finchley chapter) for purpose-built blocks and new schemes.

Whetstone

Totteridge becomes Whetstone when **Totteridge Lane** reaches the tube station, just W of the **High Rd** (A1000). Housing becomes more affordable by the average family at this point, and the word 'million' ebbs away from the house particulars. In **St James's Avenue**, for example, a typical if well-presented 3-bed semi might be £495,000, with terraced cottages in nearby streets well under £300,000. For smart homes, look to **St James Close** and **Friars Avenue**, opposite Friary Park and golf course.

The workaday **Whetstone High Rd** gives the area a more down-market appearance than the surrounding streets and properties (some 6-bedroomed) really deserve. Though there are plenty of modern, purpose-built blocks along the High Rd itself, to the E there are some wonderfully characterful semis and detached houses, such as the spacious Edwardiana on the elegant-sounding **Athenaeum Road** and **Chandos Avenue**. Many of these houses have their own garages – something rarely seen in nearby Finchley. **Church Gate** is a 1980s cul-de-sac of 5-bed houses behind electronic gates off **Church Crescent**.

Heading S along the **High Rd**, past the parade of shops is Oakleigh Park, with its own station. **Oakleigh Park Gardens** has terraced older houses and family-style semis, while **Oakleigh Park North** and **Oakleigh Park South** are quiet, leafy and well located, as are the surrounding streets: large houses, a mixture of mainly semi-detached homes with good gardens – and some flats. **Oakleigh Park North** (especially favoured) has some big individual detached homes and, nearer the High Road, fine purpose-built blocks.

Oakleigh Rd North/Oakleigh Rd South – similar in name, but not in stature, to the 'Parks' – form the main road from Whetstone to Southgate. A development of 4- and 5-bed houses appeared in 1998, but generally it's a mixture of small houses and shops, and prices hereabouts tend to be cheaper than elsewhere in Whetstone; a 3-bed terraced cottage close to the High Rd was £295,000 in late 2004.

Friern Barnet

Running off **Whetstone High Rd, Friern Barnet Lane** leads past the North Middlesex Golf Course and lovely Friary Park, a green and leafy start to the northernmost edges of Friern Barnet proper. Here homes overlooking the golf course and similar greenery command prices holding steady over the past year at between £850,000 and £1.5 million.

The rest of the area is similar in feel to next-door Finchley with its mix of 1930s semis, smart purpose-built flats and maisonettes, but lacks the Northern Line. Prices are thus lower than for equivalent homes in surrounding areas, especially in the sweeps of ex-council housing, such as the roads between **Woodhouse Rd** and **Summers Lane.**

The great landmark of Friern Barnet is the (listed) former Colney Hatch psychiatric hospital S of **Friern Barnet Rd**. The asylum building itself is now 'Princess Park Manor', a luxury block of 260 1-, 2-, 3- and 4-bed flats by Comer Homes, complete with fitness centre – and shuttle bus to the tube. Guards in uniform, too – but these days to keep troublemakers out, not in. . . . Manor flats were £300,000–2.5 million last winter. The 30-acre grounds have been split between three big new homes schemes. The developers (Barratt, Bellway, Martin Grant) have all focused on 2-, 3- and 4-bed modern houses and town-houses (a euphemism for terraced), with a couple of extra luxury flats blocks. The street maps now show a maze of winding Avenues, Drives and Closes (23!) set between **Friern Barnet Rd, Colney Hatch Lane** and the **North Circular**. These new homes cover a wide range of sizes, levels of luxury, and prices: you can pay over £600,000, but a more typical mid-terraced version is much less. Here, too, in the former hospital grounds, is the borough's newest open space: Friern Village Park (named by locals bent on expunging the name Colney Hatch, with its lunatic associations).

All told, then, a wide range of homes: small terraces, purpose-built flats and plenty of Victorian and Edwardian conversions. As we've seen, there are fine large semi- and detached houses around **Friern Barnet Lane**, the prime street. **Friern Barnet Rd**, towards New Southgate, has cheaper Victoriana/Edwardian homes; still c. £130,000 for 1-bed flats here, well under £200,000 for 2-beds. **Woodhouse Rd**, en route to Finchley, has 1930s semis and terraces, plus ex-council; **Hornbeams Rise**, modern 1-bed 'starter homes'. Close to the **North Circular** and with trains to King's Cross, Friern Barnet is a good hunting ground and something of a contrast to well-established Whetstone and Totteridge. Look here for less expensive, smaller homes that attract first-time buyers.

Transport Tubes: Totteridge & Whetstone (zone 4, Northern). Oakleigh Park, New Southgate (both to King's Cross, 15–20 min). To Oxford Circus 45 min (1 change), City 45 min, Heathrow 90 min (1 change).

Convenient for North Circular, M1/M25, Brent Cross. Miles from centre: 9.

Schools Local Authority: Ravenscroft School, Friern Barnet School, Queen Elizabeth's (b), Queen Elizabeth's (g), Dame Alice Owen, Copthall (g). Private: Mill Hill, Haberdashers, Aldenham, Queenswood.

SALES

Flats	S	1B	2B	3B	4B	5B
Average prices	120–150	125–225	150–400	200–500	250–500+	–
Houses	2B	3B	4B	5B	6/7B	8B
Average prices	230–400	275–500+	350–800+	475–1M+	700–1.5M	–

RENTAL

Flats	S	1B	2B	3B	4B	5B
Average prices	110–180	130–200	180–275+	225–350+	350–500+	–
Houses	2B	3B	4B	5B	6/7B	8B
Average prices	200–425	275–500	300–600+	400–1000	1000+	–

The properties Totteridge has grand 5–8-plus bedroom houses set in near-countryside. Amenities anything from a swimming pool to a sunken recording studio. Whetstone also has luxury houses, though slightly smaller, and smart p/b flats. Friern Barnet has a range from ex-council and smaller terraces to large detacheds – plus the huge cache of new homes on the former hospital site.

The market Totteridge is peopled by smart professionals, showbiz/sports celebs, with children, ponies, nannies, cars cars cars. Whetstone: wider range of people and homes; Friern Barnet is more urban: scope for the less-well-off. Young couples, single professionals, retired couples all eager buyers at the old asylum site.

Among estate agents active in this area are:

- Anscombe & Ringland
- Austin Chambers
- Simon Clarke
- Statons
- Hunters
- Maunder Taylor
- Martyn Gerrard
- Jeremy Leaf
- Barnard Marcus
- Winkworth
- Bairstow Eves
- Haart

TWICKENHAM AND TEDDINGTON

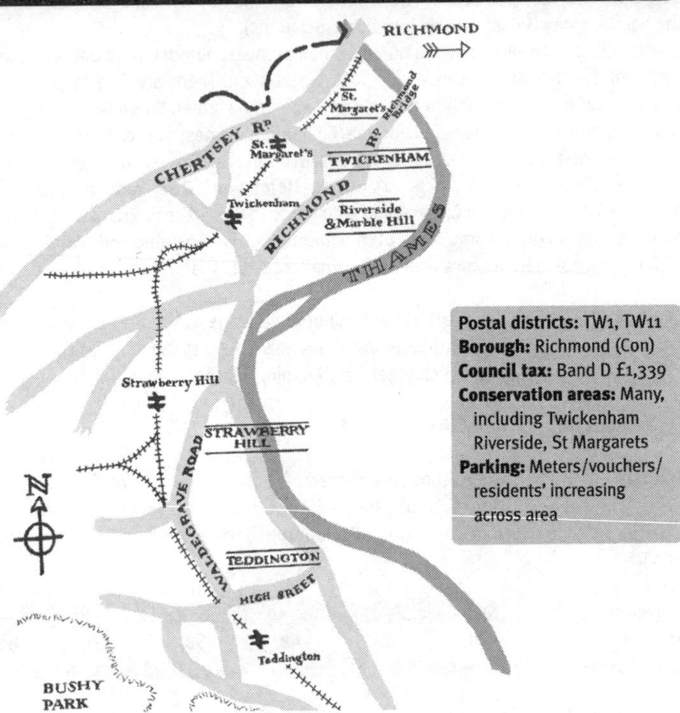

Postal districts: TW1, TW11
Borough: Richmond (Con)
Council tax: Band D £1,339
Conservation areas: Many, including Twickenham Riverside, St Margarets
Parking: Meters/vouchers/ residents' increasing across area

A 'village remarkable for an abundance of curious seats', noted a visitor to Twickenham, across the river from Richmond, in 1720. Georgian grandees built their country mansions here, along the rural reaches of the Thames upstream – and upwind – from the city. Marble Hill, Orleans House, Strawberry Hill, York House, still stand stately hereabouts; amid them on a lesser (and still lived-in, not museum-piece) scale in **Montpelier Row, Sion Rd** and more are a hundred other lovely old Georgian homes.

Essentially today these suburbs are a rich cache of family homes, from mock-Tudor to mansions, from semi-rural riverside grandeur to humdrum little 1930s semis gazing across a dual carriageway. Flats, too: purpose-built along the river and in the town centres, and many another converted from monstrous Victorian houses. If homes have, historically, cost less than those across the river, the gap has now closed considerably. But here you can often find the more modest homes – later terraces, 20th-century infill – rubbing shoulders with the grander ones: streets can be enjoyably mixed. Once happily ensconced here – amid leafy greenery and river scenes, but with good state and private schools, shops and trains all to hand – families tend to stick.

Twickenham

If it lacks the sophisticated unity of Richmond, a bridge-span away, Twickenham's locals feel they have the best of both worlds. They can, after all, enjoy all Richmond's amenities (including the District Line), while Twickenham is itself a useful little town, with High St shops. Kingston, a major shopping centre, is close, Heathrow not far; there are riverside walks with views of Richmond and Petersham Meadows. As well as the Thames, there's the wide expanse of Bushy Park; beyond lies Hampton Court, set in its own deer park.

The western boundary is the (very busy) A316, which leads in to central London, out to the M3; the eastern, the Thames. The famous Twickenham rugby stadium (actually at Whitton, across the A316), can attract vast crowds – the traffic jams are epic.

Opposite the Stadium, the Crane Valley holds a clutch of sites 'likely to come forward in the next five years', say the council: a new planning framework encompasses Richmond College – it could get new buildings, and housing may replace its existing ones – the rugby ground, a depot and the post sorting office. Watch this space. . . .

Meanwhile, the area's wide range of homes takes in quite a selection of good family houses in the £340–650,000 bracket in pleasant locations, though million-plus prices are not rare; the increase in the number of upper-six- and seven-figure homes in the past few years is in part because people have been extending and upgrading at a brisk pace. Two-bed cottages are dotted throughout the area; bungalows, too, crop up – though these, often in good-sized plots, are increasingly apt to disappear and small develoments spring up in their place. Flats in a range of styles, including riverside-smart, abound – blocks, conversions, mansion flats – and sizes from studios at c. £120,000 on up to million-plus prices for the biggest, smartest modern flats along the river. Bargain-hunters should look to the **Chertsey Rd/Staines Rd** area with its 3-bed 1930s semis, c. £350,000. Lower prices are also to be found in Whitton (you should love rugby) and on the W side of Twickenham, where there are 1920s terraces.

East Twickenham/St Margarets

Tucked into a loop of the river opposite Richmond and with its own station, St Margarets runs the gamut from convenient cottages to house-sized mansion flats, glitzy riverside new-build to the hidden secret of the St Margarets Estate which gave this corner its name.

Richmond Rd leads away S-W from Richmond Bridge, flanked by red-brick mansion flats which overlook gardens leading down to the Thames, and by small shops, open late and with flats above. (Here, and in **Crown Rd** which joins it, are the style-conscious cafés and chi-chi lifestyle/gifts/interiors places.) Turn S off Richmond Rd into the triangle between it, the river and Marble Hill Park, with the cool cream symmetry of Palladian Marble Hill House. Here **Cresswell Rd** has Victorian semis with huge bay windows (a 4-bed, £775,000); **Morley Rd** and **Denton Rd** carry on the style on a smaller scale (a 4-bed in Morley, £675,000 last autumn); Denton Rd leads to the river: here Edwardian Richmond Mansions has flats with fine views, and prices to match. On the riverbank itself, on **Clevedon Rd**, is 'Richmond Bridge', a big complex of five apartment blocks plus town-houses (a 3-bed, £775,000), which replaced the much-loved Richmond Ice Rink. Think half a million up for the flats. . . £1.25 million for a 2/3-bed penthouse recently. Traditionalists might prefer the large Edwardian mansion flats in **Cambridge Rd.**

Curving around Marble Hill Park, **Cambridge Park** has big double-fronted mansions that yield good-sized flats (a 2-bed, £295,000), mixed with small modern schemes set back behind trees. An 1860s house is the latest conversion: Birnam House is now six flats, with four more and two £310,000 2-bed cottages in new wings; flats are £430–465,000. The coveted **Meadowside** enclave down towards the river offers flats in acres of grounds. **Cambridge Park Court** has a row of 3-storey semi-detached Victoriana, also mostly flats.

Back to **Richmond Rd**, where Laing's six, 2001, town-houses plus flats overlook the park; nearby, a Georgian/early-Victorian 3-bed house – with 85ft garden – was £765,000 last winter. **St Margarets Rd** branches off and swings on NW, lined with 1930s semis (a 3-bed, £498,000) on one side; big Victoriana (most now flats) on the other. **Crown Rd**'s eclectic shops are at its N end; it and **Sandycoombe Rd** have 2-bed cottages and pleasant 3/4-bed red-brick family houses (one, an end-of-terrace, £900,000); Sandycoombe Lodge, Turner's country retreat, is here. **St Stephen's Gardens** has big 5-bed semis (c. £1.4 million); **Kings Rd**, handsome Victorian houses. **Marble Hill Close** has neat 1930s semis.

The Barons, near the station, curves down past Twickenham Film Studios: its 3-storey houses, all pillared porticoes, cluster round what may once have been a communal garden, but now holds a block of flats. **Rosslyn Rd**'s enormous double-fronted Victorian houses are now mostly flats or offices. Behind lies **Riverdale Rd**, where the 1870 Gothic mansions, shaded by trees, give a touch of the Sir Walter Scotts. **Park Rd**, too, has some big 5-bed Victorian semis (a smaller, 3-bed: £775,000). This corner is a fine example of a Victorian suburb, harbouring homes of all sizes from 1-bed flats at c. £235,000, to 5-bed £1.75 million detacheds. Down towards the bridge, **Willoughby Road** has big riverview mansion flats. For later homes, see **Ravensbourne Rd**, with its half-timbered post-war houses, and **Park House Gardens'** fine whitewashed Art Deco semis running down to the Thames. Here is **Duck's Walk**, where homes with moorings face the river. Six big two-millionish town-houses in 'Richmond Bridge Moorings' were added in 1998.

But it is the northernmost corner of St Margarets that gave the area its name. Stretching up from the rail line is a cache of roads – **The Avenue, St Margarets Drive, Ranelagh Drive, St Peter's Rd, St Georges Rd, Ailsa Rd, Kilmorey Rd, Heathcote Rd, Cassilis Rd** – in an exclusive estate laid out by a trust in 1854: huge houses that either face grandly onto the road or are hidden by high walls. And between the curving streets lie 'the Trust Grounds': nine acres of secret, private pleasure gardens: some 145 houses (c. £1.5–2 million) back directly onto the three separate gardens, one of which, behind St Peter's Rd, has a gate onto the towpath. Here owners' children play contentedly, adults use the tennis courts and summer barbecues are held. At the head of this select enclave lies the 14-acre riverside Gordon House site off **Ranelagh Drive**, being developed as 'Richmond Lock' by classy Octagon with 171 homes (70 Affordable), in new and listed buildings: first releases are 5/6-bed houses in 'The Laceys' and 'Chapel Square' (£1.65–2.75 million). Cross to Richmond *proper* via a daylight-hours-only footbridge.

The busy **St Margarets Rd** in 2002 gained four Charles Church 4-bed 3-recep town-houses: stylish modern counterparts to the big Victorian semis with large gardens, front and back, on the E side of the road. West of St Margarets Rd are less-dear streets such as **Ailsa Avenue** and **Gordon Avenue**, with 3-bed Victorian terraces (c. £495,000) and semis (a 4-bed, £625,0000); **Haliburton Rd** has smaller Victorian cottages.

Winchester Rd runs S from (but does not join) the A316 roundabout; it has Victorian/Edwardian flat-fronted houses and 2-bed maisonettes. Between it and the open space of Moor Mead Ground is a grid (inevitably, a 'toast rack'; also called by some the Moormead estate) of popular streets handy for St Margarets station: a densely packed corner of maisonettes and terraced houses. People pay a premium for the 2/3-bed maisonettes in prettier, tree-lined **Sidney Rd. St Margarets Grove** and **Brook Rd** have neat little 2-bed cottages (£375,000 for a bigger, end-of-terrace): some are so small the bathroom's downstairs – but your garden can back onto the River Crane.

Cole Park Rd twists up the E side of Cole Park and is lined with 6-bed detached double-fronted Edwardian – prices hover either side of a million – 1930s and modern houses.

Across the tracks **Amyand Park Rd** hugs the railway from close to Twickenham station up to St Margarets Rd. A mixed bag of 3-storey houses with basements (now mostly flats: a 1-bed, c. £200,000) is to be found, though some face the rather busy railway.

Riverside and Marble Hill

The prestige homes of Twickenham can be found to the W of Marble Hill Park. **Montpelier Row** (1724) skirts the park: a fine example of a Georgian terrace, with the rare sale around the £1–1.3 million level. **Chapel Rd** with its cottages leads on to equally cottagey (that's £600,000 cottages) Georgian **Orleans Rd**, shaded by huge chestnuts, which swings around Orleans House Gallery into pretty **Riverside**, winding up to The White Swan past some spectacular late 18th-century white, or pastel-washed, houses. These Thames-side delights almost never appear for sale. North of Riverside is **Lebanon Park**, where you can expect to pay handsomely for the 3/4-bed, red-brick Edwardian family houses.

Parallel to this runs **Sion Rd**, with a terrace of 12 splendid Georgian houses running down to the river. Cross a footbridge and Eel Pie Island has some modern houses with moorings for those who reckon boats are more important than cars. There's a working boatyard, too.

Central Twickenham

Few areas have such varied housing: styles, sizes, periods change markedly even within streets. Between the railway and **Heath Rd/King St** are some pretty, small-scale corners such as **Albert Rd**, with its tiny cottages, off **Lion Rd** (with Simba Court), and the even smaller ones of **Staten Gardens**, where paths lead between the gardens to little pairs of brick cottages. **Clifden Rd** has pairs of handsome, 1860s 4-floor villas, while **Queens Rd**'s high-Victorian Gothic houses with pointy-topped doors yield flats (2-bed, £230,000). **Grove Avenue** brings us down to earth with standard-issue Fulham-type 1890s terraces.

South of Heath Rd, **Cross Deep Gardens** and **Tennyson Avenue** have 1920s semis and 1914 terraces: one of the more humdrum corners. **Upper Grotto Rd** is more congenial, with un-twiddly Victorian rows and recent town-houses (c. £370,000). **Popes Grove** has large family Edwardiana; W, beyond the rail bridge, you're in Strawberry Hill. **Cross Deep** (a busy road linking to Teddington) has houses with lawns down to the river, and modern flats.

King St is the main shopping street of Twickenham. To the S is a pleasant old quarter running down to the river, with small-scale, interesting shops, pubs and cafés in pretty **Church St**. After near on a quarter-century of planning rows, at last a modest interim scheme is replacing the splendidly sited but derelict swimming pool on the **Embankment** with a children's play area and landscaped space. The sixth in a sequence of grand designs was thrown out in 2002; a seventh will no doubt appear one day. . . .

Heath Rd feeds into **The Green**, a tree-lined triangle with white 18th-century cottages to the S; these then give way to modern flat developments. More pretty little Georgian homes to the W. **First Cross Rd** and **Second Cross Rd** (two of six: imagination failed in the names department) have some sweet little cottages (a 2-bed, £290,000), some with garages at the end of the garden. To the N, **May, Knowle** and **Colne Rds** have a mix of doll-sized cottages and modern houses. First-time buyers search here for affordable flats. The Cross grid gets more suburban as it spreads W, though some 1950s Span flats and houses are worth seeking out. West again towards Hanworth prices drop, but rise in the S at Hampton Hill, where the million-ish 5-bed family houses start to crop up again.

Strawberry Hill

This prettily-named neighbourhood forms the S edge of Twickenham. Horace Walpole's 18th-century Gothic mansion of Strawberry Hill is now a college (though you can visit), and its grounds are streets of suburban houses. Tree-shaded streets such as **Waldegrave Park** are lined with big detached Victorian villas, some now flats (a split-level 4-bed, £550,000), and batches of 1950s–1970s infill: town-houses, mostly, including more of the Span ones that excite architects. There is a lot of inter-war housing: smart semis ranging down-scale to rather tired-looking 1920s terraces. The infilling continues, with the occasional new family home: the latest four semis by Charles Church on the corner of **Strawberry Hill Rd**, which match in style if not size the monster 1890s red-brick arts-and-craftsy houses in the rest of the street.

Smaller, cheaper homes are found in **Church Rd** and adjoining little streets, W of the railway. Just because you have crossed the tracks, it does not mean everything's cheap: St George added a row of 3,000sq ft, 5-bed semis in **Wellesley Rd**, W of the station. The same road has plenty of 1960s flats and a tract of 1930s suburbia by the school playing fields. **Spencer Rd** and **Walpole Gardens** mix more 1930s homes (plus golf course to go with them) and 1885 mammoths (a 2-bed flat, £335,000) plus a few pairs of handsome 1910 villas. **Popes Avenue** and **Popes Grove** offer big Victorian villas, some split into flats; an intact one, a detached 7-bed, £1.3 million last winter.

Teddington

Teddington, S of Twickenham, shares river and schools, but mostly lacks the architecture. It has a station, a few lovely Georgian homes, and some arty shops and cafés are cheering its humdrum centre in **High St/Broad St**. Bushy Park to the S is a great asset, and in 2000 Laing seized the chance to build on its fringes: **Admiralty Way** is a handsome if tightly-knit clutch of houses and flats, some with mock-Victorian towers and park views. Recent prices: £430,000 (3-bed tower house), £725,000 (4-bed town-house). Also off **Queen's Rd** lovely bow-ended, Regency, North Lodge has just become 2-bed flats: £350–375,000. And round the corner in **Park Rd** pretty, Gothicky Little Lodge (1816) is yours for £675,000.

The best roads lie to the E – towards the river. Here, **Lower Teddington Rd** forms the spine of a district of moderately smart homes set in plenty of greenery – but a longish way from shops or transport. We suggest buying one with a mooring, and shopping in Kingston by boat. There's Thameside Place: 10 flats (riverside 3-bed, £1.1 million) and three cottages (£445–570,000) newly carved from a fine old mansion.

Go N and complexes of flats and town-houses line the river, many in private estates. The most interesting houses are late 19th-century and 1930s ones in **Melbourne Rd** and **Trowlock Avenue**, which lead down to the river and share a private riverside green. **Bucklands Rd** is flat-roofed, 3-storey '60s council-build – but a row of some half-dozen smart dark-brick and wood-balconied homes hidden at its foot back onto a tiny public green – reached only by river. Beyond is a true oddity: **Trowlock Island**, a long, thin strip packed with bungalows. Most started as shacks, many are now very smart; all (when and if sold), expensive. This is true off-shore living, moorings included – and you'll pay for it. Sole access is by a hand-operated chain ferry; flood warnings are listened to avidly.

Broom Water and **Broom Water West** have some of Teddington's smartest houses: big, £1.7 million-ish, with gardens down to a private creek. To the W of **Broom Rd** and **Lower Teddington Rd** are 1991 flats in leafy grounds at **Trematon Place**, plus streets, such as **Munster Rd** and **King Edward's Grove**, of tall, gabled 1890–1910 semis (c. £670,000; a million for one 5-bed detached) and 1960s town-houses.

East of **Kingston Rd**, which leads to Hampton Wick and Kingston Bridge, lies the leafy ex-Normansfield Hospital, by far the area's biggest site: Laing/Wilson Connolly's Langdon Park – 80 flats, 41 houses, 70 Affordable Homes. Releases so far include 2-bed flats, £300–365,000, and a row of 4/5-bed town-houses (£785–799,000) in French-chateau style. A hotel is to come. Across **Kingston Rd** to the W, popular roads include **Langham Rd**, **Kingston Lane** and **Udney Park Rd**, all running N–S from **Teddington High St**. These quiet streets have a mix of 4- to 7-bed Edwardian semis and detacheds.

Down on the Thames, beside the weir, are Thames TVs' studios, with commemorative plaques of famous comedians – no news yet on proposals for development (part could become housing). On the inland side is **Rivermead Close**, a big estate of 1970s dark-brick houses and flats. **Ferry Rd** leads down to the footbridge over the lock, and two popular pubs. It has a few Victorian homes – cottages and converted houses – and the entrance to one of the many riverside flats blocks. Teddington Wharf, a St George's development of recent 1- to 3-bed flats and penthouses, is all angled rooflines (in one block, Fairmile House, a 2-bed was £290,000, a 3-bed £545,000, last winter). Its quay is home to the lifeboat. The rest of Thames-side Teddington, along a road that swaps its name from (N–S) **Strawberry Vale** to **Twickenham Rd** to **Manor Rd**, is a mix of flats from the 1930s to today, Victorian and earlier villas, and inter-war suburban detached. Many have moorings, and fine views over the water to Ham Lands and Richmond Park.

Inland lies a big tract of mixed 1880–1910 and 1930s homes – everything from handsome Arts-and-Crafts detacheds to little rows of cottages, smartened-up ex-council, 1970s town-houses. A similar mix appears W of the railway, which runs behind **Waldegrave Rd**. The handsome double-fronted (though semi-detached) Victoriana in **Cambridge Rd** is popular. Cheaper homes are further W: ex-council houses, Victorian cottages.

Borders: Isleworth

North from St Margarets, into Hounslow borough, you find Isleworth, a quirky mix of old riverside village, modern office development and standard-issue suburbia. The river sports a large wooded island (with working boatyard); Syon Park is a green backdrop. Old Isleworth has 1990s town-houses in **Heron's Place**, an enclave of stockbrick-and-stucco, and there a few lovely old riverside houses in **Church St**, including a fine if fake (it's 1970s) Regency-Gothicky one next to the touristy London Apprentice pub. **Mill Plat**, just inland, has a handful of million-plus Georgian homes. The rest of the old village isn't: a few buildings aside, it was rebuilt in the 1980s as smart offices plus a few flats.

Persimmon's Mill Park adds 99 new flats to Mill Plat on part of the West Middlesex Hospital site. Winter 2004/5 prices: 2-beds from £225,000; 3-beds £265,000-plus.

South St bounds the old village; on S are mid-Victorian terraces (**Algar Rd**, the W side of **Worple Rd**) and cottage-council houses. Homes become more suburban, 1930s semis mostly. The giant drainage works at Mogden lie W, which can be bad news on a hot day.

Transport Trains: Twickenham, St Margarets, Teddington, to Waterloo via Richmond or Kingston. Twickenham to Waterloo 25 min.

Convenient for Heathrow, Richmond, River Thames, Kingston shopping, roads to West. Miles from centre: 9–10.

Schools Richmond Education Authority: Teddington, Waldegrave (g), Whitton, Orleans Park. St Catherine's RC (g). Private: Hampton (b), Lady Eleanor Holles (g), St James (b).

SALES

Flats	S	1B	2B	3B	4B	5B
Average prices	100–170	160–260	175–500+	270–600+	→1M	–
Houses	2B	3B	4B	5B	6/7B	8B
Average prices	225–375	285–750	400–775+	500–1.5M	750–2M+	–

RENTAL

Flats	S	1B	2B	3B	4B	5B
Average prices	120–210	150–250	230–400	250–420	–	–
Houses	2B	3B	4B	5B	6/7B	8B
Average prices	220–350	260–450+	350–900	350–1000+	→2000	–

The properties From riverside splendour – 18th- and 19th-century mansions plus luxury new-build – to railway cottages, with plenty of suburbia of most sizes and vintages in the hinterland. Flats line the river, and there are conversions carved from the big old houses.

The market Big premiums paid for best riverside locations, while mainstream homes are (a bit) cheaper than Richmond. Good schools attract families, whose breadwinners find City and Heathrow easy to reach.

Among estate agents active in this area are:

- Featherstone Leigh
- Philip Hodges
- Jackson-Stops
- Dexters
- Chase Buchanan
- Milestone & Collis
- Hamptons
- Fitz-Gibbons
- Milestones
- Your Move
- Jardine & Co
- Chancellors
- Snellers
- Churchills
- Townends
- Barton & Wyatt
- Your Move
- Lauristons

WANDSWORTH

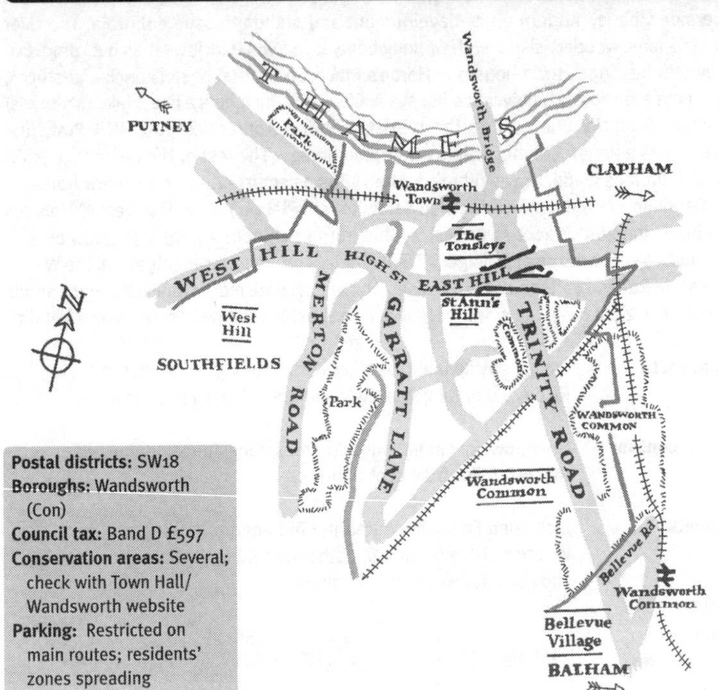

Postal districts: SW18
Boroughs: Wandsworth (Con)
Council tax: Band D £597
Conservation areas: Several; check with Town Hall/ Wandsworth website
Parking: Restricted on main routes; residents' zones spreading

Wandsworth is a mixed-up sort of place. A lot of people say they live here, but don't: it is both a borough (big, taking in Putney, Balham and Tooting) and a place (quite small, squeezed between Common and river). And if you do live in Wandsworth *proper*, home can be a dignified Victorian villa in a leafy enclave or a designer-smart riverside flat in a year-old 16-storey tower. The Wandsworth Common area attracts professional families in numbers from the cramped streets of Clapham and Battersea, drawn by the spacious houses, large gardens and good schools. Their younger colleagues go for the riverside flats, which have also been popular of late with buy-to-letters.

Smart flats are normal now: indeed, you have a choice of about a thousand brand-new ones, not counting the re-sales as investors who snapped up previous offerings take their profits. Or not. Not long ago, the riverside was a derelict wasteland. Home in Wandsworth was, for many, a council flat – some in towers as tall as the latest crop – or a cheap, skimpy, Victorian converted flat. Thanks to a council which pioneered Right to Buy, most of the council homes are now private. Thanks to three decades of growing wealth, most of the Victorian homes are now returned to a smartness perhaps only dreamed of by their builders.

What magic has transformed Wandsworth from a scruffy, traffic-choked suburban centre, crammed in between a brewery, a smelly creek and a 1970s shopping mall? The local council like to take much of the credit. So it should, for an inspired mix of efficiency, half-decent schools, self-promotion and low taxes attracted the middle classes across the river at the start of the 1980s. Then, Wandsworth (the place, not the wider borough) was a poor alternative to Battersea Park or Clapham Old Town. But once the momentum built up, the news spread that there are streets of solid family houses around the leafy Common. The neat cottages of 'the Tonsleys' attracted young City commuters. Next, incomers found the pleasant, sloping roads of East Hill, and the rather swanky suburbia over towards Putney.

The fad for riverside living adds a whole new layer of flats to what was predominantly a family-house district. Where there were once wharfs, distilleries, the untidy side of commerce and industry, now there rears a rampart of gleaming blocks with balconies and that vital river view. What matter to the developers if the glint of water leads your eye to equally anodyne blocks of 'river view apartments' in Fulham? That there is no tube for miles, and that car (and bus) access is via the nightmare Wandsworth one-way system? That 'minutes to Chelsea' means crossing one of two equally busy bridges? That your neighbours may well be a rubbish depot, and the only boats on the river are the yellow barges that convey the waste?

One should not carp: land dotted with derelict freight containers is better turned to productive use. There will be riverside walks, parks, even a pier 'for any future riverbus use'. And 2,000 new flats (1998–2005) certainly add to buyers' choice around here, even if the sellers of dowdy conversions inland find the competition a bit stiff. It's worth noting though that the riverside developments vary in smartness, degree of security and amenities: buyers, you have plenty of choice.

Wandsworth *borough* takes in a wide swathe of South-West London from Putney to Streatham. At its heart is the tightly-knit former village where the River Wandle meets the Thames. The centre is best-known today for its snarled-up one-way system, in the midst of which lies the monumental 1930s-heroic town hall, and for the recently-transformed shopping centre. The centre apart, Wandsworth lacks amenities: the inhabitants look for money-spending opportunities to **Bellevue Rd**, a chi-chi strip of shops and bars S of the Common, or to much-changed, bar-bedecked **Northcote Rd** between the commons in Battersea ('most people', sniffs a local, 'would say it's in Clapham' – an example of Neighbourhood Creep).

The Wandsworth Common tract further S is at first sight uninspiring: a prison looms on the horizon, a 6-lane road funnels traffic up from the gigantic intersection at the S end of Wandsworth Bridge, the green space is bisected by a railway line. But the open space, is there, it is green and undulating (unlike Clapham's shaved billiard-table), it provides an attractive frame for the mature and leafy streets of Victorian and Edwardian houses. And there are trains into Victoria and Waterloo from nearby Clapham Junction and the Common's own station. The Common streets share a plethora of prep schools and designer shops with the neighbouring 'twixt the commons' bit of Battersea.

The town centre mall has dropped the name 'Arndale' in favour of 'Southside', £95 million is being spent on it, yielding a 14-screen cinema, a Virgin health club and (yes!) a Waitrose. There is a large Sainsbury's in **Garratt Lane**. A landmark in the town are the Victorian buildings of the Ram Brewery (Young's). Looking ahead, how long will the brewery remain? Its 5-acre site could provide the chance for a *real* town centre. . . .

Central and riverside

Over 1,000 flats are being built, or have planning permission, on the riverside strip between Wandsworth Park in the W and Battersea in the E. The River Wandle, which flows into the Thames, provides extra sites running S to **Armoury Way**: much land here has been derelict, or in temporary uses, for 20 years. The council's vision of 'the Wandle delta' as a 'new riverside quarter' is coming to fruition, though how the new inhabitants will get in or out of their smart enclaves remains to be seen. While millions have been and are being spent on the flats, nothing has gone on the roads or railways, and Wandsworth Town station is pretty crammed at morning rush hours. There is, though, a new foot/cycle bridge over the creek, linking **The Causeway** with **Enterprise Way**.

Starting in the E, the biggest scheme is St George's 'Battersea Reach', where 658

new homes (157 Affordable) are arising in ten towers, up to 16 storeys high (we preferred the original, more apposite name: Gargoyle Wharf). It is on Wandsworth's Battersea borders, next to Wandsworth Bridge, and still in SW18. The first of five phases welcomed inhabitants last November; they will not see the last of their new neighbours till 2007, and the health centre/shops/hotel may take till 2010. Prices in the first two phases start at £249,000 for 1-beds, with 2-beds from £369,000 and penthouses (sold, it is said) at £2.3 million. On the other, W side of the bridge, past The Ship pub, is St George's vast 517-home 'Riverside West' in **Smugglers Way**. Resales examples: 2-beds £275–550,000. Beware the planned doubling in size of the next-door Solid Waste Transfer Station to the W. (If you don't know what one of those is, take a look.) Health club, restaurant, crèche complete things. To the S, next to B&Q, is a Holiday Inn hotel.

Further W, beyond the rubbish depot and the mouth of the Wandle, is the former Shell depot site accessed via **Point Pleasant** and **Osiers Rd**. This is 'The Riverside Quarter' where LCR/FairBriar are building 422 flats (107 Affordable), ranging up to 11 storeys, with restaurants and a new public plaza. Oh – and 16 moorings. Prices start at £305,000 for a 1-bed, 2-beds from £430,000, 3-beds up to £1.3 million. Or you can make an offer on a residential mooring (c. £120,000 for a 60-year lease, provide your own boat). Note that this scheme, unlike most on the river, has a decent view, across to the bosky banks of the Hurlingham Club and along W towards Putney.

Next upstream, towards Putney, is Prospect Quay: two new riverside flats blocks, an office/leisure block and a restaurant. Quay, houseboats and a 'drinks pontoon' add to the amenities. Inland, the 52-flats Parkland Square block in **Northfield Rd** dates from 2000. Another inland site in **Osiers Way** has planning permission for 52 flats, (another) health club/gym and some business space. Plans for 35 flats, shops and offices on the big gas-holder site on **Armoury Way** seem moribund.

Back in the real world, there are plenty of good buildings and an interesting townscape in the old centre, Wandsworth town. The problem is of course the traffic, which (as the council's own Conservation Area profile glumly observes), makes it hard to stand back and appreciate the buildings. Property here is mainly commercial with some small industrial premises (and of course the Brewery). Beautiful early-Georgian houses are to be found in **Wandsworth Plain** and **Church Row**. There are also privatized blocks of modernized '30s council flats that are set well back from the road. Behind is **Frogmore**, with its flat-fronted cottages and a modern, private development. **Sudlow Rd** joins Frogmore to North Passage and has a mix of mid-Victorian cottages and modern homes. Between **Hardwick's Way** and **Buckhold Rd**, SW of the centre, is 'Centre Square', with 14 flats (£215–510,000), a big restaurant and offices.

The Tonsleys

This relatively quiet enclave is tucked away between **Old York Rd**, **Trinity Rd**, and the relentlessly busy **East Hill** and **Fairfield St**. Known for attractive little Victorian cottages (mainly 2- and 3-bed), plus some large 4- and 5-bed houses, the name comes from the quartet of streets called, respectively, **Tonsley Rd**, – **St**, – **Place** and – **Hill**. A new one-way system has eased traffic somewhat in these narrow roads.

The Tonsleys is near Wandsworth Town station (12 min to Waterloo via Clapham Junction), and was first 'discovered' by '80s yuppies. **Old York Rd**, once a busy, scruffy through-route, is now a bijou cobbled backwater ('so smart now, but not *too* smart'). Restaurants, a Pizza Express, trendy bars and amusing shops burgeon. Estate agents cluster. Four 3-bed/2-bath town-houses were recently squeezed into a new mews, **Lovetts Place**, off Old York Rd. South of the road is **Alma Rd**, with large 3-storey Victoriana and a pub at the junction with Fullerton Rd. Especially pretty streets in this NE corner are **Dalby Rd** and **Bramford Rd**, which run down the fairly steep hill from Dighton Rd. Bramford Rd backs onto the dualled stretch of Trinity Rd, and **Podmore Rd** overlooks the railway. **Tonsley Place** (a leafy avenue, but joins Fairfield St) and **Tonsley Rd** have much chi-chi'd 2- and 3-bed cottages. Mixed blocks of '30s council and private flats (Fairfield Court) front **Fairfield St** (very heavy traffic: it's part of the one-way system) along with four large, semi-detached Victorian houses. Two-bed modernized Tonsley cottages are now £400,000-plus, while larger 3-bed homes are £400,000-plus (some try for more; £500,000 for extended homes, £750,000 for the few genuine 4-beds).

There are larger, 3-storey 4/5-bed houses in **Dempster Rd, Fullerton Rd** and **Birdhurst Rd**, N of East Hill. Birdhurst Rd overlooks six-lane Trinity Rd, but it's in a cutting at this point, so noise is no great problem. A 1990 Victorian pastiche on **East Hill** backs onto **Fullerton Rd**: 64 flats and six houses known as 'Tonsley Heights' are grouped round a new street called (why?) **Bloomsbury Place**. A new flats complex, Almand House, is just down **East Hill**. The Vauxhall car showrom at the E end of East Hill has been bought by Laing, who plan 66 flats for sale in a 16-storey tower, plus 22 Affordable Homes in a lower building. **Huguenot Place** is popular, but not quite as nice as it sounds: heavy traffic maroons the attractive 18th-century church, Book House and the Huguenot cemetery. There are some flats and houses, including Huguenot Mansions.

St Ann's Hill

South of **East Hill**, between **St Ann's Hill, Allfarthing Lane** and **Wandsworth Common Westside**, homes are mainly well-sized, late-Victorian and Edwardian with some modern infill. (These include low-rise council-built flats, most now privately owned.) Prices rise as you move E towards the Common. This neighbourhood has become a popular choice with families: prices are less than around the Common, and most homes are bigger than the bijou Tonsley cottages.

Popular roads on the eastern, generally more expensive, side include those around **Geraldine Rd, Melody Rd** and **Cicada Rd**. The architecture is mixed but most houses are large, late-Victorian 2- and 3-storey. When thoroughly worked over (as most are) they offer 4 beds, a double living room and the ubiquitous big-kitchen-with-glassed-over-side-passage. In this state they command £600–700,000, though 5-beds in **Geraldine** and **Eglantine** Rds can ask over £1 million. Smaller, 3-bed, houses in the same streets start below £500,000. Four homes on the corner of **Rosehill Rd** were virtually rebuilt in 1999 behind their Victorian brick facades, with splendid double-height extensions at the back to maximize space. The 1990-vintage town-houses and flats of The Washhouse are in **St Ann's Crescent**, partly overlooking the unusual, late-Georgian 'pepper-pot' church. Here, some of the houses are of the same date as the church, while others are Victorian.

Houses on and surrounding **St Ann's Hill** are mainly Edwardian 3-bed terraces, but there are some '30s-built semis. Between St Ann's Hill and Garratt Lane are plenty of purpose-built late-Victorian maisonettes and flats, and some 3-bed houses. Prices are a bit lower here. A council-built estate runs along the lower end of **Allfarthing Lane** (**Iron Mill Rd, Vermont Rd**) and up to the Wandsworth end of St Ann's Hill: look here for cheaper homes. Allfarthing's Victorian 4-bed houses can be £400,000. **Kingham Close** has modern town-houses and 1-bed flats. Allfarthing School and St Anne's C of E are popular primaries. **Earlsfield Rd**, busy though it is, has some smart conversions of big old houses, some of which survive intact to offer 6-bed space to those who grow out of the nearby streets.

West Hill

This neighbourhood is SW of Wandsworth town centre and is bounded in the N by the endlessly jammed **West Hill**, which funnels traffic from the A3 into the maw of the Wandsworth one-way system. West Hill merges into Southfields, which shares the SW18 postcode and has a tube station (District Line), which Wandsworth lacks. **Merton Rd** branches off West Hill, and features some good mid- and late-Victorian semi-detached and terraced houses. Many of the houses are set well back from the road with off-street parking. **Wimbledon Park Rd** leads down through the neighbourhood to Southfields tube station, lined with a mix of Victorian houses and low-rise council-built flats. **West Hill Rd**, running from Merton Rd to West Hill, mixes early, mid- and late-Victoriana with some 1930s and '50s homes – many detached or semi-detached. Prices are on a par with Putney: think £450–500,000 for a '30s semi, seven figures for the big ones – such as the double-fronted Victorian 5-beds in **Melrose Rd**. Houses in **Sispara Gardens** and **Viewfield Rd** are set well back and have off-street parking. **Lebanon Rd**, **Amerland Rd** and **Ringford Rd** all lead off West Hill and are more East Putney than Wandsworth: pay £500,000 for a 3-bed house, 10 per cent more for another bedroom. There is a small council-built, mostly privately-owned, infill in **Lebanon Gardens** with some 4-bed houses.

Further E, where **Broomhill Rd** meets **Merton Rd**, is an attractive, simple clutch of mews-style town-houses. Older and larger 2- and 3-storey late-Victorian houses follow from this more peaceful point on **Merton Rd** to the junction with Buckhold Rd.

Just to the W, in Sutherland Grove, is St Cecilia's, a new Church of England secondary school; also the big Whitelands homes scheme (see Southfields chapter).

A small council-built cottage-style estate off **Buckhold Rd** has mainly flat-fronted traditional-style houses. These homes now appear on the market. The large gardens of those on the eastern side of **Longstaff Crescent** back on to King George's Park.

Wandsworth Common, Spencer Park & the 'Toastrack'

Wandsworth Common Westside (the street) is protected from the traffic of Trinity Rd, (dual-carriageway at this point) by a slice of the Common, wide at the junction with Earlsfield Rd and narrowing to the junction with East Hill. Westside offers large 4- and 5-bed mid-Victorian houses; especially attractive is the row of ornate Gothic-style houses between Quarry Rd and Heathfield Rd. Further along Heathfield Rd is **Heathfield Gardens**, a secret row of enchanting Regency cottages of varying sizes, overlooking the common. Tree-lined **Westover Rd** has some very large Victorian semi- and detached houses: last winter a showbiz mogul's 6-bed was £4 million. **Crieff Rd**'s 4-bed houses seem reasonable by comparison at £650,000 – 1.5 million.

Across Earlsfield Rd and further along **Heathfield Rd** is another local landmark: Wandsworth Prison – which, believe it or not, is a listed building. There are occasional rumours of redevelopment. Just opposite is Heathfields, a 'mews' development of flats and houses, with 2- to 4-bed houses. Across the road, **Wilde Place** has 29 2- to 4-bed town-houses. Past the prison lies the pretty 1850s, flat-fronted cottages of **Alma Terrace** facing open land. Beyond, to the S and W of the prison, are 1920s and '30s blocks of flats. Some, built as homes for prison officers, now come up for sale. A block of 20 flats on **Heathfield Square** is new – with restrictions on windows looking towards the prison!

Next, to the area's gem: secretive **Spencer Park**, overlooking the Common from the N side, has a stunning range of large detached and semi-detached houses, built in a variety of styles in the 1870s. Some are now flats, or are used by institutions, but a number remain (or have been restored to) large family homes: prices of over £3 million have been mooted, though most are a lot less, especially the 1950s houses that replaced some of the Victoriana. Their secret is that they encircle, and have direct access to, their own private communal garden – a young park, really. Spencer Court on **Windmill Rd** is a 1930s flats block (1-bed £200,000) overlooking the tracks and the Emanuel School (independent, mixed) beyond.

Wandsworth Common Northside forms part of the traffic-plagued South Circular. Many houses have been converted into flats and those on the S side of the road are popular for their views over Wandsworth Common. Behind, in contrast, lie **Elsynge Rd** and **Spencer Rd**, where there's a mixture of exceptionally large, fine Victorian houses

with enormous gardens, smaller late-Victorian houses and double-fronted 'cottages'. Prices for the better houses range from £1–2 million. **Spanish Rd** has some lovely terraced houses; on **Northside** itself, half a dozen large 5-floor Victorian houses were extensively restored by Fairview in 1998: 5-beds, plus au pair flat and garage. **St John's Hill** is now much smarter than it was: new bars and shops are opening.

Approached from **Fitzhugh Grove**, an easy-to-miss turning off Trinity Rd, is the spectacular, splendidly Gothic Royal Victoria Patriotic Building. Built to care for orphan daughters of servicemen killed in the Crimean War, it stands proudly apart and now houses a theatre school, restaurant, design studios and quirky flats (some in towers and turrets), popular with artistic and media types. It is, though, set rather unfortunately between a major railway and an estate of council towers and is perhaps more fun to look at than out of. Not many come up for sale, however. A new bridge over the railway off Windmill Rd gives access to **John Archer Way**, a 1990s Fairview development of 200 flats and 65 houses. One-bed flats here are £200–220,000. Security is rather a feature: railway cuttings on two sides and the Emanuel School grounds on the third.

The more traditional charms of 'The Toastrack', a grid of streets surrounded on three sides by the Common, have been attracting family buyers since the 1980s. This group lies off Trinity Rd and takes in **Dorlcote Rd**, **Nicosia Rd**, **Baskerville Rd**, **Henderson Rd**, part of **Routh Rd** and **Patten Rd**. Here are large, detached or semi-detached 5/6-bedroom late-Victorian houses, some with exceptionally big gardens; some flats, too, in Greenview Court on **Baskerville Rd**. Houses on **Dorlcote Rd** overlook the Common from the front, while gardens in **Routh Rd** and **Baskerville** back onto the Common – which adds £200,000 to their prices. 'Toastrack' family homes hit half a million in 1989, our 1990 edition recorded: six times that is now asked for a top one, like the 6-bed in Routh Rd marketed last winter for £3.25 million (though £1.2 million is more typical). The (private) school in **Patten Rd** makes parking problematic.

West of Trinity Rd from the 'Toastrack' are some unusually large, often double-fronted century-old houses with good-sized gardens. The area is known as the Magdalen Estate: that Oxford college was the original landlord. The biggest houses are to be found in the roads adjoining Lyford Rd, most notably **Herondale Avenue**, **Loxley Rd**, **Frewin Rd** and **Burntwood Rd**. **Lyford Rd** is a no-through road running N–S between Magdalen Rd and Burntwood Lane. Prices of around a million are not uncommon (in 1990 £350,000 was regarded as the top) and a 6-bed in half an acre on **Magdalen Rd** was asking £4.25 million last winter. Houses that lie between **Routh Rd** and **Lyford Rd** back onto a wild and overgrown extension of Wandsworth Common, adding to the rural illusion beloved of many of the inhabitants (and adding c. £200,000 to the prices). To the W, the Beatrix Potter primary school (in Earlsfield) acts as a magnet, raising the profile of the roads W of Lyford such as **Loxley Rd** where 4-bed houses are £650,000-plus.

Bellevue Village

We are now at the foot of the Common, where Balham, Tooting and Battersea meet. However, the *borough* is still Wandsworth, and the useful little railway station's name is Wandsworth Common, all of which allows the denizens of the select streets of the 'Bellevue Village' neighbourhood so to think of themselves. If they are really, strictly speaking, in Tooting and in SW17, it would not be wise to say so locally. After all, Bellevue has been called 'the new King's Rd'. Hmmm. . .

The Village, bordered by **Trinity Rd**, **St James's Drive** and the Common, is a tiny, cut-off corner of streets of pretty, mid-Victorian stock-brick cottages, some flat-fronted and larger than they look. Gazing out over the Common, **Bellevue Rd** itself is lined with galleries, chi-chi delis, bars and restaurants. None of this existed 20 years ago: Bellevue was a quiet suburban parade of butchers, bakers and junk shops. The Lucky Parrot, the antithesis of all chain stores, started the change. Happily it's still there; so's the parrot.

Expect to pay £400,000-plus for a 2-bed Village terraced, £700,000 for a 4-bed. As an alternative, try the 'Bonner Building' flats carved out of the Surrey Tavern on the corner: £265,000 for a 1-bed, £685,000 for a 2-bed/2-floor. Two houses are yet to be released.

St James's Drive has larger mid-Victorian terraced houses, some semi-basement and stuccoed: 5-beds up to a million, but 3-beds £550,000-plus. The former St James's Hospital site is now housing-association homes. The streets on E, S of Balham Park Rd, are really Balham (which chapter see) but they are boosted by the Bellevue factor.

Those who need more space also venture across **Trinity Rd**, where **Brodrick**, **Wandle** and **Hendham Rds** have large, late-Victorian mainly 3-storey terraced and (just) semi-detached houses, with prices these days of £1–2 million, and £2.5–3 million in Brodrick. These are popular with families, as many have very large gardens.

Transport Trains: Wandsworth Town (Waterloo 12 min), Wandsworth Common, Clapham Junction.

Convenient for Wandsworth and Clapham Commons, Clapham Junction, Fulham. Miles from centre: 4.

Schools Local Authority: Burntwood (g), ADT College (b), Southfields College, St Cecilia's C of E. Private: Emanuel. Many prep schools.

SALES

Flats	S	1B	2B	3B	4B	5B
Average prices	120–150	200–270	250–400	290+	380+	–
Houses	2B	3B	4B	5B	6/7B	8B
Average prices	250–390	350–500	450–600	600+	750+	1.5M

RENTAL

Flats	S	1B	2B	3B	4B	5B
Average prices	150–190	200–240	250–350	320–380	400+	–
Houses	2B	3B	4B	5B	6/7B	8B
Average prices	250–400	350–500	400–700	600+	650+	1000→

The properties Wide range, but main type is Victorian in a range of locations, with cottage-style in the Tonsleys and Bellevue, grander ones near the Common, stratospheric ones in Spencer Park, 'Toastrack'. Some '30s and '50s suburban in SW of area. New flats aplenty by the river.

The market While the town centre stays forever Wandsworth, the fashionable enclaves – Tonsleys, Bellevue, 'Toastrack' (all close to stations) and Common – are established, attracting space-hungry families, and the riverside is a whole new district. Beware overhang of investor-bought riverside flats.

Among estate agents active in this area are:

- Robert Trindle & Co
- Bells
- Realm Estates
- Barnard Marcus
- Raymond Bushell
- Savills
- Friend & Falcke
- John D Wood
- Cound & Co
- Hamptons
- Douglas & Gordon
- Edwin Evans
- Vanstons
- Sullivan Thomas
- Kinleigh Folkard & Hayward
- Winkworth
- Courtenay
- Foxtons
- Craigie & Co
- John G Dean
- Curzon Wilson
- Bairstow Eve
- Townends

West Hampstead

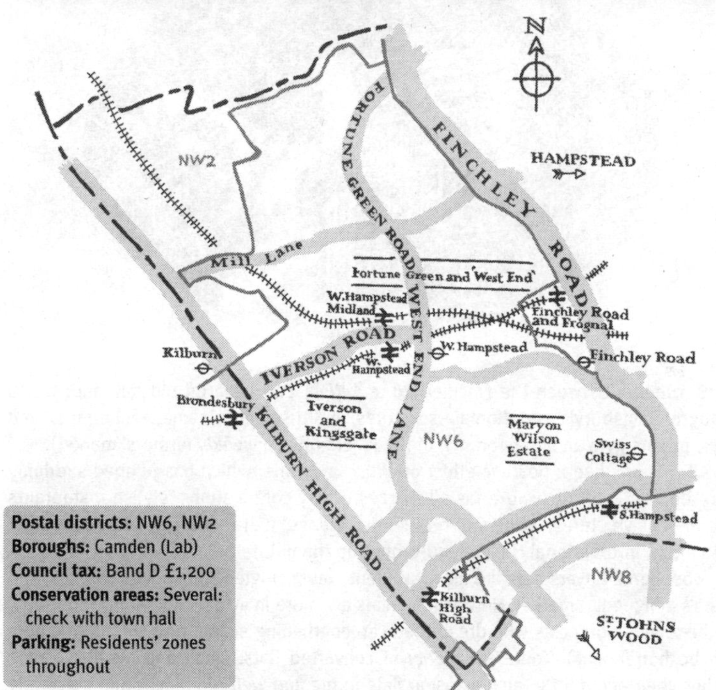

Postal districts: NW6, NW2
Boroughs: Camden (Lab)
Council tax: Band D £1,200
Conservation areas: Several: check with town hall
Parking: Residents' zones throughout

West of Hampstead, but east of Kilburn: guess which neighbour gets to name this tract? Yes, Hampstead is the name that sells, even if the hilltop village is these days stuffed with bankers and their free-spending wives, with nary an intellectual in sight. Kilburn, on the other hand, carries an aura of downmarket tat, these days far from deserved. There's a move afoot to revive Kilburn's name: the priory of Kilburn stood in what is now Priory Rd, and East Kilburn is historically a truer name than West Hampstead. An agreeable thought, but we suspect it won't catch on. . . .

West Hampstead (or East Kilburn. . .) grew fast on open fields once the railways made it commutable from 1860 on. The hamlets of West End and Fortune Green were submerged, traceable now only in the street pattern. The Priory had long gone, replaced by a pub. Victorian builders blanketed the fields with terraces, the next generation added great blocks of mansion flats, and the 20th century knocked down what it could and stuck up council blocks, and converted most of the remaining Victorian houses into flats. So much, so normal for inner London. What West Hampstead had, and has, was excellent transport and that tenuous but vital name-tag, linking it with prosperous, glamorous *echt*-Hampstead on the other side of the Finchley Rd.

Transport still attracts people to West Hampstead: the three stations (Jubilee Line, Thameslink, North London Line) form a messy, at times chaotic, hub. Plans to redevelop the whole complex (and gain a little more land to squeeze in a few more flats and offices) have been floated but seem far off. At present, passengers switching routes have to struggle out of one station, along crowded pavements, and into the next. . . .

The O2 shopping centre did get built: first mooted in the late '80s, it opened in

1998, running between the Finchley Rd and West End Lane on old rail land. It has brought Sainsbury's and Homebase stores, multi-screen cinema, restaurants and bars, private gym and huge branch of Books Etc (plus a weekly farmers' market).

All this has had a positive effect on West End Lane, which has jumped suddenly into the 21st century. It now has all the customary coffee shops, stylish restaurants and expensive stores, while still retaining a 'village' feel that locals like to contrast with glitzy, international Hampstead-proper up the hill.

Most home-buyers here are newly affluent young singles and no-kids couples, and there's a big rental market. However, families are more in evidence now, it's reported – to the anguish of locals who dread the ever-lengthening school-run jams (traffic here can be horrendous). There are plenty of converted flats, small and medium, some feeling their age a little; also mansion flats in big and well-run blocks and a growing number of £1 million-plus houses, especially in the smart South Hampstead enclave bordering St John's Wood.

The spine of the area is **West End Lane**, which leads S into **Abbey Rd** and **St John's Wood Rd**; it has stations, plenty of restaurants and bars, and the sort of shops that cater for the single and footloose. As well as the mobile young, a settled tranche of people with interesting jobs (the media, the stage, etc, increasingly joined by City and business people) give a more stable, community feel.

The development of the area took place on the large tracts of land owned by the Maryon Wilson and Eyre estates, which to this day hold the freeholds of large areas of leasehold property. A few of the streets (on the E, or Hampstead, side, such as **Crediton Hill** and **Alvanley Gardens**) were built with the relatively well-heeled in mind, but most of the area was designed to cater for the needs of the Victorian age's growing lower middle class. The result was large numbers of 2-storey, 2- and 3-bed terraced houses and semis. The area was also among the first to see the erection of those large blocks of purpose-built flats called mansion blocks – the word 'mansion' possibly designed to salve the blighted aspirations of those who could not afford whole houses. Paradoxically these flats, with their many, spacious and elegant rooms, are among the most popular homes today.

The change in the area over the last 30 years has been dramatic. Steeply rising prices and the spillover effect from Hampstead have proved an irresistible temptation to the traditional inhabitants. From the 1960s on, properties were converted into flats at a brisk rate – fewer than 10 per cent of the original houses remain in single occupation.

Recent prosperity has seen a new generation of flat conversions, smarter and more spacious, emulating the loft aesthetic in place of the inept and pokey carve-ups of the

1970s–1980s. Chipboard partitions are out, mezzanines and decked roof-terraces are in. Look hard at particulars when seeking a flat: older conversions can be both tired and cramped, though they are naturally cheaper than the airy new ones. Developers are recycling flats at a brisk pace, so the older sort is becoming scarcer. Beware, say agents, the less formal roof terraces: some are without benefit of planning or building regs, and it can cost up to £10,000 to make honest patios of them – and some are even banned.

Fortune Green and 'West End'

West Hampstead is bisected diagonally by **West End Lane** leading, at the N end, into **Fortune Green Rd**: this gives access to a whole group of roads rather marooned from the rest of the suburb by the Midland rail line. These include some quiet and peaceful enclaves compared with the bustle and congestion of the rest of the area.

Behind the pleasant open space of Fortune Green itself there lies the Hampstead Cemetery, which casts a protective shadow over streets like **Gondar Gardens** and **Hillfield Rd** – one of the few corners in the area where the Victorian builders produced family houses of any size. Many have now been converted (examples: 1-bed up to £290,000, 3-bed duplex c. £420,000), but occasional 4- or 5- or even 6-bed houses do still come onto the market. Gondar Gardens has some mansion blocks as well.

Also interesting is the group of streets known as 'The Greeks' – not surprisingly, since they include **Agamemnon Rd**, **Ajax Rd** (these two back onto greenery), **Ulysses Rd** and **Achilles Rd**. These are still well supplied with family-sized (3-, perhaps 4-bed if loft converted, a few 5-beds) houses: perhaps the best-preserved corner of the entire suburb, though this year seeing much building activity. Agents cite this as the 'best' part of West Hampstead, especially for families – though it's not that close to transport. Pay £650–700,000 for a 5-bed. On **Fortune Green Rd**, the 1930s Cholmley Gardens mansion block has sought-after, spacious flats – a 4-bed was £525,000 last winter – which share gardens and tennis courts. New homes here: an old garage site on Fortune Green Rd is now flats; in **Parsifal Rd**, more by developers Theobald. **Burrard Rd** has smaller houses than in most of the area.

Closer to **Finchley Rd** is the area once known as 'West End', now dominated by the large mansion blocks in **West End Lane**, **Mill Lane**, **Lyncroft Gardens**, **Cannon Hill** and **Honeybourne Rd**: these include Buckingham Mansions, Marlborough Mansions, Yale Court and Harvard Court. You pay more for a mansion flat than for a conversion, and they are back in favour after a period when buyers steered clear, worried by service charges. The best blocks – with good maintenance, porterage, heating and lifts – are much in demand: Buckingham and Marlborough Mansions have large flats and are the priciest (in Buckingham, a 4-bed/2-recep can reach up to £650,000; a 2-bed needing work in Lyncroft Gardens, £360,000). Pay less – c. £285,000 for a 2-bed – for flats above the shops on West End Lane. Avenue Mansions, despite being in **Cannon Hill**, gets an NW3 postcode but suffers from proximity to the busy Finchley Rd. Some houses remain in these streets: five or six survive in **Honeybourne Rd** (a 6-bed needing work was £1.4 million last autumn), and a few in **Lyncroft Gardens**.

The smartest streets in West Hampstead are as close to Hampstead as you can get. **Alvanley Gardens**, with its large detached houses, grandly overlooks the grounds of Cumberland Tennis Club and Hampstead Cricket Club in **Lymington Rd**. **Weech Rd** also has some 6- to 8-bed houses: expect to pay up to £2 million. At the **Finchley Rd** corner of **Lymington Rd**, Regime have built 'The Pulse': 55 2- and 3-bed flats around a courtyard (though some rooms overlook the busy Finchley Rd): prices from £470,000–£1.2 million, plus another £25,000 to park your motor.

Mill Lane's bars, antique shops and the like reflect to some extent the inhabitants of the area; here flats above shops are to let. To the S are streets such as **Sumatra Rd**, **Broomsleigh St**, **Solent Rd**, **Narcissus Rd** and **Pandora Rd** – all typical of the 2- and 3-

storey terraces that West Hampstead has to offer. **Solent** is considered one of the better streets: quite a few whole houses here, priced at c. £650,000 for a 4-bed (a stable price). Most of these houses have been split into flats: they are cheaper than the 'mansions' at c. £220,000 for a 1-bed, perhaps cheaper at the railway end of the streets. **Dennington Park Rd** has yet more conversions: some are showing their age (and older ones tend to be small – one big house has nine flats in it). A typical 2-bed garden flat here might be £320,000-plus.

One interesting enclave of semis, in streets including **Menelik Rd**, **Somali Rd** and **Asmara Rd**, are close to the open spaces of Fortune Green. These claim the West Hampstead name, though they are in NW2 and are as close to Cricklewood.

Iverson and Kingsgate

This is the triangle between the Midland railway line to the N, **West End Lane** and **Kilburn High Rd**. There's a steep gradient of respectability and price between West Hampstead (good) and Kilburn (not so good). Towards the N, busy **Iverson Rd** leads past light-industrial areas and large modern council estates to the slightly less smart but on-the-move area of **Maygrove Rd**, **Loveridge Rd** and **Fordwych Rd**. Once you cross the rail bridge on **Iverson Rd** you are in Kilburn, according to locals. Here the restaurants are cheaper, the streets livelier. There's a price gradient, unchanged over the last year: you might pay £270,000 for a 2-bed flat at the E end of Iverson – but £250,000 at the Kilburn (and train stations) end.

Further S, **Sherriff Rd** and **Hemstal Rd** lead W from **West End Lane**, enclosing a clutch of streets (**Lowfield**, **Kylemore**, **Gladys** and **Hilltop Rds**) that command West Hampstead prices. **Hemstal Rd** is still un-smart. 'Oppidans' in **Linstead St** is an old school split into flats (around £365,000 for a 2-bed).

South again, the densely-packed streets E of **Kingsgate Rd** have mainly small 2-storey terraced houses, with a number of council estates. There are, however, pleasant corners well worth seeking out. Roads such as **Messina Avenue**, **Gascony Avenue** and **Mazenod Avenue** hold 3-storey Victoriana, some split into flats: 1-beds at £200–220,000-ish, 2-bed £255–265,000. There are also blocks of purpose-built flats.

Cross the **Kilburn High Rd** to the W and you are still in NW6 – but not in West Hampstead: see Kilburn chapter. Up the High Rd is Kilburn tube which, like West Hampstead, is on the Jubilee Line.

The southern strip of the area, between a railway line and **Boundary Rd**, is dominated by very large council blocks, including the Abbey Estate and the extraordinary, 1,000ft-long concrete sweep of Camden's Alexandra Rd Estate in **Rowley Way**.

The Maryon Wilson estate/South Hampstead

The area bounded by **Broadhurst Gardens**, **Finchley Rd**, **Belsize Rd** and **Priory Rd** is part of the estate laid out by Sir Thomas Maryon Wilson, Lord of the Manor of Hampstead, between 1874 and the late 1890s. A glance at a street map shows a more spacious, curving street pattern, betraying larger – and better-built – homes. Nevertheless, after the war this became bedsit-land, and remained so right up until the 1970s; these days it contains some of the most attractive, most popular and most expensive properties in West Hampstead (the name South Hampstead having fallen almost out of use except for the train station). Whatever you call it, here the streets are wide and quiet, the properties gracious. Residents' parking has helped too. Think £800,000 for a 4-bed house here.

Particularly attractive, in streets such as **Canfield Gardens**, **Compayne Gardens** and **Fairfield Gardens**, are the red-brick mansion blocks, which often sport endearing turrets on the corner properties. The homes along **Fairhazel Gardens** and the streets off it share large communal gardens. Some of the best of these properties are owned by the pioneering Fairhazel Housing Cooperative (the first of its kind), and thus have not been available on the open market. But there are other elegant roads, including **Broadhurst Gardens, Greencroft Gardens, Aberdare Gardens, Cleve Road** and **Goldhurst Terrace,** where there is a brisk trade in both purpose-built and converted flats – including some luxurious recent conversions. Here and there you might even find the odd large, still whole, house: **Priory Rd** and **Terrace** both have more enviable, million-plus houses. Flats vary widely: 2-beds are, as last year, £300–375,000-plus. New-build is scarce in this crowded corner – it is a conservation area – but Barratt found space for 23 houses in Rosemount Mews off **Rosemount Rd** in 2001, and then for the handsome Highfield Mews.

Transport Tubes: West Hampstead, Kilburn (zone 2, Jubilee); Finchley Rd (zone 2, Jubilee, Metropolitan). From West Hampstead: Oxford Circus 15 min (1 change), City 30 min (1 change), Heathrow 60 min (1 change). Trains: West Hampstead (King's Cross 10 min, Thameslink and North London Line/Silverlink).

Convenient for Hampstead Heath, West End, M1/A1. Miles from centre: 4.

Schools Local Authority: St George's RC, Hampstead School, Quintin Kynaston Comprehensive.

SALES

Flats	S	1B	2B	3B	4B	5B
Average prices	100–170	165–280	220–400	300–500+	400–1M+	550–1.5M+
Houses	2B	3B	4B	5B	6/7B	8B
Average prices	300–500	400–600	500–700+	600–1M+	600–1.5M	700–2M

RENTAL

Flats	S	1B	2B	3B	4B	5B
Average prices	150–190	180–300	220–400	300–650	375–750	550–1000
Houses	2B	3B	4B	5B	6/7B	8B
Average prices	250–400	320–650	400–750+	500–1000	–	–

The properties Victorian terraced homes, most now converted to flats, which vary from the smart and spacious to the dated and cramped. Lots of big mansion flats, some almost St John's Wood-smart, some almost Kilburn-scruffy. Some surviving family houses, at a (slight) discount to NW3 prices.

The market Rapid turnover of flat-buyers, who use the area as a staging-post before moving on to family homes, plus more established (and childless) professionals. Families more in evidence of late.

Among estate agents active in this area are:

- Kinleigh Folkard & Hayward
- Harris & Co
- Greene & Co
- Parkheath Estates
- Brian Lack & Co
- Paramount
- Bairstow Eves
- Foxtons
- Cedar Estates
- Goldschmidt & Howland
- Anscombe & Ringland
- Storm Estates
- Fairbrother
- Dutch & Dutch
- In London Properties
- Arlington
- Winkworth
- Livitup

West Norwood, Norbury and Gipsy Hill

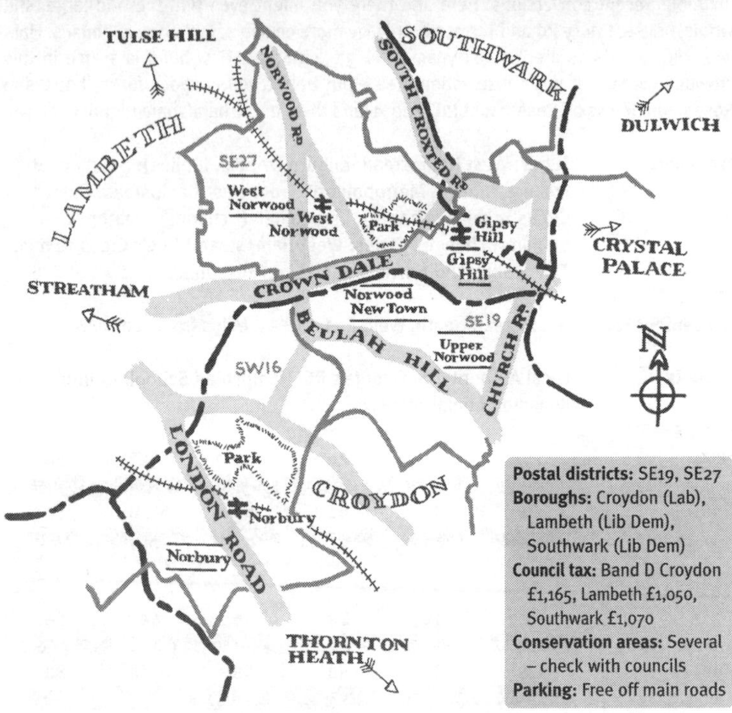

Postal districts: SE19, SE27
Boroughs: Croydon (Lab), Lambeth (Lib Dem), Southwark (Lib Dem)
Council tax: Band D Croydon £1,165, Lambeth £1,050, Southwark £1,070
Conservation areas: Several – check with councils
Parking: Free off main roads

Tumbling down from the heights of Crystal Palace, the South London suburbs of Norwood and Gipsy Hill lie on Sydenham Hill's western shores. A glance at a map shows the unusually large amount of green pockets, parks, playing fields here – even without the vast Crystal Palace Park that crowns the hill. Clues to the area's past are found in its names: Norwood is the old North Wood, which blanketed the hills S of the Thames basin. Tracts survive to this day, most notably **The Lawns'** woodland and **Sydenham Hill**'s patch; gipsies, who gave Gipsy Hill its name, considered these woodlands their own until forced out by the 19th-century enclosure acts.

Ambitious plans in the early 19th century to establish a Regency-style spa town around a mineral-water spring on Beulah Hill never materialized. The spa itself quickly failed thanks to a change in fashion (seawater cures became the latest craze). Later, however, the arrival of the illustrious Crystal Palace gave the area an enormous boost – equally enormous and splendid Victorian mansions emerged, plus a cascade of more modest houses. But 80 years on, the palace burnt to the ground – the oldest locals can still just recall that vivid 1936 night. So now the facilities of the National Sports Centre are the star local attraction. Happily, money has beeen found to restore the athletics track, and the London Development Agency is to take over the sports centre.

The future for the entire area has never been more in the balance than it is today: see the Crystal Palace chapter for the latest in the long-running, bitter battle over what will fill the empty plinth where once Paxton's graceful glass Palace stood. After the resounding defeat (locals 1, developers 0) of a truly awful scheme, hope dawns that a building of real imagination and importance will again fill a site as commanding as Hampstead's.

As things stand, the area has plenty of attractions for home-buyers, with a wide range of flats and houses, and fast rail links to Central London. House-hunters spill over from pricier Dulwich, Balham and Streatham; first-time buyers come for the many flat conversions in large Victorian houses. Agents say that people rent here, get to like the area, then buy. When looking, bear in mind that, along with the choice of roads and types of property comes the choice of boroughs: Lambeth to the N or Croydon to the S, while Southwark covers one corner. (In all, no fewer than five meet at the hilltop.)

Here a humble flat can be made special by spectacular views of London and outlying areas – most rewarding at sunrise and dusk. Larger houses are usually found on the high ground, legacy of the affluent Victorian suburb that the Crystal Palace engendered; but there are also some sensitive council-built estates, chiefly on **Central Hill**.

The northernmost, and most inner-London, neighbourhood is West Norwood (broadly, SE27), with a shopping street running N towards Tulse Hill, a rail station and the unusual combination of church and cemetery at its urban centre. Its outer reaches, W towards neighbouring Streatham and E towards Dulwich, are more popular.

Gipsy Hill (SE19), running up the W side of the commanding Crystal Palace heights, has some attractive Georgian homes – building began in 1806 – and startling views of the City. Its centre, near the **South Croxted Rd/Dulwich Wood Park** roundabout, has a pleasing, urban character largely untypical of the area. It, too, has a rail station. The SE19 area as a whole is attractive for families, with some good state schools, relatively reasonable 3-bed houses – and Dulwich's private schools just over the horizon.

Upper Norwood (see also Crystal Palace) is in Croydon Borough though still in SE19: as high as its name implies. The houses slope on S and W towards Norbury – which is a southern outlier of Streatham, and shares its SW16 postcode – and Thornton Heath (like Norbury with a station), which borders on Croydon.

Upper Norwood

Church Rd is the local high street: it declined in recent years, and in an attempt to revive it landlords have been encouraged to rent or sell empty shops, and smarten up shopfronts, by the Crystal Palace Partnership. There are now realistic hopes that the East London Line extension will reach Crystal Palace (see Transport chapter), and that the Tramlink may climb the hill from South Norwood, taking pressure off crowded roads.

The NW end of **Beulah Hill** starts modestly with a 1930s parade of shops (flats above these), then a large church and St Joseph's College. Victorian semis occupy the left side, 1960s town-houses the right. As the road ascends to leafier heights, these give way to large 1930s semis and detached homes, some in mock-Tudor style. Interesting buildings crop up, such as No. 17, an 1860 villa, and sweeping views: from the rear flats of Dorring Court, for example. Top homes here, and in **Woodfield Close**, command top prices. **Convent Hill** runs off to end in Convent Wood (there's many an outbreak of green space, if not woods, hereabouts); a 4-bed detached £545,000. Set back from the road are walled-off groups of 1960s town-houses on sites of long-gone mansions: the maps show these as closes and crescents. Then, in 1999, came eight detached half-million-plus homes luxuriating in a 2.4-acre site; in 2001 **Matilda Close**, a dozen new town-houses. More large, detached 1930s Tudor-timber-style and Victoriana complete the road.

From **Beulah Hill**, detached, garaged inter-war houses tumble S down **Spa Hill**, with its local shops and little Rising Sun pub. It fringes a park and another surviving pocket of woodland – site of the ill-fated spa. A cottagy lodge by Decimus Burton also survives. **Norbury Hill** has popular, comfortable 4-bed semis, and 5-bed detacheds that go for half a million-plus. On the corner of **Beulah Hill** and **Church Rd** stands the early 19th-century All Saints, with rural churchyard. By night the spire which, before the TV masts, dominated the skyline, is lit up. **Church Rd** has some 1930s semis, council-built blocks, big Victorian red-brick mansions (a 2-bed flat carved out of one such house, £170,000; a 5-bed detached £650,000) and a school. Again, closes and curvy roads lead to 20th-century replacements for the Victorian villas. Among the 1990s contributions, a clutch of 4-bed houses in **Turkey Oak Close**, a quiet cul-de-sac, are popular, an alternative to the Victorian 4-beds. **Old Vicarage Gardens** also runs off Church Rd: an enclave of 1- and 2-bed retirement flats set in gardens. Despite all the infilling, some of the houses date from the early 19th century. The dignified stucco of the Queen's Hotel, which was visited by all the notables of the Victorian age, has gained a modern annexe.

Roads off to the N of **Beulah Hill** are mainly 1930s residential. There's an absence of shops that would build a community; they revolve instead round the greenery of recreation ground and tennis courts. A 1-bed modern flat in one of the little cul-de-sacs was £140,000 last winter. **Hermitage Rd** has semis and council houses; **Ryefield Rd** has recent detached houses. Larger 1930s semis look over the greenery in pleasant **Eversley Rd**. So, too, do some houses in **Harold Rd** – which also gives its name to a conservation area running N that includes many fine late-Victorian houses (a studio flat in one of these, £140,000). This area takes in **Bedwardine Rd**, part of **Central Hill, Gatestone Rd, South Vale** – the attractive 1860s houses of which are about the area's oldest – **Vermont Rd** and the recreation ground. Many flat conversions in this corner.

Central Hill has Norwood Park and the imposing gothic-style Fidelis convent. Further up the hill there's a mix of 1920s and post-war council-built housing (2-bed house £177,000, 3-bed £245,000) and recent terraced town-houses. Also large Victorian houses, some split. Roads to the S such as **Essex Grove** and **Gatestone Rd** slope down attractively with Victorian semis (plus the flats of Essex Court). Victorian detached and semis overlook the vast, but carefully crafted, hillside Central Hill Estate to the N.

Gipsy Hill

Proximity to the Upper Norwood 'Triangle', with its villagy shops (see Crystal Palace) is a bonus for Gipsy Hill, a popular neighbourhood that tumbles attractively down the slopes from the road (and station) of the same name. Some Georgiana survives, large-scale Victorian villas yield serious-sized flats; even humdrum homes are made special if they share the wonderful views. It borders West Dulwich to the N, and usefully is fare zone 3. It is not peppered with new homes: they'd have a hard time competing with the range (from 1-bed flat c. £150,000 upwards), room sizes and service charges that period conversions offer. Large single homes are hunted out by professional couples, often wanting to work from home as well as raise a family. A 4-storey, 4-bed house was £450,000 last winter.

There's a magnificent view of London, with City skyscrapers prominent, from **Gipsy Hill**. Highlights of this busy street are the white stuccoed terraces and red-brick Victorian mansions. Roads leading off such as **Camden Hill Rd** and **Highland Rd** have period houses (some 3-storied, many split into flats, 1-bed c. £160,000): lots of refurbishment – and room to park – here. Also Highland Court, a wooded estate of 1930s flats (plus one 1990s block), with parking. Admire the wide-eaved houses of **Victoria Crescent**, or go for the modern: gated New Green Place with its 3-storey blocks.

The Paxton pub, shops, cafés and wine bar make an attractive start to **Gipsy Rd,** a gently rising road of varied Victoriana: you find flat conversions larger than some houses, terraced homes, purpose-built flats with views to the London Eye, plus some council-built 20th-century estates (with many homes now for sale). More variety yet: The Vestry, a recent church conversion, added six 2-bed flats.

Kingswood Primary is on the corner of **Salters Hill**: council-build with occasional Victoriana, overlooking Norwood Park). **Oaks Avenue** curls back up to **Gipsy Hill**: here, too, a good range of homes, from ex-council flats to 1930s 3-bed semis.

West Norwood

Between Streatham to the SW and West Dulwich to the NE, West Norwood has good bus as well as train links to Brixton (with its Victoria Line tube) and the West End. The spine of the neighbourhood, **Norwood Rd**, also called The Broadway, is Victorian red-brick, smartening over the last couple of years. There's a modern library next to the 39-acre West Norwood Cemetery of 1836. Across from it **Bloom Grove**, a cul-de-sac with a green amid some attractive Victorian houses (most now flats), runs down to the rail tracks; new flats fitted neatly between the period homes shows how developers search out the smallest of sites.

By St Luke's Church, with its Corinthian six-columned portico, the main road forks: the triangle of **Norwood High St/Ernest Avenue/Knights Hill** here makes a giant roundabout, in effect, round West Norwood station (Victoria 18 min). In the cosmopolitan streets around the station, good-quality Victorian houses can be found at reasonable cost, and flats over shops start around £125,000. The E fork off Norwood Rd becomes **Norwood High St**, low-rise with few shops. Off it, **Dunbar St** has a cul-de-sac of 3-bed 1970s ex-council houses; **Dunelm Grove** is an attractive, modern cottage-style council estate. **Auckland Hill** has newish homes, plus bungalows – a 5-bed chalet-style at £375,000.

Elder Rd, the continuation of the **High St**, starts off with ugly grey council blocks, but improves. There are some shops, 1930s semis with neat gardens, and the 'House of Industry for the Infant Poor': now flats. Behind this splendid piece of Georgiana, a popular, mewsy scheme in **Elderwood Place** (3-bed mews house, £245,000), overlooking the park; next door is Norwood School. Conservatory Court's post-modern flats, too, get park views. **Eylewood** and **Norwood Park Rds** have 1930s 3-bed terraces and semis (c. £270,000); the Woodvale Estate, a clutch of high-rise council blocks up by **Bentons Rise** and **Aubyn Hill**, has been smartened up. Nearby is Norwood Park (tennis courts). **Knights Hill** is Victorian, and tidying (5-bed 1920s house £500,000). Promisingly named **Rothschild St** is a let-down: a sad mix of industry and wasteland redeemed only by recent flats and 3/4-bed town-houses by Fairview. Also the bus station.

To the E of **Norwood Rd** are the 'posher' streets: we are en route to West Dulwich. The closer, the pricier: half-million-plus houses appear, and an 1860s 6-bed (**Maley Avenue**) was asking £625,000. Look at **Lancaster Avenue**'s family-sized Victoriana with pleasant front gardens; Rosemead mixed prep school is at the West Dulwich end. Lancaster Heights is a dozen flats just converted from a period house: from £200,000 for a 1-bed. Parallel, and a short walk from Tulse Hill station, **Elmcourt Rd** boasts a new, gated enclave of six flats, six town-houses and two larger semis. **Hawkley Gardens** is a cul-de-sac of town-houses; **Tulsmere Rd**, 1930s 3-bed bay-fronteds. **Chatsworth Way** is mainly Victorian (up to £600,000 for a detached), but has a modern church with a needle-like spire; a housing association added 2-bed flats and houses at the High St end. **Idmiston Rd**'s very nice Victoriana boasts fancy wrought-iron balconies: a big semi sold for £900,000 recently. The road ends modestly with period terraces; a 3-bed Edwardian house, close to £500,000. **Chancellor Grove** is similar. The cemetery's high wall and railings occupy the S of **Robson Rd**, but the cottagy Victorian rows on the N side are popular.

West of **Norwood Rd**, council houses and blocks, being done up, start **York Hill**, where a 3-bed semi might be £270,000. **Knollys Rd** – 1930s terraces, Victorian and recent blocks – has seen much renovation; two recent flats blocks grace the York Hill end, and eight housing association fair-rent flats for locals. **Pyrmont Grove** and surprising **Royal Circus** have pleasant Victorian terraces and early 20th century semis (a 3-bed Circus semi £250,000); in the centre of the Circus, fenced-off Tonge House is run by the Portal Trust. Mount Villas, small late-1970s terraces (a few are housing association) popular with first-time buyers, is off **Lansdowne Hill**, a road that boasts a bustling weekday market at its bottom end. Terraces in **Glennie Rd** (mostly 1920s, 3-bed £285,000); also **Broxholm Rd** (potentially very nice, popular with first-timers, lots of refurb going on), which mixes late Victorian through to 1930s. Larger houses are found at the higher points of these hill roads. **Canterbury Grove**, split by the tracks, has large 19th/early 20th-century semis that make big flats (a whole house c. £270,000); also every-period terraces, including 1960s **Yeoman Close**, some council, some new fair-rent flats. Pleasant **Rockhampton Rd** and **Close** are 1920s/1930s. Tree-lined **Uffington Rd** has mainly Victorian houses – and the imposing entrance to the **Chichester Mews** development (big, attractive, parking). **Wolfington Rd**, **St Julian's Farm Rd** and **Thornelaw Rd** are popular and pricier: all three lead E to the station, while Streatham lies to the W. St Julian's wide mix of sizes and periods include some big Victoriana (5-bed £380,000 recently); also a good local primary which sparks waiting-lists of would-be home-buyers. A striking modern white flats block on **Casewick Rd** boasts a lighthouse-style turret. Quiet pre-war suburbia includes **Lamberhurst Rd** (bay-fronted semis), **Greenhurst Rd** (terraces), **Cheviot Rd** (both; 3-bed semis £275–320,000), hilly **Roxburgh Rd** (semis). Near the **Knights Hill** end, **Lakeview** and **Truslove Rds** have large areas of council: much upgrading going on; more needed.

Leigham Court Rd on the Streatham borders has 1930s semis (**St Julian's Close**), mansion blocks (built high for the views) and many a new home; look, too, at **Chestnut Close**, a pleasant cul-de-sac by the Chichester Mews developers. Victorian detacheds and imposing red-brick mansions precede Fern Lodge council estate, recently renovated, and a weathered 1930s block before ending at **Streatham Common North.**

Norbury

As Londonwide prices shot up over the past few years, families began to follow the A23 down into Norbury (seen as more upmarket than Thornton Heath), particularly from Streatham and Tooting. Developers are following, and **London Rd** gained a cache of 103 new flats. The road's humdrum Victorian aspect and everyday shopping give way to the office blocks that signal the approach to Croydon.

Most of this area was developed between the wars; leafy, big-gardened **Ardfern**, **Melrose**, **Ederline** and **Dunbar Avenues** set the tone. Across Norbury Park and quiet **Green Lane** (3-bed house £295,000), **Gibsons Hill** (in part still an unmade road), **Norbury Hill** (wide, tree-lined, tidy; 3-bed house £375,000) and well-kept, leafy **Virginia Rd** (semis) are of the same period, and relieve the monotony by gazing up towards the wooded slopes of Beulah Hill. **Kensington Avenue** also has a post-war council estate – and a recent cache of Affordable Homes.

The area's gem is Norwood Grove Mansion (nowadays three flats), standing in parkland at the top of **Gibsons Hill** on the site of a Charles II hunting-box. Generally, homes to the E of **London Rd** are more sought-after than the streets down towards the Mitcham border. West of London Rd, however, find **Pollard's Hill**, a splendid eminence crowned by a small common, hidden in a curling enclave of individualistic houses laid out in the 1920s/1930s (a 4-bed semi in **Beatrice Avenue**, £385,000). **Ena Rd**, one of the few ways in, has a 1-in-4 gradient: 1930s 3-bed terraces here c. £230–240,000.

Croydon borders: Thornton Heath

In this area W of South Norwood, first-time buyers find affordable purpose-built and conversion flats; families find a range of late Victorian and Edwardian terraces and inter-war semis. This corner has yet, however, to attract much attention from outsiders.

Suburban Thornton Heath is very much a 19th-century creation spurred on by the arrival of the railway. Good rail links to town and proximity to Croydon are still the chief draws. The more expensive homes are found in the upper reaches towards Norbury – in the pleasant, well-kept 'America' roads – **Florida, Maryland, Georgia, Carolina** (3-bed 1930s semis here, c. £300,000), **Virginia Rds.** These lead to similar **Springfield Rd.**

Popular, too, are the 3-bed houses across the tracks in and around nice, quiet

Winterbourne Rd, with its 1930s bay-fronted terraces (a garden flat in one £170,000), infant/junior school and convenient shopping in **London Rd**. Larger and older homes (4-bed detached) in **Warwick Rd**, plus new flats. Flat-hunters should concentrate on **Mersham, Hythe, St Paul's** and **Liverpool Rds** – mostly 1- or 2-beds – plus **Moffat Rd**, smartening up, and with shops and some modern terraced houses. Families may have better luck towards Mitcham. Busy **London Rd** and **Brigstock Rd** are worth investigation for conversions. The less popular roads S of the **High St** (such as **Ecclesbourne Rd, Kynaston Avenue, Bensham Lane**) comprise former council houses and also older-style terraces (3-beds c. £200–240,000).

Roads closest to Crystal Palace Football Ground in busy **Whitehorse Lane** are best avoided – though, more usefully, there are also buses and a Sainsbury's superstore. The influx of fans does influence prices (e.g. 3-bed Victorian terraced house £195,000). **Cuthbert Gardens**, though, between the Lane and Ross Rd, is a pleasant 1980s cul-de-sac of flats and town-houses. **Ross Rd** homes have the park opposite and fine views behind. Across the park in **Grange Rd**, a small clutch of recent terraced houses.

Transport Trains: West Norwood, Gipsy Hill, Thornton Heath to Victoria and London Bridge. Norbury to Victoria. The East London Line may make it to Crystal Palace by 2012. . . .

Convenient for Crystal Palace, Dulwich, Croydon. Routes S. Miles from centre: 5.5.

Schools Local Authority: Harris City Technical College, Stanley Tech (b), Selhurst High (b), Westwood Girls High, St Joseph's College RC (b), Norbury Manor (g), Virgo Fidelis RC (g).

SALES

Flats	S	1B	2B	3B	4B	5B
Average prices	95–110	120–165	140–200	150–225	–	–
Houses	2B	3B	4B	5B	6/7B	8B
Average prices	150–250	160–300	250–400	300–500+	→	–

RENTAL

Flats	S	1B	2B	3B	4B	5B
Average prices	100–140	115–160	150–210	175–270	210–370	–
Houses	2B	3B	4B	5B	6/7B	8B
Average prices	185–210	200–300	275–450	→	→	–

The properties Popular Victorian/Edwardian homes are the staple. Many larger houses now flats, and lots of family homes with good gardens: Victorian, semis, 1920s, 1930s Tudor, 1960s. On Gipsy Hill, mansion and p/b flats. Upper Norwood mainly flats; Thornton Heath/S Norwood a hunting ground for smaller, cheaper houses.

The market First-time buyers find relatively inexpensive flats, good rail links to town; families come in search of more home for their money.

Among estate agents active in this area are:

- Galloways
- Haart
- Wates
- Nicholas Ashley
- Stapleton Long
- Winkworth
- Conrad Fox
- Barnard Marcus
- Your Move
- Lynx
- Kinleigh Folkard & Hayward
- Harvey & Wheeler
- Gale
- Madisons

Willesden and Brondesbury Park

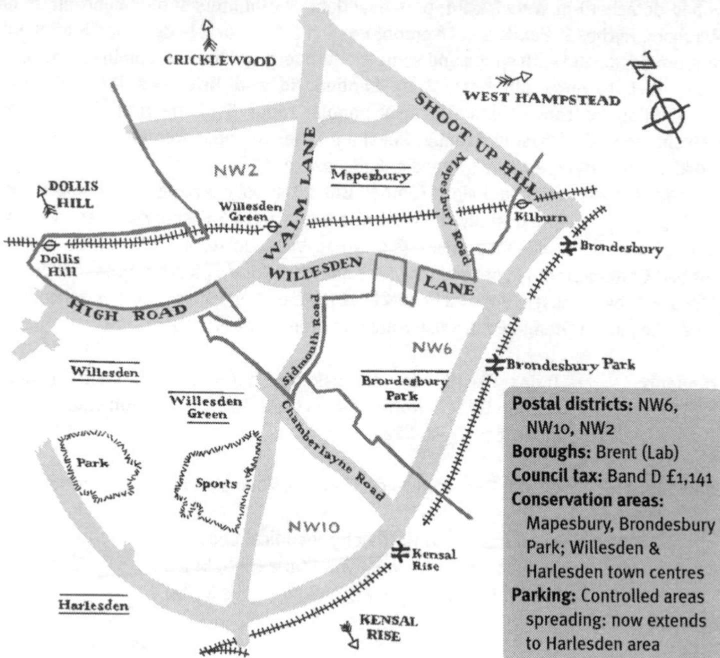

Postal districts: NW6, NW10, NW2
Boroughs: Brent (Lab)
Council tax: Band D £1,141
Conservation areas: Mapesbury, Brondesbury Park; Willesden & Harlesden town centres
Parking: Controlled areas spreading: now extends to Harlesden area

Here's an area with some very large houses, some very nice neighbours: those are the shores of West Hampstead just across the Edgware Rd. This is the old lady of NW London suburbs, a faded beauty now staging a comeback. Her bone structure is good – pockets of tree-lined Willesden are still elegant, Brondesbury Park is a *very* acceptable address – and her horizons have broadened: Paddington is her nearest major station (Heathrow 15 min) and she's on the Jubilee Line, joining her to the West End and also Westminster, Waterloo, Canary Wharf. You still get more for your money than in areas close by such as Kilburn's Queen's Park, or Maida Vale – but the gap has narrowed: despite last year's halt in the giddy price rises, first-timers still need to buy with friends, or with 'key-worker' loans and/or family help, and/or let out the spare room.

Willesden and Brondesbury Park cover three postal districts: NW6, the most desirable, covers Brondesbury Park; then comes NW2 and the part of Willesden towards Dollis Hill and Cricklewood; and finally NW10, where the area merges with less-classy Neasden and to the SW, Harlesden – still a drawback, but agents tip the fringes: prices have risen smartly in better streets. A number of rail lines carve up the area; prices can differ considerably from one end of a road to the other, one side to the other. Grand houses stand in close contrast to council blocks; most homes are Edwardian or 1930s.

The property hotspots are around Willesden Green tube station, flats in the **Chapter Rd** area on the Dollis Hill side, and the Mapesbury Estate and Brondesbury Park in particular, which attract families: huge houses here that also convert well into large flats. Flats supplies have been helped by small investors baling out of buy-to-let.

When it comes to amenities Willesden has plenty to offer. Willesden High School has now been reborn as a City Academy, specializing in sports and the arts, and Norman Foster, no less, designed its state-of-the-art theatres, studios etc. Next door, Willesden

Sports Centre has shut for a £13-million rebuild: a 25-metre pool, indoor track and courts, floodlit athletics stadium; also a play area, open space to wander in. The huge 1989 library complex boasts public halls, cinema, café-bar, bookshop and gallery; next door, a new building for the local history museum will include 16 social flats.

With the vast Brent Cross centre up on the North Circular, the shops, centred on **Willesden High Rd**, tend to be local, rather than big-name – good, small and specialized stores where shopkeepers remember your face and often stay open late (also, a 24-hr Budgen). Amid hardware and grocers' shops are sprouting trendier places catering for the denizens of the many flat conversions around Willesden Green: The Green gastro-pub draws folk from further afield, and the Sushi Say restaurant has been much reviewed.

Willesden

Willesden was given to the Dean and Chapter of St Paul's Cathedral by King Athelstan in 938 – hence names such as **Chapter Rd**; a visit to the local archive, at Cricklewood library in **Olive Rd**, will fill in more details. The area is more compact than sprawling Willesden Green; Church End is to the W; **Robson Avenue**, running up between Roundwood Park and Willesden Sports Centre, marks the E divide with Willesden Green, and the Jubilee Line is at the top. Much is green open space: Roundwood Park and its popular café with play area, schools/sports fields – and the expanse of the New and Jewish Cemeteries; S of this green belt lies Harlesden. The part of **Willesden High Rd** in the Willesden area is rather shabbier than the section towards Willesden Green, but the small shops are varied. Homes include the occasional small development: Ealing Housing Association built 32 Affordable Homes for rent here. Long, popular **Chapter Rd** in the N parallels the Jubilee Line: Dollis Hill station is at one end, Willesden Green's not far from the other. A good hunting ground (though harder now) for first-timers, homes here sell at £150,000 upwards for a 1-bed flat, c. £180–220,000 for 2-beds, £280–350,000 for a 3/4-bed house.

Willesden Green and Mapesbury

Willesden Green used to be a place where well-established Jewish families lived until they moved to leafy suburbs such as Wembley and Stanmore. These days the ethnic and religious make-up has broadened (there's a sizeable Polish community, and many an Antipodean rents, then buys, here); parts became conversion territory in the '80s, with houses split into flats. Houses tend to be larger in Willesden Green than in Willesden, and agents' boards make the place red, yellow and pink as well as Green. The general rule is that the closer to Willesden Green station (Jubilee), the better – although the best area, the large, well over the half-million, houses of the Mapesbury Estate breaks this rule.

The Mapesbury Estate lies in the triangle formed by **Chichele Rd/Walm Lane**, the A5 **Shoot Up Hill** and **Willesden Lane** (though note that the conservation area is slightly smaller – from **Anson Rd** to the tube line – while the active residents' association counts in roads across **Walm Lane** as far as **Riffel Rd**). This is the 'West Hampstead overspill', and residents would love Kilburn tube re-named – at least (correctly) as North Kilburn, if not Mapesbury. Wide, leafy **Mapesbury**, **Dartmouth**, **Teignmouth** and **Chatsworth Rds** are names to look out for if you want a well-located, roomy conversion in a stylish Victorian property – you can find 3-bed garden flats c. £360–400,000. Or, indeed, a 4-bed house (expect to pay £700,000). The larger, 5-plus bed conservation-area houses are anything up to a million. Less conventional homes 'with lots of odd-shaped rooms' in the old Baptist church on the **Anson/Sneyd Rd** corner: a 1-bed here, £200,000.

The 1980s mania for splitting houses into flats gave way, in the '90s, to converting commercial buildings – as evidenced by Jubilee Heights on **Shoot Up Hill**, at the SE border of the Mapesbury Estate. Known until '98 as Telephone House, it became 77 flats with all the trimmings: pool, gym, Jacuzzi, 24-hr porterage. A 2-bed here, c. £250,000. Behind, in **Exeter Rd,** Cedar Lodge added 30 more homes in '99, including 2-bed/2-bath houses; In **Cavendish Rd,** Chatsworth Court's four small blocks of 1- and 2-bed flats sit amid the Victoriana. Cavendish runs by the tracks, but Brondesbury station is at the end.

Out of the estate, across Walm Lane, **St Paul's Avenue** and **Blenheim Gardens** are also popular with flat-hunters thanks to Willesden Green tube. Nearby, on the corner with Willesden Lane, **Mapeshill Place** is a development of flats and 2-bed town-houses. On **Walm Lane,** Rutland Park Mansions – once known as the biggest squat in London – is nowadays housing-association flats. And more have just been added on the Lane: 54 studio and 1-bed flats for shared ownership – 24 allocated for key workers.

South of Willesden **High Rd** yet another telephone exchange, on the **St Andrews Rd/ Harlesden Rd** corner, will proved 23 Affordable Homes; five more, plus 12 private flats, are ordained for the site behind the church in **St Andrews Rd.** Finally, some low-level, industrial-chic homes are being wedged between **Harlesden Rd** and **Cornwall Gardens** in a scheme going under the name 'Oasis': three £425,000 4-bed houses, a 1-bed flat (£175,000) and a 2-bed (£240,000), plus a couple of skylit 'lofts' for £325–335,000.

Another clutch of prestige roads also lie S of the High Rd – the Dobree estate, built in the 1930s: **Bryan, Rowdon, Dobree, Alexander** and **Peter Avenues.** The estate did not, alas, prove lucky for its builders, two brothers who went bankrupt and were forced to sell off the commodious homes they had created as a job lot. It is still possible to find un-done-up homes here, and prices vary with the condition: think in terms of £350,000-plus for an un-swanked 3-bed semi, on up to a 5-bed detached for £600,000-plus.

The 'royal roads', which lie N of **Willesden High Rd,** are also popular and should satisfy a tighter budget. Roads such as **Sandringham, Balmoral** and **Windsor Rds,** between Dollis Hill and Willesden Green stations, have 3-bed terraced houses. Depending on condition, they are c. £280–330,000 (2-bed flats from c. £180,000), but prices vary a good deal (pricier towards Willesden Green). There can be £100,000 between a smart 2-bed flat on the Mapesbury Estate and one on the 'wrong side' – i.e. backing onto the tracks – of **Chapter Rd.** To the N, Willesden Green becomes Cricklewood, and prices dip again.

All Souls Avenue (the Oxford college was a major landowner here) runs N–S through Willesden Green and has small, semi-detached houses. At the N end lies Clarendon Court, a big 1930s block on the corner of **Chamberlayne Rd** and **Sidmouth Rd.** Sidmouth is a busy road, home of South Hampstead Tennis Club. On the corner with **Willesden Lane,** De Paul Trust has just done up an original building and added four new-build flats.

Spreading down towards Kensal Rise is a real enclave: the triangular grid of peaceful, orderly roads that fans out between **All Souls Avenue** and **Chamberlayne Rd** is disturbed by **Chelmsford Square,** a charming oval of semi-detached homes around tennis courts: its 4-bed houses aspire towards half a million. More modest, pretty streets are to be found in this direction.

Willesden Lane, a busy road linking Willesden and Kilburn, has a wide variety of flats blocks, among them Marlow Court (where tenants have share of freehold), Belvedere, Beechworth, Hadleigh and Bramerton Courts; agents warn of high service charges and/or short leases in some blocks – but the enticement of secure parking is irresistible to many. And still they come: the past few years have seen the two blocks of McAlpine's Manor Lodge: 1- and 2-bed flats plus penthouses; Barratt's Chatsworth Place – again, 1- and 2-beds; nearby, Banner's **Cavendish Place,** a clutch of 4-bed (up to c. half a million) and 6-bed (£800,000 has been asked, but not achieved) houses in a gated cul-de-sac off **Deerhurst Rd.** On the corner with **Willesden Lane,** ten recent 1-bed housing-association flats for rent; down towards the High Rd, Paddington Churches Housing Association added Sheil Court, an attractive flats block.

The Willesdenites, it should be noted, are a spiritual people: a Hindu temple, a Buddhist temple and a Jewish school are to be found on the Lane, while **Walm Lane** has a church and a synagogue, **Chichele Rd** a mosque and Islamic youth centre, Brondesbury Park a synagogue. The registry office sees a great range of marriages.

Brondesbury Park

Brondesbury Park is more exclusive than Willesden Green. Like Willesden Green, the district used to be very Jewish; nowadays Brondesbury Park mansions attract residents as disparate as foreign diplomats, an international footballer, a high-profile musician. Houses date from the 1930s or later; roads are wide and tree-lined, parking is not as problematic as in West Hampstead and Swiss Cottage. Communications are good – the A5 and Kilburn tube (Jubilee) giving access to West End and beyond.

Manor House Drive, off **Brondesbury Park** (the road) is a beautiful crescent, the best street in the area. Many of its detached houses are double-fronted; all have gardens front and back, often security gates. Six-bed properties complete with swimming pools along **Christchurch Avenue** and **The Avenue** expect to sell for £700–900,000 or so; (asking prices still pass the million, but most actual sales achieve less). That said, there are some even bigger 7- and 8-bedroomed monsters ('parking for five . . .'), and price tags all the way up to a couple of million in **Aylestone Avenue**, with its views across London (Queen's Park Community School is here). **Christchurch Avenue**, **Cavendish Rd** and **The Avenue** also have very attractive conversions in large Victorian houses. In an imaginative conversion, Christ Church itself became flats (plus small chapel) in the 1980s: original stained-glass and vaulted stonework guard your sleep . . .

Brondesbury Park (the road) has seen changes; some of the large detached houses here have been converted into flats, and purpose-built blocks have been built. One, Limes Court, is in Swiss-chalet style, recently refurbished. Also in the road is one of the most substantial developments in the area: the **Honeyman Close** gated cache of 43 town-houses – 2-, 3- and 4-beds, decorated in the spirit of the Arts-and-Crafts designer Charles Rennie Mackintosh – and a leisure/swimming-pool complex. The 3- and 4-bed houses are in the £440–490,000 range. On the corner of **Brondesbury Park** and **Coverdale Rd** stand Kingsbridge and Westwood Courts, three Wates blocks of 2-bed flats.

Parts of Brondesbury Park are indeed very expensive, but a house with garden may still be bought in this corner for the sort of money that buys a decent flat in Maida Vale.

Harlesden

Harlesden was once avoided, and the Stonebridge Estate in Craven Park feared as a blight on resale. This Guide has been reporting the steady change being wrought by the replacement of the estate's grim tower blocks with good new low-level flats – and a vast improvement has taken place. Tenure is now mixed, too, with private buyers doing up some of the remaining stock and letting it in their turn. The town centre, too, has been improved, as has the nightmare parking (with more zones to come).

Harlesden also has some lovely houses, Edwardian and Victorian, most with original features. With an improved Bakerloo Line service, and despite some spectacular crime stories in the papers, the area's potential is slowly being recognized – not least by buy-to-let types looking for cheaper prices and scope to do up homes. You'll find parts described as 'Kensal Rise borders' to entice Ladbroke Grove trendies.

And new people are moving in: staff from BBC Wood Lane or Virgin's Kensal Rise offices, junior City workers, a brace of recognizable celebrities, people in search of housing-association fair rents and shared-ownership deals. They find a melting-pot area, reflected in Caribbean restaurants, Portuguese cafés and more. Agents look hopefully at the major office development emerging at Park Royal, but it's the long-discussed (but not imminent) development of the Old Oak Triangle, a wilderness of railway freight depots to the S, that will one day set the seal on regeneration here.

The better Harlesden roads are **Springwell Avenue**, **Harlesden Gardens**, **Ancona Rd**, **Cholmondeley Avenue**: some larger, 4/5-bed houses here (c. £400–450,000) and agents also cite wider-than-average **Lushington Rd**, **Monson Rd** and **All Souls' Avenue**. Harlesden prices are the lowest in this area, but have risen steadily; the more standard-sized houses in the popular streets above are between £300–400,000, but you can buy a 3-bed terraced Victorian across in, say, **Oldfield** or **Brownlow Rds** for c. £265,000. Recent new homes include studio and 1-bed flats in **Trenmar Garden**, the **Dairy Close** houses and flats near the park, plus housing-trust schemes: 56 Affordable Homes in **Harlesden/ Wrottesley Rds**, seven houses for shared ownership in **Harlesden Rd**, more in **Station Rd.**

Hidden among the sidings near Willesden Junction station is a cache of Victorian railway cottages: little streets off Old Oak Lane that include **Stoke Place, Goodhall St** (the two most popular), **Crewe Place, Stephenson St.** This enclave holds out the lure of a small house rather than a flat; the little 3-bed terraces go for £210–250,000, landscaping has been appearing in some of the former alleyways, children can safely play in the street.

Regeneration of the Old Oak rail lands to the S give every sign of still being a long way off, though. The boroughs meet here: Brent wants to safeguard the remnants of industry,

Transport Tubes: Willesden Green, Kilburn, Neasden, Dollis Hill (zones 2/3, Jubilee); Harlesden (Bakerloo). From Willesden Green: Oxford Circus 25 min (1 change), City 35 min (1 change), Heathrow 1 hr 10 min (1 change). Trains: Harlesden, Willesden Junction, Brondesbury, Brondesbury Park, Kensal Rise.

Convenient for North Circular and Edgware Rds. Miles from centre: 5.

Schools Local authority: Willesden City Academy, Cardinal Hinsley RC (b), Convent of Jesus & Mary (g), Queens Park Community School. Private: Bales College, Islamia High (g).

SALES

Flats	S	1B	2B	3B	4B	5B
Average prices	130–170	120–240	145–340	160–450	160–490	–
Houses	2B	3B	4B	5B	6/7B	8B
Average prices	180–270	220–450	300–600	350–1M	650–1M+	–

RENTAL

Flats	S	1B	2B	3B	4B	5B
Average prices	110–175	135–230	180–300	220–370+	280–500+	350–550
Houses	2B	3B	4B	5B	6/7B	8B
Average prices	220–300	230–400	320–450	350–650	–	–

The properties Large blocks of flats, late-Victorian villas, plus many streets of terraces and later semis. Larger Edwardiana. Brondesbury Park has some big, imposing late-Victorian houses as well as '30s semis and detacheds. Harlesden is improving at last.

The market Willesden Green's fast tube attracts young flat-buyers. Elsewhere still a family neighbourhood – houses from modest rows, up to million-plus Brondesbury mansions. Developers turn ex-churches, offices etc. into flats, and squeeze more in wherever possible.

Among estate agents active in this area are:

- Ellis & Co
- Gladstones
- Empire Estates
- Bairstow Eve
- Hodders
- Rainbow Reid
- Camerons
- Harris & Co
- Peter Carrol
- Brian Lack
- Lewis Estates
- Wenlock Taylor
- Camerons Stiff
- Churchills
- Margo's
- Haart

WIMBLEDON, RAYNES PARK AND MERTON PARK

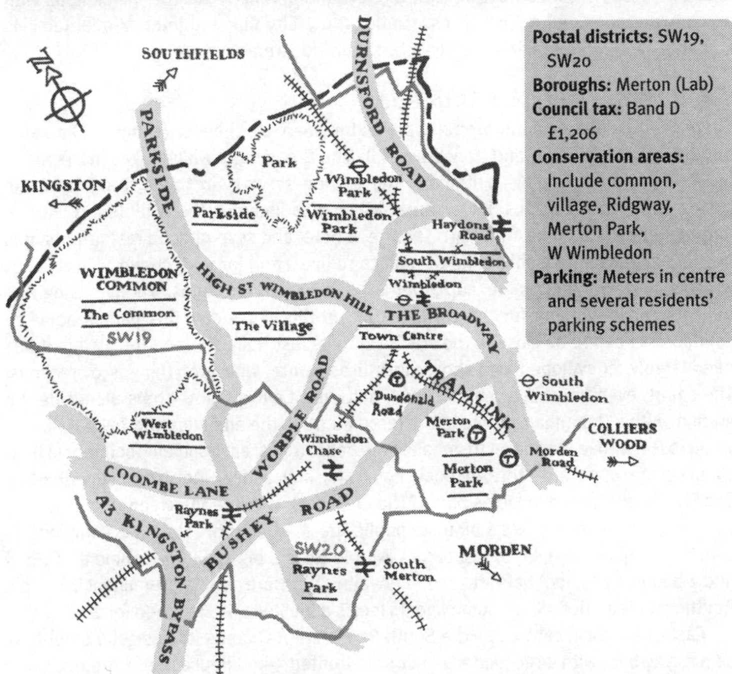

Postal districts: SW19, SW20
Boroughs: Merton (Lab)
Council tax: Band D £1,206
Conservation areas: Include common, village, Ridgway, Merton Park, W Wimbledon
Parking: Meters in centre and several residents' parking schemes

Wimbledon has a claim to be the closest village to Waterloo. Enclaves in Battersea or Clapham may assert 'village' status, but here in SW19 there's the real thing: little girls on ponies, village pubs, lots of green space for muddy walks. And it's just 19 minutes from Waterloo, even under Southwest Trains' new timetable.

This is not a village as Hardy or Trollope or even addicts of The Archers would understand it. The school-run vehicle of choice is still a 4x4, but that's as far as the rural idyll goes. Just about every village shop in the High St is there to sell you something unnecessary. Style-conscious, yes; expensive, very; useful, no. This is English village life as lived in the minds of American advertising moguls and Spanish or Swedish bankers. Which is fine because that's who lives here.

Luckily, there is much more to Wimbledon. It is a self-possessed, prosperous, south-west London suburb, with its vast common and (quite separate from the Village) busy, bustling Broadway, its town centre. Here are smart shopping mall, high-street shops, theatres, offices; also the station, a real hub: main-line, underground – and trams.

The fortnight of tennis-tournament mayhem – traffic chaos, packed tubes, no-parking signs everywhere – is but an annual blip. The rest of the year, Wimbledon is a place to live and shop. And to breathe a little fresh air: it's the first place going SW out of London where the trees seem to outnumber the houses. The 1,100-acre common – no urban park, but rough grassland and copse – stretches to Putney Vale. For centuries it was used for cattle grazing, duelling, archery and rifle practice. Today it is patrolled by rangers and is a haven for joggers, horse riders, ramblers, golfers, dog walkers, cyclists and nature lovers – the trees and scrub harbour more than 60 species of birds, as well as squirrels, badgers, rabbits, foxes, weasels and natterjack toads. Not surprisingly, houses bordering this semi-wooded expanse (mainly mansions built by Victorian merchants) and luxurious modern flats with views across the common command the area's highest prices. Competing with the loyal, long-time locals (the place hops with amenity societies and residents' associations) are City folk and international families who look here for good-sized homes a fast train-ride from town.

Town centre/South Wimbledon

There is still a big divide in property prices between 'Up the Hill' (common, Parkside and the original village) and 'Down the Hill' (the Broadway), which takes in the main, much-improved shopping centre and the station serving up trains, trams and the District Line tube. But this 'lower' area, which also includes the Wimbledon Theatre and the renowned Polka Children's Theatre, a hotel and several good restaurants, has become increasingly fashionable as a place to live – and far from cheap.

This 'new' Wimbledon grew up around the railway in the 1850s, when housing was built for those working for the carriage-folk up the hill. Today, this part is home to commuters keen to be close to the station with its fast trains to Waterloo. Its heart has been largely redeveloped as a shopping/offices centre, with everything a town needs. The smart, even imposing, mall – called, naturally, Centre Court – runs alongside the station, with a Debenhams store and a Tesco Metro in the adjoining Old Town Hall.

Across the road, narrowed to enhance the pedestrians' environment (or improve their chances) are a record store, a bookshop/café, and a new Morrisons supermarket. Cannons health club opened as part of The Crescents, with the 12-screen cinema not far behind – and a piazza offers a bit more public space. West of the station is Wimbledon's own department store, Ely's; just across **Worple Rd** is a big 1998 development of 1-bed and 2-bed (c. £350,000) flats and another health club. More new flats imminent in Worple Rd: the mooted price, which some agents feel is a bit steep, is £450,000 for 2-beds.

East of the town centre lies the South Park corner: **Queens Rd** has solid older-type semis, 3/4-bed, with large gardens (a double-fronted 3-bed house here £800,000), and joins **Haydons Rd** to South Wimbledon; both streets offer plenty of flats conversions. Quiet **King's Rd** runs parallel, its double-fronted Edwardiana match Queens Rd prices; some have views over South Park Gardens, some are now flats. At the junction of Trinity Rd and **South Park Rd**, Nairn Court is 23 flats with parking in secluded courtyard. In South Park Rd 3- to 4-bed houses are priced from £585,000 to £685,000. Mead Park off **Haydons Rd** offers 1- and 2-bed flats and a few houses. The streets in this corner between The Broadway and Haydons Rd – either side of **Evelyn Rd** and **Ashley Rd**, which are typical – have 2- and 3-bed terraces with small gardens. New houses in a gated mews off Evelyn Rd were £460–500,000 last winter (3/4 bed with garage)

The area E of Haydons Rd is no longer the wrong side of the tracks: Wandle Park, which is along the river, and a nature-reserve walk add a green note; the station is on Thameslink, there's a smart new health club – and a cache of new homes by big builders on **North Rd** and **East Rd**. Prices have risen briskly, though it is still rated affordable (when compared to the rest of Wimbledon). In North Rd, too, is Connolly House – a new block of 20 flats by First Property Investment. Off Merton Rd, 'Orton Place' offered four new 2-bed-plus-garage houses last winter at £362,000. N of the rail line and S of Gap Rd, a couple of streets are also close to Haydons Rd station: **Cromwell Rd** has 4-bed double-fronted houses at c. £600,000.

Modern flats blocks on the **Broadway**, on either side of Montague Rd, have been added by Thirlestone and Charles Church. Roads S of the busy Broadway are quiet, residential and handy for the station. This used to be bargain corner for first-time buyers, but no more. Locals (or perhaps just tidy-minded estate agents) distinguish the 'Ministers' streets (they run E from Gladstone either side of Pelham: choose your

Victorian) and the 'Battles' E of **Merton Rd**. These would better (in this anniversary year) be called the Nelsons: there's Trafalgar, Victory, even Hamilton. To live in the former group you pay £265–285,000 for a 2-bed flat, while a 2-bed Nelson cottage might be £300,000. A red-brick school building in **Pelham St** was recently converted into 30 flats, with 64 new ones on the old playground. In a quiet cul-de-sac off **Hartfield Rd** is Hartfield Court, with two large modern 5/6-bed, 2-bath houses with garage and garden. New homes here are more likely to be flats: just opposite the station at the N end of Hartfield Rd there are 2-and 3-bed ones, with ten more due on the site of a razed house.

Hartfield Crescent leads W over the tram lines to **Dundonald Rd**, and a peaceful neighbourhood with a school, a park – and its own tram stop. Rows of Edwardian terraces offer 3-bed houses for c. £325–400,000; more if overlooking the park.

Back in the town centre, **Wimbledon Hill Rd** ('The Hill') leads up from the station, and is lined with mansion flats – some 1930s, some new but in retro style. A vast flat in one of the vast Edwardian houses on the Hill can be house-sized (and priced). **Alwynne Rd** and **Compton Rd**, off the Hill and close to the town centre, hold solid 1930s semis with gardens. Climbing further, Wimbledon Girls' High School is on the left, and to the right are terraced town-houses. Higher left is **Draxmont Approach** (luxury balconied flats); right, **Belvedere Drive**, with large houses and the 'Bluegates' estate.

Wimbledon Village

The High St begins at the top of the hill and runs through the village – still Georgian in feel, if a lot more film-set than it used to be. Smart (they used to be quaint) shops on either side sell high fashion, luxury gifts and interior-designer services. There are restaurants, bars and two historic pubs – the Rose & Crown, where the poet Swinburne drank, and the Dog & Fox; the village riding school is at the rear. Life gets really hectic here in Wimbledon Fortnight, when the world descends upon Wimbledon. The rest of the year, the biggest excitement is usually a tussle over parking spaces.

Many charming artisan cottages – lovingly renovated, expensive, no room to park – lie off **Church Rd**, **Belvedere Square** and **Lancaster Place.** You'll be asked £600,000-plus for 3/4 beds. Several caches of new homes are squeezed into every square inch of available space behind the shops. **Haygarth Place** has 24 1980s red-brick, 4-bed town-houses, underground car park (plus four original cottages, modernized). Behind historic Eagle House (1613) lurk 14 4-bed 1990s houses in **Leeward Gardens.**

The Common

At the War Memorial a left turn takes you towards **Southside Common**: here pretty Victorian villas face out over the greenery in the first of a clutch of streets that run out into this corner of the common. **West Side Common** strikes out across the grass towards the furthest-flung, **North View**, past Chester House (Georgian), some 1930s houses and a cul-de-sac of council-built (most now, unsurprisingly, owner-occupied) flats and houses. Stately Cannizaro House is now a luxury hotel. A pair of 18th-century mansions, The Keir and Stamford House – split into flats – both gaze out across the common. **North View**, **Camp View** and **West Place** form a square of tall red-brick Victorian houses surrounded by common and golf course: rarely for sale, but think £1.8 million for a 5-bed. Along **Camp Rd**, and in the midst of the common, popular **Eversley Park** (by Octagon) is set in landscaped gardens. Next door is **Kinsella Gardens**: eight rather special 1999 houses (five detached, three terraced) on a grand scale, which now sell for £2.5 million-plus, and a converted Victorian coach house.

From **Southside Common** long, tree-lined roads run down to **The Ridgway**: homes in **Lingfield Rd**, **The Grange** (family houses here, £800,000–£3 million-plus), **Murray Rd**, **Lauriston Rd** and **Clifton Rd** are a mixture of styles, mostly Victorian; many reverse conversions here, with houses which had been poorly split into flats from the 1950s onwards reverting to single homes, while others are redivided into modern-standard flats. In **Lingfield Rd** Brackenbury Lodge mirrors the Victorian style: a double-fronted gabled house, purpose-built to contain six roomy flats. At Woodhayes Rd is **Peregrine Way**, a modern group of detached Colonial-style 4-bed houses among mature trees.

This corner also provides some exceptionally large mansions: in the millions, if they come up for sale. All the coveted houses and flats here are within walking distance of King's College Boys' School. Opposite, across little **Crooked Billet** green, stand the delightful old Crooked Billet and Hand in Hand pubs, surrounded by tiny, former farm labourers' cottages. Tucked just behind the pubs are a few 3- and 4-bed houses.

Parkside

Return to Parkside, which runs along the E side of the common and leads, eventually, to Putney. With the common on your left, on the right is the enclave of premier roads (**Marryat Rd** to **Bathgate Rd** on the map). These are lined with solid houses of every period over the past 100 years, varying widely in their size and state of luxury. The largest and most opulent top £3 million, even four, and even those 'in need of comprehensive remodelling' can approach £2 million. There have been several instances of clumsy flat conversions being removed, and the houses returning to single-family occupation. However big flats, or sections of mansions, are around and they command prices little different from nearby whole houses. One or two enormous new homes, some in a very transatlantic taste (Weybridge opulent?) have been added at the 'price on application' level. Octagon *are* telling about their two 4/5 bed houses off Parkside, new this spring: they're priced at £2 million. To the E of this favoured group of roads, away down the hill, is the All England Tennis Club.

On the corner of **Somerset Rd** and **Parkside**, an enclave of late 1980s flats boasts balconies, underground car park, electronic gates. On the opposite corner, an annexe to the Parkside private hospital (this neighbourhood has it all, from its own hospital to the Papal Legate's house). Near the village end of Parkside is an elegant conversion of a mansion into five flats. **Alfreton Close** is an attractive cul-de-sac of Scandinavian-style family houses in woodland. Opposite, in **Windmill Rd** on the site of the Clock House are 12 ultra-luxurious flats with underground parking and porter. Nearby **Clockhouse Close**, built on common land, has six detached family houses.

For new homes, though, look to the Putney/Wimbledon border – hilly, leafy if dominated by council-built flats (see Southfields chapter). This is the scene of the largest development in the area. Wimbledon Parkside, by Laing, has transformed the vast, pleasantly hilly site of the old Southlands College at the junction of **Parkside** and **Queensmere Rd** (which has the new Wimbledon Synagogue).

The development began with **Southlands Drive**, a rather cramped enclave of Victorian-style houses behind smart railings. Things then got better: a large, good-looking flats block emerged on the hillside, with its grounds running up to the council houses that run along the leafy ridge; a refurbished listed building now provides flats. The main part of the site, **Chapman Square** off **Inner Park Rd**, has 2-bed/2-bath and 3-bed/2-bath flats in the central, 6-storey apartment blocks, with their living rooms set in the octagonal corner turrets; pay c. £450,000 for a 3-bed here. Then came Hightrees, a flats block on **Queensmere Rd**. Up to a million has been asked for the 4-bed town-houses; the same for the 6-bed semis which form part of the scheme.

Off **Somerset Rd** is the modern Oakfield estate; Cedar Court is high-density town-houses and flats; some flats in the towers of Burghley House and Somerset House have views of the Wimbledon centre court. . . . All these roads suffer an annual invasion (30,000 visitors daily) during Tennis Fortnight. Oaklands Park in **Bathgate Rd** is a recent clutch of 13 5-bed houses. **Church Rd** and **Burghley Rd** cross a hilly neighbourhood of more large houses, some of them older than the Parkside ones. Off **Burghley Rd** is St

Mary's Parish Church, leading into **Church Rd** and **Welford Place**, a group of terraced town-houses sharing children's play area and indoor swimming pool. These represent what Wimbledon sees as good value, with a 4-bed house £750–850,000.

West Wimbledon

The Village is linked to West Wimbledon by the **Ridgway**, Wimbledon's oldest road, running parallel to Worple Rd down the Hill. **Oldfield Rd**, to the left, has a row of delightful 2-bed cottages with long front gardens but no parking. **Sunnyside**, next, has large 4/5-bed homes and also holds Sunnyside Place: 3-bed 1960s town-houses: not the apogee of architecture, but a quiet cul-de-sac – and note that '1960s town-house' translates as 'with garage'. Then **Ridgway Place**, with a group of houses on both sides built by the Haberdashers' Company in 1860. Further along is a villagey area comprising **Denmark Rd, Thornton Rd** and **Hillside** (2-bed flat, converted from a house, £285,000). There is a row of small shops, two pubs and livery stables here, plus little (but £400,000) cottages. **Berkeley Place** and **Ridgway Gardens** are cul-de-sacs with large conversion flats. **Edge Hill** is popular with Catholics thanks to nearby Wimbledon College RC Boys' School and the large Sacred Heart Church. There are plenty of flats here; Edge Hill Court, a 1930s block, is a popular example. Pay £260–280,000 along Edge Hill for a 2-bed flat (though they have been known to top £400,000 for the more opulent, multi-bathroomed versions).

The Downs has purpose-built 1930s flats on either side; in blocks such as Ravenscar Lodge you get a garage with your 2-bed apartment. Marian Lodge is a 1997 scheme of 31 flats with underground parking and gym. On the site of St Teresa's Hospital, **South Ridge** is an enclave of 4-bed town-houses. Claremont Lodge by Ruskin Homes is part conversion of an old convent building, part new-build. The Ursuline Convent School for Girls and The Hall School are neighbours. Higher up **The Downs**, Blenheim Place is a recent cache of three houses and six flats. New here is 'Lanherne Gate', where 36 flats will share gym, concierge, movie screening room and library, no less.

On the corner of The Downs and **Worple Rd** is the smartly detailed Lantern Court with 23 flats (basement parking). **Lansdowne Rd**, a cul-de-sac which holds both purpose-built and conversion flats, leads to **Cumberland** and **Lansdowne Closes**: family town-houses, some with roof terraces with spectacular views.

Arterberry Rd has the Norwegian school and older-type family houses with spacious gardens. Chimneys Court, on the corner of **Ridgway**, has ten 2-bed/2-bath flats and a 3-bed penthouse, all with underground parking. Near the corner of **Woodhayes Rd**, next to the King's College School playing fields, is **Rydon Mews**, built by Michael Shanley in 1999 with a dozen town-houses, four big semis and six flats.

The line of **The Ridgway** is now continued by **Copse Hill**. The 18th-century house, which is all that's left of

Prospect Place, the area's Big House, has been restored and the lodge cleverly split into two homes. On its land classy Octagon built seven £2 million-ish detacheds in 1998.

On the common side, **Ernle, Wool, McKay** and **Dunstall Rds** form an enclave that boasts 4- and 5-bed up-to-a-million (and occasionally over it) detached houses with big gardens, some backing onto the golf course or woodland. Also off Copse Hill to the right is **Rokeby Place**, more detached, 4- or 5-bed family houses. Two of **Copse Hill**'s Victorian mansions became flats recently. **Cedarland Terrace** consists of five Georgian-style town-houses with wide sweeping drives.

Facing the Atkinson Morley Hospital is Thurstan Rd, off which is **Grange Park Place** with detached 5-bed/5-bath houses backing onto the golf course, built on the site of the old Cottage Hospital. **Drax Avenue** is a leafy private road of Sussex-farmhouse style and mock-Tudor 5-bed detached houses, as is **Ellerton Rd**, where exceptional homes ask well over £2 million: most here are more like £1–1.5 million. Leading down to Coombe Lane, both sides of **Copse Hill** have solid 1930s 3/4-bed semis with garages. A small group of 5-bed, 2-bath semis with stunning views and £900,000 price tags in **Cottenham Park Rd**; Cottenham Place is a pair of recent 5-bed proto-Edwardian properties. **Durham Rd**, which runs down the hill, has some solid Victorian houses.

Raynes Park

Raynes Park lies at the bottom of the hill from the Common; it is split in half by the railway line and by crossing it (from N to S) you can save £100,000. Once this was little more than a backwater of Edwardian cottages and purpose-built flats and maisonettes in wide, tree-lined streets. Then (around 1990) it was 'discovered' and much of the N side was annexed, if you believe agents and newcomers, as 'West Wimbledon'.

Worple Rd, a busy main thoroughfare with blocks of new flats, conversions and small hotels, leads back from Raynes Park centre to Wimbledon. Ruskin Homes slipped in a row of three handsome new 4-beds. Roads S of Worple Rd have good small semis with prices dictated by the closeness of the railway: in **Southdown Rd**, the side backing onto the tracks is considerably cheaper. **Abbotts Avenue**, also beside the tracks, gained seven new 2- and 3-bed houses in 2001. West of Worple Rd are very desirable family houses in roads such as **Thornton Hill, Denmark Avenue** and **Spencer Hill** (where 2-bed flats hover around £300,000, while big houses can command £1.2–2.5 million). These roads climb the hill to **Ridgway** (by which time they have joined Wimbledon Village); the higher up, the better the views.

Hollymount School (primary) is in leafy **Cambridge Rd**, together with 3/4-bed family houses. **Amity Grove** has mainly 2-bed Edwardian bay-window cottages. Just to the E is the popular **Lambton Rd** conservation area, where Edwardian 3-bed terraced houses can fetch £450–550,000. The larger, later houses off **Pepys Rd** can be £750,000-plus.

South of the railway, on **Kingston Rd**, Sovereign Row by Try Homes is a new terrace of four 4-bed houses. Running from Kingston Rd down to **Bushey Rd**, 'The Apostles' are 12 long, parallel cul-de-sacs (**Gore Rd** to **Bronson Rd**): a mix of 2-bed Edwardian terraced and semi-detached, some 1930s; street parking, tiny front gardens – the glimpse of the open green space of Prince George's playing fields at the end of many of them (up to **Vernon Avenue**) adds appeal. The Apostles is considered an undervalued corner, selling for £270–295,000 for a 2-bed with loft conversion, five minutes from the station. Go N of the tracks and you incur that hundred-grand hit for very similar houses 200 yards away. The Thameslink service at Wimbledon Chase station has also drawn attention to nearby roads such as **Rothesay** and **Oxford Avenues** (3-bed houses).

Crossing Bushey Rd, busy **Grand Drive** leads S with inter-war 3/4-bed semi- and detached family houses, many with views over playing fields. To the E of the fields is a big sports and leisure centre. Houses in streets off Grand Drive, built in the 1930s by builder George Blay, are popular: £250–365,000 for 2- and 3-beds; terraced 3-beds in **Westway** and **Greenway**, £270–285,000. Off **West Barnes Lane**, a cut-off clutch of roads close to playing fields (**Somerset, Taunton, Camberley Avenues**) offer the next step for families who've outgrown The Apostles. However, traffic noise from the ever-busy A3 Kingston Bypass echoes across the playing fields. Plans by Barratt for 111 flats on the London Electricity playing fields, off Grand Drive, were thrown out last year by an inquiry.

Merton Park

Merton's main claim to residential fame is the Merton Park Estate, one of the first garden suburbs, developed in the last three decades of the 19th century. John Innes, a millionaire property developer and horticulturalist (you've used the compost), laid out the estate. The area's green appearance survives, and many homes have large gardens.

Now, the opening of the highly successful Wimbledon–Croydon tram line behind **Dorset Rd**, bringing easy journeys to the E side of the area, has attracted renewed attention to this verdant corner. The earliest streets, built in the 1870s, were **Dorset Rd**, **Mostyn Rd** and **Kingswood Rd** – where recent sales have seen prices of over £1 million for 5-bedroomed houses (all vary in size considerably). Later in the 19th century, and into the 20th, larger houses of the Arts-and-Crafts and other styles were added. The details are reminiscent of Bedford Park, but the styles are more mixed. So, too, is the scale: Innes decreed that cottages as well as solid villas be built.

Development continued into Edwardian times, as the houses in **Melrose Rd** and **Watery Lane** show. The most sought-after homes are those built by Henry Quartermain, in streets such as **Wilton Crescent** and **Mostyn Avenue**: £850,000 for a 5-bed. Building went on until the 1930s, with the opening of the tube at Morden a renewed spur. A little developing has gone on more recently: off Dorset/Erridge Rds, in a quiet cul-de-sac, are the 14 3/4-bed detached houses of **Hazlebury Close**, while Ruskin added 21 mainly 2-bed, c. £280,000, flats on **Kingston Rd** – along which shops are noticeably smartening. Even the old Merton Park station building has become a house.

Wimbledon Park

The rolling, leafy roads of Wimbledon Park contain some large, discreet and enviable houses, in a corner that centres on a big park complete with lake. It's just down the hill E of Wimbledon Village and the common, and has its own tube station on the District Line. The All England Club is here, but except for Tennis Fortnight the hilly roads that spread out S of the park are a peaceful and select neighbourhood. On a map the street pattern betrays the spacious layout of roads such as **Home Park Rd**, **Arthur Rd** and **Leopold Rd** – and the consequently very large gardens.

To the E of the railway line, between Durnsford Rd and the tracks, the roads N of Wimbledon Park station (District Line) such as **Melrose Avenue, Braemar Avenue, Normanton Avenue** and **Ashen Grove** are a continuation of the Southfields 'Grid' to the N (see Southfields chapter), over the borough and postcode boundaries at Revelstoke Rd. These are mainly long terraces of neat, solid, 2/3-bed late-Victorian/ Edwardian houses, with rear gardens and street parking; they are snapped up because they are relatively inexpensive (bordering Wandsworth), convenient (the tube) and close to the park and schools. 'Cheap' is, indeed, relative here: agents in Wimbledon enthuse over the 'great value' of 5-bed houses in **Melrose Avenue** at £550,000 (it backs onto the tube tracks, is why). You can drop the price by £100,000 for each fewer bedroom, they say. Lots of loft conversions going on in the 'Avenue Grid', expanding the 3-bed (£400,000-plus) Victorian terraced homes.

To the S, down by the tube station is a varied and useful row of shops. **Arthur Rd** winds uphill towards a different world, all the way from Durnsford Rd via the station to Wimbledon Village, becoming more and more tree-lined, with larger and larger detached houses in secluded grounds, some becoming flats.

Curving N from Arthur Rd, **Home Park Rd** houses gaze out over Wimbledon Park and the Tennis Club: expect to pay £1–3 million. In the angle of **Leopold Rd/Lake Rd** are Ricards Lodge girls' high school and well-regarded Bishop Gilpin primary. There are some 3-bed ex-council houses in Lake Rd which are sought after. **Vineyard Hill Rd, Dora Rd** and **Kenilworth Avenue** have a variety of family houses ranging in price up to £1 million – a 5-bed semi £895,000 last winter. The Edwardian 4-bed semis in Kenilworth fall into the £600–800,000 bracket.

Transport Tubes: Wimbledon, Wimbledon Park (zone 3, District); South Wimbledon (zone 3, Northern). Oxford Circus 35 min (1 change), City 35 min, Heathrow 1 hr (1 change). Trains: to Waterloo 12 min. Tramlink from Wimbledon via Merton Park to Croydon.

Convenient for Common, Heathrow and Gatwick Airports. Miles from centre: 7.

Schools Merton Education Authority: Wimbledon College RC (b), Ursuline Convent School (g), Rutlish School (b), Ricards Lodge (g). Private: Norwegian School, Wimbledon High (g), Hall School, King's College School (b).

SALES

Flats	S	1B	2B	3B	4B	5B
Average prices	110–180	165–280	180–500	250–700	–	–
Houses	2B	3B	4B	5B	6/7B	8B
Average prices	250–500	300–700	350–800+	500–1.5M	750–2.5M	–

RENTAL

Flats	S	1B	2B	3B	4B	5B
Average prices	140–185	175–275	230–450	275–550	–	–
Houses	2B	3B	4B	5B	6/7B	8B
Average prices	250–450	300–700	350–925	450–1100	→1600	–

The properties Homes (and prices) range from 3-bed terraces and modern flats near town centre ('down the Hill') via the cottages of the village to the swimming-pooled mansions near the common ('up the Hill'). Also flat conversions, Edwardian villas, 1930s semis, new town-houses, flats and more flats. Further Victorian/Edwardian charm in Raynes and Merton Parks.

The market Something for everyone – at a price. Fast trains for commuters, good schools for families. Locals stay loyal and move within area: competition, therefore, for big family homes. Overseas buyers favour Wimbledon – as do investors, especially in the village and West Wimbledon. Once here you're hooked, whether heading up to a large family house or trading down to a smart flat.

Among estate agents active in this area are:

- Robert Holmes & Co
- Hawes & Co
- Kinleigh Folkard & Hayward
- Lauristons
- Bairstow Eves
- John D Wood
- Chesterton
- Quinton Scott
- Hamptons
- Knight Frank
- Ludlow Thompson
- Haart
- Foxtons
- Townchoice
- Cross & Prior
- Courteneys
- Finch

Index of streets and areas

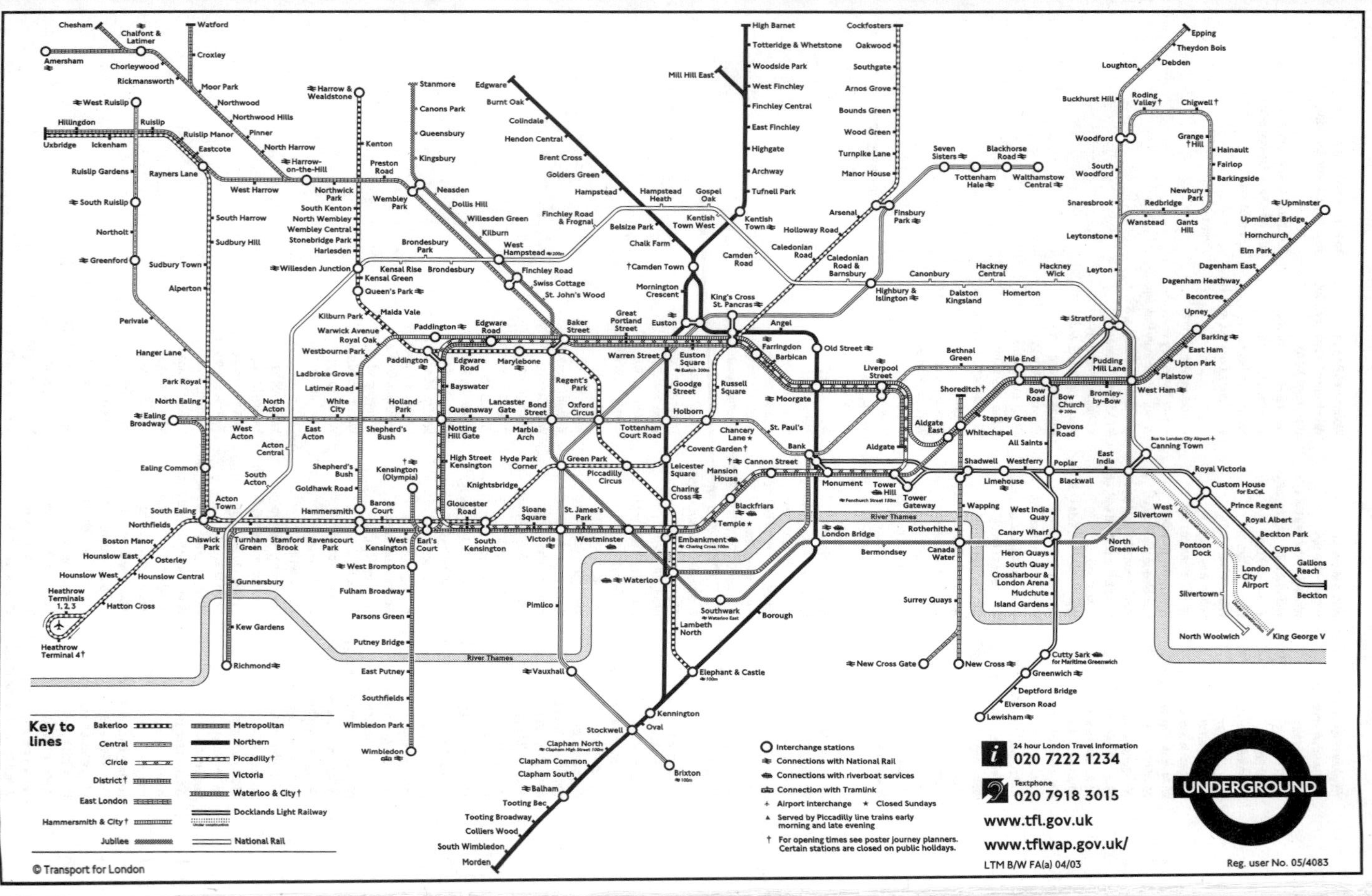

Chesham
Chalfont & Latimer
Watford
Croxley
Amersham
Chorleywood
Rickmansworth
Moor Park
Northwood
Northwood Hills
Pinner
North Harrow
Harrow-on-the-Hill
West Ruislip
Hillingdon
Ruislip
Ruislip Manor
Eastcote
Uxbridge
Ickenham
Ruislip Gardens
Rayners Lane
West Harrow
South Ruislip
Northolt
Greenford
South Harrow
Sudbury Hill
Sudbury Town
Alperton
Perivale
Hanger Lane
Park Royal
North Ealing
Ealing Broadway
Ealing Common
South Ealing
Northfields
Boston Manor
Osterley
Hounslow East
Hounslow Central
Hounslow West
Hatton Cross
Heathrow Terminals 1, 2, 3
Heathrow Terminal 4†
Harrow & Wealdstone
Kenton
Preston Road
Northwick Park
South Kenton
North Wembley
Wembley Central
Stonebridge Park
Harlesden
Willesden Junction
Kensal Green
Queen's Park
Kilburn Park
Maida Vale
Warwick Avenue
Royal Oak
Westbourne Park
Ladbroke Grove
Latimer Road
White City
East Acton
North Acton
West Acton
Acton Central
South Acton
Acton Town
Chiswick Park
Turnham Green
Stamford Brook
Ravenscourt Park
Gunnersbury
Kew Gardens
Richmond
Stanmore
Canons Park
Queensbury
Kingsbury
Wembley Park
Neasden
Dollis Hill
Willesden Green
Kilburn
Brondesbury Park
Kensal Rise
Brondesbury
West Hampstead
Finchley Road
Swiss Cottage
St. John's Wood
Edgware
Burnt Oak
Colindale
Hendon Central
Brent Cross
Golders Green
Hampstead
Finchley Road & Frognal
Belsize Park
Hampstead Heath
Gospel Oak
Kentish Town West
Chalk Farm
†Camden Town
Mornington Crescent
High Barnet
Totteridge & Whetstone
Woodside Park
Mill Hill East
West Finchley
Finchley Central
East Finchley
Highgate
Archway
Tufnell Park
Kentish Town
Camden Road
Caledonian Road
Holloway Road
Arsenal
Caledonian Road & Barnsbury
Cockfosters
Oakwood
Southgate
Arnos Grove
Bounds Green
Wood Green
Turnpike Lane
Manor House
Finsbury Park
Seven Sisters
Tottenham Hale
Blackhorse Road
Walthamstow Central
Highbury & Islington
Canonbury
Dalston Kingsland
Hackney Central
Homerton
Hackney Wick
Epping
Theydon Bois
Loughton
Debden
Buckhurst Hill
Roding Valley†
Chigwell†
Woodford
Grange Hill†
Hainault
Fairlop
Barkingside
South Woodford
Newbury Park
Snaresbrook
Redbridge
Wanstead
Gants Hill
Leytonstone
Leyton
Stratford
Upminster
Upminster Bridge
Hornchurch
Elm Park
Dagenham East
Dagenham Heathway
Becontree
Upney
Barking
East Ham
Upton Park
Plaistow
West Ham
Pudding Mill Lane
Bromley-by-Bow
Bow Road
Bow Church
Devons Road
Mile End
Bethnal Green
Stepney Green
Whitechapel
Shoreditch†
Aldgate East
Aldgate
Liverpool Street
Old Street
Angel
King's Cross St. Pancras
Euston
Euston Square
Great Portland Street
Baker Street
Paddington
Edgware Road
Marylebone
Bayswater
Regent's Park
Warren Street
Goodge Street
Russell Square
Farringdon
Barbican
Moorgate
Holland Park
Queensway
Lancaster Gate
Bond Street
Oxford Circus
Tottenham Court Road
Holborn
Chancery Lane
St. Paul's
Bank
Shepherd's Bush
Notting Hill Gate
Marble Arch
Covent Garden†
Cannon Street
High Street Kensington
Hyde Park Corner
Green Park
Piccadilly Circus
Leicester Square
Mansion House
Monument
Tower Hill
Tower Gateway
Kensington (Olympia)
Goldhawk Road
Hammersmith
Barons Court
Gloucester Road
Knightsbridge
Sloane Square
St. James's Park
Charing Cross
Blackfriars
Temple
West Kensington
Earl's Court
South Kensington
Victoria
Westminster
Embankment
London Bridge
West Brompton
Fulham Broadway
Parsons Green
Putney Bridge
East Putney
Southfields
Wimbledon Park
Wimbledon
Waterloo
Pimlico
Southwark
Lambeth North
Borough
Vauxhall
Elephant & Castle
Kennington
Stockwell
Oval
Clapham North
Clapham Common
Clapham South
Balham
Tooting Bec
Tooting Broadway
Colliers Wood
South Wimbledon
Morden
Brixton
River Thames
Bermondsey
Canada Water
Rotherhithe
Wapping
Shadwell
Limehouse
Westferry
All Saints
Poplar
Blackwall
East India
Canning Town
West India Quay
Canary Wharf
Heron Quays
South Quay
Crossharbour & London Arena
Mudchute
Island Gardens
Surrey Quays
New Cross Gate
New Cross
Cutty Sark for Maritime Greenwich
Greenwich
Deptford Bridge
Elverson Road
Lewisham
North Greenwich
West Silvertown
Pontoon Dock
London City Airport
Silvertown
North Woolwich
King George V
Royal Victoria
Custom House for ExCeL
Prince Regent
Royal Albert
Beckton Park
Cyprus
Gallions Reach
Beckton
Key to lines
Bakerloo
Central
Circle
District†
East London
Hammersmith & City†
Jubilee
Metropolitan
Northern
Piccadilly†
Victoria
Waterloo & City†
Docklands Light Railway
National Rail
Interchange stations
Connections with National Rail
Connections with riverboat services
Connection with Tramlink
Airport interchange
Closed Sundays
Served by Piccadilly line trains early morning and late evening
For opening times see poster journey planners. Certain stations are closed on public holidays.
24 hour London Travel Information
020 7222 1234
Textphone
020 7918 3015
www.tfl.gov.uk
www.tflwap.gov.uk/
LTM B/W FA(a) 04/03
UNDERGROUND
Reg. user No. 05/4083
© Transport for London